The
ANN LANDERS
ENCYCLOPEDIA

The
ANN LANDERS ENCYCLOPEDIA
A to Z

Improve Your Life Emotionally, Medically, Sexually, Socially, Spiritually

DOUBLEDAY & COMPANY, INC., GARDEN CITY, NEW YORK   1978

Library of Congress Cataloging in Publication Data
Main entry under title:

The Ann Landers encyclopedia, A to Z.

Includes index.
1. Conduct of life—Dictionaries. 2. Success—
Dictionaries. 3. Medicine, Popular—Dictionaries.
I. Lederer, Esther Pauline.
BJ1581.2.A56   170′.202
ISBN 0-385-12951-3
Library of Congress Catalog Card Number 77–25601

TO MARY LASKER
AN EXTRAORDINARY WOMAN AND A CHERISHED FRIEND
WHOSE IDEA IT WAS THAT I WRITE THIS BOOK.

Foreword

Between these covers you will find no magic solutions or capsulized panaceas —no short cuts to peace, prosperity, contentment or mental health. To suggest that this book contains the answers to all of life's problems would be fraudulent. You will find, however, a wealth of information on an enormous range of subjects—some about which you couldn't care less.

This is not a book you will want to read from the beginning. If you have no interest in diabetes or cancer or VD or high blood pressure or suicide or stuttering or drugs or how to overcome shyness, how to get a raise, what to do with the old folks, or sex after sixty—skip these pieces. But *don't* skip Father Ted Hesburgh's essay on "Forgiving." We all need to read that one.

Dr. Karl Menninger's piece on "What Causes Crime" is another must. Ditto Dr. Eugene Kennedy's essay on "Loneliness."

If you don't know the difference between a homosexual, a bisexual, a transvestite, a transsexual, a child molester and an exhibitionist, by all means read every one of these articles and learn something. I learned a great deal about dreams from Dr. Francis Braceland, Hartford, Connecticut; about writing a will from Harold Katz, a Chicago attorney; about the importance of death with dignity from Elisabeth Kubler-Ross; about headaches from Dr. Stanley Lesse of New York; "Sex Among the Handicapped" by Dr. Henry Betts of Chicago was extremely informative and written with great sensitivity.

Generously sprinkled throughout this book you will find Ann Landers' columns. Some are my favorites, others may be yours—at least they were the ones most frequently requested for reruns.

In many instances the columns will help you understand more clearly the point of the pieces they accompany.

Obviously I needed a great deal of help in order to put this book together —and I got it. The biblical directive "Ask and ye shall receive" certainly held true for me. And, at the risk of sounding corny, I'd like to quote another timeworn adage—"If you want something done, ask a busy person to do it."

The people I asked are the cream of the crop, incredibly overcommitted, and the demands on their time are outrageous.

Many of the country's most distinguished physicians, psychiatrists, business people, lawyers, teachers, clergymen, psychologists and sociologists spent long hours on manuscripts written especially for this encyclopedia. And such graciousness you wouldn't believe! Along with the articles came dozens of notes thanking me for the opportunity to contribute to a book that was "sure to help a great many people."

It has taken me nearly eighteen months to put this encyclopedia together. I wore out eight typewriter ribbons and developed a callus on my left ear lobe from using the telephone. Suddenly it occurred to me that since I am such a good customer, I should get something out of AT&T, so I asked my friend John deButts, chairman of the Board, to write a piece on "How to Manage Your Time." He came through with a beauty—three days before his deadline.

The first piece in was a dead heat between Senator Bill Proxmire on "Jogging" (naturally) and a piece on sexual promiscuity by Dr. Shervert Frazier, chief of McLean Hospital in Boston.

The last article in under the wire was "Insurance—What Every Wife Should Know" by Frank Sullivan, president of the Mutual Benefit Life Insurance Company, Newark, N.J. Frank was not delinquent. I returned his original piece and asked for "beefing up" on various points. He complied with my request while on vacation in Palm Springs.

The funniest piece is a tie between Art Buchwald's "Religion in the Airports" and "Laughter and Wet Pants" by Russell Roth, M.D. (urologist), Erie, Penn.

The longest piece is a tossup between "Alcoholism" (many contributors) and "Drugs" ("Street Drugs" by Edward Senay, M.D., Chicago, and "Therapeutic Drugs" by Nathan Kline, M.D. and psychiatrist, New York).

In an effort to remain even-handed, you will find two opposing views on abortion, one by Planned Parenthood-World Population, the other by Reverend Jim Burtchaell, Professor of Theology, University of Notre Dame.

The two authors who needed the most nagging were Edward Newman, M.D., Chicago ("Vitamins—The Giant Rip-Off"), and Edmund Klein, M.D., Buffalo, N.Y. ("Body Odor"). Understandable. Both are 'round-the-clock doctors.

Special mention should go to a couple of attorneys, who, coincidentally, are in the same law office in Chicago—Newton Minow, who wrote on "The Living Will—Or The Right to Die," and Morris Leibman—"How to Pick a Lawyer." I didn't need to alter a single word in either of these two pieces.

On the other end of the spectrum you will see two pieces written by a distinguished heart surgeon and one of the world's sweetest people, Dr. Michael DeBakey of Houston. If you've had two years of medical school or if you teach heart surgery, by all means read Dr. DeBakey's articles. I found them totally incomprehensible.

The piece closest to my heart is "Politics as a Career" by Senator Hubert H. Humphrey. That magnificent man wrote the piece during the last days of his illness. He phoned repeatedly to say, "Don't worry, Eppie, it's coming. I'm just putting on the finishing touches."

It has been said that I have a direct line to the masses—to the average person. But I have never met a "mass" and I have yet to know anyone who considers himself average. People who suffer, suffer alone.

The purpose of this book is the same as the philosophy behind the column I've been writing for twenty-three years—to provide correct information, separate fact from fiction, give hope, understanding, and encouragement to those who need it. And who is there among us that does not need it from time to time?

I have learned how it is with the stumbling, frightened people in this world who have no one to talk to. The fact that my column has been a success underscores for me, at least, the central tragedy of our society. The loneliness, the insecurity, the fear that devils, cripples and paralyzes so many of us.

I have learned that financial achievement, academic honors, social or political status do not automatically ensure peace of mind or contentment. I have come to know that many people who appear self-assured and serene are filled with doubts and loaded with anxieties. The masks people wear! The fronts they put on! The world is indeed a stage, as Shakespeare said, and we are all players.

It is my hope that this encyclopedia will help you understand that trouble is not a sign of inadequacy, stupidity or inferiority, but rather an inescapable part of life—proof that you are a card-carrying member of the human race.

If this book can shed a little light in some darkened corner, plant hope where there is despair, replace anxiety with courage and open a door to self-understanding, the eighteen months invested will have been well spent.

ANN LANDERS

Acknowledgments

Never in the history of the written word has an individual imposed on more busy people in pursuit of the best available information, in an effort to produce a single volume.

Any similarity between my conduct and civility is purely coincidental. I shamelessly telephoned and wrote to the top authorities in every conceivable field and asked, "Would you be willing to write a piece for a book I am putting together?"

The responses were magnificent. Only two said, "Sorry, I don't have the time." Over three hundred said, "Yes, I'd be happy to. How many words do you want and how soon do you need it?"

"Thank you" is a phrase so lame and hackneyed that it barely scratches the surface. There are no words that adequately express my appreciation to the extraordinary men and women who gave so generously of their time, energy and wisdom.

Almost all who wrote pieces are personal friends. No one was paid. The list of contributors will appear elsewhere between these covers, and every piece carries a signature.

A warm and special thanks to my editor at Doubleday, Ferris Mack, whose expertise and professionalism were invaluable. Ferris went over every word (and there are 660,000 of them)—often working far into the night and sacrificing weekends. He is the editor all writers dream about but seldom meet.

A low bow to my twin Popo Phillips ("Dear Abby") for putting her book in cold storage so that I might have a clear field for mine. How's that for sisterly love?

Gem-studded halos to my two principal assistants, Marcy Sugar and Kathy Mitchell. In addition to their daily office duties, they made hundreds of telephone calls, checking facts with authors, and with the help of four other heroic secretaries, Carmella De Santi, Robin-Sue Herberger, Polly Passis and Georgette Panutsos, typed manuscripts until they were cross-eyed.

A special citation to Adrienne Starkman, Ferris Mack's able assistant, for spending hours on the phone with my office, attending to endless details with rare, good humor.

Gold-plated angel wings for Sara Charles, M.D., Assistant Professor of Psychiatry, University of Illinois Medical School; Dan Herr of Thomas More Association, Chicago; and William Hausman, M.D., chief of psychiatry at the University of Minnesota, for coming to the rescue on a moment's notice with special assistance.

And finally, my thanks to Doubleday for their splendid co-operation and competence. A girl never had a better publisher.

Contents

Contributors and Sources

Adams, Theodore
Addison, Robert G., M.D.
American Fertility Society
American Medical Association
American Psychiatric Association
American Society Health Association
American Telephone and Telegraph
Ames, Louise Bates, Ph.D.
Appelbaum, Ann Halsell, M.D.
Arena, Jay M., M.D.
Barrett, Stephen, M.D.
Bart, Pauline B., Ph.D.
Begley, Kathleen
Beiser, Helen R., M.D.
Bensinger, Peter
Betts, Henry, M.D.
Blakemore, James G.
Blakeslee, Dr. Alton
Block, Jordan C., D.D.S.
Bluefarb, Samuel, M.D.
Bombeck, Erma
Borges, Albert F., M.D.
Boulware, Marcus H.
Braceland, Francis J., M.D.
Bradley, Dr. Preston (Pastor)
Brady, Robert R.
Breo, Dennis
British Intelligence Service
Brooks, John R., M.D.
Brosin, Henry W., M.D.
Brown, Murray C., M.D.
Bruch, Hilde, M.D.
Buchwald, Art

Bunn, H. Franklin, M.D.
Burtchaell, The Reverend James Tunstead, C.S.C.
Butler, Robert N., M.D.
Bynum, Loyce W.
Cahan, William G., M.D.
Cahill, George F., Jr., M.D.
Cain, James C., M.D.
Caine, Lynn
Calhoun, Calvin L., Sr., M.D.
Campion, Frank D.
Caras, Roger A.
Castelnuovo-Tedesco, Pietro, M.D.
Chappell, Ann Laycock, M.D.
Charles, Allan G., M.D.
Charles, Sara, M.D.
Chicago Lung Association
Children's Hospital Medical Center
Children's Orthopedic Hospital and Medical Center
Clarke, Ann
Codi, Michael
Cody, John Cardinal
Control Disease Center of Communicable Diseases, Atlanta, Georgia
Converse, John Marquis, M.D.
Cronin, Thomas D., M.D.
Custer, Robert L., M.D.
Cystic Fibrosis Foundation
Danish, Roy
Davies, Elam (Pastor)
DeBakey, Michael E., M.D.
deButts, John D.
Densen-Gerber, Judianne, J.D., M.D.
Diagram Group, The
Diamond, Leon, M.D.
Dickinson, Peter A.
Dogon, I. Leon
Dolan, Paul R.
Donohue, Phil
Drescher, Marlene
Edey, Helen, M.D.
Edwards, Jane D.
Eichorn, Rabbi David Max
Eisenberg, Leon, M.D.
Epstein, David I., D.V.M.
Failing, R. M., M.D.
Farber, Eugene M., M.D.
Farnsworth, Dana L., M.D.
Farrell, The Reverend David
Feibelman, Rabbi Julian B.

Feinberg, Samuel M., M.D.
Fischer, Edward
Frazier, Shervert H., M.D.
Freedman, Daniel X., M.D.
Freeman, Sean
Freese, Arthur S.
Froehlich, Edwina
Garrard, Judith McKinnon, Ph.D.
Geaney, Dennis J.
Gerbie, Albert B., M.D.
Giarretto, Henry, Ph.D.
Giffin, Mary, M.D.
Goldberg, Ellen May
Goldhaber, Paul, D.D.S.
Gordon, Gene, M.D.
Gordon, Sol, Ph.D.
Greeley, The Reverend Andrew M.
Green, Elmer, M.D.
Greenberg, Dan
Greenblatt, Milton, M.D.
Greenson, Ralph R., M.D.
Grinker, Roy R., Jr., M.D.
Gromoll, Henry F., Ph.D.
Guest, C. Z.
Hahn, Mrs. Jean
Halberstam, Michael, M.D.
Halleck, Seymour L., M.D.
Hammond, E. Cuyler, Sc.D.
Hanna, Wafik A., M.D.
Harrelson, John M., M.D.
Hastings, Donald W., M.D.
Hesburgh, The Reverend Theodore M.
Hirsch, Barbara B.
Hirschberg, J. Cotter, M.D.
Hoving, Walter
Howard, Ray and Barbara
Humphrey, Frederick G., Ed.D.
Humphrey, Senator Hubert H.
Hurley, Harry J., M.D.
Hutchinson, Stephen, J. D.
Huttenlocher, Dr. Peter R.
Ingelfinger, Franz J., M.D.
Janus, Sam, M.D.
Jenkins, Gregory L., M.D.
Jenkins, M. T. Pepper, M.D.
Johnson, Nicholas
Katz, Harold A.
Katz, Jerome B., M.D.

Keller, William K., M.D.
Kenna, Marita D., M.D.
Kennedy, Eugene, Ph.D.
Kenney, Asta-Maria
Kilkeary, Nan
Kirsner, Joseph B., M.D., Ph.D.
Klein, Edmund, M.D.
Klein, Stanley D., Ph.D.
Kline, Nathan S., M.D.
Kling, Ruth
Kliot, David A., M.D.
Knight, Gilda
Knode, Robert E., M.D.
Knowles, John H., M.D.
Kovler, Peter
Kübler-Ross, Elisabeth, M.D.
La Leche League
Landers, Ann
Lasker, Mrs. Albert D.
Layman, Dale, Ph.D.
Lebensohn, Zigmond M., M.D.
Lederberg, Joshua, Ph.D.
Leibman, Morris I.
Lepper, Dr. Mark H.
Lerner, Aaron B., M.D.
LeShan, Eda J.
LeShan, Lawrence, Ph.D.
Lesse, Stanley, M.D., Med. Sc.D.
Levy, Edwin Z., M.D.
Lewis, Myrna I., A.C.S.W.
Lichtenstein, Lawrence M., M.D.
Lilly, Sue
Littner, Ner, M.D., S.C.
Long, John S., M.D.
Lowman, Josephine
MacVicar, Jean
Martin, Peter A., M.D.
Masserman, Jules, M.D.
Masters, William H., M.D.
Mayer, Jean, Ph.D.
Mazzanti, Deborah Szekely
McGuire, Julie
McNally, Randall E., M.D.
Mead, Margaret
Menninger, Karl, M.D.
Menninger, Robert, M.D.

Menninger, Roy W., M.D.
Merrill, J. Robert
Merrill, John P., M.D.
Mikulski, Barbara A.
Miller, Daniel M., M.D.
Minow, Newton N.
Mirabella, Grace
Modlin, Herbert C., M.D.
Moore, Judy
Moore, The Rt. Reverend Paul, Jr.
Morgan, Mary Lynn, D.D.S.
Moss, Stephen J., D.D.S.
Nahmias, André J., M.D.
Najarian, John, M.D.
Napolitane, Catherine
National Commission on the Observance of International Women's Year
National Foundation March of Dimes
National Foundation for Sudden Infant Death, Inc., Washington State Chapter
National Funeral Directors Association
National Kidney Foundation
National Multiple Sclerosis Society
National Safety Council
National Sudden Infant Death Syndrome Foundation
Newman, Edward A., M.D.
Nicholas, Leslie, M.D.
Norins, Leslie, M.D.
O'Brien, Joseph P.
O'Neill, Mrs. Mary Jane
Ordway, John, M.D., and Janet E., M.D.
Parade Magazine
Park, Benjamin B., M.D.
Paton, David, M.D.
Paul, Most Reverend John J., D.D.
Pellegrino, Victoria
Pietropinto, Anthony, M.D.
Pildes, Judith
Pilling, Loran, M.D.
Planned Parenthood
Plum, Fred, M.D.
Pollock, George H., M.D., Ph.D.
Porter, Sylvia
Providence Evening Bulletin
Proxmire, Senator William
Quint, Barbara Gilder
Rabinowitz, Rabbi Stanley

Raether, Howard C.
Rensberger, Boyce
Ringer, Robert J.
Roach, Deborah
Robin, Milton, M.D.
Robison, Helen
Rome, Howard, M.D.
Rosenfeld, Arthur
Rosenfeld, Isadore, M.D.
Ross, David, M.D.
Roth, Russell B., M.D.
Rovner, Ilana Diamond
Rovner, Richard N., M.D.
Royko, Mike
Rusk, Howard A., M.D.
Rutledge, Aaron L., Ph.D.
Rutlege, Arnold, Ph.D.
Safirstein, Samuel L., M.D.
Schepens, Charles L., M.D.
Schiff, Harriet Sarnoff
Schmitt, Barton, M.D.
Schoenbaum, Stephen C., M.D.
Scofield, Jack, M.D.
Scott, F. Brantley, M.D.
Sehdev, Harcharan, M.D.
Senay, Edward C., M.D.
Shambaugh, George E., Jr., M.D.
Sherline, Donald M., M.D.
Shields, Nelson
Shumway, Norman, M.D.
Simpson, David
Simpson, William S., M.D.
Skinner, David B., M.D.
Sklansky, Dr. Morris A.
Smithson, Al
Snider, Arthur J.
Solomon, Brenda Clorfene, M.D.
Spellberg, Mitchell A., M.D., M.S.
Spiegel, David, M.D.
Spiegel, Herbert, M.D.
Spohn, Herbert E., Ph.D.
Stamler, Jeremiah, M.D.
Stamler, Rose, M.A.
Stanley, Bessie Anderson
Stare, Frederick J., M.D.
Steinfeld, Jesse L., M.D.
Stolar, Robert, M.D.

Stoller, Robert J., M.D.
Stoner, Carroll
Sullivan, Frank
Sullivan, James
Swartz, Robert M., M.D.
Taylor, Jack N., M.D.
Taymor, Melvin L., M.D.
Tighe, Patti, M.D.
Ullman, Samuel
Ultmann, John D., M.D.
University of Washington, Seattle
U. S. Department of State, Washington, D.C.
Van Gelder, David
Van Geldor, David
Van Orden, James Hill
Varro, Barbara
Viorst, Judith
Visotsky, Harold M., M.D.
Vogue Beauty & Health Guide
Voth, Harold M., M.D.
Walters, Barbara
Wangensteen, Owen H., M.D.
Warrick, Pamela
Weekes, Dr. Claire, M.D., D.Sc.
Weinberg, Peter E., M.D.
Weinstein, Louis, M.D.
Weisberger, Eleanor
Welch, Claude, M.D.
Wells, Joel
Wheeler, Joe, Ph.D.
Whelan, Elizabeth M., Sc.D.
Whitcomb, Meg
Wilson, Charles B., M.D.
Wolkonsky, Peter, M.D.
Wood, Bruce T. (podiatrist)
Woods, Richard
World Book Encyclopedia
Zimbardo, Philip G.

The

ANN LANDERS
ENCYCLOPEDIA

Abortion

When a woman becomes pregnant, the fertilized egg attaches itself to the inside wall of her uterus and begins to grow. Initially, it is just a tiny bit of tissue. But, in due course, this develops into a fetus which is nourished by the *placenta* (afterbirth) and surrounded by a protective mass of fluid.

In an abortion, the uterus is emptied before the fetus is fully developed and ready for birth, leaving the woman non-pregnant. Some abortions occur naturally. These are known as miscarriages. To the medical and scientific world they are *spontaneous abortions*. What most people think of as an abortion, the intentional termination of a pregnancy, is known to the medical community as an *induced abortion*. Our subject matter here is induced abortion only.

Today, in the United States, abortion, in the first twenty-four weeks of pregnancy, is a legally permissible medical procedure performed by licensed personnel in clinics, hospitals and doctors' offices. During the first twelve weeks, the abortion decision is a private matter between the woman and her physician. In the second twelve weeks, the state may impose some restrictions —but only in the interest of the woman's health.

Legal abortion is a safe, simple procedure when performed early in pregnancy. Later abortions are more complicated and may be more risky. However, overall, abortion is still safer than pregnancy and childbirth.

ABORTION PROCEDURES:

The medical procedure used varies with the duration of the pregnancy. Only the two most commonly used procedures are considered here.

Early Abortion:

Almost 90 percent of all abortions are performed in the first twelve weeks of pregnancy. Under these circumstances, it is a simple, quick, painless and safe procedure. The abortion visit itself requires only three to six hours at the medical facility and costs about $150–$250 (in 1978). Usually the woman receives only a local anesthetic, although some facilities offer general anesthesia.

The procedure most widely used in the first twelve weeks of pregnancy—and, sometimes, up to the sixteenth week of pregnancy—is the *vacuum aspiration* method, which sucks up the contents of the uterus.

Before the abortion, the woman receives counseling, her medical history is taken, tests are made and she is given a physical examination. If there are no problems the procedure begins.

First, the physician inserts a *speculum* (an instrument that holds the walls of the vagina apart) into the woman's vagina. Then, he/she holds the cervix steady with a scissor-like instrument called a *tenaculum*. The speculum and the tenaculum remain in position throughout the procedure.

The woman is given a local anesthetic to numb her cervix. Then the physician begins to stretch (or dilate) the narrow neck of the cervix. A series of *dilators*—thin plastic or stainless steel rods, each one a little thicker than the last—is used for this purpose. This takes only a couple of minutes. When the neck of the cervix is dilated, the physician has access to the uterus.

When the opening of the cervix is wide enough, the physician inserts a *vacurette*—a thin plastic or steel tube attached to the vacuum suction machine—into the uterus. In less than five minutes the contents of the uterus are gently extracted. Then, the physician will often insert a *curette*—a spoon-shaped instrument with a small hole—into the uterus to remove any remaining tissue.

After the procedure, the woman rests for about an hour, observed by medical personnel. For a few days, she should not engage in strenuous activities, and for two or three weeks, she is usually instructed to refrain from sexual intercourse and from using tampons. She is also required to make a follow-up visit to a physician, at which time contraception will be discussed.

Many women experience no discomfort after the abortion. Some experience bleeding and decide to rest for a day. However, complications necessitating medical attention do occur on rare occasions. For example, a few women may experience hemorrhage, an infection or a perforation of the uterus.

Late Abortion:

Abortions performed between the fourteenth and twenty-fourth weeks of pregnancy are more difficult to obtain, more expensive (in 1978, prices began at approximately $400 but were sometimes substantially higher), more risky and more unpleasant than early abortions. They entail two to three days in a hospital and a process similar to labor.

After the preliminary counseling, medical exam and tests, the physician uses a local anesthetic to numb a tiny area of the abdomen just below the woman's navel. A needle is inserted through the abdomen and a small amount of fluid is withdrawn from the sac surrounding the fetus. This is replaced by an equal amount of a saline or prostaglandin (or other) solution which is injected into the sac. This part of the procedure takes up to a half hour. Approximately eight to twenty-four hours later, the solution brings on contractions of the woman's uterine muscles. These contractions may last from eight to fifteen hours before the fetus, the placenta and the fluid are expelled through the vagina. The abortion is then complete.

A late abortion patient is generally required to spend twenty-four hours in the hospital after the abortion. Aftercare is the same as for an early abortion.

Complications following a late abortion occur more frequently than during an early abortion. The risks, however, are no greater than for pregnancy and childbirth. In a very few instances, heavy bleeding may occur and minor surgery may have to be undertaken to complete the abortion—or the saline or prostaglandin solution may be accidentally injected into the bloodstream.

The abortion decision is rarely an easy one and patients' reactions to the experience differ widely. However, most women feel a sense of relief at no longer carrying an unwanted pregnancy as well as pride for having gained control over their lives and following through on a difficult decision.

While most abortions are simple medical procedures, it is important to choose the medical facility carefully. It is advisable to consult a reputable agency or individual before making a choice: a physician, a member of the clergy, a Planned Parenthood or other family planning clinic can probably help. (Look in the phone book under Planned Parenthood or call Community Referral Service and ask for the number of a family planning clinic.)

ABORTION—LEGAL:

Until the nineteenth century, American common law, like English common law, tolerated abortion until the fetus was "quickened" (when a woman "feels life") at about five months. In the course of the nineteenth century, however, states began to enact laws making abortion a criminal offense except when the woman's life was seriously threatened. It is often suggested that these statutes were in no way related to morality, but enacted to protect maternal health. The death rate associated with gynecological surgery was approximately 30 percent in the nineteenth century. In all probability, however, these laws can be attributed to legislators' concerns for public morality *and* public health as well as other considerations such as a desire to expand the work force for growing industrial concerns. It was not until the late 1960s and early 1970s that individual states began to repeal their criminal abortion laws, and only in 1973 did the U. S. Supreme Court strike down restrictive abortion laws throughout the country.

In the years preceding liberalization of the abortion laws, women who had money and sufficient sophistication to know how things are done in our society could obtain safe abortions from competent physicians at home or abroad.

Less fortunate women crept off to the back alleys, submitting to the so-called "surgical skills" of non-medical abortionists in anything but sterile surroundings. Or they attempted to abort themselves with a lye douche, a clothes hanger or other sharp objects. It is estimated that as many as one million pregnancies each year, one in every five, may have been terminated by illegal or self-induced abortion. Small wonder, then, that hospital wards were crowded with women sick and dying from hemorrhage and infections resulting from botched abortions. Illegal abortion was the largest single cause of death to pregnant women. Between five thousand and ten thousand died each year. Of those who survived, many suffered lasting physical and psychological harm.

It was in recognition of the fact that abortions *do* take place, whether or not the procedure is legal, that progressive state legislatures and the Supreme Court determined that public policy has an obligation to protect maternal health by making safe, legal procedures available. Thus, the primary effect of the legalization of abortion has been to replace illegal and self-induced procedures with legal, medically supervised procedures.

SUPREME COURT ABORTION DECISION:

On January 22, 1973, the Supreme Court, in two landmark decisions—*Roe* v. *Doe* and *Doe* v. *Bolton*—overturned restrictive abortion laws wherever they still existed in the United States. It held that:

"The right of privacy . . . is broad enough to encompass a woman's decision whether or not to terminate her pregnancy."

The abortion decision was placed in the hands of the pregnant woman and her physician and performance of the procedure was placed in the hands of trained medical personnel. The Court held that states might regulate abortion in three ways:

(1) They might require that all abortions be performed by physicians.

(2) In the second three months of pregnancy, they might regulate performance of abortions in the interests of the woman's health.

(3) In the final three months of pregnancy, they might regulate abortions in the interests of the woman's health or the state's interest in potential human life.

In subsequent decisions, the Court elaborated on the 1973 rulings. In 1976 (*Planned Parenthood of Central Missouri* v. *Danforth*) it held that states could not condition a woman's abortion on the consent of her husband, if she is married, or of her parents, if she is a minor. In 1977 (*Beal* v. *Doe, Maher* v. *Roe* and *Poelker* v. *Doe*) it ruled that states are not required to subsidize abortions which are not "medically necessary" and that public hospitals may choose not to provide abortions.

ABORTION SERVICES:

Although the Court's decisions paved the way for the establishment and expansion of abortion services throughout the country, the availability of services has grown up unevenly. In some places, there are only a few physicians trained or willing to perform abortions. In others, hospitals have been reluctant to provide the service. In addition, community opposition to this newly legal service has also deterred many providers from meeting the need. Abortion services are concentrated primarily in metropolitan areas and only one in five public hospitals provides abortion services. Thus, poor, young women who live in small towns are likely to encounter substantial difficulties in obtaining a needed abortion.

In 1976 it was estimated that between 143,000 and 654,000 women in need of abortions were unable to obtain them. Approximately 1,115,000 legal abortions were performed in approximately 2,400 facilities during 1976. Women who obtain abortions come from all socio-economic, religious, cultural and ethnic backgrounds. In 1975, for example:

(1) One third of abortion patients were teenagers; one third were aged twenty to twenty-four and one third were aged twenty-five or older.

(2) Two thirds of abortion patients were white; one third were black.

(3) Three in four abortion patients were unmarried; one in four was married.

(4) Almost half of abortion patients had no living children—fewer than one in five had more than two living children.

(5) Four in five abortion patients had never had a previous abortion.

OPPOSITION TO LEGAL ABORTION:

A vocal minority of the American public, calling itself "right-to-life" or "pro-life," is opposed to legal abortion for moral reasons. These individuals subscribe to the theory that the fertilized egg in a woman's uterus is every bit as human as a fully developed newborn baby. Accordingly, they consider abortion murder. Their long-term goal is to pass a "human life amendment" to the U. S. Constitution, which would declare the fetus a legal person from the moment of conception.

While the "right-to-life" groups are laying the groundwork for passage of a "human life amendment," they are working aggressively at the federal, state and local levels to limit abortion in any possible way. They have succeeded in restricting public funding for abortion—including the exclusion of abortion from U.S.-funded family planning programs overseas and banning use of public funds for abortion-related legal action. In addition, they have initiated bylaw changes in some communities, preventing the establishment of abortion facilities. Several of their efforts, however, have been thwarted: Attempts to require parental or spousal consent for abortion and to convict physicians of manslaughter for performing legal abortions have failed in the courts.

There is no scientific or legal basis to consider a fetus capable of sustained and meaningful life prior to the final three months of pregnancy. The concept of a fetus as a person can be justified only on the grounds of an individual's belief. This moral principle is held by the Roman Catholic hierarchy and shared by some non-Catholics, but many other religions do not subscribe to this viewpoint. Even among Catholic laity, the majority believes abortion should be legal—at least in some circumstances—and, among women who choose abortion, the proportion of Catholics reflects their proportion in the community at large.

Attempts to outlaw abortion would, in effect, coerce all of society to act in accordance with the religious beliefs of a minority of the population. In a democratic society, this is clearly intolerable. In this country, it also violates the doctrine of separation of church and state.

The abortion decision is best made by each individual. And public policy has a responsibility to respect that fundamental individual liberty, except when it conflicts with public health and welfare.

CREDIT: *Asta-Maria Kenney, Associate Coordinator for Public Affairs, Planned Parenthood-World Population, 810 Seventh Avenue, New York, New York 10019.*

Another Point of View

Opposition to abortion has been identified in the popular mind with Catholics. Polls shows, however, that the opinions of Catholics on this matter do not vary much from those of the public at large. I offer here, at Ann Landers' invitation, not *the* Catholic viewpoint, but *a* viewpoint of a Catholic scholar who wishes that our reputation for repugnance to abortion were better deserved than it apparently is.

To begin with, since the abortion debate is such an antagonized one, we should try to set aside those matters that need not be argued, either because they are granted by thoughtful persons on all sides, or because they are well-established facts rather than judgments subject to dispute.

First, then, let it be agreed that some people turn to abortion as a measure of relief from serious tragedy: danger to a mother's life; sure or likely deformity of the child; pregnancy from rape or incest; pregnancy of a very young, disadvantaged and naive teenager. Women and men do face these and similar misfortunes, which should command sympathetic and patient (and financial) support.

It is an equally true and verified fact that few—very few—of the abortions in America today are motivated by any such misfortune. For example, only about 1 percent are performed because of the mother's serious medical needs. The overwhelming majority of abortions are performed simply to avoid an undesired childbirth.

A third matter about which there should be no legitimate doubt is the sincerity of many partisans on both sides of the argument. Despite their energetic, bitter disagreement, many supporters of abortion liberalization and of the pro-life movement rival one another in their dedication to human need and in their records of service.

Fourth, it is possible to ascertain fairly accurately—for what it is worth— where public opinion stands. National polls commissioned over nearly two decades by social scientists favorable to abortion have shown repeatedly that a strong majority of Americans hold these convictions:

(1) Human life and personhood begin before birth (most say at conception).

(2) Abortion should be a crime except to save the mother's life or if the child is deformed.

(3) After the third month it should be unlawful in any case.

(4) It should be unlawful without the husband's consent.

(5) It should not be permitted except in hospitals.

These judgments are expressed by males and by females, by Catholics and by non-Catholics. These are the judgments which Anglo-American common law, the elected legislators and governors, and in some states the ballots of the voters at large had formed into the law of the land in forty-six states— until those laws were set aside by the Supreme Court decisions of 1973 and since. I mention these measurements of public opinion not because public opinion is a sure guide to right and wrong, but because in a democracy we insist that the laws follow the will of the majority in defining rights and crimes against those rights.

Fifth, despite the creation, by the 1973 decision, of an abortion industry staffed by medical personnel, most persons in the medical profession resist abortion as a procedure alien to their pursuits. Most physicians will not perform them. There is an even firmer refusal among nurses, mostly women. And abortions are still, in the face of the Supreme Court's decision, tolerated in only about one fifth of the country's hospitals.

Having acknowledged these points at the start, how should one make a moral judgment about abortion? I hold that the life of every fellow human must be respected, preserved and even protected. We must defer to others' lives, not simply to gain and repay a like protection from others, nor just to avoid the penalties of the law, nor merely because every human being has a right to his or her life, a right which deserves priority over every other human right, need or desire. We must defer for still another reason: If we deal unjust injury or violent death to others, we shall bring upon ourselves a death of the spirit—a violent death. Those who kill, die.

I hold that so far as we best can tell, a human person's life begins at conception. Neither birth nor any transition leading up to it serves as a true beginning, unless we talk biological nonsense. Of course an unborn child does not speak or work or give her or his life to others (nor does a newborn child; nor, for that matter, some people long since born). But it is terribly important that we give the basic protection of life-loyalty to *all* fellow humans, not only to those who suit us as valuable contributors to society. The Final Solution to the Jewish Problem of the Third Reich rested on the belief that it was never enough simply to be a human to keep the right to live. One had to have certain other qualities. Hitler decided what those qualities were to be, and since Jews and Gypsies lacked them, they were destroyed. My position is that no one should have the right or power to decide what qualities or what usefulness others must have to avoid being killed. It is enough to be *any* human being, no matter how burdensome or troublesome, to merit the right to life.

Abortion, then—the willful and violent killing of an unborn human being —is homicide. By this neutral term I mean simply the killing of a human. We talk of accidental and deliberate and justifiable homicides. Is there such a thing as a justifiable abortion? Here I would argue that if we claim any honesty we must hew to the same principles in evaluating abortion as govern our judgments on any other form of homicide.

Some maintain that all deliberate killing is wrong. Better, they argue, to accept violence at the hands of others than to take up weapons and end ourselves as death-dealers. Others, likewise committed to life, would say that homicide could be justified under certain conditions, e.g., to protect oneself or some innocent third party from mortal, undeserved attack. On the latter view it might be justifiable to destroy a child were that clearly the only way to save his or her mother's life. But there is no consistent, responsible moral way, from either point of view, to justify the killing of innocent offspring to relieve his or her elders of any inconvenience, no matter how severe the distress.

It is no less savage to abort a deformed child than to exterminate a retarded adult. It is no more justifiable to abort a child in order to conceal adultery than to murder a witness about to give evidence in a trial. One cannot fairly allow a child to be destroyed because he or she was conceived by rape or incest, without also allowing the elimination of illegitimate children.

My argument is straightforward. Abortion is homicide—the destruction of a child. Save for the rare, rare instance when it is a mortal threat to a mother's life to carry her child to birth, there is no abortion that is not the unjust taking of another's life because it is a burden to one's own.

Someone has reckoned that about 70 percent of the murders in this country find close family or business associates as victims. We have in us this strange and desperate ability, this selfish madness, to blind our mind's eye toward those nearest us, to see them as insignificant, as nothing really human. We depersonalize our victims before killing them. So with abortion.

In opposing it I am in *no way* insensitive to the plight of mothers who are frightened thirteen-year-olds, or supporting six children on welfare, or having to drop out of college because of one night's foolishness. I simply say that these are not misfortunes that justify anyone in raising his or her hand to kill. They are not trivial miseries. But to allege them as cause for abortion reminds me too much of the excuses for the massacre at Mylai, and for the bondage of the slave trade, and for the industrial poisoning at Minamata.

I do not wish to donate on Tuesday to the March of Dimes for medical research on the health of the unborn, and on Thursday to Planned Parenthood to keep crippled children from ever surviving till birth. I want no part of the insanity that sends police into the privacy of homes to stop parents from battering and scalding their four-month-old babies to death, and then uses the same force of law to guarantee the "privacy" of parents to grind up their babies four months before birth. I have no stomach for a society which sees that in many of its homes children are unwanted, and would rather exterminate the children than heal the parents. And though I try to be patient, I do become exasperated when told that since I am a Catholic I have somehow lost my civil right to make public and legal appeal for the lives of the young marked down for death, or that I am imposing my private religious notions on the majority of my fellow citizens, when it is clear to anyone willing to inquire that it is the minority of citizens that presently uses the law to kill.

Women have the right to reproductive freedom, I hear it argued, and I agree: *all* women, even little girls yet unborn who have the right to be free to grow to the age when they in their turn can make love and have babies. Women should control their own bodies, it is said, and I agree; but not over the bodies of their children (and in the case of male children, who ever heard of a male part of a female body?). Make abortions illegal, we hear it said, and they will still go on, but in the back streets, and I agree. Yet rape goes on despite our laws; should it no longer be a crime? And if the day came when the nation was no longer willing to go on record that rape was criminal, would there not be more of it? Can anyone who knows that we record 1,115,000 abortions a year in America imagine that most of these have occurred without the legal protections of 1973? Drive abortion underground, it is said, and young women will die by the coat hanger. Yes, just as the young women of the Weather Underground who blew themselves up making bombs. I mourn them all, but I mourn more for their innocent victims—and differently. Make abortion a criminal act, we hear it said, and only the rich will be able to afford it. Yes, but then the rich have always been better able to afford their vices. I would as soon buy abortions for the poor as buy them heroin. Abortions *will* go on! Why not at least see that they be done cleanly and safely? Yes, say I, and so shall hatred and murder go on, but I shall not use the tax moneys to give sniper-scopes to the Klan or dumdum bullets to the Mafia.

But back to the *point,* the chief and only point, the much-avoided point, the only point at issue: To abort is to destroy one's son or daughter.

I need no particular religious doctrine to make me fear for my people, when we want no children born, and then when they come, we smother them with possessiveness or raise them by hired hands, we send them to schools where there is no discipline from homes where there is none, we pay for their psychiatrists instead of loving them, and then send them off haphazardly into frivolous affairs and marriages. America does not love children. Hardly a surprise we should be killing them. But it is by our love for the children, as much as any single duty, that we shall be judged.

CREDIT: *James Tunstead Burtchaell, C.S.C., Department of Theology, Notre Dame University.*

Accidents to Children

What Causes an Accident?

More children die from accidents than from a total of the next five most frequent causes of childhood death (cancer, congenital malformation, pneumonia, stomach trouble and meningitis).

Few people are aware that accidents don't "just happen." They are caused. Perhaps as many as nine out of ten accidents to children could be prevented if parents (and others who care for children) were better informed about the "psychology" of childhood safety.

What causes accidents to children? To answer this question, a research team of doctors, psychologists and social workers made a detailed study of pre-school children admitted to the Children's Hospital Medical Center in Boston for treatment of an accidental injury. In addition to investigating the facts surrounding the accident, the research team looked into the child's family, his relationship with his parents, brothers and sisters, his environment and daily routine. The research findings showed that "simple" everyday events and troubles in family life set the stage for almost every childhood accident.

Most accidents to children are the result of a minor family illness, a parent who is overly tired, a child who is very hungry, etc. Small troubles and irritations pile up until a mother (or father or grandmother or baby-sitter) is so exhausted or worried that she hasn't the energy to take the usual precautions. For example: An aspirin bottle is left within a child's reach; a sewing kit is left on a coffee table; a boiling teapot is left on the front burner of the stove. Hazards of some sort exist in every home but it is not the "ordinary" hazard that causes the problem, it is a chain of happenings that place an extra strain on family members and increase the possibility of an accident to a child.

When are accidents most likely to occur? Based on the Children's Hospital study, the conditions below are those that most often precipitate accidents to children. Be aware of these conditions. Any single factor might not cause an accident; but two or three factors combined can greatly increase the chances.

Accidents occur more often:

(1) When a child is hungry or tired.
(2) When any hazard—a sharp knife, a busy street, a knitting needle—is too accessible, or when a bottle of colored pills is too attractive for a small child to resist.
(3) When a mother is ill, about to menstruate or pregnant.
(4) When there is no safe place to play.
(5) When a child is considered hyperactive by his parents.
(6) When the relationship between parents is tense.
(7) When a child's surroundings change, often at moving or vacation time.
(8) When other family members are ill or the center of the mother's attention.
(9) When the family is rushed—particularly on Saturday (the most dangerous day of the week).
(10) When parents lack understanding of what new activities to expect at each stage of a child's development.
(11) When a child is in the care of an unfamiliar person or a brother or sister too young to be responsible.

CREDIT: *Jay M. Arena, M.D., Department of Pediatrics, Duke University Medical Center, Durham, North Carolina, author of* Child Safety Is No Accident, *with Miriam Bachar, M.A., Durham, North Carolina: Duke University Press, 1978.*

Accident Prevention for Children

Be aware of potential dangers as you work in and around the house. Look for "ordinary" things that could lead to trouble. Imagine what you might get into if you were a child.

Slow down and take extra precautions if the pressure of everyday problems begins to get to you. Simplify your daily chores if you or other family members are ill, worried or upset.

Protect your child, but don't overprotect him so much that he is unaware of dangers. Remember, all children must be taught to protect themselves. If a small accident occurs, discuss it with your child so he will learn from it.

Don't rely on explanations, warnings or discipline to prevent accidents to pre-school children. A child's memory is short. He may forget words or not fully understand their meaning. Even discipline may be forgotten quickly by a very young child. Many accidents occur because parents genuinely believe they have "taught" pre-school children about dangers.

Try to understand your child's needs at each stage of his growth and development. If you can, anticipate what he'll do next.

WHAT TO DO IF AN ACCIDENT DOES OCCUR

If an accident occurs, don't underestimate the injury. In the accident study conducted by the Boston Children's Hospital, fewer than 50 percent of the parents said they were aware of the extent of their child's injury. Try to stay calm if your child has an accident, but don't ignore or underestimate it. Follow this general procedure:

Don't do anything until you have observed the situation carefully. For example, grabbing up a child who has suffered a fracture or who has internal injuries will do more harm than good. Observe the child's symptoms closely. If you have any questions about what to do, don't do anything until you have telephoned your doctor or the emergency ward of the nearest hospital for advice.

Above all, try not to panic if your child is injured. Children are alert to adult reactions. If you panic, your child may panic, too. An injured child needs a calm, reassuring manner to help him overcome his natural fear.

If you do not have your pediatrician's phone number and the number of the nearest hospital's emergency room taped on your telephone—do it today.

CREDIT: Accident Handbook, *Department of Health Education, The Children's Hospital Medical Center, Boston, Massachusetts.*

Accident-Prone

We all know individuals who seem to have "rotten luck." Whenever we see them they have an arm in a sling, a patch over an eye, they are limping on a cane or hobbling on crutches. How much of a coincidence is it that these same people seem to have so many accidents?

The following letter is a good example:

DEAR ANN LANDERS: What is wrong with our seventeen-year-old daughter? In the last year she has fallen off a horse and broken her collarbone, tripped on the dog's leash and sprained both ankles, fractured her jaw in a volleyball game (collided with another girl) and just last week she totaled the car and was lucky to escape with minor back injuries.

Mary Lou is a good student but she is hotly competitive. When she loses a contest, an election or a boyfriend, she gets depressed and then something happens. Either she gets the flu or a skin rash—or she has an accident.

The car wreck occurred the day she didn't make the May Queen finals. When I told my wife there has to be some connection between Mary Lou's disappointments and her injuries, she said I was crazy. What do you think?
CONCERNED DAD

I told Concerned Dad he was not crazy and suggested that Mary Lou get counseling. Often when people are helped to recognize the relationship between anger, frustration, disappointment and their accidents (and illnesses), they have fewer misfortunes and enjoy better health.

For many years it has been known that a high percentage of accidents are limited to a comparatively small number of individuals. In a study for a major insurance company, it was discovered that 10 percent of the employees of a large manufacturing firm were responsible for 75 percent of the accidents. Another study revealed that 12 to 15 percent of the employees of a tool and dye company were responsible for 100 percent of the accidents.

In the U. S. Army, similar observations were made. Thousands of soldiers were wounded because of their emotional state. Under stress of battle, many individuals used poor judgment because of tenseness and fear.

In *Psychiatry in a Troubled World,* Dr. William C. Menninger wrote, "Accident proneness is often due to an emotional state present prior to the injury. Deep-seated personality traits (such as an unconscious wish to be punished) can lead to repeated accidents."

I have received many letters from readers who are victims of other people's "accidents." Here's one that illustrates the point well.

DEAR ANN LANDERS: I have this problem I don't know how to deal with. Seems every time I'm with my boyfriend I get injured. I mean physically. It's never anything serious but bad enough so that I'm concerned.

I've been hit in the head with a Frisbee (twice), had a car trunk slammed on my shoulder, been burned by his cigarette and knocked out of a swinging hammock. I can't count the number of times I've been clipped by his elbow or stepped on.

My guy enjoys a few beers but he never gets drunk or out of control. Somehow I feel his beer-drinking might have something to do with these accidents. What do you think, Ann? . . . OUCHING BUT NOT GROUCHING

DEAR OUCH: His beer-drinking could be a factor. Alcohol (yes, beer is an alcoholic beverage) releases the inhibitions and the more primitive behavioral patterns take over.

Freud says, "There are no accidents." You can take it from there.

Here's another:

DEAR ANN: I was amused by all those women who wrote to tell you that their husbands accidentally hit them in their sleep. It set me to thinking. My husband always seems to be hitting me accidentally—when he's awake.

For example, recently we took an auto trip and stopped at a service station to get a map. When Al unfolded the map he socked me in the jaw. I saw stars.

Last week Al was undressing. He whipped off his belt and the buckle caught me in the mouth. He said he didn't realize I was so close. Yesterday he was hanging a picture and dropped the hammer on my head.

Al has burned me with cigarettes several times and it's always the same excuse—he didn't know I was there. Do you think this means anything? KITTY

DEAR KITTY: It means Al is careless, awkward, accident-prone and possibly venting some subconscious hostilities in a manner which leaves him blame-free.

Your best protection is to be doubly alert when you're around him—and signal your position frequently.

Dr. Quinn G. McKay of American Enterprise Management at the School of Business, Texas Christian University, in Fort Worth, Texas, made the following remarks in an article entitled, "People Just Don't Want to Be Safe."

"If we want to learn why people have accidents it is important to understand certain concepts about human nature.

"The accident-prone individual is often regarded as a luckless sort who was born that way! More thoughtful people, of course, realize this is not so.

"There is evidence that accident proneness is a matter of personal habit. There seems to be some relationship between people who are erratic in keeping appointments, people who are careless in the way they keep their clothing, people who drop lawn tools haphazardly in the garage. They are also the ones who have a disproportionate share of accidents in the mine, or in the home, or wherever they happen to work.

"If one could perfect a measure, there is a possibility that, in the selection process, one could identify before hiring those individuals who have personality traits that lead to accidents. This may also suggest that, rather than just preaching safety to those who tend to be accident-prone, they should be encouraged to look at safety from a point of view of general carefulness and general concern about things.

"Developing in a person a degree of meticulousness about his general life and orderliness may result in an automatic spillover into improved safety behavior.

"Another factor relating to the accident-prone is the desire for daring. In the lives of most men is the desire to live dangerously, to take a risk—get a new thrill.

"When a group of truck drivers get together for a bull session, the man who holds the center place in the conversation is the one who can string out the most hair-raising driving experiences. The hero of many stories and TV shows is the one who is exposed to danger—auto accidents, shootings, etc.— and still comes out alive.

"Being a nation of hero worshipers, we must tend to emulate unconsciously, if not consciously, the daring of these idols. Usually, these idols are not good examples of safe practices, but they do suggest manliness.

"This is important, especially in a society where daily opportunities to display physical prowess—an evidence of masculinity—are becoming fewer and fewer."

CREDIT: *Ann Landers.*

Acne

DEAR ANN LANDERS: I am an 18-year-old normal, healthy guy who has had only three dates in my life. It's not because I am shy. It's acne.

There are times when my face is so horrible I wouldn't inflict myself on a girl. I never know when the acne is going to be better—or worse—so I'm afraid to set up anything for the future. When my complexion is bad, I just stay home. This can be very lonely.

I've tried several ointments, soaps and so-called "cures" advertised in magazines. Nothing works. I have spent at least $200 on this useless junk and would gladly spend $500 more on something that could clear up my face and shoulders. (P.S. Some guys have told me what certain girls think of me and that should give me confidence, but it doesn't. I don't need compliments. What I need is a cure. Thanks.)   HENRY THE HERMIT

DEAR HERM: If you do not know of a good dermatologist (skin specialist) call the County Medical Society and they will suggest a couple. Then go—and quit horsing around with the junk you see advertised. It's worse than useless. It's a gyp. Get going and good luck.

Acne is a skin problem that plagues approximately 80 percent of adolescents and young adults. There is no known way to prevent it, especially if it runs in the family. Heredity is definitely a factor. If both parents had it, there is a very good chance that their children will have it.

For most people, acne is a temporary nuisance and a minor embarrassment, but for those who have severe cases, acne can be a living hell. I have received thousands of letters from teenage acne victims who feel so ugly and hideous that they become social drop-outs—not wanting to inflict the "horrible sight" of themselves on others.

There are many false notions about acne that have been repeated so often, most people believe them. For example: For generations adolescents have been warned to stay away from chocolate, nuts, French fries, potato chips and soft drinks. There is absolutely no proof that these foods cause acne—or make it worse. If a person is allergic to any of the aforementioned foods, a skin problem may develop, but there is no scientific evidence that any food produces acne.

Another old wives' tale is that people who masturbate get acne. This is scare stuff. Pure baloney. Acne has nothing whatever to do with sexual activity.

As far back as when I was a teenager (and that's *way* back) teenage boys tried to convince girls that having sex was good for the complexion and *not* having sex was bad for the complexion. It was a popular selling point, but no girl who had any sense bought it. Another myth is that girls who have acne should not wear makeup. I checked this out with five fellow board members of the Dermatology Foundation. They all agreed that makeup on a girl with acne, provided, of course, she keeps her face clean, will not make her acne worse.

Acne is an inflammatory condition of the skin involving those areas where the oil glands are the most active and numerous. A definite connection exists between acne and the hormones. For this reason young girls with acne suffer with it most just before their menstrual periods.

Most acne occurs between ages fourteen and twenty-four; however, it can show up anywhere from the first year of life to the mid-fifties—and in a very severe form.

Usually the eruption shows up around the nose, on the cheeks, spreading to the forehead and chin. It often appears on the neck, around the ears, on the back and chest. The earlier treatment is sought, the less chance for permanent skin damage.

Teenagers who suffer from acne often become self-conscious and despondent. I urge them not to try to treat themselves. For one thing, not all skin eruptions are acne and a diagnosis should be made by a skin specialist. Anyone who thinks he has acne should make an appointment with the family doctor or a dermatologist.

Acne is not contagious. For mild cases, simply keeping the face very clean will solve the problem. Stubborn and unsightly cases of acne can be treated with antibiotics (pills or shots), steroids (salves and injections). The medication must be prescribed by a physician and taken under his supervision. For severe cases, ultraviolet ray, cryotherapy (freezing technique) and X-ray treatment may be recommended. Exposure to the sun for limited periods of time can also be helpful.

Avoid "sure cures" advertised in newspapers and magazines. Hygiene is important in treating acne but there is no evidence that special soaps will cure the disease. Squeezing the bumps can irritate the skin and spread infection, so *keep your hands off*. Opening the pimples, blackheads and boils should be done in a special manner with sterile instruments by trained, professional hands.

The aftermath of acne can be devastating. Sometimes deep pits and scars remain. These pits and scars can be greatly diminished by a peeling treatment given by a skin specialist. Or, in some instances where the scarring and pitting are severe, a technique called dermabrasion can be extremely helpful. Sandpaper is used on an electrically controlled wheel and several layers of the skin are removed. This can be done under a local anesthetic in a doctor's office or, if a general anesthetic is used, in a hospital. Only a specialist who is skilled at this technique should be engaged to do it. If you do not know a dermatologist who does dermabrasion, phone your County Medical Society.

This technique is somewhat painful but well worth the discomfort if the desired results are obtained. For about two weeks the skin will be fiery red and then it becomes pinkish. Finally in about a month or five weeks a healthy, normal skin color appears and the pitting and scarring may be greatly reduced or completely gone.

Before you consider this procedure, ask the skin specialist if you can see some of his former patients who have had it done. As with anything else, a botched job will cause much dissatisfaction and endless complaining. When well done, the individuals are extremely pleased and will be happy to encourage others to undergo this surgery.

CREDIT: *Robert Stolar (M.D. Dermatology), Washington, D.C., and information from the American Academy of Dermatology, Inc.*

Acupuncture

Question posed by Arthur Taub, M.D., Ph.D., Professor, Clinical Director, Section for the Study and Treatment of Pain at Yale University School of Medicine: "Did acupuncture relieve you of your problem?"

Answer: "No. It just relieved me of my money."

Acupuncture is the ancient Chinese practice of piercing the nerves with needles to relieve pain. It is also used as an "anesthetic" for patients undergoing surgery. Acupuncture has been credited by Chinese physicians with "curing many diseases and psychological disorders" although there is no clinical evidence to support these claims.

Hundreds of American physicians have traveled to the People's Republic of China since Richard M. Nixon's historic visit in February 1972. While some American physicians reported favorably on some aspects of Chinese medicine, the majority came away highly skeptical of the claims made by their Chinese colleagues regarding acupuncture.

Missionaries, traders, physicians and other travelers brought knowledge about acupuncture to Europe as early as the seventeenth century. At that time, the reporting physicians recommended acupuncture for the treatment of arthritis, gout and rheumatism. And, in fact, it is for these diseases, still today, especially in Japan, that acupuncture is recommended.

On July 9, 1974, a sixteen-member delegation of the American Medical Association entered the People's Republic of China. I was a member of that delegation. We were guests of the Chinese Medical Society, and as such, were treated as dignitaries and permitted to visit hospitals in eight major cities as well as a number of rural medical installations.

After three weeks of studying medical care in the People's Republic of China, a statement on acupuncture prepared by the delegation was transmitted from Hong Kong via telephone to the American Medical Association headquarters in Chicago. It read as follows:

"Acupuncture is to be regarded as experimental medicine, legal in the United States only in investigational settings in the hands of licensed physicians, dentists and research scientists. Acupuncture should not be permitted to become a new kind of quackery in the Western world, used for exploitation of the public.

"Acupuncture as a method of reducing pain perception during surgery is used in less than 15 percent of Chinese major surgery and presents features which should be further studied since it may reduce some complications of surgery, but its widespread use in Western surgery seems highly unlikely.

"Acupuncture as treatment for a wide range of common medical complaints has been in use for thousands of years. It has not produced satisfactory results in past treatment and there is no scientific evidence to show that anything has changed in present treatment. Every effort should be made to guard against the conversion of acupuncture into a new kind of quackery in the Western world. In China, acupuncture is not practiced for money. In our Western society, it should not become a technique for exploitation of the public."

When we returned from the People's Republic of China I wrote a series of articles which reflected my views of various aspects of the trip. Here is the column on acupuncture. It appeared on September 5, 1974:

"Today I saw it for the first time. As a delegate of the American Medical Association, I witnessed an operation performed under acupuncture. It was a thyroidectomy. The patient was a woman, age thirty-four. She had one needle between each thumb and index finger, and one in each wrist, all connected to an electric stimulator. The operating room was not air-conditioned, it was mid-July, and the patient was perspiring profusely. A nurse periodically mopped the patient's face with a damp cloth. Although I was dressed in surgical garb and mask, they allowed me to carry a fan—the same one I had used the previous day when we visited a pigsty in a commune.

"I was standing less than a foot from the patient's head and proceeded to fan her. She gave me a pleasant smile and said in Chinese, 'Thank you very much.' I asked her if she felt any pain. She replied, 'No, just a little numb.'

"Dr. Claude Welch, the distinguished surgeon from Massachusetts General

Hospital in Boston, and former president of the American College of Surgeons, said the goiter was very large and the surgical team was doing a fine job."

We witnessed other acupuncture operations, however, one of which did not go so well. The patient was having part of her lung removed. Dr. M. T. Pepper Jenkins of Southwestern Medical School and Parkland Memorial Hospital in Dallas and former president of the American Society of Anesthesiologists stood at the elbow of the doctor in charge of monitoring the electro-acupuncture equipment. When the pleural cavity was opened, allowing the lung to collapse, since it was not supported by positive-pressure breathing as is usually done by an anesthesiologist, it became apparent that the patient was in serious trouble. She developed an ominous cardiac arrhythmia (irregularity) and began to turn blue. Dr. Jenkins immediately became part of the team. He helped administer the oxygen. With him continuing this support throughout the operation, the patient survived in good shape, though it was a close call. Dr. Jenkins felt that this patient had come to the hospital only the day before and had not been adequately indoctrinated. She was unprepared for the use of acupuncture preceding and during the operation. The patient failed to experience a reduction of pain through the acupuncture administered her. Dr. Jenkins felt that had the Americans not been in the operating room the Chinese anesthesiologist would have changed his plans from acupuncture anesthesia to Western or chemical anesthesia even before the operation started.

I also wrote: "Much has been written about acupuncture as the new miracle anesthesia. The members of our delegation agreed unanimously that it has merit in selected cases, but they believe acupuncture is more of an analgesic (pain reducer) than an anesthetic, and it is not likely to become widely used in Western surgery.

"Dr. Michael DeBakey, the distinguished heart surgeon from Houston, pointed out when he visited the People's Republic several months ago that fewer than one third of the surgical patients are suitable candidates for acupuncture. They must be stoic in nature, have a suggestible bent of mind (in the same sense that some people are suitable subjects for hypnosis) and they must be in reasonably good physical condition.

"It should be remembered that acupuncture has been used as a 'cure' in China for centuries, but as an anesthetic it has been in use only since 1958. Moreover, it was virtually discontinued in 1960 when Liu Shao-ch'i and other counter-revisionists deemed it 'unscientific and of no practical value.' In 1966, Mao Tse-tung ordered the technique revived and used in all hospitals and rural areas.

"The Chinese physicians with whom we spoke made no extravagant claims. They told us they use acupuncture for surgery in only about 15 percent of their major operations. 'How does it happen that you have six going on this morning?' asked Dr. John Cowan, former Navy admiral, now AMA's director of international medicine. 'Because you American doctors are visiting us,' was the frank reply.

"The only time we felt the Chinese enthusiasm greatly exceeded any possibility of reality was in their use of acupuncture in an attempt to cure congenital nerve deafness. We visited a school for deaf and mute children who were adorable. The electrical gadgets and other paraphernalia used in conjunction with acupuncture were presented as 'deaf cures.' Although our delegation saw no evidence at all, and no audiometric verification of any success in reversing nerve deafness, we were impressed with the talent and high esprit de corps of the teachers in this school. Their great progress in treating the children may be due to the high motivation which they instilled.

"Dr. Jay Arena, the world-famous pediatrician from Duke University, said, 'There is a possibility that a child whose hearing has been damaged might be helped somewhat by nerve stimulation, but to date, there is no way that a child born deaf can be made to hear with acupuncture treatments or anything else.'"

Arthur Taub, M.D. (identified at the beginning of this piece), went to the People's Republic of China as a member of the Acupuncture Study Group in May of 1974. He wrote in a book called *The Health Robbers* (published by George F. Stickley Co.) the following:

"Acupuncture has not merely failed to demonstrate significant benefits, it has in some instances been extremely dangerous. Needles, up to one foot in length, are sometimes inserted deep into the body. Serious harm may result when they penetrate vital structures.

"In one case of back pain and burning around the mouth and vagina, needles were inserted through the skin of the chest. The lung was penetrated. It collapsed, filling the chest cavity with almost a pint of blood. The patient required two weeks of hospitalization which was complicated by pneumonia."

Death from puncture of a coronary artery has been reported. Other reports mention puncture of the liver, spleen, bladder, kidneys and the pregnant uterus.

Since classical Chinese medicine does not recognize that germs cause disease, acupuncture needles need not be sterilized. Lack of sterile technique can cause bacterial infections. In China today, acupuncture needles are stored in alcohol solutions. Since alcohol does not kill the virus which causes infectious hepatitis, contaminated needles can spread this serious infection from patient to patient.

Some acupuncture needles are poorly made and tend to break. One scientist suffered excruciating pain when during an acupuncture experiment the needle broke off in his foot. An operation was performed to remove the needle.

According to Dr. Taub, many American physicians who practice acupuncture in the United States are not adequately trained in acupuncture or in medicine. They have attended "quickie" courses lasting only a few days. Chiropractors are taking these courses in large numbers. (A distinguished physician who read Dr. Taub's statement said "Since acupuncture is mainly hokum, it would be impossible to outline any course of instruction that would be of value. Some boards of registration in medicine are being asked to do this and it is an impossible task.")

One chiropractor who travels around the country teaching "quickie" courses was asked, according to Dr. Taub, "How long would it take to obtain a working knowledge of acupuncture?" The reply, "I can teach you all you need to know in ten minutes."

CREDIT: *Ann Landers. Reviewed by Claude E. Welch, M.D., Clinical Professor of Surgery Emeritus, Harvard Medical School and Senior Surgeon, Massachusetts General Hospital, and M. T. Jenkins, M.D., Chairman, Department of Anesthesiology, University of Texas, Parkland Memorial Hospital.*

Adolescence

According to psychoanalyst Erik Erikson, the major task of the adolescent and the most fervent wish of his parents is that he "become someone." Adolescence is a period of Becoming Somebody. This must be thought of as a continuing process. Like all processes, it sometimes moves in jerks, spurts and bursts and "gets stuck" at various plateaus. It must be viewed as a whole so that the adolescent can both endure and enjoy this turbulent period.

HEALTHY INDEPENDENCE

Actually, becoming somebody develops in steps. The first is the struggle to achieve healthy independence. This is not rebellion. It is only rebellion when the independence overreaches itself. For independence to be healthy it must be achieved with the support of the parents. But parents sometimes are reluctant to realize how they can contribute to this normal growth process.

They seldom realize how they hold on too long and too tightly. The dilemma lies in the fact that no one can tell a parent the proper degree of holding nor can they tell at what pace independence should be achieved. This is where the parents and the adolescent have to reach their own delicate balance of holding and letting go.

This also is a time when the adolescent is achieving his own delicate balance. In a sense he uses his parents as a rock to swirl around. It's not that he wants his parents to give up their parental roles. He wants them to hold firm

—to be the kind of persons one can both leave and return to. He needs the firmness that his parents represent. He needs the strength he derives from what they value and believe.

Researchers estimate that for each twenty years since 1900, adolescence has occurred about one year earlier. This means parents must be prepared for an earlier beginning for the kinds of struggles we are talking about.

TWELVE RULES FOR RAISING DELINQUENT CHILDREN

(1) Begin with infancy to give the child everything he wants. He will then grow up to believe the world owes him a living.

(2) When he picks up bad words, laugh. This will make him think he's cute. It will also encourage him to pick up cuter phrases that will blow off the top of your head later.

(3) Never give him any religious training. Wait until he is 21 and then let him decide for himself. (Don't be surprised if he decides to be "nothing.")

(4) Avoid the use of the word "wrong." It might develop a guilt complex. This will condition him to believe later, when he is arrested for shoplifting or stealing a car, that society is against him and he is being persecuted.

(5) Pick up everything he leaves lying around—his books, shoes and clothing. Do everything for him so he will become experienced in throwing all responsibility on others.

(6) Let him read any printed matter he can lay his little hands on. Make sure the silverware and glasses are sterilized but allow his mind to feast on garbage.

(7) Have plenty of knockdown, drag-out fights in the presence of your children. Then, after you are divorced, they will not be surprised.

(8) Give the child all the spending money he wants. Never let him earn his own. Why should HE have things as tough as YOU had them?

(9) Satisfy his every craving for food, drink and comfort. See to it that every sensual desire is gratified. Childhood should be FUN! Denial may lead to harmful frustration.

(10) Take his part against neighbors, playmates, friends, teachers and policemen. They are all prejudiced against your child.

(11) When he gets into real trouble apologize for yourself by saying, "I never could do a thing with him."

(12) Prepare for a life of grief. You are apt to have it.

CREDIT: *Houston Police Department, Houston, Texas.*

THE STRUGGLE

How does the adolescent express his desire for healthy independence? One way is by denying what his parents believe in. Again this is done, in part, for the purpose of struggle, for conflict. Sometimes the parents deal with the rejection of their standards and beliefs by abandoning the adolescent. To do this overlooks the fact that the very purpose of emancipation is struggle. The adolescent *must* have something to struggle *against* or struggle *with*. Parents must realize this struggle is uncomfortable not only for them, but for their teenagers as well.

One common way the teenager expresses emancipation is by making full use of his peer group. The tough part, as far as the parents are concerned, is that there are times when the adolescent values his peers more than he values his parents—times when the standards and beliefs of the group are more important than the standards and beliefs he grew up with.

This period is both necessary and temporary. Parents must realize, however, that for a period of time they will not be heard to the extent that the group is heard.

At this time the task of the parents is survival—and I can say with assurance that most parents do survive their children's adolescence. The main thing to be aware of, when peer groups are so important, is that the role of the parents is a difficult one. It requires patience and fortitude and an awareness that their patience and fortitude will pay off—that the child will return to them stronger and more mature.

The adolescent has to be able to achieve the developmental process of becoming a young adult within the group. He cannot do it in a vacuum. He cannot do it without experimentation. He cannot do it without risks. The group is, in a sense, a tool for achieving the kind of role the adolescent eventually will occupy within his own society. And of course, it has to be a mixed sex group.

One must be able to take risks and experiment with relationships with the opposite sex, as well as with one's own sex. It is hoped that out of the group comes the recognition of the value of other points of view coming from one's own equals, not from authority or from authority with whom one struggles.

Still another way the adolescent attempts this task of emancipation is by searching for identification. Teenagers search about for ideals. Usually these ideals are not just persons, they also can be causes. They search for ways in which to invest themselves. The young person is asking bluntly, "What can I get out of life?" And he is asking this in a specific, non-selfish sense. This is a question about ideals, causes, people, identification. The adolescent, in essence, is asking, "What *can* I or what *may* I contribute to life?"

STANCES

Part of the parental dilemma and frustration arises because these questions are accompanied by some normal and sometimes trying attitudes. I want to stress how common they are so you can view them with more understanding.

One of the most common stances adolescents take is that of *asceticism*. Probably at no other time in life does the genuine internal meaning of what is going on in other people, or in other areas of the world, have as much impact and as much growth potential as it does in adolescence. Incidentally, the asceticism they experience at this time is idealistic. This idealism is common during adolescence and is the reason why so many teenagers paint and never paint again or write poetry and never write poetry again. It is because they are using this ascetic, idealistic stance as a way of *temporarily* coping with some of the drives they must learn to handle.

Another frustrating stance the teenager takes is one of extreme *intellectualism*. This often is one of the most difficult for parents because, as adults, we often don't learn quite as fast as we used to or as fast as the adolescent. At this time nothing the parents say is bright enough, nothing they do is clever enough and no amount of understanding they have matches the understanding "other people" have. It helps if one recognizes that this is an adolescent search for the best one can achieve intellectually and, although it can be frustrating to the parents, to the adolescent it is very meaningful.

A third stance that poses still more problems occurs as the adolescent struggles with his feelings of *inadequacy* or *inferiority*. This again is normal and usually transient. The adolescent needs to learn humility but sometimes he goes to extremes. At times these feelings are expressed in a fourth and very distressing stance—*transient depression*. This depression is genuine although time-limited. It is an expression of a number of things the adolescent struggles with as he tries to understand what is going on about him.

A final stance the adolescent uses might be called a *counter-phobic attack*. This attitude in essence says, "There's nothing I think I can't do; there's nothing I don't want to try." Again one must remember that this is a temporary character style that has validity, although it may be difficult to see at the time. The purpose of this stance is to see what happens to problems if one throws himself into them and this, too, is a normal part of the learning experience.

PREPARING FOR A VOCATION

The first part of learning to become someone is through emancipation. The second part is achieved by visualizing and deciding on a vocation—then doing something to prepare for it. The second way an adolescent becomes somebody is to learn the value of work. There is no way to avoid this. Many adolescents attempt to postpone it as long as possible, but eventually he or she must come to grips with the inevitable.

Teenagers like to feel that the world is an available area in which they can do or be whatever they'd like. For a period of time, and to an extent, this is a healthy, useful view. But eventually choices must be made.

The value of work for the adolescent lies in the fact that work brings about a much tighter amalgamation of thinking and acting. But work serves still another purpose. If well chosen, it serves as self-realization for the adolescent. Many adolescents exasperate their parents because they go off in a hundred directions at once. It's not always easy to handle a daughter who wants to be an actress today, a model tomorrow, a biochemist the next day and a philosopher the next. Parents must leave open the extent of these choices so that the adolescent feels that his or her choice can lead to self-realization; that there is a *fit* between him and his choice.

IDEOLOGIES

Still another way the adolescent becomes somebody is by achieving an ideology which may not be the same as that of the parents. The adolescent needs a devotion, not in the religious sense. He needs a devotion to causes— to individuals. Often it is a devotion to faith, but remember, the important part isn't the faith—it's the devotion, the ideology. It's a way of life, a world view he is building within himself.

There's a fascinating fact that accompanies this concept—a fact that most of us have forgotten about our own adolescence. If one is free to choose an ideology, one must also be free to repudiate other ideologies. And sometimes the things that are being repudiated are dear to the hearts and feelings and beliefs of parents. One must not forget that the adolescent is trying to strike a balance between his inner feelings and outer reality.

LOVE RELATIONSHIPS

A final way one goes about becoming somebody is by achieving a mutual stable, satisfactory love relationship—a relationship not achieved through imposition but developed by including the other person in the experience.

Incidentally, it's quite normal for the adolescent to be interested in his own self—in his own body. At no other time in our lives are we as acutely aware of ourselves physically as during adolescence. I spent three weeks with one adolescent girl working on a very important issue—whether her one eye was level with the other. Of course it was, and the issue could have been settled by standing in front of a mirror and looking. Naturally it wasn't.

Part of achieving a satisfactory, stable, mutual, loving relationship is that it also has to be chosen and developed within reality, not fantasy. And it cannot be achieved solely through defiance, which is not love. It has to include the ability to sustain frustration as well as gratification. It has to include the experience of mutual growth and mutual achievement. And it has to include the ability to love someone other than oneself.

However, in these developing relationships, one must leave room for error. I am reminded of the ninety-year-old man who was asked, "If you had your life to live over, would you make the same mistakes again?" And he answered, "Yes, but I'd make them sooner."

The point is that adolescence is a fine time for experimentation—for making mistakes as part of the developmental process. And if parents realize there are going to be mistakes, they will be ahead of the game.

THE FAMILY

Accomplishing the tasks of *becoming somebody* can best be done in the context of the family structure for several important reasons. The first is that the family usually represents a dependable set of relationships. In other words these people—this family group, this clan—have learned to depend on each other. They have learned to live with each other. They have learned that there are certain things that one gives and certain things that one takes.

There are no perfect successes in this world, but neither are there any perfect failures. This also relates to dependability. No family is totally dependable. No family is totally consistent. No family is totally reliable. What one needs to know is that, *in the majority of cases,* the dependability is there.

Probably the best reason so much of the work of becoming an adult is done within the family is that it is within the family structure that argument, hostility and aggression can best be tolerated. Learning to become an adult is learning to deal with one's aggression, one's anger, one's hostility. In a sense, the adolescent fears these feelings within himself, and he struggles with them. He has to experience the give and the take. He has to experience how hostility is dealt with and faced. It is the family's responsibility to handle the inevitable hostilities and aggressions.

THE SOCIAL WORLD

The adolescent must be given the opportunity to discover his or her own motivations and learn that the concept of responsibility includes responsibility for others. Unfortunately, there is no solution to the ambiguities in this world. Things are never clear. There is no such thing as totally good or totally bad. The idea that ambiguity must be tolerated, that compromise does not corrupt but is a structure upon which one lives, is an important lesson to learn.

What is the adolescent striving for in the world today? The first is to learn that the life process doesn't start at twelve and end at nineteen, but that it has a beginning and a following. There are certain things one achieves during adolescence and one of these achievements is learning to continue the life process with vigor, with confidence and self-esteem.

Remember, one has to look at the total functioning of the adolescent. So often parents decide that some behavior is bad because it makes them uncomfortable. But one must look for the preponderance of the favorable over the unfavorable to assess the ultimate outcome.

I would like to end with something by Hillel. Hillel lived about two thousand years ago and was a prophet struggling with his conflict with the affluent decadent Rome of his day. This is what he had to say and this is what adolescents today are saying to you and me: "Be of the disciples of Aaron, loving peace and pursuing it. Loving one's fellow creatures and, in doing so, in loving them, bringing them nigh unto the Torah."

Hillel also said: "He who aggrandizes his name loses it. He who does not increase his knowledge decreases it. He who does not seek to acquire wisdom forfeits his life. And he who makes unworthy use of the crown of learning is wasting his powers."

CREDIT: *Dr. J. Cotter Hirschberg, M.D., William C. Menninger Professor of Psychiatry at the Menninger Foundation, Topeka, Kansas.*

How to Tell a Child He Is Adopted

There have been more changes in adoption in the past few decades than in any other aspect of childraising.

Immediate family and close friends should certainly be told about the adoption. With acquaintances, it is appropriate when something comes up that is related, but I do not believe it is necessary to talk about it compulsively—telling every teacher, etc. This is just as foolish as trying to keep it a secret.

All adopted children must be told that they are adopted. But in order to figure out the "how" and the "when," it may be helpful to have a little background on this subject.

During the nineteenth century people believed that how a human being "turned out" was almost entirely based on heredity. Adoption, therefore, was a risky business because it was impossible to know in advance what inborn traits a child might have. The fact of adoption was kept a secret. Families went to great lengths not to let *anybody* know, least of all the child. Parents lived with considerable anxiety about whether or not their adopted child would turn out to have good traits or bad ones. Under such circumstances adoption was not very popular.

In the twentieth century, because of the work of Dr. Sigmund Freud, there emerged a vast new field of psychology. It caused a major revolution in attitudes. Heredity was no longer considered important; instead the experts on childraising insisted that everything depended on environment—whether or not a child grew up to be a happy, decent, successful adult depended almost entirely on how he was treated.

People now felt more confident about adopting children, adoption agencies began to flourish and an entirely different approach to adoption emerged. For the past fifty years adoption experts have urged parents to tell the child he or she is adopted as soon as the child could understand—surely by the age of three or four. A number of children's books appeared to help parents tell the story of adoption. It was considered essential to keep the records of the adoption secret to protect the rights of the biological parents, but it was felt that the child could be helped to make an excellent adjustment to this fact of life, so long as he or she felt totally loved and accepted by adoptive parents.

I became an adoptive parent in 1950, at the peak of this period of thought. I also met with groups of adoptive parents and I wrote a pamphlet on the subject. Since my professional field was child psychology, I was greatly influenced by the emphasis on environment. If my husband and I were understanding, sensitive parents (I was sure we would be) our adopted child would never have any problems about being adopted.

We began using the words "chosen" and "adopted" when our daughter was about two and a half years old. We read her the stories. We brought up the subject frequently. We made no secret of this fact with anybody. What happened to us happened to thousands of other adoptive parents. We were to learn that we had greatly oversimplified a very complex situation.

It was not difficult to adopt children during those years and the adoption field flourished. The agencies told all the parents that whether or not their children were well adjusted depended on parental attitudes and behavior. By the time most of our children were ten and twelve years old, a great many of us knew that our simple-minded optimism contained a great many flaws.

We found that many adopted children became increasingly disturbed by the knowledge that at some point in their history they had been given away. In those days, out-of-wedlock births were still considered something decent people could not talk about. We avoided that issue and told our children that their biological parents loved them and wanted what was best for them, but could not take care of them. When our children were very young all they wanted to hear and all they could understand is how they came to be our children. But by the age of five or six many of these well-informed children began to wonder why they had been given away. Because there was nothing in their experience or level of understanding to handle the "real" problems, they assumed there had been something wrong with them. That is the way young children think. If anything goes wrong which they cannot understand, they feel responsible because their experience in living is so limited.

Child guidance clinics and individual therapists gradually realized that a disproportionate number of their clients were adopted children, and that in most cases their parents did not seem different from most other parents. It was hard to blame their behavior for the child's problems.

What we all learned was that first of all, heredity and environment are of equal importance and secondly, that many children were far from delighted to learn that they had been given away. Tense, sensitive, high-strung children tended to be upset, while more placid, easygoing children seemed far less troubled, irrespective of how well the subject of adoption was handled. We have learned that while it is necessary for this information to be given, and that children must learn the facts from their parents and not casually and unexpectedly from others, some serious thought must be given to the best possible time. Many of us now feel that while a child ought to know he or she is adopted and that the truth should never be avoided, it is a good idea to study a child's nature and to postpone giving a great many details to sensitive, worrying children until a child is six or seven years old and has a solid foundation of security and identity.

Children are influenced by how their parents feel about themselves. If parents feel they have failed because they cannot have biological children, the adopted children see themselves as "second-best." If, for example, a child says, "I wish I had been born to you," parents can be most helpful by agreeing that they understand and share such feelings, and will be glad to talk openly about it—but that their feelings about the child are as genuine and loving as if the child had been born to them. Parenting is raising a child, not merely conceiving one.

We now assume that to some degree, most adopted children will inevitably have some feelings of having been abandoned and rejected and that these feelings can be handled more easily and successfully if the child has had a few years of happy and successful living before having to deal with this fact of life.

There have been other dramatic changes in adoption. In the past it was not too difficult to adopt an infant and to carefully match the child to the adoptive parents in terms of background and appearance. The advent of the pill, the availability of legal and safe abortions and the changing social attitudes about children born out of wedlock (more single mothers are keeping their babies) have sharply reduced the number of children available for adoption. As a result, when couples want to adopt a child they now must consider taking older children, children with physical or psychological problems, or children of mixed races or foreign background. All this has lead to healthy new attitudes. Young adoptive parents today seem to be prepared to accept and deal with hereditary factors as influencing a child's personality. They feel comfortable about giving children the realistic reason why most adoptions are possible—that the biological parents were unmarried and not prepared for a wide variety of reasons to raise a child.

Adopted children are now far less likely to be preoccupied with the idea that there was something wrong with them and that they were rejected. White parents adopting a black or partially black child, or a Korean or Vietnamese child, know that they will have to deal with heredity directly and openly. Parents who adopt older children and children with special problems know that they may need professional guidance and they do not feel guilty or that they are failures as parents if there are aspects of adoption with which they need help.

There are some things about adoption that have *not* changed. It is still important to remember that very young children are confused by facts because their fantasies are still more real to them. We told our three-year-old that a lady brought her to us on an airplane when she was a tiny baby. We also explained how babies are born. She drew a picture of a plane, with a uterus in the middle containing a baby and a social worker. All this confusion meant we should be prepared to repeat the facts many, many times.

In many families there are adopted as well as biological children. This has become increasingly true as young parents decide to have one or two children and then adopt several others who need loving care.

All brothers and sisters have feelings of rivalry which may be intensified in such situations. But the answer to this question which was told to me in the mid-fifties seems as valid today as it was then. A mother heard her children fighting in the living room. The biological children were saying the parents loved them more; the adopted children yelled that at least they were chosen. Mother came in, told each of the four children to go out of the room, into different rooms in the house. Then she called them back, one by one, and ended up on the sofa, hugging them all. "Here we are together," she said. "A family. What difference does it make which door you came through to get here?"

What also remains unchanged is that adolescence is a time of upheaval and uncertainty. All teenagers wonder about who they are and who they will become, and the fact of adoption may sometimes accentuate the more painful aspects of this self-searching. It is not an appropriate time to allow a child to go in search of his or her biological parents. The child is too young to make sound judgments about a natural but complicated wish, one which may lead to disastrous results. It is a time to share and talk and understand—and if necessary, see that a young person gets special help in understanding that feelings of insecurity, rebellion against parents, wild swings in mood are all a part of adolescence and may have little or nothing to do with being adopted.

What today's adoptive parents must face is that one of the most dramatic changes to take place in the past ten or fifteen years has to do with the rights of adopted adults and/or their biological parents to search for each other if they wish to do so. It seems to me that this has occurred for two major reasons. The first is the general concern with human rights for those who feel disenfranchised, particularly black people and women, and the second is that because we live in a time of confusion and danger, there is a great hunger to find one's identity in biological roots.

My personal opinion (and that of Ann Landers) is that searching for one's roots is more than likely to create additional problems, in most cases. It seems to me that the most constructive help adoptive parents can give if this issue should arise is to point out all the hazards and to encourage the adult child to examine his or her psychological motives. Then, if that does not prove to be a sufficient deterrent, make it clear that the adoptive parents do not feel threatened by this need, and do not view it as a failure on their part, and that they will give loving support and understanding whatever the decision may be.

With all of these changes, certain things remain fundamental truths in all human relationships—adoption included. These are: being honest with one's children, allowing for the expression of real feelings, encouraging each child to fulfill his own unique interests and talents, offering loving guidance when children experience the normal failures and problems of growing up, and not feeling guilty, because no parent can be perfect.

CREDIT: *Eda J. LeShan, author of* You and Your Adopted Child, *Public Affairs Pamphlet, No. 274.*

Adoption
of the Retarded Child

In many states over 25 percent of the children available for adoption are labeled as mentally retarded. Retardation describes a wide range of achievement, from those who are simply slow learners to those profoundly retarded individuals who need extensive support and training to perform even the most basic tasks.

What kinds of people adopt the retarded? Often they have relatives or neighbors who are retarded and have learned to look beyond the label to see individuals who need the support, warmth and strength that a family environment can provide. For many, seeing the gradual but satisfying progress made by the retarded child is an extremely rewarding experience.

Couples who place a high value on human life often recognize that a child's handicap is only a superficial distraction which may mask basic abilities to learn and to love.

Adopting a retarded child should never be a "second choice" for a family unable to find a "normal" child. It is essential that the child feel that he or she was chosen by parents fully prepared for the special responsibilities of raising a retarded child.

How do parents choose a retarded child? Often families "fall in love" with a child after seeing a videotape, photograph, or reading a case history. It is important that families, in consultation with adoption case workers, carefully discuss special schooling arrangements, medical care, financial assistance or any other necessary support.

Qualities demanded of parents who have adopted a retarded child include patience, a sense of humor, flexibility and openness.

Parents should discuss their plans fully with any other children.

Adoption workers often point to "the need to be needed" as the motivation most expressed by parents. Parents adopt retarded children to meet their own human needs, not just those of the child.

Some resources available to parents faced with the critical decision of adopting a retarded child are:

Adopting Children with Special Needs, a brochure available from the North American Council on Adoptable Children, 6 Madison Avenue, Ossining, New York 10562.

The Council on Adoptable Children, 2 Park Avenue, New York, New York 10016, (212) 889-7720, has lists of various state and local adoption groups that can provide information and support.

North American Center on Adoption, 67 Irving Place, New York, New York 10003.

One major question asked by couples considering adoption of a retarded child is: "What will happen to this child if he or she is not adopted?" For some, only large, more impersonal institutions are available. For others, a growing national network of small, community-based family-like homes will provide care. In addition, many family-care or foster families provide a home for retarded children, adolescents and adults.

It is essential that a family make this difficult decision out of knowledge, confidence and caring, not out of sympathy or guilt.

Parents can be encouraged by the increasing availability of early education and special educational programs in the public school system. No longer do parents of most retarded children have to rely on special and often distant schools for education.

The national emphasis on education for all children and on "mainstreaming" and including the retarded child in local recreational, educational and other services are positive signs that retarded children can be accepted members of society; they can be provided with the right to education, to interact with other children and to live in a regular family environment.

How will other children react to having a retarded brother, sister or neighbor? How well a parent prepares the other children will play a large part in their welcoming the retarded child. Public attitudes are slow to change, and neighborhood children can occasionally be cruel. They should be confronted, educated and made aware of the special needs and abilities of the retarded child. In addition, schools should make every effort to make all students aware that retarded children are more like others than they are different.

What will happen to the retarded child when the parents die? Like the natural parents of the retarded child, the adopted parents face a painful question: "Will there be only institutions to care for my child?" The answer to this question varies considerably from state to state. Families should be aware of the quality and availability of long-term care institutions for the retarded, community residences and other services. Most importantly, families should make their adopted retarded child an active family member, not sheltered from relatives and friends. Their involvement with and acceptance of the retarded child are the greatest guarantee that concerned individuals will always be available for the retarded child.

CREDIT: *Paul R. Dolan, Executive Director, One to One, New York, New York.*

Trans-Racial Adoption

The practice of placing children for adoption regardless of race began in this country shortly after World War II when homeless Asian children were brought to the United States to be adopted primarily by Caucasian families. Then followed the Korean and Vietnam wars, when American couples either out of humanitarian concern or as a means of becoming parents were motivated to adopt orphans from those countries.

At the end of the Vietnam war, hundreds of children were airlifted to the United States, the majority of whom were adopted by white couples. The adoption of American black and Indian children by Caucasian families, beginning in Canada in the 1950s, gained momentum in the United States in the 1960s and early 1970s.

Since the middle 1950s there have been more white couples who want to adopt than there are healthy white infants available for adoption. On the other hand, the reverse has been obvious in regard to dependent black children and American Indian children. Eventually, the concern for these children, coupled with the growing recognition of their availability, by the white community, led to a movement on the part of adoption agencies and white couples which resulted in wide-scale trans-racial adoptions. While studies proved that black couples of similar socio-economic level adopted more readily than white couples, they were not adopting in sufficient numbers to meet the needs of dependent black children.

Trans-racial adoption is on the wane but most of the major adoption agencies still prefer a carefully chosen, well-prepared white family to foster care or institutionalization for minority children.

Adoption agencies are charged to consider the best interests of the child in planning for adoption. Generally it is believed that the ideal home for any child is one of his own racial and cultural group. If such a home is not available in a reasonable length of time, parents of another race, if they are emotionally stable and intelligent and attuned to his need for racial and cultural identity, are considered.

CREDIT: *Jane D. Edwards, Executive Director, Spence-Chapin Services to Families and Children, New York, and Loyce W. Bynum, Associate Executive Director, Spence-Chapin Services to Families and Children, New York.*

Adultery

DEAR ANN LANDERS: I'm in love with a married man. Our affair started innocently. I didn't mean for it to happen and neither did George.

He married a woman he didn't love because she became pregnant (on purpose to trap him, probably). They have been living like brother and sister since a year ago February. George made up his mind to get a divorce before he ever met me.

I am eager to marry this beautiful man but I don't want people to think I broke up his marriage. My reputation is important to me and I need to protect it. What do you suggest?

BROWN EYES

DEAR EYES: If the marriage is dead, and you don't want people to think you killed it, don't hang around the corpse.

Ask George to call you when he's free—and not before. But don't stand on one foot waiting for the phone to ring.

It is safe to say of adultery, as it is often said of the flu—there is a lot of it going around.

Not all adultery is as portrayed in the paperback novels—romantic and exciting. Much of it is shoddy and disappointing—a futile search for kicks, and quite sad. For many it is not a meal but a hunger.

A questionnaire filled out by 2,500 psychiatrists, judged wives in their thirties as the most adulterous. Husbands, they said, cheated more in their forties.

In response to the question "Why do married people cheat?" 41 percent said because their spouses were not "fun," congenial or compatible; 35 percent said because they wanted the experience of being with someone else—variety; 14 percent said they were hoping for a love-partner who would be more versatile—someone who might do something different than the same old thing. Only 7 percent listed good looks as the reason a married person climbed into a strange bed, and 3 percent of the adulterers questioned said they didn't know why they did it and would probably not do it again.

Some contend that adultery committed in the heart is as real as adultery committed in the flesh. Others suggest that a little discreet adultery (in judicious amounts) adds seasoning and strength to a marriage. Rationalizations abound whenever infidelity is discussed. For our purposes, we may accept the definition provided by psychiatrist Leon Salzman as "sexual behavior with other partners, either overt or covert, if married or unmarried people are exclusively committed to each other." This type of rationalization is quite common for the simple reason that it works so well. Like all defenses it enables people to reduce their feelings of anxiety or guilt while it provides justification for their behavior. Any reason is a good reason when it allows people to do as they please.

In the world of human relationships there is hardly anything that is truly casual. Interaction between two people cannot take place without making some impact or leaving some mark on one or both. This is a crucial truth about humans which must be understood in any discussion of adultery. People may insist it is good for you or bad for you but no one can claim it does not make any difference.

Neena O'Neill, co-author of *Open Marriage,* which became a handbook for experimental marital arrangements in the early seventies, turned toward the end of the decade to the necessity for fidelity in another book, *The Marriage Premise.* Adultery and fidelity are different sides of the coin of the relationship of husband and wife. There can hardly be a characteristic in one phenomenon that does not appear in the other; the quality of one's fidelity, whether flabby or robust, can be read in one's attitude toward adultery.

What constitutes adultery? Is it always destructive? The need for a careful reading of the complexities of human motivation is evident in attempting to answer these questions. It is possible that one can discover through adulterous behavior the first truly generous concern for another that the individual has ever experienced. It is possible that many marriages have never been marriages at all because the husband and wife have never been in touch with each other. Can adultery occur in the absence of a true commitment? Can one break a promise that was never mutually understood?

It is possible that adultery in these circumstances needs a new name because it is not the same as when a spouse, who knows what he or she is doing, deliberately violates a marriage vow. Between these two poles hang a thousand varieties of adulterous thoughts and actions.

Psychiatrist Bernard Greene (*A Clinical Approach to Marriage Problems,* C. C. Thomas, 1970) lists both conscious and unconscious reasons for infidelity. The conscious reasons are these:

(1) *Sexual frustration,* reported by 70 percent of the spouses and in a ratio of two males to one female, and the most common of the complaints in the 750 couples he studied.

(2) *Curiosity,* with a ratio of two males to three females and just over 50 percent of the spouses reporting it.

(3) *Revenge,* reported by 40 percent, equally divided between men and women.

(4) *Ennui,* defined as "monotonous, bored and tedious," again equally divided between the sexes.

(5) *Recognition seeking* ("I need an affair to make me feel like somebody special"), reported by 20 percent of the group, equally divided between husbands and wives.

The unconscious determinants of adultery are listed in this way:

(1) *Seeking "stroking" of the "inner child,"* a motivator of other behavior besides adultery but one usually hidden by the mask of rationalization.

(2) *Rage at partner or parent,* often the acting out of previously unresolved conflicts toward the parents and, therefore, unrelated to the spouse. Here the adultery is a symbol as well as an instrument of hurt.

(3) *Proof of masculinity or femininity.*

(4) *Expression of an immature personality.*

(5) A partner acting out an *"unconscious homosexual defense."*

Salzman approaches the complicated subject from a slightly different viewpoint, stating that the causes are interrelated and represent increasing degrees of alienation and a lack of involvement which may represent a character flaw in one of the partners. Or it may be an inability to make the relationship function properly because both are uncommitted and therefore unwilling or unable to make necessary compromises required in any stable and faithful relationship.

Obviously there is going to be more adultery than understanding of it in ordinary human experience. What is significant is the fact that it always has a meaning and that with counseling, its origins may be traced and its consequences seen more clearly. Decisions about the morality of infidelity depend on an ability to understand the psychological determinants as fully as possible. Only individuals who grasp the motivation of their actions can lay claim to moral choice.

Fidelity remains the cornerstone for a stable marriage and family life. A good marriage may survive the experience of adultery but only if the crisis causes the husband and/or wife to face up to and sort out the causes. Adultery may be understandable but in and of itself it is not a healthy seasoning for married life. Few subjects can be romanticized as successfully as adultery but it hardly stands as an example for mature choice. Adultery may be forgivable but some lessons should be learned from it because adultery can never be written off as inconsequential.

Adultery is a serious business because it centers on what, for most people, is their most important relationship, the one from which they must derive the meaning of their lives.

A question frequently posed is this: Should the adulterer confess to his or her spouse? Ann Landers, who because people expect from her a direct, nononsense answer, says *no*. In almost every instance I would agree with Ann. But let us examine this question closely, looking at the most important aspect —motivation.

Because the reasons for infidelity are so scrambled, so are the reasons for confession. The common reason, of course, is guilt. But guilt can be complicated. Psychiatrist Harold Winn sets forth a reasonable proposition. He says, "The person who wants to confess must ask himself why, if there is so much guilt, did it not prevent the infidelity in the first place?" As Dr. Winn points out, it is possible that the guilt and the relief of it may be part of a narcissistic game of doing bad, feeling remorse, confessing, then getting forgiveness, in order to repeat the manipulation over and over. Such people are game-players.

Confession may also be a means of expressing conscious or unconscious hostility. "Good for the soul" it may be, but it can also be extremely painful to the person on whom the "cleansing waters" are poured.

The adulterer who wants to "set everything straight" by telling all would be better advised to keep his mouth shut and work out his guilt by behaving in a more thoughtful, loving, considerate way and stay out of other beds in the future.

CREDIT: *Eugene Kennedy, Ph.D., author of* A Time for Being Human, *Chicago, Illinois: Thomas More Press.*

"SECRET MEETINGS"*

Ellie and Marvin
Have been having secret meetings twice a week
For the past six months
But have thus far failed to consummate their passion
Because
While both of them agree
That marital infidelity is not only unrealistic but irrelevant,
He has developed sharp shooting pains
In his chest, and she's got impetigo, and

* Copyright © 1974 by Judith Viorst.

He's got pink eye.
Ellie and Marvin
Drive forty miles to sneaky luncheonettes
In separate cars
But have thus far done no more than heavy necking
Because
She's developed colitis, and
He has developed these throbbing pains in his back, and
She has started biting her nails, and
He's smoking again.
Ellie and Marvin
Yearn to have some love in the afternoon at a Motor Hotel
But have thus far only had a lot of
Coffee
Because
He is convinced that his phone is being tapped, and
She is convinced that a man in a trench coat is following her, and
He says what if the Motor Hotel catches fire, and
She says what if she talks in her sleep some night, and
She thinks her husband is acting suspiciously hostile, and
He thinks his wife is acting suspiciously nice, and
He keeps cutting his face with his double-edged razor, and
She keeps closing her hand in the door of her car, so
While both of them agree that guilt is not only neurotic but also obsolete
They've also agreed
To give up
Secret meetings.

DISILLUSIONED "HUMANITARIAN"

DEAR ANN LANDERS: Your column is a postgraduate course in life. I wish there had been something like it when I was growing up. The young people who are reading you today are getting a wonderful education. Bless you, Ann.

Your answer to "Outside Looking In" was terrific. I'm an authority on the subject because my husband fooled around for nearly two years before I caught him. It was like a scene from Mary Hartman, Mary Hartman.

I went to a roadside motel to buy some pies. I ran smack into my husband, who was checking in. (It was Saturday afternoon and he was supposed to be fishing with the boys.) His lady friend was standing a few feet away. When I spotted them they nearly went through the floor.

My husband handed her some money and said, "Take a cab home." He then asked me to meet him at our house so we could talk. I agreed.

What an afternoon that was! He cried (I did, too) and he begged me to forgive him—swore he would never cheat on me again, would rather die than have me leave him. Our talk lasted five hours, and it really cleared the air.

The following morning the "mystery woman" phoned. She told me she was shocked to see me walking. My husband had told her I was in a wheel chair.

So you see, Ann, there's often a lot more to the eternal triangle than some people realize. The Other Woman was led to believe she was performing a "humanitarian service." Just sign me

MORE COMPASSIONATE NOW

DEAR MORE: Liars and cheats often work both sides of the streets—and sometimes the alleys. Thanks for the input. It's an added dimension to infidelity that most people don't think about.

PAINLESS ADULTERY

DEAR ANN LANDERS: You hear from so many crazy fools, I thought you might appreciate a letter from someone who is sane for a change. My story might also make some hysterical woman think twice before she takes extreme measures against a husband who is having a fling.

My wife learned from one of her "friends" that I was seeing a young lady in my office. When confronted, I admitted it and asked for time to get the young woman out of my system. My wife was very sensible and agreed to be patient.

For five months, I did my own thing. My wife never asked questions when I phoned to say I wouldn't be home for dinner. She didn't throw a fit when I was going away for the weekend.

One day, I decided my romance had run its string. I told my wife her mature behavior was most admirable and that I no longer was interested in the other woman. Our marriage is better than ever, and no one was hurt. I hope you will print this letter for all wives to read. GEMINI

DEAR G.: I have no good-conduct medals for the likes of you, Buster. Just because your wife didn't stick her head in the oven doesn't mean she wasn't deeply hurt.

Don't deceive yourself into believing your affair improved your marriage. Just consider yourself lucky your alley-catting didn't destroy it.

Aging

*How to Do It with Style**

Knowledge of life prevents one from becoming passionately concerned—from behaving madly over nothing.

Such a sense of proportion helps in accepting the thefts of time. One year, time steals a dear friend, the next, some lower teeth, and the following, a driver's license. Time steals from everyone and is not just picking on you.

Such thefts are unacceptable to the grasping. They tend to harp on the trivial. The elderly who can accept these losses bring with them the infection of courage. To be able to lack things gracefully—that's a prayer worth praying. In most books of spiritual direction, patience seems to get a good press.

It's a virtue worth cultivating for selfish reasons, if for no other. Patient people seem to have a better time.

While the elderly may enjoy various vocations, the one they share in common is that of giving courage to those who are still on the way. We all need models. Every old person can be a model to someone who will someday face the inconveniences of accumulated years.

To keep free of self-pity and bitterness means reminding yourself that the important thing is not so much what happens to you but how you feel about it. Learn to compensate. Put aside one aspect of life and turn to something still within range.

The voices and faces of old people give them away. They did not develop those overnight. All their lives they have been feeling sorry for themselves and blaming others for their plight. In old age they are the same as in youth, only more so. If they want to be looked upon as subjects rather than objects, they need to make themselves worthy of such regard. To be loved requires being somewhat lovable. Saints can love the unlovable, but there are not enough saints to go around.

Serenity and wholeness in a healthy, well-formed old age come when you sense that if you lead the life you should, everything will end well. This is a consolation, but there are no money-back guarantees. Part of being human is

* Edward Fischer, author of *Everybody Steals from God*. Excerpted from an article, "The Vocation of Aging." Reprinted with permission of *Notre Dame Magazine;* copyright © 1978 by The University of Notre Dame. Original copyright © 1978 by The Order of Saint Benedict, Collegeville, Minnesota, *Worship,* March 1978 issue.

learning to live with uncertainty. To have the courage of your doubts, as time runs out, may be more difficult than having the courage of your convictions.

The media specialize in hawking tragedies without putting them in perspective. Spinoza, who would never have been interviewed on the evening news, believed that tragedies are trivial things when seen in the perspective of eternity. Once you share that belief, troubles no longer diminish you. This insight is a grace that comes from spiritual resources beyond yourself, a comfort that can be the greatest gift of old age.

The elderly may find that their delayed vocations bring more delight than the ones they made a living by. They have reached the point in life when making full use of human faculties can be more important than making money. This new sense of purpose can give a great lift to the heart.

In retirement you need to face yourself afresh—have the courage to explore some other aspect of yourself. Try to find something you have left undone, some interest that got covered up over the years. Prove to yourself that you still have reserves, mental and physical.

Without a new vocation you might find yourself surviving rather than living. You might get the feeling that nothing in life requires your presence. The past has congealed, the present is dreary and the future is limited. So you freeze. You can learn something when you come upon someone who hoards life in this way instead of using it as an investment. Such people serve as examples of how dreary the clutched life can be. When you see the boredom that smothers them you may be jolted into doing something that you should have been doing all along.

Many people find out that they cannot endure retirement in the sense that they looked forward to it—leisure time, freedom from effort, uninterrupted loafing. They awaited the unencumbered years and dreamed of a long Indian summer with nothing to do. Suddenly such freedom is a burden. They need something to give direction to the day.

If these people see aging as a vocation it could give new meaning to life, a help to both body and soul. Dr. Victor E. Frankl, a professor of neurology and psychiatry at the University of Vienna, said as much. As a survivor of four concentration camps, including Auschwitz, he said the only prisoners who survived those dreadful experiences were the ones who managed to find some meaning in their existence. Those who could not find such meaning invariably died.

I learned of the needs of the elderly while writing a book, *Why Americans Retire Abroad*. Having heard that more than 300,000 Americans have retired overseas, I wondered why so many, so late in life, pull up their roots and try to transplant them in foreign soil. For the answer, I made several trips to Italy, Greece, England, Ireland, Portugal and Spain.

During the interviews, I learned the importance of getting ready psychologically for old age. There is no reason not to prepare the mind for it. It is not like death, standing at the elbow every minute, threatening an unannounced visit. Old age never comes suddenly.

When we speak of the need to get ready for old age, we usually mean financial readiness. We act as if someone who is without money problems has no problems at all. I met people who will never suffer a pang of hunger in the stomach but whose souls are painfully hungry. They have money to spend and time to spend it, but they lack the inner resources to spend either in a satisfying way.

To find an abiding interest that brings satisfaction, they seem to have a light with them. It is not exactly a joke, the story about the doctor saying of his patient, "She died of a retired husband."

Starting to study again is one way you can lift the heart. Classes are taught almost everywhere. Once you enroll in a class you might be surprised to find the mind more ready for an education in old age than it had been in youth. By now, you know more of what is important and what is not. Youth, with its retentive memory, is best for schooling; old age, with its understanding, is best for education. Old people used to avoid classes unless they were labeled Adult Education. Now it's common to find the elderly sitting among undergraduates.

Here are some examples of a few second careers: A retired businessman, long fascinated by animals, conducts tours at the zoo. He specializes in grade-school classes, helping the children develop a sense of wonder. A cavalry officer at age ninety-one is still teaching young people how to jump hunters in a horse show. A retired accountant took a course in income tax law and returned home to teach what he had learned to sixteen other accountants.

Much is written about how unfair our society is to the aged. But in many instances the aged are unfair to themselves. Society cannot make you a dignified, interesting person. It is something you must do for yourself—like getting your own haircut—nobody can do it for you.

Living with dignity means living with the grain and not going against the grain. Old age is part of being human. By refusing to accept it, you deny your humanity.

Anyone who sees aging as a vocation can agree with Bernard Berenson, who in his eighty-second year wrote in his journal: "There is a certain sweetness in being what one is now—not reduced but contracted—so appreciative, so enjoying, so grateful for what has been, and for what is now. It means something to be able to rise above aches and pains and inertias, and to find glory in the world."

Agoraphobia

(*Fear of Leaving the House*)

FROM FEAR TO RECOVERY

DEAR ANN LANDERS: I am writing in the hope of reaching "Housebound" and others who are afraid of crowds, other people, and have a host of fears that can't be described.

My life was good. I had every human comfort. There was no logical reason for me to have attacks of panic. But for a long time I was afraid to go anywhere for fear I'd faint or be hurt by some unknown force. It is impossible to describe the tortures I suffered because none of it makes sense.

I went to two psychiatrists. They didn't help me. I joined another church. It made no difference. Then a neighbor suggested Recovery, Inc. I thought, "What do I have to lose?" So I went to a meeting. It was like a miracle. Suddenly I knew I was going to make it. For the first time someone got inside my head and said, "You are not the only one with this problem," and told me what to do about it.

Because of Recovery, Inc., I realized I had "agoraphobia." At last my fear had a name and I knew what I was fighting.

Today I am able to go anywhere. I love life. I'm free of fear. I'm a new person. Please, Ann, I know you've mentioned this grand organization in your column before, but do it again. It— SAVED ME

DEAR SAVED: Thank you for reminding me to recommend, once again, Recovery, Inc. There are hundreds of chapters all over the United States, 70 in Canada, and eight in Puerto Rico. It costs nothing. Look in the phone book. Recovery, Inc. is for men and women who feel they need help with emotional problems of all types. Their record of success is fabulous. What more can I say?

This piece was written especially for the Encyclopedia by Dr. Claire Weekes, M.D., D.Sc., F.R.A.C.P.

Dr. Weekes is the world's foremost authority on agoraphobia. She has written three books, *Peace from Nervous Suffering, Hope and Help for the Nerves* and *Agoraphobia*.

When I recommended the first two books in my column, I was inundated with letters of appreciation from readers. A woman from Oregon wrote,

"This is the first thing I have ever read about my illness. It has kept me in the house for years. I had no idea the problem was so widespread. God bless Dr. Weekes."

Another reader, from Lansing, Michigan, wrote, "I have read both of Dr. Weekes' books and they have given me a new lease on life. I can't thank you enough for recommending them."

Agoraphobia is sometimes referred to as the fear of open spaces. It could more accurately be defined as a condition in which a person suffers incapacitating fear when away from the safety of home, particularly in crowded or isolated places where he cannot make a quick escape or get help immediately should his fears grow beyond him. This includes fear of traveling in a vehicle, especially one he cannot stop at will. In crowded places, such as a restaurant, church, school, or at a sports event he sits always near the exit "just in case."

The term "agoraphobia" comes from the Greek word *agora* meaning a place of assembly (for example, the market place), the term "phobia" from the Greek *phobos* meaning flight or panic. The word "agoraphobia" was first used by C. Westphal in 1871.

Agoraphobia is more common than one would suppose. It is estimated that approximately one million people suffer from it in the United States. More women than men are agoraphobic. In a survey I made in 1973 on 528 agoraphobic men and women in Great Britain and Canada, only 9 percent were men.

Agoraphobia develops more naturally in women because their work at home provides the opportunity of shelter. The majority of agoraphobic women (approximately 78 percent in the survey) are housewives.

Men working away from home must make the effort to leave the house daily, and therefore do not easily develop agoraphobia. If they do, they often express it as a city-bound executive syndrome; that is, they avoid traveling to other cities and some even refuse promotion if it means leaving their home town, even occasionally.

Agoraphobics complain of a variety of fears: fear of a panic attack, of collapsing, fainting, having a weak spell, of being "paralyzed" in the street, fear of entering a shop, of standing in a line at a check-out counter, feelings of unreality, loss of confidence, of harming others (especially a child) and depression. Some complain of general (free-floating) anxiety without specific cause.

Agoraphobia has no known single cause. Sometimes it follows a distressing or dramatic event. Example:

The woman as a child tended to wander away from her mother. Once, when she was eight, she wandered away from her family at the beach. To teach her a lesson, the parents disappeared. Her panic started her agoraphobia. Later her father had to take her to and from high school. Married, with two children, she was dependent on her husband to take her everywhere.

Precipitating causes of agoraphobia, given in order of frequency, in the 1973 survey were: physical illness following a surgical operation, difficult confinement, tuberculosis, infection, arthritis, domestic stress, loss of a loved one, difficulty or pressure at work, dominating parent or parents, strain of looking after an elderly parent, an alcoholic parent, a sudden occurrence of frightening symptoms while moving about socially (panic, giddiness, weakness, palpitations and so on). A few agoraphobics could give no cause for their illness. Of the 528 people in the survey, only 5 (not even 1 percent) mentioned sex as a problem.

In other phobias, extreme anxiety may occur in specific situations, but agoraphobics are subject to spontaneous panic even in the home. One patient described an attack this way:

"I was sitting at home, enjoying TV and really feeling good. All of a sudden I had an attack. I was sweating; my heart was palpitating; I felt as if I were going to die."

During the last ten years, agoraphobia has been much discussed on radio, television and in newspapers and magazines. Ten years ago, doctors were pessimistic about a cure. However, since using the practical approach of taking the agoraphobic into the places he fears and teaching him how to cope with them, cure is now frequent, especially since the introduction of treatment by remote direction: LP recordings, cassette tapes that can be played while the sufferer is trying to venture out alone.

In my experience, the great majority of people who become agoraphobic are first in an anxiety state. Their agoraphobia arises from this. So, to understand agoraphobia, one must understand the anxiety state.

Most anxiety states are of two kinds. One is relatively straightforward and the sufferer is mainly concerned with his symptoms, *the way he feels*. He has minor problems only, such as inability, because of his illness, to cope with responsibilities. He may be happy at home and at work (even happy in his sex life!).

The second is caused by some serious conflict—sorrow, guilt or disgrace. The continuous tension of prolonged anxious introspection sensitizes nerves, just as a sentry on guard becomes sensitized to the slightest noise. Indeed, our subject may eventually be more concerned with the upsetting symptoms —the state he is in—than with his original difficulty.

Three main pitfalls can lead to an anxiety state and then into agoraphobia. They are sensitization, bewilderment and fear. By sensitization I mean a state in which nervous and emotional responses to stress are greatly exaggerated and may come with alarming swiftness. In a severely sensitized person, nervous reactions to stress can be so sudden, the sufferer may think they come unbidden, as if (in the words of some patients) some "thing" was doing this to him.

There is no mystery about sensitization. Most of us have felt mildly sensitized at the end of a day of tension when our nerves are on edge and little things upset us. It's not pleasant but we don't take it very seriously. However, severe sensitization (such as the nervously ill person experiences) can be much more distressing. A severely sensitized individual may feel the symptoms of stress so intensely that an ordinary spasm of fear may seem like a whipping, almost like an electric flash of panic. This can be terrifying because panic can flash in response to the slightest shock—simply tripping in the dark —or it may flash for no apparent reason, "out of the blue."

To understand agoraphobia one must appreciate the severity and swiftness of the panic that sensitization brings and also understand how, reinforced by bewilderment and fear, the original sensitization may increase so that one flash of panic may follow the other, each flash mounting in intensity. This is why an agoraphobic is reluctant to go where he thinks panic may strike; why he sits at the back of the hall or church, always near the exit.

In this article, I will use the term "sensitization" to mean the exaggerated sensations and intense emotional responses found in people in an anxiety state as opposed to the ordinary mild sensitization that most people under stress experience from time to time. The sensitized (and by now I mean the severely sensitized person) may complain of any or all of the following symptoms: "thumping" heart, "missed" heartbeats, pain around the heart, constantly, quickly beating heart, attacks of heart palpitation, giddiness, "lump" in the throat, difficulty in expanding the chest to take in a deep breath, hyperventilation, blurred vision, aching muscles, churning stomach, intestinal discomfort. Above all, he may suffer from flashes of intense panic and, if away from the safety of home, have an almost overwhelming desire to return as quickly as possible.

To these symptoms of acute stress, the symptoms of chronic stress may be gradually added: fatigue (physical and mental), loss of appetite, headaches, sleeplessness, depression.

It is important that the doctor and patient recognize that an anxiety state may be not so much the mere presence of the symptoms of stress *as their exaggeration in a sensitized body.*

Usually people become sensitized either suddenly, as a result of a sudden shock to their nerves (as mentioned earlier, a surgical operation, accident, heavy hemorrhage, difficult confinement and so on), or more gradually, from prolonged stress (debilitating illness, too strenuous dieting, living or working with a stressful life-situation and so on).

A woman debilitated after an exhausting surgical operation may find minor shocks, such as the slight impact of a tray against the end of her bed, shoot through her "like a knife." The strain of simply waiting for visitors to arrive (or leave) may seem unendurable, as if her nerves are stretched like rubber bands. She may be so upset by such experiences that she will worry about them constantly. The added strain of apprehension about coping with housework or a job, should she feel this way when she returns home, may further sensitize her nerves until the spasm of fear becomes a flash of panic. She is caught in the cycle of sensitization—bewilderment and fear—more sensitization. The state is now set for the development of agoraphobia.

In my experience with hundreds of agoraphobic patients, the feeling of panic is the symptom above all others that keeps the sufferer a prisoner in his own home. If the sufferer is a woman with no necessity to leave the house, she may so consistently avoid going out that she may gradually become too afraid to go as far as the clothesline to hang out the laundry. She may be totally dependent on others, even a child, to do her shopping. Some women will venture out if they push a baby carriage to support themselves or they will wear dark glasses even if it is raining. Somehow they feel the glasses protect them against people who want to come "too close."

Reluctance to leave the house may be further established if, on plucking up the courage and going out alone, her apprehension about panicking, her struggle not to panic, brings the stress that invites the very panic she fears. She usually returns home quickly and, from then on, becomes adept at making excuses to avoid leaving the house. As one woman said, "We become wonderful liars!" I have known women to cling to home for years, twenty or more, and so well have they hidden their fears, their family has been only vaguely aware of their disability.

Far from being dependent types, as agoraphobics have been sometimes described, many show remarkable courage and independence, fighting their fears, often with little help from their families and, unfortunately, sometimes without adequate understanding or explanation from their doctors.

Treatment lies essentially in explaining sensitization and teaching an agoraphobic person, indeed most nervously ill people, that his symptoms are those of stress exaggerated and are kept alive by his fear of them. To put it simply, by being afraid of the symptoms of fear, he puts himself in a cycle of fear—symptoms—more fear. He must understand this and be taught how to cope with his symptoms until he is no longer afraid of them, especially of panic. It is not enough to tranquilize symptoms away. The little tablet becomes the crutch and the patient remains bewildered and basically afraid. The only way to permanent recovery is to teach the sufferer how to cope with panic and all the other symptoms—indecision, suggestibility, loss of confidence, feelings of unreality, possibly obsession and depression—so that he loses his fear of them.

The agoraphobic should also be taught to expect and cope with setbacks, because setbacks, particularly in recovery from agoraphobia, are so common. He should understand that he learns as much, if not more, in coming through a setback as when in a good spell.

So much depends on a therapist's ability to explain the nuances of this strange illness: for example, to explain why, when the sufferer is feeling better, setbacks can come for no apparent reason and yet be so devastating, as if no progress had been made at all; to explain why symptoms thought forgotten can return acutely after months, or years, of absence; why all the symptoms can so quickly appear; why such demoralizing exhaustion can so rapidly follow the return of symptoms; why, despite the right attitude, sensitization may sometimes linger.

Some people recover when they get no more than a good explanation of their symptoms. It is a revelation to learn that the symptoms they thought were unique to them are no more than the symptoms of stress exaggerated by sensitization, and kept alive by their fear of them; that fighting their symptoms and not accepting them has been creating the tension and kept them ill. One woman said, "I did not know it could be so simple! I feel like I have been let out of prison!"

CREDIT: *Dr. Claire Weekes, M.D., D.Sc., F.R.A.C.P., Consultant Physician, Rachel Forster Hospital, Sydney, Australia.*

Alcoholism

SHARING TODAY

DEAR ANN LANDERS: While going through my Al-Anon book tonight, I ran across something I believe is worth sharing. In fact, I am going to have it printed and framed for my wall so I can see it every morning. Here it is:

Today is mine.

It is unique.

Nobody in the world has one exactly like it.

It holds the sum of all my past experiences and all my future potential.

I can fill it with joyous moments or ruin it with fruitless worry.

If painful recollections of the past come into my mind or frightening thoughts of the future, I can put them away.

They cannot spoil today for me.
                                    POSITIVE THINKER

DEAR THINKER: What an uplifting bit of philosophy! We can all use it. Thanks for sharing.

We drank for happiness and became unhappy.
We drank for joy and became miserable.
We drank for sociability and became argumentative.
We drank for sophistication and became obnoxious.
We drank for friendship and made enemies.
We drank for sleep and awakened without rest.

We drank for strength and felt weak.
We drank "medicinally" and acquired health problems.
We drank for relaxation and got the shakes.
We drank for bravery and became afraid.
We drank for confidence and became doubtful.
We drank to make conversation easier and slurred our speech.
We drank to feel heavenly and ended up feeling like hell.
We drank to forget and were forever haunted.
We drank for freedom and became slaves.
We drank to erase problems and saw them multiply.
We drank to cope with life and invited death.

(This was sent to me by a member of A.A.)

It has been estimated that approximately ninety million Americans use alcohol and one out of every ten has a problem with his drinking. Alcoholism among women in recent years has risen dramatically. Teenage alcoholism has also increased. Many young people have been frightened off hard drugs, which were the "in" thing in the late sixties and early seventies, and turned to beer and hard liquor.

Excessive drinking costs American business and industry some eighteen billion dollars a year in loss of production, time away from work, and industrial accidents.

The booze problem is not ours alone. In 1976 both Russia and France declared alcoholism the Number One Public Health Problem. Incidence of cirrhosis of the liver and alcohol-related car accidents were cited as evidence.

What is alcoholism? There are many definitions. I like this one sent to me by a reader who described himself as "a recovered alcoholic."

He wrote: " 'It doesn't make any difference whether a person drinks whiskey, gin, champagne or beer; whether he drinks before breakfast or waits until after dinner; every day or on weekends only; alone or with others; at home or abroad. If drinking continues to disrupt his life, he is an alcoholic.' " (From *Alcoholism—Challenge for Social Work Education* by Herman Krimmel.)

Here is another good definition, by Mrs. Marty Mann, the executive director of the National Council on Alcoholism:

"The victims of alcoholism rarely set out to get drunk. Usually they wish to enjoy a few drinks, 'like other people.' This, they find, is not possible. Every time they drink, they end up drunk, against their will. At a later stage in their progressive illness, they discover they have made matters even worse. By then they have vowed not to drink a drop. Before long, they find themselves drinking again to drunkenness."

Who is an alcoholic? It can be anyone—male or female, old or young, brilliant or dull, educated or illiterate. He can be extremely successful in business (or a profession) and he can be a skid row bum. Your surgeon could be an alcoholic. So could your clergyman, your attorney, the woman who does your laundry, the man who cuts your hair or the principal of your child's school.

Alcoholics become lonely people. They are denounced, ridiculed, damned, coddled and cajoled by their friends and families. They are tolerated, shunned, ignored by the public, and questioned and observed by psychiatrists. Their loved ones plead with them, lie about them, shelter and threaten them. They are preached to and prayed over by the clergy. The usual shelter and concealment, though well intended, often delay treatment until the disease progresses beyond the point of no return.

Yet all of this tumult has no effect on the alcoholic's drinking. His only source of comfort is the bottle. There he finds companionship and release from his loneliness, the courage to retaliate against those who infringe on what he believes are his rights. In the bottle he finds temporary release from his worries and fears. Escape from reality becomes his lifestyle while the chemical dependence traps him into an ever descending spiral of destruction.

For this temporary release, the bottle demands a big price: his time, his money, his health, his self-respect and often his job, his home, his family and his friends. When the alcoholic can no longer meet the demands, the bottle leaves him to the mercy of his craving, his poverty and his self-pity.

One reason it is so difficult to determine the precise number of alcoholics is because there are so many secret drinkers. Thousands of alcoholics are hidden from public notice until their disease becomes so obvious they can no longer keep it a secret. Women are especially skillful at concealing their drinking from friends and even from the members of their families.

I have read hundreds of letters from husbands who say they were unaware that their wives drank until they found gin bottles in the washing machine, vodka disguised as cough medicine and empty sherry bottles in the clothes hamper. To the woman with natural good looks and a sense of pride in her appearance, the havoc wrought by alcohol is devastating. Liquor washes out the complexion, destroys the sparkle in the eyes and accelerates the aging process. After a few years of excessive drinking, most drinking women look like the boozers they are. They know it, and are ashamed.

I am frequently asked if a man who drinks nothing but beer can be considered an alcoholic. The same question is asked about women who drink no hard liquor—only white wine. The answer is yes. While it takes more beer and white wine to get drunk than gin or vodka, the net result is the same if these beverages are indulged in to excess consistently.

Another question I am frequently asked is this: "Does alcohol enhance a male's sexual performance?"

The answer is no. In fact, the opposite is true. While alcohol may help overcome inhibitions, according to the experts, it definitely hinders a male's performance. Physicians also note that heavy drinkers become sexually impotent at a relatively early age. Recovered alcoholics regain their potency fully, along with confidence that they can perform.

Today, thanks to research and education, society recognizes that the alcoholic is ill and that his illness can be arrested. I hesitate to use the word "cured" because there is no known cure for alcoholism. Once the line has been crossed from normal to abnormal drinking, the victim can never use liquor again. It is poison to his system. But he *can* learn to live without liquor—as millions of alcoholics are proving again and again, day after day.

Many alcoholics undergo personality changes, although, according to the authorities at the Menninger Foundation in Topeka, Kansas, alcoholics probably bore the seeds of mental illness years before they became heavy drinkers. One of the marked traits of the alcoholic is lying. He becomes an expert at fabrication and deception. Alcoholics are often irritable, quick-tempered, defensive and suspicious of others, which may be symptoms of damage to the brain.

Almost all medical authorities agree that the alcoholic's life span is shortened substantially by his drinking. His appearance is altered, too. The blood vessels in the face (especially in, on and around the nose) are often dilated. The eyes are frequently bloodshot and premature wrinkles appear which tend to make the alcoholic look many years older than he is.

This letter makes the point:

DEAR ANN LANDERS: I am getting fed to the gullet with your incessant, relentless harping on the evils of liquor. You are so hipped on the subject I wouldn't be surprised if you were a closet nipper yourself.

You are forever quoting physicians as your "authorities." Have you noticed, Ann, there are more old drunks around than old doctors? Print this one, if you can think of an answer. JIM BEAM

DEAR JIM: Those old drunks you see around are a lot younger than they look. The booze is what aged them.

Why do people become alcoholics? Dr. Alton L. Blakeslee, a distinguished science writer for the Associated Press, had this to say:

"There is no *one* cause for compulsive drinking. Several years ago, the public (and many physicians) had a simple explanation for problem drinkers. They said alcoholics were weak people who had no willpower, that they could stop drinking if they had the strength of character and a genuine desire to do so. We now know this is nonsense.

"The real reason for their sickness is whatever drives them to indulge in the uncontrolled use of alcohol. Many of them have psychological or emotional problems they cannot face and are unable to cope with. They turn to alcohol as a means of escape. For a time it may work. Taking a stiff drink before meeting strangers may oil the way, if one feels a fear or uneasiness in meeting new people. 'Bottled courage' does not, of course, answer the central question, 'Why are you afraid of meeting new people?'

"If alcohol helps (and it appears to 'help' alcoholics uniquely) then it is easy to turn to it again and again. Alcohol then becomes the predominant method of dealing with personality difficulties."

Some authorities claim there may be other factors underlying the causes of alcoholism. There is some evidence that physical causes may also be involved. The individual who becomes alcoholic may have some abnormal physical reaction or an allergy to alcohol that social drinkers do not have.

It is important for the person who has a drinking problem (or is living with someone who has) to be aware that most health insurance policies now provide for treatment for alcoholism. Moreover, help is available—and it is free. I am referring to Alcoholics Anonymous. But the problem drinker must *want* it. If he is dragged to a meeting by a well-meaning friend or relative, it will probably do no good.

The following "test" to determine whether or not you have a drinking problem may be useful. It was published by the National Council on Alcoholism. If you recognize yourself, you need outside help. These are specific symptoms of early alcoholism:

(1) Gulping drinks.

(2) Making promises to yourself that you will "never again get so drunk" and discovering soon after that you were unable to keep the promise.

(3) Hiding liquor. Lying about your drinking—minimizing the number of drinks or attempting to conceal the fact that you had any drinks at all. (Mints, mouthwash, chewing gum.)

(4) Taking a drink before going to a party where you know liquor will be served. Or taking liquor along, surreptitiously, to an affair where you know liquor will *not* be served, or where the supply may be limited.

(5) Feeling the necessity of having drinks at certain regular times—must have a cocktail or two before lunch, must have drinks at 5:30.

(6) Insisting on drinks before dinner, regardless of the inconvenience to others.

(7) Needing three or four drinks before you can entertain guests in your home, or prior to introducing a speaker at a dinner, or before meeting with a difficult client.

(8) Must have drinks for "nerves" because of a shattering day at the office or a frantic day with the children.

(9) Drinking when "blue"—to forget problems.

(10) Feeling remorseful, guilty or ashamed of things said and done after a night's drinking and repeating the scene soon after.

If you recognize yourself, please accept the fact that you can't fight alcoholism alone. Write to the National Council on Alcoholism for specific information regarding help in your community. The address is 2 Park Avenue, New York, New York 10016. The National Council knows all the available sources for treatment and they are standing by, waiting to be of service. Your own community may have an alcoholism treatment or counseling services. See your Yellow Pages under "Alcoholism."

For those who want to act immediately I recommend Alcoholics Anonymous. Look in the telephone book and give them a call. Find out when and where the next meeting will be held and go. A member will come to you and discuss your problem. In all probability he will offer to pick you up and take you to your first meeting.

A.A. is free. They ask no questions and make no demands. It is an international fellowship of men and women with chapters all over the world.

No one bawls out an A.A. if he falters and slips. Many A.A. members backslide before they finally "get" the program. Their philosophy boils down to this: "If I can live through the next twenty-four hours without a drink I can stay off liquor for the rest of my life."

A.A. has the highest rate of success with problem drinkers. It has succeeded where psychiatry and religion failed. The emotional support and sincere caring of individuals who share the same problem are apparently the key. I cannot emphasize strongly enough the effectiveness of A.A. It gets my unqualified approval.

And now an added P.S. In these days of political unrest, financial crisis and emotional upheaval, a word to those of you who are trying to drown your sorrow. Please be aware that sorrow knows how to swim.

Alcoholism which often masquerades as social drinking, has ruined more marriages, careers, healthy bodies and fine minds than any single element known to man.

CREDIT: *Ann Landers. J. Robert Merrill of Chicago read this piece and offered some valuable suggestions. Mr. Merrill works with the Chicago Employee Counseling Program at Chicago's Alcoholic Treatment Center.*

A TEST FOR FEMALE ALCOHOLISM

DEAR ANN LANDERS: Millions of housewives in this country would be shocked if someone called them alcoholics. But they are. Members of the Kansas City-area National Council On Alcoholism have prepared a questionnaire (with help from the Michigan chapter), and we want to give it as much exposure as possible. We hope you'll print it.

Here are 20 questions. Any woman who answers "Yes" to more than half is probably alcoholic.

(1) Do you try to get someone to buy liquor for you because you are shamed to buy it yourself?

(2) Do you buy liquor at different places so no one will know how much you purchase?

(3) Do you hide the empties and dispose of them secretly?

[illegible] Do you plan in advance to "reward" yourself with a little drinking bout after you've worked very hard in the house?

(5) Are you often permissive with your children because you feel guilty about the way you behaved when you were drinking?

(6) Do you have "blackouts," periods about which you remember nothing?

(7) Do you ever phone the hostess of a party the next day and ask if you hurt anyone's feelings or made a fool of yourself?

(8) Do you find cigaret holes in your clothes or the furniture and can't remember when it happened?

(9) Do you take an extra drink or two before leaving for a party when you know liquor will be served there?

(10) Do you often wonder if anyone knows how much you drink?

(11) Do you feel wittier or more charming when you are drinking?

(12) Do you feel panicky when faced with nondrinking days, such as a visit to out-of-town relatives?

(13) Do you invent social occasions for drinking, such as inviting friends for lunch, cocktails or dinner?

(14) When others are present, do you avoid reading articles or seeing movies or TV shows about women alcoholics but read and watch when no one is around?

(15) Do you ever carry liquor in your purse?

(16) Do you become defensive when someone mentions your drinking?

(17) Do you become irritated when unexpected guests reduce your liquor supply?

(18) Do you drink when under pressure or after an argument?

(19) Do you try to cover up when you can't remember promises and feel ashamed when you misplace or lose things?

(20) Do you drive even though you've been drinking but feel certain you are in complete control of yourself?

Be honest. If your score says you're alcoholic, call the National Council on Alcoholism or Alcoholics Anonymous. They are listed in the phone book.

DORIS S. AND JANE J. (alcoholic counselors)

DEAR D. AND J.: Thank you. And now a word from me to those of you who flunked. These self-help groups have proven more successful than psychiatry, religion or medical help. Millions have found sobriety through their camaraderie and mutual support. You can, too. Get going.

According to a 1977 in-depth study, the areas with the most severe alcoholism problems are:

Alaska
District of Columbia
Hawaii
California
Washington

The states with the fewest:

Iowa
Minnesota
Nebraska
South Dakota
North Dakota

Advice for the Wife of an Alcoholic

DOCTOR'S WIFE ASKS HELP FROM AL-ANON

DEAR ANN LANDERS: My husband is a well-known, highly respected physician in this city of 100,000. He doesn't drink when on call, but when he's "relaxing," it's a serious problem. If it weren't for the children I would leave him. Believe me, I've given it serious consideration but decided, for a variety of reasons, to stay and make the best of it.

But how do I cope, Ann? My resentment is affecting my entire outlook on life. It has reached the point where the smell of liquor on his breath makes me want to throw up.

I have read about Al-Anon in your column and would like to join. When I told my husband, he said, "I dare you to show your face at one of those meetings. It would be the talk of the town."

Please tell me what to do, Ann. I am
—A VERY UNHAPPY WOMAN

DEAR WOMAN: Don't let him bully you. Go to the next Al-Anon meeting —and I hope it's tomorrow.

If your husband doesn't want to seek help for himself, that's his business, but he has no rights to deny you the benefits of Al-Anon.

As for "people talking," it's most unlikely. The anonymity of the members is rarely violated. And if someone does talk, what could he say? Showing up at an Al-Anon meeting is infinitely less damaging than a doctor who shows up ANYPLACE—drunk.

The wife of an alcoholic must become willing to let go of the idea that she has any control over her husband's drinking. No matter how determined, attractive, clever, knowledgeable or strong she is, she cannot overcome the force of her addicted husband's need for his fix. A modern-day Cleopatra would not have that much power. The most any wife should hope and strive for is emotional health for herself and treatment for her husband.

The thought of being alone and on her own is so terrifying to some women that they are willing to put up with what others would consider a shocking existence. No matter what their present pain, it's not as bad as the pain of being without a husband. Just having a man in the house, even though he is dead drunk every night, is, to some women, the desirable alternative.

The wives of alcoholics who pursue this course treat it as if it were a need, when, in fact, facing pain is their need. It is the only way they can reach healthy resolutions or obtain the emotional strength to cope with the recurring crises of active alcoholism.

I am not recommending pain for pain's sake, but if it is present it provides an opportunity to build emotional muscle, to acquire greater personal strength and tolerance for life's discomforts.

Yelling, screaming, cajoling and crying are the wrong techniques for trying to get an alcoholic to accept treatment. Threats from an employer are equally useless.

The alcoholic should not be catered to. Those around him must resist the temptation to adjust to the craziness of his alcoholism. Don't call his boss and say he is sick when he is really too drunk to go to work. Co-workers who want to "help" should not cover up for a lush who takes three and a half hours out of the day for a five-martini lunch.

Let the alcoholic know his behavior is not normal and that it is not acceptable. Don't allow him to control the family and make everyone miserable. Professional help is usually necessary to give the family of an alcoholic the strength to build their lives. Seek out trained psychologists, and join Al-Anon.

Responding constructively to your partner's alcoholism will require the greatest effort you have ever put into anything in your life. And it's a daily effort, not a one-shot deal. You must keep your eye on the Big Picture in order to break your life into manageable sections. With persistence and determination, you must concentrate on only those acts which you know have a chance. Pay no attention to how your alcoholic responds. You will be able to measure the effects of your new approach only in retrospect, after you've been using it for several months. It will not be the actions of one day to which your alcoholic will respond, it will be your daily actions, accumulated over a period of time, that will make the difference. Let go of yesterday. Put aside tomorrow. Today is the only day that counts.

Combating alcoholism requires enormous effort. It can also bring the greatest rewards you've ever known. Alcoholics can get "weller than well" and so can their spouses. There is tremendous help for the wife of an alcoholic at Al-Anon. Al-Anon is not affiliated with Alcoholics Anonymous, but the organizations work together. Al-Anon is a fellowship for family or close friends of a person with a drinking problem. Alateen is an organization for teenagers whose parents (or parent) are alcoholics. Telephone numbers of these organizations are listed in the phone directory. Call and ask when and where the next meeting will be. What you will learn at Al-Anon and Alateen can make you behave as you've never behaved before. You can become beautiful and free!

CREDIT: *J. R. Merrill, Chicago. From a review of* The Booze Battle *by Ruth Maxwell, Praeger Publishers. Mr. Merrill works with the Chicago Employee Counseling Program at Chicago's Alcoholic Treatment Center.*

Allergies

Some people are referred to allergists for what are clearly allergic conditions. In other instances, however, when a variety of other specialists have failed to identify the problem, it is called "an allergy." Thus, to some physicians, and to a large part of the lay public, many conditions are labeled allergies when there is no valid basis for this opinion.

Surprisingly, a great many conditions such as fatigue, stress, headaches and the like are treated by some physicians as if they were an allergy. In most instances, the allergy is blamed on food.

Food allergies do, indeed, exist but are manifested by immediate symptoms such as a skin rash or shock. Failing such immediate reaction, it has never been demonstrated that food allergies exist. The American Academy of Allergy recently treated patients suspected of being allergic to food with two diets, one which included all the so-called allergenic foods and another which contained none. There was no difference between the two groups.

If one puts aside all the strange conditions which have been ascribed to allergy, the remaining diseases are by comparison simple. Allergies are caused by certain class or serum protein called IgE antibodies. These antibodies recognize specific allergens and when they come into contact with them, lead to the release of histamine and other mediators which cause the symptoms of allergic disorders. These IgE antibodies can be detected in a variety of ways —by skin tests or by actual measurements of the serum antibody level.

Diseases which are caused by these antibodies include hay fever and other forms of allergies that affect the breathing apparatus (sometimes asthma), skin problems and shock. IgE antibodies may well be involved in a variety of skin rashes.

The symptoms of the aforementioned allergies are clear-cut. Inhaled allergens may lead to red, itchy eyes, nasal congestion, secretion and stuffiness and shortness of breath and/or wheezing. Hives are "bumps" on the skin surrounded by a red border and may occur in a variety of sizes in any number of places.

Allergies can be diagnosed by a well-trained allergist who is equipped to carry out skin tests and take historical information, which usually reveals the culprit allergens. In the hands of a competent allergist skin tests will probably be limited in number, usually no more than ten to thirty, depending on the patient's history. There is very rarely a need to carry out two hundred or three hundred skin tests. In this instance more is certainly not better.

Once an allergy has been discovered, the best treatment is avoidance. If it happens to be a food, this is relatively easy, but the labeling practices in the United States often turn the patient into a detective in order to be safe.

Some allergens, such as the pollens of grasses, trees and weeds, are difficult to avoid, although air conditioning of car and bedroom is very helpful and is a tax-deductible expense. If these measures do not suffice, there are many drugs which are useful.

The first line of defense is the standard antihistamines. Newly introduced drugs include nasal and bronchial sprays containing corticosteroids, which are extremely effective for hay fever and asthma. If all else fails, shots (immunotherapy) have proven beneficial. These shots will not *cure* the disease but they can make the patient much more comfortable. While many allergists recommend shots for asthma, the value of this treatment for prevention has not yet been established.

Hives are most often caused by foods or drugs. The most common offender is penicillin. A potential sensitivity to this drug can be detected by skin testing. Unfortunately, with most other drugs, appropriate skin tests are not available and we cannot at present diagnose them by any means until after the person has taken the drug and developed the symptoms. The only treatment is avoidance.

One of the most serious kinds of allergies involves reactions to stinging insects, such as honey bees. There has been considerable progress in this area in recent years. This is one illness in which immunotherapy appears to solve the problem. Injections with the venom of the insect to which the patient is allergic leads to a cure in over 98 percent of patients.

Thus, allergy in its true sense is no longer such a deep, dark mystery. Diagnosis and treatment have become established. There is a large gray area, however, which includes many symptoms that are not truly allergic and a variety of treatments which cannot be justified by scientific considerations.

True allergies can be diagnosed and will respond to established treatment, but as mentioned earlier, there are a number of physical problems which are called allergies when no evidence exists to justify the diagnosis—but a baffled physician often feels the need to produce some explanation for a patient's discomfort and the word "allergic" can be a convenient catchall.

Beware of quackery and bizarre treatments. Your best protection if you think you have an allergy is to go to a physician who specializes in this disorder.

CREDIT: *Lawrence M. Lichtenstein, M.D., Clinical Immunology Division, the Johns Hopkins University School of Medicine, Baltimore, Maryland.*

Anemia

Anemia, often called "low blood," is a condition in which there is a reduction in the blood stream in the number of red blood cells, or in the total amount of hemoglobin, or in both. The major effect of such a condition is to reduce the amount of oxygen that is carried to the tissues of the body. The resulting symptoms can range from mild to severe, depending on how low the number of red blood cells or the amount of hemoglobin is. Mild symptoms include pale complexion, weakness, headache, heart palpitations. Severe symptoms include dizzy spells, ringing in the ears, spots before the eyes and excessive irritability. In some types of anemia, a yellowing of the skin and eyes occurs (this is called jaundice). The spleen may enlarge. Untreated or improperly treated anemia may lead to heart failure and death.

Because of the non-specific nature of the symptoms and because anemia has a variety of causes, and because each cause requires a different treatment, the individual should seek expert advice in the diagnosis and treatment of this disease. Contrary to popular belief and advertising, not all anemias are caused by iron deficiency. Anemia can be diagnosed by a physical examination and several simple laboratory procedures. Sometimes a routine examination will reveal anemia in a person who has not noticed any symptoms. The physician may note unusual pallor or discover abnormalities in the blood tests for the amount of hemoglobin in the blood, the number of red blood cells or the volume percent of red cells in whole blood (hematocrit).

Once anemia is discovered, further diagnostic procedures are done to determine the specific cause. Initial categorization of anemia is according to the major mechanism responsible: (1) blood loss, (2) excess in destruction of red blood cells (hemolytic anemia), (3) deficiency in production of red blood cells or (4) deficiency in production of red cells combined with excess in destruction of these cells. Further analysis is needed to determine the underlying cause of each type of anemia and to determine appropriate treatment.

Blood loss anemia is often caused by acute hemorrhage and is characteristic of many severe diseases. Bleeding from the gastrointestinal tract, evidenced by vomiting blood or having bloody diarrhea, is one of many conditions that leads to blood loss anemia. Such anemia is extremely serious and requires immediate medical attention to restore blood volume and to prevent shock, heart complications and death. Transfusion of red blood cells is the standard treatment for severe blood loss anemia.

Deficiency in production of red blood cells is most commonly caused by a deficiency in iron, vitamin B-12, folic acid or a combination of these. Such deficiencies can result from insufficient quantities of each in the diet. The other possible causes of these deficiencies—inability to absorb the iron, B-12 or folic acid that is ingested; excessive body requirements for them which cannot be met by diet; and blood loss leading to a deficiency—all require further diagnostic studies to determine the cause of each of these conditions.

When a physician diagnoses iron deficiency anemia, not only is s/he obligated to prescribe the least expensive iron preparation, but also, and more importantly, s/he is obligated to seek the cause of the iron deficiency anemia. If the anemia is corrected, but its cause is not determined, serious, remediable diseases, such as gastric ulcers or colon cancer, may be missed. When symptoms of such disease are masked by correcting the anemia without seeking the cause, the disease progresses and the blood loss continues. For these same reasons, it is imperative that the lay person not try to treat anemia by him/herself. A serious disease may be overlooked.

The treatment of vitamin B-12 and folic acid deficiencies must be carried out under a physician's supervision. The symptoms of the two deficiencies are very similar, and a B-12 deficiency can be temporarily corrected with folic acid. However, under such circumstances, the B-12-deficient patient, while temporarily cured of his/her anemia by folic acid, will suffer serious central nervous system complications which could lead to irreversible dysfunction—for example, the inability to walk.

Occasionally the deficiency in red cell production is caused by bone marrow failure. In this case, diagnosis requires a bone marrow test. The administration of iron, folic acid and vitamin B-12 is usually not helpful, and may be harmful under certain conditions.

When iron, folic acid or vitamin B-12 is prescribed by the physicians, inexpensive preparations are available. Medical scientists know that any iron preparation tolerated by the patient is as good as any other. Unfortunately, high-pressure advertising tries to convince the public that certain iron preparations are better than others for rejuvenating the blood. This simply isn't true.

A large group of anemias, the hemolytic anemias, are due to excessive red blood cell destruction. These anemias are either hereditary (sickle cell anemia) or acquired due to defects that may have been caused by drugs. Symptoms of these anemias include varying degrees of jaundice and an enlarged spleen. The diagnosis of these diseases requires careful analysis by a hematologist (blood specialist). Simply taking iron or other vitamins for any of these conditions is not only inappropriate, but may be very dangerous.

Anemias may also be caused by the complex interaction of decreased production and increased destruction of red blood cells. In many cases, this type of anemia resembles an iron deficiency anemia. Yet there is actually an excess of iron in the body. Taking iron in this situation is dangerous because the body is already overloaded with iron it cannot use. This anemia is seen in chronic diseases, such as infections, cancer, rheumatoid arthritis, kidney disease and liver disease. Diagnosis requires an expert analysis of the patient's general condition as well as of the patient's specific problem.

As we have seen, anemia is a condition that often indicates the presence of complex disease processes. Recent progress has enabled the physician to determine the specific type of anemia, establish its cause and prescribe a specific treatment. The public must be warned that erroneous self-diagnosis can lead to delays in diagnosing the actual cause. Taking over-the-counter iron preparations may mask a more serious condition which demands attention. Avoid the widely advertised products and ask your physician what you should be taking.

CREDIT: *John D. Ultmann, M.D., Professor, University of Chicago School of Medicine.*

Anger

(*The Importance of Being Angry*)

A child screams with rage when her older brother takes away her favorite toy. Her mother tells her to quiet down "because the neighbors will hear you." An executive emerges from the front office, his face flushed with anger he could not vent against his boss. A woman sits in a restaurant and loudly protests her husband's lateness as other diners sympathize with the poor fellow.

In this culture, "getting mad" is considered an unpardonable breach of etiquette, a dangerous loss of control, a sign even of insanity. Yet anger is as normal and healthy a feeling as hunger, fatigue, love, sadness and joy.

Anger is a complex emotion based on deeper feelings. All people, even the tiniest baby, become angry when needs are frustrated, when they feel threatened or "put down," when they are afraid or when somebody hurts or rejects them, breaks a promise, reminds them of a failure, misunderstands or refuses to listen to them.

The problem is that many people become angry without knowing why. They prefer to ignore feelings they cannot understand. The accumulated fury, like an unopened sore, eventually poisons their bodies, minds and relationships.

Unexpressed anger can rob us of sleep or make us sleep too much. It can cause blood pressure to rise, even to the point of stroke. It can make necks stiff, heads ache and ulcers perforate the linings of the stomach. Anger, held in, can block our sexual feelings to the point of frigidity and impotence.

Gunnysacked anger also distorts behavior. One of the most universal effects is depression, or anger turned inward upon oneself. Pent-up rage can cause a frustrated wife to gossip viciously as she vents her wrath against others and makes her husband work late at the office, so he can punish her by his absence.

Anger can cause explosive temper tantrums, crying outbursts, nail-biting, anxiety, guilt, overeating, undereating, accident proneness, dangerous driving, chronic worry and sexual excess. It even plays a part in drug abuse and alcoholism. In its ultimate form, displaced anger causes people to kill themselves and others.

Many people try to mask anger by "dialing out," or resorting to sullen silence, contempt for others, bullying, phony "niceness" or denial that anything is wrong. Thus, unreleased anger blocks the good feelings people have for one another, deadening love and creativity, and causing every imaginable form of human unhappiness.

Why are we so terrified of anger? Many fear if they express it others will retaliate or stop loving them. Others are afraid to show how strongly they care or to learn why they care so strongly.

Learning to express anger directly is not easy since most of us have been conditioned since childhood to suppress it. The first step is to let ourselves really get mad. This takes courage, practice and occasionally professional counseling, if feelings are buried deeply enough.

Then we need to learn *why* we are angry, an even more difficult task because it involves looking beyond immediate irritations to deeper causes. Finally, we need to express that anger *at the moment* of anger, not three hours, days or months later. Express it loud and clear, at the real target, complete with shouting and table-pounding if the feeling is strong enough—but please no pounding on people.

There are other, healthy ways to dispel anger (provided we understand its cause). We can jog, beat a rug, work out with a punching bag, throw darts, write a letter to Ann Landers, scream or do anything else that does not cause physical harm to ourselves or others.

Small, periodic blow-ups release pressure. One great, long-delayed explosion can destroy—and the principal victim of repressed rage is most often oneself.

CREDIT: *Michael Halberstam, M.D., "Modern Medicine," New York Times Syndicate, New York, New York.*

Anorexia Nervosa

(Self-Starvation)

Anorexia nervosa is the name for a disease that usually occurs among the daughters, rarely the sons, of well-to-do and educated families, not only in the United States, but in other affluent countries.

The chief symptom is a devastating weight loss resulting from self-inflicted starvation. The illness used to be exceedingly rare, but there has been a definite increase during the last fifteen or twenty years. Its rapid spread must be attributed to psycho-sociological factors, such as the emphasis that our society places on slimness. These girls also use the new freedom for women not as a means of liberation but as a directive to be outstanding. Among well-to-do high school and college girls, the incidence may be as high as one in two hundred.

The leading symptom is a relentless pursuit of excessive slimness, a phobic fear of being fat. Paradoxically, this is coupled with an intense interest in food. However, the dramatic weight loss and food refusal are symptoms only that camouflage the real illness, which is a severe deficit in the inner sense of competence and capacity for satisfaction. Throughout their lives these youngsters have been engaged in a desperate struggle to make themselves appear "perfect" in the eyes of others. When with adolescence the need for independence and self-assertion arises they try to establish a sense of selfhood and autonomy by becoming thinner. The search for control is the basic psychological issue in anorexia nervosa. Starvation in turn creates its own symptoms and complications.

Characteristically, anorexics come from success-, achievement- and appearance-oriented families who appear to be stable, with few broken marriages. They are well cared for as children, but things are done according to the parents' decision, not geared to what the child expresses as her need; thus she will grow up deficient in her capacity for independent thinking and action. The parents take pride in the child's obedience and goodness, and seek affection and confirmation from this their "perfect child." When this role becomes too demanding, the anorexia develops like a declaration of independence that, however, miscarries.

Though there are individual differences in the way the illness manifests itself, anorexics display similarities in several areas of disordered psychological functioning. Characteristic is a severe disturbance in body image and body concept. These youngsters do not "see" themselves realistically and continue to be frantic about being fat when they are severely emaciated. They see their body as something separate, not part of "self," not their property but something over which they must exercise rigid discipline.

The symptom that arouses most anxiety, frustration and rage in the parents is the anorexic's refusal to eat. In some, abstinence from food alternates with eating binges during which the anorexics consume enormous amounts, though they claim not to feel hunger. They try to remove the unwanted foods through self-induced vomiting, laxatives, enemas and diuretics. Such practices may result in serious disturbances in the body's natural balance. The common symptom is confusion in the way they perceive and interpret hunger and other normal signals of bodily needs.

Constant hyperactivity is another symptom of false body awareness. Excessive exercise, as an effort to prove oneself competent and superior, often precedes the starvation phase. Later it becomes aimless activity "to burn off calories." There is often an absence of sexual feelings and menstruation ceases or becomes irregular.

Though anorexics give a first impression of being active and vigorous, they suffer from a paralyzing sense of ineffectiveness which pervades all their thinking and activities. Unable to solve their real problems, they gain a sense of accomplishment, even of superiority and power, from manipulating their bodies and making themselves thinner and thinner. They experience deep feelings of depression and self-hatred when they regain any weight.

Anorexia nervosa has a tendency to be self-perpetuating, leading to chronic invalidism. It is one of the few psychiatric diseases that can result in death. This tragic outcome is unnecessary and avoidable when proper treatment is begun before the condition becomes irreversible.

One early warning sign of something abnormal is the slavish devotion with which a youngster adheres to a reducing program, insisting it is easy and she is not hungry.

Another sign is a frantic increase in her physical activities, with more and more time devoted to school assignments and exercise, and less to sleep. An ominous sign is when the weight loss is accompanied by increasing social isolation. Treatment should be insisted on before this stage is reached. Unfortunately, a great many parents these days are so preoccupied with slimness and dieting that they may overlook serious degrees of malnutrition, and do not seek treatment for their child until the illness has progressed to a dangerous point.

Treatment involves two distinct tasks: normal nutrition and dealing with the underlying psychological problems, which means involvement with the whole family. Weight gain alone, without help with the personality problems, is not true progress. Psychotherapy needs to be directed toward the lack of self-awareness and the feeling of inferiority and ineffectiveness. Therapy must encourage patients to become capable of living as self-directed, competent individuals who can enjoy what life has to offer, so that they no longer need to manipulate their bodies by starving themselves.

CREDIT: *Hilde Bruch, M.D., Professor of Psychiatry, Baylor College of Medicine, author of* Anorexia Nervosa: The Golden Cage, *Cambridge, Massachusetts: Harvard University Press, 1977.*

Anxiety

Webster's dictionary defines anxiety as painful uneasiness of mind while expecting an impending event or anticipated ill; and again, as a desire one looks forward to. It gives as synonyms: concern, dread, foreboding, misgiving, worry, solicitude, uneasiness, apprehension.

When anxious we are concerned about what may happen to us. When the event occurs, anxiety is often replaced by more positive emotions—fear, shame or even joy. While holding concern for the future, anxiety can have different meanings. For example, we may be anxious about a visit to the doctor, or be anxiously pleased, looking forward to seeing a good friend.

Anxiety among the young (according to psychiatrists) is most commonly related to isolation, particularly to too little attention (or too much distance from) the mother. A small boy of five, whose parents were divorced, was collected from home each weekend by his father. He was away from his mother every Friday afternoon until late Sunday or early Monday morning. If during the week his mother went out to dinner and came home late (Grandma then looked after the boy), the mother often found the little fellow asleep in her bed. She was mystified. Was her bed more comfortable than his, or was there a deeper reason? She questioned the boy cautiously. To every question, he shook his head, looked at her solemnly and asked, "Mummy, do you and me have to be separated so much?" Anxious mothers must wonder how much freedom to take without creating future complications for their children.

Anxiety in response to a threatening danger is part of our defense mechanism. If one of our forebears had encountered a hungry alligator while swimming in a swamp and felt no anxiety, his ultimate fate would surely have been to end up in the alligator's stomach. His anxiety (and a nearby tree) saved him.

There is so much daily anxiety that most of us accept it as routine. For example, taking a child to school on his first day, we worry, "Will the teacher understand what a sensitive child he is? Will his schoolmates be cruel to him? Will he be given a seat in the draft?" Anxiety gives imagination wings.

The first baby is rarely enjoyed as much as the second. Rituals followed peacefully and automatically by our parents and grandparents are questioned anxiously today. We are even robbed of the joy of picking up a sweet-smelling bundle covered in baby powder for fear we will give him our "germs." And when, at the same age, the baby next door is standing up and ours isn't even sitting up, every imaginable disease in the family medical book is studied.

DOMESTIC PROBLEMS

Domestic problems are such a common source of anxiety it is impossible to imagine life without them. Some people feel home-brewed anxiety so constantly that they see causes for anxiety wherever they look. Just as a sentry on guard becomes sensitized to the slightest noise, acute or chronic anxiety can sensitize nerves to bring intense reactions with alarming swiftness. These are the exaggerated symptoms of stress. However, a person in an anxiety state may not recognize his upsetting symptoms. He thinks they are unique to him, that no one could have suffered this way before. His bewilderment and fear of the upsetting symptoms bring further stress and may prolong his anxiety, which is a nervous illness.

A person suffering from an *acute* anxiety state, which means sudden, periodic attacks, may have some or all of the following symptoms: constantly racing heart, "missed" heartbeats, attacks of palpitations, pain around the heart, churning stomach, sweating hands, trembling spells, breathlessness, nausea, weak spells, difficulty in swallowing solid food, and above all, panic attacks.

The symptoms of *chronic* anxiety (which means ongoing or continuing) are fatigue, sleeplessness, headaches, mental exhaustion (because so much energy is expended worrying about what is wrong with me). The combination of mental fatigue and exaggerated emotional reaction may lead to indecision, loss of confidence, feelings of inferiority, apathy and depression.

ANXIETY OF GUILT

Guilt can stand in the way of the recovery of an anxious person.

Unfortunately, being compassionate toward others is easier than being compassionate toward ourselves. We must understand that becoming a mature person means living through changes in character from year to year. We are apt to judge ourselves as if we were the same person then as we are today. We must learn to separate the two and look on the person of yesterday as compassionately as we would look upon a stranger.

As mentioned, we are especially likely to feel anxious and guilty if another person is involved. For example, many suffer because they think they could have treated someone now dead more kindly. It's easy to remember only the short-tempered flare-ups, the snappy comeback. People are lucky who have no special duty that subjects them to such a trial. Men are usually luckier than women, because too often it is the daughter, especially the unmarried one, who fulfills the family obligations, particularly to elderly parents. It is the daughter's patience that is at the breaking point and her conscience later becomes involved. She is so much more apt to remember what she failed to do than the good she has accomplished. She should be compassionate toward herself and remember that at least she took the burden.

Nervously ill people are especially susceptible to guilt. One woman said, "For many years I have felt guilty because of my illness. I am a second-class citizen, a poor fish, a weakling." The nervously ill are conditioned to think this way, because so many who have never been nervously ill regard nervous illness as weakness. How ironic this is! The bravery of so many nervously ill people is phenomenal. Day after day, they live with and try to fight nervous symptoms. Sometimes through shame or not wanting to upset the family, they don't even talk about it. They struggle on alone, bewildered, despairing, but still ready to put their head on the block and try again if life demands it, especially if their family demands it. How unfair that they, of all people, should feel anxiety-ridden and guilty!

Healthy people often lose patience with friends or relatives who are suffering from anxiety. They think, "Why doesn't he pull up his socks and get on with his work and forget all this nonsense?" That is exactly what he would like to do. But what we, the healthy ones, do not realize is that by this time the fear felt by such a sufferer is greater than any the average person has known, or has paused to imagine. Repeated spasms of panic, when accompanied by exhaustion, not only increase in intensity but need less and less to set them off. Dread of having a panic attack may bring on a whole sequence. Meeting a stranger, the thought of being left alone, even a slamming door may suffice. Also, in spite of a great desire to pull up one's socks and get to work, such frequent and intense spasms of fear seem to paralyze his will to act.

To describe the treatment of an acute or chronic anxiety state in an article as short as this is impossible. However, here are a few guidelines that might help:

(1) Face the problem as part of life.

(2) Accept it as something that will be resolved one way or another in time.

(3) Let time pass.

There is nothing mysterious or magical about these suggestions, yet it is amazing how many people sink deeper into their illness by doing the opposite.

First, the average sufferer is alarmed by his symptoms, and examines each one as it appears. He listens in on himself and tries to shake free of the unwelcome feelings by pushing them away—in other words, by fighting or running in the opposite direction.

Also, he is bewildered because he cannot find a cure overnight. He keeps worrying because so much time is passing and he is not yet well—as if his illness is an evil spirit that could be exercised if only he, or the doctor, knew the trick. He spends his time: (1) running away, not facing reality, (2) fighting, not accepting, (3) being impatient, not letting time pass.

Strange feelings may momentarily, from time to time, sweep over people who are in an anxiety state. Recovery lies in passing right through these moments—again and again, if necessary, with full acceptance.

Recovery does *not* lie in trying to switch off these anxiety states, taking tranquilizers or trying to avoid such states. Recovery lies in going *right through them* . . . with complete acceptance in as relaxed a way as possible. Keep telling yourself, "I will glide out of this state of panic and be all right again." And you will.

CREDIT: *Claire Weekes, M.D., D.Sc., F.R.A.C.P., Consultant Physician, Rachel Forster Hospital, Sydney, Australia, author of* Peace from Nervous Suffering *and* Hope and Help for the Nerves *and* Agoraphobia.

Aphrodisiacs

Aphrodisiacs are defined as anything that increases or arouses sexual desire, which therefore may include dance, drama and music as well as substances which are believed by some to have such special properties.

The search for special sexual powers reminds one of the equally futile search for the "Fountain of Youth." The myth is undoubtedly kept alive by an indestructible wish even though modern chemistry, pharmacology and dietary studies have failed to turn up evidence that any substance exists that will increase sexual desire and performance.

Modern chemistry has provided us with new stimulants, glandular extracts, hormone stimulation and surgical rejuvenation (all equally effective). The bulk of the literature on aphrodisiacs, from the Middle Kingdom of Egypt (2200–1700 B.C.) through the classics in Greek, Latin, Sanskrit, Arabic, Persian, Chinese and English, has been dominated by one substance—food.

The relationships between food and sex are many and complex, including subtle arousal by taste, smell and texture.

Obviously well-fed, well-rested, healthy, athletic persons will be more sexually capable than the malnourished, depressed, haggard and oppressed. Other than this reasonable premise, there is no reason to believe food can arouse or stimulate anyone.

Only two of many so-called aphrodisiacs receive serious attention by students in this field, namely "Spanish fly" and yohimbine. Spanish fly taken orally produces acute irritation of the gastrointestinal tract and the genitourinary tract, causing a stimulation to the urethra. In men, it may cause a penile erection but usually without an increase in sexual desire. The dangers of using it, however, are worth noting since it could do serious damage to the kidneys.

Another drug popularly known for its aphrodisiac qualities is L-dopa. Sexual activity is increased in 2 percent of the patients who take L-dopa for treatment of Parkinson's Disease. However, the increase is probably due to improvement in the patient's over-all physical condition, rather than to the L-dopa itself.

The Chinese plant ginseng and musk were once thought to be of value in sexual arousal, but neither has proven to be effective when tested by legitimate investigators.

It is a sobering insight that sexual abilities may be closely related to general healthiness and a zest for living together. The ability to perform well sexually is diminished when there are competing ambitions, conflicts and mixed emotions including ambivalence and evasion.

The magnificent breakthrough of Masters and Johnson, combined with the scholarship of the Institute for Sex Research in Bloomington, Indiana, will probably help us learn to become more understanding and compassionate with one another so that we can learn to live somewhat better. Mutual improved relations between men and women and the cultivation of the civilized arts of living, which include dining and drinking, seem to be the path to improved sexuality. But don't be fooled into believing alcohol is an effective turn-on. A moderate amount reduces the inhibitions—but as Shakespeare said, it increases the desire but damages the performance.

CREDIT: *Henry W. Brosin, M.D. (psychiatrist), Tucson, Arizona.*

Appendicitis

In the mid-1930s, during the Great Depression, two questions were asked by many love-struck males before proposing marriage.

(1) Are your teeth in good condition?

(2) Have you had your appendix out?

When money was tight, it was considered a big plus to get a girl who didn't need dental work and whose appendix had already been removed.

Small wonder: Acute inflammation of the appendix is the most common reason for abdominal surgery. Approximately 200,000 cases of acute appendicitis are recognized in the United States annually, with an over-all fatality rate of 1 percent. Every fifteenth person in the United States (7 percent) suffers from an attack of acute appendicitis at some time during his or her life. Such an attack can occur at any age but it happens most frequently to young adults and children. It can also occur among elderly people who least expect it.

Illness and death from appendicitis in children have decreased with each passing decade, thanks to more accurate diagnosis, safer anesthesia and advances in surgical technique and patient care. The most important factor in the death rate, however, was the introduction of antibiotics in 1945. Hospitals report fatality rates for children with appendicitis as low as 0.07 percent.

But beware—acute appendicitis, once a highly fatal infection, can be as much a killer today as it used to be if neglected or treated with home remedies.

Delay and self-treatment can lead to rupture of the appendix, expecially if a person mistakes the stomach cramps for constipation and takes a laxative. This may cause the infection to spread and a serious condition called peritonitis might set in.

DIAGNOSIS OF APPENDICITIS

The most common symptoms of appendicitis are nausea and vomiting, and cramping in the middle of the abdomen. The pain usually becomes more severe and more persistent and moves to the right lower part of the abdomen. A fever from 99 to 104 degrees may develop. Unfortunately symptoms vary with the individual. Sometimes the pain is felt in the back or pelvis—or it may be mild or non-existent—even after the appendix has ruptured.

During an attack of appendicitis the patient usually lies with his knees high up. He has difficulty straightening them, because moving muscles in the pelvis causes pain. A doctor should be called immediately. He may take a blood sample. A white blood count may provide further evidence of an acute infection.

Some patients have periodic attacks of appendicitis which subside on their own. These patients suffer from recurrent abdominal pain but are symptom-free between attacks. The results of a physical examination are usually normal unless the patient is examined during an attack.

Before surgery is performed, the physician should do a thorough job of investigating to make certain the problem is not in the urinary tract or elsewhere. A number of other abdominal problems can easily be confused with a mild, recurring pattern of appendicitis-like symptoms. In an emergency situation, however, the physician may decide to operate without further exploration since a ruptured appendix is much more serious than one intact. If the doctor decides to operate and discovers a healthy appendix, no great harm is done. A person can live very nicely without his appendix. Most patients are never told that a healthy appendix was removed, but the hospital's "Tissue Committee" will know. A physician who removes too many healthy organs will be in serious trouble with his colleagues.

CREDIT: *American Medical Association. Reviewed for factual content by Dr. David Skinner, Professor and Chairman of Surgery, University of Chicago.*

Arrested

(*What to Do If You Are*)

The very first thing to do when confronted by an arresting law-enforcement officer is remain silent after having given him your name and identification. This isn't easy. The first impulse is to babble away in the hope of charming the officer and "proving your innocence." Don't bother. Once he's decided to arrest you, your charm is worthless and it isn't up to you to prove your innocence. It's up to the State to prove your guilt. This does not occur on the sidewalk when you're arrested, but in the courtroom.

Your witticisms and denials will never be used by the officer to exonerate you, but anything you say that is inconsistent or frivolous may be turned into an admission which can and will be used against you later. Silence is a protected constitutional right, and, as such, the State cannot use your silence as a weapon against you claiming that you were hiding something or that your silence implied some guilt. Words, not silence, might incriminate you.

In addition to words, conduct might incriminate you. For example, if you are arrested while driving under the influence, the police can request a "breathalyzer" test. In many states, your refusal to submit to a breath analysis to determine if there is alcohol in your system may result in suspension of your driver's license. But it may be worth risking suspension of your license if the potential charge against you is reckless homicide. As a rule, the police have the right to use a breathalyzer, fingerprint you, place you in a lineup and obtain handwriting samples without violating your constitutional protection against self-incrimination. But you are not the best judge of whether you should voluntarily submit yourself to these tests. Your lawyer is.

As soon as possible contact a lawyer. It is the absolute right of any accused person to have a lawyer regardless of how petty or horrible the charge. If you are flat broke the courts must appoint a lawyer for you. The tough guys who've been in and out of the criminal court building so often they know the bailiffs by their first names call their lawyers immediately when arrested.

Only the inexperienced are shy about calling a lawyer. It's foolish to think you don't need a lawyer because you are not guilty of anything. In the first place, you may be guilty of something. In the second place, the lawyer is the expert at analyzing your situation and, it is hoped, extricating you from it. In the third place, it is the height of stupidity to try to represent yourself (especially if you accept the initial premise that you should remain silent). Finally, remember that the system sometimes fails and the innocent find themselves being sentenced. So remain silent, get to a telephone and call a lawyer.

CREDIT: *Barbara B. Hirsch is a lawyer in Chicago and the author of two books,* Divorce: What a Woman Needs to Know *and* Living Together: A Guide to the Law for Unmarried Couples.

Arthritis

One of the problems with arthritis is that most people really don't recognize what it is. In fact, it is over one hundred diseases which involve inflammation or destruction of the joint.

Everyone remembers his Aunt Tillie who had "rheumatism," or has had backaches of his own, a "trick knee" or something similar. So people tend to think arthritis isn't a serious problem.

Arthritis is the single largest crippler in the country. It affects the old (with so-called "wear and tear" arthritis [osteoarthritis]) and it affects a quarter of a million children (with juvenile rheumatoid arthritis).

Among the diseases we call arthritis are even real killers—systemic lupus erythematosus, for example, at one time had a mortality rate of 30–50 percent within five years; research in treatment has reduced that number significantly. Dermatomyositis, scleroderma and other arthritic diseases have an equally grave outlook.

In between the "simple" problem of "rheumatism" and the killers lie the most difficult problems of all, such as rheumatoid arthritis, which typically strikes young adults (women more than men) at the peak of their working careers. This disease, the cause of which is unknown, can range from a fairly mild affliction of paired joints (wrists, ankles, etc.) to a devastating problem involving all joints of the body, and causing high fever, weight loss, anemia and in some cases death from involvement of the lungs and the heart.

If we count all types of arthritis, about one fourth of the population or some fifty million people are afflicted. Of those, about twenty million are seriously enough affected that they need some kind of medical care, and yet, through lack of adequate specialists in rheumatology, and through lack of adequate nursing care, less than half get the required medical care. In fact, some 20 percent—four million people—get no care at all.

And these patients, many of them, are not just suffering from "lumbago" or "stiffness." Many are bedridden, eventually so deformed that they could never stand or walk even if a cure were found tomorrow. Even the less severely handicapped often have such joint destruction and pain that they cannot care for themselves; they can't hold a toothbrush or a hairbrush or a razor, they can't bathe themselves or even take care of bodily needs properly. Needless to say, such people are unable to be normal and productive. They cannot be happy mothers, fathers, sex partners, employees, students or human beings. They are lost, desperate and afraid.

Apart from the terrible cost in human suffering, the purely financial cost of arthritis is enormous—for example, almost three and a half million people are partially or totally disabled from work, at a cost of over $4 billion annually in lost wages alone. Add to these figures the amount spent on medical care. It is estimated that over $15 billion is lost annually to the United States because of arthritis.

At the same time, less is spent on arthritis research than on any other equally significant disease group. For example, the United States Government's own figures indicate that heart disease and arthritis have roughly the same number of cases requiring medical care (22,500,000 and 20,250,000 respectively) and cause roughly the same number of disabled (3,600,000 and 3,300,000 respectively). Yet the government spends $205,000,000 for research on heart disease ($9.19 per victim) and only $13,800,000 ($.68 per victim) on arthritis.

Comparable amounts of money are spent for cancer research, so that heart disease and cancer may be said to take a disproportionate amount of society's money. And while it may sound cruel to say, heart disease and cancer are in one sense self-limiting diseases—patients get well or they do not, and in either case, they do not become long-term burdens on society.

The rheumatoid arthritic, on the other hand, who may become totally disabled at an early age, has an almost normal life expectancy; thus, such a young man or woman bankrupts the family, or becomes a ward of society for all the years of a normal life expectancy.

Such frightening, painful and crippling diseases lead to quackery on an enormous scale. Arthritis is not caused or cured by diet, yet we have "diet cures" galore; it is not caused or cured by too little or too much radiation, or sea water, or cabbage juice, or copper, yet we have "uranium cures," ocean water cures, health food cures and copper bracelets. Hundreds of millions of hard-earned dollars are spent by desperate people on such worthless treatments. Worst of all, such treatments may delay good treatment until irreversible damage has been done.

But what constitutes "adequate treatment" for rheumatoid arthritis? Without question, the drug of choice is plain or buffered aspirin. Contrary to most people's thinking, and certainly contrary to television commercials, aspirin does not merely "relieve the minor aches and pains of arthritis." It is an effective anti-inflammatory drug, which in adequate dosage *under your physician's supervision* (sometimes as high as twenty tablets per day) can reduce the systemic symptoms of rheumatoid arthritis, such as fever, and can significantly reduce joint inflammation.

When aspirin fails to achieve or maintain the desired effect, the next line of defense is usually gold, in the form of liquid gold salts. Gold is administered by injection, and requires close monitoring of blood count and urinalysis, because of possible complications. The treatment is prolonged—the positive effect of gold may not be seen until after six or more months of treatment.

Dramatic remedies such as cortisone (now largely replaced by other so-called "steroid" drugs such as prednisone) have so many serious side effects (increased fragility of the bones, mental disturbances, high blood pressure, stomach and duodenal ulcers, etc.) that in the best hands they are used only sparingly, and only for those cases unresponsive to more conservative forms of therapy. They do lead to an initial dramatic relief of symptoms, and before the undersirable side effects were known, this response led many rheumatologists to believe the problem of rheumatoid arthritis has been solved.

For rapidly advancing or severe cases of arthritis that fail to respond to aspirin or gold, so-called "immunosuppressive" drugs may be used. These are at present the drugs of last resort, and require very careful monitoring by a physician who is skilled. Nevertheless, dramatic results have been achieved, not only in rheumatoid arthritis but in other such connective-tissue diseases.

In most patients, other drugs recently made available for the treatment of rheumatoid arthritis seem on the whole to be no more effective than simple aspirin. Among such drugs are tolmetin, naproxen, ibuprofen and indomethacin.

Nevertheless, rheumatologists feel they are close to a significant breakthrough in their understanding and treatment of rheumatoid arthritis, as well as in a number of other connective-tissue diseases.

However, while there are always new drugs being reported as "dramatic cures" for arthritis, an actual "cure," or even totally effective treatment, lies in the future.

Among new drugs currently under investigation are such things as penicillamine, already accepted for use in Europe and probably soon to be approved for use in this country. Like so many other potent drugs, penicillamine is not effective in all cases, and requires close monitoring by a well-informed physician.

New techniques of surgical replacement of damaged joints have proven to be a godsend to countless sufferers from rheumatoid arthritis and osteoarthritis. Pain is relieved and in many cases almost normal motion can be restored. As one patient said, "It is wonderful to be able to touch my face again after so many years."

Not all patients can be helped by surgery. Effective replacements are currently pretty much restricted to artificial hip joints and knuckle joints. Active research is going on, however, to improve existing replacement for elbows, knees and other afflicted joints.

So, on the whole, the outlook is good—better, in fact, than at any time in the past. If, in addition to research and purely medical treatment, we could increase the availability of known skills in physical and occupational rehabilitation, a vast amount of suffering and loss could be avoided.

For the real tragedy is that arthritis *can* be helped. For example, the old scourge of gout, which is not a joke, but a sometimes fatal disease involving severe joint destruction, no longer should cripple anyone—research has led to modern drug therapy which enables gout patients to be entirely symptom-free and without complications.

Even for diseases where we do not have a "cure," such as rheumatoid arthritis, proper medical evaluation and treatment can mean the difference between endless pain and disability and a productive working and family life.

Research is needed; training of doctors and nurses and therapists is needed; care is needed, in the form of adequate initial-care centers and convalescent and rehabilitation units.

Such efforts are being made in many medical centers, and through more than seventy local chapters of the Arthritis Foundation, but present efforts are woefully inadequate for lack of money and for lack of trained personnel.

CREDIT: *Peter Wolkonsky, M.D., Clinical Association Professor, University of Chicago School of Medicine.*

Asthma

(And Hay Fever)

Five to ten million people huffing and puffing! That's asthma in the United States. If you're one of the sufferers, you suddenly become short of breath, cough, wheeze and strain to get air in and out of your lungs. After a time—it could be a few minutes or a few days—your cough loosens, the tubes clear and you breathe freely again. Till the next spasm.

Your attacks may come occasionally, during certain seasons, or they may be continuous. In children (and some adults) asthma may show itself by a recurring cough with little or no shortness of breath. Long, continued asthma may be complicated by bronchitis or lung stretching, which is called emphysema. Many asthma sufferers are afraid they will get heart attacks. This rarely, if ever, happens.

If you sniffle, sneeze or have a stuffy nose, there are twenty or thirty million like you. Most of the sneezers are seasonal hay fever victims, but many have a chronic nasal allergy. Nasal allergy and asthma are compatible bedfellows and tend to occur in members of the same family. In about one third of the victims hay fever leads to asthma and sinus infections.

These ailments are as old as history. Hippocrates spoke of "asthma," which in Greek means panting. In the Ebers papyrus from ancient Egypt there is a series of prescriptions for the relief of a disease which is undoubtedly asthma. However, it was not until 1698 that it was noted (by Sir John Floyer) that asthma is due to "a contracture of the muscular fibers of the bronchi." In 1819 John Bostock described hay fever as a distinct ailment.

The most common causes of hay fever and asthma are pollen, molds and insect particles.

In most parts of the United States, pollen produces three hay fever seasons. The spring season (usually April and May) is caused by the pollen of such trees as maple, elm, poplar, birch, ash, oak and others. The midsummer agony is caused by grasses; namely, timothy, bluegrass, Bermuda and Johnson grass, which can be found in most parts of the world.

Fall hay fever is responsible for the most frequent and severe suffering. It is produced chiefly by ragweed and is typically American. With the exception of some sections of South America, ragweed hay fever is present only in the North American continent—almost always east of the Rockies.

Just as molds sometimes grow on food in the house, they flourish even more profusely outdoors in the warm months. Molds thrive on grains, such as wheat, barley, corn and oats. The seeds of these molds fly around in the air and produce allergies. Next to pollen, they are the most common cause of hay fever and asthma.

The scales and hairs of insects or the particles of disintegrated insects are also a common cause of hay fever and asthma. During the warm months, vegetation and soil teem with insect life. It's enough when the insects are alive, but they continue to do their dirty work after death. Their remains break up and turn to dust. This dust causes allergic reactions in susceptible people.

What can be done to relieve hay fever? An air conditioner will filter out pollen almost entirely. People without air conditioners can tack wet sheets over their windows. Drugstores sell effective face masks. Weather can make a big difference. When it is sunny, hot and windy, the pollen count is high and symptoms become severe. Cool, cloudy, rainy weather offers relief to the bleary-eyed, red-nosed sufferers. Weather changes, such as a marked fall in temperature, an approaching storm or dampness, can aggravate symptoms—particularly asthma.

If you are cursed with asthma, any of a variety of things might cause your nose to be stuffy or run out of season—or produce a "surprise" attack. House dust is one of the most common. Hair sprays, face powders, feathers in your (or your bed partner's) pillow, birds in the house or chickens (if you're on a farm) may be responsible. The dandruff of cats and dogs is a prime allergy source. Pet lovers, research workers or laboratory technicians sometimes become allergic to such animals as guinea pigs, mice, rats, rabbits and hamsters. (Furs rarely produce asthma because the finishing and dyeing remove the dandruff.)

Chalk dust, chemical fumes, tobacco smoke and other chemical irritants may trigger an allergy attack or asthma. Cold air can cause bronchial spasm. A cold will often convert an allergy into asthma. Various kinds of emotional upsets can produce the same mischief.

Don't let your neighbor or a friend make your diagnosis. If you are short-winded, or wheeze or cough, you may have something other than asthma, such as tuberculosis, enlarged lymph glands, emphysema, a weak heart, kidney disease, anemia or any of a host of other ailments. Seek a medical opinion to make sure.

If you have an allergy try to find out what causes it. Your physician will quiz you, examine you and make whatever laboratory tests are needed to chase down the culprit. He will probably make skin tests, which are not 100 percent reliable, but they usually give some clues. Skin tests are relatively simple but they require patience and sophisticated medical know-how in order to properly evaluate the results.

Supposing you know the cause of your hay fever or asthma—what good does it do? Plenty. If you are lucky, your allergy may be traced to something that can be avoided or changed—such as a dog, a cat, a pillow, a mattress or a food. Eliminating foods must be done cautiously, under the doctor's supervision. For pollen, mold or insect allergy, central air conditioning or a reliable room or window filter may help.

A change in climate is a far cry from the magic solution because a grass or tree allergy is hard to escape. Ragweed-free resorts and areas do exist, but to avoid mold allergy, one usually has to go a long way. It's best to consult your physician for information on areas free or relatively free from particular substances. Individuals have been known to make a climate change and obtain good results because they left their pets or occupation behind.

If you have chronic asthma, the problem is more complex. The change to a dry, warm and sunny climate may make the allergy less disturbing. Only after a thorough study of the patient is the doctor in a position to know whether a change of climate will help, make the patient worse, or be a gamble.

If the air-borne cause of the allergy can't be removed and the suffering is severe, the most effective treatment for hay fever and asthma is shots. This means regular injections of solutions of pollen or other allergy-producing substances, beginning with tiny doses, not enough to produce allergic symptoms.

Some individuals have been fortunate enough to get relief after three or four shots but usually its takes weeks or months to note results, and the treatment must often be continued for years to get lasting effects. After a while, some people get along permanently without treatment, others require it periodically. Still others need it on a continuing basis. If you've obtained good results and then slip, you may be picking up a new allergy and need to be rechecked.

If your symptoms are not severe enough for injections, or while you're looking for long-term relief, you will need some immediate, temporary help. A number of remedies are available for this purpose—liquids, capsules, pills, suppositories, syrups and hypodermics.

Your physician must decide the appropriate remedy for your particular problem. Antihistamines have been useful in mild hay fever, but are not very effective in severe or non-immunized cases or in asthma. Many people discover the antihistamines produce unpleasant effects. They should not be taken without a doctor's supervision. For asthma, decongestant drugs, bronchial relaxers and expectorants are most useful.

In addition to other remedies that have been tried and abandoned, asthmatics have been hypnotized, mesmerized and analyzed in attempts to cure them. Emotional states are not the basic cause of asthma, although they may aggravate it. The asthmatic person frequently becomes emotional because of his asthma.

The cortisone drugs are of great help in some types of asthma and hay fever. They are used for acute attacks that do not respond to simpler medication, also in severe cases for temporary treatment while the sufferer is undergoing desensitization. When an allergic cause cannot be found and when the asthma is severe and chronic, cortisone drugs may have to be used indefinitely.

The short-term use of these drugs presents very little difficulty. Long-term use, however, can be a problem and the drug user must watch for side effects which may produce complications. Because the cortisone chemicals are extremely potent, the sufferer who uses this drug must be under his physician's supervision at all times.

Individuals who suffer from allergies should carry some form of identification at all times alerting others in case of an emergency to the fact that they have special health problems. It can be a health card carried in the purse or a wallet, but far better is a tag worn around the neck or wrist, since it can be seen more readily. All the allergies and the drugs likely to produce a bad reaction should be listed.

Asthma and hay fever are serious problems to the individual and to the nation. Much is known about both, but most sufferers still fail to take advantage of the available remedies. There is certainly room for improvement in finding more perfect methods of understanding and treating these miserable ailments. This can be done only through research. And research can be accomplished only through an educated and aroused public that demands and supports it.

CREDIT: *Samuel M. Feinberg, M.D., Department of Health Education, Division of Scientific Activities, American Medical Association.*

Automobile Safety

If someone offered Americans a means of transportation that would cost "only" forty-seven thousand lives a year, citizens would be outraged and reject the offer.

Yet each year, the death toll from traffic accidents continues to approach the total number of American lives lost during the entire Vietnam war. More than two million Americans have been killed in traffic accidents since the first U.S. auto made its way down a bumpy country road. Another million will lose their lives in the next twenty years if present trends continue.

The injury toll from traffic accidents is equally staggering. Nearly two million Americans each year suffer disabling injuries on the highways. Many are permanently disabled, and must be supported by society's resources for the remainder of their lives. More than 50 percent of the paraplegics and quadraplegics in our country were permanently crippled as the result of auto accidents. Of course, most of those who suffer injuries recover in time, but they bear scars, emotional damage and often pain for as long as they live.

The cost of auto accidents to the public each year is more than $21 billion, and we accept this horrendous figure without giving it much thought because we assume the accident is going to happen to the *other* fellow but not to us.

Historically, the traffic safety experts have concentrated their efforts on changing driver habits, and with some good results. The United States has one of the lowest traffic fatality rates in the world, even though we have the highest ratio of automobiles to population.

Driver safety, however, as important as it is, is simply not enough. Safety experts are now convinced that the car itself and the roads on which it travels must be improved in order to give auto occupants a better chance of surviving the crashes which will inevitably occur.

Improved highway lighting, breakaway lampposts and signs, more and better guardrails and shock-absorbing abutments have all helped make our highways more "forgiving" of accidents. New designs of this sort are constantly being tested.

But the most important modern development in protecting drivers and passengers is technology which makes the interior of the car safer.

The first step in this direction took place in the mid-fifties when the auto makers offered seat belts on an optional basis.

Congress subsequently passed the National Traffic and Motor Vehicle Safety Act, which was designed to implement the obvious need to protect auto occupants from the dangers of the "second collision"—the collision of the human body against the interior of the car. It is the second collision, not the collision of the car itself, which so often proves fatal or injurious.

The installation of seat belts became mandatory.

There is ample evidence that safety belts will significantly reduce accident death and injury, if worn. But despite long-term and expensive efforts, more than four out of five Americans still refuse to wear their seat belts.

Many people concerned with auto safety have suggested that laws requiring everyone to buckle up are the answer, but no state legislature has yet passed such a law, and for practical political reasons. In countries where such laws exist, seat belt usage climbed to a high level when the law was passed, only to drop again when it became apparent that the law was virtually unenforceable.

Fortunately, American technology has again come to the rescue. We can now protect car occupants automatically with protective devices which are built into the car itself and require no action on the part of the occupant, in the event that protection is needed.

Dual brakes, headrests to prevent whiplash injuries, safety glass windows, padded steering columns and dashboards, and safety-locked doors are all safety systems developed through the technology of the auto industry and finally mandated by the Department of Transportation so that they would be available on all cars.

On June 20, 1977, Secretary of Transportation Brock Adams issued a rule requiring that passive restraint systems—either air bags or seat belts—be installed on all new cars by 1984 (installation will begin with larger cars in 1982).

Of all the passive restraints yet developed, air bags show by far the greatest promise in reducing the enormous human cost of our nation's highway accidents.

The Department of Transportation conservatively estimates that the air bag system in all cars would save nine thousand lives each year, prevent tens of thousands of crippling injuries, and will be available at a modest cost—about $110, or less than the cost of a vinyl roof or many other luxury items.

The air bag is the most thoroughly tested of any safety device ever to be included on new cars. Air bag cars have been on the road since 1972. Twelve thousand air bag cars have now logged more than five hundred million miles.

Research evidence, however, is often less believable than the personal testimony of individuals who have escaped death or serious injury in air bag cars. For example, Dr. Arnold Arms, a Kansas City physician, survived a 35 mph crash into a city bus, which suffered $15,000 damage, yet Dr. Arms was able to get out of his car immediately and treat one of the passengers. His car was totaled, and he testified that he could not believe he had survived the crash.

The protection the air bag offers children clearly shows the need for automatic protection. Ninety-three percent of all children in cars are unrestrained, primarily because they are too large for infant seats or too small for seat belts. To those who say they have a right to choose whether or not to protect themselves by buying a car with or without air bags, we can only ask why their so-called "right" should mean that thousands of our children will die an early death or live a crippled life.

Until our cars and highways are built to protect us from our own lapses, what can you, as a driver, do to protect yourself?

If you drink, don't drive. The National Safety Council estimates that more than 50 percent of all fatal accidents on our roads involve a drinking driver. Unfortunately, drinking drivers injure and kill other people as well as themselves. Most studies indicate that the average person can tolerate one ounce of alcohol an hour without a change in reactions. If you've had more than that, don't drive, or wait until your body has had a chance to readjust.

A survey of court cases indicates that most alcohol-related accidents are caused not by social drinkers but by chronic drinkers, a small percentage of the population that causes a great percentage of accidents. Support legislation to get the drinking driver off the road.

Wear your seat belt. Until better protection is available, the seat belt is your best protection in frontal, side and roll-over crashes. If everyone who could wear a seat belt did so there would be a major reduction in traffic fatalities.

The Insurance Institute for Highway Safety reports that more than 90 percent of the child passengers in automobiles are unrestrained. When an accident occurs, they are often thrown wildly around the interior of the car. An unrestrained child should never ride in the front seat of the car, and should never be allowed to stand in the car. For smaller children, effective safety seats are available for a minimal cost. Older children should follow their parents' example and buckle up.

Keep your car in good condition. A well-maintained car is your best defense against being stranded away from home. It also reduces your chances of having an accident through malfunction of the vehicle.

Check your safety equipment often. With a friend, run a check on all light systems—headlights, brights, taillights, backup lights and turn signals. Check your horn frequently.

Make sure your car will start by keeping the battery in good condition.

Worn tires should be replaced. You'll not only prevent unwelcome flat tires and blowouts (a major cause of breakdown) but you will increase your stopping ability if your tires have good treads. Keep the tire inflation at its proper level, as specified in your owner's manual, and you'll reduce tire wear and tear. Make sure there's a jack in the car in case you have a flat.

Periodically inspect—or have your mechanic inspect—all fluid levels in the car, including oil, coolant, transmission fluid and brake fluid. Overheating on the highway, frequently caused by underfilled coolant systems, is still a major cause of breakdown. Keep the gas tank filled. Better to spend a few minutes at a gas station than be stranded for hours on a strange highway.

And lastly, keep your windows clean, your windshield wipers in good condition and your windshield washer full. Seeing is surviving. If you're traveling at 55 mph, the road is passing at 80 feet per second and your peripheral vision suffers. Give your eyesight every chance to detect obstacles by making sure your field of vision is as clear as it can be.

Drive defensively. Always be alert for the accident that's going to happen *to* you in addition to the accidents that you might cause through your own error.

Studies show that the majority of deaths occur in accidents at higher speeds. The national 55 mph speed limit may be an annoyance, but it has reduced the number of lives lost on the highways, and we should all be thankful for that. The highway speed limit saves both lives and energy. Speed limits on other roads are set to prevent accidents as well. Obey them, and other traffic laws. We'd have far fewer accidents if everyone obeyed traffic laws.

Always have an escape plan to avoid potential accidents. Constantly think of what might happen if the driver in front of you, coming towards you or beside you suddenly makes an erratic turn or stop. Plan to handle the situation ahead of time.

Driving involves your personality as well as your co-ordination. Keep your emotions away from the wheel of the car. Experts tell us that certain types of personalities cause traffic problems. Angry, hostile, short-tempered people are dangerous drivers. Too often the man who has had a fight with his wife takes out his feelings on the driver ahead of him or—heaven forbid—the driver who tries to pass him.

Stay alert. If you've been driving for more than two hours, chances are your reaction time has slowed. Sluggishness, inattention and drowsiness impair your ability to handle emergencies. If you can't pull off for a nap or a cup of coffee and rest break, try in-the-car exercises.

Wiggle your toes every few minutes to flex your leg muscles and stimulate circulation. Ease stiffness and tension in your hands and arms by gripping the steering wheel until your knuckles turn white, then relaxing.

Change your eye focus every thirty seconds. Rotate your head in a circle without taking your eyes off the road. Take deep breaths, then exhale and let your shoulders drop heavily and slump into the seat. Change your seat position, or adjust accessories within your reach. Simple exercises like these can help keep you alert . . . and alive.

Support all efforts to make our cars and highways safer. The vocal response of a citizenry concerned with the increasing toll in lives and dollars being wasted needlessly on our highways can bring about significant change in safety standards. Only when our autos and highways forgive our own driving inadequacies will we be able to significantly reduce highway deaths and injuries and their human and financial costs.

CREDIT: *Nan Kilkeary, Allstate Insurance Company, Chicago, Illinois.*

HE'S IN LOVE WITH HIS CAR

DEAR ANN LANDERS: My boy friend asked me to write this letter because he wants to know if someone besides me thinks he is crazy.

It's Tom's car. He treats it like a person—or as if it were the Hope Diamond on wheels. When he first bought it, he laid down the rules: Don't put your fingers on the glass when shutting the door. No crossed legs, both feet on the floor mat. No smoking, eating or drinking in the chariot.

He washes it every day and waxes it every week.

When we go out he parks as far away from other cars as possible to avoid nicks on the doors. This means we often walk several extra blocks, no matter what the weather.

Other than being hung-up about his car, Tom is a great guy and very normal. Will he outgrow this love affair with "Wheels" or am I stuck forever?

NO. 2

DEAR 2: You'd better learn to live with it, dear. Most guys who are car-crazy stay that way.

One suggestion: If he insists on parking a considerable distance from "the place" to avoid nicks on the car doors, ask him to drop you off and pick you up. You'll feel less imposed on, even though the exercise would be good for you.

CAR CRAZY

DEAR ANN: We've been married 13 years and my husband has owned 14 different cars. We have five children and it's a struggle to make ends meet.

My husband is a nut on the subject of motors. Whenever he hears an odd hum he takes the car apart and spends money for new parts. Our two older boys had hacking coughs all last winter but he was deaf to those sounds. He said, "Why throw away money on doctors? They'll be all right."

The middle son has a paper route and wanted a bike badly. He'd been using a wagon. His dad said he couldn't afford it and suggested the boy save his money and buy his own bike. This burned me up so I wrote my father and he sent a bike as a birthday gift.

My husband says cars are his greatest pleasure and he enjoys trading up and down, whatever that means. I'm sick to death of it. Can you help me? DUMB DORA

DEAR DORA: Your husband sounds like a spoiled kid. Some of those "odd hums" are probably under his own hood.

He needs to hear from an outside party (preferably a clergyman) what his selfish, car-crazy attitude is doing to his family relationships. A man who puts a hunk of tin and four wheels before his children builds a foundation for a very lonesome old age.

Automobile Thefts

There's a 20 percent chance that your car could be stolen this year. The National Automobile Theft Bureau says that if you live in a large city, the odds range from 1 in 50 to 1 in 5. Nationally, chances are 1 in 150.

Nearly a million motor vehicles are stolen each year in the United States —one every thirty-two seconds. Only 14 percent result in arrests; 68 percent are recovered. Most auto thefts occur after dark. The most popular month for stealing cars is August. The total economic loss is over $1.6 billion, counting the value of the cars and the cost of trying to find them.

The type of car most likely to attract a thief's attention is the new, expensive, flashy model. Targets are most often high-line cars such as the Cadillac, Continental Mark IV and Corvette. One insurance agent in New York City admitted that there are seventeen models of cars that his agency won't even insure due to their high theft risk, but he declined to reveal them. Some insurance companies build theft probability into their rates for specific makes and models. However, your car doesn't have to be new or high-priced to appeal to a thief. He may be part of an organized ring that has an "order" for your particular model of auto.

Another frightening possibility is that your car could be used in another crime. If that's the intent, an ordinary, inconspicuous car appeals to the criminal.

The auto theft racket increased approximately 20 percent a year until 1969. The rate has slowed down since the auto companies introduced the steering column lock.

The latest FBI figures show an over-all increase of 5 percent for 1972–76, with a 1 percent drop in 1976 compared with 1975.

This doesn't mean the auto thief is giving up. It means he has switched his primary target. He still steals cars, but has found an even more lucrative market—for the auto parts and accessories and personal property you leave inside your car.

In the 1976 report, the FBI says that since 1972, personal property stolen from autos was up 67 percent. Theft of motor vehicle parts and accessories increased a whopping 90 percent during that period. The average value per incident was $216. Stripping a car of its parts brings a higher return than selling the car in its entirety. A $5,000 auto built entirely from replacement parts would cost more than $25,000. During the New York blackout in July 1977, fifty cars were stolen from a Bronx Pontiac dealership. The cars' carcasses were found the next day—with every removable part gone. A thief doesn't even have to move your car to steal its parts. He can strip it to its bare bones in minutes.

A profile of the typical car thief, as described by the FBI, is a white male between the ages of thirteen and seventeen. Those arrested are usually amateurs; some are kids out for a joy ride. But some juveniles, presumed to be amateurs, are really working for a professional network. They are assigned to do the actual stealing because, if caught, the punishment is less severe than for an adult.

Some thieves will go to great lengths to get a particular car. A man in a Chicago suburb installed an alarm system in his Cadillac. A thief attempted to steal the car, parked outside the owner's home. He fled after setting off the alarm. The owner, finding no evidence of a break-in, assumed the alarm had malfunctioned. He disconnected it so it wouldn't disturb the neighborhood. After he re-entered his house, the thief returned and stole the car.

What can you do to protect yourself? Here are some suggestions:

Always lock your car and take the keys. It's astonishing how many car owners are careless (or trusting). Eighty percent of the cars stolen last year were unlocked and 40 percent had the keys in the ignition.

Lock your car and close all windows tightly. Park in a well-lighted area or locked garage.

Remove temptation by putting packages and valuables out of sight (CB radios and tape decks are prime targets).

When you park in a commercial lot or garage, leave only the ignition key with the attendant. Make sure your key number does not appear on the key you leave, to avoid possible duplication. Don't reveal how long you intend to be gone.

Keep your driver's license and auto registration in your wallet or purse. If left in the car, these papers can be used by thieves to sell your car or to impersonate you if challenged by police.

Install several anti-theft devices and activate them when you park your car. Many people prefer to install custom-tailored deterrent devices. These, being unique, give added protection since their operation is unfamiliar to both amateur and professional auto thieves.

If you replace standard door locks with the slim, tapered headless kind, it's almost impossible to force them open with a coat hanger. Other suggested devices might include a hidden kill switch (the car won't start unless the secret switch is on), or a fuel switch that closes a valve to shut off the fuel supply.

Alarms, sirens and flashing lights are often quite effective. Advertise the fact that your car has protective devices. Put a sticker on your window or bumper to warn a would-be thief. He may decide that your car is not worth the challenge and go on to someone else's. Usually a thief will choose a car that looks easy to break into, since he must work rapidly.

There are also things you should do to aid in your car's recovery in case it is stolen.

Since professional thieves frequently remove manufacturers' identification numbers from automobiles and component parts, you should put some personal "brand" on your car in a hidden place.

CREDIT: *Ray and Barbara Howard, columnists on consumerism, Chicago* Sun-Times.

Baby-Sitting*

My mother never heard of a baby-sitter. If you are over fifty, your mother never heard of one either.

In those days, it was unthinkable that "a stranger" would be called in (and

* *Dangers to Children and Youth* by Jay Arena, M.D., Chief of Pediatrics, Duke University, Durham, North Carolina. Copyright © 1971 Moore Publishing Company, Durham, North Carolina.

paid!) to stay with small children when parents went out for an evening. Grandma, Aunt Tillie or a cousin—some kind, dependable relative—could be counted on. Moreover, there wasn't much leaving of children before World War II. Recreation was a family affair.

In the early 1940s family life in America underwent some radical changes. Women who had gone to work in defense plants, as well as offices, shops and factories, liked not only the money but the freedom. They decided to keep on working. Enter the Sitter, first to be on hand when the children came home from school, then to stay one or two weekend evenings. After all, if Mama works at a job all day, she's entitled to some social life. And so it began.

Baby-sitting has become big business in America. In large cities, some sitters are paid as much as $2 an hour. In small towns, the going rate is from $.50 to $.75 an hour, depending on the number of children and what is expected in addition to sitting. Often the rate goes up after midnight.

First: I offer guidelines for the woman who needs the services of a sitter. Second: Guidelines for the sitter.

GUIDELINES FOR PARENTS

(1) Check the qualifications and health of the baby-sitter. Although friends, relatives and neighbors are the best sources for sitters, you may have to look beyond. Churches, high schools, colleges, nursing schools and youth organizations—such as 4-H clubs, Girl Scouts, Campfire Girls, and YWCAs —may be able to offer recommendations. Another possibility is to join a baby-sitting co-operative made up of parents.

(2) When you call a sitter, tell her how many children you have, their ages, what you expect in terms of service, what time you want her to arrive and approximately how many hours you will need her services. Establish the fee and let her know you will provide for her transportation. (I shall use the feminine gender throughout this piece because most sitters are females, but males [especially young college students] can serve well in this capacity.)

(3) Before your sitter arrives, prepare two cards. One should have the address and telephone number where you can be reached, and full instructions if the sitter is to feed, bathe or put the child (or children) to bed. The other card should list phone numbers of (a) the children's physician, (b) the police, (c) again, where you will be and (d) the phone numbers of two neighbors who can be reached in case of an emergency.

(4) The sitter should know the location of all exits, telephones, stairways, bathrooms, play areas, "off limits" areas, and which neighbors are available for assistance if needed. If your sitter is new or if you've moved, have her show up early so you can point out these locales. Even your veteran baby-sitter should arrive at least fifteen minutes early in case you have special instructions. The transition time between the sitter's arrival and the parents' leaving should be as orderly as possible to avoid upsetting or confusing the children.

(5) If your children are not permitted to do something during your absence which they have permission to do when you are home, tell them in the presence of the sitter so there will be no misunderstanding.

(6) If you have a pet, tell the sitter. If the dog has a jealous nature, confine it, and tell the sitter where the animal is.

(7) If your sister, friend or neighbor asks if she can bring her child (or children) to your home to be "sat" with, you or your sister, friend or neighbor should pay the sitter extra for this additional responsibility.

(8) The parents should warn the sitter that certain small, hard foods like nuts or popcorn can be dangerous for a baby or young child because of the possibility of being inhaled, which could result in choking.

(9) The parent should make sure no firearms are accessible for a child (or a young sitter) to get at.

(10) The sitter should understand that she is not permitted to entertain guests. Her full attention should be focused on the children who are in her charge.

(11) Don't expect your sitter to do extra chores such as dishes or ironing. Her primary concern should be your children's safety.

(12) No sleeping. Ask her to tour the house and the children's rooms every half hour.

(13) Make it clear that under no conditions should the sitter open the door for any stranger, regardless of what they say. ("I'm a friend of the family" or "My car broke down. May I use the phone?")

(14) Most sitters appreciate a late-night snack. Ask your sitter what she would like and have it on hand. Let her know you have provided her with the treat of her choice—the unspoken message being she is not to help herself to whatever she sees—such as the cake you baked for the bridge club tomorrow. If she doesn't get the message—tell her before you engage her the next time. It is important to have a meeting of minds on this matter. Sitters who eat everything in sight are one of the principal complaints according to my mail.

(15) Once parents have left home, their concern for the children should not vanish no matter how capable the sitter. A phone check should be made at least once during the evening to see how things are going.

(16) Parents should phone to let the sitter know if it appears they will be unable to be home at the time agreed upon. This is no more than common courtesy.

(17) If baby-sitting chores take place during nighttime hours, a parent should walk or drive the sitter home.

GUIDELINES FOR THE BABY-SITTER

(1) Be sure the parents give you full instructions. If you are unsure about something—*ask*.

(2) Have an understanding in regard to fee, starting time, the approximate time of the parents' return and arrangements for being escorted home—*before* the parents leave.

(3) Have an understanding about snacks. (See guidelines for parents.)

(4) Find out about the animals that are in the home.

(5) If more kids are included (friends' or neighbors') this means additional responsibility so the price goes up.

(6) Have an understanding about the use of the telephone. A major complaint against sitters is that the parents tried to reach the sitter to learn if everything was okay, and the phone was busy, busy, busy.

(7) Have an understanding about household work. Most sitters resent being asked to wash dishes, do "a little ironing" or clean up a messy house. If you don't want to do anything extra, say so.

(8) It goes without saying that a sitter does not leave a mess (orange peels, Coke bottles, etc.) for the lady of the house to clean up.

(9) A sitter should never help herself to perfume, cosmetics, hair rollers —anything that belongs to the lady of the house. Nor should she snoop around in closets or drawers.

(10) All play for small children, both inside and outside, should be closely supervised.

Constant vigilance is the answer to keeping creepers and toddlers out of danger. Special points to keep in mind:

(1) Don't let a creeping child or toddler play on stairs or other high places (like porches and window sills) from which he could fall. Bar top and bottom of stairs with latched gates. Keep the older children off the railings of second-story porches, too.

(2) Medicine and cleaning cabinets are dangerous for a child to get into, as well as tubs of water into which he might fall and drown or be scalded.

(3) Don't let a baby or toddler pull on a lamp, table or anything that he might pull over. No youngster should be allowed to play under something that might fall on him.

(4) Keep a young child away from heaters, radiators, electric wires and appliances (especially electric fans, laundry equipment, machinery with moving parts). When outdoors, keep children away from railroad tracks, high banks, wells, cisterns, garden pools, piles of rock and playground equipment that may be unsafe for their age, etc.

(5) Keep children out of the street. If it is necessary to cross a street with a child, do so at intersections only and always after traffic has stopped. Never cross the street from between parked cars.

About Playthings

(1) Never let a child run with anything that might hurt him if he fell on it.

(2) Don't let a child touch or get too near a strange dog or other animal.

(3) If you see cigar and cigarette butts or ashes left lying around in trays or wastebaskets, dump them. Nicotine is poisonous when eaten.

(4) Do not let a child play with matches, scissors and other sharp instruments or anything small enough to swallow or that might poison him.

(5) Let a young child play only with those toys which have smooth surfaces, safely rounded edges and corners, colors that don't come off and parts that can't be pulled off and swallowed or put in ears or nose.

(6) Never allow a baby to play with a can or box of powder (like talcum), as it can be breathed into his lungs or eaten with serious effects.

MEALTIME

(1) If small children must be in or near the kitchen during food preparation, keep them in a playpen or high chair and away from the stove. Older children should be warned not to touch hot things in the kitchen.

(2) Handles of kettles, pots and pans must be turned away from the stove edge so they cannot be reached and pulled over by a toddler.

(3) Use a potholder when handling a hot dish so you won't drop it and burn a child or yourself, and never pass a container of hot food or liquid over the head of another person.

(4) Check the gas burners frequently so that if the flame is blown out by a draft you can relight it before too much gas escapes. If considerable gas already has escaped, turn off all burners and open windows and the door immediately, taking the children outside. If the gas still leaks, leave children with a neighbor and call the gas company. Never turn on electricity in a gas-filled room, as a small spark may cause a terrific explosion.

(5) Store sharp knives, matches, etc. beyond the reach of young children. Broken glass should be wrapped in newspaper before discarding and glass and tin cans should be discarded where children can't get at them.

(6) If a slippery substance is spilled on the floor, wipe it up immediately so it cannot cause a fall.

BATHTIME

(1) Make sure the bath water is not too hot. Test the temperature with your elbow. Babies can drown in a few inches of water—use a small amount.

(2) Don't allow the baby to put soap into his mouth. Keep it off the bottom of the tub so it cannot cause slipping.

(3) Never leave a small child alone in the bathroom even for a minute, and make sure pills and other medicines, razor blades, etc. are beyond his reach.

(4) Never touch a switch with wet hands or while standing on a damp floor—electric shock may result. Be aware that if a TV set falls into a bathtub it can electrocute a person.

(5) Always keep a firm grip on a baby while he is in the tub or in a bathinette, and again—do *not* leave him alone for an instant. Support a baby along one arm to protect his head and keep it out of the water. Have all the supplies you need at hand when you start. Do not answer the telephone or doorbell at this time. Keep a youngster far enough away from the hot water faucet to prevent his turning it on and being scalded.

(6) Hold him firmly while putting on his clothes so he can't slip from your hands and fall. Never leave safety pins open or within his reach.

ADDITIONAL ADVICE TO BABY-SITTERS FROM ANN LANDERS

I have received so many letters from baby-sitters who tell me, "Mr. ———— made a pass last night when he was driving me home. I was so shocked I didn't know what to do. I had no idea he was that kind of a person."

The sitters ask for advice. Should they tell his wife? Should they tell their parents or other sitters? Should they sit for the family again?

Usually, the wife is "a lovely person." Often the sitter goes into detail: "The children are adorable. I'd hate to give up sitting with them." Or: "Mrs. ———— would be heartbroken. I'd rather die than hurt her feelings."

Sometimes they say, "I need the money, but I'm scared. What should I do?"

My advice is as follows: Do *not* tell the wife. It could create a great many problems and would serve no useful purpose.

Do *not* mention the incident to your parents or friends. Again, it would not help the situation and it might stir up real trouble and do irreparable damage.

If you are under fifteen, do not sit for the family again (just say you are booked) unless arrangements can be made for you to be driven home by Mrs. ———— or one of your own parents. This means you would have to contact Mr. ———— privately and tell him *he* will have to suggest to his wife that she drive you home because you could not do so without putting him in a bad spot.

If Mrs. ———— doesn't drive or if Mr. ———— is unwilling to ask her, no more sitting for that family.

If you are sixteen or over, you should be mature enough to handle the situation. Tell Mr. ———— in no uncertain terms *hands off*—and if he makes another pass you will refuse to sit for the family again and his wife will be left to draw her own conclusions.

The important thing to remember is this: *Keep cool.* Let Mr. ———— know you are in command of the situation—that you will not mention the incident to anyone because of your regard for his wife and family. Chances are he will gain a great deal of respect for you and you will not be bothered by him again.

BABY-SITTING BLUES

DEAR ANN LANDERS: Please help a group of sincere, conscientious young people who are being taken advantage of. I refer to the baby-sitters across the country.

Here are our major complaints—each and every one out of my own experience—and there are more like me.

(1) Wages. We know times are hard. But inflation has hit us the same as everyone else. A dollar doesn't buy what it once did. Instead of getting raises, we are asked to take cuts because "money is tight." If people can spend money to go out, they should be able to pay a sitter.

(2) Not getting paid. Sometimes they say, "We'll pay you next time," and then they "forget." The girl hates to ask for it, so she has worked a whole evening for nothing.

(3) Late, late hours. They say they'll be home at a certain time, and come in three hours later. This makes it bad when you have school the next day.

(4) Adding other people's children to the job. I've had as many as four extra kids to sit for which means extra work. No additional pay, of course.

(5) Last-minute cancellations: After having refused two other dates, I've been canceled with half an hour's notice. This costs me money.

(6) Maid service expected. Some people ask if you'd mind doing a few dishes, and when you go into the kitchen every dish and pot and pan in the house is in the sink.

(7) Some people come from a party cockeyed drunk and we have to let them drive us home.

Thanks, Ann, for your help.

BABY-SITTERS ANONYMOUS

DEAR BABY-SITTER: I have dealt with various aspects of your problems, but now that you have listed several complaints, I'll deal with them all at once, and I hope you girls out there will clip this column and use it as a guide.

Most of your problems result from your failure to establish guidelines and stick to them. If a girl takes her job seriously she should have, in advance, an understanding with her boss on all the issues raised in your letter. If the woman does not live up to her word, the girl should not sit for her again.

(1) Wages. Establish your fee and stick to it.

(2) If you do not get paid the night you sit, remind the woman the next time she calls that you didn't get paid for last time and that you'll be expecting double money, so please have both fees ready.

(3) If the couple comes in "three hours late" on a school night more than twice, don't sit for them again. They are not reliable people.

(4) Make it plain when you talk price that the fee includes her children only and extra children mean extra money.

(5) Have an understanding in advance that unless you get three days' notice for a weekend cancellation, the woman will have to pay you half of a normal night's sitting fee.

(6) If you don't want to do dishes, say so. Tell her you have homework to do—which of course you have.

(7) Never get into a car with anyone who is "cockeyed drunk." Phone your parents or take a taxi and inform the people that the taxi is on them.

Baldness

DEAR ANN LANDERS: I'm a 17-year-old guy who has asked at least 50 people if they know of a solution to my problem. No one does. You are my last hope.

Is there any way to prevent baldness? My hair is getting awfully thin and I just hate to see it go. My father was completely bald at an early age and I'm afraid I'm going to be, too.

What causes baldness? Can anything be done to prevent it? An answer from you would be greatly appreciated by me and thousands of other guys who read your column.—
SOUTH CAROLINA BLUES

DEAR S.C.: Some hair loss is temporary, if it is caused by illness or anxiety. But usually baldness that comes on gradually, and begins at an early age, is hereditary and permanent.

For centuries men have tried everything from herbal ointments to sheep dung. Nothing works—so save your money. If you become deeply depressed, you might consider transplants. But it is an expensive, painful, time-consuming procedure and doesn't always come out satisfactorily.

Some women think baldies are sexy —so if you can psych yourself out and learn to like your shining dome, it would be the best solution of all.

Dermatologists see little chance that one day soon a "magic formula" will be discovered that will grow hair on a bald head. Baldness has a low priority in medical research. It doesn't kill people. It only hurts their pride. If there is such a discovery, it will probably come as a spinoff of research into genetics.

Baldness is part of the individual's inheritance but little is known about its transmission. The widespread belief that the mother carries the dominant genes is now in doubt.

Once baldness begins (as early as the late teens) nothing will stop it, says dermatologist Robert Stolar of Georgetown University Medical School. Brushing, frequent or infrequent washing, keeping hair long or short, massage and electrical stimulation—nothing will make a difference. Hair "restorers" benefit only the promoters.

Baldness can accompany certain diseases. When the body recovers and the hair grows back, whatever hair treatment one happens to be undergoing at the time is unjustly credited.

Progression of baldness can be slowed by administering female sex hormones, but the cure may be worse than the disease. Men who have tried it find they lose their beards and develop secondary female sex characteristics, such as enlargement of breasts, as well as sexual impotency.

Transplantation of hair is a well-established procedure and Dr. Stolar provides it only when a patient insists it is important.

"We do a large number of transplants, but I do not recommend it. To me it's a highly personal decision that should be made by the individual. If he feels he needs it, I think a doctor should give him that service. If the individual can adapt to the loss of hair and feel comfortable I would say don't go in for transplantation."

In Dr. Stolar's view, baldies can take comfort in the likelihood that their day will return.

"I have lived long enough to have people shave their scalps and their beards," he said. "Now we have reversed that trend and gone back to the hairy phase of the cycle. It may well be in another five years we will go back to the hairless state again."

CREDIT: *Arthur J. Snider, Science and Medicine, Chicago* Sun-Times.

Barking Dogs

Not a week has passed since I have been writing my column that I have not received at least fifty letters about barking dogs. Some letters are several pages long. All are filled with anger and frustration—the culmination of bottled rage. Not infrequently these letters end with threats. Example: "If something isn't done I'm going to buy a gun and kill that mutt."

I print a barking dog letter about twice a year but the problem continues to show up in the mail regularly. I sometimes wonder if anyone is reading my column. Here is a typical complaint:

DEAR ANN LANDERS: We are beginning to hate our neighbors because of their dog. The animal starts barking about 8:30 at night and keeps it up until dawn. This horrible racket began six months ago and it is driving us out of our minds.

We have tried earplugs but they don't block out the sound completely. A few weeks ago we tried turning on the radio, but the radio keeps us up so this is no solution.

We own our home and used to love it. Now we are miserable. Is this fair? What can we do?   OHIO SUFFERERS

DEAR OHIO: Anybody who would tolerate all-night barking for six months is not playing with a full deck.

Go to the neighbors and tell them their hound is keeping you up nights. They should take the dog to a veterinarian and learn why he barks for hours on end. If the barking cannot be stopped the animal should be sold or given away. The neighbors must be told that all-night barking might be judged "disturbing the peace," in which case the law is on your side.

And another:

DEAR ANN LANDERS: A word to Ohio Sufferers, who were nervous wrecks from lack of sleep due to the neighbors' barking dog. Perhaps it will help them to know how *we* solved the same problem.

We put up with our next-door neighbors' barking dog for two weeks. Finally I telephoned (at 2 A.M.) and told them their dog was keeping us up and would they please do something about it. For the next three nights, the dog was quiet. Then he started barking again. I phoned the neighbor once more (this time it was 3 A.M.). She said, "We are heavy sleepers over here and we don't hear anything." I replied, "How nice for you. But we are light sleepers over here and we hear everything."

From then on, whenever the dog started to bark we telephoned and woke them up regardless of the hour. We figured if we couldn't sleep, why should they?

It paid off. The dog doesn't bark at night any more. OXNARD, CALIF.

DEAR OX.:   Your solution is the best one yet. I recommend it.

CREDIT: *Ann Landers.*

Battered Woman

WHAT IS THE PROBLEM?

There is a huge billboard in Detroit constructed by the side of an expressway running from the city to the suburbs. It is an advertisement for a bowling alley, and thousands of people drive past it every day. It pictures some bowling pins being knocked over by a bowling ball, and reads: "Have some fun. Beat your wife tonite."

The designers of this billboard are not actually advocating the use of violence against women. But it lets us know that woman beating is still considered a laughing matter.

Fifty years ago the wife was regarded as the property of the husband. He had a right and possibly a duty to beat her. In fact, in the isle of Sark husbands are still allowed to beat their wives as long as they don't "damage the eyes, break the arms or legs, or make blood run." This is a dangerous rule to allow when it is known that 60 percent of severe beatings occur when the man is drunk and unable to judge the amount of force he is using. Serious injuries and even murder may result.

Woman abuse is the most often committed crime in the country. It occurs among every class, race, religion and ethnic group. I am not referring to an occasional slap in the face. I'm talking about brutal beatings that continue over many years.

The tools of violence may include pots, pans, lamps, table legs, guns and knives. Many women require surgery, casts for broken bones and long hospital stays. Some women are permanently injured and must spend the rest of their lives in wheelchairs. The problem is like an ever-present boil that seems to come to a head whenever we hear newspaper accounts of grotesque intrafamily homicide.

WHAT IS THE EXTENT OF THE PROBLEM?

A study in Hartford, Connecticut, found that 45 percent of all married women are physically abused by their husbands. Within these families, 29 percent of the men also abuse their children. In Brooklyn, New York, 54 percent of all women seeking divorce claim their husbands have battered them. In Chicago, over half of all police emergency calls concern domestic violence, the overwhelming majority being complaints of wife beating.

Contrary to common belief, the problem does *not* exist only in the lower and working classes. Although poor women have fewer options and resources available to them, woman abuse among the middle and upper classes is also a serious problem.

A Scandinavian woman who lived with a now-deceased shipping magnate for twelve years described an incident in which he beat her severely until *he* quit from exhaustion. He laughingly explained the next day, "All Greek men beat their wives. It's good for them."

Further proof that the problem is not restricted to the poor is the results of a study conducted in Norwalk, Connecticut, a community of wide socioeconomic range. There were roughly as many cases of wife abuse reported there as in a Harlem precinct of the same size.

WHO ARE THE ABUSERS AND WHAT MAKES THEM DO IT?

Men who physically assault women may be husbands, ex-husbands, boy-friends, jilted lovers, fathers and even sons. The only thing these men have in common is a real or imagined motive to beat the woman, and access to her when she is vulnerable and unprotected.

The most common reason for the beating is jealousy on the part of the man, almost always grossly exaggerated in his mind. He may fantasize that his wife is seeing other men behind his back or that she has betrayed him in some other way.

One woman reported that her husband accused her of being pregnant with the child of a national political figure. His insane jealousy over this fantasy led him to severely beat her. This jealousy often extends to the man's own children, when he demands that his wife pay attention only to him when he's at home and attend to all of his needs first. It is appalling how often men will punch and kick pregnant wives in the abdomen. This is another form of jeal-ousy and hostility toward what is considered a "rival." It can also be a method of terminating an unwanted pregnancy.

The compulsive wife beater is considered by Dr. Jensen of the Clarke In-stitute of Psychiatry in Toronto to be a pathological personality. His unresolved Oedipal complex causes him to regard women as extensions of himself, his property, which no one else can touch. This leads to pathological jealousy and physical abuse. On the other hand, Greenlands of McMaster states that the wife beater and his wife are usually normal, but the husband is usually frustrated or drunk, or both, and an astonishing percentage of men work at jobs they dislike. They take it out on their wives, who are weaker, handy, and anyway many consider wife beating an aspect of masculinity. If you're displeased, use your fists. It's the only thing to do. Yet the average wife beater was usually a child who was battered and nobody helped, or he watched others being beaten. One report states that of children taken from wife-beating homes, the boys are aggressive fighters whereas the girls are pas-sive-submissive; thus each sex is taking on the role of the matching parent.

In some cases, a man will beat a woman only when he is drunk. Certainly alcohol breaks down inhibitions and sometimes produces irrational behavior. But there are a great many other instances when the man will beat his wife while he is sober. For example: only before sex, only on Saturday night, and on and on. So alcohol alone cannot be considered the cause of violence, but merely an excuse for such behavior. In other words, the man drinks in order to have an excuse for woman beating; he can then disclaim responsibility for his behavior.

Another common explanation is that men beat their wives because they saw their fathers beat their mothers and they were taught at an early age that this is normal behavior in marriage. There is no data to support this notion, but it is true that in some cases I have seen a woman suffer beatings from both her husband and her son when the boy is in his teens.

Often a man will deliberately beat his wife in front of the children, and sometimes even encourage his son to take a swing at his mother. But just as there are sons who learn violent behavior from their fathers, so are there sons who abhor the violence they see in the home. They end up hating their fathers and grow up to be gentle and loving husbands.

Violence toward women can easily be picked up outside the home by exposure to the media. I refer not only to TV, but movies, books, rock albums, and even bowling alley billboard advertisements.

The most harmful rationalization for woman abuse is blaming the woman herself. There is psychiatric jargon, the use of which is fortunately now declining, about the "needs" of inherently masochistic women to be beaten. This theory, however, does not account for the millions of women who are crying out for help. Even if a woman does have masochistic fantasies, it does not mean she wishes to be beaten. The crucial difference between fantasy and reality is that the fantasizer has *complete* control over the fantasy, and ultimately manipulates the imaginary characters in a way that is pleasing to her. In real life the victim of a physical attack is in a desperate situation where she has no control over a man who is larger, stronger, possibly drunk and brutal, and perhaps has a knife or a gun.

Another example of blaming the victim is as follows: The woman saw her father beat her mother as a child, and wishes to be in the same situation herself. But it is equally likely that girls who witnessed violence against their mothers in fact are affected in an entirely different way. They may spurn all relationships with men in adulthood and frequently are reluctant to marry at all.

None of the above theories can account for the widespread practice of battering that occurs in this country. The idealization of the aggressive macho male reinforced by violent role models in life and in the media makes it easier for a man to grow up violent. But the fact is that battering occurs under any circumstances where the man wants to show that he is "the boss." He may be upset about something that has absolutely nothing to do with his wife, but she is an easy target and he can always find an excuse to direct his anger at her.

Story after story is heard of a woman beaten or killed when she burned the roast, failed to sew a button on his shirt, wore her red dress or *didn't* wear her red dress.

WHAT ARE THE RESPONSES OF OUR SOCIAL AND LEGAL INSTITUTIONS?

The sanctity of the marital home is protected by the Supreme Court's right-to-privacy decisions. It is common knowledge that "a man's home is his castle." These notions of privacy, however, sometimes are used as an excuse to ignore violence that occurs within the family. Often we have newspaper accounts of children literally tortured to death by their parents. Neighbors and teachers knew what was going on but they didn't report it because it was "none of (their) business."

Shame is one of the principal reasons beaten women do not go for help. Shame is hard to understand unless you have been a victim of abuse in marriage. But imagine that the man you married suddenly starts using you as a punching bag for no apparent reason. Maybe there are problems in the marriage, but you have done nothing to warrant a beating. Perhaps he was drunk the first time—you can make an excuse for him and just stay indoors or wear dark glasses to hide your black eyes. After all, he brings home a paycheck every week, and the kids need a father. You will try being sweeter, kinder, a better sex partner.

But it happens again, a third time, then too many times to count. You don't talk to your neighbors any more because you're embarrassed about all the screaming and crying that comes through the walls. You cancel visits to relatives because they've seen you with bruises too often and look at you with pity. You lie to friends, saying you bumped your head on the kitchen cabinet—that you're always bruising yourself because you're so clumsy. Most of all, you lie to yourself. You are sure things will get better once he gets transferred out of that department where his boss is always picking on him. You tell yourself, when the baby no longer wakes you both up for night feeding he will be in a better mood. And you believe him when he says he's sorry. "It won't happen again. I must have been out of my mind."

Sometimes he is nice, and you enjoy his companionship. You can't imagine living alone. You're sure you could never make enough money to support yourself—and child care is expensive. Also a divorce means your marriage has failed (and therefore you are a failure). Actually, the two of you have only one problem—he beats you.

A woman in this situation feels trapped. If she goes for counseling the counselor can only suggest things *she* can do to change, and of course, *her* behavior is not the problem. The man almost always refuses to go for counseling. If she is ashamed, he is ten times more so. If she goes to a clergyman, she may get sympathy, but little else. Up until recently, it was thought by most clergymen that a marriage should try to be saved at any cost.

If it's beginning to appear to you that the cards are stacked against the abused wife, you're right. But there are a few social workers, doctors, family medical centers and women's shelters where a woman can find support and help.

Usually a woman has already tried to get help through several social agencies before she calls the police. This is the last resort for a desperate woman caught in the middle of a fight. She believes the police will immediately come to her rescue and stop the fight. The police, however, are notorious for their unsympathetic behavior toward the beaten woman. At the time of this writing, class action lawsuits have been filed against police departments in New York, Cleveland and California for flagrant refusal to enforce the laws dealing with battered women. Since police officers are more likely to be wounded or killed when answering calls concerning domestic violence than at any other time, their reluctance to intervene can be explained in part by their interest in self-preservation. But battery is a criminal offense just as bank robbery is, and the police have a duty to intervene.

The fear of injury also does not account for the cop's refusal to arrest when he is already present at the home. Police were repeatedly called to the home of a well-known football player who was beating his wife. They did nothing but talk to the man about football, and then left. This pattern continued until the wife could no longer suffer the continual abuse. The police were finally called one last time—to pick up the dead body of the football player.

A Kansas City Police Department study showed that in 85 percent of the cases of domestic homicide the police had been called at least once before the actual murder took place. In 50 percent of the cases, the police had been called five times or more. A recent survey revealed that 40 percent of the women in Chicago Cook County jail for killing a spouse or boyfriend had suffered abuse by the man they finally killed.

There are many reasons why the police fail to respond effectively to calls for help from abused wives. In most police departments there is no training program that deals with domestic violence. In my experience, it appears that the police simply identify with the man, and tend to believe his side of the story, even with overwhelming evidence to the contrary.

The Chicago police recently believed a man who said his wife had merely "hit her head on the dresser" when in fact he had cracked her skull open when he pushed her against a radiator. The officer may also identify with the man because he treats his wife the same way. A Boston cop shot his wife with a service revolver in a fight that began because she accidentally broke the egg yolks as she was preparing breakfast for him.

Pilot programs have been developed in a few cities which involve special training for police in domestic violence problems. These units are generally effective when the women have access to them and are able to get in touch with them. But part of the problem is that battered women rarely know these services are available. The other part of the problem is that the pilot programs are so small they just serve as models for what should be developed. In a city the size of Chicago, for example, one would need a force of fifteen thousand trained police officers to effectively deal with battered women.

WHERE CAN A BATTERED WOMAN TURN FOR HELP?

If there is a women's center in your town or city, they would know what resources are available locally for battered women. Feminists have organized emergency shelters, legal services, counseling and support groups in many cities.

Crisis hot lines often have reference files for many social problems, and they may be able to direct you to help. The Salvation Army can usually put you up for a few nights on an emergency basis. Your local YWCA may be able to help you. Some cities have organizations designed to help victims of crimes. (In Chicago, it's called the Victim-Witness Program.)

If you want to pursue legal remedies, you have the following options available:

(1) You get an emergency temporary restraining order. This is a court order signed by a judge that says the man cannot molest, harass or injure you for a specified period of time (usually ten days).

(2) You can get an emergency injunction, which is a court order forbidding the man from entering your home or apartment, and from molesting, harassing or injuring you.

(3) You can get a legal separation. This means you are still married, but live apart. The man is still legally obligated to support you.

(4) You can file for divorce.

You will need a lawyer to assist you in all of the above actions. If you cannot afford to hire a lawyer, ask Legal Aid to help you. (It's in the phone book.)

Without a lawyer you can press criminal charges against the man. Usually the offense will be battery, but it may also be aggravated battery, assault, unlawful use of a weapon, or some other offense. If the police will not arrest the man at the time of the beating, you can sign a warrant the next morning at the police station. When you go to trial, it is best to bring a friend who will support you in the face of hostile judges and State's attorneys. If possible, have photographs taken of your injuries soon after the beating, and bring them to the courtroom, along with medical records, and a witness. Don't let anyone intimidate you into dropping charges—you have a constitutional right to be protected by the law. If you don't want your husband or boyfriend sentenced to jail, you can ask the judge that he be placed on probation, with the condition that any further beating is a violation of probation.

Legal remedies are just pieces of paper from a court, and may further enrage the abusive man. Even a jail sentence may not stop some men from beating their wives and girlfriends. We need to open up options for battered women—to give them avenues of escape from physical torment. Shelters are a good first step, and equal economic opportunities are vital to keep women from feeling chained to an abusive man. Most of all, we need to educate the public about this problem, and make this a society where it is not acceptable for men to beat women.

CREDIT: *Marlene Drescher, Legal Center for Battered Women, Chicago, Illinois.*

DEAR ANN LANDERS: My wife insists she knows some women who have beat up their husbands during a heated argument.

I can understand a woman emerging victorious in a tennis match or a golf game or even being a better bowler or skier than her husband, but the thought that a man would marry a woman who could physically over-power him is utterly inconceivable to me. I don't believe it is possible. Do you? KEYSTONE L

DEAR K.: Of course it's possible. At this very moment I'm sure some-where in the world several wives are beating up their husbands.

Many women are in much better physical condition than their mates. They can pack a mean wallop and are faster on their feet. That's all it takes, Mister.

Bedwetting

(*Enuresis*)

Bedwetting (or enuresis) may be a symptom of a deeper problem. There is no single solution or treatment since there are a number of situations that might cause a child to wet his bed.

The cause most parents hope for is some disease of the bladder which can easily be cured by their doctor. In fact, some parents talk about bedwetting as "a weak bladder." Inflammations of the bladder may indeed cause bedwet-ting, as well as daytime wetting, since the irritation produces a symptom called urgency, or a sense that the bladder must be emptied immediately. Since inflammation of the bladder is more common in girls than in boys, and bedwetting is more common in boys than in girls, this obviously cannot be considered a common cause.

More important than the bladder is the muscular ring at the mouth of the bladder called the sphincter. At birth this muscular ring operates automat-ically, opening up when the bladder reaches full capacity. The infant is not constantly wet, but urinates at intervals without any voluntary control.

Toward the end of the first year of life, as the nervous system develops, the sphincter gradually comes under the control of the child, along with some influence of the parent.

At first, with the encouragement of the mother, urine is held back until the clothing can be removed, and the toilet is available. Slowly, as it becomes easier to contract the sphincter, and the bladder capacity increases, it becomes possible for the child to remain dry through the night, although there may be some "accidents" after a stressful day.

The ability to voluntarily relax the sphincter is a later development, so that the child cannot urinate unless the bladder is close to capacity. An infrequent cause of bedwetting is some neurological defect of the spinal cord interfering with sphincter function. This rarely results, however, in just bedwetting. There would more likely be a general problem in sphincter control, with both wetting and soiling during the day as well as during the night.

A more common cause of bedwetting lies in the area of parental attitudes to toilet training. On the one extreme there are families where almost everyone wets. If this is expectable behavior, the child will follow the family pattern. No message has ever been given that it is both possible and desirable to have a dry bed. Many children learn this only when they want to stay overnight with friends, go to camp or even enter the army. I have also seen this "no training" attitude in "liberal" families who are afraid any training is harsh, and fostered by pediatricians who assure them that it is best to ignore the wet bed and "eventually it will go away by itself." Some children may be constitutionally slow in developing urinary control, and may spontaneously stop wetting at age six to seven, or else at puberty. Some attempt should be made to help them, however, because they do feel embarrassed.

"Magical" cures may sometimes occur by simply informing the child that he is old enough to go through the night without urinating, or else he should get up and go to the toilet if he feels the urge.

At the other extreme, which is not common at present, is the overly conscientious mother who makes a big deal out of training and control. If control is attained at the earliest age when it is physically possible, it is easily broken down by illness or stress. It then becomes much harder to re-establish, because both the child and mother feel like failures.

Some years ago, a urologist pointed out that the child who is placed on the toilet very frequently may fail to develop the bladder capacity which makes it possible to stay dry through the night. Also, because of the delay in the ability to relax the sphincter voluntarily, the child who is urged to urinate before bedtime or a trip, even though he had urinated a short time before, and cannot may be viewed as stubborn, and become involved in a power struggle with the parent. Urinary control then becomes a battlefield.

This power struggle is certainly an important part of bedwetting. Sometimes the act is conscious and deliberate, occurring when the child is awake, although usually the loss of sphincter control occurs on waking from the deepest stage of sleep.

In the very young child who has just attained control, the most frequent stress is the birth of a brother or sister. Wetting may be seen as a plea to remain a baby, or an expression of anger at the parents and the new baby. The older child has trouble understanding why the baby is excused from the controls which are expected of him.

In later childhood there may be more difficulty in determining the "message" of the symptom. Usually the child has been dry for some time, and the parent tends to concentrate on controlling the symptom and loses sight of the situation or the event that triggered it.

The parent often tries punishment or various commercial devices, ignoring the symptom, calling the child a baby, etc., before seeking professional help. The parent needs help to get out of a power struggle which he cannot win without the co-operation of the child. There are a number of methods, including electric conditioning devices, which may succeed in stopping the wetting symptoms. In children who are constitutionally slow, these may have some value, and they feel better in being able to visit away from home. However, if the wetting has been a symptom of a power struggle, or a neurosis, then professional help for the total situation will be necessary.

The professional investigation starts with a careful history, to determine if there might be some physical problem that requires medical treatment. It should also include a history of the toilet training experience, and significant events relating to the beginning of the bedwetting.

Somewhat more difficult to determine are the attitude and behavior of family members toward the child. Sometimes there has been actual physical abuse, and wetting is the child's revenge. There may be sexual stimulation not suitable to the child's age, with a reaction in that organ of the body which has a sexual as well as urinary function. There may be loss of a parent, or a more subtle loss of support from a parent, with greater demands for mature behavior than the child can comfortably deliver. Bedwetting is very common in children's institutions, where the loss of parents for various reasons has required children to depend on themselves and strangers.

I do not wish to imply that every case of bedwetting needs psychiatric treatment. For the well-meaning parent, the first task is to prevent the wet bed from becoming a battleground.

It is necessary to hold to the idea that each child will one day be able to have a dry bed. This can be done in a positive manner by sensing when the child can respond to the desire to be more mature, usually toward the end of the second year of life. Girls are often ready sooner than boys. It may take a year to establish a reliable habit.

Praise for success is usually more effective than shame or punishment for failure. If bedwetting develops after dryness has been attained, some attention should be paid to the stress which may have triggered the backward step.

In a case of the birth of a sibling, the loss of a parent or an illness in the child, it is best to be patient, allowing time for the child to express his feelings, then gradually encourage an effort to have a dry bed.

Sometimes reducing expectations in the area of school achievement or household chores temporarily will allow for progress to resume. If it does not, after a period of a month or two, the symptoms may be addressed more directly by offering rewards for dry nights until the pattern is established. If this is not successful, professional help should be sought. A consultation may be sufficient to suggest to parents a more effective approach. However, if the child has complex problems relating to immaturity, sexuality or hostility which no longer respond to good parental handling, treatment of the child may need to be long-term and intensive.

CREDIT: *Helen R. Beiser, M.D., Chicago Institute for Psychoanalysis.*

Bicycle Safety

The bicycle, like a car, is not inherently dangerous unless, of course, it is mechanically deficient. It's bicyclists who cause accidents. In fact, bicyclists appear to be at fault in nearly 80 percent of all collisions with motor vehicles, according to the Insurance Institute for Highway Safety.

Bicycle safety must be learned and practiced by the bicyclist. In one respect, the bicyclist faces a greater challenge than the motorist: He must not only know all motor vehicle safety regulations, but also those which apply to bicycling.

Over half of all bicycle/car accidents occur at intersections, reports the National Safety Council. Why? Because either the driver or the bicyclist failed to yield the right of way.

WHAT ARE THE OTHER CAUSES?

Riding too close to the center of the road, ignoring traffic signals and signs and moving against the flow of traffic follow in that order.

The U. S. Consumer Product Safety Commission lists the following causes:

(1) Loss of control (caused by difficulty in braking, riding too large a bike, riding double, stunting and striking a bump or obstacle).

(2) Mechanical and structural problems (such as brake failure, wheel and/or steering mechanism faults, chain slippage and pedal and spoke breakage).

(3) Entanglement (of feet, hands or clothing).
(4) Foot slipping from the pedal.

DO BICYCLISTS EVER HAVE THE RIGHT OF WAY?

By law, they have the same right to the road as motorists—as well as the same responsibilities. But don't dispute the law or the right of way with the motorist. Besides having the advantage of their vehicle's weight and size, most motorists are unaccustomed to seeing anything on the highway smaller than a motorcycle. Face it, the bicyclist is vulnerable.

WHAT LAWS MUST THE BICYCLIST OBEY?

The bicyclist shall be granted all the rights and shall be subject to all the duties applicable to the driver of an automobile. This means the bicyclist must:

Obey all traffic signs and signals.
Ride on the right side of the road, single-file.
Never hitch a ride by attaching the bicycle to a motor vehicle.
Never carry more riders than the bicycle is designed to hold.
The bicycle must:
Be equipped with white front and red rear lamps (if ridden at night) capable of being seen from a distance of 500 feet (a red reflector may also be mounted on the rear).
Have sufficient braking power to make the tires skid on dry pavement.
Have a warning device that can be heard 100 feet away.

WHAT ARE THE "UNWRITTEN" RULES OF BICYCLE SAFETY?

Ride Defensively—As in driving an automobile, remember to be on the defensive—not on the offensive.
Ride a Straight Course—Stay as close to the side of the road as possible and ride in a straight line. Stay out of the flow of traffic, but far enough from the curb to avoid sewer drains or car doors that open.
Read the Road—Learn to simultaneously scan the road immediately in front of the bicycle for unexpected hazards—potholes and bumps, glass, pedestrians, car doors opening and others—and the road ahead for distant traffic situations.
Pretend You Are Invisible—By assuming you cannot be seen, you are more likely to anticipate the motorist's driving behavior and moves.
Know Yourself and Your Bicycle—Compensate for lack of speed and visibility by forethought and strategic planning. Test yourself to find out how fast you can pedal should you have to flee an approaching vehicle or

swerve around a car leaving the curb. Apply your brakes evenly when stopping, and apply the brakes repeatedly to dissipate heat when riding downhill. (If you have hand brakes, the front brake usually makes contact with the wheel before the rear brake.)

"See" with Your Ears—Consciously listen for approaching traffic—try to visualize what's happening behind you.

Plan Your Rides—Select roads to ride on that are relatively free from traffic (particularly trucks). By avoiding congested arteries you usually can make better time and arrive less harried.

WHAT HAZARDS CONFRONT THE BICYCLIST?

Car Doors Opening—Your first reaction to a car door opening in your path is to swerve to the left—a deadly response, especially if a car is approaching from behind. A safer move is to stop. If you have to, turn toward the curb.

Broken Glass and Gravel—It is safer to run over objects than to swerve out of their way into traffic. Bicycle tires and gravel don't mix. If you must ride on gravel, approach it head on, avoid changing course and go slowly.

Wet Roads—Not only will your tires slide on slick pavement, but water on the rims reduces and wipes out braking power. Also, your vision may be impaired when raindrops land in your eyes. (Be careful that your raincoat doesn't get caught in the spokes or chain.)

Dogs—If attacked, stop and get off the bicycle—this will usually end the assault. If it doesn't, use the bike as a barrier between you and the dog. Never try to outdistance the animal—you will only make him more determined.

Bugs—It isn't unusual to have a fly, gnat or bee hit you in the face, causing you to lose control. Avoid taking your hands off the handlebar to rub a sting. Instead, steer to the roadside and attend to the problem.

Pedestrians—Pedestrians, especially at intersections, must be allowed the right of way. Bicycle/pedestrian accidents don't occur very often, but when they do it's usually because neither saw the other approaching.

SHOULD YOU USE HAND SIGNALS?

State law says you should. Before you turn left or right, or stop, you should give the same signals which are required for motorists who do not have turn signals.

However, bicyclists with drop-style handlebars will need extra practice with this difficult maneuver. In fact, using a hand signal at the wrong time may cause the rider to lose balance in a turn, or not allow the use of both hands should sudden braking be required.

The point is, signal with your hands but do so well in advance of your turn —do not take your hands off the handlebar while you are turning or braking.

WRONG-WAY BICYCLING IS DANGEROUS

Drivers tend to look left first at intersections, then right, before they pull out. If you are coming toward the driver from his extreme right, he will probably hit you before he sees you. Riding on the left exposes you to possible head-on collisions with oncoming vehicles, the impact of which may be several times that of being struck from the rear. (A head-on collision between a bicycle and a car, where the two vehicles are traveling at 20 mph, would result in an impact speed of 40 mph.)

RIDING TWO ABREAST IS UNSAFE

When bicycling two abreast, the rider on the traffic side is vulnerable to passing cars. It's safer to ride single-file. When following other bicyclists, stay at least two bicycle lengths behind and in an offset position (slightly to one side of the rider in front). Use an "early warning" system whereby the first and last riders signal the others of approaching vehicles.

FLAGS AND REFLECTORS MAY NOT MAKE YOU SAFE

Bicycling is safer when the rider equips his bike with a pole-mounted flag and reflectors. But don't be lulled into thinking that these are all that is needed to be safe. Flags and reflectors have not reduced bicycling accidents —but awareness of safety rules on the part of bicyclists and motorists will.

ARE YOU PEDALING PROPERLY?

It isn't uncommon to see a bicyclist with his feet planted flat on each pedal, the pedals nestled under each instep. This position is tiring and reduces the power of each leg stroke. By pedaling with the balls of the feet one can extend each leg farther and allow the thigh and calf muscles to push harder. (If your bicycle has toe clips, practice loosening them several times before you ride in order to be prepared for emergency dismounts.)

WHAT SHOULD YOU WEAR?
BRIGHT CLOTHING: BE CONSPICUOUS!

If you are a beginner or haven't ridden in a long time, wear long, thick pants (an old pair) to protect your legs from bruises or scrapes. (Roll up your right pant leg or wear an elastic band to keep the fabric from catching in the chain.)

Tennis sneakers or shoes with light soles are best. Always wear shoes with shoestrings—the slip-on type of shoe is too loose and may come off while pedaling.

Shirts with several pockets allow you to carry such items as tool and patch kits, snacks, maps, etc. Often you will start your ride wearing a jacket or sweater, only to take it off after a few miles of riding. Put the jacket in a saddlebag rather than tying it around your waist—loose items of clothing somehow always get caught in the spokes.

In cold weather you may want to wear thermal underwear in addition to heavy outerwear. Also, wear gloves, a scarf, a tight-fitting hat and wool socks. The wind can make it a lot colder than it really is.

Experienced bicyclists wear riding helmets to protect their heads during falls. The head is the most vulnerable—and most important—part of the anatomy. Protect it at all costs!

WHAT SHOULD YOU DO ABOUT BICYCLE REPAIRS?

Ask the dealer for the information/repair manual that comes with your bike. It should cover everything from fixing a flat tire to tuning the gear mechanism.

Take time to learn how to repair a flat tire. The dealer will show you how, as well as sell you a spare tube and patch kit. If you bicycle long distances, carry these items with you. Also, bring along a set of small wrenches, a screwdriver and a pair of pliers.

To avoid tire failure, keep the tires inflated to the pressure suggested by the manufacturer (look on the sidewall of the tire) and examine them for cuts after each ride. Exert great caution when using a gasoline station air pump. They can fill your tire too quickly, causing the tube to explode and the tire to blow off the rim. Fill by holding the hose on the valve for short periods—better yet, use a bicycle hand pump.

Leave the intricate repair jobs to the dealer. Bring the bike back to the dealer for routine maintenance at the specified intervals.

HAVE WE FORGOTTEN ANYTHING?

In summer bicycling, do not ride in direct sunlight for extended periods. Dizziness and fatigue are signs of heat stroke. It's best to cool off and relax when you feel hot or tired.

Always carry adequate identification, as well as extra money for emergencies.

Carry a small first-aid kit and a plastic bottle filled with water (frame-mounted).

Avoid busy county and state roads. Many freeways prohibit bicycles—be sure to check which ones.

Bikeways are safer than public roads, but don't let your guard down. Be prepared for careless bicyclists and pedestrians, as well as poorly marked or prepared paths.

Use extreme caution when carrying children—even when using a specially designed seat. The weight of the child may cause you to lose balance, or the child may distract you.

When carrying packages, distribute the load evenly in baskets mounted on both sides of the rear wheel. (Avoid front loading—it affects steering.)

Make sure your wheel reflectors are mounted opposite the valve stem—this will provide better balance of the wheels at certain high speeds.

Be cautious when riding on wide, well-paved shoulders. Shoulders often narrow down and force you onto the main part of the road anyway. Besides, it's illegal to ride on the shoulder. (Shoulders are for emergency use only.)

Alcohol and medicine affect your judgment while driving. Just imagine what it does to you while riding a bicycle.

If you must ride at night, stay on well-illuminated but less-traveled roads.

CREDIT: *Written by James Hill Van Orden for the New Jersey Office of Highway Safety.*

Biofeedback

If you want to demonstrate how biofeedback works,

—Tape a thermometer to your middle finger; the bulb to the fat pad. Make good skin contact but do not constrict circulation.

—Sit still for five minutes with your eyes closed. Note the temperature of the finger.

—Then while still sitting quietly, with eyes closed, repeat a few autosuggestion phrases to yourself slowly. Such as "I feel relaxed and warm. My hands feel heavy." Repeat the phrases slowly, allowing the suggestion to take effect. Every 5 or 10 minutes take a temperature reading.

Most persons will show a rise in finger temperature after 10 to 20 minutes, some increasing their finger temperature 3, 5 or even 10 degrees, some only a degree.

By so doing, you will have demonstrated to yourself all the basic elements of biofeedback.

If you stand on a bathroom scale and look at your weight in the little round window, that is one kind of biofeedback. The machine tells you something about your biological condition, it feeds back to you information about yourself. If you want to lose weight you can use this information every day to guide your diet.

If you want to learn to warm your hands or feet at will, you can tape the bulb of a tiny thermometer loosely to a fingertip or to a toe (the inexpensive room-temperature kind of thermometer that is sold at supermarkets) and practice warming. The thermometer, a biofeedback device, feeds back information about success or failure, and from this information you learn how to control the temperature, which means controlling the flow of blood through that part of the body. One way to learn to warm your hands is to imagine you are lying on a sunny beach with your hands buried in warm sand. Try to get the feeling of warmth. The trick in biofeedback is to *imagine the feeling of what you want the body to do—and then totally relax and let the body do it*. If you "try harder" it is less likely to happen, like trying to force yourself to go to sleep.

After several fifteen-minute practice sessions with temperature feedback, the average person will observe that the temperature is beginning to respond to mental commands. At first such an unusual exercise is likely to make the temperature of the hands drop a couple of degrees, but with practice most people can learn to raise the temperature from the seventies or eighties to around 95 degrees F. Even easier is learning how to make your mouth water —by imagining you are biting a big juicy pickle. A biofeedback instrument is not needed in this case to tell you that the visualization was successful.

If you want to do something more difficult, such as making your right knee get warm, usually it is necessary to become physically and emotionally quiet first, with relaxation exercises, and then *feel* warmth flowing into the right knee. Make no attempt to force it. Just imagine it happening, and then let the body do it.

Since 1960 several hundred research and clinical projects have demonstrated that through the use of different forms of biofeedback the average person can voluntarily regulate a number of body processes that were previously thought to be involuntary, such as heart behavior, blood pressure and skin voltage, as well as blood flow in specific parts of the body. This capability may not be of much importance to a healthy person, but to someone who suffers from erratic heart behavior or high blood pressure, or some other blood flow problem, it can be of great importance. The "discovery" of this human capability (the knowledge of which apparently is as old as Yoga, perhaps 3,500 years) was new to Western science in 1960 mainly because few persons previous to 1960 attempted to determine with scientific instruments whether or not the heart and other body organs could be self-regulated.

Biofeedback training is expected to be of considerable importance to medicine in the next decade. Physicians generally agree that 50 percent to 80 percent of adult illnesses result from improperly handled stress. These ills are not diseases as much as they are undesirable physiological reactions to emotional stress that we have allowed to get "under our skins." For instance, migraine headache is often triggered by stress. Fortunately, it is possible for most migraine patients to learn to change their normally unconscious reaction to stress and handle the pressures of life without headache.

Some of the medical problems that can be handled fully or in part with biofeedback training include anxiety tension, migraine and tension headache, hypertension, cardiac arrhythmias, Raynaud's disease, gastrointestinal difficulties such as stomach ulcers and colitis, and neuromuscular disorders such as functional paralysis, torticollis and stroke paralysis. Technical information on biofeedback and the names of professional therapists in various parts of the country can be obtained from the Executive Secretary, Biofeedback Society of America, Department of Psychiatry, University of Colorado Medical Center, 4200 East Ninth Avenue, Denver, Colorado 80262.

CREDIT: *Elmer Green, M.D., the Menninger Foundation, Topeka, Kansas, author with J. D. Sargent and E. D. Walters of "Psychosomatic Self-Regulation of Migraine Headaches," Seminars in Psychiatry, Vol. 5, No. 4, 1973.*

Birth Defects

A BIRTHMARK THEORY

DEAR ANN: Our son was born with a purple birthmark on his neck. The mark is the size of a dime.

My mother's aunt, who came here from another country, insists that the birthmark is a punishment because my wife stole some plums from a market when she was a child. We know this is nuts, but please comment. R. AND L.

DEAR R. AND L.: You've already said it's nuts, and I can't improve on your evaluation.

See a dermatologist about new techniques for removing "port-wine stains." This sounds like it might be one.

More than 200,000 babies are born in the United States every year crippled, mentally retarded, blind, deaf, seriously anemic, diabetic, or defective in hundreds of other ways. That's about one baby in every fourteen.

Many of these children die in infancy, particularly those who are born weighing less than five and a half pounds. The others, with medical help and rehabilitation, may overcome their defects and lead useful, though often limited lives.

There are now fifteen million Americans whose daily lives are in some way affected by birth defects. Some birth defects can be prevented or corrected by present medical knowledge. Most can't. By funding clinics and medical research projects around the country, an effort is being made to: (1) discover the basic causes of various birth defects, (2) apply those discoveries to prevent the disorders, (3) improve present methods of treatment, (4) make treatment more widely available, (5) provide families with genetic information and counseling, (6) find cures for defects which up to now have been incurable, (7) find ways to prevent birth defects from happening in the first place.

What is a birth defect? A birth defect can mean either brain damage or an abnormality of body structure or function. Either can be caused by heredity or the result of environmental influence on the unborn baby, or both.

One might say that everybody has a birth defect of some kind—crooked teeth, a birthmark, or nearsightedness. But here we are concerned with the more serious kinds of defects, the ones that can either kill or substantially interfere with the normal life of an individual.

Many defects are recognizable at birth; many are not. Diabetes, for instance, may not appear until a child is eight to ten years old, or until age fifty. Huntington's disease is another example in which the symptoms of nervous system degeneration do not show up until early middle age.

A growing national concern is the problem of low weight at birth. Underweight newborns generally have a lower survival rate. (This is commonly due to circulatory and respiratory problems.) These babies are also more likely to develop brain damage. Some 85,000 babies are born each year weighing less than four and a half pounds. They are in grave risk of early death or long-term physical or mental impairment.

It is useful to categorize birth defects by the general ways in which they affect the individual. An infant may have more than one defect. When several defects occur they are called a "syndrome." Down's syndrome (mongolism) is an example. Those affected are mentally retarded and have physical characteristics different from those of a normal child.

Some infants with birth defects have parts of their bodies missing, misshapen, or duplicated. Examples are open spine (spina bifida), water on the brain (hydrocephalus), clubfoot, cleft lip or palate, extra fingers or toes, and dwarfism.

What causes birth defects? More often than not, the answer is unclear or unknown. But we do know that some defects, about 20 percent, are inherited. Another 2 percent are thought to be caused by environmental influences on the fetus. The rest may result from heredity and environment acting together.

Some traits, for instance, are strongly associated with others. Color blindness and hemophilia symptoms usually show up only in males. Other traits may be linked to racial or ethnic characteristics of the parents, such as sickle cell disease, most commonly found among blacks; Tay-Sachs disease, most prevalent among Jews of Eastern European ancestry; and thalassemia, whose victims are mostly Italians or others of Mediterranean origin.

Other examples of inheritable birth defects include Huntington's disease, diabetes, and cystic fibrosis.

The Forming of the fetus. Especially crucial is the first month and a half, when the embryo grows from a microscopic single cell to an odd-looking creature the size of a nickel. During these forty-five days, major body parts and systems are taking shape: arms, legs, hands, and feet; muscles and a soft skeleton; liver, pancreas, digestive tract, and kidneys; eyes, ears, and facial features; brain and beating heart. For the next seven and a half months, more specialized parts appear and the fetus grows in over-all size.

It's an incredibly complicated and fast-paced period of development. The wonder is that it comes out so well most of the time. One might compare it to building a city from scratch, using millions of inexperienced workers guided only by blueprints telling them where to go and what to do.

At any time, interference from outside—such as the mother's smoking cigarettes and the use of hard drugs—can affect the normal development of the fetus. Generally, the effect is greater earlier in pregnancy.

The most sensitive period is the first six weeks, when the basic fetal framework is being built. A serious blow, a fall, or an accident can cause gross deformities which may result in fetal death and subsequent miscarriage or stillbirth. Or, the baby may survive pregnancy and be born with defects.

Maternal age. Stillbirths are more frequent among young teenage mothers than in women past twenty-one years of age. Miscarriages and Mongoloid babies occur more commonly among women thirty-five years and older. In the first case, it is thought that the girl's reproductive system may not have fully matured; in the latter, the system may have begun to break down. The ideal ages for bearing children are from twenty-one to thirty-five.

Number and spacing of prior pregnancies. Having several children in close succession can affect the mother's health, which in turn can affect the fetus. Ideally, children should be two years apart.

ENVIRONMENTAL CAUSES ACTING ON THE MOTHER DURING PREGNANCY

These are influences brought to bear upon the unborn child as a result of the mother's getting sick, eating poorly, or taking harmful drugs. They include:

Viral disease and infections. German measles (rubella) is perhaps the best-known. Depending on when during pregnancy the infection occurs, the virus can cause deafness, heart defects, cataracts, glaucoma, and central nervous system damage in babies.

Venereal diseases can cause birth defects, too. In the case of syphilis, the child may be born with bone malformations and infection of many body organs. Gonorrhea can cause eye infection, which may lead to blindness if the baby is not promptly treated at birth.

Drug use. Practically any kind of drug can potentially affect the development of the fetus. Thalidomide caused numerous limb deformities in newborns during the 1960s. Evidence is accumulating against such everyday drugs as alcohol and nicotine. They too may affect the outcome of pregnancy.

The mother's use of narcotics can definitely affect a baby's health. If she is addicted, the baby may be addicted also. Researchers don't yet know for sure whether hallucinogens like LSD can cause birth defects.

It is wise to avoid any unnecessary drugs during pregnancy. A woman's doctor is the best judge of which drugs and medicines she may safely take, since he knows her case history.

Smoking. Stillbirths, early infant mortality, and low birth weight occur more frequently among the babies of women who smoke during pregnancy. The degree of the effect appears to depend on how much the mother smokes. A recent study indicates that the risk may be lessened if smoking is stopped by the fifth month of pregnancy.

Diet. Maintaining a balanced diet plays a vital role in having a healthy baby. Stillborn, premature, and underweight babies are associated with poor nutrition of the mother. Because of inadequate brain development and growth, the child may be mentally deficient.

Effects of the larger environment. These include elements in the mother's general environment to which she may or may not know she has been exposed. One common example is:

Radiation: X rays and other kinds of radiation have been linked with deformities to varying degrees.

HEREDITY AND ENVIRONMENT

Less than half of all birth defects can be attributed to a single environmental or hereditary cause. The majority are thought to result from an interplay between the two.

Rh disease is one example. It occurs when a mother without the Rh factor in her blood conceives a child who does have the factor, inherited from its father. No damage is usually done to the child born of the first such pregnancy. Following delivery, however, the mother develops antibodies in her blood which will attack the red blood cells of subsequent Rh-positive fetuses. The result of the next pregnancy could be an anemic or jaundiced baby which may die shortly after birth unless given a massive blood transfusion.

DETECTION AND DIAGNOSIS

A great many defects are readily apparent at birth, such as clubfoot, cleft lip, or Down's syndrome. Others, affecting internal body structure or chemistry, may be less immediately obvious.

Some defects can be diagnosed while the baby is still in the uterus, using several techniques. One of the most useful of these is called amniocentesis. It involves taking a sample of the amniotic fluid surrounding the fetus, using a hypodermic needle passed through the mother's abdominal wall and into the uterus. The fluid contains castoff fetal cells, which when grown in culture can be used to detect a number of defects. The fluid itself can also be tested.

Other methods include ultrasound, a kind of harmless radar; fetal blood sampling; and late in pregnancy, when it is least dangerous, X ray.

Other defects only show up much later and, unfortunately, cannot be detected until the individual develops the symptoms. By then it may be too late for treatment, even if it were available; doctors often can only alleviate the symptoms, or keep the condition from getting worse. Birth defects in this category today include Huntington's disease, diabetes, and gout, but tomorrow the story may be different.

Detection is only a first step in combating birth defects. There remains the problem of how to treat them so as to minimize their effects.

TREATMENT

Only a few disorders, mostly structural malformations, can be cured today. We simply have no way of eliminating the basic abnormality of most birth defects.

The majority of cases can only be treated to reduce harmful effects, or to keep them from getting worse. For many individuals, this enables them to lead fairly normal lives.

Among the types of therapy available for children born with birth defects:

Corrective surgery. Particularly effective for structural defects, such as cleft lip, clubfoot, and some heart malformations. Also includes tissue grafts and organ transplants.

Rehabilitative training. Can aid the blind, deaf, crippled, mentally retarded, or others with physical handicaps. Includes the use of mechanical or cosmetic prostheses, such as artificial limbs, braces, hearing aids, and glass eyes.

PREVENTION

To this point, I have described the things that can go wrong with a baby and what can be done about them. It adds up to a bleak picture, but there are bright spots.

Only 10 percent of all babies born in the United States suffer birth defects. Nine out of ten are born perfectly healthy. Cure or effective treatment does exist for some of the more common defects. Finally, many defects can be prevented if prospective parents seek timely counseling and if pregnant women get good prenatal care.

Prenatal care is many things: a balanced diet, exercise in the right amounts, good personal hygiene, avoidance of stress, and above all, regular visits to the doctor.

"What can a doctor tell me?" a pregnant woman may ask. "With or without him, I'm going to have a baby."

When a woman seeks medical care as soon as she thinks she is pregnant, the doctor can tailor a regimen for her which will guide her through those crucial early months with a minimum of risk. As the pregnancy continues, he can regularly check her health, personal habits, and the development of the baby to make sure that things are going normally. If at some point he finds that they're not, he can take steps to deal with them.

During the pregnancy, the doctor is compiling information which will later aid in the delivery of the baby. Important factors are the baby's growth rate, its position in the uterus, the location of the placenta, and any maternal illnesses which might affect the delivery. Knowledge of these factors enables special arrangements, if necessary, to be made—as in the case of twins, premature babies, Rh babies, or deliveries requiring Caesarean section.

Prenatal care is the mainstay of prevention. But other newly developed techniques and services play a part, too.

Within the last five years vaccines have been developed to combat German measles and Rh disease. The rubella vaccine is given to children under twelve years of age. This prevents the spread of rubella in two ways—it immunizes young girls who may someday be mothers, and it keeps children from getting the disease and passing it on to non-immunized women. It is never knowingly given to pregnant women, and generally not to women of childbearing age, because even the weakened vaccine virus could adversely affect the developing unborn child.

In the few years it has been available, the rubella vaccine is thought to have cut the number of reported congenital rubella cases substantially.

The Rh vaccine, if given to Rh-negative mothers within three days after a birth, abortion, or miscarriage, prevents the buildup of antibodies in her blood which threaten the health of subsequent children. The vaccine is considered almost 100 percent effective.

Genetic counseling is available for couples who suspect that their future children may have a chance of inheriting a disorder. One or both parents may know of birth defects in their family history. They may belong to a racial or ethnic group at relatively high risk for a specific defect, or they may have already had a defective child.

In any of these cases, a genetic counselor will analyze the medical histories of the parents and their families. Blood samples may be taken for chemical and chromosomal studies.

If the counselor finds there is some risk of a birth defect occurring, an attempt is made to define the odds as precisely as possible.

A genetic counselor doesn't tell the couple what they should do. She (or he) provides facts. It is then up to the parents to decide what they will do about having children.

This information was provided by the National Foundation—March of Dimes, founded in 1938 by President Franklin D. Roosevelt. Its original aim: to find a cure for polio. That goal was realized in 1955 with the licensing of the Salk vaccine.

The Foundation then turned its energies and resources toward an even greater task: the prevention and cure of birth defects.

March of Dimes chapters also sponsor medical service programs relating to birth defects at more than 150 medical and health centers throughout the country. In some, a defective child and his family can get expert diagnosis and treatment by specialist teams. Other programs support newborn intensive-care nurseries, and treatment during pregnancy and at delivery of women of high risk. Many supply genetic counseling and other genetics services.

The National Foundation—March of Dimes helped build and continues to support the Salk Institute at San Diego, where a multidisciplinary group of scientists pursues the answers to basic questions of human biology. A number of Salk scientists are Foundation grantees.

The Foundation also helps spread the latest information on birth defects, their treatment and prevention, to the health professions and to the public. The Foundation educates doctors and other health professionals through printed materials, audiovisual aids, and scientific conferences. Public awareness is raised through articles in newspapers and magazines, and on radio and television. In addition, the Foundation distributes pamphlets, audiovisual and other educational materials to the public through local chapters, health organizations, and community service groups.

For those wishing specific help or more detailed information, write to the National Foundation—March of Dimes, Box 2000, Whites Plains, New York 10602.

Animal Bites

Over 600,000 humans in the United States are bitten and treated for animal bites each year. Probably two or three times that number are never reported.

Dog bites are, of course, the most common, but there are many other animals that bite, among them cats, bats, skunks, raccoons, squirrels, monkeys, rabbits, foxes, rats and mice.

First and most important: Remember that all bites should be reported to a doctor at once. Even if you feel there is no chance of rabies, the animal may be carrying tetanus germs and a tetanus booster may be needed. If you are able, try to catch the animal. If that isn't possible, try to have an accurate description for the police. Do *not* kill the animal. It must be kept under observation for ten days for the possibility of rabies. Dogs in the United States carry less rabies than rats and foxes.

The wound should be washed gently with soap and water. The victim should then go to a physician or a medical facility for evaluation.

Since the human is the most intelligent of all animals, something should be said here about human bites.

The mouth of every human contains a great number of bacteria capable of producing serious infection. If you are bitten by a human, the wound should be washed thoroughly with soap under running water. Tight bandages should not be used. A sterile, loose dressing can be applied. See a doctor. A tetanus booster may be needed.

CREDIT: *Jay Arena, M.D., Chief of Pediatrics, Duke University, Durham, North Carolina, author of* Safety Is No Accident; A Parents' Handbook, *Durham, North Carolina: Duke University Press.*

DEAR ANN LANDERS: My boyfriend, Buzzy, is a sweet guy, but now and then I see signs of a terrible temper.

Last Friday night when we were horsing around on the floor, I got a toe-hold on him. (I learned it from watching wrestling on TV.) I think he went a little crazy, Ann. The guy actually bit me on the hand. I don't mean just a nibble, I mean a real bite that broke the skin. When I saw the blood I nearly fainted.

Buzzy said he was sorry—that he lost his head, and promised never to do such a thing again. I forgave him. The next day my mother saw the teethmarks and asked what happened. I was going to put the blame on Tuffy (our dog), but decided I'd better tell the truth. When I told Mom Buzzy bit me she was horrified—said a human bite can be very dangerous. Is this true? So far I am O.K. Please tell me if Mom is right. NIPPED BY NICK

DEAR NIPPED: Yes, she is right. You were lucky. Every human mouth has a good bit of bacteria. You could have gotten a bad infection.

If that clown ever bites you again, wash the wound with soap and water and see a doctor promptly.

Insect Bites

If you are stung by a bee, promptly and carefully remove the stinger, getting root and all.

For other insect bites—spiders, scorpions—or unusual reactions to other stinging insects such as bees, wasps, hornets, etc.:

(1) Do not allow the victim to walk. He should be kept quiet and inactive.

(2) Place cold compresses on the bite to reduce swelling. Use calamine lotion to relieve itching. Also, a paste made of Adolph's Meat Tenderizer applied to the bite will often reduce the swelling and itching.

(3) If the victim stops breathing, use artificial respiration.

(4) Call a physician, hospital, poison control center, or rescue unit and take the victim promptly to a medical facility. Persons with known unusual reactions to insect stings should carry emergency treatment kits and an emergency identity card at all times.

CREDIT: *Jay Arena, M.D., Chief of Pediatrics, Duke University, Durham, North Carolina, author of* Safety Is No Accident; A Parents' Handbook, *Durham, North Carolina: Duke University Press.*

Bleeding

NOSEBLEEDS

Nosebleeds are usually easy to control by pressure. Bend over the washbasin and blow your nose to remove all clots and blood. Immediately insert into the bleeding side of the nose a piece of cotton which has been wrapped around itself several times to make it firm. Insert the cotton with a twisting motion. Put one of your fingers against the outside of the nostril, pressing on the cotton. Hold your finger there for five to ten minutes. Do not lie on your back. In that position it is impossible to tell if your nose is still bleeding. Either sit with your face toward the ground or lie on your stomach so that you can see if your nose continues to bleed. If it persists, call a doctor.

BLEEDING FROM THE EAR

Following a head injury, blood or watery fluid running from an ear is a dangerous sign. If these symptoms develop, go at once to the emergency room of the nearest hospital. Never put any fluid or medicine of any kind into your ear unless directed to do so by your doctor. Cover the ear with a clean handkerchief or cloth to absorb the fluid or blood until you get medical attention.

BLEEDING FROM CUTS AND SCRATCHES

Bleeding from minor cuts will usually stop without first aid. However, to help clotting and prevent infection, wash the cut thoroughly with soap and water and apply a sterile and tight dressing and bandage. Do *not* apply a tourniquet.

SEVERE EXTERNAL BLEEDING

The sight of spurting or fast-flowing blood is, of course, frightening for both the person who is injured and the person who is with him. If you remember that even extremely severe bleeding (hemorrhaging) can almost always be controlled, it will be easier to stay calm.

First, place a sterile compress or a clean cloth directly on the wound. Press your hand firmly on top of the cloth, directly over the wound. When applying pressure to the injury, do not let up; keep the pressure firm and steady. Continue firm and unrelenting pressure for ten minutes. If the bleeding saturates the dressing, apply additional layers of cloth but do not remove the original layer of dressing.

Watch for signs of shock. They are: (1) a general weakness—inability to stand; (2) cold, pale, moist skin—perspiration often appears on forehead and above the lips; the palms of the hands are likely to become clammy and wet; (3) nausea, sometimes vomiting; (4) thirst; (5) dull, vacant eyes; (6) irregular, shallow breathing; (7) weak but rapid pulse.

If you believe shock is setting in, take the person to a hospital emergency room at once.

INTERNAL BLEEDING

Internal bleeding requires urgent medical care and must be suspected if you notice any of the following symptoms: (1) coughed-up blood; (2)

vomited blood—it may be bright red or the color of coffee grounds; (3) stools that are streaked with bright red blood; (4) stools that are jetblack—the color of tar; or (5) all or most of the symptoms of shock. If any of these symptoms are present, take the person to the nearest doctor or hospital immediately.

CREDIT: Accident Handbook, *Department of Health Education, the Children's Hospital Medical Center, Boston, Massachusetts.*

Blindness

PROBLEMS OF THE BLIND

DEAR ANN: When my blind friend asked how she could wage a campaign to educate people about problems a handicapped person must face, I told her I'd write to you. Will you help? These facts need to be known:

(1) Blind people carry a white cane with a red tip. (She is certain many people don't know this because she didn't know it until she became handicapped.)

(2) If you see a blind person standing somewhere, looking bewildered, chances are he is lost. Ask if you can help. Generally all he needs to know is where he is.

(3) Guide dogs are allowed in areas other dogs aren't. Recently, a woman came up to my friend complaining because the management had allowed her guide dog into the grocery store, "And they wouldn't let me in with my poodle. I was carrying him."

(4) Guide dogs are highly trained animals with a job to do. PLEASE DON'T PET OR TALK TO THEM. THIS IS VERY IMPORTANT. The owner's life depends on the dog's concentration.

(5) Smoke bothers many blind people. If you are going to smoke and are near a blind person, tell him. He will be glad to move.

Thanks for your help.

CALIFORNIA

DEAR CAL: Thanks for your letter. We educated a few million people today.

BLINDNESS AND VISUAL IMPAIRMENT

Government estimates indicate that at least ten million (one out of twenty) Americans have a serious problem with eyesight. Fifteen percent of these people are unable to see well enough to read a newspaper. Seven percent are legally blind.

While most eye problems are not life-threatening, they create stress and frustration. In fact, among chronic diseases that prevent people from leading a normal life, blindness ranks third after heart disease and arthritis.

The cost of treatment and rehabilitation of the visually handicapped is staggering. The National Eye Institute reports that in 1972, direct costs of eye care (visits to ophthalmologists, eye surgery, optometric services, hospital and nursing home care, etc.) came to $3.6 billion. Indirect costs (loss of earnings) added up to a whopping $5.1 billion.

While a great deal of progress has been made in both the prevention and treatment of eye disorders over the past twenty years, cataracts, glaucoma, diabetes, and vascular diseases are still the major causes of blindness. This is true even though cataract surgery is one of the most successful operations performed, and glaucoma, if detected early, can be controlled. Blindness from diabetes still baffles the experts because they lack the knowledge of the fundamental processes underlying retinal function. Many eye diseases are associated with the aging and since more people are living longer we must expect these figures to increase.

Public health and safety measures, industrial as well as school safety programs have sharply curtailed the incidence of blindness due to accidents. Still, the problem of eye injuries is a major one.

Since World War II, there has been a dramatic change in the composition of the blind population. This is the result of medical research zeroing in on the high death rate of newborn babies and concentrated efforts to help people live longer.

Some of the best work was done at the Lighthouse, the New York Association for the Blind, 111 East 59th Street, New York, New York 10022. They pioneered a new approach for training and educating blind youngsters. This involved a team of medical and paramedical specialists and consultants who joined teachers and social workers in developing a new concept of education for the handicapped and sightless.

AGENCIES SERVING THE VISUALLY IMPAIRED

A wide variety of direct services to blind persons is provided in all large cities (and many smaller ones).

Local voluntary agencies (usually financed through contributions by private groups or individuals and United Funds) offer a wide range of services. All states and U.S. territories have established a separate unit to help the blind.

In addition to the direct services available on a local level, there are national agencies, both federal and voluntary, which also offer a variety of services to the blind. The Library of Congress, through its Division for the Blind and Physically Handicapped, conducts a national program (Talking Books) to bring free reading materials to those who cannot use ordinary printed materials. The Veterans Administration provides non-vocational rehabilitation services for blind veterans and members of the Armed Forces as well as dog guides for eligible blinded veterans.

Some of the better-known national voluntary agencies are:

The American Foundation for the Blind, 15 West 16th Street, New York, New York 10011, which serves as a national clearinghouse for information about blindness and conducts and stimulates research to determine the most effective methods of serving visually handicapped persons.

The National Society for the Prevention of Blindness, Inc., 79 Madison Avenue, New York, New York 10016, which conducts educational programs and research into the prevention of blindness.

Recording for the Blind, Inc., 215 East 55th Street, New York, New York 10022, which tapes and loans educational books to visually and physically handicapped students and professionals.

National Industries for the Blind, 1455 Broad Street, Bloomfield, New Jersey 07003, which co-ordinates the production of eighty-nine associated workshops for the blind in thirty-six states and allocates federal purchase orders among them.

In the area of medical research there are such institutions as National Eye Institute of the National Institutes of Health; Eye-Bank Association of America, Inc., which supplies corneas for transplantation free of charge throughout the United States (the surgeon must be paid, however); Fight for Sight, Inc., which finances eye research; and Research to Prevent Blindness, which supports clinical and basic eye research.

Dog guide schools which provide dogs to blind people who can use this mobility aid are located throughout the country. The oldest is the Seeing Eye, Inc., in Morristown, New Jersey.

A number of associations of professional workers, agencies and blind people have formed consumer groups. These include the American Association of Workers for the Blind, the Association for Education of the Visually Handicapped, the American Council of the Blind, Blinded Veterans Association, National Federation of the Blind, etc.

HOW TO FIND SERVICES FOR THE BLIND IN YOUR COMMUNITY

(1) Consult your local Health and Welfare Council or the United Fund, listed in the telephone directory.

(2) The American Foundation for the Blind has two publications that would be helpful: *Directory of Agencies Serving the Visually Handicapped in the United States,* revised and updated every two years, which contains state-by-state listings of federal, state and local services with names, addresses

and telephone numbers, $6; and *Where to Find Help for the Blind,* a free flyer listing names, addresses and telephone numbers of all state and territorial agencies for the blind.

CREDIT: *Mrs. Mary Jane O'Neill, Lighthouse for the Blind, New York, New York.*

Blood Pressure (High)

Myths versus the facts:
  (1) *Myth:* Control equals cure.
       Fact: Control requires daily regimen; there is no permanent cure.
  (2) *Myth:* Hypertension is nervous tension, so pills only need be taken when the patient feels nervous.
       Fact: Feeling tense is not a symptom; medicine must be taken every day.
  (3) *Myth:* Patients may select their treatment (medicine or careful diet or healthier lifestyle).
       Fact: Treatment requires a regular daily regimen of medication and dietary and smoking modification, depending on the individual.

People who have high blood pressure must consult their doctors and get on a program of daily medication. Medicines should be taken as prescribed. As yet, high blood pressure cannot be cured, but it can be controlled.

High blood pressure (hypertension) is a major public health problem in the United States and throughout the world. About twenty-four million Americans with high blood pressure is the current estimate. It is a major cause of sickness, disability and death—among the young and middle-aged as well as the elderly.

It is a disease that is easily detected, yet at the start of the seventies, surveys noted that about half of those with hypertension had no idea they had it. It is a treatable disease, yet at least half of the *known* hypertensives were found to be without any treatment.

BLACK-WHITE DIFFERENCES IN HIGH BLOOD PRESSURE

The toll of hypertension is not equally shared in the U.S. population. For reasons that are not understood, blacks have a much heavier burden of the disease, so that it looms as the number one health problem in the black community. They have *more* hypertension, they develop it younger, it is more severe, and they die from it more frequently and at an earlier age.

Controlling hypertension, once it is discovered, involves a lifetime commitment. But if you and your doctor work together, the prospects for controlling your blood pressure are excellent. Your faithfulness in following his advice will pay big dividends in terms of a longer and healthier life.

WHAT CAUSES HIGH BLOOD PRESSURE?

To pin down the cause of high blood pressure is not easy. Most people agree that the insurance companies know their business. Their fortunes have been built on actuarial record-keeping and evaluation over decades, all aimed at finding out who is more likely to die and who is a good risk for life insurance. They have had records of millions of people to look at, to determine what medical findings, recorded at the time people applied for their policies, were good predictors of future life expectancy.

The most recent report by the Society of Actuaries compared twenty-year survival rates for persons classified according to blood pressure level when first examined at various ages. It is clear that each step upward in diastolic or systolic blood pressure means less chance for survival.

If your doctor cannot find an underlying cause for your high blood pressure (such as kidney infection or disorders of the adrenal glands or nervous system), then you are considered to have *essential hypertension*. You have a lot of company. About 90 percent of people with high blood pressure have essential hypertension. While the cause of essential hypertension is unknown, certain factors—emotional stress, obesity, salt, and cigarette smoking—may aggravate blood pressure.

WHY HYPERTENSION CAN BE DANGEROUS

If your doctor discovered your hypertension during a regular checkup, and you felt fine when you came to see him, you may be tempted to ignore his findings. But remember that uncontrolled elevated blood pressure will harm your vital organs. High blood pressure and hypertensive heart disease cause about sixty thousand deaths annually in the United States and contribute to strokes, heart attacks and kidney failure.

In untreated hypertension, the course from onset to death is about twenty years. Yet, except for elevated blood pressure readings, no warning signs or symptoms are likely to appear for the first two thirds of this time, after which failure of one or more vital organs begins. Once organ failure starts, the average survival time of the untreated patient is only about six years. However, even after organ failure begins, effective treatment can add years to a patient's life.

HIGH BLOOD PRESSURE AND THE HEART

The heart is the organ most commonly damaged by hypertension. When blood pressure is high, the heart must expend more energy to pump the blood through the body. In response to this increased effort, the heart muscle itself increases in size and needs more oxygen and nutrients. If the blood pressure rise is uncontrolled and the strain on the heart muscle continues for a long time, the heart eventually is unable to meet the extra demands and *heart failure* results.

In some patients the burden on the heart is so great that the need for oxygen and nutrients to nourish the heart muscle itself cannot be met. As a result, coronary insufficiency with chest pain (angina pectoris), or damage to some tissues in an area of heart muscle, or even death may occur.

HIGH BLOOD PRESSURE AND THE BRAIN

Brain: A cerebral vascular accident (stroke), a disruption of the brain's blood supply, may occur as a result of continued blood pressure elevation. The severe strain, which has been imposed on the arteries in the brain by persistent increased pressure within them, finally ruptures a weakened artery and produces brain hemorrhage. A stroke may also be caused by a blood clot disrupting the blood supply of the brain. Paralysis or death may follow.

HIGH BLOOD PRESSURE AND THE KIDNEYS

The kidneys are another prime target of hypertension. The principal site of damage is in the arterioles that supply the kidneys. Increased pressure from hypertension causes damage to these arterioles and the blood supply to the kidneys is gradually reduced. They can no longer function at full capacity. If the remaining work capacity of the kidneys is not enough to meet the needs of the body for removal of waste, *kidney failure* results.

TREATMENT

Some of your doctor's most important advice will concern drugs that control hypertension. Even if your physician does not know the cause of your high blood pressure, he can recommend specific drugs that, combined with moderation in your lifestyle, can reduce your blood pressure virtually to normal.

A number of drugs have been developed in the last twenty years that are effective in controlling blood pressure. But remember that each patient responds to the various drugs in different ways; and few drugs of any type have only one action. The drugs used in the treatment of hypertension act primarily to reduce blood pressure, but in some patients other actions may also become apparent because of individual responses to a particular agent. These other actions are called *side effects*. While your physician knows they are possible, he usually cannot know beforehand if you will experience any of the side effects (or how severe they might be).

For these reasons your doctor needs your help to develop a drug program that is tailored specifically for you. His object is to control your hypertension with the fewest and mildest adverse reactions. You can help by taking your medication exactly as directed and reporting your reactions to your doctor. He may have to try different dose levels of one drug or combinations of several drugs at different dose levels before he finds the program that works best for you. A suitable drug program with very minimal adverse reactions is possible for most patients.

If your hypertension is considered mild to moderate, your doctor may begin treatment by prescribing an oral *diuretic* drug. The diuretic drugs help rid the body of salt and water and appear to have other useful actions as well. Diuretic drugs have a low incidence of side effects so they are often given in conjunction with other antihypertensive drugs to help reduce the dose requirements of drugs that are more likely to cause adverse reactions in patients.

Patients who are taking diuretics find that they have to urinate more frequently than usual. Some may also experience weakness, fatigue and gastrointestinal irritation. The doctor will want to know about these reactions if they occur.

A diuretic may be combined with *reserpine,* which, in addition to lowering blood pressure, has a tranquilizing effect that is sometimes desirable. But reserpine can cause an undesirable depression in some patients, first noticeable as early morning insomnia. Other possible side effects include a stuffy nose, drowsiness and lethargy.

Methyldopa is another drug that may be combined with a diuretic to treat hypertension. It is usually well tolerated, although a patient may notice signs of drowsiness and dryness of the mouth. These side effects rarely persist for more than three or four days.

Another drug usually used in combination with other agents is *hydralazine,* which directly dilates the blood vessels and increases blood flow in the kidneys while increasing the volume of blood pumped by the heart. Adverse side effects possible with this drug include headaches and rapid heartbeat.

Propranolol is still another drug that has effective antihypertensive properties. Originally developed for its actions on the heart, this drug now is used alone or in combination with other drugs to treat hypertension.

If you have severe high blood pressure your doctor may prescribe *guanethidine* in addition to one or more of the less potent drugs already mentioned. The dose level of this powerful drug must be carefully regulated because as part of its action it causes orthostatic hypotension, which results in dizziness and nausea when a patient stands up. This effect can be especially troublesome in the morning when getting out of bed. Diarrhea is also a side effect of guanethidine experienced by some patients.

Many other drugs useful in treating hypertension have not been mentioned. However, your doctor knows them and if he feels that they are better for your situation he will, of course, prescribe them for you.

You can help your physician by following his advice and reporting the effects of the drugs you are taking. You may have to tolerate some annoying side effects but usually these can be minimized. These discomforts are the small price paid for extra years of living because you have brought your blood pressure under control and spared vital organs from further damage.

YOUR LIFESTYLE CAN MAKE A BIG DIFFERENCE

Your daily living habits can aggravate your hypertension. In addition to the drugs he prescribes for you, your doctor may suggest some modifications in your lifestyle in order to bring down your blood pressure.

Anxiety, frustration and anger aggravate hypertension. Your doctor knows that it is impossible for you to avoid emotional tension completely, but it is advantageous for you to avoid situations that put you under an emotional strain. Some adjustments in your way of life, perhaps in your job, may be indicated. A recent study showed that persons in certain occupations are four times as likely to develop high blood pressure as individuals in less stressful jobs.

DIET

Obesity tends to exaggerate high blood pressure. Your doctor is aware that sticking to a low-calorie diet is not always easy, but the benefits gained from having normal weight and lower blood pressure are considerable.

Long before medical science had developed effective antihypertensive drugs, restriction of salt intake was a useful method of reducing high blood pressure. Since introduction of effective drugs to combat hypertension, it generally is not necessary to reduce salt intake severely. Your doctor will tell you how much salt is allowable in your diet.

SMOKING

Cigarette smoking can elevate the blood pressure of some hypertensive patients. Your doctor may suggest that you quit smoking to see if your blood pressure goes down. In most cases it will go down. If it does in *your* case, *stop* smoking at once.

EXERCISE

Exercise can add tone to the mind's outlook and spice to living. If exercise gives you an opportunity to act out the many internal forces that would not be released otherwise, it may be extremely valuable. Your doctor can advise you about how much exercise is appropriate.

MEASURING YOUR BLOOD PRESSURE

Blood pressure is the force exerted by blood against the walls of the vessels that carry it. Generally, the blood pressure in the arteries varies as the heart pumps: (1) when the heart contracts the pressure is increased (*systolic pressure*); (2) when the heart relaxes between contractions, the pressure is decreased (*diastolic pressure*). The difference between the systolic pressure and the diastolic pressure is termed the *pulse pressure*. A pressure measurement from $\dfrac{110}{60}$ to $\dfrac{140}{90}$ is usually considered within normal limits, depending on certain other factors, such as age.

CAN HIGH BLOOD PRESSURE BE PREVENTED?

Even though, in most cases, the causes of high blood pressure are unknown, it has been learned that certain people are more vulnerable than others. Traits found to be related to hypertension are:

(1) Family history of hypertension.

(2) High normal blood pressure in youth and young adulthood or the occasional "spike" of abnormal pressure in a young person who is usually normal.

(3) Overweight in youth, young adulthood, or middle age, or a sizable gain in weight in the years from young adulthood into middle age.

(4) Rapid resting heart rate.

In addition, three other traits—tendency to *elevated blood glucose, elevated blood uric acid,* and *elevated blood cholesterol*—may be associated with increased proneness to high blood pressure. All of these are in turn more likely to occur in overweight people.

CONCLUSION

The joy of finding, evaluating and treating over twenty million hypertensives is a huge and challenging one which needs doing. But the challenge should not blind us to a basic fact: in the long run, the ultimate solution of the hypertension problem is *prevention,* not case finding and drug treatment, as important as they are at present.

It is clear that the whole program—the education of the doctor and the public, the finding of new cases, the effective treatment of elevated pressure, the reduction of other cardiovascular risk factors—needs to be developed side by side with continued research to clarify the causes of essential hypertension.

Such an extensive program requires a system of medical care delivery that ensures every American equal access to the best care for hypertension currently available. This in turn requires a commitment—especially a government commitment—to a program, to planning, to funding.

The challenge of hypertension is a very great one in the country. If it is met successfully, it will be one of the biggest contributions in this century to the better health and longer life of Americans.

CREDIT: *Rose Stamler, M.A., Assistant Professor, and Jeremiah Stamler, M.D., Professor and Chairman, Department of Community Health and Preventive Medicine, Northwestern University Medical School, Chicago, Illinois.*

BLUSHING

DEAR ANN LANDERS: I started to work in this office six weeks ago and I love my job. But the men I work with have discovered I blush easily.

Now I'm the prime target for off-color jokes and crude gimmicks sold in cheap novelty shops. One guy springs this stuff on me and the whole group gathers around to watch my face turn red.

I am 20 years old and no prude, but I don't like barroom stories and crummy gadgets. Is there any way I can learn to control my blushing? TOMATO FACE

DEAR FACE: Blushing is an involuntary act and can't be controlled.

It's refreshing to know there's a girl around who can still blush. View it as an asset, honey. You are one of the last of a vanishing breed.

The following week I received a letter from a reader who gave me some fresh insight into the problem. This is an excellent example of how I learn from my readers. Here is his letter and a more enlightened response from Yours Truly.

DEAR ANN LANDERS: This letter is for "Tomato Face"—the girl who was miserable because the men in the office told off-color jokes and used shocking language—they loved to watch her blush.

Honey, I'm a 33-year-old male who used to be a blusher, too. A friend proved to me that involuntary responses can be controlled. If you will do some programming you can prevent

the blush mechanism as I did. An appropriate message to repeat to yourself might be: "CANCEL THE BLUSH, I WILL NOT PUT ON A SHOW FOR THESE JERKS."   V-8

DEAR V-8: In technical language your suggested approach is called "biofeedback." If it can lower one's blood pressure (and it can), it certainly should be able to squelch a blush.

Body Odor

Body odor is a very common problem. While there are many sources of normal and abnormal odors which arise from the human body, the term "body odor" usually refers to the odors generated from perspiration.

Some body odors come from human waste, such as fecal matter or urine which have soiled the skin or the clothing. Other body odors may be caused by various illnesses, such as the "fruit" odor emanating from patients with severe diabetes who have acetone on their breath or the "mouse" odor of patients with advanced kidney disease and the accompanying accumulation of waste products in their blood, which produces an illness known as uremia. Other sources of abnormal odors due to illness are infections ranging from multiple boils to gangrene. However, patients with these severe illnesses are rarely able to carry out normal everyday activities and are usually confined to bed, frequently in a hospital.

The normal type of perspiration is odorless. The usual type of body odor produced from perspiration is the result of the action of microorganisms, mainly bacteria, which live on everybody's skin and change the composition of the perspiration. It is the result of bacterial action that creates the odors.

Under normal conditions, heat, physical exercise, and nervous tension, and less commonly, spicy foods, alcoholic or hot beverages, and a number of less common factors stimulate the activity of the glands which produce the perspiration. The perspiration due to warm weather is less commonly associated with body odor unless other factors are involved.

There are two kinds of sweat glands. One, the eccrine glands, are distributed all over the body surface. The less common apocrine sweat glands are abundant in the armpits, around the nipple of the breast, in the area of the genitals, and between the buttocks, particularly around the anal orifice. It is the latter type of gland that contributes a considerable part of the perspiration in these regions.

Body odor which arises from perspiration originates predominantly in those areas where bacteria which cause the odors are most active. Those regions are the moist, warm areas where the perspiration is abundant, such as the armpits, the groin, the genital area, and the region between the buttocks. These are the same warm, moist areas in which the activity of the bacteria is increased. These anatomical areas are, therefore, commonly associated with undesirable body odors. In the anal-genital area, for obvious reasons, poor hygiene can contribute sources of undesirable odor both from the genitals and from the anus.

The development of the apocrine glands (in the armpits, the groin, and around the nipple) is closely associated with the development of hair in those regions. Both are under the control of sex hormones. Body odor, at least the major component which is associated with the apocrine perspiration, is therefore rarely a problem in children before puberty or in people who have reached menopause. However, even in the young and older age groups, eccrine perspiration is present, can be abundant, and as a result of increased activity of bacteria in the underarm and anal-genital areas, can produce body odor of considerable significance. Both the anal and genital areas, at all ages, harbor large numbers of bacteria, which are normal inhabitants of the gastrointestinal tract, and responsible for the production of odors usually associated with those of bowel excretions.

Various methods have been employed to control body odor. None of them are wholly satisfactory. The principal methods for controlling body odor fall primarily into three groups:

(1) Control of bacteria is probably the most effective method. Thorough washing and close attention to personal hygiene are the obvious way to reduce the number of bacteria and the amount of perspiration. Women should use mild soap in the genital area to avoid irritation. Inhibiting the bacterial growth or action is the primary function of deodorants. These preparations range from such generally available agents as rubbing alcohol, soaps, and lotions to the commercial deodorants found in drugstores.

(2) Covering the body odor with a more acceptable and potent scented preparation, such as various perfumes, aromatic substances such as mentholated or camphorated preparations or pleasing plant odors, such as pine or other evergreen extracts, or odors associated with strong antiseptic agents, such as Lysol.

(3) Another widely attempted approach is to reduce the amount of perspiration and thereby the amount of material available for the bacteria to create undesirable odors. While some antiperspirants inhibit the activities of the bacteria, their primary function is to reduce the flow of perspiration, primarily in the underarm region and the anal-genital areas.

Almost every dermatologist has had at least one or two patients who come for help insisting that they have an offensive body odor and "no one can help them." They say they have a terrible odor which is ruining their lives and they have been to several doctors but to no avail. Actually there is no offensive odor. The problem is imaginary. Such patients should seek psychiatric help.

CREDIT: *Edmund Klein, M.D., Assistant Chief of Dermatology, Roswell Park Memorial Institute, Buffalo, New York, and Research Professor, School of Medicine, State University of New York.*

Boredom, American Style

Boredom afflicts the rich more than the poor, the adult more than the child, and the so-called healthy more than the neurotic.

Boredom is often blamed on the external world ("I'm not bored—it's this lousy town . . . my stupid friends . . . this miserable job . . . my dull husband [or wife]"). The mechanism of projection helps one feel that he is the victim and not the cause. There are, indeed, boring people and situations, but frequent and long periods of boredom, no matter what the cause, are an indication of an emotional problem. This becomes evident in people who, despite frequent changes of cities, husbands, wives, friends and jobs, remain bored.

Let me try to define boredom. It is a state of dissatisfaction accompanied by a feeling of longing and an inability to identify what it is one longs for. There is a sense of emptiness, frustration and restlessness. The bored person waits for someone or something to provide the solution. Unfortunately, when someone does offer a plausible suggestion, it usually turns out to be little more than a time killer. There is another characteristic of boredom. Time seems to stand still. The German word for boredom is *Langeweile,* which means "long time."

The sense of painful emptiness, characteristic of the bored, stems from the fact that most of his fantasy life is repressed or inhibited. His imagination is stultified or blacked out in the major areas of his life. He would rather feel empty than miserable. It is for this reason that he turns to the external world, hoping it will "guess" what he wants and provide it.

A typical statement of a bored person is: "I can't get with it," or "I am nowhere." His language indicates that he is out of touch with his fantasies and thoughts.

People who are severely and chronically bored and are aware of it suffer great pain. Many years ago I treated a patient who made a serious suicide attempt because of her unbearable boredom. In the hospital and during treatment, she felt depressed, but her depression was a welcome relief from her intolerable boredom.

In studying such patients it became apparent that chronic and severe boredom is a defense against an underlying deep-seated depression. They attempt to avoid the depression by plunging into a variety of intense activities or by lapsing into a state of lethargy. These solutions are never truly satisfactory.

As long as there is an inhibition and blocking of fantasy thought and imagination, there are no connecting links between instinctual drives, emotions and human relations. These people may go through the motions of living and loving but it is essentially a charade, or a desperate search for something on the outside which can only be found on the inside, and then only after suffering through their depression.

Teenagers are an excellent example. They are usually filled with sexual and aggressive tensions—complain of having no friends—say they can't communicate with their parents—lie around the house brooding, listening to records. Inevitably they say, "Gee, I'm bored." The best way to help a teenager move out of this condition is to recognize the cause of his boredom and then give him some direction to help him find activities that will offer him an opportunity to release his tensions.

Boredom also may serve an adaptive function, particularly when it is recognized as boredom and is only temporary. It is a kind of local anesthetic dulling the pain in a particularly sensitive psychic area while natural healing takes place. Any change of routine, like a weekend away from home, a poker game, talking seriously with one's wife, or skiing, may be sufficient if the underlying conflicts can be faced consciously. Sometimes boredom may also serve as a period of germination before the birth of creative ideas. When the pathology is more serious, then boredom becomes a form of hibernation, a kind of self-preservative trance-like state, an attempt to wait out or ward off the stormy depression which howls below. I have seen such apathetic states in prisoners of war who survived years of imprisonment in World War II.

Boredom is primarily an affliction of the successful and the affluent. There are millions of these people walking, or rather, running around the country attempting to conceal their boredom from themselves and the world.

R'S OF BOREDOM

Bored people try to escape emptiness and loneliness by establishing routines. Married couples who have blocked out their marital misery will schedule social events months in advance. They have a horror of free evenings because they would then have to face each other and it would be intolerable. By issuing invitations long in advance they manage to ensnare people who would otherwise claim to be busy. Moreover, a full calendar proves to them that they are popular and "in demand" socially.

They have long lists of people to choose from because they do not discriminate among friends, acquaintances, relatives, enemies, business contacts and strangers. Guests are chosen according to tested recipes containing various social ingredients. One couple may be picked because they are, at the moment, socially prominent. Then come the couples they "owe" a dinner party to. To this group is added other couples who are "fillers"—people whose function is to add social bulk to the room. To this concoction one may add a dash of "glamour" in the form of an entertainer, a foreign couple, or a psychoanalyst. When this collection of humanity is placed in a crowded room, served strong drinks and delicate hors d'oeuvres, the noise and confusion give the appearance of excitement. Before the dinner is served, everyone eats ravenously to keep from passing out from the alcohol or from sheer hunger. The food is praised because the guests can no longer taste, and are grateful for having been saved from paralysis. Having overeaten, everyone is too tired to leave, so they linger on until early morning, which proves the party was a smashing success.

The hostess records the dates each person was invited because most of them belong to the "you remember good old what's-his-name" group. The guests are rotated regularly, new names added (after a few drinks at someone else's party), and no one is dropped unless he has committed a mortal sin like spilling red wine on an expensive tablecloth or vomiting on the hostess's new Bill Blass gown.

The sex life of people who cannot stand not standing each other is also ruled by routine and recipe. One does not have intercourse on the spur of the moment—at least not with one's own husband or wife. Spontaneity and improvisations might break through the protective wall and ward off the underlying miseries. Marital sex is carefully scheduled for a certain day. In this way, neither party has to take the initiative and run the risk of being rejected. If Sunday night is the night—that's it.

Bored couples in desperate search for sexual excitement may resort to artificial aids such as marijuana or cocaine, pornographic magazines, or X-rated films.

In recent years mechanical gadgets such as vibrators and Jacuzzi baths add spice to the agenda. Both partners may become so lost in their own fantasies that they are startled after orgasm to see who is actually in bed with them.

Bored people are frequently promiscuous because they keep searching for ways to fill up their internal emptiness. They are not able to love because they cannot communicate either verbally or emotionally. They use physical contact and sensations as substitutes for meaningful human interaction. They are alienated from a vital part of themselves and hope that physical contact with a new person will give them the feeling of being whole or in touch. Unfortunately, as marvelous as an orgasm may be, it is no substitute for love or intimacy.

Such sexual affairs do not last long and have no important emotional impact. These people continue to remain on each other's guest lists, they meet as though nothing happened, and, sadly enough, they are right.

THE PURSUIT OF TRIVIAL PLEASURES: FAVORITE PASTIMES OF THE BORED

I refer here to vast numbers of people who spend a great deal of time seeking superficial satisfactions. There are women whose major delight is shopping, without any specific need or objective. They may even accompany a friend on a shopping tour when they themselves have nothing to buy. They do this as other women might go for a walk or have a cup of coffee so they can talk. The advantage of shopping is that it makes it impossible to engage in any serious or meaningful conversation.

These women are often dependent on beauty salons, which they visit with the same regularity that wealthier women go to their psychotherapists. They study their faces in the mirror every morning so they won't miss a wrinkle, blemish, or unwanted hair. They are equally scrupulous about their figures and are constantly weighing and measuring themselves. They get facials, hot packs, ice packs and massages. They spend several hours every week at the hairdresser's being shampooed and set, combed and curled, tinted, mani-cured, pedicured, tweezed, and getting their legs "waxed." All this is time-consuming and these ladies come home exhausted.

At bedtime they put on a variety of skin creams and body oils, and end up donning hair nets and eye shades and applying skin de-wrinklers. If they would spend as much time looking inward instead of outward, their faces would undoubtedly look less artificial and strained. But to look inward means to be willing to suffer and perchance to cry, and this might produce bags under the eyes, so they stay with the beautician, the hairdresser, and the masseur.

Bored ladies talk a lot, mostly trivia and gossip—and their phone bills are enormous.

The male counterparts of the women described above are the country club addicts. The rich play golf, take a massage and a sauna bath, after which they play cards until they are late for dinner. They often dine at the Club, in fact, they spend more time at the Club than at home. They remain members of golf clubs long after they have given up golf. In a sense, many country clubs serve as a sanitarium for the rich.

Those who must work for a living stop off at a bar for a few drinks with the boys. "Boys" refers to acquaintances of any age whom you never really get to know because you meet them only in crowded bars where the noise is so loud that conversation is impossible and the smoke is so thick you couldn't recognize your brother.

Besides getting bombed, the major activity is verbal horseplay which is unrepeatable at home because it makes no sense when repeated sober.

THE BORED PERSON'S SEARCH FOR MEANING

There are people who never seem to have an ordinary experience. What-ever happens to them is the greatest, the best, the worst, the most horrible, or the most fantastic. In any case, it is the "most."

Some of them work at creating these situations. They are the life of the party, or the death of it. They are cut-ups, jokesters, storytellers or confessors. Interestingly, they can admit in a group what they cannot say in private. They laugh loud and long and cry easily and without shame. They often confuse loudness with sincerity, tearfulness with intimacy, and obscenity with passion. They love crowds because they give them the feeling they are "in"— that they belong. At parties they overdress, overeat, overdrink and overtalk.

A recent addition to this forlorn group may be seen at encounter groups, and at touch therapy and nude therapy sessions. These sad souls are out of touch with their emotions and very lonely. They hunger for contact and warmth and hope they can be achieved by artificial togetherness. Their attempts are doomed to failure. If one is unable to make contact with his own feelings and thoughts, he cannot accomplish it with an outsider.

THE DRUG TAKERS: THE SEARCH FOR OBLIVION, MINDLESSNESS AND DEATH

This subgroup is enormous and complex. In this limited space, I shall attempt to describe some outstanding characteristics because drug taking is on the increase at all age levels.

Alcohol makes time pass. It is one of the greatest of all time killers. The elation produced by booze can temporarily relieve monotony and loneliness. Alcohol, however, can also break the defensive barrier around depression, and destructive brutality may emerge as well as terrible sadness.

Sleeping pills block out a high percentage of night dreams. Tranquilizers and sedatives dull the imagination and produce peace of mind which is actually more a piece of mindlessness.

In recent times sedatives also have been used as "downers"—a means of counteracting the ill effects of such stimulants as amphetamines, such as Dexedrine and Dexamyl. The latter are euphoriants, which means they produce a temporary mood of elation. If taken to excess they produce extreme restlessness, agitation, irritability, palpitations and insomnia—a vicious cycle.

Marijuana is also a euphoriant, but it acts differently inasmuch as it stimulates the imagination and permits repressed fantasies to break through into consciousness. This is why marijuana is appealing to the bored. It also enhances certain perceptions—sound, for example, and if taken with a group it gives a feeling of belonging and creates the illusion of closeness.

The physical proximity and the communal use of pot do not break down the feeling of loneliness and isolation. While sexual capacity seems to be enhanced, this too is an illusion. The number of orgasms in women may increase but the quality of the orgasms goes to pot with pot.

The most outstanding difference between users of alcohol and marijuana is that alcohol tends to make people violent while pot makes people good-natured and lovers of loud music.

Cocaine is now the "in" thing. "Coke" also produces a synthetic good mood but the high lasts only twenty or thirty minutes if sniffed—and another rush is needed to sustain the "joy." Since cocaine is costly only the rich can afford to stay on it for long periods of time.

LSD is the most dangerous drug of the lot. It can produce psychotic break-downs which may be irreversible. It is appealing to those who search for new and vivid sensations because the old ones have failed to give them pleasure and satisfaction. It also is a way of daring to face death or insanity, a form of playing "chicken." LSD attracts people who place little value on sanity or life.

I put television in the category of drugs because TV is addictive. It dulls the intellect and artificially stimulates certain senses while it blurs one's own identity. All bored people are drawn to the tube and are prone to take over-doses. The fascination of television is complex, but it provides ready-made fantasies in living color for those with an inhibited fantasy life. They do not have to use their imaginations. TV does it for them. One of the most unfortunate side effects of television is that it makes real life seem even more drab for the person who is bored.

BOREDOM AMONG THE YOUNG—UN-AMERICAN STYLE

While large numbers of teenagers smoke pot to escape boredom, many more are attempting to escape the purposelessness of their lives. The majority are more depressed than bored. From 1968 to 1969, there was a rise of 100 percent in the suicide rate of people between the ages of thirteen and twenty-nine. Incidentally, the most prevalent instrument with which to end life was not drugs but guns.

THE CURE AND CONCLUSIONS

I hope that I have made it clear that boredom is a state of mind which is the result of blocking the thoughts and fantasies that would otherwise lead to the recognition of conflict, frustration and unhappiness and coping with them.

On occasion we all may need some boredom as a respite from struggle and misery, but it can become a serious problem when distractions and diversions replace the basic elements of life. Life is to be lived and to live a life of meaning we must contend with the painful aspects of our existence.

All people are full of loving and hateful impulses. That is the human con-dition. It is as true for the rich as the poor, the black and the white, the American and the Oriental. To know ourselves we must be willing to face and acknowledge our strengths and weaknesses. To form meaningful and en-during relationships we must be willing to share this awareness with those who matter to us. Honesty and humility are prerequisites for relating in a significant way. We change and the world changes too. It is painful to find oneself old, or out of step, or ignorant or weak. Yet, if we want to be part of the world, we must face these eventualities. If we do and are willing to endure some suffering, we shall be able to love and work with our fellow man. We may be unhappy at times but we shall never be bored.

CREDIT: *Ralph R. Greenson, M.D., Clinical Professor of Psychiatry, U.C.L.A. School of Medicine Training, and Supervising Analyst, Los Angeles Psychoanalytic Institute, Co-President, The Anna Freud Foundation, California Chapter.*

Bragging

I have never sat on a bus, at a dinner party, by the pool or in a doctor's office in my entire life that I didn't find myself next to the parent of a college overachiever.

You know the ones I mean. The parents whose son or daughter was the recipient of a four-year, all-expense-paid scholarship to one of the Big Ten schools that is recognizable by a single letter on a T-shirt.

The kid who turned down twelve other schools because they didn't offer Conversational Arabic, didn't graduate one Secretary of State and discriminated against accepting thirteen-year-olds in the freshman class.

I have the kid who, sometime during the last two weeks of August, rolls out of bed and announces, "Hey, college starts in another two or three weeks, I'd better get it on."

After polite but firm refusals from Harvard, Yale, Duke and Dartmouth, they work their way across the country . . . Ohio State, Missouri, Colorado, Tulane and San Diego.

As the time gets shorter, catalogues start coming in from places I never knew existed: Alpha Frisbee College (a free car tune-up for every sixteen credit hours); Eddie's Business School of Massage and Acupuncture; Guam School of Technology for Losers.

One day I picked up a catalogue from a school in Hawaii. Under "Location of Campus" were explicit directions for jumping from a boat in a cork vest and swimming ashore with your luggage.

"The trouble with you," I told my son, "is that you don't plan ahead. You knew you were going to graduate at least three hours before they awarded the diplomas. You should have . . ."

"Don't worry, Mom. I have found a college. It's accredited, has absolutely no standards whatsoever, and is small enough to give individual attention."

"When do classes begin?"

"Whenever I get there."

"Is it in the Free World?"

"Let me just say that it accepts five major credit cards."

I don't mind wearing a T-shirt with a big D on it, but I feel like a fool driving around with a bumper sticker reading, "SEND DOO DAH TO THE ROSE BOWL!"

CREDIT: *Erma Bombeck, Field Newspaper Syndicate.*

Brain Tumors

Brain tumors are abnormal masses of tissue in which the cells grow and divide without restraint, apparently unregulated by the mechanisms that control normal cells. Customarily, tumors are considered either benign or malignant, but in a sense all brain tumors are potentially malignant because they may lead to death if not treated.

Certain tumors occur almost exclusively during childhood and adolescence, whereas others are predominantly tumors of adult life. The age of the patient appears to correlate with the site where some tumors develop in the brain.

Most of the primary tumors attack members of both sexes with equal frequency. Some, such as meningiomas (slow-growing benign tumors that may appear in many places throughout the head), occur more frequently in women; others, such as medulloblastomas (rapidly growing tumors, some of which are curable by surgery and radiation therapy), more commonly afflict boys and young men.

Pathologists classify primary brain tumors into two groups: the gliomas, which invade the surrounding brain; and the non-glial tumors, which compress rather than invade the adjacent brain. Metastatic (or secondary) tumors arise when abnormal cells that have developed elsewhere in the body are carried to the brain by the blood flow. Lung cancer in men and breast cancer in women are the original sources of almost 70 percent of all brain tumors.

By invading the neighboring structures, the tumor expands to produce increased pressure within the skull. Certain signs of a brain tumor reflect the pressure exerted on the brain by the tumor growth, and symptoms usually point to its location in the brain. The rate at which these symptoms progress is determined by the rate of tumor growth.

Depending on the size of the tumor and the parts of the brain it affects, an individual may suffer persistent headaches, paralysis, personality changes, loss of vision or visual hallucinations, speech difficulties, or behavioral disorders, at times accompanied by seizures. It is not surprising that individuals who have been confined to mental institutions occasionally turn out to harbor brain tumors.

Unfortunately, symptoms of a brain tumor often mimic those of other diseases, causing a delay in diagnosis. Although the doctor may elicit from the patient's previous history symptoms suggesting the presence of a tumor, the diagnosis is often not suspected until it becomes apparent that, in spite of treatment, the patient's condition is becoming worse. Certain conditions resulting from head injuries also may pursue a course similar to that of brain tumors. If the patient's course leads the doctor to suspect a tumor, neurologic examination, skull X rays, an electroencephalogram (EEG), radioisotopic brain scans and a computerized tomographic (CT) scan are used to determine if the patient should undergo more definitive procedures.

Increased pressure has many causes and therefore does not always signify the presence of a brain tumor. Among children, certain diseases and, on very rare occasions, medical therapy for an illness can produce increased intracranial pressure. "Benign brain edema," which affects some adolescent and young women and also some women taking contraceptive pills, is a swelling of the brain that may produce pressure resembling that of a tumor. The patient's history, a neurologic exam and special neuroradiologic tests usually can distinguish between increased intracranial pressure caused by these other conditions and that caused by a brain tumor.

The most accurate diagnosis of a brain tumor can be made by surgery that permits the neurosurgeon to see the tumor and obtain a specimen for examination. However, diagnostic surgery is not without risk, and there are now several diagnostic procedures for detecting brain tumors without resorting to surgery. The CT scanner provides many X-ray views of thin sections of the brain, increasing the likelihood that a tumor can be detected at an early stage. Other diagnostic procedures may provide evidence of a brain tumor that might otherwise go undetected; these include angiography, in which contrast material is injected into an artery, flows with the blood into the brain, and demonstrates on an X-ray picture the area where the tumor has developed; and pneumoencephalography, in which air is injected into the spinal fluid that circulates around the brain and spinal cord. While CT scans have reduced the necessity for pneumography, in certain conditions, such as tumors around the pituitary gland, air contrast is the procedure that affords the best information.

Many advances have been made in radiation therapy and chemotherapy for treating certain brain tumors, but these techniques are still of limited value. Both have side effects and, because they cannot be directed exclusively to the tumor, they have the potential to damage healthy as well as diseased tissues. Radiotherapy is used primarily for tumors that cannot be removed completely, or for cases in which surgery involves a great risk to the patient. In general, radiation therapy and chemotherapy are used as secondary treatments for tumors that cannot be cured by surgery.

Brain tumors that can be removed surgically lie just outside the brain or in parts of the brain that can be removed without causing significant neurological damage. Because a tumor will recur if any tumor cells are left behind the surgeon's goal is to remove the total tumor whenever possible. If the location or size of the tumor, or its relationship to the blood supply within the brain, preclude a safe removal of the entire tumor, partial removal may be all that can be accomplished by surgery alone.

One of the most important advances in the surgical treatment of brain tumors is the operating microscope, which can magnify the area to be surgically removed to many times its actual size. This instrument affords the neurosurgeon a clear view of the smallest area, and a greater precision in performing delicate operations.

While the operating microscope and microsurgical techniques have afforded a greater chance that many tumors can be removed totally, most types of invasive tumors still cannot be cured by operation alone. However, using these techniques, the neurosurgeon can now approach and remove tumors that were formerly inoperable, and patients having certain types of tumors that were once considered incurable now have an excellent chance of recovery. One such case is the benign craniopharyngioma, which often attacks children. While this tumor was considered rarely curable by surgery only a decade ago, it now can be removed with minimal or no brain damage in many cases.

Research into new methods of radiotherapy, chemotherapy, and the relation of the body's immune system to tumor development is yielding new insights into the basis and treatment of this disease. In addition, because of new methods of diagnosis and a greater awareness of the symptoms of tumor development, people having brain tumors are being referred for proper treatment earlier in the course of their disease, when there is a greater chance of cure. Although brain tumors are a major cause of death, particularly among children, these diagnostic and therapeutic advances and the wide application of microsurgical techniques promise that surgeons, radiotherapists and chemotherapists may be able to control, if not cure, many more tumors at some time in the foreseeable future.

CREDIT: *Charles B. Wilson, M.D., Department of Neurological Surgery, University of California School of Medicine, San Francisco.*

Breast Enlargement

A SILICONE QUESTION

DEAR MISS LANDERS: I'd appreciate it if you would tell me the names of the states where silicone shots to enlarge a woman's breasts are legal. Also, will you please give me the name of a doctor who gives these shots? Thanks a lot. FLAT FAYE

DEAR FLAT: There is no state in which silicone shots are legal for breast enlargement. This is a dangerous procedure which can cause serious trouble. Silicone implants, however, are legal in every state.

Sorry, I never recommend doctors. Call your County Medical Society and ask for the names of two or three plastic surgeons. Then take your pick.

For many years, women who were self-conscious and felt unfeminine because of very small breasts did a variety of little tricks to camouflage their "inadequacy." They stuffed cotton or toilet tissue into their brassieres, creating the illusion of larger breasts.

Later, brassiere manufacturers produced padded bras and filler cups to slip inside the bra. While these techniques were satisfactory for some, many women longed for something more "real"—and the medical profession did indeed come up with the answer—the silicone bag enclosing a silicone gel.

Following that major development, breast enlargement (augmentation) has been done in increasing numbers each year. The estimated number of breast enlargement procedures done in the United States is approximately 120,000 yearly.

Confusion exists among lay persons in regard to injections of silicone to enlarge a breast and the use of a prosthesis or implant to accomplish the same effect. To date, the Food and Drug Administration has not permitted the sale or use of injectable silicone in the breast because of the pain, lumps, and a tendency of injected silicone to move around. Criminal indictments have been filed against people who have injected silicone, many of whom were not physicians.

Following the major breakthrough of the development of a silicone bag encasing a gel of silicone, variations in the type of prosthesis have evolved. To date, no type of implant is superior. All the problems that will be noted below may occur with the use of any of the prostheses.

The commonly used prostheses include one similar to that first developed but with a thinner bag encasing a gel of silicone. Another common prosthesis is a silicone bag with a valve which can be used to inflate the bag with salt water. A combination of these—an inner bag of silicone and an outer bag filled with salt water—may also be used. The implants are inserted by surgery.

The ideal candidate for surgery is a healthy, thin or moderately thin person who will not expect a miraculous change in her life as a result of the alteration in her figure. She should not be younger than eighteen and there is actually no age limit on the other end of the age spectrum so long as the woman is in good health.

Situations which may make breast enlargement surgery undesirable are:

(1) Prior existing breast problems such as frequent occurrences of breast cysts.

(2) The presence of scar tissue from previous biopsies.

(3) And most importantly, breasts that sag a great deal. In sagging breasts, the nipples are, of course, lower and often need to be transplanted. There is a chance that in the transplanting, the nipple may become permanently numb. To a younger woman, this loss of sensation can be important. In the case of an older woman, it may be of small significance. In any event, the woman should be aware of the risk.

Occasionally women come in with one breast larger than the other. The surgeon can place an implant in the smaller breast, or he can place implants in both breasts, using a larger implant in the smaller one, so the result will be two breasts of the same size.

Every woman who considers breast enlargement should be fully aware that the size of a woman's breasts will not change her life. It will not cause a philandering husband to stay home, nor will it attract eligible swains. No man worth having will suddenly take up with a woman because she is a 38-D cup. The ideal candidate for breast enlargement is the woman who is realistic and understands that after surgery the only thing that will change is the size of her brassiere cup. The usual change is one cup size—such as A to B, or B to C.

The procedure itself may be done as an inpatient or, in increasing numbers, as an outpatient with the basic reason being cost, to be discussed later. The surgery also may be done under general anesthesia or local anesthesia, again as an inpatient or outpatient. The risk of anesthesia is greater with general rather than local anesthesia. Several incision sites are available to the patient and her surgeon. The choices basically are: in the armpit, in the pigmented area surrounding the nipple, or in the fold beneath the breast. The most commonly used incision is the fold beneath the breast.

Loss of nipple sensation may occur with any of these incisions. As in most surgery, considerable time is spent controlling the bleeding. The implant is then put in and the wound is repaired in layers. Strap support is applied to the breast, or a brassiere is put on the patient. Most surgeons have instructed their patients to be on a limited activity regimen for ten to fourteen days after surgery avoiding the use of the shoulders for such things as lifting. The average student or employed person would miss ten days of regular activity. No vigorous physical activity for six weeks is the recommendation of the majority of surgeons.

Standard risks of all surgery are bleeding and infection. Profuse internal bleeding of the breast area may require reoperation. Infection is rare, and at worst, would cause removal of the prosthesis and eventual replacement after a few months. Rejection of a prosthesis because of allergy to silicone is extremely rare. A scar is the aftermath of all surgery, but all three areas of standard incisions are favorable. Because of the development of the pocket and the stretch of the soft tissues, diminished or absent nipple sensation is thought to be a less than 1 percent risk. The rupture of a prosthesis is even more rare than this, as patients have incurred severe auto accidents, skiing injuries, etc. without that occurrence. Sagging of the breast is thought to be not increased as the weight of the prosthesis approximates that of normal breast tissue.

Pain is not a significant feature of this operation. Many patients have pain medication the first day or two following surgery, and none thereafter. Most patients forget about the presence of the breast implants after a matter of weeks. The most common complication following breast implant surgery is the development of excessive firmness caused by the overdevelopment of scar by the tissue surrounding the implant. Because many of the patients are thin, this would result in a breast that is firm to touch, and to sculptors, too firm in appearance. This development usually occurs months after breast surgery. This situation can be remedied by the doctor using his hands to soften the area. This can be done with or without anesthesia depending on the threshold of pain of the patient.

Breast feeding is possible after surgery because the prosthesis is placed behind the normal breast tissue and ducts. An almost unique aspect of breast enlargement surgery is that for any of these above complications, including the complication of being too large or too small or the appearance not fitting one's own body image, removal is possible. (The surgeon cuts along the same incision line and takes out the implants just as he put them in.)

According to the statistics of the American Cancer Society, the incidence of breast cancer is one woman in fifteen. It is unknown if breast implant surgery alters that percentage risk. The insertion of prostheses does not interfere with the ability of the doctor to do a breast examination.

The result of enlargement surgery is extremely gratifying to most patients. The expression of many patients after surgery is that they wish they had had the surgery several years earlier. With proper patient election, the good to excellent results estimated by the patients is about 95 percent, despite the complaint of excessive hardness present in 15 percent or more of the patients.

The surgical fees involved may vary from $1,500 to $2,000. The outpatient hospital costs approximate $500, and the inpatient hospital costs approximate $1,200 to $1,500. Generally the fees are higher in California and New York.

The largest protesters against breast implant surgery are the women who are naturally endowed. For some reason they resent it when a "flat" sister suddenly appears with a beautiful figure.

CREDIT: *Randall E. McNally, M.D., Associate Professor, Plastic Surgery, Rush-Presbyterian-St. Luke's Medical Center.*

A SENSITIVE SPOT

DEAR ANN LANDERS: I've never written to a column such as yours, but that letter from the secretary who was desperate to increase the size of her breasts really got to me.

I have always been small-busted and know how self-conscious and inadequate it can make a woman feel. It only takes one lousy, insensitive jackass to give a woman like me an inferiority complex forever.

Just last week a supposedly sophisticated man-about-town told me to put some calamine lotion on them and they would be gone by morning. I was so humiliated and hurt I almost bawled. What I had hoped would be a delightful weekend at the gentleman's summer home turned out to be a miserable flop.

I hope you'll print this letter so the men out there will realize there are certain things you just don't kid about.
                    CRUSHED IN CINCINNATI

DEAR C.: A pox on both his houses—the cad! Put this column in the mail. Maybe he'll learn something.

Breast Feeding

The birth of a baby signals the start of a remarkable process in the mother's body. A hormone is released from her pituitary gland which starts milk production in her breasts. Her nipples, small protrusions of skin, tissue and muscle at the outer edge of the breasts, contain a number of very tiny holes through which hairlike streams of milk flow when the baby sucks at the breast. The flow of milk increases as the baby extracts the milk by sucking. If the milk is not extracted, the body will stop manufacturing the milk and the mother will probably experience discomfort of the breasts as the body adjusts to the fact that the milk is not being used.

Women from the beginning of mankind have been able to feed their babies at the breast. The modern woman is no different from her ancestors in this respect. If she is not separated from her baby at birth and is allowed to offer him unrestricted feeding, she will be capable of breast feeding.

Mother's milk provides for her baby a food that is perfectly suited to his developmental needs. Though all mammals feed their young from their bodies, the content of the milk differs according to the kind of development that is expected to take place in the particular mammal. The natural milk of each species provides the kind of nutrition needed by the young of that species. For example, the milk of the cow has a great deal more protein (and of a different kind, as well as calcium) than the milk of the human mother. Since the calf walks from birth the calf's growth need is protein for increased musculature and calcium for bone development.

Moreover, the calf gains a great deal of weight during the first year of life. The cow's milk is well suited to that kind of development. The milk of the human mother, on the other hand, is uniquely suited to the needs of the human infant. In the human baby, huge bodily growth and instant motor development are not desirable in the first months of life. Rather, enormous brain growth must take place, as well as a myelization (insulating the nerves with a covering) which is necessary for co-ordination of the muscles, which in turn makes sitting up and walking possible. Not much intellectual development is expected or needed in the cow; a great deal is required in the human.

In addition to offering the baby superior nutrition, the milk of the human mother also provides striking immunological benefits, supplying the baby's intestines with bacteria protective against certain gastrointestinal and nutritional diseases to which human infants are susceptible. These defense mechanisms also include protection against viral and bacterial disease of the lungs and nervous system.

There are psychological benefits also for both infant and mother. Because breast feeding usually requires the mother to feed the baby frequently (at least eight to ten times in a twenty-four-hour period during the early weeks) it helps to ensure that the baby receives the fondling, caressing, and affection from the mother which provide the stimulation the human infant requires for good emotional development. It also establishes the bonding or attachment which enhances the maternal qualities of the mother and produces in the infant feelings of security which play a lifelong role. This kind of stimulation can be accomplished also by a mother who feeds her baby artificially. However, the frequent handling of the baby required in breast feeding is a foolproof way of accomplishing this, especially in the first-time mother, who may not as yet realize the extent of the one-to-one communication her baby needs for healthy emotional development. It takes time and experience to develop the art of mothering. It has been found that the female hormone prolactin is an enormous help in developing maternal feelings. Prolactin is present in extremely large amounts in a woman's body only when she is breast feeding. It is part of nature's way of assuring protection for the helpless infant.

An important basic fact to understand about breast feeding is that nature has arranged it so that the more the baby sucks at the breast to extract the milk, the more milk the mother's body will manufacture. The reverse is also true. A common frustration for the woman trying to breast-feed in a bottle-feeding society such as the United States is the worry that she will not have enough milk. Physicians educated to be experts in artificial feeding, and who perhaps never saw a baby at the breast, frequently advise mothers to follow the schedule that was worked out for bottle babies—usually a feeding every four hours. Medical schooling failed to teach physicians that human milk is digested by the baby much more quickly than the heavier curd cow's milk, which normally requires about four hours for the infant to digest. As a result, when the breast-fed baby cries with hunger after two hours or less, the mother may be told that she does not have sufficient milk, or that the milk she does have is not of good enough quality to sustain her baby. Babies by the thousands are switched after a few days from natural feeding to artificial feeding because of lack of knowledge about the functioning of the mammary gland and the content of human milk.

Between 1920 and 1950, extensive studies on artificial feeding were undertaken by the scientific community. Thus an acceptable method of artificial feeding—formula based on cow's or goat's milk—was developed which enabled the mother to share the feeding of the baby with others and to spend less time in the care of her infant, not, however, without certain disadvantages to the baby. Since the composition of cow's milk is vastly different from that of the human mother, even when watered down and scientifically adjusted in an attempt to suit the human baby's needs, the product frequently produces allergies in the baby which often persist throughout life. Moreover, the baby on artificial feeding is deprived of the immunological protections offered by natural milk and the psychological benefits associated with breast feeding.

The art of breast feeding is quickly lost once artificial feeding is started. When some women in the United States in the 1950s first began to breast-feed their babies again, they found they needed help in doing so. Since the physicians and nurses in whose care these women were placed at the time of giving birth had become experts in artificial feeding only, the help the breast-feeding mothers needed was not available to them, and many women were bitterly disappointed. This led to the development, first, of a lay group (La Leche League) prepared to offer this help, and second, a renewed professional interest in breast feeding.

It is interesting that the trend toward a desire to suckle their young was beginning about the same time women were clamoring to be liberated in other ways. To the woman who desired to breast-feed it was a form of liberation to be able to feed her baby the way she wanted to, rather than the way the professional community (at that time predominantly male) dictated she should because that is what had been taught in medical school.

The 1970s produced exciting new research on the value of human milk including its medicinal value in the prevention and cure of an increasing number of diseases. As a result, the number of mothers in the United States who are breast feeding when they leave the hospital after giving birth has increased from 18 percent in 1966 to close to 50 percent in 1977. This increase in the United States typifies the renewed worldwide interest and appreciation for one of the world's most valuable natural resources—human milk.

CREDIT: *Edwina Froehlich, La Leche League International, Chicago, Illinois.*

Breast Reduction

PROBLEMS WITH A LARGE BUST

DEAR ANN LANDERS: I find it hard to sympathize with "Crushed in Cincinnati" and her small-busted sisters. My problem is just the opposite and I'll trade with her.

Ever since I was 14, I've known that most boys are interested in one thing. Or should I say two?

When "Crushed" shops for a blouse or a dress she can wear any style. I must avoid low necklines, clingy fabrics and knits. The brassiere problem is simply awful. Mine have special pad-ding on the strap, and still they cut into my shoulders.

A woman can always make herself look larger, but to accomplish the reverse requires surgery, which is painful and expensive. "Crushed" should count her blessings.—TOO MUCH IS NO GOOD

DEAR T. M.: I've heard from many women who have had the surgery you speak of. They say it was worth the money and pain. Reconsider.

In our society a great deal of emphasis has been placed on the appearance of the female breast. Very small or very large breasts may be damaging to a female's self-image. These variations from the "normal" can affect how a woman interacts with her friends, husband, family and co-workers.

The problem of the small breast is one that deals mainly with this self-image concept. In contrast, a female with unusually large breasts must also deal with physical problems which are, in many situations, incapacitating, and limit her ability to live a normal life. This breast enlargement (or mammary hypertrophy as it is termed medically) is therefore considered more of a "disease" than is the small breast. In light of this fact, many insurance companies will pay for surgical operations to reduce the size of the breast in contrast to the breast enlargement operations.

The actual cause of breast enlargement is a mystery. It is known that even male breast tissue will respond to large doses of the female hormone estrogen. However, in almost all cases of unusually large breasts in the female, the estrogen levels are within the normal range. It is believed that the mammary gland tissue in these women may be especially sensitive to normal amounts of female hormone and therefore become markedly enlarged. An unusual type of breast enlargement can occur in younger females going through puberty. It is called virginal hypertrophy and may result in truly gigantic breasts. Certainly, heredity does play a role. In many instances large breasts follow a family pattern.

It is erroneously believed by many that large breasts are related to being overweight. Whereas this may be true in a few cases, women with true mammary hypertrophy will persist in having large breasts despite a weight loss. Of course, this leads to frustration and disappointment when weight loss is not accompanied by a corresponding decrease in breast size. It further cripples a woman's self-image and frequently she will attempt to camouflage her problem in the cloak of obesity.

The physical symptoms of mammary hypertrophy are many and are all related to the abnormally enlarged mass and increased weight of the breast. The increased weight itself leads to an aching in the breast which becomes more painful over a period of years. This excess weight also accelerates the degree of sagging and requires more supportive brassieres. The result is marked grooving and discomfort in the shoulders from the brassiere straps. In extreme situations, arthritis in the shoulder joints may result.

This abnormally positioned weight also places undue stresses on the spine and may result in a progressive and possibly irreversible curvature of the upper spine. Aching muscles of the lower neck and upper back and shoulder areas are also common complaints of heavy-breasted women.

The abnormal weight can also hinder breathing and in the older patient may cause a significant problem. The enlarged bulk of the breasts frequently interferes with arm motion, thereby limiting vocational and recreational activities.

Moisture retention from inadequate ventilation may result in irritation in the skin folds around the breast. Inability or unwillingness to appear in bathing suits or other sporting garments, because of appearance alone, can be psychologically crippling, especially to the teenager.

For these reasons reduction of breast size should ideally be carried out once the condition has established itself, usually by sixteen to eighteen years of age. It can, however, be performed at any age.

Economic factors cannot be ignored. Untold amounts of money are spent on special garments for additional and more comfortable clothing. Often this outlay is more costly over a period of time than having the problem corrected surgically.

The operation involves a total restructuring of the breasts and almost always includes repositioning the nipple, reducing the nipple size, and reducing the mass of the mammary gland itself. The supporting skin is also modified, resulting in a pleasing contour, size and appearance.

In mythology, the Amazon women would amputate a breast if it interfered with the use of the bow and arrow. Today, few women would accept amputation of the breast as a solution to such a problem. Over the years, plastic surgeons have developed various operative techniques for reduction of the breast mass so that the qualified plastic surgeon today can select a procedure for the patient that best suits her specific situation.

As with any surgical procedure, scars result. The configuration of the breast in most cases allows the plastic surgeon to place these scars in locations where they are relatively unnoticeable. Of necessity, there must be a scar around the nipple complex. This is in a location that tends to become less visible with time because of the difference in skin coloring. The majority of the available procedures then result in an upside-town T-shaped scar running from the nipple complex downward to the fold area beneath the breast and there joining a scar that runs in the fold area. Other procedures may result in a scar running from the nipple complex outward to the side of the breast. This scar has a shorter over-all length but does tend to be more visible because of its location.

The placement of the scars allows them to be hidden by most bathing suit tops. The presence of these scars must be accepted by any person contemplating this type of surgery as they are of a permanent nature. However, they tend to become less apparent with the passing of time. The final appearance and the time necessary for this to be achieved vary with the individual.

The operation takes approximately three hours to perform and the patient is often able to leave the hospital one to two days after surgery.

Most often discomfort after surgery tends to be related to the skin incisions and is not severe. Soreness may persist for two to three weeks but limits only strenuous activities. Most patients are able to return to their usual jobs one to two weeks after surgery.

As with any surgical procedure, complications may occur. Fortunately, with this type of operation they are most often minor problems and easily managed. The most common problem relates to bleeding causing temporary discoloration and swelling. Usually no treatment is needed but occasionally a collection of blood may require drainage. Infection is not frequently encountered following breast reduction.

The most serious potential complication is total or partial loss of the nipple tissue itself. In most of the operative procedures, the nipple is left attached to the breast tissue to provide continued blood supply. During the operation it is repositioned upward. The greater the distance the nipple must be repositioned, the more strain on the blood supply. This could possibly result in death of the nipple tissue due to inadequate blood supply. If this does occur, a new nipple can be reconstructed. In massive breasts, nipple grafts similar to skin grafts may be required for repositioning.

A change in sensation or sensitivity of the nipple is to be expected after surgery. However, most patients with mammary hypertrophy tend to have diminished nipple sensation already and often this sensitivity is improved following surgery. In some cases, however, the sensation may be further diminished after surgery. With the passage of time, this generally improves, but in a few cases, the sensitivity may never return to normal.

Many women are concerned about the possibility or advisability of breast feeding following breast reduction surgery. Frequently women with excessively large breasts are unable to breast-feed. Such women, after their breasts have been reduced, are better off not trying to nurse because their breasts may again become larger and have increased sagging.

Since the normal aging process has a tendency to place stress on the human skin, one must expect, after any kind of surgery, that time will make some changes. The breasts, like any other part of the body, will, as the years go by, sag a little. When this occurs, if it is of concern, comparatively minor procedures with further adjustment of the supportive skin can be performed. Further breast enlargement occurs only in rare specific disease situations or to a minor degree with weight gain.

There is a great deal of satisfaction following this type of surgery because of the immediate and complete disappearance of the pre-operative physical symptoms. The improvement in self-image is apparent when the patient views herself as a much more attractive individual.

The most frequent complaint is, "Why didn't I have this done years ago?"

CREDIT: *Robert E. Knode, M.D., Associated Plastic Surgeons, Chicago, and Arlington Heights, Illinois; Clinical Assistant Professor of Surgery, Division of Plastic Surgery, University of Illinois, Chicago.*

Budgets For Married Couples*

HIS-AND-HER BUDGETS

America is a land of working couples. Tens of millions of you who are and will be brides will continue working long after the wedding. Millions of you will quit working for pay only during the years your children are babies. Most of you will return to work when your children go off to school.

Money management takes on a special aspect in today's two-paycheck American homes. With both of you earning salaries, specific questions are bound to come up:

How do you divide the money you bring in? Who pays for what around the house? If you had an ideal partnership, who would pay for what—how and why?

Here are ten basic rules I've worked out over years of discussions with experts on family finance, interviews with husbands and wives in every income bracket across the country, my personal experience as a working wife through my entire adult life. These are *my* rules, no one else's, but I'm sure all of you can benefit from some of them, some of you can benefit from all of them, and any one of them can be revised to fit your individual circumstances.

(1) Make your marriage a *financial partnership;* discuss your income and plan your spending as a husband-and-wife team.

The wife who insists she should pay for only the part-time housekeeper and put the rest of her paycheck in her savings account is selfish and wrong. If you're a team in other ways, be a team financially as well. If your mutual decision is that the wife's paycheck should be saved, excellent—but make the decision as a couple. Otherwise, deceit and suspicion are virtually inevitable. This is a fundamental rule.

(2) Pool part of your individual paychecks in a family fund which is to be used to cover essential household expenses.

In many households, the pooling will be automatic, for both paychecks are being used to buy things and non-things the family wants. *It should be automatic.* How much of the wife's paychecks will go into the pool may vary from home to home, depending on the wife's income and the family's circumstances, but the key point is that there should be a pool.

* From *Sylvia Porter's Money Book.* Copyright © 1975 by Sylvia Porter. Reprinted with permission.

(3) Decide which of you will be responsible for paying specific bills out of the pool. As a husband you might take over payment of the "big bills—rent, mortgage, insurance, taxes, the like. As a wife, you might take over management of the "household bills"—food, entertainment at home, ordinary household overhead. To me, this is a logical division of responsibility. It's entirely okay if you have other ideas, but talk them out to your mutual satisfaction.

For instance, some experts say a woman who has been accustomed to her independence for a long period may be actively unhappy unless, as a working wife, she continues to have "my" telephone, "my" bank account, etc. So be it —as long as she and her husband agree on the division and there is no secret resentment of the situation.

(4) Use the combination savings account and checking account method as your money control.

If you don't carefully separate your savings from your regular checking account, your savings easily can dribble away without your knowing just how or why. For most couples, the two-account "control" works best.

(5) If the wife's job necessitates the added expense of household help, the wife's paycheck should cover it. This is a rule I came to instinctively, for in most homes, if the wife did not hold an outside job, she could, if she had to, get along without any extra help. Thus, this is "her" expense which she should handle. If the expense is to be paid out of the family pool, the wife should directly make the payment. Or the wife may withhold a specific part of her earnings for this expense. Whatever the details, it should be understood that this expense is in the wife's department.

(6) Extra expenses for entertainment at home should be handled by the wife, but when you go out, it's the husband's deal. Again, this is my viewpoint only.

(7) If you're a young couple planning to have children, the husband's paycheck should cover all basic household expenses, and part of the wife's earnings should be earmarked for the initial expenses of a baby. You must be prepared for the time when, for a while at least, you'll scale down to one paycheck. You may decide to share this planning by earmarking funds out of each paycheck—but at least *plan*. A couple without the financial responsibilities of children obviously has more leeway to shift spending and saving.

(8) With both of you earning money, you'll really benefit from spreading payment of your big bills so that each month bears a share.

In addition, plan your installment buying as a team and with caution so that even if you're hit by an emergency your total monthly bills will be well within your capacity to repay. Under no circumstances take on *any* installment debt without a joint agreement.

(9) The rules on personal allowances are particularly vital for you. If you want to do something absurd with your personal allowance, that's your business. Your allowance is yours alone.

(10) Make a pledge to each other today that when you get into a squeeze in the future—which you will, for nearly everyone does—you'll choose a

quiet evening alone to argue it out and decide how to escape from it. And when you talk about it, call it "our" squeeze, not "yours."

A superficial point? Oh no. The wife who in the heat of a money fight says, "We wouldn't have any savings at all unless I worked," is begging for resentment and the retort that she wouldn't have any home unless he paid for the rent or mortgage. It's imperative to avoid discussing your money mess when you're both frantic. If you can't figure a way out, take your problem to the service department of your bank or savings institution and ask for guidance on where and how you might get help.

A BUDGET IF YOU'RE JUST LIVING TOGETHER ("MINGLES")

What if you're among the millions of young Americans who today are just living together under one roof ("mingles")—with no legal ties, no established rules for behavior except those you and your peers agree are okay, and certainly no guidelines for management of your individual incomes and expenses?

You could easily and successfully follow the rules in the preceding pages for a working man and wife. But you may be far more fascinated by the following real-life system of budgeting created over the past two years by a young technical consultant and his schoolteacher living companion. The two insist that, once their system was perfected, it ended two years of destructive fighting about money (an even more brutal cause of split-ups among the nonmarried than among the married).

"Basically," says Dick, "the system consists of four (yes four) checking accounts which we call 'yours,' 'mine,' 'ours,' and 'car.'

"In addition, we have savings accounts. We keep a minimum balance of $100 in each checking account to avoid service charges, which would run between 12 and 18 percent for us, but higher for frequent check writers. To reduce the temptation to dip into the $100 minimums, we delete the balances from our records and pretend they don't exist."

Here are details which are provocatively similar in many ways to the his-and-hers budgets:

(1) All income from both individuals goes into the "ours" account. Each has a checkbook and the money deposited is arbitrarily split in half between each checkbook as a hedge against overdrawing. If either book runs dangerously low, temporary transfers are made. Then, at the end of each month, the books are balanced and the joint bank statement reconciled.

(2) Out of this "ours" account come virtually all living expenses—food, rent, utilities, etc.—which these two have agreed to share on a regular basis.

(3) Once a month, $50 is transferred from the "ours" account to each individual account ("yours" and "mine") as each person's personal allowance. "This figure was chosen arbitrarily and is still experimental," says Dick. "We expect to adjust it after we have had more experience with it." The personal allowance covers clothes and other items "which have a large potential for

conflict over what is or is not extravagant" and for "simply spending as we please." Neither accounts to the other for what happens to each month's personal allowance.

The special account for the car is an ingenious twist. "This is the largest single expense we have, costing more than rent and food combined," says Dick. "And we feel that it's important for us both to be conscious of what cars really cost." They are making a vital point. Also, watching the real costs of their car tends to discourage excessive driving.

A simple record is kept of the number of miles driven and deposits of $.10 per mile are regularly transferred from the "our" account. The $.10 covers all operating expenses, plus a margin of $.05 a mile for depreciation. (This figure is subject to revision upward as costs dictate.) The "car" fund includes forced savings for a new car in the future.

Another ingenious system for food shopping involves the initialing of all store register tapes or chits and periodic checking and reconciling of the records.

There are many gaps in this couple's system—but if you add their hints to all you've read so far, you will be way, way ahead of the vast majority of budget-keepers.

Without any difficulty, you can shift the details to fit your own situation. You, for instance, may prefer to contribute equal amounts—rather than all— of your income to your joint checking and savings accounts. Whether you're a married couple or merely living together, you may feel it's unfair for both of you to bear an equal share of the food costs if the man regularly eats far more food and far more expensive food than the woman. Or you may argue that it's unfair for both of you to bear an equal share of the phone bills if the woman does most of the long-distance talking.

Whatever your own decisions, I guarantee that personal budget-keeping will help you curb your living costs—and help bring you peace of mind.

Budgets

How a Woman Can Look Her Best on a Limited Budget

The bedroom closet is filled with clothes, but most of the garments are useless.

A five-year-old black cocktail dress is too short, too snug and out-of-date.

A pink puffy-sleeved two-piece outfit with ruffles down the front (left over from co-ed days) would look adorable on your twelve-year-old daughter, but what thirty-four-year-old wife and mother of three wants to dress like a pre-teen?

A provocative red number with a neckline that plunges nearly to your navel was a great buy ($75 marked down to $20), but it doesn't fit your life-style.

Dozens of other dresses hanging in your closet are just as useless and a waste of precious closet space.

The reason you have very little to wear is that there was no planning.

A person isn't born with fashion sense. It takes practice and knowledge to pull together a versatile, all-occasion wardrobe—and it can be done with relatively little money.

Before spending another dollar on a new dress or accessory, set aside a couple of hours. You will also need a pencil and a pad of paper to map out a personal fashion chart. If you don't trust your own judgment, turn to a friend or relative whose taste you admire and help get to the root of your clothes crisis.

For starters, go through the closet bit by bit. Weed out items and put them in different piles on the floor. One mound should be clothes that are abso-lutely useless. Later, separate these items into trash and items that are in good condition and can be donated to charity.

Recently I cleaned out the master bedroom and hall closets and donated two dozen pieces of men's and women's clothing, jewelry, shoes, handbags and other accessories to a local hospital service league thrift shop. Three weeks later, an appraisal form stating that the items were worth $367 arrived in the mail. The $367, I learned, was a legal tax deduction. This was an un-expected surprise.

Don't chuck out all the old clothes in the closet. Sort out items that are reusable—garments that can be made longer or shorter—or wider with the help of fabric inserts, lace trims, false hems or other clever alteration tricks.

The uses for old clothes, still in good shape, are limitless. Old mini-dresses can be converted into cropped tops for color-matched pants. Wide crepe party pants can be snipped apart and turned into a long or mid-calf skirt sim-ply by adding a triangle of fabric in the front and back center of the lower half of the skirt. No one will ever suspect that the newly formed top and up-dated skirt had a past.

Unimaginative souls unable to figure out refurbishing tricks can turn to how-to books for help. A variety of publications on the market show readers what to do—step-by-step instructions, easy-to-follow diagrams, and before and after photographs.

Finally, set aside clothes that are still usable, but cannot stand alone. A pair of pants may need to be updated with a cowl neck blouson top and a tweed hacking jacket or blazer. A wool tent-shape jumper needs a print shirt underneath and a narrow stretch belt to add definition to the waistline.

As you work your way through the "usable but needs help stack," jot down exactly what is needed to put each item to good use.

When trying to color-match an item, it's a good idea to snip out a smidgen of fabric from the seam and carry it with you on the shopping expedition. It will save a return trip to the department store to exchange the item for a more flattering color.

A well-rounded wardrobe revolves around a handful of pieces that can be mixed or matched depending on your mood or the occasion.

If your cleaned-out closet lacks the basics, shop for clothes that can be used in more ways than one. For instance, a dress should be able to stand on its own or double as a jumper or as a long tunic over pants.

Dozens of looks can be achieved by switching around six basic fashions—a sleeveless jersey tent dress, a surplice top, a T-shirt, a scoop-necked peasant blouse, a skirt and pants. The component look is available both in ready-to-wear or in easy-to-sew patterns for those who know how.

The ability to switch pieces around will give you more value per dollar. The mix-and-match items are also a boon to travelers since they cut down on packing space.

How much you spend on new clothes depends on your budget. But it is not necessary to go overboard in order to dress in good taste.

Simplicity is the code word. Search for a look that will be just as useful five years from now as it is today. Avoid extremes. They don't last and they strain the budget.

One way to determine a timeless look is to scan old fashion magazines. Try the local public library if old fashion publications cannot be unearthed at home.

Safe investments that defy style changes include silk Ascot tie skirts, mid-calf A-line wool skirts in dark colors, and plain white all-cotton or linen peasant-style shirts and blouses.

These items may cost more than man-made synthetic items, but the natural fabrics and classic lines eventually pay for themselves because of the wear you will get out of them.

To choose clothing that will last for five years or more, it is necessary to be aware of the direction fashion is headed.

An easy way to research style trends is to read leading fashion magazines published in America, France, Italy and England for insight on what designers are showing both here and abroad.

If price is no object, fine—pay full price for these items. If money is scarce, search out lower-priced copies or the real thing in discount houses or on sale racks of name designer boutiques in specialty shops and leading department stores.

It's amazing how much one can save at an end-of-the-season close-out when retailers are anxious to clear the racks.

Don't be a snob and pass up a visit to a resale shop. A good percentage of items for sale at these shops have usually been worn only a few times by some well-to-do woman who refuses to be seen in the same outfit more than once.

If a garment fits, looks great on you, and the price is well below the original cost, buy it. Have it dry-cleaned and it will look and feel like new. Name designer suits and dresses often go for as little as $10.

Occasionally labels may be snipped out of designer garments by the original owner. It takes a sharp eye to tell chic items from the schlock. One has to be able to tell the well-made clothes from the not-so-well-made.

Learn how to distinguish cashmere from Orlon or genuine leather from the stiffer man-made stuff. It should not be necessary to depend on labels to tell if the garment is top quality.

How does one learn the differences? For starters, go to top quality stores, even though you have no intention of paying the steep prices. Try on fashions you cannot afford. It will give you the opportunity to touch and study the fabric so you can tell one material from another.

Examine the way the seams are finished—how the neckline zipper starts several inches below the neckline, rather than at the top of the neckline. Notice how the hem is finished with fine hand stitches rather than by machine— or how the hemline has been weighted, so the garment hangs smoothly. These fine, and expensive, details are what add to the price of high-quality clothes.

Accessories are an important fashion ally. Start collecting the little touches in the natural tones—black, brown, beige, rust—so they can be put to work with everything in your wardrobe. Look for the following accessories:

Scarves: An assortment of silk and/or cotton squares and oblongs in plaids, stripes, geometrics and tiny floral patterns.

Bags: A roomy leather or canvas tote bag. One or two clutch bags. A dressy evening bag.

Belts: Narrow leather, linen, and canvas belts that are tasseled, banded, braided or rolled. A stretch belt and a fabric sash would also be handy.

Shoes: A classic leather kiltie to wear with pants or casual skirts. One pair of dressier beige shoes that can go just about anywhere. A pair of black fabric sandals, perhaps with wrap-around ankle ties, that can be worn during the day or evening.

Write down what you need and how much your budget allows before setting foot in a store. It will save time, leg work, and money. Don't deviate from the list unless you stumble across a fantastic bargain that fits your lifestyle.

The key to organizing a well-rounded wardrobe is to focus on one or two colors that compliment your skin tone and hair shade.

When trying on new clothes, size up your figure in the mirror. Height, weight, proportions, and any figure problems should be considered in the final decision.

Here are some guidelines:

Petite Figure: Choose one color and tiny patterns. Avoid fussy "little-girl clothes" and bulky fabrics. Accessories should be kept small and in scale with your small figure.

Tall Full Figure: Choose dresses, skirts, tops, and pants that don't cling and are cut along classic lines. Semi-fitted shifts and dress and jacket ensembles are flattering. Understated patterns are most becoming.

Short Full Figure: Choose vertical lines and one-color outfits minus collars, but with open necklines. Avoid horizontal stripes, gigantic prints, two-tone tops, and skirts cinched with wide belts. They will make you look dumpy. A turtleneck or cowl neckline will bury your neck from view.

Tall Slim Figure: You can wear just about anything. Best styles include soft silhouettes and fabrics, bold patterns, pleated or gathered skirts, two-tone blouses, blouses with long puffy sleeves and tailored pleated top pants.

Very few of us are born with perfect figures. However, even certain figure flaws can be made less noticeable. Here is how it's done:

Short Neck: A V-neckline adds length to a short neck. Avoid turtlenecks, neck scarves and chokers.

Thin Neck: There are dozens of ways to knot or wrap a glamorous scarf around the neck. Learn some of the scarf tricks. It will give the appearance of having a fuller neck.

Heavy Legs: Wear pantyhose or stockings that match or blend with your skirt or dress. Avoid pants that cling to the leg or short skirts that make heavy legs look heavier. Wear simple shoes that are sturdy-looking enough to balance the proportion of your legs.

Thin Legs: Wear pantyhose or stockings in a pale shade. Stylish boots with wider tops will also add width to thin legs. Never wear dark seamed stockings that will appear to cut the width of the leg in half.

Extra Big Bosom: Square, V-neck or oval necklines are most flattering. A properly fitted bra is a must. Avoid clingy sweaters. To balance a big bosom, wear skirts that are semi-full, perhaps with big pockets to detract from the bosom.

Flat Bosom: A padded bra will help. So will wearing a cropped vest over a turtleneck sweater or dress or a blouse with a pleated front.

Narrow Shoulders: Choose dresses, jackets, or blouses that emphasize shoulder width with wing collars, boat necklines, and extended or padded shoulders. Set-in sleeves are more flattering than raglan sleeves, which make narrow shoulders look even narrower.

Wide Hips: A-line skirts and pants cut straight from a natural waistline, both in non-cling materials, are most flattering. Avoid too tight or too full skirts and wear loose pullover tunics that hit mid-thigh.

Above all else, learn what looks best on *you* and stick to those basic styles. Every woman feels better when she has confidence in her appearance. If you lack a sense of style listen to someone whose fashion sense you admire. Loads of compliments mean you've done the right thing. Stony silence means —well—don't go in *that* direction again.

CREDIT: *Judy Moore, Chicago* Sun-Times.

Burns

If your clothing catches fire outside, do *not* repeat *not* run for help. *Roll on the ground.* If you are in the house, roll on a rug. If a child's clothing catches fire, smother flames by wrapping the child in a rug or blanket.

FOR MINOR BURNS INVOLVING SMALL AREAS

To relieve pain, hold burn under cold water for a few minutes or apply ice cubes. Wash skin surrounding the burn with soap and water, but not the burn itself, which is sterile. Apply Vaseline or vitamin A and D ointment (to prevent dressing from sticking to burn) and cover with a sterile gauze square. No ointment is needed if you use non-sticking plastic-covered gauze, such as Telfa. Do *not* use Grandma's old stand-by—butter. It is the one substance that will cause the skin to blister.

FOR BURNS INVOLVING LARGE AREAS

Cover burned areas with Saran Wrap or a similar thin plastic wrapping (it won't stick to burn) or a clean sheet. Cover a child who has been burned with blankets and take him to the nearest hospital.

Do not apply ointments or salves. Because shock may occur quickly, the person should be in the hospital as soon as possible; prompt medical help is essential.

ELECTRICAL BURNS

If electrical current at the outlet is controlled by a wall switch, turn it off. If not, pull the person away from the outlet or appliance with a non-conductive material (such as a board or *wooden* chair). *Do not use bare hands.*

If the person is not breathing, apply mouth-to-mouth resuscitation. Always consult a doctor for electrical burns. They can permanently deform the face, mouth or hands.

Two types of extension cords, those with pronged plugs at both ends and those with a pronged plug on one end and a bulb socket on the other, are extremely hazardous. Remove them from the home. If you have small children, put safety caps (available at hardware stores) on *all* unused outlets.

CHEMICAL BURNS

Chemical burns require prompt treatment. Instructions for treating burns are often printed on the chemical's container. If instructions are available, follow them. If not, wash away chemical with large amounts of clean water; if possible, put the burned person under the bathroom shower. When chemical is washed away completely, treat burn as a fire burn.

Chemical burns of the eye require instant treatment. If a faucet is nearby, hold the person's head under it, turn on cool water at medium pressure. Rinse the eye for ten minutes, directing the water away from the unaffected eye. (If water isn't available, use milk or another bland liquid.) After all chemical particles are washed away, cover the eye with a sterile compress and take the person to a doctor or hospital.

CREDIT: Accident Handbook, *Department of Health Education, the Children's Hospital Medical Center, Boston, Massachusetts.*

Bursitis

Bursitis is due to inflammation of a sac-like cavity called a bursa which is filled with a fluid. The bursae are located at places in the tissues of the body where friction and irritation would otherwise develop, between tendons, bones, and the overlying skin.

As a result of repeated and excessive irritation and friction or pressure, the bursa becomes inflamed, the wall of the sac thickens, and an increased amount of fluid develops. Motion of the affected area or limb is difficult because of the excruciating pain that sometimes occurs.

The most common example of bursitis is that which is caused by pressure and friction of tight shoes over the prominence at the base of the large toe which is known as a bunion.

Specific occupations may produce friction over the bursa, e.g. pre-patellar bursitis (housemaid's knee, nun's knee); ischial bursitis (weaver's or tailor's bottom); olecranon bursitis or bursitis of the elbow (student's elbow), or pressure over the elbow as a result of leaning on the elbow; subdeltoid bursitis, bursitis of the shoulder produced by athletics like golf, tennis, as well as by occupations like paper hanging, painting, carpentry. Bursae can also become infected by bacteria.

In subdeltoid bursitis any motion of the arm causes severe pain which is greatest over the front part of the shoulder. The pain may radiate up to the head, the back of the neck and down to the fingers. Raising the arm and turning the arm outward are the most painful movements. X ray of the shoulder may show a calcium deposit in the bursa of the shoulder.

The symptoms of bursitis of the hip are pain on passive motion outward of the flexed hip and tenderness behind and slightly above the hip.

Pre-patellar bursitis is characterized by tenderness and swelling in the front of the knee and below the kneecap.

Calcaneal bursitis (soldier's heel) is characterized by tenderness to palpation and swelling over the back of the heel as well as tenderness and pain at the bottom of the heel.

Bursitis is not a life-threatening disease and responds to treatment rapidly. It may occur at any age in both males and females. Emotional factors are not considered a cause or precipitating factor for this condition.

The treatment of bursitis is directed toward the underlying cause under the supervision of your doctor, of course. Friction must be eliminated. Local anesthetics and cortisone injections may be of value. Sometimes the chronically infected bursa needs to have surgical drainage. On other occasions the bursa may have to be cut out by surgery.

CREDIT: *Daniel M. Miller, M.D., F.A.C.S., Associate Professor of Surgery, University of Nebraska College of Medicine, Omaha, Nebraska.*

Business

Your Career

"My object in writing you," the letter stated, "is to inquire about the possibility of a position for my son. He has just finished college and is now twenty-two. I shall greatly appreciate an interview . . ."

This letter is not vastly different from many I receive every month dealing with the problems of the young person out of school and trying to find a job. In the interview that followed, and in other similar interviews, it became apparent to me that most college graduates have given little or no thought to the career they wish to pursue. Instead, they seem to feel that they will just fall into a job. They do not know themselves or their capabilities, and have given little thought to the skills required or functions performed in the various sectors of business. This haphazard approach is the reason so many young people in business today are floundering and why those who are looking for jobs today will have difficulties tomorrow. The following advice is offered in an effort to help young job-seekers overcome the hurdles that face them.

Simply defined, business is the process that brings to people the things they need, both material goods and various services. It is divided into several broad categories: manufacturing, distribution, transportation, publishing, insurance, mining and banking, to name only a few. Each area of business calls for specific skills, a fact overlooked by job-seekers, many of whom end up trying to do a job for which they are poorly suited.

As a first step in looking for a job in business, take stock of yourself, your skills and your goals. Getting a job often depends on the first impression you make. Let's examine a list of factors that combine to form that first impression.

(1) Personality. How do you come across? Are you friendly, open, pleasant, comfortable with yourself?

(2) Intelligence. Because levels of intelligence vary greatly and jobs in certain kinds of business may require one sort of intelligence rather than another, it is important to determine the nature and direction of your intelligence.

(3) Humor. The ability to laugh at yourself is a big plus. A good sense of humor will enable you to deal with people more effectively.

(4) Outgoingness. Whether you are an extrovert (outgoing) or an introvert (inward-looking or shy), be sure you know which you are. Some jobs are best suited to extroverts; some, to introverts. Don't get caught in the wrong groove.

(5) Tact. The ability to deal diplomatically with others is an extremely valuable asset.

(6) Good manners. Closely akin to tact, good manners are essential to smooth modern business relationships. Make sure yours are in top form when interviewing for a job.

(7) Standards. The worthwhile person will set for himself high standards of conduct, values, judgment, speech, appearance, and, most importantly, honesty (which always has been, and still is, the best policy). Avoiding half-truths, presenting facts in a real and unemotional manner, and, above all,

being honest with yourself are essential if you hope to be charged some day with responsibility over others.

(8) Maturity. An important factor in the well-integrated, stable personality, this quality is crucial in determining the kind of job you can do and how well you can do it.

(9) Sense of responsibility. Many people are afraid of responsibility or tend to underrate the degree of responsibility necessary to do a particular job.

(10) Shrewdness. By this I do not mean cunning. Shrewdness is the possession of a penetrating mind and the ability to make sound judgments about people and situations.

(11) Imagination. The basis of all creative work, this quality, like intelligence, is directional. It is necessary to determine that direction and follow the career that best utilizes your creative abilities.

In addition to these intangible personality traits, there are several more easily identifiable basic skills necessary to get a start in business. Even in the creative fields you will be required to do some routine addition and subtraction. Almost any job will entail speaking and writing clearly and coherently. You must pay particular attention to your enunciation when speaking and to grammar when writing. Some jobs will demand a special skill in reading aloud, for the presentation of reports, the delivery of speeches, etc. And, without exception, the person who pays attention when spoken to will inspire confidence in a prospective or present employer.

Now that you have a fairly complete list of aptitudes and basic skills, the next step in preparing for a career is to investigate various types of businesses and determine which skills are required by each. A good way to do this is to contact people in different fields in your own community. Ask them about their business. What kinds of activities are involved? What kinds of people do they employ? What skills and qualities do they look for when hiring personnel?

You might also keep in mind the usefulness of summer jobs as an investigative tool. By working for a month or two in the field you think you like, you may quickly find out that it is not for you. On the other hand, you will also pick up valuable experience and contacts.

As you progress with your research, keep in mind the following questions: "How able a person am I?" "What are my aptitudes and abilities?" "What should my business specialty be?" Remember also that a major function of education is not so much to fit you for a job as to enable you to discover what kind of job you are best fitted for. The sooner you can discover the right direction, the sooner you can focus your energies and begin acquiring the specialized knowledge you will need.

Even though you have finished your formal education, continuing studies will be beneficial in any job. Some businesses require their employees to take specialized courses as a prerequisite to career advancement. But even if this is not the case in your field, continuing education is essential to your growth as a person. Make the most of libraries, radio and television, books, magazines, newspapers, university courses and in-house training programs. They are there for your benefit. Another important reason to continue your studies is the development of taste and aesthetic standards, important factors in many modern businesses as well as in the public consciousness.

Having determined your career goals, you now face a difficult task—that of finding and getting the job you want. You should have a well-thought-out plan, a campaign, to accomplish this and an important part of this campaign is learning to sell yourself. Practice reciting your reasons for wanting a particular job, so that when you are being interviewed you will be coherent and convincing. If, after you have been your most persuasive, you are not hired, try to find out from the interviewer the reasons why. Use that information to appraise yourself and your skills constructively. If the interviewer indicated that he wished he had a job for you, but is unable to provide one at the present time, don't give up. Pursue the lead he has offered you. Before you talk or write to him again, learn more about his business and demonstrate this new knowledge at your next meeting. Don't neglect the possibility of jobs in a field closely allied to your chosen one—the experience can prove most helpful later on.

When your campaign pays off and you have the job you were looking for, there are almost as many things to think about as there were during the planning stage. For instance, the job might be different from what you had imagined. You may find that the job lacks sufficient stimulation. It may seem routine, rigid in schedule, a long way from the executive suite. The people you are working with may not be very congenial. You can, however, put these experiences to good use. The degree to which you co-operate with co-workers, the efficiency with which you handle the routine tasks, and the goodwill and ambition you demonstrate will help you advance in that company or facilitate finding a new job.

Constructive ambition can be a very strong motivating force. It is the kind of ambition that does not waste time complaining about routines or conditions that cannot be changed, but instead takes things as they are and looks for ways to work with them. With this quality, you can be a planner, not just a dreamer, someone who perseveres and is determined.

If you are going to be ambitious and successful, a very important person to consider is your boss. It is vital to find the right boss, i.e., one who is enlightened enough to recognize the importance of rewarding good service and who advances his employees according to their merit and their value to his business. The wrong boss is one who exploits his people—"uses them up," in other words. He is usually (but not always) recognized by the fact that there is an excessive turnover of personnel in his department and that his employees are often disgruntled and discouraged.

At all times in your search for a job and on the job itself, keep a goal firmly in front of you. The main part of that goal should be to broaden your horizon and sharpen your leadership skills. Investigate the policies of your company, in order to understand them better; develop an interest in something other than your job; talk to—and listen to—many different kinds of people. Travel if you can. Read for information as well as pleasure. The more you see, read, and experience, the broader and better developed you will become and the better prepared you will be to move forward.

The talent to manage entails good judgment, the ability to plan ahead, the courage to make decisions and the possession of a deep sense of ethics. It also means having the willingness to put more effort, time and thought into a job than is required.

Business exists to serve its customers and to make a profit. To be successful, you must contribute as much as possible to the customer, the stockholder, the community and your fellow employees. Keep stretching yourself and developing as a person. Remember that real success is measured not only in terms of dollars earned, but in the utilization of all your capabilities to their fullest extent.

CREDIT: *Walter Hoving, Chairman, Tiffany and Co., New York.*

HER HUSBAND CONTINUALLY CUTS DOWN HIS EMPLOYER

DEAR ANN LANDERS: My husband is a good man but he has one fault that bothers me terribly. Whenever we are out with friends he speaks in a very disparaging way about the man who owns the company he works for. He doesn't realize how bad it makes him look.

Will you please say something to him, and to others who have this fault?
—WIFE OF A KNOCKER

DEAR WIFE: Elbert Hubbard, an old-fashioned philosopher and one of my long-time favorites, said it best.

"If you work for a man, for heaven's sake work for him. Speak well of him and stand by the institution he represents.

"Remember, an ounce of loyalty is worth a pound of cleverness. If you must condemn and eternally find fault, resign your position and when you are on the outside, damn to your heart's content. But so long as you are a part of the company, do not condemn it. If you do, the first high wind that comes along will blow you away and you will never know why."

Cancer

Cancer, the most terrifying of all diseases, is surrounded by so much anxiety and fear that millions of people will not take the steps necessary to protect themselves against dying from it.

Cancer is actually not a single disease. It is a group of diseases with one common characteristic—the uncontrolled growth and spread of abnormal cells. If the spread is not controlled, the results are fatal. But many cancers can be cured if detected early enough and treated properly. Today more than three million people in the United States are alive after having been treated for cancer.

In the 1930s, science began to report impressive progress against cancer. One out of five patients treated with surgery at that time was saved. Within the next twenty years, the ratio of patients saved rose one in four. Today it is one in three. So much knowledge about early detection and proper treatment has been accumulated that if the patient and physician would take the necessary action based on that knowledge, one out of two patients could be saved today.

HEALTH

Ella Wheeler Wilcox wrote, "Laugh, and the world laughs with you; weep, and you weep alone." She also wrote this:

> Talk health. The dreary, never-ending tale
> Of Mortal maladies is more than stale:
> You cannot charm or interest or please
> By harping on that minor chord, disease.
> Say you are well, or all is well with you,
> And God shall hear your words and make them true.

Your chances of getting cancer are influenced by a wide range of factors—where you live, what you do for a living, your medical history, the medical history of your parents and grandparents, and your personal habits. Cancer is *not* caused by fluorides in the drinking water, cooking in aluminum pots and pans, or taking smallpox, measles, mumps, or any other kind of immunization.

Mormons and Seventh-Day Adventists have less cancer than other people, possibly because they adhere to restrictions in lifestyle and diet. (Their religion prohibits the use of tobacco and alcohol.)

One in four Americans can expect to develop cancer, most often between the ages of sixty-five and seventy-five. But cancer is also the leading cause of death—except for accidents and homicides—among Americans from one to thirty-five.

Women generally get cancer at a younger age than men, but cancer appears more frequently in men than in women, and men have higher cancer death rates.

In the United States, poor people tend to have more cancers and more cancer deaths than the financially well-off. Precisely why this is we do not know.

Cancer death rates are higher in the Northeast and Middle Atlantic states, lowest in the Rocky Mountains, the Southwest, and the South (except the Gulf Coast states and the Mississippi Delta).

Worldwide, between five and six million people get cancer each year.

One third of everyone who is treated for cancer *will* be saved, and half of the remaining two thirds *could* be saved with early detection and proper treatment.

For example, Charles Hoyt lost a vocal cord to cancer twenty-eight years ago. After treatment, he ran his own business, was an elected trustee of his suburban New York village, learned to fly a plane and was able to communicate without difficulty over the aircraft radio. Now retired, Mr. Hoyt and his family travel extensively.

Mrs. Charles Taylor was a homemaker and the busy mother of three young children in upstate New York, when she found she had cancer of the thyroid. She had surgery and follow-up radiation therapy. That was in 1954. Subsequently, Kay Taylor had five more children. Today, a grandmother, she runs her own dress shop.

Show business celebrities John Wayne, Beverly Sills, Richard Rodgers, Arthur Godfrey and Bill Gargan are just a few of the well-known personalities who have been successfully treated for cancer—proof that having cancer does not mean the end of a career—much less the end of life.

WHAT CAN YOU DO TO PROTECT YOURSELF AGAINST CANCER?

(1) One simple step would prevent more than 30 percent of cancer deaths among U.S. men and women: *STOP SMOKING!*

(2) Avoid overexposure to the sun. If you must be out in the sun a great deal, use a sunscreen lotion.

(3) Women should practice breast self-examination monthly and have an annual "pap test."

(4) Both men and women should have a "procto" exam of the rectum regularly (approximately every other year) especially after age forty. Because the exam is somewhat uncomfortable, many people avoid this basic precaution which can uncover precancerous polyps in the colon, as well as cancer. These polyps can be removed by a simple office procedure. A very important test is the hemocolt slide in which a stool specimen is deposited on a thin white piece of paper after a three-day, meat-free diet.

(5) Check the causes of occupational cancers—discover whether your job has a cancer risk. If so, be sure your employer protects you and that you have frequent regular examinations.

(6) X rays are important for diagnosis. However, these should be done only when necessary and fluoroscopy in particular should be reduced to a minimum.

VITAL TESTS TO DETECT EARLY CANCER:

(1) Breast self-examination is very important. The simplest safeguard against dying of breast cancer, and one that is available to every woman, is breast self-examination. This is an easy procedure by which a woman checks herself for lumps in the breast. Although any breast abnormality should be brought to the doctor's attention, women should be reassured by the knowledge that almost 80 percent of breast lumps turn out to be non-cancerous.

Performed regularly, breast self-examination can provide an effective early warning. Your doctor can show you how to examine your breasts, or a pamphlet is available from any office of the American Cancer Society. If you want a free pamphlet, write to your local unit of the American Cancer Society. (Check the phone book.)

In recent years valuable new techniques have been developed to detect breast cancer at a very early stage. One is called mammography—a low radiation X ray of the breast which can reveal a tumor so small it cannot be felt. The American Cancer Society recommends this technique for women over fifty and for women who have a high risk for developing breast cancer.

(2) Microscopic examinations of sloughed-off cells from the cervix, lungs and bladder.

(3) X-ray examination of the colon by barium enema.

(4) Lighted instruments which can be inserted into parts of the body that are difficult or impossible to reach with standard equipment.

(5) Laboratory tests of blood in the urine or stool.

Find out whether your community has an Early Warning System to screen for cancer. Programs such as CANSCREEN in New York, Philadelphia and Omaha; and in Chicago, the George and Anna Portes Cancer Prevention Center offer periodic examinations designed to uncover cancers.

In between checkups, all adults should be on the alert for early cancer symptoms. Knowledge is protection. Arm yourself. Here are the signs:

Change in bowel or bladder habits.
A sore that does not heal.
Unusual bleeding or discharge.
Thickening or lump in the breast or elsewhere.
Indigestion or difficulty in swallowing.
Obvious change in wart or mole.
Nagging cough or persistent hoarseness.

If you have any of the above symptoms see your doctor immediately. It is amazing how many people write to me and say, "I'm afraid to go to a doctor because he might give me bad news!" I respond immediately: "Go to your doctor at once. If there is no bad news, you'll feel like a million. If the news is bad, early treatment might save your life. Get going!"

WHAT ARE THE MOST COMMON TYPES OF CANCER?

The types of cancer that are the most common are in these organs of the body: breast, colon-rectum, prostate, stomach, pancreas, bladder, lung, skin and womb or uterus.

BREAST: It goes without saying that if you detect anything irregular, any kind of discharge or lump, you should see your doctor at once.

"High risk women" are those who have a personal history of cancer in one breast, lumps and thickenings in the breast, nipple discharge and other abnormalities, a family history of breast cancer on the mother's side, or in sisters, late menopause, no childbirth, first child at age thirty or over, and early onset of menstruation.

COLON-RECTUM: In addition to the warning sign of any change in bowel habits, an instrument has been developed to enable a doctor to find cancers of the rectum and colon in the very early stages. Called a proctoscope (procto for short), it is a hollow lighted tube through which a doctor can inspect the lining of the colon and rectum. Medical authorities say the procto can help save more lives from cancer than any other procedure in a physical checkup.

LUNG: Lung cancer is largely a preventable disease, since approximately 90 percent of all lung cancer is caused by cigarette smoking. Yet every year approximately ninety thousand Americans die from this form of the disease.

About thirty million Americans have quit smoking cigarettes. However, thousands of young people are taking up the habit each day. According to a recent survey, 30 percent of all teenage boys and 27 percent of all teenage girls smoke cigarettes. So long as the smoker is portrayed by the advertising media as sexy, virile, sophisticated and "cool" we will see a continued increase in teenage smokers. I am in favor of an intensive nationwide campaign which presents smoking as a stinky, dirty, offensive, dangerous, expensive and a dumb thing to do.

An annual chest X ray is of great value in detecting early lung cancer, particularly in heavy smokers. An early cancer may not show up on the X ray (but will be reflected in the sputum—or coughed-up phlegm—where cancer cells can be found). With improvement in early detection and treatment techniques, the cure rate for lung cancer, which is only 10 percent at present, will improve gradually.

MOUTH: Since mouth cancer (including cancer of the tongue) may be painless or without symptoms in the early stages, regular and complete oral examinations are essential. This means scheduled periodic visits to the dentist so he can inspect the entire mouth. Sores that don't seem to heal should be seen immediately by a dentist or physician. Cigarette smoking and chewing tobacco are causes of mouth cancer. So is poor oral hygiene and lack of regular dental care. Excessive exposure to the sun is a factor in lip cancer.

SKIN: The most virulent form of skin cancer is melanoma. It usually appears as a black or dark brown mole. All such moles should be checked the moment one is noticed, especially if they darken in color, enlarge or bleed and are located in friction areas: neck (collar), bra, belt, soles of feet. The risk of skin cancer is highest among farmers, sailors and others with outdoor occupations which require frequent sun exposure. This is particularly true for those with fair complexions.

WOMB OR UTERUS: Death from uterine cancer is declining. The death rate has dropped 65 percent over the past forty years. Much of the credit for this dramatic decline is due to the Pap test, named after its discoverer, Dr. George N. Papanicolaou.

The Pap test consists of an examination of cells shed from the uterus and taken directly from the cervix. It is a painless test, easily done in the doctor's office, and can detect cancer at an early stage when it is highly curable before a woman has any symptoms.

The Pap test is almost 100 percent accurate in detecting cervical cancer and should be included in every regular health checkup. However, it is found to be only about 60 percent effective in revealing cancer of the upper part of the uterus. Additional procedures which can be done in a physician's office have been developed to help find this type of cancer in an early stage.

Women who have made sex a part of their lives at a young age and have had several sex partners are more likely to develop cervical cancer.

HOW IS CANCER TREATED?

Surgery, radiotherapy (use of X rays and radium) and anticancer drugs and hormones are the principal methods used in treating cancer today. Advances and improvements in these techniques have increased their effectiveness and safety and many more patients are being saved. The management of cancer by combining various methods of treatment has contributed greatly toward the saving of lives.

SURGERY: A patient undergoing surgery can count not only on the skills of the surgeon but also on a variety of supportive treatments and equipment. Improved means of controlling infection, more effective anesthetics, wider use of blood substitutes (materials which can replace blood temporarily if necessary) are just a few of the advances. Emphasis, too, is now placed on the recovery phase of surgery—intensive care units and sensitive equipment for monitoring the patient's postoperative condition.

RADIOTHERAPY: In radiotherapy, too, remarkable strides have been made, thanks to the development of machines that produce beams of electron volt energy in the multimillion range. These megavoltage devices can now attack and destroy a cancer deep inside the body.

CHEMOTHERAPY: Chemicals have proved capable of curing certain cancers and greatly extending the remission periods of others. About one third of all cancers are responding to chemotherapy. Unlike surgery or radiotherapy, which require precise location of a tumor, chemicals can spread throughout the patient's body and destroy cancer cells which the physician cannot locate.

Cancers controlled by chemotherapy chemicals for five years and longer:

(1) Choriocarcinoma, a highly malignant, if rare, type of cancer in pregnant women.

(2) Burkitt's lymphoma, a cancer found mostly in African children.

(3) Hodgkin's disease.

(4) Acute lymphatic leukemia.

(5) Wilms's tumor, which occurs in the fetus and may not be apparent for years.

(6) Superficial cancers of the skin.

(7) Some cancers of the testicles.

(8) Rhabdomyosarcoma, a cancer of the muscle fiber.

Today hope is high that more drugs will be found to cure specific cancers.

Combination therapy, the use of not one drug but several, in varying dosages, has proved highly successful in treating cancer. It has proved effective in treating Hodgkin's disease in 70 percent of patients. Chemotherapy is also combined with other forms of treatment such as surgery and X-ray therapy with good results in many other types of cancers such as lymphomas, advanced breast cancer, Wilms's tumor, colon and ovarian cancers, and two types of bone cancer found primarily in children.

WHAT HAS RESEARCH ACCOMPLISHED IN HELPING THE CANCER PATIENT?

Research has already developed improved treatment, examples of which have been mentioned. Other aspects of research show continued promise. For instance, the Pap test is being applied to analysis of sputum (coughed-up phlegm) among persons having a high risk of developing lung cancer. This may lead to earlier diagnosis. New methods of X ray are being developed to examine the brain and other parts of the body more accurately than with present conventional methods. Some bone cancer patients are being treated by removal of bone sections instead of amputation. Ultrasound uses high-frequency sound waves instead of X rays to locate tumors deep in the body.

Immunotherapy holds out hope of harnessing the body's own disease-fighting immune system to combat cancer. The idea is to stimulate the body to reject cancer cells—the way it rejects other foreign substances. Although investigators have not yet found the best techniques to help the body resist cancer's invasion, research is being done with various cancers, usually combining immunotherapy with other modes of treatment. BCG, a vaccine against tuberculosis, is a chemical currently being tried somewhat successfully to bolster the body's defenses against cancer.

Research into the relationship between viruses and cancer holds promise. We learned years ago that viruses can cause cancer in certain animals and the suspicion has grown that they may also cause cancer in some humans. If a particular virus should prove to be the cause of a certain type of cancer, the next step would be the development of a vaccine to protect people against that virus.

Thousands of scientists throughout the world are working on leads to discover causes and prevention of cancer.

If your physician wants information on the most recent drug therapy for treatment of cancer, suggest that he write to the Chief of the Treatment Division of the National Cancer Institute (part of H.E.W.) in Bethesda, Maryland.

Don't worry about offending him. It will be to his advantage as well as yours. To assume that any doctor knows everything about medicine is a mistake. Also be aware that there are nineteen comprehensive cancer centers in the United States which screen and treat cancer patients:

University of Alabama
205 Mortimer Jordan Hall
Birmingham, Alabama 35294

University of Southern California
University of Southern California
  Cancer Center
1721 Griffin Avenue
Los Angeles, California 90031

UCLA Comprehensive Cancer Center
924 Westwood Boulevard
Suite 650
Los Angeles, California 90033

Colorado Regional Cancer Center
165 Cook Street
Denver, Colorado 80206

Yale University
333 Cedar Street
New Haven, Connecticut 06510

Howard University
1825 Connecticut Avenue, N.W.
Suite 218
Washington, D.C. 20009

Comprehensive Cancer Center for the State of Florida
University of Miami School of Medicine
Jackson Memorial Medical Center
2 S.E. 13th Street
Miami, Florida 33131

Illinois Cancer Council
36 South Wabash Avenue
Chicago, Illinois 60603

Johns Hopkins Medical Institutions
Johns Hopkins Cancer Center
550 North Broadway
Baltimore, Maryland 21205

Sidney Farber Cancer Center
44 Binney Street
Boston, Massachusetts 02115

Minnesota Cancer Council
Mayo Clinic
Rochester, Minnesota 55901

Roswell Park Memorial Institute
Buffalo, New York 14203

Memorial Sloan-Kettering Cancer Center
1275 York Avenue
New York, New York 10021

Duke University
200 Atlas Street
Durham, North Carolina 27705

Ohio State University Comprehensive Cancer Center
McCampbell Hall, Room 357
1580 Cannon Drive
Columbus, Ohio 43210

Fox Chase & The University of Pennsylvania Cancer Center
7701 Burholme Avenue
Fox Chase—Philadelphia, Pennsylvania 19111

University of Texas System Cancer Center
Texas Medical Center
Houston, Texas 77025

Fred Hutchinson Cancer Research Center
University of Washington
1102 Columbia Street
Seattle, Washington 98104

University of Wisconsin
1900 University Avenue
Madison, Wisconsin 53705

Most Cancer Information Services have toll-free telephone numbers. If the number of the Cancer Information Service near you does not have such a listing, you may call the national toll-free operator at (800) 555-1212 and ask for the listing. Or write to the Office of Cancer Communications of the National Cancer Institute, Department of H.E.W., in Bethesda, Maryland.

HOW DO YOU SPOT A CANCER QUACK?

Here are eight characteristics of a cancer quack:

(1) He says there's only one way to treat all kinds of cancers—his way. (The fact is that no single form of therapy is effective against *all* cancers.)

(2) He avoids and is shunned by established medical facilities and reputable physicians.

(3) He uses unorthodox methods of publicizing his discoveries. His cure appears in popular magazines but not in scientific journals.

(4) He claims that organized medicine or science is persecuting him, that the "establishment is out to get" him.

(5) He uses secret methods, doesn't name the compounds in his medicine and is reluctant to let legitimate practitioners try his procedures.

(6) Medical records are kept inadequately or not at all. Phony diagnostic tests (blood or urine tests or even a machine) take the place of biopsy and other recognized diagnostic techniques.

(7) He gets testimonials from patients and celebrities who have no way of scientifically evaluating his methods.

(8) He challenges all established theories and scientists—claims they don't really want to cure cancer. He compares himself to other scientific greats who were first persecuted then proved right.

A quack will not only take your last dollar, he will waste precious time that should be spent getting legitimate treatment.

HOW TO RECOVER FROM CANCER

Rehabilitation starts at the time of diagnosis and must continue physically and psychologically to help the patient return to normal. The American Cancer Society's Reach to Recovery program, for example, helps women who have lost a breast to cope with emotional problems—which can be considerable. I have received hundreds of letters from women who fear their husbands or lovers will view them as "mutilated" or "disfigured" and it will put an end to their sex life. These women need reassurance to overcome the emotional trauma. Frequently the husband is less concerned about the distortion than he is about causing pain to his wife.

WILL YOU BE ABLE TO PAY FOR CANCER TREATMENT?

One way to insure yourself against the cost of cancer, or any major illness, is to check your insurance policy carefully. Here are four ways your insurance can give you better cancer protection:

(1) A policy should cover at least thirty days in the hospital.

(2) Be sure it includes outpatient coverage for such things as chemotherapy and radiation therapy.

(3) Try to include home health benefits, such as visiting nurses and home health care services.

(4) Take a policy which has a high initial deductible—$500 or $1,000—and continues to cover you for catastrophic illness. You can usually handle that initial payment if long-term expenses will be paid.

HOW TO HELP A PATIENT COPE WITH CANCER

Reactions to cancer vary according to age, type of cancer, prognosis and type of treatment required. But a patient's hope can be kept alive regardless of the outlook. Learning to live with cancer is an art, not a science. Each must find his own way in his own style. The best advice for everyone is to live one day at a time. Once you can help a cancer patient do that, the battle is won. No matter how few or how many years he has left, they will be happy ones.

HOW THE FAMILY CAN COPE WITH CANCER

Until new treatment, cures and preventative measures are taken, cancer will eventually strike two out of three American families. The family plays a vital role in the patient's adjustment. With cancer of a child, many problems arise. For example:

Communication between family members, especially parents, often breaks down.

The mother concentrates exclusively on the sick child. The father feels neglected. The other children are resentful.

Sometimes parents feel guilty, believing the child became ill from being punished or due to some inherited problem.

The parents refuse to accept the seriousness of the situation and do not get the best medical care available.

The parents shop around for doctors, faith healers, quacks, any promise of a cure.

One final word: Cancer research and educational material cost money. Urge your congressmen and senators to pass legislation that will enable us to continue cancer research on a large scale. We *can* conquer cancer in our lifetime if we have the tools to do it.

You Can Fight Cancer and Win, by Jane E. Brody of the New York *Times* and Arthur I. Holleb, M.D., of the American Cancer Society, is well worth reading.

CREDIT: *My thanks to Theodore Adams, Editorial Consultant to the American Cancer Society, for his invaluable assistance in gathering information for this piece. Some statistical material reprinted from the New York* Times, *April 29, 1977. Checked for accuracy by Mrs. Albert D. Lasker. Final draft reworked and alterations made by William Cahan, M.D., Attending Physician, Memorial Sloan-Kettering Cancer Center, New York.*

I'M DYING, YOU'RE DYING

DEAR ANN LANDERS: This may be one of the most unusual letters you have ever received. You see, I am dying. But don't become alarmed, and please don't feel sorry for me. After all, we are all dying. From the moment we are born, we are headed toward inescapable death.

Three years ago I learned I have chronic leukemia. (I was 31 then.) The doctor told me the truth at once because I insisted on knowing. The news came at a crisis time in my life. (I had just gone through a divorce and had young children to raise.)

Would you believe I had to move out of town to a larger city because people would not accept me as a normal person? I was devastated, not by the disease, which has been controlled by drugs, but by the way I was treated. Although I could play tennis, ski, dance, hike and take part in community activities, the people at work made my life miserable. (One woman refused to use the same washroom!) Men wouldn't date me. I was treated like some sort of social outcast—a pathetic, hopeless case.

After I moved to this distant city my life changed dramatically. No one here knows of my illness and I am keeping my mouth shut. I work part-time, attend college, have many friends, am involved with community activities and participate in sports. What a pity that I had to move to a town where nobody knew me in order to live a normal life!

Although I feel well, look fine and am managing beautifully, I know it can't last forever. I dread the day my friends must be told of my illness. I don't want to be pitied. And of course I fear that I may be deserted as I was once before.

The purpose of this letter, Ann Landers, is to help educate people, should they encounter someone in their life's pattern who is in the same spot I'm in right now. Yes, folks—you can help. How? Here are the ways:

(1) Treat me the same as a well person. Don't ask me, "How are you doing?"

(2) Include me in your activities. I need friends just as you do.

(3) Stay off the subject of funeral arrangements and insurance. (Relatives are especially guilty of this.)

(4) Forget I have a disease. I'll do better if I don't know it's on your mind.

(5) Ask me out. Develop a relationship with me. You can even marry me. I might live another 20 years. (Today that's longer than most couples stay together!)

(6) Hire me. If I'm productive I will live longer. If I'm forced to go on welfare or disability, it will raise your taxes.

(7) Give to the American Cancer Society. They support research and alert the public to cancer signs.

(8) Get a checkup this week. Many forms of cancer can be cured if caught early.

(9) Treat me as you would like to be treated under the same circumstances.

(10) Love me! Enjoy me! I have a lot to give.

I COULD BE ANYBODY

DEAR ANYBODY: What a beautiful and courageous letter! Thank you for educating millions of people today. You've made an enormous contribution.

Breast Cancer

Breast cancer is the most common malignant growth in women. One out of thirteen women, or about 7 percent, will develop breast cancer during her lifetime. In 1975, there were nearly ninety thousand new cases in the United States alone. Breast cancer is also the leading cause of cancer death in women, as well as the leading cause of death from all causes in women forty to forty-four years of age. Every fifteen minutes, one woman dies of this disease. Nearly thirty-three thousand deaths in the United States during 1975 can be attributed to breast cancer.

So much for the "bad news." The "good news" is that if cancer of the breast is detected and treated early, when the cancer is less than one inch in diameter and the glands in the armpit are not also affected, there is a better than 90 percent chance of cure.

The point is to discover it and to take care of it promptly and properly. To this end, there have been many efforts made by the American Cancer Society and others to teach patients the technique of self-examination (most breast cancers are discovered by the patients) and to encourage *regular* visits to physicians for professional help. These visits should normally take place every year until the age of fifty and then twice a year thereafter. This regimen is particularly important in those who (a) have a history of breast cancer in their family; (b) have had their first child after the age of thirty; (c) have never been pregnant.

As an aid in early detection, mammography has been used. This is an X-ray examination of the breast which is capable of uncovering very early cancers too small to feel with even the most careful examination.

There has been some concern about the use of mammograms in that the exposure of the breasts to X rays might, of itself, help to initiate a breast cancer at a future date. To some extent, this concern has been reduced by decreasing the amount of irradiation used during the examination. This is accomplished by the use of more sensitive X-ray film which requires less exposure.

The most recent opinions also maintain that mammograms should not be used routinely before the age of fifty unless there is good reason to suspect that the individual has a tumor which needs clarification, or is in one of the groups described that is more liable to develop breast cancer.

Its routine use on a biennial (every two years) basis is suggested for women over the age of fifty.

The use of thermography, which is the recording of temperature differences in the breast (an increase in temperature suggesting the presence of cancer), is a less reliable test for early detection and should not be used as a substitute for a routine physical examination plus mammograms.

As a result of these methods, breast cancer is being discovered at much earlier stages than a generation ago. This has helped influence the type of surgery used to treat the cancer.

Considerations of appearance and its attendant sexual implications have naturally concerned women, even though, of course, they are anxious to be cured.

For generations, cancer of the breast was treated by a classical radical mastectomy, which is the removal of the entire breast, the pectoral muscles beneath it and the glands in the armpit. The resulting deformity often caused reduced ability to move the arm and occasional swelling.

Recently, surgeons have become involved in less radical surgery, made possible as a result of the early detection of breast cancer. It is also, in fact, due to the insistence by women that less disfiguring surgery be tried.

One result of these influences is a modified radical mastectomy in which the entire breast is removed together with the lymph glands in the armpit but leaving the muscles underlying the breast tissue intact. The value of this operation lies in the excision of all breast tissue plus the glands, which are sent to laboratory for analysis. It is less disfiguring than the classical radical operation, although some lymph glands and channels that carry cancer cells are not as thoroughly eliminated by this modified method.

Even more conserving of breast tissue is the use of lumpectomy, which removes the known cancer locally and leaves the remainder of the breast intact. The virtue of this relatively small and cosmetically acceptable operation is tempered by concern that cancer may still be present in microscopic size in the same breast and that it could grow into a larger, more dangerous size and spread to other organs.

Yet another method uses X-ray therapy (Cobalt) either alone or in combination with chemicals after the biopsy of the breast has been performed.

The effectiveness of these techniques is being studied and compared with the older, more classical procedure to determine which method is the most reliable for *cure,* which is the most important consideration.

Trustworthy results of these studies will not be available for many years. In the meantime, it is unwise to insist on an operation that, although cosmetically attractive, may conceivably jeopardize the chances of cure.

For those who have had or will have to have a breast removed, there are some established and some new approaches to relieving the impact of the surgery.

The substitute of breast-shaped forms fitted into special bras is well established. These forms are now being improved upon and the right size and consistency is obtainable at most large department stores or at private corsetières who specialize in such prostheses. Bathing suits and dresses have been made especially for this purpose.

An increasing number of women have had a substituted "breast" (a silicone bag—same as used for breast enlargement) inserted beneath the scar of the mastectomy. This is usually performed by a plastic surgeon months (or years) after the original breast surgery. The result seems to be more satisfying than the external adjustment. Although it is not a perfect match for the opposite breast, it does permit greater ease of motion and is more readily adapted to clothes. In addition, the woman feels psychologically better with the accustomed "bulge" than without it.

The return of full function of the arm has received a great deal of attention. Exercises used to encourage return to normal activity begin while the patient is still in the hospital. Classes of instruction are attended by women who learn the exercises which they will continue at home. In the meantime, they gain comfort by seeing and associating with others who have had similar operations.

The psychological impact of this type of surgery has also been studied and a great deal has been learned about the anxieties it produces.

These considerations of vanity and arm function have been discussed but there is also concern about the future love life of the patient. With this in mind, classes are now held for husbands (and lovers) to enlighten them about what to expect and to allay some of their fears of "hurting" their wives. (Many husbands mistakenly believe that if they accidentally touch the area where the breast has been removed it will cause pain to the wife.) By attending these classes together, the women and their partners arrive at a much better communication and understanding. As a result, an unhappy or even tragic love life has been avoided.

Single women have a problem in this regard, but attraction between the sexes is most often not dependent solely upon bodily configuration or symmetry. Love, indeed, does find a way and conquers all.

CREDIT: *William G. Cahan, M.D., Attending Surgeon, Thoracic Service, Memorial Sloan-Kettering Cancer Center, New York.*

DEAR ANN LANDERS: Can a man get into the act? I have read your column every day for years and although you've come pretty close to hitting me on a few occasions, you never quite scored a bull's-eye until you printed that letter from the woman who had a breast removed and was afraid no man would want her "mutilated body."

My wife had a beautiful body. Could easily have been a brassiere model. She was proud of her figure and I enjoyed her womanly curves. Five years ago she went to the hospital to have a lump biopsied. I held her hand when she came out of the anesthetic and realized she had had her malignant breast removed. She shed many a tear that week, but I let her know that I was so thankful to have her alive that it made no difference to me—and I can truthfully say it never has. We've laughed a lot since about the line I used when I drove her home from the hospital—"Forget it, dear. All I need is one." IN LOVE

DEAR LOVE: What a beautiful letter! You sound like a prince of a fellow—a model for all men.

Cankers

Canker sores can be extremely painful. They occur inside the cheeks and lips, on the tongue and soft palate or at the base of the gums. The rare canker sore on the lip affects only the red part. I want to make it clear, by the way, that this piece concerns only canker sores, not in any way related to the chancres of syphilis, described elsewhere in this book.

Canker sores resemble craters and range from one-eighth inch to more than an inch in diameter. They often cause a burning sensation and are aggravated by the touch of a finger, food or toothbrush. Severe canker sores can become excruciating because they enflame large areas of tissue and nerve endings. They can even deepen to expose the muscles and bone.

Although the exact cause of canker sores is not known, any kind of injury or aggravation of the mouth can trigger them: impacted food, cheeks bitten accidentally or from nervous habit, or cuts inside the mouth. Canker sores also occur after fever, upset stomach, colds or eating acidic foods such as citrus fruit, walnuts, tomatoes and hot, spicy dishes.

These sores form rapidly and should heal rapidly. They tend to recur at least once or twice yearly. The problem almost always runs in families. Women have canker sores twice as often as men. Children and students taking examinations are especially prone. One study of medical, dental and nursing students showed that half of the group developed sores.

Untreated canker sores usually disappear in four to eight days. The discomfort can be relieved in the meantime by rinsing the mouth for several minutes with various home remedies: salt water, baking soda, milk of magnesia and even sauerkraut juice.

Doctors sometime prescribe commercial mouthwashes or tetracycline mouthwashes and, in severe cases, order steroid hormone ointments. But most victims have no recourse but to grin and bear it, if they can bear grinning.

CREDIT: *Dr. Michael J. Halberstam, Senior Medical Editor of Modern Medicine and author of a syndicated medical column.*

Cataracts

Despite the availability of surgical procedures that are about 95 percent successful, cataracts are one of the leading causes of visual impairment in the United States. Ironically, although surgical treatment of cataracts can save a significant amount of vision, some people, in their attempt to avoid the frightening prospect of blindness, neglect cataracts and may eventually lose their sight.

A cataract is a cloudiness or opacity in the lens of the eye which interferes with vision. The lens is located just behind the colored iris and in front of the clear jelly-like material that fills the back portion of the eye. The word "cataract" comes from a Greek word that means a "falling down," like a waterfall or a portcullis gate in a castle. The ancients who first recognized cataracts in people's eyes more than four thousand years ago thought that a "vile humor" was actually flooding down over the opening into the eye (the pupil).

A cataract is neither a tumor nor an infection. It is not contagious, nor can it be "cured" today with medication, eye exercise, or gadgets. There is no indication that exposure to a reasonable amount of light or using one's eyes (such as in reading and writing) has any effect on the production of cataracts. Scientists have determined that cataracts probably result from a change in the biochemistry of the lens, but what causes this change is unknown. It is certain that a cataract may be caused by different types of biochemical changes. Therefore, all cataracts do not result from the same cause. The only treatment available at the present time to maintain or restore vision to a victim of cataracts is surgery by legitimate and skilled eye surgeons.

Cataracts are classified in different types. The most frequent is the senile type, which occurs after age sixty. Other types of cataract may be caused by injury and are called "traumatic." A congenital cataract is that which is noted at birth, or soon thereafter. A cataract may follow another eye disease and is then called secondary. Finally, certain types of cataract are due to a poisoning or the intake of certain medications.

The senile type of cataract accounts for better than two thirds of cataract operations. It has been theorized that if people lived long enough, everyone would eventually develop senile cataracts. It seems to be one part of the aging process that occurs faster in some people than in others. Fortunately, in the United States, less than 15 percent of people over the age of sixty-five will develop cataracts severe enough to interfere with normal activity.

Because there is no inflammation or pain connected with cataract formation, it is especially important to have regular eye checkups. A cataract begins to develop long before a person is aware of any symptoms, but it can be detected in a regular eye examination. The symptoms which a person may have as a result of a cataract developing are: fuzzy, blurred vision (like looking through a film); double vision; seeing spots; dazzling glare from lights at night; and need for frequent changes of eyeglass prescription.

The cause of senile cataract remains unknown. However, the causes of other types of cataracts, which can occur in the very young and among diabetics, are better understood. Someday, researchers may discover the causes of cataracts and preventive measures. For now, however, surgery is the only proved treatment. Cataract surgery is a relatively simple but precise and delicate procedure. It is done under either local or general anesthesia. There is little or no discomfort during the procedure, which usually takes less than an hour. Most patients are up and walking within twenty-four hours after surgery, and out of the hospital very shortly thereafter.

Removal of the cataractous lens from the eye has an effect similar to removing a lens from a camera. The ability to focus is lost. A substitute must be provided so the person can see and function. Today the ophthalmologist has three procedures to offer that can provide this substitute lens capacity: cataract eyeglasses, contact lenses, or lens implant. None of these options restores 100 percent of the vision for a patient, but they are continuously being improved. At this time each of them makes it possible to live an almost completely normal life: working, reading, watching television, driving, etc.

A lens implant is a tiny lens that is fixed inside the operated eye, where it replaces the surgically removed opaque lens. Eye surgeons are heatedly debating the advantages and the potential danger of lens implants. Prior to cataract surgery, consult the eye surgeon of your choice for the latest advice on this matter.

The ancient Egyptians made the first attempts at cataract surgery—with little success. We have come a long way since then in perfecting the surgical techniques and in providing comfortable vision after surgery. With this hope, there is little reason for fear if your ophthalmologist recommends surgical treatment for cataracts. This specialist is the best source of guidance on the latest advances, and on the most appropriate treatment for you.

For everyone, eye examinations should be a part of health care and regular checkups. After age forty, have your eyes checked once a year—more frequently if you have an eye problem or a family history of eye disorders.

CREDIT: *Arthur S. Freese,* Cataracts and Their Treatment, *Public Affairs Committee, Inc., New York. Reviewed for accuracy and additional material added by Charles L. Schepens, M.D., President, Eye Research Institute of Retina Foundation, Boston, Massachusetts.*

Cerebral Palsy

WHAT IS CEREBRAL PALSY?

Cerebral palsy is a group of medical conditions—not a disease—characterized by nonprogressive dysfunction of the motor centers in the brain. It's usually due to complications of pregnancy or delivery and is seen most commonly in children that are born prematurely. Sometimes cerebral palsy shows itself only by a slight awkwardness of gait. More severely involved children may be unable to walk because of weakness, increase in muscle tone (spasticity), or involuntary movements (choreoathetosis). One's ability to co-ordinate hand movements may be similarly affected. Other handicaps may coexist: seizures; the inability to see, hear, speak or learn as other people do; psychological or behavioral problems. It is important to remember, however, that *cerebral palsy is not progressive; it will not become worse with age.*

HOW IS IT TREATED?

The emphasis is on helping the child in his growth and development. Physical, occupational, speech and hearing therapy by skilled professional personnel are important features of the treatment program.

Orthopedic surgery helps to improve muscle co-ordination in some cases. Braces reinforce a muscle group in certain types of cerebral palsy, and can prevent or correct deformity. Drugs may be effective in reducing muscle tone and in limiting other problems connected with brain damage. The earlier treatment begins, the better for the child.

Home care is important. Family members may need to help the child with dressing, toilet training, self-feeding and control of drooling. They may find it beneficial to adapt the child's environment to make him more comfortable and safe: armchairs for support, the use of a standing table to prevent him from falling.

IS A CEREBRAL PALSY CHILD MENTALLY RETARDED?

Not necessarily.

Often a cerebral palsy child functions on a retarded level because, given his physical condition, he has not had the opportunity to interact with his environment, be it things or people. When one cannot move independently, one does not know about space—about the feel or surfaces, the differences in textures. Just as the normal child learns and practices through his play many of the movements he needs for everyday activities, so can the handicapped child. He must have the help of inventive adults, the encouragement of other children and the support of his family. The inability to speak or to move gracefully often makes the cerebral palsy child appear retarded, even when he is not.

WHAT TYPE OF HELP IS AVAILABLE?

UCP community services aim to meet the lifelong needs of those with cerebral palsy. There are programs of detection, treatment, care, education and psychological counseling. Teenagers and adults may receive job training and guidance, as well as sheltered workshop experience, leading to competitive employment.

Recreational opportunities are provided through camps, hobby groups and sports programs. For older patients, there may be residential facilities for independent living. Parents are helped through counseling and instruction. Developmental day care centers work to help cerebral palsy children adjust to everyday life and to relieve parents of the constant care demanded by many handicapped children.

Parents need not worry about extra expenses for special education because all cerebral palsy children are eligible for, and have the right to, a public school education. For facilities nearest you, contact:
United Cerebral Palsy, 66 East 34th Street, New York, New York 10016
Easter Seal Services, 2023 West Ogden Avenue, Chicago, Illinois 76011
Your local university, for child assessments or development centers.

CREDIT: *Dr. Peter R. Huttenlocher, Professor of Pediatrics and Neurology, University of Chicago, Pritzker School of Medicine.*

Cheating

(Among Students)

Cheating in high school and college has been common for a long, long time and no amount of punishment for offenders seems to prevent other students from cheating when the opportunity arises.

Nearly every time youngsters in high school and college get caught cheating a wave of criticism and disillusionment goes through the community carrying the implication that the ethical standards of young people are deteriorating.

Publicity by the mass media tends to exaggerate the unethical behavior in such a way as to obscure the reasons for it. Indeed, if one follows the behavior of all people, it soon becomes apparent that the young who cheat are imitating much of what they see in the behavior of their elders.

The explosive outbursts of college students, beginning with the Berkeley disturbances of 1964, the Columbia riots of 1968, the militant protests at Harvard and finally the tragedy at Kent State raised the question as to how to develop idealism in young people.

In 1956 Robert C. Hendrickson, then a senator from New Jersey, chairman of a Senate Committee on Juvenile Delinquency, published a book outlining his committee's findings in a series of hearings. In it he stated that more than a million youngsters in America were in trouble and that the number is increasing. (Perhaps this is because there are more people in the world today—both old and young.) His committee worked diligently to find out why. In the subsequent investigation his committee discovered a "training ground" for crime in the form of lack of supervision by parents, use of alcohol at an early age, use of drugs for nonmedicinal purposes, horror comics and a glut of TV violence. This supports data collected two decades later by Peggy Charron, founder and president of Action for Children's Television.

Recent experiences in the larger cities (New York in particular) suggest that the judicial system, supposedly designed to be considerate of young adolescent offenders, is so inflexible that it protects and encourages them toward crime rather than encouraging them to be honest and law-abiding.

In recent survey of the books in my library dealing with the "revolt" of college students during the decade of 1964–74 (about 150 in all), it became clear that the dissatisfaction that motivated them to condemn college policies through noisy mass meetings was based on legitimate complaints. Education was becoming too impersonal. Contacts with faculty members were too limited. Many students thought that a number of their teachers were "only textbooks wired for sound."

Cheating occasionally spreads in a particular institution in somewhat the same fashion as a contagious disease. A particular student may be observed cheating on an examination by other students and, if he is not apprehended, other students may be encouraged to do likewise. Thus the awareness spreads that one can get away with cheating and get higher grades.

Unfortunately, such phenomena all too often occur in military academies, following gross speculation by the mass media with too few facts to verify the opinions expressed by reporters.

Too often parents come to the defense of their children who have been accused of cheating by making counteraccusations against teachers and other school authorities rather than keeping an open mind and emphasizing to their children that honesty must be practiced at all times.

Parents are often puzzled as to what to do when their child has been caught cheating in school or college. Perhaps the least desirable way to deal with their son or daughter is to condemn him or her and make threats as to what will happen if it happens again. A warm, thoughtful discussion of the complications of such behavior, together with an exploration of how dishonesty can be avoided in the future, is far more effective. In a real sense the child can then be comforted by the fact that his parents love him even when they strongly disapprove of some of his behavior. In short, a crisis has been transformed into a constructive learning situation.

If the offender repeats his offense, a much more disapproving course of action becomes necessary, possibly including talks with the teacher or a school counselor, a psychiatrist, an understanding minister or priest, or withdrawal of some prized privileges. Perhaps a worthwhile work project could be given to the young person, which would involve making retribution for his offense. What must not be withdrawn is basic respect and confidence in his ability to shape up.

Cheating is prevalent in many schools, colleges and universities. Whether it is more prevalent now than several decades ago is difficult to prove, but I believe the evidence suggests that it is not on the increase. When I have raised this question with deans and other counselors during the past few months they agreed with my conclusions. Perhaps the fact that dishonesty in high places is so all-pervasive probably leads many people to believe that students must be following their example.

It may be that disgust shown by the American people toward the flagrant lying and cheating of those involved in the Watergate affair and the fact that the perticipants did not get away with their misconduct have given young people hope that the old principles of morality still hold, and the conclusion drawn is that in the long run the cheater turns out to be the one who suffers the greatest loss of all.

CREDIT: *Dana L. Farnsworth, M.D., Editorial Director,* Psychiatric Annals; *Consultant on Psychiatry, Harvard School of Public Health, retired.*

EVERYBODY DOES IT, BUT A CHILD CHEATED IN LIFE

DEAR ANN LANDERS: These days, when one hears so much about cheating and lying and crooks in high places, will you please rerun a column that appeared 10 years ago? It had to do with a boy named Johnny and the example his elders had set for him from the early days of his life. I believe it might help a great many parents understand why their kids "went wrong." I've carried that column since 1966, and I'll bet you've added a lot of readers since then. Thanks, Ann.

ST. PETERSBURG FRIEND

DEAR FRIEND: I know precisely the column you want and here it is, with my thanks for asking.

IT'S OK, SON, EVERYBODY DOES IT

When Johnny was six years old, he was with his father when they were caught speeding. His father handed the officer a bill along with his driver's license. "It's OK, son," his father said as they drove off. "Everybody does it."

When Johnny was eight, he attended a family get-together, presided over by Uncle George. All the relatives were instructed on the best techniques for chiseling on their income tax returns. "It's OK, kid," his uncle said. "Everybody does it."

When Johnny was nine, his mother took him to his first theater production. The box-office man couldn't find any seats until his mother discovered an extra $2 in her purse. "It's OK, son," she said. "Everybody does it."

When Johnny was 12, he broke his glasses on the way to school. His Aunt Francine persuaded the insurance company that they had been stolen and they collected $27. "It's OK, kid," she said. "Everybody does it."

When Johnny was 15, he made right guard on the high school football team. His coach showed him how to block and at the same time grab the opposing tackle by the shirt so the official couldn't see it. "It's OK, kid," the coach said. "Everybody does it."

When Johnny was 16, he took his first summer job at a supermarket. His assignment was to put the overripe tomatoes in the bottom of the boxes and the good ones on top where they would show. "It's OK, kid," the manager said. "Everybody does it."

When Johnny was 18, he and his buddy who lived next door applied for college scholarships. Johnny was a marginal student. His neighbor was in the upper 10 per cent of his class, but he couldn't play right guard. Johnny made it but his buddy didn't. "It's OK," he told himself. "Everybody does it."

When Johnny was 19, he was approached by an upperclassman who offered him the answers to an exam for $10. "It's OK," he told himself. "Everybody does it."

Johnny was caught and sent home in disgrace. "How could you do this to your mother and me?" his father said. "You never learned anything like that at home." His aunt and uncle were also shocked.

If there's one thing the adult world can't stand, it's a kid who cheats. . . .

Chicken Pox

Chicken pox is a very mild but highly contagious illness caused by a virus. It is most common in children from three to eight years but can occur in infants and adults. It usually begins with a rash and lasts from seven to ten days.

(1) What does the rash look like?

The rash develops over a two- to seven-day period and appears in three different stages. First, the child will develop "red spots" or "pimples" that may appear in groups on the face, arms or stomach. These "red spots" then develop into "water blisters" that become crusted scab-like pimples. The rash may spread to legs, scalp, inside the mouth and is usually very itchy.

(2) Are there other symptoms?

Your child may develop a headache, loss of appetite, tiredness and fever. Fever can reach as high as 105° but usually the fever is mild.

(3) How do children catch chicken pox?

The virus is spread by your child having direct contact with other children who have chicken pox such as in a family or school. Your child will usually develop the rash about two weeks after contact with an infected child.

(4) How long will my child be contagious? When will he/she be able to return to school?

Chicken pox is contagious until all the "water blisters" have crusted over or dried out. This will occur about seven to ten days after the rash first appears. Your child should stay at home, out of school and away from newborn infants until *all* the pox have dried out.

(5) Will other members of my family get chicken pox?

Most adults have had chicken pox as children. Once a person has had chicken pox, it is extremely unlikely that he or she will have it again. It is not necessary to separate other children in the family from the infected child, because they will probably get chicken pox anyway. It is better to get chicken pox as a child than as an adult.

(6) How can I take care of my child with chicken pox?

The infected child should be given appropriate amounts of aspirin or Tylenol for fever. A bath in lukewarm water or application of calamine lotion (available at any drugstore) may relieve the itching. Fingernails should be kept short and clean to help reduce the chance of infecting the skin due to scratching. If the itching is severe, your doctor may prescribe medicine for relief.

(7) Will the chicken pox cause scars?

Most scarring is caused by scratching the rash. It is very important to keep your child's fingernails short and clean. Most pox will gradually fade within a few weeks.

(8) Are there any shots that will keep my child from getting chicken pox?

At present, there is no vaccine that will prevent chicken pox.

Complications with chicken pox are rare. Your doctor should be consulted if:

a. some of the pox seem swollen, hard, hot with yellow drainage or yellow crusting;

b. an infant under three months old develops chicken pox;

c. your child develops unsteady walking, high fever, severe headache, stiff neck and/or change in behavior;

d. there is fever for more than a week.

CREDIT: *The Children's Hospital Medical Center, Boston, Massachusetts.*

Child Abuse

Help for Parents Who Want to Stop Beating Their Kids

A nineteen-year-old mother of three "just couldn't take it any more" and nearly flung her infant daughter out a fourth-floor window.

A single father handcuffed his young son to a bedframe for fear he would kill the boy if interrupted once more while reading.

A mother of two teenagers suddenly found herself screaming into a generation gap.

A couple can't remember who started hitting first, and now can't remember how to stop.

They are abusive parents. For them and their children, life can—quite literally—be brutal.

But for hundreds of families, stress will be eased by an organization that spends every day of the year helping parents who want to stop hurting their children.

Parents Anonymous, a free self-help program started by an abusive mother in California, now has twenty-five chapters in the Chicago area. And, like the problem it addresses, the organization involves parents of all ages, incomes and neighborhoods.

Parents Anonymous is open to anyone who wants to be a better parent. Many of its members, in fact, are not "child beaters." Some have joined for fear they may become that. Others, because they know they already are abusing their children verbally or emotionally.

All are parents who feel overwhelmed, frustrated and, often, angered by the tasks of parenting.

For Anne, who is pregnant with her third child, Parents Anonymous was a last resort. It may be her unborn child's last chance.

"I'm so scared. Scared of what my husband is doing, scared of how I'm getting so much like him," she said softly. It was when her husband doubled his belt and "started in" on her eighteen-month-old daughter that she decided to seek help.

The hitting had begun years ago, when her first child was just a year old. "Funny thing is," said Anne, "he was a real easy baby. But it seemed the more spankings he got, the more he'd cry."

"I decided to get some help for us for the new baby. . . . I want this one to come out in a calm environment."

Anne's husband, Phil, still thinks of Parents Anonymous as more of a social group, a time once a week to get out of the house and talk with other parents.

But Phil said, "The group has opened some doors for me. I see the problem might be me, not the kids. We had like an overreaction to normal things they would do . . . crying or messing with the TV.

"My wife used to think I hit 'em too hard. But then, I'm the type of parent, I tell you to do something and you don't do it, I get the belt . . . I still believe in whipping when they need it."

Phil and Anne, like all the names of parents quoted here, are pseudonyms for real Chicago-area parents.

Some are known to the police. Some are familiar faces in hospital emergency rooms. Many of them are involved in Parents Anonymous or one of the other programs sponsored by Parental Stress Services, an arm of the nonprofit Citizens' Committee for Children and Parents Under Stress.

A few of the parents, primarily those who have killed their children, are sent to the organization by law enforcement agencies. But most join voluntarily and remain with the group for years.

Benjie Barrett, a director of Stress Services, said that hotline volunteers answer four hundred to five hundred calls a month from troubled parents. In January and December, the number swells.

"It happens after Christmas a lot, when it's snowing outside and the kids are stuck in the house and the toys are broken," said another staffer, Pat Higgins. "The Walton family Christmas never materialized and they're devastated."

For single parents, the specter of spending New Year's Eve alone can send an entire household into turmoil, according to JoAnne Shanberge, Parents Anonymous director.

"When you're by yourself, all your energies during the holidays are going to make your kids happy," she said. "You want someone to make you happy and when that doesn't happen, you want to strike out. . . . The kids are the only ones there."

Financial troubles during the holidays can be another source of stress for parents.

It was the inability to give her children all they wanted that pushed May, a thirty-two-year-old mother of five, to the brink and over the edge.

"It was like they were always nagging me for this thing or that thing they saw on television. I'd been on my own trying to take care of the kids since my husband left me," she said. "I didn't blame him. I wish I could've left too. So there I am on welfare and I can't give them what they want. I feel like the worst mother in the whole world."

Two years ago, a week before Christmas, she locked her children in the apartment and left, though her eldest was just eight.

When she returned nearly two days later, child welfare authorities had placed all her children in foster homes. "I love my children and I want them back. I just can't seem to do the right thing," she said.

Although Parents Anonymous officials believe helping parents help themselves saves far more children from abuse than many other methods, the group is, first and foremost, a parent-advocate.

At the weekly group talk sessions, the participants remain anonymous and their conversations completely confidential. The success of the program derives from its dual service to troubled parents: It supports them as "good persons who can be good parents" while offering alternatives to the poor parenting techniques they learned from their own parents.

Almost without exception, abusive parents were themselves abused or neglected children. With that in mind, Parents Anonymous groups concentrate on breaking the cycle. It's not always easy.

For the teenaged mother from the North Side who got pregnant to escape life with her own mother, parenthood backfired.

She didn't know how to care for her baby. All she knew was how her mother treated her. So when her baby cried, she cried. One day, she carried the baby to an open window. A friend stopped her from flinging the child to the street forty feet below.

A few months ago, welfare authorities took her child away from her. Ironically, they put the child in the "protective custody" of the girl's mother.

For Phyllis, a west suburban divorcée, mothering became "a living hell" when her children reached adolescence. "My son was swearing at me constantly," she said. "My daughter [who was later hospitalized for mental illness] went into a rage at the least little thing. . . . One day she came at me with a kitchen knife because I told her she couldn't use the car."

Phyllis doesn't hit her children, but she realized she might hurt them when she found herself one day with her hands around her daughter's neck. "I didn't strangle her, but God knows I could have. I certainly wanted to," she said.

Some children are abused by parents who tell them they are "dumb," "fat," "lazy," or "worthless." That is verbal abuse, and it can be as damaging to a child's psyche and future development as beating is to his body.

Do you withhold affection as punishment? Do you "get back" at your child by calling him or her names? Do you simply wish you had a better relationship with your child, that you could really talk together instead of yelling at each other?

The volunteers who answer the Parental Stress hotlines can relate many stories of parents who called after just such near misses as Phyllis'. A distraught father who called in tears after handcuffing his son to a bedframe told a volunteer he was "ready to kill" and terrified of his own anger.

For those parents who call the hotline after they've hurt their children, there are trained staffers to accompany the parent and child to the emergency room.

"Parents don't want to hurt their children," said Ms. Barrett. "And we want to help them stop. . . . Often at Christmas time, parents say to themselves, 'This year I'll start being nice to my kids.' It's not that easy. That's why we're here."

CREDIT: *Pamela Warrick, reporter.*

Child Molesting

(*A Message to Mothers*)

This is a difficult problem to deal with because it embarrasses most people. Your best bet is preventive. If you and your child or children have good communication, enjoy one another's confidence, and can talk frankly about sex, you will be in a favorable position to handle this problem should it rear its ugly head.

Hopefully, the child molester is a stranger, a Funny Uncle, a friend or a neighbor. You can best protect your child by warning him or her at an early age (five is not too soon) about the general topic of child molesting. Discuss it as calmly and unemotionally as possible. (The calmness is most easily achieved if this talk takes place before, rather than after, an unfortunate incident.)

Explain to your child that some people, even grownups, are confused about sex and sometimes they approach young children. Tell them that the person might start by kissing, touching or hugging when no one else is around. This, they should understand, is a danger signal. Advise them if this happens, they must get out of the situation and away from the person as quickly as possible.

Suggest that they do so without hurting anybody's feelings if they can; but hurt feelings or not, it is important to say "No" to any advance and to let the person know you mean it. Explain that even though it might be easier to forget about the incident, they *must* tell you about it.

An informed boy or girl, knowing what might happen, can often spot an advance very early in the game and turn it off completely.

If the person who makes the advance is a stranger, you may be tempted to call the police and try to track him down. If this is the course you choose to follow, be aware that the children are often more upset by a follow-up of this sort than by the incident itself. You will have to use your own judgment as to whether or not you do wish to subject your child to this kind of trauma.

If the man (it usually seems to be a man) is a close friend or a relative who is likely to be around often, there is no alternative except for you, or the man in *your* family, to warn the offender that a repetition of the episode would mean he is no longer welcome in your home. (Fathers often become very angry and will not give a second chance. If your husband takes this position, respect his wishes.)

No reasonable talk is going to change the behavior of a person in such serious trouble that he must molest the young, but you *can* get him out of your house and you should.

And now for the most devastating situation in which it is the children's own father who molests them. Difficult as it will be to do, a mother must take this as an indication that her husband is seriously disturbed. If she cares what happens to her children she must get help at once.

The ideal solution would be to enroll the entire family in family therapy. Family therapy, if it could be arranged, would be the best approach for several reasons. The main reason is that a "sick" family situation is not made up of one lone, deranged individual plus several "good," well-adjusted people. When a family is in such serious trouble as this, more often than not, everybody is involved in one way or another.

Thus in cases of child molestation, a female child, for example, may be behaving in an overly seductive way (parading before Dad unclothed or scantily clad . . . sitting on his lap and kissing him a great deal, etc.). A mother who may be far from satisfying (or satisfied) in her own relationship to her husband, makes it easier for him to look elsewhere for gratification. The person who looks like the villain is often not the one at fault—obvious as his or her wrongdoing may seem. Good family therapy can unwind the tangled skein of family relationships and help the whole family to more satisfactory ways of behaving.

However, the chances of a man who is so disturbed taking part in family therapy are not very promising. The next best approach would be to urge him to go for therapy by himself. Here, too, it is unlikely that he will agree.

The common sense solution, as seen by an outsider, would be for the mother to lay down the law. This is an oversimplistic solution for so serious a problem. When the person who is most in trouble refuses to get professional help, somebody *else* in the family must get not only psychological help but practical suggestions as well.

If you can't afford a psychologist in private practice, check with your local Mental Health Association or Family Service Association to see what kind of help is available in the bracket you could afford. Most mental health clinics charge according to what the person can pay. Be aware that the prospect of improvement for a man so seriously disturbed and the likelihood of smooth and successful family functioning are limited. But you must try.

If professional help seems beyond your reach, you may have to do what women did before this kind of help was available. You may need, at least temporarily, to send any child or children who are "at risk" to live or board with some other family. Or you may be forced to break up your own family. You must start with the premise that any man who, for any reason whatever, molests his children is a very sick person, indeed, and any wife who aids, abets or permits such a situation is in trouble herself . . . more than she realizes.

Incest is nothing new; in fact, it was an acceptable practice among certain cultures centuries ago. In our society, however, it is against the code of acceptable conduct. Mothers who tolerate such behavior, or are too passive to do anything about it, are failing their children badly. A mother's first and foremost position must be: *This cannot go on.* Then she must work it out from there in a manner that protects her children.

CREDIT: *Louise Bates Ames, Ph.D., Co-Director, Gesell Institute of Child Development, New Haven, Connecticut 06511.*

Child Pornography

also known as "Chicken Porn" and "Kiddie Porn"

DEFINITION: Films, photographs, magazines, books and motion pictures which depict children under a certain age (usually sixteen) involved in sexually explicit acts, both heterosexual and homosexual.

The American attitude towards its children manifests itself in many ways, including, unfortunately, a tolerance for child abuse and neglect in significant proportions and varieties. One form of mistreatment is the exploitation of children used in the production of sexually explicit films and magazines. This statement is offered to acquaint the reader with the nature of the commercial sexploitation problem, and the impact of these activities on the children involved. As far as pornography is concerned, it does not consider the much larger problem of child prostitution, which probably involves as many as 1.2 million children nationwide.

THE SEXPLOITATION PROCESS

The use in commercial pornography of children ranging in age from three to sixteen has become a mulitmillion-, perhaps billion-dollar industry in the United States. By recent count, there are at least 264 magazines being produced and sold each month in adult bookstores across the country dealing with sexual acts between children or between children and adults. These magazines—slickly produced—sell for prices averaging over seven dollars each. This number of 264 does not include the vast number of films or other media.

Until recently, it was incorrectly assumed that child pornography was produced mostly in Europe. Investigations have now revealed that much of it is produced in the United States—even some materials which are packaged in such a manner as to give the impression they are of foreign origin.

Film makers and magazine photographers have little difficulty recruiting youngsters. Some simply use their own children, or buy the children of others. Some rely on runaways. Recent findings of a U. S. Senate subcommittee on juvenile delinquency indicate that more than one million American children run away from home each year, often for good cause, having been victims of intolerable conditions, with physical and sexual abuse present. From this vast army of dispossessed children, exploiters select literally thousands of participants for their production needs and prostitution rings.

Los Angeles police estimate that adults in that city alone sexually exploited over thirty thousand children under seventeen in 1976, and photographed many of them in the act. Five thousand of these children were under twelve.

In 1975, Houston police arrested Roy Ames after finding a warehouse full of pornography, including fifteen thousand color slides of boys in homosexual acts, over one thousand magazines and paperback books, and a thousand reels of film.

In New York City, Father Bruce Ritter of Covenant House, a group of shelters for runaway children, has reported that the first ten children who entered Covenant House had all been given money to appear in pornographic films. These children, in their early teens, could not return to their homes because of extreme conditions of abuse and neglect, and could not find jobs or take care of themselves other than in illegal ways. There is no other way for a child of twelve to support himself or herself, and, sadly, too few sheltering alternative environments are provided by our communities.

Many are not runaways, but come from broken homes. They can be induced to pose for five dollars or a trip to Disneyland, or even a kind word.

Sometimes the mothers are porn queens; often parents or guardians are addicts or alcoholics. Approximately 2.8 million children are in the sole custody of substance abusers, and 2.2 million are with parents involved in sex for sale.

In 1977, at the Crossroads Store in New York's Time Square, we purchased *Lollitots,* a magazine showing girls eight to fourteen, and *Moppits,* children aged three to twelve, as well as playing cards which pictured naked, spread-eagled children. We also looked at film depicting children violently deflowered on their communion day at the feet of a "freshly crucified" priest replacing Jesus on the cross. Next, we saw a film showing an alleged father engaged in urolagnia with his four-year-old daughter. Of sixty-four films able to be seen, nineteen showed children, and an additional sixteen involved incest.

THE VICTIMIZATION OF CHILD-PORN STARS

Despite the highly secretive nature of the recruitment and sexploitation process, a growing body of information about the children involved confirms that psychological scarring and emotional distress which occur in the vast majority of these cases lead to significant other problems.

Prepubescent sexual activity, especially in conditions of exploitation and coercion, is highly destructive to the child's psychological development and social maturation. Psychiatrists report that such inappropriate sexuality is highly destructive to children. It predisposes them to join society's deviant populations: drug addicts, prostitutes, criminals, the promiscuous and pre-adult parents. Over seventeen thousand babies were born to mothers under fourteen years of age in 1976. Venereal diseases in children have now reached epidemic figures. Although there may not be a proved link between adult pornography and sexual abuse, beyond a doubt this degradation of children scars them usually for life.

There have also surfaced a number of children and young adults who have been involved in posing and/or performing for sexually explicit films and magazines. These children are now or have been in treatment programs for substance abuse, delinquency or other aberrant behavior. Some of these children have voluntarily recounted their experiences to law enforcement and news media persons who are attempting to learn more about the recruitment process and the type of activities involved.

Many are victimized in more brutal fashion. Los Angeles Police Investigator Jackie Howell rejects the commonly stated belief that nude posing is harmless to the children. "We have found that a child molester is often also the photographer. Photography is only a part of it, a sideline more often than not, to prostitution, sexual abuse and drugs."

It is important to note that the victimization in the child pornography process goes beyond the child actor. For example, authorities in Rockingham County, New Hampshire, reported recently that in 1977 every one of the twenty-seven cases of incest reported in their jurisdiction included child pornography preceding and accompanying the assaults on the children. Many more such cases are beginning to surface, with recent reports from Ohio and California.

Dr. Henry Giarretto, one of the nation's leading experts in incest, who works directly with the Probation Department of Santa Clara County, California, reports that he saw fifty cases of incest in 1975, had over 350 in 1976, and predicts that 800-plus will be referred in 1977.

The men who support this billion-dollar industry do so because they are seeking justification and rationalization for their deviant behavior. Indeed, one magazine in the Odyssey Institute files, *Lust for Children,* is a primer for the sex molester, teaching him how to go to the park and pick up two little girls, what games to play to induce them to co-operate, and what acts to perform which will have the least evidence for the police should the children report him. Another, entitled *Schoolgirls,* instructs a father in text and photographs as to those positions for intercourse best used with prepubescent girls (in this instance a girl of nine) and still another book shows how to affix a lock to one's daughter's genitals so that no other man may "get to her." Such sadomasochistic activities are part of the "kiddie porn" market.

Furthermore, not only are these activities harmful emotionally, developmentally and psychologically to the child actors and children subsequently sexually abused, but physically, as many suffer lacerations of the vagina and rectum. Additionally, the research of Dr. Malcolm Coppleson, one of the leading gynecologists in Sydney, Australia, has shown the vaginal pH of the prepubescent female is not sufficient to neutralize infectious agents that come with intercourse, so that she is subject not only to vaginitis, but early onset of cervical cancer, often necessitating hysterectomies prior to attaining thirty years of age.

It is obvious that children were not meant to satisfy the sexual needs of adults, and such use of them is, like rape, a crime of power and abuse.

SOLUTION:

There are many parts to the solution of this problem. This menace will not be removed by simple changes in law or harsh penalties, although these are essential components of the complete strategy.

There must be first a public awareness in each community that child porn exists, that it is very big business, in large part run by organized crime, that it victimizes children in every community, that it can be stopped and that it will only be stopped by a commitment to the children of the community manifested in explicit actions:

(1) Amendment of child abuse and neglect statutes to include sexual exploitation, and to prescribe harsh criminal penalties for offenders.

(2) Amend Civil Codes to provide for licensing of all children used in commercial modeling or performing, with carefully worded proscriptions and substantial sanctions against the use of such children in sexually explicit activities.

(3) Extend criminal liability to promoters and distributors of child pornography, without whose promotion and marketing of the finished product there would be no financial motive for the sexploitation of children in the first place.

(4) Develop intervention and treatment models for children victimized by this process, to mend their emotional and psychological injuries and to return them to the mainstream of society.

As Erik Erikson wrote: "Someday, maybe, there will exist a well-informed, well-considered, and yet fervent public conviction that the most deadly of all possible sins is the mutilation of a child's spirit; for such mutilation undercuts the life principle of trust, without which every human act, may it feel ever so good, and seem ever so right, is prone to perversion by destructive forms of consciousness."

CREDIT: *Judianne Densen-Gerber, J.D., M.D., F.C.L.M., President and Chief Executive Officer, Odyssey Institute of America and Australia, and Stephen Hutchinson, Esquire, Vice President and General Counsel, Odyssey Institute of America and Australia.*

Child Prostitution

Definition: The use of, or participation by, children under the age of majority (or sometimes defined as under sixteen years of age) in sexual acts with adults or other minors where no force is present. Prostitution differs from statutory rape and incest in that there is an element of payment, usually in money, but often in drugs, gifts, clothing, food or other items. Prostitution is "the oldest profession" and a lifestyle for women, men, adolescents and now, sadly, children, some as young as three. Occasionally, parents who are involved in the sex-for-sale industries sell their daughters who are too young to know right from wrong. Child prostitution is closely allied with child pornography, incest, drug addiction, child abuse, and generalized family disruption and juvenile delinquency.

HOW MANY CHILDREN ARE INVOLVED?

Experts in the field of juvenile delinquency have shown that in the United States there is a minimum of three hundred thousand active boy prostitutes under the age of sixteen. Approximately thirty thousand of these are located in New York City, with at least two thousand concentrated in the Times Square area. The Los Angeles Police Department has identified thirty thousand boys working as prostitutes within that city, of whom five thousand are under fourteen years of age, and several hundred are as young as eight. No one has counted the number of girls involved in sex-for-sale, but most authorities agree that there are probably as many girls involved as boys. In other words, there are more than a half million children in the United States who are actively engaged in prostitution. Some experts estimate the number is easily twice that number—1.2 million—and this includes only children under the age of sixteen. The number nearly doubles again if sixteen- and seventeen-year-olds are added.

Odyssey Institute has consulted on this problem in Atlanta, Boston, Chicago, Detroit, Houston, Los Angeles, Milwaukee, New Orleans, New York and San Francisco to name but a few cities. It touches all the cities of our nation and all walks of life. Child prostitution has occurred in church-affiliated boys homes (Tennessee), independent schools (Massachusetts) and Boy Scout troops (Louisiana). It has reared its ugly head in the Roman Polanski case (California); in the making of a major movie, Pretty Baby (Louisiana), whose storyline is legalized child prostitution at the turn of the century in Storyville; in the recent death of a twelve-year-old prostitute (New York) who fell or was pushed from a window of a "quick-turnover" hotel; and in the Ms. and Mr. Nude Teeny Bopper Contest, scheduled to be held at Naked City (Indiana). There, children were to be paid ten dollars each—as were their parents—to enter the contest naked, and observers, fully dressed, were to pay fifteen dollars to photograph them. An unexpected visit in the summer of 1977 to one of the truckers' stops at Naked City by CBS Television, Chicago, uncovered eleven- and fourteen-year-old girls waiting, stark naked, for eighteen-hour shifts, for which they were paid fifteen dollars a day. These circumstances were found to be violations of the minimum wage law, the child labor law, and the liquor licensing regulations. There were no laws to address the matter of their nakedness. However, we are delighted that community and official action in the state of Indiana has halted many of these objectionable practices. But much still remains to be done.

An interesting sidelight is that in Victorian England a group of concerned women organized to raise the ages of girls within the brothels from nine to thirteen. They were successful.

Children engaged in prostitution often are recruited from rural areas or midwestern cities. There are more than one million runaway children each year, many of whom turn to prostitution for survival. Many leave homes of violence and sexual abuse, others are lonely because of neglectful personally preoccupied families. Still others are overwhelmingly bored and unchallenged. A few are severely mentally ill but untreated.

The longing for adventure and to be rid of parental abuses leads hundreds of thousands of children into the streets, brothels and bus terminals. Their common needs are affection and attention. These needs make them vulnerable to smooth-talking pimps, who woo them with pretenses of love and promises of fun and big money. For some, drugs and alcohol are part of the enticement. For others, these habits follow. Most are involved in drug abuse sooner or later. The habit ensures their captivity in the lifestyle of domination by the pimps.

Many child prostitutes travel from city to city. In some cases, this travel is due to their being employed by organized prostitution rings, which often carry the children's vital statistics on computers in order to efficiently meet customers' demands. Boston, Chicago and New Orleans have eliminated such technologically advanced rings in recent months. Child prostitutes are rotated around the country like circuit riders because the men who desire children also desire variety. These men need the illusion of innocence and virginity. One child I treated literally claimed to have sold her maidenhood forty-four times. In other cases, the wandering is to avoid arrest or territorial disputes with local established prostitutes. Still others follow conventions of professional and business groups.

WHAT HAPPENS TO THESE CHILDREN?

The life of a child prostitute is generally very different from what may have been promised or anticipated by the child victim. Besides the drug and alcohol abuse, there are frequent beatings by pimps, violence from customers, and conditions of slavery. If the girl has a child, her pimp often takes her baby from her. He sends the infant out of state to be cared for by one of his relatives whose name or whereabouts she does not know. If the prostitute tries to leave his stable (the name for a pimp's group of girls) he threatens her with the reality that she may never see her child again. The youngest mother I personally delivered during my medical training was nine years and eight months old. She had been prostituted by her own mother from age three. When delivered of a son, she thanked God that it was not a female who would have to experience a life similar to what hers had been.

There is physical damage to the child arising from the premature and inappropriate sexuality of child prostitution. Nature did not intend for children to have sex with adults. In addition to lacerations of the genitals, venereal diseases, pregnancy, etc., there are local infections of the genitals and a well-established correlation between precocious sexuality and cervical cancer in young women under thirty, necessitating hysterectomies. When a child's normal physical development has been punctuated by extensive premature sexual activity a total disruption of emotional development usually occurs as well. How can we expect a child to trust an adult world which sexually exploits him or her?

WHAT KIND OF PEOPLE USE CHILDREN SEXUALLY?

They are almost exclusively men. While occasionally I have treated mother-daughter incest and, even more rarely, mother-son, when I have consulted on child-sex-for-pay, the buyer has always been male. The men come from all classes and races though there is a marked Caucasian preponderance. Many are married—even those primarily interested in boys—and a surprising number are middle or upper class. Many are men of prominence and power. Some are jaded and bored, but almost all feel inadequate and unable to meaningfully relate to peer sexual partners. They see sex as something one person does to another, not as a mutually reciprocal relationship. Sexual activity equals a performance, and they relish an inexperienced child as the judge. Persons who use children are called pedophiliacs. Pedophiliacs frequently feel disquieted with themselves and punish themselves with degrading sexual acts that the children have to perform—acts often sadomasochistic in nature or involving urine and feces. We must never confuse healthy adult human sexuality and our own experiences with the activities these children must experience. The size discrepancy alone is cause for pain and fear.

Incredibly, during the British Psychiatric Society's meetings in Wales in May 1977, the first meeting of the International Paedophilic Information Exchange was held. This is a group of persons who believe that sexual conduct between child and adult is perfectly permissible behavior. This society is working for the rights of adults to so use "consenting" children. Children, in my opinion, do not have the capacity to judge the consequences, or give consent in the true sense. There are many American sympathizers with this newest rights movement and, indeed, one association, the Rene Giuon Society in California, claims to have 2,500 members who have filed an affidavit that they have each deflowered a child under eight (male or female). The motto of this group is: "Sex by eight or it is too late."

WHAT CAN BE DONE?

First, we must recognize that a sexually permissive society without humanistic caring contributes to the defective values presently being developed in children. Children need structure. They must learn that sex is more than just doing what feels good or earns them money. Sex is part of a relationship —a special kind of friendship which is not exploitative. Second, children must be given attention and affection in the home. This includes loving, cuddling, warmth and concern—basic psychological needs devoid of genital sexual overtones. If these warm touching experiences are missing in the home, the child may seek them elsewhere, becoming vulnerable to sexual exploitation by others with their own agendas.

Third, we must develop and provide all children with sex education—not simply information about human sexuality, but including the preciousness of human relatedness, caring and commitment. Anatomy and warnings about masturbation are not a substitute for dealing with the very real concerns and frustrations of adolescence, and all information shared with our young must be appropriate for them, not for sophisticated adults.

Fourth, when a child gets involved in prostitution, authorities should recognize the behavior as a symptom of more serious problems. The juvenile justice system or other strictly legalistic approaches cannot alone prevent or stop the problem. We must take a comprehensive look at the child in trouble, including psychological, medical, educational, legal and intra-family issues.

Fifth, communities must recognize that child prostitution and pedophilia are very serious threats to all children in the community and to the community itself. Community resources must be organized to maximize the impact of appropriate skills and resources to return the victimized child to a happy, healthy and appropriate lifestyle. At the present writing there are no treatment centers specially designed to treat child sex abuse victims. Much remains to be done, but at least we have begun by identifying that these problems exist. Now we must create a society where children can enjoy love and affection without being subject to sexual abuse. All children should have an inalienable right to love and affection.

CREDIT: *Judianne Densen-Gerber, J.D., M.D., F.C.L.M., President and Chief Executive Officer, Odyssey Institute of America and Australia, and Stephen Hutchinson, J.D., Vice President and General Counsel, Odyssey Institute of America and Australia.*

Child Safety

DEAR ANN: You have, in the past, printed some very useful suggestions and guidelines sent in by readers. As superintendent of the Allegheny County Police, I would like to share some literature put out by the Boys and Girls Crime Prevention Corps. We hope young people everywhere will profit from these rules:

(1) Keep out of wooded areas, empty lots and empty buildings.

(2) Do not talk with strangers or get into a car driven by a person you don't know.

(3) Never thumb rides.

(4) Don't permit anyone you don't know to touch or handle you.

(5) Turn down any offer by a stranger who asks you to sell things or pass things out.

(6) Do not take candy or money from strangers.

(7) Keep away from strangers who get friendly in a movie, park, swimming pool or other public place.

(8) Never eat anything or puff on anything given to you by a stranger.

If someone should grab hold of you, do the following:

(1) Scream as loud as you can. Keep screaming. Don't stop.

(2) Jerk free and run as fast as you can.

(3) Run to the nearest home or building and tell the first person you see what happened.

(4) Call the police and your parents. Remain there until someone comes for you.

(5) Try to remember the description of the person who bothered you.

ROBERT G. KRONER, SUPERINTENDENT ALLEGHENY COUNTY POLICE, PITTSBURGH.

DEAR FRIEND: Thanks for the expert advice. I hope parents everywhere will go over your suggestions with their children and re-emphasize the importance of each one. It could mean the difference between life and death.

CREDIT: *The above article appeared in the Providence* Evening Bulletin *on June 25, 1975.*

PREPARING JOHNNY FOR SURGERY

DEAR ANN LANDERS: Our 8-year-old son must go to the hospital and be operated on for a hernia next month. I feel we should tell him in advance and prepare him for what is coming. My mother says we should keep quiet about it. According to mother, kids are never happy about going to the hospital and the less time they have to dread it the better. "Just tell Johnny you are going for a ride and take him to the hospital" is her advice. Is my mother right or wrong?

DARNDIFIKNOW

DEAR DARNED: Your mother is wrong. Tricking a child is the worst possible approach. It is far better to tell Johnny in advance (three days is enough) that he is going to the hospital and that the doctor is going to make him 100 per cent well. You might even make it sound like an exciting adventure. The doctor will be glad to brief you on what to say if you need his help.

Child Safety

Very Young Children and Alcohol

The party's over and the guests have left. Happy but beat, host and hostess survey the litter of glasses, bottles and ashtrays. "Wanna clean up?" asks one. "Yech!" says the other.

So they lock the door, put out the lights, look in on their sleeping children and go to bed.

It was a great party. But great everything isn't. Two potential hazards have been overlooked and there is plenty of trouble ahead. The hazards:

(1) The threat of fire and (2) the danger of their children swallowing a deadly poison—alcohol—*a poison that has no antidote.*

Dr. Richard W. Moriarty, director of the National Poison Center Network headquartered at The Children's Hospital of Pittsburgh advises: "Alcohol poisoning is becoming more and more common among children under five. We call it 'The Sunday-morning Syndrome' because children often get up early on Sunday morning, before their parents are awake, and discover bottles and unfinished drinks left over from a Saturday-night party.

"It doesn't take much alcohol to kill a child. It doesn't take many ounces to depress the nervous system or drop the blood-sugar level low enough for death to occur.

"And there is no antidote—nothing you can do to increase the metabolism or break down the alcohol in the body. That's why it's so dangerous."

The ability to metabolize alcohol is directly related to body weight. The more you weigh, the more you can drink without experiencing side effects. "But when it comes to young children," Dr. Moriarty points out, "you're dealing with a very small package."

As for The Sunday-morning Syndrome, he adds: "A child has nothing in his stomach when he first gets out of bed, so the rate of absorption is further increased."

Precautions: Before going to bed after a party, empty all glasses and place liquor bottles out of the reach of children.

If, despite your precautions, your child swallows alcohol, immediately telephone your local poison center, physician or hospital emergency room. Give details and follow instructions. If you do not have these telephone numbers taped to your phone, I urge you to attend to the matter at once. You may never need them, but if you do, time wasted can spell the difference between life and death.

Do *not* induce vomiting unless you're told to. If it's a severe case and your child is brought to a poison center or hospital emergency room, the alcohol may be removed from the bloodstream by dialysis—a procedure similar to that of an artificial kidney machine.

A sobering footnote for parents with children over five; keep your guard up. According to Dr. Moriarty, "Alcohol is already the number-one drug of abuse among adolescents between the ages of ten and sixteen."

The other hazard after the party is over is fire—caused by cigarettes or their embers smoldering in sofas and chairs after you've gone to bed.

A party increases the danger of fire, according to Rexford Wilson, President of Firepro Incorporated, a technical consulting center for fire protection. His reasons:

"People are less alert when they are drinking. Alcohol dulls the senses. Fire consumes oxygen, creating carbon monoxide and carbon dioxide, which further dulls the senses.

"Moreover, drinking guests are often careless while smoking. They may jar a cigarette off an ashtray and not realize it—or mildly inebriated guests might bump into each other and knock ashes and burning coals off cigarettes and into sofas and easy chairs. Should those incendiaries fall on a rug or carpet, you might smell smoke fairly soon. But if they drop into the upholstery, it could take forty minutes or more to smell danger."

According to Wilson, "Most fires that cause multiple deaths in the home occur during the sleeping hours—10 P.M. to 6 A.M." During those hours, he says, you and your family are highly vulnerable because "fire gets a foothold before anyone awakens. Then time for escape is short—sometimes too short."

Precautions: Before a party, provide plenty of large, deep ashtrays. If wastebaskets are in the area, remove them; they are a target of opportunity for a thoughtless or careless intoxicated smoker.

After a party, remove all cushions from the furniture and feel around for cigarettes and ashes with your hands. Hundreds of fatal fires begin in sofas and chairs.

Finally, gather up all ashtrays, dump the contents on a sheet of newspaper, wrap them up, run them under the faucet in the kitchen and leave them in the sink. Nicotine, when eaten by children, is poisonous.

Empty all cocktail glasses and lock up the alcohol.

If you follow these precautions the next time you have a party, you can sleep like a baby and not be concerned if your young children might get up before you do.

CREDIT: *National Safety Council.*

Childbirth Without Pain

The Lamaze Method

Until relatively recent times, the experience of childbirth, no matter how different it may have been for each woman, included one constant factor: pain. The pains of labor were viewed as an inescapable ordeal, the heritage of Eve, as the religious-minded put it. From the late nineteenth century on, anesthesia offered an alternative to pain—but at a price. Anesthetized women become removed from active participation in the birth of their children and their babies sometimes show the results of the drug for weeks after birth. In the 1920s a group of Soviet physiologists, foremost among whom was Ivan Pavlov (whose experiments in conditioned reflexes in dogs are well known), addressed themselves to the question of pain in childbirth. It was discovered that much of the difficulty of labor and parturition is due to the mother's fears (often stemming from ignorance) compounded by voluntary muscular contractions which work against the involuntary contractions and dilations of the uterus and birth canal. At first, hypnosis was used with a fair degree of success as an antipain device, but its applicability was limited and it treated only the symptoms rather than the root causes of pain. Through a process of trial and error, the Russian doctors developed a program of prenatal education and a series of breath and muscle exercises designed to build up conditioned reflexes which would enable the mother, almost instinctively, to work with her body rather than against it during labor. The result of this program was a painless delivery.

By the early fifties, the "Pavlovian Psychoprophylactic Method of Childbirth" was widely established in the Soviet Union. At about the same time, a French physician, Dr. Fernand Lamaze, impressed by the successes of the Russian system, introduced it to France where it underwent certain modifications and refinements. Despite the rigidity of the French medical establishment and initial political objections to a "communist" technique, "accouchement san douleur" or childbirth without pain, as the Pavlovian method is now commonly called, began to attract a growing number of expectant mothers in the West.

In essence, Dr. Lamaze's method is fairly straightforward. It consists in the first place of a thorough education of the expectant mother in the process of childbirth and in the bodily changes it brings about. Secondly, she is taught a number of stretching and posture exercises which have no direct bearing on the actual delivery but which serve to improve her muscle tone and to prepare her body for the crisis of delivery. Finally, the mother is given a set of breathing and muscle control exercises which she will use during the four stages of the delivery, a brief description of which follows:

(1) The Flattening of the Cervix. In this preliminary stage, the opening of the uterus (cervix) assumes the shape of a ring. This is accompanied by mild contractions of which the mother often remains unaware.

(2) The Dilation of the Cervix (to a diameter of about ten centimeters). This process starts slowly and gradually accelerates. It is accompanied by contractions of increasing intensity which the Lamaze-trained mother assists with a combination of deep chest breathing* and short, superficial panting.

(3) The Transitional Period. At this point, the mother first feels the urge to push even though the cervix is not fully dilated. To the breathing combination described above are added forceful exhalations which prevent the mother from pushing prematurely and thus slowing up the final dilation of the cervix.

(4) The Expulsion. This is the hardest part of the delivery and calls for great concentration and work on the part of the mother. The contractions are at their most intense and the mother must assist them with strong pushes of her own. A combination of inhalations, held breaths, exhalations and pushing plays a crucial role in the smooth and painless delivery of the child. After the baby has emerged, one final push usually suffices to expel the afterbirth or placenta.

Another Lamaze technique, used to relieve muscle tension during uterine contractions, is a light massage of the area above the pubic region towards the hips. This should be done only during contractions and in conjunction with the breathing exercises outlined above.

This has not been meant as a textbook guide to childbirth without pain, but rather as a general exposition of the principles and techniques involved. The important thing to remember is that the primary purpose of the Lamaze method is to build up, through *daily* exercise and training sessions, conditioned reflexes which enable the mother to respond automatically during labor to the signals given by her body, her doctor, her "monitrice" (a Lamaze-trained guide or monitor), and, more often than not, her husband.

Although the Lamaze technique has encountered strong resistance from the American medical establishment (as it did initially from the French), interest in it is growing for a number of reasons. In the first place, its effectiveness against pain has been well proven. Even with Lamaze training, labor entails very hard work but it no longer has to mean excruciating pain or drugged oblivion. Secondly, since the mother is not anesthetized, she remains alert and aware of every step of her baby's birth. This is not only satisfying in

---

* Note the emphasis on chest breathing; abdominal breathing, often taught in American natural birth courses, interferes with the work of the uterus and can lead to pain.

itself but the mother's increased mental activity and physical involvement serve to lower her sensibility to pain. And finally, the father in a Lamaze delivery is encouraged not only to witness the birth of his child but to participate in it actively. Simply put, the Lamaze technique offers both parents the opportunity to experience more fully the joy and fulfillment that should be a part of every birth.

For those wishing further information on the Lamaze method of painless childbirth, there are a few excellent books on the subject available in the United States, among which are *A Practical Training Course for the Psychoprophylactic Method of Childbirth* by Elizabeth Bing and Marjorie Karmel, A.S.P.O., and *Thank You, Dr. Lamaze* by Marjorie Karmel, Lippincott (hardcover) and Doubleday/Dolphin (paperback).

CREDIT: *Ann Landers.*

Childbirth Without Violence

The Leboyer Method

In 1975, a French obstetrician, Frederick Leboyer, wrote a book entitled *Birth Without Violence* (Alfred A. Knopf, Inc.) which revolutionized many people's thinking about a baby's entry into the world. His central thesis is that "babies are persons" endowed with a full complement of sensory and psychological vulnerabilities. Even a fetus, according to many psychologists and biologists, is sensitive to its prenatal environment. Yet, in the majority of hospitals, newborn babies are thrust from the comfortable environment of the mother's womb into a harsh world of bright lights, noise and the often brusk handling of attendants. The cries of the newborn, which are ordinarily greeted with joy, are actually screams of anguish. As Dr. Leboyer puts it, ". . . this little creature, so sensitive to the light, is removed suddenly from its dark cavern. Its eyes are exposed to floodlights! The infant howls. Why should this surprise us? Its eyes have been burned."

Another common hospital practice is to suspend the baby by its ankles immediately after birth. "Suddenly nothing is supporting the infant's back. And it is in this paroxysm of confusion and distress that someone seizes the baby by a foot and suspends it over a void. The spinal column has been strained, bent, pushed and twisted to the limit of its endurance and is then robbed of all support. The head, also, is dangling, twisting."

Essentially, Leboyer's method is designed to ease the baby's transition into the world through three basic modifications of the traditional childbirth procedure:

(1) The birth room should be dimly lit and quiet, thus eliminating the "blinding" surgical lights and traumatic noise.

(2) At the time of birth, the baby should not be held up by its heels or ankles and stimulated to cry, but rather placed, with the umbilical cord intact, on its mother's abdomen, where it is gently massaged.

(3) After this period of tender caressing, the umbilical cord is cut and the baby bathed in a basin of warm water.

The Leboyer method does not preclude any of the standard medical practices for predelivery or postpartum care. In fact, Dr. Leboyer stresses the importance of these procedures in ensuring the health of the mother and child.

In the United States, reactions to Leboyer's ideas vary from ignoring the subject, to amusement, to open hostility. Critics feel that these modifications are at best unnecessary, and at worst, dangerous. Another factor in this critical reaction is that Dr. Leboyer presented no technical data to support his assertions, since he felt that his procedures were a natural extension of safe routines.

Recent physiological studies by Drs. David Kliot and Max Lilling show, however, that the Leboyer method is both safe and beneficial. They have proven that, following the Leboyer techniques, babies will expel mucus when placed in a head-down position on the mother's abdomen, thus eliminating the need for active suction. The baby's body temperature will remain in a safe range thanks to heat induction from the mother's abdominal skin. And most importantly, Dr. Leboyer invites the father to be present at the birth, thus turning a routine hospital event into a family-centered one.

These simple innovations entail no extra hospital costs and only a small amount of extra time on the part of the hospital personnel. While the Leboyer method is frequently used in "home deliveries," it can greatly enhance the experience of a "hospital delivery." Mother, father and baby all interact much more closely than in a "normal" delivery, thereby strengthening what psychologists call Family-Newborn Bonding.

In a study of sixteen men who had committed violent crimes, Dr. Arthur Janov discovered that fifteen of them had "had the most horrible possible conditions at birth." In his conclusions, Dr. Janov wrote, "Doctors must remember that they are delivering a live, sensitive human being, not a blob of protoplasm. They should know that their actions during delivery may have something to do with the later neurosis of the child. Gentle handling is of the utmost importance."

A retrospective study by Dr. Rappaport, a French psychologist, revealed that the "Leboyer" babies were normal or above normal in psychomotor testing; they were ambidexterous (able to use left and right hands equally well) and significantly more alert (and had longer concentration spans) than other children. They also had fewer sleeping and feeding problems. Since these children were more relaxed and agreeable, the parents were also more relaxed and a better parent-child relationship was established.

Most parents described the Leboyer birth as a profound experience. They liked all aspects of the delivery and expressed a desire to have any future children the same way. The usual sensation of emptiness that follows birth was compensated for by placing the infant on the mother's abdomen. In addition, fathers seem to take an exceptional interest in their children if they are permitted to be in the delivery room.

Modern obstetrical methods now virtually guarantee the health and safety of both mother and child. Obstetricians and hospitals have therefore shown a reluctance to modify proved safeguards. At present, however, the Leboyer method and modifications of it are being tried by many doctors with the approval and understanding of their patients. As studies of these methods are published and reviewed, Dr. Leboyer's ideas will probably be practiced more widely. Unfortunately, the threat of malpractice suits will undoubtedly prevent many obstetricians from deviating from the old routine. They are afraid to do anything different and, of course, everybody loses when medicine is practiced in a climate of fear.

CREDIT: *David A. Kliot, M.D., F.A.C.S., F.A.C.O., Clinical Assistant Professor, State University of New York, Downstate Medical Center, New York.*

Children in Trouble With the Law

INTRODUCTION

Today, children under eighteen years of age commit 50 percent of all serious crimes, and a greater percentage of lesser crimes such as school vandalism (which alone annually costs our society $600 million). Many parents are stunned by calls from the local police department informing them that their son or daughter is in custody. Perhaps you have received such a call—or will, in the future. This article is designed to help you and your friends who have children in trouble. The children represent all segments of the community, all races and creeds, every economic and educational level.

YOUR INITIAL RESPONSE IS VERY IMPORTANT

Admittedly, the first response is surprise and shock, followed by denial and shame. But it is essential that parents with children in trouble with the law accept the fact that there is a problem. It is too easy and very destructive to blame Johnny or Janie's friends. Children choose friends who meet their own needs. The cliché "Birds of a feather flock together" may be corny but it's true.

It is important that parents be concerned about their teenagers' choice of companions. Adolescence is the time of life when the young are weaned from the values of their families. They must replace these familial values with those of their peer group in order to choose mates with whom they will establish their own family units. This is a normal development, but it is an extremely stressful time for both generations. I have always considered my children's friends the clearest barometer of their well-being or difficulty.

Parents must guard against overreacting, blaming or avoiding the problem. There is a natural tendency in all of us to deny the possibility that our children are lawbreakers or involved in criminal activity, particularly activity as life-threatening as taking drugs. Denial arises from the need of the parents to protect their self-image, even though the consequence of such denial is to deny the child help.

The nature of the specific complaint or event is not the most important criterion for attention. Indeed, adolescent "acting-out" behavior is almost always symptomatic of significant underlying feelings and problems. The behavior, including criminal activity, is a "distress flag" raised by a child who is often confused, angry and out of control. "Beating the rap" can frequently worsen the problem. A youngster in difficulty needs help. The problem is not the arrest, but the child behind the arrest. The arrest must be considered a signal of underlying emotional distress in the same way that fever is a symptom of physical illness.

PARENTS MUST BECOME PART OF THE SOLUTION

Once you as parents are made aware of a problem, you must co-operate in the resolution of both the legal and personal issues confronting your child. Hostility towards either the child or the authorities prevents an accurate assessment. Acceptance and justification of the child's situation is also non-productive. A parent must walk a thin line between rejection and abandonment on one hand and excuse and rationalization on the other. Parental assumption of all responsibility for the child's actions is equally destructive. The parent must be firm but supportive and often needs counseling and understanding, in this time of stress, as well as the child.

CHECKLIST FOR PARENTS

In addition to maintaining the aforementioned attitudes, there are several steps to be taken when your son or daughter is in trouble with the law.

First, promptly seek out the person with the immediate responsibility for your child. In most cases, he or she will be a juvenile officer assigned to the regular police force. Begin by listening carefully to his or her understanding of what has happened. Then, sit down with your child, even if he or she is sullen and uncommunicative, which often occurs as a coverup for fear, shame and confusion. The child must hear that the parents understand there is a problem, and that correcting the situation is mutually of primary importance. Differences in facts must be resolved as best as possible, and good legal counsel should be engaged, preferably a lawyer experienced in handling juveniles, and who understands that getting help for the child emotionally is as important as "beating the charges." Often the court and law enforcement officers may be helpful in recommending legal assistance, as may the family doctor or clergyman who has helped other families in like situations. You must realize that your difficulty is not the first time that this problem has occurred. You must guard against shame and the need to hide the situation. At times like these, true friends emerge and you and your child need the help and closeness of concerned others.

Second, all concerned must discuss with the juvenile officer the seriousness of the charge(s) and what counseling services are available. Most juvenile or district courts which handle the bulk of juvenile offenses request a prejudgment evaluation as well as the probation department's recommendation. Juvenile officers or probation officers can refer you to community resources, and they will often make the initial contact and referral. The sooner corrective action begins, the better. Don't wait! The closer to the time of the criminal action the initial assessment process is completed and treatment begins, the better, because the child is more willing to make changes in lifestyle, when the impact of the arrest is still remembered and felt. The passage of time allows a dangerous distance to set in for all concerned.

Often parents must accept the hard fact that they have been part of the problem that led to the "acting out" of their child and they too must change for total rehabilitation to occur. You must listen to what trained personnel have to say and don't waste time defending past events. Most probably the time has come for change on the part of all members of the family unit.

Third, both parent and child must capitalize on the court's placement decision or disposition of the case. Accept it and work with it. Don't rant against the system! Depending upon the seriousness of the offense, youth offenders can be released in custody of their parents with the charge(s) dropped; found guilty but placed on probation; or sentenced to a training school or youth detention center (the present euphemisms for reformatories). Occasionally, in the most serious cases, an adolescent will be tried as an adult and if found guilty sentenced to an adult prison. Even if it comes to this, some good can result. Out of traumatic and negative experiences, the entire family can commit to a plan which assesses family relationships, sets appropriate limits for the child, and builds supportive bonds throughout the entire living unit. While previously we have focused on the parent-child-in-trouble relationship in the solution of these problems, it is important to include all members of the family living or playing a role together. Brothers and sisters tend to be forgotten in the immediacy of the courtroom, as well as grandparents. Attention must be paid to all significant others.

Fourth, follow up with long-term caring, concern and commitment. Do not return to the old ways of relating. Prove you *all* have learned a lesson. The situation does not return to normal ("as before") because the charges are dropped or the child is let out on probation. The reasons the child got in trouble must be understood and corrected. Remember, the crime is only a signal, not the issue.

Numerous states offer the court alternatives to incarceration or reformatories such as diversion to private or state-run residential treatment programs. Most authorities in the juvenile justice field agree that the latter programs afford a better chance for successful rehabilitation than public training schools. If no such alternative exists in your locality, ask the juvenile officer, probation officers, the judge, community counselors, or other local resources to find out where there are such programs willing to take your child. If your state or community has not made such arrangements for the treatment of its juveniles in trouble, contact and complain to your local state assemblyman, senator, governor and other politicians. Furthermore, join with other parents to insist that such services be provided to the children in your community. The federal government has allocated monies to the states for these services.

Fifth, participate in and support the therapeutic services provided. Once your child has been placed, visit whenever you are permitted. Write letters and call whenever possible. Be cheery, and don't burden the child with your problems. Remember, the staff who operate reform schools and rehabilitation centers are frequently up against enormous odds; probably you found your own child more than enough to handle. Workers in these centers must cope with twenty to fifty youngsters and their families daily, plus inadequate funding and often hostile environments. At all times try to make their job easier because, in the long run, they are working for, not against, you and yours. Be co-operative and seek their advice about ongoing problems. Inform them if difficulties arise that they might not know about. After all, they are on *your* family's team. Be guided by what they think is best. Constant intruding or making life hard for staff creates unnecessary complications.

Sixth and lastly, consider the interests of the child in all decisions. When necessary, parents of a child in serious difficulty must accept that their home and its dynamics may not be the best place for the child to return to upon completion of treatment or prison. The child may be welcomed by relatives, foster parents, or juvenile group living situations. Your own feelings of guilt or inadequacy should not be the guiding principles. What matters is that your child is in an environment which offers the best opportunity for him/her to grow into healthy young adulthood. Too often the parent's need to be loved, or to appear normal to the world, outweighs the child's legitimate demands. Don't be afraid of losing your child's love—that is selfish on your part— think only of what is best for the child. However, don't sacrifice the entire family's well-being for the demands of a disruptive youngster. Children must learn to respect the needs and rights of others within their circle of experience.

SUMMARY

A key to eventual success is the child's being willing to accept responsibility for what has happened and committing to making changes. Given the support of the parents and other important figures involved in his or her life, there is an excellent prognosis.

Remember, solving personal problems for all of us is difficult and painful, even more so for adolescents just emerging from the protective nest of home into a frightening hostile world. Pain is an essential part of the healing process; we can neither protect ourselves nor our children from experiencing it; "growing pains" are part of the human reality. There are no easy answers or quick cures. The determination to see things through despite pain or difficulty must be developed. The parent should not shield the child, but stand alongside the child in trouble. The Odyssey Institutes throughout the United States stand ready to work with you if difficulty arises. The long-term effects of the personal crisis are determined more by the manner in which the parents and child respond to the problem than by the act of delinquency itself or even the deposition by the authorities.

CREDIT: *Judianne Densen-Gerber, J.D., M.D., F.C.L.M., President and Chief Executive Officer, Odyssey Institute of America and Australia, and Stephen Hutchinson, J.D., Vice President and General Counsel, Odyssey Institute of America and Australia.*

Children of the Super-Rich

DEAR ANN LANDERS: My wife and I never had the opportunity to be around children till we had our own. What should we do about childhood nudity in the home?

We have a girl, 10, and two boys, 8 and 6. They love to run around naked. Now and then they ask if they can bathe together.

My wife and I believe this is innocent childhood behavior that will pass in time. But how long should we allow it to continue? Please advise.
—PARENTS WHO NEED GUIDANCE

DEAR PARENTS: If the kids were all the same sex, it wouldn't make any difference, but nudity among brothers and sisters should not be allowed after five years of age. (Coeducational bathing should be stopped, also.)

In most instances, nothing need be said—especially to girls. They usually develop a sense of modesty a few years before bodily changes occur. A girl of 10 who is still romping around nude with her brothers should be told her baby days of running around naked are over.

If you catch the kids "playing doctor," don't take the roof off the house. Simply explain that their bodies are private and no one should be allowed to fool around with private parts.

In recent times there has been an increase of interest in the problems of minority groups. One group that has been grossly neglected is the children of the super-rich. The super-rich are defined as those with personal fortunes of many millions. These individuals are not ordinarily thought to be in need, but they are deprived in a very real sense and little has been written about them.

THE PATIENTS

Children of the super-rich usually come for psychiatric treatment out of whim, boredom, a desire to do the "in" thing, or because of behavior considered bizarre or "too far out." They often lack motivation of anxiety, and do not seem to suffer greatly. They may be single or married, in school or out, but all have one or more of the following symptoms: chronic mild depression, emptiness, boredom, superficiality, low self-awareness, lack of empathy, intense pursuit of pleasure and excitement, the belief that they can only be happy with people like themselves. They also show very little interest in work, goals, or ideals, and a belief that buying or spending or travel will solve any and all problems.

They are generally not the children of hard-working parents who "have made it" in the new country, but the grandchildren of that group. The parents of the patient group are usually closer to *their* parents in values and ideals, having seen poverty or struggle and work-ethic attitudes. They too may have struggled hard, although their goals were power or fame, as well as amassing more wealth. They often suffer from typical neurotic conflicts, such as depression, phobias, compulsions, and the like. Even though they might not have seen a great deal of their parents, there was a strong bond and identification with parental values.

The children of the latter group, the third generation, were usually raised by servants, tended to see little of their parents, had fewer and less-clear role models with which to identify and were keenly aware that money was plentiful. In general, the parents were busy, socially active, traveled a great deal, and left the child-rearing to servants.

Not only did the children have unlimited freedom, but relatively few close friends. Most of their relationships were superficial, with individuals who came from the same type of background.

Society is replete with figures that contradict the above description. As an example, the five Rockefeller children all have been hard-working and productive in government, banking and philanthropy. To say they have no problems would be incorrect, but to say they are like the patients above would be untrue. They have ethics, morals, values, ideals and intense commitments to goals. Most other children of the super-rich have not been so fortunate.

The patients to whom I refer have severe emotional problems, and scant awareness of themselves and others. They cannot tolerate frustration and are unconsciously so overwhelmed by anxiety, rage, shame or guilt that they operate with every possible defense. In addition, we see chronic failures, personal attachments with great ambivalence, absent, perverse or compulsive sexuality.

With the majority of these patients, the villain is not money, but the parental relationship. The children are truly underprivileged. What the family has gained in money it has lost in feeling, and at times even common sense. Some of the most simple sensible child-rearing practices are beyond the parents' imagination.

The patients show evidence of the typical narcissistic character: easy frustration, self-centeredness, shallowness, rage, vindictiveness, lack of shame or embarrassment, low empathy, little tenderness and, of course, difficulty in establishing an honest relationship with a therapist.

THE PARENTS

Before therapy, the parents do not seem to understand the deficiencies in their children. As one father said to me (his daughter at thirty had not one single friend or activity), "Thank God, she's not a lesbian." That was his only concern.

Certain qualities of the parents often become clear. They may be jaded, see the world as corrupt, with money as power, and job or outside interests as unimportant. Even when the parents are hard workers, they do not expect a similar work-ethic in their children. Always the focus is on what one *has,* not on what one *does* or how he does it. The exceptions occur in those families where creativity or hard work is an independent tradition.

Often the parents are "unavoidably" absent. More often they are disinterested in their children, self-absorbed, immature and tend to repeat patterns of their own childhood experiences, including frequent absences and shifting parent-substitutes. The manner in which they use money as a weapon or a token of love creates further distortions.

The similarity between the children of the super-rich and the children of the poor is startling. The poor suffer from discrimination as well as inadequate parenting or despised models for adult behavior. Their parents are often absent, depressed, action-oriented, angry and antisocial. They tend to feel frustration, hopelessness, boredom, cluster in groups of "like" people, have little tolerance for frustration, low empathy and have a poor sense of "self." There is a greater tendency towards antisocial activity, but otherwise the similarities are far greater than the differences.

A supportive doctor-patient relationship, if it can be developed, has considerably more to offer than psychoanalysis. Ego-strengthening and models of behavior and values may be provided. A strong identification with the therapist or a substitute parent may be fostered. There is a latent hunger for feelings and ideals so that a desire to become a member of a meaningful group may appear. This may reveal itself in the form of a radical group, a religion, a political belief, an interest in power or philanthropy, and sometimes a strong interest in business and making money. Signs of progress are many but the most important are increase in self-esteem, humor, empathy, less narcissistic object-choices, more compassion, the development of true interests leading to activities that are maintained over time, lessened impulsivity and more introspection. Interest in children, animals, sexuality or marriage are all signs of development.

The latent hunger for relief from boredom and depression may be satisfied by belonging to groups that provide a useful service, a shared belief or a common interest. These groups develop and enhance a capacity for trust self-esteem, self-discipline and, above all, the capacity to endure frustrations separations and loneliness.

Cardinal signs of improvement are: increased involvement with others, the appearance of a sense of humor, the capacity for sympathy and empathy, and a realistic perspective of one's life, past, present and future. With hard work, gains are available and significant.

CREDIT: *Roy R. Grinker, Jr., M.D., Attending Physician, Michael Reese Hospital, Chicago; Training and Supervising Analyst, Chicago Institute for Psychoanalysis.*

Children Who Won't Eat

No well child ever starved to death in the United States when adequate supplies of food were available and his parents were reasonably intelligent.

Very few normal and well children between the ages of one and five are going to eat three square meals a day. One full meal a day is the limit for most, with considerable dawdling and picking over the other two meals.

In this age range, growth and development continue at a slow pace, with a total weight gain of four or five pounds a year. This is reason enough for a child's finicky appetite and "not eating enough to keep a bird alive." Usually, he will eat enough snacks throughout the day to compensate in calories for the incomplete and poor meals.

Concern about a "balanced diet" and forcing, cajoling, begging or bribing a child to eat a helping of vegetables, fruits and meats accomplishes very little. It even produces harm, in that it conditions the child early against certain foods and may give him a sense of satisfaction from the increased attention he is receiving.

Children are creatures of habit. They resist the new and unusual. Most small children prefer the same old things rather than accepting or even tasting new and unfamiliar food. They also are "streak eaters," preferring and eating the same foods for weeks on end and then suddenly refusing to touch the favorite food.

Mealtime should be a happy time for the child and parents. The following simple do's and don'ts will be helpful in achieving this goal:

(1) A quart of milk a day is great for the milk industry but not necessarily so for your child. One pint of milk a day—about six ounces at each meal—is sufficient. Too much milk fills the stomach, dulls the appetite, and leaves little room for other important foods.

(2) Serve small, attractive portions, emphasizing meat, eggs and cheese. Don't expect him to eat all of each food served.

(3) Serve raw vegetables; many children prefer them to cooked vegetables.

(4) Don't allow him to refuse what had been placed before him and then expect something different prepared for him alone, such as a bowl of fruit or cereal to sustain him through the night or until the next meal.

(5) Thirty minutes is time enough; end the meal bravely and without emotion.

(6) Don't use dessert as a bribe or reward for eating. If a dessert is part of his planned meal, don't insist that he clean up his plate or eat his other foods first.

(7) Vitamin supplements do not take the place of food.

CREDIT: *Dr. Jay Arena, Chief of Pediatrics, Duke University Medical Schools, Durham, North Carolina.*

Illegitimate Children

(*Their Rights*)

Approximately 10 percent of all newborn children in the United States today are born out of wedlock. Because the number has grown to such great proportions in the last decade, there have been many changes in the law of illegitimacy.

Numerous court cases have been brought into this area of the law and because of recent legal decisions the illegitimate child and the legitimate child now share legal equality.

An illegitimate child has the right to support from his father. The father's liability to an illegitimate child is no different from the father's obligations to a legitimate child.

The father of an illegitimate child cannot be denied visitation rights. Court decisions have on occasion given custody to such fathers and permitted them to adopt their illegitimate children.

An illegitimate child has been held entitled to collect Workmen's Compensation benefits related to his father and an illegitimate child has also been held entitled to recover for his father's wrongful death.

One case granted Social Security benefits to an illegitimate child whose father had conceded paternity.

The Supreme Court has held that illegitimate children can inherit from a father who has left an estate but no will.

The latest cases decided by the courts are noteworthy for their humanitarian aspects. The rationale behind the humane thrust of the law is best summed up by the following quote from a 1972 case:

> The status of illegitimacy has expressed through the ages society's condemnation of irresponsible liaisons beyond the bonds of marriage. But visiting this condemnation on the head of the infant is illogical and unjust. Moreover, imposing disabilities on the illegitimate child is contrary to the basic concept of our system that legal burdens should bear some relationships to individual responsibility or wrongdoing. Obviously, no child is responsible for his birth and penalizing the illegitimate child is an ineffectual—as well as an unjust—way of deterring the parent.

CREDIT: *Ilana Diamond Rovner, attorney, Assistant Deputy to Governor James R. Thompson of Illinois.*

Mean Little Kids

We have all seen cartoons portraying the theme of the pecking order for expressing anger. In the barnyard the strongest chicken pecks the next strongest and on down the line to the weakest chicken, who has no one to peck. Similarly, the father who is angry at the boss comes home and yells at mother who screams at daughter who hits her brother who bites the baby who kicks the cat.

The difference between chickens and humans is that older and bigger humans fool themselves into believing that the target of the hit (whether verbal or physical) provoked it.

Little kids do not have that skill. When we see children hitting or biting others or torturing animals we often think they do it for no reason at all. Aggressive acts for which adults cannot see a reason arouse fear. This fear is often stated as: "If I cannot control him when he's little, how will I control him when he's big?" From this fear comes inappropriate punishment that not only fails to get rid of the problem but often perpetuates it. Biting the child who bites another in no way conveys the message, "You're not allowed to bite."

Almost everybody feels and acts like a baby at times. For example, when we are sick. A biting child tells us that he feels very babyish. It is a sign that he has not passed babyhood in his image of himself or that he has regressed to feeling like a baby. Parents feel frightened because it has gone on too long and efforts to stop it have failed.

With a tone of helplessness parents say: "We've tried everything from punishing to being extra nice." They often feel guilty because, while their heads tell them the child has no reason for acting so mean, they feel uneasy about it. "Tell us what we're doing wrong," they say.

Even though the reasons for biting and hitting people or hurting his pets are not apparent, we can be sure reasons do indeed exist.

These are the ingredients of the problem:
(1) The child feels frustrated and angry.
(2) He cannot verbalize his feelings.
(3) He is impulsive, that is, he acts quickly on a feeling.
(4) He has not learned more socially acceptable ways to discharge his feelings or to get rid of the causes.

When we understand this we are on our way to helping the mean little kid change into the wonderful little human that he really is.

How can a much loved child feel so frustrated and angry? One of the most observable causes is a sudden change of expectation. For example: A new baby arrives. Suddenly he is supposed to give up his position as center of attraction and be the "big brother." Or there may be sickness in the family, or lack of sufficient help for the mother to cope with all the demands in her life. The child is expected to understand and be good.

This does not mean that parents must cater to the demands of the child. They should think about whether their expectations have jumped from little to much. The child could feel rejected, not because it is so, but because he perceives that brother or sister is more in favor. The possibilities are too numerous to itemize, but you should ask yourself whether it might be hard to be this particular child in this particular family at this particular time.

There are many reasons why a child cannot express how he feels in words. One is obvious. He has not yet learned to talk. Another—he feels it isn't safe to speak. Still another—he feels he would be "bad" if he made his parents feel guilty.

The young child does not know how to use himself well, that is, his eyes, ears, hands, feet and powers of speech. Often, we expect children to go from not knowing how to do something to knowing how, without helping them learn to do it; moreover, we do not provide models to imitate, or tools to practice with. We expect them to get along well with others but offer few opportunities to practice doing just that.

Start with recruiting help for the mother, who really should not have to shoulder all the work of raising a child. Fathers can help a lot. The littlest children can use a pounding toy and graduate to hammers and other tools for fixing and making. Parents can take children to where other children are playing to watch and participate. All kinds of games with balls help relieve frustration because they allow for throwing, kicking and hitting.

Expose your child to many kinds of experiences—the greater the variety the greater is the possibility that one of them is going to strike him as *his* thing. For example: Grampa playing chess; the naturalist in the local park teaching about flowers and trees and birds; kids playing baseball, football, tennis or cheerleading; a cousin making music on a piano or a wind instrument; men working on the streets; and women doing needlework. They all plant seeds of future careers and hobbies.

Turn off the TV and become an active, interacting, and socializing family. It is a good bet then that your destructive, mean little kid will turn into a constructive likable kid. The famous deaf, blind Helen Keller was a mean little kid. Anne Sullivan helped her to great achievement through first teaching her to use her hands well. Knowing how to *do* opens acceptable channels for discharging aggressive feelings.

If the problem continues, don't be reluctant to seek professional help. Sometimes when our own emotions are caught up in a problem we cannot see it clearly. You don't have to wait until you feel desperate. A little help early can save a lot of time and expense later. It may be distressing to discover that a child may be acting out the anger that one or both of his parents have bottled up.

You have probably read the saying "Tall oaks from little acorns grow." Did you know that it comes from a poem called "Lines Spoken by a Boy of Seven Years," written by David Everett in 1791? The middle of it goes like this:

> Large streams from little fountains flow:
> Tall oaks from little acorns grow:
> And though I now am small and young,
> Of judgement weak and feeble tongue,
> Yet all great learned men, like me,
> Once learned to read their A B C.

The poet wrote these words with a deep sense of understanding of the feelings of children and what they want adults to know about them.

The hitting, biting little kid is saying by his actions, "I am having trouble learning the A B C of loving and being loved. I need a helping hand, not a heavy one." Don't be reassured by people who say "he'll grow out of it." Fulfilling a wonderful potential is too important to count on that.

CREDIT: *Marita D. Kenna, M.D., child psychiatrist, Assistant Professor, University of Pittsburgh.*

HOW SAD NOT TO HAVE ANY CHILDREN

DEAR ANN: Now that so much has been said about your survey that revealed 70 per cent of America's couples would not have had children if they had it to do over again—please rerun that great column, "Musing Of A Good Father On A Bad Day." BALTIMORE FAN

DEAR FAN: I thought you'd never ask! Here it is:

There's nothing sadder than the childless couple.

It breaks your heart to see them stretched out relaxing around swimming pools in Florida and California, sun-tanned and miserable on the decks of boats, trotting off to Europe like lonesome fools—with more money to spend, time to enjoy themselves and nothing to worry about.

Childless couples become so selfish and wrapped up in their own concerns, you feel sorry for them. They don't fight over the kid's discipline. They miss all the fun of "doing without" for the child's sake. They go along and do as they darn well please. It's a pathetic sight.

Everyone should have children. No one should be allowed to escape the wonderful experiences attached to each stage in the development of the young. The happy memories of those early years—saturated mattresses, waiting for sitters who don't show, midnight asthma attacks—rushing to the emergency room of the hospital to get the kid's head stitched up.

Then comes the payoff—when the child grows from a little acorn into a real nut. What can equal the warm smile of a small lad with the sun glittering on $1,500 worth of braces—

ruined by peanut brittle—or the frolicking, carefree voices of 20 hysterical savages running amok at a birthday party?

How sad not to have children to brighten your cocktail parties—massaging potato chips into the rug, wrestling the guests for the olives in their martinis.

How empty is the home without challenging problems that make for a well-rounded life—and an early breakdown. The end-of-day report from mother, related like strategically placed blows to the temple. The tender, thoughtful discussions when the report card reveals that your senior son is a moron.

Children are worth every moment of anxiety, every sacrifice. You know it the first time you take your son hunting. He didn't mean to shoot you in the leg. Remember how he cried? How sorry he was? So disappointed you weren't a deer. Those are the memories a man treasures.

Think back to that night of romantic adventure, when your budding, beautiful daughter eloped with the village idiot. What childless couple ever shares in such a wonderful growing experience? Could a woman without children equal the strength and heroism of your wife when she tried to fling herself out of the bedroom window? Only a father could have the courage to stand by—ready to jump after her.

The childless couple lives in a vacuum. They try to fill their lonely lives with dinner dates, the theater, golf, tennis, swimming, civic affairs, and vacation trips all over the world. They contribute nothing to humanity.

The emptiness of life without children is indescribable. But the childless couple is too comfortable to know it.

Just look at them and see what the years have done. He looks boyish, unlined and rested. She is slim, well-groomed and youthful. It isn't natural. If they had kids, they'd look like the rest of us—tired, gray, wrinkled and haggard. In other words, normal.

The Terminally Ill Child

Parents and children are faced with great tragedy when a terminal illness is diagnosed. They must deal with two traumas. First the shock at the time of diagnosis and second the shock at the time of death.

As opposed to a sudden death such as an accident, murder or drowning, a terminal illness can give a family only one positive thing: the opportunity to do things correctly.

Parents can help the child deal with the medical aspects of the illness, care for the child and, most important, show their love. Parents grieve differently because they are battling a foreign invader and each must handle it in his own way.

When a child dies suddenly, it is difficult to forgive one's self for harsh words spoken, or punishment, perhaps too harsh, given in the past. There may be some guilt, too, about words of praise, or love not verbalized.

When feasible, even ill children should have chores and responsibilities and the knowledge that they must not use their illness to take unfair advantage of others. There is security in discipline for all youngsters, sick or well.

Strong and honest medical backup at such a time can be the difference between falling off or hanging on. Parents and children have a right to expect a show of concern, and understandable explanations from a doctor.

If a family turns to religious leaders for help, clergy should understand the dynamics of a family unit that is threatened—the fears, the neglect of other children.

Because there is time, with guidance from trained personnel, the problems of coping with a terminally ill child should be handled as a total family. Sisters and brothers should be included in helping to feed the sick child and spend time with him. This will benefit not only the sick child but also the brothers and sisters, who later will have feelings of having helped.

There is a growing move toward honesty with children about their terminal illness. Many parents are beginning to feel the need to answer frankly when asked questions by the dying child. When possible, straight answers can help the youngster talk openly about his or her own fears and thoughts.

Although not every family can be completely honest at this time, more and more psychiatrists and social workers trained in grief therapy are advising parents to do so. They believe even young children suspect, through nonverbal communication, when something is being hidden from them. Secretiveness tends to make the child extremely apprehensive and insecure. The unknown can be frightening. Although it may be difficult to face, try to understand the value of these words: "and the truth can set you free."

CREDIT: *Harriet Sarnoff Schiff, author of* The Bereaved Parent, *New York, New York: Crown Publishers.*

Unmotivated Children

Lack of motivation occurs among school children with frequency in our society, and a variety of forces produces this lack. Motivation seems to require at least two ingredients: (1) the desire within the child to achieve and (2) the expectation by the child that he can and will succeed. The unmotivated do not meet these requirements.

All learning is motivated and there are essentially two methods of participating in this process. In one, the learning takes place for someone else (such as parents or teachers), or for honors or rewards, and is called extrinsic learning. Intrinsic learning, on the other hand, is done for oneself, is inner motivated, gives pleasure, and may take place in any setting at any time. When life is going well in a loving and accepting atmosphere, both the actual process of learning and the accomplishment of having done a good job brings pleasure. However, when the child becomes unmotivated, his ability to learn becomes impaired.

Superimposed on the child's motivation are the expectations of society, the school, the child's family, and the child's teacher or teachers. Today, whether it is in the best interests of the children or not, it is expected that all children will complete their high school education and that one third to one half of them will go on for further education beyond high school, in vocational schools, junior colleges or colleges.

In the past the less academically motivated students often planned apprenticeships with their father, relatives or others with skills which the adolescents needed or wanted. This apprenticeship often occurred between the eighth and tenth grades and offered an easy transition from school to craft or trade. The academic skills that had already been acquired were sufficient for them to go successfully through life.

In today's higher technical society, the jobs that require little or no training or skills are being done more and more by machines. This eliminates work formerly done by people with little academic training. Since many of these jobs which demand little training no longer exist, schools take the former apprentice population and force it towards higher academic attainments, whether the individuals have an aptitude for higher learning or not.

When a child who is unmotivated for learning is evaluated, one must be aware of what is going on within the child, within the family, within the school environment and within his society. Such scrutiny usually requires a team of specialists in all these areas in order to determine whether the problem lies within the child, the family, the school or parts of all three. Beyond these factors, within the child's body itself there may lie constitutional defects that lead secondarily to emotional problems, including lack of academic motivation.

Some organic factors which may reduce motivation will be briefly mentioned since they must be ruled out.

(1) *Mental retardation* may be caused by birth injury, prematurity, convulsions, infections, malnutrition (both in the child after birth and also during pregnancy when the child is developing), biochemical or endocrine disorders such as hypothyroidism, viruses such as "German" measles and hepatitis in the mother during pregnancy, and various blood incompatibilities between the blood factors of the father and the mother.

(2) *Visual problems or deafness* may cause the child to appear unmotivated when in fact he cannot see or hear properly, and therefore gives up the attempt to keep up with his classmates.

(3) *Specific degenerative diseases* which show up after infancy or in childhood, such as Tay-Sachs disease or Friedreich's ataxia or endocrinological disorders such as hypothyroidism, may hinder a child's academic progress.

(4) *Chronic fatigue* may affect the child. If he has been deprived of sleep for long periods of time, he may become apathetic in the classroom.

(5) *Poor nutrition:* too little or the wrong kind of food can affect learning.

The unmotivated student in whom organic causes have been eliminated and who has, or appears to have, a learning problem will demonstrate (1) a decrease in ability to acquire knowledge (broadly defined as learning skills) or (2) a decrease in ability to impart or demonstrate this knowledge. Eventually he develops negative feelings about school, about learning, and about himself. He often reaches a point where he either does not want to learn, or in some cases actively tries not to learn.

Usually an unmotivated child comes to the attention of the school or parents when he is more than an academic year behind where he should be for his intelligence level. He may be considered a slow learner, or underachiever. In a conference about the child a teacher may say, "Well, he is bright enough, but he just doesn't try." It is frequently at this point that the school psychologist, school principal, child's parents or a school evaluation team is consulted and the child's skills, abilities and problems are assessed. Such an assessment may lead to consultation with a pediatrician, psychiatrist, or neurologist.

What are some of the symptoms or signs of poor motivation?

(1) Short attention span.

(2) Hyperactivity or sometimes underactivity.

(3) Failure to finish tasks or assignments.

(4) Negative behavior such as tantrums, teasing, bullying, or distracting other children in the classroom.

(5) Developmental lag in which the child appears to be emotionally less mature than his peers.

(6) Unwillingness to become involved because past involvement has resulted in failure.

(7) Feelings of being picked on by teachers and peers.

(8) School attendance problems such as "sickness" or truancy.

In looking for the causes of these signs and symptoms, there are four major psychosocial areas to explore for problems that may be affecting the child's motivation:

(1) What is going on within the family which is not directly related to the child or child's learning? Is there severe marital discord, overly large family size, overcrowding, psychiatric disorders of other family members, or poverty?

(2) What are the family's spoken or unspoken attitudes towards learning?

a. Disapproving facial expressions, a shrug of the shoulders, walking away from the child and his problems cut the props out from under any child struggling with school.

b. A family that openly says, "School won't help you in life," deals motivation a severe blow.

c. Pressures to have the child achieve at a level which is too high for that particular child can be exhausting. One often hears parents say their child is going to learn all the things in school that they didn't. This then becomes a struggle between parents and child with the parent saying to the child, "Study harder, get higher marks, do better or else." External familial pressure of this kind can leave the child feeling that his chance of success is so small he simply gives up.

d. Children who view their parents as "super-successful" sometimes give up rather than try to equal that success. The fear of failing or suffering from comparison is so great they retreat from the challenge. Parents who are achievers should make a strong effort to let their child know he is loved, respected and is "okay."

e. Sometimes the child does not have aptitudes in the areas of parental competence but he does have talents or competence in other areas which are not understood or given encouragement by his parents. He may be seen therefore by his parents (or by himself) as "dumb"!

f. The family may be impatient with the child because he may learn more slowly, or in ways different from the ways in which they learned. This can turn off his motivation.

(3) What are the child's expectations of, or attitudes towards himself?

a. There may be an expectation of failure, since there have been multiple failures in the past.

b. Often a child fears success. This is manifested as a fear of competition and responsibility, or a fear that he cannot master a skill.

c. There may be a desire to rebel and show his parents "who is the boss" by getting whatever darned marks he pleases.

d. The child may find that he can get attention (however negative) by refusal to involve himself in school activities or by misbehavior in school.

e. A child may not want to show that he is smarter or more competent than his peers because he may be teased by them. Therefore he will take on the attitudes of his peers who regard academics as "square."

(4) What about the teacher or teaching process?

a. The teacher must have knowledge and be able to impart knowledge.

b. The teacher must realize that there are different speeds of learning and ways to learn, and should try to tailor his teaching to the child who is a little slow.

c. Children usually want to identify with a teacher whom they like and who likes them.

Two special categories of the learning child must not be overlooked: (1) learning disabilities, and (2) giftedness. Both categories may produce the same picture of low motivation.

Children with specific learning disabilities, which are popularly called by various names such as dyslexia or minimal brain damage, show difficulties in school, usually in the areas of reading, writing and spelling. They also manifest dysfunctions in the area of motor activity and co-ordination, attention and perceptual functions, interpersonal relationships, impulse control and emotional control.

Boys more frequently than girls (4:1) are learning-disabled and are often not recognized until entering school. At this point they are often seen by their teachers as problem children because of their short attention span, inability to sit still and inability to easily follow directions. They are easily distracted by noise and visual stimuli and frequently have trouble stopping one school activity and switching to another. Letter and number reversals, mirror-reading or mirror-writing, lasts long after the other children in the classroom have established reading and writing patterns which have a firm left to right flow.

Some children seem to have behavioral difficulties, others seem to have trouble comprehending something that is quite simple.

Some gifted children appear unmotivated because they are academically unchallenged in settings where their special needs are unmet. Contrary to the belief that "smart kids can take care of themselves," it has been shown that there are over two million children in the elementary and high schools in this country whose needs are not being met and that many of them are high school dropouts for this reason. These children are especially unrecognized in the inner city and rural populations and comprise up to 15 percent of their school population. Programs which are designed for the average student will cause frustration, boredom and sometimes failure for the gifted and talented. It is important that these children be identified and their academic needs met, as they are our future scientists, scholars, philosophers and statesmen.

What can be done to help the unmotivated psychosocial, learning-disabled and gifted children? A warm, accepting school environment may be provided which gives direction, realistic and specific goals for the particular child. Simultaneous changes at home can provide the same modifications, along with love and recognition of the child for what he is and what he believes in. This may or may not include psychotherapy for the child and his family. The goals should be meaningful for each unmotivated child and should be tailored to his specific needs—his interests, his rate of learning, his strengths and weaknesses. Co-operation between the parents and the school is vital for a child's development. As he has a chance to experience success he then will attempt things that he previously was unwilling or unable to do, which then improves his self-esteem. Such things as prescriptive teaching, remedial education, one-to-one tutoring, participation in after-school activities such as scouting, or summer programs such as Outward Bound stimulate happy motivation. The feedback to the particular child is a continuous sense of *his* ability to meet first the short-term goals and later the longer-term goals. This has direct impact on the way he views himself and his increasing self-confidence and self-esteem. He then gets into the "success breeds success" cycle.

In summary, an unmotivated child is one who, for various reasons, does not have the desire to achieve, or who does not expect probable success. Review of the demands of the school, the home situation and the learning patterns of the child are necessary before changes are introduced. Changes should be made in any or all of these areas simultaneously in order to increase the motivation of the child. Hopefully he will get into a successful self-confident position where again learning can effectively occur.

CREDIT: *Janet E. Ordway, M.D., Ordway Professional Association, Bangor, Maine.*

Chiropractic

Harriet Cressman is a lovely lady who lives with her husband on their farm in Pleasant Valley, Pennsylvania. Early in 1963, she developed a backache. Thinking that chiropractors were "bone specialists," she went to one. He did not disappoint her. After examining her and taking an X ray, he said that her spine was "tilted" but could be corrected by spinal "adjustments." The adjustment took place three times a week for several months. As her back symptoms improved, her treatment was reduced to twice a week, then once a week and then once a month. At this point, although Harriet felt completely well, the chiropractor suggested that she continue adjustments regularly for "preventive maintenance." She did so faithfully for ten years and had no further trouble with her back—as far as she knew. In November 1973, however, the chiropractor took another X ray and gave her bad news: the X ray showed "eighteen compressed discs and progressive osteoarthritis of the spine which was spreading rapidly." It would make her a helpless cripple if she did not have immediate treatment. He reassured her, however, that his new machinery could correct her disc problem and stop the spread of her arthritis.

Staggered by the news, Harriet went home to discuss the matter with her husband. But the chiropractor's receptionist had already telephoned Mr. Cressman to ask him to bring Harriet back immediately to the office. Because of the serious nature of the case, the chiropractor wished to begin "intensive treatment" that same day. The treatment would be in day-long sessions, alternating complete bed rest with "Diapulse" and "Anatomotor" therapy, spinal adjustments and acupuncture. Its cost would be $11,000, but with payment in advance, the doctor would accept an even $10,000.

Because of her long association with the chiropractor, and because she was in no mood to trifle about her health, she unhesitatingly went about raising the money. Supplementing her life savings with a bank loan, she paid in advance.

For the next few months, as far as she could tell, Harriet's treatment proceeded smoothly. Every week another full spine X ray was taken. Each time the chiropractor pointed out on the X ray how she improved. He also discussed other patients with her and asked her to help talk them into treatment with him. Advising Harriet that her condition might be hereditary, he suggested that other members of her family have spinal X rays.

Harriet's son Donald did have an X ray and was told by the chiropractor that he had a "pin dot of arthritis which, if untreated, would spread like wildfire and leave him crippled within a short time." Donald's cost? With the usual 10 percent discount for advance payment—a mere $1,500!

In May 1974 the chiropractor suddenly informed the Cressmans that he was moving to California. "What about us?" they asked. "Don't worry," he answered, but their worry increased and turned to suspicion when his answers became contradictory. Pressed by Harriet for the name of another chiropractor who could continue her treatment, the chiropractor named one. "Don't bother to call him before I leave," he said, "because he has already gone over your records and X rays with me." Harriet did contact her chiropractor-to-be, however, and was told that her name had been "mentioned" but that no record or X-ray review had taken place.

Shocked by the turn of events, the Cressmans consulted medical and legal authorities, who suggested that they file criminal charges for "theft by deception." They did. Investigation by the Northampton County District Attorney's office uncovered other patients of the chiropractor who had similar experiences. A medical radiologist X-rayed the spines of Harriet and Donald and offered to testify at trial that neither had any condition which could possibly be helped by chiropractic treatment. When news of the arrest became public, a third patient filed a criminal complaint. The chiropractor, he claimed, had cheated him out of $2,075 by promising to cure his arm and leg which had been paralyzed by a "stroke."

Now it was the chiropractor's turn to be stunned by the turn of events. He disappeared from public view and communicated through his attorney. He was innocent, he claimed, but was anxious to leave Pennsylvania as soon as possible. (He could not do so until the criminal cases were settled.) If the three complainants would drop their charges, he would return their money. Under supervision of the Northampton County Court, the $13,575 was returned and the charges were dropped.

Do you wonder whether Harriet Cressman had to be very gullible in order to part with $10,000 for such questionable treatment? Please let me assure you that she is a very intelligent person who is not at all gullible. Until the chiropractor announced that he was leaving, she simply had no reason to be suspicious. Though generally well informed, she had never encountered criticism of chiropractic in any newspaper, magazine, book or radio or television program. Like all chiropractors, hers was licensed by the State *as a doctor*. He seemed warm, friendly and genuinely interested in Harriet. And he did what she would expect a doctor to do. He examined her, took an X ray, made a "diagnosis" and prescribed a "treatment" plan. She was happy to feel better and, like most people, gave no thought to whether the "treatment" had cured her or whether she would have recovered just as quickly with no treatment at all. Nor did she give any thought to the nature of chiropractic itself, how it began, how its practitioners are trained or what they usually do. She certainly did not suspect that chiropractic is based on the mistaken beliefs of a grocer and his son.

THE DEVELOPMENT OF CHIROPRACTIC

Chiropractic is said to have begun in 1895 when Daniel David Palmer restored the hearing of a deaf janitor by "adjusting" a bump on his spine. Palmer thought he had helped the man by releasing pressure on the nerve to his ear. A grocer and "magnetic healer" by profession, he did not know that the nerve from the brain to the ear does not travel inside the spinal column. But no matter—he soon became certain that he had discovered *the* cause of disease.

At first he kept the "discovery" secret, but by the end of 1895 he set up the Palmer College of Chiropractic to teach it. One of his early pupils was his own son, Bartlett Joshua, better known as "B.J." The boy began to help his father run the school soon after it opened. Gradually, however, B.J. took over. In 1906, Daniel David was charged with practicing medicine without a license and went to jail. When he was released, B.J. bought out his interest in the school. Business boomed, and many Palmer graduates opened schools of their own. Cash was the basic entrance requirement for most of them and some even trained their students by mail.

As competition among chiropractors grew, and as many were jailed for practicing medicine without a license, they began to pressure state legislators to license them. Responding to this pressure, perhaps with the hope that licensing would lead to higher standards of education and practice, states began to pass licensing laws. Chiropractors would be allowed no drugs or surgery. Most states limited chiropractic treatment to "spinal adjustment." *But for what?* If all disease was caused by spines which need adjustment, couldn't chiropractors treat everything?

They could. And they did. Over the years, many cases have come to light where chiropractors treated patients for cancer and other serious diseases which should have had medical attention.

THE SCOPE OF "MODERN" CHIROPRACTIC

Does this mean that no matter what is wrong with you, if you go to a chiropractor today, he will diagnose your problem as a "pinched nerve" and want to treat you with spinal adjustments? According to chiropractic officials, the modern chiropractor most often treats musculoskeletal problems such as backaches and stiff necks. In 1974, Stephen Owens, D.C., Past President of the American Chiropractic Association, was asked by *Medical Economics* magazine what chiropractors do. Said Owens: "A chiropractor would be silly to take on a disease that's not susceptible to his kind of treatment. He'd just be inviting failure."

Owens' statement was similar to what chiropractors told Congress as they lobbied for Medicare inclusion. In 1970, for example, William Day, D.C., President of the International Chiropractors Association, was questioned by U. S. Senate Finance Committee Chairman Russell Long:

LONG: The medical profession says that your profession claims to treat all sorts of things for which it can do no good whatever.

DAY: Let me state categorically that the chiropractor does not claim to be able to cure all conditions . . .

LONG: How about migraine?

DAY: No.

LONG: You don't treat ulcers?

DAY: No, sir.

LONG: What about hepatitis?

DAY: Hepatitis is an infectious disease. We would refer it to a physician.

Such answers from top chiropractic officials sound quite reasonable and easy to believe. After all, who nowadays could accept Palmer's original belief that all disease had just one cause or that one method of treatment can cure everything? But many studies suggest that official chiropractic is not willing to admit what chiropractors are actually doing.

In 1963 the American Chiropractic Association asked its members what conditions they treated. Of those responding, 85 percent said that they treated musculoskeletal conditions most frequently. However, the following percentages reported treating other conditions:

Asthma	89%	Pneumonia	32%
Gallbladder	82%	Acute heart conditions	31%
Ulcers	76%	Appendicitis	30%
Chronic heart condition	70%	Pernicious anemia	24%
Tonsillitis	67%	Cerebral hemorrhage	18%
Impaired hearing	59%	Fractures	9%
Goiter	48%	Leukemia	8%
Diabetes mellitus	46%	Cancer	7%
Rheumatic fever	37%	Diphtheria	4%
Hepatitis	32%		

In 1971, skeptical about Dr. Day's testimony, the Lehigh Valley Committee Against Health Fraud sent the following inquiry to 130 members of his organization selected at random from its Directory:

"I have been suffering from ulcers and sometimes migraine headaches for many years. I am going to this chiropractor near my home now and he is helping me. But I have not finished my treatments and my husband has a job near you. Do you treat these conditions? Do you think I can finish my treatments with you?"

Of the 110 who replied, 75 percent offered treatment. A similar letter asked ninety-two other chiropractors whether they treated hepatitis. Only one of seventy-two who replied answered negatively—that he might not be able to take the case because his state law required reporting of communicable disease. However, another chiropractor from the same state said that "chiropractic offers the safest and best care for hepatitis, as well as many other conditions."

In 1973, Dr. Murray Katz, a Canadian pediatrician, surveyed chiropractic offices in Ottawa, Canada. Seven out of nine displayed pamphlets which exaggerated what chiropractors can do. When a chiropractic official responded that use of such pamphlets would cause automatic thirty-day license suspension, Katz noted that no chiropractor had ever been suspended for their use.

Additional evidence that chiropractors do not know their limitations comes from advertising. The Lehigh Valley Committee Against Health Fraud has collected hundreds of chiropractic ads which contain false claims. Among them:

"There are very few diseases . . . which are not treatable by chiropractic methods."

"Diabetes . . . the chief cause lies in displaced spinal vertebrae . . ."

"QUESTION: If a surgeon cuts out a tumor of the stomach, does he not remove the cause?

"ANSWER: No, he may have removed the cause of the distress in the stomach, but he has not removed the cause of the tumor and it will probably grow again. A chiropractor adjusts the cause of the tumor."

"If every person were under regular chiropractic care, the incidence of cancer would be reduced by 50 percent in ten years."

"There is hardly an illness that does not respond to chiropractic care."

During the past six years, I have collected chiropractic journals and textbooks, listened to chiropractic lectures, spoken and corresponded with hundreds of chiropractors and interviewed many of their patients. My effort to define the scope of chiropractic has led me to three conclusions:

(1) Many chiropractors do not know their limitations.

(2) What chiropractors say about what they do depends greatly upon who they think is listening.

(3) Chiropractors themselves are confused and cannot agree about either what they are actually doing or what they should be doing.

There are undoubtedly some chiropractors who make a sincere effort to quickly refer people who need medical attention to an appropriate physician. Doing this well, however, requires a good medical education.

Which brings us to the question of what chiropractors learn in school.

CHIROPRACTIC EDUCATION

If D. D. Palmer could look at current chiropractic schools, he would be surprised. In his day, chiropractic training lasted two weeks to one year and covered just spinal analysis and treatment. Today, chiropractic school takes four years and includes many subjects which Palmer would think were not related to his "great discovery." Among these are "basic sciences" such as anatomy, biochemistry, bacteriology and pathology, and clinical subjects such as psychiatry, study of X ray, obstetrics (delivery of babies) and pediatrics. Standard medical textbooks are used in many of these courses.

There are several reasons for these changes. As licensing laws became stricter, many states required testing in basic sciences. Chiropractic schools which could not prepare their students for these exams could not remain in business, and an estimated six hundred of them have closed. Thirteen schools exist today.

Because Palmer's basic theory is false, chiropractic has been under continual attack from the scientific community. Since few people nowadays could believe that all diseases have just one cause or cure, many chiropractors have modified their philosophies. "Modern" chiropractic, its leaders claim, recognizes the value of modern medicine and refers patients who need medical care to proper physicians. "Modern" chiropractors, their leaders claim, recognize that factors such as germs and hormones play a role in disease. "We would like to work together," they say. "While the medical doctor gives antibiotics to kill germs or insulin to control diabetes, we will eliminate pinched nerves so the body can heal itself."

Unfortunately, despite the "new" look of chiropractic education close observation suggests that much of it is a hoax. In 1960, for example, the Stanford (California) Research Institute published a study which included inspection of two chiropractic schools. They noted that although certain scientific subjects were part of the school programs, the school libraries and laboratories did not appear to be in actual use.

In 1963, the AMA Department of Investigation sent applications from nonexistent persons who did not appear to meet admission requirements listed in chiropractic school catalogues. Only two out of seven were rejected.

In 1966 the AMA published a study of the educational backgrounds of teachers at chiropractic schools. Fewer than half had graduated from college and many who taught basic sciences did not even have degrees in the subjects they taught. When I examined current catalogues four years later, I found that little had changed. Since that time, some chiropractic schools have affiliated with nearby colleges so that students can get training in basic sciences from properly trained instructors. Other chiropractic schools have added teachers who have degrees in these subjects. But neither of these changes will greatly increase the quality of chiropractic training. Basic science courses merely prepare students for the *study* of disease. They do not prepare them to make diagnoses or to prescribe treatment.

In 1968 a large-scale study by the U. S. Department of Health, Education and Welfare concluded that "chiropractic education does not prepare its practitioners to make adequate diagnoses or to provide appropriate treatment." The HEW Report quotes many chiropractic statements which helped to bring about this conclusion. Among them:

"For the chiropractor, diagnosis does not constitute, as it does for the medical doctor, a specific guide for treatment . . ." ("Opportunities in a Chiropractic Career," 1967, prepared by American Chiropractic Association and International Chiropractors Association).

". . . chiropractic adjusting is efficacious in handling both the acute and chronic cases of coronary occlusion . . ." (*Neurodynamics of Vertebral Subluxation,* 1962, by A. E. Homewood, D.C. The most widely used chiropractic textbook).

"Q. Do you think that if an acute appendicitis was identified early enough in the disease process, chiropractic can cure it?

"A. Yes, I do. I say this strictly from experience. I don't say it only from my experience but from the experience of all who practice." (1968 Testimony of II. R. Frogley, D.C., Dean of Academic Affairs, Palmer College of Chiropractic.)

Chiropractic attacked the HEW Report as "biased," and implied that HEW failed to look at "modern" chiropractic. Considering that the Report was based primarily upon information submitted by leading chiropractic organizations, these charges seem odd. Actually, they are true to form. Whenever chiropractic is attacked by an outsider, it claims its attacker is "biased." Whenever it is embarrassed by quotes from within its own profession, it claims they are not representative.

HOW DANGEROUS IS CHIROPRACTIC?

It should be obvious that to help you, doctors must first be able to figure out what is wrong with you. Yet chiropractors who believe that spinal problems cause all diseases may not even try to make medical diagnoses. According to Reginald Gold, D.C., "If you were to come to my office, I wouldn't want to know what is wrong with you. I wouldn't want to know what your symptoms are. I would want to do one thing . . . examine your spine." Gold said this at a public meeting in 1971 after a colleague introduced him as "one of the country's leading authorities on chiropractic" and a lecturer on the faculty of three chiropractic schools. Currently, he is Vice President of Development of the Sherman College of Chiropractic.

Although many chiropractors share Gold's philosophy, the majority probably do try to determine whether their patients need medical treatment. Most patients protect themselves from misdiagnosis by consulting medical doctors before they go to chiropractors. Those who start with chiropractors, of course, take a greater risk. Not only are chiropractors poorly trained to make diagnoses, but they are prohibited by law from doing some tests which may be crucial to medical investigation.

Although spinal manipulation has a small place in the treatment of back disorders, in the hands of chiropractors it can be dangerous. I know of one man who was paralyzed from the waist down after a spinal manipulation. Unknown to his chiropractor, spinal cancer had weakened the patient's spinal bones so that the treatment had crushed his spinal cord. In another case I investigated, a patient who took anticoagulants (blood thinners) had serious bleeding into his back muscles after a manipulation. Surgery was required to remove the collected blood.

From time to time, broken bones, paralyses and strokes have been noted in court cases and medical journals. So have deaths from cancer and infectious diseases where chiropractors did not know enough to make medical referral in time for proper medical treatment. Although such serious cases are relatively rare, they are inexcusable. Lesser complications such as sprains are more common, but statistics are hard to collect. Some patients are too embarrassed to publicize them. Some do not realize that their extra discomfort is the result of inappropriate treatment. And others are sufficiently fond of their chiropractor that they cannot believe he has mistreated them.

X rays by chiropractors are a leading source of unnecessary radiation. A full-spine X ray exposes sexual organs to from ten to a thousand times as much radiation as a routine chest X ray. This is dangerous because it can lead to increased numbers of birth defects in future generations. Most chiropractors use X rays. A 1971 survey of the *Journal of Clinical Chiropractic* suggests that more than ten million X rays were taken each year by U.S. and Canadian chiropractors. Of these, two million were the 14×36-inch full-spine type. Chiropractic inclusion under Medicare, which began in July 1973, will probably increase these numbers greatly.

Chiropractors claim that X rays help them locate the "subluxations" which D. D. Palmer imagined were the cause of "pinched nerves" and "nerve interference." But they do not agree among themselves about what subluxations are. Some chiropractors believe that subluxations are displaced bones which can be seen on X rays and can be put back by spinal adjustments. Other chiropractors define subluxations vaguely and insist that they do not show on X rays. But what chiropractors say about X rays also depends upon who asks.

When the National Association of Letter Carriers Health Plan included chiropractic, it received claims for treatment of cancer, heart disease, mumps, mental retardation and many other questionable conditions. In 1964, chiropractors were asked to justify such claims by sending X-ray evidence of spinal problems. They submitted hundreds, all of which were supposed to show subluxations. When chiropractic officials were asked to review them, however, they were unable to point out a single subluxation.

Some chiropractic textbooks show "before and after" X rays which are supposed to demonstrate subluxations. In 1971, to get a closer look at such X rays, our Committee challenged the Lehigh Valley Chiropractic Society to demonstrate ten sets. They refused, suggesting instead that we ask the Palmer School to show us some from its "teaching files." When we did, however, Ronald Frogley, D.C., replied, "Chiropractors do not make the claim to be able to read a specific subluxation from an X-ray film."

Frogley might have answered more cautiously had he anticipated the wording by which Congress included chiropractic under Medicare. Payment would be made for treatment of "subluxations demonstrated by X-rays to exist." To help chiropractors get paid, the American Chiropractic Association has issued a *Basic Chiropractic Procedural Manual* which defines subluxations as anything which can interfere with spinal function and says, "Since we are obligated to find subluxations before receiving payment, it behooves us to make an objective study of what films show in the way of subluxations . . ." Referring to the Letter Carriers experience as "an unfortunate debacle which almost destroyed chiropractic credibility in Washington," it cautions, in italics, "The subluxations must be perfectly obvious and indisputable."

If a chiropractor limited his practice to muscular conditions such as simple backaches, if he saw patients only on referral from medical doctors after medical diagnosis has been made, if he were not overly vigorous in his manipulations, if he consulted and referred to medical doctors when he couldn't handle a problem, and if he avoided the use of X rays, his patients might be relatively safe. But he might not be able to earn a living.

THE SELLING OF THE SPINE

A chiropractor's income depends not only on what he treats but on how well he can sell himself. The American Chiropractic Association estimates that the "average" chiropractor earns about $31,000 per year, but the meaning of this figure is not clear. Many chiropractic graduates do not remain in practice and others are forced to practice part-time. Top chiropractic salesmen can earn a fortune.

Intensive selling of the spine begins in chiropractic school as instructors convey the scope and philosophy of chiropractic to their students. Chiropractic graduates can get help from many practice-building consultants, the most expensive of which is Clinic Masters. In 1973, Clinic Masters estimated that fifteen thousand chiropractors practiced actively in the United States and Canada and said it represented more than eighteen hundred of them. Its fee is $10,000—$100 on entrance and the rest payable as income rises. In 1973 its directors said, "Many of our clients have moved right on up through the

$50,000, $100,000, $150,000 income levels to $300,000 and above," and that "before long practice incomes of $500,000 will not be rare."

Clinic Masters promotes the idea that higher income means greater service to patients. Such service includes charging for each adjustment or other unit of treatment instead of a flat office fee, an overall "case" fee instead of charging per visit, and "intensive care," which adds room or ward fees to the bill. In 1974, 132 of its clients reported charging an average of $129.43 per day for intensive care.

Clinic Masters apparently wants the details of its advice to remain a private matter. Its clients sign a secrecy agreement and new applicants are checked against directory lists to make sure that they really are chiropractors. It also offers a $10,000 reward to anyone who is first to report "disparaging statements about Clinic Masters or its clients" which lead to a successful lawsuit.

The largest practice-building firm appears to be the Parker Chiropractic Research Foundation of Fort Worth, Texas. Its founder, James W. Parker, D.C., claims that "more than thirteen thousand chiropractors, wives and assistants" have attended his four-day courses. Unlike Clinic Masters, Parker has not been cautious about revealing his techniques to outsiders. In 1968 an investigative reporter named Ralph Lee Smith gained admission to Parker's course by pretending to be a chiropractor and paying its $250 fee. Emerging with a diploma that he had "completed the prescribed course of study at the Parker Chiropractic Research Seminar," Smith published what he observed.

Parker's course is built around a 335-page *Textbook of Office Procedure and Practice Building for the Chiropractic Profession*. Parker appears to believe that the scope of chiropractic is unlimited. The *Textbook* suggests that patients be offered a "free consultation" but led into an "examination" which costs them money. It suggests that "One adjustment for each year of age is a rough thumbnail guide of what people will willingly accept and pay for," but "If in doubt about the payment or the return of the patient, take only the smaller X-rays on the first visit but ostensibly X-ray fully."

Share International, Parker's sales organization, sells a wide variety of practice-building aids. One is a chart which pictures a spine and claims that more than a hundred diseases are related to nerve pressure at its various parts. Included are: hernias, appendicitis, crossed eyes, diabetes, anemia, gallbladder conditions, hardening of the arteries and thyroid conditions.

For about twenty dollars, chiropractors can get copies of 107 advertisements to "guide" preparation of their own ads. Most of the ads are case histories, and the instructions which accompany them suggest: "Re-type each ad on your own stationery for presentation to the editor. This would indicate that they are your own creations, and that the cases mentioned . . . are from your own files." For about forty-five dollars, graduates of Parker's basic course can purchase a set of ten cassette tapes which give additional advice. In *Sentences That Sell,* Parker describes how chiropractors associated with him test ideas scientifically and report back to him how they work. In *Ways to Stimulate Referrals,* he tells how to steer conversations to sick people. "In a casual, natural way," patients should be asked about the health of their families, friends and neighbors. Should any be ailing, patients should be urged to be "Good Samaritans" by telling them about "all the wonderful things" that chiropractic might do for them.

Despite his questionable methods, Parker appears to be a highly respected and integral part of the chiropractic world. He is a welcome lecturer at chiropractic schools. In fact, in 1970, when one of my Committee members merely requested a catalogue from the Texas Chiropractic College, he received a letter from Parker telling how chiropractors often reach incomes of $50,000 to $100,000 per year.

Sid Williams, D.C., of Atlanta, Georgia, is another leading promoter. His many enterprises include a chiropractic supply house, several publications, practice-building courses, and the recently opened Life Chiropractic College. According to a College booklet, "thousands" of chiropractors follow his philosophy. Known as Life Fellows, they appear to believe that virtually all conditions should be treated by chiropractic methods. His practice-building techniques appear to stress mass-production. Ads for his seminars boast that their top instructors see six hundred to a thousand patients per week. And at a 1973 hearing for deceptive advertising, one Life Fellow testified that he "adjusted" 593 patients in a single day!

Many chiropractors recommend regular "preventive maintenance" to increase resistance and prolong life. Reginald Gold, for example, hopes that "every man, woman and child will see his chiropractor once a week for life so that they can live 120 to 150 years." Other chiropractors have told me that all people, sick or well, should have regular chiropractic care. Wondering what approach chiropractors would take toward healthy people, our Committee once sent a perfectly well four-year-old girl to five chiropractors for a "checkup." The first said the child's shoulder blades were "out of place" and found "pinched nerves to her stomach and gallbladder." The second said the child's pelvis was "twisted." The third said one hip was "elevated" and that spinal misalignments could cause "headaches, nervousness, equilibrium or digestive problems" in the future. The fourth predicted "bad periods and rough childbirth" if her "shorter left leg" were not treated. The fifth not only found hip and neck problems, but also "adjusted" them without bothering to ask permission. Unfortunately, the adjustments were so painful that we decided to end our experiment.

Chiropractic has been described as the "greatest tribute to applied public relations that the world has ever known." Despite its shortcomings, millions of people have tried it. Chiropractic's ultimate goal is inclusion in national health insurance. And unless concerned citizens can find ways to organize and protest, your tax dollars will wind up paying for D. D. Palmer's dreams.

OVERVIEW

In 1895, modern medicine was in its infancy. Many of its theories were just as ridiculous as that of Palmer. Since that time, medicine has become a science. Chiropractic, however, has not. The only science chiropractic has developed is that of salesmanship.

Chiropractors, of course, will deny this. They will say that since I am "biased," this chapter is deliberately slanted to make them look bad. But what I have reported comes mainly from its schools, its organizations, its recognized leaders and its official publications. My data truly represent chiropractic as it is today.

This book will tell you about many practitioners who have gained large and faithful following even though their theories make no sense at all. Such practitioners rely upon salesmanship and the fact that most people get better without treatment.

Chiropractors win many friends with their warm manner, their seductive techniques, and their physical therapy and massage. But going to a chiropractor is a distinct gamble.

CREDIT: *Stephen Barrett, M.D., Chairman, Board of Directors, Lehigh Valley Committee Against Health Fraud, Inc., author of* The Health Robbers, *Philadelphia, Pennsylvania: George F. Stickley Company.*

Choking on Food

How to Help Someone Who Is in Distress

Every year scores of healthy people die in restaurants, at home, at the tables of friends and relatives because no one knows what to do when a chunk of food becomes lodged in the throat.

Dr. Henry Heimlich, Director of Surgery at The Jewish Hospital in Cincinnati, has devised a simple technique which has saved countless lives since he made his routine known in 1974. These instructions should be posted in the kitchens of every restaurant in the world. They should be taught in the classroom.

The technique is called the Heimlich Maneuver. It compresses the air in the lungs so that the plug of food pops out like a champagne cork. It can be applied whether the victim is standing or sitting.

If no help is at hand, victims should attempt to perform the maneuver on themselves by pressing a fist upward into the abdomen as described.

WHAT TO LOOK FOR

The victim of food-choking:
—Cannot speak or breathe
—Turns blue
—Collapses

For a standing or sitting victim:
(1) Stand behind him and put your arms around his waist. Allow his head, arms and upper torso to hang forward.
(2) Place a fist thumbside against his abdomen, slightly above the navel but below the rib cage.
(3) Grasp that fist with your other hand and press into his abdomen with a quick upward thrust.
Repeat several times if necessary.
When the victim is sitting, the rescuer stands behind the victim's chair and performs the maneuver in the same manner.

For a victim lying on his back:
(1) Facing him, kneel astride his hips.
(2) With one of your hands on top of the other, place the heel of your bottom hand on the abdomen slightly above the navel and below the rib cage.
(3) Press into the victim's abdomen with a quick upward thrust.
Repeat several times if necessary.

CREDIT: *Ann Landers.*

Cigar and Pipe Smoking

Is it true that if you give up cigarettes and smoke cigars or a pipe you need not be concerned with cancer? The answer is no.

Death rates from cancer of the mouth, pharynx, larynx and the esophagus are about as high among cigar and pipe smokers as they are among cigarette smokers.

Cigar and pipe smoke contains more alkaline properties than cigarette smoke and is therefore not so pleasant for the smoker to inhale. This is why cigar and pipe smoking causes few cancers of the lung. If, however, cigar and pipe smokers *do* inhale, they will suffer the same risks as cigarette smokers.

Among men who smoke cigars and pipes only cancer of the mouth and larynx are more frequent than lung cancer. Larynx cancer is found most often among men from fifty-five to seventy years of age. The odds of a pipe or cigar smoker dying from this disease is about the same as if he smoked cigarettes. It is also important to note that pipe and cigar smokers die of cancer seven to ten times as often as nonsmokers.

Larynx cancer is often cured by surgery, but it means losing one's voice box. The patient can be taught a new method of speech but must live with a permanent opening in his throat.

Mouth cancers include cancer of the lip, tongue, the floor of the mouth, hard palate and pharynx. Lip cancer has long been associated with pipe smoking.

Cancer of the mouth seems to strike (more frequently) those who both drink and smoke heavily. This is also true of cancer of the esophagus.

If words like larynx and pharynx and esophagus throw you, let me put it simply. There is no way a person can smoke anything—cigarettes, cigars or a pipe—and not risk getting cancer.

Aside from the health risks involved, cigar smoking is considered extremely offensive by a great many people. The following letter says it better than anything I could say:

DEAR ANN: Over the years I've put up with some rather inconsiderate people, but someone just left my home who made me furious. It was a cigar smoker, one of those terribly stinky ones. Now my house smells like cigars. I have an allergy headache that will last for hours. I would have kicked him out the door but he is my husband's business associate so I couldn't say a word.

How can we get it through the thick skulls of cigar smokers that they are infringing on other people's rights? Are they too gross to care, or don't they know what they are doing?

We read and hear a lot about the evils of cigarette smoking but how can we get through to the cigar freaks? Cigars are not labeled "hazardous to your health" but they really can foul up a place and are a definite infringement on the rights of others. Please print this and comment. WHERE'S A CLOTHES-PIN?

DEAR PIN: More and more we are seeing signs that say "No Smoking." This means cigars and pipes as well as cigarettes.

I share your disgust in regard to cigars, but I'm not allergic to them. Since you ARE, your husband should ask his business associate not to smoke them in your home. Doctor's orders!

CREDIT: *E. Cuyler Hammond, Sc.D., Vice President for Epidemiology and Statistics, American Cancer Society, Inc., New York, New York, and Theodore Adams, Editorial Consultant, American Cancer Society, Inc., New York, New York.*

Cigarettes

Each cigarette you smoke shortens your life five and a half minutes. This is what came out of a major British study. The results were released June 1, 1977.

The study, *Smoking or Health*, is by the Royal College of Physicians, its third such study in fifteen years. It was prepared in co-operation with all Britain's medical colleges.

The Royal College, a leading medical institution that dates back to 1518, called for tough, new antismoking measures, including a ban on tobacco advertising to end what it called the "lethal epidemic" caused by tobacco.

The Royal College called for withdrawal of all but lower-tar cigarettes, higher prices for cigarettes and a far stronger health warning than now appears on cigarette packs.

The study says roughly one in three smokers dies because of smoking, that a smoker who quits gains immediate benefit, that within ten to fifteen years the extra risk of dying early disappears, and that in Britain fifty million working days a year are lost through illness caused by smoking.

If the Royal College's proposals were adopted, millions of Britons would have to change their smoking habits. Withdrawal of all but lower-tar cigarettes, for example, would force an estimated 80 percent of smokers to switch brands if they didn't quit.

The Royal College called current government action against smoking "paltry and hesitating."

To bring the problem closer to home, I obtained help from my friend Ted Adams, Editorial Consultant for the American Cancer Society.

If no one smoked cigarettes, 250,000 people in the United States would not die prematurely each year. Cigarette smoking remains the largest, single, unnecessary and preventable cause of illness and early death. Yet 53 million persons still smoke. A recent poll showed that 25 million of these smokers would like to quit.

Most smokers know the habit is harmful to their health. But do they know *how* harmful? These are the facts: A twenty-five-year-old who smokes two packs a day has only a 50 percent chance of living to be sixty-five because he smokes.

What is the relationship between cigarette smoking and lung cancer and heart disease?

Today more than 100,000 American men and women are suffering from lung cancer. Another 100,000 are stricken each year. About 90,000 die each year. Ten percent of those who develop lung cancer are saved—a very low survival rate when you consider that other equally common types of cancer are cured in almost 50 percent of cases.

A unique study by the American Cancer Society produced evidence that no major cause other than cigarette smoking was related to lung cancer. The study involved 36,975 pairs of male smokers and non-smokers. These pairs were matched to be as nearly alike as possible in every way except their smoking habits. They were matched by race, height, place of birth, occupation, education, marital status, consumption of alcohol and other criteria. The only aspect of their lives that was notably different was that half of them smoked cigarettes and half of them didn't.

After three years of follow-up, twice as many of the smokers had died— 1,385 against 662. There were 110 cases of lung cancer deaths among the cigarette smokers, contrasted with only 12 among non-smokers; 654 of the smokers died of coronary heart disease compared with 304 non-smokers. This is only one example of the thousands of studies showing the relationship between cigarette smoking and death.

The next letter reveals some interesting insights:

DEAR ANN LANDERS: I'd bet 98 percent of your cigarette-smoking readers have been telling people exactly how they feel about their enslavement by those small cylinders of paper wrapped around a mixture of nicotine and tar-filled weeds: It goes like this:

"I could quit in a minute if my doctor told me I had to, or else."

"I go through maybe two or three packs a day, but I don't actually smoke more than a third of 'em. I light them up and they burn in the ashtray."

"I suppose I should quit smoking, but a person has to die of something. Besides, I enjoy it."

These same people are saying something quite different when they talk to themselves. Here's the truth:

"These damn things have to be bad for me or else why would I hack and cough every morning—and sometimes during the day?"

"Gee, how I envy Bill. He's been off 'em for five years. How come he can do it and I can't?"

"The fact that I have to race out of a theater at intermission to get a nicotine boost is a sure sign I'm hooked. I hate being so weak."

After forty years of puffing away, by simply comparing the two types of statements you just read, I tossed my last pack into the ashcan sixteen months ago and haven't lit up since.   WEST OF CHICAGO

DEAR WEST: Everyone who reads this column recognizes himself sooner or later. I hope those who recognized themselves today will do something about it. Thank you for putting their feet to the fire.

What are the dangers for women of developing lung cancer from cigarette smoking?

Of the 90,000 deaths from lung cancer each year, over 20,000 are among women. The death rate for women lung cancer victims has doubled in the last ten years, and it continues to rise. The highest lung cancer death rate is among women fifty-five to sixty-nine, who have smoked up to one or more packs of cigarettes a day, or among women who have been smoking since before age twenty. Women in these groups are five times more apt to die of lung cancer than women who never smoked.

Isn't it true that air pollution is a major contributor to disease and death from lung cancer?

In Iceland, which is largely free of air pollution, it was found that with the rise in cigarette consumption during and after World War II, lung cancer incidence between the mid-fifties and mid-sixties (ten to twenty years later) rose about 30 percent in men and 52 percent in women.

In the rural areas of the United States, where there is also little air pollution, heavy smokers have from ten to fifteen times as much lung cancer as non-smoking rural residents. On the other hand, studies were made in Los Angeles, where air pollution is the worst in California. It showed that the risk of lung cancer was no greater in Los Angeles than in any other California city.

What changes are there in the smoking habits of young people?

While studies show that about thirty million adult smokers have quit cigarettes, there is an alarming increase in cigarette smoking among teenagers, ages thirteen to seventeen, particularly teenage girls.

In 1969 the percentage of teenage girls smoking cigarettes was 22 percent; by 1975 the percentage of smokers had risen to 27 percent. During that same period the percentage of teenage boys smoking remained steady at 30 percent.

Since smoking habits are established in the teens, there is particular concern that these teenage girl smokers will become adult women smokers. In another ten years there may be as many adult women smokers as there are men smokers.

What are the dangers of cigarette smoking for young people?

While the problems of disease resulting from cigarette smoking and premature death seem distant to young people, there are other problems of immediate concern. First, the earlier you start smoking cigarettes, the more difficult it is to quit and the greater the danger to your health.

However, there are immediate bad effects of cigarette smoking. To quote one California doctor, when asked how long it takes for one cigarette to harm you, he answered, "About three seconds."

Smoking a cigarette starts your heart pounding an extra fifteen to twenty-five beats per minute and raises your blood pressure by ten to twenty points. It leaves behind cancer-causing chemicals in many parts of your body. It cuts your wind. It begins to neutralize the defenses of the lungs against the poisons being drawn in. There are tiny hairlike structures lining the airways to your lungs called cilia. They beat back and forth as one swallows or breathes. They clean the mucus in your throat of germs and foreign particles. Cigarette smoke destroys the cilia and thus robs the lungs of their best defense against foreign substances. This is why so many smokers cough.

Cigarette smoking is especially hazardous for pregnant women and their unborn babies. Nicotine and carbon monoxide from cigarettes can retard the growth of the fetus. The resulting lower-than-normal birth weight can affect a child's physical and emotional development. Women who smoke during pregnancy also increase their chances of having a stillborn infant or a baby who will die soon after birth. If a woman quits cigarettes during pregnancy, it is easier to stay off cigarettes after the child is born.

Studies show that the number of high school students who smoke cigarettes is twice as high if their parents smoke.

Aside from living longer and enjoying health, what are the other benefits from quitting cigarettes?

If no disease is present, your lungs begin to return to normal almost immediately after you quit smoking. The cilia repair themselves. Blood vessels and arteries constricted by cigarette smoke begin to return to normal, lessening the likelihood of heart attacks and strokes. Chronic cough, sinus condition, fatigue, shortness of breath disappear.

What is the best way to go about quitting cigarettes?

The following letter tells how one man did it:

DEAR ANN LANDERS: When I read your articles against smoking I just shake my head and say, "Isn't it a shame there are so many gutless wonders in the world?"

People will fight with each other at the drop of an adjective, but they can't stand up to a four-inch cigarette.

I smoked heavily for twenty-one years. When I decided to quit here's how I did it. I carried a pack of cigarettes in my pocket. Whenever I got the urge to smoke, I reached into my pocket and asked, "Who's boss—you or me?" Then I'd answer, "I am," and jam the pack back into my pocket. After three weeks, I kicked the habit for good.

Either you're boss or you're not. You wouldn't let another person push you around, would you? So why let a lousy cigarette rule your life?

You don't need pills, a hypnotist, clubs, pacifiers, or any of that junk, all you need is to really want to quit smoking.   ONE WHO DID IT

DEAR ONE: You're beautiful! But unfortunately, not everyone is made of such stern stuff. Some folks need outside help. And if they do—so what? It's the results that count.

First, you must believe you can do it. Thirty million adults have already quit. Of the 53 million still smoking cigarettes, 25 million have said they would like to quit. There is no one way that works for everybody. Many commercial groups claim success. Hypnotism works for some. Your doctor can recommend a hypnotist if he believes one might help you. Certain personality types do well with hypnosis, others do not. There are also various programs country-wide that assist smokers trying to quit. Some of these are SmokEnders, Inc., 3435 Camino Del Rio South, Suite 216, San Diego, California, 92108; St. Helena Hospital and Health Clinic, Deer Park, California, 94576; and Seventh-Day Adventist programs available throughout the country.

Many smokers have quit through guidelines offered by the American Cancer Society, which has free Quit Smoking Clinics in many communities.

If you decide to do it on your own, here are some suggestions which have proved helpful to others:

For many smokers an important first step in the process of giving up cigarettes is to set the date for Q (quitting) Day, when you are going to stop completely—perhaps four weeks in the future. As that day approaches, gradually reduce the number of cigarettes you smoke, day by day, or week by week.

A good system is to decide to smoke only once an hour—or to stop smoking between the hours of nine and ten o'clock, eleven and twelve, one and two, three and four, etc. Then extend non-smoking by half an hour, an hour, two hours. You may decide to halve the cigarettes you smoke week by week, or smoke only half of each cigarette.

In the process of reducing smoking keep your pack of cigarettes in a different pocket or place than has been your habit. This way you'll be reminded you are quitting; also make it tougher to smoke. Wrap your pack in several sheets of paper with an elastic band around it. Shift from a brand you like to an unpalatable brand. Ask yourself, "Do I really want this cigarette, or am I acting out of habit?"

How can I strengthen my decision as Q Day approaches?

Think over the reasons why you should not smoke: the risk of disease, the bad breath, the cough, the cost, the morning-after ashtrays, your own slavery to the habit.

Concentrate each evening before you fall asleep on one good result of quitting. Repeat and repeat that single fact. Drive home another fact the next night, etc.

Review the facts about the risks. Remind yourself that you could be the one dying early, cutting years off your life. Be aware that 100,000 doctors have quit cigarettes and ask yourself, "Why?" The answer, of course, is: "They see first hand what happens to thousands of cigarette smokers."

On Q Day drink lots of liquids, nibble fruit, celery, carrots, candy, or chew gum. Take vigorous exercise. Avoid places where people smoke. Go to the movies where there's a No Smoking section. Instead of a cigarette after meals, try a mouthwash. Reward yourself. Give yourself all the things you like best. Buy yourself a present with the cigarette money you've saved. Put your arms around someone you love and say, "Our chances for having many more years together are a lot better now."

CREDIT: *Theodore Adams, Editorial Consultant, American Cancer Society, New York, New York.*

CIGARETTES
A PERSONAL TESTIMONY

DEAR ANN LANDERS: This letter is based strictly on my own feelings about cigarettes, after twenty-four years of smoking. I'm ashamed to admit I'm still at it. I doubt that my words will have the slightest impact on the heavily addicted. For me, all the words in the world will not take the place of that first cigarette in the morning.

I'd rather address myself to your readers who are seventeen, as I once was, with a set of healthy lungs, white teeth, clean blood coursing through my veins—and in my pocket my first package of cigarettes.

How was I to know that twenty-four years later I'd be so hooked that any thought of quitting would be out of the question? How could I know, at seventeen, that I'd be waking up each morning to a mouth that tastes like the bottom of a bird cage? How could I know my teeth would be stained dark brown and my chest would feel as if it were filled with cement dust?

All I knew was that smoking was the cool thing to do. It made me feel grown up.

Although I have never seen my lungs, I know how they must look. My uncle, who is a surgeon, once showed me some "before" and "after" pictures. "Sit in on an autopsy one of these days," he said. "You'll see that the non-smoker's lungs are a bright pink. When I open the chest cavity of a smoker, I can at once tell about his habit, because the entire respiratory system is nearly black, depending on how long he has smoked." (Mine must look like lumps of coal.)

Still I continue the filthy habit, going half-crazy on mornings when I'm out of cigarettes. I go digging through ashtrays and wastebaskets for a long butt to satisfy my craving. I pace the floor like a hungry lion, waiting for the store to open. Then I hurry, unshaven, and hand over another fifty-five cents for a package of suicide.

With that first puff I realize nothing about it tastes good. Those ads are a lot of malarkey. But the people who sell cigarettes couldn't care less about me. I'm hooked and they love it. They run those sexy ads, telling you to "C'mon." But don't be fooled, Seventeen, it's not a bandwagon you'll be hopping on. It's a hearse.

If I could write cigarette ads, I'd show you pictures of myself, coughing till the tears come, gargling away a rotten taste that keeps returning, spending money I can't afford—stupid me, sucking on a little white, stupid pacifier.

Then I'd show you pictures of the clothes I've burned, and the people I've offended with my breath, my smoke, my ashes, my matches and my butts.

This is me, Seventeen, a rasping, spitting, foggy-brained addict who has let the habit consume me, a "can't quitter" who creates his own air pollution, who prefers carbon monoxide to oxygen, whose sinuses are constantly draining. Me, with the yellow fingers and the foul breath, smoking more and enjoying it less—telling you that I wish to God someone had wised me up when I was seventeen.   A DAMNED FOOL WHO HATES HIMSELF

DEAR FOOL: Your signature reveals the reason you continue that filthy, expensive, offensive and destructive habit. Get some professional help. When you like yourself better, you might decide you're worth saving. Good luck, junkie.

DAUGHTER SMOKES, MOTHER FUMES

DEAR ANN LANDERS: Two weeks ago, our 14-year-old daughter, Maria, came to me and asked for permission to smoke. She said all her girlfriends were smoking and their parents knew about it. She didn't want to sneak behind my back.

I admired her integrity and said, "All right, on three conditions." They were as follows:

(1) She wouldn't smoke more than four cigarets a day.

(2) She would not inhale.

(3) She would pay for her own and not "borrow" mine.

Unfortunately, I discovered that Maria broke two of the promises yesterday. I found 10 cigaret butts in her wastebasket and one floating in the toilet. I noticed too that she had taken three cigarets out of the pack in my purse. (I remembered I had just opened a fresh pack and smoked only one.)

I smoke too much and know what a terrible habit it is. I've tried to quit many times but can't. How can I help my daughter avoid the trap that I am now in? Please advise me. I feel
HELPLESS

DEAR MOTHER: Your first mistake was giving Maria permission. Those conditions didn't mean a thing, as you well know.

I've said repeatedly that smoking is a habit. The health authorities have made it abundantly clear that a strong connection exists between cigaret smoking and lung cancer and heart disease.

Smoking among teenagers is at an all-time high. I don't know what else can be done to get the message through to these kids. The bodies they now have must last them all their lives. If they don't take care of them, they may be in big trouble eventually. As for Maria, I suggest the firm, hard line, "No. You do not have my permission to smoke. I am 100 percent against it." Of course, it would help a lot if you would quit with her.

AN APPEAL FROM ANN: STOP SMOKING TODAY!

DEAR READERS: Please forgive this personal reference but I must share with you, my millions of friends, what is on my mind and in my heart.

A few weeks ago, our family gathered in Omaha to bury one of the dearest, most gentle people I have ever known. He was David Brodkey, married for 43 years to our eldest sister, Helen.

Dave was a delight. We adored him. He was meticulous about detail, the perfect choice to take charge of any family project. Dependable. Industrious. Thorough. "Integrity" was his middle name.

Dave cherished Helen, and well he might. She was a devoted wife, the beauty of the family, a talented pianist, a superb cook, and a leader in community affairs.

But Dave, the Perfectionist, the man who did everything right, did ONE thing wrong. He smoked at least two packs of cigarets every day for 30 years. This senseless addiction deprived him of the joy of seeing his grandchildren marry. And it will deny those who loved him of the pleasure of his beautiful presence.

So often I have heard smokers say, "Well, you have to die from something." True. But please, friends, if you can help it, die from something else and don't rush the event. Lung cancer is a horrible way to go. While non-smokers, too, die from lung cancer, the evidence is irrefutable cigaret smoking does cause lung cancer. The more we study it, the more certain we become. Smokers are the leading candidates for this dreaded disease and heart trouble and emphysema as well.

One out of every four Americans alive today will have some form of cancer during his lifetime. One out of six people who get cancer will die from it unless, of course, we learn more about how to prevent this scourge and how to cure it.

The economic cost of cancer in our country is $20 billion a year, to say nothing of the agony and suffering. The life of every person who reads this column has been touched in some way by cancer. It is the second biggest killer in the United States.

Almost the last words Dave uttered to his wife were these: "I should have listened to you years ago when you begged me to stop smoking." But like so many others, Dave believed cancer happens to other people.

And now, all you wives who are nagging your husbands, and all you husbands who are pleading with your wives to throw away those filthy killers and all you young people who are turning your healthy pink lungs into tar pits at 65 cents a pack, for God's sake, for the sake of those who love you, STOP SMOKING TODAY. Do it for yourself. Do it for the people who care about you.

ANN LANDERS

Circumcision at Birth

Circumcision, or surgical removal of the male foreskin, has been practiced since biblical times. The covenant between God and Abraham recorded in Genesis 17:10 instructed Abraham to "circumcise among you every male." It is fair to say, however, that the procedure has never been as common in other cultures as it is in the United States today. In some hospitals of the United States, 90 percent or more of the male infants are circumcised at or near the time of birth.

Practices vary around the world, in different cultures and in different areas of the United States. On the subcontinent of India, Hindus don't, but Moslems do. Jewish people do, most eastern Europeans don't. In the United States it is more common in urban areas than in rural and in the North than in the South and is the subject of much controversy today.

Circumcision done at or near the time of birth is a relatively simple procedure and usually carried out with one of three instruments: a metal instrument with a slit in it, a metal bell clamp, or a plastic bell that falls off after eight or ten days. Serious complications are unusual. Small amounts of bleeding, an occasional infection, swelling or the removal of too much or too little foreskin are the more common complications.

Why are infants circumcised? The reasons vary. The ritual circumcision among Jews (Bries) done on the eighth day of life is well known and an example of ritual circumcision accompanied by prayer, feast, a joyous occasion and an opportunity for the entire family to be together.

For years, cleanliness has been used as a reason for this procedure. It is easier to keep the circumcised penis clean and odor free.

Uncircumcised males occasionally have a painful swelling of the foreskin when it is retracted (phimosis) that necessitates emergency circumcision at any age.

Smegma, the white material that accumulates under the foreskin, has been cited as a cause of cancer of the penis in the male and cancer of the cervix (neck of the womb) in females. Cancer of the penis is very rare in the circumcised male, and the wives of males circumcised during infancy have an extremely low incidence of cancer of the cervix.

The usual question of whether sex is more pleasurable when the male is circumcised will probably never be answered. Some people feel that constant exposure of the end of the penis after circumcision to the irritation from clothes makes it less sensitive than the tip protected by the foreskin. The conclusion drawn by these individuals is that the circumcised male gets a little less sexual satisfaction.

Last we should consider the circumstances in which the boy is to grow up. It is not good to be the only circumcised boy in a locker room full of uncircumcised males or vice versa. In communities where circumcision is not regularly carried out the circumcised male is viewed as something of a freak and can be the object of ridicule.

"Now what do I suggest for my patients?" I tell them everything that I've presented in this article. I strongly recommend that if they are considering circumcision that it be done before the infant leaves the hospital. I also tell them that circumcision in infancy presents fewer complications and is a much simpler procedure than if done in adulthood.

CREDIT: *Donald M. Sherline, M.D., Professor and Director, Perinatal Biology, Department of Obstetrics and Gynecology, Rush-Presbyterian-St. Luke's Hospital, Chicago.*

Circumcision of Adults

Adult circumcision has been practiced for many generations. It is probably becoming progressively less frequent since circumcision at birth, at least in this country, has been rapidly increasing over the past thirty to forty years. However, there still are many men who have never been circumcised and who in later life desire or are advised by their doctors to undergo circumcision.

Some men elect to have the foreskin removed for cosmetic reasons. They think the penis looks better without the foreskin which cloaks and hides the head of the penis.

The most common reason for circumcision in the adult male is to improve hygiene. The foreskin permits the accumulation of smegma and moisture which produces an undesirable odor and also may cause irritation and inflammation of the penile head and the undersurface of the foreskin. This is painful and discourages sexual intercourse.

Similar infection is more frequently seen among patients with diabetes. Sugar in the urine trapped under the foreskin promotes bacterial growth. In some cases the foreskin may be torn—usually during sexual intercourse—

and these tears usually occur on a fold of skin on the underside of the penile head. This area is stretched when the penis is erect and the foreskin retracted. The resultant bowstring effect can then be more easily torn. Frequently this may recur and each time the scar tissue thus formed makes the bowstring more taut and the scarred tissue is also more easily torn. Understandably this phenomenon is most unhappy for the bearer since intercourse and even erection may cause much pain until the tear is healed. Circumcision also includes cutting out the fold and replacement with penile skin that is more easily stretched and much less subject to tearing.

In some individuals the foreskin cannot be retracted or can only be done with great difficulty because the opening is too small or contracted to slip back over the head of the penis. This situation is undesirable for several reasons. It discourages or makes it impossible to clean under the foreskin. With erection and/or sexual intercourse the skin at the opening is more subject to tearing, and sexual intercourse is less pleasurable due to the presence of the foreskin over the sexually sensitive head of the penis.

Finally, and most important, individuals who don't or can't retract their foreskin may harbor cancer of the penis. Hidden from sight and painless, this malignant growth may go undiscovered too long with tragic consequences. Partial or total amputation of the penis may be required for cure. If unsuccessful, it will ultimately lead to death because of the spread of this disease. Circumcision in the adult may not prevent penile cancer but the disease is more quickly recognized and hence treated earlier.

Circumcision is a minor operation. It may be performed in the doctor's office under local anesthesia or in the hospital under general anesthesia. It is not a difficult operation but best results are probably obtained by someone who does this operation frequently. There is definite tenderness at the line of cutting and suturing. In addition, the previously unexposed head of the penis is much more sensitive for a time to touch of clothing. This problem can be overcome or minimized by covering the sensitive area with a gauze bandage for as long as the doctor and the patient desire.

If there is no wound infection and normal healing occurs, sexual intercourse is usually comfortable and without risk of injury in six to eight weeks. Even then liberal use of lubrication is advised.

I have no idea as to the number of adult circumcisions performed annually. I would guess that the majority are performed by urologists. These specialists may well average fifteen to twenty cases per year.

CREDIT: *Jack N. Taylor, M.D., Associate Professor of Surgery (Urology), Ohio State University College of Medicine, Columbus, Ohio.*

Class

Class never runs scared. It is surefooted and confident that it can handle whatever comes along.

Class has a sense of humor. It knows that a good laugh is the best lubricant for oiling the machinery of human relations.

Class never makes excuses. It takes its lumps and learns from past mistakes.

Class knows good manners are nothing more than a series of petty sacrifices.

Class bespeaks an aristocracy unrelated to ancestors or money. A blueblood can be totally without class while the son of a Welsh miner may ooze class from every pore.

Class can "walk with kings and keep its virtue and talk with crowds and keep the common touch." Everyone is comfortable with the person who has class because he is comfortable with himself.

Cleft Lip and Palate

Clefts of the lip and palate are congenital separations in the muscle and skin of the lip, and of the structure of the palate (upper gum and roof of mouth). These problems are the result of an "accident" in development and occur in approximately one of every six or seven hundred live births.

The appearance of the cleft in the lip and palate is, of course, of great concern to the families of these infants. The deformity often evokes feelings of rejection, guilt, recrimination and anger. The family's stability is severely tested as blame and responsibility are divided. Whereas heredity does play a part, other causes of this deformity can of this date only be characterized as accidental. Extensive research suggests possible causes such as vitamin deficiency, drug usage, viral infections, nutritional disorders, mechanical factors and oxygen deficiency affecting the embryo during the critical fifth to tenth week following conception. None of these factors, however, has been proved as a cause of the cleft deformity.

Heredity does play a role in the occurrence of cleft lip and palate. The chances of a cleft lip occurring in a child of parents, one of whom has a cleft, is about 2 percent. This increases to 14 percent if there is already a sibling with a cleft lip. If two normal parents have a child with a cleft, there is said to be a 5 percent chance that subsequent children will have the deformity. Clefts of the lip alone are more common in males and clefts of the palate alone are more common in females. Both of these deformities can, however, occur in either sex separately or combined. The cleft deformity can also affect either one or both sides of the lip and palate.

The clefts may be partial or complete, involving various portions of the lip, gum and palate. The full deformity involves a total separation of the lip, gum and palate with flaring out of the affected nostril, protrusion of the middle of the face and distortion of the involved side. Few would suspect from a casual glance that in actuality nothing is missing. The deformity consists of a lack of fusion in the developing parts and herein lies the methods involved in repair and the hope for a good result in appearance and function. By surgical means the parts are rotated and repositioned to a more normal relationship and surgically repaired.

The major responsibility for surgical correction rests with the plastic and reconstructive surgeon, but the over-all treatment of the problem involves a "team of experts," each with his important part to play. The team consists of the pediatrician, orthodontist, otolaryngologist (specialist in diseases of the ear, nose and throat), speech therapist, social worker, psychologist and others.

Only with the advice of all these can the proper sequence and timing of treatment for the individual patient be outlined and planned. Basically, lip repair is carried out from the time of birth to three months of age, and repair of the palate from six months to eighteen months of age. The timing of these repairs and methods used is open to wide differences of opinion and must be individualized with each patient. More than one operation may be required for the original defect and others later for revision, resulting in refinements of appearance and function.

Several areas of function and development are involved in the over-all scheme of rehabilitation. These areas include cosmetic appearance, speech function, dental development and hearing function.

Cosmetic considerations in the patient with clefts of the lip and palate primarily involve the form and shape of the lip and nose area. A great deal can be accomplished in achieving good cosmetic appearance at the time of the initial closure of the lip cleft. Secondary revisions of the scar and later nasal plastic surgical procedures may be necessary to give the ultimate benefit in final appearance.

Speech function is in all likelihood the most important area of concern in the patient with the cleft palate. Efforts are directed at prevention of the characteristic "nasal speech" pattern so frequently associated with cleft palate patients. Many studies have shown that early closure (by twelve to eighteen months of age) of at least the soft palate cleft greatly contributes to the production of good speech. Generally, it can be said that about two out of three cleft palate patients will have a very satisfactory speech result. Persistent nasal speech may occur and require extensive speech therapy and in some cases a secondary surgical procedure. In these operations, a pharyngeal flap (tissue from the back of the throat) can be rotated into place at the back of the palate to diminish the nasal air loss and thus decrease the nasal quality of the patient's speech.

Dental development is often distorted by the presence of the cleft through the gum area, abnormal development of the maxilla (upper jaw), and at times by scar tissue present as a result of the surgical closure of the cleft. Treatment should consist of a co-ordinated effort involving both the pediatric dentist for general dental care and an orthodontist for bite readjustment and the recording of key measurements of facial bone growth.

It has been said that careful examination of cleft palate patients will reveal that 90 to 100 percent of them have abnormal fluid behind the eardrum even during infancy. This is felt to be due to a malfunction of the Eustachian tube leading from the middle ear into the throat area. More often than not, tiny plastic drainage tubes must be inserted through a small incision in the eardrum and left indwelling to allow for the evacuation of this fluid. Forty to 50 percent of the children with cleft palates had significant hearing loss because of recurrent ear infections prior to the utilization of these drainage tubes. This has eliminated the problem of hearing loss, but ear infections must still be carefully watched for and promptly treated.

In summary, clefts of the lip and palate occur as accidents of development. Some hereditary factors do come into play and parent counseling is thus beneficial. Most patients following treatment obtain gratifying results in appearance and function, allowing them to lead normal and productive lives.

CREDIT: *Robert M. Swartz, M.D. (Reconstructive Plastic Surgery), Arlington Heights, Illinois.*

Clubfoot

Just a few decades ago, if a mother had been informed that her child was born with a clubfoot, she would have been terrified and would have envisioned her child with a deformity, limping and handicapped through life.

The last thirty years has changed all that. Clubfoot is now no longer considered a tragedy. Medical science has learned what to do about it. Techniques and management have been greatly improved.

The cause of clubfoot (an extreme twisting of the foot is probably a combination of events. We are not really sure. Other coexisting limb and muscle deformities may be subtle and are not always immediately apparent. Therefore a careful and thorough examination should always be made.

The pressure of the feet against the womb is a definite factor, but there may also be an inherent weakness, an inability of muscles to withstand such pressures. Thus heredity has a part in clubfoot, especially if it occurs in others in the family.

The good news, of course, is that almost all cases of clubfoot can be cured without so much as a snip of surgery.

If therapy is begun early, sometimes in the hospital nursery, complete recovery often occurs.

Verifying diagnosis is the important first step. The treatment is two-pronged: to correct the deformity and to build up muscle strength to maintain that correction. As the child gets older the good corrective therapy—casts, braces, etc.—becomes even more effective. Surgery, however, may be needed if the muscles do not respond adequately to conservative therapy. Each child should be evaluated individually because there are varying degrees of severity of clubfoot, and in the more severe cases surgery may be required.

CREDIT: *Jay M. Arena, M.D.; Department of Pediatrics; Duke University Medical Center, Durham, North Carolina; author of* Child Safety Is No Accident, *with Miriam Bachar, M.A., Durham, North Carolina: Duke University Press. John M. Harrelson, M.D., Assistant Professor of Orthopedics, Duke University Medical School, Durham, North Carolina.*

Cold

(*The Common Cold*)

The famous physician Sir William Osler once said, "There is just one way to treat a cold and that's with contempt." Few Americans heed this advice. Instead, they spend over half a billion dollars a year for non-prescription decongestants, antihistamines, and other cough and cold remedies. At this very moment, thirty million Americans are suffering with a cold. If you are not among them, chances are three out of four that you will have a cold at some time during the year.

The common cold is caused by a virus, which is picked up from someone who has it. There is no sure way to avoid catching cold. Some people seem to catch colds frequently. Others seem rarely or never to have one. The best protection is to get enough rest, eat properly and stay at arm's length from anyone who is sneezing, blowing or coughing.

It is important to be aware that a variety of viruses may cause what feels and looks like a common cold but exposure to allergens and irritating substances may produce the same symptoms. There is no evidence that going without a hat, getting your feet wet, sitting bare-armed in an air-conditioned room, or exposure to cold winds will bring on a cold. Excellent studies by W. E. C. Andrews in England point out that patients who are not carrying one of the viruses that cause the common cold can be exposed naked and soaking wet to icy gales and not get a cold. However, they may experience some stuffiness of the nose when they return to a warm room. This is not a cold but is due to changes in the degree of nasal congestion as they shift from cold to a warm environment.

A recent Food and Drug Administration report noted that cold medications relieve certain symptoms but do not prevent, cure or shorten the duration of the "common cold." It lasts seven to fourteen days no matter what you do.

Still, most of us must "do something" even though we have been told repeatedly it won't make much difference. For this reason, many physicians recommend cold remedies, even though they are rarely dramatically effective. Certain medications, however, can make you feel better if they are used properly.

For example, locally applied decongestants in the form of nose drops or sprays can unplug a stuffed nose whether caused by a cold or an allergy. These preparations shrink the dilated blood vessels and temporarily reduce swelling in the mucous membranes that line the nasal passageway. This makes breathing easier.

But there is a hazard. Often as the effect wears off, the membranes swell again, sometimes worse than before. After about three days, this condition, known in medical jargon as the rebound phenomenon or, more elegantly, as rhinitis medicamentosa, may develop.

To break this vicious cycle, some physicians advise discontinuing the nose drops or sprays on one side for several days, and then on the other. This allows breathing on one side while the other recovers from the rebound effects of the decongestant. Avoid the rebound phenomenon by using topical decongestants no more than three days at a time at recommended intervals.

Oral decongestants do not cause the rebound phenomenon but still should not be used longer than a week. These medications are not recommended for people with high blood pressure, heart disease, diabetes or thyroid problems.

Antihistamines help relieve runny nose, sneezing, and itchy eyes and nose caused by allergies, but they do not relieve the cold itself.

A precaution: Antihistamines may actually increase and thicken the mucus in your lungs and set the stage for bronchial complications. People with high blood pressure, diabetes, glaucoma or prostate disease should check with a physician before taking any cold remedy.

Another warning: Antihistamines may cause drowsiness which might make it dangerous to operate automobiles or machinery.

Cough suppressants (antitussives) temporarily relieve the urge to cough, but sometimes the cough reflex is essential for clearing secretions from the lungs and should not be suppressed. Anybody with a persistent cough should consult a physician. A fever of over 100° F. is *not* part of an ordinary cold in an adult and should be reported to a doctor.

Various cold remedies may cause minor side effects such as drowsiness, excessively dry nose and mouth, nervousness and sleeplessness if taken before bedtime.

One of the worst things that has happened to the common cold since the pharmaceutical industry has come up with "packaged relief" is that people tend to ignore the old-fashioned home remedies which are much less expensive and equally as effective. I refer to bed rest, hot tea with a teaspoon of honey, hot milk with egg yolk, sugar and a little vanilla (in Yiddish it's called a "gawgell-mauggel"—which is delicious), warm baths and the old stand-by, chicken soup. Aspirin is still good for relieving minor aches and fever.

In 1975 Linus Pauling, the distinguished scientist (twice winner of the Nobel Prize), came out with the theory that massive doses of Vitamin C would prevent (and cure) the common cold. Needless to say, the manufacturers of vitamins profited handsomely from the statement, but after a few months many True Believers were sniffling and blowing in spite of the massive doses and some had come down with something worse than a cold— kidney damage. So much for that "magic formula," although many people insist that Vitamin C has alleviated the discomfort to a noticeable degree.

The best way to keep from getting a cold is (a) get sufficient rest, (b) eat a balanced diet, (c) don't get chummy with someone who has one.

CREDIT: *Louis Weinstein, M.D., Peter Bent Brigham Hospital, Boston, and Visiting Professor of Medicine, Harvard, Cambridge, Massachusetts.*

Colitis

Colitis by definition means "inflammation of the colon." The colon is the part of the gut extending from the upper end of the large bowel down to the rectum, which is the lower end of the large bowel.

Only acute inflammatory conditions of the colon should be termed colitis. The inflammation can begin suddenly and appear a few hours to a day or so after eating contaminated foods, water, etc. It is called "acute colitis" or "acute enterocolitis" if the small bowel is also inflamed. It is generally due to a virus, bacteria, or parasites (or the by-products of these). If a specific causal agent is known, it is usually included in the description of the acute colitis, for example, "amoebic colitis." The specific "acute colitis" may subside in a few days without treatment, for example, "Tourista," "Montezuma's Revenge," etc. In some instances, however, the inflammation may be rampant and the bowel movements torrential, containing blood and pus. These stools should be examined in a laboratory, the specific causal organism isolated, and its sensitivity to various medicines tested. Patients with this type of acute colitis may require hospitalization and treatment with intravenous fluids and antibiotics. A colon X ray and a rectosigmoidoscopic examination may help to establish a specific cause.

"Acute colitis" is seldom a serious, life-threatening problem, but it may carry some risk in the very young and the elderly. It is primarily a problem in the United States in patients who have recently traveled to foreign countries. Treatment consists of avoiding solid foods and taking fluids to combat dehydration. If fever of 101 degrees is present or if there is blood in the bowel movement, the advice of a physician should be promptly sought.

Often a *"nervous bowel"* or "irritable bowel" is erroneously called colitis, for example, "spastic colitis," "mucous colitis," etc. Patients with these problems who may well have loose, urgent and watery stools do not have "colitis," for there is no inflammation of the colon. It is a mistake to label these patients under the category of colitis. This problem can be worrisome and frightening and require extensive and expensive medical investigation to exclude true colitis. It is a derangement of the bowel motor function and is not due to disease. It is not a precursor to a diseased bowel nor is it a symptom of cancer.

Chronic ulcerative colitis is a serious disease of the large bowel. It is a chronic, non-specific inflammatory and ulcerative disease of the colon. Its cause is not known, but much research is being done and hopefully we may have an answer in the not too distant future. It is not infectious nor does it seem to be inherited. The patient usually has frequent bowel movements— small in amount—often urgent, and the stools frequently contain red blood and pus. The patient is ill, has a poor appetite with weight loss, often to the point of emaciation. Fever of a low-grade character is often present and abdominal cramping is common. It may begin abruptly and persist for months, but often it starts insidiously and may come and go only to gradually worsen and become persistent.

This illness seems more likely to begin in youngsters of either sex, but may start in middle or even old age. Severe attacks may be associated with leg ulcers or joint problems, especially a low back pain, or eye symptoms. It can be a life-threatening disease.

The weight loss and general deterioration cause the patient to feel ill and the disease may progress to marked enlargement of the bowel and even rupture. Some patients do well, but many experience recurrent flare-ups. Patients seldom develop cancer during the first ten years of the disease, regardless of the severity of the inflammation. However, any patient who has had ulcerative colitis for ten years or longer regardless of the severity has a definite increased risk of developing cancer. Cancer risk is especially great if the patient developed the illness as a child and has had it for ten or more years.

Diagnosis is made by proctosigmoidoscopy and colon X ray. A relatively new procedure using a flexible colonoscope allows for visual inspection of the entire colon and this may on occasions be needed. Treatment consists of a high protein, low residue diet. Sulfasalazine is often helpful and can be used over long periods with benefit. Cortisone preparations are frequently used, but these have many side effects and should be used with caution.

If the disease is not responding to medical treatment, surgical removal of the entire colon and rectum is the treatment of choice and the results are very satisfactory. Unfortunately, even if the patient has done well after a period of ten years, the risk of cancer looms great and removal of the colon must be given serious consideration. Removal of the colon and rectum means there must be an opening of the small bowel to the abdominal wall. The contents of the small bowel then empty either into a sack or into an intestinal internal pouch (Brooke ileostomy). The surgery is quite successful and many patients live their normal life expectancy and do not find their lifestyle greatly restricted. Surgery, of course, precludes the risk of cancer of the colon, which is a major threat if the patient retains the large bowel. This is a serious disease and chronic ulcerative colitis should be treated only by a thoroughly competent physician, preferably a gastroenterologist.

Crohn's disease (inflammatory bowel disease, regional enteritis, segmental colitis) is often classified as colitis. It is frequently confused with chronic ulcerative colitis. If it involves the terminal part of the small bowel, it may be called terminal or regional ileitis ("President Eisenhower disease"). It may or may not be limited to the small bowel, but can involve the small and the large bowel or just the large bowel. The distal large bowel (rectum) is often spared in Crohn's disease whereas this is nearly always involved, very early, in ulcerative colitis. The patient usually has abdominal cramps and symptoms much like those of chronic ulcerative colitis except that bowel movements usually occur less frequently, perhaps only two to five a day, and may have no red blood. The disease is often discovered when an operation is performed for supposed appendicitis. These patients heal poorly and may develop fistulas (openings from the bowel to the abdominal wall), etc. Often the patient with Crohn's disease may have abscesses and fistulas about the rectum and this may be the first hint as to the diagnosis. A proctosigmoidoscopic examination may be negative. A colon and small bowel X ray are often needed for diagnosis. A colonoscopic examination may be helpful.

In general, the same treatment advice is often given as that described above for ulcerative colitis. However, there seems a little more rationale for not removing the whole colon and rectum in Crohn's disease and the threat of cancer that is such a major problem in ulcerative colitis is very minimal in Crohn's disease and perhaps can be ignored.

Unfortunately, Crohn's disease does have a tendency to recur after surgery, whereas this seldom is the case in ulcerative colitis. Crohn's disease is not a condition that should be treated by a lay person or druggist. The patient with this condition should seek a highly competent physician, preferably a gastroenterologist.

CREDIT: *James C. Cain, M.D., Gastroenterology and Internal Medicine, Mayo Clinic, Rochester, Minnesota.*

Conduct

(*How to Get Along with Others*)

(1) Keep skid chains on your tongue. Say less than you think. Cultivate a pleasant voice. How you say it is often more important than what you say.

(2) Make few promises and keep them faithfully, no matter what the cost.

(3) Never let an opportunity pass to give a well-deserved compliment.

(4) If criticism is needed, do it tactfully. Don't use a sledgehammer when a fly swatter will do the job.

(5) Be interested in others—their work, their homes and families. Let everyone you meet feel that you regard him as a person of importance.

(6) Don't burden or depress those around you by dwelling on your minor aches and pains and small disappointments. Everyone has something in his life that is not exactly as he would like it to be.

(7) Discuss, don't argue. It is a mark of a superior mind to be able to disagree without being disagreeable.

(8) Let your virtues, if you have any, speak for themselves. Be constructive. Don't indulge in gossip. It is a waste of time and can be destructive. People who throw mudballs always manage to end up getting a little on themselves.

(9) Be respectful of the feelings of others. Wit and humor at the expense of a friend is rarely worth the small laugh, and it may hurt more than you know.

(10) Pay no attention to derogatory remarks about you. The person who carried the message may not be the world's most accurate reporter. Simply live so that nobody will believe him. Insecurity (or a stomach-ache, a toothache, or a headache) is often at the root of most backbiting.

(11) Do your best to forget about the "rewards." If you deserve credit someone will "remember." Success is much sweeter that way.

(12) Keep in mind that the true measure of an individual is how he treats a person who can do him absolutely no good.

CREDIT: *Ann Landers.*

Constipation

Once upon a time a young lady consulted an eminent specialist for headaches. The great man gave her a laxative. "But, doctor," she said, "I move my bowels every day." "I know," he replied, "but you are always twenty-four hours late." This story epitomizes the problem of defining a "normal" frequency of passing feces. For babies and natives of the tropics, three to four stools daily are common. Many healthy Westerners defecate once every two or three days. In general, bowel habits ranging between one movement every three days and three movements per day are compatible with health. The idea that a daily stool is necessary to avoid "intestinal toxemia," with headaches, tiredness, apathy and old age, is a myth.

TYPES OF CONSTIPATION

Three major varieties of constipation exist. The first (and most serious) is caused by gradual narrowing and obstruction of the colonic tube, where the feces become more solid. Cancer may be responsible. In others, colonic narrowing is caused by a chronic inflammation, usually *diverticulitis*. This disorder may develop in numerous little colonic pouches known as diverticulums which commonly form as people grow older. The narrowing, whether cancerous or inflammatory, causes increased blockage of the bowel. Its main feature, therefore, is a *change* in bowel habits over weeks to months and usually affects those past middle age. Symptoms are: increasingly infrequent stools, straining, lack of that good feeling after bowel movement, and cramps. Progressive constipation of this type means you should seek medical advice right away. Furthermore, if any such symptoms occur, examine your bowel movements carefully to see if there are any flecks of blood. Blood in the stools should also get you to the physician's office immediately. The cause *may be* no more than hemorrhoids that bleed when a hard stool is passed, but you should check regardless.

The second type of constipation is known as *spastic constipation*. The muscular walls of the colon, especially the sigmoid, instead of providing a relaxed reservoir between peristaltic waves, stay in a contracted state, or a "spasm." This holds up the passage of feces and they dry out and form little hard pellets (like rabbit dung). Difficult and incomplete evacuation of the rectum is common, and the spastic sigmoid is often sore and tender to touch. Straining to produce a few mucus-covered pellets is typical. The causes of spastic constipation are not absolutely known, but irregular bowel habits (not heeding an urge to pass feces), no breakfast to stimulate a bowel movement, nervous tension, laxative abuse and a variety of dietary habits are often the cause.

The third common type is atonic constipation. The rectum fills with feces but there is no urge to move the bowels. As might be expected, it is a disorder principally of old age, but persistent failure to respond to "nature's call" as well as dietary practices may play a role. In a few cases, a severe psychiatric disorder may be responsible. Essentially, the muscles of the colon gradually give up their normal function.

TREATMENT

Symptoms of the first type of constipation, with bowel habits changing over weeks to months, means you should see a doctor right away.

Regular Bowel Habits. Spastic and atonic constipation benefit from attempts to move the bowels regularly, preferably at the same time daily. People with conventional working hours should get up in time to have some breakfast and then, shortly after, go to the toilet and try to have a bowel movement. Straining is inadvisable, but intermittent and voluntary "bearing down" may be attempted. Obviously, regular bowel habits cannot be established by half-hearted and brief attempts. A month or two may pass before there is even partial success.

Diet. A few years ago a "low roughage diet" was recommended for spastic constipation, but current medical thought favors a high fiber (in the past called "high residue" or "roughage") intake for both spastic and atonic constipation. The idea is that food residues in the colon should be bulky: The colon likes to stay in trim by having something to work on. The eating of high-fiber content food like bran, unrefined flour products, leafy vegetables, or fruits—all of which contain substances our small intestine cannot digest or absorb—means that the huge bacterial population of the large bowel has the food needed to produce gas bubbles that prevent feces from compacting, and to release products that have a slight laxative action. Fruit juices, especially prune juice, may also be helpful. It is also a good idea to drink at least five or six glasses of water every day.

Laxatives. Laxatives as a rule should be avoided by those who have spastic constipation. If a laxative habit has already been established, it should be broken. Laxatives in general are of four types:

(A) Stool softeners containing mineral oil. The trouble with mineral oil is that in large amounts it may interfere with absorption of some vitamins. After prolonged use, the oil may fail to mix with the stools. Leaking may occur and cause embarrassment.

(B) Non-irritant bulk producers and stool softeners. Some of these substances, which absorb and hold water, swell up in the bowel to produce, it is hoped, a soft bulky mass.

(C) Salts that are poorly absorbed and retain water in the colon. The most common are magnesium salts such as magnesium sulfate, carbonate, or hydroxide (milk of magnesia).

(D) Irritants. These contain substances that stimulate the intestinal muscles and nerves. Phenolphthalein and cascara are common ingredients in many widely advertised preparations. Use of this type is in general inadvisable, because it tends to make the bowel dependent on an artificial stimulant to get into action. Castor oil, of course, is a famous old-time irritant laxative but not intended for prolonged use.

Types A and B are to be preferred if any laxatives are used. The irritant type (D) should be particularly avoided by those with spastic constipation, for these medicines may produce muscular colonic spasms which are at the root of the trouble. In spastic constipation, attempts to establish regular bowel habits may have to be encouraged by initial use of laxative types A or B. The ultimate objective, however, is to wean the patient off all laxatives.

In atonic constipation, all types of laxatives may have to be used, especially by the elderly sedentary person. In fact, one may hold that in such persons continued use of laxatives, including types C and D, is necessary and not really harmful.

Enemas. Like laxatives, enemas can act as bulk producers, irritants, or both. The mildest enema is one teaspoon of salt added to a pint of warm water. One quart of this solution, can be run in slowly, held five minutes, and then passed. Plain water is less desirable. Soap enemas are irritating. (Note: If you are on a salt-free diet, do not add salt to the water if you take an enema!)

Enemas of all types have no place in the prolonged treatment of constipation. They can be used as semi-emergency procedures if the patient is very uncomfortable and after three days finds it is still impossible to defecate.

Constipation existing for years is in itself no cause for concern. It causes no symptoms except abdominal discomfort and difficult evacuation of the rectum. A regular daily bowel movement is nice but not necessary. The treatment of constipation depends on establishing regular bowel habits and heeding, not postponing, going to the toilet if an urge to move the bowels is felt. Good dietary habits, including breakfast which consists of high fiber foods, are important. The laxatives or occasionally enemas should be used only as crutches if other measures fail. Don't forget, however, that constipation coming on over a few weeks or months, blood in the stools, or both, may mean more serious trouble and requires medical attention.

Laxatives and enemas should *not* be used when constipation accompanies abdominal pains that are sudden, unusually severe or complicated by nausea, vomiting or fever. See a doctor and make sure the discomfort is not a symptom of a more complicated problem.

CREDIT: *Franz J. Ingelfinger, M.D., Editor,* New England Journal of Medicine, *Cambridge, Massachusetts.*

Contraceptives

No method of contraception is perfect for every woman all the time. This doesn't mean that the available methods don't work—they do. But a method which works perfectly for one woman may not be suitable for another. How, then, can you find out which method is right for you?

There are several considerations:

Safety: The ideal method of preventing pregnancy must be safe to use. All of the methods mentioned here have a high degree of safety.

Effectiveness: Will the method do what it's supposed to? Will it work? While any method is better than none, not all are equally effective. Furthermore, effectiveness depends in large part on whether or not any method is used properly and regularly.

Medical Desirability: Some methods are not suitable for women who have had certain ailments, or whose present health is not good. Other women may find one method causes discomfort while others do not.

Convenience: The less the method interferes with your normal life, the better it is.

Cost: None of the methods discussed here can really be called expensive, though some cost more than others. Women who cannot afford a private doctor can usually pay the lower fees at clinics or obtain the services free if they are public aid recipients or visit public health departments.

Personal Feelings: This is important too. Any method which you find unpleasant, uncomfortable, or embarrassing may not be right for you. Don't hesitate to discuss your feelings with your doctor. He or she will help you select the best method for you.

Note: Two methods of birth control not covered here are voluntary sterilization and abortion. Sterilization of both men and women should be regarded as a permanent form of birth control. Vasectomy and tubal ligations are reversible in only a small percentage of cases. Abortion is considered a "backup" method when regular contraceptives fail.

EFFECTIVENESS

How effective a method of birth control is depends on how well the method itself works, and how correctly and regularly it is used. For example, the condom or rubber sheath is a relatively effective method if used properly. If, however, it is put on at the wrong time, it may not be effective at all.

Because a birth control method is only effective if it is used properly, the method that makes the couple feel the most natural and comfortable is often the "best method."

THE PILL

The pill works by imitating some of the normal body reactions that take place during pregnancy. When a woman becomes pregnant, her body stops producing eggs until after the baby is born. When a woman takes birth control pills, much the same thing happens even though she isn't pregnant. That is, the hormones contained in the pill "signal" the body not to produce an egg (or ovum), just as naturally produced hormones act during pregnancy. With no egg present for the male sperm to meet and fertilize, a woman cannot become pregnant.

The medical practitioner decides which kind of pill is best for each woman, as there are different kinds of pills. Pills vary in chemical composition, so side effects can sometimes be removed by changing to another type of pill. If the pills are started on the correct day they are effective immediately.

ADVANTAGES

(1) When used properly, this is the most effective method next to sterilization.

(2) No special preparations necessary before intercourse.

(3) Provides protection against pregnancy at all times.

(4) No special training required to learn to use the method. Pills are taken just like aspirin or any other tablet.

(5) Since pills are taken daily whether intercourse takes place or not, there is less temptation to take a chance on going without protection "just this once"—a very real danger with some methods.

(6) No need to insert anything into the vagina either before or after intercourse, or even to touch the female organs.

(7) Allows a woman to regulate and plan her monthly cycle.

(8) Usually causes a lighter menstrual flow.

(9) Often clears complexion.

(10) It's a good method for the woman whose partner does not want to accept responsibility for contraception, or may not want her to use another method.

DISADVANTAGES

(1) Pills must be taken regularly whether intercourse takes place or not. Women who have intercourse infrequently may prefer another method, feeling pills an unnecessary precaution or the expense not worthwhile.

(2) Possible trouble remembering to take a pill at the same time each day.

(3) Some women have a fear of swallowing pills or any other medications, feeling all drugs are "unnatural."

(4) A medical examination and a prescription are necessary.

(5) Pills should not be taken while breast-feeding.

(6) Side effects are a possibility. Some—though not all—women, during the first month or two of pill-taking, experience minor discomforts similar to complaints women have in early stages of pregnancy (nausea or morning sickness, spotting or bleeding between periods, gain or loss in weight, tenderness or enlargement of breasts). These side effects almost always disappear during the first few months.

(7) It has been estimated that about one woman in two thousand on the pill is hospitalized for a blood-clotting disorder. For this reason, women who have had blood clots should not use this method.

(8) Women who have had migraine, fibroids of the womb, heart or kid-

ney disease, asthma, high blood pressure, mental depression, diabetes, sickle cell anemia or epilepsy should be sure to tell the doctor. As these conditions may be aggravated by the pill, some other method of birth control will usually be recommended.

(9) More serious complications, encountered by a small percentage of women taking the pill, include eye trouble, stroke, liver tumors, decreased sex drive or high blood pressure.

IUD (INTRAUTERINE DEVICE)

The IUD, also known as the "coil" or "loop," differs considerably from the other methods discussed here because the woman using it bears almost no responsibility for its effectiveness. In fact, she need hardly be concerned with it at all, once it is inserted.

The IUD is a small, white, soft plastic device that is inserted into the uterus (womb) by a physician and left in place for as long as the woman desires to prevent pregnancy. No other contraceptive is necessary once the IUD is in position, and the woman wearing it should be totally unaware of its presence. The woman should, however, examine herself after each menstrual period, at the least, to make sure the device is still in place. This is done by inserting the index finger well into the vagina to feel for the short nylon threads protruding from the cervix.

There is some uncertainty as to exactly how the IUD works, but there is no doubt about its effectiveness. While some women using IUDs have become pregnant, the actual number is quite small.

A small amount of copper wound around certain IUDs seems to increase their effectiveness.

ADVANTAGES

(1) Once inserted, little or no thought need be given to contraception by either the woman or the man.

(2) Can be left in place for years without apparent harm. The copper IUD must be replaced every two years because the copper gradually loses its effectiveness.

(3) Apart from the initial cost of the IUD itself and the medical fee for insertion, there are no additional expenses. (A medical checkup once a year is advisable but this should be standard procedure for a woman whether she is using an IUD or not.)

DISADVANTAGES

(1) It is common for women to have a heavier menstrual flow with the IUD, especially during the first and second periods after the insertion.

(2) Some women are unable to retain the device and it is expelled by contractions of the uterus. This is more apt to happen to women who have had no children.

(3) Cramps and backaches may occur during the first few days, particularly in women who have not had children. They usually disappear within a week, but if they do not, the woman will usually prefer to have the device removed.

(4) Temporary spotting or bleeding may occur between periods during the first few months—an inconvenience but no cause for alarm.

(5) There is a slight risk of infection; rejection of the device by the body; perforation of the uterine wall; septic abortion; or an undiscovered allergy to copper.

(6) Insertion of the IUD must be done by a medical practitioner and is a delicate and initially uncomfortable procedure. The fee varies, so it is wise to discuss this with your practitioner in advance, if cost is important.

(7) For greater effectiveness—close to 100 percent—foam may be used as a reinforcing method of contraception during the most fertile days of the monthly cycle (mid-cycle).

DIAPHRAGM

The diaphragm method is highly effective and has been used successfully for more than eighty years. It involves the use of a contraceptive cream or jelly in combination with a device called a vaginal diaphragm, which is made of soft rubber, shaped like a shallow bowl, with a flexible spring rim.

When properly placed, the diaphragm fits securely and comfortably between the rear wall of the vagina and the upper edge of the pubic bone. In that position, it completely covers the cervix and holds the contraceptive cream or jelly tighty cupped over the entrance to the womb. This provides a chemical barrier that acts to kill the male sperm.

After the diaphragm is removed, it should be washed with a mild soap and water, dried and powdered with cornstarch and returned to the case. Occasionally it should be held up to the light or filled with water to see if there are any cracks or leaks.

ADVANTAGES

(1) Women using the diaphragm need only concern themselves with being protected at those times when they expect to have intercourse.

(2) Diaphragm and jelly need not be inserted just before intercourse. A woman may insert them as much as two hours beforehand and still be protected.

(3) When it is properly positioned, the woman should not feel the device,

no matter how active she may be. (If she does, it is either the wrong size for her or has been inserted incorrectly.)

(4) No need to get up after intercourse to douche or remove the device. In fact, the diaphragm should be left in place for at least eight hours after intercourse.

(5) Whether or not intercourse takes place, the diaphragm may be safely left in place for twenty-four hours or even longer. However, if intercourse is delayed more than two hours after insertion of the diaphragm, additional jelly or cream should be inserted. (It is not necessary to remove the diaphragm.) If intercourse is repeated, insert more cream or jelly and leave diaphragm in place.

DISADVANTAGES

(1) Women must first be "measured" by a medical practitioner. The proper size must be determined if the method is to be at all effective. The practitioner will then instruct her on how to insert and remove it properly.

(2) Cannot be obtained without a prescription.

(3) Must be used whenever intercourse takes place. Sometimes this means an interruption in order to insert the diaphragm, if intercourse at a particular time was not anticipated.

(4) Women who have a strong aversion to inserting a device into the vagina will obviously not be happy with this method.

(5) Women must be measured following pregnancy, miscarriage, abortion, gynecological surgery, or weight gain or loss of at least ten pounds.

CONDOM

The condom, or rubber, is made to be placed over the male organ (penis) just before sex relations. It keeps the man's fluid (semen) with its sperm from getting into the woman's vagina.

Originally designed as a prophylactic to guard against contracting venereal disease, the condom has gained popularity steadily as a contraceptive device as well. Improved production methods and materials plus federal government quality control checks have greatly reduced the possibility of defects and made this a good, effective method, if properly used.

The condom may be used by itself, or the woman may use contraceptive jelly, cream or foam at the same time for added protection.

When putting on the condom, at least a half inch of space should be left at the tip to collect semen, if the type of condom being used does not already have a nipple-like "sperm bank" at its tip. To ensure that the condom doesn't slip off as the male withdraws, he or his partner should hold on to the top (open end).

ADVANTAGES

(1) Best method for the man who prefers to be in complete charge of contraception.

(2) Guards against VD.

(3) Handy as a supplementary method for the balance of a monthly cycle of pill-taking if the woman forgets to take a pill.

(4) A good method to use after childbirth, before the woman has had a chance to have a diaphragm refitted, or before her medical practitioner thinks it wise to prescribe pills or insert an IUD.

(5) An effective alternative when the woman is reluctant to equip herself with any birth control device—for whatever reason.

(6) Inexpensive, conveniently available in every drugstore (no prescription needed), easy to carry.

DISADVANTAGES

(1) Care must be taken in putting it on properly, which may interrupt love play.

(2) Withdrawal must take place fairly soon after the man's ejaculation so the condom does not loosen and slip off, or fluid escape into the vagina.

(3) Some men report dulling of sensation during intercourse.

(4) Prelubricated condoms may seem to the user to be somewhat "messy."

(5) After long shelf-life, latex may tend to dry out and tear during use unless used with jelly or cream.

FOAM, JELLY OR CREAM

A simpler technique for the woman to use than inserting a diaphragm, though not rated as effective. The spermicide products are designed to be used without a diaphragm or other contraceptive device.

The woman merely inserts a measured dosage of the spermicide into the vagina, just prior to each intercourse, with a special plastic applicator provided for that purpose.

The contraceptive action of these preparations is twofold. The spermicidal ingredients work to kill the male sperm while the foam, cream or jelly base provides a "barrier" over the cervix that helps prevent sperm from entering the womb.

These products are not the same as the creams and jellies intended for use with a diaphragm.

ADVANTAGES

(1) Can be bought without a prescription. However, since not all products are equally effective, it is still wise to ask a doctor's advice as to which is best.

(2) No fitting is necessary, such as that done before obtaining a diaphragm.

(3) The woman needs no special training in how to use the method. The instructions that come with each product provide complete directions for use.

(4) Nothing to remove after intercourse.

(5) Douching is not necessary. But if a woman does desire to douche, she should wait six hours after intercourse.

(6) Need be used only at those times when intercourse takes place.

(7) Is an inexpensive method to use.

(8) Products are mildly lubricating, which may be an advantage in some cases.

(9) Provides some protection from VD.

DISADVANTAGES

(1) Must be applied just before intercourse, which may mean interruption of love play.

(2) If intercourse is repeated, another applicator full must be inserted beforehand. One application provides protection for only one intercourse.

(3) Applicator must be washed with soap and water after each use.

(4) Some women experience itching, burning, or soreness of the vagina after use of a spermicide. Changing brands may help.

RHYTHM ("NATURAL" METHODS)

The rhythm method is perhaps the simplest of all contraceptive procedures. It is also the most difficult to use effectively because of the complex problem of determining the "safe" days.

Three biological facts provide the basis for the rhythm method:

(1) A woman normally produces only one egg during each menstrual cycle.

(2) This egg lives only about twenty-four hours, and it is only during this period that it can be fertilized by the male sperm.

(3) The sperm lives for only forty-eight hours, so it is only during this two-day interval that it can fertilize the female egg.

The obvious conclusion from these three facts is that there are really only seventy-two hours—a mere three days—each month when intercourse can lead to pregnancy; the two days before the female egg is released, and the full day afterward. If a woman could avoid having intercourse during this time, she would be in no danger of becoming pregnant.

That is the idea behind the rhythm method. A woman using this method must refrain from having intercourse on the days when she can become pregnant. Put another way, she must limit her sexual activities to the days during each monthly cycle which are known to be "safe."

The "ovulation" or "mucus" method refers to a way a woman can determine between periods whether or not she is in her ovulatory, or unsafe, phase, by paying close attention to sensations of wetness or dryness from the vagina.

This method is sometimes called the Billings method, after the Australian doctor who first described it.

Note: It is important to have instruction from a clinician to apply this method to your body.

ADVANTAGES

(1) No prescription is necessary, nor is any sort of "fitting" required. Medical guidance, however, should be sought, for without it your chances of success with this method are apt to be slim.

(2) No special equipment or contraceptive materials are necessary. You do need a calendar, of course, and possibly a thermometer.

(3) It is not necessary to take any drugs or to insert anything into vagina.

(4) There is no need to interrupt relations to arrange for adequate protection. (It is absolutely necessary, though, to avoid intercourse completely on those days which are suspected of being unsafe.)

(5) No side effects or allergic reactions from contraceptive materials.

DISADVANTAGES

(1) A written record of periods must be kept for at least a year prior to attempting to use the rhythm method since success depends on accurate prediction of time of ovulation.

(2) A daily record of body temperature (taken immediately upon awakening with a specially marked "basal body temperature thermometer") is also advisable. This record alone is not enough, however, since illness or other factors may affect body temperature.

(3) It is not safe to use this method during the first few months after childbirth.

(4) If a woman has vaginitis, which produces its own discharge, the ovulation (mucus) method cannot be used.

WITHDRAWAL

Withdrawal, or coitus interruptus, refers to the withdrawal of the male organ (penis) before the man "comes," so that sperm are not deposited in or near the vagina. This method is not too reliable and should be used preferably only when no other method is available.

ADVANTAGES

(1) No drug or chemical is needed to use this method.
(2) It is available any time, anywhere.
(3) It does not cost anything.

DISADVANTAGES

(1) Failures may occur because of poor control, carelessness or because sperm are sometimes released before the man's orgasm, or climax.
(2) Worry that withdrawal will not take place in time may lessen enjoyment of intercourse for either or both partners.
(3) The woman, if she is slower to reach orgasm than the man, may be left unsatisfied or frustrated after withdrawal takes place.

QUITE INEFFECTIVE METHODS

Vaginal foaming tablets, sold at drugstores, are inexpensive and no prescription needed. They are simple to use. The high failure rate of this method is due to the fact that the spermicide does not get evenly distributed through the vagina. The tablet should be moistened with saliva or water and immediately inserted deep into the birth canal at least fifteen minutes before each sex act so it has time to dissolve. A new tablet should be used before each sex act. Tablets lose their effectiveness one hour after insertion whether intercourse has taken place or not. Douching, if desired afterward, should be postponed until at least six hours after the last sex act.

Vaginal suppositories are small and waxy, and sometimes contain a sperm-killing chemical. A suppository is inserted into the birth canal ten to fifteen minutes before each sex act so it has time to melt at body temperature. Sometimes it will not melt quickly enough, or it may be incorrectly inserted. It is not reliable enough to be recommended.

INEFFECTIVE METHODS AND MYTHS. BEWARE OF BOTH

Douching as a method to avoid becoming pregnant is risky. Douching consists of washing out the birth canal with a solution of one kind or another in the hope of removing the sperm. Since sperm enter the womb seconds after a man "comes," it is impossible to wash them out with a douche, even if immediate. Sometimes the force of the water actually helps to wash the sperm into the womb.

Some believe that if they "hold back" during intercourse, not allowing themselves to reach orgasm, pregnancy is impossible. This belief is based on the misconception that women, like men, ejaculate in orgasm a substance which is necessary for fertilization. This is not true.

There is no truth, either, in the belief that as long as a woman is nursing a baby she cannot conceive. Because of hormonal balances, during early months of breast feeding ovulation may be delayed, but this protection does not last long, nor is it reliable.

Certain products—sprays, douches, suppositories—are sold as aids to "feminine hygiene." In some cases, these widely advertised products hint at birth control in order to fool buyers. Many women buy these products in the mistaken belief that they will prevent pregnancy. Not so!

If you want more information about birth control, pregnancy detection, sterilization, infertility referral, problem pregnancy counseling and referral, or any other matters relating to reproductive health care, Planned Parenthood Association can help you.

CREDIT: *Deborah Roach, Planned Parenthood Association/Chicago Area, 55 East Jackson Boulevard, Chicago, Illinois 60604.*

DESTROYING THEIR MORALS WITH CONTRACEPTIVES

DEAR ANN LANDERS: Your agreeing with the high-school student who believed it should be legal for him to purchase contraceptives (he lives in Massachusetts) was shocking.

People expect you, Ann Landers, to uphold the moral standards. Instead you go along with the weaklings who will surely destroy our civilization by their hedonism and decadence.

You ought to be telling high-school kids to pay more attention to their studies. Young boys should be advised to treat girls with respect. Young girls should be instructed to think of their bodies as holy temples. Our teen-agers need to be told sexual promiscuity begets disgust, disease, unhappiness and misery.

When I was growing up only the crudest boys and the cheapest girls (we called them "tramps") had sex just for the fun of it. All this looseness has come about since World War II, thanks to advertising, pornography, trashy movies and the affluent society.

I think you could do a lot to stem the tide if you had the courage to speak out and didn't worry so much about being called a square.

Tell your young male readers that self-control is a wonderful thing and when they have the urge, a cold shower can do wonders to get their minds up above the belt and back on the books where they belong. ANOTHER VOICE FROM MASSACHUSETTS (WORCESTER)

DEAR VOICE: I agree that self-control is a wonderful thing. I also believe that virginity is beautiful—if a girl can hang on to it. But to tell a high-school senior who is trying to buy contraceptives in a drugstore that he should take a cold shower and forget about it is ridiculous.

Once a teen-ager (male or female) has crossed the line and experienced sex, he or she is not about to stop just because contraceptives are illegal. What they are apt to do is go ahead and take a chance on disease, pregnancy and a whole host of unfortunate events—such as a sudden end to their education, a too-early marriage, an unwanted child or an abortion.

The drive to reproduce is second only to the instinct for survival. It is inborn, demanding, persistent, compelling and it will not go away.

I say it is far better to permit sexually active young people to buy protection than to deny it to them and let them (and us) suffer the consequences.

Conversation

In her book, *How to Talk with Practically Anybody About Practically Anything,* television's "first lady," Barbara Walters, shares some of the secrets of her success in interviewing and talking with a wide variety of people, including celebrities, scientists, politicians and authors. She says at the outset that she's not concerned with conversation between friends—few of us have problems there—but even gracious and poised people tend to become rattled by the very famous, the very rich, the highly intellectual, or those in positions of power. And many people have difficulty talking with any stranger in a social setting.

After an awkward pause, one might make a comment about the weather, but such forced attempts are usually doomed to lead right back to uncomfortable silence because they open no new conversational territory.

It is necessary to take yourself in hand at the outset, and cross the "shyness barrier." One way to do this is to realize that everyone is self-conscious and afraid of saying something foolish. Since everyone has the same fear, why worry about it? Barbara cites the formula that Abigail McCarthy used to combat needless nervousness when she first came into the public spotlight. Before any interview she told herself: "I am the way I am; I look the way I look; I am my age."

The old line that the secret of being a good conversationalist is to be a good listener is only partly true. This may work among friends or relatives, but it's no way to break the ice and get a conversation going with strangers.

Start with the premise that everyone likes to talk and there is plenty to talk about. The trick is to hit on a subject of mutual interest. No one is ever bored by a genuine compliment followed by a sincere question. Something as simple as, "That's a very attractive tie (or dress). Would you mind telling me where you found it?" is better than, "It certainly is hot, isn't it?"

Easy openings are usually blocked by the real or imagined gaps which people sense between each other. These gaps can be religious, political, racial and generational. Many adults have trouble talking to anyone under thirty without becoming condescending, defensive or hostile, and—there's something about approaching a stranger sitting behind a big desk that gives a person who is usually confident and poised a feeling of inferiority.

In recent years a trend has developed among business executives to eliminate this discomfort. Their offices now have sofas and upholstered furniture which create a casual living room atmosphere. The executive moves from behind his desk and asks the visitor to join him in the less formidable setting.

Perhaps the most commonly experienced conversational block results from "the accomplishment gap." Americans may not be intimidated or impressed by nobility or titles or wealth, but they do tend to measure worth by status and achievement. Even though that person may not be famous, the salesman, housewife, or office worker often becomes tongue-tied (or worse yet, excessively verbose) when he must engage in conversation with a professor, a doctor, a scientist, etc. This is ridiculous when one stops to think about it. He is not going to be taking a competitive exam in that person's specialty, nor will he be comparing incomes. In short, there is no need to feel outclassed, overpowered or struck dumb.

You cannot go wrong if you are sincere, pleasant and natural. Try to come up with a genuine, non-obsequious opening line which has been run through the tact test. This means don't put people on the defensive. If you are going to deliver a compliment, keep it light and brief so the recipient will not be forced into a frozen smile waiting for you to finish. Long-winded praise can be as embarrassing as an insult.

We have been warned repeatedly against talking about religion or politics in a social setting. My personal opinion is that these two subjects are extremely interesting and can be a perfect bridge between individuals who are meeting for the first time. It goes without saying, one does not launch into an attack with an individual who is sure to have another point of view. For example, to open a conversation with a Catholic priest by asking what he thinks of abortion would exhibit extremely poor judgment. By the same token, don't expect a friendly response from a notoriously conservative, male chauvinist type by asking, "What do you think of the Equal Rights Amendment?" In other words, for openers, stay off subjects you know will create discomfort or a hostile response.

Needling, baiting and arguing is not conversation. Remember, it is a mark of a lady or a gentleman to be able to disagree without being disagreeable.

High-level conversation at stand-up cocktail parties is virtually impossible. Small talk is the order of the day, and, of course, this is what most people get at such affairs. One of the hazards of the stand-up cocktail party is being cornered by an interminable bore. In addition to being unable to extricate oneself, it is often difficult to hear at such parties, particularly if there is music.

So, what does one say at a cocktail party where 90 percent of the conversation is meaningless? A question is always a good opener and the best questions deal with topics of the day. A person who reads at least one newspaper daily and two or three magazines a week should be adequately informed on what is happening in the world to ask a provocative question about world affairs. ("What do you think about . . . ?") I recommend, as conversational ice-breakers, questions on current events rather than current gossip. It is never in good taste to ask questions about recent illnesses, operations, divorces, business failures, jail sentences or other unpleasantries.

One question which should *not* be asked when meeting an individual for the first time is, "How many children do you have?" It may well be that the person to whom you are speaking has no children and is unhappy about it. Another is, "I notice you aren't drinking. Is there any special reason?"

If you are seated at a dinner party and have strangers on both sides, remember to divide your time, even though one may be utterly fascinating and the other a certifiable idiot. If the idiot seems to be monopolizing you (and they invariably do), grasp the opportunity while he is taking a breath or sipping wine (or coffee) to say, "Excuse me. I must speak to the person at my right (or left). He seems to be lonely."

A good conversationalist knows how to listen. We all have experienced situations where one person's voice seems to be heard over all others. The clod with the overpowering voice invariably has no terminal facilities. He has a talent for interrupting but cannot be interrupted. If, as you read this, you are wondering, "Am I guilty of this social sin?" you probably are.

As Dear Abby says, "The person who takes over the conversation and does all the talking is as much of a pig as the person who comes to a party and eats all the food."

A sign of graciousness is to allow others to speak. The quiet one can be brought into the conversation by asking him a direct question. Everyone feels flattered when asked for his opinion.

My favorite hobby is conversation. I have learned a great deal of what I know by listening to others. When I find myself in the presence of people who have achieved success in a special field, I make it a point to be a listener, not a talker. My father used to say, "You'd be surprised how much you can learn by keeping quiet. Nobody ever learned anything while he was talking."

CREDIT: *Ann Landers. Some material derived from Barbara Walters' book,* How to Talk with Practically Anybody About Practically Anything, *Garden City, New York: Doubleday & Company, 1970.*

Convulsions in Children

If a child has a convulsion (as a result of a head injury or for other reasons) the most important thing to do is to stay with the child and watch the convulsion carefully. Try to remember that the convulsion, in and of itself, is rarely a threat to the child's life nor does it require immediate medical care.

Protect the child with pillows or blankets to keep him from hurting himself and make sure he can't fall off the bed, couch or car seat.

Turn the child on his side so saliva or vomit will run out of his mouth, not into his lungs. If the child is wearing a tight collar, loosen it. It is not necessary to place a pencil or other firm object between the child's teeth. In fact, doing so may cause more harm than good. Do not worry that the child will "swallow his tongue." This is an old wives' tale.

A convulsion can be frightening, but try to stay calm. The child will usually lose consciousness; his limbs will stiffen and then jerk; his lips and face may turn blue; his eyes may roll upward and his breathing will probably be heavy. The convulsion will probably last only a few minutes (two to ten minutes in most instances), but because of your anxiety the time will seem much longer.

Watch the child carefully so you can describe the convulsion to the doctor. If possible, notice where the convulsion starts (for example, on one side of the face, or in one arm or leg; with stomach pains or with one eye blinking, etc.). Your description will help the doctor diagnose the trouble.

When the convulsion is over, and the child is resting comfortably, call your doctor or a hospital emergency ward for further advice. Make certain the child is not left on a surface from which he can fall.

CREDIT: Accident Handbook, *Department of Health Education, the Children's Hospital Medical Center, Boston, Massachusetts.*

Coping

Ann Landers' Advice on How to Handle Crises

FOR TODAY ONLY

DEAR ANN LANDERS: Three years ago, I clipped my favorite column and carried it in my wallet until it is just barely legible. You called it "How to Get Through the Day," and it helped me more than anything I have ever read in my life. Will you play it again, Sam? LINDA

DEAR LINDA: With pleasure.

Just for today I will live through the next 12 hours and not tackle my whole life problem at once.

Just for today I will improve my mind. I will learn something useful. I will read something that requires effort, thought and concentration.

Just for today I will be agreeable. I will look my best, speak in a well-modulated voice, be courteous and considerate.

Just for today I will not find fault with friend, relative or colleague. I will not try to change or improve anyone but myself.

Just for today I will have a program. I might not follow it exactly, but I will have it. I will save myself from two enemies—hurry and indecision.

Just for today I will exercise my character in three ways. I will do a good turn and keep it a secret. If anyone finds out, it won't count.

Just for today I will do two things I don't want to do, just for exercise.

Just for today I will be unafraid. Especially will I be unafraid to enjoy what is beautiful and believe that as I give to the world, the world will give to me.

Be bigger than what happens to you.

If I were asked to give what I consider the single most useful bit of advice for all humanity it would be this: Expect trouble as an inevitable part of life and, when it comes, hold your head high, look it squarely in the eye and say, "I will be bigger than you. You cannot defeat me." Then repeat to yourself the most comforting of all words, "This too shall pass."

Maintaining self-respect in the face of a devastating experience is of prime importance. To forgive oneself is perhaps the most difficult of life's challenges. Most of us find it much easier to forgive others. I've received letters brimming with self-recrimination—letters that prove no punishment is so painful as the self-inflicted kind. Here are a few examples:

"I let my boyfriend go too far. Now, when he sees me, he looks the other way. I'm so ashamed of myself I could just die."

"I threw a dish towel in my mother-in-law's face. She was trying to be helpful and I lost my temper. I hate myself."

"I got caught cheating in a history exam today. All the kids know about it. I feel rotten."

"I'm not used to liquor. I only drink to celebrate something. Last night was my birthday and I got disgustingly drunk. I insulted people, became sick in the car and disgraced myself. I wish I was dead."

I've written this advice thousands of times:

"It's done. Finished. Over. There is nothing you can do to change the past. Take heart from the knowledge that something good can come of it if it teaches you a lesson. Profit from it—then forget it."

Most people with normal intelligence learn from experience. A white rat will refuse to follow a piece of cheese along a maze if he discovers after a few attempts that the maze will lead him into a puddle of cold water. Some humans, unhappily, don't have the common sense of a white rat. They make the same mistakes time after time. To them, experience merely helps them to recognize the mistake when they make it again. My mail is heavy with examples. A St. Louis woman writes:

"I married an alcoholic. He is brutal and I'm scared to death of him. This is the third time I've picked a loser. I knew Steve drank a little, but I had no idea he was a drunk. Why do I have such miserable luck with men?"

Specialists in the field of human behavior tell us that people who repeatedly bring disaster down on their heads are self-destructive. They feel unworthy and are unconsciously seeking punishment. Professional help must be sought to end this self-flagellation. Experience, they say, is the best teacher, but we get the grade first and the lesson later.

As a youngster I was effervescent, outgoing, and I talked too much. I had a talent for saying the wrong thing at the wrong time. By the time I was a high school freshman, I was better able to synchronize my mouth and my brain, but still I made mistakes and tortured myself because of the foolish things I had said.

One day a high school English teacher taught me with a single dramatic act the futility of rehashing the past. As the students filed into her classroom, we noticed on her desk a quart bottle of milk standing in a heavy stone crock.

"This morning," she announced, "I'm going to teach you a lesson that has nothing to do with English, but it has a lot to do with life." She picked up the bottle of milk, crashed it against the inside of the stone crock, and it splintered into small pieces. "The lesson," she said, "is, don't cry over spilled milk."

Then she invited us to look at the wreckage.

"I want all of you to remember this," she said. "Would any of you attempt to restore the bottle to its original form? Does it do any good to wish the bottle had not been broken? Does it help to get upset and tell yourself how good the milk might have tasted if this hadn't happened? Look at this mess! You can moan about it forever, but it won't put the bottle back together again. Remember this broken bottle of milk when something happens in your life that nothing can undo."

I've reminded myself of that broken bottle of milk in the stone crock time and time again. It has helped me remain steady and calm as well as physically sound. Our bodies take a beating when we put ourselves through an emotional wringer. To try to undo what has been done or agonize about opportunities missed it not only foolish, it's futile.

Omar Khayyám put it eloquently:

> The Moving Finger writes; and, having writ,
> Moves on: nor all your Piety nor Wit
> Shall lure it back to cancel half a Line,
> Nor all your Tears wash out a Word of it.

Most of us have been victimized in one way or another by an unscrupulous opportunist. Even the experienced can be taken in by a clever operator. In many instances we can't control what happens to us, but we can control our own *reactions* to what happens to us. We can stay down for the count and be carried out of the ring or we can take the beating and pull ourselves back to our feet. Sometimes the choice isn't even a conscious one.

Many crises seem insurmountable, but time and again we have seen ordinary people display genius in turning a hopeless situation into something tolerable or even good. There should be a special citation for the little guy who manages to keep going when he has every right to crack up.

When Jesus said in Matthew 5:4 "love your enemy," He was not only suggesting that we make life easier for them but He wanted to make life easier for us. Some contend that such advice is folly. Why give our enemies goodwill in return for treachery? Should we not try to crush those who try to destroy us?

But by "love your enemy" Jesus did not mean that we should "grapple them to our soul with hoops of steel." He did mean that to preserve our own mental and physical well-being we should refuse to allow ourselves to be consumed with hatred or bitterness. We must refuse to give evil people the power to break our spirit, make us physically ill, and perhaps even shorten our lives. Any doctor will tell you that worry, anxiety, tension and anger can make you sicker than a virus. As far back as Plato man knew that what took place in his mind produced physical changes in his body.

We are all acquainted with examples of such emotional phenomena. The sight of an accident can cause nausea or fainting. Stage fright can cause a pounding of the heart, excessive perspiration and butterflies in the stomach.

During the First World War thousands of soldiers were incapacitated because of "shellshock." Many of the afflicted had never been near a shell. In World War II they called it "battle fatigue," although many of the men stricken had never been in combat. They collapsed and were unable to function because of fear and anxiety.

The expression "nervous breakdown" suggests that nerves have broken down, but the problem is purely emotional. Organically the nerves are healthy. A doctor on the staff of the Mayo Clinic has said the majority of patients in hospital beds today are there because of illnesses which were psycho-generated. This means the sickness was triggered by an emotional problem.

So, when you find that someone has "done you wrong," say to yourself, "I will not spend one extra minute hating or trying to get even. It's too expensive." Hatred is like an acid. It can do more damage to the container in which it is stored than to the object on which it is poured.

TROUBLE BEYOND HUMAN CONTROL

"I am the master of my fate; I am the captain of my soul." These words by William Henley offer courage to the faint of heart. It's comforting for man to feel that he has the power to chart his own destiny, but it isn't always true. Even though we may lead the good life and fight the good fight, we are sometimes tripped up by the process of living. Call it bad luck, fate, or whatever you choose, but man is at the mercy of trouble beyond human control.

Death and tragedy touch us all sooner or later. When it comes, it reminds us of our own frailty, and it makes us all brothers and sisters. Shortly after World War II, I was the chairman of a tea for Gold Star mothers. Some women arrived in chauffeured limousines. Others came on foot, not able to afford bus fare. Some wore mink stoles, others, woolen jackets. Their backgrounds and daily lives couldn't have been more different, but their heartache was the same. As they sat side by side, their differences disappeared. The tragedy each shared united them for a time at least. Never before or since have I seen more dramatic proof that trouble is the great equalizer.

I believe in blind faith. I have known people who have suffered deep personal tragedies and they believe in it too. But, I also believe in the efficacy of positive action to overcome grief. Time is a healer, but those who help time by using it wisely and well make a more rapid adjustment.

Grief, in part, is self-pity turned inside out. The widow who wails, "He was everything to me. How can I go on without him . . ." is crying for herself, not for him. Death is sometimes a merciful release from suffering and misery. The one who survives must struggle with the problem of living.

The mourner who wears his grief interminably eventually isolates himself from his friends. The world may stop for a few hours (or perhaps a few days) to hold a hand or to wipe away a tear, but friends and relatives have problems of their own. Life goes on—and those who refuse to go on with it are left alone to wallow in their solitary misery.

The best prescription for a broken heart is activity. I don't mean plunging into a social whirl or running off on trips. Too many people try to escape from their heartache by hopping on planes, trains and ships. They succeed only in taking their troubles with them. The most useful kind of activity involves doing something to help others. I have told thousands of despondent people, "Enough of this breast-beating. What will it accomplish? No matter how badly off you are there is someone who is worse off—and you can help him."

Most touching to me is the heroism, the courage and faith of the average people in the world. Often readers who write about a problem will add something about their personal lives. I am moved by the magnificent people who write such lines as: "My husband lost his sight shortly after we married, but we manage beautifully." Or: "I've had two operations for cancer, but I know I'll be able to attend my son's graduation in June and I'm so thankful for that."

No one knows why life must be so punishing to some of God's finest creatures. Perhaps it is true that everything has a price and we must sacrifice something precious to gain something else. The poets and philosophers say adversity, sorrow and pain give our lives meaning—an added dimension. Those who suffer deeply touch life at every point; they drain the cup to the dregs while others sip only the bubbles on top. Perhaps no man can touch the stars unless he has known the depths of despair.

CREDIT: *Ann Landers from* Since You Ask Me, *Englewood Cliffs, New Jersey:* Prentice-Hall.

Cosmetics

How to Enhance Your Looks

There are no ugly women—only lazy ones. A woman, no matter how much God has blessed her with good looks, can improve on or detract from them with the proper or improper use of cosmetics. The purpose of this article is to help you learn about cosmetics, and how to use them. It will not be easy. It takes practice—knowing where to begin and what tools to use. Each face is unique. A careful study of *your* face is the key to enhancing your beauty. Let's get started.

STEP 1—A GOOD HARD LOOK: Pull your hair straight back from your face. Better yet, put on a scarf and tuck all the hair in. Look straight ahead into a mirror. Be sure to use a mirror that is magnified in a room with lots of natural light.

If you own a makeup mirror with lights, you have a definite advantage. I prefer to sit while I do my makeup; it can be relaxing and fun, like painting a picture. Study your features, decide which are your good points and which are bad. Then accentuate the positive and camouflage the negative.

Take a moist bar of soap and draw on the mirror the shape you are seeing. Study that shape—is it round, square, oblong, triangle, a heart or the perfect oval? This will help you not only in selecting cosmetics, but also in choosing a hair style that will best suit your features.

STEP 2—AND THEN: Cleanliness is next to godliness; never put new makeup on over old. Use a cleanser or cold cream to remove old makeup, followed by a thorough washing with warm water and a non-alkaline soap. Many women do not feel clean without using soap; however, it must be pointed out that soap does not dissolve makeup; only cleansers can do this. Never rub the face; pat and stroke gently and use only the little fingers around the eyes. Follow the cleansing by dabbing an astringent on a cotton ball and patting it on the face. This ensures complete removal of all makeup.

Moisturizer comes next, vitally important under makeup from sixteen years of age to grandmother, as well as when not wearing makeup and at bedtime. Never go to bed without removing all makeup and using the procedures mentioned above, as well as a night cream. If you are applying makeup for the day, moisturizer will help seal the look and prevent your makeup base from turning orange or streaking.

STEP 3—THE BASE: Selecting a base is extremely important. Remember, expensive does not always mean best. The color must blend with your natural skin tones. You don't want to look as if you have painted your face. Choose a liquid or cream base that can be applied with a wet sponge for a natural look. Choose a color by dabbing the makeup on the outside of the hand near the thumb and blending it to the wrist. Seek a professional in the cosmetic department of a store to help you. They have been trained by cosmetic manufacturers and do not charge for their services.

When applying makeup, use the dot method—putting it on the forehead, nose, cheeks and chin, blending it in, especially at the neck. Nothing looks more amateurish than a visible makeup line. To ensure a perfect blend, pat a water-saturated cotton ball around hairline and neckline and through the eyebrows.

STEP 4—THE BLUSH: Color selection of cream or powdered blush is the next step. Choose a bronze shade if your hair is brown, red or brunette; a rose-pink shade if you are blonde or graying. To apply, smile—it feels good and helps you place the color properly. As you smile, you will see what we will call the apple of the cheek. Place the blush in the center of the apple and blend upward to the temple. Do not go below the nose or around the eye area.

STEP 5—EYES: Add sparkle to tired eyes with eye drops, and a moist tea bag can do wonders for puffy eyes if you lie back with one on each eye for ten minutes. Dark circles can be camouflaged with coverup or illusion cream two shades lighter than your complexion. Place it under the eyes and directly under the brow, blending it to the temple.

The brow comes next—the shape of the brow is critical. Determine the shape for your eyes and face. Do not follow fads. I stress again that God made each face unique, and trying to look like a picture of someone else is a mistake. You must establish your own look and stick to it. Fashion can dictate a few minor changes but not totally. Perhaps a new eye shadow color or lipstick shade will do the trick. To determine the shape of your brow, look straight into the mirror and use your eyebrow pencil to make three marks. Mark the brow at the outer corners of the iris (this determines the arch), lay the pencil to the side of your nose to the temple and mark it. This is the length. Lay the pencil along the nose to the inner corner of the eye and mark it. This will determine how far the brow should come to the nose. Now take a tweezer, preferably the scissor type, and tweeze a few hairs from the arch at the mark. If you have brows extending past the mark at the nose, remove the hairs there. Use the pencil to lightly fill in the area of length to that mark. Rubbing the brow area with an ice cube will cut the sting if this is your first attempt at tweezing. If possible, it would be good to go to a professional for the first arching. Never tweeze above the brow or use a shaver. Select a brow pencil or brush and brow color to blend with your hair (never black, charcoal or brown/black for brunettes). Use auburn or light brown for redheads and blondes, medium brown for shades of brown hair.

Everyone wants long thick lashes. If you have been blessed, lavish them with a coat of mascara—uppers only. Very few women can use mascara successfully on the lower lashes. The problem is—(even with the waterproof non-smudge-promising brands)—the mascara almost always has a way of flaking off onto the face. It's wise to carry a magnifying makeup mirror in your purse at all times and check out the upper mascaraed eyelashes. A single fallen fleck can ruin the entire effect.

For special occasions try a light pair of false lashes trimmed to fit your eyes. Black mascara is good for most everyone except blondes and certain shades of red and gray (they must use brown). The same applies to the false lash color.

Eye shadow is next. Select a color that highlights your eyes, again no fads —blue and violets and aquas for blue eyes; frosted grays, beige and pink for brown eyes. I prefer the powdered to the creams for a lasting effect. Apply only on the lids—never put colored shadow to the brow. As you become more experienced, you may want to blend colors to the brow, but to be safe, only on the lid at the beginning. Cotton swabs are excellent for repairs. Go to a professional salon if you wish to learn more glamorous eye techniques. Liners and smudging can add dimension if applied with extreme care. Practice and experiment before you make this part of your daily routine.

The same caution would apply to contouring the face, shortening or narrowing a less than perfect nose, working on more specific problems such as birthmarks, moles, freckles, pitted skin, scars, removal of unwanted hair on the face, etc. A professional beautician's advice would be money well spent.

The eyes are everyone's most important feature. If you must wear eye frames, select them with care. The new designer frames are very flattering and most optical shops have an experienced consultant to help you.

STEP 6—LIPS: Lips are the second most important feature. Using a lip brush assures properly applied lip color. Choose a lipstick that is moist and creamy; this is no time to be stingy. A good lipstick is a sound investment in good looks. Select a color that is fashionable and blends with your skin tones. A touch of lip gloss or Vaseline gives you a polished look.

STEP 7—THE FINAL TOUCH: To complete your total look, apply a translucent medium-shade powder with a powder brush or cotton ball lightly over the entire face. This will set your makeup and you will look fresh and lovely for hours.

STEP 8—THERE'S MORE THAN A PRETTY FACE: Don't forget your fingernails and toenails. Clean and shape with clippers and an emery board. Remember to file in one direction only and remove the dead cuticles. Clear polish or a base coat followed by a color to co-ordinate with your lipstick completes your look.

Polished teeth, a sweet breath, a good deodorant and a spray of your favorite cologne add the finishing touches.

Touch-ups with powder, blush and lipstick are acceptable in public if done quickly.

Remember that genuine beauty comes from within. Cosmetics cannot make up for loss of sleep, poor diet, or a negative attitude. A happy smile, sparkling eyes and a positive outlook help make you beautiful.

When you have done your best to look your loveliest, forget about yourself and concentrate on others. After all, isn't that what life is all about?

CREDIT: *Sue Lilly, TV Show Host, WHIO-TV, Dayton, Ohio.*

Makeup
for the Mature Woman*

Here are ten do's for a better makeup for the mature woman:

(1) Do makeup in the proper light. Use daylight directly on your face and, if possible, a magnifying mirror. After the makeup has been applied, check it with a regular mirror in artificial light.

(2) Apply moisturizer to a clean face. Use a foundation to give even color and tone down small brownish spots that may appear after forty.

Be sure the color you wear is the same as your skin tone. When purchasing colors, try them first on your neck, not the back of the hand. Try to get to daylight to see the color. Avoid dark or muddy colors.

A thinner base should be used as lines start to appear; the "let's cover them up" concept is wrong for the older woman. The denser bases accentuate the lines, making them appear deeper.

(3) Cover lines with a lighter colored base, a little bit heavier in texture. It can be as much as three shades lighter. Apply the lotion to such wrinkled areas as those beneath the eyes, and the lines from the nose to the chin. Apply before and after the foundation, blending carefully to avoid any line of demarcation. Never use white, it's too strong.

(4) Next to the eyes, eyebrows are the most important facial feature because they control the expressions. Pluck the hairs underneath the brow and where they straggle out at the end. Consider the shape of the eyes and the position of the brow bone.

(5) Don't use greasy eye shadow. Powdered is more attractive.

The safest color for the older eye is a soft, light brown or mushroom. This is the color of the eyelid skin and does not draw attention to eyelids as bright blues and greens do. A pink shadow is right for rosy-toned complexions.

(6) Eyeliner is subject to fashion changes. Right now, almost no liner and no mascara is being used, which is good for the older woman. A soft shade of a thin line blended above and on the lower lid can help change the shape of the eyes.

(7) Mascara. Black, brown or blue are the only colors to be considered. Most over-forty women wear glasses, which magnify eye makeup, especially

---

* Ruth Kling, "How to Catch a Man After You're 40," copyright © 1977 New York News, Inc. Reprinted by permission. Reviewing the book *Beauty for the Mature Woman,* Dorothy Seiffert, New York: Hawthorn Books.

mascara. If mascara is worn during the day, blot it with thumb and forefinger while it is still wet to separate lashes.

(8) False eyelashes. Use a sparse strip, cut shorter than the eyelid. Avoid too heavy or coarse a lash. Remember to apply a liner before applying lashes. Mascara blends well with false lashes, giving a more natural look.

(9) Rouge. For the older woman, creams seem to work very well. They don't blotch or cake. Avoid all purplish, bluish tones. The color should match the skin tones, giving a rosy, healthy, natural hue. The new earth tones may be used if they are not too dark for the complexion.

(10) Lipstick. Older women should wear lipstick stronger in intensity, not darker in color. Learn to use a lipstick brush to control contours of lips. The new pencil outliners are good in light brown, avoid the strong reds. Fill in with lipstick and cover with lip gloss; it's great for keeping lips shiny-looking and moisturized.

If the mouth is too small or too large, use soft, light shades of lipstick. If wearing a dress in the purple, orange, pink, red or peach shade, be certain lipstick doesn't clash. Keep lipstick and cheek color in the same shade.

Skin care is another important factor in keeping mature skin looking good. Know your own skin type and use products designed for normal, dry or oily skin.

The nightly routine should include a freshener or astringent for toning. Use a heavier moisturizer at night, one that is easily absorbed and gives a resiliency to the touch. This works as well for the mature skin as expensive creams with exotic names and promises.

Several of the old standbys are great since many women in this age bracket are on fixed incomes. Witch hazel is a fine astringent, while Vaseline Petroleum Jelly can act as a night cream. Simply wipe off the excess to save the bed linens. There are really no miracle wrinkle removers that have any permanent effect.

Cousins

(*Should They Marry?*)

We are not going to delve into questions such as "Should anyone marry, and worsen the population problem?" or "Is it better to marry than to burn?" Any couple contemplating marriage needs to confront a wide range of pressing questions, and we hope that whether cousins or not, a couple will be asking themselves these questions with great seriousness, deliberation and hope.

In addition to all the ordinary problems, cousins inherently face additional challenges that come out of their prior family relationships. These special problems are the only ones that will be dealt with here.

Two things come to mind: the issues that arise from family tradition, and those from genetic or biological relatedness. I do not know of any factual data on the extent to which the success or failure of marriages depends on the common traditions of the mates. Common sense would say that large differences in economic, social and religious outlook may be sources of misunderstandings in the later married life of a couple. Since cousins are more likely than the average couple to come from homes with similar economic, social and religious backgrounds, they may be relatively free of those burdens.

Common sense also suggests that mates may become bored if there are no differences; but even cousins are likely to have different life experiences and perspectives. There is some danger that cousin marriages have been arranged to suit the convenience of others, but even here there is little factual evidence on how this affects the outcome. Obviously such matters will vary enormously with the cultural background that the couple brings to the marriage, and the setting of their future life.

The more obvious question is, "What about the children?" There are many taboos about close marriages in many cultures and religious faiths. In many states first-cousin marriages are not permitted.

First, it should be stressed that inbreeding does not in any way generate "bad genes" or create genetic factors that may cause disease or impair the functioning of the child. This is a superstition that has grown over the centuries, from the observation that inbreeding tends to expose the genetic defects already carried by almost every individual of the species. These defects are the result of evolution, the mutations without which higher organisms and human beings could never have emerged out of the primeval ooze, millions and billions of years ago.

The exposure of previous mutations is not to be taken lightly. Everyone of us is carrying two or three "bad genes" in a masked condition, in a way that might only be revealed by the bad luck of meeting a partner with a similar defect.

In practical terms, first cousins who marry must face the fact that they will have about twice the risks of bad luck with the genetic dice as do unrelated partners when they have children.

It has to be said that women who have children after age thirty-five, or couples who have children knowing that there are definite hereditary problems in their ancestry are taking similarly increased risks.

Whether cousins should marry (and have children!) in the face of these concerns is an ethical problem they alone must answer. However, the risks of disaster are greatly increased for cousins who are also carriers of known genetic diseases, such as cystic fibrosis, sickle cell anemia, etc. They may be increasing the odds of a bad result from less than one out of a hundred (the general average) to over one out of four. For that reason, it is important that cousin-mates, before they have children, visit a genetic counselor and get informed advice about their own specific situation, rather than try to play the odds that apply to the whole average population.

For genetic counseling contact your nearest sizable university or your county medical department.

CREDIT: *Joshua Lederberg, Ph.D., Professor, Department of Genetics, Stanford University Medical School, Stanford, California.*

Crabs

(*Pubic Lice*)

Reliable statistics on the number of people who have pubic lice (crabs) are very hard to come by. I decided to ask for the help of a distinguished physician, Dr. Leslie Norins, at the Center for Communicable Diseases in Atlanta. I discovered Dr. Norins had moved from the Center to become President of American Health Consultants. He informed me that the most dependable indicator of louse activity is the sale of medication for this annoying affliction. Dr. Norins also disabused me of a notion I had believed for years—that pubic lice and head lice were the same—found in different places. Not true. They are two different species.

Public health authorities believe the principal reason for the increase in pubic lice is the widespread practice of communal living among the young and increased sexual activity at all age levels. They also point out that the social prestige of the pubic louse has been elevated these past ten years. It is no longer an affliction of the ghetto. Pubic lice can now be found in the best social circles.

Sales of over-the-counter lotions for treating both head and pubic lice increased 1,200 percent from 1963 through 1975. When school is in session, in some college towns, the sale of anti-louse medication is almost equivalent to that of mouthwash.

Based on the total sales per 1,000 population, the lousiest cities in the United States for 1975 are:

(1) Providence, Rhode Island, (2) Corpus Christi, Texas, (3) Albany, New York, (4) Troy, New York, (5) Orlando, Florida, (6) Boston, Massachusetts, (7) Fresno, California, (8) Eugene, Oregon, (9) Manchester, New Hampshire, (10) Las Vegas, Nevada.

Almost all pubic lice are "caught" from someone who has pubic lice. It is unlikely but possible to pick up lice on a bedsheet, a bath towel, a gym mattress, or a sleeping bag.

It takes from seven to ten days from the time of exposure till the itching begins. Pubic lice are prolific breeders and their eggs are cemented to the hair shafts and cannot be eliminated by normal washing or scrubbing.

Lice vary in size, but the average louse is about twice as large as a pinhead. They are brownish in color and may look like freckles at first glance. Since lice feed on human blood (like mosquitos) the miserable little creatures penetrate the flesh and are difficult to identify as living things, unless you catch one that is ambulatory. The alternative is to scratch one off for examination —preferably under a magnifying glass. It looks like a crab. Final evidence is the wiggling of the legs. Freckles do not wiggle.

Once it has been determined that you have pubic lice, check the eyebrows, eyelashes, underarms—any area where hair grows. These creatures are "good travelers" and set up housekeeping rapidly.

Here are the Do's and Don'ts of eliminating pubic lice, courtesy of Norcliff Thayer, Inc., manufacturers of A-200 Pyrinate, a leading, non-prescription medicine which eliminates lice.

SOME DO'S

(1) *Seek assistance.* The first sign of lice is usually intense itching. Get a magnifying glass and explore. If you see lice or grayish eggs attached to hair shafts pay a hasty visit to your local health department (city, county or state), take your problem to the school nurse or go to your pharmacist.

(2) *Treat quickly.* Once lice infestation starts, it can spread like wildfire. Shampoo the infested area with a modern proved product. Many are available without prescription at most drug counters.

(3) *Protect others.* The entire family, or others who have had contact with an infested person, should be inspected. If they too are lousy they should undergo treatment at once.

(4) *Sanitize personal items.* Boil, steam or dry-clean all clothing and personal items, such as combs and brushes. Bedding and the backs of upholstered furniture, car seats, etc. should be thoroughly vacuumed and disinfected, where possible.

(5) *Re-treat to be sure.* It is a good idea to re-treat the infested area after seven days to eliminate any lice that might have hatched after the first treatment.

SOME DON'TS

(1) *Don't be embarrassed.* All people, regardless of their sanitary habits or station in life, can get lice. The important thing is to get rid of them.

(2) *Don't attempt home remedies.* Some home remedies can be ineffective or dangerous. The most effective non-prescription drugs for treating pubic lice are A-200 Pyrinate and Cuprex.

CREDIT: *Leslie Norins, M.D., Ph.D., President, American Health Consultants, Atlanta, Georgia.*

Cremation

Cremation as a way of final disposition of the body at death has not been widely practiced in the United States. In comparison with Japan and England, where over half of the people who die are cremated, recent statistics indicate that less than 5 percent of American families choose cremation. The reason for this is a matter of custom when formerly it may have been religious. Today there is more acceptance of cremation by the public and less resistance by religious authorities.

The fact that you are reading this brief piece of information about cremation indicates that you are more than curious about its subject. You are probably the kind of person who is open to different ideas. Perhaps you also feel some responsibility to help your family by suggesting a preference about the final disposition of your body after death.

WHAT IS CREMATION?

Cremation is an alternative method of the disposition of the human body at death. Through intense heat, the body of one who has died is quickly reduced to ashes. In contrast to earth burial, which is a gradual process of reduction to basic elements, cremation accomplishes the same thing in less than a couple of hours.

There may be a psychological advantage to cremation for some persons. The idea of a quick, clean incineration of the body is preferable to the slower process of reduction in a grave.

What's involved in cremation?

It's reassuring to know that most of the customs and rituals we have come to expect with a funeral are not significantly altered if you request cremation.

There can still be a visitation and viewing of the deceased. A worship service or ceremony with the body present can be held. There can also be some form of committal service for the cremated remains.

The body, instead of being taken in a procession to a cemetery or a mausoleum, may be accompanied by the family in procession to a crematory in a casket or other suitable container. There, usually in a chapel setting, the casket is placed into a retort. The retort is a specially designed furnace capable of reaching extremely high temperature. All smoke and gases are recirculated through the heat chambers, so there is very little discharge into the open air.

In less than two hours, the body, which is cremated in a casket, is reduced to a few pounds of bone fragments and ashes. Each body is cremated separately.

The cremated remains are then placed in an urn or in a canister and carefully identified. Your funeral director or the crematorium selected will have a variety of urns from which a family can make a selection.

What happens to the cremated remains?

A family has several options available. One is *inurnment*. Here the cremated remains are put into a small metal or other type container. The urn can then be permanently located in a purchased niche. Many cemeteries have such facilities ranging from the simple to the elaborate. There are usually perpetual care agreements in force and certain regulations regarding the use of flowers.

Burial: A second option involves placing the cremated remains in an earth grave in the simple canister or urn in which they are delivered from the crematory. Some cemeteries require that the urn be placed in a vault-like container. Such burials of cremated remains can be in a family plot or a special area available within some cemeteries. This burial can take place immediately after the funeral and the cremation, but the usual custom is to make such burial several days following the cremation.

Scattering: Strewing the cremated remains is a third option. This requires some pulverization because usually there are some larger fragments of calcified bones after cremation. The cremated remains are then distributed on the surface of the ground, into a flowing stream or over the ocean. Most crematories have a special garden and will dispose of the cremated remains according to a family's request.

Other families may wish to scatter the cremated remains in some place of particular sentimental attachment, providing there are no local legal prohibitions. Your funeral director can advise you about any such restrictions.

Are there special ways of remembering someone who has been cremated?

If the cremated remains of the deceased are put in a grave, a plaque or marker can be used. When the ashes are strewn, it is still possible to have some marker or memorialization if it is so desired. Since there is no final resting place, a memorial plaque may be used to indicate the general location of the ashes. A tree or shrub might be planted and dedicated as a tangible memorial. In other instances, crematories provide Books of Remembrance in which the name of the deceased can be suitably inscribed or displayed.

Sometimes a committal service is held with the family present when the ashes are finally disposed of by any of these means. This brief way of honoring the deceased completes the process of separation.

Are there economic advantages to cremation?

Costs are related to the way cremation is utilized. There are several alternatives. It is not possible to estimate actual costs or savings in comparing cremation with an earth burial because they vary with locality and patterns of custom.

However, if economic considerations are of utmost importance, cremation may be an alternative to be considered. Cost may also be affected depending on whether or not a family grave plot is already owned and by the charges for opening and closing a grave. Your funeral director can discuss with you the alternative patterns of arrangements and their related costs.

Where can we get more information about cremation?

Your local funeral director is the most knowledgeable resource for any questions you might have about post-death activities, including cremation.

CREDIT: *Howard Raether, Executive Director, National Funeral Directors Association of the U.S., Inc., Milwaukee, Wisconsin.*

Crime *

(*What Causes It?*)

Anyone concerned with the study of crime and criminals is familiar with the challenging question: "Well, doctor, what *is* the cause of crime?" Of course, he means, "Let's stop talking about our crimes against criminals and talk about what they do to us and why."

Every human event has many determinants and surely this is true of crimes. The question should be worded: What are the *causes* of crime—or what are the causes of criminals, for every one is different.

To accept the challenge is to first tick off the textbook "causes": Hunger, poverty, ghetto living, drugs, anger, jealousy, hate, fear—any or several of

* Copyright © 1978, Karl Menninger, M.D.

these. "But," the inquirer persists, "are there causes we can do something about?"

Crime—the thing we all want to do something about—means, to the average citizen, familiar kinds of violent lawbreaking, like killing and raping and bank robbing. But each of these categories has many complexities. Bank robbing often means guns and masks and "stick 'em up," a loot sack, a waiting car, a chase and great excitement. That's crime! But the crime of bank robbing is more frequently a quiet, long-undetected inside job—a covered-up affair.

Take murder, or rape, or vandalism: exciting, ugly, violent, fearsome behavior that interests the newspapers. These are crimes for sure—crimes that are ruining our cities. (There is no substantial evidence that crime is increasing any faster than the population.) But the legislators want to do away with mandatory sentences, nix on paroles, bring on double-time sentences or triple, solitary confinement, and capital punishment if we can get it by the sentimentalists. They believe terror is the way to stop terror; violence requires counterviolence! "Never mind the *causes* of those crimes—just get the criminals!"

They tell us we need more policemen, more jails, more prisons, more helicopters, more mace, more "security," more tough guys to deal with tough guys. Let's drown the tongues of fire and preserve our peace and way of life!

Look at rape and treason and kidnapping and child abuse and wife abuse. They're not as evil as murder, but they are multiplying, which murder is not! Vandalism, the destruction of beautiful and valuable things, is ruthless, ugly, costly, violent. And mugging, stabbing, assaulting, maiming—all these aggressions against fellow creatures, especially weaker or less defensive ones, are surely crimes.

What does cause all this perversity, this antihumanity? Who are these villains? They were all children once. What made some of them turn against their fellow man and do forbidden things?

We know this behavior isn't exactly inherited, but can it be perhaps congenital, an innate streak of wickedness? The laws stating the limits of social behavior, forbidding violence and expressing our common disapproval and dislike of it, weren't laid down long ago by us—nor by those trespassers either. To "keep the peace and punish the evildoers," lawmakers wrote down a code. In olden times, it was the *King's* peace that was important to preserve, even by force; later the peace and safety of the King's subjects assumed some importance. We think of law as a community's conscience, a duty to maintain safety for all members.

We accepted those laws as facts; they were *there,* written in the book. We didn't *promise* to obey then; in fact, we weren't asked to. We were *told.* We grew up impressed with the importance of power and possessions, not law abidance. "Them as has gits!" Life gets constantly more complicated and stressful and all through it "someone" tells us what we must do, or may not do. The stress, the pressure of this compulsion weighs heavily on some already pressured individuals. Some of us are under more (conscious) pressure than others. And some yield to those increasing pressures at the weakest point in our "defenses," as the psychologist calls them. Others reach out a hand and take, or strike.

From a statistical point of view, those personal physical rebellions against accumulating pressures with the consequent injury of someone else are not the bulk of "crime." They are crimes, to be sure, but not *crime*. Violence characterizes *a very small proportion of the detected criminal acts* in any community. The noisy and newsy lawbreakings, unpleasant and frightening, are not the main bulk of lawbreaking. Crime is not simply a collection of killings and rapes and beatings interspersed with a few kidnappings. Crime is mostly a great mass of *stealings,* small and great, secret and overt, bloody and "clean," sneaking and spectacular, nice and nasty. Crime is *mostly* someone taking for himself, without permission, the money or property of someone else.

Shoppers do it, clerks do it, deliverymen do it, secretaries do it, storehouse men do it, cashiers do it, lawyers do it, presidents do it, corporations do it, land companies do it. Let's face it, nearly *everyone* does it once—twice, occasionally, repeatedly, or constantly. Theft is a universal crime, committed by nearly all of us sometimes and by many of us all the time, daily, everywhere.

Some people use their hands to steal. Some use their tongues, and swindle. Some do it with pen and ink, some with satchels and purses, some with dollies and trucks. There are hundreds of methods of stealing, cheating, robbing, thieving and swindling. Only a fraction of them are ever detected.

I know a millionaire who brags about never paying any income tax. He makes good use of the blessings provided by his government but he never returns anything to it or to anyone else. He regards himself as shrewd and clever, even. I know (and you know) many friends whose cheating and stealing are no secret. We stole much of our American land from the Indians and Mexicans. Do we generally acknowledge it, or even think about it? Do we feel guilty? Neither, apparently, do many people we know to be stealing from us.

Do you ask why people do this, why so many of us steal and cheat? Is it just people who need something who take it? Do you wonder if so many of us are "naturally dishonest?" Do you ask if cupidity is a disease or a normal response to something?

I read the following in a newsletter yesterday: "An employee of a northern book company admitted to making a tidy sum for himself by stealing Bibles from his company's warehouse, then reselling the stolen goods to churches, happy to get the books at a reduced price. A special agent, posing as a warehouse employee, discovered that five employees had been regularly stealing whole sets of books. One employee, who had been working there five years, had been doing this for a year."

Don't ask me why we steal; *tell* me! Because we want to have something that isn't ours and have never acquired the conscience or wisdom or the ability to resist the infantile temptation of grabbing.

What are the causes of all these other less numerous but more disturbing crimes, the violent ones, the scary ones? Have I, as a psychiatrist, seen many of these offenders "up close"? Yes, I have, and I can generalize about them. Some of these acts are defensive measures against detection or recognition. Some of them are spurred by needs the doctors can't identify. Some people actually do snatch purses or steal food because they are hungry and penniless, or their dear ones are. So—put poverty on the list, in great big letters. Add unemployment which threatens poverty. Put down the desperation of some poor devils who had gotten hooked on a drug habit. They *have* to steal, or suffer grievously. Don't forget the stressed and strained and worried housewife who has no excitement in her life except a visit to the store!

But most stealing is done by people who don't need the things they steal. Many of my daughter's clothes were stolen by college classmates. How about them? Why is this? We do have to have some rules and moral standards and laws to keep organizations, communities and nations together. If anyone is going to defy them, defy proprieties and good taste and law and order, defy even his conscience and common sense, he'd better be quick and clever, or expect to be caught and "dealt with." This dealing—in most countries—means jail or probation. Most people avoid jail the first and second time they are caught. But to be sure of avoiding jail, the offender had better have some friends who will "do something for him." If not, he's going to be arrested, booked as a criminal, and we're going to have to punish him. He's a bad man. But we'll "larn" him. At any rate, we will slow him up. He won't steal so much again—soon.

Some people need what the stolen object symbolizes or enables or gives evidence of—power, knowledge, expertise. I know one individual who stole much and frequently, discarding what he acquired, but he was immensely proud of his skill in avoiding detection. Some people steal to hurt the person or organization stolen from. None of these motives should have prevailed over the resolution to be honest—but they did. Why do people take this chance? What impels them? All those drugs, of course. Including alcohol, in a big way. Depressed, anxious, worried people shouldn't take alcohol. Alcohol leads to such things as beating up babies and stomping wives and steering automobiles into the wrong lane, and getting the red light mixed up with the green, and even getting mad and shooting a brother-in-law.

Anger causes crime, too. Can we give that up? Everybody gets mad now and then—sometimes awfully mad. Some of us do things we regret. Minor (or major) frustrations, illnesses, continuous toothaches, no money for dental care, persistent backaches, recurrent arthritis, debts unpaid and mounting, disagreeable family members, obnoxious relations, annoying fellow workers. All kinds of things happen to people now and then. We get tired, and sometimes our feet hurt. Feet hurting a cause of crime? How ridiculous! Yes, it's ridiculous always to single out one cause. But such things as hurting feet and hurting feelings can contribute much to a disorganization of personality and self-control.

Too, there is such a thing as sex, a complicated web of impulses and restraints, temptations and punishments. All kinds of mix-ups, disappointments, jealousies, angers, fears and sorrows. Those are among the disturbers of one's equilibrium, the co-operating causes of crime. Jealousy was the cause of the first murder—Cain and Abel—and in many others since then.

Many times it is a choice between committing a crime or committing suicide. Sometimes it may be between committing a crime or going crazy. People steal (or commit other crimes) when to do so seems to them the lesser of two or more evil courses toward which they feel driven or pressured.

Some people have no consciously perceived need to take, to snatch. Others are obsessed by it and are tempted to steal big with tax evasion, property rip-offs, frauds and other sorts of cleverness. I know that some of my friends are at it right now, and some of yours too. Why this ambition to pile up more money than friends or neighbors? What are the causes of hoarding, of cheating, of lying?

What kind of crime and punishment are we talking about when we use such general terms as "the causes" of crime? Are we talking about the big shots or about poor people's crimes? Or are we just talking about jails' populations?

Of course, one of the great, comprehensive universal human "causes" of crime is simply *greed*. Overweening greed in the adult is an uncontrolled persistence of infantile *grasping* and sucking. One *learns* to be considerate and fair. Greed in an adult is a good old-fashioned sin—one of the classical carnal sins or immaturities. It has surely existed as far back as history records anything. It was a specific sin forbidden the children of Israel—on the tablets of Moses. With it go covetousness and acquisitiveness, and all the unlovely emotions that accompany them. Offered an opportunity to *acquire* something without being observed, these traits make for an obvious likelihood of a crime.

The causes of being in jail are not the causes of crime. You can't just get envious and steal Mrs. Smith's diamond ring and get put in jail for it. To get there, you have to be caught.

There are, of course, good lawyers who can keep you out—but can you get one? There are bail bondsmen; can you afford one? Property crimes are a kind of rich man's game or a poor man's gamble. If they win, fine. Who cares? If they lose, the rich get a lawyer and the poor go to jail. Everybody knows this. Everybody knows it's wrong. Everyone knows that prisons make people worse and cost the state lots of money. It isn't fair to lock some of these men up. But, as our President said, "Life is unfair."

So we keep up this expensive farce. It's expensive, it's cruel, it's barbaric, it's dirty, it's vile and it's mostly undercover. It provides a living for a lot of people. They will take care of these jailbirds—a dreary and dreadful job. They'll see that these villains don't trouble my fair lady.

The other great cause of crime, in a single word, is vengeance. Most violent and many non-violent crimes are committed in a spirit of vindictiveness —for revenge. Revenge often against non-guilty people for pains and indignities suffered way earlier. That usually means by parents and teachers and stepparents. The fright and pain suffered by children can't be assuaged at the time they are beaten and slapped and kicked. But children have memories. Freud said that neurotics suffer from reminiscences. Criminals suffer from memories. Cruelty to children—and we know how evil and covert it is—is not forgotten. It is stored until an opportunity and a provocation to replay it on a substitute object, a "symbolic" substitute, presents itself.

Then the abused child can exert *his* power and pay back his weaker victim the debt of days long ago when *he* was the weaker victim. He takes his revenge for those beatings, those jerkings, those slappings, those cursings.

Then comes society's turn. The criminal "justice" system takes *its* revenge; later the repayment will be made to society by the embittered man, and the vicious circle continues.

Our original question was, "What are the *causes* of crime?" We haven't touched on the things a psychiatrist is supposed to know about—defective will power, lack of proper training, evil nature, basic wickedness. As long as we, society, handle the disobedient ones in the unjust, cruel, dehumanizing way I have described, society itself is going to maintain a stream of criminals by adding to the causes and reasons for crimes by the very devices it pretends to think are curing them. "Prisons manufacture criminals," said Ramsey Clark one day in my hearing, "like Detroit manufactures automobiles."

Instead of any effort to discover and correct the vicious circle, what the system does is continue to give prisoners the motivation for going out and doing more of the things they did to get themselves jailed in the first place. Jails and prisons are re-enforcers and re-motivators. They constitute case-hardening machinery for making criminality. Prisoners are released from them full of bitterness, fright, resentment, fears, regrets, heartbreaks. The ex-prisoner re-enters a cold, hostile, suspicious world which doesn't want him, which has few jobs ready for him, which expects him to find and keep one of those few jobs nevertheless, and pay his "way," buy his food and shelter, re-establish his life and restore his sources of biological, psychological and social survival. I repeat: The greatest single cause of crime is the machinery that we have developed in "civilized society" to "control" it.

CREDIT: *Karl Menninger, M.D., M.A.C.P., Menninger Foundation, Topeka, Kansas.*

Criticism

Whether criticism is strong or mild, direct or implied, most of us have one immediate, strong reaction: resentment verging on anger. We tend to take critical remarks as a direct attack on our total worth, our taste, our mental and physical abilities, our appearance and our very souls—and this holds true whether the offending comment pertains to the color of our socks or to our total lifestyle.

If a person could discover the neurological patterns which criticism seems to activate, he could get rich overnight. People who are prone to forget their own telephone number or what they ate for breakfast never forget a critical word—ever.

There are many shades and degrees of criticism, but really only three kinds: (a) that which is justified and fair; (b) that which may be justified but is delivered in a snide or hostile manner; and (c) the unjustified or brutal put-down.

Most people react badly to all three, though the first is obviously the least irksome and can often be tolerated after the initial sting of resentment subsides.

People in the arts and professions, if they are good at what they do, use constructive criticism to their advantage. But most of us will go to absurd lengths to avoid getting criticized.

The first step in learning to handle criticism: Be sure you are really being criticized. Half the time, if you bother to examine the situation and the source, no criticism was intended—perhaps just careless or ambiguous use of words was involved. Also, don't invite criticism by such asking insincere questions such as, "Did you really like it?" or "How did I do?" If you can't take an honest answer to such questions you're better off not asking them.

Secondly, if a criticism is justified, see it in its proper perspective. Don't interpret a remark about your appearance as a total put-down of your talent, brains, personal worth, etc. Also, be sure about the specifics and intent. Criticism is often intended by its giver as a backhanded compliment; that is, you look bad today, compared to how well you usually look; or, this effort of yours is inferior when compared to the high standards of everything else you do.

If a criticism is unjustified, or given snidely, it will make you feel better if you react immediately. Don't give the person who has unfairly gored you the satisfaction of knowing he or she has scored. Practice control. Stay cool. Of course, if you keep getting the same criticism from a number of people you should accept the fact that there is some justification to it.

Finally, consider the source. Criticism always hurts, but it shouldn't hurt coming from the ignorant, the rude, the uninformed, the constant commentor who has a rotten tomato for everybody.

Above all, don't brood on criticism. Dispose of it instantly by judging it as either deserved or gratuitous. If it's deserved, make a resolution to correct the fault then forget it. Don't let criticism poison a whole day or week. And, bearing in mind how it rankles, think twice before you criticize others.

CREDIT: *Joel Wells, staff of The Thomas More Association, Chicago.*

Custody

(*When a Father Gets Custody*)

So you're a divorced man who got custody of the kids:

First, the bad news: You are not as good and great as people will tell you. More than anything else you are probably lucky. The next time someone says how wonderful you are for raising your kids alone, remember that almost no one compliments a single woman for doing the same thing.

Now the good news: You're going to find the experience very exciting. If you don't enjoy this opportunity to get close to your kids, share feelings with them, and enjoy the noise in the house, then you really ought to give the opportunity to one of the millions of lonely divorced fathers who are reduced to weekend visitation.

You may already know that you can't take a marriage and the kids away from a divorced man, place him in a bachelor apartment and tell him to "go play." While this may be the fantasy of many unhappily married men, it doesn't translate into reality. You are raised in a "Very Married Culture" and you cannot expect yourself to immediately adjust to single parenthood. Keep in mind that no matter what your age, you are probably an "old dog" and the new tricks are not going to be mastered during the first week.

Some non-romantic, nitty gritty, free advice to the single father:

(a) Your biggest headache will be finding help. If you can afford it, your help should live in. This gives you the freedom to accept last-minute dinner invitations, cope with responsibilities that may require your attention in the evening, or occasionally do an evening with friends that wasn't planned. Remember, no matter how firm you resolve to be the World's Greatest Father, you are going to need time to cater to *your* needs.

Be aware that moving a stranger into your house to care for your kids is a complicated maneuver. Everyone brings a certain amount of "excess baggage" into a relationship. No matter how thoroughly you've "screened" your help, there is no way to anticipate all the things that you and the kids do that will annoy the new "Nanny." No matter how hard you try, there will be certain aspects of your parenting that "Nanny" will not approve. Be ready for this. You'll be surprised at her disapproval, because she seemed so absolutely perfect during the job interview.

(b) "Nanny" will probably develop a large "crush" on you. In a world of hard-drinking men who seldom show affection for their kids, you are consciously trying to be a decent father, and you are clearly inept at it. Your little-boy-lost posture will be very attractive to her. Establish an employee/employer relationship immediately and maintain it. This means her quarters are absolutely private and not to be trespassed by either you or the kids. Always address "Nanny" as Mrs. ——— or Miss ———. First names breed contemptuous familiarity and can diminish the children's respect for the new authority person.

(c) "Nanny" must be supported at all times by you when the children are present. Never, repeat, Never take the children's side against her. On the other hand, make sure your "housekeeper" (as you'll probably refer to her) understands that there is only one parent in the house, and it is *you*. Tell her you feel obligated to support her in raising the children, but under no circumstances is she to force the children to do anything. That's your job. If she begins with a whole bunch of "shoulds" for the kids, they'll draw imaginary venetian blinds on her. All "shoulds" must come from you.

Nevertheless, your housekeeper is human and you must allow her the freedom to become discouraged, angry, sad and all the other human emotions that accompany child-raising. Your live-in help must know that she can communicate all anxieties regarding the children with full confidence that you will take her seriously. Her grievance must be discussed with the children immediately and you must be supportive of her. If you find yourself consistently in disagreement with her then you must get another housekeeper.

Under no circumstances should a housekeeper be given permission to administer physical punishment to your children. When a real parent does it, it's tough enough on kids. They certainly don't need or want a "hired hitter."

(d) Never speak critically about your ex-wife. She is still their mother, and you owe your kids a genuine effort to present her in a positive way.

(e) Your main task as a parent is to make clear to your children in countless ways that they are loved. Psychiatry, analysis and research may occasionally develop contradictory conclusions, except for one tenet about which there is no argument: *Your kids must know they are loved.*

(f) You owe them every effort to make visitation by your ex-wife convenient. She should be welcome according to the agreement, but she should not be encouraged to spend the night in your house with your kids. This could cause confusion to your children (especially the younger ones). You know your marriage is over, your wife knows it is over, and your kids should know and understand it as well. Providing live-in accommodations for your ex-wife could blur the separation, which may be damaging to young children, who often harbor fantasies about a reconciliation.

(g) If you are worried about the well-being of your kids, let them know it. You don't have to drive them crazy, but, remember, being reasonably anxious about their health and welfare is a sign of love. Of course, you have a right to know where your kids are at all times.

(h) If you are back in the social whirl, make sure your kids meet your friends of both sexes. If you are dating, bring her home, avoid theatrical niceties, allow for imperfect human behavior, and avoid dramatic demonstrations of affection. If you are involved with a woman and expressing yourself intimately, you are now coming face to face with single parenthood's most distracting problem: whether or not to share the same bedroom. Now the ball is in your court. Your decision should be based on your own moral code and your evaluation of your feelings about your partner.

Questions to help you decide should include: Is this relationship going to last? If it ends, how soon can the kids expect you back with another woman? With how many women can you share a bedroom in front of your kids without affecting their moral perception? Remember also, if you choose to reserve your intimacy outside your home, your kids are going to draw their own conclusions before too long. When do discretion and dishonesty begin?

I never said it would be easy.

CREDIT: *Phil Donohue, TV host of "The Phil Donohue Show."*

Cystic Fibrosis

Millions of American children suffer from lung-damaging diseases.

Of illnesses treated by pediatricians, 75 percent involve respiratory problems. Of illnesses which strike children, lung disease is the second major cause of death. It is a health problem of frightening proportions.

The most serious chronic lung-damaging disease is cystic fibrosis. It can affect not only the lungs, but also the gastrointestinal system. Other serious lung-damaging diseases affecting infants and children include hyaline membrane disease, severe asthma, chronic bronchitis, bronchiectasis, persistent pneumonia and a condition resembling adult emphysema.

WHAT IS CYSTIC FIBROSIS?

CF, a genetic (inherited) disease, is a leading cause of death in children and young adults. In CF, chronic lung infection produces sticky mucus which clogs the lungs and airways, creating breathing difficulties, high susceptibility to further infection and lung damage. The mucus may also interfere with digestion by preventing the flow of enzymes from the pancreas into the small intestine, causing malabsorption of food.

CF happens approximately once in every sixteen hundred births, when a child inherits two genes for CF, one from each parent. In each pregnancy, a child born to parents with the CF gene will have a 25 percent chance of having the disease, a 50 percent chance of being a symptomless carrier, and a 25 percent chance of escaping both the CF gene and the disease. When only one parent has the CF gene, none of the children will have the disease itself, but they could be symptomless carriers.

Research developments may soon make it possible to detect symptomless carriers. Research is trying to identify characteristics in the cells and blood of both CF patients and their parents that could be isolated to provide accurate testing. When such a test is perfected for practical screening, prospective parents could learn if they are among the ten million CF gene carriers in the United States.

A "sweat test" for measuring salt content in the sweat is a major tool in establishing the diagnosis of CF. Sweat in CF patients has an abnormally high salt content, a condition not occurring in other lung-damaging diseases. The earlier a child is diagnosed and treated, the better his chances for improved health, stable lung condition, and prolonged life. Diagnosis in infancy, whenever possible, is strongly recommended.

Treatment for CF children varies with each individual child and is determined by the attending physician. Treatment often includes postural drainage, a type of therapy which helps the patient cough up mucus from the lungs and bronchial tubes; inhalation of aerosols to loosen thick mucus; and special medications and diet supplements such as antibiotics, pancreatic enzymes and vitamins. Some children with CF take as many as forty or fifty pills a day. Children with other lung-damaging diseases benefit greatly from some of the same treatment as those with CF.

Little more than a decade ago, most CF babies died in pre-school age. Thanks to improved therapy and expanded research, increasing numbers of individuals with CF are surviving into adolescence and adulthood with the ability to lead more normal and active lives than ever before. The Cystic Fibrosis Foundation conducts a CF Adult Program to help those fifteen years and older with physical, emotional and career development.

More than a hundred CF centers associated with the Cystic Fibrosis Foundation offer the services of respiratory specialists and the latest therapy for CF and other children's lung diseases. CF centers screen and evaluate children with lung-damaging diseases, offering diagnosis, patient-referral and care. Precise diagnosis of lung-damaging diseases requires specialized knowledge as the symptoms of CF and other lung-damaging diseases are often similar and can be misleading.

Center personnel train parents in administering the home care therapy and medication needs of lung-damaged children.

Hyaline membrane disease occurs in the first days of life of some prematurely born infants. It may resolve completely, or lead to prolonged respiratory distress.

Asthma with lung damage: An allergic condition, common in childhood and frequently outgrown, can occur seasonally or throughout the year. It is characterized by labored breathing, wheezing, coughing and mucus production. Associated infection can cause chronic bronchitis and damage to airways. It is frequently familial.

Chronic bronchitis: Prolonged irritation and infection of bronchial tubes with progressively severe attacks of coughing, production of mucus and loss of weight. Can be very serious if of long duration. Smoking in parents may aggravate this condition in the children who live in the same household.

Bronchiectasis: Caused by long-term bronchitis, asthma, pneumonia, whooping cough, cystic fibrosis or lung collapse. Involves breakdown of bronchial walls and even cartilage. Children may have fever, are underweight. Very rare, and may be serious.

Childhood emphysema: Name given to overinflation and destruction of lung tissue resulting from chronic respiratory disease, with obstruction and hyperaeration. Can result from previous treated lung disease, such as some viral pneumonias.

Disorders of lung development: Many children are born with abnormal size or placement of one or both lungs. In addition, the breathing tubes or blood supply to the lungs may not have developed properly before the baby was born, leading to respiration difficulties throughout life.

Recurrent or persistent pneumonia: Some children, because of abnormal structure of their lungs, or because of a malfunctioning system of immunity to infection, suffer repeated episodes of pneumonia. If not properly treated, permanent damage to the lung develops.

Recurrent wheezing; persistent coughing/excessive mucus; pneumonia more than once; excessive appetite/poor weight gain; clubbing (enlargement of fingertips).

Additionally, signs of cystic fibrosis may include: salty taste of the skin, nasal polyps, and persistent, bulky diarrhea.

Any child with one or more of these signs should be examined by his or her physician or at a CF center.

Because someone you know—perhaps you—may be one of the estimated ten million CF gene carriers in the United States. You may have or know a child with a chronic respiratory problem who could greatly benefit from prompt diagnosis and expert treatment. It is important because there are millions of children struggling for the breath of life, and they need you.

The Foundation, established in 1955, is dedicated to the research and clinical care which is essential for children with lung-damaging disease. CFF grants to scientists and researchers are bringing us closer to the primary objective of the organization: finding a cure or control for cystic fibrosis. It is also leading to better understanding of the causes and controls for all diseases which affect the lungs of children. CFF training and sponsorship of CF centers is continually improving the quality of care—indeed, the quality of life—for children with respiratory problems. The Foundation also conducts public and professional education programs, sponsors medical and scientific symposiums, and acts as a source of assistance and guidance to its chapters. The CFF co-operates in a worldwide effort toward better understanding of genetic problems and pediatric pulmonary illnesses.

There are one hundred local chapters of the CFF, many of which have branch operations in major communities. Manned by volunteers and professional staff, local chapters conduct the annual CF Breath of Life Campaign to provide funds for chapter activities and the National Foundation's programs. Chapters provide informational assistance to families of lung-damaged children and can make referrals to various local agencies for financial aid. (Many states include cystic fibrosis under the Crippled Children's programs.) The total care of a CF patient can cost $5,000 yearly in drugs, dietary supplements, equipment, hospitalization and clinic evaluations. Chapters are a source of information on available CF center care and conduct year-round public information activities on the problems of lung disease in children.

CREDIT: *Cystic Fibrosis Foundation, Atlanta, Georgia. Checked for accuracy and amended by Mary Ellen Avery, M.D., Physician-in-Chief, Children's Hospital, Boston, Massachusetts.*

Dandruff

It has been said that nothing stops dandruff like a blue serge suit. Actually, dandruff can be "stopped" by prescription preparations, antidandruff shampoos and rinses, but so far there is no known cure for the pesky condition.

The only thing dandruff is good for is the economy. Last year Americans spent nearly $75 million trying to get rid of it.

What is dandruff? Dandruff in its simplest form is flaking and itching of the scalp. It can become a social or cosmetic problem when many large flakes hang loosely in the hair or fall onto the shoulders.

In simple dandruff there is no inflammation, swelling, or redness. If any of these symptoms develop, it usually means that a more severe form of dandruff has developed. This goes under the medical name of seborrheic dermatitis.

Psoriasis and ringworm of the scalp can also cause scaling that may look like dandruff. If recognized, this condition should be treated by a physician immediately.

Who gets dandruff? Practically everyone feels that he or she has had a dandruff problem at one time or another. Only 6 percent of a representative sample of U.S. citizens claim never to have had dandruff. Cradle cap of infancy is a form of dandruff. Otherwise, dandruff is seldom seen in children before the age of eleven or twelve.

Observations made during clinical trials of shampoo products show that when a large group (4,000) was examined seven days after each had had a shampoo, 10 percent of the group had enough scalp scaling to be concerned about it as a cosmetic problem. Another 13 percent was close to this level.

What causes dandruff? Medical science cannot yet answer this question. Until recently many medical authorities did not recognize simple dandruff as a disease. Today, thanks to work made public within the last few years, it is known that skin from scalps of people with dandruff is abnormal.

Simple dandruff is a low-grade inflammation of the skin in areas of the body with increased oil production. That is, it occurs in areas with increased numbers of sebaceous glands with its oily product, sebum. Dandruff will flare up during times of increased sebum production. One of the most popular theories for the cause of dandruff is that microorganisms (the bacteria and yeast-like fungi that live on the scalp) cause dandruff. Many of the antidandruff products on the market are based on this theory. However, this theory has not been proved.

Dandruff is definitely not contagious. It is also not a ringworm or fungus infection. It is not a malignancy or an early form of skin cancer.

Dandruff comes and goes, but no ones knows for certain why. One investigator believes the severity of dandruff may increase during spells of emotional stress or following respiratory infection. In general, dandruff will often flare up during the winter, with pregnancy, lack of sleep, or overwork, and at times of excessive alcohol consumption. For unknown reasons, it often appears with certain neurologic diseases.

Dandruff is not an allergic condition and, contrary to popular opinion, does not lead to baldness.

One of the confusing things about dandruff is that the skin may seem dry and flaky even though the rash occurs in oily areas. This is explained by the fact that the oily sebum in some way causes inflammation in the skin, which in turn irritates the skin and causes the flaking and itching.

Dandruff is often patchy. A person can have noticeable dandruff on one part of the head and no scaling on another part. Dandruff can also commonly occur in other areas of the body, such as the eyebrows, sides of the nose, beard area, ears, central part of the chest, armpits and groin. Dandruff can appear at any age after adolescence, either gradually or quite suddenly. It may last for years or may disappear after a few weeks. Even though it is a chronic condition, it can usually be completely controlled without an outright cure. While there is no final cure, proper action can control the problem.

What can be done about dandruff? Despite the fact that the cause of dandruff is unknown, dandruff can be managed.

If there is nothing on your scalp but loose flakes, with the skin beneath it appearing normal, improvement may result from a program of improved scalp hygiene.

Many dandruff remedies are sold without a prescription. They are available as shampoos, post-shampoo treatments, or hairdressings. Which form is chosen is a matter of personal preference. Frequent shampooing is always the initial step in dandruff treatment. For some people once a week is enough, though for many people two or three times a week is much more effective.

If there is any redness, swelling, oozing or scabbing, the condition is probably more than simple dandruff. It is best managed by a physician. Dermatologists have traditionally treated dandruff in its severe forms with sulfur, cortisone, salicylic acid, resorcinol, tar and, more recently, selenium sulfide. The concentration of the medication and the frequency of use depend on the severity of the condition, as determined by the physician. These medications are available on prescription as a cream, lotion or spray. Daily shampooing may be necessary to control the oiliness, itching and scaling.

Once under control, you find out by trial how often to use the medications.

Treatment is necessary more often during flare-ups but can be tapered off when it subsides.

In addition, ample rest and recreation will help. Sunlight is often beneficial and summer may bring a spontaneous remission. Scalp massage and medications that claim to improve scalp circulation are without benefit.

A word about effectiveness. Published information is scarce. It is difficult, therefore, to assess the effectiveness of the many products available. A physician (preferably a dermatologist) can help you decide the best method of treatment.

CREDIT: *Gregory L. Jenkins, M.D., dermatologist, San Jose, California.*

Death and Dying, Made into a Human Experience

Many books and papers have been written in the last decade dealing with the issue of dehumanized care in hospitals and nursing homes with patients who are chronically incapacitated—especially those who have an incurable illness and face imminent death.

Not too long ago, these patients were given sedatives rather than told the truth and given a chance to deal with their emotions. They received excellent nursing care in order to prevent bedsores and dehydration (loss of fluids) by being put on intravenous feedings when they became too weak to drink or eat. No one, however, dealt with the emotional and spiritual aspects of these lonely and often isolated people who spent their last days or weeks in a strange, unfamiliar environment with a change of nursing shifts and a medical staff whose names the patients did not even know.

Children are usually not permitted to visit hospitals, especially for critically ill patients. Visiting hours in Intensive Care Units are often restricted to five minutes every hour. Dying was—and still is—in many hospitals a lonely ordeal alternating between excruciating pain and strict orders "not to make a dope addict" out of patients, to have sedation where the patient drifts in and out of a semiconscious state and is unable to communicate his needs or share his wishes or personal experiences.

No wonder people dread entering a hospital, which instantly sees to it that they receive a plastic armband on which is printed their name but has the staff call patients "honey" and "sweetie" and say, "Let's see if we can have a bowel movement now," as if the patient was a helpless child, deferring to the convenience of the staff when to perform the most natural of bodily functions.

Staff come and go without knocking at the door, without asking for permission to examine them. They stick needles in arms or legs and tell them when they are allowed to sit, walk, visit or eat.

For many patients this is a tremendous shock and adjustment. But they tolerate it out of fear—with much repressed resentment, guilt and shame. Hospitalization is a great financial burden to most families. It places an enormous amount of stress on people at a time when they should mobilize all their energies to fight against disease.

When a terminal illness has been verified and the treatment has been exhausted, the family is often much better informed than the person whose life is at stake. The behavior of staff and relatives changes in a subtle way. Visits become shorter and less frequent and dialogues more shallow. Rules are broken. Relatives visit from faraway places with excuses of "being in town for a day or two." The patient is naturally aware that the anxiety level increases the moment he makes an attempt to discuss the true state of affairs. When he dares to ask the physician about his outlook, he may get a remark like, "Well, today you sure look much better than last week," and the real issue is avoided. When he finally corners his favorite nurse with a complaint that "no one 'levels' with me," the nurse, embarrassed about her own apparent impotence, replies, "You'll have to ask your doctor." Later, when the patient confronts his wife, she smilingly projects her own despair and hope by saying, "Now, honey, don't think about such things. All you have to do is eat a little more and you will get stronger soon."

While all this game-playing is going on, the patient goes quietly through his own adjustment. At first he may not want to accept the fact that he is dying. He may pass through a stage of denial and seek out another doctor who will tell him the first doctor was wrong. But soon he is aware that it is his own despair that prevents him from facing the truth. Gradually, he drops this defense, knowing that he will not be able to take care of his unfinished business as long as he cannot mobilize enough courage to face the outcome.

Many a patient goes through a period of rebellion and anger, a sense of deep resentment directed at those who are well, those who play games and remind him of his previous ability to function and tell him that in time he will again be in control of his life. Rather than take this anger personally, the family and staff should facilitate the expression of these natural emotions, thus helping them to empty the pool of repressed anger and resentment, freeing all the energy that could be used for positive rather than negative fighting.

While children with leukemia may grieve the loss of their hair (due to the treatment), a man may mourn his inability to be productive and a mother her separation from the children. These natural grief reactions again have to be ventilated rather than repressed. It is only by encouraging the open expression of anger, grief, guilt and shame that we can help our fellow man to free himself of all this energy-consuming negativity and assist him toward the true and genuine feeling of wholeness, pride and self-acceptance.

These patients should not be put on valium or other antidepressants to sedate their feelings when they finally have the courage to face the real loss and impending separation. It is a genuine loss and tears are the healthiest means of expression of this natural grief.

When a patient is supported without criticism of his behavior by an understanding member of family or staff, the process of anger followed by acceptance will require a very short time and enable the patient to live free of anxiety and fear for whatever time he (or she) has left.

When all treatment has been exhausted, it has become our procedure to ask the patient and family if they will take the patient home to die. Most families are grateful for the opportunity.

The use of the Brompton Mixture has facilitated this move.

The Brompton Mixture is a fully acceptable and legally permissible pain cocktail which requires a physician's prescription and can be mixed by any local pharmacist. Details are available through Mr. Gregg Humma, Department of Pharmacy, Methodist Hospital, Indianapolis, Indiana, or Dr. William Dugan, distinguished cancer specialist at the same address. Be sure to enclose your physician's name and address. He will receive a brochure and instructions.

We are now able to keep our cancer patients free of pain and fully alert and conscious with the use of this oral pain-cocktail. It eliminates injections, and makes it possible for patients to communicate without difficulty until the last moments of life.

When a patient dies at home, we usually make a few house calls to assure that everything necessary is being done to keep the patient comfortable and that the emotional and spiritual needs of patient and family are being met.

Since our research has verified the death experience as a painless, anxiety-free shedding of the body with emergence into a different form of life with continued consciousness and growth, we usually explain this experience to small children in symbolic language like the emergence of the butterfly out of a cocoon "when the time is right." This reflects simultaneously our own philosophy that there is a time to be born and a time to die and that we should neither shorten life nor artificially prolong the dying process because of our own fears and inability to let go.

Our own Growth and Healing Center, "Shanti Nilaya"—which means The Home of Peace—in Escondido, California, is the first retreat center of its kind in the United States where people of all ages, creeds and cultural or economic background can come in order to pass through this process without waiting until they are faced with a terminal illness. It has been proved through many workshops with a variety of people across the world that we have the ability to conquer our greatest fears about death and eliminate negative feelings such as shame and guilt, which prevent us from living fully and from learning to love without strings, conditions and claims on others.

Our tendency in the past has been to protect our children and patients from facing such difficult and painful issues as death and dying. We believe that this is a protection for ourselves and not an act of love. As one of our greatest teachers once said: "To truly love means to live without fear of life's storms, knowing that should you shield the canyons from the windstorms you could never enjoy the beauty of its carvings."

CREDIT: *Elisabeth Kübler-Ross, M.D., Flossmoor, Illinois, author of* On Death and Dying, *New York: The Macmillan Co., 1969.*

Death of a Child

(*How to Deal with It*)

FOR BEREAVED PARENTS

DEAR ANN LANDERS: May I respond to "Sinking," the grieving mother who had lost a child? She inflicted herself on a casual acquaintance who had suffered the same tragedy because, as she put it, "No one else understands. A person has to experience it." Sixteen months ago, our 8-year-old son died of a brain tumor. I can tell you that losing a child is life's most punishing sorrow. I'm writing to inform that woman (and others) of an organization called Compassionate Friends. It saved my sanity.

The purpose of Compassionate Friends is to offer support and understanding to any bereaved parent. We have sharing groups where we both talk and listen. At our meetings, "Sinking" will become acquainted with parents whose grief has softened. They have found new hope and the strength for living.

Since I don't know where "Sinking" lives, I'm sending the address of the national headquarters. Anyone who wants information about us and our branches should write to Compassionate Friends, Box 3247, Hialeah, Fla. 33013.

N.C. OF CHICAGO

When your parent dies you've lost your past, but when your child dies you've lost your future.

It is precisely this loss of future, this sense of seeing one's continuity buried, that makes the death of a child the ultimate tragedy.

Beyond the pain, which to many bereaved parents is like a physical amputation, a number of problems surface. A numbness, exhaustion, the brief attention span, anger and guilt—they all play a part in increasing an already agonizing situation.

One of the most serious problems is the sense of helplessness that overtakes a parent at this time. Somehow, there is a sense of having failed to have performed one's principal duty—that of preserving your own child's life.

In the natural sequence of life, people grow older, marry and ultimately they are buried by their children. When a child dies, this natural life cycle is reversed. The parents are bitterly resentful. They feel cheated. Life has handed them a raw deal.

When a child dies, most couples encounter devastating marital problems. Society has erroneous notions that bereaved parents can at least look to one another for support and that sharing a tragedy brings them closer together. In most cases this does not happen. Within a matter of months 90 percent of all bereaved couples are in marital crisis.

The problems most frequently encountered are (a) sexual dysfunction, since grief sharply diminishes the sex drive or kills it altogether, (b) a sense of pervasive doom and the feeling that one's mate is somehow inadequate because he or she is unable to help.

The most insidious difficulty of all is the inability to deal with day to day annoyances. Compared to the magnitude of a child's death, messiness and uncooked meals are trivialities. Grieving couples frequently stop verbalizing the daily irritations that are a part of marriage. Things are swept under the rug so often that what started as a trash pile ends up becoming a garbage dump.

There are times when spouses blame one another for the child's death. When this happens psychiatric counseling should be sought.

It is important to become associated with other bereaved parents once you have buried your own. Great comfort can be derived from the presence of those who have been there and are now functioning. You can then tell yourself, "If they can get over it, I can too."

Because we live in an instant society—one in which we expect instant coffee, instant headache cures and instant stain removers—bereaved parents are thrown into further despair when they see that their grief does not disappear as soon as they expected it might.

Parents must understand the healing process after the death of a child is a long-term procedure. They must not despair because it goes on and on and seems endless.

Another problem of bereaved parents is the unfortunate fact that the entire support system in this country is centered around the mother. She receives comfort and warmth from friends and family along with a greater outward manifestation of caring. The father, on the other hand, is expected to make the funeral arrangements, and go back to work as usual.

Because of business pressures, many fathers do not have sufficient time to grieve. This can produce the feeling that his life is not synchronized with his wife's. There are instances where two or three years after a child's death the father begins delayed mourning. He then becomes resentful of his wife's ability to cope, not realizing that she is years ahead of him in the process. The wife, on the other hand, may become resentful because her husband is pulling her back to where she was in her grieving years.

While we live in an age where we attempt to address ourselves to the problems of racism and sexism, grieving stands out as the last bastion of true chauvinism. Not only do we fail to address ourselves to the needs of bereaved fathers, we fail to accept the fact that such needs exist.

I feel the story I am about to relate is rich in significance for all grieving parents:

The man, seeing his son near death, changed from his rich robes to sackcloth and from his diet of plenty to fasting, hoping his sacrifices would help the boy he dearly loved. When, seven days later, the youngster died despite the finest medical attention of his day, the man once again put on his luxurious garments and sat down to an abundant feast. When friends asked him how he could eat with his child newly dead, he replied he had done all that was humanly possible while the boy was alive and now that he was gone, it was time to pick up the pieces of living and go on with life.

The man was King David.

The wise King had come to a truth that countless parents in their pain have also found.

The living must go on with life.

CREDIT: *Harriet Sarnoff Schiff, Birmington, Michigan, author of* The Bereaved Parent, *New York: Crown Publishers.*

Death of a Sibling

Because a natural rivalry is built into the relationship between brothers and sisters, it is a great burden to bear when a sibling dies.

Most surviving children are convinced that their negative feelings about a dead brother or sister actually caused the death.

This is a serious and only recently defined problem. Children are taught from early childhood that if they are good, think nice thoughts and do fine deeds the Good Fairy will grant their every wish. This concept is called magical thinking.

They also believe the reverse is true—that if they are envious, angry, or have any of the feelings that are normal among brothers and sisters, that somehow they are to blame if a brother or sister dies. When they quarrel one may say or think, "I wish she was dead." If that child should die, the effects on the one who did the wishing can be devastating.

The problem compounds itself because the parents are usually so immersed in their own grief that they fail to recognize the problems faced by their children.

Parents sometimes make the mistake of comparing the dead children to the living. The surviving children often stop achieving when this occurs.

Children are criticized for the manner in which they grieve. Onlookers tend to keep opinions to themselves about adults, but they do not feel reticent to comment about children who laugh and play when a sibling has died. They fail to understand that everyone needs a break from grief.

Discipline within the home frequently takes on different characteristics at this time. Parents shift from leniency to strictness—or the reverse. This is common after tragedy.

Children can become terrified at seeing their father cry for the first time unless it is carefully explained and handled. Of course, if it is properly handled, both boy and girl children can come to more positive conclusions about tears.

Because so much raw emotion is exploding within the heads of bereaved parents, living children rarely receive the type of support they have a right to expect. It is imperative to reopen a dialogue and tell children truthfully that you were unable to help them because you were drowning in your own grief.

Ask if there are questions. Ask if there are memories they would like to share. Explain that the dead child was mortal with a combination of both good and bad qualities.

This conversation can free up suppressed feelings of a surviving sibling. When told there is anger in all loving relationships, youngsters begin to accept that there was nothing wrong with how they felt about their dead sibling.

The question of whether siblings should attend the funeral is one that should be discussed with funeral directors or clergy. Generally, psychologists claim that a child of five understands death is final, at six they are emotional, at seven they are curious and at eight they are coping.

Most important to recognize is that siblings are the forgotten mourners and often carry problems into adulthood because they were not given their due at the time a brother or sister died.

CREDIT: *Harriet Sarnoff Schiff, Birmingham, Michigan, author of* The Bereaved Parent, *New York: Crown Publishers.*

Explaining Death to Children

Children today are more aware of death than their parents realize. Despite a strong movement to curb violence on television, death is still commonly portrayed (and often in a rather gruesome manner) on TV and in films. Yet it is surprising how many parents try to shield their children from the realization that death is an inevitable part of life.

The death of a loved one is a traumatic experience for all the survivors—children included. Youngsters react to these stressful situations just as adults do, with disbelief, anger, guilt, anxiety, panic and, sometimes, physical illness. But children are not as well equipped as adults, emotionally and intellectually, to understand, express and eventually resolve these conflicting feelings.

The best thing a parent can do to help a child through the difficult times following the death of a loved one is to be honest. Children have an uncanny ability to detect deception. They receive messages through non-verbal communication and sense instinctively when someone close to them is troubled. Don't try to hide the fact that someone has died and you are upset about it. Explain to the child, in terms he will understand, exactly what death is. Tell him that people die when the heart, brain, lungs, etc., can no longer continue to function, usually as a result of accident, illness or extreme old age. Emphasize that old age is the most frequent cause of death and that children and parents rarely die young. There is every reason to believe that all of us will live to a ripe old age. There are exceptions, of course, but the best thing we can do is to live our lives fully and not worry about the exceptions.

In order to avoid what could be a painful explanation of death, parents often resort to associating death with sleep, a tactic which could have unfortunate consequences. The prayer that starts "Now I lay me down to sleep" and ends with "If I should die before I wake . . ." has caused nightmares for many children. It is important to make a clear distinction between death and sleeping. Explain that sleep helps the body build up strength so it can work better and has nothing to do with dying.

After the death of a close relative or friend, children often begin to wonder where people go when they die. Abstractions are confusing to young children. Parents who believe in heaven and in a God who watches over us might do well to delay teaching these doctrines to their children until they are at least six or seven years old. Or, if you do introduce your child to the concept of heaven, do so in terms he will understand. Warn him that it is a difficult idea and that he will grasp it better when he is older. Children tend to make abstractions concrete. Heaven to a child can be very much like the street on which he lives. If you tell your child, "Grandpa is looking down from heaven and watching you," he might believe that his grandfather is watching every move he makes. This becomes a tremendous burden and might destroy the loving memories he has of his grandfather.

A good way to help a child understand the concept of immortality is by using an example from his own experience. Emphasize the fact that a person's good deeds continue to influence other people's lives long after that person has died. Likewise, point out that love between people extends from one generation to the next. Because memories and love are real to a child, they are more useful than abstractions, which should be taught later in life.

Another important reason for being honest with children about death, aside from the fact that they easily recognize dishonesty, is that a child's imagination can produce concepts that are far more frightening than reality. In one family, an infant, dead at birth, was cremated. The parents thought this would be too difficult to explain to a four-year-old, so they avoided the issue altogether. Weeks later, after the child had shown signs of emotional disturbance, the parents sat him down and explained in detail the various ways in which the dead are buried or cremated. The child sighed with relief and said, "I'm glad you told me. I thought the baby was somewhere in the house."

A common misconception held by children is that they are somehow responsible for the death of a loved one. It is normal for a child in the heat of anger to wish his parents dead, and an outburst of this sort is usually followed by severe guilt. After the child has cooled down, and perhaps been reprimanded for his temper tantrum, explain to him that people who love each other often do get angry at one another and that death is never caused by angry words or thoughts. A little boy of four suffered terribly when a baby brother died at the age of three months. What later came out, after weeks of terror, was that he was sure his thoughts had killed his little brother. Like every normal child, he had resented the baby's arrival, and in his jealousy he wished that the baby would be taken back to the hospital. When the baby actually died, the boy was convinced that he was responsible. This type of thinking is normal for all children up to the age of nine or ten. Understanding parents can help the child resolve these guilt feelings.

There is no way to protect a child from the experience of grief. It is the normal reaction to death. Parents are mistaken when they think that any child above the age of two can be spared it. One young mother went to stay with her sister when their mother died. "I didn't want my three-year-old to see me cry," she explained. "It would have upset her too much." The mother did not realize that a parent's sudden, unexplained disappearance is far more frightening to a child than the sight of her tears.

Parents should neither disguise their grief in front of a child nor should they encourage a child to suppress his own. Proper mental health, for both adults and children, depends on the acknowledgment of tragedy, not its denial. Exhortations to "be brave" or, to a son, to "be a man," place enormous burdens on a child and seem to minimize his sense of loss. It is more realistic to tell the child, "Yes, it is sad and I am feeling the same things you are." Do not reprimand your child when he cries. He obviously loved the person who died, misses him, and tears are a natural and therapeutic expression of grief. Children who are made to suppress their tears may later find a release in a more serious emotional explosion. Communicate the fact that it is all right to cry. Let your child know that it is normal to feel shock and disbelief, to feel sad and deserted. Adults and children often become angry at the person who died for leaving them. They may also feel guilty about not having been "nicer" to the person who died. Discuss these feelings openly with your child. Remember: If adults need the experience of mourning, so do children—perhaps even more so.

One of the major childhood fears (usually aggravated by the death of a loved one) is that of being left alone. Reassure the child that he will not be abandoned; that even though Grandpa, Daddy, or whoever, has died, he is still surrounded by people who love him and who would never let him come to harm. Demonstrate this to the child with words and touch. Encourage him to talk and hold him lovingly when he cries.

From about age seven, a child should be encouraged to attend the funeral of a close relative if he wishes to do so. Younger children should also go if they are accustomed to attending church services or other public gatherings. Parents often think funerals are too harsh an experience for children and discourage their own from attending. Many child psychologists disagree. A funeral is a shared community experience and a crucial occurrence in the life of a family. A youngster should have the same right as any other family member to be present at the funeral and to express his emotions. To deprive a child of a sense of belonging at an emotionally trying time could have harmful psychological consequences.

When parents are open and direct with their children about death they are giving them a message about how precious life is. When they avoid the subject, they deprive children of an opportunity to understand the miracle of being human and alive. The knowledge of death affirms the wonder of life, and helps us all to realize that we should make every one of them count.

CREDIT: *Eda J. LeShan, author of* What Makes Me Feel This Way? *and* Learning to Say Goodbye: When a Parent Dies, *New York: The Macmillan Co.*

What Not to Say at the Funeral

Some feel that they must deliver a deep philosophical and theological message to the mourners. More often than not, profound words are meaningless because they are not comprehended when there is suffering and emotional turmoil.

Be cautious about using phrases that may be misunderstood. Implying that the death was "God's will" or telling a son or daughter when a parent has died, "Well, you were lucky to have him as long as you did." They do not consider themselves "lucky," no matter how long the loved one lived.

On the other hand, do not talk about every subject except the reason for your coming together—the death of the person loved. The mourner wants and needs to talk about his loss and all that it means to him.

It is no help to say, "Don't talk about it." The survivor may be going through an intense emotional crisis. He may need to speak and act out his feelings of denial. He needs to weep and confront the truth of his loss.

If the person who mourns suppresses his feelings he is adding one more burden to the many he already has. Studies of mourning show it is therapeutic to talk about the deceased. The visitor may also want to recall some valued memories of the person who has died.

Too often, well-meaning people say: "Be brave! Don't cry! Don't take it so hard!"

But why not? Tears are the most sincere tribute that can be paid to the one who is gone.

Emotions of grief are normal reactions necessary for health. Death has so many overtones: loneliness, fear, ambivalence, anger, guilt and hostility. There is nothing shameful or unacceptable in these feelings.

The mourner who denies them or keeps his emotions bottled up may find release later in a damaging psychic explosion. It is good to encourage outward expression of feelings. Just as joy shared is joy increased, grief shared is grief diminished.

Encourage the mourner to tell you what he feels, rather than trying to tell him how he should feel.

It is not necessary to say a great deal to the bereaved. The most significant approach may be non-verbal. A firm shake of the hands, a look into their eyes, will show you care. By your presence, you affirm that they are not alone in their grief.

Conversation should be natural. Interest must be genuine and sincere. A most important method of encouraging the natural outpouring of grief is by responsive listening. If possible, let the sorrowing people talk. Many callers are worried about their ability to say the right thing when it is far more important to give the mourner an understanding ear. The aim of any conversation should not be only to recall the past, but to help the bereaved adjust to the present.

Never underestimate the value of the condolence or sympathy visit. As has been written: "No man is an island . . . Any man's death diminishes me."

CREDIT: *National Funeral Directors Association, Milwaukee, Wisconsin.*

Dental Health

The American mouth is a disaster area. At least twenty-five million people in the United States put their teeth in a glass at night. Seventy-five percent have gum disease and 98 percent have at least one cavity.

Researchers have been looking diligently for ways to stop tooth decay. Some progress has been made by adding fluorides to drinking water, "glazing" the teeth with laser beams, encasing them in plastic-like chemicals, even vaccines that would affect bacteria in the mouth have been proposed. Despite the experimentation, the exploration and an intensive campaign designed to educate the public to the value of brushing and flossing, the nation's dental problems are far from solved.

NURSING

Young mothers must not allow their children to use a nursing bottle as a pacifier. Children who sleep with a bottle in their mouth or walk around with a bottle very often develop early cavities. Children should be held in an upright position when nursing from a bottle. This allows the facial muscles to assume the position as if the child were nursing from the breast. In this way, many dentists believe you can prevent the development of crooked death since the muscles will develop properly and move the teeth later in life into the proper position.

FLUORIDE—THE MOST IMPORTANT ASPECT IN A PROGRAM OF CAVITY PRE-
VENTION

This is a complicated and important subject in preventive dentistry.
Fluorides are a large group of chemical compounds formed when fluorine
combines with other elements. They are found everywhere—in soil, in the
air, in plant and animal life, in foods, and dissolved in water. Fluoride works
like this: When the teeth are forming, fluoride becomes incorporated into the
enamel of the tooth. The resulting tooth is stronger, and more resistant to
dental decay. The period between birth and three years of age is especially
critical because during this time the permanent teeth are forming. Dentists
today recommend early use (from one year on) of a fluoride toothpaste. Parents should talk to their dentists about various ways of getting fluoride into
their children's teeth. In addition to the water supply, children can get
fluoride through toothpastes, mouthwashes, and applications at the dentist's
office.

DIET AND CAVITIES

A basic principle for parents to remember is that the best way to change
their child's dental health is not to change *what* the child eats, but *when* he or
she eats it. This does *not* mean that parents should permit their children to
eat candy, cookies, and other sweet snacks all day long. Snacking on sweet
foods (such as candy and cookies) or sticky foods (such as potato chips)
can be disastrous. The job of the concerned parent is to control the number
of times during the day the child's teeth come in contact with sugar.

Foods containing sugar trigger acid formation almost immediately. And
this acid often causes decay. The number of times during the day that the
child has sugar-containing foods, as well as how long the sugar remains in
contact with the teeth, are the two important factors in cavity development.
If the parent can restrict the child to three meals a day, the child's teeth will
only be subjected to this acid three times a day. Every time a parent lets a
child snack on sweet or sticky foods, the danger is multiplied.

Parents should teach their children these three rules: (1) If it's sweet and
sticky, it's bad for your teeth. (2) It's better to eat sweet and sticky foods
at mealtime than in between meals. (3) If you eat something sweet and
sticky, you *must* brush your teeth immediately afterward. If children understand these rules, parents will find they will often decide on a celery stick
rather than a cookie. It saves them having to brush their teeth!

CLEANING

Just as a mother cleans the body of the child, she should learn how to clean her child's mouth. In the case of infants, this should be done twice a day, after breakfast and after the evening meal. The child should be placed on its back on a dressing table. The parent should then take a small piece of gauze between thumb and forefinger and with it wipe over the gum ridges of the top and bottom jaws. As soon as the teeth start coming into the mouth (somewhere between nine months and one year of age) each day, before the child falls asleep, a parent should take a piece of gauze and wipe the newly erupted teeth clean. This prevents the build-up of bacteria which can cause cavities. As the child gets older, the parent should begin to use a toothbrush for these daily cleanings.

Although children can start trying to use a toothbrush around the second birthday, they can't be expected to do an adequate cleaning job before the age of seven. This means that up until that time, parents must assist in the toothbrushing process. Even when children brush their own teeth, parents should check to make sure they have done a good job.

Toothpicks and Water Piks are devices that are used by adults to get food out from between their teeth. The food sticks there because as people get older, their gums recede (generally because they fail to remove the plaque on a routine basis), causing spaces between the teeth. Children do not have this problem since it takes a number of years for the gums to recede, generally in their late teens or early twenties. So, toothpicks and the Water Piks do nothing except give children something to play with. In the case of the Water Pik, it will get their pajamas and the bathroom floor wet.

CHOOSING A TOOTHBRUSH

Deciding which toothbrush is right for a child is an individual decision. Remember, the objective is getting the crumbs and plaque off the teeth. With a regular toothbrush, it doesn't matter whether the child uses a nylon or a natural bristle. A brush with a small head, straight handle, and flat brushing surface is fine. Parents will probably want the child to have two brushes, so that one is always dry and ready to use.

FLOSSING

The daily practice of flossing is essential for the removal of pieces of food and plaque which forms between the teeth. Plaque is an almost invisible film which coats the gums and teeth, setting the stage for dental decay and gum disease. Again, the parent must teach the child this procedure. For very young children, take a piece of floss about twelve or fourteen inches long and knot the ends together so that the child has a circle of floss to work with. This is easier for young hands to manage. In children, the most important place to floss is between the last two molars in each jaw.

DISCLOSING TABLETS

In addition to daily brushing and flossing, parents might want to use disclosing tablets to help show their children how effectively they are cleaning their teeth. These tablets, available at any drugstore, are made from harmless vegetable dyes. When chewed, they temporarily color plaque red so the child can see how well he or she has brushed. Use of disclosing tablets encourages children to make a special effort to clean the hard-to-get-at areas—between the teeth, along the gum line, or any rough surface or crack.

VISITS TO THE DENTIST

The first dental visit should occur between ages two and three years, then again at five, seven, and nine years of age. Application of fluoride in a dental office twice a year is a highly effective and economical way of preventing cavities. The use by dentists of plastic sealing materials on the biting surface of permanent molar teeth is another effective way of preventing dental cavities.

A CAVITY PREVENTION PROGRAM

Have child brush twice a day, use dental floss once a day.
Use a fluoride toothpaste.
Control sugar snacks as much as possible.
Take child for dental checkup which includes cleaning and a fluoride treatment twice a year.
At least once a week, give child plaque-disclosing tablets as a self-check to see how good a cleaning job is being done.
Here is a word for parents whose hearts land around the ankles when little Horatio comes home with part of his front tooth knocked out during a game of football.
New materials make it possible to paint on layer after layer of a kind of cement until you've got the volume of the original tooth. And then it is molded and shaped and in four minutes it is dry. This is called enamel bonding. This technique is also used to broaden teeth that are widely spaced, extending them to fill the space.

For those parents of older children, a few words on wisdom teeth. Don't remove them unless they are causing trouble.

CREDIT: *Stephen J. Moss, D.D.S., Professor and Chairman, Pedodontics, New York University College of Dentistry; author of* Your Child's Teeth, *Boston: Houghton Mifflin Company.*

Dentures

Question 1: What should people do when they have dentures made and the damn things don't fit?

First of all, let me point out that the "fit" of dentures depends not only on the dentist, but on the patient as well. Every mouth is different and changes in response to a variety of factors.

Full dentures "stick" because of the vacuum or "seal" made by the denture in contact with the tissue. In general, upper dentures are more stable than lower dentures because the upper denture covers a larger area, the alveolar bone of the upper jaw is broader and higher, and the peripheral seal is more readily maintained than in the lower jaw. It is for this reason that dentists will frequently recommend retaining several lower teeth, even though not in ideal condition, in order to allow the construction of a lower *partial* denture (instead of a *full* denture) whose additional retention may be gained by metal clamps around the few remaining teeth.

The ability to get full dentures to stay in place is helped by the presence of saliva in the mouth. A dry mouth, brought about by the normal process of aging, salivary gland disease, emotional disturbance, some types of medication, or irradiation of the head and neck area for cancer without adequate shielding of the salivary glands, create conditions that make for a poor "fit." Finally, the bony ridges of the jaw gradually shrink with time and dentures that fit when they were first made might not fit months or years later.

The dentist, for the most part, should be able to determine in advance whether or not the patient has any obvious problem that might cause difficulty in adapting to full dentures. All patients should expect some difficulty in fit and function, but by working closely with the dentist a satisfactory result can be attained. It is unrealistic to assume that artificial dentures can fully replace the natural teeth.

It is virtually impossible to satisfy every denture wearer. Under ordinary circumstances, however, we would expect the dentures to fit. There are conditions, as mentioned previously, where difficulty should be anticipated. I would think that running off to another dentist after only four visits is premature. At least three to four months should be allowed for necessary adjustments of the dentures by the dentist and for accommodation by the patient. The time to consider seeing another dentist is when the first dentist throws up his hands and says he has done as much as possible and the patient is still unhappy with the result.

Question 2: Will you please tell people why their dentures hurt and the importance of wearing dentures every waking moment?

Dentures may hurt if they are overextended and irritate the soft tissue on which they press. This frequently occurs immediately after the dentures are made but should be overcome after several visits to the dentist. Similarly, old dentures may irritate the tissue due to the shrinkage of the underlying bone, and the manner in which the teeth fit (lower against upper) is also important since excess pressure in one area on closing may "tip" the dentures leading to pressure spots on the soft tissue and possible displacement of the dentures. This unevenness in the "bite" can be overcome with judicious grinding of the "high" teeth by the dentist. Dentures should be kept in the mouth during the day and not in the pocket or drawer because the tissues do adapt to the denture and because the dentures will warp if not kept in a moist environment all the time.

Failure to wear dentures leads to a vicious cycle: the tissues change, the denture warps, and the "fit" deteriorates, making it more difficult to wear.

Question 3: Please emphasize the importance of keeping dentures clean and suggest how this should be done.

If one of the reasons for going to the trouble and expense of obtaining dentures relates to appearance and interpersonal relations, it makes no sense for the individual to neglect the care and cleaning of those dentures. Bacteria, food debris, and tartar form on dentures just as readily as they form on the natural dentition. "Bad breath caused by decaying food and bacterial growth is as common and repulsive in denture wearers as in individuals with natural teeth. Clean dentures depend on frequent removal, rinsing and brushing after meals, particularly at night prior to retiring. Special cleansers, more abrasive than toothpaste, may be needed to help remove adherent food debris, bacteria and tartar. Such cleansers may be purchased at any local drugstore.

Question 4: What about dentures that slip? How good are the products we see advertised in newspapers and on television to keep dentures in place?

Slippage of dentures is probably due to shrinkage of underlying bone and soft tissue. Such shrinkage occurs most rapidly immediately after teeth are removed and accounts for the former practice of waiting several months after all the teeth are removed before taking impressions for dentures. However, most people are unwilling to face their family and friends without teeth during this "waiting period" while the tissues are healing and reshaping themselves. Instead, they obtain "immediate" dentures as soon as the remaining front teeth are removed and wear these during the the the initial "shrinkage" period with the understanding that new dentures or a relining of the "immediate" dentures by the dentist will be necessary several months later. Unfortunately, the tissues under the dentures continue to shrink subsequently over the years, albeit at a slower rate. At present this biological process is not fully understood, nor can the dentist predict in advance the rate of tissue shrinkage for a given patient. Although denture adhesives and denture liners for home use are advocated by various commercial concerns, there is no worthwhile research evidence to indicate whether or not such products are harmless. The best analogy I can think of would be, if one's feet were shrinking with advancing age, to advocate wearing two, three or four pairs of socks to take up the increasing space rather than buying a new pair of better fitting shoes. In other words, if one's dentures were loosening, I would suggest consulting the dentist and considering the possibility of having a new set of dentures made. In the end, this last approach may be the least expensive.

One word of caution: Don't go to a dental laboratory for denture adjustments. It is illegal for a laboratory technician to take care of patients. If you succumb to the temptation to get dental care in one of the illegally operating dental "parlors," you are a party to a crime. There are a few such establishments around. The best way to put them out of business is not to give them any.

CREDIT: *Paul Goldhaber, D.D.S., Dean of Harvard School of Dental Medicine, Cambridge, Massachusetts.*

Depression

The term depression has many different meanings. It is a feeling that may be thought of as a mood, an emotion, or an illness. There are few people who at one time or another have not felt depressed or "down." Depression can be mild in its intensity or may be of such depth as to immobilize and inhibit all social and individual functioning. It may color how one feels about oneself or how one sees the world. It may refer to a particular state of feeling on a given day or it may be specifically associated with a particular event or period in one's life.

For most of us, depression is an unpleasant feeling and as such is related to, although different from, other unpleasant feelings such as shame, guilt, anxiousness, or general non-interest in one's self, one's family, one's work or one's community. The feeling is usually brief and frequently leaves without our knowing why it came in the first place or why it disappeared.

For a few, this state may be present on an almost permanent basis. When depression continues, or when it seems to become worse, we no longer are dealing with a normal mood or state of emotion but with an illness that can have serious consequences and which requires professional assistance. At times the unpleasant feeling of depression comes as a direct reaction to a disappointment—the loss of one's job, not getting a promotion, the breakup of a love affair or a marriage, the serious illness of a child, parent or mate. These reactive depressions are quite normal.

When we do not have control of external situations that frustrate us or have no chance of undoing a hurt, we get depressed. Usually feelings of depression can be directly linked to external events. However, when the outside "triggers" are relatively mild or disappear without a lifting of the depressed feelings, one must look further and try to determine what underlying problems have been uncovered. Severe and long-lasting depression is an illness that requires help. If nothing is done, the illness may become worse and may ultimately result in suicide, a major cause of death in the United States today.

A related type of illness requiring psychiatric assistance is depression that alternates with periods of overexcitement and excessive good feelings. This alternation of extremes of good and bad feelings is called a manic-depressive disorder. It fortunately can be treated today with specific drugs that prevent the mood swings from high to low. So the term depression is used in many different ways and the feeling can be a symptom of a psychiatric illness or of a normal mood.

The mourning reaction, commonly seen after the death or loss of a meaningful person, is to be distinguished from depression, although in feeling the two are similar. Mourning is usually directly related to a loss; it is a normal reaction; it usually is overcome as the reality of the loss is realized, accepted, and other individuals and activities are found which bring renewed interest and pleasure in life. But depressive illness may not be overcome and in such cases may require active treatment by a professionally qualified individual.

The symptoms of depression vary. Unpleasant feelings, physical symptoms for which there are no organic causes, a withdrawn feeling about oneself and at times about life itself are common. The individual feels miserable, hopeless, helpless, worried, unhappy. Physically the depressed person feels tired but cannot get refreshing sleep or rest. There may be a loss of appetite, constipation, weight loss, and a lack of interest or diminished capacity for sexual activity. Crying may easily be set off by events which ordinarily would not cause such a reaction. In more serious instances, individuals feel negatively about themselves. This self-dislike, increased tension, profound sense of worthlessness and an inability to do anything about the situation can stimulate ideas and acts of self-destruction. Emotional withdrawal from work, close associates, friends and intimate family members occurs. Activities that previously brought pleasure, fun, joy or laughter bring gloom. Indecisiveness, loss of motivation, constant negative expectations, and lack of incentive are additional indicators of serious difficulty. Preoccupations with punishment, thought disturbances that include ideas of serious deprivations where these are not realistic, constant involvements with unrealistic ideas of repentance, where the world is seen as desolate and empty or where actual hallucinations occur—all these symptoms indicate serious illness and require immediate professional attention.

Increasingly we are finding that children, adolescents and the elderly are as susceptible to depressive illness as are the young middle-aged adults. We know all human beings regardless of sex, age, race, culture, religion, education or economic status can be depressed and have serious depressive illness. As we examine individuals more closely we are detecting more depressive disease that requires attention.

Suicide among adolescents has reached serious proportions, and the disappointed, disillusioned, disrupted, isolated, abandoned and helpless elderly may also suffer from severe depressive disorders. Mid-life crisis in males, menopausal symptoms in women, the "empty nest," all contribute to depression in the middle-aged. In many ways depression now constitutes a major social issue as well as a serious psychiatric disturbance.

All people get depressed at times. Depression is normal and does not require treatment if it is short-lived, infrequent and is self-limiting. For the more serious depressive illnesses, different treatments can be utilized depending on the type and degree of the disturbance. Currently individual psychotherapy, drugs prescribed by a physician, marital-family-group psychotherapy, electroconvulsive treatment, psychoanalysis and counseling are the major forms of treatment utilized in the care of depression.

The understanding of the problem, the diagnosis, the severity and the duration of the illness are some of the critical determinants as to which treatment is best. At times treatment should be handled in the hospital. On other occasions in the therapist's office. As we understand more about the causes of depression we are in a better position to try preventive measures before going ahead with drastic and costly forms of treatment. Research is constantly needed to increase our understanding of this psychological problem from which so many of us suffer.

CREDIT: *George H. Pollock, M.D., Ph.D., Director of the Institute of Psychoanalysis, Professor of Psychiatry, Northwestern University, Chicago, Illinois.*

Depression After Childbirth*

(*Postpartum Depression*)

Postpartum depression, or "baby blues," is rapidly being acknowledged as a significant aftereffect of childbirth. Though its intensity ranges from mild anxiety to severe psychosis, most women experience depression of some kind after a child is born.

This state is not confined to first-time mothers. Some women become depressed after the birth of each of their children.

Almost every mother goes through a "low" period about three days after the birth, roughly coinciding with the time the breasts begin to produce milk rather than colostrum. Many more women, however, experience severe depression when they leave the hospital. These feelings may last only a few days, but if a woman is physically run down, they may persist for several months.

Among the feelings most commonly experienced during depression are confusion, shock, insecurity, inadequacy, fear of inability to cope with the baby, and even disappointment about its sex or appearance. Many women are frightened because they cannot understand their feelings and terrified at the thought that their marriages are in jeopardy.

Postpartum depression is often attributed to hormonal imbalance following childbirth, but evidence is as yet inconclusive since depression has been noted in adoptive as well as natural mothers. Probably the single most important cause of postpartum depression is society's glorification of motherhood. When the realities of the situation do not compare with the glowing picture portrayed by the advertisements for baby powder, the mother feels that something must be wrong with her. She begins to question her ability to be a loving mother and feels guilty about it.

Some physicians prescribe drugs to help a woman who is in such a state but usually it is preferable to treat the cause rather than the symptoms. If the mother receives emotional support and constant reassurance from her family, friends and other mothers, the chances of a rapid and complete recovery are good.

* From *Woman's Body: An Owner's Manual* by the Diagram Group © 1977 The Diagram Group, published by Paddington Press.

Diabetes (Mellitus)

The word "diabetes" comes from the Greek word for "siphon" or waterspout. The second part of the medical term for the disease, "mellitus," comes from the Latin word for honey or sweet. Thus, "diabetes mellitus" refers to sugar in the urine, a major component of the total picture.

Historically the disease was known to the Ancient Egyptians and was also described by physicians in India over two thousand years ago. Sugar appears in the urine because there is too much sugar in the blood and the kidney is unable to retain it. To put it simply, diabetes is the inability to keep blood sugar levels within normal range. It becomes elevated, particularly after meals, and spills into the urine, carrying with it much water and essential minerals. The reason this occurs is because the body's regulator of sugar levels, which is insulin, is defective.

Diabetes is one of the most common of all diseases, and it is estimated to affect between five and ten million Americans. The majority of these, perhaps 80 to 90 percent, have a form of the disease called by physicians "the maturity-onset type" and most are overweight. This type of diabetes is due to a partial deficiency to make insulin in the body. It is believed that the relationship between being overweight and having diabetes is not that people who develop diabetes are usually fat, but rather that being overweight can indicate a predisposition to diabetes.

Included in this five to ten million Americans are 100,000 children of school age who have "the juvenile-onset type" of diabetes and therefore require at least one daily insulin injection, since in this form of the disease, the insulin-making machinery is totally and permanently lost.

Although juvenile-type diabetes tends to afflict mainly children, as the name suggests, there are some children who also have the mild maturity-onset type diabetes which can be handled by diet alone, or by weight reduction if they are obese.

That diabetes runs in families has been known for thousands of years, but the exact mode of inheritance is a mystery. In general, someone in mid-life who has a brother or sister or a parent with diabetes has at least one in ten chances of having diabetes.

Anyone who suspects the presence of diabetes should request a glucose tolerance test, which consists of the following:

A sample of blood is taken from the arm. The individual is then given a measured quantity of sugar by mouth. Every thirty minutes up to approximately two or three hours, another sample of blood is taken. The blood sugar is being measured periodically. If it is higher than what is considered the usual level, the doctor has evidence that the patient is diabetic.

The symptoms of diabetes are numerous. If the insulin deficiency is marked, and the individual has juvenile-onset type of diabetes, there is a noticeable increase in thirst and frequent urination with a craving for sweets and usually cold beverages.

With increasing severity of the disease, there is weakness, loss of muscle, and in children, irritability, poor performance at school and a noticeable lack of energy. Thus a typical child will have weight loss, marked increase in thirst and urination. He may even get up at night to drink water and urinate, and often wet the bed. As the insulin deficiency becomes more severe, organic acids appear in the blood due to the breakdown of body fat. These acids are called ketoacids. As they accumulate the body becomes more acid and may progress to dehydration, collapse of the circulation and death unless treated.

Again this type of diabetes most frequently occurs in children, but it can occur at any age. In the adult, since the insulin deficiency is usually less severe, the symptoms may vary from minor manifestations to severe.

Diabetics have a tendency to pick up infections, particularly of the skin. These infections may develop into abscesses or boils. In the female, there may be fungus infections with itching and redness in the vaginal area.

The dentist may be the first to discover the signs of diabetes because of marked infection around the gum margins of the teeth with premature loss of the teeth due to gum abscesses.

Complications may involve either the small blood vessels, which lead to problems in the eyes and the kidneys, or to the larger blood vessels, which results in poor circulation in critical areas of the body. These areas are the brain and heart, which may cause stroke or heart attack, or the blood vessels leading to the lower extremity. Poor circulation may intensify ulcers or infections and eventually lead to gangrene of the toes or foot.

High blood sugar also affects the nervous system, especially the nerves going to the lower extremities. The diabetes may be indicated by a numbness or tingling.

Sometimes a sudden loss of a single nerve such as one of the nerves to the face, resulting in Bell's palsy, may signal diabetes. Thus, in summary, the symptoms of the disease can be varied and depend on both the degree and duration of the insulin deficiency.

The treatment of diabetes is mainly directed to the major problem, the insulin deficiency. If the deficiency is severe, as usually occurs in young people, one or more insulin injections must be taken every day. If the insulin deficiency is mild, as usually occurs in most older individuals, the first approach is to decrease the need of the body for insulin. This is achieved by making the individual lose weight if he is obese, and usually he is.

Thus the individual is placed on a "diabetic and hypo-caloric" diet, which means eating smaller amounts, several times during the day. There is also a limitation on foods that contain sugar—pastries, sweetened beverages, candy, syrups, etc.

Some diabetes specialists believe that as many as 75 percent of all individuals in the United States with diabetes would lose their diabetic predisposition if they were simply made to lose weight and eat more sensibly.

Approximately one million Americans take diabetic pills, daily, which lower blood sugar presumably by making either more insulin available or by making the insulin more effective.

There are now at least five different kinds of pills on the market but they fall into two categories—one the sulfonylureas and the other the biguanides (of which only one preparation is available in the United States, and this is currently under attack by the Food and Drug Administration and will probably not be available). Diabetes experts disagree regarding the role of these pills in the treatment of diabetes. Some feel that only diet should be used. Others feel that if the patient is unable to stick with the diet, then the pills should be added. All agree, however, that the diabetic diet, particularly if the individual is overweight, is the best therapy.

The diabetic on insulin must inject himself or herself with insulin and then eat the meal to match the insulin intake. Thus the diabetic on insulin must learn not only how to use the needle to inject himself, but also how to judge diet, its caloric content and its distribution of carbohydrate, protein and fat, in order that the right-sized meal can be eaten to match the insulin injection schedule.

Teaching the diabetic to learn the dietary requirements and inject insulin usually requires a combined effort of dieticians, nurses and physicians. Sending children to diabetic camps has also proven very successful.

LIVING WITH DIABETES

Diabetes, depending on the age of onset and severity, may produce some changes in lifestyle. Frequently there is diminished sexual potency in the male. Believe it or not, studies have shown *no* changes in the females.

The youngster who has developed diabetes and has learned to take care of his insulin injections as well as his diet can manage extremely well. There are many young professional athletes who have diabetes—including hockey stars, football and baseball players, boxers and world tennis champions. Likewise, there are diabetics in all walks of life, including members of the U. S. Senate and House of Representatives, successful individuals in theater, films and leaders in business and industry.

The majority of diabetics, mainly those with the maturity-onset type, die of major blood vessel problems, most frequently a heart attack, but at an earlier age than the non-diabetic. The juvenile-onset diabetics may also have large blood vessel problems, with premature heart attacks. Over the past few decades, however, nearly half of these diabetics have died of kidney failure due to problems of the very small blood vessels, with an average survival of approximately forty years from the time of diagnosis.

There is, however, mounting evidence that the closer the diabetic can make his blood sugar match that of the non-diabetic, by adjusting diet and insulin to very fine limits, the less chance there is that he or she will have these tiny blood vessel complications—namely problems of the eye and kidney.

It takes a great deal of diligence and education for most insulin-requiring diabetics to achieve this degree of expertise.

It also requires that they check their urine samples throughout the day in order to detect when their blood sugar is above the level at which the kidney is able to retain the sugar in the body. It also means they will have times when their blood sugar may fall too low, and they will require a little food containing carbohydrate in order to bring the blood glucose back up to the normal range.

These episodes (when the blood glucose is too low) are called "reactions" and are exactly the reverse of diabetic acidosis. Whereas diabetic acidosis takes days to weeks to develop and the individual is chronically ill, the diabetic on insulin may go into "reaction" literally within minutes from otherwise being completely alert and functioning. These situations will be discussed below under *Emergencies*.

EMERGENCIES

The first emergency is diabetic acidosis, but since this takes days or weeks to develop, it is not usually an acute emergency unless a major error or oversight has been made. Thus an individual, especially a child, who becomes severely ill with marked thirst, increased urination and dehydration followed by nausea, vomiting and perhaps even progressing to stupor and coma, is an almost certain candidate for a severe diabetes emergency.

Any infection in any diabetic must be considered a dire emergency. This is particularly true of even the smallest cut or injury to the leg. If not appropriately cared for it may result in a rapid-spreading infection and even loss of the leg, or it could prove fatal.

The type of emergency which many diabetics experience is "insulin reaction." Usually the person first experiences symptoms such as hunger, sweatiness, rapid heartbeat, fatigue and cold skin. Once he or she is aware of this, he should eat crackers, or bread, or a little bit of sugar or candy carried in the pocket for this purpose. Thus the blood sugar will be brought back up to its usual level.

Unfortunately some diabetics will be unaware or will overlook these symptoms and the blood sugar will fall lower and lower and their thinking processes become disturbed. This can produce a memory loss or totally irrational behavior, occasionally even combative.

For the reasons stated above, diabetics should have in their wallet as well as around their neck or wrist a tag stating that they are diabetic and if found incoherent or wandering aimlessly around should be given sugar-containing foods or beverages. It is not uncommon for a diabetic to be picked up by the police and charged with being drunk or psychotic.

If the individual, however, has had such a severe fall in blood sugar that he becomes unconscious or goes into convulsions, food or sugar-containing beverages should not be given, since it may end up in the lung and cause choking or subsequent pneumonia.

The patient should be brought immediately to a physician or hospital and glucose given intravenously.

Families of some diabetics may be taught by their physicians how to fill a syringe with glucagon. Like insulin, glucagon can be purchased by a prescription at druggists'. When injected into the unconscious diabetic it produces an increase in blood glucose within a few minutes. The individual then is able to take things by mouth and bring the blood sugar back up to an acceptable level.

Since exercise increases the effectiveness of insulin, insulin reactions are most frequently experienced between meals, especially when the diabetic is exercising, particularly if the exercise is unexpected, such as changing a flat tire or having to walk up several flights of stairs because an elevator is not working. Again, diabetics should carry extra carbohydrate in their pockets to be able to keep their blood glucose in an acceptable range should they encounter unexpected exercise. Many diabetic athletes drink sugar-containing beverages to improve their activity and prevent a reaction.

Although we know that heredity is an important factor in diabetes, certain measures can be taken to prevent the probability of getting the disease. The most important is not to overeat and to use sugar sensibly. This does *not* mean you must eliminate sugar completely. (Sugar is an excellent source of energy.) It means refrain from stuffing yourself with candy, cakes, pies, doughnuts, pastries and all those luscious desserts that are so appealing and which are the major contributions to overweightedness.

For more information write to: The American Diabetes Association, 1 West 48th Street, New York, New York 10020.

CREDIT: *George F. Cahill, Jr., M.D., Professor of Medicine, Harvard Medical School, Director, Elliott P. Joslin Research Laboratory, Diabetes Physician, Peter Bent Brigham Hospital, Boston, Massachusetts.*

Diets—Watch Out!

(*Phony Diets Can Be Dangerous*)

Let us assume you have a weight problem, not an imaginary one but due, in truth, to more fat than you should carry for your health, comfort and beauty. What is the answer? Certainly not the succession of faddist diets which, season after season, claim they will enable you to lose weight and yet eat as much as you want. I marvel at the gullibility of my fellow citizens for believing that it is possible to flout the laws of nature on the basis of principles which change from year to year. I can remember diets founded on the following principles:

The low protein diets: The "rice" or "Duke" diet was originally developed for the treatment of high blood pressure. It consists of white rice (boiled, unsalted) and those fruits lowest in calories. It is low in iron, contains no vitamin B-12 or vitamin D and is a highly unsatisfactory diet in the long run. Another variant was the "Rockefeller" diet (developed at the Rockefeller Institute for an experiment; it was not meant to be a reducing diet and has been disowned by the Institute for this purpose).

The "high protein" (in fact, high fat) diet: This is a diet which comes and goes—but not, each time, without bringing notoriety and riches to somebody. It first appeared in the 1860s as the "Banting" diet and has reappeared in this era as the "DuPont" or "Pennington" diet (so named after a Doctor Pennington who used it on executives of the E. I. DuPont de Nemours Chemical Company), the "Mayo Clinic" diet (disclaimed by the Mayo Clinic), the "Air Force" diet (disclaimed by the Surgeon General of the U. S. Air Force), the Stillman "Doctor's Quick Weight Loss" diet (with eight glasses of water), the "drinking man's" diet (with martinis), and Atkin's "diet revolution" (a particularly extreme form). All of these diets advocate an avoidance of foods containing starches or sugar, and claim, in effect, that protein foods, meat in particular, are essentially calorie-free or thinning. The fact is that protein, like carbohydrate, contains four calories per gram, and fat contains nine calories per gram. The calories from meat, incidentally, are derived from fat more than protein (about 75 percent calories from fat in hot dogs, 60 to 75 percent in most hamburgers, at least 50 percent in "lean" steaks). Eliminating carbohydrates causes a certain body dehydration, with rapid weight loss in the first few days due to loss of water rather than loss of "unwanted fat." (This weight, obviously, can be regained as rapidly.) Thereafter, weight loss proceeds only to the extent that you eat less than you expend —as is true in every diet. (A loss of one pound corresponds, on the average, to a cumulative deficit of 3,500 calories over the course of days of dieting.) Drawbacks to this diet are: (1) the absence of carbohydrates (the nearly exclusive food of the brain) means that protein has to be made into blood sugar, a process which often leads to levels on the low side, tiredness and headache; and (2) the high saturated fat and cholesterol content of the diet is dangerous for those people who have a tendency to high blood cholesterol to start with, particularly overweight middle-aged men and older women.

The "grapefruit" diet: This is "based" on the supposed ability of grapefruit, or the organic acids thereof, to eliminate the calories in the rest of the diet. While grapefruit is a good food *per se,* this theory is pure drivel!

The "hard-boiled egg" diet: You can eat all you want as long as it is a hard-boiled egg. Eggs are a good source of almost all nutrients (except vitamin C and—unless you eat the shell—calcium!). And they contain only 80 to 90 calories. After a dozen hard-boiled eggs, you should be pretty sick of them—and yet you have eaten less than 1,200 calories, so you should lose weight. At the same time, this variant of the high-protein, high-fat diet is extremely high in cholesterol (250 to 300 milligrams per egg) and is therefore potentially quite dangerous in the long run.

What should you do? If you want to lose weight, there are five principles you should keep in mind:

First, remember that losing weight is a matter of arithmetic. Any diet (including a sane, complete, well-balanced diet) which has less calories than you expend will lead you to lose weight. A deficit of 500 calories per day will yield a weight loss of one pound a week. If you think that's not very much, remember it is fifty-two pounds a year—and that should be enough. Losing weight slowly means that you will not get tired in the process, stop menstruating if you are a young woman, become anemic, or generally buy a lot of trouble for yourself.

Second, remember that your diet should be balanced with enough fruits, vegetables, milk or cheese, good sources of iron, such as liver, some eggs (particularly for women) and enriched or whole grain cereals.

Third, remember that a diet is not a list of "permitted" foods which are "not fattening." Portion size is the key. Bread is only worth 70 calories per slice. Ten slices may be too much but only one or two slices a meal would be all right. Ditto for potatoes, meat, etc.

Fourth, avoid "empty calories," those foods that contribute nothing or almost nothing to your nutrition except calories.

And, finally, remember that increasing energy expenditure is just as useful as cutting down calories—and much more fun. You can increase your energy expenditure by 200 to 300 calories per hour by walking, 400 to 700 by playing tennis or swimming. Like a bank account, what is taken out is just as important as what goes in. And it has the additional advantage of making you look taut and fit. It's much better for your health and looks to be thin and firm than simply thin and flabby. Occasional brief bouts of exercise won't do it, but a well-established daily routine of walking and more active exercise several times a week is the basis of lasting fitness—and lasting looks.

"Amazing diets" of one kind or another produce amazing profits for their promoters. They are all based on the fantasy that a magic combination of ingredients can cause you to lose weight no matter how much you eat. Use one and you are more likely to shed dollars than pounds.

The American Medical Association Department of Food and Nutrition lists some clues which can help you to recognize a "kooky" book or diet promotion:

(1) It uses bad biochemistry.

(2) It makes a heated attack on carbohydrates as bad for people.

(3) It claims to be a revolutionary new idea.

(4) It reports testimonials rather than documented research.

(5) It refers to the author's own case histories but does not describe them in detail.

(6) It claims 100 percent success.

(7) It claims persecution by the medical profession.

Amphetamines (e.g., Dexedrine) are sometimes used to suppress appetite at the beginning of treatment. Their effect is temporary and they can have unpleasant side effects.

Artificial bulk-producing agents frequently are sold with the claim that they will curb appetite by tricking the stomach into thinking it is full. Your stomach won't be tricked, so don't you be tricked either.

Artificial sweeteners, used in place of sugar, provide another means of reducing calorie intake.

"Cellulite" spot-reduction plans are supposed to get rid of "unsightly, unevenly distributed pads and lumps of fat which dieting and exercise will not dissolve." The plans consist of diet plus exercise and massage. Exercise and the recommended diet are good for general weight-reduction, but the "cellulite" concept is mere window dressing.

Counting calories. Safe and effective, the low-calorie balanced diet is ranked highest by professional nutritionists.

Counting carbohydrates. Studies show that counting carbohydrates goes hand-in-hand with counting calories. A balanced diet that relies on lowering carbohydrate intake is fine.

Diuretics can make you lose weight by causing your body to shed water. This effect is short-lived; the weight will come back when you stop the pills. Diuretics can have bad side effects. If you want to lose fat, not water, stay away from diuretics as a "weight reducing" pill.

Exercise machines tend to be overpriced and most people find their use monotonous. Good exercise programs can help you burn up calories and improve your body tone. Passive machine exercise, however, will do little more than reduce your chances of being mugged in the park.

Formula diets (usually liquid) containing specified numbers of calories offer a simple regimen which does not require much knowledge of nutrition. They may substitute usefully for one meal a day, but most people find them too monotonous to use more often.

HCG (Human Chorionic Gonadotropin), a hormone derived from the urine of pregnant women, is neither safe nor effective. The 500-calorie diet which often accompanies injections is a semistarvation one which is likely to result in protein loss.

Kelp, lecithin, cider vinegar and B_6 accompanied by a 1,000-or-so calorie diet will cause weight loss—as a result of the diet alone. The kelp and other supplements are of no benefit in a weight reduction program.

Low-calorie foods can give you a bit more food with fewer calories. Noncaloric sweeteners and low-calorie dressings may make your food more interesting, but their nutritional value is negligible. People on low-calorie diets must pay close attention to the nutritive content of their foods. Choosing foods by calories alone is not a useful approach.

Obesity specialists should be approached with caution. Some are excellent, but many are overpriced and follow questionable nutritional theories. Membership in the American College of Nutrition or the American Society for Clinical Nutrition is a good sign. So is medical school affiliation. But make a fast retreat if a "specialist" suggests any of the systems criticized in this book!

Reducing clubs often offer needed moral support and nutritional information. If you join a weight-reducing club, make sure it has a consulting nutritionist.

Reducing pills (non-prescription type) imply or state outright that you can eat all you want and still lose weight. This type of false claim has made millions for some of its promoters. (Regimen tablets, claimed to shed pounds without dieting, sold for an estimated $16 million between 1956 and 1962. In the court case that ended in conviction of the manufacturer and the advertising agency, it was shown that TV models who reduced during an advertising campaign had done so by *dieting*.)

Reducing salons may give you moral support in keeping to your program of exercising, but if you can't afford one, don't use one. Exercise at home on a regular basis, but beware of overexertion.

Solo diets—such as the fruit diet, the macrobiotic diet, or any diet restricted to one food—are unhealthy because they do not provide adequate nutrition.

Spot reducers, such as creams, sauna belts and electric shock devices, may *appear* to work by causing water loss or muscle contraction. These are temporary effects. Spot reducers do *not* roll it off, rock it off or bake it off!

Starvation diets can cause protein breakdown and are potentially dangerous.

Surgical procedures which bypass part of the small intestine are in the experimental stage. So far, the results are unsatisfactory.

Thyroid hormones in large amounts can cause you to burn calories faster, lose weight and *strain your heart.* If your thyroid is normal, small amounts of prescribed thyroid will simply cause your body to produce less of its own. Thyroid preparations must carry a label statement that they are not for use in weight reduction. If you suspect "hypothyroidism" (underactive thyroid gland) as the cause of your overweight problem (a very rare disease, by the way), have it diagnosed at once by a physician who does not rely on the basal metabolism test (BMR) to make his diagnosis.

Vitamin supplements are not necessary if you eat a balanced diet.

"Wrapping" your body so that a concentrated salt solution can take the water out of the outer layers of your skin can produce only temporary shrinkage at best. At worst, if enough of you is wrapped, you can get seriously ill from dehydration.

Your doctor may be able to help you plan a proper diet or refer you to someone else for that purpose. Registered dietitians of the American Dietetic Association are trained in dietary counseling.

CREDIT: *Jean Mayer, Ph.D.; President, Tufts University, contributor to* The Health Robbers: *George F. Stickley Company, 210 West Washington Square, Philadelphia, Pennsylvania 19106.*

Discipline*

Do Your Children a Favor—Say No!

What *do* kids want anyway? Never in the history of our country have children had so much money to spend and so many things to spend it on. In 1976, teenagers shelled out between $16 and $18 billion on record albums, magazines, soft drinks, cigarettes, junk food, chewing gum, cosmetics, fad clothing, jewelry, hair dryers, stereo sets, pocket radios and other assorted gadgets.

What kids really want is not more *things,* nor do they want more freedom to do as they please. Although they frequently complain that their parents treat them like babies, they hunger for firm guidelines. The child who does

* Reprinted from "Do Your Children a Favor—Say No!" by Ann Landers. *Family Circle* magazine, September 1976 issue, copyright © 1976 by The Family Circle Inc. Updated.

not hear the word "no" from his mother or father has a good chance of growing up to be a problem to his peers, his teachers, law enforcement officers, society—and himself.

Children want someone to set up well-defined limits that say, "These are the boundaries. You may go so far—and no further." Even the youngest child is keenly aware that discipline is a special kind of love. It says, "I care about you. I will not let you get into trouble. My judgment is better than yours. You can trust me. I have been down that road and I know it well. I will protect you against your impetuosity and your lack of experience. Rant and rave, call me 'square' and insist that I am living in the 'olden days' but the answer is *no*—and it's final."

One of the favorite cries heard throughout the land is, "Everyone in our crowd gets to do it but me. I'm the only one who can't." This allegation is often a gross overstatement designed to make parents feel they are out of tune with the times.

An excellent response to that ploy is this: "I don't care what the other kids are allowed to do. Their parents are responsible for them. I care about *you*. The answer is no and the subject is closed."

Every child knows whether or not he has "collapsible parents." He learns from experience if haranguing and nagging will wear a parent down and make him change his mind. If this technique has proved successful in the past, he will use it in the future. Children learn, too, whether or not it is possible to work both ends against the middle. Example:

"If Dad says I can go to the hockey game with Brad, is it okay?" Mom knows the hockey game is rarely over before 10:30 P.M. and there is school the next day. The correct answer is: "You can't go to the hockey game on a school night, so don't bother to ask your father. He knows the rules because we set them up together."

Setting up rules together is extremely important in presenting a united front. Parents should agree on a fair and reasonable curfew for each child, allowances, purchasing privileges, number of nights out, duties, responsibilities and penalties. No fair changing the rules without consulting the other half of the team. And punishment, especially, should be meted out as soon as possible after the offense has been committed. No "wait-till-your-father-comes-home" routine. This casts Father in the role of chief executioner, and it is unfair.

One of the most vital aspects of good discipline is consistency. Parents who say "no" today, "yes" tomorrow and "maybe" three days later are asking for trouble. While a changed verdict might create temporary joy, it invariably produces endless confusion and a sense of "Where am I?" It's like playing tennis without a net.

Once the decision has been made, stick to it, even if after thinking it over you decide you were too strict. There will be another opportunity to be more lenient. You can then say: "I believe you are able to handle the situation now. You have proved that you are more mature. I feel more comfortable about it than I did a few weeks ago." Parents can always give their children a longer leash. It's infinitely more difficult to tighten up and give them *less* freedom than to loosen up and give them more.

In the years between fourteen and seventeen, there are bound to be "I hate you" days. If you understand what is behind these outbursts you will feel less hurt.

When a child says, "I hate you," it means he hates himself, too. He is unhappy and frustrated. His feelings of conflict are puzzling and frightening to him. While teenagers insist they are eager for independence, they are also afraid of it. They aren't certain they can handle all the freedom they ask for.

This brings us to the most challenging aspect of raising children. How much freedom *should* I give my child? When do I let go? There are no pat answers. Some girls at thirteen are excellent baby-sitters. Others at thirteen need a baby-sitter themselves. I have known fifteen-year-old boys who handle a car with far more skill than their forty-five-year-old mothers. Other boys at seventeen are so erratic and reckless they should not be permitted to get behind the wheel.

The measure of freedom and independence must be determined by the dispassionate evaluation of what your teenager is like. I don't mean what he *says* he is like or what you *wish* he were like—I mean his record of performance. Does he do his share of work around the house without griping? How well does he perform in school? Are his grades respectable? After all, going to school is his job. How is he managing it? Can he be trusted with the family car, or do mysterious dents appear in the fenders? Does he return it with an empty gas tank? Is your teenager reliable and truthful? Does he respect the curfew agreed upon or do you walk the floor at night worried sick because he should have been home hours ago?

Children should understand that they will be given privileges in direct ratio to their ability to handle responsibilities.

Let them know freedom is a privilege. It must be earned. A twelve-year-old girl who leaves her coat on the bus and her shoes on the beach is not grown up enough to have her own telephone. A thirteen-year-old boy who tells the teacher, "The dog ate my homework," should not be permitted to go to the movies on Saturday with his chums.

If someone were to ask, "Are you more lenient with your children than your parents were with you?" chances are you would have to say "yes." There are several reasons for this.

Forty years ago more mothers were at home baking bread, doing the laundry, scrubbing the linoleum, making slipcovers and taking care of their children. There was very little "debating of issues" and no smart-mouth talk from the peanut gallery. The answer "You can't go because I said so" was common. I heard it often when I was growing up and it signaled the end of the discussion.

Since World War II, the domestic scene has changed dramatically. Today over 40 percent of the work force in this country is made up of women. Many working mothers feel guilty because they can't spend the time with their children they feel they should; consequently they want the time they do spend together to be pleasant. No hassling. No long faces around the house.

Naturally, the best way to avoid arguments and unpleasantness is to be agreeable—which, of course, means to let the precious little darlings do as they please. The word "no" can ruin a child's day.

Unfortunately, during that period in our history large numbers of psychiatrists were turned loose and anointed as "saviors" of the new generation. Spanking was out. Freedom of expression was in. The answers to all child-rearing problems were in books. Mothers were "dumb" and the professionals took over. The competent therapists with whom I consult today deplore the damage done by their colleagues in the fifties.

I firmly believe that a mother's instinct is better than all the outside advice in the world. But she must have the wisdom to trust her instincts and the courage to do her children a favor and say, *"No!"*

DEAR ANN LANDERS: Dr. Thomas P. Johnson, a psychiatrist who works with the San Diego County Probation Department, wrote the following guidelines for parents. I hope you will print them in your column. Thanks, Ann. A Parent Who Needs All The Help She Can Get

DEAR PARENT: Dr. Johnson's guidelines are well worth printing. I appreciate your sending them on.

1. Don't disapprove of what a child is—disapprove of what he does.

2. Give attention and praise for good behavior—not bad behavior.

3. Encourage and allow discussion, but remember it's the parents who should make the final decision.

4. Punishment should be swift, reasonable, related to the offense and absolutely certain to occur—it need not be severe.

5. Throw out all rules you are unwilling to enforce and be willing to change the rules if and when you think they need changing.

6. Don't lecture and don't warn—youngsters will remember what they think is important to remember.

7. Don't feel you have to justify rules, although you should try to explain them.

8. As your youngster grows older, many rules may be subject to discussion and compromise. The few rules you really feel strongly about should be enforced no matter what rules other parents have.

9. Allow a child to assume responsibility for his decisions as he shows the ability to do so.

10. Don't expect children to demonstrate more self-control than you do.

11. Be honest with your youngster—hypocrisy shows.

12. The most important factor in your youngster's self-image is what he thinks YOU think of him. His self-image is a major factor in how he conducts himself.

CHILDREN NEED BETTER MODELS

DEAR ANN LANDERS: I write this out of genuine concern for today's youth.

Parents, have you found your son or daughter, grade school and up—

Lying—but overlooked it?
Cheating—felt a little disappointed?
Swearing—got a little upset?
Smoking—got quite upset?
Stealing—gave a lecture?
Drinking—grounded him for a week?
O.K., Mom and Dad, just who set the examples for these children? Was it those bad kids at school or you in your own home?

What you do speaks louder than what you say! If the youth of today are going to get straightened out, the adult generation had better start setting standards kids can look up to.

What images do your children have of you? Puffing on a cigarette, sitting around before dinner with martinis, cheating on your income tax, telling a few small lies, swearing at them and each other? Not a very pretty picture, is it?

What is life like at your house?

BOCA RATON

Diverticula of the Colon

Diverticula are pockets or abnormal pouches protruding from a hollow organ such as the intestine. True diverticula include all layers of the bowel wall, as in a birth defect. "False" or acquired diverticula lack the muscle layer.

Diverticula occur throughout the length of the digestive tract but more often in the colon, and especially in the sigmoid portion, on the left side. The caliber of the bowel normally decreases from right to left and is narrowest in the sigmoid. Three longitudinal bands of muscle (taeniae) overlay the powerful circular muscle coats and together they enable the bowel to contract vigorously (peristalsis). Normally, the colon contracts in segments, propelling the bowel contents onward against mild and yielding resistance. Excessive muscular contraction and intense spasm result in pronounced segmentation, with temporarily closed areas of pressure within the bowel. These "segmented" pressures cause the inner layer of the bowel to herniate through points of weakness, i.e., between muscle bundles and where the nutrient arteries enter the bowel wall. Sustained muscular activities also leads to muscle thickening, commonly associated with diverticula. Thus, diverticula of the colon are acquired herniations, occurring in parallel rows on each side of the bowel, although in some patients they are distributed throughout the colon.

An important factor in some patients with colon diverticula is prolonged nervous tension, causing the irritable bowel syndrome, a situation characterized by irregular, intensified bowel muscular contractions and spasm. The emotional difficulties arise from the many usual problems, frustrations and anxieties of life, rather than from significant psychiatric abnormalities. The accentuated nervous stimulation increases the motor activity of the bowel. Another very important cause is prolonged insufficiency of natural fiber or bulk in the diet. Inadequate bulk results in small hard bowel movements which are difficult to propel onward and require the colon muscles to work harder than usual. A third factor in some patients appears to be age, since colon diverticula are found in only about 8 percent of the population under sixty but in at least 40 percent of individuals over the age of sixty-five.

Interesting geographic differences highlight the incidence of colon diverticula. The condition is almost unknown in rural Africa and is rare in Japan, India and Pakistan, countries where the diet contains large amounts of fiber; bowel movements are large and numerous, and bowel transit time is relatively short. Diverticula disease of the colon is very common in Western countries such as the United States where the diet is less abundant in natural fiber; bowel movements tend to be small and hard, transit time is prolonged and bowel movements are less frequent. Since 1900, colon diverticula have become more frequent in the United States and in other Western countries.

Colon diverticula fill readily but since they lack a muscle layer they tend to empty less easily. Retained fecal material, in approximately 25 percent of patients, may cause inflammation and microperforations of the diverticulum, resulting in diverticulitis and pericolitis. The symptoms include lower abdominal or left-sided cramping pain and tenderness in the lower abdomen, increasing constipation and low-grade fever with malaise and occasionally chills. The development of an abscess within the bowel wall may lead to perforation and peritonitis. When penetration occurs adjacent to the urinary bladder, an abnormal communication (fistula) may develop with the colon (approximately 5 percent of patients). Symptoms then may include painful, frequent urination, pus and blood in the urine and, infrequently, the passage of air or feces through the urinary orifice (urethra).

The combination of muscle enlargement, inflammation and scarring results in a partial obstruction of the bowel on the left side (sigmoid) in about 20 to 25 percent of patients. Symptoms include severe lower abdominal cramps, nausea and vomiting, abdominal distension and the temporary cessation of bowel activity.

Erosion of blood vessels in and around the diverticula by the inflammation results in bleeding; a situation encountered in 5 to 25 percent of patients, especially among older individuals in whom arteriosclerosis increases the vulnerability of the blood vessels. Usually the blood loss is small and slow, causing no special symptoms. More extensive loss of blood is associated with the usual manifestation of hemorrhage from any source.

In the absence of inflammation or other complications, colon diverticula are not accompanied by symptoms, and many people are unaware of their presence. Frequently, the symptoms are those of the associated irritable bowel, with abdominal discomfort or pain, distension, gas, cramps, and constipation, and less often diarrhea. Symptoms otherwise relate to the presence and the type of complication.

Colon diverticula are diagnosed by the barium enema examination of the large bowel. The X rays demonstrate small, grape-like protrusions of bowel wall along either or both margins of the colon, a characteristic muscle thickening, and an associated spasm and irritability, creating a saw-toothed appearance. Rectal and proctosigmoidoscopy examinations are of value chiefly in excluding other conditions. Occasionally, the openings of the diverticula containing fecal material may be seen, but these are visualized better by the longer fiberoptic colonoscopy, permitting inspection of the entire colon, a diagnostic procedure rarely necessary for the diagnosis of diverticula.

The medical management of diverticula of the colon depends upon the individual situation. For many patients without bowel symptoms and in whom colon diverticula are an incidental finding, no treatment is necessary other than maintenance of bowel regularity.

For patients with an associated irritable bowel and constipation, the addition of bulk to the diet (fruits, vegetables, bran and other whole grain cereals, psyllium hydrophilic colloid and similar preparations) in combination with regular eating and bowel habits may suffice to relieve symptoms. Additional dietary measures in the high roughage diet are: (a) Substituting whole wheat flour (instead of white flour) for bread, cakes, pastries, etc. and (b) Reduced intake of sugar. A mild antispasmodic (e.g., tincture or extract of belladonna) alone or together with a mild sedative, as prescribed by the physician, helps to relax muscular tension, decrease pressure within the bowel and relieve abdominal discomfort.

For mild diverticulitis, temporary limitation of diet, bed rest, heat to the abdomen, antispasmodics and antibacterial drugs usually control the problem. In severe diverticulitis, associated with partial or complete obstruction, additional measures are required; e.g., nothing by mouth, fluids, minerals and nutrients intravenously, and intensive antibacterial medication. Since the initial attack of diverticulitis, in approximately 50 percent of patients, may be the only such episode, prompt attention to the earliest presentation of diverticulitis is important. Medical treatment otherwise is determined by the presence or absence of obstruction, bleeding, abscess or fistula formation.

Operation usually is required for persistent or recurrent diverticulitis, perforation of the bowel, abscesses or fistulas, uncontrollable bleeding, and when a cancer in the involved bowel cannot be excluded completely. Elective prophylactic surgery may be indicated in patients below the age of fifty and otherwise in good health, prone to recurrent attacks and complications, and usually leading to eventual operation at a time when surgery is more difficult and complicated. The usual procedure is removal of the diseased segment of bowel and re-establishment of normal bowel continuity, preceded or accompanied by a temporary opening located higher in the colon (colostomy). A procedure of incising the thickened bowel muscles to relieve excessive muscle contraction and decrease colon pressure (colomyotomy) is under evaluation.

If the concept of insufficient dietary fiber as a major cause of colon diverticula is correct, a general program of providing adequate bulk in the diet from childhood on eventually may decrease the incidence of colon diverticula and obviate the need for extensive medical and/or surgical treatment.

CREDIT: *Joseph B. Kirsner, M.D., Ph.D., M.A.C.P., The Louis Block Distinguished Service Professor of Medicine, University of Chicago.*

Divorce

"THE OTHER WOMAN"

The Other Woman
Never smells of Ajax or furniture polish.
She was bored with Bobby Dylan
A year before we had heard of him.
She's a good sport
Because it's easier to be a good sport
When you're not married.
The Other Woman
Never has tired-blood.
She can name the best hotels in Acapulco
As readily as we can name the best detergents.
She wears chiffon peignoirs instead of a corduroy bathrobe,
Because it's easier to try harder
When you're not married.
The Other Woman spends her money on real furs
While we spend ours on obstetricians.
She knows how to make a husband feel wanted
Because it's easier to want a husband
When you're not married.

* "The Other Woman," copyright © 1968 by Judith Viorst.

In 1977 there were over a million divorces in our country. It appears that 1978 will see at least as many splits, if not more. The bars and cocktail lounges are jammed with married men and women having "a quick one" before heading home, anesthetizing themselves against the battle—or the boredom—that awaits them. Too often they end up seeing double and acting single. Women's magazines continue to print "helpful" articles on "How to Hang On to Your Husband" while thousands of wives write to me and complain that "hanging is too good for 'em."

According to a Gallup Poll, one of the principal reasons for the high divorce rate is the economic independence and improved status of women. Forty years ago if Grandma was galled by Grandpa's stinginess, his alcoholism, his roving eye, or a tendency to be quarrelsome, profane or violent, she put up with it and hoped the neighbors didn't hear. Grandma had no marketable skills. She was dependent on her husband for the roof over her head and food for the table. If there were children, she stayed "for their sake."

What's more, divorce laws were designed to make marriage permanent. Unless the wife had uncommon courage or family money to fall back on, she was hopelessly trapped.

Today when a marriage turns sour, most women have options. Vocational school, a college degree or on-the-job training can be her ticket to freedom. No longer is an unhappy wife locked into a wretched, anxiety-producing marriage for "room and board." She can tell the bum to get lost. And more and more women are doing just that.

By the same token, the husband whose dearly beloved has turned into a shrew, nag or a lazy slob and views him only as a meal ticket has a way out too. He can extricate himself without producing rigged photographs to prove adultery. Can you believe adultery was the *only* grounds for divorce in New York State until 1967! Thousands of women and men were forced to take this duplicitous route because it was the only way to legally terminate a marriage.

No-fault divorce laws are among the most civilized pieces of legislation passed in the last twenty years. Today almost every state has some form of "no-fault" divorce. I am ashamed to say my own state, Illinois, was not among them in October of '75. It was painful for me to sue my former husband for "cruel and inhuman treatment" when he asked for his freedom. He was neither "cruel" nor "inhuman." But like thousands of others, I sought the least destructive grounds—and that was it.

Another reason for the increase in the divorce rate is the admission (at long last) that it is perfectly possible for well-intentioned, intelligent people to make a mistake. People *do* change. The man or woman you took for better or worse in 1952 is not the same person you see across the breakfast table in 1977. If you don't believe it, just get out the old wedding album and take a look.

Furthermore, times have changed. Before World War II, a divorcée was considered—well, not exactly a scarlet woman, but she did pay a price. In small towns, particularly, if she was Catholic or Jewish, she was made to feel like a pair of brown shoes worn with a tuxedo.

When Adlai Stevenson was being considered as a Presidential candidate there was concern about his chances for the nomination because he was a divorced man. When Stevenson received the nomination in 1952, it was a giant step toward making divorce "respectable." Interesting that in 1946, James M. Curley, the Mayor of Boston, was re-elected while in jail. Had he been divorced, he wouldn't have had a chance.

Has the cultural shock knocked us crank-sided? Are we punchy from the radical changes that have occurred these past thirty years?

I don't know if these are the best of times or the worst of times, but I do know they are the only times we have. In my view, anything that allows people to be more honest and true to themselves is good. Life is too precious to waste years in a joyless marriage—or worse yet, a miserable one.

Do I sound as if I am championing the cause of divorce? Let me assure you such is not the case. I am, however, making a strong plea in behalf of integrity, courage and self-respect. This is what the good life is all about. Nothing is so joyous or energizing as a healthy marriage—nor as draining and nervous-making as a sick one.

Divorce does not necessarily mean failure. It can mean victory, an indication that there has been growth. It takes courage to change one's life, to say, "We are no longer good for each other so let's not continue to cheat ourselves by putting up a false front for people who couldn't care less."

CREDIT: *Ann Landers.*

'THE OTHER MAN' PAINTED BY ONE WHO KNOWS HIM

DEAR ANN LANDERS: You recently had a column describing "The Other Woman." Why is it no one has ever described "The Other Man"? He is everywhere. Places you'd never suspect. I'd like to try my hand at it since I know him well. My wife knows him even better.

The Other Man is never seen in the morning unshaven, with hair disheveled, in a ratty bathrobe, groping for his glasses. He appears in the morning (at work) or in the evening at a favorite rendezvous, looking perfectly groomed and very appealing.

The Other Man is not puttering around the house in torn trousers and an old shirt, trying to fix the plumbing or a garage door or a leak in the roof. No hint of perspiration from mowing the lawn or washing the car. He smells of cologne, toothpaste and after shave.

The Other Man is always in a good mood. When he is with you, he is out for a good time. He leaves his worries at home.

The Other Man invariably has a wife who has back trouble, is emotionally disturbed, frigid and a terrible nag. She doesn't understand him and talks of nothing but bills, unmanageable kids, bothersome relatives and things that are depressing. But he can't leave her to marry you—for a while—because of financial circumstances, the children, his aging mother, his religion or his boss. His list of excuses is endless.

The Other Man doesn't care that he has caused his wife untold hours of anguish, that she has become a guilt-ridden nervous wreck, confused and unsure of herself. He doesn't give a thought to the fact that his children have heard rumors, or sense something is terribly wrong in the family. He is having a great big round ball—concerned only with himself, his pleasure and his ego, in spite of what he has led his playmate to believe. Do you know him? Look again. WATCHING ALL FROM UP CLOSE.

DEAR WATCHING: Thank you for an insightful description. It's bound to hit a lot of people where they live—or at least visit.

MIDDLE-AGED PLAYBOY'S A CLOWN PRINCE

DEAR ANN LANDERS: Here are some questions all married men over 50 should ask themselves while slapping a little extra after-shave on their faces in preparation for a clandestine date with a cute young thing:

(1) When was the last time you heard of a young woman sneaking around with a married man twice her age who was poor?

(2) Have you ever noticed that the "Glamor Puss" invariably has bills that must be paid, or she is always in desperate need of something she can't afford? Who was the last solvent chick you ran around with?

(3) What would you think if your daughter or your son's wife was involved in the type of relationship this woman is carrying on with you?

(4) Have you ever considered the possibility that your affair is not as private as you think?

Wake up, idiot. Nobody is envying you. Your friends think you've lost your marbles. A SEX CLOWN'S WIFE

DEAR WIFE: Here's your letter. And now a word to the Clowns: Please don't write and ask me where that letter came from. I'm not talkin'.

A RERUN ON 'TEN WAYS TO BREAK UP A MARRIAGE'

DEAR ANN LANDERS: Please repeat that great column, "Ten Ways to Break Up a Marriage." I need it NOW. SOS

DEAR SOS: Here it is. Thanks for asking.

1. When sons or daughters let you know they plan to be married, show open hostility to the person of their choice. After all, marriage means less love and attention for parents and they have a right to resent it.

2. Expect your married children to spend every Sunday and holiday at your home. Act hurt if they have other plans.

3. If your married children have problems with their mates, encourage them to come home, no matter what. Listen attentively to all complaints and point out additional faults that may

have gone unobserved. Remember, single drops of water can wear away a rock if the drops keep falling long enough.

4. When your married children have financial problems, rush in with the checkbook. If you are having financial problems yourself, borrow, if necessary, but let them know they'll never have to do without anything so long as you are around.

5. If a married child has a drinking problem, tell him his mate drove him to it. It will make him feel better. Everyone needs someone to blame.

6. If your married son gets an opportunity for advancement that takes him to another city, tell him "family is more important than money." If he leaves anyway, remind him that God punishes those who ignore the commandment, "Honor thy father and thy mother."

7. If there are grandchildren, smother them with gifts. If the parents object, tell them to keep out of it.

After all, grandchildren are to spoil. Sneak money to the little ones secretly if you have to. They'll love you for it.

8. If your married child has a difference of opinion with his mate, get into the act and give them both a sample of your wisdom born of years of experience. What do THEY know? You've lived!

9. When your married sons or daughters visit with their children, make a point of how thin and tired the kids look. Get across the message that you don't like the way your beloved grandchildren are being cared for. Ask repeatedly what they eat and why they have so many colds. If a kid breaks a tooth or is injured during play, get all the details and place the blame on lack of maternal supervision.

10. If your son has a button off his shirt, say something. Also mention the hole in his sock or the spot on his coat. It will fan the flames of self-pity and could start the final fight that ends in the divorce court.

The Divorced Mother

Bringing Up Children on Your Own

When you're first separated, your children usually seem like an added burden. In the beginning, you are frightened and overwhelmed, and you can hardly think of anyone but yourself. But as time goes on, life gets easier.

What stops you from enjoying your role as a single mother? Basically, five things:

(1) *The poisonous pattern of guilt*

All parents probably feel to some degree that they have failed their children when they divorce.

The brand of guilt can deprive you of satisfaction, peace of mind and the pleasure you should get from your family. Instead of feeling guilty, tell yourself you did the best you could with your marriage and you are doing the best you can *now*.

Don't communicate your guilt to your children. Take the positive approach that this new, single lifestyle has many advantages. Now that you are a single parent, there won't be any arguments with their father over how to raise the children. If your husband ruled with a heavy hand while you were married, there is now an opportunity for flexibility and freedom of expression.

(2) *Depriving yourself in order to give the children more*

Divorced mothers are the biggest patsies in the world. This is ridiculous. You have just as much right to enjoy life as your children. Don't give up your bedroom. Don't chauffeur the children around to make their lives easier at the expense of making your life more difficult. Don't spend your last dime to buy your child luxuries. It's better to lean on the side of doing more for yourself. Life can be grim for those who are overly generous to others and not generous enough to themselves.

(3) *Trying to be two people—both husband and wife*

Remember, you are only one person; you can't be two. Substitute other relationships to replace the absent father. Don't be reluctant to call on uncles, friends, grandparents. You'll be surprised at how delighted they may be to be asked to "pitch in." Remember, there are others who can offer your children emotional support besides you and your husband.

Encourage a spirit of co-operation in your children. Decide who will do the dishes, run the errands, carry out the trash, do the grocery shopping, and fold the clean clothes. Explain that if they help with the chores, you will have more time to do fun things with them.

Children of divorced parents usually become infinitely more self-sufficient than children of two-parent homes. This is an enormous advantage when they become adults.

(4) *Feelings of hate toward your husband*

It's damaging to your children to hear how much you hate their father (if you do). Half of them *is* their father and they're bound to be confused when they hear you talk against him. They might even get the notion you hate them too. Most children want to love their father. Your verbalized hostility will make them feel guilty and confused.

You can say, "I'm upset with Daddy now," or you can convey your disappointment that the marriage didn't work out, but do avoid expressing strong negative feelings about him. If he treated you shabbily, they *know* it. They were *there*.

(5) *Resentment over having kids at all*

We all have it, to some degree, especially if we have custody of the children. What your resentment is telling you is not that you're a bad mother who doesn't love her children, but that you are overwhelmed with too many problems.

The answer to this is to make your life as easy as you can. Try everything. For example:
—get a mother's helper
—organize a day-care center
—organize a baby-sitting co-operative
—get a housekeeper or a live-in student
—let your husband share more of the responsibility
—live communally or with another woman
—get help from parents or other relatives
—exchange services with relatives, neighbors or friends

As a single woman you need outside interests, emotional support and time away from the kids so you can renew your spirit and meet some interesting people.

You must stop thinking in terms of being able to do everything by yourself, especially if you are working outside the home. And you must also get over the idea that you owe your children every minute of your free time.

FATHER'S VISITATION DAYS

These days are important and should be encouraged. It is in your best interests to make these days as pleasant as possible for your ex-husband as well as your children.

Why?

—Because your husband will probably only keep a relationship with your children if he enjoys being with them.

—Because your kids will resent you later if they feel you ruined their relationship with their father.

—Because, when you have a gentleman friend or a new interest, and would like your husband to spend more time with the kids, he'll be happy to do it.

—Because if he has a good relationship with the children, he'll be more likely to send support money.

—Because, when problems with your children arise (and you can be sure they will), you'll have an interested party who will be willing, even eager, to help you.

Encourage your children to tell their dad what they want to do when they have a day—or weekend or a vacation together. The best kind of day for the children will be a natural one—in which they can talk to Daddy, perhaps watch TV with him, eat with him, argue with him—anything that makes up a normal day. Some fathers feel guilty about having divorced and they try to "make up" to their kids for their absence by entertaining them on a grand scale, or buying them expensive gifts. Kids "get the message" and are uncomfortable about it. They don't like to feel that they are ripping off their father, and would prefer that Dad just help fix their bicycles or go to the shoe store with them to buy a pair of sneakers.

Make Dad's visiting day a good one for you too. Planning is the key. Don't just sit home and feel lonely and left out. Schedule something that is fun. Shop with a friend. Go to the beauty salon. Take a course in an adult education class or a swimming lesson. Play tennis, or bridge, or take in a movie. Go to the theater. Get a massage or attend an exercise class. Even if money is tight, do something that will lift your spirits. It will be well worth the expenditure.

P.S. Some women (especially those who were displaced by another female) try to turn their children against their father and often they are successful. But this can be damaging to the children and as the bitterness is reduced, these women invariably admit they were shortsighted and ungenerous.

It's a myth that any closeness or co-operation between the ex-husband and wife is neurotic—in fact, the opposite is true. Not only is it emotionally healthy, but it is always in the best interests of the children, if their divorced parents have a civilized relationship. Divorce doesn't necessarily mean war! It can and *should* mean peace.

CREDIT: Living and Loving After Divorce *by Victoria Pellegrino and Catherine Napolitane, New York: Rawson Associates.*

Income Taxes and Divorce

After the emotional trauma and guilt trip have begun to fade, husbands and wives going through divorce proceedings are faced with the hard reality that two separate households are not as cheap as one. Who will help you pay alimony and child support? Who will help you keep up the house payments on the family home while paying the rent on the new singles flat? None other than our Uncle Sam.

Congress has given alimony payers a deduction to help them foot the high cost of living apart. In 1976 the tax reform act made that deduction even better. For convenience, let's call the person who receives alimony the wife and the person who pays it the husband.

Periodic alimony, that's alimony that is paid until the wife dies or remarries, is deductible from the husband's income on his federal income tax return.

Temporary alimony, the support payments made to the wife while the divorce case is pending in the courts but not yet decided, is also deductible but only if there is a written support order signed by the judge. The money a husband pays voluntarily (or out of guilt) while the case is pending but where there is no court order is not deductible. Of course, if you are still married on December 31, you and your spouse may still file a joint tax return for the whole year.

Lump sum alimony—that's alimony that is paid in a specific sum in installments until it's paid in full whether or not the wife remarries—is deductible by the husband only if the pay-out time is longer than ten years.

The wife who receives alimony which is deductible by her husband is receiving income and must pay income tax on that alimony. But if the wife is in a lower tax bracket than her husband, it's Uncle Sam that comes out on the short end and so it's Uncle who makes it easier to pay a bit more in alimony.

Child support is not deductible, but the person who provides more than one half to the support of the children is entitled to take them as dependents on his tax return.

There is, however, one means of the husband's deducting child support. This method is called "unallocated alimony and child support." Here's how it goes. If the husband pays $4,000 a year in alimony and $3,000 more a year for his child's support he deducts only the $4,000 he has paid in alimony and has one child dependency exemption on his tax return, but if he pays unallocated alimony and child support he pays the same $7,000 each year and deducts the full $7,000 on his tax return. His wife pays the tax on the whole $7,000 and his wife is entitled to take the child as her dependent on her tax return and, as an added bonus, she may file as a single "head of household" at a lower tax rate. If the wife is in a lower tax bracket than her husband, then, lo and behold, the Internal Revenue Service gets less tax money and the husband is less strained in making his payments.

So, with divorce as prevalent as it is and the obligations so acute, it is at least helpful to know that the Internal Revenue Service is taking a smaller share in divorce situations and, indirectly at least, it's helping the husband to pay alimony and the wife to receive a bit more.

CREDIT: *Barbara B. Hirsch, attorney, Chicago, Illinois.*

You and Your Ex-husband

A formerly married woman's feelings about her ex-husband are usually terribly complex. She may be angry or bitter, or she may yearn for a reconciliation. The range of feelings is wide, but *all* these feelings are so common as to be almost predictable.

For example, the enormous anger that so many newly divorced women feel is perfectly normal and it is healthy to admit to it. Covering up anger can lead to depression. It's best to express anger through physical activity such as tennis, swimming, jogging—or even pounding a pillow with your fists. Talking honestly about how you feel, preferably to a therapist or a trusted friend, can do a world of good.

If you're angry because your husband is disappointing your children and not living up to his obligations (this is one of the principal complaints of divorced mothers) it is best not to attack the father for his negligence or lack of consideration. Tell him in a non-judgmental way how the kids feel. "Jimmy cried when you didn't show up. He really wanted to show you his new hockey stick."

Many women find that after time has passed, and bitterness and anger subside, a wellspring of loving, caring, positive feelings for the ex-husband emerges. Many women have been told that these feelings are destructive, foolish, or neurotic, but, the fact is, they are normal. If you have lived with a man and perhaps had children by him, it is natural to have some positive feelings about him, and just because you may want them to vanish doesn't mean they will.

However, just because you have some good feelings toward your former husband doesn't mean you should go back to him—assuming you can. You must evaluate the situation carefully. Ask yourself: Has he really changed? Have I? Am I reconciling out of guilt? Or because I want to win? What bothered me about him? About the marriage?

If you do decide to try for a reconciliation, do it with a minimum of exposure. Keep the children from getting their hopes too high.

Let us say that in your particular case, the marriage bond is so strong that you have an enormous need to maintain contact with your ex-spouse, because of the "game-playing." Some of the most common games are:

(1) *Look how I've changed*

Dull old Harry was overweight and used to sit in front of the TV all weekend. Now he's lost weight, has acquired a tan and three smashing new suits. He tells you he's learning to dance and to ski—things you wanted him to do while you were married! This is typical of the kind of changes men make after they're divorced.

Many women react violently to changes of this kind. ("Why did he wait till *now* to do these things?") They may become furious and bitter. It is unwise to assume that these outward changes are proof that the man really got hold of himself and shaped up. The "new" fellow may have opted for the change because he needs to hide his pain, keep busy or feel better about himself.

The best way to deal with your anger when you think of "the new improved product" is to concentrate on your own life and what you are doing to improve yourself. Recount to yourself the *real* reasons you got out of your marriage—even if he left you. The pain should be enough to bring you back to your senses.

(2) *See if you can get the money*

Because the men are usually in control of the money, they may try to manipulate, threaten or frighten you with it.

If this is what your ex is doing, ask yourself why. Is he holding back the money to prove he's still the boss? Is he trying to maintain contact? Does he want to punish you? Once you figure out his motives, you will be in a better position to deal with him.

You can always involve your lawyer and take your ex-husband to court. The courts are your legal weapon and you shouldn't hesitate to use them. You can also appeal to his family or his boss for help. He may pay up to save face.

On the other hand, the better the relationship you have with your ex-husband, and the more involved he is with the children, the better your chances are for getting the money that is rightfully yours.

It's easy to stop paying an enemy. Therefore, even if being nice to him goes against your grain, be practical. If you are not financially self-sufficient, don't be so quick to ventilate your hostile feelings.

It's best to make a strong appeal to the man. Example: "I need you to be a father and the kids need your support." This is a sound approach and one that has worked for many women. Most people want to be liked—and that includes your ex-husband. If you can allow him to see himself as a good guy, you can benefit in the long run.

(3) *The kids love me more than you*

In many divorces, each parent wants to prove he or she is the best parent —and the children become the victims of the competition.

Some fathers, for instance, use money as the trump card to win over the children. They buy gifts, clothes and toys to score points. If this happens to you, don't let your child see that you are angry. It will confuse him and make him feel guilty for accepting Daddy's gifts. Try to talk it out instead with your ex—and explain that time means more to kids than gifts and he is wasting his money.

(4) *Let's see if she's still interested in me*

Why is he flirting with you? Many times it's a game. Some men allow their ex-wives to cling to the hope of a reconciliation when it isn't possible just to reassure themselves that they've still got the old "zing." It will help if you can talk over your feelings with someone who knows you both well—someone who will be honest and tell you if he (or she) believes he's *really* interested. There is no end to the number of games that ex-wives can play.

Some women manage to look as seductive as they can when their husbands come to pick up the children. Others make it a habit of being as nasty as possible or imposing ridiculous rules, such as not letting him see the children if he's late in bringing them back. Women who play these games are angry and want to punish the so-and-so, but the benefits of the game aren't worth the price they pay.

With time, game-playing lessens and that's good, because game-playing often keeps the relationship alive when we should close that chapter in our lives.

DEALING WITH HIS NEW WIFE

This isn't easy. You probably feel hostile and hurt. These feelings aren't "nice" but they are very human. The adjustment to a new wife takes time, even if you're glad you're divorced.

What can you do to make your adjustment easier? As a general rule, especially if you have children, you're better off to establish a distant but cordial relationship, especially if you are still dependent on your ex-husband financially, and/or if you want your children to have a good relationship with him.

If the new wife resents the money her husband owes you (and this is common), don't fight with her or them. If they don't want to send the check, your nastiness can give them the excuse they've been waiting for. Instead, take a businesslike attitude—perhaps the check has been lost in the mail? Inadvertently forgotten? Appeal, too, in terms of the children and how they need the support.

Above all, don't become too deeply involved with his new family. Don't try to butter up his wife. It will look phony and you will look foolish. Remember, you have your own new life to build so use your time and energy doing just that.

CREDIT: *Victoria Pellegrino and Catherine Napolitane, authors of* Living and Loving After Divorce, *New York: Rawson Associates.*

Do-It-Yourself: Should You?

When money is tight, you learn to do a lot of things yourself. And, of course, when people are laid off work they have more time on their hands and often use that time to repair and improve their homes. Hopefully.

This year home improvement work is expected to top $30 billion, up $8 billion over last year. It is estimated that Do-It-Yourselfers use more than 40 percent of all paint sold in the United States. They buy 33 percent of all power tools.

Another economic indicator is the boom in rental tools and equipment. Look in the Yellow Pages of the phone directory under "rental" and you will find companies that rent everything from air compressors to tar kettles.

Accident statistics prove that "do-it-yourself" can sometimes mean "do-it-to-yourself." To keep from becoming a statistic, ask yourself these important safety questions. By answering yes to each, you'll prevent accidents—if you remember to ask-it-yourself before you do-it-yourself.

Are you physically up to it?

Don't be a victim of false pride. At sixty, you can't do some of the jobs you easily handled at thirty-five. Some people are subject to dizzy spells and should avoid heights such as ladders and roofs. Others have allergies and should be careful in selecting solvents, adhesives and other chemicals that might produce a reaction. Still others have physical handicaps such as a heart condition, tricky backs, knees or hernias. They should stop to think before they lift and exert themselves.

Do you have sufficient technical knowledge for the job?

Some electrical, plumbing and heating projects are not for amateurs, even if they have a little savvy. A man in a Chicago suburb did a makeshift job on his furnace and his children were killed by carbon monoxide.

A New York man decided to install an attic fan in his home, to save the cost of an electrician. His hands were wet with perspiration when he touched a live wire. He was electrocuted.

In the Midwest, another Do-It-Yourselfer spent weeks installing an oil heater in his garage. After he finished, a building inspector drove by, noticed the burner and stopped to check. The unit was improperly installed and had no fire-resistant partition. This violated the building code and constituted a fire hazard and had to be removed. The Do-It-Yourselfer was forced to call in a licensed heating man to transfer the burner to the basement. Cost: $300.

If he had used a knowledgeable craftsman in the beginning the bill would have been no more than $150.

Do you have the proper tools and equipment?

Few homeowners own all the tools needed for a specialized job. Not having the proper tools often leads to a sloppy, make-do job—or even an unsafe one.

The classic case is the home plumber who doesn't own a large pipe wrench and slips a section of pipe over the handle for increased leverage.

Using an improvised tool may cause frustration and tension that can lead to an accident. Often you can get advice on how to fit the right tool to the right job from your local hardware store.

Do you have enough time?

Many jobs can be done at your leisure without disrupting the household. But if, for example, it's a plumbing emergency that takes the bathroom or kitchen out of service, you may not have the necessary spare time to do the job. This can also lead to sloppy and unsafe work. If it's an emergency, hire a pro. If it isn't an emergency, allow enough time to do the job properly. As time runs out, the accident rate goes up.

Do you go by the book?

Many homeowners fail to acquaint themselves with the possible hazards of the products they work with. They open a can of tile cement and read the instructions on how thick to apply it and what kind of trowel to use, but they stop reading and never get to the sentence that says, "Use with adequate ventilation and keep away from open flame."

A number of Do-It-Yourselfers have installed counter tops with volatile, flammable mastic. This can cause a flash fire and result in serious injuries.

The rules and regulations should be known and thoroughly understood, particularly when working with electricity, gas, solvents, adhesives and power tools. Always go by the book!

Will you avoid the make-do solution?

Many Do-It-Yourselfers are concerned only with whether the appliance or plumbing works, not whether the job is done right. But right means safe.

If, for example, you connect black (hot) wires to white (neutral) wires the light will go on or the appliance will work. So far so good? Wrong. So far so bad. You may have created a shock hazard. The home electrician who installs a three-wire outlet without connecting the ground wire can set up a booby trap. Years later someone may plug in a defective tool with a three-wire plug and be electrocuted.

Will you get the help if it is needed?

A Midwestern Do-It-Yourselfer will never forget the time an aluminum ladder slid out from under him and left him dangling from his roof. Fortunately, a neighbor heard his yells and rescued him.

When the load is bulky, when the ladder is on a questionable footing, when the task calls for more than two hands, regardless of the job, don't be afraid to ask for help when you aren't sure you can handle it yourself.

That's what the pros do. When the going gets tough, substitute "Do-It-Together" for "Do-It-Yourself."

CREDIT: *National Safety Council, Chicago, Illinois.*

Doctor

How to Select Yours

Medical schools have been in existence for a long time. However, well into this century apprenticeship was the usual manner in which physicians gained their initial training in practical medicine. The protégé attached himself to someone knowledgeable and experienced in practice.

All this has changed. Today Qualification Boards have been established in all areas of medicine demanding that recent graduates seeking approval of a Medical Board pass the examination in the discipline of that Board in order to achieve recognition. These Medical Boards have done a great deal to upgrade medicine in all its disciplines, especially in its scientific aspects. Today's graduates from American medical schools with Board training enter practice far better trained than in any period of history. Combining the art of medicine with its science, the young doctor gradually acquires an expertise far superior to that of his forebears trained essentially by apprenticeship.

Medicine has advanced greatly through the agency of research and its liberal support by our Congress and the American people since World War II. Physicians in greater medicine and its many disciplines have at their disposal helpful tools unknown to the physician of 1930. In recent years, there has been a worldwide interest in better dispersion of medical care, greatly increasing the availability of competent physicians. In the United States, with its 220,000,000 people there are approximately 350,000 physicians, a ratio of a physician to 628 people, perhaps the highest in the world. In Scandinavia the ratio is one physician for approximately 1,400 people.

Still, many small towns and villages in every country of the world are without a single physician. In our country, telephones and suitable means of transportation are available to bring patients anywhere within an hour's time to well-established clinics of the Mayo pattern which cover most specialties of medicine. A worthy feature of group practice is the readily available opportunity for consultation.

All patients like to feel that they are in the hands of the most competent person available in their community. The enduring attachment of a patient to his doctor is dependent upon many considerations, including sympathetic and mutual respect, similarity of interests, reciprocal attitudes of kindliness and friendliness, as well as success of the treatment. Frankness, honesty and sincerity are qualities that all patients welcome in their physicians.

Baffling diagnostic problems demand a ready willingness on the part of the doctor to seek consultation. In the early decades of this century, it was not an uncommon practice for the doctor to dispense medicines from his office rather than through the local pharmacy, a scheme that perpetuated the practice of providing patients with medicines from the first point of contact. The emphasis of today's physician is upon diagnosis, medication being deferred, save in emergencies, until the nature of the illness has been definitely established.

An obvious interest in and concern for the patient's welfare are attributes that inspire confidence in the physician. Ready accessibility, gentleness, integrity, and competence are also qualities that patients appreciate in their doctor. How to find the professional skill and talent that best meets the needs of the individual patient is a recurring question, for which there are no specific guidelines. It is like choosing one's friends: affinity of interests, mutual confidence and respect are the essential factors in establishing lasting friendships. These same qualities help the patient in the selection of a doctor. Consulting the employer in a new environment is sound counsel, or asking one's friends or fellow workers for the names of doctors in whom they have confidence.

Competent physicians, combining a balanced knowledge and experience in the science and art of medicine, are available in every sizable community today. The patient should remember too that the best-trained physicians in the community are usually no more expensive than the less-accomplished practitioner.

The public image of the physician has greatly improved over the years that have elapsed since World War II, largely because creative research has greatly improved his accomplishments. Sworn allegiance to the Hippocratic Oath binds all physicians to a concerned, kindly and generous attitude towards our fellow voyagers. Physicians who exhibit greater concern over personal remuneration than over the patient's welfare, and occasionally exact inordinate fees—and there are few such—tarnish the image of the physician and should be shunned. Even in this materialistic age, the doctor does well to remember the altruistic background of his profession and the motivation to do good—not for himself—that originally attracted him to the profession of medicine.

CREDIT: *Owen H. Wangensteen, M.D., Regent's Professor, Department of Surgery, University of Minnesota, Minneapolis, Minnesota.*

Dogs

Picking a Family Dog

What kind of a dog should a family get? There are a number of considerations whether you are seeking a specialty breeder and buying a pure-bred
dog or going to the pound and saving a random-bred animal from the
euthanasia room.

First, what do you want in a dog? Companionship? At what level? A big
thumper to run beside you in the woods and fields, or a snug little cushion-
sitter? There is a world of difference between maintaining a Yorkshire Terrier and a Labrador Retriever, yet both are superb companion animals. Is
your life sedentary or are you very active? Do you like tossing a ball to a
wildly cavorting Terrier or do you want a Basset Hound that will sit by your
side while you stare at the fire and sip your port?

The first step, then, is to ask yourself do you want a great lumbering Teddy
bear dog or a dog that will be a child in your home and never grow up. That
is what the toys are and other breeds like the Boston Terrier. Is the dog for
your children? If so, how old are the kids and how well-behaved? Do they
need a Newfoundland that can hold its own against a thundering herd of little
savages, or are your kids basically gentle? If the latter, a Whippet might do.
The first step is to carefully and honestly analyze your lifestyle and determine
what you are going to expect of the dog you get.

How about size? Dogs range from tiny toys like the Chihuahua and the
smaller Yorkshire Terriers, through the small Boston Terriers, smaller Spaniels, through the medium-sized, the Basset and the Bulldog, to the large, the
Retrievers, Setters and working breeds like Boxers and Shepherds, all the
way to the giants like the Bull Mastiff on up to the Irish Wolfhound. That is
an enormous range. A St. Bernard or a Wolfhound can weigh close to eighty
times as much as a Yorkshire Terrier. But size is not a factor to be taken
alone because size may not tell you the animal's exercise requirements. A
small Fox Terrier needs more running than a Mastiff. These two things must
work together, size and exercise.

Be honest with yourself. How much room can you spare? How much trouble will you have stepping over and around a Great Dane that is spread out
across your living room and how much exercise are you going to want to give

your pet? And what kind of exercise? A German Shepherd and a Mastiff will want to be walked several miles a day. It will be good for both of you. A Golden Retriever is going to want to fetch, especially from water, winter and summer. A Whippet is going to want to really run and an Italian Greyhound is going to want to sit home and pose. What kind of attention can you give? Don't get a dog that is so big it will be in the way and eventually resented. And don't get a dog that will go stir crazy with the kind of lifestyle to which it will have to accommodate itself. Remember, too, don't count on opening the door and having the dog exercise itself. That is not exercise, it is dogicide. Dogs should not be allowed to wander. There are exceptions, of course. On a farm or ranch, you don't have to leash your dog and walk it around the back forty, but in the city you do, and in the suburbs certainly and in many rural areas where there are highways. In most situations, then, the exercise your dog gets will be up to you and other members of the family. How much and what kind can you provide?

We have discussed your expectations of a dog and also the dog's expectation of you when it comes to exercise, touching on the needs of the dogs and also their size. What about other aspects of care? How about the dog's coat? Some people really like to fuss over their pet but lots of people don't. Before buying a dog, you had better decide where you stand on this matter. Of course, you can always get a dog whose coat needs a lot of care and then give out the contract. Many grooming services pick up and deliver, so all you have to do is pay the bill. Your dog is picked up at the door and then brought back all shiny and renewed. That can be expensive. From $10 a time to $50. It depends on where you live and what you want in the way of services.

If you are going to groom your dog yourself, be sure you want to do the learning and the equipment-buying that goes with it. Take, for example, a Poodle. It takes more than brushing. There is trimming and designing. It's a hobby in itself if done well and if the Poodle is to look smashing at all times. With other breeds brushing is the thing—Spaniels and Setters, for instance. They have feathers on their legs and their ears are subject to terrible tangles. They really must be brushed very often, vigorously, too. And not just for a minute or so. Is that what you want to do with your dog? The shorter-haired dogs, those with hard, close coats, need a quick going over from time to time but nothing compared to what we have been talking about. A sloppy dog is like a sloppy house, an unmade bed, a soiled rug or a spot on your tie. It reflects on you.

Be honest with yourself. How much coat care do you want to give? Bloodhounds, Boston Terriers and Bulldogs need almost none. The Borzoi, the Cocker Spaniel and the Schnauzer need a lot. Pick your place in that spectrum and keep it in mind. It is a very important factor in picking your breed.

Sit down with your family and look them over. The decision you are about to make is an important one—not only for the family but for the dog you choose. Out there, somewhere there is exactly the right dog for you. But before you know him you must know yourself.

CREDIT: *Roger A. Caras, author of* The Roger Caras Pet Book, *New York: Holt, Rinehart & Winston, Special Correspondent, ABC-TV and CBS Radio Commentator.*

Dreams and Dreamers

HUBBY GETS HIS LUMPS IN DREAMLAND

DEAR ANN LANDERS: My husband has a problem that is so weird he's afraid to tell anyone.

Recently he dreamed he took a bite out of a bar of soap. For several hours after awakening he felt nauseated and couldn't eat. Last week he dreamed he had his appendix removed and when he woke up he not only felt as though he had been through surgery, but he looked like it.

Last night he dreamed someone slammed the car door on his foot. This morning he's limping and swears he's in physical pain. Is this possible? I say NO. After all nothing actually happened to his foot. What should he do —see a doctor? It all sounds so foolish. Please help. SHOOK

DEAR SHOOK: It is possible that your husband is in pain and he should see a doctor—not a foot doctor but a head doctor. An imagined pain can be just as severe as a "real" one.

Since your husband is so good at dreaming, it's too bad he doesn't treat himself to something better than an appendectomy or a smashed foot.

A Dream which is not interpreted
is like a letter which is not read.

Talmud: Berakoth
IX55b

Dreams are mental activities that occur during sleep and though they are embellishments of fantasy life, they generally are experienced as if they were real. Everyone dreams—and the dreams are believed to describe the inner situation of the dreamer. They have both psychological and biological purposes. They permit the partial resolution of conflicts too difficult to deal with in waking life; and they are thought to be the guardians of sleep which the mind and body require in order to function in the waking hours. Investigation has proved that all dreams are in color although most people are not aware of it.

Dreams can be regarded as a commentary on recent and past events that arise from the individual's unconscious life, for it is there that memories of the more distant past are stored. The relationship between the 25 percent of our sleeping time, during which we dream, and the state of our emotional health during waking moments is being intensively examined by countless "Dream Laboratories" around the world. Research is also being done to help people who suffer from recurring nightmares.

Repetitive dreams are of particular significance, for they often portray evidence of long-standing conflict and may even aid in the reconstruction of events which contributed to the conflict. All moods and feelings contribute to dreams and should a person be devoid of one of the senses (blind or deaf) he will have dreams that are lacking in that particular sense.

Dreams can have a profound effect on a child's behavior—particularly during the child's first few years when he is unable to tell the difference between reality and fantasy. The dream may be thought to be true and the child can have strong reactions of pleasure or of fear, the latter being the most often reported. All parents know that in some instances the child becomes so frightened that he will not return to sleep unless he is comforted and lights are left on in halls, etc.

DREAMS IN ANTIQUITY

Man has been interested in and puzzled by dreams since the dawn of recorded history. The oldest dream book is the Egyptian papyrus of Deral-Madineh, 2000 B.C. It has to do with divine revelations. Kurland, who explored dream literature back to the fifth century B.C., in addition to examining scrolls and hieroglyphics of ancient and primitive cultures, has noted that generally dreams were used to foretell the future and to divine the will of the gods. Apparently this was common practice and an important part of society.

It is important to note that dreams must be interpreted in the context in which they occur. Also, it is well to remember that one can easily go astray in interpreting one's own dreams or following the advice of so-called "Gypsy Dream Books." This is no pastime for amateurs.

The Greeks had their dreams interpreted at the Temple of Apollo and physicians were the official dream interpreters to the courts. Hippocrates was aware that dreams were meaningful and that knowledge of their symbols was valuable. He believed the powers of the mind were increased during sleep and at that time the psyche became its own master. He also believed dreams had the ability to indicate bodily states of health or illness.

DREAMS IN THE BIBLE

The Bible is replete with dreams and references to dreams. One of the most famous of the dream interpreters was Joseph who, while in prison, interpreted the dreams of a hapless butler and an unfortunate baker who were in prison with him. His most famous interpretations, however, were those of the dreams of Pharaoh in which he correctly foretold the seven years of famine and the seven years of plenty.

Another biblical figure was the prophet Daniel in the court of Nebuchadnezzar. Daniel's role was comparable to that of a court psychiatrist or advisor. Dreams were then thought to be divinely inspired and therefore a holy man was needed to decipher them. Daniel's method of interpretation was somewhat like the methods utilized by present-day analysts. He listened to the dream, and since he knew the King's background and was aware of his influences, he was able to put the King's dream in proper perspective.

At the turn of the present century, Sigmund Freud, an unknown thirty-nine-year-old Viennese physician, began to write about and interpret his own dreams. He wrote: "Some sad secrets of my life are being traced back. The humble origins of much pride are being laid bare." In his book he concluded that dreams can be interpreted, that a dream represents fulfillment of a wish (usually an infantile wish), and that dreams represent a regression to an earlier form of mental functioning.

Freud described the dream as partly a hallucinatory experience made possible because the dreamer is unable to carry out the motions he dreams about. When the results of his work were published he called the book *The Interpretation of Dreams*. It was ignored for the most part and not taken seriously by the scientific community. Fewer than five hundred copies were sold. That book, nevertheless, was the basis for modern dream research.

Freud considered the basic function of the dream the gratification (through fantasy) of unacceptable, unconscious, wishes. This is the meaning of his statement that all dreams are disguised wish fulfillments. He cautioned against prolonged exhaustive translation of every dream. "Dreams," he said, "are to be taken up and considered day by day. Dreams left aside at one session represent no loss since the same unconscious wishes and conflicts will appear again in a later dream."

Symbols as expression of hidden or secret ideas play an important role in dreams. Freud discovered that ideas or objects represented in this way are highly charged with inappropriate feelings and laden with conflict.

Night, said Freud, was the time when repressed drives of all kinds can be symbolically satisfied. Sex, being the most repressed drive, is the most common focus of dreams. All weapons and tools, from umbrellas to daggers, are symbols of the male sex organ, as are asparagus, airplanes, snakes, fish, snails, cats and mice, while female genitals are represented by, among other things, rooms, windows, jewelry, landscapes and churches. Riding a horse, plowing a field, climbing stairs are all symbols of sexual intercourse.

Freud's Swiss rival, Carl Jung, strongly disagreed with him about the nature of dream images. Instead of seeing them as a secret code for sex organs and sexual acts, Jung believed that most dreams symbolized ignored or rejected aspects of our own personalities.

Alfred Adler, also a Viennese psychiatrist, saw dreams as an integral part of the thought processes. He stressed their relationship to the lifestyle of the individual.

Adler believed the dream has a useful purpose—that it puts the burden on the dreamer for the solution of a problem in his own particular way. Dreams seen in this sense are geared towards humans as problem-solving creatures who are continually evolving new solutions as the daily demands of living change.

In Adler's framework the dream becomes a means of examining the problem and trying out possible solutions without the risk of doing so in life. In one sense the dream could be described as a rehearsal for the real thing. Adler also believed that self-deception is part of the intent of the dream because one's private goals are usually not in line with reality. He concluded that dreams ordinarily do not lead to direct solutions of problems, rather, upon waking, the dreamer is in a certain frame of mind. The dream creates an attitude. Adler points out that some famous men have found solutions to vexing problems in their dreams. He further stresses that valid and correct dream interpretation must be tailored to the individual and that there are no pat guidelines for "dream interpretations."

In 1886, W. Robert had already written in a German publication that dreams were the safety valve of the mind, allowing tensions accumulated during the day to be discharged. He foresaw serious problems for humans deprived of the possibility of dreaming. Current research has shown that there is indeed a definite need for dreaming. Within limits a certain amount of dream (D) time is required by the body each day.

MODERN VIEW OF DREAMS AND DREAMING

In the middle of this century it was said that little new had been discovered about dreams for the preceding fifty years. Whether that was true or not, a whole new era of dream research began in 1953 when Nathaniel Kleitman, a University of Chicago professor, noticed a series of movements under the closed eyelids of a sleeper. It was a slow, drifting movement which occurred immediately after the onset of sleep. Eugene Aserinsky, a graduate student, was given the task of observing sleepers during a number of nights in a sleep laboratory. He noted still more active movements in dreamers at times and when the sleepers were awakened they generally reported that they had been dreaming. Kleitman named this rapid eye movement phase of sleep REM sleep and the dream period later came to be known as (D) sleep, and the remainder or non-(D) sleep to be called (S) sleep, and while there is no finding which says one cannot dream during (S) sleep, the accent is on the so-called (D) period.

Interestingly, the very young spend more time in the (D) state than does the adult. In the infant there is a dream cycle of 45 to 60 minutes, gradually increasing in the adult to a 90-minute cycle.

Accompanying the striking irregularity of the pulse, blood pressure and respiratory rate, there are some additional findings of great interest. One study links dream content with full or partial erection in the male. Fischer in 1965, and in a more recent study, has shown that there is a similar congestion of the blood vessels in the pelvic area of the female, indicating that the sexual response is more nearly identical for males and females than has been suspected.

Interestingly, Whitman reports that a number of disturbances have been studied in various stages of sleep; for example, bed-wetting occurs early in the night during (S) sleep, talking and walking also occur in the (S) period, as does a particular type of nightmare.

Thus, by a fortuitous set of circumstances (the Kleitman and Aserinsky discovery) the way has been opened for the most exciting field of dream research. The field, therefore, has become an attractive bridge between the mental and the physical aspects of the human being. But the bridge is still quite shaky and most people would prefer not to cross it but rather to remain on their own side.

The future of dream and sleep research, therefore, obviously holds great promise. Interestingly enough, more has been discovered about dreaming in the last quarter century than had even been thought of in all the years that had gone before. It does seem that dreams are truly the "Royal Road to the Unconscious" and present-day research will undoubtedly learn more about how and why we "manufacture" dreams and what they mean in our lives.

CREDIT: *Francis J. Braceland, M.D., Senior Consultant, The Institute of Living, Hartford, Connecticut.*

Street Drugs

More has been written about "street" drugs in the last ten years than in the previous two hundred. Some of the information represents the work of dedicated researchers, but much of it is just plain garbage.

Before discussing drugs further we should define the term "drug." A drug is any chemical that changes the structure or function of the cells of the human body. Alcohol is, of course, a drug. From the point of view of an individual or a family, excessive use of drugs or drug abuse, must be viewed as an emotional problem.

Television commercials promise instant solutions to indigestion, headaches, sleeplessness, fatigue, backache, nervousness and unpopularity. ("If you're lonely, change soap.") With this type of exposure, day in and day out, is it any wonder millions of viewers see no danger in popping pills or smoking pot to relieve anxiety, to escape reality, or to turn on?

Who are the drug abusers among us? Are you one? If you started to take diet pills two years ago, lost the weight you set out to lose, but continue to wheedle the doctor into refilling the prescription because you "need the pills for energy," you are a drug abuser.

If your husband needs a tranquilizer or two every day to calm him before a business luncheon, and then takes a Seconal to assure himself of a good night's sleep, then he is a drug abuser.

If Grandma gulps cough medicine, although she hasn't had a cough in years, she is a drug abuser.

If your brother-in-law, Joe, started to take antihistamine pills for his hay fever and is still taking them long after the hay fever season has ended, then he is a drug abuser.

A drug abuser is someone—anyone—who is hooked on something that makes him feel better than he felt before he took it. By "hooked" I mean he doesn't have the will power to stop, even though he tells himself and others that he can kick the habit any time he wants to.

Drug abuse in America (and in most of the rest of the world) is an ever-increasing threat to the quality of life. It destroys individuals, divides families and corrodes the social structures of our cities and communities. In the past ten years, drug use has reached into the fourth grade. Both sexes are now equally affected and the pattern of multiple abuse has replaced the historic pattern of abuse of one drug. Almost certainly we are generating larger numbers of people with drug problems. The economic cost alone, in terms of lost productivity, narcotics-related crime and drug abuse prevention programs, is estimated in excess of $10 billion a year. The toll of human suffering is beyond calculation.

This section of the Encyclopedia will contain detailed information about a variety of drugs. Much of it is technical, boring (unless you have a special interest) or simply more than you want to know. Scan it—or skip it.

NARCOTICS—BEWARE!

Narcotic drugs relieve severe pain and cause feelings of intense pleasure and sleepiness; continued use is associated with tolerance, which means it takes more of the drug to achieve the same effect, and dependence. The person taking the drug needs the drug to feel normal, and if this person stops he or she will suffer from nausea, bone aches, sweatiness and restlessness.

The initial effects of narcotics are often mixed, being composed of feelings of nausea and intense pleasure. To the extent that the response is pleasurable, its intensity may be expected to increase with the amount of the dose administered.

Methods of taking narcotics include oral ingestion (by mouth), sniffing or smoking, and the needle, which is known as "mainlining" and "skin popping."

It doesn't take long to change from an abuser of narcotics—one who uses these drugs for pleasure instead of for relief of pain—to an addict—one who needs the drugs to feel normal. Daily use for a period of three to six weeks is enough to get the job done. Then a number of things happen.

Since addicts become preoccupied with the procuring and taking of drugs, they often neglect themselves and suffer from malnutrition, infections and unattended diseases or injuries.

Among the hazards of addiction are contaminated drugs and needles, resulting in abscesses, blood poisoning, hepatitis and infections of the heart.

Since there is no simple way to be sure of the purity of a drug sold on the street, effects of illicit narcotics are unpredictable. This compounds the danger of overdose and death.

A person suffering from a mild overdose may slip into a deep sleep. Larger doses may induce a coma and shallow breathing. The skin becomes cold and clammy, the body limp, and the jaw relaxed. The tongue may fall back and block the air passageway. Convulsions might occur. Death will follow if breathing problems become severe.

When the addict cannot get morphine or heroin, the first withdrawal signs are usually experienced shortly before the time of the next scheduled dose. Complaints, pleas and demands by the addict increase in intensity and peak from 4 to 72 hours after the last dose.

Symptoms such as watery eyes, runny nose, yawning and perspiration appear about 4 to 6 hours after the last dose of heroin. The addict may then fall into a restless sleep.

As the abstinence syndrome progresses, there is restlessness, irritability, loss of appetite, insomnia, goose flesh, tremors and finally violent yawning and severe sneezing.

The patient is weak and depressed from nausea and vomiting. Stomach cramps and diarrhea are common. Heart rate and blood pressure are elevated. Chills alternating with flushing and excessive sweating are also characteristic symptoms. Muscle spasms and pains in the bones and muscles of the back and extremities occur. Without treatment the syndrome eventually runs its course and most of the symptoms will disappear within seven to ten days. How long it takes to restore physiological and psychological equilibrium, however, is unpredictable. Many experts believe that the changes in the body caused by the narcotics are not back to normal for twelve to eighteen months after the addict stops taking the drugs. Other experts, such as Dr. Vincent Dole of Rockefeller University in New York, believe that these addicts never return to the normal, healthy condition they enjoyed before they messed around with narcotics.

For a few weeks following withdrawal, the addict will continue to think and talk about his use of drugs and be particularly susceptible to an urge to use them again.

The withdrawal syndrome may be avoided by reducing the dose of narcotic over a one-to-three-week period. Detoxification of a heroin addict can be accomplished by substituting oral methadone for the illicit narcotic and gradually reducing the dose.

It is not possible to discuss every narcotic drug, for there are too many, but the following information highlights major points about some of the most frequently used narcotics.

OPIUM

Opium is a gum produced by poppy flowers. It is made by making slits in the capsules of these flowers and collecting the sticky substance along the slit.

The plant was grown in the Mediterranean region as early as 300 B.C. At various times it has been produced in Hungary, Yugoslavia, Turkey, India, Burma, China and Mexico. There were no restrictions on the importation or use of opium in the United States until the early 1900s. Patent medicines in those days often contained opium without any warning label and many persons became physically dependent on medicines that were bought and sold without restriction over the counter in drugstores and through Sears, Roebuck catalogues.

Today, state, federal and international laws govern the production and distribution of opium and drugs made from it.

About 240,000 kilograms of opium are legally imported into the United States annually. Although a small part of this is used to make antidiarrhea preparations (such as paregoric), most of the opium is processed by U.S. pharmaceutical and chemical firms for the manufacture of morphine and codeine. Abuse of opium is rare in America, but in Iran and other countries it is a social problem of significance. In these countries, opium is eaten or smoked. Addiction occurs in many people even though they do not "mainline" the drug.

MORPHINE

Morphine is one of the most effective drugs known for the relief of pain. It is marketed in the form of white crystals, hypodermic tablets and injectable preparations.

Morphine is odorless, tastes bitter and darkens with age. Most addicts in America and in Western Europe inject morphine into their bodies with a needle. They take the powder, put it into something small (like a bottle cap) and mix the powder with a small amount of water. Next, they draw up the dissolved morphine into a syringe and inject it intravenously. Because they do this without proper sterile precautions and often share needles, liver problems and blood infections occur frequently.

Long-term symptoms of morphine addicts are similar to that of the heroin junkie—loss of appetite and an uncontrollable craving for another fix.

The dependency pattern is the same with all narcotics. An overdose will cause death by slowing the lungs until they stop functioning.

The primary destructive effect of morphine is psychological. If taken under sterile conditions even with large doses over long periods of time, morphine does not cause death of cells or organs in the human body, but the sex drive is decreased and production of sperm is diminished. The menstrual cycle may be thrown off or menstruation may stop altogether.

HEROIN

Heroin was synthesized at the beginning of this century. The Bayer Company in Germany first started commercial production of the new pain remedy in 1898.

The medical profession for years remained unaware of its potential for addiction. Many doctors considered it a blessing for patients who suffered intense pain, but with increasing experience the abuse potential of heroin was recognized.

In the decades following its discovery, intravenous heroin use began to occur among the poor and socially disadvantaged in the United States. Following the Harrison Narcotic Act of 1914, it became illegal for doctors to treat addicts for their addiction. The problem was defined in criminal terms. This contrasted sharply to the view in England which defined the problem in medical as well as legal terms.

By the 1930s, heroin addiction was part of the scene among the big city's poor. Gradually, the numbers of heroin addicts increased until it involved about ¼ to ½ of 1 percent of the entire population of the United States. This growth was not paralleled in England, where the number of addicts remained quite small until the last ten years, in which there has been a modest increase, but by no means to the extent seen in our own country.

One of the most significant developments in America has been an official change in the definition of heroin addiction, which has permitted legal narcotic substitution. This has been a godsend for tens of thousands of addicts because they have been able to change their lifestyles by going to methadone maintenance centers. From a social point of view, however, the addiction problem has not been greatly affected. Recruitment of addicts by the drug culture continues to keep pace or exceed the rate at which addicts are rehabilitated.

Some experts feel that in 1965 there was a sudden upsurge in heroin addiction in New York City and elsewhere in the United States, with the age of "beginners" dropping from about nineteen, to thirteen or fourteen. At first it was the underprivileged in the ghettos. Soon it spread to the suburbs and middle- and upper-income groups. A similar epidemic has been seen in Washington, D.C., where the number of addicts rose from about 4,000 to over 16,800 in three years. Other experts feel that for the past forty years there have always been substantial numbers of narcotics addicts and that the sixties increased the numbers somewhat, but not greatly. They insist that our progress in the field of communication made people more aware of the drug culture.

The U. S. Bureau of Narcotics and Dangerous Drugs reported 75,000 narcotic addicts in 1972. These figures are low since they include only those who had been reported to the Bureau. The New York State Narcotics Control Commission reported 65,000 addicts in New York City alone. More than half of these addicts were under thirty years of age. Mr. John Finlator, who was at that time Deputy Director of the Bureau, estimated there were approximately 320,000 heroin addicts in the United States at that time.

Pure heroin is a white powder with a bitter taste. Illicit heroin may vary in color from white to dark brown, because of the impurities left from the manufacturing process.

Pure heroin is rarely sold on the street. A "bag" (slang for a small amount) may weigh about 100 mg, usually containing less than 10 percent heroin. To increase the bulk of the material sold to the addict, other ingredients (sugar, starch, powdered milk, antihistamines, quinine) are mixed with the heroin in ratios ranging from 9 to 1, to as much as 99 to 1.

Heroin has a high potential for abuse. People in control of their lives do not experiment with it. Those who do usually recognize the risks but are convinced that they possess "extraordinary strength" and can handle it. Needless to say, it is unusual to be able to control use of this vicious drug and these people find themselves, sometimes in a matter of weeks, at the mercy of a dangerous, energy-consuming, expensive and illegal habit. It can cost a junkie from $70 to $100 a day to stay on heroin. Attempts to stop are extremely difficult because of the pain and agony of the withdrawal syndrome.

The Committee on Mental Health Services of the Group for the Advancement of Psychiatry reported in their booklet "Drug Misuse: A Psychiatric View" that an acute hazard faces the newborn infant of a drug-dependent mother. The child will have withdrawal symptoms at birth, and if the condition is not recognized and the baby does not receive proper treatment, it will die.

This description comes from a distinguished psychiatrist at the Mayo Clinic; it is the verbatim report of a twenty-year-old heroin addict: "The first time I shot up I felt a terrific high, a real rush. It was the most exciting feeling I ever had. After the excitement died down, I felt relaxed and easy, like I was in a dream world. Life was beautiful. All my troubles and worries disappeared."

Sound good? Well, here's the rest of the story: If, within ten or twelve hours, an addict doesn't get another shot, he becomes irritable. He yawns, shakes and perspires. His eyes and nose run. He begins to vomit. His muscles ache and he gets severe stomach cramps, chills and diarrhea. Hallucinations and terrifying delusions often follow. The only relief is another fix.

Some people are more vulnerable to drug addiction than others for reasons we don't understand, but in general they tend to be lonely, angry, unable to function, except in the deviant subculture. Such individuals are apt to be concerned only with the pleasure of the moment. They appear not to care about their future or anybody else's.

The general health of a drug addict ranges from poor to terrible. He rarely eats properly and frequently suffers from malnutrition. One day he might be sick from withdrawal symptoms and the next day he could be sick from an overdose. It is unusual for a junkie to stay in school for long or to hold a steady job. Statistics indicate that the life expectancy of a heroin addict is reduced by many years.

It is difficult to cure a heroin addict, but it is not impossible. Self-help groups have proved useful for some, and narcotic substitution programs, using methadone, are useful for others. Synanon, in Santa Monica, California, was the first of the self-help efforts, but Odyssey House, Phoenix House, Delancey Street and the Gateway System in New York and elsewhere have been effective. Private hospitalization and psychiatric therapy work for a few, but this therapy is costly and it can take several years. The Narcotic Addict Rehabilitation Act of 1966 gives certain addicts a choice of treatment instead of imprisonment, and, if they are not charged with certain classes of crime, they have the right to receive treatment.

An addict already convicted of a crime can be committed to the Attorney General for a treatment period of no more than ten years, or for the maximum period of sentence that could be imposed for his conviction.

An addict not charged with an offense can be civilly committed to the Surgeon General for treatment upon his own application, or that of a relative or friend.

To understand the obstacles faced by law enforcement officers, one should appreciate the fact that heroin is ten to twenty times more valuable per ounce than gold. There is enormous profit in heroin traffic and detection is extremely difficult. The United States imports over 100,000,000 tons of goods of various kinds every year. Five tons of heroin is more than enough to satisfy the needs of all the addicts in the entire country, even allowing for seizures by the police. The fact that we live in a free society also makes it almost impossible to catch the top dogs in the criminal distribution system. All they do is "lend a friend some money." There is no way to prove the money was loaned with criminal intent. Moreover, there is no way to stop the top dogs except by pressuring their underlings. Since the top dogs are usually very well connected politically, law enforcement officers have a difficult job indeed.

The treatment methods for heroin addicts developed in the past decade; most notably, methadone maintenance programs and therapeutic communities have raised the treatment success rates about ten times. Addiction treatment in the now-defunct government-run centers at Lexington and Fort Worth was effective in only two to five addicts out of one hundred. Modern treatment programs, combining all known methods of treatment, are successful in helping twenty to fifty addicts out of one hundred. So while we are ten times better at treating addicts than we used to be, we still have a long way to go.

METHADONE

In response to a shortage of morphine during World War II, German chemists created methadone. Although chemically unlike morphine or heroin, it is a narcotic.

Methadone was introduced in the United States in 1947 as an analgesic and distributed under such names as Amidone, Dolophine and Methadon. Since the 1960s it has become widely used in the detoxification of heroin addicts and in methadone maintenance programs. Its use as a legal narcotic substitute is based on the fact that it is effective by mouth (no needles— sterile or unsterile—are involved) and its effects last from ten to twelve hours. No other narcotic possesses these two characteristics.

Methadone is very cheap, and if the addict obtains it from a legal program, he or she is freed from the necessity of spending large amounts of money for illegal heroin. This means that many addicts stop their criminal activities. Those who went into crime to support their addiction often reverted to straight living. They may have to take the drug for long periods of time, *perhaps the rest of their lives,* but their families and neighborhoods and they themselves report satisfaction at their return to a normal life.

One of the problems with methadone maintenance programs is that many patients cannot be completely or even partially recruited back to "straight" living, and they sell their methadone on the street. It, like heroin, is more valuable ounce for ounce than gold. The new long-acting form of methadone promises to do away with this problem, since addicts can receive treatment at the center and "take-home" doses are not given.

CODEINE

Codeine was first isolated in 1832 as an impurity in a batch of morphine. It is widely distributed in tablet form for the relief of moderate pain or combined with other products such as Empirin Compound. Codeine is effective in relieving coughs.

Liquid codeine preparations for the relief of coughs became very popular among high school students as a "legal" high in the 1960s. Codeine use can lead to dependence and in high-enough dosages it can produce severe dependence rivaling that of morphine or heroin.

Codeine has a high potential for abuse although it is not as risky as other opiates such as morphine or heroin.

DEPRESSANTS OR "DOWNERS"

Depressant drugs (referring to their action on the brain), when prescribed by a physician, can be beneficial in the treatment of insomnia, relief of anxiety, irritability, and tension. In excessive amounts, however, they produce a state of intoxication that is remarkably similar to that of alcohol. If used regularly, even in amounts not much higher than necessary for medical reasons, physical dependence may occur.

In marked contrast to the effects of narcotics, intoxicating doses of depressants or "downers" invariably result in impaired judgment, slurred speech, and an often unrealized loss of co-ordination. They may also bring on drowsiness, sleep, stupor, coma and, possibly, death.

The abuse of depressants falls into several distinct patterns. Intoxication is found most commonly in young adults or teenagers, whose source of supply may be the family medicine cabinet, the illicit market, theft, or illegal prescriptions.

In addition to the dangers of disorientation which may result in accidents on the highway or death by an overdose, habitual users incur high risk of developing dependence. Tolerance to depressants develops rapidly. This means a person who is hooked must keep increasing the dosage to achieve the desired effect. The difference between an "adequate" dose and enough to cause death becomes smaller and smaller.

The person who is unaware of this danger will often obtain prescriptions from several physicians. After a while, he may be taking a daily dose of ten or twenty times the recommended amount. Observers may not recognize the person's problem until he or she exhibits extreme confusion, an inability to do one's work, or repeated episodes of intoxication.

Members of the drug scene often use depressants to "come down" or soothe "jangled nerves" brought on by the use of stimulants. Or, they may use them to quell the anxiety of "flashbacks," or to ease the withdrawal agonies of heroin.

The dangers of depressants, it should be stressed, multiply when used in combination with other drugs or alcohol. Depressants also serve as a means of suicide, a pattern more common among women than men.

The depressants vary with respect to their overdose potential. A moderate depressant overdose closely resembles drunkenness from alcohol. The symptoms of severe depressant poisoning are a cold and clammy skin, a weak and rapid pulse, and a slow or rapid but shallow respiration and unconsciousness. Death may follow if the breathing difficulties and low blood pressure are not remedied by prompt and proper medical treatment.

Anyone who ceases to take, or abruptly curtails, the amount of a depressant on which he has become dependent will suffer from anxiety, accompanied by a loss of appetite, nausea, vomiting, a palpitating heart, excessive sweating, fainting, insomnia, tremulousness and muscle spasms.

If the individual is dependent on a large amount of the drug, delirium, psychotic behavior, convulsions and even death may occur. People don't generally understand that withdrawal from "downers" can result in death for both adults and infants. Withdrawal from opiates rarely results in death for adults although the fetus and the infant are liable to die from narcotic withdrawal.

It is recommended that withdrawal from depressants be supervised under the controlled conditions of a hospital. The withdrawal program usually consists of the substitution of a long-acting barbiturate for the depressant, followed by a gradual decreasing of the dose.

Among the depressants that most commonly produce the symptoms described above are chloral hydrate, a broad range of barbiturates (Doriden), glutethimide, methaqualone (Sopor, Parest, Quaaludes), the benzodiazepines (Valium, Librium), meprobamate (Milltown, Equanil), ethchlorvinyl (Placidyl).

BARBITURATES

Among the drugs most frequently prescribed to induce sleep by both physicians and veterinarians are the barbiturates.

Approximately 2,500 derivatives of barbituric acid have been created by chemists, but only about fifteen remain in widespread use. The legitimate uses for barbiturates are to treat epilepsy, relieve anxiety, calm patients before surgery, and to bring sleep to individuals who are faced with a life crisis.

As with alcohol, some people may experience a sense of excitement before sedation takes effect. If the dosage is constantly increased, the effects of the barbiturates may go beyond producing sedation and sleep. The person may slip into a coma and death may result if a serious breathing problem occurs and medical attention is not at hand.

Barbiturates are produced in tablet or capsule form. In tablet form they are sometimes sugar-coated. According to law, barbiturates are supposed to be obtained only through prescription, but in too many instances they are available for the asking.

Veterinarians use barbiturates as an anesthesia for operating on animals and for putting them to sleep—permanently.

Barbiturate misusers are often involved in traffic accidents because their reactions tend to be sluggish. The effects of barbiturate overuse resemble alcoholic drunkenness—slurred speech, staggering, inability to concentrate and a breakdown of inhibitions. Users become lethargic and drowsy and finally fall asleep.

Accidental death from overdoses are common because users become disoriented, confused, and can't remember how many pills they have taken. The combination of alcohol and barbiturates can be lethal. Several celebrities have died because they took sleeping pills after a night of drinking. A few of the better-known victims are Alan Ladd, Marilyn Monroe, Dorothy Kilgallen and Judy Garland.

If taken in high-enough doses for a period of weeks, barbiturates are physically addicting. If they are taken regularly, the body may need increasingly heavier doses to achieve the desired effects.

If the drug is withdrawn abruptly, the physically dependent person will suffer withdrawal symptoms—cramps, nausea, delirium, convulsions and, in some instances, death.

Withdrawal should take place preferably in a hospital, under the supervision of a physician, over a period of several weeks, on gradually reduced dosages. Some physicians say it is more difficult to get a patient off barbiturates than heroin. Small wonder that barbiturate overdose is the most common method of suicide in North America.

METHAQUALONE

Methaqualone is a synthetic sedative "downer" chemically unrelated to the barbiturates, glutethimide, or chloral hydrate. It has been widely abused because it was once mistakenly thought to be safe, non-addictive, and to have aphrodisiac qualities—a "love" drug. It is taken orally. Actually, methaqualone has caused many cases of serious poisoning. Large doses can result in coma and may be accompanied by thrashing movements or convulsions. There is no question that it has a high abuse potential and much more of it is produced than is needed for valid medical needs.

Continued heavy use of large doses of methaqualone leads to tolerance and dependence. It has been marketed in the United States under various brand names such as Quaalude, Parest, Optimil, Somnafac and Sopor.

David Simpson, the son of a psychiatrist at the Menninger Foundation, who worked at the Naval Regional Medical Center at Camp Pendleton in

Oceanside, California, saw many cases of drug abuse, including some who died. Simpson said: "The most dangerous aspect of methaqualone is the extent to which it distorts the judgment and interferes with depth perception. Driving a car while under the influence of methaqualone is suicidal as hell."

STIMULANTS OR "UPPERS"

All drugs which have an effect on the human brain are depressants. Antidepressants or stimulants or "uppers" differ from depressants or "downers" that the tranquilizing effect is preceded by an excitement phase—usually quite brief in comparison to the length of the tranquilizing phase.

Although stimulant abuse does not cause addiction in the same sense as narcotics or barbiturates, users who attempt to stop taking "uppers" abruptly report extremely strong episodes of paranoia, deep depression and anxiety— more severe than coming off narcotics or barbiturates.

Some commonly abused stimulant drugs are discussed below:

AMPHETAMINES

Physicians sometimes prescribe amphetamines to curb the appetite, relieve minor cases of depression, calm hyperkinetic children and combat narcolepsy (an illness which causes patients to sleep a great deal). Like so many other drugs, amphetamines are produced in quantities that cannot be justified for legitimate medical needs.

Amphetamines are used as "helpers" by truck drivers, entertainers, athletes and professionals whose work demands spurts of energy or long periods of wakefulness. Students who cram for finals often lean on amphetamines. Too often, users don't understand that amphetamines are effective only in combating performance problems related to fatigue. Amphetamines will not improve performance and may create serious problems of another kind if fatigue is not present.

The pills or capsules are taken orally, but for those who want a stiffer jolt, the pill is dissolved in water, heated in a saucepan and injected into the veins. When the needle gets into the act, it's an entirely different ballgame, which we'll explore later.

Amphetamines are a relatively new class of drug, first used for medical purposes in 1935. They were popular among the Beat Generation after World War II. They were known then as Bennies. Americans buy about twenty billion—that word is billion, not million—amphetamines a year.

Some of the users are under a physician's observation and take the pills for medical reasons, but most of the pills are taken to get high. This moved the American Medical Association's House of Delegates to adopt a resolution, in June 1971, to support the proposal of the Bureau of Narcotics and Dangerous Drugs to transfer amphetamine and methamphetamine from Schedule III to Schedule II. This placed these drugs under strict government control (same as morphine) in regard to manufacturing and distribution.

The American Medical Association further resolved to bring pressure on physicians to prescribe amphetamines and other stimulant drugs only to patients who need them for specific medical reasons.

How amphetamines work: The prescribed dose of a tablet called a White Cross will tame the appetite. A second dose soon after will produce a high. A person who is revved up on pills is abnormally cheerful, hyperactive, and behaves like a happy drunk. Later his speech becomes unclear or rapid, his hands shake, his pupils become enlarged and he perspires profusely. Some users go on to another stage which is not so pleasant. They may become jumpy, irritable, aggressive and sometimes violent. An additional dose may produce hallucinations and finally a psychotic episode.

A person on amphetamines often feels intensive sexual excitement, but finds it difficult (usually impossible) to culminate a satisfactory sexual experience because of the inability to climax. This can lead to physical exhaustion, as well as social and psychological problems. Many college students who have used "uppers" during finals say it's a lousy idea to mix sex with Bennies. "It's a killing combo," wrote a male junior at Yale.

The following letter illustrates how a teenager became innocently hooked on amphetamines:

DEAR ANN LANDERS: I'm a sixteen-year-old girl who didn't mean to get involved with drugs. I've never been a wild kid, in fact, I'm considered sort of a mouse. I did turn on, in an innocent or stupid way, and now I know what drugs can do—even to a person who isn't looking to freak out.

My weight was getting out of hand, so I went to a doctor. He gave me a diet and some pills to curb my appetite. I was supposed to take one pill a day. To make sure I killed my appetite real dead, I took an extra pill whenever I felt like it. Soon I ran out of pills, and asked the doctor for a refill. No problem.

Suddenly I found myself crying for no reason. I'd go into a depression and want to jump out the window. Then I began to have dizzy spells and I felt like I was floating. Once when I was driving on the highway my eyesight became blurred and I almost ran into a kid on a motorcycle.

I knew I was zonking out on the diet pills, but I was losing weight and getting whistled at for the first time in my life, so I didn't want to stop. Then one day I hit a "bummer." I went into a laughing jag, then a crying fit, and finally I passed out. Lucky for me I was at home in my own room. When I came to, I swore I'd never touch another pill—ever. I flushed all the pills down the toilet and vowed to diet with will power, not drugs. That was three months ago. Today I feel like the luckiest girl alive. I owe it to the world to tell my story, so print it please, and sign me. RABBIT'S FOOT

My reply:

DEAR R.F.: Thanks for your letter. There's a lesson to be learned from it. Pills are pills—and they don't know what you're taking them for. The chemical reaction is the same whether you're trying for a trip or hoping to lose weight. Benzedrine and Dexedrine (the most popular diet pills) are amphetamines. They can raise your blood pressure, louse up your mental machinery and lead to addiction. No teenager should take these pills unless he or she is suffering from a specific illness for which a doctor has prescribed them. Even then, if he finds himself getting zonked, he should inform the doctor so the dosage can be cut or another medication substituted.   ANN LANDERS

"Speed" is amphetamines injected into the vein for a bigger jolt. The most common variation (and the most dangerous) is methamphetamine (meth) which is severely addictive. When injected, it is called "mainlining."

It doesn't matter how a user starts to mainline, the results are almost always the same. Body weight decreases, malnutrition occurs, and the user needs more and more of the drug to stay "wired," or stimulated. In the 1960s, during the heyday of Haight-Ashbury, the hippie district of San Francisco, users of amphetamines were injecting 5 grams or more per day into their veins. The usual medical dose by mouth is from 10 to 30 milligrams. This means the amphetamine user had developed tolerance by a factor of hundreds or thousands.

"Speed kills," but "it could make you crazy first." If you think this information is propaganda put out by an Establishment Square who is trying to scare you, read this quote from Allen Ginsberg, hippie poet and superstar of the far left:

"Speed is antisocial. It will make you paranoid. It's a drag. It's bad for your body, bad for your mind. The only people who can stand Speed freaks are other Speed freaks—and then, not for long."

Here is an interesting description of the Speed freak by Dr. Sidney Cohen of the Center for the Study of Mind-Altering Drugs at the University of California at Los Angeles:

"The Speed freak is overactive, irritable, impulsive and suspicious. He may sit and take his clock apart and put it together a dozen times, or he may become abusive without apparent cause. He is unpredictable. He is a nuisance. He is completely unreliable and irresponsible. Those who try to help him receive no gratitude. Let him into your home and soon you will be crowded out by a swarm of other Speed freaks who will come at his invitation. When they leave, you will have a sizable mess on your hands and a telephone bill which looks improbable."

Here is a transcript of what it feels like to freak out on Speed. This track was made in a drug treatment center in Chicago. The boy is eighteen years old and a high school senior:

"I started to pop these pills for kicks and, man, were they a groove. After two pills, I thought I could lick Muhammad Ali. I also thought I could make it with any girl in the crowd, but I was wrong on both counts. A kid half my size knocked my brains out when I called him a couple of names which reflected on his mother. Then this chick that I got the hots for was willing, but I couldn't hack it with her after I took a second Co-Pilot. I don't know why, but I just couldn't. She got disgusted and told me to buzz off. This made me depressed so I took another couple of Co-Pilots and backed it up with a shot of gin that just happened to be sitting there.

"For some crazy reason I began to get the shakes, so I grabbed a couple of 'downers' to get me calmed. Man, I started to dive like on a roller coaster. I never wanted it to stop, so I got myself a packet of crystal (more Speed) and sniffed it like cocaine. It was like an atom bomb exploded in my head. I found the bed and enjoyed the fireworks for what must have been a couple of hours. When I saw it was light outside, I knew it was the next day.

"I mainlined it to keep the ride going and all sorts of scary things began to happen. I heard a knock on the door and I was sure it was the FBI. It was really my buddy who came to check on me. I was sure he came to turn me in. I begged him not to. I promised him half interest in my airplane factory and I offered him my Mercedes-Benz. Of course, I was imagining I owned these things. If my buddy hadn't come when he did, I think I would have killed myself." (End of transcript.)

The physicians at the drug treatment center in Roxbury, a section of Boston, say the most treacherous aspect of Speed freaking is that the user will do anything to stay "up." He often injects more Speed which launches him into a "run" that could last for seven or eight days. During this time, the drug user rarely eats or sleeps. You can imagine what this does to his body.

Some kids took Speed in the late sixties and early seventies (they told themselves) as a protection against the Establishment. Here is such a letter, and my reply:

DEAR ANN LANDERS: I am getting fed up with your remarks about drug users. You give your readers the impression that drug users are mentally ill. This is a Fascist lie. Drug users are the only sane people left in this crazy world.

I'm a Speed freak, and I defy anyone to prove I am mentally sick. I *am* sick, however, of war, conflict between black and white, and sick of seeing poor people live in hovels that aren't fit for pigs. I'm also sick of phony politicians, filthy water and polluted air. The only way a person can keep from cracking up these days is by getting stoned or spaced out.

People say the youth of our country are rebelling. Well, who can blame us? We are creating our own world because we can't live in your world of war, racial strife, phony politicians, poverty and pollution. Anyone who can tolerate what is going on is crazy.

I don't expect to see my letter in print because you have no answer. DR. LOVE.

DR.: I, too, am sick of war, conflict between black and white, shameful housing for the poor, phony politicians, filthy water and polluted air. But I'm hanging in there, without drugs, thank you, trying to keep it all together, attempting to cope with problems and looking for solutions.

Unfortunately, the world you escape to is a private world, imaginary and temporary. It's only a place to visit. You can't live there. It takes guts to keep your head on straight, to fight ignorance, prejudice and injustice. But it's the only chance the good guys have to win. President John F. Kennedy said, "The most valuable natural resource of any nation are its young people." If the youth of our country opts to cop out (and drugs *are* a cop-out), this country is finished. The next ten years will be a period of crisis in world history, and you and your contemporaries will be in leadership positions. We can't meet the challenge of the future with a generation of fried brains. ANN LANDERS

AMYL NITRITE (POPPERS)

Amyl nitrite is a liquid which, when exposed to the air, becomes a vapor. It has strong effects on the human brain.

Amyl nitrite is a street drug, often stolen from a pharmacy or laboratory, or created by chemistry students in their own kitchens. Some use it for the rushing sensation which follows inhalation. What it does is dilate the blood vessels. This causes an increase in blood flow which usually produces a splitting headache and a drop in blood pressure. Athletic trainers used to administer a low dose of the drug to athletes who were temporarily stunned by a fall or a blow to the head. It helped them regain consciousness almost immediately. It is no longer used by knowledgeable trainers because of the risks of possible bleeding within the skull.

When pleasure is the goal, amyl nitrite can be extremely dangerous. It can cause lowering of the blood pressure with unpredictable consequences to the heart, kidneys, liver and brain.

Sometimes this drug is used by urologists to prevent an erection after surgery for circumcision or prostate operations. In the hands of a competent physician for medical purposes, the drug is perfectly safe.

Amyl nitrite is not habit-forming and can be stopped without suffering withdrawal symptoms.

ANORECTIC DRUGS
(APPETITE SUPPRESSANTS)

In recent years a number of drugs have been manufactured and marketed to replace amphetamines as appetite suppressants. These so-called anorectic drugs include benzphetamine (Didrex, etc.), chlorphentermine (Pre-Sate, etc.), clortermine (Voranil), diethylpropion (Tenuate, Tepanil, etc.) fenfluramine (Pondimin), mazindol (Sanorez), phendimetrazine (Plegine, Bacarate, Melfiat, Statobex, Tanorex, etc.) phentermine (Lonamin, Wilpo, etc.) and methylphenidate (Ritalin).

These drugs produce many of the effects of the amphetamines but are generally less potent. There is no question but what they have a very real abuse potential, however—especially when combined with wine.

Too often physicians recommend these drugs to fat patients half-heartedly. They know the weight will not stay off unless the patient changes, for all time, his eating and exercise habits. This is called behavior modification and it rarely succeeds unless there is a strong incentive.

COCAINE

Cocaine has been called the most expensive high in the world. It is also the strongest stimulant produced by Mother Nature.

A report, *Cocaine: 1977,* prepared by the National Institute of Drug Abuse, under the supervision of Dr. Robert L. DuPont, director of the Institute, ran for 223 pages. It cost $4 million and took four years to complete. Findings from the report are as follows.

Death "from snorting" is rare but there are some cases on record.

Dr. DuPont said he was concerned about the increase in the number of cocaine users over the last five years and estimated that at least eight million Americans had tried the drug and approximately one million have used it within the last month.

Among high school seniors, a nationwide study showed that 9 percent of the class of 1975 and 9.8 percent of the class of 1976 reported having tried cocaine—mostly all by snorting.

There is nothing new about cocaine. For centuries the Indians in the Andean highlands, where the coca plant has been cultivated since prehistoric times, chewed the leaves for refreshment and relief from fatigue, much as North Americans once chewed tobacco. In Europe and America in the late 1880s, many doctors recommended cocaine as a "lift." Sigmund Freud recommended cocaine as a cure for depression, and considered it a great help to people with asthma, stomach problems, morphine and alcohol addiction and he even suggested it as an aphrodisiac.

Cocaine became extremely popular as a remedy for everything and anything and before long people were brewing it in tea, sniffing and snorting it, using it in nasal sprays, smoking it in cigarettes and injecting it into their veins. It was available at pharmacies, in grocery stores and just about anywhere, including mail order houses. No prescription was needed. Only money.

When a good friend of Freud's took cocaine to overcome morphine addiction and developed a psychosis and died, Freud quit recommending the drug.

While most of the crop serves the needs of South Americans, some cocaine is legally exported to the United States. In this country, the leaves (after they have been decocainized) yield flavoring extracts for cola beverages. The pure cocaine extract supplies a dwindling world market for medical purposes.

Cocaine as a local anesthetic has been largely replaced by synthetic substitutes. Its medical use is now mainly restricted to ear, nose and throat surgery. While the demand for licit cocaine has been decreasing, the supply of illicit cocaine in recent years has been rapidly rising.

Virtually all the cocaine available in this country today is of illicit origin. It is sold on the street in the form of a white crystalline powder containing usually from 5 to 10 percent pure cocaine "cut" with other substances, such as procaine, baby laxative and lactose. It is generally administered by sniffing or "snorting." For heightened effect it is sometimes injected (by needle) into a vein. This produces intense euphoria along with increased heartbeat and a rise in blood pressure and body temperature.

Cocaine is called the rich man's high. The current price is about $2,000 an ounce or $10 for a single dose—the effect of which generally lasts for less than thirty minutes. Most snorters use two, three or four doses for a full evening's entertainment. Dr. DuPont deplored the constant glamorizing of the drug because of its use by jet setters, Rock musicians and high rollers. "Young people especially tend to imitate people they admire." DuPont adds: "While the 'beautiful people' do use cocaine, probably to some degree because of its snob appeal, many people who get into trouble with it are just ordinary folks, three-to-one are males, as with most other illegal drugs." "Cokies" experience terrific "highs" and explosive spurts of energy called "rushes." One researcher reported that repeated massive doses lead to intense excitement, bizarre convulsive movements, violent nausea and hallucinations. Some users become aggressive and violent and can go for three or four days without sleep if the drug is continued in massive doses.

Withdrawal from cocaine can produce extreme fatigue, depression, paranoia and even psychosis. Death may result from the inability to breathe. If the cocaine is injected into the bloodstream, it may cause heart failure. There is wide disagreement among the authorities as to whether or not a person can stop taking cocaine—cold turkey—and not suffer withdrawal symptoms. All authorities agree, however, that cocaine can cause serious damage to the nostrils (if sniffed over a prolonged period of time) and that it is psychologically addictive to a very high degree. Many street users report that they have seen people die soon after "mainlining" coke. Such cases are often attributed to heroin overdose.

As with the amphetamines, large degrees of tolerance can develop in the frequent user of cocaine. An ordinary dose is in the range of 10 to 30 milligrams taken by sniffing. Some cocaine users who go on "run" (frequent daily intravenous use day after day) often develop a tolerance which is ten to a hundred times higher than the ordinary dose. When this occurs, the cokie is in very serious trouble.

CANNABIS-MARIJUANA AND HASHISH

I know of few subjects that have been discussed more and understood less than marijuana. In my search for "the facts," I have discovered that they vary—according to who is doing the talking. Some authorities say marijuana is relatively harmless and should be legalized. Others insist it is an insidious and dangerous drug and the penalties for pushing should be life imprisonment.

My mail reflects every conceivable point of view. Here are two examples:

DEAR ANN LANDERS: When are you going to stop kidding people? Your stand on marijuana is absurd.

I am a seventy-three-year-old man and I have been smoking marijuana since 1921. There is nothing wrong with it. I am living proof. I would also like to point out that in the fifty years I have been smoking pot (both in a water pipe and in cigarettes) I have never gotten into trouble, nor have I had the desire to try anything stronger.

Pot relaxes me and gives me a pleasant glow. The only thing wrong with it is that it's illegal. This should be changed. That person who wrote to you and said he heard such stupid talk at pot parties, why didn't you tell the idiot that those same people would have talked stupid without pot. Marijuana doesn't make people smarter or dumber. It just makes them more like what they are.

I'll bet you a $20 bag of grass, you'll never print this letter.   BUFFALO BILL

I did print his letter and it produced an avalanche of mail both for and against Buffalo Bill's position. Here's another point of view:

DEAR ANN LANDERS: My boyfriend and I had a terrible hassle tonight. It might be our last. The fight was about the same old thing. Marijuana. I want Mike to quit smoking. He refuses. He also refuses to admit that he is hooked. He insists the only thing wrong with pot is that it's illegal. I told him that's reason enough for me, and if he doesn't knock it off, we split. Actually, there are *other* reasons, and this is what I'm writing about.

I can see a big difference in Mike when he smokes, but I can't get through to him. After a couple of joints he gets dreamy-eyed and lazy, doesn't want to talk or go anyplace—he just sits and stares into space. His grades are slipping because he "forgets" to do his homework—or he loses it.

Mike isn't as neat about his personal appearance as he used to be. He doesn't think it's important how a person looks. I told him it's a matter of respect for other people to shower and shave and wear clean clothes. He doesn't see this either. Please, Ann, tell Mike what pot is doing to his life. He thinks you're cool, and maybe you can get through to him. Thanks. SICK AT HEART

Since man has existed on the face of the earth he has discovered (and used) a product of nature to ease the pain of day-to-day living. There is no question that temporary relief can be helpful, but too much relief can be harmful. People need to be prodded by curiosity and motivation if they are to be creative. They must have challenges in order to learn how to cope with difficult situations. They must also keep their brains intact so they can cope with the inevitable problems of everyday living. Since marijuana is a common tranquilizer used by young people today, and the fastest growing in terms of numbers of young people using it, it should be carefully examined.

All marijuana comes from the cannabis sativa plant. The active chemical ingredient in this plant is known as THC (tetrahydrocannabinol). The exact identity of this chemical was established in 1964 by Dr. Raphael Mechoulam in Israel. The ordinary joint, made by chopping up parts (or all) of the plant, contains about 2 to 10 mg of active drug. Hashish, made from the sap of the plant, is much more powerful.

In low doses (2–10 mg) THC causes relaxation and a pleasant feeling; perception of sight and sound may be changed, usually in a pleasant direction. In higher doses (15–30 mg or more), as in hashish, freak hallucinations may develop. Soldiers in the U. S. Armed Forces who used up to 50 grams per month were observed to develop serious disturbances of behavior. The basic question about the effects of pot cannot be discussed without discussing the dose and frequency. All of the psychiatric problems and/or disturbances of mental functioning cited by doctors below developed in people using high doses on a daily or near daily basis. There is no question but that high doses taken frequently do impair mental ability and co-ordination. There is nothing unique to pot in all this. The same is true of the person who drinks four or five double vodka martinis every day. They are also impairing their judgment and co-ordination. Make no mistake about it, in high enough doses, taken frequently, pot, more accurately THC, causes problems.

There is another factor in the pot question and that is the so-called placebo effect. Some experts believe that 2 mg of THC is not sufficient to have an effect on the brain and that the entire experience reported by smokers at this level are attributed entirely to the "set" or "expectation" that they bring to the experience. If others assure you that you will see things more clearly, sure enough, you will believe you are seeing things more clearly.

One of the current myths concerning pot-THC is that it reduces aggression. The experimental evidence for this is non-existent and the evidence in experimental animals is that a combination of stress and pot is associated with more aggression than is caused by stress alone.

As is reviewed below, humans under stress react badly to a drug like THC, especially in high doses. THC, however, is not harmful to the body.

There is no known lethal dose of THC. Overdoses of hashish oil observed in people trying to smuggle balloons filled with this oil (in their stomachs) have come close to being lethal, however.

Recent research suggests that specific chemical components of marijuana may be useful in the treatment of glaucoma and asthma. It has also been used (on an experimental basis) to combat nausea and vomiting produced by anticancer agents. But all this research is in an early stage and at present marijuana does not have any proved medical value.

The recreational use of marijuana provokes the fear of progressing from one drug to another. All studies to date indicate that experimental use of THC is not associated with such a progression but recent studies show that there are indeed stages in the onset of drug abuse. Most young people do not begin with marijuana. The typical adolescent starts with beer and wine. The next step is hard liquor. If the young person goes on to further drug use, it is almost always marijuana.

The next step is to other illicit drugs, usually "pills" such as tranquilizers, amphetamines and barbiturates. Those who are inclined to try for a "bigger belt" experiment with LSD and other hallucinogens. The next (and final) progression is the most dangerous drug of all—heroin.

Dr. Seymour Halleck, Chief of Psychiatry at the University of North Carolina, says drug education isn't doing the job.

The current format of drug education these days is to "scare the hell out of the kids," and it's a flop. The program often consists of a meeting, at which a local physician, a law enforcement officer and a former addict engage in endless dialogue about the horrors of drugs. The physician talks about freaking out and deterioration of the mind. The law enforcement officer speaks gravely about the pot smoker who became a heroin addict, turned to a life of crime and was finally gunned down in an alley during a holdup. Sometimes the officer brings slides. The former addict (who by this time has become an Academy Award performer) recounts the details of his harrowing experiences and tells the audience how his life changed when he was rescued from the gutter by a social worker who virtually snatched him from the jaws of death.

Most of the high school and college students in the audience have already experimented with marijuana and none of these things ever happened to them or to anyone they know. They snicker, elbow each other in the ribs and conclude that since the information on pot was phony, the word on LSD, Speed and heroin is also bull.

Now let's listen to some of the experts. Dr. Zigmond M. Lebensohn, Emeritus Chief of Psychiatry at Sibley Memorial Hospital in Washington, D.C., and Professor of Clinical Psychiatry at Georgetown University, School of Medicine, has this to say:

"Marijuana is not the innocuous drug many would have us believe. Nor is it the deadly poison that scaremongers describe. However, all agree that it is a *drug,* which acts on the brain. *In sufficient doses* this drug induces confusion, disorientation, hallucinations and delusion. In my long experience working with Peace Corps returnees and other patients in their teens or early twenties, marijuana *in sufficient doses* has the capacity to trigger serious mental illness in susceptible persons.

"These psychotic episodes, some of them lasting for months, would never have occurred had the person not been exposed *to substantial amounts of marijuana.* Although alcohol and marijuana act somewhat differently on the central nervous system, they are both toxins (or poisons). Just as people who don't drink alcohol don't get D.T.'s (delirium tremens), emotionally unstable people who stay away from marijuana *in high doses* reduce their chances of spending some time in a psychiatric hospital. It is true that some people can indulge in occasional or periodic use of marijuana without noticeable ill effects, but the emotionally unstable young who use it are playing Russian roulette."

Who smokes pot? There is no classic pot smoker. Some are as young as nine years of age. Recently a pot smoker turned up in a Detroit home for the aged. He was celebrating his hundredth birthday. (He attributed his long life to "a shot of bourbon every day and a reefer [pot] whenever I felt like it.")

In-depth interviews on college campuses turned up the following facts: At least half of the students admitted they tried pot at least once. (My own hunch is that the figure is closer to 85 percent.) Almost every student who said he had tried pot said he did because he wanted to be part of the scene or "to see what it was like." When asked if pot made them horny (interested in sex), most said no but some said yes. While talking to college students about pot, one interviewer noted a sharp division between the social smoker who lights up at weekend parties and the head who has made marijuana an important part of his life. These kids were as different as night from day. They not only looked different and sounded different, but they smelled different.

Is marijuana physically addictive? There is almost unanimous agreement on this question. The answer is no for people using low doses on occasion as a recreational drug. But when the dose rises as with the use of hashish, some experts feel that dependence does occur in mild form.

Dr. Francis Braceland, former President and Director, now Senior Consultant of the Institute for Living in Hartford, Connecticut, points out that marijuana can be psychologically addictive, and this may be as compelling a force as physical addiction. The desire to experience again and again the high feeling or the release of tension can be "habit-forming" in a very real sense.

Some psychiatrists say the users who become psychologically hooked on pot are people who have difficulty handling their problems and had they started on alcohol, they would probably have become alcoholics.

The real question is whether or not most marijuana smokers go on to use other drugs. The answer is no. Most marijuana smokers do not go on to harder drugs. But the facts when viewed from the other end of the telescope are a bit scary. Almost every survey and study reveals that approximately 90 percent of the heroin addicts when questioned about the history of their drug addiction say, "I started smoking pot."

Is marijuana harmful? Smoking it probably carries the same lung risks as would occur with the use of an equivalent number of cigarettes.

Driving a vehicle under the influence of pot is definitely dangerous. With higher doses (hashish) the risks of developing psychological dependence increases and psychotic episodes can occur.

The most important factor is the emotional stability of the smoker. All authorities whom I respect agree that an emotionally healthy person who has a reasonably high degree of self-esteem will not get into serious emotional or physical trouble if he smokes pot on occasion with friends. The problem lies in the stability of the user. But if the dose and frequency increase, the risk of problems in functioning vocationally, socially and sexually increases exactly as is the case with other drugs. The most intact person in the world should not smoke hash or have two martinis and attempt to fly a jet.

The strongest evidence of the harmful aspects of marijuana were cited by Dr. Harvey Powelson, chief of the Department of Psychiatry at the University of California at Berkeley. Dr. Powelson said:

"Five years ago I testified before the state legislature that marijuana was harmless. I have changed my mind. At that time my experience with users was limited and literature was sparse. Most of what I had read and heard led me to the conclusion that there was no proof of long-term harm. The Psychiatric Clinic in Berkeley sees approximately three thousand students a year. My thinking began to shift when I noticed that formerly bright students were finding it difficult to concentrate, to memorize and to think straight.

"They would insist that they were feeling things more acutely, getting unusual insights into situations and loving humanity more. But I could see no evidence that any of this was true when those students spoke to me. I heard patches of lucidity and sometimes brilliance. Suddenly they would fall into a hole of confusion and be unable to extricate themselves. A common statement from such a student: 'I am lost.' Or: 'I forget what I was trying to prove.'

"I have now come to believe that the effects of marijuana are cumulative, that after a period of prolonged use, say, six months or a year, if pure marijuana is *used in frequent dosage,* chronic changes can occur which are similar to those seen in organic brain disease."

A striking confirmation of Dr. Harvey Powelson's testimony was presented in a study by two Philadelphia psychiatrists, Dr. Harold Kolansky and Dr. William T. Moore. Their statement in the *Journal of the American Medical Association* reported that all thirty-eight patients in their study were adversely affected by smoking pot (lots of it, frequently). Of eight who became psychotic, four tried to commit suicide, and of the thirteen unmarried girls who became sexually promiscuous (some with other girls), seven became pregnant. Eighteen developed anxiety, depression, apathy and had trouble remembering and distinguishing fact from fantasy. *None of the patients, who were from thirteen to twenty-four years old, used any drug but pot, and none had a history of mental illness.*

Some psychiatrists did not believe Dr. Kolansky and Dr. Moore had proved anything. One of the principal critics was Dr. Lester Grinspoon, a Harvard psychiatrist. He warned against "alarming reports based on slim data." He said, "Such reports widen the credibility gap between doctors and adolescents." Dr. Grinspoon, who believes marijuana should be legalized, strongly opposes the use of marijuana by teenagers. He said, "Many ordinarily harmless drugs can set off a psychosis in people who have shaky egos, and in adolescence, a shaky ego is a normal condition of life."

TAKING POT LUCK

DEAR ANN: Please publish this for young people who think pot is so great:

Philosophy of a Pot-Head—
Or Nothing Matters

My pockets are empty—*SO WHAT?*

I owe everybody—*LET 'EM WAIT.*

I have no job—*LET OTHERS WORK.*

My car broke down—*DAD'LL GET IT FIXED.*

I dropped out of school—*WHO NEEDS IT?*

My life is a mess—*ISN'T EVERYBODY'S?*

But I have good friends—*COP-OUTS LIKE ME.*

And I'm happy—*AM I??? Yes, but give me a few minutes to get high first.*

DEAR FRIEND: I'm sure a lot of marijuana users will laugh their heads off and call the poem ridiculous, but now it seems pot is turning out to be riskier than ever.

Lately I've been hearing from teenagers who are getting Angel Dust mixed in with their pot. (Street dealers can be pretty scummy.) The kids are ending up in emergency rooms of hospitals, freaked out like you wouldn't believe. So—watch it, out there.

Advice from Ann Landers— and I'm No Authority I'm Just a Columnist Who Happens to Love Kids and Cares What Happens to Them

I have tried to present both sides of the marijuana story. You have here scientific data and opinions of physicians, academicians and psychiatrists, and some of them are poles apart in their thinking. Here's mine:

At this writing, I am fifty-nine years old. People tell me I look like forty and I can tell you I feel like twenty-one. I believe my youthful appearance and enormous energy has a lot to do with the fact that I have never smoked cigarettes or messed around with alcohol or drugs.

When I was a high school freshman (age fifteen) I realized God had been very good to me. He gave me a healthy body and a pretty good set of brains. I wanted to count for something—to make a contribution to society. I decided I needed all the energy and brainpower I could muster in order to make it in a competitive world. I made the decision then, at age fifteen, no booze, no drugs, no cigarettes. It was one of the best moves I've ever made in my life.

I am opposed to any and all mind-altering agents, "drugs," "alcohol," whatever you call them, especially for teenagers. Pot can make you passive, lethargic, unmotivated and can be, if nothing else, a terrible waste of time.

In the years (junior high and high school especially) when you should be absorbing knowledge, getting it all together, setting goals and planning your future, smoking pot will not help you see things more clearly.

Some kids say they don't want to be the "oddball," that the social pressures to smoke are great, they need to be part of the crowd. My answer is: You will never be looked down on or respected less because you stuck to your principles. In fact, the opposite is true. They may call you "chicken" or a "nerd" but deep down, they will admire your independence. They know it takes guts to split with the crowd and go your own way.

The final findings on marijuana are still being examined. My guess is that when all the clinical facts are in, it will be decided that for well-adjusted adults low-dose occasional use of pot is relatively harmless, and may even be a suitable relaxing agent, comparable to low-dose occasional use of alcohol. For others, it could be quite damaging. My advice is—leave it alone. Don't take any chances with your health or your head. You need them both. They are irreplaceable. There's a lot to be said for being in complete control of yourself at all times. I like the feeling.

CREDIT: *Ann Landers.*

HALLUCINOGENS

These drugs usually stimulate the brain before producing the depressant effect, but in addition they produce a false sensory experience, usually of a visual nature.

Primitive tribes occasionally use these drugs but use in these societies does not result in abuse, for the occasions of use are controlled by traditions which prescribe certain times, usually religious ceremonies and certain group conditions, which result in control of the extraordinary experience undergone by those taking these drugs. We will discuss only a few members of this large class of drugs.

LSD

LSD (lysergic acid diethylamide) is a man-made chemical developed in 1936 by Dr. Alfred Hoffmann and a colleague, both chemists for Sandoz, Ltd., a Swiss pharmaceutical company. LSD is a derivative of ergot obtained from a fungus that grows on rye and wheat. This fungus is considered an agricultural disease. In 1943, Dr. Hoffmann accidentally ingested LSD and here is his description of how it affected him:

"I noted with dismay that my environment was undergoing progressive change. Everything seemed strange and I had great difficulty expressing myself. My visual fields wavered and everything appeared deformed, as if I was looking in a faulty mirror. The faces of those around me appeared as grotesque, colored masks. I shouted half-insane, incoherent words. I was overcome by a fear that I was going crazy."

LSD is a hallucinogenic drug and, like most illegal drugs, much of it is manufactured in underground laboratories—often the kitchenette of a chemistry student's pad. This means a wide range of quality and no dosage guides. LSD is colorless and tasteless. It can be prepared in liquid form, powder, capsules or pills.

Illicit peddlers can transport LSD in candy, aspirin, liquor or sugar cubes, and even on the backs of postage stamps. Known in the late sixties to the hippie cult as acid, a dose of 50 to 200 micrograms (no larger than the point of a pin) can produce a trip.

Why do people take LSD? The early use of LSD was solely for investigation of schizophrenia and associated psychotic states. Its effects appeared to simulate the disassociation of the personality from the body which is characteristic of acute schizophrenia. The earliest glowing reports of its mood-altering and exciting extrasensory effects were first publicized by Aldous Huxley.

Later Timothy Leary and a group of psychologists used LSD as a research tool in psychology at Harvard University and elsewhere. Leaving the world of reality and escaping to a dream state of screaming colors and total abandon appealed to young students who were bored and having difficulty coping with daily problems. LSD became the "in-trip" as a result of Leary's endorsement and encouragement, which went far beyond accepted standards of academic and research integrity.

To date, the studies done on LSD indicate that most users tried it for the first time "to see what it was like" or "to understand myself better" or "because I didn't want to be chicken." Some said they were in search of religious insights and were told that LSD would free them from the world of reality, which they decided was "rotten, corrupt, polluted and hopeless." The drug, they were told, would open doors to a world of creativity, exciting color, sound, fabulous geometric visions and unbelievable ecstasy.

What are the physical effects of LSD? An average dose of LSD, which is no more than a tiny speck, can produce an eight-hour trip. The blood pressure and temperature go up, the heartbeat is accelerated and the pupils become dilated. Often the hands tremble, the palms become clammy, breathing is labored and chills develop. Waves of nausea sometimes occur. If the trip is a "good" one, it is called a "joyride" and the "passenger" comes down okay. If the trip is a "bummer" he will "think he has died and gone to hell"—in the words of a user who described his experience.

Repeated LSD use is associated with tolerance if the doses are taken fairly frequently. This means the user will need a higher dose to get the same effect, but there is no development of physical or psychological dependence.

Here is a letter from someone who has been there:

DEAR ANN LANDERS: If you think my letter is too far-out to print, please think again. More kids are into LSD than adults realize. Some have had LSD slipped into their drinks without knowing it. This is what happened to me. The following information is for every cat who attends rock festivals or hangs out with drug users.

LSD takes about forty-five minutes to connect. Before you start tripping, you'll feel a knot in the back of your head. It's a definite pressure. When you realize you've been drugged, don't panic. Relax and keep your cool. Don't go off alone. Ask someone to stay with you. Don't drive a car. Your sense of distance and timing are off. Also your vision is sure to be temporarily out of whack.

Don't look at the sun. It might result in serious eye damage. You can expect the average trip to last about ten hours. When you come down, you probably won't remember much, so don't try.

Be prepared for flashbacks. They are fairly common. This means an unexpected trip, weeks or even months after you've dropped acid. If you feel a flashback trip coming on, call a friend immediately.

If you've never had an LSD experience and are considering one, remember that nobody knows for certain what LSD does or if the damage is permanent. I've had my experiment and I'll never touch it again. My advice is to learn from somebody else's experience. It's cheaper. If you've *got* to try it, happy landings, Brothers and Sisters, and good luck to you. You'll need it. BUTCH (South Carolina)

What are the psychological effects of LSD? Interviews with hundreds of LSD users have brought the researchers to these conclusions: The effects vary from person to person and one individual can experience a wide variety of trips. The effects of LSD depend on the emotional stability of the user, the dosage taken and the quality of the acid. If the dose is taken by mouth, the person begins to feel the effects in about thirty minutes. If it is injected into a vein, it takes less than half that time.

The "bummers" or "bad trips" usually occur because the user takes too much acid in the hope that he will have an unusually groovy trip. "Bad trips" also are related to the user's emotional stability. Individuals with a history of mental illness can be seriously damaged by the use of LSD and the damage may last for months or even years.

Most users remain conscious throughout a trip and will respond to questions. The responses are often illogical, but there is evidence that the tripper hears voices and is aware of the presence of others.

The impact of LSD on the visual senses is striking. The user may notice a sharp intensification of color. Pink appears to be flaming red, lavender is described as "passionate purple," pastel green becomes "brilliant emerald." The outline of objects becomes liquid. The frame of a picture suddenly appears to be wavy. The colors in a painting seem to run together. Ordinary objects take on a luminous glow. In several interviews, users who were thousands of miles apart insisted that they had spoken with Jesus or the Virgin Mary and described a glowing halo around the head, "just like in the religious paintings."

Persons under the influence of LSD often laugh uproariously for no apparent reason, or they can become very sad, weep uncontrollably and sink into a deep depression.

The tripper may become paranoid, convinced that someone is trying to control him. (This is because he has lost control of himself.) The danger of accidental death is ever-present during a trip. The possibility of an accident is so well known that most trippers provide themselves with a "guide"—someone who will stay with them to see that no harm will come. But even the presence of a "guide" is no sure safeguard against trouble. A guide may be able to prevent a tripper from jumping out a window or rushing into traffic, but he can't prevent death from an overdose of acid to which a lethal foreign substance has been added.

LSD distorts the user's sense of time. The person who returns from a trip may believe he has been out of this world for several months. Other users, after a twelve-hour trip, express disappointment that "it lasted only a few seconds."

Often a tripper will become fascinated with a single object such as a vase or a bowl of fruit, and rave endlessly about the extraordinary beauty of it. When the drug wears off, he may or may not notice anything unusual about the object.

The mental picture of one's own body frequently becomes grossly distorted. Arms and legs seem to be separated from the body and the victim is convinced that the dismemberment is permanent. According to several researchers, this experience is unique to LSD users. These fears can be so terrifying that they produce a severe and prolonged state of anxiety.

One of the most dangerous aspects of LSD is that it creates delusions of super-strength and indestructibility. Several deaths have occurred because trippers thought they could fly and leaped out of high-rise buildings to prove it. Others have walked into heavy traffic, convinced they could stop oncoming vehicles with their bare hands. One acid head told his companions he could twist a railroad train "like a toy." He ran out of the house before he could be stopped, raced down the tracks to catch the train, and was killed instantly.

Does LSD increase creativity or self-understanding? People who have experimented with LDS often claim the drug expanded their consciousness and opened new worlds to them, but there is no evidence to support these claims. Comparative studies of the writing and painting of LSD users proved to be, in most instances, not superior but inferior after drug use. The acid head is in the same boat as the lush or the user of marijuana who believes that his drug makes him witty, brilliant and charming, or a better musician or a more sensitive poet. The mind-altering agents remove inhibitions, but this in no way enhances the personality; in fact, it often brings out unguarded traits which can be crude and unattractive. One thing is certain—a person who is under the influence of alcohol or any other drug is no judge of how he appears to others.

Does LSD produce deformed babies? A number of reputable scientists, notably Dr. Joshua Lederberg, Nobel Prize-winning geneticist of Stanford University, have reported chromosomal fragmentation in connection with LSD exposure in the test tube in animals and in man. A number of highly capable scientists have been unable to confirm these findings. So one must say, in all honesty, that this question remains, as of now, unsettled. The answer is "perhaps LSD produces deformed babies." Until further research throws additional light on the subject, medical authorities warn that the drug must be considered a definite risk in this regard. Women of childbearing age should be aware of the possible dangers.

In this connection, I was interested to see if Gracie Slick, the singer with the Jefferson Airplane (now Starship), would produce a normal child when she became pregnant by a musician with the group. Grace referred frequently to her use of LSD and other drugs, but announced she was laying off all dope during her pregnancy. Gracie produced a normal child.

Does LSD have any medical value? So far, there is no evidence that LSD has medical value, but it is still under investigation and some optimistic researchers claim it is too early to tell.

Some scientists say LSD is potentially valuable in psychotherapy. Under proper conditions, a controlled and measured dose of LSD can release long-buried, deep-seated wishes and bring them to the conscious level. This exposure might make it possible for the patient to recognize and then, hopefully, to deal with the true nature of his problem. But to date, no solid evidence of successful use of LSD in medicine or psychiatry has been produced.

Is LSD dangerous? The answer is *yes*. LSD is a powerful drug which is still under investigation. Flashbacks are a frightening side effect which users report with increasing frequency. Some users who have not touched LSD for as long as six months report unexpected trips after smoking one marijuana cigarette, or after taking an antihistamine pill for hay fever. Former users who have sworn off all drugs have experienced unexpected trips during periods of emotional strain—such as a death in the family, a divorce or the loss of a job.

Increasing numbers of acid heads are seeking psychiatric help from private physicians, campus counselors and mental health clinics. The University of California at Los Angeles studied seventy LSD users under treatment at its medical center. The findings revealed that, in every case, the LSD user had experienced one or more severe reactions after the effects of the drug should have worn off. This supports other evidence that LSD may cause serious psychiatric disorders.

Dr. Roy Menninger, President of the Menninger Foundation in Topeka, Kansas, had this to say:

"The use of LSD is declining because more and more users are experiencing unpleasant results. There is no question but what LSD must be considered a dangerous drug because of its total unpredictability. The person who is about to trip, even though he has tripped before, has no way of knowing whether he will have a pleasant journey, or hit a 'bummer' which might lead to serious injury or death."

LSD use seems to decrease with age. Most people who use it give it up as they mature because of the unpredictability of its effects and because sooner or later they have a scary experience.

BABY WOOD ROSE SEEDS

The following item appeared in the ACTION column of the Chicago *Sun-Times* on June 29, 1976:

My son sent for some Baby Wood Rose Seeds not long ago. He got a paper explaining how to plant and care for them. There was a history of the plant that said East Indian natives used the seeds for ceremonial purposes. To produce a relaxed and euphoric feeling, it said, they would wash, crush and eat four to ten seeds. Sometimes the drug-like effect would be strong enough to cause hallucinations. Is this legal? The paper that came with them said, "These seeds are being sold as a novelty." That doesn't sound all that novel.   D.H., Burbank

We asked the Illinois Drug Abuse Program (IDAP) your questions. While its director, Dr. Edward Senay, told us a chemical analysis of the seeds would be required for positive identification, the effects probably are similar to those of nutmeg or LSD. These can cause pleasurable feelings and possible hallucinations, if the dosage is high enough.

"What the flyer accompanying the seeds does not tell you," Senay said, "is that the natives (in the East Indies where the seeds originated) had cultural and psychological controls that protected them from lasting harmful effects. [A strong "national" religion such as Hinduism can be a cultural control.] Unfortunately, we do not have such cultural controls in our society. Therefore, your son should be advised that the potential risks have not been identified in the flyer. Certainly, large numbers of these seeds should not be taken, if indeed they are to be taken at all." But what about the legality? The IDAP's lawyer said it is legal to mail the seeds.

According to *High Times,* a magazine read by people who want to know the latest on drugs (prices, availability, etc.), Baby Wood Rose Seeds sell for $300 a pound. (A pound is approximately four thousand seeds. Twenty seeds is enough for a trip.)

MESCALINE OR PEYOTE

Mescaline or peyote comes from the buttons of a cactus plant. It is usually ground into powder and taken orally. For centuries mescaline has been used in religious ceremonies by the Indian tribes of Central America, and by some tribes in the southwest of the United States. The first references to "cactus magic" describe the plant that can "take a person to another world."

Mescaline has been used in experimental psychiatry to produce a state of semiconsciousness during which a person will remain for hours with his limbs in a fixed position. Psychotic patients sometimes enter this state (it is called catalepsy). Researchers have discovered that mescaline also can produce this condition.

Mescaline, like LSD, is a hallucinogen. It can result in a high and sometimes a trip. The major danger from mescaline is not the development of dependence, either physical or psychological. It is the bad trip, during which the user may endanger his life.

Mescaline is illegal in the United States and Canada, but the law-enforcing agencies have had a difficult time keeping it out of the hands of users because it grows wild near the harmless cactus plants and can easily be obtained in the raw state.

PHENCYCLIDINE (PCP)
(ANGEL DUST)

Phencyclidine, developed in the 1950s, is now legally manufactured as a veterinary anesthetic under the trade name Sernylan. The street name is angel dust.

Since 1967, it has also been produced in "underground" laboratories, frequently in dangerously contaminated forms. Although most angel dust is snorted, taken orally or injected, it is most often sprinkled on marijuana, mint leaves or parsley, then smoked.

This dangerous drug is sometimes sold to unsuspecting consumers as LSD, THC or mescaline. In low doses the experience usually proceeds in three stages: First there is a change in body image, sometimes accompanied by feelings of separation from one's self. Next the visual distortions occur—hallucinations take place and the user "sees" and "hears" things that do not exist. Finally, the feeling of "I don't care about anything" takes over.

The angel dust experience often produces drowsiness, inability to verbalize, and feelings of emptiness or "nothingness." Reports of difficulty in concentrating and making decisions are common. This is sometimes followed by a preoccupation with death.

Many users have reacted to its use with an acute psychotic episode. Common side effects of angel dust include profuse sweating, the inability to feel pain, involuntary eye movements, muscular inco-ordination, double vision, dizziness, high blood pressure, nausea and vomiting. The person may report later that he could feel nothing and was unable to talk. The most serious aspect of using angel dust is that the user can commit some heinous crime, such as murder, and later he has no recollection whatsoever of what he has done.

Prolonged psychotic reactions of repeaters has been noted. These patients require many months of treatment before any improvement takes place.

There is no question about the fact that this drug is extremely dangerous.

MORE ADVICE TO PARENTS

Here is a sensible answer to a question that has appeared in my mail frequently these last several years. The question: "If your teenage child came home and said, 'I am going to take one of the three—booze, cigarettes, or marijuana, which one would you choose?"

The answer was provided by Dr. Robert L. DuPont, who was the director of the National Institute on Drugs in 1975:

"Marijuana use, an issue once marked by emotionalism and scare tactics, is today being examined thoughtfully. Much remains to be understood; marijuana does not lend itself to simple answers.

"Marijuana has been used for over three thousand years as a medicine. It comes from a plant called *Cannabis sativa,* which grows as a weed in many regions of the world. Some of marijuana's properties—notably its psychoactivity—are undesirable for most medicinal purposes. But marijuana has one highly desirable property: there is no known lethal dose, and even after very large doses, the user does not die.

"Although it now seems unlikely that marijuana will ever be used widely in modern medicine, recent research suggests that specific chemical components of marijuana may be useful in the treatment of severe medical illnesses such as glaucoma, asthma, and for the nausea and vomiting often produced by anticancer agents.

"Recreational use of marijuana provokes the fear of progression from one drug to another, from marijuana to more dangerous drugs. Recent studies show that indeed there are stages in the onset of drug-using behavior as adolescence progresses. But drugs for most young people do not begin with marijuana.

"For the majority of illicit drug users, however, marijuana is indeed a step on a staircase. It appears that adolescents typically begin their drug consumption with beer and wine. The next step is to cigarettes or hard liquor. If the young person goes on to further drug use, it is almost inevitably marijuana.

"The next step is to other illicit drugs—most often to "pills" such as tranquilizers, amphetamines and barbiturates. Then—for those comparatively few who go on—the next drug used is LSD and other hallucinogens, followed by final progression to the use of what is generally known as the most dangerous drug, heroin.

"Currently, 33.6 million Americans have used marijuana and 13.3 million continue to use it on a regular basis. Clearly many of these people will not progress beyond marijuana; in fact, many will give up marijuana altogether.

"Marijuana may be less harmful than cigarettes or alcohol. But since marijuana is an illegal substance, the parents of the more than 50 percent of the teenagers in America who have tried it face a tough dilemma. Should they condone their child's use of marijuana or condemn it, perhaps even turning the child in to the nearest police station?

"My view is that a parent has to approach the drug problem as a whole and not pick out any particular drug for special condemnation. One should recognize the fact that most adolescents are going to be exposed to a wide variety of substances. It is important for the parent not to get too uptight about whether the child does or does not use a particular drug once or twice, or even a number of times, recreationally.

"The parent should talk with the young person about the consequences of the decisions that he or she is making, in the context of his adolescence.

"Personally, my advice with respect to any of these substances would be, 'If you are not using them, I would recommend that you *not* begin. Drug use is expensive, it's messy, it's of very limited value in terms of the person's lifestyle, and there are serious health risks associated with all the drugs.'

"One reasonable position parents can take is to realize that *no* drug use is always better than *some* drug use, but that if the youngster is to use *any* drug he should use as little as possible.

"Unfortunately, everybody does not have the ability to control their consumption. This is the point I was making about marijuana earlier, about the likelihood of going on to heavy stuff. The same thing is true of alcohol. Before they start drinking, [there is no way for them to know] if it will have a disastrous effect. They may not be able to control their consumption. So I would say this is one of the things I'm concerned about.

"If a young person uses any of these drugs, I want to help him in a non-hysterical, non-scary way. We must remain calm and not become hysterical. I've heard people say, 'Well, if my child used one marijuana cigarette, I'd throw him out of the house.' I think this is ridiculous.

"Although we need to know more about the health consequences of marijuana use, we already have two areas of major concern. The first is impairment of co-ordination in the marijuana smoker which—like drunkenness —may lead to car accidents. The second is the tendency for a sizable minority of marijuana users to use the drug very frequently and to let their lives revolve around the drug. I would add the risk of developing the same lung problems as cigarette smokers have.

"'Decriminalization' has become a scare word that polarizes people and induces a fighting and contentious attitude. That is probably the biggest problem we have right now. We should step back and ask simply: What do we really want to do with the person, young or old, who is caught by the police with a small amount of marijuana? Put him in prison and label him with a criminal record?

"Locking up marijuana users makes little sense to me. Neither does it make sense to treat marijuana as we now treat alcohol and tobacco.

"A modest fine for marijuana use seems to make the most sense.

"A fine signals to the public that society is opposed to the use of marijuana, but that we do not consider the possession of small quantities for personal use a problem to be dealt with by putting people in prison."

The key principle for parents assessing their child's drug use is the success or failure of his or her general adaptation. How well is he doing in school? How well does he or she socialize? Do they have reasonably healthy future goals toward which they are able to work? If things are all right in general, probably the parents should not hassle the child. But if drug use is frequent and doses are clearly affecting adaptation, then there is a problem. In general, the real dialogue with children ought to be about adaptation, not about a specific behavior such as infrequent marijuana use. But use of heroin or other high risk drugs, such as barbiturates or diazepam (Valium), should be cause for concern.

GLUE-SNIFFING

Many preteen drug abusers go for glue-sniffing because the stuff is easy to obtain. No pushers. No needles. No big outlay of money. Neat.

This is especially distressing because preteens cannot possibly comprehend the risks they run or the extent of the physical and mental damage that can result from such recklessness.

Although model airplane glues are the best-known compounds having organic solvents that will produce a high, there are approximately thirty other substances which will also produce intoxication and exhilaration. The most popular are fingernail polish remover, cigarette lighter fluid, lacquer and varnish thinner, gasoline, antifreeze and cleaning fluids, such as naphtha, benzene, and carbon tetrachloride. At this writing some manufacturers of glues are trying to find less toxic and less volatile materials.

The feeling of excitement and exhilaration is fairly prompt. The sniffer feels as if he were intoxicated from alcohol. In addition to the exhilaration, there is a sensation of detachment, disorientation and confusion. One ten-year-old girl said, "I thought I was Peter Pan. It was like I was floating in air."

Blurred vision, dizziness, slurred speech and a ringing in the ears are common symptoms of sniffing. The judgment is impaired and often the sniffer has delusions of superior strength or unusual athletic ability. These delusions have resulted in serious accidents and some deaths. The earlier phases of intoxication usually last from thirty minutes to one hour, depending on the strength and amount of the substance inhaled and the physical tolerance of the user. The feeling of intoxication is often followed by a period of drowsiness which lasts about an hour. When a heavy amount of inhalant is used, the sniffer could have convulsions, or slip into a stupor, or unconsciousness. The final result in some cases is death.

Solvents when inhaled in large amounts can cause severe kidney and liver damage and heart trouble. They can also damage the central nervous system.

There have been several cases of permanent brain damage due to lack of oxygen. Deaths from glue-sniffing have been reported in almost every one of the fifty states. Like LSD, abuse of solvents is more frequent among younger age groups. As youngsters mature, they tend to give up use of solvents, although a few cases are known in which solvent abuse for over a decade has been reported. Solvent abuse is dangerous. The most effective prevention is to remove dangerous solvents from commercial preparation.

I am grateful to the U. S. Department of Justice (Drug Enforcement Administration) for providing me with literature on which this portion of the Encyclopedia is based.

Glossary of Slang Terms for Drugs

Amphetamines—Beans, Bennies, Black Beauties, Blackbirds, Black Mollies, Bumblebees, Cartwheels, Chalk, Chicken Powder, Co-pilots, Crank, Crossroads, Crystal, Dexies, Double Cross, Eye Openers, Hearts, Jelly Beans, Lightning, Meth, Minibennies, Nuggets, Oranges, Pep Pills, Speed, Roses, Thrusters, Truck Drivers, Turnabouts, Uppers, Ups, Wake-ups.

Barbiturates—Bars, Block Busters, Bluebirds, Blue Devils, Blues, Christmas Trees, Downers, Green Dragons, Marshmallow Reds, Mexican Reds, Nebbies, Nimbies, Peanuts, Pink Ladies, Pinks, Rainbows, Red and Blues, Redbirds, Red Devils, Reds, Sleeping Pills, Stumblers, Yellow Jackets, Yellows.

Cocaine—Bernice, Bernies, Big C, Blow, C, Coke, Dream, Flake, Girl, Gold Dust, Heaven Dust, Lady, Nose Candy, Paradise, Rock, Snow, White.

Glutethimide—C.D., Cibas.

Hashish—Black Russian, Hash, Kif, Quarter Moon, Soles.

Heroin—Big H, Boy, Brown, Brown Sugar, Caballo, Chinese Red, Chiva, Crap, Doojee, H, Harry, Horse, Junk, Mexican Mud, Powder, Scag, Smack, Stuff, Thing.

LSD—Acid, Beast, Big D, Blue Cheer, Blue Heaven, Blue Mist, Brown Dots, California Sunshine, Chocolate Chips, Coffee, Contact Lens, Cupcakes, Haze, Mellow Yellows, Microdots, Orange Mushrooms, Orange Wedges, Owsley, Paper Acid, Royal Blue, Strawberry Fields, Sugar, Sunshine, The Hawk, Wedges, White Lightning, Window Pane, Yellows.

Marijuana—Acapulco Gold, Broccoli, Bush, Dry High, Gage, Ganga, Grass, Griffo, Hay, Hemp, Herb, J, Jay, Jane, Mary Jane, Mota, Mutah, Panama Red, Pod, Pot, Reefer, Sativa, Smoke, Stick, Tea, Weed.

MDA—Love Drug.

Mescaline—Beans, Buttons, Cactus, Mesc, Mescal, Mescal Buttons, Moon.

Methamphetamines—Crystal, Meth, Speed.

Methaqualone—Quas, Quads, Soapers, Sopes.

Morphine—Cube, First Line, Hocus, Miss Emma, Morf, Morpho, Morphy, Mud.

Phencyclidine—Angel Dust, DOA (Dead On Arrival), Hog, Killer Weed (when combined with marijuana or other plant material), PCP, Peace Pill.
Psilocybin/Psilocyn—Magic Mushroom, Mushroom.
Tetrahydrocannabirol—THC, TIC, TAC.

DEATH FROM DRUGS

Drug abusers die of pneumonia, hepatitis, overdoses, hotshots, violence and traffic accidents. Fatal doses may be accidental or intentional. Accidental deaths occur when the addict unknowingly gets a stronger dose of drugs than he had been accustomed to taking. It is impossible to know how much the drug has been cut or if the peddler has added milk, sugar, arsenic or strychnine.

If an addict accustomed to taking 5 percent heroin takes a dose containing 75 percent heroin, it will kill him. It is not unusual for an addict to deliberately take an overdose. When a junkie realizes that his health is ruined, and the future looks black, he may choose death as a welcome release.

Criminal dealers have been known to add poison to the drugs they sell to customers they suspect of giving information to the police. These poison mixtures are known as hotshots. Recently in Los Angeles a heroin addict was found dead, sitting on the edge of his bed with the needle still in the vein of his leg, indicating almost instant death. Hotshot or overdose—who can say?

The drug addict faces other dangers. Pain, which the body uses as a warning signal that something is wrong, is deadened by the effect of drugs. An addict may develop acute appendicitis or some other serious illness and, since he is unable to feel the warning pain, he fails to get treatment—which could be fatal.

Drug addicts are often burned seriously when they drop off to sleep while smoking. They are also subject to falls and other accidents while in a stupor.

The prolonged use of narcotics gradually causes an impairment of the addict's memory and destroys his initiative. He has a very short attention span and is unable to concentrate or reason. Self-respect disappears as well as honesty. Regardless of whether the mental and moral breakdown is a result of the chemical action of drugs on the brain, or because addicts stop using their minds for normal thinking and behavior, the result is the same—disaster.

The following facts were reported after a thorough investigation of the two thousand drug-related deaths in Chicago, Cleveland, Dallas, Los Angeles, Miami, New York, Philadelphia, San Francisco and Washington.

Of the two thousand drug-related deaths, nearly two thirds were among males and were associated with narcotics, homicide and other forms of violence. Female drug-related deaths were more often associated with barbiturates and suicides.

There were more Whites than Blacks.

Approximately one third of the victims were unemployed.

Over 50 percent had been arrested at least once, and one third had been convicted of felonies.

Over 70 percent were heavy drinkers and heavy smokers.

Except for Cleveland, Dallas and Miami, narcotics or barbiturates were involved in the majority of the deaths.

Narcotics-related death victims were generally poorer than the users of other drugs. They were more involved in street buys and most often died accidentally from drug overdose.

People whose deaths were barbiturate-related tended to be older, more often they obtained their drugs by legal prescriptions and frequently they used these drugs to commit suicide.

Barbiturate users were shown to have less involvement with heavy drinking than narcotics users and fewer records of arrest.

Depression, divorce and marital separation were the most frequently noted stresses or problems.

Suicide victims more often lived alone.

SOME GOOD ANSWERS TO COMMON QUESTIONS

From Special Action Office for Drug Abuse Prevention
Washington, D.C.

(1) Why are drugs used?

There are many reasons, ranging from the belief that "medicines" can solve all problems, to "peer pressure," the wish to be accepted by the group that uses drugs.

(2) How can misuse of legally obtained drugs be controlled?

The medicine chest at home may be the first source of drugs misused by young children and teenagers. All members of the family should use drugs only as prescribed by a physician. These drugs should be destroyed when they are no longer needed. Doctors and druggists should pay close attention to the renewal of prescriptions that might cause dependence.

(3) Is it possible to seek help for drug problems without risking getting into trouble with the law?

Doctors, psychologists or drug treatment centers can assure patients that their record of treatment will be kept strictly confidential. There are important legal safeguards for the confidentiality of patients who undergo treatment.

Federal law *requires* that patient records be kept confidential. However, under certain conditions the federal law allows information to be disclosed but the patient must give written consent.

Information can be given, however, to authorized researchers, auditors, or program evaluators, but they are required to keep the information confidential. It is possible to obtain information by a court order, but courts must show good cause for requesting such information.

It may be necessary for the doctor who is treating the patient to see the background information. Also, it needs to be seen by authorized personnel for obtaining benefits (such as insurance). In any event—repeat—permission, *in writing,* must be given by the patient.

State laws may provide *additional* protection for the patient, but the state law cannot reduce the protection provided by federal law.

(4) What is the effect of drugs on sexual response?

Very little reliable information exists on this subject. No drug seems to be a "true" aphrodisiac (that is, capable of "creating" sexual desire), although various substances have been considered to be aphrodisiacs throughout history. Present knowledge suggests that the expectation of the user is probably more important than the action of the drug itself. If the user is convinced that a certain substance will improve his (or her) sexual performance, it might do so. Some drugs, such as narcotics and alcohol, are known to hinder sexual performance.

(5) Is it unsafe to use drugs during pregnancy?

Women should be extremely cautious about taking any drug during pregnancy. Some babies born to narcotic- and barbiturate-dependent mothers have shown withdrawal symptoms. Excessive use even of socially and legally acceptable drugs such as tobacco and alcohol may be harmful to the unborn child.

(6) What is drug overdose, and what can I do about it?

An "overdose" of drugs can be defined as an amount of drugs taken which causes a severe and unexpected reaction to the user. A drug overdose can often be recognized even by a non-medical observer because it often produces stupor or coma, and sometimes serious breathing difficulties. Medical help should be sought immediately if any of these symptoms occur. First-aid measures that can be taken while waiting for medical help to arrive include artificial respiration to restore breathing.

Sometimes hallucinogens, marijuana or stimulants will produce a so-called panic reaction. The person may be frightened, and suspicious. He may believe someone is attempting to hurt him. It is very important that all concerned remain calm and reassure the person that his fears are drug-related and will subside. I repeat—help should be sought as soon as possible. It is usually available from community drug hotlines, drug crises or treatment centers, and hospital emergency rooms.

(7) What is wrong with taking any drug so long as no one else is hurt by it?

It is difficult for an individual to do something to himself that will not affect others. The drug abuser touches the lives of those who are close to him—especially those who depend on him. Society is affected as well. People who become physically or emotionally disabled as a result of drug abuse are generally dependent upon society for their subsistence. Even more important, a drug-dependent person usually represents a human loss to himself, to his family and to his community.

(8) What are the legal distinctions between possession, dealing and trafficking in drugs? What are the penalties for each?

Legally there are distinct differences between these three terms. Illegal possession means that the drugs were not obtained from a doctor, or from a pharmacist by virtue of a valid prescription. A dealer is a drug supplier on a small scale. A drug trafficker manufactures and sells illicit drugs on a much larger scale. Possession of small amounts of legal drugs unlawfully obtained, or of an illicit drug, generally calls for lesser penalties than dealing or trafficking. Penalties in these instances vary widely from state to state.

WHERE TO GO FOR HELP

Hundreds of drug abuse clinics have been set up in the United States and Canada. They are waiting to serve individuals who want to kick the habit. Many of these treatment centers are government-funded. Others are run by organizations such as the Salvation Army, Family Service or church-sponsored groups. It would be impossible to list these centers, their addresses and their telephone numbers, but let me assure you they do exist, and can point to a remarkable record of success. Many large cities have hotlines for emergency situations. Call Information or the Police Department if you need help in a hurry.

If you or someone close to you is on drugs, and wants to get off, I urge you to call your city, county, or state mental health organization. Look in the Yellow Pages of your phone book under Mental Health or Drug Abuse and Addiction. You can also call any hospital connected with a university. Almost all these hospitals have an excellent drug abuse treatment center, or someone in the medical school who can direct you to one.

The important thing to know is this: There is free help available for anyone who wants to get off drugs. Most of it is paid for by your tax dollars, so don't feel as if you are freeloading. If you need it, *get it!*

CREDITS: *Mr. Peter Bensinger, Chief, U. S. Department of Justice, Drug Enforcement Administration. Edward C. Senay, M.D., Associate Professor, Department of Psychiatry, University of Chicago; Executive Director, Substance Abuse Services, Inc. (A special word of thanks to Dr. Senay, who put in more hours than I want to think about. He read my material, corrected the errors and added information on his own. Once again I saw living proof of that old adage, "If you want to get something done, ask a busy person to do it.") Additions by David Simpson, Medical Technician, Coffey County Hospital, Burlington, Kansas.*

Therapeutic Drugs

FOR EMOTIONAL ILLNESS

Physical illness was once regarded as punishment for sins. Even today some superstitious attitudes continue towards illness, especially mental illness.

For the past twenty-five years, medications have been available to treat many psychological disorders and there is increasing evidence that there is a physical cause for such diseases. At least one in every five persons has a psychiatric disorder during his or her lifetime and probably half the population will be given one of the "minor tranquilizers" at one time or other.

Decisions about who should be treated and with what medications (also for how long) should be decided by a physician.

The descriptions of drugs given here is to help you understand what they do. This is *not* a substitute for a visit to your doctor. Never take drugs given to you by a well-meaning friend who had "similar" symptoms. This is asking for trouble.

If you have been helped by a particular drug but more than six months have passed since you have seen the doctor, go back. Your condition may have changed or a better and more effective medication that wasn't available on your last visit may have been developed. Also, some drugs may produce side effects not known about when the medication was first prescribed.

VALIUM, LIBRIUM, SERAX AND TRANXENE

We all suffer from anxiety, tension or nervousness from time to time. ("Will I get the job?" "Will I be fired?" "Will the blind date turn out to be what I had hoped for?" "Will our child be born normal?" "Will the person I love recover from his or her illness?")

Frequently "help" for stress can be provided by a minister, a social worker, a counselor, a psychologist or a psychiatrist. Discussing the reasons for the anxiety and ways of dealing with it may be sufficient. When the anxiety is so overwhelming that the patient can talk of nothing but the symptoms (difficulty in getting to sleep, the shortness of breath, the perspiring, pains for which no physical cause can be found, the diarrhea, the loss of appetite, the irritability, etc., etc.) a physician should be consulted. A medication such as Valium can provide relief of the symptoms—then something constructive can be done in psychotherapy.

A certain amount of anxiety is a normal and healthy part of life. To take medication to relieve the first signs of anxiety would be to misuse the medication.

How should the decision be made as to whether medication should be given? If the discomfort is so intense it becomes impossible for the person to work effectively or to be an adequate father, mother, husband or wife, medication may prevent a bad situation from becoming worse.

Most patients will respond to Valium (as they will to any of the so-called "minor tranquilizers"). At times, Valium, instead of reducing tension and anxiety, may cause additional stimulation—a rapid heartbeat and insomnia or, at other times, excessive sleepiness or cause an allergic reaction. In such cases, one of the other "minor tranquilizers" may work better.

Valium comes in a variety of doses ranging from one milligram to ten milligrams. Some people believe that the less medication they take the better off they will be. At times this kind of thinking results in taking so little medication that it is not effective. The dose of Valium (or whatever drug is given) should be sufficient to relieve the anxiety or there is no point in taking it.

The opposite error is based on the concept that if a little medication is good, more is better. This reasoning can be dangerous since the side effects are often greater at higher doses. In addition, the procedure is self-defeating since tolerance develops fairly rapidly and the higher doses are no more effective than the ones prescribed. It is therefore of great importance to take the medications AS PRESCRIBED.

If you find that the dose prescribed begins to lose its effectiveness, *do not increase the amount of medication without orders from your doctor.* Increasing the dose may result in your becoming dependent on the medication.

The time of day at which the medication is given is important. For some conditions a divided dose taken every three or four hours is most effective. In other circumstances, the dose may be given once or twice a day. Sometimes the medication is prescribed only at bedtime, in which case it may serve as a sleeping aid.

Patients undergoing operations do better if their anxiety level can be reduced. For this reason, Valium is frequently used just before surgery.

DALMANE

Some people get along well on three or four hours of sleep, while others require nine or ten. Most of us have a fairly set pattern. Certain individuals are slow to get started in the morning, while others wake up rapidly and cheerfully.

If fatigue and sleepiness occur after a normal night's sleep, there may be some underlying illness such as anemia. It is wise to consult a physician if you are in this category.

If you have trouble getting to sleep and wake up tired, sleeping medication may be indicated. Insomnia may be the result of anxiety. If this is so, medication can help. One of the best medications for sleep is Dalmane.

At one time, barbiturates such as Seconal and Tuinal, were very widely used. Barbiturates tend to be cumulative and also they may produce confusion. Dalmane (and related drugs) does not present these problems as often. In a number of studies it has been shown that the number of individuals who die from overdose of sleeping medications (whether deliberate or accidental) has been greatly reduced (to about 25 percent of the old number) since Dalmane and related drugs have come into use in place of barbiturates.

One of the reasons for overdosage is that the person using a sleeping medication often loses track of time. The person who is half-asleep may believe he has slept for several hours, when in fact he has slept only ten minutes. He may then take another sleeping pill before the previous one has a chance to work. If this confused dosing occurs three or four times during the night, the combined dosage may be enough to cause serious trouble or even death. This is often made worse by the addition of alcohol, which should never be used with sleeping medications.

The only really safe procedure is to put on the night table only the maximum number of sleeping pills allowed and then put the bottle back in the medicine chest.

Under no circumstances should more sleeping medication be taken than has been prescribed by the doctor. The increased dose may work for a few nights but then tolerance develops and the dosage would have to be increased once again. This often leads to dependence. Another caution—if a sizable dose of medication is being used, it should not be abruptly discontinued since it may produce withdrawal symptoms.

MAJOR TRANQUILIZERS

Thorazine, which is the brand name for chlorpromazine, was the first of a group of drugs of which there are now eight or ten offshoots available. The decision as to which one ought to be used depends on how agitated the patient is, how sensitive he or she is to side effects, and a variety of other factors which the physician must consider. Since chlorpromazine is often used to treat serious mental and emotional disorders, the person for whom it is prescribed may conclude that there must be something seriously wrong. This is not correct. Thorazine can also be used for much less serious illnesses.

One major use of chlorpromazine is in the treatment of schizophrenia. The diagnosis of schizophrenia at times is more frightening than the disease. With presently available treatment, many of these patients are able to live a normal existence, hold a job and have families. At times, the physician is reluctant to tell the family or the patient of the diagnosis.

Medication is not indicated for all schizophrenics, but when it is needed, it is especially important. Experience has shown that, when patients go off medication, they may get along satisfactorily for a few weeks or months but eventually the number who must be readmitted to the hospital is four times as great as for those patients who remain on medication as it is prescribed.

Chlorpromazine is also used for any marked or uncontrolled degree of excitement or agitation. For instance, it might be used for an acutely disturbed and excited state in a manic-depressive. Such individuals sometimes have episodes of feeling excessively good (high) and as a result may behave in a foolish and even dangerous manner.

There are also a variety of other uses for chlorpromazine and other medications in the same group. For instance, a closely related medication, Compazine, can be applied for the uses above. It is also very useful in the treatment of nausea and vomiting. Some of the drugs in this group, known as phenothiazines, are sedating (chlorpromazine for one). Others, to varying degrees, may be less sedating or even somewhat stimulating. The medication should not make you feel "zonked out" or so "dopey" that you cannot perform. There should be a decrease in agitation, anxiety and overactivity, but not to a degree that incapacitates you. Certainly there may be a period of a few days when you first start taking the medication that you are definitely slowed down, but if this persists beyond a week, it is important for you to let the doctor know, so he can change the medication or dosage if it is needed. The reverse is also true. If the medication does not relieve the anxiety or overactivity, it is equally important to have the amount of medication adjusted. To give up "in disgust" because the effect is not immediate, or because there are some annoying side effects, is a bad mistake.

Some dryness of the mouth is extremely common. Occasionally a patient will develop an allergic rash and, if the diet is not watched carefully, there may be weight gain.

There is one side effect which you may not connect with the medication. The clinical term to describe this condition is akathisia—the patient's inability to sit quietly. Patients with akathisia are extremely restless and will often spend most of their waking hours pacing about. When they sit, they keep shifting their legs about and jiggling their feet. There may be tremors of the hands, legs or even the lips. In severe cases, the movements of the hand may interfere with writing or eating. These symptoms can easily be removed.

One other occasional symptom in this group is muscular rigidity, which can be frightening unless you know that it is related to the medication. Like the other symptoms described, this can be cleared up within a few hours by using any of the anti-Parkinson medications. In the extreme case, the muscular rigidity may affect the neck or tongue. In such cases, an intravenous injection of the same medication will bring relief in a matter of minutes. None of these conditions are dangerous, but they can be extremely uncomfortable. Be sure that you let the doctor know should any of these occur, since they are easily corrected.

One less dramatic symptom can be more serious—constipation. This condition is correctable but can cause real trouble, especially in older people, if something is not done about it. Your doctor should be notified.

Another effect of the medication which may be overlooked is sensitivity to sun. This is more true of chlorpromazine than with other members of the same group, and, should it occur, all that is required is a change in medication.

Other medications such as antibiotics can, at times, cause a similar reaction. Be careful if you are on vacation that you do not stay too long in the sun the first time, even though in the past you had no trouble. An overheated kitchen, boiler room or similar overheated environment may also bring on a rash.

As is the case with all medications, one must balance the advantages to be gained against possible undesirable effects. This is true with chlorpromazine and the other phenothiazine derivatives, since in a small percentage of patients a persistent side effect may develop for which at the present time we have no adequate treatment.

LITHIUM

Lithium is a natural element like sodium or potassium. It is an excellent drug for treating certain types of emotional disorders. Even more remarkably it can reduce or eliminate the symptoms of other conditions when taken regularly. However, it *must* be taken under medical supervision since the dosage is not the same for everyone. Too small a dose may be useless and too large a dose may cause serious side effects. A blood test can determine whether the amount of lithium is in the safe and effective range.

The first major use is for the treatment of *manic* conditions. A person in a manic state has the problem of feeling "too good." As a result of this feeling of abnormal elation, the person's thinking and acting may become so severely distorted that eventually they are out of touch with reality.

There is a very special problem treating these patients, especially in the earlier, milder stages of the disease when the patient is hypomanic (just below being manic). The difficulty is that the person feels extraordinarily well and often will not believe that there is anything wrong. Often such patients will spend much more money than they can afford, will monopolize the conversation, become irritable and angry if anyone contradicts them and will wear everyone else out since often they can get along with only a few hours of sleep every night.

In extreme cases, the patient may even have auditory hallucinations (hear voices that aren't there) and suffer from a variety of delusions. Frequently, the delusion is that they are actually a very important person—the reincarnation of one of the saints or even Jesus Himself.

Since the patient does not usually recognize when he or she is becoming hypomanic, it is extremely useful if a friend or family member who knows the situation can be on hand to monitor the situation. Since it is almost impossible to convince the patient that something is wrong, the best way of handling the problem is to try to persuade the patient to go see a doctor and let him make the decision. Since such episodes tend to recur, an agreement to go to the doctor can often be worked out after treatment or hospitalization from the first episode.

In the early stages the patient can be treated with lithium, which usually takes from four to ten days to become effective. Under medication the patient's mood gradually returns to normal and, by remaining under treatment, it is usually possible to prevent a recurrence. If the condition is moderately advanced or the onset is rapid, it may be necessary to use other medication along with the lithium at the beginning. The usual dose of lithium is three capsules or tablets, but this can vary from one patient to another. Usually, but not always, older people do not need as much medication. Sometimes, six or eight medications a day may be necessary to control the situation.

If the dosage is properly regulated, there are usually very few side effects. Occasional patients feel lightheaded and there are some who develop sleepiness, but this usually disappears after a few days. If it does not, the doctor should be promptly notified. If the dose is too high, the usual effect is to produce thickness of speech and an unsteady gait. In those individuals who have a tendency to low thyroid, the condition may become exaggerated after the patient has been on medication for several months. Therefore it is important to see the doctor regularly and report any changes.

Some patients also develop extreme thirst and have to urinate frequently. This is not dangerous and is not a reason for discontinuing treatment.

USE IN PREVENTING MOOD SWINGS

Most of us undergo mood swings—periods of a few days or even weeks when we feel better than usual, and other periods when we tend to be gloomy, lack energy and have less interest in what is happening. It is possible for these mood swings to become exaggerated and reach a point where they interfere with normal functioning. Such patients are labeled manic-depressive. Lithium, in addition to its usefulness in treating manic states, has also been found valuable in preventing their recurrence. Interestingly it is *not* the best treatment for a person who is *in* a depression, but if given when the patient has recovered it will often prevent another depression from occurring.

The ability of a drug to prevent these extreme mood swings is of great importance. It obviously is better to prevent a disorder than to treat it after it occurs. In addition, a patient with these marked ups and downs is unable to plan for the future since he does not know how he will be feeling.

DRUGS FOR DEPRESSION

The most frequent of all psychological disorders is depression. This presents a particular problem since all of us become depressed from time to time as a normal part of existence. In fact, to distinguish it from the disease (which can be treated with medications) we will refer to this condition as existential depression (which should not be treated with medications). There are ways of distinguishing the two types of depression.

First, let us look at the characteristics which most depressions have in common. This is important because often the early symptoms are such that frequently the fact that someone is depressed can be overlooked. The typical picture of sadness, dejection, slow movement and gloomy or even suicidal thoughts occurs fairly late in the course of the disorder.

The earliest symptom is usually anhedonia, which means the absence of joy and pleasure in those things which in the past provided great satisfaction. Food, sports, company and even friends and family leave the patient feeling indifferent so that they don't really care one way or the other.

Another of the early symptoms of depression is fatigue, especially if no other medical reason can be found to account for it. Less commonly recognized as a symptom of depression is difficulty in concentrating and also difficulty in making decisions. Anxiety, irritability as well as forgetfulness may also occur. There is a tendency to think about the past, remembering things that one should have done and didn't do or regretting things which had been done. At times the situation may seem hopeless and life not worth living. Even though the person doesn't think of committing suicide, he or she may wish "that I won't wake up in the morning."

In more severe cases not only does the patient neglect personal appearance but may even believe he has a fatal disease which the doctors and the family won't discuss. In the most severe cases the patient may even hear voices that aren't there and be convinced that all sorts of terrible things are about to happen.

It cannot be too strongly emphasized that every normal human being experiences depression from time to time. Often this is due to a particular life situation. A dear friend or relative may have died or may be very ill. The job, whether as a housewife or company president, may be extremely boring. There may be financial problems. A love affair or a marriage may be going badly. And, from time to time, we may feel depressed and sad for no particular reason that we know of. Although medications for certain types of depression will be discussed below, it must be strongly emphasized that *most depressions should NOT be treated with medication.* In fact, most depressions don't need to be treated at all since they disappear when the situation that is causing them changes or when the person accepts the fact that for the time being nothing can be done to make things better.

If, after weeks or months, there is no improvement and the situation is still producing great unhappiness, it is sometimes useful to consult with someone experienced in such matters. This might be a minister, a marriage counselor, social worker, a psychologist or a psychiatrist. Such discussions, counseling or therapy may lead to the person's either accepting the situation or doing something to change it.

Once again, after weeks or months of "treatment," there may still be no real improvement. It is usually at this point that medication should be considered. There are conditions when it might be given even sooner, but this usually depends on the severity of the illness. If the degree of suffering is extreme and lasts for more than a week or so, if the depression is so severe that the person cannot function in his or her job, or if there is a preoccupation with suicidal thoughts, then medications may be indicated.

There are other signs and symptoms which may also provide clues as to when medication is indicated. One of these is called "early morning insomnia." In this condition the patient is able to get to sleep without much difficulty but awakens at two or three or four o'clock in the morning feeling miscrable and is unable to get back to sleep. Another characteristic has to do with the time of day which is most unpleasant. Often those conditions which eventually require medication are ones in which the patient feels worst in the morning and may show some improvement as the day progresses. Another important clue is that usually there is no relief from the sadness and depression. Even at funerals the bereaved person may smile when reminded of some pleasant or humorous event, but with the type of depression which often necessitates medication, the person may go for weeks and months with absolutely no break in the continuous unsmiling sadness and depression.

One of the difficulties in getting such patients to accept medications is that they almost always can provide a "reason" why they should feel depressed. Often the depression they have is out of all proportion to the reasons which they provide. Someone may argue that although they just received a raise "the supervisor doesn't like them" and the next time there are layoffs they will be fired. Or they may argue that because their child or some other loved one only phones them once a day that "they really don't care any more." There are very few of us who do not have a variety of circumstances which if only slightly exaggerated could provide a "good reason" for us to feel sad and depressed. Often such conditions have existed for years and it is only when the patient develops this type of depression that the condition which they were able to live with in the past suddenly seems of exaggerated importance.

The Medications

These medications are very slow to work and it is usually three weeks before there is any noticeable change. Anyone using the drug for a "quick lift" will find that he is going to be disappointed. As indicated above, one of the medications should only be used for certain types of depression.

There are two major types of medication: the tricyclics and the monamine oxidase inhibitors (MAOIs). There are several different medications in each of the two groups. Patients who are on monamine oxidase inhibitors must avoid certain foods, alcohol and certain medications. Therefore, it is customary to start with the other group of drugs, the tricyclics.

The decision about which tricyclic antidepressant to use is usually dependent upon how much anxiety is present. If the amount of anxiety is not excessive, the most commonly used medication is imipramine (Tofranil, etc). Also used for cases of this type is desipramine (Norpramine, Pertofrane, etc.). When there is a fair amount of anxiety, another group of tricyclics is used such as doxepin (Sinequan, Adapin) or amitriptyline (Elavil, etc.) or nortriptyline (Aventyl). In those cases when there is a retarded depression, that is, when the person is very much slowed down, protriptyline (Vivactil) may be the medication of choice.

The monamine oxidase inhibitors (Marplan, Nardil, Parnate) are often effective when the tricyclics do not produce the desired results. Great caution must be used with alcohol and wine. Most cheeses should be avoided. (Cream cheese and cottage cheese are permissible.) Certain other medications are potentially dangerous in combination (these include Contac and similar preparations used for a stuffy nose or a cold). The physician who prescribes the monamine oxidase inhibitor will usually give you a complete list of such medications. If you have any questions, do not hesitate to call the doctor and ask him.

Side Effects:

With the tricyclic antidepressants in particular, dryness of the mouth is common. There is also at times some slowness in urinating and for certain types of glaucoma the tricyclics are not desirable. The monamine oxidase inhibitors, in addition to placing restrictions on certain foods, alcohol and medications as noted above, may also tend to lower blood pressure and thus certain patients may become slightly dizzy or lightheaded, especially when they first stand up.

As is true with all medications, the benefits must be weighed against the side effects. In cases of severe depression, these side effects are insignificant compared with the relief of the depression.

The introduction of medications in the early 1950s completely changed the situation in respect to mental, emotional and psychological illness. At that time over half the hospital beds in the United States were for psychiatric patients. The number of patients was increasing each year and, had it continued at the rate at which it was going, approximately one million beds would have been needed for such patients. The medications were an essential factor in reducing the hospital population in 1977 to about one third of what it had been in 1956.

Similarly, the patients seen in private practice who did not require hospitalization could also be treated much more effectively and rapidly in most cases.

With the successful use of medications came better understanding of the biochemical factors in mental illness. This in turn led to improved medications. Recently there has been a burst of new knowledge and the prospects are very good that we will have even more effective medications in the near future and possibly be able to treat some of those conditions which we still cannot deal with successfully.

CREDIT: *Nathan S. Kline, M.D., Clinical Psychiatrist, New York, New York; Director, Rockland Research Institute, Orangeburg, New York; Professor of Clinical Psychiatry, Columbia University, New York, New York.*

Dyslexia

Dyslexia is a term that has been used in many different ways in recent years. The word dyslexia derives from two Greek word stems: *dys* meaning difficulty and *lexis* meaning word.

Dyslexia was originally a medical term used to label a condition in which an individual is unable to read as a result of damage to a specific part of the brain.

This definition is no longer useful, for today the label dyslexia is likely to be pinned on any child who has trouble reading. As a result of this indiscriminate usage, consumers (parents, teachers, children) have no way of knowing exactly what dyslexia means when it is used in reference to a specific child.

A teacher, physician, psychologist or other professional may use the term dyslexia when, by a process of elimination, he or she has ascertained that a child

(1) is of average intelligence,

(2) does not have any major emotional problems that might interfere with learning to read,

(3) has good vision and hearing,

(4) does not have any major brain injury,

(5) has had adequate educational opportunities,

and therefore that the child's reading problem must mean that something in the brain is not working correctly when it comes to understanding written symbols. The "something" is *not* a major brain injury; what a practitioner believes it *is,* however, varies widely from practitioner to practitioner. One dilemma here is that no one practitioner is equipped to evaluate all of the above five components.

Some practitioners are overzealous in seeking out dyslexia in young children. They overlook the fact that many of the symptoms (e.g., reversing letters, confusing "d" and "b") in this or that theoretical "dyslexia package" are also normal, temporary phenomena in children's development. Other practitioners simply find it convenient to have technical-sounding labels to use in trying to pin down an elusive disability.

There may be a substantial difference of opinion among professionals about the cause of reading difficulties in any individual child. Even when practitioners agree about the cause(s) they may not agree about ways to help the child read better.

There are many possible causes to consider when a child has difficulty learning to read. Reading is a highly complex skill. Learning how to read requires that the child muster the following tasks:

(1) Recognize and differentiate letters.

(2) Understand that groupings of letters (words) stand for things in the world as well as for sounds in the language.

(3) Understand and remember specific words.

(4) Know the rules of reading (read from left to right on a line of print).

Problems with vision or hearing, intellectual deficits, emotional problems or problems in the functioning of the brain can all, individually or in combination, interfere with the child's efforts to learn to read.

At the same time, the child who is trying to learn to read is interacting with teacher(s), teaching methods, teaching materials and a learning environment. These factors may also make learning difficult. Finally, while most children in our society do learn to read, they learn at different rates and in different ways.

Today, learning disability is a popular label for children who have difficulty learning in school. Although learning disability is perhaps an even more vague term than dyslexia, I think it is preferable since—unlike dyslexia —it does not imply a specific medical condition.

Parents and professional consumers are well advised to be wary of the practitioner who uses dyslexia as if it were a precise condition "cured" via a precise treatment program. Children with reading problems are best served by a comprehensive assessment by a number of different practitioners who together can assess educational, medical, psychological and environmental factors that may singly or collectively result in reading difficulties or other problems in school.

CREDIT: *Stanley D. Klein, Ph.D., Clinical Psychologist; Editor,* The Exceptional Parent *magazine, Boston, Massachusetts.*

Entertaining

Drunk Guests and What to Do with Them

Did it ever occur to you that perhaps people get drunk at your parties because there is nothing better to do? Good hosts or hostesses make sure their parties are sufficiently lively so that a person need not become anesthetized by alcohol in an effort to avoid the pain of boredom.

A good host does not push drinks on guests. Too often this is done in the spirit of generosity and graciousness. Remember—alcohol is a drug.

It is also a good idea to serve some food with the drinks if dinner is to be delayed by thirty or forty minutes. Food slows down the rate of alcohol absorption into the system. You need not serve caviar or lobster tails. Carrot sticks, celery, bits of cauliflower, any fresh vegetable with a low-cal dip will do.

Also make sure there are plenty of non-alcoholic beverages available. Fruit juices, vegetable juices, soda water, and carbonated drinks give the guests some options.

If you, the host, are fixing drinks, remember—alcohol never should be poured unmeasured from the bottle. Add plenty of ice, soda or water into the mixed drinks.

A meal will generally sober up a group unless there is wine served with the meal—in which case, a slightly tipsy person may get a good deal drunker.

When serious drinking occurs after dinner, real trouble is indicated. If you see a guest who is heading in that direction, offer him a substitute drink such as coffee.

What should be done about a guest who shows visible signs of intoxication —staggers, picks up the wrong coat, puts his hat on sideways—says goodnight and heads for his car to drive himself and perhaps his wife home? It is the responsibility of every host or hostess to offer to arrange with another guest to drive the inebriated guest in his own car, or call a taxi. This may result in some profanity or even some harsh language. But it is better to have a tiff than to allow a drunken guest to get in his automobile and kill himself and three or four innocent victims.

One often wonders why the wife of a drunk doesn't insist on taking the wheel. The answer is that she is afraid of causing a scene. Frequently I have received letters from women who say something like this: "I'll never forgive myself. I knew he was cockeyed drunk and I let him drive because I didn't want to look like a bossy wife when he left the party. That accident took his life and put me in the hospital for four months."

I always advise young girls whose escorts get drunk at parties to call a taxi or ask a sober friend for a lift. If the fellow becomes angry and upset, so what?

Over 50 percent of all fatal automobile accidents in this country are alcohol-related. Don't let your party be "the scene of the crime." A host or hostess who values his friends should be willing to risk the wrath of a drunken guest by refusing to allow him to drive himself home. The drunk may be very annoyed by such action, but the next morning, he'll view the situation differently.

CREDIT: *Ann Landers.*

How to Entertain with Ease

THEY LIKE TO DROP IN

DEAR ANN LANDERS: Last week you printed (for the third time since I've been reading your column) advice to the effect that it is rude to drop in on friends (or even family) uninvited.

My sister and I are maiden ladies. We never call anyone in advance. We just drop by when we feel like being friendly. No one has ever said they weren't glad to see us. You must be very lonely, Ann. I'll bet if you printed your address you'd have lots of company. How about it? WANT TO BE NEIGHBORLY

DEAR NEIGHBOR: I'm sure I would. Thanks for your concern. I've got all the friends I can handle and nobody drops in on me. EVER.

We all know people who have a special gift for entertaining. They know how to make people feel at home. They seem to produce spectacular meals or refreshments effortlessly and still manage to enjoy themselves and their guests. Others go rigid with tenseness at the very prospect of having people into their homes. This may be understandable in the classic case of the new bride entertaining her husband's boss for the first time, but it is sad, unnecessary and counterproductive.

Sad, because entertaining can be as much fun for the host or hostess as for guests; unnecessary, because anyone can learn to entertain well; and coun-terproductive, because entertaining is a way to make new friends and deepen and enrich existing relationships. Entertaining is a personal gift which amounts to more than food and drink. It is the care expressed in preparation, in opening one's home, in serving others, which makes people value an eve-ning or afternoon with you. By giving them a good time—not necessarily a lavish or expensive meal—you are giving of yourself and showing regard for others in a special way that they value. A tense, nervous hostess or host wastes all that potential. It becomes so obvious that they want the occasion to be over and done with that the guests feel the same way—and may go away wishing they hadn't come.

Countless books have been written on the "art" of entertaining but there are only three basic rules anyone needs to follow—*think, prepare, relax.*

Thinking begins with people and then goes on to food and drink. Spend a little time pondering your guest list. (Often this is not a factor, since you have a particular person, couple, or group in mind.) People with wildly different lifestyles and religious, political, or socal convictions will not always mix well. It may be better to entertain thcm at different times. Pick a time that is convenient for both you and your guests. Make your invitation clear as to whether a meal (or substantial food) will be served. (Woe unto the hostess who asks people for cocktails at 5:30 P.M. and doesn't indicate that it's *only* cocktails and no food.) Don't plan exotic dishes unless you are sure all your guests are experienced gastronomical swingers (six plates of un-touched snails can be depressing as well as wasteful). Great parties and good dinners are not made by simply spending lots of money, but whatever you plan, serve the best food you can afford. Special little flourishes and condi-ments add a lot. Make your main course something you are sure you can prepare well. If you've never made a cheese soufflé or pressed a duck, it's not a good idea to experiment when you have guests. If you have a few time-tested specialties, plan your meal around them. Think about your time schedule—make it generous—allowing for the late arrivals and animated pre-dinner conversation that can cause your roast to burn and your peas to turn to mush. Plan as many dishes as possible that can be prepared ahead of time and will go that extra hour with you. Avoid menus that require three si-multaneous photo finishes in order to serve them well. Get any advice you need on special cuts of meats, what wines to serve, etc. Ask someone whose dinners seem to go well.

Prepare. Everyone cleans and dusts, but take a few minutes and pretend you're a stranger coming into your place for the first time. Are there stains and frays that suddenly appear obvious? Better see these now than with sud-den clarity through the eyes of guests. Rearrange seating if necessary. Can-dles and a few flowers do wonders for any room. Think of any and every thing you can do ahead of time. Everyone remembers to set the table, but glasses can be set out and inspected; butter dishes, cream and sugar containers filled; condiments and even salads arranged and covered and put into the refrigerator; dessert, with thought, can be rendered fairly painless to serve. Get plates, silverware, cups and saucers counted and ready. If you're still not sure of yourself, make a checklist for step-by-step progress and post it someplace (inside a cookbook, where you can consult it but wandering guests can't); check the bathroom. Open the wine. Have enough coat hangers. Make it a contest with yourself to see how many steps and seconds you can save in advance.

Relax. Having done all you can, devote the rest of your energy to enjoying yourself and keeping calm. If something goes wrong, you're now in a position where so much has to go right that it won't matter. Don't be a fusser. Don't search guests' faces for reactions to each sip and bite they take. Don't make apologies for the appearance, quality or condition of anything. Don't take the apparent casualness with which some people will consume your prize recipes as indifference or criticism. Some people enjoy everything without making a single comment. Serve as casually as you can and keep that smile on your face. And, after everything has been served, sit down and join your guests. The dirty dishes will be staying, the guests won't. Finally, accept departing compliments gracefully—and give yourself a big one as well.

CREDIT: *Helen Robison, White Plains, New York.*

PARTIES—NO SHOWS

DEAR ANN LANDERS: Last night my husband and I gave a party—no special occasion—just a get-together for friends. Twenty-five couples were invited. Six couples showed up.

We sent the invitations in the mail two weeks ago with "Regrets Only" printed at the bottom. Two couples called to say they couldn't come. The morning of the party, my husband ran into one of the couples we expected and said, "We look forward to seeing you at our place tonight." The wife replied, "Sorry, we're having a party of our own."

We spent a lot of money and time getting the house ready. Now we feel insulted and worn out. The 12 people who came had a wonderful time, but they hardly put a dent in the food we prepared for 50.

I wanted to call the rude ones at 8 this morning and ask why they didn't show up. My husband said I'd better not. How can a hostess protect herself against such a catastrophe? HURT IN HATTIESBURG

DEAR HURT: Too bad there are so many inconsiderate slobs in the world but I get this question at least a dozen times a week. The solution is simple: three days before the party telephone those who haven't responded and ask if they plan to come.

You will then have some idea as to how much food to have on hand and spare yourself a big let-down.

Epilepsy

PARENTS FINALLY DISCOVER HARD-LUCK SON'S AILMENT

DEAR ANN LANDERS: I read the letter from "Hard Luck Harry" and had to write. I hope his parents read this.

We, too, have a son 19 years of age. We also thought he was accident prone. Like the other lad, our boy totaled a car and was a "regular" in the emergency room of the hospital. A collar bone or an arm had to be set, a head needed to be stitched up—I can't count the number of injuries. Our doctor would just say, "Oh, no, not again."

Then a serious illness turned into a blessing. An abnormal EEG showed up. We tried for months to find out what was wrong. Then a wonderful team of doctors at a children's hospital in Memphis, Tenn., made an exception —they took in our 18-year-old college freshman. The diagnosis was epilepsy.

It was a shock, but we calmed down when the doctors assured us his illness could be controlled by drugs. They were right. He hasn't had an accident since. It breaks my heart when I recall the physical and mental anguish our boy went through before we got to the real problem.

Please urge all parents who have "accident prone" children to seek good medical help immediately. It might be something else besides bad luck.

ARKANSAS MOTHER

DEAR MOTHER: Thank you for an enlightening letter. Problem: Most people think they HAVE good medical help until it turns out to be bad. My advice is get ANOTHER opinion.

The true tragedy of epilepsy lies not in the physical impairment of the disease, but in the stigma—the misunderstanding—attached to it.

It is especially sad when children are the victims. Throughout this nation there are children who have normal or above normal intelligence who are being raised as "retarded" or mentally deficient because they are epileptics.

Since biblical times, epilepsy has been surrounded with a stigma which grew out of the superstition that people who had seizures were possessed by devils. Even today the public continues to regard epilepsy as a curse rather than an illness.

This misunderstanding has extended to obvious prejudice against epileptics in obtaining jobs, insurance or advancement.

What are the facts?

First: Epilepsy is not rare. Over four million people in the United States have epilepsy.

Second: Epilepsy is not caused by insanity or mental illness. Epilepsy is only a symptom—like a headache—rather than a disease. Usually it is not related to brain damage.

Third: Persons with epilepsy are not retarded or intellectually inferior. Many prominent people have had epilepsy, including Julius Caesar and Alexander the Great. The vast majority of those who have it do not suffer any intellectual impairment.

What is epilepsy?

Epilepsy is a term used to describe the sudden, explosive electrical discharge from the brain which produces recurrent changes in consciousness, behavior, sensation or muscular activity. It is a symptom rather than a single disease and represents an abnormal electrical discharge only. There are many types of epilepsies, from grand mal where loss of consciousness, jerking movements or frothing at the mouth may occur to petit mal where a brief loss of consciousness occurs, unassociated with other symptoms.

The most common form of epilepsy seen in adults is the psychomotor attack in which there is a characteristic "aura" or warning—usually a sinking abdominal sensation accompanied by fear, followed by repetitive, automatic movements, such as lip smacking, swallowing, hand movements, or other more organized behavior which may appear purposeful, but isn't. A simple jerking of one hand or arm may be a seizure of the focal type with the discharging area being located in the appropriate portion of the brain.

What is the cause of epilepsy?

Since the term epilepsy is actually a description of a symptom rather than a disease, there are many possible causes. Anyone is capable of having a seizure if sufficient stimulus exists to excite the brain cells and produce this electrical discharge. However, most of us have a built-in resistance to such overexcitability. Where this resistance is lowered by direct damage to the brain because of head injuries, birth defects, brain tumors, infection (encephalitis and meningitis); or when this resistance is lowered by the genetic makeup of the individual, the susceptibility to this abnormal brain cell excitation is present.

This will show up on the electroencephalogram (equipment which measures the activity of the brain waves) as an abnormal discharge which may well trigger a seizure as the discharge spreads. The result is what we call epilepsy.

Can epilepsy be cured?

When the seizure is the result of a known cause, such as a focal lesion of the brain, like a tumor, or a generalized illness like encephalitis, surgery or treatment of the illness may remove the cause of the epilepsy. However, for the bulk of patients, the cause is usually not surgically accessible and may represent a scarred area of the brain or simply a genetic tendency. The object of medical treatment then will be to prevent and control further seizures through the use of medication. With the use of anticonvulsant medication, seizures can be completely controlled in 60 to 70 percent of persons with epilepsy. Another 20 percent will experience at least partial control.

Initiation of the drug program should be done under the close supervision of the physician. The physician will usually proceed by obtaining a series of tests to rule out the possibility of any underlying focal lesion of the brain which may require surgical removal.

Following this, an electroencephalogram is obtained to help decide which medication will be most effective since this will aid greatly, along with the patient's description of the attack, in establishing the type of seizure disorder. Medication is then selected along with careful follow-up, which now includes the obtaining of serum anticonvulsant levels. The patient is instructed to avoid alcohol, get adequate sleep, avoid excessive stimulants, such as coffee and cola drinks, and report all attacks, even the most minor, to the physician. Serious consequences can result if medication is decreased or stopped without the knowledge or advice of the physician.

What should you do for a person experiencing grand mal seizures?

Witnessing a grand mal seizure for the first time can be frightening. Such seizures involve unconsciousness, falling to the ground, deep and slow breathing, breath holding, frothing at the mouth, rapid jerking of the limbs, rigidity, and eyes rolling upward. The seizure is usually self-limited and in no way will the victim hurt an onlooker. During the seizure the unconscious person is not in danger of dying. It is also unusual for him or her to suffer serious injury as a consequence of a seizure.

However, laceration of the tongue or cheek, caused by jaw clenching, often occurs. In falling the person may strike a sharp or hard object. Therefore, the onlooker should assist by keeping the person away from sharp objects that might cause injury during the seizure. Tight clothing, especially around the neck, should be loosened. A person who has not had special training should not attempt to place objects in the victim's mouth to prevent tongue biting. Such attempts have resulted in injury to both the patient and the onlooker.

Most importantly, the observer should remain calm and reassuring once the patient has regained consciousness. Dealing with the anxieties of both the patient and the witnesses is aided greatly by a calm and reassuring manner, with the realization that the event observed is not life-threatening unless a series of such attacks goes unattended. Should the patient have more than one seizure he should see a physician or be taken to the nearest hospital for evaluation.

For further information write to:
  The Epilepsy Association of America
  111 West 57th Street
  New York, New York 10010

CREDIT: *Richard N. Rovner, M.D., Associate Professor Clinical Neurology, Director, Epilepsy Clinic, Northwestern University Medical School, Chicago.*

The Importance of Exercise

There is a rhythm to human life, just as there is in the movement of the earth and the sea. The need to move is as basic as breathing or hunger, thirst, sleep and even growth.

Nature created man as a seed-gatherer, a nomad who spent the day seeking food. In no way could it be foreseen that our brains would develop until they would make a world where movement became a luxury.

In Nature's original plan, man's mental and physical functions complemented each other. There was an inherent balance; to the degree that the mind was used, so was the body. Today, the mind often spins like a wheel without brakes. At the same time the body is continually slowing down. The distance between mind and body has become a chasm.

When confronted with the need for action, your body automatically releases adrenaline, which in more primitive times was a signal for flight or fight. In today's world, you do neither. Your muscle tension may produce anxiety, headache, upset stomach, ulcers or high blood pressure. Buildup of tension can best be relieved with exercise, so that adrenaline-induced fatty acids are put to good use and not stored to become future health hazards.

Consider one widespread ailment. Statistics show that 80 percent of lower-back pain has no organic cause. Most backaches result from disuse, nervous tension and anxiety.

In so many diseases the underlying culprit is lack of exercise. When the balance of mind and body is restored and nourished with the proper fuel, we may achieve physiologic and psychologic health. The ancient Romans said it in one phrase which is as valid today as when it was coined by Decimus Junius Juvenal (A.D. 50–130): *"Mens sana in corpore sano"*—a sound mind in a sound body.

Just as Nature programmed you to move, you must program your days with heart-and-lung-strengthening movement. You can live with nary a tooth but as the cardiovascular/pulmonary system deteriorates, so will every aspect of your existence. So brush your heart twice a day with great gobs of life-giving oxygen.

If you have doubts about your physical condition, if you are obese, a heavy smoker, or in any other respect belong to the coronary-risk group, begin your program under the supervision of your physician, exercise physiologist, YMCA or YWCA, university extension service, or similar experts. Once you begin, you will commence a new love affair with life.

At the start of each day, awaken every part of your body. While still in bed, stretch. Wriggle. Now, deliberately take your body out of bed and into the day. First, to your full-length mirror for two minutes of eyes-wide-open nude stretching, alternately flexing and relaxing the muscles from your scalp to your toes. No matter what you see in your glass today, you will like the reflection better tomorrow, and the day after. Next, into your warm-up suit for thirty minutes of wake-up-the-body routine.

Certainly, if often will be a bore and a nuisance. Of course you are tired— your body has been comparatively still for six or seven hours. That's why, when you set your alarm clock to go off a half hour earlier, you must remind yourself that thirty minutes of exercise are more energy-boosting and vital to your life than thirty extra minutes of sleep.

Fringe benefits from an early morning exercise routine are limitless. Paramount will be your awareness of your body. Learn to listen to it. Practice your exercise scales faithfully and your body will literally sing as you release locked-up tensions. All experts agree that exercise gives a definite high. It provides that step upward so that you can enjoy the self-fulfilling prophecy of successful goal setting.

Now you have wound up for the day. After high-tension mornings, work out those tensions at midday. (A workout also is a great substitute when you crave a snack or cigarette—often simply a desire for a change of pace, since our bodies weren't constructed to sit hour after hour.) Business deals of the future may be conducted along jogging paths, a life-giving alternative to the two-martini luncheon. Good decisions are made more quickly when the whole body is alert and functioning.

In the evening you tell yourself you are exhausted, and this is partly true. Your mind is tired after working all day. Your body too is tired but not from use. It is tired from at least eight hours of sitting. This is the time to unwind with twilight exercises. Twenty minutes of a walk-jog-run continuum is usually the easiest answer. Comfortable shoes and your neighborhood streets are the only equipment you'll need. Blustery weather? A happy habit is a jump rope, or a stationary bike in front of the TV or with a radio handy.

Consult the dozens of superbly written, easy-to-follow books by experts. Particularly note the ones that include excellent pre-exercise warm-ups. You must always stretch and warm the muscles before putting any stress on them. Learn to do this properly. Just as important are the simple cool-downs which are a must after vigorous movement. Experiment until you find the exercise routine you feel happiest with.

The best exercises are both *isotonic* and aerobic combined. An *isotonic* exercise is one that involves rhythmic, repetitive tensing and relaxing of muscles. The repeated squeezing of the muscles helps your blood flow and promotes cardiovascular/pulmonary fitness. An aerobic exercise is one in which you sustain exertion for more than a few minutes; during that time, oxygen is being supplied to the exercising muscles and the heart. Walking, running, jogging, swimming, bicycling, dancing, rowing, skipping rope, and working out on a mat are aerobic. Sprinting, for example, is not aerobic because the average person cannot run full blast for more than a few seconds.

Health clubs with machines are fine if *you* act as the motor, for the value of exercise can be measured only by the amount of work your own body performs.

Surveys show that more and more people are exercising, and this is encouraging. However, upon study it is found that not enough people are exercising long enough to give the heart real benefits. Any exercise must be carried on daily, preferably twice a day, no less than twenty minutes, in a prolonged huffy-puffy state in order for cardiovascular-pulmonary improvement to be obtained.

Increasing energy expenditure is the healthiest and the only permanent way to normalize weight. A daily exercise routine will gradually recontour the body as it recontours your life.

Join the fit people who as a statistical group tend to live longer, to enjoy their lives more, to have greater job satisfaction and less illness. There's overwhelming proof correlating your body's fitness to your ingathering of the good things of life. We must accept that fitness is a vital biological need. Its neglect handicaps the total effectiveness of the individual and thus our society, which is comprised of such individuals.

Inactivity must cease. Or we will.

CREDIT: *Deborah Szekely Mazzanti, Escondido, California, founder, The Golden Door, author of* Secrets of the Golden Door.

Exhibitionism

DEFINITION: Exhibitionism is a sexual deviation or sexual perversion in which the primary satisfaction is derived from exposure of the genitals (usually male) to a member of the opposite sex.

Synonyms: (1) Indecent exposure.
                (2) "Flashing" (slang).

PSYCHOLOGICAL CONSIDERATIONS: All so-called "normal" people (both male and female) have a certain amount of the show-off or the exhibitionist in them. The exhibitionism of the normal infant who has no awareness of the social significance of nudity and exposes himself with reckless abandon in such an innocent way is considered charming. However, what is appropriate and charming behavior for a ten-month infant is highly inappropriate and sick for a grown man.

Many exhibitionistic tendencies found in the normal individual become sublimated or refined as we grow up. For example, the urge to show off may manifest itself in a socially acceptable form by going on the stage, lecturing, or dressing in a flamboyant manner to attract attention.

A few years ago "streaking" (running naked in public) was a popular fad. Since it was considered a "fun thing" and streakers could run faster than fat police officers, very few were arrested.

Most exhibitionists are male. Authorities in the field of human behavior have various theories as to why this is so. The most obvious reason is that the male has an organ which is easily visible. The female, on the other hand, like Hamlet, has ". . . that within which passeth show." Theoretically, the blurring of sex differences which has been taking place in recent years should have produced a greater frequency of female exhibitionism. However, there is no solid data to support this. The increased number of go-go girls, strippers and topless waitresses are excluded from the ranks of true exhibitionists because their primary reason for engaging in these activities is to make a living.

Another reason for the preponderance of males and the low incidence of females is that a certain amount of sexual exhibitionism in the female (plunging necklines, see-through blouses, slit skirts, and mini-miniskirts, etc.) has been accepted and even encouraged by society and by the setters of women's fashion. Hence, a certain amount of built-in, socially acceptable exhibitionism is considered "normal" for the female.

TYPICAL CLINICAL HISTORIES: Exhibitionism occurs at almost any age. The typical exhibitionist, however, is a male who has been unable to establish a satisfying sexual relationship with a woman and feels so insecure in his sexual role that he is compelled to show off his genitals to prove he is a man.

Many exhibitionists are married and resort to episodes of exhibitionism after being rejected by their wives. They feel a compulsion to exhibit themselves in order to reassert their so-called masculinity. To the exhibitionist, asserting his masculinity by exposing his genitals may be a perverse symbol of power and control, reminiscent of the behavior of animals who use sexual display to establish their dominance.

A common practice for exhibitionists is to drive to a park or near an apartment building and wait for a woman to appear. At that moment the exhibitionist opens the car door, revealing that he has dropped his trousers and underwear to the floor, exposing himself. Many exhibitionists labor under the mistaken belief that such a sight is sexually stimulating to the woman and that she enjoys it. Instead, what usually occurs is that the woman finds such behavior repulsive and frightening and calls the police, who if they arrive in time, take the man into custody.

Even though many exhibitionists may abstain from their practices for months or years, there is a definite tendency for recurrence. In addition, many exhibitionists have a compulsion to return to the scene of the crime, where the chances of being caught are great. It is almost as if, on an unconscious level, they *want* to be punished.

EXHIBITIONISM: DANGEROUS OR HARMLESS?: Exhibitionism is one of the least dangerous of the sexual perversions, especially if it is confined to adults. When children are involved, trauma may result and the situation is more serious. In such cases, legal action and treatment are called for. Most exhibitionists are harmless. There is no body contact, only visual contact. They do not rape or molest and they have no explanation for their aberrant behavior. In fact, most of them will attempt to deny the extent of their exposure or minimize it by saying, "I forgot to zip up my fly. Good God, that's no crime!"

EXHIBITIONISM IN THE ELDERLY: Although exhibitionism occurs in the elderly, many such cases often result from complete misinterpretation. Dr. Robert Butler, an expert in mental illness of the older age group, reports instances in which old people were picked up for molesting young children and booked for "indecent exposure" when in fact they were merely confused, needed to urinate, and picked the most convenient spot.

TREATMENT: I have never known an exhibitionist who volunteered for psychiatric treatment *prior* to being picked up by the police. Thus, the only rational treatment for exhibitionism, even though it is not entirely satisfactory, is psychotherapy during a period of probation. Much can be accomplished in psychotherapy, especially if the man is married and the wife can be brought in for joint therapy. Placing exhibitionists in jail with hardened criminals should be considered "cruel and unusual punishment." It is totally counterproductive as far as the exhibitionist is concerned. Many exhibitionists lead otherwise respectable lives, are active church members, and hold down responsible positions.

CREDIT: *Zigmond M. Lebensohn, M.D., Chief Emeritus, Department of Psychiatry, Sibley Memorial Hospital, Clinical Professor of Psychiatry, Georgetown University School of Medicine, Washington, D.C.*

Eye Banks

An eye bank is a local organization created to obtain human eye tissues to be used for cornea transplantation and other surgical grafting procedures for research.

The cornea is a clear tissue covering the front of the eye like a watch crystal. It can become clouded as a result of disease, degeneration, or injury from an accident. Modern surgical techniques make it possible to replace the damaged cornea with tissue obtained from another healthy human eye.

Human eyes used for this purpose are normally obtained from deceased persons who have generously arranged during their lifetimes to donate their eyes after death for this purpose. Nearly every ophthalmologist or eye surgeon has a list of patients who are in need of corneal transplants to restore the sight of one or both eyes or to prevent blindness. The need for eye tissue is always greater than the supply or availability.

Local eye banks distribute information and pledge cards, urging donors to pledge their eyes to the bank upon death. When eyes become available to the bank through this means, a local surgeon is immediately notified. He alerts his patient for the impending transplant operation. There is normally a sense of urgency since the eye tissues should be used as soon as possible, usually within forty-eight hours of the removal from the donor. The eyes should be removed within six to eight hours after death.

Local eye banks are normally voluntary efforts organized and run by volunteers on slim budgets. They maintain constant contact with hospitals and other institutions where human eyes pledged for another's use may become available. They also maintain contact with the eye surgeons.

The eyes are provided at no cost to the recipient and eye donors receive no financial compensation. The expense of running eye bank operations is financed by means of local fund-raising drives and through contributions of interested charitable groups and individuals.

Donating one's eyes is a simple procedure. Age is no barrier as the years have practically no effect on the quality of the cornea. Even persons who have had eye problems or worn eyeglasses can donate their corneas in most instances.

The eyes can be removed swiftly with no damage and no evidence that they have been removed if the body of the deceased is to be displayed after death. If the eyes for some reason are unsuitable for transplant, they can be used for valuable research.

One of the most important allies of the eye bank (and the recipient waiting for the tissue) is the relative who knows the deceased has pledged his eyes and informs the doctor or hospital or attendant, who in turn can alert the eye banks. A next of kin can arrange to donate the eyes of a deceased relative with no prior arrangements having been made.

In order to pledge one's eyes, a card should be obtained from a local eye bank (see telephone directory) which should be filled out and carried on one's person. In some states, provision is made on driver's licenses to indicate the holder has pledged his or her eyes. The Lions Club of America as well as Rotary organizations are active in eye bank support. The local club can usually provide information about banks in the area. Medical centers and hospitals are also knowledgeable about where eye banks are in operation.

There is an Eye Bank Association of America (3915 Maplewood Avenue, Winston-Salem, North Carolina 27103) comprising seventy member banks which work to promote eye bank activity and to establish high professional standards among its member banks. There is also an International Eye Foundation (7801 Norfolk Avenue, Bethesda, Maryland 20014), which has helped to establish over thirty eye banks in foreign countries. The Foundation works with U.S. eye banks in sending tissues abroad where needed and until the new banks overseas can arrange to obtain tissue among their own populations.

CREDIT: *Michael Codi, International Eye Foundation, Bethesda, Maryland.*

Eye Care

Your eyes may be your most priceless possession. They are irreplaceable—so take care of them. Here is some excellent advice from one of the nation's most distinguished ophthalmologists.

(1) If an irritant such as a household chemical solution gets splashed in your eyes, wash out with water immediately! The damage to your eyes may be greatly minimized or even avoided by the promptness with which you get to a water supply such as the kitchen sink, shower, garden hose, etc. Thousands of persons have unnecessarily become blinded because they did not know what to do in a simple emergency. By the time they got to a doctor, the damage was irreversible.

(2) Never use someone else's eye medicines.

(3) "Tired eyes" and dull headaches can be caused by prolonged reading and poor light, the wrong pair of glasses, or the lack of glasses when needed. Such use of the eyes may produce discomfort and a sense of "strain" but will not cause actual damage to the eyes. Looking at an extremely bright light, such as the sun or that involved in arc welding, can cause damage to the eyes. Be aware that not all dark glasses are effective in cutting down the damaging glare.

(4) Many elderly persons (particularly women) have a chronic irritated sensation in their eyes resulting from inadequacy of the tear fluid that normally bathes the surface. Such dry eyes usually can be made much more comfortable by the use of artificial tears, available without prescription at most drugstores. Rather than using these tear substitutes, however, it is better to have an ophthalmologist make the diagnosis to be certain that something else is not causing the discomfort.

(5) "Pink eye" (technically termed conjunctivitis) has many different causes ranging from highly contagious bacterial infection to the more benign but troublesome allergy to pollens, medications, etc. The more discharge and matting of the eyelashes, the greater the likelihood that the cause is an infectious disease that should be treated by an antibiotic. Chronic and/or recurrent redness of one or both eyes can be caused by virus infections. The leading responsible virus is herpes simplex, which is the same agent that causes cold sores near the mouth and nose. Because the herpes virus can cause severe eye damage, a mother with a cold sore near her mouth should be careful not to kiss her infant near his eyes. (Better not to kiss him at all until the cold sore is gone.)

(6) Protect your eyes with goggles when working near a grinding wheel, riding a motorcycle, or hammering with metal on metal. Blindness from accidents is woefully common and when this lesson is learned from experience it can be a costly one. Firecrackers and other explosives are particularly devastating causes of eye injury.

(7) Cataracts can occur at any age and have many causes. A cataract is a cloudiness of the lens located within the eye; the more cloudiness the worse the vision. Thus, cataracts do not "grow," they simply increase in cloudiness. It is just as easy (and as difficult) to perform cataract surgery on an early cataract as on a late cataract. Nowadays, there is no reason to wait until a cataract is "ripe," but as with all surgery, there are risks and potential complications. Thus, cataract surgery should not be performed until changes of glasses fail to provide adequate vision for his/her daily purposes. Some people need more vision than others. After cataract surgery, the eye no longer has a lens within it. This means the power of that lens must be duplicated by thick spectacle lenses or a contact lens, or a plastic lens placed within the eye to substitute for the lens that has been removed. Spectacle lenses are heavy and cause distortion of peripheral vision and false enlargement of objects.

Contact lenses (both hard and soft) avoid these difficulties but can be troublesome to put in and remove. It is safe to predict that before long, we will have contact lenses that can be worn twenty-four hours a day. At present, many ophthalmologists are offering their patients the option of having an intraocular lens placed within the eye at the time of cataract surgery. These can produce excellent vision (although ordinary distance and/or reading glasses are still required) but the presence of these plastic devices within the eye increases the chance of operative and postoperative complications. It remains to be seen if eyes will tolerate these implants over a period of many decades when used by young adults.

There are numerous techniques of cataract surgery. Each person should depend on the advice of the ophthalmologist as to which technique is best for him or her. Some cataracts are removed in their entirety through a moderately large incision. Other cataracts are removed by ultrasound-fortified needle systems that dissolve the cataract and remove its substance through the bore of the needle, thus accomplishing the surgery through a very small incision. There are advantages and risks to both techniques. It is most unwise for a person to insist on one or the other means of surgery based on information from newspapers and magazines. The best surgery is that which can be accomplished with the least risk of immediate and long-range complications.

(8) Glaucoma means increased pressure within the eye that leads to a progressive damage of the retina and optic nerve. There are many causes of glaucoma and it may occur at any age, but like cataracts it is more common in the older age groups. There is one basic principle in the management of eyes with glaucoma: reduce the pressure within the eye to a tolerable level. (Some eyes tolerate elevated pressure better than others.) In most cases, glaucoma is managed by eye drops and sometimes by the additional use of medication by mouth. Some types of glaucoma require eye surgery and others require surgery only if medication alone is inadequate. Every citizen over forty should have his/her eye pressure measured every few years because most forms of glaucoma are symptomless and cause a gradual irreversible loss of vision. This loss affects the peripheral vision and progresses to the point where only a small central field of vision remains. Glaucoma invariably can be controlled by medication or surgery if necessaary. Having glaucoma is often similar to having diabetes in that it requires constant medication to lower the ocular pressure. For a diabetic person it is a small price to pay to watch his/her diet and take prescribed medication. Life itself is dependent on such management. For the person with glaucoma, it is just as important to take medications as prescribed and to accept the recommendation of the ophthalmologist if surgery is advised. Following those instructions will preserve eyesight in almost every instance.

(9) There are numerous diseases of the body which are in some way related to the eyes. For example, diabetes is associated with a greater incidence of cataracts and glaucoma.

It is also associated with an acquired abnormality of the blood vessels of the retina after diabetes has existed for approximately fifteen years or more. In the majority of cases, when the so-called diabetic retinopathy is diagnosed promptly, it can be controlled or delayed in its progress by the use of the laser beam and other forms of medical management.

High blood pressure, too, will cause a higher incidence of blood vessel problems within the eye. This constitutes only one of numerous reasons why people with hypertension should be under constant observation of a physician. There is hardly a disease of other body organs that is not reflected in the condition of the eye. An ophthalmologist is a medical doctor and has the responsibility for detecting and diagnosing abnormalities and specific diseases of the eye. An optometrist does not have this responsibility—and rightly so, for his training has not been in medicine. Most ophthalmologists and optometrists are fine professional people and they will refer their patients to a specialist when necessary. However, there are some fundamental disagreements between the ophthalmologist and optometrist. The former believes that the latter (who is concerned largely with glasses and contact lenses) should refer to an ophthalmologist all patients whose vision does not correct to a normal level. Ophthalmologists believe that the responsibility for diagnosis and management of disordered eyes should lie with the medical profession. Unfortunately, the laws in many states do not support that position. Optometrists in such states are beginning to use and prescribe medication. It will be interesting to see if the public is best served by these new laws. What a shame that all eye care is not brought under the single umbrella of medical practice and that all practitioners at various levels of training are not equally responsible to the same system of regulation.

(10) The retina is the light-sensitive layer of tissue on the inside back surface of the eyeball. It "records" the visual message transmitted by light that is focused on the retina by the refractive power of the eye's surface (the cornea) and the lens of the eye itself. There are many forms of retinal disease. Extremely severe nearsightedness can eventually lead to degeneration of the retina and even to holes in the retina which in turn can produce separation of the retina from its proper position (retinal detachment). Another common "cause" of retinal detachment is a history of cataract surgery. Once the lens of the eye has been removed, there is a greater chance that in some future year, retinal holes will develop and a retinal detachment will follow. Fortunately, almost every retinal detachment can be cured by surgery. There is great importance in knowing the symptoms of a retinal detachment so that prompt eye examination and appropriate management can be carried out. Often, a person with a retinal detachment in one eye will notice a curtain-like defect obscuring a small or major portion of his/her visual field. Lying flat on one's back often diminishes this curtain-like field defect. Light flashes and floating spots may accompany or precede the field defect produced by a retinal detachment. Once the loss in visual field has extended to the center

(loss of central visual keenness), the chance of complete restoration of vision by successful surgery is reduced significantly. Thus, prompt examination by an ophthalmologist is imperative when such symptoms occur. Of course, most adults note "floaters" in their field of vision and some may experience the occasional lightning flash in the far periphery of the visual field. In many cases, these symptoms alone are not indicative of serious eye disease but they are sufficient reason for having a careful examination of the retina.

(11) Many forms of eye disease "run in the family." Cataracts, certain forms of retinal degeneration such as retinitis pigmentosa, types of glaucoma, and even "crossed eyes" are related to the person's genetic background. It is helpful for the ophthalmologist to know as much as possible about family history. At times such knowledge can even be lifesaving. For example, there is a form of tumor that occurs within the eye known as a retinoblastoma. Survivors of this malignant tumor have a much greater likelihood that their children will be similarly affected and those children, in turn, can usually have their lives saved by early recognition and treatment of the tumor.

(12) Strabismus refers to eyes that are not synchronized in their movements so that one eye turns in, out, up or down. Strabismus also is referred to as "squint." It can occur at birth or at any time in childhood. It may also occur as a result of the loss of vision in one eye throughout adult life. A child's eye that sees poorly usually turns in. An adult's eye with poor vision often turns out. The most common form of strabismus is crossed eyes in childhood. The most common remedy for this is the prescription of eyeglasses which in itself may be sufficient to provide the child with straight eyes. If there is a child in your family with strabismus, do not assume that the management of another ophthalmologist treating his patient by surgery necessarily implies that your child being treated with glasses and/or an eye patch is incorrect. Every case is different. This is the most important information for you to remember. Most pairs of eyes that do not work well together have one eye with vision that is less good than the other. This is referred to as amblyopia. In most cases amblyopia can be treated by the use of eyeglasses and putting a patch over the other eye to reverse the "laziness" of the amblyopic eye. After early childhood, amblyopia no longer responds to such patching and an eye may be irreversibly "blind" as a result of inadequate treatment in the crucial earlier years. Seldom do eye "exercises" help a person with strabismus. Not all forms of strabismus can be cured and not all amblyopic eyes can be given back normal vision—but almost all can be helped when recognized and treated promptly.

(13) Finally, a word about cosmetic surgery of the eyelids. By all means, have your eyelids tightened and the wrinkles reduced if you are self-conscious about the aging appearance of your lids. However, as with all surgery, be prepared for the possibility of complications. Cosmetic lid surgery is not a minor procedure. Slight asymmetry of the postoperative results, healing deficiencies and complications that affect the eye itself are highly unlikely but

are a part of the chance that you take even in the skilled hands of a surgeon. Generally speaking, cosmetic lid surgery can make a person feel rejuvenated. There are numerous varieties of lid surgery performed by either ophthalmologists or plastic surgeons. Discuss the pros and cons with your surgeon. Be aware of risks but also be aware that cosmetic surgery has no stigma, for if a good result makes you look and feel better, it can have a very good effect on your emotional life.

CREDIT: *David Paton, M.D., Professor and Chairman, Department of Ophthalmology, Baylor College of Medicine, Houston, Texas. Director of Cullen Eye Institute of Neurosensory Surgery of Houston.*

Face Lift

Aging suggested wisdom in days gone by. This attitude still exists in many non-industrialized countries today. In America, however, and in some countries in Europe, the development of modern society and the competition for employment as well as the contemporary emphasis on youth, beauty, and success have caused patients to seek means of removing or lessening the signs of growing older. In response, various types of cosmetic or aesthetic operations were devised.

Patients may be moved to seek corrective surgery for signs of aging by a desire for self-improvement or the wish to preserve a youthful appearance. These requests may also reflect a desire to be a useful member of society after the arbitrary age of retirement.

Various names have been used by the medical profession to define the face lift operation. Rhytidectomy, from its derivation, indicates the removal of wrinkles, and rhytidoplasty implies an operation to remove wrinkles. The term face lift has come into common usage.

The importance of aesthetic surgery of the face to psychological well-being and vocational success was slow to be recognized by the medical profession at large. Operations to correct nasal deformities were more quickly accepted because many of these deformities were related with functional problems, such as difficulty in breathing, that required correction in conjunction with the surgical correction of the nasal deformity. It is true that aesthetic surgery, in its early stages, was performed most often by unqualified and often unscrupulous surgeons who used unethical means such as newspaper advertisements to recruit patients. Even today it is not infrequent to receive patients in consultation with unsatisfactory or even disastrous results following operations by unqualified surgeons.

Patients often ask, "How do I find a good plastic surgeon?" The answer is to ask a family doctor, who usually knows of a qualified plastic surgeon. If he does not, one should look in the phone book and call the County Medical Society. They will offer guidance.

Aging of the face usually parallels aging of the body. The facial skin, however, being exposed to sunlight and other extraneous factors, is apt to show signs more rapidly than unexposed areas. Aging of the face varies from person to person because of lifestyle, illness, environmental influences including exposure to sunlight and many other factors, among which heredity plays an important role.

The patient consults the surgeon for a variety of motives; the motive may be a simple one, the desire to improve his appearance. The motivation may be quite different, however. It is important to make the patient understand that aesthetic surgery will not necessarily solve such problems as loneliness, inability to make friends, the threat of losing a job because of the signs of aging or recapturing the affections of an unfaithful spouse.

The result the patient can expect to obtain is related to many factors, but one of the most important is the quality of the patient's skin. Often the elasticity of the skin of the face is not directly related to the patient's age. A patient in his or her forties or fifties has a better and more durable result than a patient of advanced age with loose and some damaged skin.

Surgical improvement of the signs of aging include two areas of the face, the eyelids, upper and lower, and the face and neck. These two areas of the face may be operated on in a single operative session, thus saving the patient the time and expense of undergoing two separate operations and hospitalizations.

A corrective operation on the nose is usually not performed at the time of a face lift and eyelid operation. If there are some very minor defects of the nose, the two operative procedures might be done in the same stage. I have developed a new technique to modify the shape of the nose without the resulting bruising around the eyes that has been common in the past. The reason for not performing a corrective operation on the nose during the same stage as a face-lifting operation is that the diminution of the size of the nose results in a redistribution of the skin of the face. It is therefore best to perform the nasal operation in a first stage prior to a face lift operation. Corrective operations of the nose are usually done in young patients who do not require a face-lifting operation. Corrective operations of the nose in older individuals must be done with a certain amount of prudence and rather conservatively because the skin does not redistribute itself in the same way as it does in a young person.

The patient's attitude about his or her weight is important in assessing the anticipated degree of improvement and provides a clue to the patient's self-image. If the patient is overweight, the required weight loss is recommended before surgery. Considerable weight loss following surgery results in a disappointing sag of the face and neck.

Clinical observation has shown that the patients who undergo cosmetic surgery for the aging face at a relatively young age obtain a more satisfactory and durable result than patients in their late fifties or even older. The results obtained by operative procedures done by the plastic surgeon do not provide a permanent result because the aging process continues. After a number of years, a secondary operation will be required. Some of the most remarkable results have been obtained in patients who, for professional reasons, have undergone operations in the thirty-year age group in order to maintain a youthful appearance and in whom additional operations have been performed to maintain their appearance.

Bruising and swelling following a face lift operation have been largely eliminated by the use of very fine suction tubes that are left in place under the skin for forty-eight hours. Many of the patients have hardly any black and blue marks following the operation. The average hospitalization time is from twenty-four to forty-eight hours after the operation.

Patients usually ask, "Doctor, how long will the face lift last?" The answer to this question is a difficult one, as the duration of a satisfactory result depends on so many factors that a precise figure cannot be given. Five to six years is an average figure. At the end of this period the patient's face is still vastly improved in appearance in comparison to the original condition.

Aesthetic surgery of the eyelids is performed for two specific reasons: (1) excess skin of the eyelids may reach such proportions in older patients that it obstructs vision when the skin of the upper eyelids falls downward over the eyelashes; (2) protrusion of fat which surrounds the eyeballs and forms fat pouches or pads, particularly in the lower lids. Both of these deformities make the patient look older than his age as well as dissipated. The fatty pouches or "bags" under the eyes result in the patient being accused of "staying up all night."

The condition often referred to as "baggy eyelids" or fat pads under the eyes is caused by a weakness of a delicate membrane which normally maintains the fat around the eyeball. This membrane may be weak as the result of a hereditary condition and the fat which normally surrounds the eyeball protrudes beneath the membrane causing the deformity, which manifests itself as a bulge under the eyelid skin. It is often observed in young people when the condition is a hereditary one. In older individuals the gradual relaxation of the skin which is characteristic of aging is usually combined with the relaxation of the membrane which maintains the fat around the eyeball and a combination of excess skin and fat pads is present.

There are a number of other conditions which are responsible for the abnormal appearance of the eyelids. One of them is the increase of the size of the muscle which closes the eyelids. This condition is often seen in people who squint habitually in the sun, sometimes referred to as "tennis player's eyelids."

Aesthetic surgery of the eyelids is often referred to as blepharoplasty. The operation is done as a separate procedure or often in conjunction with an operation for face lifting.

Before the operation the excess skin is gently pinched with small forceps until the border of the upper lids begins to raise. This procedure indicates the amount of excess skin. Using some surgical ink, the outline of the excess skin is carefully traced. Thus the surgeon knows how much skin to remove. After the skin has been removed, protruding fat, which is usually located in the portion of the upper lid nearest the nose, is teased out by making a small opening through the membrane (the orbital septum) which retains the fat around the eyeball (the orbital fat). A similar procedure is then performed on the opposite upper eyelid.

The lower eyelids are then operated upon. An incision is made through the skin immediately below the eyelashes and is extended for a short distance into one of the crow's-feet. The skin is carefully raised from the muscle for a variable distance depending upon the extent of the deformity. By exerting slight pressure upon the upper lid the protruding fat of the lower lid becomes easy to locate. It is usually distributed in three pockets, one central, one near the nose, and the third in the outer portion of the lower lid. Small incisions are made through the muscle and the membrane retaining the fat and the excess fat is extracted in a manner similar to that described for the upper lid. The careful removal of the excess skin is the key to the success of the operation. When performed by an expert this portion of the operation offers no problem. Unfortunately inexperienced surgeons often remove too much skin. This results in a downward displacement or even eversion (turning inside out) of the lower lid. If this condition does not improve spontaneously after a period of time skin grafting may have to be resorted to to correct the deformity.

There are a number of variations of the operation to correct aging eyelids depending on the type of the deformity.

The incisions for the face lift operation are made in areas which are not visible after the operation, in the scalp above the ear, immediately in front of the cartilage of the ear down to the earlobe, within the fold behind the ear and back into the scalp. The skin of the face and neck are then raised from the underlying tissues and the skin is retracted upward and backward. The required amount of skin is removed and the mound is carefully sutured in order to avoid any visible scarring.

Patients with badly sun-damaged skin may require a later planing (chemical peel or dermabrasion). A chemical peel of the lips and the forehead is feasible in conjunction with a face lift operation; a full-face chemical peel, however, is contraindicated in conjunction with a face lift operation.

In a patient with a double chin it may be necessary to make a short incision along the lower border of the chin in order to expose the fat and remove it. In addition to removing fat, excess skin is also removed through this incision and the muscles are tightened by suturing them together.

In some patients the muscle of the neck (known as the platysma) must be tightened in addition to the resection of the excess skin. Depending on the type of deformity the platysma muscle is incised and it is displaced backward to a point situated behind the ear in order to tighten the muscle and improve the neck contour.

Another problem is present when the patient has a poorly developed chin. In these patients skin and fat accumulate below the small chin and the patient has no angle between the chin and the base of the neck. In such patients a silicone chin implant can be placed over the tip of the chin, thus increasing the forward position of the chin. In conjunction with the face lift operation this will result in the restoration of the angle and the jaw line.

CREDIT: *John Marquis Converse, M.D., Director, Institute of Reconstructive Plastic Surgery, New York University Medical Center.*

Fatherhood

On Being a Father to Boys

I am a psychiatrist and psychoanalyst in my early fifties, and my wife, of similar age, is a guidance counselor in a junior high school. We have four sons, ranging from twenty to twenty-four years. The editor of this book, Mrs. Eppie Lederer, our friend for fifteen years, is well acquainted with our sons. She asked me to contribute my thoughts about the role of a father in rearing sons, as she believes that these young men have turned out quite well.

Of greatest importance in being the father to sons is to pick the right wife to be their mother, and I have been very fortunate in this respect. Our sons have had the opportunity to observe the love and respect that exists between their parents.

As was the custom during the early to late 1950s (during which these children were born), my wife did not work outside the home, but completely devoted herself to being a housewife and mother. Like most fathers during this era, I took little part in the day-to-day raising of the children as infants. I cannot remember even learning how to change a diaper. I was busily occupied with my professional training and the advancement of my career, which at that time was considered to be the main business of a father. Though I was not uninterested in the children as infants and very young children, my interest in them was not thoroughly aroused until each of them began to reach the age of about two or three, when, in a sense, I began to feel that they really were "boys," and that I had a real part to play in helping raise them. Though the amount of time I had available to spend with them was limited due to the pressure of my work, I saw to it that the available time was of high quality, and thoroughly directed toward them. During other times when I was at home, reading or studying, I also made myself accessible. Much free time was spent with them particularly in physical activities involving running, swinging, teaching them to swim, taking them to parks, taking them on hikes and similar activities. I can seldom remember having to resort to physical punishment to maintain discipline. It is probably because of this that when I asked my sons what adjective they would choose to best describe me, they each replied that I was a "gentle" man.

The sons were exposed at an early age to a father whom they saw working not only in an intellectual way, but also in a physical way. They would see me mow the lawn, plant trees, shrubs, and flowers. One of them had a toy lawn mower, and when I would mow the lawn, he would follow behind me with his toy lawn mower, identifying himself with me.

The famous psychoanalyst Erik Erikson wrote that it is important for children to learn good work habits starting between the ages of about six and ten. While my sons were in this age group, I formed with them a small family business. I bought lawn mowers, one by one, until we had four. I actively participated with them as the administrator and co-worker in a neighborhood lawn-mowing business. We would all work together, with my carefully seeing to it that none of them got too tired. Whenever any one of them would show signs of fatigue I would take over his place so he could rest. A good deal of money was made from this business—money which was paid to me directly. I saw to it that the children received an appropriate reward, for example, a large ice cream cone, but the rest of the money I placed secretly in a bank account in the sons' names.

When Christmastime approached, I informed them of the amount of money that had accumulated in the account, and asked them what they wanted to spend it on. They elected to spend it on a color television set. In subsequent years, when enough money had accumulated again, another color television set was bought. Through this mutual activity among these sons and their father, they learned co-operation, collaboration, working toward a common goal, the establishment of regular and persistent work habits, and the necessity to work even when they didn't feel like it. I believe this early discipline has resulted in their subsequent persistence and stick-to-itiveness in their own personal work habits. As they grew older, they established their own individual lawn-mowing business to keep themselves in pocket money.

Another area of shared work was that of cutting firewood. We live in a large old house with a fireplace that requires a lot of wood. At first, while the children were quite young, I would have professional tree services leave trees at my home which had been cut down within the city and would ordinarily have gone to the city dump. The tree service men cut the trees into lengths appropriate to be split. I did the sledge and wedge work, and the young boys would haul away the cut wood in their play wagons and stack it in a woodshed.

As they grew older and stronger, they gradually took over some of the splitting themselves. As they grew into their teens, I bought a chain saw, and we would make forays into a wooded acreage owned by a friend of mine. We divided the tasks of using the chain saw, splitting the wood, piling it, cutting down trees, and building fires in which we would burn the unusable branches of the felled trees. This work was uniquely satisfying to the boys, working in a co-operative way toward a common goal. It had an additional value in having them come to appreciate the fireplace and all that it came to stand for as symbolic of their home and the part they had played in making it a warm, comfortable, and attractive place through their own physical efforts. It was interesting to me years later, when one son performed some scientific research on himself on brain theta wave and dream imagery training, to find in his images such very strong and close associations between the experiences that he had in cutting wood, the love he had for his home, and the identification that he had with me.

As the children passed into junior high school, it of course became necessary for them, for the first time, to do school homework. This immediately set up a conflict within the household, as the children prior to then had been accustomed to watching television after dinner. When homework became a necessity, an iron-clad rule was laid down: no television watching after dinner from Sunday evening through Thursday evening. This was met with outraged howls at the onset, but since my wife and I held absolutely firm, the howls died down in two to three weeks. Once they had finished their homework, they were still not allowed to watch television, but had to spend their time reading.

As teenagers and pre-teenagers, family vacations were spent on camping trips in the United States and Canada visiting national parks. This activity contributed to their love of nature and the outdoors and their increasing senses of self-reliance.

As the boys grew up, three of them showed great interest in athletics. I encouraged their participation in sports, and whenever it was appropriate, I engaged in the same sport with them. Every conceivable kind of support was given to them in the form of transportation to swimming meets and turning out as a spectator in sports in which they participated. I particularly encouraged two of the boys who showed talent in swimming, even though I had given it up myself when I was fourteen years old. As they became more outstanding, I began to take a personal interest again in swimming, becoming a Master's Swimming Association member at the age of forty-seven. By age fifty-one, I was an All-American Master's swimmer myself. One of my sons had already become an All-American swimmer and later on set a swimming record when he was a student at Yale.

You win some and lose some. As a youngster, I had had a great interest in band music, and saw to it that each of the boys took up an instrument. In order to encourage them all the more, I bought a trumpet myself and began to relearn this instrument, in order to be able to play with them and to help them play better. I spent countless hours with them in this activity. By the time they had reached high school, however, all but one lost interest in this activity. The remaining one, and I, joined a fifteen-piece stage band, playing trumpets in adjacent chairs for several years.

As youngsters, the four boys were enrolled in Sunday school in our church. Although they are not now regular churchgoers, they show evidence of practicing the values taught in the church and their home, and probably later on in their lives they will become more active in this area when they have children of their own.

As the boys developed, I did my best to find out what their individual talents and interests were. Each child comes into the world with a certain set of potential talents and proclivities. I felt it my task to try to find out what special talents my sons might have. As these interests were identified, I did everything within reason to support them in developing these talents.

As they entered and finished college or went on to other careers, my wife and I sacrificed so that each son received the very best education we could afford.

As our sons grew up, they were taught the values which had been taught to my wife and me by our own parents and they now espouse these values as their own. They are devoted to each other, and as time goes on, are more and more openly expressive of their affection and appreciation for each other and their parents and of the home in which they were brought up.

There comes a time when every child must leave home and go out on his own. Our sons seem to have been able to make this transition with very little discernible difficulty—doing so gradually. At the same time, they know they are always welcome whenever they wish to return.

In every home, decisions must be made, some of which have to be made by the parents, but some of which ideally should be made with the full participation of the children. In our home, whenever anything of major consequence was to be undertaken, a "family conference" would be held at which time each individual had his say regarding the matter, although the ultimate decision was left to the parents.

Every effort has been made, in spite of the fact that great distances separate us from the other members of our extended family, for the sons to become better acquainted with their cousins, aunts, uncles and grandparents. A number of them have taken trips to visit their relatives, and have invariably returned to us to tell us of the fine people they have found their relatives to be, and the great hospitality with which they were welcomed.

In the process of writing this article, I asked the children what they believed to be the greatest influence they felt I had had on them. They all said that I had served as an example. They had been able to establish identities of their own, had excellent work habits, were engaged in personal physical fitness programs in lifetime sports which would keep them fit as long as they live. They have become self-sufficient, autonomous, goal-seeking, down-to-earth young men and have many friends with whom they share similar characteristics.

As my wife and I grow older, we look forward to the boys' having their own homes and children, visiting them frequently, and taking a grandparently interest in our grandchildren and a continued interest in our children. We believe that they in their turn will always look forward to coming home to visit us.

CREDIT: *William S. Simpson, M.D., Psychiatrist, Menninger Foundation, Topeka, Kansas.*

DEAR ANN LANDERS: The piece I send was printed in *Newsday* a few years ago. I came across it again and send it to you to share with your readers—with the author's permission. His name is Martin Weinstein.

ON BEING A FATHER

I was the product of a broken home. I grew up without the physical or spiritual presence of a father, without the comforting knowledge that, at home, there was a strong figure I could turn to for solace, warmth, and discipline—someone who would be glad to share the joys of childhood and shield me from the minor hurts.

I am now a middle-aged man, the father of three, but I can still feel the pain of being fatherless—as if I just had a tooth extracted. That void in my life has never been filled.

Growing up alone forged my character and my personality.

It taught me to look only to myself for aid and comfort.

But it denied me an emotional haven, the one thing a young person needs if he is to grow up whole.

How vital it is for a child to have a shoulder to cry on in crisis. He needs a place to go—so he can close his eyes and shift the burden of woe or responsibility, even for a moment, to someone who really cares. Only a father can fill this role. Only a father can create the ambience that grounds the emotional security that young people require if they are to become mature adults and, in turn, pass on to their children the warmth and love that make for stability.

I love my children and I care about them. This means, in addition to attending PTA meetings and open school nights, I give of myself. I do not try to enter their world as a peer. I want to be a father, not a friend.

I establish order in my home. This means discipline—swift, certain, consistent and, above all else, loving.

I strive to transmit waves of concern without creating neurotics. This means setting standards and insisting on achievement within the framework of my child's capacity to perform. It means sharing the victories and helping to pick up the pieces after a failure.

Being a father also means nights under a sheet with billowing steam to cure the croup and more nights trying to decipher the new math. It means museum time and romp time, family singing, dinner table discussions, reading Edgar Allan Poe by candlelight in the den, sacrifice without histrionics, conveying the fact that parents are human and, therefore, fallible. It means saying "I'm sorry" when you're wrong, even from your exalted position as head of the house.

The job is full-time, Saturdays and Sundays included.

It can be open to anyone who cares to apply and is willing to work to qualify, and it is not necessarily limited to natural parents. Stepfathers, adoptive fathers, even strangers who care, can enter the arena and carve out a relationship with a child that will be filled with rewards and, yes, sorrows and disappointments. For the sum total of all these things is a father.

Fire Safety

Unlike death and taxes, fire doesn't necessarily have to strike us all, but there is dangerous human tendency to think that fires are disasters that happen to *other* people. That is probably what the approximately 6,500 children, men, and women who were killed by home and apartment fires last year thought, too. Fires rank third to auto accidents and falls as the major causes of accidental death. The annual tragedy is compounded by the fact that most of these deaths could have been prevented.

Here is a checklist for minimizing the risk of fire and its deadly consequences, drawn up with the help of publications issued by the National Safety Council, Chicago, Illinois:

(1) *Have a workable escape plan.*

The best approach is to sit down and draw a plan of your home (don't forget to show porch roofs, etc.). Try to discover two exit routes from each room and mark them. Then walk through them all seeing that exits are clear and that windows work freely. If you discover places that offer only one exit, such as a second- or third-story room with no porch roof beneath it, consider purchasing an emergency rope or chain ladder. Post fire/emergency numbers at or on each telephone.

(2) Hold a fire drill.

Yes, an actual, serious fire drill. Test your escape plan in action. Work the windows, walk the routes, explain how to break out glass using an object other than your hand. Emphasize the importance of clearing all jagged edges from the opening. Urge everyone to keep doors closed at night to prevent the spread of smoke and gases. (Show how to test a closed door with the palm of the hand laid near the top of the door to feel for external heat. Explain that a door should never be thrown open wide but braced against blowing in with a foot so that you can open it just a crack for observation.) Tell children never to hide in a closet or under a bed in the event of fire. (In a quick check of rooms, firemen have failed to find potential victims because they were hiding.) Demonstrate how to crawl down a smoke-filled hall or stairway while keeping nose and mouth covered with a cloth or piece of clothing soaked in water if possible. Set up a definite place (a neighbor's porch, perhaps) where everyone should meet immediately after escaping from the home so a headcount can be made quickly. Forget about your prize possessions and once out of the home, *never go back in.*

(3) Install smoke/heat detectors and fire extinguishers.

Experts say that half of all home fire deaths could be prevented by properly installed electronic smoke/heat detectors. Those cost from $25 to $50, and are easily installed, offering the greatest protection during those deadly hours from 10 P.M. to 6 A.M. when everyone is asleep and when most fire fatalities occur. Gases and smoke from fires actually kill 80 percent of victims and the detector signals their presence long before most sleeping people could become aware of their presence.

Small fires that have just started can often be dealt with by a good UL (Underwriters' Laboratory)-approved fire extinguisher. Dry chemical or CO_2 types are best for the home. Ideally there should be an extinguisher in the basement, the kitchen, near or in all bedrooms. Don't, however, linger to extinguish any major blaze. *Get out.*

(4) Check heating and electrical systems.

People are naturally reluctant to spend money on purely preventive maintenance but an annual professional check of your heating system is well worth the money. The tragic headlines as the heavy-heating season begins each winter offer all the evidence that's needed to convince even the most frugal of home or apartment owners. Electrical shorts and overheated wires, faulty plug-ins, overloaded circuits connected to inadequate fuse boxes are among the chief causes of fires. Wiring gets old, insulation dries and cracks, more and more appliances are added, overloading the circuits. All spell potential trouble and require a professional inspection at least every few years.

(5) Toss it out.

At least once a year go through your house or apartment and throw out the accumulated papers, old clothing and junk that inevitably end up in closets, crawl spaces, and basements—the unnoticed corners where fires can start and be fueled to destructive fury by such materials.

(6) Sort it out.

The typical modern home is filled with highly incendiary materials—cleaning agents, lighter fluid, gasoline for the power mower, wax, oil, paint, alcohol. All too often these are stored haphazardly under sinks and on basement shelves where they are easily knocked over and readily accessible to feed a spark of static electricity. Gasoline should be kept in properly marked cans and kept out of the house altogether, if possible. Like all volatile fluids, it should be tightly capped. Keep all such fluids out of harm's way, capped and upright in a place where they are not routinely shuffled around with the soaps and powders. Guard especially against leaving oily cleaning rags stored away in closets, since the right combination of heat and air will cause spontaneous combustion—that is, heat builds up to the point where fire starts itself.

(7) Kids, matches, smoking.

Everyone knows that these are obvious sources for fires, but we tend to get careless. A book of matches or a cigarette lighter left on a table starts hundreds of fires each year. Don't leave young children alone. They have a nose for matches left in coat pockets and table drawers. Smoking in bed, especially lying down, is begging for trouble. The same goes for tossing cigar or cigarette butts into wastebaskets. Half of the ashtrays in the country are too small to be safe. The other half seem to be stored away in cupboards.

(8) Don't panic.

Statistics show that plain old panic in the event of fire probably kills nearly as many people as smoke and flames. In the event of fire, take a precious second to get yourself in hand. Now is when the plan and drills pay off. You have alternatives if only you will keep thinking. Blind panic causes people to rush into flame-filled hallways and stairways, jump out of windows and cut arteries on jagged glass. Fire is bad enough; don't make it worse by losing your head and depriving yourself of the chance to make lifesaving choices.

CREDIT: *Sean Freeman, staff writer for The Thomas More Association, Chicago, Illinois.*

CLIP AND SAVE YOUR LIFE

DEAR ANN LANDERS: How would you like to save some lives today?

Millions of people read your column. Plese print these suggestions on what to do in case of fire. Ask your readers to post them somewhere in the house for all to see. Taping them to the refrigerator is a good idea.

I read these suggestions in Look magazine in 1971. I then had them retyped when the article became too ragged to read. Now I'd like to clip it from Ann Landers' column and post it again. How about it? FAITHFUL FAN

DEAR FAN: Here it is: Start clipping. And thank you in behalf of those whose lives may be saved because you took the time and trouble to write:

(1) When a fire breaks out in your home or office, get out immediately. A fire can spread faster than you can run. Even if you smell smoke, get out.

(2) If you find smoke in an open stairway or hall, use another preplanned way out.

(3) If you escape through smoke, stay near the floor where the air is better. Take short breaths. Breathe through your nose, and crawl to an exit.

(4) Make sure your family knows the quickest and safest ways to escape from every room in the house. Keep a flashlight in all rooms to help escape at night. Make sure children can open doors, windows and screens to the escape routes. Teach your children how to use the phone to report a fire. And they should know where the alarm box is in the neighborhood.

(5) Head for stairs—not the elevator. A bad fire can cut off the power to elevators. An elevator could also deliver you to the fire floor.

(6) Don't jump. Many people have jumped and died without realizing rescue was only a few minutes away.

(7) If you are trapped in a smoke-filled room, stay near the floor where the air is better. If possible, sit by a window where you can call for help. Open it at the top and bottom. Heat and smoke will go out the top. You can breathe at the bottom.

(8) Feel every door with your hand. If it's hot, don't open it. If it's cool, make this test: Open slowly and stay behind the door. If you feel heat or pressure coming through the open door, slam it shut.

(9) If you can't get out, stay behind a closed door. Any door will serve as a shield.

(10) If there is a panic for the main exit, get away from the mob. Try to find another way out. Once you are safely out, don't go back in. Call the fire department. Use alarm box or telephone. In the country, be sure you know the number of the closest volunteer fire department. Never assume someone else has turned in the alarm.

Flu

(*Influenza*)

In ancient times Italian astrologers thought this illness came from an influence of the heavenly bodies. They attached to it their word for "influence"—*influenza*—and the name stuck. Today we know the flu is not caused by the stars but by a group of viruses.

Is having the flu like having a cold?

No, it's worse.

A cold usually means frequent sneezing, a stuffy nose, and a scratchy throat. Flu (influenza) means sickness that makes you go to bed. And it may keep you there for a while. Flu can be a fatal illness if other trouble complicates it.

Influenza is usually a fairly brief but severe sickness and it is highly contagious. If you must be in close contact with a flu patient, wear a surgical mask.

WHAT DOES INFLUENZA DO?

When flu strikes, tissues become swollen and inflamed. The throat becomes sore and hot and the muscles become achy. Cells may die and little sores are formed, causing the discharge from your nose or throat to be streaked with blood. Flu may damage the lining of your breathing equipment and spread to your lungs.

But these tissues are not damaged permanently. They are repaired after nine to fifteen days as replacement cells are formed—provided no other germ takes over.

WHO GETS INFLUENZA?

Anyone can get flu—especially when it is widespread in the community. It can be a serious illness for those with a lung problem or chronic diseases. Flu can also be dangerous for older people and pregnant women. In large worldwide epidemics many healthy young adults have been fatally stricken.

HOW DOES INFLUENZA ATTACK?

Flu takes from one to three days to develop but the symptoms appear abruptly. They may vary according to the individual, but most flu victims suffer from chills and fever, headache, backache, muscular pains, a dry cough, nausea, loss of appetite, and a sensitivity to light.

The temperature goes up quickly during the first day—usually to 101 or 102 degrees. It peaks the first twenty-four to forty-eight hours and often stays up for three to five days. It may go down gradually and then rise again on the third day. Fever usually lasts three or four days, but it may persist for as long as seven days even in uncomplicated cases.

As your temperature begins to go down, you'll probably notice more stuffiness in your nose. Your cough may get worse. There may be pus in the discharges from your nose or throat, but these unpleasant symptoms are signals that you are getting well. Don't be surprised, however, if you feel tired for a week or more. A lingering cough for two or three weeks is also common.

WHAT ARE THE EFFECTS OF INFLUENZA?

In most cases, flu leaves no permanent aftereffects. But too often people develop other complications, the most common of which is pneumonia. When your body is weakened by an illness like flu, pneumonia germs find it easier to invade your lungs. There are different strains of pneumonia and one is uncommon but extremely serious. This type is caused by the flu virus itself. It gets deep into the lungs and can result in death among presumably healthy young people.

Other complications that follow flu are not life-threatening but can be very annoying. They are a persistent cough or bronchitis, sinus trouble and ear infections.

HOW IS INFLUENZA TREATED?

Your doctor almost always suggests bed rest. If he doesn't you'll probably feel like going to bed anyway. He may also tell you to take something like aspirin to ease the pain and bring down the fever. He may urge you to drink a lot of fluids to replace the loss produced by fever. Follow his advice.

If the sickness you have is really flu, penicillin and other wonder drugs will not help because they are not effective against viruses. But the doctor may give you one of these drugs if he thinks you are getting another kind of infection as a complication.

It is wise to stay in bed as long as the sickness is severe and probably for two days after the fever is gone. The temperature of your room should be moderate and the humidity should be kept high. If you are a smoker, stop smoking during this illness. If you want to do yourself a real favor turn your flu into a blessing and stop smoking permanently.

HOW CAN INFLUENZA BE PREVENTED?

Vaccination is the only satisfactory way to prevent or control flu. The vaccines are made from strains of the virus that are currently causing illness.

The public health officials in the United States and Canada advise the drug companies on the makeup of the vaccine, which usually includes several strains. This affords a high degree of protection against the disease. Chronically ill and elderly people especially need this protection.

Sometimes the virus abruptly changes its nature and a new strain sweeps across the world so quickly that there is not sufficient time to include it in the vaccine. Of course the vaccination will not work as effectively against that strain. Nevertheless, people at high risk—susceptible because of advanced age or chronic illness—are urged to make use of the vaccine in the fall, when the "flu season" begins, since the new strains occur about once a decade but the old strains cause the sporadic cases every year.

The high-risk group also includes people who have chronic bronchitis, emphysema or other lung diseases, heart trouble, high blood pressure, or selected other chronic illnesses. They should be vaccinated every year. So should people over forty-five and patients in nursing homes or crowded home conditions.

Ask your doctor whether you should get the vaccine.

IF YOU HAVE SYMPTOMS OF INFLUENZA, YOU SHOULD:

(1) Call your doctor.

(2) Go to bed. Even if your aches and pains and sore throat turn out to be nothing but a cold, bed rest will help you get well sooner.

(3) Keep warm and drink plenty of liquids. A washcloth wrung out in cold water and placed on your forehead may relieve the discomfort of fever.

(4) *Do not* take medicine suggested by friends. Let your doctor prescribe.

(5) Stay in bed except for necessary brief periods until the doctor says you can get up. He will probably tell you to stay in bed for at least two days after your temperature returns to normal.

(6) Eat what you want. At the onset of flu you will probably be content to stay with tea and toast. If nausea is severe stick to fluids for twelve to twenty-four hours.

CREDIT: *Chicago Lung Association. Reviewed by Dr. Mark H. Lepper, Vice President of Rush-Presbyterian-St. Luke's Medical Center, Chicago, Illinois.*

Flu Shots

During the past ten years, about twenty million "flu shots" have been given to Americans each year. The discovery of the swine flu virus at Fort Dix, New Jersey, and the resultant National Influenza Immunization Program doubled the number of flu shots given in 1976 to forty million. It also stimulated widespread controversy about vaccines in general and flu shots in particular.

Flu shot recommendations are already being hotly debated by the experts. The controversy makes it difficult for most people to decide whether or not to get the vaccine.

Dr. Stephen Schoenbaum, a specialist in infectious diseases and a former physician at the U. S. Center for Disease Control, supplies the following information about flu shots:

WHAT IS INFLUENZA?

The symptoms of influenza are those of many short-lived viral infections: fever, fatigue, muscle aches, cough, headache, etc. While it is popular to refer to any bout with these symptoms as "the flu," most flu-like episodes are caused by viruses other than true members of the influenza family of viruses. Only influenza viruses, however, are responsible for the large epidemics that occur periodically. Influenza A viruses, which commonly affect all ages, are usually responsible for the largest epidemics, while influenza B viruses usually cause more limited epidemics among children. Influenza vaccines (flu shots) are effective only against members of the influenza family of viruses; they offer no protection against the common cold or other "flu-like" illnesses.

WHAT ARE FLU SHOTS?

The flu shots currently used consist of large quantities of influenza viruses which have been grown in eggs, killed, and purified. Being dead, they cannot reproduce within the body to cause disease. But they will stimulate the body to produce antibodies which will protect against similar live viruses. A full-blown infection can be prevented—or at least curtailed.

WHY ARE FLU SHOTS CONTROVERSIAL?

First, the influenza vaccine is only 60–70 percent effective in preventing illness, while vaccines for polio, measles, and some other viruses are over 90 percent effective.

Secondly, influenza vaccines seem to lose their effectiveness after one year —though the exact duration of their effectiveness is unknown. For this reason, annual immunization is advised.

Thirdly, there is a high reaction rate associated with influenza vaccines. Sore arms are common after a shot, and some people will have a fever for a day or two. More importantly, the surveillance program for vaccine reactions resulting from swine flu shots uncovered a previously unknown problem—the occurrence of the Guillain-Barré syndrome in about one out of every 100,000 recipients. This neurological illness, which often seems to follow naturally acquired virus infections, is fatal in about 5 percent of cases and causes some degree of permanent paralysis in another 5 percent. Despite the widespread publicity given to three deaths from heart attacks in Pennsylvania early in the swine flu program, there is no evidence that fatal illness other than Guillain-Barré syndrome is associated with influenza immunization.

WHO SHOULD GET FLU SHOTS?

Current evidence still suggests that it is important for certain individuals to receive the vaccine—those in the so-called high-risk groups (persons with chronic diseases, persons over sixty-five, and people in high-risk occupations, such as hospital employees).

Each time there is a large epidemic caused by an influenza virus, an excess number of hospitalizations and deaths beyond that normally expected occurs. These flu-related deaths are most common among high-risk groups.

The question is whether the benefits from vaccination outweigh the risks and the costs involved. *It appears the most sensible policy is yearly immunization of high-risk groups with vaccine made from viruses similar to the strains expected to be prevalent during the winter season.*

Vaccination of the entire population is recommended only in years when very large epidemics are expected. When the outbreak occurred at Fort Dix, the best guess at the time was that the swine flu virus might represent a major change. In retrospect, it is obvious that the Fort Dix outbreak was an isolated occurrence, but that was not predictable at the time. The irony of the swine flu episode is that in other years such as 1968 when Hong Kong flu was first detected, there was great indignation over shortages of vaccine, whereas the failure of an epidemic to materialize from Fort Dix led to claims of a fiasco because so much more vaccine was made than consumed.

It is obvious that much more research is needed to improve influenza vaccines and to exploit other approaches to control influenza—such as the use of antiviral drugs. Nonetheless, I feel that annual immunization of high-risk groups is justified, and, in fact, should be implemented to a much greater extent than in the past. *Such an immunization program won't prevent epidemics, but it should reduce their impact.*

CREDIT: *Stephen C. Schoenbaum, M.D., Assistant Professor of Medicine at the Peter Bent Brigham Hospital, Harvard Medical School, Boston, Massachusetts. Taken from* Harvard School Health Letter, *September 19, 1977.*

Foot Problems and Care of the Feet

"When my feet hurt, I'm sick all over" is a frequent complaint heard by podiatrists, doctors who specialize in diseases of the foot. To a great extent, it is true. Our feet are subject to many common problems, and most are closely related to our general health.

Many of these problems are due to inherited or acquired changes within the bone structure of the feet. When feet with structural irregularities are subjected to pressures and stress, they develop some of the common foot problems. These stresses are often aggravated by "stylish" shoe fashions and the nature of the surface we walk on.

CORNS AND CALLUSES

A callus is a hard thickening of the skin and is a normal development which serves as a protective mechanism. In some situations our bodies are unable to control the amount of callus development. When the callus becomes very thick it causes pain or burning. A corn is similar except it is usually much harder and has a center or core extending into the skin. The simple removal or trimming of the corn or callus usually will not result in a permanent "cure." The typical painful corn or callus most frequently develops over a prominent bone or joint where the skin is subject to significant friction and pressure from shoes while walking or standing. The underlying causes must be determined before a definite treatment is given. In some instances an orthotic, a device worn within a shoe to alter the stress of walking and standing, may be used. When the corn or callus is significantly painful or disabling, it might be treated with surgery. This would involve removing or relocating the bony prominence or deformity. Growths which are not correctable with orthotics and not severe enough to treat surgically require periodic trimming or cutting by a podiatrist. This procedure is best left in the hands of a skilled professional, as improper self-care may cause problems. Similarly, the use of non-prescription medicines and chemicals intended for treatment of corns and calluses is potentially hazardous. However, pumice stones and other non-cutting fine abrasive products may be safely used.

PLANTAR WARTS

Plantar warts are often confused with corns and calluses but are a distinct benign growth found on the sole of the foot. These painful growths are caused by a virus and most frequently seen in young adults between the ages of sixteen and twenty-two, although they may occur at any age. In structure, they are similar to other common warts but due to their location and the stresses of weight-bearing they become embedded within the skin rather than on the surface. There is no totally effective treatment and the skin specialists (dermatologists) and foot specialists (podiatrists) who treat plantar warts often have their own favorite treatment. Common treatments include freezing with liquid nitrogen or "dry ice," burning with an electric needle, applications of various types of acids and surgery. Surgical treatment must be done carefully to avoid leaving a scar which may become a further source of pain on the sole of the foot. In some instances, warts will reoccur no matter what treatment is used, while occasionally they will disappear without any treatment. The use of X ray in the treatment of plantar warts is not advisable.

INGROWN TOENAIL

The term "ingrown toenail" means that one or both of the edges of the nail have cut into the adjacent skin and flesh, resulting in a painful infection. A common underlying cause is a nail which, either through inheritance or injury, is improperly shaped. Tight shoes and stockings, improper nail cutting, or recent injury are also factors. The treatment for this problem is for the embedded or "ingrown" part of the nail to be removed. A podiatrist or general surgeon should perform this procedure. If the problem is chronic, reoccurrences can be prevented by surgically removing a portion of the nail matrix or root. The cutting of a V at the end of the nail is of no value either in the treatment or prevention of this problem.

As a result of injury or disease (especially a fungus infection) toenails may become extremely thick and hard. To prevent both pain and infection this type of nail is often removed along with its root. In some instances this problem can be managed by filing or grinding the nail to maintain a more normal thickness. It should be noted that removal of a nail does not correct these problems unless the root of the nail is also removed.

ATHLETE'S FOOT (TINEA PEDIS)

During the past several years, newer medications, including creams, oily liquids, and powders, have been on the market, making the prevention and treatment of this condition easier than it once was. However, if athlete's foot, especially between the toes, results in open sores, bleeding, swelling or pain, a person should seek professional help. Prevention is aided by alternating shoes, avoiding vinyl or plastic shoes, wearing clean socks daily, and keeping the feet clean and dry.

BUNIONS AND HAMMERTOES

A group of frequent and often painful deformities sometimes occurs in the front part of the foot. These conditions, known as bunions, hammertoes, and prominent bones in the ball of the foot (metatarsals), may be related to one another. Bunions are prominent and often painful bumps of bone located at either side of the foot alongside the great toe or just behind the little toe. Hammertoe refers to a bending of the toe at the joint causing a bump on the top of the toe which rubs against the shoe. The causes for both are complex but many people are susceptible to these deformities because of their inherited foot structure. Shoes are rarely the cause but they certainly can aggravate and complicate these conditions. Some of the causing factors can be at least partially controlled with padding that is fitted into a shoe. If these measures fail to improve comfort and function, surgery may be required. (A bunionectomy will keep a patient off his feet for six weeks but is sometimes the only way to end the painful problem.)

ARCH STRAIN

Pain in the long arch at the inner side of the foot may be due to improper shoes, obesity, prolonged periods of standing, or weakness and irregularities of the bone structures in this part of the foot. Frequently the pain is due to a strain or attempt to stretch the ligaments, which hold the foot bones together. This ligament strain is most frequent in the so-called "flat foot." Treatment often involves the use of shoe padding, losing weight, changing shoe styles, standing less and sitting more.

RELATION TO GENERAL HEALTH

There are many instances in which the feet can alert us to the fact that something else has gone wrong and a doctor should be seen at once. Symptoms which may show up in the feet first often signal heart and kidney disease, diabetes mellitus, gout, arthritis, and certain disorders of the vascular (blood vessel) and nerve systems.

The following are among the foot symptoms which require attention: swelling; pain; change of color (from pale to red or vice versa) which happens either at rest or with activity; changes in sensations which may include numbness, burning, itching, tingling and occasionally shooting pains; slow-healing cuts, bruises and sores.

SHOES

Proper shoes are essential if one is to enjoy the comfort of healthy feet. The stylish, slender-appearing shoe with elevated heels and thin soles is suitable for sitting but will not provide comfort or adequate support for walking or standing. In general the most comfortable shoe is made of soft, pliable leather with the least amount of stitching and decoration possible, and a cushioned, resilient sole thick enough to protect the foot from rough and hard walking surfaces. Crepe rubber between one quarter and one half inch thick is a good sole material. There should be ample room in the front to allow easy movement of the toes without pressure or irritation. Shoes should be about one half inch longer than the longest toe. For men shoes with laces are generally preferable to the loafer type.

CARE OF THE FEET

Proper care of the feet should include the following:

(1) Good hygiene. Keep nails, skin, shoes and stockings clean.

(2) Properly fitted shoes, chosen to be appropriate for the activity or occasion.

(3) Nails cut straight across or contoured slightly to correspond to the shape of the toe.

(4) Exercise. The best exercise is walking in properly designed and fitted shoes.

(5) Avoid excessive dryness of skin especially in colder winter climates. Apply skin cream lightly after bathing, except between the toes. This area should be kept dry. Powdering between the toes after a bath or shower is a good idea.

CREDIT: *Bruce T. Wood, Podiatrist, Peter Brent Brigham Hospital, Boston, Massachusetts, Robert Breck Brigham Hospital, Associate Professor, Orthopedics (Podiatry), Harvard Medical School.*

Forgiving

This essay on "Forgiving" was written especially for this encyclopedia by the Reverend Theodore M. Hesburgh, president of the University of Notre Dame.

HOW TO FORGIVE

Of all the human qualities that make men and women godlike, none is more divine than forgiveness. Jesus told many stories, but none more touching than that of the Prodigal Son. In a true sense, it ought to be renamed "The Prodigal Father," so magnanimous and generous was his forgiveness.

The son was not unlike many sons—greedy, anxious to get his hands on wealth he had not earned, so humanly foolish in the way he spent it on fast living with those who exploited him and left him in his misery when the money ran out. How slowly he came to his senses, dying of hunger in a pigsty that mirrored his life. Then the awakening. "My father's servants live far better than I," he told himself. Yet he did not really expect forgiveness from his father, just the chance to say what a bum he had been and ask if he could be —not his son any longer, for he knew he had forfeited that privilege—but one of his father's servants. All he wanted was a roof over his head and better food than the pigs were getting. He started on the road back.

Now Jesus teaches us how to forgive. Don't even wait for the sinner to arrive. When you see him coming, yet far away, run out to meet him. When he starts to say he is sorry, do not even give him time to finish. Embrace him, love him, put him into your best outfit, put your ring on his finger, get the best meat out of the freezer, cook up the best meal you can put together, start the music, rejoice with your friends, and proudly invite them to meet your returned son.

The Lord also warns us that acting this way will be greatly misunderstood and unappreciated, even by one's own family. The faithful son will pout and call you a fool for forgiving his stupid wastrel brother. He ought to be sent back to the pigsty of his own foolish making, not forgiven!

The forgiving father can only say that he loves and will always love his son who has no need to be forgiven. But as for the other one, rejoice. He was lost and is found; he was dead and is alive again because he was forgiven.

Is it any wonder that when the Lord taught us how to pray, the best words He could think of, for us who have so much to be forgiven, were: Our Father. The Lord's Prayer does not ask for much: daily bread, freedom from evil, and *forgiveness*. How the Lord puts into our mouths words that are not easy to live with: "Forgive us our trespasses, *as we forgive those who trespass against us.*" Those words really put our feet to the fire. We ask God to forgive us as we forgive others, and vice versa by implication. As St. James puts it in his New Testament letter (2:13): "There will be judgment without mercy for those who have not been merciful themselves. The merciful need have no fear of judgment." Or as it is said in the Beatitudes: "Blessed are the merciful for they shall obtain mercy."

Why should we be forgiving and merciful without measure? Maybe the simplest answer is that we are all in such need of mercy and forgiveness that we can ill afford not to be merciful and forgiving to others.

A foolish question: Why didn't Our Lord entitle the story "The Prodigal Daughter"—forgiven by her mother? Maybe because sons are harder to forgive than daughters and mothers are generally more forgiving than fathers. Anyway, I believe He wanted us to see forgiveness in its most difficult mode.

CREDIT: *The Reverend Theodore Hesburgh.*

Forgiving

Ann Landers' Thoughts on Forgiving

While forgiving may seem to be a generous, magnanimous thing to do, it is also self-serving in a very real sense. Forgiving promotes good fellowship, it strengthens ties with family and friends, and best of all, it is good for one's blood pressure, digestive system and general health.

Many years ago, I read a book by Dale Carnegie, *How to Stop Worrying and Start Living*. He said, "When we hate our enemies we give them power over us . . . power over our sleep, our appetites and our happiness. They would dance with joy if they knew how much they were upsetting us. Our hate is not hurting them at all but it is turning our own days and nights into a hellish turmoil."

When Jesus said, "Love your enemies," He was not only preaching sound ethics but good mental health. Hate is corrosive and destructive. It can ruin your good looks. We all know people whose inability to forgive—especially women who have been dumped by lovers or husbands—causes them to look angry and bitter. The agony and hostility show on their faces. They look defeated and sullen, hard and unsmiling. Their eyes are dead—their jaws are set. Their heads are down, their shoulders slump. They lack grace when they move. They look like losers—and that's what they are.

Shakespeare said it best: "Heat not a furnace for your foe so hot that it do singe yourself."

CREDIT: *Ann Landers.*

DEAR ANN LANDERS: Funny how your advice for somebody else had a message for me. I took it eight years ago, and I am writing to say thank you. It was the "forgive and forget" answer you gave to a woman with small children and a husband with a "wandering eye."

You said, "If there is a light in the window, and the man has any good in him, he'll be back." Then you added, "Don't be stubborn or proud. Take him back. I promise you won't regret it."

When I read that letter, my husband was living away from home and he wanted to come back, but I just couldn't bring myself to accept him. Your advice to that woman seemed somehow as if it was meant for me. So I took it. The eight years that followed were our happiest.

Three weeks ago, death took my darling, very suddenly. The days and nights are lonely, but the warmth of the memories of our last years together will sustain me forever. So, Ann, I want to thank you for helping me, even though I didn't write to you. YOUR FRIEND IN MARSHFIELD, WIS.

DEAR FRIEND: Your heart-warming letter reminded me of those wonderful words by Robert Frost:
"Home is where, when you have to
go there,
They have to take you in."
I'm so glad I helped. Thank you for letting me know.

DEAR ANN LANDERS: My husband and I have been married 15 years. We have two wonderful children and a beautiful home, many friends and no money trouble. There's only one problem and it's MINE, not OURS.

Walter and I were married only a year when he was drafted into the Army and sent to Korea. He was gone 13 months. Not a day went by that we didn't write to each other. When he returned we were like newlyweds.

Several times during these last 14 years, Walter has asked me if I ever cheated on him when he was in Korea. I did not and told him so repeatedly. Last year he became unusually persistent in his questioning. Suddenly I understood why. He was feeling guilty about something. Well, I was right. Walter confessed that he and several buddies went to a Korean house of prostitution to relieve a physical need.

That ended our marriage in my heart. I am crushed. I think about it day and night. I don't trust him to go for a newspaper. I feel totally betrayed and can't shake this depression. Why, oh why did he have to tell me? Please help if you can. WHAT I DIDN'T KNOW DIDN'T HURT ME

DEAR DIDN'T KNOW: Your attitude is immature and lacking in compassion. Moreover, your inability to forgive and forget has made you sick. I suggest counseling at once.

WEDDING BELL BLUES

DEAR ANN LANDERS: I haven't spoken to my brother's wife in seven years. It would take the whole newspaper to tell you the entire story, so I'll just say she did me unbelievable dirt and I have never been able to forgive her.

My daughter is getting married in a few months and I want the wedding to be a happy occasion. I know my mother will be sad if my brother and his wife are not present. (He refuses to come without her even though he knows she was in the wrong and has told me so.)

My other two sisters say she (the one who did me the dirt) should apol-

ogize and then I should invite her. But the girl is as stubborn as a Missouri mule. I'm sure she'd die first. What should I do? OPEN FOR SUGGESTIONS

DEAR OPEN: Don't let the Missouri mule spoil a beautiful day. Go to her and say, "Let's forget the past. I want you to attend my daughter's wedding and make it a happy day for everyone —especially Mother."

It takes a big person to make the first move and mend a rift when he (or she) has been wronged. But I can tell you for sure, it's the thing to do.

Freckles

Freckles are the flat, irregularly shaped light to medium brown spots found on the skin of many fair-skinned people, especially redheads and blondes. They generally appear in early childhood after the earliest significant sun exposure, and tend to fade in late adult life.

Freckles usually fade and sometimes disappear during the winter months when there is no exposure to sun or other sources of ultraviolet light. Following exposure to sun or ultraviolet light, the brown color of freckles deepens, often within a few hours. The fluorescent lights used to illuminate offices and homes may also cause freckles to become more prominent.

Freckling is apparently an inherited tendency, but not all fair-skinned individuals will develop freckles. Freckles are different from moles and liver spots, which are growths or tumors of the skin. Freckles are simply the result of the increased formation of brown melanin pigment in small skin areas.

Although freckles can be removed by surgical dermabrasion (sandpapering the skin while under anesthetic) and by chemical peeling, they often recur. These methods of treatment are performed by dermatologists and some plastic surgeons. Prevention of freckling can be accomplished by avoiding the sun and ultraviolet light and by using protective sun-screening preparations. Appropriate makeup can help hide freckles very effectively.

CREDIT: *Harry J. Hurley, M.D., Professor of Clinical Dermatology, School of Medicine, University of Pennsylvania, Philadelphia, Pennsylvania.*

Freeloading

DEAR ANN: I'm ashamed to discuss this problem with anyone I know. It's my husband. He is a chronic check-dodger and I don't know what to do about it.

When we go out for dinner or an after-the-movie snack with other couples, he manages never to pick up the check. He is a master at being "out-fumbled." What is even worse, I've seen him leave for the men's room when he spots the waiter approaching with the check.

We aren't hard up for money. There is no excuse for his freeloading. I'm sure our friends think we are terribly cheap. Please come up with a solution. I am M. BARRASSED

DEAR M.B.: Since your husband seems to have trouble finding his pockets, I suggest you step in and give him some help. Next time the situation arises say in a loud voice, "It's our turn, dear." Then take the check from the waiter and hand it to him.

If he happens to be in the men's room when the check arrives, *you* should take the check and present it to your husband when he returns.

I frequently hear from readers who complain about being taken advantage of by people at work. The following letter hits my desk, in one form or another, at least once a week:

DEAR ANN LANDERS: This is no big deal but it bothers the hell out of me because I hate to be taken for a fool.

I'm 28, female, self-supporting and barely able to make ends meet. I work as a secretary in a large office. The problem: two women, one married, one divorced. Both of these dames have a habit of sponging small amounts and "forgetting" to pay me back. It's "Bring me some coffee and a Danish from the cafeteria—as long as you're going. I'll pay you back tomorrow."

Well, "tomorrow" never comes and a coffee and Danish cost 45¢.

Or, "I'm out of cigarettes and haven't got the right change for the machine. Will you let me have a couple of quarters?" I say, "Sure," and I'm out 50¢.

Three weeks ago there was an office collection for flowers. The manager's wife died. I put in $2 for one of these gals. The following Friday was payday. She "forgot" and I was too chicken to remind her.

The way I figure it, I am out about $30 this year (and it's only May) because of these two freeloaders. What can I do without looking cheap? TAPPED OUT IN TALLAHASSEE

The advice I gave to "Tapped" was the same advice I give to hundreds of readers who write annually with variations on the same theme.

Keep track (date and amount) of any loan or monies advanced for a friend, relative or colleague—even if it's only a Coke or bus fare.

Don't feel you are being petty or cheap. In a few days if nothing is said about repayment, or if no effort is made to reciprocate ("It's my turn"), *remind* the person about the indebtedness ("It's *your* turn").

If the answer is, "Sorry, I'm broke," or "I'll pay you next week," make a note. When "next week" rolls around and you again encounter total amnesia, get your small speech ready for the next pitch and *use* it when the freeloader puts the bite on—for whatever amount, no matter how small. Say, "I'm sorry. You still owe me from last time and I can't go for another dime until you improve your credit rating."

From then on, say no to every request, no matter how insignificant. The freeloader will get the message and find another sucker—if he can.

CREDIT: *Ann Landers.*

Frigidity

Frigidity is a subject that reflects the way a culture stumbles through the half-light of prejudice, rumor and fragments of knowledge toward understanding itself. As a scientific term, frigidity has all but lost its usefulness; it is too oversimplified to apply to the complicated situations it was once thought to describe. Frigidity is still used as a label for a variety of female problems with sexual response, a label that permits the male to comfortably distance himself from the blame while, with overtones of shame and guilt, it places the responsibility largely on the woman.

The uninformed use of the term "frigidity" works the same mischief as the rumor and old wives' tales. Not until the research of Masters and Johnson have we had an organized body of knowledge about the common but extremely disruptive problems of human sexuality. Masters and Johnson not only reject the term "frigidity" as vague and meaningless, they also emphasize the reciprocal nature of sexual problems between spouses. Thanks to them and other contemporary researchers, we also know that persons with sexual difficulties can be successfully treated through a variety of therapeutic approaches.

Masters and Johnson place the notion of frigidity under the heading of orgasmic dysfunction. They view sexual functioning as the interaction between two systems, the biophysical and the psychosocial. The biophysical system refers to a reasonably healthy body and anatomically functional sex organs; the psychosocial system describes a set of values and attitudes relating to sex. These systems are closely interrelated. Significant negative signals from either of the two can cause dysfunction for a person of either sex.

The causes of sexual problems identified by other researchers—some organic, some psychological, and some from cultural conditioning—all can be placed within this framework. Such a backdrop enables us to move away from the one-dimensional view that the female is solely responsible for the dysfunctions that were once classified as frigidity.

What are the most common forms of sexual dysfunction in women? A. A. Lazarus, avoiding the term "frigidity," names them: "(1) complete or partial absence of sexual arousal; (2) total or partial aversion to sex (despite feelings of arousal); (3) loss of sexual interest or arousal before achieving an orgasm; (4) inability to have an orgasm; (5) absence of pleasure during sex; (6) various degrees of pain or discomfort during coitus, not due to organic disorders."

An important note is added by Philip Polatin, M.D., who observes that "a woman without orgasm is not necessarily lacking in sexual responsiveness. Consequently, achieving orgasm should not be considered the full and final aim of sexual gratification for the otherwise responsive female."

Perhaps Ann Landers' summation pulled these concepts together as well as anyone when she wrote, "Many are cold but few are frozen."

The incidence of orgasmic dysfunction varies according to the scientific understanding of the experts. Those who echo an older tradition have reported that nearly 80 percent of women have such problems. More recent views, however, based on broader definitions and deeper research, have lowered that figure considerably. They also have emphasized the positive statistics of the number of women who report the experience of orgasm on a fairly consistent basis. It should be no surprise (except in an unrealistic culture that demands machine-like sexual success in every performance) that the range and quality of sexual experiences vary widely.

Despite research advances, there is still a great deal we do not know about human sexuality. All human beings will experience variation in sexual responsiveness and performance, including failures.

When the difficulties are chronic they can be understood and treated, especially when viewed within the relationship of the concerned couple. Masters and Johnson have reported several causes for orgasmic difficulties in women. Chief among these is religious prohibitions, which, according to the researchers, arise in rigidly religious families and result in major social and emotional deprivation. Obviously, this category refers to a distorted and guilt-laden religious orientation and the influence of the parental figures who transmit it.

These latter can also be responsible for what has been called a "protective vacuum" in which a young woman can arrive at physical maturity without developing the emotional maturity necessary to successful female identification.

Orgasmic problems have also been related to the "second-best" mate syndrome—a situation in which the partner is not the ideal spouse the wife once had or sought. The inability of the woman to identify with her partner in a loving manner is probably the most frequent cause of her own orgasmic dysfunction. Closely related to this is her inability to let him know what in his lovemaking is pleasurable and what is not. The causes in the male's sexual dysfunction may be varied but the effect on the woman is the same. She may experience such anxiety about the performance of her partner that it can prevent her from responding.

Masters and Johnson report "situational orgasmic dysfunction" which can be related to the woman's dislike for her spouse because of his crudeness or selfishness, or other qualities which turn her off. When a sexual problem exists there is a definite need to view the couple in relationship to each other rather than focusing solely on the man or the woman.

The complaint of "frigidity" is most often associated with a sexual difficulty reported by the husband, yet the most frequent of problems (107 out of 223 couples treated in one research report) involved premature ejaculation.

Successful treatment for what was once termed frigidity include psychotherapy and behavior modification. Successes have also been reported through group counseling and the use of hypnosis to uncover the sources of inhibition.

Sexual dysfunction clinics have been established throughout the country and many are good. The credentials of the therapists should be carefully checked, however, as this is an area where people are extremely vulnerable and quacks abound.

A change in attitude has taken place and a beginning has been made at understanding more deeply and providing greater help for women who experience orgasmic dysfunction. It is, however, only a beginning, and despite the massive information about human sexuality now available, rumors and prejudice and old-fashioned "common sense" remedies for what was once termed frigidity are still plentiful.

Nothing is worse, for example, than the notion that all a woman needs is a good man to take care of her and all her problems will disappear. Human beings need a sensitivity to their difficulties, as well as patience and compassion. They also need to know that a new day has dawned and it is no longer necessary for couples to live in painful silence when sex is unrewarding, boring, or non-existent.

CREDIT: *Sara Charles, M.D., Assistant Professor of Psychiatry, Abraham Lincoln School of Medicine, University of Illinois in Chicago. Eugene Kennedy, Ph.D., Professor of Psychology, Loyola University, Chicago, author of* Living with Everyday Problems *and* A Time for Being Human, *Chicago, Illinois: Thomas More Association Books.*

The Funeral

(*And Other Arrangements Following a Death*)

Most funerals in the United States, except for those of native Americans, include much of what was brought to this country by the people who settled it. There are distinct ethnic and religious customs and symbols. There are also funeral directors, morticians and embalmers. They all help meet the needs of the survivors in caring for the dead. These licensed and trained individuals do for the survivors what they cannot do for themselves because they lack the facilities, equipment and skill—and often emotional strength.

During and since the 1960s the splitting up and mobility of the families, extension of the life-span, segregation of the aged, and a lessening of the influence of religion have brought about some changes in funerals. There are "newer" parts of the country, where fewer family and religious ties exist. All of these have brought about some alternates to the funeral, explained by the following definitions:

Funeral: A funeral is an organized, purposeful, time-limited, flexible, group-centered response to death. It involves personalized rites and/or ceremonies with the body present, to commemorate that a death has occurred and that a life has been lived. It includes a time ranging from a couple of hours to two or more days when the body is "in state" for the purpose of a "visitation" or "wake."

Memorial Service: A memorial service involves rites and ceremonies and commemoration without the body present. These could be held before or after disposition of the body.

Direct Disposition: Direct disposition of the body is most times without any rites or ceremonies. When there are ceremonies they are usually associated with the scattering of the cremated remains, sometimes into an ocean or river.

Body Donation: Donation of a body to medical science is deemed an alternate to the funeral when there is no funeral held with the body present prior to delivery of the body to the medical school. There can be a memorial service, a committal service of the residue after use, or direct disposition to the medical institution.

There are psychological, philosophical, sociological, theological, and financial aspects of post-death activities. To some, the cost is of prime importance. They feel they can resolve their grief by intellectualizing their emotions. They reason that when a life has ended it is impractical and useless to spend money on what they call "pageantry."

The following facts, however, should be considered by all who will experience the death of someone loved and be involved in the decision-making process as to a funeral or alternate to it.

Most bereaved are helped when family, friends, neighbors and colleagues gather around to show they care.

The embalmed body in an open casket viewed prior to final disposition is helpful for most persons affected by the death. It provides realization, recall and expression. Seeing is believing. And this believing is often essential to proper grief management. However, some feel or their religious beliefs dictate that viewing the casketed body is inappropriate. Whether viewed or not, the presence of the body provides a climate for mourning.

A religious service meets the spiritual needs of most. For those of religious orientation, the clergyperson acts in the dual role of minister and officiant. There can also be a non-religious or humanist ceremony.

Regardless of the type of ceremony it should be adapted to the lifestyle of the deceased and the survivors.

Children should be encouraged to participate in post-death activities but not against their wishes.

Those who wish to express their sympathy should be able to do it as they prefer. The bereaved should not direct what type of remembrance should be made nor exclude any form of expression.

If a body is being donated to medical science information should be obtained in advance of delivery to the medical institution as to whether it will be needed and acceptable.

Prearranging and prefinancing a funeral is a method some people choose to assist their survivors after death occurs. Careful counseling with an experienced person such as a funeral service licensee can avoid unwise planning or even fraudulent schemes involving the financing of funerals in advance of death.

Arranging for any form of post-death activities involves some or most of the following expenses:

Those of the funeral director—staff, facilities, equipment, casket and other items that may be selected from him.

Those involving final disposition of the body—cemetery, crematory, mausoleum, columbarium, or of the direct disposure or for burial at sea.

Memorialization such as a monument or marker for the grave.

Miscellaneous charges such as clergy and musicians' honoraria, paid newspaper death notices, additional transportation and flowers. These may be paid by the family directly or through the funeral director.

Most deaths touch and affect relatives, friends and associates of the deceased in a direct and forceful way. Those arranging for a funeral or alternate should consider the feelings of others who shared in the life of the deceased even though some may not be known to the survivors. They should also be aware of the outlet that post-death rites and ceremonies provide, encouraging expression of grief which if bottled up could be physically or mentally harmful or both.

After the rites and ceremonies or lack of them, one cannot then do what was not done. Nor can one undo or change what has been done. That's why thinking and talking about death and how it will be dealt with when it occurs is of importance.

CREDIT: *Howard C. Raether, Executive Director, National Funeral Directors Association.*

LAST RESPECTS

DEAR ANN LANDERS: I'm sure I'm not the only person who's had this problem, and I'd like your opinion on how it should be handled.

My brother is dying. He was my favorite and I am very sad. Before he passes on I would like to know if it would be all right if I did my mourning at home and skipped the funeral. I would prefer to remember my brother as he was and not see him laid out in a casket.

Funerals have always been depressing to me. I do not care for the "social" luncheons that follow. The sobbing of relatives is out of place since their grief never seems to interfere with their appetites. Sign this NEEDING TO KNOW

DEAR N.T.K.: Go to the funeral, since it will be your last act of respect for your dear brother. You can simply avoid the casket. Also—you can skip the luncheon.

Your absence from the funeral would be an affront to your brother and to the other members of the family.

FUNERAL FAREWELL WILL PREVENT DENIAL OF DEATH

DEAR ANN LANDERS: Our San Antonio Press printed the letter critical of you for suggesting counseling to a 17-year-old girl who refused to attend her best friend's funeral. You replied, "A funeral provides proof that the deceased is gone. It helps the bereaved to overcome denial mechanisms."

You are dead right, Ann. Don't let anyone change your mind. I learned the lesson from bitter experience.

My husband was declared missing in action over France on June 10, 1944. In January of '45 he was declared dead after his crashed plane was found.

I refused to believe it. News items about lost flyers who were found alive in unexpected places kept my hopes alive. Finally I was forced to make the decision and I requested that my husband be buried in France. A flag came home. Almost 20 years later I took my son to France to visit his father's grave. When the kindly custodian asked us whose grave we had come to see my throat closed. I couldn't speak or eat for 48 hours. I grieved as if my husband had just died. Even now, as I write these words I can feel my throat tighten. I realize I suffered all that agony because I had never witnessed the final farewell. I should have requested that my husband's remains be sent home and had a funeral.

So please keep telling it like it is, Ann. People need to hear it.   K.N.F.

DEAR K.N.F.: I appreciate your letter more than I can say. You made the point far better than I. Thank you, in behalf of all those you have helped.

A WORTHY PROFESSION

DEAR ANN LANDERS: As you undoubtedly are aware, a great deal is being said against the funeral-service profession of late. I would like to present the other side of the controversy since almost everything I have read casts the funeral director in the role of the rip-off artist who takes advantage of poor people by making them feel guilty if they don't put Pa or Ma away in a $4,000 bronze casket.

The charges against the profession are based on an infinitesimal sampling of families, made in one small area of the United States. The statistics I have seen indicate that there were approximately 100 complaints from nearly a million families who were served. This compares very favorably with any profession in the United States. In fact, I believe it's a testimony to the integrity of the profession. Will you please comment?   UNJUSTLY MALIGNED

DEAR U.M.: Every profession has its chiselers, con artists and incompetents. Funeral directors, along with the physicians, lawyers, bankers, etc., have their share. But I'm sure the overwhelming majority of morticians are honorable people who perform a service we could not do without. Moreover, they perform it with dignity and sensitivity and are extremely evenhanded in that they offer a wide range of financial alternatives for people of every economic level.

I know of a funeral director in Chicago whose family has been in business since 1864. Rarely does this firm charge more than a token fee for the burial of an infant and in cases of financial hardship they either donate their services or they will accept as a fee whatever the family can afford.

Gallbladder Disease

An inflamed gallbladder and the gallstones affecting the gallbladder and the bile tubes are common troublemakers.

The usual treatment for acute gallbladder disease is to remove the gallbladder and any stones that may be found in the tubes that carry bile from the liver to the intestine, as well as to and from the gallbladder. This is the usual treatment but frequently variations are necessary.

THE PATIENT'S DECISION

Since each person's medical history is unique, individualized treatment is essential. The surgeon recommends what the treatment should be. His advice is based on studying his patient's history, physical examination, laboratory tests, and X rays in terms of his understanding of this disease and his experience with it.

An operation will not be performed without your consent, but the recommendation of your surgeon should be given careful consideration. His training and experience qualify him to best evaluate your health needs. If you are not completely satisfied with your physician's evaluation—get another opinion.

IS SURGERY ALWAYS NECESSARY?

In some cases an operation may not be necessary. In some cases gallbladder disease may be controlled for a while with medicine and special diets.

Generally, however, a patient with gallbladder disease sooner or later must have his gallbladder removed.

DELAY OF SURGERY?

Some patients may experience an attack of gallbladder pain for a few days, then later appear to be quite well. During this well period a patient may decide not to follow his physician's advice. Such delay may be unwise, since the disease may then damage surrounding tissues. If gallstones are present, delay could lead to plugging of the bile tubes by these stones, a condition requiring emergency surgery.

EMERGENCY OPERATIONS

A dangerously ill patient may require an emergency operation that merely drains the gallbladder. For some other patients the surgeon may remove the gallbladder and any existing gallstones. An operation on a dangerously ill person naturally involves more risk than one performed in the more or less "well" period between attacks.

Very ill patients may require more than one operation. Some patients are too ill to undergo the immediate removal of the gallbladder. In such cases the only possible operation is to open and drain the gallbladder and then at a later date remove the diseased organ.

Approximately 10 percent of the U.S. population has gallstones. Stones are more common in Caucasians, Mexicans and Indians than in Negroes and Orientals. They also are more common in women than in men, especially in fat women and those who have had pregnancies.

THE TROUBLED GALLBLADDER

The physician uses a number of methods to identify the gallbladder and the bile ducts as the site of a patient's trouble. Among these are laboratory and X-ray tests, jaundice or yellowing of the skin and the location and character of the pain. Your physician will study all of these factors as well as other signs or symptoms he may observe to determine what treatment is needed.

The patient with gallbladder disease may experience some or all of a variety of signs and symptoms including pain, swelling and tenderness in the abdomen, jaundice, indigestion, vomiting and a loss of appetite. Usually patients experience a combination of these disturbances. They may occur at any time of day but discomfort is most often felt after meals, especially after heavy meals containing fat and fried foods.

IN BRIEF

Gallbladder disease is not uncommon. A chronically infected gallbladder usually is not functioning and is filled with stones. When acutely inflamed it may become a surgical emergency. Gallstones are prone to cause emergencies by obstructing the neck of the gallbladder or the bile ducts, which results in jaundice and liver damage. Chronic inflammation in a stone-filled gallbladder may lead to cancer of the gallbladder.

There sometimes are good reasons for not performing surgery at any particular time, but almost all patients with gallbladder inflammation or gallstones will eventually need surgical removal of the offending gallbladder.

CREDIT: *American Medical Association.*

Gambling

Billions of dollars—exactly how many no one knows for sure—are lost annually on crap tables, roulette wheels, slot machines, at race tracks, dog tracks, around poker tables, mah-jongg tables, at bingo, bridge, backgammon, checkers and chess. Some people will bet on whether the sun will rise tomorrow.

All too often the people who can least afford to lose are the ones who do it. It's the rent money, the kids' shoes, the wife's dental work, the grocery bill, etc.

Here are a few samples from last week's mail:

"We are drowning in debt but he can't stay away from the track. Last week he lost his whole paycheck. He promised—'No more. I've had it.' Well he's gone again today."

"She's hooked on bingo and there's nothing I can do to keep her from going to the games. It's every night—and she has to play four cards at a time."

"He makes a good living but loses everything on the crap tables. I've cried, begged and pleaded, but it doesn't do any good."

"If it's not mah-jongg, it's canasta or bridge or pam. That woman can't stay away from the cards. We'll be eating hot dogs and hamburgers for two weeks."

"His poker losses have kept us broke. And it's got him in with bad company. He plays with a very crummy bunch of guys. I think they are racketeers and I'm worried sick."

And so it goes. Week after week I get these heartbreaking letters. I'm convinced that gamblers, like alcoholics, are powerless against the compulsion they know will ruin them.

There's a streak of self-destruction in these people—along with the thrill of risk-taking. They need help as surely as the alcoholic. The following letter and my answer will tell you what you need to know if you or someone close to you has the problem.

DEAR ANN LANDERS: I am a compulsive gambler and a member of Gamblers Anonymous. I read about this wonderful group in your column eight years ago, went to a meeting and have not gambled a penny's worth since.

Please tell your readers again about Gamblers Anonymous, Ann. It is a unique fellowship of men and women who share their experiences and their strength in an effort to solve a common problem. It costs nothing to join. The only requirement is the desire to quit gambling.

I hope you will print my letter, Ann. Millions of people need help, and they don't know what to do or where to turn. You can tell them. Sign me   SAM G.

DEAR SAM G.: May I add a word? Any reader who flunks the Gamblers Anonymous test (see article on Pathological or Compulsive Gambling) is invited to write to the National Headquarters of Gamblers Anonymous, P. O. Box 17173, Los Angeles, California 90017, for information on how to join your local chapter.

This group has performed miracles and changed thousands of lives. It has my solid backing.

CREDIT: *Ann Landers.*

Gambling

(*Pathological or Compulsive*)

Compulsive gambling is a behavior disorder which disrupts or destroys the gambler's personal life, family relationships, or vocational pursuits.

To understand compulsive gamblers, one needs to know what other types of gamblers there are. There appear to be four broad, distinguishable categories of gamblers, with some overlapping. In order of frequency, they are:

The social gambler—the most common and the widest variability of gambling behavior.

The compulsive gambler.

The antisocial (criminal) gambler.

The professional gambler, the least common type.

The social gambler gambles for recreation. He pays for his entertainment —sometimes he wins but most often he loses. Once the gambling ceases to be pleasurable (or becomes too painful) he stops and returns to more satisfying or less uncomfortable behavior. He knows he is playing a game and he has a totally separate life. He may wish to return to gambling but his sense of balance steers him to activities that provide him with a sense of achievement and comfort.

How much money, or the amount of time spent on gambling, has very little bearing on whether or not a person is a compulsive gambler. The reason a person gambles is the determining factor. Amounts of time and money are minor indicators, but more revealing is what they don't do in regard to family, work and interpersonal relationships.

Social gamblers do not disrupt other areas of their life with their gambling. The professional gambler approaches gambling as a business. He receives gratification only if he wins. He is a student of the game, highly disciplined, patient, and receives little pleasure from gambling except for winning. He analyzes his losses and learns from them. He accepts losses as a part of his business. Professional gamblers invariably have other business interests.

The antisocial (criminal) who gambles has certain unique characteristics. He will cheat whenever possible. He will do anything to win. He believes his losses are the result of someone's cheating. If he wants money for gambling, he will take it in any manner possible with no intention of repaying it. Losing stimulates blaming and violence. He rarely has any feelings of remorse or guilt. He has been in trouble with the authorities virtually all of his life.

The compulsive gambler gambles to minimize discomfort and for pleasure. Gambling or the anticipation of gambling gives him excitement as well as an escape from the discomfort. Winning, of course, is the objective—not so he can keep what is won but to assure him of continued gambling. There is no fun, relaxation, or recreation as with the social gambler. The compulsive gambler cannot stop. His life centers around gambling. Other aspects of his life gradually diminish in importance. Ultimately, other aspects of his life become intolerable and devoid of emotional concern and response. With heavy losses, there is depression and remorse. The only way he can get relief is to return to gambling. The consequences become insignificant. Gambling has become his world—his reason for existence. To not gamble means despair because he feels he cannot exist without gambling. The compulsive gambler develops an irrational optimism which is based on previous big wins and bailouts. Big wins produce an exciting expectation. The compulsive gambler is protected from reality by any friend or relative who is foolish enough to pay off all of his debts on the promise that he will stop gambling. This gives him the illusion that nothing painful can really happen to him.

Here is a composite picture of a compulsive gambler as he might appear when he asks for help:

A male in his thirties who is without any financial resources. He is deeply in debt to banks, loan companies, credit card companies, friends, business associates, and family. He is behind in mortgage payments, car payments, utility payments. He has no life insurance, disability insurance, or hospitalization insurance. The family's basic needs are provided by parents, welfare, or income from the wife's employment. His employment is lost due to absences, inefficiency, irresponsibility, or theft. He has lost his business due to legal action by unpaid creditors. He may have a history of bankruptcy in the past.

His wife is regularly threatening divorce. She complains about the family's deprivation, persistent calls from creditors and his lack of communication. There are discipline problems with the children. He must avoid encounters with most acquaintances due to unpaid loans. He is away from home for prolonged unexplained periods of time. Siblings are alienated as are his parents, who have possibly paid off his debts at least once. There is threatened or real prosecution for unpaid loans, IRS demands, forgery, or theft.

He sleeps poorly, eats irregularly, and is indifferent toward sexual activity. He is drinking alcohol more. He and his family have no social life. He is tense, irritable, critical, and not concerned about his personal appearance. He has thought of suicide, of running out on his family. He spends most of his time frantically searching out sources of money. He thinks about gambling constantly. He gambles and loses regularly. If he should win, he does not pay debts except those from illegal sources.

He doesn't want to admit his losses. He dreams of the big win, the only comfort for his depression. The tension increases and the desperation drives him on. His only relief from the pressure is gambling.

One out of four will deny a gambling problem at this point.

The study and treatment of compulsive gambling is perhaps one of the most intriguing but also one of the most neglected problems of human behavior. Gambling is generally accepted as a recreational activity although it is closely linked to the attitudes, folkways, symbols, mores, taboos and laws of culture and subculture.

Nothing will stop the compulsive gambler, unless the environmental pain becomes greater than the internal pain. Once the environmental pain is gone, so is the stimulus for stopping. The environmental pain can make the compulsive gambler stop for short periods of time, but he cannot stay stopped unless he develops satisfying substitutes for the feeling that gambling provides.

Punishment is ineffective since it rarely is as painful as the personal internal discomfort. Punishment also provides no substitute. The rehabilitation of the compulsive gambler is like a three-cornered stool: (1) stop gambling, (2) make restitution and (3) get treatment.

If he does not stop gambling, he cannot think straight, moreover he is unable to learn, grow, solve problems, or make decisions. If he does not make emotional and financial restitution, he has no true remorse. He is actually encouraged to be irresponsible if he does not make restitution.

Treatment is directed toward the search and finding of adequate substitutes for the feelings and escapes which gambling had tried but failed to provide. Without the use of all three of these legs, the compulsive gambler remains exceedingly vulnerable.

The compulsive gambler, unlike the social gambler, has to gamble—it is not a game and he is not just playing. The compulsive gambler, unlike the professional gambler, doesn't want control, he wants relief. The compulsive gambler, unlike the criminal who gambles, doesn't want to hurt others, he cares what others think about him.

The compulsive gambler goes to great lengths to prove he is not a compulsive gambler, that he is in control. As with other aspects of his life, he is constantly acting as a defense attorney in his own behalf. The compulsive gambler gradually develops a distinct lifestyle that marks him. He is not only a stress seeker, he becomes a stress creator—in relation to his family, his work, and his friends. He takes irrational risks. He takes chances with his family's affection, his employer's consideration, and his friends' kindness. He exaggerates, distorts and lies—as weapons of self-defense.

He demands honesty, trust, loyalty, affection, praise, appreciation and admiration. In return, he gives criticism to others for not doing more or not understanding. As the compulsive gambler becomes more and more alienated from his family, friends and work associates, his life values become less and less stable.

Life risks increase until these values are compromised and he commits acts which are alien to his basic value system. Unfortunately, he does not recognize that his course is clearly destructive so he becomes more reckless, which leads to more senseless gambling. The process is progressive and accelerates at a frantic pace. He begins to think of suicide as a way to "get away from it all."

The compulsive gambler is not the only victim. His spouse suffers—also his children, his parents, friends, employer and society.

The climb back is excruciatingly painful, humiliating, depressing and discouraging—and it takes time. The mere cessation of gambling is only the beginning. He must earn the respect of himself and others by a responsible and realistic approach to life. The only one who can more fully understand and share this burden is a recovering compulsive gambler. The compulsive gambler himself must make the decision that he needs help. He must admit that he cannot do it alone. Compassionate and knowledgeable others, like Gamblers Anonymous members, make the irresistible resistible—by offering an alternative approach to life.

The interview data, observations, and psychological testing indicate that compulsive gambling provides an escape or relief from underlying psychic pain. The intensity of the gambling in respect to its psychological impact was made apparent when compulsive gamblers who stopped experienced physical symptoms such as cold sweats, tremor, headache, abdominal pain, diarrhea, confusion and insomnia that persisted for about one week. The pattern and duration of withdrawal symptoms were similar to the withdrawal symptoms seen during mild to moderate alcohol detoxification.

The psychological and sociological data further suggested that the compulsive gambler experienced some deprivation throughout his childhood and adolescence and frequently had a model of pain avoidance such as alcoholism or compulsive gambling within the family. He also had early exposure to a strong money ethic and an availability to gambling activities especially through and with his peers. Most compulsive gamblers began in legal gambling establishments before reaching the legal age.

Of approximately 250 compulsive gamblers interviewed, the following demographic, psychological, physical and social characteristics were found:

1. AGE:
Range   16 to 53 years of age
Average   38 years of age

2. SEX:
Male   94%
Female   6%

3. NATIONALITY BACKGROUND:
Jewish
Italian
Irish
Black   90%
Puerto Rican
Oriental
Other   10%

4. RELIGION:
Jewish   30%
Catholic   42%
Protestant   25%
Other   3%

5. MARITAL STATUS:

Married	52%
Divorced	16%
Separated	16%
Single	16%

6. EMPLOYED:

Yes	80%
No	20%

7. MILITARY SERVICE:

Veterans	52%
Non-veterans	48%

8. EDUCATION:

Less than High School Graduate	8%
High School Graduate	60%
Some College	22%
College Graduate	10%
Average 2 years College	

9. AGE:

First Gambled	12
First Won or Lost $20 Gambling	18

10. FAMILY HISTORY OF SUICIDE:

Yes	8%
No	92%

11. FAMILY HISTORY OF ALCOHOLISM OR COMPULSIVE GAMBLING:

Yes	32%
No	68%

12. LOSS OF PARENT BEFORE AGE 15:

Yes	17%
No	83%

13. AGE AT ONSET OF GAMBLING:

Before age 21	96%
After age 21	4%

14. SERIOUS SUICIDAL THOUGHTS:
Yes   36%
No   64%

15. HISTORY OF SUICIDE ATTEMPTS:
Yes   20%
No   80%

16. CONSIDERED SELF COMPETITIVE:
Yes   92%
No   8%

17. CONSIDERED SELF ATHLETIC:
Ycs   62%
No   38%

18. HIGH ENERGY LEVEL:
Yes   79%
No   21%

19. ADMITTED TO COMMITTING A CRIME:
Yes   53%
No   47%

20. ARRESTS:
Yes   23%
No   77%

21. IMPRISONED:
Yes   9%
No   91%

22. DECLARE BANKRUPTCY:
Yes   21%
No   79%

23. WON AN AMOUNT EQUAL TO ANNUAL SALARY:
Yes   44%
No   56%

24. HAD A BAIL-OUT (someone who paid his debts
    on the promise that he would quit gambling)
    Yes   91%
    No   9%

25. DID GAMBLING CAUSE FAMILY PROBLEMS:
    Yes   99%
    No   1%

26. BORROW MONEY FROM ILLEGAL SOURCES:
    Yes   50%
    No   50%

27. BRAG THAT WINNING MONEY WHEN ACTUALLY
    LOSING:
    Yes   75%
    No   25%

28. DEFAULT ON DEBTS:
    Yes   66%
    No   34%

29. LOST A JOB BECAUSE OF GAMBLING:
    Yes   60%
    No   40%

30. PREFERRED FORMS OF GAMBLING:
    Horse Racing   20%
    Harness Racing   15%
    Sports Betting   21%
    Card Games   23%
    Dice   15%
    Dog Racing   2%
    Bingo   1%
    Other   3%

GAMBLERS ANONYMOUS

There is no question that GA has been responsible for the effective treatment of more compulsive gamblers than any other method—social, religious,
or medical.

GA is a voluntary fellowship of compulsive gamblers gathered for the sole
purpose of helping themselves and each other to stop gambling and stay

stopped. It is not involved in any movement to combat or restrict gambling in general. GA espouses no causes, not even causes designed to help compulsive gamblers. This policy does not, however, restrict its individual members from becoming involved in community activities or services concerned with compulsive gamblers. In fact, GA members are often in the leadership of such activities.

There are, at this time, 206 chapters of GA in the United States, 11 in Canada, 59 in the United Kingdom (which includes England, Ireland, Scotland and Wales). There are also groups in Australia, Belgium, Brazil, New Zealand, Israel and Japan.

There is only one condition for membership in GA—being a compulsive gambler who wants to stop gambling. Membership is never solicited—but when it is asked for it is given unstintingly. There is an absolute principle, however: direction to GA can be given by anyone, but this help is given only at the request of the compulsive gambler. GA is effective because it: (1) undercuts denial ("I am not a compulsive gambler"); (2) undercuts projection ("Everybody drives me to gambling"); (3) undercuts rationalization ("I really don't gamble too much"); (4) identifies the serious realistic implications of gambling; (5) demands honesty; (6) demands responsibility for the person to do something about it; (7) identifies and corrects character defects; (8) gives affection, personal concern and support; (9) develops substitutes for the void left by stopping gambling; and (10) is non-judgmental.

Gam-Anon is a fellowship for the families of compulsive gamblers. Families of compulsive gamblers have found living with a compulsive gambler to be a devastating experience. With Gam-Anon, they learn to cope with problems in the face of disaster. They hope to and do accomplish many things. They understand the compulsive gambler. They learn to talk out feelings and deal with guilt. They do things for others, set priorities, learn to plan, and by so doing, see that some of their own needs are met. It is a place where they are understood.

Gam-Anon is the largest and most effective group to be of help to GA— and it is the most effective group to help the families of compulsive gamblers.

Gam-Anon is the most effective group, outside of GA, to attract compulsive gamblers to GA—and to retain GA members.

The family in GA learns how *not* to hinder the GA members' recovery and growth. They must learn that they can hinder the compulsive gambler's recovery but they are not the reason he gambles. It is a fact that a family member can drive the compulsive gambler *toward* gambling—but the compulsive gambler himself must assume the responsibility for the decision to return to gambling.

Gam-Ateen is a fellowship for the children of compulsive gamblers.

Gamblers Anonymous has a list of twenty questions which will assist a person in learning whether or not he/she is a compulsive gambler. Anyone who answers "yes" to seven of these questions is probably a compulsive gambler.

The following are the questions and how known compulsive gamblers frequently answer them.

		Yes	No
(1)	Do you lose time from work due to gambling?	85%	15%
(2)	Is gambling making your home life unhappy?	99%	1%
(3)	Is gambling affecting your reputation?	93%	7%
(4)	Have you ever felt remorse after gambling?	99%	1%
(5)	Do you ever gamble to get money with which to pay debts or to otherwise solve financial difficulties?	93%	7%
(6)	Does gambling cause a decrease in your ambition or efficiency?	94%	6%
(7)	After losing, do you feel you must return as soon as possible and win back your losses?	97%	3%
(8)	After a win, do you have a strong urge to return and win more?	98%	2%
(9)	Do you often gamble until your last dollar is gone?	97%	3%
(10)	Do you ever borrow to finance your gambling?	99%	1%
(11)	Have you ever sold any real or personal property to finance your gambling?	79%	21%
(12)	Are you reluctant to use "gambling money"?	93%	7%
(13)	Does gambling make you careless of the welfare of your family?	94%	6%
(14)	Do you ever gamble longer than you had planned?	98%	2%
(15)	Do you ever gamble to escape worry or trouble?	92%	8%
(16)	Have you ever committed or considered committing an illegal act to finance gambling?	86%	14%
(17)	Does gambling cause you to have difficulty sleeping?	72%	28%
(18)	Do arguments, disappointments, or frustrations create within you an urge to gamble?	92%	8%
(19)	Do you have an urge to celebrate any good fortune by a few hours of gambling?	84%	16%
(20)	Is gambling, especially winning, an ego-building activity?	96%	4%

NATIONAL COUNCIL ON COMPULSIVE GAMBLING, INC.

The NCCG, Inc., represents one of the major accomplishments in the efforts to help the compulsive gambler since the birth of GA on September 13, 1957. The Council was established on December 8, 1972, and incorporated as a voluntary, non-profit agency on May 6, 1975.

This Council was organized to disseminate information and education on compulsive gambling as an illness and public health problem.

It seeks to stimulate the concern of the medical profession, educators, legislators and the criminal justice system in the nationwide problem of gambling by supplying community services and medical treatment for compulsive gamblers—and their families.

Information about compulsive gambling can be obtained through the National Council on Compulsive Gambling, Inc., 142 East 29th Street, New York, New York 10016; telephone (212) 686-6160.

CREDIT: *Robert L. Custer, M.D., Chief Treatment Services Division, Mental Health and Behavioral Sciences Service, Veterans Administration, Washington, D.C.*

Gardening

How to Care for Favorite Flowers and Plants

> The Kiss of the Sun for Pardon
> The Song of the Birds for Mirth
> One is nearer God's heart in a Garden
> Than anywhere else on Earth.

There are so many different and interesting hobbies, but as I or any other gardener will testify, there is none as delightful or rewarding as tending flowers and plants. Rewarding is the key word. Other hobbies can be fun, but when the needlepoint pillow is finished, your work is done; when the painting is completed, your work is done; when the game is over, your work is done; but in the garden, your work is never done. You are creating and caring for a living thing—a work of art in its own right.

Having a plant or garden is like having a good and loyal friend. The fabulous thing is that absolutely anyone can do it. Gardening is a joy to those who are lonely, relaxing to those who are nervous, and a lesson for those who are always in a hurry. You can't rush Mother Nature! Her seasons come and go as they please—not even politicians can tamper with the seasons. Caring for plants and flowers demands discipline, but they will return all the love and attention you give them. If you help them grow, they will never disappoint you.

Gardening can be done on many different levels. If you are out in the country and have an acre plot, you have a variety of choices, but if you are a city dweller with just a tiny ray of sunshine peeking through an apartment window, you must choose carefully.

One of the easiest flowers to grow inside is the African violet. It doesn't need full sun or a lot of water. Speaking of water, most house plants need very little—especially in the winter. At least a million plants are drowned annually by overenthusiastic "caretakers." Remember, plants are not fish! Watering twice a week is plenty. A neat trick that I use for watering my house plants is to drop three or four ice cubes into each pot twice a week. The plants seem to love this slow, seeping method of nourishment.

Temperature is important too. Most house plants do best when the temperature is between 60 and 70 degrees. If the room is too warm, some plants will become annoyed (and stubborn) and simply refuse to bloom.

Another lovely house plant—one of my favorites—is the geranium. It comes in so many different sizes, shapes, and delightful fragrances. There is a geranium to please every eye and every nose! Like most plants, after blooming all summer long, the geranium will need to take a rest. Don't worry, there are flowers for every time of year.

The beginning of autumn is the time for chrysanthemums. They are one of the few house plants that really love water. They have a tendency to dry out, so do water them *a little* every day—enough to keep the soil moist. The minute a chrysanthemum gets thirsty, he'll tell you. His leaves become limp and he starts to wilt. The chrysanthemum, like all flowers, does not like to be in a draft.

As you move through the fall on towards Christmas, your flowers can become more festive. The amaryllis comes in gay oranges, reds, and even stripes. The poinsettia, which has become the symbol of Christmas, comes in lovely shades of pink, red, and white. After Christmas, you have your bulbs; narcissus, crocus, daffodils, tulips, and hyacinths. Most of these bulbs are pre-potted when you buy them, with explicit instructions on every package. Things have become so easy today! Just unwrap the plant, water a little, put it in a sunny window, and sit back and watch it grow. These bulbs will bloom clear through spring and then it's time for your geraniums to start again.

For those of you with outdoor gardens, I have a few tips on cutting and keeping your flowers fresh. All flowers will last longer if picked in the early morning when the dew is still on them. The rose needs special attention when being cut. It should always be cut at an angle just above the stem which has five leaves. This way, a new shoot will sprout from where you have cut and your rose blooms will increase. Just after cutting, pull off the leaves and plunge the roses up to their necks in lukewarm water for a few hours. This should help them last for several weeks.

When you cut hollyhocks, put Clorox in the water (a tablespoon of Clorox to a quart of water). It also helps to pound the bottom two inches of the stem with a hammer. The water can then seep in more easily.

If poppies are your flowers, be sure to burn the bottom two inches of the stems before putting them in water (use either a cigarette lighter or a gas stove). You will be amazed at how much longer they will last.

One last gardening lesson—anyone who has an outdoor garden should realize that he or she has a double responsibility. Not only must the flowers be cared for—so must the birds! How lonely the garden would be without a bird! Put up a bird feeder, or just sprinkle some seeds around and see what a lively and popular spot your garden becomes. You can bring beauty and happiness to yourself and others through gardening. It will help you realize and appreciate how truly exquisite nature is.

Happy gardening.

CREDIT: *C. Z. Guest, Palm Beach, author of* First Garden (*paperback*), *New York: Chelsea House. C. Z. Guest and Elvin MacDonald,* Weekly Garden Planner, *New York: Chelsea House.*

Gay Bars

Most homosexual persons—about nine out of ten, according to a recent study—have never seen the inside of one, but the gay bar has become the institutional symbol as a major recreational and social institution. So successful are the bars that in larger cities "superbars" are opening which draw not only gay crowds by the hundreds, but almost as many straight customers, eager to capitalize on the farthest-out variety of "radical chic." A city the size of Los Angeles, New York, or Chicago can support several superbars and as many as one hundred or more regular gay bars.

Most gay bars are pleasant places, more so than the majority of straight and "singles" bars. They are less violent, more congenial, livelier, and in better repair. Many have restaurants and a place to dance. Some are raunchy, others discriminate against straights or even other gays, depending on whether a bar caters to the S&M (sado-masochistic) crowd, "cowboys," lesbians, blacks, Puerto Ricans, or just males. Lesbian bars tend to be smaller and less elaborate than male bars, partly because fewer lesbians make the bar scene, and partly because the real money and power in the gay world are in male hands.

The main function of the gay bar is to provide an open environment for drinking, mixing, cruising (looking for partners), and often dancing and other forms of entertainment. Gay bars are, of course, moneymaking enterprises and most do well.

While gay bars may be a mecca for lonely homosexuals, it must be remembered they are first of all bars, and alcoholism can become a serious problem if a bar becomes the focal point of one's social life. Further, despite the recreational benefits bars provide, they are intended to be cruising grounds and thus contribute to promiscuity.

The pressure exerted by the need to appear young and attractive, in addition to the "mating rites," sexual competition, frustration and loneliness, make the bars a highly mixed bag for gays attempting to create a lifestyle of integrity and dignity.

CREDIT: *Richard Woods, author of* Another Kind of Love, *Chicago, Illinois: Thomas More Associates.*

Gay Couples

(*Legal Options*)

Same-sex couples are not recognized as legally married, therefore their legal relationship is often characterized as "strangers" to each other under the law. Gay couples do not benefit from the tax advantages of joint tax returns. They have none of the property ownership protections and inheritance tax reductions offered other "families."

Since gay surviving spouses have no legal standing as heirs, it is absolutely essential that gay couples protect each other with mutual and reciprocal wills in which they name each other as the executors and beneficiaries of their estates. Having no community property rights or dower estate interests in each other's property, generally gay couples should own their property in some form of joint ownership.

A surviving joint tenant property owner succeeds to the decedent's share of joint tenancy property outside of probate. But ask your attorney if this is the law in your state. Some states restrict the survivorship rights of joint tenants to spouses and heirs at law. By contrast, tenants in common do not have survivorship rights and the decedent's share goes to the beneficiaries under a will or the heirs at law if the decedent dies intestate; that is, without a will. Moreover, in the absence of a will, all personal property not jointly owned, including cash, bank accounts, and securities, goes to the heirs at law, i.e., the "relatives." Proof of joint ownership of personal property can be a difficult, tedious, and emotionally distressing task. Therefore, even when property is jointly owned, a will is still essential. It not only guarantees the proper succession of the decedent's property, but it places the so-called "stranger" spouse in charge as the executor of the estate.

Gay couples can provide protection for each other with life insurance policies. They can specifically name each other as the beneficiary of the policies and thereby keep the insurance proceeds out of probate, which will save on probate fees (*not* to be confused with inheritance taxes). If, however, they are hesitant to name a non-related "stranger" as beneficiary of a fringe benefit policy at their place of employment, they can name their "estate" as the beneficiary and then bequeath the proceeds in their will to their surviving gay spouse. The tax ramifications are generally the same either way and most states provide substantial exemptions for insurance proceeds.

To handle ongoing legal and business matters in the event of an emergency or absence of the other, gay couples should execute reciprocal general powers of attorney to each other. If this involves banks or government checks, it should likewise be duplicated on their prescribed forms.

The inheritance tax rates of most states are based upon the blood or marital relationship of the beneficiaries to the decedent. Since gay spouses are neither, but are "strangers" by category, they find themselves in the highest-taxed and lowest-exempt category—taxed several times higher than their straight married counterparts. On the federal side of the estate tax coin, the results are largely the same, but are arrived at somewhat differently. Surviving spouses get whopping federal marital deductions of one half of the taxable estate or as much as $250,000 deduction—whichever is greater! Gay widows and widowers receive no such tax break.

Even if a gay person is so fortunate as to have owned their property jointly, and is thereby protected from greedy and long-lost "relatives," the death tax burden remains. In most states, jointly owned property is presumed by the taxing authorities to be owned entirely by the decedent—and, therefore, fully taxed to the survivor. Unless capable of adequately documenting the proof of contribution to the acquisition and upkeep of the property, the survivor faces the classic inequity of paying to inherit back one's own property.

In cases of long-established stable relationships, couples might consider adult adoptions of each other. This effectively changes the relationship from "stranger" to "parental." This not only gives them a legal relationship to each other, but in most states will reduce the inheritance tax bite by moving it to a lower-taxed "family" category. However, most states require adult adoptions to be in effect several years before they reduce inheritance taxes. One final warning about adoptions—they are difficult, if not impossible, to undo. So they should be reserved for only the most stable and time-tested of relationships.

Purchasing a home together is often more difficult for gay couples because lending institutions most often refuse to recognize the combined incomes of both persons for the loan qualification. Since the marital nature of the relationship is not recognized, the lenders consider the "friendship" too tenuous to support a loan. In light of the soaring divorce rates, the illogic of this irrationale is indeed ironic.

Once a home is purchased, gay couples find themselves deprived of "head of household" and "husband and wife" advantages offered to homeowners by many states. For example, creditor's exemptions and property protections such as "homesteads" are often *twice* as great for married couples as for "unmarried" joint property owners.

When those "irreconcilable differences" arise, and a gay couple decides to dissolve their relationship, they may be faced with a myriad of complex legal machinations which make the divorce courts look like kindergarten by comparison. A gay dissolution involving family assets requires imaginative, difficult, and often long-drawn-out legal maneuverings involving potential law suits over property rights, dissolving partnerships (actual and de facto), joint tenancy partition actions, and damages from breach of implied contracts.

Retirement benefit plans and medical plans provide for various protections and benefits for spouses, but not for an unmarried life partner. Likewise, there are no special reduced premiums for gay spouses on home mortgage insurance premiums, nor extended insurance coverage upon the death of the principal insured family member.

Gay spouses have no standing to sue in wrongful death suits and no recoverable damages for loss of consortium of an injured spouse. Needless to say, gay surviving spouses are denied Social Security and V.A. survivor's benefits. They are likewise denied company family benefits—ranging all the way from the proverbial vacation in Hawaii to family night at the movies!

CREDIT: *Al Smithson, attorney at law, San Diego, California.*

Gay Marriages

The Metropolitan Community Church of San Diego offers a religious ceremony called the "Rite of Holy Union" to same-sex couples under the following conditions:

(1) The couple is required to have *lived* together under the same roof for a *minimum* period of six months to one year.

A same-sex couple who have chosen to share each other's lives and who have lived together in an atmosphere of mutual love and respect for a period of six months to one year have demonstrated their ability to communicate, adjust and compromise in order to preserve their relationship.

(2) The couple must participate in counseling sessions with the minister to determine their understanding of the seriousness of such a step and to ascertain as nearly as possible the stability and mutuality of their relationship as well as the depth and nature of their commitment to each other.

The same-sex couple, in counseling sessions with their minister or pastor, are often able to pinpoint potential problem areas in their relationship and to determine to what extent they are willing and/or able to cope with them. In addition, they are often able to verbalize and thus better define for themselves the exact nature of their commitment.

(3) The minister must be satisfied that the couple understand that this religious ceremony has *no legal significance*.

The same-sex couple, in recognizing the absence of *legal* significance, will understand that the only acceptable motive for entering into this ceremony is to seek God's Blessing and Presence in their lives and in their relationship. Further, they will not be misled into believing that the legal rights and privileges that accrue to opposite-sex couples in "marriage" are being automatically conferred upon them. They should be advised of various *legal* steps which may be taken to protect their mutual interests.

(4) The minister and the couple must have a mutual understanding that the Rite of Holy Union is a means of asking God's Blessing upon their relationship and a public declaration before God, minister, witnesses and friends of the nature of their feelings towards each other.

The Rite of Holy Union is taken very seriously by our Church (the Metropolitan Community Church Of San Diego, California). It is not to be entered into capriciously. It is, in fact, a Service of Worship, in which prayers are offered, vows are exchanged and a Blessing is given. Therefore, every possible effort is made to ensure that all parties concerned approach the service with attitudes of respect and reverence.

(5) The minister should be certain that the couple understand that this ceremony does not bind them together "until death do us part" but is valid only so long as mutual love exists between them.

The soaring divorce rate in our country might lead one to believe that "marriage" is often entered into lightly, or, at best, prematurely. The climate of testimony in divorce cases sometimes seems to indicate that one or both parties have misunderstood the intent of marriage and have viewed it as a means of "tying up" or "binding" another human being to them regardless of later circumstances.

Partners in Holy Union must understand that *mutual* love and respect and a willingness to share each other's lives are *essential* to maintain a productive and rewarding relationship. The absence of this mutuality may cause the relationship to become unrewarding, if not actually *destructive,* to both parties. We believe that in such cases a termination of the relationship serves the best interests of the human beings involved. Therefore, we allow for a "Dissolution of Holy Union" after counseling with the minister reveals that the essential elements to a Christian partnership/union are no longer present. The trauma of "guilt trips" arising from having vowed before God to remain together "until death do us part" is thus avoided. We maintain that *love* is the only bond which *truly* unites people in the sight of God.

It is significant to note that the Rite of Holy Union is in no way a parody of the institution of marriage. Obviously, there is no intent of procreation, and likewise, no legal recognition of the union exists (at least not at this point in history).

Why have it then?

For years, homosexual or "gay" people have been subject to argument that they are overly promiscuous and are unwilling or *unable* to form stable relationships. These arguments are advanced despite the fact that our religious institutions and our political/governmental structure have consistently denied them any of the legal, societal and, perhaps especially, religious support systems upon which heterosexual marriages absolutely depend for stability or permanence.

We assert that the Rite of Holy Union, i.e., the seeking and acceptance of the Blessing and Presence of God in relationships of same-sex couples, adds an importance of spiritual dimension to their lives. This added spiritual dimension, along with the supportive fellowship of other Christian gay couples, singles and understanding heterosexual friends, relatives, etc., has already begun to demonstrate a stabilizing influence on many Christian gay unions. The knowledge that God's Love, Strength and Grace are available to them is an important beginning toward the building of supportive systems for gay couples and toward a truly Christian understanding of the homosexual in today's society.

CREDIT: *The Reverend David Farrell, Pastor, Metropolitan Community Church of San Diego, San Diego, California.*

Germs

DEAR ANN: I'm the mother of two young children. My neighbor has three. Her kids are permitted to go barefoot from May to October. Of course their noses run constantly. They are never without colds.

My two children caught measles from them last year. At present they are both ill with chicken pox, which they got next door.

I dress my youngsters properly and do everything within my power to keep them well. But it seems hopeless with the kids next door sneezing and coughing on them.

The situation is very touchy because they are great pals. I'd start a war if I suggested they not play together. Please tell me what to do. I keep praying the neighbor kids don't get leprosy or polio because if they did our kids would surely get it, too.   DISTRAUGHT DOLLY

DEAR D.D.: The world is filled with germs of every imaginable type. The best protection against illness is ample rest, proper food and normal precautions. When you know the neighbor children have severe colds insist that yours stay away from them.

Stop worrying about leprosy. Chances for the neighbor kids getting it are very slim. Leprosy is one of the least contagious of all diseases. As for polio, the Sabin vaccine has produced a virtual miracle. It doesn't guarantee 100 percent protection, but it offers a high degree of immunity.

You can't raise children under a glass bell. See that they get sufficient rest, wholesome food and are inoculated against polio, smallpox, diphtheria, measles, mumps, whooping cough and rubella.

Gossip

DEAR ANN LANDERS: Our sixteen-year-old daughter is a nervous wreck and my husband is so burned up he can't see straight. Three weeks ago someone started the ugly rumor that Janet is pregnant.

There is absolutely no truth to this vicious story but once something like this gets loose, it's impossible to trace it—or stop it. Janet wants to change schools. She says everyone stares a hole through her and she just dies when she sees them whispering behind her back.

My husband feels we should go to the principal and ask for permission to transfer her to another one on the other side of town. Janet would prefer to leave town. She could go to live with her married sister, who has a nice home about 70 miles from here. We await your counsel. DAYTON PARENTS

DEAR PARENTS: The best way to prove the story is a lie is to have Janet stay right where she is—and maintain a perfect attendance record. To allow her to leave town and run from the gossip would suggest that it might be true.

SURGEON 'CUTS' HIS PATIENT'S NOSEY FRIEND

DEAR ANN LANDERS: A woman I've known for years told me she couldn't attend my dinner party next week because she's going to the hospital. When I asked what for she replied, "A little surgery." I asked what kind of surgery and she answered curtly "minor," and changed the subject.

This brushoff over my deep concern for her welfare made me so mad I called her doctor, who happens to be a social friend also. I asked him what was wrong with Mrs. So and So.

The doctor insulted me by saying it was none of my business and that it was pretty nosey of me to call him. This cut me deeply, as we are all good friends.

I'd like you to tell me, Ann Landers, why in the world should a person be ashamed of having an operation?
FRIENDSHIP UNRETURNED

DEAR UNRETURNED: Some people take pleasure in regaling one and all with details of their poor health. They are happy to give an organ recital to anyone who will listen.

People of taste and judgment, however, consider such conversation brutally boring. They spare their friends.

You were rude to press for details of the type of operation when your friend volunteered none. And phoning the doctor to pump him for information was indefensible gall. You earned whatever sharp criticism he ladled out.

DEAR ANN: Love you. Love your column. Heard you speak in Huntington, Long Island, and can attest to the fact that you are a Dynamite Lady. Let there be no mistake about it. I'm on your side. But I wonder if you have a clear picture of what your column is all about? Your response to "Tell Someone Else" raises some serious questions in my mind.

You said, "Superior people talk about ideas. Mediocre people talk about things. Little people talk about other people." Surely you must realize that each and every one of us enjoys a little gossip. In fact, your column is the most widely read gossip column in the world. People can't wait to see what their neighbors, friends, relatives, colleagues and fellow workers are up to.

The saving grace is that all who write in are protected by the merciful cloak of anonymity. At least nobody is hurt. Just sign me. A LITTLE PERSON WHO LIKES TO TALK ABOUT OTHER PEOPLE

DEAR PERSON: If one considers other people's problems "gossip" then I am guilty as charged. But I view this column in quite a different light.

To me, it represents an opportunity for anyone and everyone to unload anger, fear, hostility, guilt, frustration —the full gamut of human emotions. I try to print letters that deal with every aspect of life. Although some of them may seem bizarre, let me assure you nothing is so outrageous or crazy that somebody won't do it.

The service aspect of this column is the most important. We have on file in Chicago the names and addresses of the agencies and self-help groups in every one of the cities that print this column. We offer guidance to thousands of people every month so they can get the continuing help they need.

Of course there are those who read Ann Landers for laughs, and I have no objection to this. (It may be their only laugh for the day.) Humor can take the sting out of misery.

Anyone who reads this column regularly cannot help but recognize himself —or his son, or his wife, or his daughter or his boss—eventually. Trouble is the common denominator of living. It is also a great equalizer. When we share the same kind of trouble we become brothers and sisters under the skin. That, to me, is what this column is all about.

Gout

Gout is a disease with an impressive history. Its earliest account appears to be in the scriptures (II Chronicles 16:12), where Asa is described as "diseased of foot." Years before the birth of Christ, Hippocrates termed the malady "the unwalkable disease." The list of gout sufferers is long and illustrious. Alexander the Great, Lord Chesterfield, Charles Darwin, Benjamin Franklin, Oliver Cromwell, Dryden, Lord Beaverbrook, Cardinal Wolsey, Isaac Newton and Alexander Hamilton.

What is gout? Gout was originally called "podagra" from the Greek words "pous" meaning foot and "agra" meaning attack. The name now in use is from the Latin "gutta" which is a broad reference to an abnormal amount of uric acid in the bloodstream.

Gout is caused by defective purine metabolism, in the body. Purines are the end products of nucleoprotein digestion. They break down to form uric acid. Everyone has uric acid in his bloodstream. The disease called gout results when the body produces an excessive amount of uric acid or when there is a decreased excretion of the uric acid by the kidneys. It is then that gout manifests itself by attacks of acute joint pain. Chalky deposits may form in the cartilages of the joints, or a buildup of uric acid crystals which are not excreted by the kidneys can produce kidney stones and/or damaged kidneys.

For many centuries, gout was considered a disease of the upper class. Artists of the day delighted in drawing cartoons portraying a paunchy nobleman slumped before tables overladen with food, his bandaged feet propped on a "gout stool." (Such severe cases are seldom seen today because gout is preventable.)

Nineteenth-century physicians believed that gout was caused by the use of alcoholic beverages, especially port wine and sherry. Modern physicians know that gout can also be precipitated by foods high in purines, which the body converts to uric acid. Certain blood conditions and some medications (including many diuretics) may cause an acute attack.

Purine-rich foods include beer, wine, liver, kidney, heart, sardines, anchovies, fowl, gravies, and other meats and seafood. Consider what Samuel Pepys' diary tells us he ate for dinner on a typical day in March 1660: "Home from my office where my wife had got ready a very fine dinner, viz. a dish of marrow bones, a leg of mutton, a loin of veal, a dish of fowl, three pullets and two dozen of larks all in a dish, a great tart, a neat's tongue, a dish of anchovies, a dish of prawns and cheese." A full service at the table of the well-to-do might consist of thirty-two dishes, including sixteen different kinds of meat.

The poor, meanwhile, dined mainly on low-purine foods: cheese, dairy products, vegetables, bread, tea and very little meat except, perhaps, beef at Christmas. Thus a typical menu for the affluent was laden with purines, which explains why gout became associated with rich food, high living and wealth.

Gout is most common in males by a ratio of 20:1 and particularly in the over-forty age group. In women, it usually occurs in the post-menopausal age group.

What are the symptoms of gout? An attack of gout usually occurs in the middle of the night, most often starts as an acute joint pain in the large toe. However, it may affect other joints in the body, the instep of the foot, the ankle, knee, wrist, or elbow. The skin is hot, red-purple, swollen and exquisitely tender. The area cannot tolerate any pressure and the pain becomes increasingly unbearable. The patient with gout may feel ill with chills, headache, mild fever, weakness and loss of appetite.

There is no cure for gout; but this disease is not serious if treated promptly by a physician and kept under control. The problems occur when it is *not* kept under control, and complications result in severe kidney and joint damage.

It is important to treat elevated uric even without the acute symptoms of gout. It is also known that an elevated uric acid may be a factor in the later production of heart attacks since elevated uric acid also seems to occur in individuals and people who are very aggressive. Your physician can easily check the uric acid level in your body by a simple blood test.

Gout can be effectively controlled by medication and acute attacks of this disease can be relieved within twenty-four to forty-eight hours.

CREDIT: *Daniel M. Miller, M.D., F.A.C.S., Omaha, Nebraska, Associate Professor of Surgery, University of Nebraska College of Medicine, Omaha, Nebraska.*

Grandchildren

How to Get Along with Them

Love them. Love them a lot. Wholeheartedly, without reservation. Let them know you care. Treat them with respect and tenderness. Grandparenthood has got to be the best of all possible times.

Loving someone without reservation means doing the best for that individual's growth and happiness. It means full acceptance of that person as an individual, with his own personality and feelings.

It means not trying to change Danny into someone he isn't, just because you wish it. It means looking at Susan when she's seven, with her front teeth missing, and not laughing. It means suffering in silence when fourteen-year-old Jimmy's face is a mass of acne. It means accepting Janie's changing hair styles, long, short, or falling over the eyes. She's sixteen. It means enjoying the funny and often ridiculous clothes—Marc's T-shirts that say "Bullshirt" or "Dangerous Curves Ahead," or "I'm with Stupid," with an arrow pointing to whoever is standing nearby. It could be you.

Loving a grandchild means understanding the long silences when he can't think of a thing to say except "yep" and "nope." That happens around thirteen. And at sixteen, when your grandson gets up from your dinner table and says, "Excuse me, but I have plans with some of the guys," you shouldn't feel hurt. He's trying to tell you something. You're not in his world any more. Swallow hard. Understand.

Loving that child means you know he still cares for you whether or not your letters to him at camp or college are answered. It means not taking sides or interfering when he's in a head-on collision with his parents, even when you know the parents are wrong. You can speak your piece later, when you're alone with them and the heat's off.

Getting along with your grandchildren means not playing favorites with the one who appeals to you most. It means not giving gifts to one and not the others; not talking about Jack's athletic ability to friends while his brother, Bill, stands there, listening. "She never talks about what I can do," Bill is thinking. What he really feels is, "She doesn't really love me."

The parents of your grandchildren set the tone and influence their attitudes about you. You are fortunate if your son and daughter teach your grandchildren courtesy and consideration towards the older generation. It's not done by scolding and haranguing after you've left, but by family discussions beforehand. "Grandma and Grandpa are coming for dinner tonight. Remember, Grandma is hard of hearing. Sit close to her and talk slowly and loudly. It will make the evening more pleasant for her." "Grandfather falls asleep after dinner. Sometimes he snores. I know it's funny, but try not to laugh. Old people get tired early." These are suggestions that will help children learn kindness and consideration.

What if grandchildren don't write or call to say thank you for a gift? Should you remind them? Scold them? Tell on them or feel hurt?

If your grandchild lives out of town, drop him a note, asking him if he got your gift and if he did, did he like it. That's all. If he lives nearby, call and ask the same question. Mention it to his parents privately. They need to learn how to help their child show appreciation by saying thank you.

The next birthday or holiday, send a card—not a gift. You might write, "I wanted to send you a gift because I love you, but it's no fun when you don't write back to let me know whether or not you received it." See what happens.

When grandchildren are little, it's easy to get along with them. Their games, music and toys are fun to share. One grandchild, curled up in your lap while you read his favorite story, is worth more than the Shah of Iran's fortune. A surprise treat, like an ice-cream cone, can light up the whole afternoon. A trip to the zoo or playground is a joyful, shared experience.

It's when grandchildren grow older that the communication breaks down. Then the challenge is yours. Read some of their books, watch some of their favorite TV programs. Listen to their music, whether you can stand it or not. Go to some of their school football or basketball games. Invite them to a movie. You'll find you have something to talk about together.

Help your grandchildren know something of their heritage. Show them photographs from your old family albums. Read them letters if you've saved any. Talk to them about their forebears' struggles and challenges. Bring your parents and grandparents into your grandchildren's world so they can feel related. The important thing is not that they were rich or famous, but that they once lived and represent your "roots."

Be proud of the word "family." Help your grandchildren realize that the world doesn't begin and end with them—that all those relatives who lived before them were links in the family chain—and in their own lifetime they have a link to forge.

CREDIT: *Ellen May Goldberg, columnist for the Chicago* Sun-Times.

Grandparents

Our Greatest Unused Resource

When my grandmother died in 1928 at the age of eighty-two, she had seen the development of the horseless carriage, the flying machine, the telegraph and Atlantic cables, telephone, radio and silent films.

In my lifetime, I have lived through driving a horse and buggy, making butter, going to bed with a kerosene lamp and the appearance of great airships.

Because I have been able to go back and forth to the world of peoples still in the stone age, I have also been a participant in their leap into the modern world. Grandparents—and great-grandparents—have now become the living repositories of change, evidence that humans can adjust—witness the enormous changes that separate the pre-1945 generation from those who were reared after the war.

Under simpler conditions, it was the child who was more likely to accept change. Today the reverse is true. Parents of young children were born into the world of TV, computers, space exploration and the bomb. They have seen much less change than their parents and their grandparents. Many of them learned in school that the only safe way to keep from being overwhelmed by the knowledge of their teachers was to refuse to deal with history. If all the adults in the community are in the same age group, have the same ethnic background and approximately the same income, their children grow up to accept the small world in which they live as the only version of reality.

When the Peace Corps began sending suburban-reared middle-class young people to remote parts of the world, a great deal was made of "culture shock," a term invented by anthropologists to describe the impact of a foreign culture. Actually, what was called "culture shock" was more accurately described as "life shock" to overprotected, middle-class youngsters who had never seen an open sore or a completely disoriented person, or a birth or a death. The children of the slums see more of the seamy side of life, but their experience too is confined and limited.

Often one of the barriers to employment is the lack of experience in traveling more than a few blocks from home. Consequently, the last decades have given us an increasingly present-bound generation, a generation who assume that the world is somehow finished, although possibly finished wrong.

Somehow we have to get the older people, grandparents, widows and widowers, spinsters and bachelors, close to growing children if we are to restore a sense of community, a knowledge of the past and a sense of the future to today's children. While better-proportioned communities are being built, there are many things a school system itself can do. Older people, even if they have been segregated in some distant housing, can be brought into nursery schools, day-care centers and kindergartens, if only to watch the children play and be ready to answer their questions. In this way, children learn to relate to older people, to make allowances for their deafness and poor eyesight and failing memories. They will then be able to learn from them and not recoil in horror when they meet old people for the first time later in life.

A second important way in which the two-generational gap can be bridged is by developing ways in which both parents and teachers, after graduating or retiring from their earlier responsibilities, can resume contact with the next generation of schoolchildren. At present, active workers in the PTA retire when their youngest child graduates from the local school system. Most of them are initially very glad to do so. They rejoice that there will be no more frantic calls just as dinner is ready to go on the table, no more frustrating committee meetings, no more scrambling about for the last few dollars needed for a project. But after that wonderful respite, many of those once-active members will miss the organization that occupied so much of their time and effort.

Retired teachers may be asked back to lunch once a year or for a single social evening. A boys' club may give a lunch for the retired teachers. In some places retired teachers are participating actively in day-care programs for children of working mothers. But for the most part there is no continuity. The retired teacher may be smiled at and greeted wherever she goes, and her heart may be wrung when three of her former students yield to temptation and become thieves. But students rarely keep in touch with their former teachers. The older, retired teachers avoid former students because they feel that young people don't like older people. The young people, in turn, feel that older people don't like them. Each act of hesitation increases the mutual shyness.

One of the greatest challenges to contemporary education is how to impart a knowledge of the immediate past—ten years, twenty years, thirty years. The lament of the parents who find it hard to explain the Depression to their children separates old and young who have not talked enough together through the years. Many of us, particularly my age, when we heard that President Kennedy was shot, thought of the assassination of Lincoln. The reaction of the younger generation was, "Who would have believed that this would happen in America?" The gap between generations is wide.

In the schools there are beginning to be many young teachers who are on the same side as their high school students. But if they make common cause against the older teachers, there will be no real communication across the gap. Older teachers, younger teachers and students alike will all lose. Long conversations in small groups, looking at old movies and new movies together can start up communication again and keep our social system and our own minds from cracking under the strain of rapid change.

CREDIT: *Margaret Mead, Curator Emeritus of Ethnology at the American Museum of Natural History and Adjunct Professor of Anthropology at Columbia University, author, among other volumes, of* Culture and Commitment: A Study of the Generation Gap, *Garden City, New York: Doubleday, 1970.*

Grief

Grief is a catchall word for the feelings and altered behavior that one experiences from a significant loss.

The grief process is the movement through which one lives as one experiences the loss day by day. Hopefully it is a healing process as one goes from one stage to another. It must be emphasized that grief is not pathological but a healthy response to the ebb and flow of life.

Bereavement is often viewed narrowly as the state of the survivor after the death of a person who is loved, highly prized or held very dear. When we see a boy suffering from acne after his steady has deserted him, or a young adult has a puffy face and is red-eyed from nights of crying over the breaking of an engagement, we do not refer to them as bereaved, but the sorrow is physically visible. Physically and emotionally they are in real pain.

Some of the physical symptoms of acute grief are: sensations of distress occurring in waves lasting from twenty minutes to an hour at a time, a feeling of tightness in the throat, choking with shortness of breath, need for sighing, an empty feeling in the abdomen, lack of muscular power and an intense subjective distress described as tension of mental pain.

This discomfort can be caused by visitors who mention the deceased. There is a tendency to refuse to see people lest they bring up old memories.

The grieving person may try to keep away deliberately from all thoughts and references to the deceased. Some fear they are going insane. For example, the young navy pilot who lost a close friend with whom he had eaten, slept and discussed all his personal problems—for six months after his death, he would not admit that his friend was no longer with him.

One of the major obstacles is that many grievers try to avoid both the intense distress connected with grief and the necessary expression of emotion. The male victims bereaved by the Cocoanut Grove fire in Boston in 1942 appeared in the psychiatric interviews to be in a state of tension, with tightened facial muscles, unable to relax for fear they might "break down." They required considerable persuasion to yield to the grief process which would enable them to accept the discomfort of bereavement, to accept the grief process and embark on a program of dealing in memory with the deceased person. As soon as this change was accomplished there was a rapid relief of tension, and the subsequent interviews were animated conversations in which the deceased was idolized and in which misgivings about the future adjustment were worked through.

The most disastrous symptom of unresolved grief is "agitated depression" with tension, insomnia, feelings of worthlessness, bitter self-accusation and obvious need for punishment. Such patients may be dangerously suicidal.

While the intensity of interaction with the deceased before his death seems to be significant, the interaction need not have been one of affection. It may be the person who died invited hostility which could not be expressed because of his status or a feeling of family loyalty on the part of those who hated him. Thus two middle-aged men were overheard in a hospital corridor discussing the rapidly approaching hour of death of their elderly father, a person they regarded as a self-centered, hateful old tyrant. They had instructed the medical staff to spare no cost in prolonging their father's life—a procedure carried out with the usual oxygen masks, blood transfusions, drugs, intravenous feedings and succession of operations. As death drew near, one said to the other: "They really gave it to the old blank, blank, blank, didn't they."

They did not like their father, they despised him and used the hospital procedures to spit out their poison.

Acting out one's hate is not an appropriate way to resolve grief. Hate produces guilt, which calls for forgiveness and reconciliation.

We say we grieve over the loss of another, but we really grieve for ourselves.

It helps to see life as the flow of a river which is always moving, never the same. Life is a process in which death and rebirth are natural and normal. The pain of loss does not make the process less human. Good grief is good health, or more simply, being human.

CREDIT: *Dennis J. Geaney, author of* Living with Sorrow, *Chicago, Illinois. Thomas More Press.*

The Grieving Spouse*

Mourning is an inevitable part of the human condition. To quote one psychiatrist, who dealt extensively with widows, "You really don't get over it, you just get used to it."

SIGNIFICANCE OF THE LOSS

A rough estimate of the size of the problem by a worker in Canada is that 10 percent of Canadian women of adult years are widowed at any one time and that the ratio of widows to widowers is four to one. Bereavement may occur at any age, and many losses of a spouse occur in young age groups; for example, one fifth of all widows created in any one year are under forty-five years of age.

Mourning for a spouse, then, is a problem that affects mainly women because of their greater longevity. Moreover, they are usually younger than their husbands and their marriage rate after bereavement is lower than that of widowers.

Bereavement is, of course, a tragedy of major proportions. A widow is not only faced with loneliness, loss of companionship and unmet sex needs, but she now lacks the comfort, information and support of a partner of many years.

If her income is reduced, as is often the case, the widow may have to move to a smaller place. This introduces the trauma of relocation on top of the trauma of loss. Her grown children often have moved away. Family attention tends to fade after the first few weeks or months. The widow may be regarded as a threat to her married women friends or looked upon as a "fifth wheel."

Some friends may expect the widow to move through her grieving process too rapidly. At times, in order to avoid their own painful memories of the deceased, they may withdraw from her at the very time when her need for emotional support is most acute.

* Milton Greenblatt, M.D., Professor of Psychiatry, University of California at Los Angeles. (*American Journal of Psychiatry,* Vol. 135, pp. 43–47, 1978), Copyright 1978, the American Psychiatric Association. Reprinted by permission.

RISKS TO HEALTH

Apart from psychological and social distress, bereavement may pose a serious risk to physical health and even to survival. In many studies of the stresses, the loss of a spouse rates the highest of all stresses. Widows under sixty-five, during the first year of widowhood, consulted physicians at three times the expected rate. Physical symptoms were prominent. Sedation was used sevenfold more than normal. Widows spent more time in bed and in hospitals.

It is estimated that at least one bereaved person in five will suffer substantial health deterioration during the first year of bereavement. In one series, at thirteen-month follow-up, 32 percent showed deterioration of health. (Health deterioration was more prominent in widowers than in widows.)

Widows tend to drink too much. They lose weight and often take more drugs than are good for them. The risk of mortality is greater. The death of widows is mainly due to heart disease. Their illnesses often mirror the illnesses of the spouses they lost.

Even in the second year, mortality is higher when compared with married women.

Although the mechanism responsible for producing serious illness is not known, it is assumed that physiological stresses related to loss of a life partner are very great. One study of parents mourning the acute loss of their children by leukemia revealed highly significant physical deterioration.

GRIEF AS A PROCESS AND THE PHASES OF MOURNING

Grieving is not a steady state. It is a process . . . one phase fading gradually into another. Manifestations may vary greatly according to level of education, personality, rituals and culture. The time it takes to move from one phase to another also varies greatly.

In adult mourning the situation is somewhat different. The following phases can be noted:

Shock, numbness, denial, disbelief. The most distressing manifestations of shock and numbness last only for a short period, perhaps a few days, but the process of struggling with denial and disbelief runs through many days and even months.

The next phase, that of *pining, yearning and depression,* is most characteristic of the grief process. This starts within a few days of the loss and reaches its height in about five to fourteen days but may continue. This is the phase of *learning to live with the loss.* Weeping, sighing, hopeless feelings, feelings of emptiness, of distance from people, lack of interest and preoccupation with the image of the deceased are common during this period.

Physical symptoms of distress may come in waves. Many symptoms of this period may be interpreted as an alarm reaction due to a heightened stimulation of the sympathetic nervous system and accompanying feelings of danger.

The major symptoms that may be attributable to sympathetic stimulation include anger, irritability, fear, sleeplessness and loss of weight. Another group of manifestations may be related to the conscious and unconscious search for the dead object—crying and calling out for him or her, vivid dreams of the departed one, even hallucinations during which the deceased is "seen and spoken with." Sometimes there is a compulsion to visit the graveside day after day . . . with the mourner spending many hours "talking" to the departed one.

A process of *emancipation from the loved one and readjustment to the new environment* is the next phase. In this stage, calling upon one's inner resources and the help of all possible supports of family and friends are important. This period may take several months.

The final stage may be called *identity reconstruction* when the formation of new relationships and the development of a new role in life without the partner become crystallized. But even many months after the acute loss has occurred, studies show that a significant percentage of people remain depressed. Although many continue to mourn, few of the bereaved are suicidal. This is an important finding in relation to the diagnosis of pathological grief.

Several authorities claim that intense grief lasts longer in those who have had a sudden loss. This is particularly true for young widows, who, as we have noted, are also more prone to suffer greater deterioration of health following bereavement.

On the other hand, others observed that those who anticipated the loss, and therefore grieved before the loss, were less acutely distressed after the loss. However, the literature is not altogether clear at this point and at least some individuals who suffered anticipatory grief felt worse after the death had occurred. Aged persons who suffer losses after living through a chronic, fatal illness of their spouses often show a poor adjustment, probably because during the illness they felt "useful"—they had a function. After the spouse died they were no longer able to do anything meaningful.

Family members and friends can help a great deal to relieve the pain of grief. This is especially true where there has been a close-knit family and communication has been good. Under these circumstances, outside help seems to be less necessary.

Unfortunately, however, families often do break up rather early and many friends and relatives move away. Under these conditions, emotional support is not even present at the funeral, let alone after the funeral.

Delayed or suppressed grief. There is much evidence that delayed or suppressed grief means serious trouble later. Some of the factors that operate to delay or suppress grief are:

(1) The loss may be socially stigmatized, as in abortion or suicide.

(2) Mortality may be due to a drug overdose.

(3) There may be uncertainty as to whether or not there is an actual loss, as in the case of soldiers missing in action.

(4) The awakening of old losses that have been unresolved.

(5) Multiple losses suffered in the past make normal grieving difficult.

(6) Trivial factors such as an unappealing or overcrowded cemetery may inhibit grief.

(7) A grieving widow's great concern about the health and welfare of her young children may make it difficult for her to express her own feelings.

Other factors that may be operative are lack of finances, lack of religious support, difficult relationship between the widow and mother and/or other family members. Again, when bereavement strikes, as indicated above, widowers are at greater risk than widows.

RECOGNITION OF PATHOLOGICAL (ABNORMAL) GRIEF

It has been estimated that 98 percent of the bereaved do not seek outside help and 81 percent begin to improve in six to ten weeks. However, at any one time in a thirty-eight-bed psychiatric unit this author finds one or two individuals locked in his or her grief process. It is difficult to arrive at figures for incidence of pathological grief; however, in a study of 109 randomly selected widows and widowers, it was found that 67 percent had mild or severe *anniversary* reactions, which is often regarded as one clue to excessive stress.

Failure to grieve and delayed grieving are also regarded as clues towards pathological (abnormal) mourning.

Signs of pathological grief are excessive sorrow which goes on and on; irrational despair, severe feelings of hopelessness and loss of identity, impaired self-esteem; blaming oneself for the death; loss of interest and planning for the future; development of symptoms similar to those of the deceased; apathy, irritability or hyperactivity.

RESOLUTION OF GRIEF

Shakespeare proclaimed, "Give sorrow words. The grief that does not speak whispers the o'erfraught heart and bids it break." Modern writers and clinicians agree with this statement.

Unfortunately, well-meaning friends or relatives may have their own ideas of how grieving should be done and become irritated when it goes slowly.

Participation by the bereaved in funeral arrangements can help. Faith in God and church or synagogue attendance may be supportive. Often pastoral counseling is the appropriate support, and trusted religious advisers may be more helpful in situations of bereavement than physicians.

Some physicians recommend tranquilizers if anxiety, restlessness and insomnia become severe. Some physicians recommend electrotherapy if the mourner presents significant suicidal trends. Fortunately, both suicidal trends and psychoses are rare.

More grief therapists warn that the final adjustment, even in normal grieving, requires about two years. This is longer than we have been led to believe through the researches of earlier pioneers.

Identity reconstruction takes a long time. The scars of the loss heal slowly or may remain throughout life. The field literally cries out for further research.

Guilt

One of the most painful, self-mutilating, time- and energy-consuming exercises in the human experience is guilt. There are two varieties. Both bad.

First: Earned guilt. It can ruin your day—or your week or your life—if you let it. It turns up like a bad penny when you do something dishonest, hurtful, tacky, selfish or rotten. Any act, ill-conceived, can make you feel unworthy, ashamed and then, heaven help you, the guilt moves in like an unwelcome house guest.

Every one of us has, at some time or another, behaved badly and suffered the consequences. Never mind that it was the result of ignorance, stupidity, laziness, thoughtlessness, weak flesh, or clay feet. You did wrong and the guilt is killing you. Too bad. But be assured the agony you feel is normal. What's more it may even be a sign of nobility. It proves you have a conscience.

But—and here's the clincher—know when to stop suffering. (I'd say two hours is plenty.) Tell yourself, "Enough of this hairshirt already. I did something I'm not very proud of, but I learned from it."

You can't relive the past so put it out of your mind. It takes energy to beat yourself over the head. What a waste of life's most precious commodity!

So much for earned guilt. Now comes the variety from which nothing can be learned. Unearned guilt. This is the stuff other people lay on us. It's a bad trip and should be avoided at all costs. But first we must learn to recognize it.

One of the funniest books I ever read was, *How to Be a Jewish Mother* by Dan Greenburg. His chapter which describes a fail-safe technique for instilling guilt in a child is hilarious. Greenburg suggests the following:

Give your son, Marvin, two sport shirts as a present. The first time he wears one, look at him sadly and say in your Basic Tone of Voice, "The other one you didn't like?"

Borrow a tape recorder and practice the following key phrases until you can deliver them with eye-watering perfection:

(1) "Go ahead and enjoy yourself."
(2) "Don't worry about me."
(3) "I don't mind staying home alone."
(4) "I'm glad it happened to me and not to you."

Remember, the child is an emotionally unstable, ignorant creature. To make him feel secure, you must continually remind him of the things you are denying yourself on his account. It is best to do this when others are present, if possible.

Greenburg lists four basic sacrifices to make for your child:

(1) Stay up all night to cook him a big breakfast.
(2) Don't let him know you fainted twice in the supermarket from fatigue. (But make sure he knows you aren't letting him know.)
(3) When he comes home from the dentist take over his toothache.
(4) Open his bedroom window wider so he can have more fresh air. Then close your own so you don't use up the supply.

And while we are discussing guilt in the family, let's not forget that children can give their parents a bad case of it. These days especially. Working mothers are particularly vulnerable. Often they are loaded with guilt because they are not at home taking care of the little ones.

The same goes for fathers who put in long hours at the office or the store —or travel for business. Frequently guilt-ridden parents try to make it up to their kids by buying them expensive gifts or giving them extra privileges. The result: spoiled brats. Gimmee pigs. They grow up unmotivated and shiftless, having learned early if they laid on the guilt they could get whatever they wanted.

The most insidious form of unearned guilt (and the most difficult to get rid of) is the brand instilled during childhood. It is the twisted legacy left over from the mid-Victorian era—that anything connected with sex is bad.

This notion is often put into the head of a child by a parent who says, "You mustn't touch yourself there. It's nasty." (Or "It's a sin.")

Of course, the warning does no good. We continue "to touch ourselves there" because it feels good. But once the seed of guilt has been planted, it's hard to get over feeling that sex is dirty or wrong—something nice people don't do.

I have encountered just about every sexual hang-up you can imagine in my daily mail. One I run across quite often is the madonna-whore syndrome. These males cannot enjoy sex with a respectable woman (a wife). The wife is the Madonna. With her there are strong inhibitions and very little satisfaction. In order for this male to give full vent to his sexual feelings, he needs a whore.

What some people do with guilt is fascinating. They drive it underground (where it festers and surfaces on demand). It can be expiated through suffering and self-flagellation ("I'm rotten. I'm no good. I deserve this.") Or it can be passed on to others.

Example: While hurrying toward a crowded theater exit, you accidentally dig your heel into an elderly woman's instep. You look straight ahead as if nothing happened—hoping she doesn't know it was you. A moment later a gentleman steps on *your* foot—just barely. You let out a bloodcurdling yell. He turns around and says, "I'm so sorry." You bite your lip, manage a weak smile and reply, "Oh, that's all right. It's been two weeks since I had the cast taken off." You limp slowly up the aisle—steadying yourself against the rows of seats.

Got the picture? Good. (This is what is known as projecting your guilt onto the next guy.) It's a nifty trick if you can find a sucker. The major drawback is that you can pull it only a few times and then the smart ones get your number.

One of the most effective guilt producers is illness. A bad back is the best because the "victim" just lies there—helpless. The unspoken message is, "You did this to me, you S.O.B. You know when I get tense my back goes out —and it's all your fault for upsetting me."

Asthma attacks, high blood pressure and headaches are also wonderful aids to keep a parent, a grown child, a husband or a wife "in line." Sample sentences when an argument is lost or expectations not met: "I think I'm getting a heart attack." Or, "Will you please bring me my migraine medicine? I can't make it to the other room."

An undefined illness can be even deadlier. Nothing much is said. She languishes on the sofa, hair askew, pale as a ghost (no makeup), and sighs, "Go without me, dear, and have a good time. I feel a little dizzy—can't keep my balance. I'm sure it's nothing serious. I didn't get much sleep last night worrying about you. Next time please phone when you're going to be late."

Resolve—when you finish reading this piece—that:

(1) You are not going to spend more than two hours feeling guilty even though what you did was dumb, foolish, mean, petty—whatever. Admit you were wrong, that you behaved badly and vow you aren't going to let it happen again. Then lock the incident out of your mind and never let it creep back in.

(2) Refuse to let anyone send you on a guilt trip by making you believe you made him sick. Nobody makes anyone sick. People make *themselves* sick.

(3) Let the characters in your life who try to manipulate you by pouring on the guilt know you are capable of handling their wrath, their anger and

their disappointment. When you louse up their guilt-producing equipment you free yourself from a treacherous form of tyranny and create a far healthier climate for growth toward maturity. Remember—guilt is a pollutant and we don't need any more of it in the world.

CREDIT: *Ann Landers.*

Guns

(*A Serious Problem*)

90 MILLION GUNS

DEAR ANN: Tonight at 9:55 p.m. our phone rang. Dad answered. We could tell from his responses that it was bad news.

It was the mother of a dear friend who had just died. The week before, HER phone had rung. It was the sheriff asking her to come to the hospital. Her son had been shot in the head while driving down one of the main streets in Omaha.

He was only 33—a wonderful person, no enemies, no reason why anyone would wish him dead. But someone took a shot at him—and now he is gone forever. The agony of this man's parents is unbearable. He was their only child.

There are no clues as to who committed this senseless murder. They will probably never find the killer. It makes me sick to know that whoever did this awful thing is out there somewhere— walking around with that gun. God knows who will be next. AMERICA, WHAT'S HAPPENING TO YOU?

DEAR AMERICA: That's a good question. One of the answers is this: There are at least 90 million guns out there and many are in the hands of crazy, irresponsible people. Again I am asking all concerned citizens to urge their congressmen and senators to pass a strong federal gun law. Every poll taken shows that the vast majority of Americans want it. Are the gun manufacturers and lobbies in Washington stronger than the voice of the people? Let us make ourselves heard.

Do you have a handgun in your home or in the glove compartment of your car to protect yourself against assault or robbery? If the answer is yes, here are a few facts that deserve your consideration.

In 1976 approximately 25,000 Americans were murdered by guns. To put that figure in its proper context, here's another way to look at it. During our ten-year involvement in the Vietnam war, over twice as many Americans were murdered by guns at home than were killed in that war.

So much for the heartbreak that goes hand in hand with loss of life. Here are some financial facts:

Gun killings and wounds cost the United States taxpayer at least $4 billion a year, according to the U. S. Department of Justice. Crimes committed with guns account for a large share of the cost of law enforcement, justice, prison upkeep, welfare to dependents, insurance premiums, medical expenses, recuperation time, losses in talent and experience, permanent disability, workmen's compensation and property losses.

How do we compare with other countries in this regard? I don't want to burden you with statistics, but this one will give you a fairly good idea. From 1946 through 1967, 19 policemen were killed by guns in England, as compared with 1,014 policemen killed in the United States. No country in the world approaches us when it comes to shooting one another to death. We are the gun-happiest people in the world.

Why? Because guns are available almost anywhere, to anyone who wants them. This means minors, idiots and people with criminal records. Anybody who wants a gun can walk into a store and buy one (or ten). In fact, you don't even have to go out of your own home. Guns are available through mail-order house catalogues. (The gun that killed John F. Kennedy was purchased from a Chicago mail-order house.)

In Japan the private ownership of pistols is forbidden to everyone except the police, military and a few competitive marksmen. In France all guns must be registered and their owners licensed. In Sweden applicants for gun ownership licenses must prove their need for a gun and their knowledge of the weapon.

Guns are big business in the United States. Many powerful interests would hate to see them go. Those who are fighting gun control legislation have for years been bankrolling a powerful lobby in Washington. Their motto is, "Guns don't kill people—people kill people." Whenever I print a letter urging gun control laws, that motto pops up in my mail at least 25,000 times. My response to these people is, "Yes, of course people kill people, but it's a lot easier if a person has a gun."

Part of the gun problem exists because we are afraid—and we have a right to be. Man can now walk on the craters of the moon, but he cannot walk safely after dark two blocks from his own home. Many people insist they need a gun for protection. They say if guns are outlawed, only the criminals will have them. The response to that statement is "Yes, the criminals—and the police." The war against crime would then be waged by those best equipped to do the job. And the police would win.

Citizens who keep guns in their homes to protect themselves against intruders would do well to keep these facts in mind: 98 percent of burglaries are committed when no one is at home. The burglar often adds insult to injury by making off with the handgun—along with the silverware.

A Chicago study showed that citizens who resisted being robbed by brandishing a weapon were eight times as likely to be killed. The average person is not adept at handling a gun. He is slower on the draw and more easily rattled than an experienced thug (U. S. Mayors' Conference, 1976).

If you wish to protect your home there are several things you can do:

(1) Install a security system.

(2) Get a dog. It doesn't have to be a large dog. If he barks and calls neighborhood attention to the fact that something is "wrong," he'll serve a very useful purpose.

Ordinary, everyday citizens like you and me must keep in mind this important fact. Almost 70 percent of the people who are shot to death in the United States year after year are *not* killed by robbers or rapists. The murders are committed by husbands, wives, in-laws, brothers, sisters, lovers, neighbors, friends, employees and other acquaintances. They are crimes of passion resulting from old grudges, new arguments, lost tempers. Often booze or drugs are involved.

If there were no gun handy, the victim would have been clobbered by a fist, a club, a piece of pipe or stabbed by a kitchen knife. His chances for survival would have been infinitely better.

In addition to crimes of passion, approximately fourteen thousand Americans shoot themselves to death intentionally. Some psychiatrists argue that if a person wants to commit suicide he will do it—somehow. This may be true, but when a deeply depressed individual has a gun in his bedside table, it is easy to pull the trigger while in a state of anxiety. Often a suicide attempt is a cry for help. If pills are taken, the stomach can be pumped and the person may be saved, but when a bullet blows off a head or pierces the heart, no second chance is possible.

Accidental gun deaths are another tragedy. Last year nearly four thousand people lost their lives in the United States because they "didn't know it was loaded." Can you imagine the excruciating guilt of a parent whose pre-school youngster found a loaded gun on a shelf and accidentally killed his four-year-old playmate? This occurred in Chicago recently.

Every poll taken in the United States has shown that the American people are strongly in favor of handgun registration or an outright ban against their sale or possession. It's up to us to let our representatives and senators in Washington know how we feel about this vital issue.

CREDIT: *Checked for accuracy by Nelson Shields, Executive Director, National Council to Control Handguns, Inc. James Sullivan, National Committee for a Responsible Firearms Policy.*

Hair Care for Men

When the crew cut of the fifties went out and the long hair of the middle sixties came in it created a revolution in men's hair styles. At first the older generation despised it. Then they imitated it. Full heads of hair, long sideburns, moustaches and beards cropped up everywhere. Hair was definitely "in." At this writing, it is still "in," although the trend is toward shorter hair than in the early seventies.

Just as a male would seek a qualified doctor for help with a medical problem he should find a good professional hair stylist if he feels he needs advice on what to do with his hair. If you are one of this group, make an appointment for a consultation and go on from there. Don't be afraid to ask questions. Today hair stylists with professional expertise are not hard to find. The best way to select a hair stylist is to ask someone whose hair styling you admire. Ask, "Who is your barber?" Then make an appointment.

A good stylist takes into consideration: hair type—straight, wavy or curly; density of hair—the number of hairs per square inch; hair texture—fine, medium or coarse; the growth directions of the hair. The stylist will study the shape of your face and head, your ears (size and degree of protrusion) and the set of the mouth and type of chin. Perhaps he'll suggest a beard, moustache . . . or perhaps both to enhance your appearance. He will consider your height, girth and general physical posture. He will inquire about your daily grooming habits, your needs relating to recreational and business lifestyle.

What would be appropriate for an introverted man could be all wrong for an active "macho" personality.

A competent hair stylist has knowledge of the chemistry and physiology of the body and of the many new products that are available. Don't back off if he recommends a permanent or a straightener to achieve a certain style that would be good for you—or color. If you aren't ready for silver threads among the gold, he can do something about it.

Many men today don't realize that their hair is subject to damage by wind, sun, blow-drying and sprays. A hair-conditioning agent is as important for men as for women. If hair is left in a dry state of abuse it can lead to severe hair and/or scalp problems. Weather is a big factor in playing havoc with hair and scalp. Conditioners are plentiful. Your stylist will be happy to suggest the type best suited for your needs.

BASIC PROBLEMS AND POSSIBLE SOLUTIONS:

(1) Dull, lifeless, fine and flyaway hair: Keep it short. Use conditioners, grooming aids, or perhaps a series of herbal henna treatments (neutral or colored).

(2) Matting hair, fine or coarse: If the hair is too oily, check your shampoo. If high in alkaline it will cause the body to produce more oil to regain acid balance. Hair should be cut shorter, in layers, to lift off the scalp, away from the oil, for easier management.

(3) Coarse hair: Keep it conditioned regularly and use a creme rinse along with your acid-balanced shampoo. A longer style is advisable because of the additional weight to keep hair smartly in place.

(4) Dandruff: Whether it is flaking and itching (known as dry dandruff) or redness and inflammation plus flaking and itching (called wet/oily dandruff), the problems are the same. There is no known cause and it can appear on other parts of the body. No one has proven that germs are the primary villains. If daily cleansing with a good acid-balanced shampoo doesn't alleviate the problem consult a dermatologist. Dandruff can easily be confused with psoriasis or eczema. A word of caution: dandruff shampoos (commercial or professional) can be damaging to the scalp and should be used as instructed by a knowledgeable stylist or doctor.

(5) Baldness and receding hairlines: On Yul Brynner, baldness looks good, but most men are distressed when they discover their hair is going. What causes it? Mainly it's an inherited tendency but there are other factors as well. Often illnesses, nervous conditions and bacteria can cause the loss of hair. We also know that the buildup of androgen, the male sex hormone in the body, causes the follicle to become dormant. In many cases the hair can be restored to its original glory by the injection of estrogen, the female sex hormone, but this may cause the body to develop breasts and other female symptoms.

The loss of hair need not mean the loss of manly pride. There are many alternatives, but investigate before you invest. Full wigs, partial hairpieces, implantations, weavings and transplants are available. Decide with your hair stylist which is best for you. Generally when the hair begins to go it is best to keep it cut short. Remember, when you try to conceal a receding hairline or a balding area you merely draw attention to it. "Less is definitely more!"

CREDIT: *Robert R. Brady, Obelisk Studios for Men, Chicago, Illinois.*

Hair Care for Women*

Man's first miracle fiber was hair. It survives washing, drying, cutting, curling, burning, teasing, stripping, dyeing and straightening. What man-made material can tolerate such torture?

While hair may survive, it does not always thrive. The abuse suffered by the average head of hair is incredible. Before thinning begins and split ends appear, something should be done lest woman lose her crowning glory.

Beautiful hair begins with good health. It needs loving care and protection. What you don't know about hair care can hurt you. What you *do* know can mean the difference between having a magnificent mane and a dull, straggly mop that you'll want to cover with a scarf or a turban when you desire to look your best.

ABOUT SHAMPOO

How often? Often as you like, but the more you do it, the milder your shampoo should be; if you're a frequent shampooer, it might be wise to dilute the shampoo with water before applying. To forestall as much tangling as possible comb or brush your hair before you wash it, smoothing it in the appropriate direction—forward if you dunk your head into a washbowl, back if you're shampooed in a salon, down if you shampoo in a shower.

Many shampoos offer extras now, in the form of lemon, balsam, herbs or protein. These contribute their own natural benefits—the first three offer fragrance, and protein seems to join forces with the protein hair is made of. The water should be anything but hot—lukewarm to cool is best for hair, and most shampoos work just as well in cooler water. Most, also, do their job in hard or soft water.

ABOUT CONDITIONERS

Conditioners make hair easier to manage and reduce static "flyaway" electricity. Some conditioners are rinsed off right away; some are rinsed off after a little longer time; some stay on and become setting lotions. Labels will tell you which does what. Most conditioners, now, also have the extra benefits of

* Grace Mirabella, *Vogue Beauty & Health Guide*, Copyright, 1973, 1974 The Condé Nast Publications, Inc.

lemon, herbs, balsam or protein. Conditioners should be applied two inches from the scalp, then down to the ends of the hair—it's hair, not scalp, that needs this therapy. As you work in the conditioner, separate strands of hair with your fingers then comb through them with a wide-toothed comb to distribute the conditioner evenly. After this, loads of rinsing, in fresh-flowing water. Wet hair should look shiny before it dries—if it's dull while wet, there's still too much conditioner left. This can weigh down hair (especially fine hair) and make it limp. One solution: use all the conditioner you need—but no more—to get your comb through without damage; after combing, use a little vinegar in the near-to-last rinse water to counteract the conditioner's limping effects. Final rinse should be as cold as you can stand it—this firms up hair.

ABOUT CUTTING

A skillful cut makes thin hair appear thicker, limp hair bouncier, thick hair more manageable. For stronger, healthier hair, the blunt cut is your answer. Here's why: The weakest area of hair is the ends, the portion of hair not covered by protective outer cuticle and the only area where the hair shaft is completely exposed. When hair is cut at an angle, even more of the inner hair shaft is exposed, so more protein and moisture can escape (same principle as cutting rose stems on a slant to take up more water; but with hair, nourishment goes out instead of in). A good haircut has other advantages. The hair can be washed and blown dry, worn loosely avoiding the torture treatment of teasing, tight clips and rollers and overspraying—all things that could damage hair. Speaking of hair spray—no need for hair to be drenched in it right down to the skull—it's only the top layer that needs it. And if you use spray, be sure to comb it out before going to bed so hair will be unbrittle and unbreakable overnight.

ABOUT BRUSHING

Forget that hundred strokes. Do it just enough to loosen hair, start it bouncing, but don't overdo. Brushing hair promotes oiliness, so well-oiled hair can do with even less. Before you buy a brush, feel its bristles; if they hurt your fingers, they'll hurt your hair. Same applies to combs. Make sure the teeth won't bite.

TWO MODERN PROBLEMS FOR HAIR

One is pollution—bad air promotes bad hair. City hair needs washing and conditioning frequently to rid it of fumes and soot. Country hair is luckier, gets cleaner air, is probably attached to a healthier scalp. Another problem is tension. According to one hair expert, tightened-up shoulder and neck muscles restrict the flow of blood (and its accompanying oxygen) to the scalp, where it's needed for hair growth and health. The moral: When it comes to hair, relax and enjoy it—more.

DIET

Your general health will be reflected in your hair. Plenty of protein is good for all of you, hair included. Too many fats and oils, if your skin and hair are oily, will make your hair greasy. It matters what you eat—so eat sensibly.

WEATHER

Hair grows faster in warm weather than in cold and is more apt to get oily, since oil glands and blood circulation are more active then. Cold weather is harder on hair, makes it less lively; also, in winter, heads are more often covered so hair is squashed and less air gets to the scalp. Excesses of wind and sun are drying to hair just as to skin. Very hot hair dryers are as harmful as strong sun and wind, so if the hairdresser, in an effort to get you out in a hurry, puts you under a very hot dryer, move the dial to medium or cool. At home hold your hand dryer a foot away from your head—and keep it moving around.

There is a natural tendency for hair to become thinner as the years pass, but with good tender, loving care your hair can remain your crowning glory.

Hair Transplants

Unless you're the Telly Savalas type, losing hair on the head can be traumatic. We live in a society where hair loss is often associated with loss of youth, power and self-esteem. In fact, hair loss and its roots (pardon!) reach back into mythological times.

When Delilah cut Samson's hair he could have put on a curly wig, but today's Samsons have much more going for them. They can have a hair transplant.

More than a hundred thousand men have had transplants. They are not only our most visible politicians and entertainers, but more often the neighbor down the street. Medical authorities agree that hair transplantation is the most effective, safe and permanent method for replacing lost hair. Although it won't look exactly like the hair one had at eighteen, it's the next best thing.

Male pattern baldness looks much like a monk's haircut; hair growth at the sides and back of the head, but not at the top. It can begin in a young man just out of his teens or occur ever so gradually over the years.

Causative factors point to a combination of hormonal and hereditary influences. Some men have more of the male hormone androgen than others. Add this to a hereditary disposition for baldness, and you are dealing against the odds.

Hair loss can also be caused by burns, radiation treatments, accidents or surgery. Other reasons can be glandular disorders such as diabetes, system infections, medications and chronic, physical scalp abuse. Women especially should vary their hair style every few years. Ponytails should not be a habit because continued tension or pulling on the hair impairs the blood circulation at the hair roots. This could cause the root to die and the hair would then fall out.

Many of the above conditions can be cured or corrected, but medical science still cannot prevent the hair follicle from dying. Once the root dies, no hair will grow naturally on that spot and there are no medications or commercial products that will grow hair.

The one way hair will grow, oddly enough, is if hair plugs are transplanted from the area of the scalp where hair is seldom lost. That location for most men is at the sides and the back of the head.

Some doctors bypass the plug technique at the hairline, and place a strip graft there. Too often this type of graft doesn't take. It frequently becomes infected and leaves visible scarring. It's not worth the trouble.

Women, too, can be helped by hair transplants as long as they have an adequate amount of healthy donor hair.

A consultation with a qualified doctor can provide the best answer. Those physicians performing hair transplants are cosmetic surgery specialists in ear, nose and throat, plastic surgery and dermatology. Recommendations from your family physician or the County Medical Society are most helpful in selecting a doctor. Most doctors who do this type of work are kept busy through referrals—people who have been sent by grateful patients.

Hair transplants are most always done in the doctor's office. There the doctor evaluates his patient's health. A blood test for bleeding tendencies is performed, another for the blood sugar level. The doctor makes sure his patient understands what is to be done. The number of total plugs and transplant sessions is discussed. With a pencil, the doctor then draws the future hairline in and takes photographs.

Placement of the hairline is important. Some unfortunate individuals have had their hairlines put in straight across their foreheads or too near the eyebrows. Most of the botched jobs occur because people patronize unqualified practitioners, some not even in the medical field. If you admire someone's hair transplant, find out who did it! If you see a botched job, it might be useful to find out who did *that* one—and stay away from him.

Once the surgery date has been arranged, the patient is cautioned not to take any aspirin (or its derivatives) ten days prior to that time. He should have no alcohol twenty-four hours before and after the procedure.

The patient shampoos his hair the night before and can eat a light meal on the day of surgery. A pre-operative medication is given before the transplant begins; this minimizes the anxiety.

The hair at the donor site (usually the back or side of the head) is cut to a 3-mm. length and cleansed with an antiseptic solution. At the recipient site, the scalp is cleansed again and the hairline is penciled in.

The next step is about as painful as having a tooth frozen at the dentist's. A local anesthetic is injected into the scalp which minimizes bleeding and dulls sensation. Once done, the patient feels only slight pressure.

Then by means of a 5-mm. circular punch, the doctor removes the donor plugs at the proper angle so as to include the hair follicle. Each plug, containing from eight to fourteen hairs, is cleansed, trimmed and put into a "waiting" solution.

The recipient site at the top of the hair is prepared with a 4.5-mm. punch. This assures a good fit; and as the hair plugs are inserted, the doctor must carefully note in what direction he deposits them. Hair at the hairline grows forward so it must be placed that way. Otherwise, the hair will grow in the wrong direction and tangle badly.

The plugs are spaced one plug diameter apart in order to assure a good blood supply. Fifty to sixty plugs are grafted in one session which takes one half hour to one hour. A mild pressure bandage is then applied on the head and changed the following day. A mild analgesic or sedative can be prescribed if needed. It is advisable to avoid alcoholic beverages for twenty-four hours after transplantation and to avoid severe or strenuous physical activities for seven days after the procedure.

The patient is told not to disturb the plugs for two weeks although he can shampoo in five days. A few days later, the patient can wear a loose-fitting cap or toupee, but when new hair growth begins, a toupee should not be worn.

Crusts will form on the affected areas, but will fall off in about two weeks. Because the hair follicles go through a shock period, the transplanted hair falls out. No cause for alarm because in about three months, hair begins to sprout. This transplanted hair lasts a lifetime or as long as the unaffected hair remains in the donor region, which, as mentioned earlier, most men never lose.

The next transplant session comes in three weeks. Subsequent sittings can be three weeks apart or longer. This depends on the patient's new hair growth and his own needs. Generally, the doctor will not space the sittings too close together. He needs to observe the new growth rate and make any needed corrections.

The donor sites heal and shrink to a pinhead size which are amply disguised by the surrounding hair. The same happens to the recipient sites.

Depending on the stages needed to suit each patient, the entire transplant procedure can be completed in six months or less. Health insurance will cover the cost if, for example, the hair loss was caused by a burn, but not for purely cosmetic reasons. Most doctors charge between $8 and $35 for each hair plug, and the total cost can be $1,000 to $4,000. The entire cost is now tax-deductible.

CREDIT: *Wafik A. Hanna, M.D., facial cosmetic surgeon, Hinsdale, Illinois.*

Unwanted Hair

DEAR ANN LANDERS: Will you please tell me why Americans are so hung up on hair? In Europe women do not shave their armpits or their legs and nobody gives a damn. In this country, if a woman has hair any place but on her head, she is considered some sort of freak.

It so happens I am a brunette lady—and a hairy one at that. I shave my legs because society says I must. When I wear a sleeveless dress, I also shave under my arms, which is a nuisance. Now my husband tells me if I want to go swimming with him this summer I must shave the tops of my legs, both front and back, from the knees up.

I resent his male chauvinism and told him I'd be happy to oblige, provided he shaves the tops of *his* legs also—front and back. His reply was, "You're nuts."

Am I? I tried shaving the tops of my legs four years ago and ended up with a half-dozen ingrown hairs. Please settle this. HIRSUTE HANNA FROM URBANA

DEAR HANNA: If your legs are shaved from the knees down and you have an abundant growth from the knees up you would be something of a conversation piece around the pool.

Since shaving causes you to have ingrown hair, try a depilatory or a wax job. Either will take more time than shaving but the results last longer and you won't get cuts, infections or ingrown hairs.

That letter and response produced this—from Toronto:

DEAR ANN LANDERS: I was very much offended by your reply to "Hirsute Hanna from Urbana," the woman who hated to shave her legs and armpits.

Why is it that women are made to feel ashamed of any hair that grows on them except that which is on the head? Meanwhile, men who walk around looking like gorillas are considered "sexy" and "virile." Hair on a male is touted as a great turn-on.

I live in Canada and it gets mighty cold up here in the winter. Last year I had a long talk with my boyfriend about the shaving bit. I pointed out that hair helps keep a person warm and it would be real considerate of him if he'd revise his attitude. He said my request sounded reasonable and would you believe he actually grew to like my hairy legs?

It's a relief not to be shaving all the time and I couldn't care less what other people think. Please, Ann, encourage your women readers to accept themselves as they are. Society has already imposed so much on us.   ALL HUNG UP AND TRYING TOO HARD

DEAR TRYING: Any woman who has the desire (and guts) to face the world with hairy armpits and legs to match, deserves high marks for having the courage of her convictions. Speaking strictly for myself, I'm not quite ready for such heroics.

And then came this—from San Diego:

DEAR ANN LANDERS: I was disturbed by your regressive and insipid advice to the hairy lady whose husband insisted she shave her legs and armpits before donning her swimsuit. Our culture is screwed up, not the lady. Hair removal is not the answer. Education is.

You have done a disservice to your readers by not pointing out that this practice of self-mutilation is not only demeaning but anti-erotic.

I'm a middle-aged man, happily married, and unashamedly confess I am turned on by the unshaven good looks of women. Females must be perpetuating this silly practice of hair removal because I have yet to meet a man who doesn't think a woman's hairy legs and armpits are sexy. Shaving is a nuisance. It's up to each and every woman to decide for herself whether or not she wants to do it. For those who don't I hope this letter will give them the courage to combat criticism.   I LIKE HAIR

DEAR I.L.H.: American women with hairy armpits and legs will need more than courage. I can't imagine a less appetizing sight.

Granted, shaving is a nuisance, but it's one of the more rewarding things a woman can do to help herself look feminine and attractive. You've stated your opinion. This is mine.

More and more, especially in the United States, women have come to look upon the removal of leg, underarm and facial hair as an essential part of good grooming. Most women feel that leg hair and underarm hair look masculine. Moreover, studies show that women who shave almost always have a higher opinion of themselves than women who do not.

Unwanted hair presents more than a grooming problem since it can be caused by a variety of factors. Medical consultation is often necessary to determine the origin and nature of excessive unwanted hair. There are two kinds of unwanted hair—that which is simply cosmetically unappealing and that which grows in excessive amounts, or in unusual textures, or in areas where it is not usually found or wanted. Treatment for both types overlap, but women should know the difference.

It is important to determine first if the excess hair (called hirsutism) is a sign of an internal physical disturbance. (Its recognition and investigation will require observation and testing until a diagnosis is made.) Treatment may be medically or surgically directed depending on the cause. When no internal cause is discovered, cosmetic treatment of unwanted hair—from bleaching to electrolysis—is available, depending upon the individual's concern.

Family and racial characteristics influence hair growth on the head, face and body. A Greek or Sicilian woman living in a community of Norwegians may consider herself abnormally hairy, although she has only the average amount of hair growth for a woman of her racial stock. Mediterranean and Semitic peoples are hairier than those of Nordic or Anglo-Saxon strains. Caucasians are more hairy than Negroes. Orientals and American Indians are the least hairy.

HORMONAL INFLUENCE IN HAIR GROWTH

In addition to familial traits and racial characteristics, sex hormones influence hair growth. In both men and women, different types of hair respond to sex hormones in four different ways: hair on the eyebrows and fringe of the scalp is uninfluenced by sex hormones; pubic hair is very sensitive to androgens (male hormones); hair on front and top of the scalp may be retarded by male hormones; hair growth around the mouth and chin is considered true female hirsutism.

Both male and female hormones are produced by men and women. The average woman produces about two thirds as much male hormone as the average man. If a woman has some malfunction or a tumor in the adrenal glands or in the ovaries it will cause her to produce an excess of male hormone. Signs of masculinization will appear, such as coarse hair on the face, chest, lower abdomen and extremities. If a woman without a strong family history of excess hair growth has a sudden or rapid increase in hair on these body areas, prompt investigation should be made to determine if an endocrine disorder is present. Should excess hair growth appear during childhood, in either girls or boys, tests for disease or malfunction of the endocrine glands are definitely indicated. If an endocrine disorder is found and corrected either by medical or surgical treatment, the excessive hair growth may lessen or return to normal over a period of some months, although it may take one to two years. Occasionally, excess hair persists despite correction of the glandular condition, but at least it does not continue to increase.

Most cases of excessive hair growth in adult women are definitely not associated with any other outward signs of masculinization, nor with any detectable internal disorder. Many women troubled with excessive hair are entirely feminine in physique and mental outlook. Usually, their menstrual cycles and fertility are normal, and laboratory tests indicate no excess of male hormones. Hirsutism does not usually imply that there is a serious endocrine malfunction, but if it becomes a cause of concern, it should be medically evaluated. Some investigators in the field of endocrinology believe there are subtle hormonal differences between women with excessive hair growth and other "normal" women. These findings need further observation and verification before they can point to any dramatically successful medical treatment for hirsutism.

Again, in the area of drug therapy for excess hair *not* linked to an endocrine disorder, there is controversy. Some studies indicate that there is a possible benefit in giving hormone therapy. Others report no success along these lines. No medical treatment capable of effectively reversing excess hair growth in otherwise normal individuals is available. The problem of getting rid of the unwanted hair cosmetically is another matter.

COSMETIC MANAGEMENT OF EXCESS HAIR

There are several methods women may use to conceal or remove excess hair. Superfluous hair may be concealed by bleaching or removed by plucking with tweezers, clipping with a scissors, waxing, shaving, chemical depilation, mechanical abrasion and electrolysis.

All these methods (except electrolysis) have a temporary effect, and each method has advantages and disadvantages. The choice of method should be made depending on the consistency of the hair, the area and amount of growth, and personal preference.

REMOVAL OF EXCESS HAIR BY SHAVING

The most popular way of removing unwanted hair on the legs and underarms is shaving. In fact, shaving of legs and underarms has become a standard grooming activity for most American women.

According to one major manufacturer, about 98 percent of all American women between the ages of fifteen and forty-four shave.

Women account for 16 to 18 percent of razor blade consumption and about 27 percent of electric shaver sales. Nearly 80 percent of women who remove hair from legs or underarms use razor blades; 20 percent use electric shavers; and approximately 4 percent use depilatories, waxes and electrolysis.

(Percentages total more than 100 because some women use one method for underarms and another for legs.)

Most women shave about twice a week, more often as summer and bathing suit time approaches. In spite of the widespread practice of shaving by women in this country in other countries shaving is decidedly limited. However, there are signs that it is becoming more popular in many European countries.

Because shaving is the most popular way of dealing with excess hair, many questions and misconceptions have arisen about its effects and about how it should be done. Dermatologists point out that most of the time there is no harm in shaving—men have been doing it for thousands of years with few side effects. As for the myth that shaving makes new hair grow faster and thicker, they claim shaving has no structural effect on hair because the hair papilla which determines the structure of the hair is located below the surface of the skin and is not affected by anything done to the dead hair shafts above the surface of the skin. Temporary methods (including shaving) seem to thicken hair because a short hair is less flexible than a long hair and, therefore, feels more bristly. Here are a few suggestions to make shaving more comfortable, safe and effective:

First, never shave dry. Hair can soak up to one third of its own weight in water, and wet hair is soft and pliable and easier to cut. The most convenient way to shave is during or directly following a warm shower or bath.

A shaving cream or lather is recommended. It will lubricate the skin and keep the all-important water from evaporating. Use a clean razor and a sharp blade. Many used blades can be dull, causing discomfort and irritation. Use long, upward, even strokes when shaving the leg.

Do not wipe a razor blade dry since this will dull its keen shaving edge. Simply loosen the razor and rinse with hot water, then shake it and let it drain. If your skin is irritated due to shaving, shave in the direction of hair growth. If shaving is extremely irritating consult a dermatologist. Occasionally women find that applying an antiperspirant shortly after shaving causes irritation. In such cases, it is better to wait a few hours or until the next day before using the antiperspirant; a mild medicated powder can be used meanwhile.

Most nicks and scrapes caused by shaving are due to haste or carelessness. When bleeding occurs apply pressure on the nick with a dry, clean (preferably sterile) cloth or pad until the bleeding has been stopped (one to two minutes usually). Apparently only a negligible number of women use styptic pencils. Surveys conducted by the Gillette Safety Razor Company show that more than half of women blade users use toilet soap to prepare for shaving; of the remaining, 25 percent shave dry, 17 percent use a shaving preparation and 7 percent use plain water or some other method. Probably the reason so many women use toilet soap as a shaving preparation is because most shaving is done in conjunction with bathing.

Ladies' electric shavers are preferred by some women because they give a fairly close shave with less irritation. Most manufacturers of electric shavers for women warn "use on dry surfaces for best results."

Few women remove facial hair by shaving. Most women do not have serious excess facial hair problems until after the menopause, at which time this hair may begin to grow longer, darker and sometimes thicker.

Surprisingly, there are no actual medical reasons why a woman should not shave to remove hair from the face. Contrary to popular belief, neither shaving nor other methods of temporary hair removal affect the texture, color or rate of hair growth. However, facial shaving has masculine connotations for many women, and those who are troubled by dark or excessive facial hair prefer other methods of cosmetic treatment.

REMOVAL OF EXCESS HAIR BY BLEACHING

Bleaching is the simplest cosmetic aid for the common, mild "peach fuzz" variety of excess hair so often found on the upper lip, as well as hair growth on the arms.

Commercially prepared bleaches are available or a preparation can be made at home. For a home treatment, make a paste of baking soda and 6 percent (bleaching strength) hydrogen peroxide (ask your druggist for this strength). Then add a few drops of household ammonia, apply and leave on for about ten minutes. Another simple bleach preparation is a paste of soap chips and bleaching peroxide plus a few drops of ammonia.

Bleaching has certain advantages over other methods because it is painless and harmless to the average skin. (Occasionally there are reports of irritation.) Another advantage is that repeated bleaching damages the hair, which then tends to break off. The disadvantage of bleaching is that the hair is still present, although less obvious. If temporary irritation occurs, experiment with a less concentrated solution to find the preparation best suited to your skin. Consult a physician if irritation continues.

CHEMICAL DEPILATION

Chemical depilatories are preferred by some women for temporary hair removal, but should not be used on the face unless the label specifically states that the product can be used there.

Chemical depilatories contain alkaline agents that break down the structure of the hair, so that it detaches easily from the skin at the surface. Skin irritation may develop after use of these products because hair and skin are similar in composition, and any compound that has a destructive effect on hair will also affect the skin to some extent.

Skin irritation may be minimized by following instructions and observing the time schedules indicated in the instructions. Dermatological consultation is advised if irritaton is a problem.

Because they work by chemical action, depilatories usually take about ten to fifteen minutes to work on some areas of the underarms or legs. Many women consider this an inconvenience and prefer to shave, because it's faster. It is claimed that the results from depilatories last longer than shaving because the hair is removed closer to the surface of the skin, but the difference, if it exists, is probably slight.

Depilatories gained a "bad name" when they first came on the market, because many women disliked their chemical odor and the length of treatment. However, modern depilatories have overcome the odor problem, and some new foam depilatories have reduced the waiting period to five minutes or less.

WAXING

This is one of the oldest methods of temporary hair removal and one of the least popular. Most waxes must be heated. A thin layer of melted wax is then applied to the skin, allowed to cool and quickly stripped off in the direction of hair growth. The hairs are embedded in the wax and plucked out as the wax is removed. A few "cold" waxes are available. A strip of cloth or some other material is applied over a thin layer of wax and "zipped" off, removing hairs embedded in the wax. While waxing can be used to remove leg and arm hair, it is most often used to remove facial hair, such as on the upper lip or chin.

Because the hairs are plucked out below the surface, the results from waxing last longer. It takes several weeks for a new growth to become evident. On the negative side, waxing may be painful and cause skin irritation, particularly if the wax is too hot when applied. Because one must wait for hair to get long enough for wax applications, a stubble will show for a short time. Waxing kits are available for home use, but most waxing is done in beauty salons because the technique of application and removal requires a good amount of experience.

ABRASIVES

Abrasives, such as pumice, are among the oldest devices employed for temporary hair removal. Rubbing the pumice over the skin on the site of hair growth produces friction which wears off the hairs at the surface of the skin.

These devices have the advantage of being inexpensive and easy to use. They are not as likely to cause skin irritation as chemical depilatories and may remove hair closer to the surface of the skin than shaving. They have the disadvantage of being somewhat slow and tedious and are impractical for large areas. If the abrasive is rubbed too vigorously the skin will be irritated.

Once the hairs are removed, regular treatments may take less time, since the new hairs will be short. It is possible that the hair growth may become less coarse or dense after years of using a pumice, but this procedure cannot be considered a permanent method of hair removal.

After using a pumice it is advisable to gently massage a mild cream or lotion into the area to lessen skin irritation produced by the abrasion.

OTHER METHODS OF TEMPORARY REMOVAL

Plucking with tweezers is the preferred method for temporary removal of scattered hairs on the face or chest. It is obviously impractical when the growth is extensive, such as on the legs and arms. Plucking may be somewhat painful, but has no other adverse effects. Regrowth sufficient to require repeated plucking may occur anywhere from two to twelve weeks, depending on the density and speed of hair growth in a given area. It is interesting to note that women do not hesitate to pluck eyebrow hairs but believe it is harmful to pluck hairs elsewhere.

Clipping (with a scissors) may be satisfactory for removing hair from the upper lip and the chest, the only disadvantage being that it is temporary.

PROFESSIONAL ELECTROLYSIS

The only safe method for the permanent removal of superfluous hair is by electrolysis, or destruction of the hair root with electric current. This is done by introducing a very fine wire probe into the opening of the hair follicle. The electric current destroys the hair root and loosens the hair, which is then removed with tweezers.

This can be done either with galvanic current (electrolysis proper) or by modified high-frequency current. With galvanic current, a proficient operator is less likely to produce scarring and the incidence of regrowth is less. With a modified high-frequency current, more hair can be removed in each session. A newer system of professional electrolysis called photo-*depilation* (destruction of the hair root by pulsed and guided light beam) appears to be limited in performance, at least with present equipment.

Most professional machines today utilize the high-frequency current, which has led some electrologists to advertise that they do not perform electrolysis, implying that they have a unique system of hair removal. Technically, they do not perform electrolysis but use a particular brand of machine that works with high-frequency current. The safety and effectiveness of the technique depend on the expertise of the operator, not on the machine.

As with any procedure, the competence of non-medical electrologists varies widely. In many states there are no minimal training and licensing requirements. Physicians rarely do electrolysis themselves, but they may have a technician proficient in the technique, or they may refer patients to a competent electrologist. Electrolysis can be a long, tedious, uncomfortable and expensive process and is not suitable for all cases of excess hair. Extensive hair growth may involve treatments (usually half an hour) once or twice a week for as long as two years, because each hair root must be treated individually.

For this reason, electrolysis is generally recommended for removal of facial hair, while temporary methods are considered more practical for the arms and legs.

If performed improperly, the electric current may damage the skin and result in scarring. Other temporary complications from electrolysis may be irritation, infection and patches of discoloration. Satisfactory results, with minimal post-treatment reactions and danger of scarring, are produced by using fine wires and the smallest amount of current that is effective and by limiting the number of hairs in close proximity removed in each treatment. It is better to "thin out" the area than to concentrate on one spot. Some skins do not tolerate electrolysis even with the best technique.

A certain amount of hair regrowth will always occur after electrolysis even when it is performed by a skilled operator. Most experts estimate that about 40 to 60 percent regrowth is normal.

Some hair growth recurs because the procedure is necessarily "blind." Some follicles are crooked or grow at an angle and it is not always possible to be certain that the needle and sufficient electricity touched and destroyed the hair root. It is not possible to determine immediately whether the hair root has been permanently destroyed. If the hair has simply been plucked, the root will remain intact and the hair will regrow within several weeks and require new treatment.

HOME ELECTROLYSIS DEVICES

Various types of home electrolysis devices are advertised for permanent removal of hair by self-treatment. The basic procedure is the same as for professional electrolysis. Complications would also be comparable to those that may occur from professional electrolysis. Except for cost, home electrolysis has all of the disadvantages of professional electrolysis, plus others.

Inexperienced users of home electrolysis devices may have more difficulty than a skilled professional operator in determining the direction of the hair follicle and the amount of current that is needed.

More than one treatment is necessary to destroy many hairs permanently, and the limit on the money-back guarantee is often too short to permit adequate evaluation.

In contrast to professional treatments in which an experienced, skilled operator may remove several hundred hairs per session, the inexperienced operator of a home device will probably be able to remove no more than thirty to forty hairs per hour. Older people may not be able to sustain use of the device for a long period of time.

Home devices are better suited for removal of hair from areas such as the lower parts of the arms and legs which are readily accessible, while professional electrolysis is best suited for removal of facial hairs. Self-treatment of facial hairs requires the use of a mirror, which means the movements are reversed, and this is not easy.

The degree to which safe and satisfactory results may be obtained through self-electrolysis treatments depends to a large extent on the condition of the hair and skin, the equipment and the skill of the individual. By carefully following the manufacturer's directions, with patience, time and development of skill, removal of some hair by home electrolysis may be achieved.

CREDIT: *American Medical Association. Reviewed and checked for accuracy by Milton Robin, M.D., dermatologist, Chicago, Illinois.*

Hairy Chests

One of the more common myths is that hairy-chested males are more virile, "manly," sexually active, etc. The unspoken implication is that the male who has little or no hair on his chest is less virile, less "manly" and an underachiever sexually.

The response to the following letter contains a good deal of valid information on the subject.

DEAR ANN LANDERS: The letter to Elmer's wife was my laugh for the day. Why any woman would attach so much importance to the hair on a man's chest is a mystery to me.

My brother happened to have a very hairy chest and he was so proud of it he showed it off at every opportunity. He especially enjoyed displaying his bountiful growth in the presence of my husband, who had very little hair on his chest.

One day I happened to run across a magazine article that surprised me. It said men with hairy chests were fooling themselves if they considered it a sign of manliness. The more hair on the chest (according to the person who wrote the article), the more female hormones the man had. He went on to say the hairy-chested male is more likely to produce female children while the less hairy-chested man is more apt to have sons. (My brother has four girls and one boy. We have three boys and one girl.)

After I showed that article to my brother he strutted a lot less and kept his shirt buttoned more.   LAST LAUGH

DEAR L.L.: That article may have solved an irritating problem for you, dear, but according to Dr. Norbert Frinkel, director of the Center for Endocrinology at Northwestern University Medical School, there is no convincing evidence that links the quantity of chest hair with the level of female or male sex hormones—or, for that matter, virility or sexual performance. Also, it has nothing whatsoever to do with the ability to have either girl or boy babies.

CREDIT: *Ann Landers.*

Halitosis

(*Bad Breath*)

Halitosis, fetor oris, malodor, bad breath are terms used for the emittance of putrid odors from the mouth. Normal exhaled air has generally a very faint sweetish smell which is by no means offensive. Halitosis, on the other hand, is of great social significance in modern American society. This is well borne out by the amount of money spent on mouthwashes, gargles and breath sweeteners. There is little evidence, however, that any of these products have much value in preventing or making bad breath less offensive, except perhaps by masking the unpleasant odor temporarily.

The causes of halitosis can be placed into two categories; those of intra-oral origin, that is from within the mouth itself, or those from extra-oral origin, arising from areas other than the mouth.

INTRA-ORAL CAUSES

By far the most significant causes of halitosis are those which occur in the mouth. Poor oral hygiene, which allows food debris to collect and stagnate, and dental plaque, which adheres to teeth or dental appliances as well as to the tongue and other structures in the oral cavity, are the most important factors contributing to bad odors. Other local oral factors include stagnant saliva (contributing to early morning bad breath), dental decay, periodontal (gum) diseases, dehydration, oral infections and smoking.

Researchers have shown that odors may arise from the decaying action of the bacteria in the dental plaque, saliva, on the tongue, etc. Other research workers have also shown that certain substances found within the dental plaque and in debris found in saliva and coating the tongue are capable of giving off volatile sulfur compounds such as hydrogen sulphide which account for the unpleasant odors in halitosis.

EXTRA-ORAL CAUSES

Common extra-oral causes of halitosis include diseases of the respiratory tract such as chronic sinusitis, post-nasal drip, pharyngitis, tonsilitis, lung infections, bronchiectasis and malignant tumors. Certain odors may arise from the stomach but are generally only detectable during belching or vomiting. Certain substances such as garlic or onions even if swallowed whole without chewing are soon detected in the breath, after being absorbed from the digestive tract and exhaled through the lungs. These odors disappear once the causative agents have been cleared from the blood circulation.

CONTROL OF HALITOSIS

As the retention of food debris and the collection of dental plaque on the teeth and dentures are the primary causes of unpleasant odor from the mouth, it stands to reason that their removal by toothbrushing is the most effective means of reducing halitosis. Brushing after every meal is ideal but many people find this impractical. It goes without saying that the teeth should be brushed every morning and before bedtime. Flossing nightly is highly recommended.

The bacteria in plaque also cause dental diseases such as dental caries (decay) and periodontal (gum) diseases. Therefore, having your dentist remove plaque periodically (at least once a year) will also prevent these diseases which contribute markedly to the cause of halitosis.

CREDIT: *I. Leon Dogon, head, Department of Operative Dentistry at Harvard School of Dental Medicine; head, Department of Dental Materials, Forsyth Dental Center, Boston, Massachusetts.*

Handicapped

How to Best Help the Handicapped Adjust to a Normal Life

My life as a physician has been dedicated to the rehabilitation of disabled people, and I am asked many times for advice by anxious families, friends and bewildered and frightened people who do not know how to deal with the disabled. The basic principles are very simple: common sense, good manners and sensitivity.

Disabled individuals are just people, who because of their disability have packs on their mental backs and packs on their physical backs. However, if through courage, opportunity and hard work they conquer their disability and get back into the mainstream of life, they have a quality of spirit the average person knows little about.

You don't get fine china by putting clay in the sun. It must go through the white heat of the kiln. But once it goes through the fire, it is porcelain, not clay. And so it is with the disabled. Able-bodied individuals must understand that this is a basic principle. These are special folks. They may look different, walk differently, speak in a different way, but they are people—sensitive people, brave people—who want to live the best lives they can with whatever they have left. Enlightened, sensitive friends can help make this possible.

Most disabled people, especially those who have been through rehabilitation, do not like to be helped unless it is absolutely necessary and they ask for it. Years ago at the Institute we established a policy: if a patient fell, we waited until he asked to be assisted. Part of his training was to learn to get up after a fall and do it with pride. Blind people waiting to cross the street often must have assistance and appreciate a courteous inquiry. They prefer to take your arm rather than for you to grab theirs and propel them across the street. Again, the same rules—sensitivity, common sense and good manners.

I remember a boy in the Air Force who was shot down in the Battle of Britain. He had lost both hands. His face was horribly scarred and he was blind. The young man had been married only a month when he left for combat. He was afraid his wife would be frightened when she saw his severely scarred face. He refused to see her for many months after his return to the United States. One day she came to the hospital and demanded to see her husband. He was terrified—like a small child—and shook with fear when she walked in the door. She took one look at him, ran across the room, threw her arms around his neck and said, "Honey, you never needed to worry about me. I married a man, not a face."

That woman typifies the spiritual relationship that so-called "normal" people should have with the disabled, whether it is a facial disfigurement, a limb off, blindness or any other type of disability.

Since World War II, attitudes toward the physically handicapped throughout the world have changed radically. I remember two severely disabled airmen who came to me shortly after the war and asked for help in finding jobs where they might go to work after dark and return to their homes before daylight. It seems on several occasions, when they walked out in the street, people stared, and sometimes even screamed. I was able to find employment for both men. They went to work and learned to understand why people were so upset and felt sorry for them. Before long they were able to establish themselves in a life that provided self-sufficiency and dignity.

When children are born without a limb, we teach them very early to understand that in some ways they are stronger than their so-called "normal" peers. I remember an instance in Korea in 1953 when I visited an orphanage. There were able-bodied children, sick children and disabled children. But they were all homeless and hungry. When they sang, however, they were all happy, except for one little boy who had lost an arm. He just sat there and looked at the floor. At the end of the meeting I went over to the lad and put my hand on his. "Is it because you only have one arm?" I asked. He replied, "Yes," with tears in his eyes. I said, "But you know that one arm is much stronger than the other kids' because you do twice as much work with it, and you should show them how strong it is. Wrestle with them if necessary. When I get back to the United States I am going to send you a new and special arm."

I did send him a special arm several weeks later and when I returned to Korea the following year, the young lad was in the group that met the airplane. He gave me a big smile and proudly shook my hand with his artificial one. That once withdrawn, forlorn boy had become a leader in the school.

We have learned through the horrors of war that arms and legs and eyes and ears and muscles and bone do not make a man. It is the spirit that counts and if people would just remember this there would be no problems understanding and helping and loving our handicapped friends.

CREDIT: *Howard A. Rusk, M.D., Director, New York University Medical Center, Institute of Rehabilitation Medicine, New York, New York.*

Hangovers*

Every weekend, six million Americans shudder and shake their way through that morning-after-the-night-before feeling.

Hangovers are nothing new, but what causes them is—and it's not just booze. According to the Yale Center of Alcohol Studies, a host of emotional and psychological factors go into the making of a Class A hangover—and you don't have to drink all the booze in town to get one.

It's not how much or what kind of alcohol you drink, it's what it does to

* By Meg Whitcomb, copyright © The Star-World News Corporation, July 6, 1976 issue.

you that brings on a hangover. If you can get drunk on two scotches, your hangover can be just as bad as if you'd had ten.

And it doesn't matter if you prefer ouzo, vodka, sake or good old American brew. If you get drunk on it, the consequences are the same.

"Hangover is the direct result of a disturbance to the nervous system, but not of any injury to it," says Dr. Seldon Bacon, former director of the Yale Center of Alcohol Studies.

"Only in the last twenty years has much been learned about hangovers.

"Before that, it was considered a minor and humorous irritant, not serious enough for scientific study."

But during World War II and the Korean war it was seen that the hangover was responsible for a huge wastage of manpower in the factories and defense plants.

Today most of the nation's big corporations have programs to deal with the heavy drinker and his hangover.

"The half-man who comes to work the next morning accomplishes nothing," says Dr. Bacon.

"For practical purposes he isn't there at all. From the viewpoint of performance it would be far better if both halves stayed home."

To understand how alcohol works on the body we must first realize that it is a drug. It contains no vitamins, minerals or proteins, so it requires no digestion.

Alcohol passes directly through the stomach wall into the bloodstream in pure form. It reaches the brain quickly and goes to work on the nervous system.

This is when you feel your first reaction, usually lightheadedness—that "high" feeling.

So begins what often ends in a hangover, unless you stop right there.

Why does a hangover bring on unslaked thirst, thundering headache, the jitters, depression and fatigue? Let's take them one at a time:

THIRST: Contrary to popular belief, alcohol does not "dry out" the body. We are all 70 percent water. Two thirds of this water lies in individual cells, the rest helps make up the bloodstream.

Alcohol upsets this balance; the cell water shifts to extracellular body areas and is discharged in the urine, causing those frequent trips to the john. This loss of cell water creates thirst.

HEADACHE: Experts at the Yale Center believe that psychological causes are central to the blistering headache known to all hangover victims.

Anxiety, remorse, worry, guilt cause fluctuations in blood pressure which, in turn, cause headache.

SHAKES: These result from the state of extreme anxiety and tension in which the hangover victim finds himself on returning from the non-reality of drunkenness.

Dr. Georgio Lolli of New Haven, Connecticut, says: "The general psychological picture in hangover is that of a person saying, 'The world doesn't offer me anything. I am worth nothing.' The hangover is a time of sorrow."

DEPRESSION AND FATIGUE: Depression is also a psychological reaction to overindulgence. It relates directly to guilt and remorse.

There are countless hangover cures floating around. The most venerable of all, of course, is the hair of the dog—drinking whatever it was you got drunk on.

This will temporarily ease hangover misery. It momentarily anesthetizes a headache, quiets the nerves and also provides a spurt of energy.

But too much hair of the dog and the whole vicious cycle can start all over again.

There are a lot of preventative theories around, too. One of the most popular theories rests on the premise that certain drinks are safer than others.

Millions of drinkers are positive that scotch is safer than rye, bourbon is gentler than gin, or highballs are safer with water than soda.

The fact is that any intoxicating beverage will produce a hangover if enough alcohol gets into the blood.

Alcohol is no more potent in whiskey than it is in beer or wine.

Regardless of the form in which it goes down, it always takes the same person the same amount of time to oxidize it and eliminate it from his system.

The same applies to the wrong-headed notion about mixing drinks.

A cocktail is a mixed drink but it's not the fact that gin and vermouth are mixed in martinis that makes them so lethal.

Mixed or not, it's all still alcohol.

One popular belief is that a hangover can be prevented by swallowing a few ounces of olive oil or cream before drinking.

Both olive oil and cream will line the stomach walls, thereby slowing the absorption of alcohol. This will indeed retard intoxication, but not the hangover.

Hangover remedies range from milk, ice cream and strong coffee to concoctions like the white of an egg, vodka, sugar and Pernod mixed to a froth and downed in one gulp.

These do offer relief, but only momentarily.

Meanwhile the same old treatments prevail. Aspirin, rest, a warm bath and hot meals.

Food is important, especially food rich in carbohydrates, for the hangover sufferer is a victim of fatigue, and needs to increase the sugar content in his blood as rapidly as he can.

Most important of all is rest—not exercise or sweating in a steam bath—and better yet, sleep. There's truth to the words "sleeping it off."

HOW TO CURE HANGOVER

A hangover is nature's way of telling you that you got drunk. I've never understood why nature goes to the bother, since millions of wives pass on the information.

Except for abstinence or moderation, there is no way to completely avoid a hangover. But certain rules, if followed, will ease the discomfort.

First, stick with the same drink you started with. By that I mean that if you started the evening drinking champagne, beer and frozen daiquiris, stick with champagne, beer and frozen daiquiris the rest of the evening.

Drink quickly. If you can do most of your drinking within the first hour of the party and quickly pass out, you will have regained consciousness and be well on your way to recovery while others are still gadding about. By the time the Rose Bowl game comes on, your eyeballs will have come out from behind your nose.

Be careful what you eat, especially well into the night. Especially avoid eating napkins, paper plates and pizza boards.

It should be remembered that part of a hangover's discomfort is psychological. When you awaken, you will be filled with a deep sense of shame, guilt, disgust, embarrassment, humiliation and self-loathing.

This is perfectly normal, understandable and deserved. To ease these feelings, try to think only of the pleasant or amusing things that you did before blacking out.

Block from your mind all memories of what you later did to your host's rug, what you said to that lady with the prominent cleavage that made her scream, whether you or her husband threw the first punch. Don't dredge up those vague recollections of being asleep in your host's bathtub while everybody pleaded with you to unlock the bathroom door.

These thoughts will just depress you. Besides, your wife will explain it in detail as the day goes on. And the week, too. If anything, you should laugh it off. It's easy. Using your thumb and forefinger, pry your tongue loose from the roof of your mouth, try to stop panting for a moment and say: Ha, ha.

The other part of a hangover is physical. It is usually marked by throbbing pain in the head, behind the eyes, in the back of the neck and in the stomach. You might also have pain in the arms, legs, elbows, chin and elsewhere, depending upon how much leaping, careening, flailing and falling you did.

Take two aspirin and hold your tongue under the kitchen faucet. Or rest it in the freezer compartment of your refrigerator. If you don't like to take pills, the headache can be eased by going outside and plunging your head into a snowbank. Be sure it isn't a snow-covered hedge.

Most experts recommend physical activity, such as blinking your eyes during the Bowl games and moving your lips just enough to say to your wife: "Later, we'll discuss it later."

On the other hand, you might consider leaping out of bed the moment you open your eyes, flinging the windows open to let the cold air in and jogging rapidly in place while violently flapping your arms and breathing deeply and heavily.

This will make you forget your hangover because it will bring on a massive coronary.

CREDIT: *Mike Royko, Associate Editor and columnist, Chicago* Sun-Times.

Headache

Headache, or cephalalgia, is one of the most common symptoms which afflict mankind. Medical specialists and general practitioners are constantly confronted by patients to whom headache is a serious problem. It is a rare individual who at some time or another has not had a headache.

Headaches may vary widely as to severity, location, quality and duration. Some that seem horrendous to a patient (or to the patient's family) may not be caused by a serious illness at all. On the other hand, certain headache patterns when evaluated by a skilled diagnostician may turn out to be a symptom of a severe disorder. It is important that an individual who experiences acutely severe or chronic or recurrent headaches consult a physician.

In taking a history from a patient with headache one must ask detailed, specific questions in order to obtain a clearly defined clinical description. These include questions such as: When did the headaches begin? Are they constant or intermittent? If intermittent, how long do they last? How severe are they? What is the quality of the pain (i.e., sharp, stabbing, throbbing, pressing, exploding, burning, sticking, etc.)? What is the location of the pain; does it spread or radiate? Does it fluctuate in severity? What precipitates the pain? What makes it worse or better? Are the headaches associated with neck stiffness, scalp sensitivity, nausea, vomiting, dizziness? Does a change in body position affect the pain? Does coughing, sneezing or straining increase the pain? Does the headache respond to pain medications? Does the headache interfere with routine functioning?

A careful study of a patient with severe or persistent headaches includes, in addition to a detailed history, a study of vital signs, especially blood pressure, and general, neurologic and psychologic examinations. In addition to general laboratory studies specific testings should include skull films, sinus X rays (if indicated), an electroencephalogram and brain scan. With increasing frequency computerized tomograms (multidimensional X rays) of the head are being utilized. In the not too distant future these will become routine procedures in patients with significant headache. Arteriography (dye study of arteries) and pneumocephalography (air study) are reserved for more esoteric problems.

CAUSES OF HEADACHE

Headache pain may be caused by a wide variety of processes. These vary from psychologic stress to organic lesions of the intracranial structures to lesions of other organs.

Headache of Psychogenic Origin

Fortunately most headaches are caused by emotional stress. These are commonly called "tension headaches" and vary from mild to excruciating. While the discomfort may be located in any part of the head, it is often described as a "bandlike" squeezing sensation. At times a patient feels as if he or she is wearing a hat that is too tight. Some patients with tension headaches may also complain of having a sensitive scalp or a tightness of the muscles of the back of the neck.

A careful history will usually reveal the relationship between anxiety-producing situations and the onset of the headache. Most headaches that persist without letup over a period of many years are usually caused by continued anxiety. However, there are exceptions to this rule; chronic headaches at no time should be taken lightly. Some individuals with tension headaches complain of nausea, vomiting and dizziness.

Most tension headaches disappear with the passing of the stressful situation. Other patients require mild analgesics such as aspirin or aspirin substitutes to relieve muscle tightness; some require tranquilization. A smaller number may require professional counseling.

Headaches may also be a reflection of a more severe psychologic disorder. This has been called "masked depression" and occurs primarily in middle-age women. The patient is commonly seen by a large number of physicians before a correct diagnosis is made. The underlying depression may be of severe proportions. Such patients require intensive psychiatric care including the use of antidepressant drugs and psychotherapy.

Intracranial Lesions (Abnormalities Inside the Head)

There is a wide variety of intracranial lesions. These include: (1) cerebrovascular disorders (abnormalities of blood vessels); (2) intracranial tumors—these tumors may originate in the skull, meninges (tissues covering the brain), various portions of the brain, the blood vessels, the intracranial nerves, the pituitary gland; (3) head trauma—this may vary from concussion, contusion of the brain, skull fracture or damage to the blood vessels, meninges or the brain proper; (4) infections—there may be infections of the meninges (meningitis) or the brain (encephalitis); (5) interference with the flow of cerebrospinal fluid—the excessive accumulation of cerebrospinal fluid may cause hydrocephalus, which may produce intense headaches.

There are a number of mechanisms to explain how these lesions cause head pain. One or more of these mechanisms may play a role in a given patient with a given lesion. For example, head pains associated with arterial hypertension, fever, allergic reactions and anoxia (lack of oxygen) are usually related to dilatation of the blood vessels inside the head. Patients with arterial hypertension may complain of a throbbing or pounding headache over the back of the head. Others will complain of a discomfort over the top of the head. Still others will feel a haziness or a diffuse fullness. A throbbing sensation that is co-ordinated with the pulse is another common complaint.

In contrast to this mechanism, the headaches caused by most space-occupying lesions such as tumors, abscesses, infections and hemorrhage commonly are secondary to displacement, traction or compression of large vessels or intracranial nerves. Rapidly growing tumors, abscesses or hematomas (blood clots) are often associated with a marked amount of edema (swelling). The combination of the primary lesion plus the additional swelling can result in a massive displacement and compression of blood vessels, nerves and normal brain tissue accompanied by massive headache. These headaches are at times associated with violent vomiting and dramatic localized neurologic abnormalities, such as paralysis, loss of feeling, etc.

Infections of the meninges (meningitis), which may be due to viral or bacterial infections or a chemical irritation, are usually associated with severe headache. In addition there is a stiffening of the neck due to spasm of the paraspinal muscles that may be very profound. Meningitis is usually associated with high temperatures and other manifestations of severe illness.

Other Causes of Headache

Headache may be due to neuritis or neuralgia of the nerves of the scalp. At times there is a combination of scalp pain and pain over the face, depending on which superficial sensory nerves are involved. Trigeminal neuralgia, which involves the fifth cranial nerve, may produce agonizing brief bursts of pain involving the frontal area of the head but more commonly the cheek or lower jaw. Shingles (herpes zoster) may at times involve the forehead and the eye and may be a source of chronic, nagging head pain. On other occasions it may involve the region below the eye.

Headaches may also be caused by ailments involving the eyes, sinuses, auditory canals, teeth and jaws. Arthritic changes in the top bones of the neck may at times also cause head pains. Eye problems such as eye strain, glaucoma and double vision are among the abnormalities that can cause headaches. Nasal obstruction and sinus trouble may cause severe pain across the forehead or cheekbones.

Head injuries, particularly those of a more severe nature, are common causes of headaches. At times, in the initial stages, they are masked by impaired levels of consciousness. The amount of headache does not necessarily reflect the severity of the injury. Chronic head pains sometimes result from a head injury and may be associated with irritability, anxiety and limitation of functioning for months and even longer.

MIGRAINE

Migraine is a common syndrome characterized by headaches that are periodic and recurrent. The pain may be generalized or on only one side of the head. A migraine may or may not be preceded by warnings. Not infrequently, the warnings come in the form of "flashing lights," blind spots (scotomata) or a more extensive loss of vision. Less commonly there may be warnings in the form of a feeling of weakness on one side or a loss of sensation or a "pins and needles" feeling. Some patients may have warnings in the form of dizziness or vertigo (sensation of rotation).

Migraine headaches are classically pounding and throbbing in nature. They are often incapacitating. Nausea and vomiting frequently accompany such headaches. The patients may retch to the point of exhaustion. Photophobia (sensitivity to light) is a frequent complaint. Most patients will prefer to lie in a dark, quiet room until the pain subsides. The headaches themselves are often associated with dizziness, vertigo, diarrhea or complaints of chilliness. The pains may last for hours or even days.

Migraine headaches may occur at any age. They are seen in children often in a modified form. In my experience the majority of patients are past twenty years of age when the headaches begin. This ailment is more common in women than in men. In my practice the ratio of women to men is 6:1. Very frequently there is a family history of migraine in which a parent and one or more siblings will have headache patterns similar to those found in the patient.

Migraine patients commonly have a specific personality profile. They are usually highly intelligent, perfectionistic, superconscientious, aggressive, strong-willed and sensitive. Usually at least one parent will have a similar personality. The episodes of migraine may be precipitated by stressful situations, anger, head injuries or taking of oral contraceptives. In women who have a propensity to migraine headaches they frequently occur during the pre-menstrual period. Less commonly they may occur during menstruation.

There are many theories as to the cause of migraine. The most common theory holds that the warnings, many of which I have already described, are secondary to constriction or narrowing of the arteries within the brain. In contrast to this, the headache itself is due to dilatation or stretching of the arteries of the covering tissue of the brain or scalp. There is some evidence that a neutral transmitting biochemical substance, serotonin, may play a role in the headache mechanism.

Migraine headaches may often be treated successfully. The treatment has two phases: (1) the treatment of the attack and (2) the prevention of recurrent headaches.

Mild migraines can often be relieved by taking medication such as aspirin or aspirin substitutes. More commonly, however, other preparations are necessary. Ergotrates, medications that constrict the dilated arteries outside the brain, are usually necessary. The ergotrates may be taken orally, by rectum, by injection in the muscle or even in a vein. The manner in which this type of medication is given depends on the frequency and intensity of the headaches and the sensitivity of the patient to various ergot preparations. The ergot compound must be given immediately at the first warning of a headache or else it is not effective.

A common method of managing the routine migraine attack is for the patient to take two tablets containing a combination of ergotamine tartrate and caffeine (Cafergot, Sandoz) by mouth with the first warning of a headache, followed by one tablet every half hour for two hours. More severe episodes may be treated by giving an ergotrate in the muscle or in the vein. Some patients become nauseated and vomit after taking ergot preparations. I should point out that ergot preparations should not be used by pregnant women or by individuals who have vascular disease. The excessive use of ergotrates may also cause significant narrowing of the arteries of the arms and legs and the use of these drugs should be closely monitored by an experienced physician.

The prevention of migraine attacks may take a number of forms. Methysergide, which is commonly known as Sansert, often has beneficial effects in preventing or limiting migraine headaches. This preparation, similar to ergotrates, must only be taken under the close supervision of a physician because it can produce significant side effects.

Many patients with migraine require psychological help. This may simply take the form of sedation or the judicious use of tranquilizers. Other patients must be taught the relationship between their personality patterns, everyday pressures and the onset of their headaches. A significant number of individuals with migraine, particularly those in the middle-age group, may also experience underlying depressions (masked depressions) of significant intensity. In these individuals, the frequency of the migraine attacks may not be reduced until the underlying depression is treated, usually by antidepressant drugs in combination with psychotherapy.

Biofeedback, hypnotism and other forms of strong suggestive treatments have had limited effects in the long-term management of migraine headaches. There are, however, a number of patients with chronic, recurrent migraine in whom all techniques will have to be tried before a reliable control is achieved. In other words, some people must try every technique.

CREDIT: *Stanley Lesse, M.D., Med. Sc.D., Editor in Chief,* American Journal of Psychotherapy, *Associate Attending Neurologist, Neurological Institute of the Presbyterian Hospital of New York.*

Head Injuries

Instructions to Parents

SIGNS OF TROUBLE

(1) *Excessive Drowsiness*
Your child may well be exhausted by the ordeal surrounding the injury, but should be easily aroused by methods that you would ordinarily employ to awaken him from a deep sleep. If you cannot do this, take him to the hospital.

(2) *Persistent Vomiting*
Children will, in most cases, vomit one or more times following a severe head injury. Should the vomiting recur more than twice, or should it begin again hours after it has ceased, take him to the hospital.

(3) If *one pupil* appears to be *larger* than the other, take him to the hospital.

(4) If the child does not *use* either *arm* or *leg* as well as previously, or is *unsteady* in walking, take him to the hospital.

(5) Should *speech* become *slurred* or the child be apparently *unable* to *talk,* take him to the hospital.

(6) If *severe headache* occurs, particularly if it increases in severity and is not relieved by aspirin, take him to the hospital.

(7) Should the child complain of *seeing double* or should you detect any failure of the eyes to move together appropriately, take him to the hospital.

(8) Should a *convulsion* occur, place the child on his side where he cannot fall and when the convulsion ceases take him to the hospital.

On the night following the head injury, or during any nap, it is advisable to *awaken* your child every three hours and look for any of these danger signs. If you see any—guess what? TAKE HIM TO THE HOSPITAL!

CREDIT: *The Children's Hospital Medical Center, Boston, Massachusetts.*

Head Lice

Head lice have no respect for financial status or social position. They can and do show up in the best of families.

Transmitted easily from person to person, head lice spread rapidly in group situations such as schools, colleges, military and summer camps and public facilities. Outbreaks may occur any time of the year. During the summer months, lice are acquired at playgrounds, swimming pools, camps—wherever young people gather. During the winter months, when schools are in session, the incidence of head lice increases noticeably in college towns.

The presence of lice is signaled by intense itching. Another indication that lice are present is the grayish eggs (or nits) attached to the hair shafts close to the skin. The eggs hatch in seven to ten days.

Lice are sometimes difficult to spot due to their miniature size, but may be seen easily with a magnifying glass. They live on human blood which they suck through the skin. This is what produces the itching.

Lice cannot hop or jump but are transferred from person to person. Lice may also be acquired by coming in contact with lousy hats, brushes, combs, pillows, backs of chairs, car seats, infested clothing or bedding.

Somewhat smaller than the body louse, although similar in appearance, the head louse thrives best in the fine hair at the back of the head and behind the ears. Occasionally, lice wander to other parts of the body, particularly the beard or eyebrows.

While head lice do not transmit diseases, severe scratching may result in bacterial infections. Such infections should be treated by a physician. Head lice will not disappear or die of old age, nor can they be scratched out of existence.

WHAT TO DO

To eliminate a head lice problem and prevent it from spreading requires the co-operation of parents, children and school authorities. Teachers in particular should be on the lookout for children in the classroom who seem to be preoccupied with head scratching. Any such child should be examined immediately by the school nurse. If lice are detected the child should be sent home with a note to his parents urging immediate treatment and examination of other members of the family.

Parents should also be alert to head-scratching children. Grayish eggs attached to the strands of hair close to the scalp are additional evidence that lice are present.

All clothing and personal items should be boiled, steamed or dry-cleaned, including combs and brushes. Bedding and the backs of upholstered furniture, car seats, etc. should be thoroughly vacuumed and disinfected whenever possible.

School health personnel should examine other students who may have come in contact with the infested student and where necessary, urge treatment. Fortunately antilice treatments are readily available at most drugstores without prescription. Usually one shampoo treatment at home will put an end to the problem. A second shampoo is recommended within a week—just to make sure.

At this writing, the best non-prescription medications for head lice are 200 Pyrinate and Cuprex. If you go to a physician, he will give you a prescription which may be more powerful and therefore more effective than what is available over the counter.

CREDIT: *Ann Landers.*

Health

If It's Your Health, It's Your Responsibility

Prevention of disease may mean forsaking bad habits which many people enjoy—overeating, too much drinking, taking pills, staying up late at night, engaging in promiscuous sex, driving too fast and smoking cigarettes. To put it another way, it means doing things that require self-discipline—exercising, going to the dentist, getting annual physical checkups and working to maintain a harmonious family life.

The cost of sloth, gluttony, alcoholism, reckless driving, sexual frenzy and smoking is now a national and not an individual responsibility. This is justified as individual freedom. But one man's freedom in health is another man's shackle in taxes and insurance premiums. I believe the "right" to health should be replaced by the individual's moral obligation to preserve one's own health.

The individual has the "right" to expect help with information, accessible services of good quality and minimal financial barriers. Meanwhile, the people have been led to believe that national health insurance, more doctors and greater use of high-cost hospital-based technologies will improve health. Unfortunately none of them will.

The paranoid style of consumer groups demands a fight against something, usually a Big Bureaucracy. In the case of health, it is the hospitals, the doctors, the medical schools, the Medicaid-Medicare combine, the government. Nader's Raiders have yet to allow that the next major advances in the health of the American people will come from the assumption of individual responsibility for one's own health and a necessary change in habits for the majority of Americans. We spend over $30 billion annually for cigarettes and whiskey.

The behavior of Americans might be changed if there were adequate programs of health education in primary and secondary schools and even colleges—but there aren't. School health programs are abysmal at best, confining themselves to pre-emptory sick calls and posters on brushing teeth and eating three meals a day. There are no examinations to determine if anything has been learned. Awareness of danger to body and mind isn't acquired until the mid-twenties in our culture. By then set patterns of behavior are difficult to change. Children tire of "scrub your teeth," "don't eat that junk," "leave your dingy alone," "go to bed" and "get some exercise." By the time they are sixteen, society says they shall have cars, drink beer, smoke, eat junk at drive-ins and have a go at fornication. If they demur, they are sissies, queer or both. The pressure of the peer group is hardly balanced by the limp protestations of permissive parents, nervously keeping up with the Joneses in suburban ranch houses well stocked with snacks and with mobile bars.

The barriers to the assumption of individual responsibility for one's own health are lack of knowledge (implicating the inadequacies of formal education, the all-too-powerful force of advertising, and the informal systems of continuing education), lack of sufficient interest in and knowledge about what is preventable and the "cost to benefit" ratios of nationwide health programs (thereby implicating all the powerful interests in the health establishment, which couldn't be less interested, and calling for a much larger investment in fundamental and applied research), and a culture which has progressively eroded the idea of individual responsibility while stressing individual rights, the responsibility of society-at-large and the steady growth of production and consumption ("We have met the enemy and it is us!"). Changing human behavior involves sustaining and repeating an intelligible message, reinforcing it through peer pressure and approval and establishing clearly perceived rewards which materialize in as short a time as possible. Advertising agencies know this, but it is easier to sell deodorants, pantyhose and automobiles than health.

What is the problem? During the nineteenth and early twentieth centuries, communicable disease was the major health problem in the United States. In 1900 the average life expectancy at birth was 49.2 years. By 1966 it had increased to 70.1 years, due mainly to marked reduction in infant and child mortality (between birth and age fifteen). By mid-century accidents were by far the leading cause of death in youngsters, and the majority of those accidents were related to excessive use of alcohol by their parents, by adults generally and even occasionally by the youngsters themselves. While twenty-one years were added to life expectancy at birth, only 2.7 years were added to it at age sixty-five—the remaining life expectancy at age sixty-five being 11.9 years in 1900 and 14.6 in 1966. The marked increase in life expectancy at birth was due to the control and eradication of infectious disease, directly through improved nutrition and personal hygiene, and environmental changes, namely, the provision for safe water and milk supplies and for sewage disposal.

Today, the major health problems in the United States are the chronic diseases of middle and later age, mainly heart disease, cancer and strokes. Death and disability in middle age are premature and potentially preventable. For those under forty-four years, the leading causes of death are accidents, heart disease, cancer, homicide and suicide. For those under twenty-five years, accidents are by far the most common cause of death, with homicide and suicide the next leading causes. Of the roughly two million deaths in the United States in 1969, 50 percent were due to heart disease (40 percent) and strokes (10 percent); 16 percent to cancer; and 8 percent to accidents (6 percent), homicide (1 percent) and suicide (1 percent). But death statistics tell only a small part of the story. For every successful suicide, an estimated ten others, or 200,000 people, have made the attempt. For every death due to accidents, hundreds of others are injured, and many of those are permanently disabled. Over 17 percent, or thirty-six million people, have serious disabilities limiting their activities.

Dietary factors play a major role in cardiovascular disease and cancer. The major variable, as deduced from studies of migrant populations, seems to be fat content. For example, cancer of the large bowel as well as that of the breast and prostate is much more common in the United States than in Japan, and seems to be related to the difference in fat intake. The American derives 40 to 45 percent of his calories from fat, whereas the Japanese obtains only 15 to 20 percent of his calories from that source. Japanese descendants living in the United States have an incidence of bowel cancer similar to that seen in native Americans. Although the mechanism has not been established, it would appear that high fat intake (usually with resultant obesity) predisposes the American to both cancer and cardiovascular disease. Data from long-term study of cardiovascular disease in Framingham, Massachusetts, indicate that each 10 percent reduction in weight in men thirty-five to fifty-five years old would result in a 20 percent decrease in the incidence of coronary disease. A 10 percent increase in weight would result in a 30 percent increase in coronary disease.

The individual must realize that a perpetuation of the present system of high-cost, after-the-fact medicine will only result in higher costs and greater frustration. The next major advances in the health of the American people will be determined by what the individual is willing to do for himself and for society-at-large. If he is willing to reassert his authority with his children, he can provide for their optimal mental and physical development. If he participates fully in private and public efforts to reduce the hazards of the environment, he can reduce the causes of premature death and disability. If he is unwilling to do these things, he should stop complaining about the steadily rising costs of medical care and the disproportionate share of the Gross National Product that is consumed by health care.

It is his primary critical choice—either he must change his personal bad habits or stop complaining. He can either remain the problem or become the solution to it; beneficent government cannot—indeed, should not—do it for him or to him.

CREDIT: *John H. Knowles, M.D., President, Rockefeller Foundation, New York.*

Hearing

(*Problems of the Ear*)

Hearing is the hidden sense, the sense so taken for granted that few of us appreciate it until it is impaired or lost.

Hearing is with us asleep and awake, night and day, around corners and behind us. It is the sense that alerts us to danger. Who has not been suddenly awakened by a strange sound? Hearing keeps us in communication with others and soothes us with pleasant music and the familiar sounds of home and kitchen.

The organ of hearing begins with the outer ear that collects sound and directs it into the ear canal. The eardrum membrane at the bottom of the ear canal separates the outer ear from the middle ear. A blow on the ear with the cupped hand, or a sharp instrument in the ear canal, can tear this thin membrane, leaving a perforation that prevents the normal vibrations of this membrane needed to carry sound to the hearing nerve.

The middle ear cavity, about the size of an aspirin tablet, lies just beyond the eardrum membrane. It is filled with air that reaches it from the throat through the eustachian tube. Infections from the throat can reach the middle ear the same way, causing severe earache and temporary loss of hearing. A chain of three tiny bones in the middle ear transmits sound vibrations to the nerve of hearing in the inner ear. When this chain is broken by a blow on the head or by infection a severe loss of hearing results, but almost always can be restored by an operation to reconstruct the chain.

The inner ear, containing the nerve endings of both the hearing nerve and the nerve of balance, is the most delicate as well as the most important part of the ear. Encased in solid bone, the inner ear is well protected from the outside unless a skull fracture should pass through it, destroying both hearing and balance. Loud noise, especially when repeated or continued, causes a slow deterioration of the hearing nerve. Noisy industries, jet engines, snowmobiles, shotguns and amplified rock music all result in progressive loss of hearing of the nerve type which can never be reversed.

Unlike loss of hearing due to eardrum membrane perforations, middle ear infections or a break in the chain of middle ear bones, all of which can be improved by surgery, hearing nerve loss cannot be regained by treatment or operation. Therefore great care must be taken to protect the hearing nerve from damage due to noise. Ear muffs or plugs are effective protection against noise damage. A special type of cotton called Bilesholm effectively protects the ear from noise, whereas ordinary cotton is of little value. Some people are more susceptible to hearing nerve damage from noise than others.

The outer ear canal produces a lubricating ear wax that normally works its way out and needs no special attention. Sometimes a great deal of wax collects and needs to be removed by a physician who can do so without injuring the delicate eardrum membrane. The ear should be cleaned by a washcloth daily. A piece of cotton on a stick or any sharp instrument should never be used because it often pushes the wax farther into the ear.

Water in the outer ear will infect the middle ear if the eardrum membrane has a perforation. In such cases swimming or diving is to be avoided unless the ear is protected by a plug of lamb's wool with Vaseline to make it watertight.

LOSS OF HEARING

According to the Environmental Protection Agency, some eighty million Americans live in areas in which the sound often is loud enough to interfere with speech. Of these, forty million must tolerate sound levels that threaten the hearing—one out of twenty citizens has a hearing loss. Noise not only reduces the quality of city life, it can impair mental and physical health.

As a public problem, noise is nothing new. Julius Caesar wrote the first antinoise ordinance in 44 B.C. to little effect. Two centuries later, Juvenal complained of Rome: "It is absolutely impossible to sleep anywhere in the city. The perpetual traffic of wagons in the surrounding streets is sufficient to wake the dead." In a joint letter supporting an 1864 proposal to quiet London, Dickens, Tennyson and others complained of being made "objects of persecution" by "beaters of drums, grinders of organs and bangers of banjoes." But in the United States, noise as a political issue is much newer. Few ordinances are more than fifteen years old, and most deal with airplane noise.

Since World War II, the number of high-powered noisemakers, from trucks and motorcycles to air conditioners and sirens, has increased almost geometrically. It's no wonder, as EPA found, that in many areas of the country, especially in the suburbs, the average sound level has doubled in twenty years.

Loss of hearing can be present at birth and must be detected by special kinds of tests. Severe illness with high fever can injure the hearing nerve and cause a permanent loss of hearing. Certain infections such as mumps can cause severe hearing nerve loss. One in one thousand children is severely deaf and must receive special instruction and training to learn to communicate by sign language, lip reading and speech training.

During school age a frequent cause of loss of hearing is fluid in the middle ear, sometimes from a head cold, more often from an allergy. This condition is painless and may not be discovered except by school hearing tests. The child, unable to hear parent or teacher, may be labeled disobedient or stupid, until the true cause of the difficulty is discovered. Medical treatment to remove the fluid will restore the hearing. Seven children per thousand will have a hearing loss due to fluid in the middle ear.

In some adults the eustachian tube fails to equalize air pressure in the middle ear during airplane flights. This can result in pain and loss of hearing as the plane descends. If the person is unable to open the tube by swallowing hard, medical attention may be necessary to relieve the discomfort.

In adults loss of hearing can be due to old infections of the middle ear with chronic drainage, eardrum membrane perforations or a broken chain of tiny bones. Surgery can improve hearing in most of these. Especially necessary is surgery for chronic draining ears, for in these, the infection may have gotten into the bone, with the danger of extending inward to the brain.

A rather common cause for progressive loss of hearing in adults is the condition called otosclerosis. This consists of a nodule of bone that gradually closes the opening to the inner ear, with slowly progressive loss of hearing. The stapes bone, the last in the chain of tiny bones, becomes fixed or frozen so that it no longer transmits sound to the hearing nerve. Surgery in many of these cases has restored hearing.

A hearing aid can be utilized if surgery is not performed. Otosclerosis tends to be hereditary. Otosclerosis causes progressive loss of hearing in about ten adults per one thousand. Most inner ear nerve deafness cannot be restored or improved by treatment or surgery.

After age sixty-five, hearing nerve loss due to age begins to affect most people and these cases cannot be improved by surgery or treatment. An exception is Meniere's disease, a condition that affects both hearing and balance. In the early stages of Meniere's disease, medical treatment can relieve the attacks of vertigo (loss of balance) and sometimes improve the hearing. Later on, surgery may be needed to end the disabling attacks of dizziness.

Ringing in the ears is a frequent complaint in all types of hearing loss.

When loss of hearing can be restored through surgery or treatment the ringing usually subsides. When the loss of hearing is of the nerve type, treatment is useless. A bedside radio kept on at night and wearing a hearing aid during the day are helpful in lessening the annoyance from head noises.

Another common complaint is itching in the ear canals. This may be the result of a low-grade infection of the skin of the ear canal or it may be an eczema type condition due to hair spray or other skin irritants—or to a food-related allergy. Scratching the ear canal with a toothpick or hairpin can be injurious.

Modern hearing aids are helpful in nearly all cases of hearing loss due to outer ear or middle ear disease and in many cases of hearing nerve loss. Most people, however, prefer surgery to wearing a hearing aid. It should be noted that if surgery is not successful, the only alternative is a hearing aid.

In 1976 more than 600,000 hearing aids were sold in the United States. Although this figure sounds high, there are at least ten times that number who could benefit from a hearing aid, yet they will not buy one—or if they buy one they will not use it on a regular basis. The reason—vanity. Many people feel that a hearing aid will label them as "handicapped" or "older."

With total loss of hearing, an aid is useless. The government is currently involved in legislation that would require that the cause of hearing loss be investigated by a physician before a hearing aid can be sold. Such laws will not hurt the majority of hearing aid dealers. They will, however, protect the public against unethical door-to-door solicitation.

It is well to note at this point that a great many people have a tendency to shout into the ear of a person who is wearing a hearing aid. This is not necessary; in fact it is annoying to the person with the aid. Shouting in his ear has an even more unnerving effect than if you shout in the ear of a person with normal hearing because the aid amplifies the sound.

Lip reading is the use of the eyes to supplement hearing. It is used unconsciously, to some degree, by those of us with normal hearing. It becomes increasingly necessary as loss of hearing progresses. It can be taught by a lip-reading teacher, or can be learned simply by practice, watching television and keeping the eyes fixed on the speaker.

A few simple rules will help to preserve the precious sense of hearing.

(1) Draining ears must receive medical treatment both to prevent serious consequences from the infection and to preserve or restore hearing.

(2) Put nothing "smaller than your elbow" into your ears. In other words, do not try to clean your own ear canals, for you will probably succeed only in pushing ear wax farther in, or you may injure the eardrum membrane.

(3) Avoid loud noise. If you must be around it protect your ears with ear plugs or ear muffs or Bilesholm cotton.

(4) Keep water out of your ears if there is a perforation or a chronic infection.

(5) Seek medical advice if loss of hearing is suspected, if the ear drains, itches or rings.

CREDIT: *George E. Shambaugh, Jr., M.D., Hinsdale, Illinois, Senior Attending Staff, Hinsdale Sanitarium and Hospital; Professor Emeritus of Otolaryngology, Northwestern University Medical Center; past President, American Otological Society; Chief Editor, Archives of Otolaryngology, American Medical Association; and author of* Surgery of the Ear, *Philadelphia, Pennsylvania: W. B. Saunders Company, 1967.*

DEAR ANN LANDERS: This is for the woman who is tired of shouting at her deaf mother-in-law.

I understand exactly how you feel. It IS annoying. But nobody WANTS to be deaf. Here are some practical suggestions, which I guarantee will help if you will act on them:

(1) Be sure your mother-in-law knows you are talking to her. Get her attention before you start.

(2) Face her. All deaf people lipread to a certain extent and gather clues from your facial expression.

(3) Speak SLOWLY and more distinctly. Enunciate clearly. Don't slur word endings. Use your lips and your hands when explaining something.

(4) Get to the point. Like a good news story, explain first the what, who, when and where. Then go on and elaborate as much as you wish. She needs to know what you are talking about.

(5) When there are others present, help her by saying, "We are talking about 'Cousin Joe,' " This will prevent her from interrupting with inappropriate remarks.

(6) Raise your voice only when necessary. Shouting in her ear will only make her nervous.

(7) If she asks you to repeat, use a different key word. Instead of, "We bought a new car," say, "We just bought a new Chevrolet."

(8) If you have to say it again, do so graciously. She feels bad enough having to ask you to repeat. Just smile sweetly and think of the stars you are getting in your crown, dear. Signed DEAF ALSO

DEAR ALSO: Thank you for making a solid contribution to this space today. The millions of hard-of-hearing will bless you.

Heart

DEAR READERS: Within this "Heart" section there are two articles—"Coronary Arterial Disease and the Bypass Operation" and "Valvular Heart Disease and Valve Replacement"—written especially for this encyclopedia by my good friend Dr. Michael E. DeBakey, one of the world's most distinguished heart surgeons.

Both articles are totally incomprehensible to me. Unless you have had at least two years of medical school you will not be able to understand them either.

In an attempt to simplify these articles, I sat with a medical dictionary in my lap for nearly two hours. Finally I gave up. There are no simple, lay terms for "atherosclerotic plaques" or "myocardial infarction" or "electrocardiography" or a couple of dozen other words which are sprinkled generously throughout Dr. DeBakey's articles.

I'm sure his brilliant descriptions of these two surgical procedures will be greatly appreciated by countless professors in medical schools who teach heart surgery, but for the average person, like you and me—forget it.

Ann Landers

Coronary Arterial Disease and the Bypass Operation

The blood supply that nourishes the heart is derived from the coronary arteries, which are so named because they encircle the surface of the heart like a crown. There are two major coronary arteries, a right and a left, originating from the ascending aorta, which is the large, hoselike structure about one inch in diameter that carries oxygenated blood from the heart to the rest of the body. The fine network of vessels that arises from these coronary arteries serves as tributaries to feed the heart. In the average adult the lumen or bore of these arteries is about one eighth of an inch in diameter, and each hour about fifteen gallons of blood are pumped through them.

The development of atherosclerotic plaques, which consist essentially in a localized deposit of fatty material and cholesterol within the inner layer of the arterial wall, is the major cause of coronary arterial obstruction. These atherosclerotic plaques may occur in any segment of the artery, but they are usually localized to the proximal part, the distal segments being relatively healthy. This characteristic of the disease is important with regard to the bypass operation, as will be indicated later. As these atherosclerotic plaques enlarge, they project further into the lumen of the artery and thus produce a narrowing or constriction of the lumen which, in turn, diminishes the flow of blood through the artery. When the lumen becomes so obstructed that an inadequate amount of blood is available to support the needs of the heart muscle, myocardial ischemia results, a condition characterized by an insufficient supply of oxygen to the cells of the heart muscle. The victim may then experience a form of discomfort in the chest called angina pectoris, often brought on by physical and emotional exertion. The attack may begin with a choking or constricting sensation beneath the breastbone which may then extend up into the neck and down the arm. If the obstruction in the coronary artery is sufficient to produce sudden occlusion, the patient may suffer a heart attack or in medical terms, a myocardial infarction, which means death of a part of the heart muscle. The amount of muscle damaged in this way varies considerably. In some patients it may be extensive enough to cause death. From 15 to 25 percent of patients who have such an infarction die. Most patients will fortunately survive the first attack.

The diagnosis of coronary arterial disease can be readily made by a physician after examining the patient and performing some relatively simple tests, including electrocardiography, exercise electrocardiography and possibly echocardiography. Some patients, however, may also require coronary arteriography. This test is done by inserting a catheter through an artery in the arm or groin and threading it into the ascending aorta to the origin of the coronary arteries. A radiopaque material is then injected through the catheter to make the coronary arteries visible in X-ray movies. By this means the precise location and extent of the obstructive atherosclerotic plaques in the coronary arteries can be determined. This test is absolutely essential in considering the possibility of surgical treatment.

Most patients with coronary arterial disease can be adequately treated by medical means. Some patients, however, may require surgical treatment, as for example, those with severe, disabling angina not adequately controlled by proper medical treatment, whose disease is localized to the proximal segments, who have relatively normal coronary arteries beyond the obstruction and whose left ventricular function is not too severely impaired. Surgical treatment may also be indicated in certain patients who are threatened with myocardial infarction, those who have had a previous myocardial infarction and severe obstruction of the left main coronary artery and those who require surgical correction of valvular heart disease or an aneurysm of the left ventricle. Certain forms of the disease are not amenable to surgical treatment, such as diffuse involvement of the coronary arteries, particularly if there is extensive narrowing of the distal arterial segments, and extensive damage to the muscle of the left ventricle resulting in poor left ventricular function. Age itself is not a surgical deterrent since experience has shown that properly selected patients in their seventies and eighties who are in reasonably good condition may be successfully operated on.

The procedure of choice in most patients requiring surgical correction is the bypass operation. It was first performed by us in 1964, and since then, literally thousands of patients have had the operation with increasingly better results. The operation is performed with the patient under general anesthesia and supported by the heart-lung machine. A segment of the saphenous vein, which is a large superficial vein in the leg, is removed for use as a substitute artery or vein graft in the bypass procedure. Since there are sufficient other veins in the leg to replace its function, its absence causes no circulatory disturbances in the leg. The heart is exposed through a midline opening in the breastbone. Since the coronary arteries are on the surface of the heart, it is relatively easy to identify the proper segment for attachment of the vein graft as determined by the arteriogram. An incision, about one-fourth inch long, is made in a reasonably normal segment of the coronary artery beyond the obstructive process. One end of the vein graft is beveled and trimmed to fit the opening in the artery and then is attached to the edges of the incision in the coronary artery by a fine plastic suture. After this anastomosis, or attachment of the vein graft to the opening in the coronary artery, has been completed, a special partial occluding clamp is applied to the anterior wall of the ascending aorta to pinch off and isolate a part of the wall of the ascending aorta. A longitudinal incision about one-fourth inch long is then made in this isolated or pinched-off segment. The other end of the vein graft is tailored to fit this opening and is attached to the edges by a fine plastic suture. After completion of this procedure, the partial occluding clamp on the ascending aorta is removed to allow blood to flow through the vein graft into the distal coronary artery. In this manner blood is shunted around the obstructing lesion and into the relatively normal coronary artery beyond the blocked segment— hence the term "bypass operation." Additional bypasses may be performed to other coronary arteries depending on the extent of the occlusive lesions.

The results of the operation are excellent, insofar as relief of chest pain and restoration of the patients to relatively normal activity are concerned. In a recent analysis of our own experience, follow-up studies of patients five or more years after operation show that 92 percent are still living with excellent results and 80 percent have returned to work. Other medical centers have reported similar results. The risk of operation in most experienced medical centers is now only about 1 to 2 percent.

CREDIT: *Michael E. DeBakey, M.D., President, Chairman of the Cora and Webb Mading Department of Surgery; Director of the National Heart and Blood Vessel Research and Demonstration Center, Baylor College of Medicine, Houston, Texas; co-author with Antonio M. Gotto, M.D., The Living Heart, New York: David McKay Company.*

Heart Attacks and Sex

Statistics on death during sexual intercourse are difficult to obtain. The surviving partner usually will not tell the truth and physicians signing the death certificate usually describe it as occurring during sleep.

Nevertheless, Dr. George C. Griffith, University of Southern California cardiologist, believes the incidence is larger than believed and that cardiacs should receive medical counsel rather than a simple "take it easy."

They should know there is greater risk too soon after eating or drinking. It is wise to wait three hours, Dr. Griffith said.

A fatigued condition can be hazardous. The optimal time is in the morning, followed by another rest period.

Tension and fear have an impact. Coitus should take place in an atmosphere of relaxation instead of under furtive, anxious conditions. Sex with a partner toward whom there is resentment can be hazardous.

"Congenial partners who are accustomed to each other and whose technique is habituated can achieve sexual satisfaction without great strain on the heart," Dr. Griffith commented in the journal *Heart and Lung*.

"Mutual tenderness and intelligent co-operation lead to expressions of affection and relaxation."

Eighty percent of the patients surviving a heart attack can resume their normal life, including coitus, within four to eight weeks, said Dr. Griffith.

If there are complications, such as recurring pain, or abnormal heart rhythms or pump failure, then work on the job as well as sex activity must be denied for a time or severely curtailed, he said, adding, "The patient should report the following occurrences to his physician: (a) anginal pain that occurs during or after intercourse; (b) palpitation that continues for fifteen minutes or more; (c) sleeplessness caused by sexual exertion; and (d) marked fatigue during the following day."

CREDIT: *Arthur J. Snider, Science and Medicine, Chicago* Sun-Times.

How the Heart Works for You

MOST FEARED DISEASES

A Gallup poll, the results of which were reported in 1977, representing the views of 1,600 people across the United States, revealed that the ailments most feared are:

(1)	Cancer	58%	(6)	Loss of Limb	2%
(2)	Blindness	21%	(7)	Tuberculosis	1%
(3)	Heart Disease	10%	(8)	Deafness	1%
(4)	Arthritis	2%	(9)	Undecided	3%
(5)	Polio	2%			

These statistics were especially interesting when one considers that heart disease is the number-one killer in the United States—and has been since 1900.

Consider the work of the heart. It normally beats anywhere from 60 to 100 times a minute (the average rate in adults is about 75 per minute). When you're excited, when you run or exercise your heart beat may get up to 180 per minute. On the other hand, if you're a trained athlete with an efficient circulation, it may beat as slowly as 45 or 50.

Your calculator will tell you that this amounts to approximately 100,000 beats a day or 3.5 million heartbeats every year—and each contraction depends on every other part of your body. So for sixty minutes every hour, twenty-four hours every day and night as long as you live, your heart beats steadily—for a lifetime—without an oil change or the need to replace worn-out parts.

Whatever goes wrong with the heart is due to disease—and has nothing to do with wear and tear. In fact, patients with heart trouble are often encouraged to exercise. Do you know any man-made machine that can compare to this?

Now here's the paradox. Even though the heart is one of the toughest and most durable organs of the body, it is nevertheless responsible for the greatest number of deaths in the "civilized" world. Why then, despite its strength, does heart trouble cause about 650,000 Americans to die every year? What is it that goes wrong?

Most people don't really understand what heart disease is all about. Ask them, and they're apt to answer, "I have a condition. I take this little white pill every morning."

In order for you to appreciate the kinds of cardiac trouble that may affect you, you must understand how the heart is put together and what it does.

The heart muscle itself functions like a pump—and normally, a very efficient one. Its job is to deliver blood to every part of the body. The oxygen in this blood keeps us alive. The brain, kidney, liver, legs, the digestive tract, muscles—all require a great deal of energy (oxygen) to perform their life-controlling functions. They cannot tolerate more than a few seconds of interruption in that blood supply. So even when we sleep, and all our muscles are resting and relaxed, the heart keeps pumping.

The normal heart, about the size of your fist, contains two kinds of blood. There is the "used" blood from which oxygen has been extracted and to which waste products have been returned. This "used" blood is returned to the heart in order to be recirculated in the lungs, where its oxygen supply is renewed. Then, "fresh" blood, full of oxygen, is returned from the lungs to the heart, which pumps it to the rest of the body.

To keep these two types of blood separated there is a wall down the middle of the heart, dividing it into left and right sides. Sets of valves within the heart result in upper and lower chambers on each side. These valves are responsible for controlling the flow of blood within the heart. Two of them are situated where the blood exits from the heart. It is their job to make sure that none of it leaks back.

To keep itself supplied with energy, the heart has its own arteries—the coronary arteries. There are three major ones and they penetrate the heart muscle, delivering oxygen to all parts of it.

So there you have the basic structure of the heart—muscle, valves and arteries. The muscle pumps the blood, the arteries carry the energy for it to do so and the valves control the flow of blood in and out of the heart. A heart "condition" means that something has gone wrong with either the muscle, the valves or the arteries. Let's discuss each of these potential sources of trouble.

THE VALVES

When a heart valve becomes diseased, two things may happen to it. Either it doesn't open all the way (stenosis) or it fails to shut tight (regurgitation). (Often, stenosis and regurgitation occur together in the same valve.) When that happens, the heart muscle has to work harder. If the valve opening is narrow, the heart has to squeeze more vigorously to get all the blood out. If the valve leaks, some of the blood ejected from the heart returns to it when it shouldn't. This increased load or volume of blood stretches the heart. Whatever the valve disorder may be, the net result is cardiac enlargement. As this situation continues for years without treatment, the heart gets bigger and bigger. When it can no longer enlarge, it starts to get weak, and loses its ability to eject all the blood within it. When that happens the heart "fails" (heart failure).

Such valve disorders are occasionally congenital, that is, you're born that way. Or, they may become deformed during life because of some infection, the most common of which is rheumatic fever. Usually rheumatic fever occurs in childhood due to a streptococcus germ. In the usual course of events, the child has a bad strep throat. A few weeks later the joints become swollen and tender. Nobody thinks much about the heart at that point because cardiac symptoms are not usually apparent. Years later, after the "rheumatism" or "growing pains" have been forgotten, a heart murmur appears. Murmurs are due to the swirling of blood across a deformed heart valve.

When the doctor examines your heart he can tell from the quality of the murmur, its location on the chest wall and its timing in the heart cycle which valve is involved and whether it is narrowed or leaking. Regardless of how the valve becomes diseased, it can now be replaced surgically with a new artificial one. If we don't wait too long, heart valve replacement can restore normal function. This is an excellent example of how a formerly important cause of death and disability has been overcome by medical research and progress.

THE CORONARY ARTERIES

These are a network of small blood vessels within the heart which supply the oxygen to keep it pumping. The process of arteriosclerosis, popularly called "hardening of the arteries," causes fatty deposits (or plaques) to form in their walls. This makes them progressively narrower until finally they close —very much like rust depositing over the years in water pipes. When one or more of these coronary arteries are narrowed, they may still provide enough blood to take care of your ordinary needs. But when the heart has to pump a little harder or faster, for example, when you're running, making love, digesting a meal or when you get excited at a sports event, the narrowed arteries cannot deliver the extra blood required. When it lacks enough oxygen, the heart signals you to stop what you're doing. That signal is pain, pressure or constriction in the chest, and is called angina pectoris. If you stop running or whatever else you are doing, the pain goes away. Remember then that the characteristics of angina are that it is *induced by stress or exertion and relieved by rest*.

When the narrowed artery finally closes, and the blockage is complete, you are said to have sustained a "coronary occlusion." When that happens, instead of just crying out for a little more blood with the symptom of angina pectoris, a portion of the heart muscle actually dies. The death of muscle following a coronary occlusion is called a *myocardial infarction* or *heart attack*. If the diseased artery is a large one and the closure sudden, the myocardial infarction may be big enough to interfere so drastically with the function of the heart that it may cause death. Whether the heart attack is mild, severe or fatal depends on the size of the involved coronary artery, the speed with which it closed and how much damage was sustained by the heart muscle.

One reason some patients die and others survive after a heart attack has to do with something called "collateral circulation." Nature has provided us with a wonderful protective mechanism called "collaterals." When the blood supply to the heart is diminished because the coronary arteries are narrowed and diseased, tiny new vessels open up. As the months and years go by, these new smaller branches gradually take over the job of feeding the heart muscle and delivering its precious oxygen. Collaterals can be so effective that in some cases, when the final closure of the coronary arteries occurs, the collateral circulation is so highly developed that there may not even be a heart attack at all. The muscle is not deprived of oxygen and does not die.

Coronary artery disease accounts for the major portion of heart trouble and death. But that's not something you're born with. We enter this world with wide-open coronary arteries. But then, we start eating the wrong food, smoking, gaining weight, worrying, sitting around instead of exercising and raising our blood pressure. As the years go by, we gradually pay for all this by depositing sludge in our coronaries. Later fat deposits develop and go on to become hardened plaques that narrow the coronary arteries. These plaques are made up mostly of cholesterol and there is a definite relationship between how much cholesterol we have flowing in our arteries and the extent and severity of these plaques. Because of this, most doctors try to keep your cholesterol level as low as possible.

When young American soldiers killed in the Korean war in the 1950s were studied after death, it was found that many of these apparently healthy eighteen- and nineteen-year-old boys already had significant narrowing of their coronary arteries! Korean soldiers of the same age did not show evidence of this disease. The reason? Who knows for sure? Probably lifestyle and diet.

HEART MUSCLE

The end result of any trouble in the heart is weakening of its muscle. As you have seen, diseased valves can make it get bigger and thicker until it finally weakens and "fails." Similarly, narrowed coronary arteries deprive it of blood, damaging and weakening it. Another most important and treatable cause of heart muscle weakness is high blood pressure. When the heart has to pump harder to push its blood into the body's arteries against an increased resistance, the heart enlarges. Certain viruses can also attack the heart, hurting the muscle too. On rare occasions, cancers originate in or spread to the heart.

Whatever the mechanism, a damaged heart muscle ultimately becomes so weak that it cannot perform its critical function of pumping blood to the rest of the body. The organs dependent on it for energy are not properly nourished and stop functioning as they should. When the pump fails, blood backs up into the body since the weakened heart can't accommodate its return. The lungs fill up with this extra blood and shortness of breath results. The feet and later the abdomen swell. The physical ability of the patient in heart failure is drastically reduced because his muscles aren't getting enough blood and the air in his lungs has been replaced by fluid.

That gives you the spectrum of "heart trouble"—congenital (what you're born with) and acquired (what strikes you) during your lifetime. Since we control most of the processes that make the heart large, such as high blood pressure, bad valves and infections, the main problem facing us today is to understand why the coronary arteries close up and how to prevent them from doing so. Even though we don't fully understand the mechanism by which this occurs, we know that certain "risk factors" are important, in that they appear to speed up the disease. The most important of these risk factors are high blood pressure, cigarette smoking, cholesterol and triglyceride levels (blood fats), overweight, a sedentary lifestyle (lots of sitting and no exercise) and nervous stress.

High blood pressure can be easily controlled these days—if you co-operate with your doctor and faithfully take the few pills he prescribes, reduce your salt intake, take off weight if you are too heavy and keep it off. In 1975 and 1976 for the first time there was actually a drop in the number of deaths from heart disease in the United States. We believe this was largely due to a nationwide campaign urging people to get their blood pressure checked. (Half the people who have high blood pressure do not know it because there are often no symptoms.)

The relationship between cigarette smoking and lung cancer has been so strongly emphasized that we sometimes forget that tobacco is also very bad for the heart. I see so many patients with heart attacks in their forties. They are thin, have normal blood pressure and reasonable cholesterol levels. Even their family history is good. What did them in, in my opinion, was their twenty or more cigarettes a day.

Smoking is bad enough, but in addition if you have high blood pressure and an elevated cholesterol, you're really in trouble. And don't seek comfort in the fact that pipes and cigars are "okay." They may not be as dangerous as cigarettes, but you're better off without them. Doctors are beginning to practice what they preach in this regard. Most medical meetings prohibit smoking and thousands of M.D.s have kicked the habit. As a matter of fact, improved survival statistics among doctors in England are attributed to the fact that they have stopped smoking cigarettes.

CHOLESTEROL

What about cholesterol? It's true that all the evidence is not yet in with respect to what causes narrowing of the arteries, but we are certain that a high cholesterol at best doesn't help. In fact, it's looking more and more like reducing cholesterol is good for you, especially if you don't wait for your first heart attack to do it. Even if you enjoy good health, follow a prudent diet. Try to avoid an excess of food rich in cholesterol such as eggs, dairy products, fat meat and shellfish.

We've talked about prevention so far. What about the millions of people who have already been stricken with some form of heart trouble? They can slow down further progress of their disease by paying attention to the risk factors.

Then there is an operation called the coronary bypass, in which the surgeon takes a piece of vein from your leg and sews it onto the surface of the heart. This "bypasses" the blocked coronary arteries. Almost 100,000 patients are submitting to this procedure every year in the United States alone. It eliminates or reduces angina in most cases. Whether it actually will prevent a heart attack or prolong life is still not known, although we hope it will do so. The operation is safe, the risk is somewhere between 1 and 2 percent, depending on where you have it done and by whom. Stay away from hospitals that do one or two operations a week. Practice makes perfect, and the centers which have teams performing this procedure frequently provide your best chance for success. This is no time for loyalty to your community hospital. In one recent series done at a large medical center 89.6 percent of patients who had bypass operations for angina were alive and well after five years.

So what does all this mean in terms of how to conduct your life so as to avoid heart trouble? If you had rheumatic fever as a child, you should be examined at regular intervals to see whether you have developed a murmur. You should have your blood pressure checked at least once a year. A normal reading taken anytime during life is not binding forever. You can develop high blood pressure weeks or months after a normal reading just as you can develop cancer, diabetes or any other disease at any time during your life. If there is a strong family history of heart disease (parents, brothers or sisters before the age of sixty) you should be alert to your own vulnerability. Don't start smoking. If you smoke now—stop. Keep yourself physically fit. Don't take an elevator to the mezzanine. Walk. Try to avoid unnecessary emotional stress. Change your job if you have to—or your wife or husband! Maintain ideal weight. Follow a prudent, low-cholesterol diet. If you develop pain, pressure, heaviness or constriction in the chest, don't assume it's indigestion because you had a big meal with lots of wine. Check it out with your doctor. Remember that angina and "gas" are both relieved by belching.

Finally, keep your eye out on the fruits of research and do everything you can to support it—out of your own pocket, at the community level and by keeping your legislators interested and committed. Medical research is big business—your business. It will bring us new life-prolonging advances only if we pay for it. We need answers to some vital questions and we need them now. The questions are: What narrows the coronary arteries and how? How can we have new, safer and more tolerable drug control for high blood pressure and disturbances in heart rhythm? What new surgical techniques can be developed to improve operative results in congenital and valvular heart disease? How much longer must we wait for the artificial heart? How can we get everyone to stop smoking? What are the secrets of obesity and how can we control it? Answers to these and a host of other critical questions will mean that you and I will reach old age feeling and staying young. That's the heart of the matter.

CREDIT: *Isadore Rosenfeld, M.D., Clinical Associate Professor of Medicine, Cornell Medical Center, New York; author of* The Complete Medical Checkup, *New York: Simon & Schuster.*

A HEART-ATTACK SURVIVOR WITH A DEATH WISH

DEAR ANN: Will you please do a great many wives of heart-attack victims a favor and find some answers for us?

My husband, Ted, and several of his friends were lucky enough to survive severe heart attacks. Ted and two of his pals are now off their diets and even worse, they've started to smoke again. The other wives are ignoring it, but I feel as if Ted had slapped me in the face.

Isn't he saying to me, "I don't give a damn what I do to you?" Could it be that he has a death wish? This man needs every ounce of oxygen he can get, and here he is wasting it on smoking. What should I do? Every time I see Ted smoke a cigaret something in-side me dies. The love and respect I had for him for over 30 years is slipping away.

What can I do about it? HEART-SICK WIFE

DEAR HEARTSICK: Not a darn thing. So quit eating yourself up, or he'll bury YOU.

People who defy doctors' orders do indeed have a death wish. A person must want to live in order to give up smoking or drinking or eating things he shouldn't. To wives who are in your shoes, I say quit nagging. You can't inject a person with the will to live if he doesn't have it. Just keep yourself in good shape and make sure his life insurance is paid up.

Heart Transplants

In December of 1967 the first human heart transplantation operation was performed in Capetown, South Africa, by Dr. Christiaan Barnard.

In January of 1968 transplantation of the human heart was first done after a decade of significant animal research at Stanford. It was believed that the patient could survive following the removal of the heart if the healthy heart of an accident victim whose brain was dead could be put in its place.

With the worldwide publicity, it appeared to some that human heart transplantation would be the miraculous "cure" for all difficult cardiac problems. Unfortunately, this is not (and never was) correct.

The initial transplants were applied as a result of a variety of heart diseases —coronary arteriosclerosis (hardening of the arteries), valvular heart disease, congenital heart disease, acute myocarditis, and cardiomyopathy of the idiopathic variety.

Of the initial group of patients during the first two years of heart transplantation, survival was so infrequent that many respected physicians expressed the opinion that heart transplantation should no longer be permitted. Frequent pronouncements were and are still being made that coronary artery bypass graft surgery has eliminated any need for transplantation.

It is nevertheless a fact that certain cardiac patients deteriorate to a point where no conventional surgery will relieve the patient's symptoms. When the problems become so severe that the chances for survival are bleak, the patient and his family often beg the doctor for a transplant operation. Unfortunately, not every patient is a good candidate for this kind of surgery; what's more, it is not a simple matter to obtain a heart for transplantation.

Patients are selected for heart transplantation who have heart muscle damage with severe heart failure and low cardiac output. In 105 of the first 109 patients who underwent heart transplantation at Stanford University in 1968–1975 coronary artery disease or primary disease of the heart muscle contributed to the need for a "new heart." Patients with heart valve disease are not candidates for heart transplantation, and neither are patients with acute inflammation of the heart or congenital heart disease.

There are three factors which rule out selection of a patient for heart transplantation and an additional three factors that weigh heavily against a decision for transplantation. The first is a high pulmonary vascular resistance which would make it very difficult for the transplanted heart to pump against the poor condition of the small pulmonary vessels. A second is the presence of infection. Thirdly, a poor tissue match between the donor and the recipient. When the difference in genetic types is great, the transplant often fails within the first few days or weeks. Patients older than fifty years of age have a difficult time surviving the complication of infection which almost always occurs in the transplantation of any kind of tissue.

Individuals of advanced age are not promising prospects for heart transplants. Persons who have had a long-time history of heart disease with definite changes in the liver and kidneys are poor candidates for transplantation. Finally, the presence of acute pulmonary disease means a serious breathing problem, and this would rule out the transplant.

One of the interesting points in considering the Stanford University experience in heart transplantation has been the discovery that patients who have undergone *previous* heart surgery show a greater rate of survival following heart transplantation rather than to the contrary. Conventional thought would suggest that exposure to multiple transfusions during heart surgery would sensitize the patient to a subsequent tissue graft. This has definitely not been the case. Since so many patients are being presented for heart transplantation who had poor results with conventional cardiac surgery, the fact of increased survival is all the more intriguing.

All patients are treated with immune suppressing drugs. Prednisone and azathioprine or cyclophosphamide are the ones more frequently used. Rabbit antithymocyte globulin is given in the form of injection by needle during the first eight to twenty-one days after transplantation—after which the substance can be discontinued.

One half of all deaths after heart transplantation are caused by infection. Aggressive diagnostic and therapeutic measures for infection must be used, and an intensified form of medical management is necessary to assure the survival of patients following cardiac transplantation.

It is gratifying to note that patients are much less restricted after heart transplantation than, for example, after pacemaker implantation, when the heart rate is totally dependent on the pacemaker. Even though the transplanted heart is without central nervous system control, there is a compensatory mechanism for heart rate changes when the patient exercises, becomes frightened, walks stairs, makes love—the same as his own heart would do.

Retransplantation of the heart is not only feasible, but at Stanford University it has been applied in seven instances. Three of these patients are presently living, and it is probable that retransplantation will become a standard feature in the long-range plans for select patients after cardiac transplantation.

The usual period of hospitalization after heart transplantation is three months at a cost of approximately $40,000. Patients are seen and fully evaluated annually. X-ray studies of the coronary arteries in the donor heart are routinely performed at that time to rule out vascular disease in the graft.

Since the transplanted heart has no nerves, patients do not experience angina pectoris (severe chest pains) in the presence even of significant coronary disease in the transplanted heart.

Currently, 50 of 124 patients at Stanford University Hospital are alive from eight years to one month after heart transplantation. Ninety percent of the patients who live one year after transplantation are fully rehabilitated.

At present the patient following cardiac transplantation can expect a 65 percent chance for one-year survival and a 50 percent chance for a five-year survival. These figures are on the conservative side, but they do reflect rather accurately the prospects that patients have today following heart replacement.

CREDIT: *Norman Shumway, M.D., Stanford University Medical School, Stanford, California.*

Valvular Heart Disease and Valve Replacement

The valves of the heart serve the important purpose of maintaining the flow of blood through the heart chambers. There are four heart chambers, two on the right, termed the right atrium and right ventricle, and two on the left side, termed the left atrium and left ventricle. Between each of the chambers is a valve. Thus, between the right atrium and right ventricle there is a valve known as the tricuspid valve, and between the right ventricle and pulmonary artery there is a valve known as the pulmonary valve. On the left side is a valve called the mitral valve between the left atrium and the left ventricle and an aortic valve between the left ventricle and the aorta. The function of these valves may be better understood by following the circulation cycle beginning in the right atrium, which is the collecting chamber for blood returning from the body. As the muscle fibers of the right atrium contract, the squeezing motion exerts pressure on the blood in the atrium, forcing the tricuspid valve to open and allow the blood to enter the chamber of the right ventricle. After the right ventricle is filled, the muscles of this chamber contract, and in this way exert pressure on the blood in the chamber, which causes the tricuspid valve to close. Since the tricuspid valve opens only one way, there can be no return of blood from the right ventricle to the right atrium. As the pressure mounts in the right ventricle, the pulmonary valve is pushed open to allow blood to be pumped into the pulmonary artery and into the lungs to be oxygenated. The pulmonary valve also opens only one way, and after the blood is forced through it and the right ventricle relaxes, the pulmonary valve closes; this prevents blood from returning to the right ventricle. The blood, which is then oxygenated in the lung, is returned to the left side of the heart and is collected in the left atrium. Contraction of the left atrium then forces open the one-way mitral valve to allow blood to flow into the left ventricle. After the chamber of the left ventricle is filled, its muscular wall contracts and the mitral valve closes; the resultant pressure on the blood in the chamber forces open the aortic valve, and this allows blood to be pumped into the aorta. After the left ventricle is emptied, it relaxes, with the result of greater pressure in the aorta than in the left ventricle, and this differential in pressure slams shut the aortic valve so that the blood is prevented from returning into the left ventricle. Normally, these valves are delicate, thin-walled and highly flexible structures that are in the form of two or three leaflets. The tricuspid valve is so called because it consists of three leaflets. The aortic valve also consists of three leaflets, but the mitral valve consists of two leaflets.

Disease affecting these valves may be congenital or acquired. In congenital valvular disease the infant is born with the defect because the malformation occurred during the development of the fetus. The aortic and mitral valves are most commonly involved and usually result in partial or severe obstruction to the flow of blood across the valve.

Acquired forms of valvular disease may be caused by infections, such as rheumatic fever or bacteria in the bloodstream. In other cases the cause may not be determined. Most commonly affected are the mitral and aortic valves and less frequently the tricuspid valve. They may be affected singly or in combination.

Damage to the mitral valve produces thickening and loss of pliability of the valve leaflets with fusion of the edges, contraction and in some instances calcium deposits. These changes cause the opening of the valve to become narrow. This condition, known as mitral stenosis, produces obstruction of blood flow between the left atrium and left ventricle. The damage may also result in the inability of the valve leaflets to close, a condition termed mitral insufficiency. Whereas one or the other of these dysfunctions may be predominant, there is often an element of both.

Somewhat similar changes may occur in the aortic valve and produce narrowing or stenosis with obstruction of blood flow from the left ventricle into the aorta, or they may cause such severe destruction of the leaflets that incompetence is produced. Here too there is usually an element of both types of dysfunction.

The effect on heart function varies with the degree of the changes in these valves. In mild forms of the disease the heart may compensate adequately so that there is little disability. Most patients, however, suffer gradual and progressive changes over a period of years with increasing disability and ultimately heart failure and death unless proper treatment is given.

The diagnosis can be readily made by a physician after proper examination, which may include cardiac catheterization, particularly if surgical treatment becomes necessary.

Treatment may be medical or surgical depending on the stage of the disease, the effect on the heart and the degree of disability. Surgical treatment is indicated in patients who have symptoms of early heart failure and in certain patients in whom complications develop, such as the breaking off of a piece of blood clot in the left atrium, which then is swept into the bloodstream to lodge in a peripheral artery. This complication is called embolization. In addition, surgical treatment may be indicated in some patients with aortic valvular disease without symptoms but with evidence of progressive disease and a strain developing on the left ventricle.

Surgical treatment of mitral valvular disease consists in repair or replacement of the valve, depending on the extent of damage. In certain types of mitral stenosis, for example, in which the valve leaflets are not badly damaged and are still pliable, it may be possible to repair the valve by separating or dividing the fused edges. This is preferably done by supporting the patient on the heart-lung machine to allow the surgeon to make an opening in the left atrium and thus permit direct vision of the mitral valve. This enables an accurate assessment of the damage and a more precise technique for dividing the fused edges. Most cases, however, require removal and replacement of the damaged valve. Most heart centers such as ours use an artificial valve, although a few surgeons prefer to use a heterograft valve (one taken from an animal, such as a pig). Great improvements have been made in artificial valves during the past decade, and a number of different types have been developed, most of which use the ball-valve principle. The ball itself, however, may be in the form of a disc, especially when designed for mitral or tricuspid valvular replacement. In this type of valve the ball or disc is enclosed in a cage consisting of three or four wired struts with an opening at the bottom somewhat smaller than the ball or disc so that the opening is closed when the ball or disc is seated on it. With an increase in pressure on the inflow side of this opening, the ball or disc moves into the cage so that blood flows around it. With the drop in pressure that occurs in the next phase of the heart's cycle, the ball or disc drops back against the seat of the opening and prevents blood from flowing back. Thus, the artificial valve functions like the normal heart valve in having a one-way opening and thus maintaining unidirectional flow of blood through the heart.

The operation is performed with the patient supported by the heart-lung machine to permit the surgeon to make an opening in the left atrium to expose the damaged mitral valve, which is excised. Sutures are then placed circumferentially in the edges of the excised valve and are then passed through the sewing ring (made of Dacron) at the base of the artificial valve. The valve is then seated into the annulus, and the sutures are tied to firmly attach the artificial valve to the annulus. The sutures are then cut, and the opening in the atrium is closed. The operation for aortic valvular replacement is performed in a similar manner except that the aortic valve is exposed through an opening in the ascending aorta just above the valve. Tricuspid valvular replacement is also performed in a similar manner except that the valve is exposed through an opening in the right atrium.

The surgical risk for these operations ranges from less than 5 percent to about 15 percent, depending on the degree of heart damage and the general condition of the patient. Most patients can resume normal activities, and long-term results extending for more than ten years are quite good.

CREDIT: *Michael E. DeBakey, M.D., President, Chairman of the Cora and Webb Mading Department of Surgery; Director of the National Heart and Blood Vessel Research and Demonstration Center, Baylor College of Medicine, Houston, Texas; co-author with Antonio M. Gotto, M.D.,* The Living Heart, *New York: David McKay Company.*

Help

Where to Go to Get It

Barnum was right when he said, "There's a sucker born every minute." And I say there are two to take him. I know because the victims have been writing to me every day for over twenty years.

Ann Landers receives approximately seven thousand letters a week from readers who represent every conceivable socio-economic group. They live on suburban estates and in the city slums. My correspondents are from 6 to 110 years of age. They are double-dome intellectuals and borderline morons. Almost half of the letters come from men.

Every bag of mail contains at least 150 inquiries that drive me up the wall. "How can they be so stupid?" I ask myself. And then I answer the question. It's not merely stupidity. It's often a combination of desperation and wishful thinking that wipes out all reason and common sense. I become furious at the exploitation of these good people whose only crime is ignorance and vulnerability.

Here are some examples that crossed my desk just this week:

DEAR ANN: Is it true that musk oil will turn a man on? My husband is 46 years old and sexually dead as a doornail. I've seen this musk oil advertised, but $11 is a lot of money for a little bottle. If you say it will help, I'll buy it.

DEAR ANN: I'm a career girl, 28 years old, and haven't had more than three real dates in my life. The reason is because I am flat-chested. I mean I don't have any bust at all. All my life I've wanted to have nice round bosoms. Please tell me if this cream will help. (Advertisement enclosed.) As you can see, the "before" and "after" pictures are very convincing. What do you say?

DEAR ANN: Is it true that cooking in aluminum will cause cancer? A man came to the door yesterday selling cookware. He scared the life out of me. His utensils cost $450 for the complete set. If what he says is true, about cancer, I mean, it sure would be worth it. But I hate to throw out these perfectly good pots and pans I've used for 10 years.

One after another the letters come—from the "exotic dancer" who wants to grow "gorgeous nails in 20 days"—from the overweight housewife who will do *anything* to get thin except quit eating the things she loves. Then there are the females with bags under their eyes and extra chins who believe they will look ten years younger if they use the enriched cream (secret formula) for thirty days. The trouble is—it's awfully expensive. "But it would be well worth the money if it works," writes Mrs. W. from Sheboygan. "Cheaper than a face lift. And no pain."

When men write and ask if the pomade and treatments guaranteed to grow hair will help, I often reply, "Yes. It will help the manufacturer and the man who sells it. They will get rich. As for you, it will help flatten your wallet, but it won't do anything for your bald head."

The letters from teenagers are especially pathetic. "My skin is such a mess of pimples and blackheads no girl would go out with me, so I don't even ask. Please don't suggest a doctor. I can't afford one. This soap and cream combination promises results within ten days. What do you think, Ann? And while I'm at it, Ann, maybe you can tell me if this mail-order speech course will help my brother. He stutters. His grades are awful. He's not dumb, he's just ashamed to speak up in class."

DEAR ANN: Our sex life is blah after 15 years. My husband wants to try a sex clinic, but some friends of ours went and you wouldn't believe the things they were asked to do. I don't go for that far-out stuff like changing partners. Frankly, I'm scared. What do you think?

The saddest letters of all come from relatives of the desperately ill, those who are dying of cancer or kidney disease. "Our family doctor said there was nothing more he could do, so we took Mom to this wonderful chiropractor. She seems a little stronger today. Do you think, Ann, that we should have brought her to the chiropractor from the beginning and not wasted all that time and money on a specialist with a fancy diploma from Harvard hanging on his office wall?"

Every letter gets a personal reply in the mail, if there's a name and an address. I urge my readers to beware of quacks and phonies. I warn them against the charlatans and fakers. More often than I care to admit, I have received in return a seething reply. "How dare you take away our hope! I'll bet you are on the payroll of the American Medical Association. The medical doctor didn't do anything but send us big bills. Jesus Christ is the greatest healer of them all. Now that we have put our child in His hands, we know everything is going to be all right."

How can the public be protected against phonies, quacks and unscrupulous money-grubbers who prey on the insecure, the frightened and the sick? The answer is education. Ignorance is *not* bliss—and it never will be. Only the truth can set you free.

Here are the names of organizations which offer reliable health information and sometimes free services. Most of them are non-profit and non-commercial. Use them in good health!

ABORTION: Association for the Study of Abortion, 120 West 57th Street, New York, New York 10019. For information check your telephone directory, or Yellow Pages under Social Service Organizations.

ADOPTION: Check your telephone book for local agencies. For adoption of foreign children contact Compassion, 7774 Irving Park Road, Norridge, Illinois 60634.

ADULT EDUCATION: National Association of Trade and Technical Schools, 2021 L Street, N.W., Washington, D.C. 20036; Association of Independent Colleges and Schools, 1730 M Street, N.W., Washington, D.C. 20036.

AGING: Aging Research Institute, 342 Madison Avenue, New York, New York 10017; American Geriatrics Society, 10 Columbus Circle, New York, New York 10019.

ALCOHOLISM: Alcohol, Drug Abuse and Mental Health Administration, U. S. Department of Health, Education, and Welfare, 5600 Fishers Lane, Rockville, Maryland 20852; Alcoholics Anonymous, P. O. Box 459, New York, New York 10017; Alateen or Al-Anon, Al-Anon Family Group Headquarters, Inc., P. O. Box 182, Madison Square Station, New York, New York 10010; National Council on Alcoholism, 2 Park Avenue, New York, New York 10016; National Institute of Alcoholism and Alcohol Abuse, P. O. Box 2345, Rockville, Maryland 20852.

ALLERGIES: Allergy Foundation of America, 801 Second Avenue, New York, New York 10017.

American Alliance for Health, Physical Education, and Recreation, 1201 16th Street, N.W., Washington, D.C. 20036.

American College of Sports Medicine, 1440 Monroe Street, Madison, Wisconsin 53706.

American Heart Association, 44 East 23rd Street, New York, New York 10010.

American Hospital Association, 840 North Lake Shore Drive, Chicago, Illinois 60611.

American Lung Association, 1740 Broadway, New York, New York 10019.

American Medical Association, 535 North Dearborn, Chicago, Illinois 60610.

American Medical Women's Association, 1740 Broadway, New York, New York 10019.

American Medical Writers Association, 9650 Rockville Pike, Bethesda, Maryland 20014.

American Public Health Association, 1015 18th Street, N.W., Washington, D.C. 20036.

American Red Cross, 17th and D Streets, N.W., Washington, D.C. 20006.

AMPUTATION: National Amputation Foundation, 1245 150th Street, Whitestone, New York 11357.

ANEMIA: Cooley's Anemia Foundation, 3366 Hillside Avenue, New Hyde Park, New York 10040; Association for Sickle Cell Anemia, 521 Fifth Avenue, New York, New York 10036.

ANOREXIA NERVOSA: Suite 2020, 550 Frontage Road, Northfield, Illinois 60093.

ARTHRITIS: Arthritis Foundation, 475 Riverside Drive, New York, New York 10027; Arthritis Foundation, 3400 Peachtree Road, N.E., Atlanta, Georgia 30326.

Association for the Advancement of Health Education, 1201 16th Street, N.W., Washington, D.C. 20036.

ASTHMA: National Foundation for Asthma, P. O. Box 50304, Tucson, Arizona 85703.

AUTISTIC: National Society of Autistic Children, 169 Tampa Avenue, Albany, New York 12208.

BATTERED CHILDREN: See Child Abuse.

BIRTH CONTROL: National Family Planning Council, 1800 North Highland Avenue, Los Angeles, California 90028; Planned Parenthood/World Population, 515 Madison Avenue, New York, New York 10022.

BIRTH DEFECTS: National Foundation/March of Dimes, Box 2000, White Plains, New York 10602.

BLIND: American Foundation for the Blind, 15 West 16th Street, New York, New York 10011; Braille Institute of America, 741 North Vermont Avenue, Los Angeles, California 90029; Jewish Guild for the Blind, 15 West 65th Street, New York, New York 10023; Seeing Eye (dogs for the blind), Washington Valley Road, Morristown, New Jersey 07960; Dialogue (recordings for the blind), 3100 South Oak Park Avenue, Berwyn, Illinois 60402; National Society for the Prevention of Blindness, 79 Madison Avenue, New York, New York 10016.

Blue Cross Association, 842 North Lake Shore Drive, Chicago, Illinois 60611.

BREAST CANCER: Reach for Recovery, c/o American Cancer Society, 777 Third Avenue, New York, New York 10017.

BREASTFEEDING: La Leche League, 9616 Minneapolis Avenue, Franklin Park, Illinois 60131.

CANCER: American Cancer Society, 777 Third Avenue, New York, New York 10017; Cancer Care, Inc., 1 Park Avenue, New York, New York 10016; Candlelighters (for parents of cancer victims), 123 C Street, S.E., Washington, D.C. 20003.

CEREBRAL PALSY: United Cerebral Palsy Associations, 66 East 34th Street, New York, New York 10016.

CHILD, Death of: Candlelighters (parents of cancer victims), 123 C Street, S.E., Washington, D.C. 20003; Compassionate Friends, First Street and Park Avenue, Hinsdale, Illinois 60521.

CHILDREN

Child Abuse, Neglect, or Molestation: C.A.L.M., P. O. Box 718, Santa Barbara, California 93102; Parents Anonymous, 2810 Artesia Boulevard, Suite F, Redondo Beach, California 90278. To report a case of child abuse, contact your local police department.

Day Care: Day Care and Child Development Council of America, Inc., 622 14th Street, N.W., Washington, D.C. 20005.

Delinquent: National Council on Crime and Delinquency, Continental Plaza, 411 Hackensack Avenue, Hackensack, New Jersey 06701; Big Brothers/Big Sisters of America, 220 Suburban Station Building, Philadelphia, Pennsylvania 19103.

CLEFT PALATE: American Cleft Palate Association, University of North Carolina School of Dentistry, Chapel Hill, North Carolina 27514.

COLITIS: See Ostomy.

Consumer's Union, 256 Washington Street, Mount Vernon, New York 10550.

CONVALESCENT: American Nursing Home Association, 1200 15th Street, N.W., Washington, D.C. 20005; Check your telephone directory under Visiting Nurses Association, or Home Health Care Service.

CYSTIC FIBROSIS: National Cystic Fibrosis Foundation, 3379 Peachtree Road, N.E., Atlanta, Georgia 30326.

DAY CARE: Day Care and Child Development Council of America, Inc., 622 14th Street, N.W., Washington, D.C. 20005.

DEAF: Alexander Graham Bell Association for the Deaf, 3417 Volta Place, N.W., Washington, D.C. 20007; American Speech and Hearing Association, 9030 Old Georgetown Road, Bethesda, Maryland 20014; Deafness Research Foundation, 366 Madison Avenue, New York, New York 10017.

DEATH OF A CHILD: Compassionate Friends, First Street and Park Avenue, Hinsdale, Illinois 60521; Candlelighters (parents of cancer victims), 123 C Street, S.E., Washington, D.C. 20003.

DELINQUENT CHILDREN: National Council on Crime and Delinquency, Continental Plaza, 411 Hackensack Avenue, Hackensack, New Jersey 06701; Big Brothers/Big Sisters of America, 220 Suburban Station Building, Philadelphia, Pennsylvania 19103.

DENTISTRY: American Dental Association, 211 East Chicago Avenue, Chicago, Illinois 60611.

DIABETES: American Diabetes Association, 1 West 48th Street, New York, New York 10020; Juvenile Diabetes Foundation, 23 East 26th Street, New York, New York 10010.

DIET: American Dietetic Association, 430 North Michigan Avenue, Chicago, Illinois 60611; National Nutrition Consortium, 9650 Rockville Pike, Bethesda, Maryland 20014; National Nutrition Exchange, 55 Union Street, San Francisco, California 94111.

DIVORCE: Check your telephone book for listings. Also: Parents Without Partners, 7910 Woodmont Avenue, Washington, D.C. 20014.

DOWN'S SYNDROME (Mongoloidism): National Association for Down's Syndrome, 529 South Kenilworth, Oak Park, Illinois 60304.

DRUG ABUSE: Drug Abuse Council, 1828 L Street, N.W., Washington, D.C. 20036; Families Anonymous (children on drugs), P. O. Box 344, Torrance, California 90501; Narconon (drug rehabilitation), 3636 Grand Avenue, South, #303, Minneapolis, Minnesota 55409; National Clearinghouse for Drug Abuse Information, 5600 Fishers Lane, Rockville, Maryland 20852; Alcohol, Drug Abuse, and Mental Health Administration, U. S. Department of Health, Education, and Welfare, 5600 Fishers Lane, Rockville, Maryland 20852; Therapeutic Communities of America, c/o Gateway Houses Foundation, 624 South Michigan, Chicago, Illinois 60605; National Institute of Drug Abuse, Rockwall Building, 11400 Rockville Pike, Rockville, Maryland 20852.

DWARFISM: Little People of America, Box 126, Owatonna, Minnesota 55060.

DYSLEXIA: Dyslexia Memorial Institute of Chicago, 1936 South Michigan, Chicago, Illinois 60616. See Learning Disabilities.

EPILEPSY: Epilepsy Foundation of America, 1828 L Street, N.W., Washington, D.C. 20036.

EUTHANASIA: Euthanasia Educational Council, 250 West 56th Street, New York, New York 10019.

EX-CONVICTS: Safer Foundation, 343 South Dearborn, Chicago, Illinois 60604 (employment for ex-convicts).

EYE CARE: Better Vision Institute, 230 Park Avenue, New York, New York 10017; American Optometric Association, 7000 Chippewa Street, St. Louis, Missouri 63119; The National Retinitis Pigmentosa Foundation, 8331 Mindale Road, Baltimore, Maryland 21207.

FACIAL DISFIGUREMENT: Society for the Rehabilitation of the Facially Disfigured, 550 First Avenue, New York, New York 10016.
Family Health (publication), 545 Madison Avenue, New York, New York 10022.
Family Service, 44 East 23rd Street, New York, New York 10010.

FERTILITY: American Fertility Society, 1608 13th Avenue, South, Suite 101, Birmingham, Alabama 35205.

FOOT CARE: American Podiatry Association, 20 Chevy Chase Circle, N.W., Washington, D.C. 20005.

FOSTER PARENTS: Check your Yellow Pages under Social Service Organizations.

GAMBLERS: Gamblers Anonymous, P. O. Box 17173, Los Angeles, California 90017.

GENETICS: National Genetics Foundation, 250 West 57th Street, New York, New York 10019.

HANDICAPPED: American Rehabilitation Foundation, 1800 Chicago Avenue, Minneapolis, Minnesota 55404; Institute for Rehabilitation Medicine, 400 East 34th Street, New York, New York 10016; National Easter Seal Society for Crippled Children and Adults, 2023 West Ogden Avenue, Chicago, Illinois 60612; National Paraplegia Foundation, 333 North Michigan Avenue, Chicago, Illinois 60601; National Rehabilitation Association, 1522 K Street, N.W., Washington, D.C. 20005; National Wheelchair Athletic Association, 4024 62nd Street, Woodside, New York 11377; Closer Look (parents of handicapped children), P. O. Box 1492, Washington, D.C. 20013.
Health Education Council, 92 Belmont Drive, Livingston, New Jersey 07039.

HEARING: American Speech and Hearing Association, 9030 Old Georgetown Road, Bethesda, Maryland 20014; National Association of Hearing and Speech Agencies, 814 Thayer Avenue, Silver Springs, Maryland 20910.

HEMOPHILIA: National Hemophilia Foundation, 25 West 39th Street, New York, New York 10018.

HOMOSEXUALITY: Parents Of Gays, 201 West 13th Street, New York, New York 10011, or Box 24528, Los Angeles, California 90024; Dignity, 755 Boylston Avenue, Room 413, Boston, Massachusetts 02116.

HUNTINGTON'S DISEASE: Committee to Combat Huntington's Disease, 2729 West Birchwood, Chicago, Illinois.

HYPERKINETIC: Association for Children with Learning Disabilities, 5225 Grace Street, Pittsburgh, Pennsylvania 15236.

HYPNOSIS: American Society of Clinical Hypnosis, 2400 East Devon Avenue, Des Plaines, Illinois 60018.

ILEITIS: See Ostomy.

INCEST: Check your Yellow Pages under Social Service Organizations, or the Family Service Association of America.

KIDNEY DISEASE: National Kidney Foundation, 116 East 27th Street, New York, New York 10016.

LARYNGECTOMIES: International Association of Laryngectomies, c/o American Cancer Society, 777 Third Avenue, New York, New York 10017.

LEARNING DISABILITIES: Dyslexia Memorial Institute of Chicago, 1936 South Michigan, Chicago, Illinois 60616; Time Out to Enjoy (for adults) 113 Garfield, Oak Park, Illinois 60304; The National Affiliation for Literacy Advance (for adults), Loubach Literary International, Box 131, Syracuse, New York 13210; or check your telephone book under "Literacy"; Association for Children with Learning Disabilities, 5225 Grace Street, Pittsburgh, Pennsylvania 15236; National Society of Autistic Children, 169 Tampa Avenue, Albany, New York 12208.

LEGAL AID: Check your telephone book, or contact your local Bar Association.

MARRIAGE COUNSELING: American Association of Marriage and Family Counselors, 225 Yale Avenue, Claremont, California 91711.

MATERNITY: Maternity Center Association, 48 East 92nd Street, New York, New York 10028.

MEDICAL IDENTIFICATION: Medic Alert Foundation International, P. O. Box 1009, Turlock, California 95380.

Medical Library Association, 919 North Michigan Avenue, Chicago, Illinois 60611.

MENTAL HEALTH: Alcohol, Drug Abuse, and Mental Health Administration, U. S. Department of Health, Education, and Welfare, 5600 Fishers Lane, Rockville, Maryland 20852; American Psychiatric Association, 1700 18th Street, N.W., Washington, D.C. 20009; American Psychoanalytic Association, 1 East 57th Street, New York, New York 10022; American Psychological Association, 1200 17th Street, N.W., Washington, D.C. 20036; Family Service Association of America, 44 East 23rd Street, New York, New York 10010; Recovery, Inc., 116 South Michigan, Chicago, Illinois 60603; National Association for Mental Health, 1800 North Kent Street, Arlington, Virginia 22209; National Institute of Mental Health, 5600 Fishers Lane, Rockville, Maryland 20852.

MIDGETS: See Dwarfism.

MONGOLOID: See Down's Syndrome.

MULTIPLE SCLEROSIS: National Multiple Sclerosis Society, 257 Park Avenue South, New York, New York 10010.

MUSCULAR DYSTROPHY: Muscular Dystrophy Association of America, 810 Seventh Avenue, New York, New York 10019.

MYASTHENIA GRAVIS: Myasthenia Gravis Foundation, 230 Park Avenue, New York, New York 10017.

NARCOLEPSY: American Narcolepsy Association, Inc., Box 5846, Stanford, California 94304.

National Association of Blue Shield Plans, 211 East Chicago Avenue, Chicago, Illinois 60611.

National Health Council, 1740 Broadway, New York, New York 10019.

National Public Relations Council of Health and Welfare Services, 815 Second Avenue, New York, New York 10017.

National Safety Council, 425 North Michigan Avenue, Chicago, Illinois 60611.

NURSING: American Nurses Association, 2420 Pershing Road, Kansas City, Missouri 64108; National League for Nursing, 10 Columbus Circle, New York, New York 10019; National Student Nurses Association, 10 Columbus Circle, New York, New York 10019.

NURSING HOMES: American Nursing Home Association, 1200 15th Street, N.W., Washington, D.C. 20005.

NUTRITION: Nutrition Foundation, 489 Fifth Avenue, New York, New York 10017. Also: See Diet.

ORGAN DONORS: National Kidney Foundation, Box 353, New York, New York, 10016; Sibley Memorial Hospital, Washington, D.C., or contact local Medical School.

OSTEOPATHY: American Osteopathic Association, 212 East Ohio Street, Chicago, Illinois 60611.

OSTOMY: United Ostomy Association, 1111 Wilshire Boulevard, Los Angeles, California 90017; National Foundation for Ileitis and Colitis, 295 Madison Avenue, New York, New York 10017.

OVERWEIGHT: The Diet Workshop, Hearthstone Plaza Building, Suite 301, 111 Washington Street, Brookline, Massachusetts 02146; Overeaters Anonymous, 2190 190th Street, Torrance, California 90504; Weight Watchers, 800 Community Drive, Manhasset, New York 11030; TOPS, 4575 South 5th Street, P. O. Box 4489, Milwaukee, Wisconsin 53207.

PARAPLEGIA: National Paraplegia Foundation, 333 North Michigan Avenue, Chicago, Illinois 60601.

PARENTS WITHOUT PARTNERS: 7910 Woodmont Avenue, Washington, D.C. 20014.

PARKINSON'S DISEASE: National Parkinson Foundation, 1501 N.W. Ninth Avenue, Miami, Florida 33136.
Patient's Aid Society, 509 Fifth Avenue, New York, New York 10017.

PEDIATRICS: American Academy of Pediatrics, 1801 Hinman Avenue, Evanston, Illinois 60204.

PHARMACEUTICALS: American Pharmaceutical Association, 2215 Constitution Avenue, N.W., Washington, D.C. 20037.

PHYSICAL THERAPY: American Physical Therapy Association, 1156 15th Street, N.W., Washington, D.C. 20005; American Occupational Therapy Association, 6000 Executive Boulevard, Rockville, Maryland 20852.

PHYSICIANS: American Academy of Family Physicians, 1740 West 92nd Street, Kansas City, Missouri 64114.

POISON: Check your telephone book for Poison Control Centers, or call the nearest hospital.

RAPE: Call the local Y.W.C.A., or the Family Service Association of America, 44 East 23rd Street, New York, New York 10010. Check your telephone book for local organizations for rape victims.

RELIGIOUS CULTS: For distressed parents whose children have joined: Committee Engaged in Freeing Minds, Box 5084, Arlington, Texas 76011; Citizens Engaged in Reuniting Families, Box 348, Harrison, New York 10052; Citizens' Freedom Foundation, Box 256, Chula Vista, California 92012; Free Minds Inc., Box 4216, Minneapolis, Minnesota 55414; Individual Freedom Foundation, Box 48, Ardmore, Pennsylvania 19003.

RETARDED: National Association for Retarded Citizens, P. O. Box 6109, Arlington, Texas 76011; American Association on Mental Deficiency, 5201 Connecticut Avenue, N.W., Washington, D.C. 20015.

RETINITIS PIGMENTOSA: The National Retinitis Pigmentosa Foundation, 8331 Mindale Road, Baltimore, Maryland 21207.

RUNAWAYS: Toll-free national hotline: (800) 621-4000.

SEX EDUCATION AND COUNSELING: S.I.E.C.U.S., 122 East 42nd Street, Suite 822, New York, New York 10017; American Association of Sex Educators and Counselors, 5010 Wisconsin Avenue, N.W., Washington, D.C. 20016; Institute for Sex Research, Inc., Indiana University, Bloomington, Indiana 47401.

SICKLE CELL ANEMIA: Association for Sickle Cell Anemia, 521 Fifth Avenue, New York, New York 10036.

SMOKING: Action on Smoking and Health, 2000 H Street, N.W., Washington, D.C. 20006; SmokEnders, 3435 Camino Del Rio, S., Suite 216, San Diego, California 92108; National Interagency Council on Smoking and Health, 419 Park Avenue South, New York, New York 10016; St. Helena Hospital and Health Clinic, Deer Park, California 94576.

SOCIAL WORK: National Association of Social Workers, 1425 H Street, N.W., Washington, D.C. 20005.

SPEECH AND HEARING: American Speech and Hearing Association, 9030 Old Georgetown Road, Bethesda, Maryland 20014; National Association of Hearing and Speech Agencies, 814 Thayer Avenue, Silver Springs, Maryland 20910; Speech Foundation of America, 152 Lombardy Road, Memphis, Tennessee 38111.

STERILIZATION: Association for Voluntary Sterilization, 14 West 40th Street, New York, New York 10018.

SUDDEN INFANT DEATH SYNDROME (SIDS): National Foundation for SIDS, 1501 Broadway, New York, New York 10036.

SUICIDE: Suicide Prevention Center of Los Angeles, 1041 Menlo Avenue, Los Angeles, California 90006.

TAY-SACHS: National Tay-Sachs and Allied Diseases Association, 122 East 42nd Street, New York, New York 10017.

TELEVISION: Action for Children's Television, 46 Austin, Newton, Massachusetts 02166.

TRANSCENDENTAL MEDITATION: National Center for TM, 1015 Gayley Avenue, Los Angeles, California 90024.

TUBERCULOSIS: American Lung Association, 1740 Broadway, New York, New York 10019.

UNWED MOTHERS: Florence Crittendon Division of the Child Welfare League of America, 67 Irving Place, New York, New York 10003; National Directory of Services for School-Age Parents, National Alliance Concerned with School-Age Parents, 7315 Wisconsin Avenue, Suite 211-W, Washington, D.C. 20014.

V.D.: American Social Health Association (venereal disease), 1740 Broadway, New York, New York 10019.

VOLUNTEER: Big Brothers/Big Sisters of America, 220 Suburban Station Building, Philadelphia, Pennsylvania 19103; R.S.V.P. (Retired Senior Volunteer Program), c/o ACTION, 806 Connecticut Avenue, N.W., Washington, D.C. 20525.

Hemorrhoids

The word "hemorrhoids" comes from the Greek, *haima*=blood, and *haimorrhois*="vein liable to bleed." The origin of the colloquial term "piles" for hemorrhoids is not clear, but may stem from the Latin *pila* (a mass) referring to a mass or cluster of veins.

What are they? Hemorrhoids are varicose swellings of the veins of the hemorrhoidal system that drain blood from the anal area back through the liver and eventually into the heart. All normal people have these hemorrhoidal veins, which become abnormal "hemorrhoids," as we know them, when dilated and engorged, much like varicose veins of the leg that are prominent and tortuous beneath the skin of the lower legs and thighs. These veins of the leg return directly through the large vein of the abdomen to the heart. By contrast, the hemorrhoidal veins of the anal area return blood first through the so-called portal system which flows first into the liver. The liver in turn sends the blood on to the heart.

What causes dilatation and engorgement of the hemorrhoidal veins to produce hemorrhoids ("piles")? There are many theories as to the cause of hemorrhoids. Hemorrhoids are probably not inherited. Man's upright posture may have something to do with their development, for they are not found in four-footed animals. Probably most hemorrhoids have no clear cause, but we know that constipation can exaggerate them. We also know that hemorrhoids appear in the third trimester of pregnancy due to back pressure on the veins from the enlarging uterus which prevents free return flow of blood from the anus, rectum and pelvis. We also know that patients with cirrhosis of the liver, in which there is a block to the free flow of venous blood through the liver, can also develop back-up pressure in the pelvis with resulting dilatation and engorgement of the hemorrhoidal veins. Hemorrhoids usually do not turn into cancer.

The kinds of hemorrhoids. Internal hemorrhoids lie within the muscle sphincter of the anus. External hemorrhoids prolapse or fall outside the muscle sphincter of the anal canal. They may be combined in any one patient. Also, internal hemorrhoids may prolapse or fall outside the anal sphincter and appear as external hemorrhoids. Internal hemorrhoids are covered by non-sensitive mucous membrane and, as long as they remain inside the muscle sphincter of the anal canal, are pain-free. External hemorrhoids are covered by the sensitive skin of the peri-anal area and may be quite tender and painful. Both kinds of hemorrhoids may bleed and both kinds of hemorrhoids may thrombose (fill up with clotted blood) and become further distended and extremely uncomfortable. Once a cluster of hemorrhoidal veins becomes situated outside the anal muscle sphincter, further engorgement, swelling and thrombosis (clotting) occur until the veins are manually reduced (pushed up by hands) inside the sphincter muscle bundles.

A note of warning: hemorrhoids characteristically produce bright red rectal bleeding. This bleeding may occur at the time of a bowel movement or may be unrelated to it. The blood may be in the toilet bowl or may be on the toilet tissue. Characteristically the blood is not mixed with the stool, but may appear on its surface as a linear streak. However, it is important to remember that other disease in the rectum may also cause bleeding. Although the commonest cause of bleeding from the rectum or anal canal is due to hemorrhoids, nevertheless, fissures, polyps, ulcers or tumors may also produce blood from the anus and, therefore, must be ruled out before one treats rectal bleeding as if it were due to hemorrhoids. An anal fissure (ulcer) produces mild bleeding. An anal fistula may produce minimal bleeding and discharge. A rectal polyp may produce quite profuse bleeding. Ulcerative colitis, bacterial colitis, diverticulitis are all causes of rectal (anal) bleeding. These must ultimately be excluded by anoscopy (looking in the anus) or sigmoidoscopy (looking higher up into the rectum and sigmoid with a 12-inch lighted scope) before any definite treatment should be given hemorrhoids themselves.

For older people (over forty) it is appropriate also to carry out a barium enema X ray (which evaluates the colon above what can be seen with the sigmoidoscope) if the bleeding persists over a significant period of time (three to four weeks), and particularly if associated with a change in bowel habit.

Treatment. For bleeding internal hemorrhoids that do not prolapse outside the anal canal, injection of sclerosing solutions (to shrink the hemorrhoids) may completely eliminate the bleeding problem. This can be done in the doctor's office through an anoscope.

External hemorrhoids that create swelling in and outside the anal canal represent an acute problem that may require bed rest, application of cool solutions (witch hazel, etc.) and an attempt to reduce the hemorrhoids inside the anal sphincter into the anal canal. Hemorrhoids that prolapse and become dilated, engorged and thrombosed, once subsided and reduced within the anal canal, may well subside completely. An example of this are the thrombosed, prolapsed hemorrhoids that occur during the late stages of pregnancy and at the time of delivery.

Only persistent or repeated and continued prolapse and thrombosis of a significant degree of hemorrhoids require surgical removal in a hospital setting.

Clotting may occur in one or two single hemorrhoids, but not involve the whole circumference of the anal canal. This process may be solved in the doctor's office by injecting a local anesthetic solution into the tissue overlying the hemorrhoid and evacuating the clot to allow hemorrhoid decompression.

Types of Operation. Simple excision of external hemorrhoids, though indicated less frequently nowadays, is accomplished under a general or spinal anesthetic in the hospital. The operation requires excision of the hemorrhoidal clusters and suturing of the resulting defect. The post-operative course may be prolonged as long as a week or more, depending upon the severity of the hemorrhoidal condition.

A newer method of elastic band ligation of internal hemorrhoids has become popular and may be carried out in the doctor's office. The procedure virtually eliminates postoperative discomfort. The rubber band, placed at the base of the hemorrhoid, cuts off the blood supply, and the tissue sloughs off in a few days.

Local freezing and thus thrombosing and destroying of hemorrhoids, originally popular, has become less so in recent years.

Non-operative Treatment. Conservative home treatment for hemorrhoids involves sitting three or four times a day for twenty minutes in a tub of warm water (sitz bath), and taking a stool softener (Metamucil, Colace, Kondremul, etc.). The application of local anesthetizing ointments or creams such as Nupercaine, dibucaine and Obtundia or cooling applications such as witch hazel, viz: Tucks ointments or pads, and other medications to shrink the hemorrhoids will often produce subsidence of an uncomfortable hemorrhoidal condition. Suppositories (anusol with and without cortisone, etc.) can also help decrease discomfort. Preparation H contains none of the above medications.

It should once again be emphasized here that most, but not all, hemorrhoidal problems can be solved without admission to a hospital and without major surgery.

CREDIT: *John R. Brooks, M.D., Professor of Surgery, Harvard Medical School, at the Peter Bent Brigham Hospital, Boston, Massachusetts.*

Hepatitis

The dictionary defines hepatitis as "inflammation of the liver." The liver is the largest single organ in the body and performs a number of different functions, primarily aiding in digestion and clearing the blood of certain waste products.

One of these functions is removing bilirubin, a major bile pigment produced from the normal breakdown of old red blood cells. Any damage to the liver, either by toxic or infectious agents, can impair this function, causing a buildup in the body of bilirubin. It turns the skin and whites of the eyes yellow and is known as "yellow jaundice," or simply jaundice.

Any serious injury to the liver, therefore, usually produces jaundice.

For instance, alcohol in sufficient quantities can be toxic to the point of destroying enough liver tissue to cause jaundice. The damaged liver heals by scarring (called cirrhosis) which produces further liver impairment.

Certain drugs, especially those in the tranquilizer family, can damage the liver, and produce jaundice. Cancers blocking liver drainage can do it also.

A common cause of jaundice is hepatitis, which is due to an infection by a virus that injures the liver.

There are several forms of viral hepatitis but the two most common are: (1) hepatitis A and (2) hepatitis B, more commonly called "infectious hepatitis" and "serum hepatitis."

Infectious hepatitis is acquired through the ingestion of fecally contaminated material and is usually found in areas of poverty and poor sanitary facilities. It has a relatively short incubation period, two or three weeks, and will hit a whole family or group of people who have been exposed. While making you feel very sick it has a very low death rate and when well again you are left with no significant or permanent disability. At present there is no practical laboratory test to detect this virus.

Serum hepatitis, on the other hand, is a more serious disease. The virus in this case is found in the blood of the infected individual and it is transmitted by some form of inoculation such as a blood transfusion or needle injection. It has a longer incubation period, up to six months, and can cause a more serious illness. There is a significant death rate and a number of infected people are left with permanent liver damage in the form of cirrhosis. Laboratory tests can detect this form of hepatitis.

The symptoms of both forms of hepatitis are somewhat similar. There is an initial period of feeling just plain "lousy," with a headache, upset stomach, loss of appetite and vomiting. It may last one or two weeks and is followed by the onset of "yellow jaundice" which first becomes apparent to the patient in the form of a darkening color to the urine, an increased yellow pigmentation to the whites of the eyes and then full-blown yellow change in the skin color. By this time the patient is really sick. This lasts two to three weeks with continued loss of appetite, nausea, vomiting, headache, fever, etc. The symptoms gradually subside as does the jaundice and in uncomplicated cases the patient is well in four to six weeks but invariably requires several more weeks or even months to fully regain his strength and the feeling of well-being experienced during his pre-hepatitis days.

There is no specific treatment or known cure once the disease is acquired. However, one should definitely see his doctor, who will put him at bed rest with supportive care.

Certain things can be done to decrease or prevent the chance of acquiring hepatitis.

Preventive measures: In the case of infectious hepatitis, if one is traveling to an area where the disease is prevalent, serum immune globulin can be given by your local doctor or health department. This will temporarily supply antibodies to fight off the virus should you become exposed. Serum immune globulin is usually given to all members of a family or close contacts of a person who has acquired infectious hepatitis. This procedure has been proven to be effective in decreasing the incidence of or preventing the disease.

In the case of serum hepatitis there has recently been developed hepatitis B immune globulin that appears to be effective in temporarily preventing this form of hepatitis in people who have been exposed. However, the best prevention is avoiding exposure.

For example, today most blood in this country used for transfusion has been procured by either an American Red Cross Blood Bank or a Blood Bank member of the American Association of Blood Banks. Both have pretested blood to be used for transfusion for the virus of serum hepatitis. While this test is not 100 percent accurate it does eliminate the vast number of infected units of blood and thereby has significantly reduced the incidence of hepatitis from blood transfusions.

Your doctor today uses disposable needles for injections and blood tests, thereby reducing the incidence of serum hepatitis by needle stick in that the needle is used only once and then discarded.

Today, probably the largest single source of serum hepatitis is the teenage and young adult drug-oriented culture where injection of various drugs, using a common needle, is a common practice.

Another source of serum hepatitis is the tattoo parlor, where a common needle is used for tattooing numerous individuals.

If you get hepatitis, there is no specific treatment that will cure you. The disease runs its course and you will get well—much like a common cold. There are measures, however, that can be taken to make you feel more comfortable, such as bed rest and good nutrition. To protect yourself against infectious hepatitis, practice good sanitary habits and avail yourself of temporary immunization with immune serum globulin prior to traveling in an endemic area or when exposed to close personal contacts who have the disease.

In the case of serum hepatitis, *never* use a communal needle.

Research is under way to develop a vaccine that may someday protect people against hepatitis, but until we have such a vaccine, hepatitis remains a serious illness with serious complications, including death. It is not to be regarded lightly.

CREDIT: *R. M. Failing, M.D., Associate Pathologist, Santa Barbara Cottage Hospital, Santa Barbara, California.*

Hernia

Hernia is a term describing a protrusion of tissue from the compartment of the body in which it normally belongs. The most common location of hernia is in the groin and is also called a "rupture."

A person suffering from an inguinal hernia notices a bulge and perhaps an ache or pain in that area. The bulge is usually intestine pushing through the body wall inside a sac. Since the sac is part of the abdominal cavity, intestines can easily slide in or out of the abdomen into the sac.

Hernias commonly occur in the groin because a cord of tissue normally penetrates the muscle layers at this point. In males the cord includes the tube passing from the testicle to the base of the bladder through which sperm normally travel. In females the cord is a ligament which forms a normal attachment of the uterus. Since the cord has a passage through the abdominal wall, a hernia sac can push out along the cord if the passage is too large as it is in some babies, or if the opening becomes stretched by pressure from abdominal straining as it may in older people.

Besides discomfort, the danger of a hernia is that loops of intestine may become trapped in the sac. The bulge becomes persistent and cannot be easily reduced or pushed back in. The bowel may become blocked or strangulated, which is a life-threatening condition. Bowel may become trapped as readily in a small sac as a large one, so size of the bulge is not a good indication of the degree of trouble that may be brewing. It is thought that the risk of bowel being trapped in a hernia sac is about one in ten. For this reason it is advisable to have a hernia taken care of.

In some patients a truss can be worn to keep bowel from entering the sac. A truss is a metal belt-like apparatus which applies pressure over the opening in the abdominal wall. While this may control the situation in some patients, it doesn't work for all; moreover, some find the truss uncomfortable and inconvenient.

Many patients and doctors prefer surgical repair of the hernia. The hernia operation closes the defect by sewing the body wall layers back together. This operation has a 95–98 percent chance of success in preventing a reoccurrence. Risk in this operation is low for patients in otherwise good health. The operation can be done under local, spinal or general anesthesia depending on the individual circumstances and wishes of the patient and surgeon.

In older patients, a new hernia or enlarging hernia may indicate early signs of diseases of the lungs, bowel or bladder which cause increased abdominal straining. Tests may be done to be sure that such other problems are not present before the hernia is repaired.

CREDIT: *David B. Skinner, M.D., Chairman, Department of Surgery, University of Chicago.*

Herpes Simplex Virus—1 and 2

(1) What is herpes?

Herpes is the common term for two viral infections currently existing at epidemic levels in the United States.

(2) What is herpes simplex virus type 1?

It is the medical term for the virus which commonly causes "cold sores" or "fever blisters."

(3) What is herpes simplex 2?

It is the medical term for the virus which usually causes genital herpes—an infection which can cause painful sores around the sex organs. According to the American Social Health Association in Palo Alto, California, this year more than 250,000 Americans will experience this disease.

(4) Is there any difference between HSV-1 and HSV-2?

Yes. First, they are different diseases caused by different viruses. HSV-1 most often affects the parts of the body above the waist (mouth, lips, skin, eyes) and HSV-2 almost always occurs below the waist—on or around the sex organs, buttocks and thighs. Occasionally, medical investigators have reported these infections in reverse areas.

Another important difference is that HSV-2 is now being regarded by experts as a venereal disease. Please note that it is possible to get HSV-2 without having sexual intercourse. For example, if a person touches the genitals of an actively infected individual, he or she may pass the virus to his or her own genitals by hand contact.

(5) Are canker sores the same as herpes?

No. Canker sores are recurrent ulcers that appear inside the mouth and their cause is still unknown. Herpes simplex 1 can and does appear in the mouth, particularly in children as a first infection, but it shows up much more frequently on the lips as a cause of recurrent infections (cold sores).

(6) Are there any differences between HSV-2 and other venereal diseases (like syphilis and gonorrhea)?

There are many differences between HSV-2 and other venereal diseases such as syphilis and gonorrhea—differences in incubation periods, symptoms, long-term effects, etc.—but the single most important difference is that HSV-2 cannot as yet be cured, as can syphilis and gonorrhea. Unlike syphilis and gonorrhea, which are caused by bacteria that can be killed by antibiotics such as penicillin, HSV-2 is caused by a virus, and like nearly all viruses it cannot be killed by presently known antibiotics. Once infected with HSV-2, a person may have recurrences throughout life.

(7) If I have HSV-1, can I also get HSV-2?

Yes. Most individuals who get HSV-2 have had HSV-1 in the past, usually when they were children.

(8) In what way is HSV-1 spread?

HSV-1 is most often spread by close contact with an infected individual, who may or may not have visible evidence of the infection, in the form of cold sores or skin blisters. Sometimes the virus can be spread from one part of the body to the other.

(9) How can spread of HSV-2 to a newborn be prevented?

Since the most usual way that a baby can become infected is from a maternal genital infection at the time of delivery, pregnant women should avoid contact with males with genital herpes, particularly in the latter part of pregnancy. If the infection is verified around the time of delivery, the doctor may consider performing a Caesarean section so they baby will not pass through the infected birth canal. If a woman has had recurrent genital herpes, she should inform her doctor, who can tell her if a recurrence is present around the time of delivery.

(10) What happens when you get HSV-2?

Approximately two to ten days after exposure, the first symptoms may be minor rashes or itching in the genital area. The symptoms then commonly develop into one or more painful blisterlike, fluid-filled lesions or sores. (Clusters of lesions are common.) These lesions may be accompanied by swollen lymph glands, fever, aching muscles and a general "sickly" feeling. These sores will eventually dry up and disappear, usually within a week to a month, as will the accompanying symptoms. This apparent "spontaneous" cure is in fact no cure at all. Even though the symptoms have disappeared, the virus has not. The virus remains alive in an inactive (latent) form inside the body. It must be stressed that the symptoms just described apply to external sites of HSV-2 infection. A person with an internal case of HSV-2 (primarily women in whom the cervix or vagina are the sites of infection) may notice only some and perhaps none of the "typical" symptoms.

(11) If the virus is alive but inactive, can it ever "reactivate"?

Yes—and chances are that it will. Medical scientists report that only about 30 percent of all active cases of HSV-2 are new infections. The others are recurrences in individuals who have had the disease before. There is no apparent pattern of recurrent infection. The duration and frequency of recurrences vary with the individual and may be triggered by physical or even emotional stress.

(12) Is HSV-2 really dangerous?

It can be. First, there is the danger of secondary infection on top of the active HSV-2 infection. Because the blisters of HSV-2 are breaks in the skin, there is the possibility that other germs may enter the exposed area and cause another infection that can be even more serious than HSV-2.

Second, in the case of pregnant women with HSV-2, the virus, if transmitted, can prove devastating, even fatal, to the fetus or newborn infant.

Thirdly, medical scientists suspect a possible relationship between HSV-2 in women and cervical cancer. While no cause-and-effect relationship has been established, scientists report that women with HSV-2 are five times more likely to develop cervical cancer than women with no evidence of past HSV-2 infection.

(13) What should I do if I think I have HSV-2?

First and most important, get medical attention at once—while you still have the symptoms. What you suspect as HSV-2 may not be that at all. Only a doctor can make the diagnosis.

If you definitely have HSV-2, you will be advised not to have sex for at least as long as the HSV-2 is active. This advice should be heeded because HSV-2 is contagious.

You will probably be told to pay very close attention to matters involving personal hygiene while the HSV-2 is active. This is to reduce the likelihood of acquiring another infection on top of HSV-2.

You might be given an ointment or pills to help relieve the pain, depending on the severity of your infection. If you're a woman, your physician will probably reinforce the need for routine Pap smears. In the case of a pregnant woman, your physician will probably want to closely monitor the term of pregnancy and possibly take added precautions to minimize the risk to the unborn child or infection or transmission to the infant during birth.

(14) Have any forms of treatment been proven to be effective?

Although some drugs may help certain patients, no one treatment has been consistently successful for all. Many new forms of treatment (at least a dozen) are currently under active investigation. Some are aimed at cutting short the duration of the blisters, others attempt to prevent recurrences.

Again, you should appreciate that more has been learned about herpes in the past ten years than in the previous two thousand years.

(15) Can HSV-2 be prevented?

In terms of vaccines—no, at least not yet. Research to find a vaccine is presently under way, but as yet no vaccine exists in the United States. Regarding other forms of prevention, the condom (rubber sheath for the penis), as with other venereal diseases, is one way for a male to avoid exposure if he is having sex with an infected female.

As with all venereal diseases, sexual habits and patterns greatly influence the likelihood of exposure and infection. The general rule: The more frequently one engages in sexual relations with a variety of partners, the greater the risks of acquiring a venereal disease. This is especially applicable to HSV-2.

(16) Herpes and cancer: Is there any connection between them?

It should be emphasized that, at present, there is no conclusive proof that HSV-2 causes cancer in humans. Researchers have been working in this area for the past decade and believe that it will be some time before it can be said that the virus definitely does or does not cause cancer in humans. Because there is some association between HSV-2 and cervical cancer, physicians recommend at present that women with genital herpes (diagnosed as such by your doctor) should have frequent Pap smears (at least one a year). Remember that cancer of the cervix can be detected very early with a Pap smear and that whether or not HSV is related to cervical cancer, a Pap smear should be obtained at least yearly.

CREDIT: *American Society Health Association, Palo Alto, California. Checked for accuracy by Dr. André J. Nahmias, Professor of Pediatrics, Chief of Infectious Diseases and Immunology Section, Emory University School of Medicine, Atlanta, Georgia.*

Hiccups

There are dozens of "home cures" for the hiccups and many of them work. I have discovered the most effective one (for me) is to take a teaspoon of sugar and eat it slowly. If you are a diabetic (or don't want the calories) a teaspoon of vinegar will do as well.

Another cure for hiccups is to sip a glass of water from the opposite side of the glass. Bend low from the waist and drink with your head upside down. It's not easy!

Some people recommend that you put your head in a paper bag and breathe deeply.

If none of these remedies work and the hiccups persist for longer than two hours, go to the emergency room of a hospital. The hiccups may be a symptom of a more serious problem.

CREDIT: *Ann Landers.*

Homosexuality

(*One Point of View*)

IS HOMOSEXUALITY A PERSONALITY DISTURBANCE?

DEAR ANN LANDERS: I read with considerable alarm the column in which you insist homosexuals suffer from a "severe personality disorder." You refer to a number of psychiatrists who agree with you and also state that the American Psychiatric Association does not.

I would like to call to your attention that the American Psychological Association not only supports the notion that homosexuality, per se, implied no impairment in judgment, stability, social or vocational capability, but further urges psychologists to take the lead in removing the stigma that has long been associated with homosexual orientation.

I feel it is only fair that you let it be known that yours is a minority opinion.   S.F.M., PHD, CALIFORNIA

DEAR S.F.M.: Since you are a PhD perhaps you can tell me the origin of one of my favorite quotes: "One person with courage constitutes a majority."

I agree with the American Psychological Association's statement that homosexuality per se implies no impairment in judgment, stability, social or vocational ability. I am well aware that a great many homosexuals function in their jobs and interact with others far more successfully than some heterosexuals. In fact, the only difference is their sexual preference.

We part company, however, at that juncture. I believe, when an individual prefers a member of his (or her) own sex as an object of physical love, that person suffers from a severe personality disorder.

Few subjects seem to generate as much passion, controversy or misunderstanding as homosexuality. And few subjects seem to raise as many unanswerable questions. For example: Is it an illness that warrants a psychiatric diagnosis? Or is it simply an alternate lifestyle? Even the "experts" are sharply divided. Obviously, no statement will satisfy everyone.

I shall attempt to present this complex subject as clearly and objectively as possible from the standpoint of a practicing psychiatrist who has been concerned with the problem of homosexuality for many years.

DEFINITION

Homosexuality has been variously defined, but the simplest definition, with all its defects, is often the best. The Greek prefix "homo" means "the same." Hence, "homosexuality" refers to the state of being persistently attracted on both a physical and emotional level to a member of the *same* sex. An isolated homosexual experience while intoxicated, for "kicks" or in special unisex situations (imprisonment) does not justify labeling that person a homosexual.

The Greek prefix "hetero" means "other" or "different." Hence, "heterosexuality" refers to exclusive physical and emotional attraction to members of the opposite sex.

The "bisexual" is a person who is capable of having satisfying physical relations with both sexes.

However one defines "homosexuality" it is no more of a specific diagnosis than the term "heterosexuality." In some instances homosexuality is a symptom of deep underlying conflict. In other cases it is the end result of complex biological, cultural or environmental factors. There are as many varieties of homosexual behavior as there are of heterosexual behavior. The isolated homosexual experiment during adolescence, the one-night stand, the homosexual prostitute, the compulsive pickup in bars or public lavatories and/or the settled homosexual marriage are but a few examples.

In discussing terms or "labels" it is of interest to note that the Gay Liberation movement prefers the term "gay" to "homosexual." This is characteristic of other types of militant groups that strive for a new identity. Consider for example the successive use of the terms "colored," "Negro" and finally "black." Even the slogans bear a certain similarity. Compare "Black is Beautiful" with the militant "Gay, Proud and Healthy" or "Gay is Good!" This similarity should not come as a surprise to anyone familiar with the thinking of militant homosexual groups, most of whom have considered themselves (like blacks) a persecuted minority.

HISTORICAL

Whether condoned or condemned, homosexuality has been present in almost all cultures from the earliest dawn of history. In a comparative study of seventy-seven present-day primitive societies, Ford and Beach found that forty-nine of those societies accepted homosexuality in some restricted form, whereas twenty-eight societies condemned the practice. At certain times in history, such as fifth-century Athens, homosexuality was even idealized by some of the state's greatest philosophers, including Plato. In other countries with differing cultural patterns, homosexuality has been strongly condemned. Disapproval probably reached an all-time high during the Victorian period in England. Those negative attitudes were quickly imitated in America.

In recent years, with the loosening of sexual mores and greater openness in discussing and writing about previously taboo subjects, our understanding of aberrant sexual practices, including homosexuality, has increased greatly. Fifty years ago, the terms "syphilis" or "homosexual" were never permitted to appear in a respectable U.S. newspaper or magazine. Today such terms are commonplace. Fifty years ago public and official attitudes toward homosexuals were restrictive and punitive. Prior to World War II, the U. S. Navy sent convicted homosexuals to Portsmouth prison, where they served a term and then given a bad-conduct discharge.

The Gay Liberation movement, in spite of some of its tasteless extremes, has done much to make the public aware of the cruel discrimination directed against homosexuals in our society. However, the spirit of the times was also heading in that direction and many of the advances would most likely have occurred in any case, but probably at a somewhat slower pace.

WHAT CAUSES HOMOSEXUALITY?

There is no one specific cause for homosexuality. But one thing is certain, it is not inherited. In view of our general lack of knowledge, all one can say is that homosexuality may result from a cluster of causes which often differ from case to case. These include early influences in childhood, special types of fathering and mothering, exposure to homosexual activity at a vulnerable age, excessive attachment to a "smothering" mother, or a tyrannical, weak or absent father. To make matters more complicated, some persons with these very backgrounds may develop into normal heterosexual adults. Finally, endocrine (glandular) factors cannot be entirely ruled out as contributing factors in some cases.

One should remember that all of us reflect our bisexual origins by retaining some anatomical, chemical, glandular and even behavioral residues of the opposite sex. The developing fetus is so "bisexual" that its final sex cannot be determined by inspection until it is ten weeks of age. Every man retains some circulating female sex hormone in his blood; every woman has some male sex hormone circulating in her blood.

One finds homosexual behavior in almost all species of mammals. Anyone who has observed dogs or monkeys in a zoo knows that such behavior is a common occurrence. However, the relevance of such animal behavior to sexual behavior in man is open to question. At one level it may be nothing more than simple, uninhibited genital activity to obtain pleasure from any animate object. On another level, it may be nature's way of limiting population growth. In recent experiments with rat populations, they were permitted to reproduce freely within a confined living space. The rats who received plenty of food but suffered from severe overcrowding, began to exhibit abnormal sexual patterns which automatically cut down the birth rate. Does this help explain why homosexuality is most common in our large, overcrowded cities? Is homosexuality one of nature's ways of population control?

HOW MANY HOMOSEXUALS ARE THERE?

Statistics in this area are notoriously unreliable. Homosexuals who wish to lead a quiet, productive life certainly outnumber those who have "come out of the closet." They are also least likely to consult a psychiatrist or answer questionnaires. In 1948 Kinsey astonished the medical and lay public by his findings that 37 percent of all males reported at least one homosexual experience ending in orgasm and that 4 percent of them went on to an exclusively homosexual life. Other studies suggest that homosexuals comprise anywhere from 2 to 10 percent of the adult male population. As long as the subject remains sensitive we are not likely to obtain reliable data. The fact remains that there is a sizable homosexual population in the United States. This segment of our population may appear larger now because many homosexuals are identifying themselves as such, and letting the world in on their secret in an effort to give strength to their number. The unobtrusive, reasonably well-adjusted homosexual, however, continues to cherish his privacy and anonymity.

FEMALE HOMOSEXUALITY (LESBIANISM)

As fragmentary as our knowledge is in regard to male homosexuality, it is even more incomplete in the area of female homosexuality. There are many reasons for this. In the first place, our society tends to condone two women living with each other, or kissing and embracing publicly, without taking offense. Female homosexuality is, therefore, much harder to study statistically. Estimates of the incidence of lesbianism vary from a figure equal to male homosexuality to half that number. It is a curious fact that far fewer lesbians seek psychiatric treatment than do male homosexuals.

HOMOSEXUALITY AN ILLNESS? IF NOT, WHAT IS IT?

In spite of Sigmund Freud's views: ". . . Homosexuality is assuredly no advantage but it is nothing to be ashamed of, no vice, no degradation. It cannot be classified as an illness; we consider it to be a variation of the sexual function produced by a certain arrest of sexual development . . ." homosexuality, until quite recently, had indeed been classified as an illness in all official manuals of mental disorders since they were first published.

On December 15, 1973, the Board of Trustees of the American Psychiatric Association ruled that "Homosexuality *by itself* does not necessarily constitute a psychiatric disorder." In place of "homosexuality" the listing was to read "sexual orientation disturbance (homosexuality)." The reasoning which prompted this change was that the term "homosexuality" failed to meet either of the two requirements of psychiatric disorders, namely, (1) that "the condition regularly causes subjective distress," or (2) "is regularly associated with some generalized impairment in social effectiveness or functioning." The new diagnosis "sexual orientation disturbance" was to be used only if the person involved was troubled enough to seek consultation or treatment.

The APA went on to say: ". . . by no longer listing homosexuality as a psychiatric disorder we are not saying it is 'normal' or as valuable as heterosexuality."

Announcement of the new APA position created a furor in psychiatric circles and also among homosexuals. Many of the gay activists hailed it as a victory but an equal number felt that it did not go far enough and that there was too much hedging.

The division among psychiatrists was equally sharp. A distinguished group of psychiatrists, many of whom had worked intensively in this area, strenuously objected to the decision of the APA Board of Trustees and initiated a referendum of the entire Association which put the issue to a general vote. Of the approximately twenty thousand APA members, only half of them voted: 58 percent approved the new classification; 37 percent voted to keep homosexuality listed as a mental disorder; 3.6 percent abstained from voting. The referendum was both ridiculed as an unscientific "popularity contest" and hailed as a vindication of the Board of Trustees' decision.

IS HOMOSEXUALITY TREATABLE? IF SO, WHAT ARE THE RESULTS?

In order to treat a disorder there must be some complaint on the part of the person seeking treatment. The term "disease" literally means "dys-ease"; that is, not being at ease. If the person is satisfied with his lot and refuses treatment even though he may have diabetes or high blood pressure, the disease is usually untreatable. Other persons who do not have a definable illness but who may not conform to a "norm" or majority view, such as the vegetarian, the fanatic believer in an offbeat cult or the rabid racist, are also unlikely to complain and even less likely to seek treatment for their non-conformist preferences. The same theory applies to homosexuality. In order to be treated, the homosexual must suffer from anxiety related to his (or her) homosexuality before there is any chance of success.

Even if the homosexual decides to reach out for treatment the results are very difficult to predict. Evaluation is made even more difficult by the great variety of treatment methods now in use, which include (1) psychoanalysis, (2) group therapy, (3) aversion therapy and (4) the use of hormones.

An example of aversion therapy is as follows: The goal is to make the homosexual think of his condition in a distasteful, negative way—in other words to create an aversion to it. He is shown movies of homosexual activity. Whenever the act is performed, he receives a mild electric shock in the area of the penis, which has been wired for the event. The movies and electric shock are repeated several times. The homosexual then becomes conditioned to react adversely to the homosexual act whenever the thought of it enters his head.

Aversion therapy has been much criticized (especially in the Gay Liberation movement); however, it seems to be just as effective as psychotherapy and much less time-consuming. It must be noted, in order to keep the record accurate, that there is a tendency for patients treated by this method to relapse.

In my own clinical experience I find very few homosexuals who wish to change. I have known only two cases in which there have been successful and happy changes to a heterosexual way of life following several years of psychoanalysis. Homosexuals have also consulted me for a wide variety of reasons including anxiety, depression and alcoholism—the same psychiatric disorders which afflict heterosexuals.

Contrary to Gay Liberation propaganda, psychiatrists never try to make the homosexual go "straight" against his will. Only when the homosexual is desperately unhappy with his lot and strongly motivated for treatment can he be helped to achieve a good heterosexual adjustment in a certain percentage of cases, *provided he gets into competent professional hands*. If he is unwilling or unable to change, psychotherapy may reduce his anxieties and help him to make a better adjustment to his homosexual way of life.

It is bitterly ironic that the Gay Liberation movement has selected psychiatry as one of its prime targets for attack. Ironic because it was psychiatry, more than any other single branch of medicine, that tried so long and hard to understand, to help and to treat the homosexual.

Society can best understand the homosexual by viewing him as objectively as possible and by not becoming irritated with the more bizarre types we see from time to time. One should keep in mind that many varieties of bizarre heterosexual behavior can be equally offensive.

Some of the more militant members of the Gay Liberation movement preach that homosexuality is a "superior" lifestyle, which it is not. This fact is apparently recognized by homosexuals themselves. In a recent New York survey of homosexuals none expressed the wish to change his sexual orientation, but almost all stated that they would not wish their sons to become homosexual. Parents of homosexuals are anguished when they discover that one of their children is homosexual and often try desperately to get him or her to seek help.

If a homosexual is young, "on the fence," and wishes to have treatment, I believe he should be encouraged to seek help even though the chances of becoming heterosexual are extremely slim. On the other hand, if a person has decided on an active homosexual life, it he does not harm anyone, and continues to be constructive in his profession or work, he should be left alone.

This subject deserves more serious study and research than it has thus far received, so that homosexuality (however it is defined) may someday be viewed without prejudice and in a spirit of humanistic understanding.

CREDIT: *Zigmond M. Lebensohn, M.D., Chief Emeritus, Department of Psychiatry, Sibley Memorial Hospital; Clinical Professor of Psychiatry, Georgetown University School of Medicine, Washington, D.C.*

OUT OF THE CLOSET? O.K. BUT PLEASE CONSIDER THE CHILD

DEAR ANN LANDERS: I live with another woman who has a young female child. Yes, we are lesbians and I am not ashamed of it.

I am very fond of the little girl and consider myself very nearly a parent because of my relationship with her mother.

What I need to know is what I should call this child when I refer to her in conversations? I don't like to say, "She is the daughter of my roommate," because she is much more than that.

I am proud of the fact that she is the daughter of the woman I love and is as dear to me as if she were my own

child. Your suggestions will be greatly appreciated. NO CLOSETS FOR US

DEAR NO CLOSETS: The question you should be asking yourself is why do you feel the need to hit people over the head with the fact that you are involved in a lesbian relationship? It seems to me this is a personal matter. In fact, I can think of no matter that is more personal.

Since you feel compelled to cut the world in on your sexual preference, you could refer to the child as "the daughter of my female lover with whom I am living." If it's popped eyeballs you're after, you'll get them.

Homosexuality

(*Another View*)

Contrary to what the leadership of the gay liberation movement and misinformed professionals would have one believe, homosexuality is an unnatural condition, the outward evidence of a psychological disturbance. Homosexuality is rarely due to biological factors within genes, chromosomes or hormones. It is wrong to compare homosexuality with left-handedness or right-handedness, for to do so is to imply that people are born with the homosexual tendency. They are not. People do not choose to become homosexual. They may think they are making a free choice to be homosexual, but they are driven to this form of interpersonal behavior by forces within the unconscious region of their mind. It is completely incorrect to refer to this condition as a sexual preference, thereby implying free choice.

The causes of homosexuality can be readily discovered by looking in two places. One leads to an inspection of the personalities of the homosexual's parents and the nature of the family interactions and patterns during the early years of the homoscxual's life. The other area for inspection is into the unconscious regions of the homosexual's mind. The findings in both areas are consistent with each other and irrefutably establish a purely psychological basis for the condition.

Nature provides each person with enormous potentialities which the environment releases and develops. It is part of Nature's plan for the opposite sexes to mate. The kind of mothering a child receives awakens his or her capacity to experience intimacy with another human being. Good mothering creates courage, the capacity to trust and the capacity to experience intimacy. These fundamental human qualities make possible the further psychological development of sexual identity and the capacity to experience sexual arousal toward persons of the opposite sex. Fathers play a necessary role in this process. The child is thereby prepared to enter into a heterosexual relationship later on in life.

Mothers of homosexuals fail to provide the quality of mothering which fills the child with a sense of courage, self-confidence, security and an ability to experience intimacy. These women who are not fully prepared for mothering may show some or all of a variety of personality characteristics towards their infants and small children. They are one or more of the following: domineering, aggressive and even masculinized, or infantile and ineffectual. In short, they are lacking in what can be defined as mature femininity. As a consequence they tend to be overly possessive, even clinging, or rejecting and hostile, often volatile and unstable. These qualities instill great fear in the heart of an infant and child, the very last kind of feelings a child requires in order to proceed further with personality development.

The fathers of homosexuals are often physically absent, more often they are emotionally remote, and they are usually dominated by their wives because of their own passivity and weakness of masculine qualities. Such fathers tend to be openly or secretly hostile and rejecting towards their sons from early life on, and overly close and even seductive towards their daughters.

The relationship between the parents of the child who eventually becomes homosexual is far from perfect. They are frequently distant and/or openly hostile toward each other. The wives tend to demean their weak and ineffectual husbands. The emotional distance between them tends to create overt or covert alliances between mother and son and father and daughter.

Under these circumstances, little girls fail to fully develop a feminine identity, which will later make it impossible for them to enter into a committed, loving and sexual relationship with a man. Instead, they may remain infantile and childlike and become easy prey for an aggressive lesbian with whom they find intimacy which mimics the mother-child relationship. Sex becomes part of the relationship. Other little girls become "masculinized," a trait which imitates the harsh, aggressive qualities of their mothers and also incorporates elements of their fathers' personalities, with whom, as noted above, they had developed excessively close relationships.

Little boys cannot find their full masculine identity when they grow up within such family patterns and cannot enter into intimate, loving relationships with women. They are too frightened to do so. They lacked the inner courage to fully develop as young males and as a consequence they lack the inner psychological conditions to be able to relate to women. In particular, they have been short on good fathering. Much of the meaning of later overt homosexual behavior is a search for maleness which they expect to magically acquire from the homosexual act.

Homosexuals can be successfully treated by psychological methods alone, a fact which further confirms the purely psychological basis for the condition. Parenthetically, were homosexuality a "normal" condition like left-handedness, it should exist in *all* cultures. It does not. Successful treatment of homosexuals requires the removal of those unconscious conflicts (fears, guilt, confusion with regard to sexual identity, etc.) which were created by their childhood family patterns and experiences, and the stimulation of further personality development which is long overdue. Homosexuals must also be discouraged from having such relationships and must be encouraged to relate to members of the opposite sex. In order for successful treatment to occur, the treating doctor must thoroughly understand the condition, he must have mastered the required therapeutic techniques and his own personality must be mature, especially with regard to his or her own maleness or femaleness as the case may be.

The personal and social consequences of defining homosexuality as merely a matter of preference are enormous. Troubled people who might otherwise seek treatment are being misled. Society is already changing its values, e.g., homosexuals wish to "marry," adopt children. Educators are misleading the young by defining the condition as "normal." In short, to define homosexuality as "normal" is to assault the fundamental building block of all societies, namely, the heterosexual bond and the family which springs from that bond.

CREDIT: *Harold M. Voth, M.D., Psychiatrist, Menninger Foundation, Topeka, Kansas; author of* The Castrated Family, *Kansas City: Sheed, Andrews and McMeel, Inc.*

ACCEPT ME AS I AM

DEAR ANN: When I read the letter from "Why Me?" I knew I couldn't keep quiet any longer. I had to write.

I, too, am a homosexual—male, 24 years old. I was in therapy for three years at my mother's insistence and am now convinced I will never be straight. I'm not happy about the situation but I can handle it.

The problem is my family. Although my parents know, no one else does. My relatives are all ultra-conservatives —politically, socially and religion-wise. It would kill them if they knew that their brother, nephew, grandson, cousin was gay. The news nearly destroyed my parents six years ago and I'm not eager to put anyone else (in-cluding myself) through that hell again.

I hate living a lie. I don't want to deceive some nice woman, marry her and produce children (gays can, you know) just to please my family and cover up what I really am.

Unlike your other correspondent who asked "Why Me?" I am asking, "Why can't I BE me?" NEED AN ANSWER

DEAR NEED: As far as I'm concerned you CAN. I would have no trouble accepting you as you are. The question is, do you have the courage to come out of the closet? Others have. Only you can make that decision.

Hyperactivity

(*How Parents Can Help*)

Children need daily outside activities such as running, sports or long walks.

Keep the home existence organized. Predictable responses by the parents to daily events help the child become more predictable.

Avoid fatigue in these children. When they are exhausted, their self-control often breaks down and their hyperactivity becomes worse.

Avoid formal gatherings. Settings where hyperactivity would be extremely inappropriate and embarrassing should be completely avoided. After the child develops adequate self-control at home, these situations can be introduced gradually.

Maintain firm discipline. The family needs a few clear, consistent, important rules, with other rules added at the child's own pace. Parents must avoid being after the child all the time with negative comments.

Enforce discipline with non-physical punishment.

Stretch his attention span. Rewarding non-hyperactive behavior is the key to preparing these children for school.

Buffer the children against overreaction by neighbors. If he receives a reputation for being a "bad kid," it is important that this doesn't carry over into his home life. At home the attitude that must prevail is that he is a "good child with excess energy."

CREDIT: *Barton Schmitt, M.D., University of Colorado Medical Center, Denver, Colorado.*

HYPER HELP

DEAR ANN LANDERS: I had to write when I read about the woman whose lunatic husband wants to give his 4-year-old daughter up for adoption because she is hyperactive.

I am the mother of a 5-year-old hyperactive child. He used to bite, punch, kick, spit, have violent temper tantrums, and couldn't play with other children. We took the boy to several doctors before one suggested our state university medical center for evaluation. He was placed in a daily therapeutic program and the results have been fantastic. He is a different child.

I am grateful for all the help our son received there but I feel that most of the change was accomplished by love. GRATEFUL FOR HELP IN CONNECTICUT

DEAR CONN: I'm grateful to you for writing. I caught Holy Ned from hundreds of readers because I cautioned mothers against making "little junkies" out of their children. Too often a youngster is put on drugs because it's easier than taking the time to be loving and patient. I realize that some children are truly hyperkinetic and medication can be a godsend, but drugs should not be a substitute for parental time and attention. An excellent book for parents who need guidelines for raising children (not necessarily hyperkinetic, just normal healthy kids from 1 to 5 years of age) is "Your Young Child and You" (Dutton, $7.95) by Eleanor Weisberger. I've read it from cover to cover and it is superb.

The Hyperactive Child

The hyperactive (or hyperkinetic) child has been described as a child who was born running. From birth he is more active than most infants. As he grows older and is able to walk he seems to be constantly on the move. He jumps from one activity to another. His span of attention is usually brief. This condition is much more common in boys than girls.

In school he often finds it hard to concentrate and he may have great difficulty in staying in his seat. Generally he is not a behavior problem if allowed to be active but may present difficulties if he is forced to remain still. He may have learning problems in school resulting from his poor span of attention and limited ability to concentrate. These learning problems in turn may produce emotional difficulties resulting from frustration when he is unable to keep up with the rest of the class. His intelligence is not affected by his hyperactivity and is comparable to that of other children his age.

Hyperkinesis, as the condition is called technically, is not a specific disease but rather a group of symptoms. It probably is the surface manifestation of different types of underlying problems in difficult children. In some children the hyperactivity is a symptom of an underlying emotional disturbance. In these children there will be other evidence of their emotional problems in addition to the hyperactivity and difficulties.

In other children the hyperactivity is a result of minimal brain damage and there frequently will be found some neurological evidence of minimal brain dysfunction. Usually, when this is present, the damage is due to a difficult birth process or to something minimally damaging the child's brain in infancy.

Recently there have been suggestions that some hyperactive children become hyperactive because of their being poisoned by food additives. (Food additives are artificial substances added to foods for purposes of coloration, taste, preservation, etc.) As yet there is no evidence that this is true.

It was discovered accidentally that the symptom of hyperactivity can frequently be helped by the use of stimulant drugs. These are drugs that would actually produce hyperactivity in adults but in children have an opposite effect and act as tranquilizers. These drugs are Benzedrine or other substances that act like Benzedrine, for example Ritalin. Drugs that serve as tranquilizers for adults seem to have little effect on the symptom of hyperactivity.

If the child is hyperactive but shows no other problems either at home, with peers or at school, nothing need be done. The parent should learn to accept the fact that his child is simply more active than the average child.

It is important also that the parents request that the teacher of the hyperactive child show as much patience as possible, including allowing him to get up and walk around the room at intervals, provided, of course, that the child does not take advantage of this and become a discipline problem.

If, in addition to the child's hyperactivity, he also has other symptoms, then the following should be considered:

(1) The child should be given a full neurological examination by a pediatric neurologist—that is, a doctor who specializes in neurological examina-

tions of children. If he decides a stimulant drug is indicated he will prescribe it.

(2) The parent should not allow anyone but a doctor to prescribe or suggest medication for the hyperactive child. Far too many children are being given drugs without a thorough neurological examination.

(3) If the child's hyperactivity or other symptoms persist after he has been on medication for a reasonable period of time (for example, three months), the parent should consider having the child receive a psychiatric evaluation.

Most hyperactive children with problems can be helped by medication, psychiatric treatment and a great deal of patience shown by parents and teachers.

CREDIT: *Ner Littner, M.D., S.C., Institute of Psychoanalysis—Chicago, Coordinator, Child Therapy Program.*

Ten Guidelines for Living with a Hyperactive Child

(1) *Accept your child's limitations.* A parent must accept the fact that his child is intrinsically active and energetic and possibly always will be. The hyperactivity is not intentional. A parent should not expect to eliminate the hyperactivity but just to keep it under reasonable control. Any undue criticism or attempts to change the energetic child into a quiet child or "model child" will cause more harm than good. Nothing is more helpful for the hyperactive child than having a tolerant, patient, low-key parent.

(2) *Provide outlets for the release of excess energy.* This energy can't be bottled up and stored. These children need daily outside activities such as running, sports or long walks. A fenced yard helps. In bad weather he needs a recreational room where he can do as he pleases without criticism. If no large room is available, a garage will sometimes suffice. Although the expression of hyperactivity is allowed in these ways, it should not be needlessly encouraged. Adults should not engender roughhousing with these children. Siblings should be forbidden to say, "Chase me, chase me" or to instigate other noisy play. Rewarding hyperactive behavior leads to its becoming the child's main style of interacting with people.

(3) *Keep the home existence organized.* Household routines help the hy-

peractive child accept order. Mealtimes, chores and bedtime should be kept as consistent as possible. Predictable responses by the parents to daily events help the child become more predictable.

(4) *Avoid fatigue in these children.* When they are exhausted, their self-control often breaks down and their hyperactivity becomes worse.

(5) *Avoid formal gatherings.* Settings where hyperactivity would be extremely inappropriate and embarrassing should be completely avoided. Examples of this would be church, restaurants, etc. Of lesser importance, the child can forgo some trips to stores and supermarkets to reduce unnecessary friction between the child and parent. After the child develops adequate self-control at home, these situations can gradually be introduced.

(6) *Maintain firm discipline.* These children are unquestionably difficult to manage. They need more careful, planned discipline than the average child. Rules should be formulated mainly to prevent harm to himself or others. Aggressive behavior and attention-getting behavior should be no more accepted in the hyperactive child than in the normal child. Unlike the expression of hyperactivity, aggressive behavior should be eliminated. Unnecessary rules should be avoided. These children tolerate fewer rules than the normal child. The family needs a few clear, consistent, important rules, with other rules added at the child's own pace. Parents must avoid being after the child all the time with negative comments like "Don't do this" and "Stop that."

(7) *Enforce discipline with non-physical punishment.* The family must have an "isolation room" or "time-out place" to back up their attempts to enforce rules, if a show of disapproval doesn't work. This room can be the child's bedroom. The child should be sent there to "shape up" and allowed out as soon as he has changed his behavior. Without an isolation room, overall success is unlikely. Physical punishment should be avoided in these children since we want to teach them to be less aggressive, rather than make aggression acceptable. These children need adult models of control and calmness.

(8) *Stretch his attention span.* Rewarding non-hyperactive behavior is the key to preparing these children for school. Increased attention span and persistence with tasks can be taught to these children at home. The child can be shown pictures in a book; and, if he is attentive, he can be rewarded with praise and a hug. Next the parent can read stories to him. Coloring of pictures can be encouraged and rewarded. Games of increasing difficulty can gradually be taught to the child, starting with building blocks and progressing eventually to dominoes, card games and dice games. Matching pictures is an excellent way to build a child's memory and concentration span. The child's toys should not be excessive in number, for this can accentuate his distractibility. They should also be ones that are safe and relatively unbreakable.

(9) *Buffer the child against any overreaction by neighbors.* If he receives a reputation for being a "bad kid" it is important that this doesn't carry over

into his home life. At home the attitude that must prevail is that he is a "good child with excess energy." It is extremely important that his parents don't give up on him. He must always feel accepted by his family. As long as he has this, his self-esteem and self-confidence will survive.

(10) *Periodically get away from it all.* Parents must get away from the hyperactive child often enough to be able to tolerate him. Exposure to some of these children for twenty-four hours a day would make anyone a wreck. When the father comes home, he should try to look after the child and give his wife a deserved break. A baby-sitter two afternoons a week and an occasional evening out with her husband can salvage an exhausted mother. A preschool nursery or Head Start class is another option. Parents need a chance to rejuvenate themselves.

CREDIT: *Barton Schmitt, M.D., Department of Pediatrics, University of Colorado Medical Center, Denver, Colorado.*

Hypnosis

The word "hypnosis" conjures up an image of dangling watches, rotating spirals and mystery. Hypnosis is, in fact, a form of intense receptive concentration which is finding growing application in various aspects of medicine, dentistry and psychology.

Actually, hypnosis alone is not a profession. Hypnosis is always secondary to a primary professional commitment. For example, the dentist can use hypnosis to facilitate his dental work. The surgeon can use hypnosis to alleviate surgical pain. A psychotherapist can use hypnosis to implement appropriate behavior change. But none are hypnotists. They are professionals who use hypnosis.

The physicians I know who use hypnosis do not call themselves hypnotists. Usually the quacks or self-designated healers call themselves hypnotists. (It sounds better than "quacks.")

Entertainers who use hypnosis as part of a show or a nightclub act are primarily actors who use hypnosis. They are not doctors or therapists. In general, anybody who presents himself to the public as a hypnotist, implying that he is a therapist, or doctor, without having legitimate training and experience in the basic medical, psychological or psychiatric professions, is likely to be a sad sack groping for something to do to make himself feel important.

The use of hypnosis can facilitate the treatment of many common problems, including pain, anxiety, insomnia, smoking and obesity. Because there has been such widespread misunderstanding of what hypnosis is and what its appropriate uses are, we will review ten of the most common misunderstandings about hypnosis:

(1) MYTH: Hypnosis is sleep.

FACT: Hypnosis is not only *not* sleep, but actually the opposite of sleep. It is a form of intense, receptive, focused concentration. For example, none of the electroencephalogram (brave wave) findings of sleep are present in hypnosis. Instead, those tracings typical of alert concentration are found during the hypnotic state. Hypnosis is not like general anesthesia. People are aware of and remember most of what occurs is a hypnotic trance.

(2) MYTH: Hypnosis is projected onto the patient.

FACT: The hypnotist projects nothing whatever. Instead he taps into the natural capacity to experience trance, which is inherent in many people. This trance capacity is a relatively fixed ability in each adult. Some people have a very high trance capacity; others are not able to be hypnotized. Most people have a capacity to experience trance which is somewhere between these two extremes and which does not change much throughout adult life. Most older children, on the other hand, have a high trance capacity. When a doctor uses hypnosis with a patient, he simply activates this capacity which the patient uses spontaneously at other times during intense concentration.

(3) MYTH: Only mentally "weak" or "sick" people are hypnotizable.

FACT: Wrong. In fact, the opposite is true. It is the mentally healthy person who is more likely to be hypnotizable. While some normal people cannot be hypnotized, in general those who suffer from serious mental or neurological problems are more likely to be unable to concentrate well enough to be hypnotized. The capacity to be hypnotized is a statement of relative mental health. In general highly intelligent and educated people are more hypnotizable.

(4) MYTH: Hypnosis occurs only when a doctor decides to use it.

FACT: It can occur when the doctor decides to use it if the patient co-operates, but hypnosis often occurs spontaneously, especially when a hypnotizable person is under duress or is concentrating very hard. It is not uncommon, for example, for a highly hypnotizable patient to report that he often gets so absorbed in watching a movie or reading a good book that he has to take a moment to reorient himself to the world around him when he is finished. This is a kind of spontaneous trance state.

(5) MYTH: Symptom removal means a new symptom.

FACT: Not necessary. Hypnosis can be used to help in the treatment of a variety of disturbing symptoms and in most cases, if it is done in a noncoercive manner, the patient will feel better and no new symptom will occur. However, if the patient directly or indirectly learns that this is expected, a new symptom may occur as a fulfillment of that prophecy. In most cases, patients who overcome problems such as anxiety or insomnia feel better and often learn to make improvements in other areas of their life as well.

(6) MYTH: Hypnosis is dangerous.

FACT: Hypnosis itself is not dangerous, but the trance state can be used mischievously. The hypnotic state is a neutral state of attentive concentration. If a therapist introduces a therapeutically wrong proposal or unethically exploits the patient, then, of course, harm may result. A scalpel in the hands of an expert surgeon can be a powerful tool for eradicating disease. In the hands of an unprincipled practitioner, it can do serious harm. Likewise, it is the use to which hypnosis is put that counts, not the state itself.

People often fear that they can be made to do something against their will in the trance state. It is true that a hypnotized person is less likely to employ his usual critical judgment in deciding whether or not to comply with an instruction. But such a person is always capable of bringing himself out of the trance, and is likely to do so if given an instruction which runs counter to his usual moral and ethical standards. However, learning that one has a tendency to automatically accept direction from others can become an important defense against making mistakes in the future. It is essential that one choose an ethical and well-trained therapist if hypnosis is involved.

People also fear that they will become "stuck" in a trance. The entrance and exit from the trance state occur in a matter of seconds, and no one has ever been "lost" in a trance.

(7) MYTH: Hypnosis is therapy.

FACT: Not at all. At most, the use of hypnosis creates a receptive atmosphere in which treatment strategy can be used with enhanced effectiveness. Being in a state of hypnosis by itself, without an appropriate therapeutic strategy, offers no particular therapeutic effect unless the patient uses this as an occasion to bring about a spontaneous change in his life. It is especially important to note that a person who calls himself a "hypnotist" is making a statement about how limited his abilities are. One can learn to produce a hypnotic trance in a matter of minutes. What counts in choosing someone who uses hypnosis is his or her training and ability as a therapist. This could be a physician, a psychiatrist, a psychologist, a dentist or other trained and responsible clinicians. Determining therapeutic goals and strategies is what counts. The competent clinician who employs hypnosis to this end has one additional tool at his command. A person who is nothing more than a hypnotist is like a person who has access to an operating room but no knowledge of what to do with it.

(8) MYTH: The hypnotist must be a charismatic, unique or weird.

FACT: Not so. Of course if the patient senses that the doctor is charismatic or unusual in some way, he may be inclined to trust him or initially attempt hypnosis. But any sound, sober clinician can learn the techniques of induction into the hypnotic state. His manner should be natural and appropriate to the treatment setting. Trance induction is teachable and learnable. In many instances recent learners are as fully effective as experienced practitioners in utilizing hypnosis as long as they are, in other respects, sound clinicians.

(9) MYTH: Women are more hypnotizable than men.

FACT: This is also untrue. All objective studies indicate that about 70 percent of both men and women are hypnotizable to one degree or another, and the ability to experience hypnosis is an example of real equality of opportunity for men and women.

(10) MYTH: Hypnosis is only a psychological phenomenon.

FACT: There is evidence that hypnotic capacity can be inherited and that it is associated with certain patterns of brain functioning such as alpha waves on the electroencephalogram.

The ability to concentrate intently which we call hypnosis has been used in the clinical setting for many purposes, for example in helping an individual cope with pain immediately after an injury, or chronic pain associated with such diseases as arthritis and cancer. Many such patients find that by practicing self-hypnosis they can learn to pay less attention to the pain even though it may still be there.

Hypnosis should not be used to alter the perception of pain until a patient and his doctor are satisfied that they understand the reasons for the pain and have instituted the proper medical treatment. Once this has been done, however, self-hypnosis (the patient practicing his own hypnotic exercise to alter the perception of the pain) can be effective and far safer than the use of various pain medications if the individual has the necessary hypnotic capacity.

Hypnosis has also been used effectively in helping people overcome such problems as smoking and overeating. Many people find that they can learn to use the hypnotic state to reorient themselves in the direction of enhancing their sense of respect for their body and thereby learn to avoid the trap of fighting the urge to eat or smoke. Learning to use self-hypnosis can help individuals troubled with anxiety as well, although it must be noted that anxiety is a signal that something may be wrong in one's emotional and personal life, just as pain is a sign that something may be wrong in one's body. Practicing a self-hypnosis exercise can give an anxious person something to resort to when anxiety builds.

Anxiety-related problems like phobias and medical problems which may have psychological aspects such as asthma, ulcers, headaches have been successfully treated with hypnosis. When patients are taught self-hypnosis, they learn to conduct their own therapy and often one session is sufficient to teach the necessary skills to overcome such problems as smoking and pain.

Hypnosis has stirred interest in other areas as well. There has been growing use of the intensity of concentration in hypnosis to enhance the memory recall of witnesses and victims of crimes. On the other hand, it should be clear that hypnosis is not a cure-all. It is rather one means for making better use of an individual's psychological resources. Nothing can be done in therapy with hypnosis that could not be done without it, but the intense concentration of the hypnotic state can help a person with the necessary capacity achieve his goals more quickly.

CREDIT: *Herbert Spiegel, M.D., Clinical Professor of Psychiatry, Columbia University College of Physicians and Surgeons, New York, New York; David Spiegel, M.D., Assistant Professor of Psychiatry and Behavioral Sciences, Stanford University School of Medicine, Stanford, California; authors of* Trance and Treatment: Clinical Uses of Hypnosis, *New York: Basic Books.*

Hypoglycemia

Much publicity has been given to the subject of hypoglycemia in the mass media recently. It has been blamed for all sorts of difficulties such as inability to concentrate, chronic lack of energy, dizziness and uncontrollable weight problems. Although some people with these complaints do indeed have hypoglycemia, it is more likely that these symptoms are due to other causes such as depression, anxiety, poor eating habits, as well as other medical conditions. Hypoglycemia has become a catchall diagnosis. Therefore, it is important to clarify what hypoglycemia actually is.

Hypoglycemia literally means "low blood sugar" and refers to a condition in which a person experiences a certain set of symptoms because of an inadequate supply of sugar (glucose, to be exact). The body, especially the brain, gets much of its energy from sugar. It is therefore important to try to maintain a good blood sugar level at all times. Two hormones, insulin and glucagon, produced by the pancreas are primarily responsible for this important task.

When the blood sugar rises following a meal, insulin shuttles the extra sugar into various organs of the body (particularly the liver), where it is stored for future use. When there is a shortage and the blood sugar level is low, glucagon breaks down the stored sugar. The sugar released flows into the bloodstream and restores the blood sugar. Glucagon can also stimulate the liver to make sugar anew. The interplay of these two hormones keeps the blood sugar at the right level whether we eat a large meal or skip a meal.

The failure of the body to maintain the blood sugar at an adequate level results in hypoglycemia. In such a situation, a person may suffer many symptoms. A sharp drop in the blood sugar will bring forth a surge of the emergency hormone adrenaline. This surge of adrenaline in turn will precipitate many familiar symptoms such as palpitation (pounding of the heart), lightheadedness and sweating. Because of the inadequate supply of sugar to the brain, one may also have mental lapses, blank spells, and may even pass out. Some people become highly emotional and irritable and go into crying spells during hypoglycemic attacks. Severe hypoglycemia, if uncorrected, could precipitate convulsions, coma and permanent brain damage.

Two characteristic features help to distingish hypoglycemia from other conditions which cause similar symptoms. The first of these is that people who have hypoglycemia are usually free of symptoms between attacks. The second feature is that the symptoms of hypoglycemia usually disappear promptly, say within five or ten minutes, if one eats some carbohydrate such as orange juice or a candy bar.

A thorough evaluation by a physician with the use of a full glucose tolerance test will be necessary to diagnose hypoglycemia and exclude other conditions. The glucose tolerance test will help determine not only whether one has hypoglycemia, but also what kind.

There are two types of hypoglycemia, broadly speaking. The first is the so-called "fasting hypoglycemia" in which the attacks tend to occur when a person has not eaten for a while (for example, before breakfast or after skipping a meal). The second is called "reactive hypoglycemia" because in this type attacks tend to occur in reaction to a meal. A typical attack usually comes a few hours after eating a meal with a high carbohydrate content.

Most people with hypoglycemia have the reactive type. Those who have had a stomach operation for peptic ulcer disease are prone to this type of hypoglycemia. Many obese people with early, mild diabetes also suffer from this type of hypoglycemia, but do not have these underlying conditions. In such people, the cause of hypoglycemia is unknown.

Fasting hypoglycemia also occurs under many different conditions. If the liver is not working well, it can neither store nor make sugar, and hypoglycemia results. People who abuse alcohol often suffer from hypoglycemia because they don't have good sugar stores and because alcohol interferes with the liver's production of sugar. One of the most important causes of fasting hypoglycemia is a special type of pancreas tumor called insulinoma. Such a tumor produces hypoglycemia by making too much insulin.

Diabetic patients who take insulin are the single largest group of people who are subject to hypoglycemia. Severe diabetics in whom the blood sugar level swings widely during the course of a day are particularly vulnerable. Fortunately, most diabetics have warning symptoms of hypoglycemia so that he or she may be able to prevent a severe attack by eating something sweet. With a few diabetics, however, these warning symptoms do not occur, and they can get into serious trouble. This is why a diabetic should always carry sweets and also wear an identifying tag.

The treatment of hypoglycemia depends on the type and the cause. In the case of reactive hypoglycemia, avoidance of sweets is essential except during the actual attack. Food high in carbohydrates stimulates too much insulin, thereby precipitating hypoglycemia in a susceptible person. For patients with mild diabetes and hypoglycemia, a weight reduction and diabetic diet are the mainstay of therapy since many of them are overweight. Those who abuse alcohol should stop drinking and eat properly. Hypoglycemia in patients with an insulin-producing tumor can be cured by removal of the tumor. The frequency and severity of hypoglycemic attacks in diabetic patients taking insulin can be lessened by the addition of snacks between meals and by changing the dosage and type of insulin given. This maneuver can eliminate hypoglycemic attacks associated with exercise, and can be particularly important for the young diabetic who is physically active.

Self-diagnosis and self-treatment of hypoglycemia is unwise and can be dangerous. When the presence of hypoglycemia is suspected, the exact cause and type should be determined. Since insulinoma can produce severe hypoglycemia without causing any outward physical or other chemical abnormalities, its presence should be ruled out vigorously in patients with fasting hypoglycemia. Specialists in the field can make the diagnosis with new, sophisticated tests. Proper treatment of hypoglycemia can be started only after a full evaluation of its cause and the type has been made.

CREDITS:　*Dr. Benjamin Park is an attending endocrinologist at the New York Hospital-Cornell Medical Center and an assistant clinical professor of medicine at Cornell Medical School, New York. Dr. Park practices medicine in Manhattan.*

Hysterectomy

Hysterectomy is the surgical operation of removing the uterus, either through the abdominal wall or through the vagina. It is the most often performed major operation in the United States. Frequency of hysterectomy is increasing because a great many women choose to seek relief from menopausal problems, contraception worries and the fear of uterine cancer.

Hysterectomy is the procedure of choice for many benign and malignant diseases of the uterus (1) if there are definite indications that call for its removal, (2) if the woman is not bothered by the fact that she will no longer be able to produce a child, (3) if there are no medical reasons the operation should not be performed. When done under these circumstance it rids the patient permanently of her disease; it eliminates the necessity of surgical procedures in the future; it relieves the symptoms of which the patient was complaining and gets rid of the dangers of the gynecologic diseases. It also removes the principal cancer-bearing tissue of the pelvis although the procedure is not carried out for this reason. If surgery is indicated, it permits correction of other difficulties. Many times the surgeon performs several different procedures coincidentally with the hysterectomy, such as plastic repair of the vagina.

Emotional stresses which might arise in some women who are advised to have (or have had) a hysterectomy can usually be counteracted by free discussion of the function and purpose of the uterus and the role played by menstruation. All this does not mean that hysterectomy is performed without carefully considering the alternatives. It is performed if conservative management of the gynecologic disease proves inadequate. If the symptom is one of bleeding, it is performed if curettage (scraping of the uterus) or hormonal therapy fails to correct the bleeding; if due to myomas (benign fibromuscular tumors of the uterus; fibroids) if myomectomy is not suitable. Age and desire for pregnancy will certainly affect the choice of the surgical procedure. No treatment is preferable to a hysterectomy in some instances even though it is acknowledged that the latter might eventually be necessary.

The ovaries should not be removed in pre-menopausal women unless definite ovarian disease exists. Ovaries continue to function after hysterectomy. They seldom create problems if left intact.

Opinion regarding the need for hysterectomy has certainly come a long way since the mid-1800s when the *London Medical-Chirurgical Review* stated, "Extirpation of the uterus, not previously protruded or inverted, is one of the most cruel and unfeasible operations ever projected or executed by the head or hand of man." The other extreme is shown in a statement in a medical textbook published in 1969: "the uterus has but one function, reproduction, and after the last planned pregnancy, the uterus becomes a useless, bleeding, symptom-producing, potentially cancer-bearing organ and therefore should be removed." Both statements, of course, are nonsense.

The view of the situation regarding hysterectomy that best puts it into focus is by Dr. Joseph Pratt of the Mayo Clinic. He said, "Hysterectomy, removal of the uterus, is usually performed to relieve symptoms and to improve the quality of life. It does not necessarily have to be life-saving."

In spite of adverse publicity regarding hysterectomy that one reads in the media today, most women are quite receptive to the benefits of hysterectomy. The main emphasis seems to be elimination of the possibility of cervical and endometrial cancer, relief of pelvic pain, incapacitating menstrual cramps and sterilization.

Total abdominal hysterectomy, removing both the body and the cervix of the uterus, is the operation of choice for patients with benign uterine disease who have completed their childbearing and for patients with benign uterine disease that may be potentially dangerous. Examples of these diseases are abnormal uterine bleeding (which has failed to respond to simpler means of treatment either curettage or hormonal), uterine fibromyomata (fibroids), endometriosis and chronic pelvic infection. In addition, the uterus is frequently removed when the patient is being operated on for coincidental disease, particularly tumors of the ovary and lesions of the vagina. If the patient is being treated for malignant disease, particularly endometrial (lining of the uterus), then total hysterectomy and bilateral salpingo-oophorectomy (removal of both tubes and ovaries) is the recommended treatment.

Total hysterectomy is also used for treatment of pre-invasive cancer of the cervix and an extensive or radical hysterectomy with lymph node dissection may be the treatment for invasive cancer of the cervix, although radiation might be the treatment of choice.

One of the confusing terms for the non-medical person is total or complete hysterectomy. By this we mean removal of the entire uterus: neck and body. If the ovaries and tubes are also removed we call this a total hysterectomy and bilateral salpingo-oophorectomy. However, for years a complete hysterectomy to the lay public meant removal of the ovaries. It should be made clear that the ovaries are removed only if they are diseased. When they appear normal they are left alone unless the patient is postmenopausal.

Vaginal hysterectomy may be performed in preference to the abdominal operation when it is being performed in conjunction with a repair or plastic operation for the cure of prolapse (falling) of the uterus, repair of relaxation lesions of the vagina, particularly cystocele (hernia of the bladder into the vagina) and rectocele (hernia of the rectum into the vagina), or if one is simply removing a malfunctioning uterus that is not too large to be removed vaginally. The postoperative course of a vaginal hysterectomy alone without repair is more comfortable than an abdominal procedure, which necessitates an abdominal incision.

The vaginal approach is not desirable if one is operating primarily for ovarian disease, or if there are large uterine tumors which are best removed via the abdominal route and there has been extensive previous pelvic surgery or infections.

The question of hysterectomy as a form of sterilization is being asked many times today and it is our feeling that the operation is far too drastic as a routine means of sterilization. As Ralph Reis once said, "One does not crack chestnuts with sledgehammers." With tubal ligation being so readily available today—a quick, simple and easy operation, done abdominally through either the laparoscope, or a mini-laparotomy incision, or vaginally— ligation is much more sensible than the major procedure of a hysterectomy with all its inherent potential complications. However, if the patient is one who will eventually need further gynecologic surgery such as a patient with small fibroids, a moderate degree of prolapse or abnormal bleeding, it would be better to do a hysterectomy right away rather than to subject this patient to a second hospitalization, anesthetic and operation in the future.

To answer charges that too many hysterectomies are being performed, it has been shown that many of these charges are based on the lack of pathologic findings in the excised tissue. These are simply not relevant. A dysfunctional uterus, one that is either badly prolapsed and is hanging out of the vagina along the patient's thigh, or one that is bleeding profusely, would probably be considered "normal" by certain tests, but the woman who undergoes hysterectomy in such a case is *not* healthy and would have needed the operation. In addition to prolapse, other indications would of course include extremely heavy menstruation; not life-threatening, but still dangerous or partly disabling.

Hysterectomy can be a matter of great psychological consequence in the life of a woman. It is understandable that the uniquely female organ is often greatly valued. The psychologic effect of the uterus was first recognized in ancient times with the origin of the words "hysterectomy" and "hysteria" being exactly the same in the Greek, meaning "womb." In order to understand the reaction of a patient to hysterectomy, it is necessary for the patient to know the realistic anatomical and physiologic changes dependent upon a particular operation: the patient's own private physiologic and anatomic beliefs about the function, value and importance of the organ, and the patient's major patterns of adaptation that may be disrupted by both realistic and irrational effects of hysterectomy.

Delay in seeking medical care is due to a wide range of conscious and unconscious psychological factors. The loss of any organ is cause for fear. And this organ particularly (the uterus) is believed by some women to be vitally necessary to achieve complete sexual gratification. The amount of bleeding, pain and weakness that a woman ignores or tolerates before seeking medical care tells us something about her fears. Other fears which are not specifically related to the loss of the uterus are fear of surgery itself and fear of anesthesia. (Anesthesia and complications from anesthesia are now considered some of the most dangerous aspects of any operation.) Then there is the fear of cancer—some women would rather not know if they have it so they stay away from doctors.

An obvious concern about removing the uterus is the loss of childbearing ability. While many women feel it makes them less "womanly" others welcome freedom from unwanted pregnancy and the burdens of contraception. The expected termination of menstrual periods brings varying responses. Many women regard the loss of menstruation as relief. Others consider menstruation good for the body, because it's a cleansing procedure. The majority of women in one study expressed genuine regret that menstruation would cease, yet many of my patients say, "I'm glad to be through with it."

Anxiety concerning the effect of hysterectomy on sexual activity is expressed by many patients. Some fear they will lose sexual desire. Others fear they will be unable to respond to their husbands. Still others worry about the loss of sexual attractiveness. The opposite is usually true. Many women will be more interesting to their husbands because they will be able to have sexual intercourse without contraception. Moreover, the problem of bleeding will no longer be present. Nor will the pain and anxiety make for a depressing bed partner.

There are many misconceptions regarding the anatomy, physiology and function of the uterus and these must be counteracted. It should be emphasized that the uterus has essentially no hormonal function and removing the uterus will not bring on "change of life." The hormonal function is in the ovaries. If these are left in, the patient should not need sex steroid hormones. If, on the other hand, the ovaries must be removed, the hormones can be replaced by medication and the woman will still maintain her femininity. Many women have fears from talking to members of their family and friends that after a hysterectomy, they will become fat, their skin will become dry and they will look much older. They have heard that the pain of surgery is terrible and that they might go insane after the operation. All of these misconceptions are just that—misconceptions. The uterus is an organ of reproduction in which the baby is incubated and has no other function. Following a hysterectomy, the patients usually feel remarkably better mainly because they no longer have the symptoms for which they were being operated on— bleeding, pain, pressure and the dropping out of the womb.

Hysterectomies are performed in a hospital and require a stay of at least five days—perhaps six or seven, barring complications and depending on the recuperative powers of the patient. Another ten days of partial bed rest is advised, if the patient feels like it. Some patients leave the hospital after five days and within a week are back to their normal patterns of living—healthier and happier.

CREDIT: *Albert B. Gerbie, M.D., Professor of Obstetrics and Gynecology, Northwestern Medical School, and Attending Obstetrician-Gynecologist, Prentice Women's Hospital, Chicago; Chief, Division of Obstetrics and Gynecology, Children's Memorial Hospital, Chicago.*

HYSTERECTOMY IS HISTORY, BUT MATE REMEMBERS

DEAR ANN LANDERS: For several years I postponed a hysterectomy (which I needed badly) hoping the "problem" would disappear. When the situation became critical my doctor insisted I have it done. I looked forward to a better sex life with my husband after the surgery but it hasn't worked out that way.

Last night, after another failure, my husband tried again to analyze his inability to perform. I reassured him of my love and said, "It doesn't matter."

Then I asked if perhaps he felt that my surgery had made me less of a woman. He replied, "I HOPE that isn't the problem." Needless to say, I was crushed.

One thing is certain, there's no way I can put back the missing organs. Can you advise me on how to think about this shattering putdown? My husband has asked me not to mention my hysterectomy to him again. I'm afraid he thinks of me as AN EMPTY SHELL

DEAR FRIEND: A woman doesn't need a uterus or ovaries to have a completely satisfactory sex life. From the sound of your letter I suspect you've verbalized your fears repeatedly and transferred your apprehension and anxieties to your husband.

Take his advice and stop talking about your operation. Take MY advice and have a long talk with your gynecologist. You need some reassurance and emotional support and he is the one who can and should provide it.

Impotence

Sexual impotence is the term used for the condition when a man is unable to obtain a penile erection satisfactory for him to have successful sexual intercourse.

There are a multitude of possible causes of impotence, both psychological and physical. Most authorities believe the vast majority of men who suffer from the inability to perform sexually have no physical basis for it, but rather that the problem is rooted in some psychological problem.

There are various physical diseases as well as neurological diseases that could cause organic impotence. Various drugs (alcohol, antidepressants, barbiturates and others) may also cause temporary impotence.

From the psychological point of view, impotence is often very selective in nature. For instance, a man may be impotent with his wife, but with no one else. He may be impotent with women of a particular social standing, but not with prostitutes. Or he may be impotent with females, but not with males. Or he may be impotent with women, but able to obtain an erection through masturbation.

Many men may experience occasional impotence, and the full extent of its frequency is not known. Most men are too embarrassed to consult a physician about the problem, and many others simply accept an occasional incident of impotence and do not seek treatment. Actually, it is relatively common for men to have sexual failure when they are tired or upset. If he overreacts to this minor dysfunction, the symptom could become persistent, based on his fear of failure. Since the partner's understanding and support play an important part in the man's ability to perform successfully, her use of negative or belittling comments should be avoided.

Psychological impotence when persistent is usually not an isolated problem. Impotent males often have a more general problem with intimacy and closeness. The symptom may well symbolize their rage and anger at the world in general, and at women in particular. The failure in the sexual act may intensify the rage of this type of person, and perpetuate the impotence.

Many other psychological factors may contribute to impotence, including very early relationships with women, intense religious beliefs about sex, and the effects of a failure in one's first sexual experience, particularly in an insecure person.

The Women's Lib movement, with its resulting shift in the societal roles of most women, may cause an increase in the frequency of male impotence in those men already threatened by women. On the other hand, many men seem to become more virile in response to the more open sexual response of the modern woman.

Any male who is impotent should first have a thorough examination by a competent physician to rule out a physical basis. The best treatment for impotence of a psychological origin is counseling by a qualified professional. Beware of quacks. Sources of referral may include most medical societies, many medical schools (with programs in human sexuality), the American Psychiatric Association, the American Psychological Association, your local physician and your pastor.

Exploring-feeling-touching techniques, taken step by step along with counselling, can be very effective. The type of therapy depends on the clinical impression of the physician after he has done a complete examination, and the skills of the counselor to whom you may be referred.

Organic impotence can sometimes be remedied by a surgical implant of a penile prosthesis. This procedure has proven reasonably successful but it is not without problems.

CREDIT: *Dr. Robert Menninger, Psychiatrist and Psychoanalyst, the Menninger Foundation, Topeka, Kansas.*

OVER THE HILL AT 61

DEAR ANN LANDERS: I have been a steady reader for many years. Now I need your help. I am a man, 61, who does not agree with all your answers, but I respect you.

I am divorced, comfortable financially, and I enjoy the company of the opposite sex. The problem is I am over the hill sex-wise and am wondering if it would be fair to marry a woman under these circumstances.

Is it possible to have a good marriage without sex? My first wife and I were married 22 years. We had a very satisfactory sex life but little else. Now I've met a woman who has added a great deal of joy to my previously dreary existence. We get along beautifully but I don't want to be unfair to her. Is companionship enough? UNSURE

DEAR UN: I suggest that you level with your lady friend. It's the best way to find out how she feels. But don't be surprised if there are some changes in your life. The problem of impotency in the vast majority of cases is psychological and not physical. A new relationship might produce some high-octane fuel that will make you wonder what happened to those hills.

DEAR ANN LANDERS: My husband has been impotent for the past five years—which means no sex whatever. Being a loyal and highly principled woman, I could not bring myself to cheat on him. So I haven't had any sex either. Will you please educate your male readers who are in the same boat as my husband?

A wife can live without sex, if her man can't perform, but she cannot live without affection. The very least a husband can do is hold his wife in his arms and tell her he loves her.

I have never made one unkind remark to him about his inability to perform. I know it must bother him terribly and I don't want to add to his unhappiness. But don't you think I am entitled to some consideration? It would take so little for him to make me feel wanted and loved.

I have asked my husband to go to a doctor, but he refuses. He comes home from work, eats dinner (reading a newspaper at the table) and proceeds to get drunk. This goes on seven nights a week. I need some help. WITHERING ON THE VINE

DEAR W.: You sure do, honey. Why did it take you five years to write?

My advice is talk to a counselor and learn the relationship between male impotence and alcoholism. There's a definite link. Next join Al-Anon and get a new outlook on YOUR life. Al-Anon is as near as your phone book.

Many impotent husbands make their wives feel wanted and loved. Yours could, too, if he didn't get bombed every night. That's the problem.

Surgical Treatment of Impotence

No one knows how many men are afflicted with the problem of impotence— the inability to have an erection and to complete the sex act. Estimates by health care experts run into the millions.

There are many causes for this problem, both physical and psychological, and there is no one treatment method appropriate for all cases.

A surgical procedure, however, offers new hope to many of these impotent patients—particularly those whose impotence is caused by a medical condition. The procedure calls for implanting a prosthesis, or artificial device, to produce an erection in the penis. The device is called the inflatable penile prosthesis. It operates like a miniature hydraulic system and is totally implanted within the body to remain there permanently. To date, more than one thousand impotent men have received the device. I implanted the first such device in Feburary 1973, in Houston, Texas.

The device had its beginnings several years ago, when a collaborative study was initiated by myself, a neurologist at the University of Minnesota and a bio-medical engineer affiliated with the American Medical Systems, Inc. This study concerned the development of an implantable artificial sphincter (ring of muscles) to help people who could not control urination.

From the beginning, our attempts were to simulate the natural process of erection. This process depends upon the expansion of two cylindrical bodies of spongy tissue in the penis, enclosed within a thin and strong elastic tissue. In the normal male, sexual excitement causes the spongy tissue to fill with blood until the surrounding elastic tissue becomes tense. The penis is then hard and erect. In the impotent male, the flow of blood to the erectile bodies within the penis is impaired.

The process of erection by the inflatable penile prosthesis also depends upon two cylindrical bodies, but constructed of elastic silicone rubber (a medical-grade silicone rubber similar to that used for breast augmentation, facial reconstruction, heart valve replacement, etc.). These silicone rubber cylindrical bodies are surgically implanted so they lie within the erectile bodies. Since these silicone cylinders lengthen as well as expand when filled with fluid, they fill the same space that would be occupied by blood in a natural erection.

Since inflation of the cylinders causes the elastic covering around the spongy tissue to become tense (as with a natural erection), the penis becomes hard and rigid. The size of the penis and the degree of hardness when erect is quite comparable to that of a natural erection.

The pump for a natural erection is, of course, the heart, which provides the force to pump blood into the penis. The pump for the prosthesis is constructed of silicone rubber and is implanted inside the scrotum (the sac containing the testicles). This small bulb-shaped pump is connected to the penile cylinders by silicone rubber tubing, and hangs loosely inside the scrotum in a manner similar to the testicles. It is invisible but can be felt with the hand. The act of squeezing the pump with the fingers through the skin of the scrotum forces fluid into the silicone rubber cylinders. Repeated squeezing makes the penis harder, until sufficient for natural sexual intercourse.

The reservoir for the blood of a natural erection is the body's circulatory system. The reservoir for the erectile prosthesis is constructed of silicone rubber and is filled with a fluid that is compatible with the body's tissue fluid. This fluid can be made radiopaque so it will show up on an X ray. This reservoir (also connected to the pump by silicone rubber tubing) is implanted underneath the muscles of the abdomen, where it is invisible, the patient is unaware of its presence and it lies in a protected position.

After intercourse, the fluid inside the penis is released, and moves from the penis back into the reservoir until the penis becomes soft or flaccid again. To release this fluid, a release valve located in the same pump inside the scrotum is opened by pressure over a button-like spot on the pump. Steady pressure in this area for a few seconds causes the penis to go limp.

The surgical procedure is a meticulous technique, but is well tolerated by the patient since there is little loss of blood, no incisions into major organs and minimal tissue disturbance. Usually through a single incision about one inch long, the cylinders are inserted into the penis, the pump is inserted into the scrotum and the reservoir is implanted beneath the abdominal muscles. These components are connected and put in place using special surgical instruments and techniques. The sizes of the components selected are determined at the time of the procedure and will differ according to the build of the patient. The duration of the operation will vary, ranging from less than one hour to as many as three. Since the operation does not require dangerous deep stages of anesthesia, the surgeon need not feel rushed.

Implantation of the device allows the patient to achieve an erection; it does not produce orgasm or climax. If the patient could have a climax even with a soft penis before, then he can also expect this after surgery. Some patients who were unable to reach a climax can do so after surgery, because they can now have natural sexual intercourse.

In evaluating patients for this procedure, the physician must first determine whether or not the patient is indeed impotent, and if so, what is the reason. Usually a team of physicians works together to evaluate each patient. Some patients require more extensive evaluation than others. The patient must be able to withstand the stress of surgery and anesthesia. He must be emotionally stable, and he must have realistic expectations as to the purpose of the surgery. (For example, the prosthesis is not implanted unless the patient has, or expects to have, a sexual partner.) Goals are to help the patient lead a normal sex life, which may or may not require this surgical treatment.

The cause of impotency varies and is determined whenever possible so that the treatment is appropriate. The majority of patients do *not* require surgical testing and laboratory studies.

Normal diagnostic evaluation of the patient includes a routine medical and sexual history, a physical examination, psychiatric interviewing, psychological testing and laboratory studies.

To properly determine treatment, the physician needs to know whether the impotence is physical or psychological. In a case of severe psychogenic impotence, the patient would be referred for therapy before the implant would be considered. The monitoring of nighttime erections—called "nocturnal penile tumescence"—has contributed significantly to making a valid diagnosis. This diagnostic technique involves the use of a special machine that records erectile activity while the patient is sleeping, on a recording similar to an electrocardiogram tracing. Patients selected for the procedure at our medical center have included those whose impotence is related to diabetes, trauma (such as pelvic fracture), cancer surgery, neurological disease, arteriosclerosis, Peyronie's disease and psychological factors.

More than 250 patients have received the device at our medical center. Of these, over 230 or over 90 percent are now functioning successfully. The remainder have had the device removed for various reasons, some unrelated to the device. A decreasingly small percentage of patients require minor revision surgery following the original implant.

Time required for the procedure is usually seven to ten days in the hospital for work-up, surgery and recovery. Sexual intercourse is not advised until at least three weeks after surgery.

It should be noted that temporary failures are possible; however, they can be corrected. (1) Sometimes the prosthesis is rejected if the man has an infection at the time of the surgery. However, when the infection clears, the device can be reimplanted. (2) Sometimes an occasional leak is discovered. Minor surgery can replace the part that is malfunctioning, or the entire prosthesis can be replaced if necessary.

Some cases of "failure" are due to poor candidate selection (1) when the husband or wife cannot get used to the device for some psychological reason and therefore it isn't used, or (2) in a case where a man has psychogenic impotence to begin with, the device will not necessarily help the psychological problem. In these cases, the men are referred for therapy and are not good candidates for the surgery. (They should not have been selected in the first place.)

Also, if a man has a severe congenital malformation or has had previous penile operations, he may not be a good candidate for the surgery since the device may not be insertable. However, in most cases this can be rectified. The only cases where the device cannot be implanted would be where there is gangrene of the penis, or an extremely severe deformity.

In summary, the device can malfunction temporarily as with a leak, or it can be rejected in case of an infection, but these problems can be corrected. If there is a psychological problem, the device should not be implanted and the patient should be referred for therapy.

If the man discovers that he is able to have a normal erection following surgery, the device *can* be removed if the man so wishes, but there is no reason for this. In a few rare instances the device may interfere with a normal erection. In a small percentage of cases, the device would make no difference whatsoever in the man's normal erection. (It could be in a case of psychogenic impotence, the man discovers that actually having an erection [even mechanically] helps solve his original impotence, in which case the device may be removed. This has never happened so far, however.)

Since this procedure is relatively new, not all physicians are aware of it. However, information is readily available to a physician who is interested in learning about it. He should contact a urologist in his area or write to the author of this article, who will put the inquirer in touch with implanting physicians at any of the more than one hundred medical centers throughout the country where the implants have been performed.

Although the prosthesis implant operation is being done at over one hundred medical centers, I am listing twenty of the best-known. If you are interested and do not live in the vicinity of any of these hospitals, you may write to American Medical Systems, Inc., attention: Graeme Thickens, 3312 Gorham Avenue, Minneapolis, Minnesota 55426, and he will inform you of the hospital nearest you.

(1) St. Luke's Episcopal Hospital (Texas Medical Center)
   Houston, Texas 77030
(2) Mayo Clinic, St. Mary's Hospital
   Rochester, Minnesota 55901
(3) Pennsylvania Hospital
   Philadelphia, Pennsylvania 19107
(4) Stanford University Hospital
   Palo Alto, California 94304
(5) St. Louis University Hospital
   St. Louis, Missouri 63104
(6) Loyola University Medical Center
   Chicago, Illinois 60153
(7) Walter Reed Army Medical Center
   Washington, D.C. 20012
(8) Lackland Air Force Base, San Antonio, Texas 78236
(9) University of Colorado Medical Center
   Denver, Colorado 80262
(10) Latter Day Saints' Hospital
   Salt Lake City, Utah 84102
(11) Cleveland Clinic
   Cleveland, Ohio 44106
(12) Boston University Medical Center
   Boston, Massachusetts 02118
(13) White Memorial Medical Center •
   Los Angeles, California 90033
(14) University of Iowa Hospital
   Iowa City, Iowa 52242

(15) Northwestern Memorial Hospital
      Chicago, Illinois 60611
(16) Morristown Memorial Hospital
      Morristown, New Jersey 07960
(17) Lucerne General Hospital
      Orlando, Florida 32801
(18) Baylor University Medical Center
      Dallas, Texas 75246
(19) New York University Medical Center
      New York, New York 10016
(20) El Cajon Valley Hospital
      El Cajon, California 92021

Address inquiries to the Urology Department in each of the above hospitals.

ANN LANDERS' APPRAISAL

I have checked out this device with several leading urologists in addition to the authorities at Loyola University Medical Center and Northwestern Memorial Hospital in Chicago and their consensus is: This prosthesis works but it may be too expensive for the average person. It also requires a training period that many doctors find too time-consuming. Other devices less complicated and less costly are now being developed. Interested parties should check with their own urologists for further investigation and write to Dr. F. Brantley Scott.

CREDIT: *F. Brantley Scott, M.D., Professor of Urology, Baylor College of Medicine, Houston, Texas.*

Incest

Illicit Sex in the Immediate Family

Incest is defined as sexual intercourse between people related so closely that they may not legally marry. This definition, simple as it seems, is so loaded with loopholes that anthropologists and sociologists, lawyers, theologians and philosophers have puzzled over the issue for thousands of years.

To begin with, close kinship is defined differently by various societies, so that people who might legally marry in one culture may not do so in another. Sexual intercourse, too, is defined differently by different cultures; simple vaginal penetration is only one of a vast variety of sexual activities that might be considered incestuous if done with the wrong relative.

Even in our modern United States, where the legal structure is fairly consistent concerning most matters, the laws defining and punishing incest vary from state to state. Some states, for example, permit first cousins to marry; others do not. The penalties for incest range from a $500 fine and/or twelve months in prison in Virginia to a prison term of one to fifty years in California. In general, modern societies prohibit sex between blood-related people: between a person and his/her brothers, sisters, parents, grandparents, uncles, aunts and cousins.

THE INCEST TABOO

The mere mention of sexual feelings within the family or any hint of sexual activity between close blood relatives is sure to bring out feelings of fascination, anxiety, fear, anger or avoidance. This is particularly true when the sexual partners are parent and child.

Throughout the centuries, incest has served as a major theme for mythology, religion, law, literature and psychology. Its prohibition has been called "the universal taboo," and for good reason: with very few exceptions, every human society, past and present, primitive and modern, has banned incest in one form or another. Among those few societies that have permitted incest, most have permitted it only in special rituals or between certain privileged or holy members of the society. Generally speaking, incest has never been socially acceptable.

How and why did this powerful taboo originate? This question has been debated for many years by biological and social scientists, and still no one has come up with an answer that will satisfy everyone. One theory is that successive inbreeding leads to genetic weakness, so incest must be forbidden for the health of the species. Another theory is that exogamy (marriage outside the kinship group) is beneficial to the nuclear family, the extended clan and society in general.

The first theory doesn't hold together, because we know that primitive people were ignorant of biogenetics and in fact weren't even aware of the connection between intercourse and pregnancy. The second theory makes more sense, since it is reasonable to assume primordial human families were sure to learn that extended sexual relations within the family—except between husband and wife, and especially between parent and child—blurred the familial roles and led to jealousy and family disintegration. Primitive families were also bound to discover that marital contracts between families helped replace rivalry with co-operation and enhanced the ability of kinship groups to survive. For example, when Margaret Mead asked men of the Arapesh, a New Guinea tribe, why they didn't marry their sisters, they responded, "What is the matter with you anyway? Don't you want a brother-in-law? Don't you realize that if you marry another man's sister and another man marries your sister, you will have at least two brothers-in-law, while if you marry your own sister you will have none? With whom will you hunt? With whom will you garden? Whom will you go to visit?" Thus many social scientists have concluded that human society began and flourished as a result of the incest taboo.

One other thing we can say about the incest taboo is that it has never completely prevented incest from happening. If the incest taboo is "the universal taboo," then incest itself is "the universal crime." Incestuous behavior has cropped up in virtually every society ever studied. Nor is it the rare phenomenon it was once believed to be. Until recently, the incidence of reported incest in the United States and other modern nations was believed to be one or two in a million inhabitants. In Santa Clara County, California, in 1971 about thirty cases of incest were referred to the Child Sexual Abuse Treatment Program, which serves a population of just over a million. This year we have been contacted by more than five hundred families troubled by incest. Even this figure is but the tip of the iceberg. Sexual tension in various degrees exists in all families. This tension is of course more serious when it is acted out, but many children develop sexual problems from seductive parents who send subtle sexual messages and even from parents who deny them affection because they are afraid of arousing sexual feelings.

FATHER-DAUGHTER INCEST IN AMERICA

Perhaps the most common form of incest is sexual experimentation between young members of a family. But the most damaging and certainly the most frequently reported form of incest in America today is that between fathers and daughters. It is a myth that incest occurs only in lower-class families or that the daughter is a Lolita, the mother is a doormat and the father is a tyrant. The problem can and does exist at every social and economic level of society, among all races.

Many men who have incestuous relationships with their daughters do not drink, have never been in trouble with the law ("not even a parking ticket" as one father put it to me during a therapy session). He was in the $40,000-a-year income bracket.

The average child-victim of father-daughter incest is about ten years old when the affair begins, and the sexual activity involved can include anything from fondling and exposure to oral sex to full intercourse, usually at puberty.

Occurring, as this often does, just as the girl is beginning to develop sexually, it can be an intensely bewildering experience. She receives from her father attention that should suggest pleasure, closeness, approval, warmth and security but instead translates into guilt, anxiety and anger when she discovers that she is being used. At a time when she needs the warmth and guidance a father can give her, the father instead uses his position of authority to force her into sexual acts far too mature for her years or her understanding. The familial roles become terribly confused. Her father is both parent and lover. Her mother also becomes "the other woman."

What leads to this tragic breakdown in the family structure? As Tolstoy said, "Every unhappy family is unhappy in its own way." But experience with hundreds of incestuous families leads me to believe there are few recurrent themes. Often the father is going through a period of intense boredom and low self-esteem. He is unhappy in his marriage, disappointed with his career and discouraged about his future. In the midst of all this despair, the one bright spot in his life is his daughter. Usually his first approaches to her are tender, but slowly they become sexual. His guilt is soon sensed by his daughter and she finds his attentions intolerable.

The effects of father-daughter incest are nearly catastrophic. If the situation is detected and reported and the case handled along traditional punitive lines by the criminal justice system, the whole family can expect to suffer even more. The girl is often removed from her home and placed in a juvenile shelter. The father is more often than not placed in jail to await trial. The mother is stuck with the problem of raising enough money to cover legal costs and maintain the family. The family often ends up separated, humiliated and bankrupt and the child is forced to endure the ordeal of the courts.

Even when the incestuous situation goes undetected and unreported the danger of harmful effects is high. Denied her right to a normal social and sexual development, the girl is in danger of psychological aftereffects. A number of studies have shown a high percentage of former incest victims among women and girls with such problems as truancy, promiscuity, prostitution, drug abuse, sexual dysfunction and poor marriages.

CHILD SEXUAL ABUSE TREATMENT PROGRAM

In midyear of 1971 I was invited by the Juvenile Probation Department to provide family counseling to the increasing number of families being referred to the department for father-daughter incest. There was grave concern regarding the inadequate treatment these cases were receiving. I felt strongly that family therapy was needed. At the time we had no idea full-fledged programs would develop, or that in the next six years the current referral rate of thirty cases per year would jump to over five hundred per year. I started with the idea that the principles and methods of humanistic psychology would be used in the treatment of these families, similar to the approach I had been using with other relatively "normal" families I had been treating.

What are the basic premises of this humanistic approach? First, we start with the simple assumption that a person's strongest drive is to feel good. To feel good our needs must be met. These needs include the biological needs of food, clothing and shelter; they also include a need to belong, to be respected, to connect, to care and be cared for by other people. If our needs are not met, we feel bad, and if we feel bad we must find a way of discharging that agony, through hostile acts toward ourselves or toward others. People with unmet needs become social problems, and a society that doesn't provide for the needs of all its people will in time be overwhelmed with casualties. Many have pointed with alarm at the high cost of violence in our country, but little has been said about the subtler products of alienation: suicide and alcoholism, ulcers and heart failure.

Another key premise of the humanistic viewpoint is that people are what they are. We persist in our ways until we are taught better ones. Insults do not motivate us to change for the better. The father-offender already knows he has betrayed his daughter, wife and family. One of our tasks is to teach him to develop self-worth and how to meet his needs in a productive rather than a damaging and self-destructive way.

It was with these lofty notions that I began the Child Sexual Abuse Treatment Program. My humanistic convictions were quickly put to the test by my first case. Before our first appointment I read the police report: fondling at age five, oral copulation and sodomy at eight, full vaginal penetration at thirteen. I was overwhelmed with a picture of pain on the young girl's face and my first feelings toward the father were violent outrage. I was surprised by this reaction and felt like dropping the whole thing. But it didn't take long to realize that there must be repressed incestuous feelings in myself that needed attending to.

I spent a week in deep self-exploration of sexual feelings I might have felt and repressed toward my mother, sisters and daughters. Although I knew I had just begun this investigation I was able to calm down enough so that I could face the offender. This turned out to be far less difficult than I had thought. For one thing, the man's raw feelings of despair, confusion and helplessness needed to be examined. What's more, my own hang-ups were temporarily set aside. My sessions with the girl and her mother were far easier because the mother's primary interest was for her daughter.

I'm convinced that to be an effective child advocate you must be a family advocate. If you are really concerned with the child's well-being, you will do your best to get the family together.

We begin by concentrating on the mother-daughter relationship. With few exceptions most child victims wish to return to their mothers, who in turn want them back. This may not be apparent at first because the child often feels she has betrayed her mother and family and suffers from shame and guilt just as she feels anger for having been betrayed. The mother too usually feels let down by her daughter, not to mention her husband. So the child and mother normally have to be treated separately before they can be treated together. The aim here is to convince the child that she was indeed a victim—a victim of inept parenting and of a poor marital relationship. She must hear this not only from the counselor but more importantly from the mother before she will be ready to return home. The mother too must tell her that her father has assumed full responsibility for the sexual activity.

While we are working with the mother and daughter we also work with the father, who comes to us as soon he is free on bail or on his own recognizance. We continue to treat the father even after he is given a jail sentence, by special arrangement with the county jail. In addition to individual therapy, the family members usually receive mother-daughter, marriage and eventually family counseling. There are also two self-help groups—Parents United and Daughters United—which meet weekly for group therapy sessions and to assist one another through family and personal crisis.

In addition to individual and group counseling, the CSATP and Parents United provide practical assistance in the form of advice on financial and legal problems, help in finding housing and jobs, etc. But most important, the CSATP offers troubled families a supportive, caring environment where they can find hope and assistance during this the crisis in their histories and where family members can learn to lead more self-satisfying lives.

The CSATP can point to a number of successes during its first six years. No offenses have been repeated among the more than six hundred families that have been treated and formally terminated (the over-all repeat rate is less than 1 percent). About 95 percent of the girls have been returned to their homes. About 90 percent of the marriages have been saved, many couples reporting they have never been happier. The self-abusive behavior of the victimized children (promiscuity, drug abuse, etc.) has been reduced dramatically. The criminal justice system seems to recognize the value of our program, as evidenced by the increasing number of referrals each year and by the suspended or lighter sentences given to offenders who have agreed to participate. Parents United has grown from 3 mother-members to over 125 members, of which half are father-offenders. Daughters United has also grown substantially. The most satisfying result to me and the staff of the CSATP is that the child is returned to a family which can now provide a healthy, nurturing environment for her. Finally, I am gratified to see that the idea of a caring way of treating families troubled by incest is transferable to other communities. In early 1977 the Child Sex Abuse Therapy Program was established as a treatment and training center for the state of California. Our training program, like the treatment program, is guided by the principle and methods of humanistic psychology. At this writing, six months after the training project began, about ten communities are in various stages of developing their own therapy programs. It is our hope that the practical, personal and compassionate help offered to families in trouble will be made available in all American communities.

IF INCEST HAPPENS . . .

One last word for children who are being molested or who are suffering from the effects of past molestation. If you are a victim, please confide in your mother or someone you can trust. Anyone suspecting a child molest situation should contact the Child Protective Services Agency, or the police in his/her community. Also, most states have child abuse hotlines which can offer immediate help. A good general source for information and assistance is the National Center on Child Abuse and Neglect, Washington, D.C. Phone: (202) 755-0590.

Above all, the worst thing anyone can do is ignore or try to cover up father-daughter incest. If you are a mother who is afraid of the consequences to your husband, child and family if you report the problem, make an anonymous phone call to your Child Protective Services Agency. The person answering your call will explain what is apt to happen to your family if you place your problem in the hands of the agency. The chances are that your husband will be treated far less harshly by the authorities if he turns himself in than if they hear about the situation from other sources. But most importantly the situation will stop once and for all and both your child and your husband will receive help.

CREDIT: *Henry Giarretto, Ph.D., Director of Treatment and Training Center Child Abuse Treatment Program, Juvenile Probation Department, Santa Clara County, California.*

Indigestion

The word "indigestion" is a term rarely used by physicians; the synonym "dyspepsia" is used instead. However, dyspepsia, which comes from the Greek (*dys+peptein,* to digest), means a disturbance of the function of digestion. It should be emphasized that what patients call indigestion and physicians dyspepsia usually has no relationship to the inability to digest food.

INDIGESTION AS "GAS"

When a patient says he has indigestion one must ask what his specific symptoms are. What does this person mean by indigestion? One of the most frequent replies is, "I have gas." This is a poor answer since the hollow portions of the gastrointestinal tract—the stomach, small bowel and large bowel or colon—invariably contain gas. The normal person is quite unaware of its presence. People may become aware of "gas" normally present due to its marked increase in quantity. One might then describe this as bloating, or an apparent enlargement or bulging of the abdomen.

Another reference to "gas" may be defined as expulsion of gas either by belching (eructation) or by passing of flatus via the lower opening of the intestinal tract. Either way, it is never a sign of any organic disease. It may be a bad habit and is most commonly seen in nervous people or during a period of anxiety. A single eructation may expel a small quantity of gas from the stomach. This is normal after drinking carbonated beverages. However, the repeated "belching" or "eructations" do not expel gas from the stomach—on the contrary, they are accompanied by swallowing of air without relief, and increase bloating. This act of swallowing air is called aerophagia and is seen in nervous people, or people who actively swallow more air as they belch. It is a bad habit and should be treated as such. People who eat rapidly frequently swallow more air than food. Therefore, a change in eating habits is necessary to rectify this situation.

A small amount of flatus is natural, but socially unacceptable. The flatus of air swallowers does not have an especially offensive odor. If the flatus has a very offensive odor and is accompanied by frequent, foamy, watery stools (true indigestion), malabsorption may be present. Such individuals may be unable to digest and absorb a variety of substances including carbohydrates, proteins and fats. The intestinal bacteria break down the unabsorbed food into foul-smelling by-products. In this condition weight loss is the rule despite a good appetite. This is called steatorrhea, which means diarrhea with undigested fat in stools. The proper treatment can be instituted only if the exact cause is determined.

ACID INDIGESTION

This term has been popularized by TV commercials. The patient may also say, "I have acid" or "too much acid." Hydrochloric acid is a normal secretion of the stomach. The normal individual does not feel that he has acid in his stomach because acid itself produces no symptoms. On the contrary, complete absence of acid secretion by the stomach is abnormal. Normally the capacity of the stomach to secrete acid is reduced with advancing age. "Heartburn," a burning sensation under the breastbone, may be due to the abnormal location of hydrochloric acid in the esophagus. This is produced by reflux of acid into the esophagus, also referred to as reflux or peptic esophagitis. This is due to weakness of the muscle which separates the stomach from the esophagus. This condition may be accompanied by a hiatus hernia, or diaphragmatic hernia. If the burning sensation is below the diaphragm it may be due to a gastric or duodenal ulcer. All of the above-described in this paragraph are reduced or relieved by antacids. These are simple drugs that neutralize hydrochloric acid.

THE NERVOUS STOMACH

If this burning or other discomfort in the upper abdomen (pit of the stomach) is not readily relieved by antacids and is brought on by nervous tension or anxiety, there may be no organic cause for it. The stomach and esophagus are quite normal in such situations. It may be brought on by spasm of the stomach muscle at the outlet of the stomach (pylorus). This is not serious or detrimental to health, but may be quite annoying.

SPASTIC COLON

Abdominal discomfort in the lower abdomen is usually due to disturbances of the large bowel or colon. Indeed too much "gas" in the colon may be the cause of discomfort and relieved by passage of gas. The air swallowing described above may cause the accumulation of this excessive gas in the colon: A person with an irritable or spastic bowel becomes aware of normal amounts of gas because the muscles of the colon contract excessively, and unnecessarily, because of the nervous impulses brought on by tension. These individuals may be constipated or have frequent stools. This condition is not serious and does not lead to any serious organic disease. It is not caused by specific food; "it's not what they eat but what they meet." It is no longer thought that dietary restrictions will cure these people. If constipation is the chief problem, a low-fiber diet is considered harmful but high-fiber (residue) diets, including bran, should be helpful.

LACTASE DEFICIENCY

Lactose or milk sugar has to be split into two primary sugars by the enzyme lactase before it can be absorbed. Most Orientals and many black adults, as well as many Jews, but only about 1 percent of Scandinavians, have deficiency of this enzyme. When people with this deficiency drink milk or eat milk products, such as ice cream, they develop bloating, abdominal discomfort, passage of flatus, as well as diarrhea. This is a true form of indigestion of milk sugar and the treatment consists of avoiding foods that contain a large amount of milk sugar or lactose. After such restriction of diet the condition may improve, and the person may gain the ability to digest these foods in small amounts.

CREDIT: *Mitchell A. Spellberg, M.D., M.S., F.A.C.P., F.A.C.G., Clinical Professor of Medicine, the Pritzker School of Medicine, University of Chicago; Acting Chairman, Department of Gastroenterology, Michael Reese Hospital, Chicago, Illinois.*

Infatuation

Emotional involvement—that almost crazed and confused experience of absorption in another person's life, feelings and whereabouts—has been experienced by everybody. Not many of us like to talk about it because even its recollection causes us to smart with pain. We are generally glad we finally came out on the other end of it—and we promise ourselves that we will never let ourselves get involved that way again.

And yet emotional involvement of this anguished sort is a necessary experience in our journey of development. It is a hazard at the stage of learning something of the world, a problem that goes along with the wonder of discovering friendships, an almost inevitable component of first love. It seems powerful enough to destroy us and yet most of us survive and if we have been open to the experience we have grown a little and we know a lot more about ourselves. Such involvement should not be regretted. We won't recognize real love unless we experience the pain of discovering that we mistook something else for it at another time.

We start out filled with our own needs. The business of day-to-day living burns away the fatty tissue of self-concern and, as we mature, we begin to make room for other people and their needs. In other words, we break out of ourselves and respond to others for their sake rather than for our own gratification. That chink in the armor of our narcissism allows love to find a place in our hearts. We turn outward, in necessary vulnerability, toward others.

Infatuation, like a bad detour, occurs at the earliest stage of that journey. It is the experience we have before we have grown beyond concern for or understanding of our own needs. The pain of infatuation can, in fact, help to free us from these needs. Infatuation in itself is the product of these needs. It is an exciting and sometimes dizzying state, but it is not based so much on our accurate perception of and response to others as it is on a view of them that is notably distorted and distended by our emotional hunger.

There is no getting outside of ourselves without these stirrings and all the bittersweet disharmony of the soul which they generate. But the passage can be made safely because basically healthy people do survive infatuation. They learn from it, and go on to real love.

CREDIT: *Eugene C. Kennedy, Ph.D., Professor of Psychology, Loyola University, Chicago; author of* Living with Everyday Problems *and* A Time for Being Human *(published by Thomas More Association Books, Chicago).*

Infertility

The Inability to Have Children

About 85 percent of the couples who want children manage to get pregnant within the first eight months of trying.

Approximately 15 percent of the couples who want children have some sort of problem. Sixty percent of the time the inability to conceive lies with the female. The other 40 percent of the time, it's the male. Seventy percent of the couples who have trouble eventually manage to conceive. The other 30 percent need special evaluation and help. About half of the group will eventually succeed.

If the couple is thirty years of age or younger, and a wanted pregnancy has not occurred within twelve months of trying, medical help should be sought. If a couple is over thirty, help should be sought after six months. (Time becomes more valuable.)

Absolute infertility must be accepted as an irreversible fact, if the testicles of the male or the ovaries of the female were removed surgically or were not properly developed because of an inherited condition or an illness.

Relative infertility can be present in one or both of the partners. Some of these problems can be corrected easily, others require more patience.

The most common problems are a lowered sperm count, pituitary or ovarian disease resulting in infrequency or lack of menstrual periods, a blockage of the Fallopian tubes or an incompatibility between sperm and cervical secretions.

When both partners have been checked out and declared "fertile" and no pregnancy occurs, it must be suspected that there may be psychological problems—usually anxiety, overeagerness or a mental block of some sort. Such couples need counseling. In some cases, adoption is recommended.

THE EMOTIONAL ASPECTS OF INFERTILITY IN THE FEMALE

A rather wide scope of personality profiles can describe the woman who has trouble becoming pregnant. There is no one special type.

Some are extremely shy, sexually inhibited, high-strung, immature, unable to cope with daily stresses or angry with themselves or the world.

Others have been described as not really wanting a family, in spite of well-circulated claims to the contrary and repeated insistence that they would "give anything" to have a child. Some of these women have unresolved conflicts with their mothers or deep-seated conflicts about accepting the responsibilities of motherhood. Others may be afraid of pregnancy or labor. On the other hand, many are quite normal emotionally.

It is sometimes difficult to separate the emotional factors from the physical when conception does not occur. For example: A woman who is in a state of anxiety may have muscle spasms of the tubes which cause temporary obstruction. If the sexual interaction is poor, or the woman is frustrated by a partner who experiences frequent premature ejaculation, organic obstacles may be set up.

Depressions can influence the hormonal output and interfere with fertilization. Since the state of infertility can produce anxiety, frustration and depression, a vicious cycle may develop. Therefore, some women need counseling in order to help them conceive. A major danger signal is the tendency to reach for pills or alcohol in an attempt to relieve depression. Extreme anger or envy of women who are pregnant is another danger signal.

WHAT SHOULD THE INFERTILE COUPLE DO?

A couple who want a child and have been trying for well over a year with no results should seek the help of a physician who specializes in infertility. Ask your family doctor, or call the County Medical Society. If they live in a small community, it may necessitate a trip to a larger city. Expensive, perhaps, but certainly worth it.

The average sperm count for impregnation is approximately three hundred million. It is possible (though rare) to impregnate a female with a sperm count as low as one million.

Fertility specialists often recommend that men with a low sperm count who want to father a child (1) stop smoking marijuana, (2) abstain from drinking alcohol, (3) discontinue the use of non-prescriptive drugs.

Men whose occupations subject the testicles to undue heat, such as driving a truck or operating a blast furnace, may have to change jobs in order to father a child.

TESTING THE MALE

Tests for the male are painless and quite simple. Three separate specimens of semen are required to ascertain whether the sperm cells are of the quality and quantity to result in a pregnancy.

In addition to the analysis of the sperm count, a sample of the sperm is taken from the female immediately after sexual intercourse, along with the mucus from her cervix in order to determine the compatibility of the two.

TESTING THE FEMALE

There are many tests to determine whether or not a female is fertile. Most of the tests can be performed in a physician's office.

First it must be learned if the passages are free of inflammation and if the reproductive structures are fully developed and free from obstruction. The blowing out of the Fallopian tubes, which may be blocked, has been described as slightly uncomfortable by some women and extremely painful by others—depending on their threshold of tolerance. There may be bloating and shoulder discomfort.

Ovulation, or egg-cell production, must be ascertained and the exact time of ovulation in the menstrual cycle determined. It varies according to the length of the cycle. (Some women menstruate for three days, others for as many as eleven.) The best time to conceive is in the center of the month. For example, if a woman's menstrual cycle is twenty-eight days in length, and she begins on January 10, the best time to get pregnant would be from January 20 to the 27.

AN EXCELLENT ALTERNATIVE

Artificial insemination with a donor.

In cases where the husband is completely sterile, a woman can get the sperm of an anonymous donor. Selection can be made from a large number of donors, choosing from males who have the same hair and eye coloring, height, skin color and other physical characteristics of the husband. Also, a woman can choose the sperm of a male who has no inheritable diseases or incompatible blood types.

SPERM BANKS

The sperm for donor insemination can be obtained fresh or frozen from a sperm bank. Although the concept of human sperm banks dates back to 1866, the first human pregnancies resulting after insemination of frozen sperm cells occurred only in 1956. However, freezing destroys some of the cells so that the rate of successful pregnancies, even when using donor semen, is somewhat lower when frozen sperm is used as opposed to fresh sperm.

There are three commercial sperm banks in the United States—one in Minneapolis, another in Atlanta and a third in New York. The university banks usually get their semen from medical students. A donor is paid about $20 (this can vary).

In general, the banks do not engage in widespread advertising, although the commercial banks do sometimes take ads in medical journals, aimed at gynecologists who are looking for sperm for infertile couples.

There is some controversy about the testing of donors. While the banks are usually quite good on hair, eye and skin color, blood type, RH factor and family health background (looking for sickle cell anemia among blacks and Tay-Sachs among Jews), there are inconsistencies. Some banks do a chromosome check. Others do not.

There are no laws at this moment (1978) that govern sperm banks, so the opportunity for fraud is great.

If infertility is caused by the husband's low sperm count, it has been suggested that he deposit several of his semen samples in the sperm bank, where they will be frozen. At the proper time (the woman's most fertile period) the sperm deposits will be thawed out, combined and deposited in the wife's vaginal tract. However, once again, too many of the sperm are injured by freezing and thawing, and this procedure has not been too successful.

The other use of sperm banks is to store sperm for future use. In recent years, since vasectomy has become popular, many males have deposited large quantities of their sperm in these banks for freezing in the event that if they and their wives might want a child in later years, the sperm will be available to them.

FREEZING AND THAWING SPERM CELLS

A brief description of the actual method begins with the collection of the ejaculate from the donor or husband, who has been asked to refrain from sexual activity for three days. An evaluation of the ejaculate is made to determine motility, volume measurement and sperm count. Glycerol is added to the semen to prevent the formation of ice crystals during freezing.

The container, or ampul, is sealed and placed in the cold vapor coming from liquid nitrogen for about fifteen minutes. The ampul is then submerged in liquid nitrogen for storage at −196° C (−320.8° Fahrenheit). Thawing is accomplished by immersing the ampul in a water bath at body temperature (37° C). The motility, or percentage of forward-swimming sperm cells, is checked under a microscope, and the semen is ready for insemination. This is done in the office through a vaginal speculum—depositing the semen in the entrance of the womb.

At present, the number of spermatozoa exhibiting good motility is usually reduced 30 percent or more by the freeze-thaw process. Variation in the stoage temperatures of the sperm cells is highly detrimental to their survival, therefore exacting techniques are demanded of the specialists managing sperm banks.

Research has revealed numerous requirements for a good survival after thawing, including such things as a rapid freeze rate, a perfect seal on the ampul, upper and lower limits of glycerol concentrations, as well as the time when the glycerol preservative must be added. Some factors, such as the time between adding glycerol and freezing, and the thawing method, have been shown to be non-critical. Human ejaculates contain a number of abnormal sperm cells and these forms appear to survive just as well as the normal spermatozoa.

CHILDREN FROM FROZEN SPERM

Already, dozens of children have resulted from inseminations with frozen human spermatozoa. At the present time, no form of genetic damage due to frozen semen has been detected among these children.

Considerable confidence in regard to genetic safety is derived from the dairy cattle industry, which has led the way with frozen semen and artificial insemination. No genetic damage has been established after production of more than one hundred million calves by this technique.

Recently, a child was born after artificial insemination with sperm cells that had been frozen ten years. Usually inseminations are done with sperm cells stored less than a year, since research has shown some decline in sperm motility after long-term storage.

There are presently fifteen human sperm bank facilities in the United States, with several additional under way. Records and identification of semen samples are meticulously kept, and the use of such facilities is strictly confidential. These banks of human seed may be viewed as technological achievements, but for many deserving couples, they are the means of fulfilling a missing part of their lives.

CREDIT: *American Fertility Society. Checked for accuracy by Melvin L. Taymor, M.D., New England Fertility & Gynecology Associates, Boston, Massachusetts. Additional information supplied by Peter Kovler, Washington, D.C., free-lance writer.*

In-Laws

BABY, IT'S A PAIN

DEAR ANN LANDERS: I have a 5-month-old son and things are back to normal now but the first four months were a nightmare. Why? Because almost every day four or five sets of friends and relatives came to visit. Some didn't even call first.

My mother-in-law brought over a woman I barely knew. She told me how she had developed complications while nursing her baby and almost lost her breast. (A great story for a young mother just getting started.) Another woman brought her young child along and after an hour said, "I really ought to take Billy home. He had a 102 temperature this morning. I'm afraid he's coming down with something."

The constant round of company made me nervous. The baby became cranky and my husband and I started picking at each other. We realize now we were fools to let thoughtless people do this to us.

It's too late for now, but next time we'll know better. MAD IN MORTON

DEAR MAD: Relax, honey. The second baby rarely attracts crowds like the firstborn. Nevertheless, here's your letter. Maybe somebody will learn from it.

In 1961 I wrote my first book. It was called *Since You Ask Me*. In that book, I dealt with the problems that produced the greatest number of letters. Chapter Six of that book was called, "Must We Outlaw the In-Law?" Today, many years later, in-law problems still figure prominently as one of the major causes for marital bust-ups.

I am often asked, "How serious is an in-law problem? Has it been exaggerated? Has the American mother-in-law earned her black eye or is she the innocent victim of gag-writers?"

My mail provides daily evidence that the in-law problem is no myth. Experts say in-laws figure in two out of five divorces—somewhere.

Social critics insist the American matriarchy has crowded Dad so far out of the picture that he isn't important enough to make trouble. This may be more than a lame joke. My mail indicates that the mother-in-law is at least fifty times as troublesome as the father-in-law. And in most cases, it is the mother of the husband who causes the problem.

When it is the wife's mother who creates marital discord, the problem becomes extremely complicated. The Mama-dominated wife never gets over feeling like a naughty child when she bypasses Mama and puts her husband first.

The most troublesome relative, after the mother-in-law (his or hers), is the sister-in-law (usually *his* sister). The brother-in-law (*his* brother) is close on her heels, and the father-in-law (*hers*) comes straggling in—a poor fourth.

The trite phrase, "I'm marrying *him* (or her), not the family," is unrealistic. In most instances it is virtually impossible to steer clear of all relatives. But even when physical separation is accomplished, it is difficult to sever emotional bonds. Family ties are like roots. And roots lie ever present, beneath the surface.

The classic mother-in-law problem is caused by the woman who refuses to let go of her son. The young wife who understands her mother-in-law's need to cling feels less threatened and maintains a calm center. I have suggested repeatedly that married couples who are plagued with in-law problems visit a clergyman or a marriage counselor and verbalize their feelings. A third party who is unbiased and trained in dealing with family problems may give them both a fresh look at the other side.

The daughter-in-law should be tuned in and sympathetic to a mother of three or four adult children who finds herself with an empty nest. For the past twenty years she has been busy with her children. One by one, they leave. Her interests are frequently limited to club or church groups. Suddenly life becomes empty and sterile. She has nothing important or demanding to occupy her time and energy, so she turns to "helping" her married children. She means well, but a young bride who wants to do things her own way may consider it meddling.

When a mother-in-law offers suggestions to Betty on what to do about Ted's cold (after all, who knows better than a boy's mother?) Betty interprets it as "butting in." A marriage counselor or a clergyman can point out that a mother's interest in her son is normal and that a mother-in-law can be useful to a daughter-in-law who is willing to accept gracefully a few well-intentioned suggestions.

The following letter from Virginia illustrates a problem which is more complex because it involves two gravely neurotic people—a mother and her son:

DEAR ANN LANDERS: My mother-in-law is making a nervous wreck out of me. She lives in an apartment about two miles from us (the closest one she could find) and my husband is her sole means of support. Her medicine bills and doctors cost us a fortune. She takes pills to go to sleep, to wake up, to calm her nerves, balance her thyroid, slow up her breathing and pep up her blood. Three times last week she phoned us in the middle of the night to say she was dying. My husband dragged himself out of bed and rushed to her bedside. She's been pulling this same stunt for ten years. The doctors can find nothing organically wrong with her. She'll probably bury me. I've tried to tell my husband she is a clever woman who fakes illness to get attention. He says she is his mother and whatever she wants him to do, he will do whether it makes sense or not. Can you suggest a course of action for me? FED TO THE TEETH

The wife who is trapped in such a situation has a rough life. Her best hope is to persuade her husband to seek psychiatric treatment so that one day he may detach himself from his domineering and demanding mother. A grown man who says "Whatever my mother wants me to do I will do whether it makes sense or not" concedes that he is operating at an adolescent level.

If the mother-in-law is unbearably punishing, I advise the wife to tell Junior to go live with Mama until he grows up. If there are children, he can send the support checks in the mail.

The most difficult of all mother-in-law problems involves the only son of a widowed or divorced woman. Young men who grow up with no male influence in their lives are often poor marriage risks. There are exceptions, of course, but the evidence is heavily weighted on the negative side.

Some months ago, I received the following letter from a North Carolina bride:

DEAR ANN LANDERS: I am writing this letter on my wedding night. My groom and I were married this afternoon in a beautiful church ceremony. We left the hotel reception at about eight-thirty in the evening and drove to this lovely little resort hotel. The first thing my husband did when we arrived here was telephone his mother. They talked for thirty minutes and he spent most of the time comforting her and trying to get her to stop crying. After the conversation he flopped down on the bed, bawled for ten minutes, cracked open a pint of bourbon, drank it and passed out.

Her signature, several pages later, was "Unmarried Wife."

If you think such neurotic relationships exist only between mother and son, please read the next letter. This problem occurs less frequently. But it *does* happen.

DEAR ANN LANDERS: Our son went steady with a lovely girl for two years. The girl's father died when she was thirteen and she and her mother were like sisters. We knew they were close, but we didn't realize they were crazy. We should have known something was wrong when the mother moved to the college town and took a selling job to be near her daughter. After graduation B and J had a nice wedding. On the wedding night J complained of a sick headache. The next day she said her eyes hurt. That night her back ached. The next morning she scribbled a note saying she couldn't bear to think of her mother alone so she had taken the bus home. What can our son do? Shocked Parents.

Again, psychiatric help is the only solution. But too often, as I told this woman, professional help is rejected. The sick ones defend their behavior with such fancy (and even admirable) labels as "mother love," "family devotion" and "filial loyalty." When I advised a New York reader to get outside help before his mother's apron strings throttled his marriage, he replied:

"There is nothing wrong with me, Ann Landers. You are the one who needs professional help. My wife is twenty-eight years old. She has her whole life before her. My mother is sixty-four. I shall continue to spend every January in Florida with my mother as long as she lives. My wife belongs home with the children."

Some women dislike their mothers-in-law even before they meet and it's the husband's fault. He sometimes paints such glowing pictures of "dear old Mom" that he gives the girl an inferiority complex, and plants a premature dislike for this paragon in-law.

Many mother-in-law problems are bound up in some way with food, perhaps because food is an ancient symbol for love. It may be the unconscious motivation for two women who attempt to battle it out in the kitchen.

These complaints tell the story: "My husband's mother phones him at work and asks him to stop by her house for his favorite dish—meatballs and cabbage." Or, "My mother-in-law insists on bringing matzo-ball soup over here because she knows Lou loves it, and I can't make it as well as she can." A woman who had been married seven years wrote, "My mother-in-law comes over every Wednesday and takes over my kitchen. She likes to prepare special Italian dishes for her son. I've asked her for recipes dozens of times, but she claims she never measures anything."

I tell these wives they can only win by co-operating. If a mother-in-law wants to prepare special dishes and bring them over—fine. If she wants to come to the house once a week and cook a meal, what's wrong with that? Many women are happy to pay a caterer a good price to do the same thing. If a mother-in-law finds pleasure in doing these things for her son, why fly into a rage? The smart wife who permits her mother-in-law the satisfaction of mixing batter in her kitchen now and then often ensures that her mother-in-law will not mix in more vital matters.

I take the firm position that newlyweds will be happier in a one-room apartment (even if it's under a bowling alley) than in a mansion which belongs to his or her parents. Living under one roof is bound to produce a long list of small irritations. And an accumulation of irritations can add up to an atomic explosion after several months. Every young couple should be free to settle their differences privately, outside the hearing range of relatives. They should have a place of their own in which to make the transition from cloud nine to down-to-earth living.

No two women make a bed or peel a potato exactly the same way. The mother-in-law may make a better apple pie, but even if it isn't better, her son will probably think it is because Mom made it.

Newlyweds often have difficulty adjusting sexually. In-laws in an adjoining bedroom can complicate the problem. Young marrieds are frequently shy and the knowledge that parents are close by can be horribly inhibiting.

One young bride wrote from Salt Lake City:

DEAR ANN LANDERS: We moved into my mother-in-law's home because she begged us to. She said she would be lonely by herself in that big house, and explained that it would give us a chance to save some money until Jack got on his feet. After the first week I knew it was a foolish move. Our sex life was awful. His mother always managed to knock on our door at the wrong time.

If I could hand every newly married couple a framed motto as a wedding gift, it would say this: *"Your first allegiance is to each other. Let no man or woman come between you."* No, I am not suggesting that the parents of newly married couples should join the Foreign Legion. My motto, however, would spare millions of young people the agony of split loyalties.

The man who is unwilling to put his wife before his mother is not sufficiently mature for marriage. The woman who is unable to put her husband before her parents is not sufficiently grown up to be a wife.

A young wife wrote that just as she was going into labor her husband left her to drive his mother to a bridge party. I knew that short of a miracle she would feel forever second to her mother-in-law. The humiliated woman wrote: "I had to phone my neighbor next door to drive me to the hospital. I'll never get over the shame."

Realigning loyalties can be agonizing, particularly when a parent is involved. Feelings of guilt can play havoc when a choice must be made between two people who are close to us. Sons and daughters who have been reared successfully do not feel that marriage imposes a choice; there are no pangs of guilt attached to leaving Mama and Papa. The goal for all children should be independence. The successful parent prepares his child to stand on his own and be a central figure in another family. Too often the parent who refuses to let go and insists "my child needs me" is twisting the facts. What he means is "I need my child."

The adult approach is to recognize the different kinds of love. It is possible to love—and at the same time—a wife, a mother, a sister and a grandmother, cherry pie, football, Lincoln, Rembrandt and Bach. But we don't love them all in the same way. The kind of love which results in marriage should be unique. It should be a combination of admiration, respect, physical desire, mutual interests and mutual goals.

Some newlyweds as well as long-married couples create their own in-law trouble. They feel free to borrow money, accept large financial gifts, drop in on Mom for meals any old time, ask her to baby-sit and present her with their youngsters when they go on trips. If the mother-in-law is used as a sitter because she is handy and free, then the mother should be content to let her unpaid sitter discipline the children in her own way. If the disciplinary methods are not to the young wife's liking, she does not have the right to complain. I frequently receive letters from wives who say:

DEAR ANN LANDERS: My mother-in-law is ruining our children. When we leave them at her house weekends, they run wild. She gives them candy and ice cream between meals, lets them watch TV until they fall asleep on the floor, and she doesn't even insist that they keep their hair combed and their faces clean.

I tell such women to hire a sitter and give her orders. It's cheaper in the long run and it will save wear and tear on everyone.

Independence from in-laws is vital if young marrieds are to build a solid relationship. A husband and wife should not carry their personal disagreements to the homes of their parents, either individually or together. Husband and wife troubles should be settled between themselves. One wise mother-in-law from San Luis Obispo wrote:

DEAR ANN LANDERS: When my daughter-in-law and son begin to raise their voices and I see an argument brewing, I leave. I don't want to witness any quarrels. I don't ever want to be asked to take sides.

The wife who tattles on her husband and the husband who downgrades his wife are disloyal. The knowledge that a mate has blabbed about intimate family problems can destroy for all time the trust and confidence which are essential to a sound marriage.

The mature husband and wife run little danger of in-law interference because they were reared to lead their own lives. Mature people don't get that way by accident. They can make decisions, accept responsibility for themselves, and they don't whine to Mom and Dad when things go wrong.

The Bible story of Naomi and Ruth eloquently describing the devotion between a woman and her daughter-in-law has been repeated millions of times in every country in the world. Many warm and beautiful in-law relationships exist today, as my mail testifies. Often when readers write about unrelated problems, I note the line: "My mother-in-law is a marvelous person. She has helped us in so many ways. I love her dearly."

To all mothers-in-law I would like to say this: If you once had to put up with an interfering mother-in-law, try to remember what it was like. Spare your daughter-in-law the hell you endured. If your mother-in-law was wise and understanding, you know how fortunate you were. Give your daughter-in-law the same break.

Since it is the wife who most often complains to me about her husband's mother, I direct this advice to her. Think ahead. One day you will probably be a mother-in-law. You will want to be treated with kindness and understanding. Remember that every mother has an emotional investment in her children. In the evening of her life, her greatest joys and satisfactions come from the knowledge that they are content and that she is loved by them. When your mother-in-law gets you down, and granted, she may be off base a country mile, be tolerant. Be forgiving. Remember, she raised the boy you selected for a husband.

CREDIT: *Ann Landers.*

A VOTE FOR CACKLING KIN

DEAR ANN LANDERS: I envy that woman who griped because her mother-in-law laughs like a donkey. (She said it was an embarrassment to take her to the movies because the old girl hee-haws and snorts and everyone gawks to see who the jackass is.)

My mother-in-law hasn't cracked a smile in 20 years. Odd that not one funny thing has happened to her since I married her son. I am JUST COMMENTING

DEAR J.C.: Isn't it nice that you can comment to me? I'll bet when you read this letter in the paper you'll see the humor in it and feel a lot better.

A FRESH FATHER-IN-LAW

DEAR ANN LANDERS: My in-laws are both in their early 70s. I've had no trouble with my mother-in-law ever since I told her to please stop trying to shove her religion down my throat.

My father-in-law has become a real problem, however. He was always fond of me, but in the last year or so, his "fatherly" kisses have become much too frequent and not very fatherly.

He never does anything out of the way when his wife or my husband are around, but when he catches me in the back hall or behind the bushes, he gets awfully fresh. Last night, I went to the fruit cellar to get some pickled peaches. He followed me into the fruit room and kissed me on the back of the neck.

When I was dating, I knew how to deal with clowns who acted like that. I hauled off and planted one on the schnoz. But I just can't do that to my father-in-law.

My husband would be furious if he knew his dad was making passes at me. My mother-in-law would kill the old lecher. I don't want him pulverized or dead. What's the best solution? IN A SPOT

DEAR SPOT: Make it a point not to be alone with him—ever. If he follows you again and gets out of line, give him a clop in the chops. On those occasions when he forgets you're his daughter-in-law, I say it's all right to forget he's your father-in-law.

TROUBLED IN-LAW

DEAR ANN LANDERS: I must respond to one of your observations because it hurt so much when I read it. You said 80 to 90 per cent of the in-law problems that cross your desk are against the mother-in-law—and usually it's the man's mother who is under attack.

I am a mother-in-law—the man's mother. His wife is beautiful, poised and well-educated. She is a very good wife to my son. I have tried to treat her as a daughter and a friend. I hoped and prayed she would love me, but I have failed completely to achieve these goals.

I have learned that some wives can be jealous of a husband's mother. They view her as "the other woman" in his life. This fact has come out in so many ways it is unmistakable.

How easy it is to be the mother-in-law of a male! My son just eats up the attention he gets from his wife's mother. His wife doesn't object one bit to her own mother lavishing affection on him—and his returning it. But she resents it when he shows any warmth whatever toward me. Why am I the problem—just because I'm the husband's mother?　SAD FAILURE

DEAR FRIEND: Apparently you and your son's wife got off to a bad start and the situation was never set right. I suggest that you have a heart-to-heart talk with your daughter-in-law. Hand her this column and tell her the letter is yours. Ask her if she will meet you halfway. I'll bet some good will come of it.

MOTHER-IN-LAW'S RULES FROM ONE WHO KNOWS

DEAR ANN LANDERS: I am a widow and soon to be a mother-in-law. I hope I can follow these rules as a gift to my son.

(1) I will try to manage my modest income prudently so as not to be a financial burden.

(2) I will respect the privacy of his home. I will not visit unless invited. I will realize my son and his wife need time together—alone.

(3) I will not hint to go along on vacations or weekend trips.

(4) I will not present my son with chores to do on his day off.

(5) I will be kind and loving toward his wife, never critical of her housekeeping, cooking or appearance.

(6) If there are children, I will show no partiality, nor will I interfere with their discipline.

(7) In summary, I will do my best, no matter how lonely, to avoid being a selfish, domineering or clinging mother because my husband had one of those and I know what it did to my life.　BEEN THROUGH THE MILL

DEAR BEEN THROUGH: Your letter is strong testimony that experience is the best of all teachers.

I find it interesting that 90 per cent of the letters I receive pertaining to in-law problems are complaints against the mother-in-law—not the father-in-law. And 80 per cent of the mother-in-law beefs are against the husband's mother—not the wife's.

Insomnia

BED TROUBLE

DEAR ANN: My husband dared me to write you this letter. Our problem is not unique. It is one shared by thousands of women.

My kids won't let me sleep days and my husband keeps me up nights. I'm tired all the time. He's a restless sleeper, thrashes around continuously, takes his half of the bed out of the middle, wraps himself in the blankets and leaves me shivering. I've begged for twin beds but he insists the double bed is the cornerstone of a happy marriage. What do you suggest? BEAT BEVERLY

DEAR BEAT: The double bed may be the cornerstone of a happy marriage, but exhaustion could be the tombstone.

Tell your husband the average person spends one-third of his life in bed. It's an undisputed fact when THAT third is happy, the remaining two-thirds is considerably more pleasant.

Since he is a restless sleeper, yet he obviously wants you "near" I suggest twin beds (separate mattresses and box springs) placed smack together and use a single headboard. It will look like one large bed, but actually it's two—each with its own set of sheets and blankets.

Insomnia is defined as a temporary, or chronic, loss of sleep. The definition comes from the Latin *in,* meaning "not," and *somnus* meaning "sleep"—so, "not sleep." In general, temporary sleeplessness is usually caused by some transient physical condition or emotional upset. Chronic sleeplessness may be caused by persistent physical disorders, or more often, deep-seated psychological difficulties, or a combination of both.

Insomnia is one of the sleep disorders that has been studied extensively at leading universities and medical centers in facilities called "sleep laboratories." Electroencephalogram (a machine that studies brain waves) tests during sleep provide an understanding of both the normal and the abnormal variations.

Insomnia should be looked at against other factors that may affect sleep, such as season of the year, climate, social customs and occupation. People who change work shifts may have difficulty adjusting to a new sleep schedule.

There are three levels or stages of sleep depth distinguished in the normal variations of human sleep. Stage One is a very light sleep which is a transition between waking and sleeping. This represents about 5 to 10 percent of the total sleep period.

Stage Two is medium deep sleep and represents about 50 to 70 percent of the total sleep period. Stage Three, called delta sleep, or deep sleep, represents somewhere between 0 and 25 percent of total sleep. Stage Three (delta stage) is frequently subdivided into two stages so that it may sometimes be called Stage Three and Stage Four. One normally enters the deepest sleep period or delta sleep about a half hour to an hour after the onset of sleep. As the night goes on, there is less delta sleep, and more of Stage Two sleep. Delta sleep declines with age, so that many elderly people who are in good physical shape will complain of being relatively light sleepers. There is very little delta sleep after the age of sixty.

Now, alternating with normal sleep (which is technically called non-REM sleep) in about ninety-minute intervals through the night is a separate state which is called paradoxical sleep. This is called the REM state (REM stands for Rapid Eye Movement). This period of REM sleep which alternates with normal sleep accounts for about 15 to 30 percent of the total sleep period.

In theories of sleep and the studies that try to confirm them, REM sleep involves a time of psychological recovery for the sleeper. It parallels delta sleep, which is a period for physical recovery. This is just a theory, but it proposes that REM sleep is a period for psychological repair and reviewing of psychological and emotional processes during the day. It involves the consolidation of memory. It has been proven that dreams dissolve within five to ten minutes after REM sleep, unless one awakens from REM sleep and immediately fixes the dream in his waking memory by trying to remember it. What this means is that someone who remembers a dream has actually awakened from REM sleep and fixed that dream in his waking, conscious memory.

Not all people need the same amount of sleep. Many healthy adults can get along without any ill effects on three hours of sleep a night. Others need ten or twelve, and feel tired and irritable when they get less than ten to twelve. Therefore, insomnia should be defined only as it relates to an individual. A person has insomnia if his inability to sleep for as long as he needs to interferes with efficient daytime functioning, regardless of how many hours he gets.

Short-term sleep losses are only of concern with certain medical conditions such as epilepsy, where the lack of sleep will lower the epileptic seizure threshold; or in those whose jobs require attention such as air traffic controllers and persons working with highly technical and dangerous equipment.

The most common complaint about insomnia is difficulty in falling asleep. Frequently people become more and more concerned and approach sleeping periods with anxiety, which almost always assures another sleepless night. For those who have occasional nights when they have difficulty falling asleep,

I recommend a hobby, reading or some form of quiet relaxation. Some insomniacs would do well to catch up on back work rather than spend hours rolling and tossing.

Occasionally a sleeping pill will help; but for the most part, sleeping pills are virtually useless when taken on a continual basis. Most are ineffective after ten days of chronic use, although occasionally, some will show potency up to a month. Actually, for those who use sleeping medication on a regular basis, depriving them of the drugs for a night or two causes a REM rebound which may produce nightmares and disturbed sleeping patterns. Usually severe and continuing insomnia may be caused by conditioning. It may have started during a crisis in one's life, such as an impending divorce, following a death, etc. It then continues because one establishes a pattern of sleeping poorly and expects to sleep poorly. To correct this situation, the person should be taken out of his conditioned setting. Frequently these people report that they sleep better on vacation than at home—the reason being that they are out of a conditioned setting. This is called behavior modification, and incorporates the following instructions: One should not take naps during the day and should try to stay awake even when feeling sleepy after meals. One should try eating lightly during the evening meal since many of the chemicals in food induce a certain amount of sleepiness. This leads to "cat naps" rather than to a full night of sleeping. One should avoid stimulants like coffee and tea and cola drinks (all contain caffeine) or at least restrict them to the earlier part of the day.

Essentially: (1) Go to bed when you feel sleepy. (2) If you do not fall asleep within ten or fifteen minutes, get up, get out of bed and leave the bedroom and go into another room, and do what you feel like doing until you feel sleepy again. This process of returning to bed as often as necessary until you fall asleep should be repeated until such time that you fall asleep instantly when going to bed.

Every effort should be made to avoid oversleeping in the morning. What will happen is that after three or four nights of a sleepless or a disturbed routine, the patient will fall asleep on the second or third attempt and will gradually relate to the bedroom as a place for sleep, rather than sleeplessness.

Many individuals who have had high anxiety about falling asleep will fall asleep almost anyplace other than their bedrooms. They will fall asleep in front of the television, they will fall asleep reading the newspaper, etc. For these individuals, relaxation techniques, such as the practice of transcendental meditation, are useful mechanisms. Occasionally a sleeping pill may help to reduce the anxiety, if it does not lead to chronic use.

For some individuals, situational factors, such as overstimulation, excessive work demands, emotional problems, or chronic tension, will lead to chronic insomnia. Some insomniacs have been encouraged to exercise before going to sleep. In certain instances, this merely sets up an arousal pattern and stimulates them to a point where they cannot fall asleep. For such individuals, a quiet relaxation period of reading or drinking a glass of warm milk would be the better approach.

Most patients with sleep onset problems show a combination of physical and emotional problems. Fragmented sleep (sleep in which an individual may frequently get up at intervals during the night) occurs in a variety of forms of depression and the remedy is to treat the underlying depression—usually with psychotherapy and antidepressant drugs.

Many people get trapped into taking medication because they think they are not getting enough sleep, when, in actuality, they need less sleep than other members of their family. Certain types of physical illness, such as hypertension and cardiac disease, frequently will cause difficulties with insomnia or fragmented sleep.

There is another sleep disturbance in which an individual sleeps the entire night but wakes up exhausted in the morning. This is related to a condition which is called sleep apnea—usually associated with people who snore for extensive periods during the night. Their pattern can be described as follows: they snore, then they stop breathing and gasp for air; they resume loud snoring, then they breathe heavily again. The breathing interruptions are so brief that the patient can't remember them, but it does leave him exhausted and fatigued in the morning. Actually, the patient wakes up momentarily many, many times during the night. Such conditions are treated by a drug or, in a recent series at Stanford, by making a small hole in the trachea which is plugged during the day and which allows the patient to breathe more effectively at night.

In summary, insomnia is a symptom usually of an underlying emotional problem such as depression or anxiety; sometimes it is situational and transient—which means it passes.

It may also be related to certain physical conditions, all of which should be explored. Most of all, one should remember that the usual sleeping medication does not help after a period of time and may keep a person locked into a pattern which, on rapid withdrawal, will cause nightmares, teeth-grinding and other symptoms related to the disturbed sleep pattern.

CREDIT: *Harold M. Visotsky, M.D., Professor and Chairman, Department of Psychiatry and Behavioral Sciences, Northwestern University Medical School; Director, Institute of Psychiatry, Northwestern Memorial Hospital, Chicago, Illinois.*

Intercourse (Painful)

(*Dyspareunia*)

Physical and psychological factors may cause dyspareunia—painful intercourse—in both sexes. Since the condition is much more common in women than in men, we will discuss only dyspareunia in women.

In some virgins, the hymen (maidenhead) may be intact and unstretched. The first few times intercourse takes place there may be pain or even slight bleeding as the hymen is stretched or torn to accommodate the penis. A very few women have tough hymens which need minor surgery.

Burning, itching or aching pain in the vagina during intercourse often is caused by failure to lubricate. The production of lubricating materials in the vagina can be compared to an erection in a male: Without it the woman is not ready either physiologically or psychologically for intercourse. Failure to lubricate can occur when the woman has little or no love, affection, respect or trust in her sexual partner or believes he feels none of these for her. Inadequate lubrication may also result from fears (for example, of becoming pregnant) and from the aging process. Using a lubricant such as K-Y jelly or foam (available in drugstores) is often helpful in relieving a lack of natural lubrication. Lack of lubrication after the menopause is a common symptom due to inactivity of the lubricating glands.

Bacterial and fungal infections may also cause this type of vaginal pain. Douching after intercourse is popularly believed to be a hygienic practice that will help prevent infections. Actually, douching usually does more harm than good because it destroys the natural ecology of the vagina and increases its susceptibility to the growth of harmful bacteria and fungi. Women often get fungal infections after being on antibiotic therapy. The antibiotic kills the bacteria and the fungus grows wildly.

Persistent bacterial infections of the vagina may also result from anal intercourse if the penis is inserted into the vagina after being in the rectum. The incidence of this type of infection can be decreased by either refraining from vaginal intercourse after anal entry or having the male partner wash his penis well before inserting it into the vagina.

A common cause of pain in the pelvis is deep thrusting. This problem can be remedied by informing the partner, who should then proceed in a less vigorous and more gentle manner. When pain during intercourse results from scars of injuries received during abortion, childbirth or violent rape, surgical repair is the appropriate treatment.

Endometriosis is one of the most common causes of deep pelvic pain with intercourse. It is always worse just before or after a period and is not too difficult a diagnosis for your doctor to make in his office.

Some women complain of painful intercourse after hysterectomy. Although physical causes should not be ruled out, this pain is frequently caused by fear that the sex drive and orgasmic response will decrease or disappear. On the other hand, some women enjoy sex more after hysterectomy because they no longer worry about pregnancy.

Many women who have undergone radiation therapy will experience pain during intercourse due to a shrinking of the tissues.

Since painful intercourse has a variety of causes, some of them physical, a counselor's first step should be to assist the woman in obtaining a thorough physical examination, including sexual history. If no physical cause can be found, counseling should be sought. The pain may be caused by the desire to avoid intercourse. This means there is an emotional problem which needs exploration and ventilation if the woman is to have a satisfactory sex life.

CREDIT: *John S. Long, M.D., F.A.C.S., F.A.C.O.G., Associate Professor of Obstetrics and Gynecology, Rush-Presbyterian-St. Luke's Hospital; attending physician, Rush-Presbyterian-St. Luke's Hospital, Chicago, Illinois.*

Introductions

When I was growing up (back in the Stone Age, of course) I was taught a few basic rules about introductions:

(1) A child or teenager always stands when introduced to an older person.

(2) When introducing one person to another one should present the younger (or less important) person to the other. Example: "Johnny, this is my grandmother, Mrs. Jones." "Prince Philip, may I present my laundress, Ruth Smith."

(3) A woman when meeting a man for the first time does not wait for him to extend his hand. She extends hers.

Well, there's a lot more to introductions than that—as my readers have taught me. Here are a few examples of what I mean:

DEAR ANN: Many years ago an uncle of mine served in the capacity of lieutenant governor for about five weeks. He was appointed to complete the unfinished term of the lieutenant governor who died.

My husband, when he introduces me to friends, invariably says, "Meet my wife—the niece of the former lieutenant governor of the state." This embarrasses me and I become very uncomfortable and wonder what others must think.

How can I cure my husband of this tasteless habit without humiliating him before friends? He's extremely sensitive. ANNOYED

DEAR ANN: It's one of the ironies of human nature that the most sensitive people are generally insensitive to the feelings of others. Tell your husband, in private, of course, that you are perfectly content to be introduced as his wife and it's unnecessary to drag your uncle in by his heels to build you up.

As for what your friends think—they think exactly what you think they think, that your husband is an insecure clod who feels the need to impress people even if it means using a slightly fraudulent device.

DEAR ANN LANDERS: Since everyone seems to toss their pet peeves and private annoyances in your direction I think I will, too. Even if you can't help me, it will make me feel better.

Whenever my husband introduces me to anyone, or refers to me in conversation, he calls me "the wife." It's never "MY wife" it's always "THE wife." Doesn't that sound cold and impersonal?

The word "MY" is definitely in his vocabulary. He uses it in connection with his secretary, his office, his newspaper, his dog and sometimes his son.

Why does my husband do this to me? Is there a solution? ARMS LENGTH LIFE PARTNER

DEAR PARTNER: Speech patterns can mean something or nothing. Often they are established out of habit.

If it bugs you to be called "the wife," speak up, first privately, then publicly. But in a nice way. Example: "Please, dear I'm YOUR wife. Have you forgotten so soon?"

DEAR ANN: I just read the letter from the lady who complained because her husband always introduced her as "THE wife" instead of "My wife." Some people don't know when they're well off. My husband never introduces me at all, just lets me stand there like a cigar-store Indian. Print this, please. He reads you daily. MRS. INVISIBLE

DEAR MRS.: Here it is. Let me know if it helped.

'INCUMBENT WIFE'

DEAR ANN LANDERS: I just read the letter from "Mrs. Invisible"—the woman whose husband always forgot to introduce her. (She was comforting the lady whose spouse introduced her as "the wife" instead of "my wife.")

Here's a suggestion for all husbands who want to keep their wives on their toes. It certainly has worked wonders for me. I introduce the little woman as "The incumbent wife . . ." or "My first wife . . ." Every time she hears it, she tries harder.   IN CHARGE IN CALIFORNIA

DEAR CAL: Well, bully, for you! And I do mean bully. My condolences to your "incumbent wife." She sure drew a lemon when she got you, Bub.

KEEPING A TIRED OLD LINE IN LINE

DEAR ANN: I would like to comment on the slob who enjoyed introducing his wife (the only one he'd ever had) as "My *first* wife." He said it helped keep her in line. His signature was, "In Charge in California."

My father is the same kind of bully, but my mother knows how to handle him. Whenever he uses that tired old line, she responds instantly with, "And this is my *last* husband."

They have been married 30 years and I guess one of the reasons is that they both overlook a lot. Especially my mother.   LOVE COVERS A MULTITUDE OF SINS

DEAR LOVE: It sure does. In addition to being blind, love can also be deaf and dumb.

CREDIT: *Ann Landers.*

Jealousy

The universal emotional trauma called jealousy can be caused by things as well as people. Jealousy has been defined as wanting what someone else has while envy is when you don't want somebody else to have what you don't have. But most of us think jealousy exactly as John Milton saw it, "the injur'd lover's hell." The something else that another has is the attention, the regard, some portion—large or small—of the love and devotion of someone we care for and which we feel should clearly be directed exclusively towards ourself.

Like love, jealousy is involuntary. It's useless to say to yourself, "I'm not going to be jealous." Psychologists tell us that jealousy is probably instinctive as well as a lifelong conditioning process that begins in the crib. A baby experiences jealousy from the first instant she or he realizes that Mother's attention must be shared.

Jealousy can be frightening in its intensity. Its closest emotional relative is probably anger but jealousy has more staying power. Like anger, it can provoke a passion to strike out in revenge, only with the jealousy the revenge sought is usually emotional. More often it causes the jealous person to sulk and wallow in self-pity. Sometimes we complain openly of the direct cause but more often it is carefully disguised while we lash out at a baffled spouse, lover or relative about a dozen petty things far removed from the real cause of irritation.

In one sense, jealousy is a natural reaction, a warning sign that something is causing trouble in a relationship that is of primary importance. Sometimes people have every reason to be jealous. They convert their emotional energy into action to try and protect or save a vital part of their lives. But persistent, obsessive jealousy can kill that same vital relationship, as in the classic (and frequently dramatized) situation of the husband who suspects his wife of "the worst" if she so much as smiles at another male.

Such destructive jealousy usually signals deep insecurity of one whose life experiences have repeatedly lowered his self-esteem—one who has had a series of important relationships in which he has lost out to someone else. In such cases professional counseling is the sensible course. But most people can learn to cope with the periodic storms of jealousy which overtake them if they learn how to recognize and deal with the problem.

First, psychologists tell us, you must be honest with yourself. Put a specific name to the things that are making you jealous. Look at them objectively. Are they silly or trivial? Is your partner doing them deliberately or without thinking? Does your partner know that such behavior brings out the green-eyed monster in you or have you always just assumed that it should be obvious from your reaction? If the cause is chronic and the emotional pain so strong that you can't live with it, tell your partner exactly how you feel. Often once he is aware of the problem and if the relationship is a good one to begin with, the simple knowledge that certain kinds of behavior cause you pain is sufficient to cause him to stop doing it once and for all. An appeal is always better than a demand, just as a warning is better than an ultimatum.

Remember that jealousy is a two-edged sword. Don't be surprised if your partner has a small list of things you are doing that cause him just as much anguish.

CREDIT: *Joel Wells, editor of* The Critic, *a Thomas More publication, Chicago, Illinois.*

DEAR ANN: I'm engaged to a 26-year-old man who sometimes behaves like a small child. I love him dearly, but his jealousy and tantrums make me wonder if we could have a happy marriage.

During lunch hour I went with the head of the accounting department to a jewelry store to help select a gift for his wife's 50th birthday. I casually mentioned this to my fiance and he turned on me like a mad dog. He said he'd long suspected something between this man and me.

I was too crushed to defend myself. Ten minutes later when I was in tears he apologized and blithely changed the subject.

Several weeks ago he accused me of making a play for his younger brother. I was so upset I had to take nerve pills. Do you think after we're married he'll be sure of my love and stop this nonsense? Frankly, I'm worried. JOYCE

DEAR JOYCE: If you think a few words uttered by a clergyman will transform an insecure, suspicious man into a confident and trusting husband— I have news for you.

He will carry these destructive qualities into marriage and you'll wind up a steady contributor to this column.

Today he's jealous of the man in the accounting department. A few weeks ago it was his younger brother. Next week it may be the mailman. After you're married it probably will be the butcher, the baker and the candlestick maker.

Jealousy and suspicion are manifestations of insecurity. He's unsure of himself (probably doubts his worthiness) so he takes it out on you in this way. Unwind yourself from the little boy and start to date some men.

Jogging

Unless you're already a distance runner, you should approach running or even jogging with the same caution as you would a hot stove.

You can't be too careful. Many a new enthusiast, eager to get in top-notch condition in a hurry, has done himself more harm than good. One should never begin to jog or run without careful preparation.

The fact is that you can run five miles whether you're man or woman, boy or girl—if you're twenty-five, thirty-five, forty-five, fifty-five, sixty-five or yes, seventy-five. It will help you feel better than you have ever felt in your life. It might even help you to tolerate frustration at work and arguments at home, and to avoid headaches at both places. But don't expect it to happen in a week, or a month. The buildup must be gradual. The weekend crash athlete who goes all-out in competitive sport every other Sunday or even every weekend puts his heart under great tension and stress. Be good to yourself and follow my instructions.

The only equipment you need is the right clothes to keep you warm when it's cold and cool when you are warm. Footwear is very important. Don't try to save money on shoes or you may pay the difference to a foot doctor. Buy the best shoes that are made for running. Your feet will appreciate the consideration.

Discipline is vital. You must stay with your program of first walking, then running short distances at an easy pace. And you must do it every day without a miss, no matter how busy you are, or what the weather is like.

Before you go out to walk or run, make sure you have the right clothing. First—make sure you are comfortable. Almost anything that feels natural and is not too tight is appropriate for running.

To build up running you should start walking. Walk at a good, fast, striding pace. Then trot slowly and I mean slowly, taking it very easy, for a block. Walk a block, then run a block. Keep an eye on your watch, make sure you know what time you started. And when you've been out for about fifteen minutes, turn around and start back. Walk a block, then run very slowly a block, walk a block, lope very slowly a block, and get back to the house.

For two weeks just keep up your walk-a-block, jog-very-slowly-a-block. During that two weeks get an appointment with your doctor and have him give you a thorough examination, paying special attention to the heart. Make sure you are in good physical condition.

Tell your doctor exactly what you are doing and follow his advice to the letter. After two weeks, see if you can go just a little farther and I mean just a little. Not much. If you press yourself you can go a great deal farther, but see if you can go just a little farther in the same period of time. This means you will have to walk a little faster and run a little faster—not much, just a little.

For the next two weeks go one extra block in the same half hour. After this second two weeks, I have a surprise for you. Go to the same distance, but run two blocks and walk one block. Time yourself. You will be astonished at the way you are able to cover more distance in less time without walking or running any faster but simply running a little more than you walked.

Just consider the extra benefits. If you run to work and back, you immediately and directly save money on transportation by bus, taxi or automobile. If you enjoy eating, that five-mile run will enable you to eat another five hundred or six hundred calories a day without gaining an ounce, or if you want to lose, you can maintain your present diet and lose about a pound a week.

Five miles of running means you burn up 3,500 calories a week, and it just happens that 3,500 calories equals one pound. Then there's the advantage of looking better, you're bound to look better. It will show in the clearness of your skin, in the clearness of your eyes, in the serenity and relaxation, in the inches that will melt off your waist, in the strength that will come to your arms and legs.

And you lengthen the odds that you'll live longer, for running opens up additional blood vessels. Most studies indicate that those who have developed this persistent athletic capacity are far more likely to survive a heart attack.

If you stay with this moderate buildup every single day, your system will become accustomed to it. You will give your heart and your cardiovascular system the best kind of daily tonic—which is regular, moderate physical exercise day after day.

CREDIT: *Senator William Proxmire, author of* You Can Do It, *New York: Simon & Schuster.*

Kidneys

The Bashful Kidney

The term "bashful kidney" could be changed to "shy bladder," since it refers to the inability to urinate in the presence of others.

It is recognized in medicine that functional disturbances of urination may be related to emotional factors, just as the stomach may register emotional disturbances.

The function of urination is to relieve the discomfort of accumulated urine within the bladder. However, this function may also serve different psychological ends in the developing child. Gaining control over the bladder sphincter is part of growing up and a persistent defect in such control means a lack of emotional growth. This is most commonly seen in either persistent bedwetting (enuresis) or inability of the male to urinate in the presence of others ("bashful kidney").

It must be remembered that organic disease of the genito-urinary system may play a role in hesitancy of urination as well, and may be confused at times with the purely psychological condition of difficulty in urinating *only* in public.

The primary problem arises from the fact that the urinary and sexual functions are performed by the same part of the body. The inability to urinate in the presence of others, however, may have different (but related) causes. For example—a family that has emphasized absolute modesty will raise a child who will be excessively shy about his (or her) body. Consequently, this child may be unable to toilet if anyone is present.

Some individuals must always flush the toilet while urinating if others are in the bathroom, even though they cannot be seen, because they do not wish to be heard. This does not constitute a serious emotional problem but it does represent a specific behavioral pattern that suggests uneasiness or shame about a function that is perfectly natural.

Another manifestation of the bashful kidney may have more serious implications. For example, an individual who is excessively curious about another person's bodily parts or nurtures fears of his own masculinity may actually avoid using a public facility. He realizes he may be discovered if he appears too curious so he stays out of public toilets.

Also, an adult who suffered a sexual assault as a child may avoid any situation which might remind him of the earlier upsetting attack or invasion on his (or her) privacy.

Attitudes towards public toileting vary among different cultures. In France, for example, public urinals can be seen on the city's streets every few blocks.

In the United States there has been a great deal of emphasis on early control of the bowel and bladder function; consequently, if this toilet training has been too severe it may elicit negative responses to toileting in the presence of others.

How does one conquer a bashful kidney? Counseling and getting to the root of the problem might do it—if one is sufficiently bothered by it to invest the time and money. Or—just forcing oneself to do that which is extremely difficult might work for some. During World War II, I am told, many men (and women) who had mildly bashful kidneys overcame the problem because they *had* to!

CREDIT: *Richard N. Rovner, M.D., Associate Professor of Clinical Neurology, Northwestern University Medical School, Chicago, Illinois.*

DEAR ANN LANDERS: I am a 20-year-old male with a very embarrassing problem. It is also depressing because I can't talk to anyone about it. Please don't tell me to go to my doctor because it is not medical. And I hope you won't suggest a shrink. Even though I know the problem is all in my head, I don't think it warrants psychiatric treatment.

I have what is commonly referred to as "a bashful kidney." I simply cannot urinate unless I have complete privacy.

Is there anything I can do about this? Can I cure myself? I'd appreciate some advice.   B.K. IN MINNESOTA

DEAR B.K.: My consultants tell me that the harder you try, the more difficulty you'll have.

Unless you can suddenly surprise yourself and relax, your best bet is to use a private stall and accept that which you cannot change.

(P.S. There are worse things in life than not being able to urinate before an audience.)

When the above letter and answer appeared in print I heard from several hundred males whose ages ranged from the early teens through the seventies, expressing relief that someone else in the world had the same problem.

I believe one of the most valuable aspects of my column is that it lets the person who has an embarrassing problem know he isn't alone. Misery does, indeed, love company.

Many men who wrote said they had "bashful kidneys" until World War II, Korea or Vietnam. "Circumstances," confessed a former corporal from Rochester, New York, "made it impossible for me to continue living with that hang-up. When I had no choice—the problem solved itself.

Kidney Disease

More than eight million Americans suffer from kidney and other diseases of the urinary tract. About 54,000 Americans die each year because of kidney disease, and more than 35,000 need the help of the kidney machine to stay alive. At least 8,000 patients are waiting for a kidney transplant but only approximately 2,000 will receive one this year because of a shortage of suitable organ donors.

The kidneys are two bean-shaped organs, each slightly larger than the palm of your hand. The vast majority of people have two kidneys, but approximately one person in four thousand is born with only one. This need be no cause of concern since one healthy kidney can carry an individual through life. This, of course, is the reason doctors can remove a healthy kidney and transplant it to a person whose kidneys have failed.

"Functioning kidneys (or their equivalent) are essential to survival. Bones can break, muscles can atrophy, glands can loaf, even the brain can go to sleep without immediate danger to survival, but should the kidneys fail, neither bone, muscle, gland nor brain could carry on." So stated Dr. Homer W. Smith, of New York University, the foremost pioneer in kidney physiology.

The function of the kidneys is to eliminate body waste which can be poisonous if retained. These wastes result from the burning of body fuel—just as gasoline in your car produces toxic fumes which must be eliminated by exhaust. If for some reason there is failure of the exhaust system (in this case the kidneys) and the toxic products remain in the body, kidney failure occurs. A second function of the kidneys is to regulate the excretion of salt and water. In some instances, failure of the kidney to do this properly may result in retention of fluid, swelling of the ankles and marked bloating of the belly.

In recent years it has become apparent that the kidney is not only a filter for the elimination of body poison but plays a major role in the regulation of blood pressure. Many doctors believe that most, if not all, high blood pressure problems involve failure of normal function of the kidney. In addition, the kidney is critically important in producing substances which control the formation of red blood cells and vitamin D.

Many kinds of kidney disease, if discovered early, can be cured. These include infection, birth defects of the kidney or bladder and obstruction by enlargement of the prostate in men, or by kidney stones in either sex.

Pain and burning on urination or frequent small voidings, blood in the urine and difficulty in starting urination are all symptoms which should be quickly investigated by a doctor. The appearance of blood in the urine, which frequently may cause the urine to look "smoky" or "coffee-colored," may also be due to tumors of the kidney or occasionally to disease formally known as Bright's disease but more properly called nephritis.

Nephritis is the inflammation of the kidney's filtering apparatus, and in some instances, this inflammation may create scarring, much the same as a scar that is left on the skin after an injury. However, in the case of the kidney, these little scars destroy the filters and if enough of them are destroyed, the result is kidney failure, and eventually uremic poisoning. This scarring accounts for two thirds of the cases of kidney failure. It is estimated that more than thirty thousand people die of this disease every year.

One of the insidious forms of nephritis is called nephrosis or nephrotic syndrome. Here the filtering apparatus of the kidney becomes damaged so that protein leaks from the blood into the urine, thus decreasing the amount of protein in the blood. When this occurs, salt and water are retained and produce swelling. This is usually first noticed by puffiness of the eyes in the morning and later by swelling of the ankles as the day wears on. It is easily diagnosed by examination of the urine, which shows large amounts of protein. Many kinds of nephrosis in the early stages are treatable.

Another form of kidney disease which is treatable, or at least preventable, is caused by taking too many headache pills or pain-killers which contain phenacetin. Large amounts of aspirin and phenacetin taken over a period of years may cause kidney disease and kidney failure. At least seven hundred cases of this disease were reported in the United States last year. This kidney disease is particularly difficult to diagnose since it may give very little in the way of signs or symptoms even on examination of the urine until failure of the kidneys is already apparent.

The problem of kidney failure is one which has become increasingly important in the past twenty-five years since there are now specific methods for keeping the patient with kidney failure alive and well. Twenty-five years ago, kidney failure led to death. Today, however, the use of an artificial kidney machine or transplantation of the kidney can mean a useful, relatively normal life even in patients who have no kidney function whatever.

The artificial kidney is perhaps the most widely used form of treatment. It can be utilized in the hospital or in ambulatory centers where people can walk in, be treated and go back to work or home. The machine can also be used at home if there is a co-operative relative or friend. In some instances, even the patient himself can be trained to use this machine. Although the treatment is expensive and must usually be done three times a week, a federal law passed in 1973 provided that anyone eligible for Social Security will have such treatment paid for with Medicare funds. At the present time, there are more than thirty thousand patients being treated with artificial kidneys.

Transplantation of a normal kidney, however, is the treatment of choice when this is possible. The major problem is that transplanting a kidney from one individual to another is, in essence, transplanting a foreign substance. We know that if a bacteria such as typhoid is injected under the skin, the body of the person who receives the bacteria develops a response which rejects the bacteria. The same thing is true to a lesser extent of human kidneys when transplanted from one person to another.

Some kidneys are more suitable for certain patients than others. For example, a kidney taken from a brother or sister does much better than a kidney from an unrelated person. Brother and sister transplants, for example, show a 95 percent survival for a two-year period. Many of these have survived for ten to twelve years. Our oldest survivor received a transplant from his brother and is now in his eighteenth year of survival and in good health.

PRACTICAL HINTS ABOUT KIDNEY DISEASE

"Floating kidney" is a medical myth. Kidneys do not float. A kidney that is loosely attached may drop when the patient stands up and may be cause for concern. Surgery to "tack the kidneys back up" may be performed but usually this is not necessary. Pain from such kidneys is unusual although some patients who know they have "floating kidneys" may worry about it and imagine they have pain.

Many patients are told that they have three kidneys and this may be disturbing. The common explanation is that one kidney is divided somewhat more than normal but only in rare instances does this create any difficulty.

Infection of the urine may come from the kidneys or the bladder. In severe cases, high fever, chills and back pain may indicate a need for immediate investigation. In many cases, the symptoms are burning on urination and frequency of urination. Many bladder infections are caused by bacteria getting into the bladder during sexual intercourse. Therefore, careful cleansing of the female genitals should be done before and after sexual relations.

Bedwetting, particularly after the age of five, should be evaluated by a kidney specialist. Although most bedwetting is caused by emotional problems it is possible that there may be an organic problem. If there is an organic problem it should be corrected promptly. Such problems not attended to may lead to total kidney failure in further adult life.

"Foul-smelling urine" may mean simply that the normal urine is highly concentrated and therefore gives off a stronger odor and is of a darker color. On occasion, it may be due to the fact that the urine sample has been left out unrefrigerated and the bacteria have gone to work.

Kidney stones remain a problem for both the doctor and the patient. In situations where the kidney stone is formed in the kidney and remains there, the patient may have no symptoms and the stone is discovered on X-ray examination. In other instances, blood in the urine may be a clue to the stone and frequently the passage of the stone from the kidney to the bladder may produce severe pain in the back and also in the groin. Many such stones are passed in the urine but others must be removed by surgery.

What can one do to keep the kidneys in good condition? Prompt attention to symptoms of infection or obstruction may reveal preventable kidney disease. Unfortunately, most forms of nephritis are not "curable" at the present time. However, more and more of these patients are being treated successfully each year and many heal with no medical attention, particularly children.

One important thing to remember about chronic nephritis is that good results can be obtained if it is diagnosed and arrested before too much of the kidney has been destroyed. Thus, the patient whose kidneys have been 50 percent destroyed still has the equivalent of one normal kidney. A healthy life is perfectly compatible with one normal kidney. In the past few years, progress in medical science has been such that more and more of these cases are being successfully treated before they reach the stage of failure requiring transplantation or treatment with an artificial kidney.

CREDIT: *John P. Merrill, M.D., Professor of Medicine, Harvard Medical School; Director of Kidney Section, Peter Bent Brigham Hospital. Dr. Merrill perfected the kidney machine in 1948 and did the first successful human dialysis in the United States. He also directed the team that performed the first successful kidney transplant in 1954.*

Kidney Donor Plan

If you needed a kidney or other vital organ to live . . . would you be able to get one?

This question can only be answered by first answering a number of other questions:

What is the present status of organ transplantation?

Advances in medical science now make it possible to replace a variety of malfunctioning human organs. For instance, since 1954 thousands of kidney transplants have taken place. Techniques for transplanting kidneys are currently the most advanced, but progress is also being made in overcoming transplantation problems connected with the liver, pancreas, heart, bone and other tissue.

How are organs for transplantation obtained?

They are donated by individuals like yourself—with the donation going into effect at the time of death.

Is there a need for organ donors?

Yes. Thousands of lives every year are lost because there aren't enough donors of kidneys and other organs. A donated organ, successfully transplanted, is literally the gift of life—your gift of life.

How can I become a donor?

Write to: National Kidney Foundation
            P. O. Box 353
            New York, New York 10016

Is there an age requirement for donors?

Yes. Anyone eighteen years of age or over and of sound mind may become a donor by signing the card. An individual under eighteen years of age may become a donor if either parent or legal guardian gives consent.

Do I have to register with some agency?

No. Your signed and witnessed donor card is all that is needed.

Do I have to mention the organ donation in my will?

No. Your donor card is a kind of "pocket will" and is all you need. Mention it in your will if you wish. But obviously it's important to carry the card and also inform your family and physician to ensure their co-operation.

Can I change my mind later?

Yes. Simply tear up the card. Nothing else is necessary.

Can I be sure my gift will be used?

Yes, if circumstances permit and the organ donation can be used to benefit the health and life of another person.

When will my gift be used?

For purposes of transplantation, organs must ordinarily be removed within an hour after death. According to the Uniform Anatomical Gift Act (the "model law" that governs such matters in the states), the physician in attend-ance has the responsibility for determing that life has ceased and that the donor's wishes may now be carried out. The Act specifies, however, that the physician attending the dying person should not participate either in the removal process or in transplantation. That's the job of the hospital and the transplant team.

Will organ donation affect funeral and burial arrangements?

No. Removal of organs or tissue authorized by the donor will not interfere with customary funeral or burial arrangements. If a person wills his body to a medical center for anatomical study (line "c" on the donor card), arrangements must be made in advance with the particular medical center.

Will my estate be paid or have to pay for organ donation?

No.

What are the ethics of organ donation and transplantation?

Moral leaders the world over favor such donations as expressions of the highest humanitarian ideals. The gift of an organ essential to the life of another human being is consistent with virtually all religious and ethical groups. If you have any question in this regard, consult your religious leader.

What does the future hold?

As the problem of organ rejection comes under better control and as techniques for tissue-typing and organ preservation are improved, kidney and other transplants will become increasingly feasible. Thus, thousands of people who might otherwise die will live.

What else can I do to advance this life-preserving program?

Acquaint others with the donor card program. The more donors available, the more this new and important medical advance can be used for the benefit of mankind. Learn more about organ donation. Your Kidney Foundation will be happy to give you more information and to provide donor cards.

CREDIT: *National Kidney Foundation, 116 East 27th Street, New York, New York.*

Kissing

HITTING A FUNNY NOTE

DEAR ANN LANDERS: Tom Kiene, who produces a lively column for the Topeka Capitol Journal, wrote something recently that you might want to share with your readers. Here it is:

"What worries Ann Landers concerns us, too. One of her correspondents, age 19, was contemplating marriage with a French horn player. She was dismayed because her fiance refused to kiss her. He kept insisting that his lips were his only means of livelihood and he had to protect them. Said Ann, opting for the practical, 'Tell him good-by and find a guy who plays the violin.'

"Other side effects of dating a French horn player are astonishing, if not deleterious, as reported to us by John Beatty, a former press secretary to Sen. Jim Pearson. He told of a couple of Washington girls who were exchanging confidences on the kissing technique of musicians.

" 'I believe,' offered one, 'the French horn player is best.' 'Well, maybe,' concluded the other. 'But he sure does hold you funny.' " WE LOVE YOU IN TOPEKA

DEAR LOVE: Thanks for my laugh for the day. And please say hello to Tom Kiene. He's one of my oldest friends in the business—or I should say one of my best friends of long standing.

No one knows for sure when, how or why kissing started. One theory that sounds reasonable is that the first kisses were between cavemen and cavewomen, regardless of sex—licking the cheeks of their relatives and neighbors for the salt.

The early Christians were instructed by St. Paul to "greet one another with a holy kiss." Knights kissed before doing battle, just as boxers touch gloves before a fight. Lovers have kissed from the beginning of recorded history. Promises are sealed with a kiss. Children ask their mommies and daddies to kiss skinned knees, or a bump on the head to "make it well."

The late Mayor Richard J. Daley of Chicago said on live TV when criticized for giving the city's insurance business to the firm that employed his son, "What's wrong with a father helping his son? If the critics don't like it they can kiss my ass."

The custom of kissing varies from country to country. In the Arab lands the men greet each other with a kiss. Italian and French men may sometimes do this also. (Usually its both cheeks in France.) The Orientals consider kissing in public bad manners. The British are not big social kissers. The Russians, Greeks and Slavic people kiss hello and goodbye publicly without the slightest hint of embarrassment.

In the United States, there is a great deal of kissing of every imaginable kind. *Time* magazine, February 7, 1977, in an article called "The Great Kissing Epidemic" by Lance Morrow, quoted sociologist Murray Davis of the University of California at San Diego: "Increased kissing is a part of the general inflation of intimate signals. We kiss people we used to hug, hug people we used to shake hands with, and shake hands with people we used to nod to. Not to kiss or hug means one is not 'relating.' Isolated individualism is out. Today separation is not allowed. Everyone is expected to kiss everyone else."

There is no question but that kissing can spread disease. Mononucleosis is in fact called "the kissing disease."

Dr. Leslie Nicholas, president of the American V.D. Association, wrote on April 15, 1977, admonishing me for giving "incomplete and somewhat misleading" advice. I had told "Alpena": "It is indeed possible to get syphilis if you kiss a person who has an open chancre on his lip, tongue or in his mouth —if you have a cracked lip or a cut on your tongue or in your mouth."

According to Dr. Nicholas, "in the act of enthusiastic kissing, enough cells of the superficial layers of the lips or other parts may be so abraded as to permit the germs of syphilis to enter without a cracked lip." Dr. Nicholas continued: "With the increases of oral sexual activity presently practiced, you should warn your readers to address themselves to these four questions:

(1) Whom are you kissing?
(2) How are you kissing?
(3) What are you kissing?
(4) Where are you kissing?

CREDIT: *Ann Landers.*

AN OLDIE HE THINKS IS A GOODIE

DEAR ANN: I stayed home from work today because I had the flu. My wife went to the drugstore, so I answered the phone. Some man must have been trying to call the Coast Guard and got us by mistake. He wanted to know if the coast was clear. When I told my wife, she got rattled. What do you think, Annie? BENZIE

DEAR B.: I kicked the slats out of my cradle when I heard that joke for the first time, and I'm no kid. Your letter came from Boston. I trust you made the dean's list, Buddy.

Kvetching

Complaining

IF IN KALAMAZOO, IT HELPS TO HAVE A BIG OPERATION

DEAR ANN LANDERS: A few months ago I moved to Kalamazoo, Mich., from Grand Rapids. Although the cities are not far apart it's like a different world.

I have always been involved with church and club work. In Grand Rapids, I was active in many groups and the women were lovely. I've met some fine women here in Kalamazoo but they are older and seem to be pre-occupied with their illnesses and operations. I attended a lunch meeting this afternoon and the conversation was a rehash of everyone's surgery. One woman told about her ovarian cyst, "the size of a lemon." Another woman described her uterine tumor as "big as a grapefruit." A third lady, not to be outdone, said her fibroid was the largest the doctor had ever seen—"as big as a watermelon."

Such topics are boring and unappetizing. I've tried without success to turn the conversations to more uplifting subjects. What do you suggest? NEW IN TOWN

DEAR NEW: I've been to Kalamazoo and I can tell you there are many women there who can talk about something besides their operations.

If you are fed up with "organ recitals" (and who can blame you), find new friends. There are all kinds of women everywhere. People, like water, seek their own level.

DEAR ANN LANDERS: If you say I am super-critical and overly-sensitive, I will take your word for it. My husband and I are having a sharp disagreement over something and you are going to settle it.

Last night we were invited to a dinner party. The hostess is a good person. She would give anyone the shirt off her back. But she manages to turn every conversation into what you call "an organ recital." We are all sick to death of listening to her physical complaints. I call her "Mrs. Kvetch." (Not to her face, of course.)

"Mrs. Kvetch" had an operation for gallstones six weeks ago. The entire cocktail hour was devoted to the details of her operation—down to the last stitch. When she brought out the bottle of her gallstones and passed it around, I was appalled. Plus viewing the stones we had to listen to her doctor's appraisal . . . "The largest he had ever seen."

Needless to say, I had no appetite for dinner. (My husband had two helpings of everything.) What do you think about a hostess who would monopolize the entire cocktail hour with talk of her operation and display her gallstones at a dinner party?   STILL NOT HUNGRY

DEAR S.N.H.: I'm with you. In fact, I think I'll have an apple for lunch. Thanks for writing.

Laughter and Wet Pants

Wet pants is no laughing matter, especially if you are an adult woman out for an evening, socializing with friends. This is a problem I hear about frequently, and almost everyone who writes thinks she is the only one who has it. (I say "she" because I don't believe I have ever had an inquiry about this problem from a male.)

According to several urologists with whom I consulted, "stress incontinence" (a fancy term for "can't hold it") must first be differentiated from a constant wetness or dribbling, which has more serious implications. A physician's evaluation should be sought if there is any question.

Stress incontinence is common in women as a result of childbirth. It is caused by a general weakening and sagging of the muscle slings which normally hold the bladder, rectum, vaginal walls and uterus up in place. The control muscles are simply not strong enough to hold back against the sudden surge of pressure caused by sneezing, coughing, laughing, jumping or coming down from a high step.

Two things can help. First—more frequent emptying of the bladder. (Some people, especially teenage girls, are "too busy" to go.) Women who have a tendency to wet their pants when they laugh hard should urinate before they leave the house and as soon after as possible when they get to where they are going.

The second thing: Exercise the muscles and strengthen them. Here are the instructions: When you begin to urinate, make yourself stop, then start again. Then stop, and start again—all the while exercising the muscles that control the starting and stopping mechanism.

According to my consultants, this is exclusively a female problem. Any male who wets his pants during the day needs a thorough checkup by a urologist to determine the cause.

CREDIT: *Russell Roth, M.D., Attending Urologist, St. Vincent Health Center, Erie, Pennsylvania.*

HOLD IT . . . BUT SHE CAN'T WHEN SHE LAUGHS

DEAR ANN LANDERS: You will probably think this letter is a fake, but I give you my word of honor it is real.

I am 15 years old—a girl. In the last year or so, I have had a problem that has caused me a lot of embarrassment. Whenever I laugh hard I wet my pants.

Lately it has been happening almost every other day, but so far only with girl friends. If it should happen when I am with a boy, I would just die.

I asked my mother what to do about it, and she said it would go away and not to worry—that she had the same problem when she was my age.

Can you give me some advice? NORMAL OR WHAT?

DEAR N.O.W.: I took your problem to a top-notch urologist, Dr. Russell B. Roth of Erie, Pa. He called it "stress incontinence"—a fancy name for not being able to hold it.

According to Roth, this condition is common among women who have had children and experienced a general weakening of the muscle slings that normally hold the bladder in place. When these muscles become weakened, they cannot do the job of protecting against a sudden surge of pressure caused by coughing, sneezing, laughing, jumping or coming down from a high step.

First you should be examined by a urologist to make sure you don't have an organic problem. (Chances are very good that you don't.) If you are OK physically, the trouble is that you let your bladder get too full. (Some teenagers drink a lot of milk or pop and get too busy to go.)

The remedy is twofold. One: Empty your bladder more frequently. Two: Exercise the muscles of control by starting and stopping the urine flow voluntarily—several times a day. This should solve the problem.

DEAR ANN LANDERS: I have this friend who would give me the shirt off her back. She's the kindest, most considerate person I know, but she has a habit that drives me crazy. Maybe if I understood it better I could be more tolerant.

Mrs. X laughs constantly—in the middle of sentences—at the end of sentences—during moments of silence —she gives out with that little laugh that gets on my nerves.

I once had a teacher like that and couldn't figure her out either. Is there some explanation for people who laugh when nothing is funny? CLENCHED FISTS AND GRINDING TEETH

DEAR FISTS AND TEETH: Laughter can be something other than a response to amusement. It is a way to relieve tension. People who are ill at ease, embarrassed, self-conscious or at a loss for words often laugh. Laughter is better than silence, they figure, even though it may be inappropriate.

Teenagers who are struggling to master social graces laugh a lot. It's the same thing.

Lawyers

How to Select One

Law is becoming an increasingly specialized profession. The lawyer who seems highly skilled in handling the purchase of a home may be of little help in a divorce case or as a criminal defense attorney. Anyone who needs a lawyer must take this into account.

Finding an attorney who is competent to handle a particular matter requires the same sort of exploration as finding the "right" doctor. Relatives, friends or co-workers may be able to supply the name of a lawyer who has satisfactorily handled a similar matter for them. A lawyer who is highly regarded by a friend or acquaintance, if he himself is unfamiliar with the type of problem involved, may suggest a competent fellow practitioner.

If these approaches are not successful, the local bar association can be consulted. Many bar associations provide a lawyer referral service which offers a list of attorneys capable of handling particular types of problems. Then, too, it is wise to make appointments with several lawyers to discuss the problem and the amount of the fee. In most cases, there will be no charge for an initial consultation unless the lawyer is retained to proceed with the matter. Be sure to ask if there will be a charge for the consultation when you phone for an appointment.

Although lawyers are now permitted to advertise routine legal services, very few have done so. Many of the advertisements are for legal clinics, of which there are two basic types.

The first type of legal clinic is associated with a law school and is staffed by law students. These clinics do not charge a regular fee. They base their charges on the income of the potential client. Often they will not handle a case if the client can afford a regular attorney. Law school clinics are useful in dealing with routine matters, but will usually refuse more complicated cases. Most law school clinics will not draft wills, handle real estate transactions, bring suits for personal injuries or defend traffic or criminal cases. Such clinics are also frequently associated with legal aid bureaus whose purpose is to serve, without fee, people who cannot pay.

The second form of legal clinic is a private organization of practicing attorneys. These clinics are less likely to have an income limit for their clients, and will often take on complicated matters. Just as with other lawyers, however, they may not be equipped to deal with problems of particular types. Be sure to ask your lawyer whether he has had experience with your type of problem.

Some courts maintain through bar associations an in-court referral service. There are also special services for defense of prisoners. In some situations a legal problem may involve sums of money which are less than the fees a lawyer would be obliged to charge to handle the matter. Most states now have a pro se court which is intended to handle small claims, and where the presence of a lawyer is neither necessary nor encouraged. Information about small claims procedures can usually be obtained by calling the local courthouse and discussing the matter with a representative of the clerk's office.

When a lawyer is obtained, it is necessary that both the client and the lawyer understand their roles and responsibilities. The fee arrangement, in particular, should be covered and either a letter or a contract should be prepared to prevent misunderstanding.

There are three basic types of fee arrangements. First, many simple legal matters, such as the drafting of wills and the handling of real estate transactions, may be covered by a fixed charge. Second, suits for personal injuries and similar claims may be charged for on a "contingent fee" basis. This means that if the client wins the case, the lawyer receives a certain percentage of the amount recovered. If the client loses, however, the lawyer receives little or nothing. Many states require that such arrangements be formally agreed to in a signed contract and it is mandatory in federal courts. Third, there may be an hourly charge for the amount of time a lawyer (or his associates) works on a case. This arrangement is commonly used in complicated transactions or by large law firms. The client is entitled to the lawyer's best estimate of the cost in advance, but should recognize that unforeseen complications may make the estimate obsolete. Remember, since most lawyers do not record their time in segments of less than a quarter hour, a few short phone calls can be quite costly.

Any lawyer should inform his or her client of the progress being made and should also provide copies of important documents or court papers. Civil suits, particularly in large cities, may take years to come to trial; and during much of this time, little or nothing may happen. The client should recognize that this does not mean the lawyer has forgotten the case; but on the other hand the client should be advised of significant developments. Most lawyers are competent professionals who cannot guarantee success (particularly if the case goes to court) but whose responsibility it is to protect their client's interests.

Finally, it is an old maxim that the lawyer who represents himself has a fool for a client. The same is true of the client who retains a lawyer and then tries to handle the case himself.

CREDIT: *Morris I. Leibman, Attorney, Sidley and Austin, Chicago, Illinois.*

Leprosy

Leprosy is a word that even today, among enlightened people, creates feelings of fear and revulsion. This goes back to the biblical interpretation.

Before much was known about medical science, the Bible was used as the basis for evaluating and treating all diseases. Ignorance abounded and hygiene was poor. Many practices were declared sinful in order to get people to take better care of themselves.

When the Bible was translated into Greek, the word "leprosy" came into being. *Lepra* is the Greek word for skin disease. (In those days, all skin diseases were called leprosy.) Since many skin diseases (under poor hygienic conditions) were contagious, anyone who had a visible skin problem was banished from society. People fled when they saw a "leper" coming. "Unclean," they would shout—and toss a few coins. Lepers were easy to identify because in the advanced stages (before drugs) a leper was a revolting sight. Their hands became claw-like and parts of the face and body were eaten away.

There was no good definition of leprosy until about 1820, when it was defined sharply by Danielsson, a Norwegian. The organism that causes leprosy was isolated fifty years later by G. Armauer Hansen, and leprosy is now called Hansen's disease.

Estimates on the total number of cases in the world range from five to twelve million. No country has been completely free of leprosy, but six countries account for 85 percent of the total. These countries are China, Congo (Kinshasa), India, Indonesia, Japan and Nigeria. There are about two thousand cases in the United States but nearly half of these patients were born in other countries where they probably contracted the disease. In the United States, the disease occurs chiefly in California, Florida, Louisiana, Texas and Hawaii. Canada once had some cases in Nova Scotia and New Brunswick; however, the disease has almost disappeared from Canada.

Scientists believe the germ escapes from infected persons in discharges from nose and skin sores. It is possible that the germ enters the bodies of healthy people through breaks or cuts in the skin. Leprosy is contagious but the danger of getting it has been wildly exaggerated. Relatively few people exposed to the disease ever get it. To get leprosy, a person must have low resistance, poor nutrition, and live in close contact with a person who has an advanced case. In instances involving married patients who continued to live with a spouse, fewer than 5 percent of the spouses were infected. It is rare for a nurse or physician who attends to a patient to get the disease. A person who has been exposed may not get the disease for several months or in some instances for as long as twenty years. The average incubation period is from six to eight years.

Scientists believe that children are more likely to get leprosy than adults. A mild form of the disease may develop in about 30 percent of the children whose parents have severe cases. But leprosy persists in only about 20 percent of these children.

There are two major kinds of leprosy—tuberculoid and lepromatous. Tuberculoid leprosy produces patchy spots on the body but may cause inflamed nerves. Patients with this type seldom spread the disease to others.

Lepromatous leprosy causes a general thickening of the skin over most of the body, especially on the face and ear lobes. Facial lines deepen and the eyebrows fall out. Lumps appear on the skin. When the germs enter the eyes they cause a painful inflammation—and in severe cases, blindness.

Leprosy usually affects the nerve ends of the face, arms and legs. Nerve damage may cause a loss of feeling. A leprosy patient may burn himself without realizing it. Severe nerve damage may also cause paralysis.

Scientists cannot yet grow the leprosy bacillus on substances outside living things, but they have been able to grow the bacillus in the ears of hamsters and on the footpads of mice. Growing the germ is important so we can learn (1) exactly how the germ is passed from one person to another, (2) test drugs that might destroy the germ and (3) develop a vaccine to prevent the disease.

Since 1941 the use of drugs in the sulfone group has been very useful in controlling the disease and restricting its spread.

Many people fail to realize that leprosy often is a mild disease that may be arrested without treatment. Skin discoloration may disappear or leave only faint traces. If the disease is not checked, however, severe nerve damage can cause muscles in the hands and feet to become weak. As a result, the fingers and toes may curl inward. Early treatment is important to prevent deformities and other physical handicaps. Proper treatment can help these people lead an almost normal life. Bone and tendon surgery often helps to restore the use of disabled hands and feet.

Leprosy becomes inactive in almost all patients who undergo treatment from three to five years or more. But the cure is not always permanent. To prevent the disease from returning, patients must consult their doctors at least twice a year and continue to take drugs. These patients can be employed without any fear that they will spread the disease to others.

Until the late 1940s, any patient who was found to have leprosy was isolated in special hospitals called leprosariums. The United States Public Health Service maintains such a place in Carville, Louisiana.

An individual who has the disease can safely be cared for at home, or in a hospital with almost no risk to his family, the hospital staff, other patients or colleagues at work.

It is high time the public dropped the centuries-old concept of lepers born of ignorance. Individuals stricken with this illness should no longer be stigmatized and discriminated against. Today a victim of Hansen's disease is much less a threat to the classroom or community than a person with VD. In fact, the chances for getting VD are infinitely greater.

I visited a leprosarium in 1960 on New Providence Island near Nassau and saw many victims of the disease in various stages of deterioration. (Unfortunately, they contracted the illness before the sulfone drugs came into existence.) Some of the patients were extremely unsightly but all were gracious and visibly delighted that a person from "the outside" would have the courage to come and visit them.

I felt very good about that visit but confess when I returned to the hotel I scrubbed myself from head to toe—"just in case"—additional proof that although we know something intellectually we sometimes cannot accept it emotionally.

CREDIT: *Robert Stolar, M.D., Clinical Professor of Dermatology, Georgetown University School of Medicine, Washington, D.C. World Book Encyclopedia.*

The Liberated Woman
or
The Career Woman in a Changing Society

Surely by now the full-time career woman who is also a wife and mother cannot have anything to complain about. Society supports her efforts entirely. It is "good" for her to satisfy her need for achievement outside the home. Her children will profit by her independence, her husband will feel supported (emotionally, and perhaps financially) by her efforts. With everything going her way, what, if any, problems could possibly exist? Plenty!

Society is still in a state of transition in its attitudes towards and support of the full-time career woman who also invests herself fully in the roles of Wife and Mother. This transitional state has been described from a variety of viewpoints. Statistics about working mothers, research on the dynamics of marital relationships in a dual career family and psychological studies of the effectiveness of the career woman, etc., abound in social science, literature and popular magazines. While these are all valid approaches, I am especially interested in exploring what it *feels* like to be a career woman in a changing society.

This, then, is a report from a participant-observer, based largely on my own experiences but incorporating those of friends, colleagues, students and patients. Although the details of my career and family situation probably differ from those of other career women, I suspect that the feelings my associates and I experience are all too common. For the record, I am a psychologist with a full-time faculty appointment in a department of psychiatry in a large midwestern medical school where my professional activities include research, teaching and psychotherapy. I am also the wife of a professor and the mother of two children, a kindergartener and an infant. With the exception of six weeks off with the birth of each child, I have worked full time since completing a Ph.D. degree six years ago. Although I have no intention of reducing my workload in any of these areas in the future, I have considered the cost/benefit of this lifestyle and find that the price by any standards is high. To me, the decision to have a full-time career or a spouse or children (or any combination thereof) is highly personal, and the reader who seeks advice on which combination is "best" won't find it here.

Clearly there are advantages to a full-time career. Economic independence (whether actual or potential) is a prime consideration. The range of benefits from this alone is staggering—for example, the ability to contribute financially to the family as well as the freedom to consider ending an unsatisfactory marriage.

Feelings of independence, satisfaction and self-actualization are today's possible harvest for the career woman. In addition, feelings of competence and effectiveness can also be a heady brew. Ideally, these feelings can be derived from both career and family life; for example, organizational efficiency in managing a project at the office is not very different from the efficiency required to co-ordinate the Saturday logistics of car-pooling for music lessons, errand running and dinner party preparation.

On the other hand, life is rarely ideal. The hours of satisfaction are frequently bought by weeks of drudgery—emotional as well as physical. Some of the more commonly acknowledged disadvantages of attempting the impossible, such as combining several full-time activities, include lack of time for oneself (soaking in a hot tub of water is absolutely out), being unable to complete a task begun and—of course—physical exhaustion.

A different kind of disadvantage is the feeling of rage and resentment at the subtle (and sometimes not so subtle) discrimination at the office—being denied leadership in a project "because we were sure you didn't want to go out of town," or being asked to take on a larger workload "because you're so efficient at that kind of thing." Life in the changing society has not yet eliminated discrimination against the career woman—it has only been disguised.

In spite of the advantages of independence and autonomy that the career woman has, it is ironic that in some ways, she is forced to become even more dependent on others. The 7 A.M. call from the child-care provider saying she (or he) can't take the children today or the message from the weekly cleaning lady (sexist again?) canceling her commitment for three weeks because she has decided to take an unscheduled vacation are events familiar to every career woman with children and a semi-chaotic household. The system overload is on the woman who works full time, often coming from logistical breakdowns at home. The pressures at work are traumatic enough. When combined with criticism from other women who have chosen other lifestyles about "escaping one's responsibility to stay home and raise her own children," the load can become too much and the career woman may succumb to feelings of defeat and ultimately depression.

All of the above disadvantages have been mentioned by other writers, but there is yet another disadvantage rarely discussed—one that I have come to recognize only in the past few years. I refer to the feeling of apartness, of separateness from others. It is not loneliness but rather the sense of being different and unlike anyone else in practically all situations. Perhaps this sense of apartness could also be interpreted as uniqueness, and one might then wonder why it draws a negative rather than a positive response. A common example of this feeling of apartness is in a male-dominated sphere such as a medical school faculty where questions or statements by female faculty members seem to be challenged more frequently—or worse yet, ignored. The feeling of apartness includes some elements of exclusion, probably based on outdated and inappropriate mores about male-female relationships. Long-term relationships between male and female co-workers are highly suspect, and the availability of a mentor, especially in a highly competitive environment, is sheer fantasy on the part of any aspiring career woman.

Other elements make up this feeling of aloneness. In relating to other career women, even those in one's own specialty, interests and degree of investment rarely overlap sufficiently for close camaraderie. Many professional colleagues have chosen not to marry and/or not to have children. Others do not share the same interests outside of work and home (such as music, weaving, politics, etc.).

Finally, this feeling of aloneness may be exacerbated by a conscious decision by the career woman to generate more aloneness. A promising friendship with another woman may not be pursued because building that friendship requires time, and time is of prime consideration in any career woman's life. Priorities must be set and acted on unswervingly or the full-time career woman may find herself the victim of chaos.

It is doubtful that this feeling of aloneness can be alleviated by society. It does seem possible, however, that as the number of full-time career women who are also heavily invested in family roles increases, there will be more opportunity to share in solving this and other disadvantages described above. It should be obvious that a woman who chooses (or is forced) to combine several full-time and competing roles is inevitably entering an arena of great potential for both fulfillment and pain. The woman herself must weigh the advantages and disadvantages, with the knowledge that in today's changing society none of the alternatives can be described as "the best."

CREDIT: *Judith McKinnon Garrard, Ph.D., Department of Psychiatry, University of Minnesota Medical School, Minneapolis, Minnesota.*

Life Insurance

Insurance Information for Women

Life insurance makes sense for any woman, married or single, who feels she has economic responsibilities.

Deciding on what kind of and how much life insurance to buy can be a problem for the uninformed woman.

Term insurance and whole life insurance are the two basic kinds of life insurance policies. Term guarantees your beneficiaries a sum of money if you die within a stated period. Whole life or "straight life" combines insurance with "savings."

Because term insurance is so much cheaper than whole life, it is an excellent buy for someone who needs immediate protection but can't spend much. On the other hand, a woman whose beneficiaries do not need the large amount of protection required by, say, the children of a widow or divorcee might buy a whole life policy, especially if she finds it hard to save on her own. Here she gets some insurance protection for her family if she dies, plus forced savings, if she lives, that will be available to her, say, at retirement, in the form of cash values.

Avoid two typical mistakes. Don't be tempted to buy so much insurance that the premiums are more than you can comfortably afford, or you may be forced to drop the policy within a few years. And be wary about switching

from one whole life policy to another even if a better-sounding deal is offered
later on. Cash and loan values build up very slowly during the first two or
three years you own a whole life policy but fairly quickly afterward. Therefore, switching to a new policy will almost always cost you more money in
the "lost" cash or loan values that you would have otherwise earned on your
old policy than you will save if you buy a new one.

CREDIT: *Barbara Gilder Quint, "How to Get More for Your Money,"* Glamour
magazine. Reprinted from Sola.

Life Insurance*

What Every Wife Should Know

"Nobody but a life insurance salesman likes to think about life insurance. It's
depressing and complex and mystifying, wrapped in nearly incomprehensible
language. So it's not surprising that most Americans have no idea how much
they need. Most are dangerously underinsured. Even Herbert Denenberg, the
insurance commissioner of Pennsylvania, has never calculated how much he
should have. He confesses: 'When I bought it I didn't sit down and figure it
out.'

"Agents sometimes suggest rules of thumb for calculating proper life insurance coverage; they say that the husband should have four or five times his
annual income in insurance, or that 5 percent of his salary should go for life
insurance premiums. But such guidelines are worthless, because individual
needs vary greatly. A rich, elderly man with only his wife dependent on him
may not need anything like five times his income in insurance, but a young
man with a modest salary and a houseful of children may need more.

"Sometimes there is a special need—providing money to pay the death
taxes on a large estate, for instance, or protecting a partnership interest in a
business. But the usual reason for buying life insurance is to make certain
that there is enough capital to do the things a husband's income now does for
the family. Since no one knows when he will die, and since insurance is meant
to cover untimely death, the only sound assumption is that the husband will
die tomorrow. If he does, how much capital will it take to replace his income?
To arrive at the answer, the family needs to consider how many dependents
there are, how long they will remain dependent, how well they are to be provided for and what other resources they will have. Then it becomes a rela-

tively simple matter to lay out the family's needs—the immediate cash needs first, and then the future income needs—and calculate how much capital, or insurance, will meet those needs. Many insurers have developed computer programs for working out insurance plans."*

A wife should know there are many kinds of insurance and they serve different purposes. In this article we will distinguish between two major types of coverages; one that insures things (house, auto, jewels, etc.) against catastrophes that *may* happen, such as fire, accident and theft; and a second that insures persons against occurrences, at least one of which positively *will* happen, such as illness or death.

It has been observed that many wives are eager to have their homes, cars and jewelry insured and suggest that their husbands purchase insurance to cover these valuables. Strangely enough, we rarely hear of wives urging their husbands to buy life insurance.

In this discussion we would like to show the role a wife can play in helping her husband decide how best to protect his family should he become disabled or meet an untimely death. Her role is far more critical than she might realize. If her husband dies she will have to become strong and decisive. If she puts these traits into practice when he is in good health many future heartaches will be eliminated.

First of all, she must be open and candid in her willingness to discuss the fact that a husband owes it to his family to discuss the problems that would be created by his untimely death. Once the subject is opened it is relatively easy to discuss it. Unfortunately, many husbands think the topic would be stressful so they don't bring it up. So, step number one for a wife is to initiate a discussion about the income required to support the family should death or catastrophic illness occur.

When we talk of life and health insurance, we refer primarily to "income replacement" insurance. Such insurance can be studied, analyzed and purchased just as one would approach the purchase of any tangible item. These questions should be answered:

(1) What do we absolutely need to maintain our family in a minimum standard of living?

(2) How much would it cost to permit the family to continue to live in the manner to which they have become accustomed if death or catastrophic illness should strike?

(3) How should we pay for it?

(4) What options are available?

It is possible through premium life insurance to spread the costs of an untimely death over the entire lifetime of the insured, even if that lifetime is very short. There is a source from which information is available to determine how much a husband is worth—thanks to an extremely talented profes-

* Excerpted from "How Much Life Insurance is Enough" by Jeremy Main, *Money* magazine, January 1974, by special permission; © 1974 Time, Inc.

sor who taught at the University of Pennsylvania for nearly fifty years. Dr. Solomon S. Huebner became known as "the Teacher Who Changed an Industry." For its first fifty years the life insurance industry provided coverage on a "cost to die" basis; that is, people were encouraged to buy enough insurance to pay their taxes, bills and burial expenses. Dr. Huebner created a formula for determining "human life values" which is still in use today and is frequently used in court to place a "value" on a person who is injured or killed in an accident.

The Huebner method makes it possible for a husband and wife to sit down with a qualified professional life insurance person and determine exactly what it would require to keep a widow and her family in "their world" when her husband dies.

How do you make such a contract without exposing yourself to the pressures of a "come on strong" salesperson? It's simple if you go about it properly. Although there are over 400,000 people licensed to sell life insurance in America, there are some professional standards which identify those who are competent. I would not consider discussing insurance with anyone who is not a member of the National Association of Life Underwriters. This professional organization has a code of ethics and it has local associations which breed professionalism.

Closely allied to NALU is the Life Underwriter Training Council (LUTCO), the Million Dollar Round Table (MDRT), the American Society of Chartered Life Underwriters (CLU) and the Association for Advanced Life Underwriters (AALU). Any person who is a member of any one of these organizations is qualified to serve you.

How does such a professional go about determining your husband's "human life value"? It's relatively simple. Ask yourself:

(1) What do we absolutely need to maintain our family on a minimum standard of living?
   (a) What does it cost us to live now per month?
   (b) What would it cost without my husband as a "consumer"?
(2) What would be required to permit the family to continue to live in "their own world"?
   (a) Today's income less that used by the breadwinner?
(3) How much would it cost?
   (a) To provide "today's income" for X years would cost Y dollars?
(4) How should we pay for it?
   (a) There are plans to fit many situations. Examine them all.
(5) What are all the options available?
   (a) Don't be confused by the different jargon life insurance people use such as "term," "ordinary life," "limited pay life," etc. Just determine what you need and what you can afford to pay. There are enough options available to fit almost every conceivable case.

It is a determinable fact that there is such a commodity as a "human life value." When a human life is extinguished the personal value is lost forever, but the financial commitments of the deceased live on. The future must be paid for. It can be paid for in dollars deposited with an insurance company in advance of death, or it can be paid for by a mother who must go to work every day—not because she wants to—but because she has to, or by the student who drops out of college not because he wants to, but because he must go to work and help support the family.

Many people over forty can remember that when death took a husband and father, his family moved in with relatives. Although they faced many hardships they had a place to live and at least a semblance of the life they once knew.

When death strikes the head of the household in today's mobile society, the option of moving in with the in-laws is not very desirable. There is not enough room in most urban households, lifestyles are different and privacy is richly treasured.

It's too late to plan your future after death strikes. Every wife should make a commitment to review her husband's "human life value" with a competent professional life insurance person. All members of the family will profit in terms of peace of mind.

CREDIT: *Frank Sullivan, President, the Mutual Benefit Life Insurance Company, Newark, New Jersey.*

Lightning

(*How to Keep from Being Struck*)

DEAR ANN LANDERS: A neighbor of mine was struck by lightning last Friday. She was buried today.

I never knew anyone who had been killed by lightning before. Her tragic death got me to thinking. I wonder how many people would know what to do if they should get caught in an electrical storm. I'm not sure I would know. Will you please spell out some Do's and Don'ts for your readers? Thanks, Ann.   SAD NEIGHBOR

DEAR NEIGHBOR: First the Don'ts:

(1) Don't stand under a lone tree.

(2) If you are swimming or fishing, get out of the water as fast as you can.

(3) Get off bicycles, golf carts or motorcycles immediately.

(4) Don't touch anything metal, such as a wire fence, a golf club or a flag-pole. Metal objects attract lightning.

Now the Do's:

Get out of the storm promptly and go into a building or a closed automobile.

If you are in the woods, crouch in a low area under dense brush.

If you feel your hair stand on end (an indication that you are about to be struck) fall to your knees and place your hands on your knees to reduce the chances of your body acting as a conductor.

Please note: The most frequent victims are farmers, fishermen, golfers and cyclists.

LIGHTNING STRIKES AGAIN

DEAR ANN LANDERS: In a recent column you said the safest place to be during an electrical storm is in a car. A number of years ago the National Geographic Society published the results of extensive experimentation with relation to the action of lightning. A car with the driver inside was repeatedly struck with a million volts of man-made lightning. The man in the car suffered no injuries whatsoever.

The tests proved that if only the tires touched the ground and there were no loose parts or other objects in con-tact with the earth, and if the occupants did not allow any part of their bodies to touch the metal parts of the car, they could not be injured.

The National Geographic Society further concluded that the three safest places to be during a lightning storm are (1) in the furnace (2) in the refrigerator and (3) in a car. CLIFFORD H.S.

DEAR CLIFF: Thank you for the supportive evidence.

Living Together

(*The Legal Consequences*)

Unlike marriage, which has legal rights and duties, single people living together do so without the state's approval. When they decide to split they can —without a judge's intervention.

In fact, living together single doesn't even have a proper name. It is *not* common law marriage. Common law marriage is the lawful union of man and woman by declaration, intention and conduct which, in about fifteen states, can be severed only by death or divorce.

Single people living together do not pretend to be married nor do they consider themselves married. They are single, proud of it and are just plain living together, having sex and exchanging services. The law has a label for such an arrangement. It is called "consortium." So let's call the new relationship consortium and the parties to it "consorts."

Regardless of your feelings on the subject, there is no doubt that consorts have distinct advantages and disadvantages under the law.

Everyone, married or single, who earns a minimum income must pay federal income tax based on a graduated scale. This means the more money one earns, the higher the bracket he is in. Because of the graduated scale, those who earn high incomes are always trying to find ways to split their incomes and lower their taxes.

The most common way to get the benefits of an income split is through the means Congress provided—the joint income tax return. So long as there's substantial difference between the income of one taxpayer and the income of his spouse, filing a joint tax return generally saves, because it splits the higher income among two taxpayers, which lowers the percentage taxed. But the joint income tax return is available to married people—not single people or consorts.

Married couples, however, face a disadvantage that consorts do not. Married couples get only *one* standard deduction. Consorts, since the IRS considers them single taxpayers, each get his and her own standard deduction.

In dollars and cents, this means a *married* couple, both working, one earning $10,000 a year, the other earning $17,000, taking the standard deduction, will pay about $700 more in federal income tax than the same couple living together single.

While love and income taxes can help in determining whether consortium is what you're after, nothing does more to test the desire to stay together and the extent of commitment than the way you handle your money once you start living together.

Married couples, except for a little holding out, usually put the cash and property in a common pot. The status of marriage allows the husband and wife to charge their family-type expenses or "necessaries" to each other's accounts. This means a wife can charge groceries and the grocer can collect from either husband or wife, whichever the grocer chooses. These rights, incorporated in "family expense laws," are creditor's rights predicated on the marriage relationship. But lawful matrimony is not always required. If a couple holds itself out as married, call each other Mr. and Mrs., charge freely on each other's credit, then one of the pair cannot skip out on his financial obligation by simply claiming on the courthouse steps that he is not married and therefore "not responsible for his (or her) debts."

The point then is to be careful about retaining your separate names and independent credit unless you *want* to allow your partner to buy family-type expense items on your credit. Allowing your consort to charge to your account is easy. Credit managers are satisfied to have a charge account in the name of one solvent debtor. They are overjoyed to have two debtors to sue.

Banks are pleased to have *anyone,* spouse or stranger, guarantee a loan. But before signing that guarantee, think twice. Long after the romantic haze has lifted and you have slammed the door and moved out, your consort's default can bring the bank to your doorstep demanding that you pay up.

Let's assume you have the cash or the credit, and your consortium has deepened to the extent that you want to make a joint investment. There are a number of ways people can own property together whether they are married or single.

There are three major ways to hold title to property. The first, and typical consort method, is in your name alone. The second is joint tenancy and the last is tenancy in common. Both joint tenancy and tenancy in common are means of providing joint ownership and have nothing to do with marriage.

Single people, consorts, lovers, business partners and even married couples can own property in joint tenancy or tenancy in common, as they choose. The forms of joint ownership allow each joint owner to own an undivided share in the entire property with his partner. For example, if there are two joint owners of a house in the suburbs, each joint owner owns one half of the house. The only way to divide the property is to sell it and divide the cash after the mortgage company and brokers are paid.

Joint tenancy is joint ownership with the right of survivorship. That means that if there are two joint tenants and one joint tenant dies, the surviving joint tenant automatically gets the whole.

Tenancy in common is joint ownership without the right of survivorship. While tenancy in common will provide consorts with an undivided one-half ownership in the house, the house remains in their separate estates when they die. For example, if consorts Jack and Jill buy a house on the hill in joint tenancy and Jill dies, Jack gets it all. If Jack and Jill have title to the house in tenancy in common and Jill dies, he gets to share it with Jill's mother (or whoever else inherits from her). And so, your dream house becomes a partnership with the in-laws you never wanted in the first place.

All of this living and loving has so far ignored the possibility that your consortium will be fruitful and multiply. When you are worrying over abortion, adoption and paternity suits, think, too, of the bastard you bring into the world. Bastard, by the way, is the proper legal name for children born out of wedlock. His name is on the lips of every waiter you don't tip and every cab driver you cut off. The bastard's rights to support and inheritance are severely restricted and the bastard's father's rights barely exist. Historically bastards belong exclusively to their mothers, and the father's interest has been largely limited to supporting the child. While the law is making some strides in recognizing a father's rights to custody in the event the mother dies, the states can decide the father's fitness for custody of his own bastard almost as if he were a total stranger.

And we've only just begun to look at living together and the law. While the Social Security laws are making consortium respectable and lucrative for the old folks, insurance companies won't let you insure each other's lives or protect each other's health. The Army won't treat a consort as a dependent and the Mann Act is still on the books (and even sometimes enforced), making it a crime to cross state lines with an immoral intent even if you are crossing state lines totally on a voluntary basis to vacation together.

As a rule, there is neither alimony nor attorney's fees to pay when you decide to call it quits. This may be a powerful incentive for the once-burned, but now in California it appears that the courts may be requiring some consorts to pay for the value of services rendered to them during consortium.

Clearly then, living together single is at least as complicated as divorce. If this keeps up we may have to do what our grandparents did—simply stay married.

CREDIT: *Barbara B. Hirsch, Attorney, Chicago; author of* Living Together: A Guide to the Law for Unmarried Couples, *and* Divorce: What a Woman Needs to Know.

Loneliness

"The world is shrinking," Thomas Merton wrote a few years before his tragic death. "There is less and less space in which man can be alone. It is said that if we go on increasing at our present rate, in six hundred and fifty years there will be only one square foot for every person."

Merton, a cloistered monk, valued solitude and loneliness to the extent that he found too much togetherness in the silent community life of the Trappists, so he moved out to the woods to live alone in a tiny hermitage.

But for most people, loneliness is something to be avoided like the plague. Their great fear is to confront the dreadful inner bleakness summed up in the poet W. H. Auden's lines: "Alive but alone—belonging where?"

Loneliness is all around us. You see it everywhere—in the jammed streets of a strange town, in a room rocking with laughter, on planes and trains with people packed in like so many sardines with nothing to say to each other. You can be lonely in a house filled with friends and family. It is creased in faces like the lines of a weathered farmer in an Edward Steichen photograph. It is in the watery eyes of the old and the innocent eyes of the young. It is in the glances of the middle-aged, guarded against a world filled with strangers.

You can touch loneliness in the rigidity of old bodies under thin blankets, in aching limbs holding themselves tight against the cold winds of life. You can feel it in the tension of a woman turning away from pain, in the stateliness of a widow standing alone like half of a giant oak.

You can taste it in food that has no flavor because it must be eaten alone. You can smell it in the drinks the falsely cheerful raise against the New Year which they hope will treat them more gently. You recognize it in the poor appetites of those who have run out of friends or family when they say, "I'm not very hungry tonight."

You can sniff it in hospitals and nursing homes. It is the scent of cleaning agents that don't quite cover the odors of people suffering or dying by themselves. It hangs in the air around the women who were ladies before the last century ended as they cry out for their long-gone mothers and their playthings.

Walk into any singles bar and you will see the essence of real loneliness. It is not difficult to sense beneath the sophisticated trappings and snappy conversation, the fake smiles, small talk, manufactured gaiety—the exchange of a thousand glances, glazed over with more desperation than seduction. They are clues to the emptiness of the lonely heart.

Life, then, may in some way be defined as a struggle to understand and respond to loneliness. It is a task that is never fully accomplished. It is part of every man's journey toward a sense of himself, of his own human dignity and worth. Loneliness is normal for the person who tries to understand the meaning of his own gifts, his special inheritance and the unique opportunities he possesses to contribute something to humanity. We may never think of loneliness as a friend, but constant companion that it is, we cannot afford to count it as an enemy.

The proper understanding of and response to loneliness can, in fact, be an asset. Without loneliness, our journeys to self-discovery or to the heart of life's meaning would be impossible. Loneliness lights up the values that are truly significant because it is the edging of man's deepest needs. Without the spur of loneliness, man might never look more deeply into himself or begin the search for values that ultimately humanize him.

Loneliness enables a person to crack through the shield forged by the narcissism that isolates him in his own self-concern. Without loneliness a man would never sense the need to respond to others. He would never attempt to bridge the gap that makes him finally a full-grown, mature person. Being lonely can strip us of our pretenses. It forces us to feel the bite of truth, as in the words of Thomas Wolfe—it is the "surest cure for vanity."

Loneliness, then, is not all bad. It reminds us that we are alive, that we have felt the warmth of the sun, that we have been close enough to others— and they to us—to know the beauty and the agony of longing for each other. We have made a difference to someone, and they to us. Loneliness is a sign that we have been touched by love, and what can be more beautiful than that?

Loneliness has many faces. There is the loneliness of the person who is misunderstood by his colleagues or friends. Probably no experience is so devastating as being misread by those on whom we count for real under-standing. They are terrible moments and can shatter, temporarily, the lives of the best-adjusted person.

It is easy to arrive at wrong conclusions about others in this day of pop psychology and amateur analysis. The loneliness that follows estrangement is difficult to shake because the bridges to healing relationships seem to have been burned.

There is an everyday loneliness that has never been identified—the loneli-ness that fills the hours when we can do nothing but wait. It is the loneliness of lovers who are separated by jobs and miles and circumstances they cannot control; the anxiety of a person waiting outside the hospital room where a loved one is critically ill; the endless waiting in doctors' offices, in long lines for buses to come or planes to go, for the darkness to give way to dawn or for the beginning of a vacation or the end of a school year.

The loneliness of a marriage gone sour is one of the worst agonies of life. It happens when people drift away from one another because they have stopped sharing—or caring. The extramarital affair is often the result of a man or woman in search of someone who will listen to the problems that his or her spouse is not interested in. Prostitutes frequently describe how the men who buy their time are more eager to talk about their troubles than to experi-ence a sexual release.

Often the "acting out" of sexual behavior has its roots in the personalities of people who are lonely and groping for a way to make contact with some-one who will respond to their needs as humans. One should not be too hard on individuals whose chief fault is reaching out, even if they reach out in ways we do not approve of.

Such an effort is, in the long run, healthier than isolation, which charac-terizes the life of the loner who scorns friends in the name of "loftier" values. The loners practice a crippled religion. They are the most miserable of all. But they dare not let themselves feel the pain of their loneliness be-cause they cannot or will not admit it. How tragic that they do not know what it means to be close to another person.

Many sexually related behavioral patterns are the result of loneliness. Reading pornography and attending X-rated movies are the pastimes of peo-ple who have difficulty in their relationships with themselves and others. They are attempting to ignite some flame that will light the way for a short time at least, to restore a sense of warmth and remind themselves that they are human. It is not surprising that in a world which offers them so little shel-ter they should look in dark and unsatisfying places for relief.

What then is the lonely person to do? He must first come to terms with himself, with his assets, his personal worth. He must learn to value himself so he feels he is giving something worthwhile when he offers his friendship. He must not be passive, waiting on the sidelines for someone to rescue him. Nor must he allow himself to be absorbed by the crowd. He should not count on being carried along in singles bars, group sex, political demonstrations or on following the current trends and opinions of others. Life kills us unless we face it with something of our own.

A lonely person cannot, then, wait for friends to assemble around and take care of him. Friendship, for each of us, begins with reaching out. It is an active process. Those who wait to be saved from loneliness will experience even more anguish and injury than the individual who makes himself vulnerable by moving toward people. It always hurts to try to be a friend to man. It wears us down and wears us out, but it is still more rewarding and healthier to choose the active role rather than the passive one.

The concept of trying to help others as a practical approach to dealing with our own loneliness may sound corny, but it works. You need not have much to give, but whatever you have—give it freely. Volunteer work in hospitals, worthy causes, visiting the elderly, reading to crippled children, assisting the handicapped, being a good neighbor, investing ourselves in constructive activities break the shell that encases us in our aloneness.

When a person asks that age-old question, "What can I do about my terrible loneliness?" The best answer is still, "Do something for somebody else."

CREDIT: *Dr. Eugene Kennedy, Ph.D., author of* Living with Everyday Problems *and* The Trouble Book, *published by Thomas More Press.*

---

10 REASONS FOR LONELINESS

DEAR ANN: The best column you ever wrote has been in my wallet for several years. It is barely readable, but I'm sure you can make it out. Please run it again so I can carry it around for another decade.   YOUR FRIEND

DEAR FRIEND: With pleasure. Here it is:

DEAR ANN LANDERS: You get many letters from people who are lonely. They wonder why.

Yesterday, a person I work with complained that no one likes her. I sat down and listed the personality and character traits I dislike most. Strangely enough, out of the 10 traits, this person has seven. Please print the list. It might help some person see themselves as others see them.

(1) A compulsion to show off knowledge.

(2) Exaggerates to the point that it's the next thing to lying.

(3) Moodiness. Friendly one day, unfriendly the next.

(4) Bossiness. Must run everything.

(5) Not reliable. Word is no good.

(6) Chronic complainer. Inveterate crepe-hanger.

(7) Nosy. Asks questions that are none of her business.

(8) Gossipy. Knows everything about everybody. Makes you wonder what she is saying about you.

(9) Says things in anger, then tries to smooth things over by buying a gift.

(10) Always fishing for compliments but never gives any.

Sign me   H20 TOWN, S.D.

Love

ANN'S DEFINITION OF LOVE:

Love is friendship that has caught fire. It is quiet understanding, mutual confidence, sharing and forgiving. It is loyalty through good and bad times. It settles for less than perfection and makes allowances for human weaknesses.

Love is content with the present, it hopes for the future, and it doesn't brood over the past. It's the day-in and day-out chronicle of irritations, problems, compromises, small disappointments, big victories, and working toward common goals.

If you have love in your life it can make up for a great many things you lack. If you don't have it, no matter what else there is, it's not enough.

"America," a French visitor observed in the thirties, "is the only country in which love is a national problem." And so it is, because, to borrow a phrase from Dickens, love can be the best of times and the worst of times. It can be a joy and a pain, a snare and a delusion.

Love remains the one subject on which the last word will never be uttered —a mystery that seems to elude its trackers at every turn. Yet men and women have learned something about it, mostly the hard way. Perhaps the basic truth, even though it is regularly ignored, is that love is delivered not to the gods, who have no need of it, but to mere mortals, always unfinished in their growing, forever failing themselves and each other, preoccupied with unresolved conflicts and shortcomings.

Certain kinds of love can be defined and distinguished. There is the love of God, the love of friends, the love of country and the love of Eros. And yet what people long to understand is not these intellectual distinctions, but what they themselves experience and call love in their own lives.

Love's worst enemies are those who presume that it can be found and preserved in a perfect state. It can be known only by those who make mistakes and grow old. Love is friendship that has caught fire. It is found in the sweet and sour of reality rather than in the always out-of-reach stars in the heavens.

Love is the force that connects the broken parts of life, filling in the hollows and bridging the gaps. It is of its very nature to do this, and it cannot exist in any other environment. Love is not a great work of art, plastic-perfect; only cheap reproductions, mass-produced, are like that. In masterpieces, the living hand of the artist can be detected in the human touches that give the works their lasting greatness. In the same way, no great love story, in fact or in fiction, has been remembered for being flawless. Rather, it remains fresh because it is filled with the elements of human frailty that mark the course of ordinary people.

Love has a great deal to do with one's upbringing. People who were deprived of love early in life have a hard time giving it. A child cannot be loved too much but he can be overindulged. The difference between giving love and giving things is too often blurred in the minds of those who try to buy affection.

Human development is an infinitely complex process. Wholeness is an achievement rather than a gift, and no exceptions are granted. People can never know love unless they pass through the crisis of growing up and becoming independent. The problem, of course, is that many seek to avoid the necessary pain of growth. Although they yearn for love, they do it from a sheltered narcissism that prevents them from experiencing it.

The notion of romantic love first appeared when the medieval troubadours sang their courtly songs across Western Europe. It broke into a world whose institutions of authority in both the church and state exercised considerable control over the lives of people. Romantic love was the triumph of one's deepest yearnings over authority and custom. It challenged the worldwide tradition of arranged marriages in which the destiny of husband and wife was decided by parents almost from the day of birth. While no one is sure that marriage by choice has been more successful than marriage arranged by parental selection, it is clear that America is the first country that has tried to make romance and marriage work.

Americans, unlike many other nationalities, have never accepted the idea that a man should have a wife to bear his children and a mistress to provide romance. Even in the relatively new concept of couples living together without marriage, the emphasis has been on mutual emotional support. Americans want love to work. They are more committed to the ideal than any other people in history.

Unfortunately, love is in trouble. The greater the expectations the greater the disappointment. The divorce rate has sharply increased in the last twenty years and alternate living arrangements have cropped up everywhere. But living together is not marriage, and when the split comes there is often bitterness. Love has indeed become a national problem.

We have all looked into the faces of strangers and seen what they must have looked like many years before. The smiling or troubled child lives on in the adult. We carry the expressions and emotions of our earliest years throughout our lives, including whether and how we love others. Our capacity to give and receive love is shaped by the way we learn about love in infancy and childhood.

The chaos in a family that provides no models makes it difficult for children to achieve the growth necessary to sustain a love relationship. Problems caused by ineffective parenting cannot be easily remedied or reversed.

Love that is doled out conditionally from parent to children places a mortgage on the children's capacity to love themselves or others. For example, children who are loved only when they meet their parents' expectations—only on the condition that they don't cry, that they get good marks or promise to become a doctor—never feel that they are loved just for themselves.

A sense of self-worth—the ability to love ourselves—is the foundation for friendship and love. Our love relationships reflect what we feel about ourselves. It is clear that any major distortion or denial of love during our years of development will seriously cripple our ability to love as adults. These relationships are sometimes characterized by efforts to get the kind of love that was missing in childhood. The unloved devour others, taking what they can and giving little in return.

While a lack of adequate love in childhood may generate such difficulties, later life experiences of mature love can heal the early wounds and enable men and women to learn to love. Love is indeed the cure for its lack, but not everyone is so fortunate to find someone who cares enough to be patient with a defective personality and repair the early damage. It is clear that despite other seemingly pressing considerations, there is nothing more important for children than to be born of parents who are mature enough to love each other and, therefore, imperfectly but wholeheartedly to love them as well.

Love dies if people try to fix it at a certain time or place in their lives—like airplanes in different holding patterns, not close enough to crash but out of radio contact. The couple, starry-eyed on their wedding day, share quite a different kind of love after they have helped each other grow through a few children and financial reverses. People who want their love to remain the same (because change involves pain) are doomed to mourn a love whose death they never understood.

True lovers cannot pretend they are totally free of each other or that what one does has no effect on the other. Love is a claim that links two people who share a commitment. It succeeds only in relationships when the lovers acknowledge that they have made claims and counterclaims on one another. Love is not love when lovers can walk away at any moment.

The notion that love takes care of itself is another misreading of this most important of life's experiences. Love never takes care of itself. It needs constant nurturing and must be able to adjust and readjust in order to be kept fresh. Perhaps this has never been expressed more clearly than by Ann Landers when she wrote, "Marriages may be made in heaven but the maintenance work must be done down here."

Perhaps most of the current misunderstandings about love center on the desire to have the benefits of love without paying the price. The frequently repeated but meaningless phrase from the novel *Love Story,* "Love means never having to say you're sorry," is a good example. True lovers have to say they are sorry all the time because they live close enough to each other to be hurtful even when they don't mean to be. Lovers have to say they are sorry and they have to hear themselves say it because the humbling experience of putting such feeling into words can be the adhesive that holds love together.

Freud did not invent sex, but he did pinpoint it as a central and profoundly significant force in all human relationships. Despite what many say, almost everybody can tell the difference between sex alone and sex in the context of love. The problem frequently is that we don't want to get the message. We may prefer the confusion and employ rationalizations—the excuses that abound when people use others for pleasure only—with no commitment. We even work out elaborate explanations for the advantages of not being committed, or for remaining free of responsibility. Sex as bait and barter may seem to hold the promise of something lasting, but if we are honest, we can tell the difference between sex and real love. The most revealing clue is, how do you feel after it is over? Are you fulfilled, at peace, content—or would you just as soon have no caressing, no conversation or, worse yet, to be left alone? One of the tragedies of this supposedly sophisticated age is the vulnerability of people who want love so badly that they are willing to accept sex as a substitute.

Contemporary people are sometimes misled into settling for a lifestyle instead of a life, for sexiness instead of sexuality. The latter element is a rich dimension of any true love relationship—marked by tenderness and mutual concern. It reflects the mystery of love itself. Sexuality refers to a healthy dimension of human sharing that thrives when men and women love each other completely, unselfishly, and attempt to make sex a better and more expressive part of their lives together.

HOW CAN YOU TELL?

The question that many ask but few dare answer is, "How can I be sure this love is real?" Vague reassurances—"You'll know when the real thing comes along"—don't help. Hoping that it is the real thing may only indicate a longing for, rather than the possession of, love. So—how can you tell?

Perhaps the best sign that love is real is, despite the floating-on-air feeling, the stars in the eyes that characterize the early stages, real love produces a feeling that there is solid ground beneath our feet. We sense that our longing has been quieted, that a peaceful calm exists at the true heart of things.

We can tell if love is real when we want to put the needs and desires of the beloved ahead of our own. Real love can tolerate the bright lights of honesty. It does not need candlelight (or wine) or other props to make it look better.

Real love provides inner nourishment and shuns external trappings that some people seem to need for "the observers." It lets us be ourselves.

True love is present when we feel that it has made us better human beings, given us something to live up to. Love asks and finally delivers more than you dreamed possible. And, although it is fraught with risk, it keeps its promises by opening the door to the meaning of life itself.

CREDIT: *Eugene Kennedy, Ph.D., author of* A Time for Being Human, *Chicago, Illinois: Thomas More Associates.*

BUT I COULD NOT LOVE THEE, ANN, SO MUCH, LOVED I NOT HONORE MORE

Some find the world in a grain of sand,
　I in the correspondence of Ann Landers.
I eavesdrop unabashed as she spoons out her acerb sauce with even hand
　On lachrymose geese and truculent ganders.
Her desk is positively formicating, which means swarming with moving beings,
　Although I might well employ the other word that sounds like unto it.
Because her mail consists mostly of letters from those embittered ones
　Who have discovered about illicit sex that often there are more headaches
　　than fun to it.
A present-day Emma Lazarus, she cries Give me your huddled problems,
　The wretched refuse of your wrongs, unwrap for me your festering sores and
　　stigmas;
Your poison is my meat,
　Be it alcoholism, infidelity, frigidity, satyriasis, premarital pregnancy or bor-
　　borygmus.
Yes, if anyone's Gordian love-knot requires a blade more cutting than
　Alexander's,
　Let them call on Ann Landers.
No pussy-footer she,
　　no purveyor of admonitions soothing or polite;
　It's tell the bum to jump in the lake,
　　tell the old bag to go fly a kite.
If Ann of Cleves would have
　　written to Ann Landers
　I bet Henry would have thought twice before
　　calling her the mare of Flanders.
From a human comedy as varied as Balzac's I choose for you one excerpt,
　The ultimate in wails of poignant woe,
The plaint of a teen-ager who doubted the affection of her boy friend because
　　the only compliment he ever paid her was
　You sweat less than any fat girl I know.

Ogden Nash

CREDIT: *Copyright © 1971. Courtesy* Signature *magazine, Diners Club Inc.*

TO HELP YOU IMPROVE THE QUALITY OF LIFE

On This Day—
Mend a quarrel,
Search out a forgotten friend,
Dismiss a suspicion and replace it with trust,
Write a letter to someone who misses you,
Encourage a youth who has lost faith,
Keep a promise,
Forget an old grudge,
Examine your demands on others and vow to reduce them,

Fight for a principle,
Express your gratitude,
Overcome an old fear,
Take two minutes to appreciate the beauty of nature,
Tell someone you love him.
Tell him again,
And again,
And again.

Ann Landers

Love or Infatuation?

Infatuation is instant desire. It's one set of glands calling to another.

Love is friendship that has caught fire. It takes root and grows—one day at a time.

Infatuation is marked by a feeling of insecurity. You are excited and eager, but not genuinely happy. There are nagging doubts, unanswered questions, little bits and pieces about your beloved that you would just as soon not examine too closely. It might spoil the dream.

Love is the quiet understanding and mature acceptance of imperfection. It is real. It gives you strength and grows beyond you—to bolster your beloved. You are warmed by his presence, even when he is away. Miles do not separate you. You want him near. But near or far, you know he is yours and you can wait.

Infatuation says, "We must get married right away. I can't risk losing him."

Love says, "Be patient. Don't panic. He is yours. Plan your future with confidence."

Infatuation has an element of sexual excitement. If you are honest, you will admit it is difficult to be in one another's company unless you are sure it will end in intimacy. Love is the maturation of friendship. You must be friends before you can be lovers.

Infatuation lacks confidence. When he's away, you wonder if he's cheating. Sometimes you even check.

Love means trust. You are calm, secure and unthreatened. He feels that trust and it makes him even more trustworthy.

Infatuation might lead you to do things you'll regret later, but love never will.

Love lifts you up. It makes you look up. It makes you think up. It makes you a better person than you were before.

CREDIT: *Ann Landers.*

Lying

How Can You Tell?

For better or worse, lie detector tests are becoming routine in police investigations and other situations. Whether or not people still believe "it's a sin to tell a lie," science has confirmed that the truth is a powerful commodity and is not easily twisted by the human brain. The lie detector uses all sorts of sensitive apparatus to measure the real but invisible and involuntary reactions triggered in our bodies when we fail to tell the truth. Still people lie regularly and are lied to—in matters great and small. We are both the victims and practitioners of lying and it's one of life's ongoing lessons to become both better at deception and better at perceiving it in others.

Nature has equipped all of us with our own built-in lie detector. The mother who has evidence of a raided cookie jar has only to confront the possible young suspects to know immediately which one is the culprit. It is the one who fidgets and squirms and cannot look her in the eye. But it won't be so easy to spot the secret owner of a forbidden pack of cigarettes, even in the same culprit, a few years later. He or she has improved the ability to suppress the giveaway body language that identified the hand in the cookie jar.

Most adults are inexperienced liars and will give themselves away by a variety of gestures which are obvious signals to anyone who is familiar with their ordinary responses. But there are also many who, for one reason or another, become accomplished liars, sometimes for the best of reasons, as in the case of doctors, nurses and other professionals who find it kinder or more practical to withhold the brutal truth. Actors have to be consummate liars in order to fit convincingly into roles that will fool audiences into accepting them for what they are not. Criminals learn how to lie to stay out of prison and politicians do what is necessary to stay in office. Some used-car salesmen would never make a sale if they told the truth, nor could the con man ever make a crooked buck.

For the police there is always the lie detector test, but most of us have only our own senses to rely on as protection against being lied to. Recent research has come up with interesting findings about typical behavior exhibited when people lie. The accomplished liar has no difficulty avoiding twitching, shuffling or sweating. He can look you straight in the eye while telling a whopper. But while all of us tend to touch some part of our head or face while talking, there is a marked increase in mouth, nose, cheek, ear and hair touching on the part of someone who is not telling the truth—even the chronic liar.

You must have some basis for comparison of "before" and "during" lying for each individual, but such gestures should become more noticeable the closer the person comes to the heart of the lie. The same research shows that people will also exhibit similar behavior in other situations of mental stress as well. But when you're in a situation where the truth is at stake and your woman or man starts touching lips, eyebrows, pulling at ear lobes and stroking the nose, etc.—look out.

CREDIT: *Sean Freeman, free-lance writer, Chicago.*

Malpractice

Are you thinking about suing your doctor? If you are, you're not alone. A lot of people have been doing just that in recent years. No one has the exact figures, but the American Medical Association estimates that the number of medical malpractice claims has doubled or possibly tripled since 1970 to approximately 75,000 cases in 1976.

Not only has the frequency of claims increased, but the size of the awards has jumped. Ten years ago an award of $1 million was virtually unheard of. Today multimillion-dollar awards raise no eyebrows.

While the number of suits seems to be leveling off, the question nevertheless arises: Why the upsurge? Has the quality of medical care slipped? Most experts agree that, if anything, the standards of U.S. medicine have been rising, not falling. But higher bills may have something to do with the increase in malpractice suits—and the increase in daring, dramatic, new surgical procedures may also be a factor.

Doctors are by no means the only targets of a suit-happy public. Lawyers themselves are now being sued more frequently for malpractice. Product liability insurance rates for manufacturers also have skyrocketed.

Malpractice suits have the appeal, at first glance, of an everything-to-win, nothing-to-lose proposition. Most are handled by lawyers on a contingency fee basis. This means you pay a fee to the lawyer only if you win the case. If you lose, you don't have to pay the lawyer anything.

But, like many surefire schemes, thorns grow among the roses in the malpractice thicket. If you are mad enough at your doctor (or hospital) to sue, or if a friend comes to you urging a suit and asking, "What can you lose?", there are a number of things you ought to know before you go ahead.

First of all, you do not have a valid lawsuit just because you did not get the medical results you had hoped for. Not every fracture knits perfectly. Not every cosmetic procedure creates a more beautiful you. Not every individual responds in the same way to identical treatment. Even in such a simple operation as the removal of tonsils, something can go wrong without anyone being at fault.

Medical science has made tremendous strides in recent years. New machines, new drugs and new surgical techniques have added dramatically to your chances for a longer and more enjoyable life. Yet there are risks in every medical procedure, even in taking aspirin. Despite the "Marcus Welby syndrome" (the expectation of perfect results every time), malpractice laws are not intended to provide financial compensation for every medical outcome that falls short of perfection.

In order to sue successfully for malpractice, your case generally must meet two criteria. One, you must prove that the unfortunate results occurred because of negligence and not because of misadventure. Generally, you must also prove a financial loss as a result of the negligence.

If your doctor or hospital can show that the level of skill and knowledge applied in your case was the same as the skill and knowledge used by reasonably well-qualified doctors in your community in similar cases, you do not have a very good case.

To prove that the care you received did not meet the medical standards of your community or similar communities, you will have to bring in an expert witness to testify. Almost always this means another physician.

Much has been written about how doctors refuse to testify against each other. Like so many often-repeated judgments, there is more exaggeration than truth here. However protective physicians may (or may not) have been in the past, it is recognized today that physicians are getting tougher on the bad apples in the medical barrel.

The AMA reports that the number of disciplinary actions against physicians has gone from 1,200 in 1971 to 4,200 in 1976. In addition, some local medical societies, fed up with out-of-town medical authorities who make a career of traveling around to give "expert" testimony, now have pools of local physicians to give testimony in malpractice cases. This has upgraded the level of expertise and scientific objectivity.

Another thing you should consider before suing is your chance of winning the suit. According to a recent study by the National Association of Insurance Commissioners (there is an insurance commissioner for each state), the plaintiffs in malpractice cases (you) do not come out very well. In two thirds of the claims examined, those bringing suit received nothing. Another 15 percent received less than $3,000.

Most malpractice cases—94 percent—are settled out of court. In 6 percent of the cases that do go to court, the plaintiff loses four times out of five.

When a patient is successful and receives an award, he (or she) generally receives only part of it. The lawyer usually keeps a third or more as his fee. Moreover, the expenses of the suit absorb a large share. One study indicates that the patient collects only 15–38 percent of the total.

What should make you think even longer before suing for malpractice is the chance that the physician can turn around and sue you and your lawyer. This has happened, notably in the case of a suburban Chicago radiologist, Leonard Berlin, M.D. A woman patient sued Dr. Berlin, the hospital and an orthopedic surgeon connected with the case, claiming that a small fracture in her little finger incurred in a tennis game had gone undetected. She demanded damages of $250,000. Dr. Berlin instituted a countersuit. The two cases were scheduled for trial together. Just before the trial opened, the patient dropped her suit. Dr. Berlin, however, persisted with his countersuit and won a jury award of $8,000 damages.

Through late 1977 at least thirty-five other physicians have instituted countersuit actions. At least four of them have won awards ranging from $100 to $85,000.

Lawyers are quick to point out that none of those countersuits has gone through the appeal process. Nonetheless, a new element of two-way traffic has entered the picture. It is now a game two can play. Suing for malpractice is no longer the surefire, risk-free proposition it once was.

Changes in many state laws are also placing a damper on malpractice actions. Some states have set up arbitration panels or pre-trial proceedings to help screen out cases of small merit. Other states have placed limits on the percentage of awards lawyers may collect, or have shortened the period of time a patient has in which to file suit. There is evidence also that juries are scaling down the size of awards.

Malpractice suits unquestionably add to the cost of treatment. Physicians admit to ordering extra tests and X rays in order to protect themselves against a possible suit. In a 1977 AMA poll, 75 percent of the physicians polled said they now practice "defensive" medicine. The rising premiums that physicians and hospitals pay for liability insurance add to the cost of patient care.

Michael Reese Hospital in Chicago, for example, must tack on an extra $16 to the daily charge for a bed just to cover malpractice premiums. Of a typical $15 charge for a visit to a doctor, the AMA estimates that $1.24 now goes to an insurance company for the physician's protection against a lawsuit.

In the long run, it is the public who picks up the malpractice tab.

This is not to deny that medical negligence does exist or to say that people injured through medical negligence should not be compensated for damages. Such legal rights have existed in law for centuries. They come under a part of the law called torts. ("Tort" is a word of Middle English origin that means "a wrong.")

But in the instance of malpractice, the process of tort law has been stretched to cover episodes that have nothing to do with negligence. For example, in New York in 1975 a Brooklyn College sophomore who lost one eye and has only partial vision in the other filed a $2 million suit for damages. When she was born, two months prematurely, she weighed only two and a half pounds. As part of the successful effort to save her life, she was given oxygen. What is known now—but may not have been known then—is that too much oxygen for a premature infant can lead to blindness later on. That is what happened to her.

Should the physicians and hospital involved in that episode nearly twenty-one years ago now be judged negligent? If so, they would have to be held accountable for medical knowledge that was just coming to light and was not proven information until years later. In justice to the doctors and the hospital it may be hard to characterize their treatment as negligent. At the time given, the treatment was standard in the community and considered safe.

But what about the young blind woman? She lost most of her eyesight as a result of medical treatment. Should she not be entitled to compensation? In this case, she accepted a settlement from the insurance company of $165,000 just minutes before the jury was to announce an award of $900,000.

If society believes that people in such cases should receive compensation for medical misadventures which are no one's fault, malpractice suits are not the way to finance it. A new method similar to Workmen's Compensation might be more fair to everyone concerned and less expensive. A study of such a "no fault" approach has just been done by the California Medical Association and the California Hospital Association. The concept deserves serious consideration for future public policy.

As things stand today—1978—the compensation comes from professional liability insurance. The result is frustration. This present setup puts an extra strain on everyone's health bill, yet it provides uneven justice for both physician and patient alike.

CREDIT: *Frank D. Campion, Director of Public Relations, American Medical Association.*

Manic-Depressive Illness

The manic-depressive is a psychotic who differs quantitatively and qualitatively from the neurotic. His illness is a mental disorder which, when combined with schizophrenia, constitutes the bulk of severe mental illness. If one eliminates the organic mental disorders (brain damage and brain tumors), schizophrenics and manic-depressives accounted for at least 95 percent of the population of state mental hospitals until recently. Now, a great attempt is being made to treat and maintain these patients in the community after brief periods of hospitalization in a mental or general hospital, or even better, without any hospitalization at all.

Manic-depressive illness is known as an affective disorder; this means that although thinking may be impaired, the main impairment is in the area of feelings and moods. The sickness is also called the "up and down" disease because of the drastic mood swings that the patient experiences, which may run from the heights of elation (mania) to the depths of despondency (depression). The two components of the disease, the highs and the lows, may alternate, sometimes very rapidly, or they may appear as a succession of lows only, or highs only. In the former case the disease is called bipolar and in the latter case it is called unipolar (unipolar depressed or unipolar manic).

The manic phase of the illness is characterized by elation, a feeling that one can move mountains, conquer worlds, build empires. The person who carefully saved for a rainy day will suddenly spend everything he has on a luxury vacation or go into debt to buy expensive gifts. He promises the world and does not seem to have a single care in life. He may talk incessantly and not necessarily make sense. He is restless, cannot sit still, barely sleeps and is in perpetual motion. He appears witty, happy-go-lucky and enjoys every minute of the state he is in. No one could convince him that he is ill.

At the other extreme, the depressed phase consists of melancholia, despondency, a feeling of hopelessness and that the world is coming to an end. There is a general retardation and slowing down of all functions. The patient does not eat, sleep or move his bowels. In extreme cases he is motionless, sitting or lying and staring into space. He appears in severe pain and cannot tolerate the condition he is in. He seldom talks or walks and cannot be motivated to do anything. If he could move he would likely do away with himself.

It can be easily seen that in either phase the manic-depressive is dangerous to himself; in the manic phase because of overconfidence and likely physical exhaustion and in the depressed phase because of pain and the feeling that life is not worth living (possible suicide). In either phase of the illness the patient needs to be protected from himself either by hospitalization or by being watched twenty-four hours a day.

Fortunately, hospitalization need not be long because of the availability of excellent drugs for both phases of the illness. The manic phase responds in most instances to lithium carbonate, a drug that has been used successfully in this country for over a decade. Occasionally lithium may have to be supplemented with some of the major tranquilizers in order to arrest the symptoms.

In the depressed phase we have a number of energizing drugs that in most cases will bring the patient out of his depression. Occasionally, if drugs fail, electroshock will prove effective.

Although we do not know the cause of manic-depressive illness—there seems to be a genetic factor involved—we are far from helpless in treating the person suffering from it. We may not be able to effect a cure but we can effectively arrest the symptoms, restore full function in the great majority of cases and enable the person to lead a productive and satisfactory life.

CREDIT: *Samuel L. Safirstein, M.D., Associate Clinical Professor of Psychiatry, Mount Sinai School of Medicine, New York, New York; Associate Attending Department of Psychiatry, The Mount Sinai Hospital, New York, New York.*

Marriage

A Checklist for Selecting a Man to Marry

Since one out of every two marriages is winding up on the rocks—a woman needs all the help she can get. Here are some guidelines.

(1) How does he handle problems and pressure? Does he go to pieces? Blame others when things go wrong or remain calm and search for the best solution?

(2) How does he feel about women? Does he believe they are inferior to men and can't possibly make important decisions?

(3) How does he feel about housework? Does he think it is beneath his dignity?

(4) How does he feel about children? Do they annoy him or does he

enjoy them? What part does he feel a father should play in the rearing of children? Does he believe it's strictly the mother's job?

(5) Is he stingy when it comes to spending money on you but somewhat extravagant with himself?

(6) How does he feel about his job? Is he content to keep doing the same thing for the rest of his life? (If so, you can be sure he'll complain later that he never got a break.)

(7) What is your social life like? Do you find yourself spending all your spare time with his family and friends and very little with yours?

(8) Does he ask you which film you'd like to see and then somehow you end up seeing the one he prefers?

(9) How does he handle the car when he's in a bad mood? Does he drive like a crazy man when he's ticked off? (This is a real symptom of immaturity.)

(10) Does he become irritated if you are late but expect you to be understanding when he is late?

(11) How does he feel about birth control? Does he think the entire burden should be on the women? If, for example, you are unable to take the pill, would he be willing to accept the responsibility to protect you from an unwanted pregnancy?

(12) Has he ever slapped or punched you and later said he was sorry—and then done it again?

(13) Does he treat his own mother and yours with respect?

(14) How is his sense of humor? Can he laugh at himself or does he see something funny only at the expense of others?

(15) How is his credit? Is he inclined to buy things on impulse, then have trouble paying his bills?

(16) Is he truthful, or have you caught him in little lies which he has tried to wriggle out of?

(17) Do you really enjoy his company—even when you are sitting silently?

(18) Have you thought about what he'll be like in twenty-five years? Do you honestly want to live with him for the rest of your life?

If your prospective husband doesn't get a passing mark on twelve of these questions, the man is not for you.

CREDIT: *Ann Landers.*

Marriage Counseling

*What It Can and
Cannot Do for You*

Marriage counseling has been described as being as old as the institution of marriage—for the very first marriage counselors were probably the newly wed couple's respective parents-in-law. Family members and relatives have always tried to solve couples' marital problems but most people find these attempts are not very helpful. Family support and encouragement are usually welcome when one is in trouble—but families can never be neutral when marital battle lines are drawn. Realizing this, increasing numbers of couples today seek the help of a skilled marriage counselor when marital stresses become too strong for them to resolve by themselves.

What can professional marriage counselors do for you—and what can they *not* do? First, what counselors can do. They can provide couples with a place to unload their worries and hurt feelings in a confidential, dignified and "safe" atmosphere. Marriage counselors don't take sides, even though many people try to get the counselor on their side against the partner. Because the counselor is neutral, *both* the husband and the wife can be assured of being listened to. Most counselors talk to couples together (conjoint counseling) as well as individually.

Many people are troubled by "secrets" they want to discuss with a counselor without their spouse present—and counselors should be expected to honor these wishes. Counselors are good listeners—and just having someone to listen to you when your marriage seems to be falling apart can be immensely helpful.

Many marriages suffer from poor, faulty or non-existent communication between the husband and wife. These people don't know how their spouses feel about their troubles and worries. Marriage counselors, in order to overcome this, work hard to help couples talk to their spouses and listen to them. Having studied about marriage, personality, sex, religion and family life, counselors can help couples develop new ideas and new ways of thinking about their problems and of coping with their conflicts. Often people only think about handling marriage problems the way their parents did. They need to learn new and better ways of treating each other.

Frequently couples consult a marriage counselor only when their marriage reaches a crisis. They may be wondering whether they should divorce or try to "salvage" the marriage. Modern marriage counselors value marriage highly but they also realize that divorce may be the best or only reasonable solution to a conflicted marriage. In such a situation, couples find counselors helpful in sorting out mixed feelings about their partners when trying to decide whether to end a marriage or to stay in it.

Counselors try to help these clients become aware of how these important decisions may affect themselves, their husbands or wives and their children. The average person cares very deeply about how his or her actions affect others and the counselor's knowledge and neutrality are valuable assets in reaching these tough decisions.

Many couples who go to marriage counselors know what they want to do, even what they *should* do to improve their marriage, but they lack the courage to try again. To say "maybe I was wrong," or even to say and do nice things for a partner after a long period of tension and fighting is difficult. In these situations counselors are able to act as catalysts and get the marriage moving again. Often individuals who have endured unhappy marriages for a long time tell the counselor privately that they have secretly wanted to treat their spouse better but needed a way to handle their "pride." Counselors can help these people see that to "give in" or to compromise is often a sign of maturity—not of weakness. Once the couple have broken through their initial feelings of being hurt, scared and angry, counselors can help them agree on better ways of behaving toward each other that will strengthen their relationship and make it interesting. Good marriages don't just happen—and counselors spend much time "teaching" couples how to develop and keep these skills.

Often either the husband or the wife refuses to see a marriage counselor. People wonder if it is worthwhile for a married person to go by him- or herself. Marriage counselors always prefer to see both the husband and wife—as both persons' feelings and actions are vital to the success of any marriage. However, sometimes a partner doesn't believe in counseling or denies that he or she needs help. In these instances, the interested person should still seek counseling.

Marriage counselors cannot help all marriages. They can do nothing for persons or couples who don't want help, except perhaps indirectly by counseling with the co-operative spouse.

Marriage counselors cannot work miracles. They cannot undo the damage that years of nagging, arguing with or ignoring a partner may have done to love and caring. Couples who wait until it is too late to consult a counselor hurt themselves, not the counselor. Love is a human emotion that must be earned and cared for. If it is not periodically replenished by loving acts in the marriage relationship, it may eventually vanish. Some clients realize it too late to save the marriage.

Another limitation of marriage counseling is that even the most skilled professional counselor cannot change the many social ills and problems that harm the quality of married life. Poverty, severe physical or mental health problems, poor housing and chronic unemployment all interfere with constructive family life. While counselors can and usually do refer these couples to public agencies that may be able to help them, the counselor cannot change their income, living conditions and job problems.

In spite of these obvious limitations on a marriage counselor's ability to help, husbands and wives will never know how much value they can obtain from counseling until they actually try it. Problems that couples commonly bring to counselors include arguments over their children and how to raise them, handling money, in-laws, sexual adjustments, household chores and who does them, extramarital affairs, personality differences and, increasingly today, what are "women's" rights and duties in the marriage and what are "men's." Experienced counselors say the majority of marital complaints boil down to one recurrent theme—"my spouse doesn't consider my feelings on anything." Fortunately, unless all interest in the marriage has been lost by one partner, these are complaints that skilled counselors can usually help couples reduce or eliminate in their marriages.

Who are qualified professional marriage counselors? Many who advertise in the telephone book are legitimate, well-trained, professionally trained people, but others (because marriage counselors are licensed in only a few states) may have little or no training—or be outright phonies.

A well-qualified marriage counselor should have an advanced college degree in marriage and family counseling, or in a closely related field like social work, psychology or medicine, plus supervised experience under a skilled counselor. A list of qualified marriage counselors in the United States and Canada can be obtained by writing to the American Association of Marriage and Family Counselors, 225 Yale Avenue, Claremont, California 91711.

Another way to obtain qualified counselors is to go to an agency that belongs to the Family Service Association of America. Sometimes mental health clinics or centers as well as pastoral counseling centers have qualified marriage counselors on their staffs. In some areas, conciliation counselors attached to family relations courts offer similar services.

Marriage counselors in private practice all charge fees for their services, just as physicians and lawyers do. Counseling agencies, clinics and counselor training centers in colleges usually charge "sliding" fees—from no fee at all up to private rates—and set the charges on the couple's ability to pay.

Some couples want professional marriage counseling services but don't know how to pick a qualified counselor or agency from an incompetent one. Thousands of these people write to columnists like Ann Landers and ask for guidance. Miss Landers directs them to competent people from the files she maintains. It may also be helpful to talk to friends who have received counseling help. They can sometimes supply the names of helpful counselors.

Usually one's clergyman or family physician also knows which counselors and agencies in a local area have been most helpful.

In summary, professional marriage counseling can be most helpful to couples with serious marital problems who sincerely want to improve their marriage. If one partner is not motivated to receive help, the task is more difficult but not necessarily impossible. It is important to pick out a well-trained counselor, one belonging to a professional group like the American Association of Marriage and Family Counselors or one who works for a Family Service Association of America agency. Marriage counseling cannot help with all the problems affecting modern marriages but it can assist motivated couples to improve their relationship or help people who decide on divorce to plan their future lives more constructively.

CREDIT: *Frederick G. Humphrey, Ed.D., University of Connecticut, Storrs, Connecticut; President of American Association of Marriage and Family Counselors, 1977.*

The Episcopalian and Marriage

An Episcopal priest can marry any two persons if one of them is a baptized Christian. This means baptized by water in the name of the Father, Son and Holy Ghost, or words to that effect. Thus he could marry a Roman Catholic and a Jew, or a Baptist and a pagan.

The priest only needs permission from the bishop if one of the parties has been divorced. If he feels their intention is for a Christian marriage, that they attempted to do all they could to save the previous marriage and that the prospects for the anticipated marriage are favorable, he can ask the bishop's permission to grant their request to be married in the Episcopal Church.

Regulations regarding marriage are much more flexible than they used to be when the bishop could only make such an allowance under certain rather restrictive criteria.

CREDIT: *The Right Reverend Paul Moore, Jr., the Episcopal Bishop of New York.*

Marriage

How to Make an Intelligent Selection

HE'S CLEARLY NUTS

DEAR ANN LANDERS: Please tell me how certain people can appear to be perfectly OK when they are clearly insane.

Our sweet, innocent daughter was married last week to a mortician 12 years her senior. He courted her for over a year. One of the things that impressed her so favorably was this man's restraint and good manners. He never embraced her intimately nor did he try to talk her into sex, even after they were engaged.

Last night they were married. This morning our daughter phoned—in hysterics. It seems her wedding night was a nightmare. Her husband asked her to take a very cold bath before coming to bed. He suggested that she soak in the tub for about half an hour. When she came to bed he asked her to close her eyes and lie perfectly still. Then he said, "You may as well know that I am a necrophiliac as so many of my profession are. I can only make love to dead women or women who look as if they are.

Our daughter fled in panic, packed her bags and checked into another room. She is at this moment in a state of shock and under a doctor's care. Her physician has already agreed to co-operate in an annulment.

I think the man is crazy. What do you think? SAN FRANCISCO

DEAR MOTHER: I agree with your diagnosis. He is clearly nuts. And so is that statement about "other members of his profession." Report him to the National Funeral Directors at once. The address is 125 W. Wells St., Milwaukee, Wis. 53203. If your daughter's story is accurate they will boot him out of the business pronto.

Since marriage is probably the most important single decision of a lifetime, it is strange that so many people rush into it with less selectivity than they would give to the choice of a secondhand car or a winter coat.

All marriages are happy, it's living together afterward that's tough.

Thousands of letters from unhappily married people suggest one striking reason for failure. Young romanticists spin themselves into a cocoon of dreams and imagine that life together is going to be like the marriages they've seen in the movies, on TV screens and in the ads for engagement rings and silverware.

Unfortunately, a great many American movies are a far cry from life as people live it. How many husbands in the movies get up in the morning and go to work? I recall precious few. The blissfully happy couple live in a beautifully furnished home. They wear lovely clothes, drive expensive cars and are forever going to formal parties. But nobody goes to work. If there are children, they are never underfoot, sick or in faded play clothes. The maid or governess ushers them into the drawing room for a goodnight kiss and shepherds them out again. The movie wife is seldom seen wrestling with bills, shopping for groceries, harassed by troublesome relatives or involved in anything so mundane as housework.

The ads for engagement rings say "forever," but the statistics show that the divorce rate in America is at an all-time high. The chances for a lasting marriage today are approximately one half what they were thirty years ago.

When I speak to high school audiences, I emphasize the realities of married life. I tell the teenagers that marriage is the difficult business of living with another human being. It's in-laws, doctor bills, car payments, dishes in the sink and mortgages. It's disappointment and diaper rash. It's the raise or promotion that he almost but never quite gets. It's tears in the pillow at night.

If teenagers were given facts instead of fiction, they would be less shaken and bewildered when faced with some of the not-so-attractive aspects of married life. The young bride who discovers that her "dream boat" actually snores feels as if she's been robbed. One bride married less than three weeks wrote:

"I can't discuss this with anyone I know personally because I'm too ashamed. How come in the morning my husband has a beard?"

No marriage is free of problems. Be realistic, not only about marriage, but about the person you are considering as a lifetime partner. Remember that dating couples usually see each other in the most flattering light. An aura of saintliness surrounds the beloved. While love may not be blind, its vision is something other than 20/20. In the mind's eye of a high school girl, the football hero may be the most exciting prize in all the world. But the football season doesn't last forever and unless her halfback can back up his handsome physique with many character qualities, he's a poor marriage risk. The glamour of high school and college athletics has lured many foolish girls into ill-fated marriages.

My plea for realism among young couples who fancy themselves in love has met with lively opposition, particularly among university students. Many coeds with whom I spoke at Southern Methodist University in Dallas criticized my concern as "materialistic and calculating."

"Projection is of prime importance," I told them. "Try to imagine, temporarily, how you'll feel about that gorgeous hunk o' man in fifteen years, after his hair has fallen out and he has gained thirty pounds. Will you still be crazy about him even though his looks are gone and the wolf at the door has had a third litter?"

All people don't want the same things out of life, and this is good. Some women are content with a man of limited horizons who wants to work thirty-seven and a half hours a week for a modest salary. Others want an aggressive type, one who strives to scale financial, artistic or intellectual heights.

I make no plea for either the go-getter or the unambitious. I do plead, however, that those who are considering marriage think and plan ahead. You can accomplish this by discussing goals and objectives during courtship. Decide what *you* want out of life, then choose someone who shares your dreams and objectives.

What's your hurry? A great many divorces could have been prevented had the couple gone together another ninety days. They would have become better acquainted, and probably not have embarked on marriage in the first place.

In much of the mail these words appear: "I'm mad about him. It was love at first sight." I advise them to look again, they may see things they hadn't noticed before. Love at first sight is a myth, in spite of the poets' claims. Love does not konk you on the head like a chunk of loose plaster. It must take root and grow, a day at a time. Happily married people who claim they fell in love at first sight didn't really. They were smitten on first meeting and the fine qualities they imagined they saw proved to be present after they got to know each other.

Frequently a purely chemical reaction is mistaken for love. One college freshman wrote:

"I know it's love. Whenever I see her, my knees turn to water and my heart pounds like a triphammer. It's got to be love. It can't be anything else."

A strong physical reaction is a powerful plus and should be a factor in the final selection. But a compelling sexual attraction is not a substantial hook on which to hang a marriage. And this is where so many "madly in love" couples who marry in a hurry make their greatest mistake. They are unable to distinguish between love and sex. They learn too late that they can't live their entire lives in the bedroom.

There is no substitute for time in testing the durability of a relationship. A couple should go together long enough to view each other in a variety of circumstances. Complaints of this nature are numerous: "I never knew until after we were married that she had such a violent temper" . . . "I was shocked to find he was such a mama's boy" . . . "I wasn't aware that he couldn't stand children" . . . "I didn't know he was such a liar" . . . "I had no idea she drank in the daytime too" . . . "I didn't know he was so lazy."

Although it is impossible to know all about a person until you share a life together, a great many things *can* be learned during courtship if a couple will take the time. It's easy to be charming when things go well, but how does he behave when the going is rocky? Is he dependable? Does he have patience? Is he considerate? Is he understanding? Is he honest? The individual who conducts himself with maturity under stress will make a reliable marriage partner. So time—time to test him in the clutch—can be your greatest ally.

What can you share? The more you have in common with the person you marry the better your chances for a successful marriage. Although there are notable exceptions (we all have our pet examples), couples who share similar economic, religious, racial and educational backgrounds have fewer marital problems. The reason is obvious. There are fewer areas of conflict, fewer things to fight about.

There's an old joke that if the rich girls married poor boys and the rich boys married poor girls, the money would be spread around and poverty would be abolished. This is a delightful theory, but the experts know that marriage of people from opposite ends of the economic spectrum often fail.

Few principles are more deeply embedded in our society than the right to marry whom we please, and the suggestion that economic status should be considered may sound downright un-American. But problems are bound to crop up when two people who have been reared differently undertake to share a life. Surprisingly enough, my mail indicates that the partner with the money is seldom the troublemaker. The one who marries wealth usually creates the problems. He is unable to shake off the feeling of inferiority and often attempts to get off the defensive by attacking.

Educational background is an important factor often ignored when two people fancy themselves in love. One young man wrote:

"If I had been listening to the girl instead of just looking at her, I might have avoided this horrible mistake. She is a doll with a sawdust head."

Many of the letters from teenagers who want to quit high school to go to work or get married sound as if they had all been written by the same person:

"School bores me; I'm not learning anything. I can get a job and earn good money and buy some nice clothes. Why should I stay in this dumb place?"

I urge them to stay in school and get that diploma no matter how boring and pointless it may seem. I tell them about the thousands who have written to say they could kick themselves for quitting—that it was the most foolish thing they ever did. I warn them of the nagging feeling of inferiority they'll inevitably experience.

Well-educated women who marry poorly educated men seem not to notice the glaring grammatical defects and limited intellectual interests until after they marry. This strikes me as odd. It's as if they had been totally deaf during courtship.

The husband who resents being corrected and will make no effort to help himself is hopeless. Married people who write about such problems are advised to correct the grammar gently, and always in private. The ear-grating gaffes should be ignored when others are present. Play deaf. You can't divorce a man because he says "have went."

When engaged people write with this complaint, I warn them that if the beloved's poor grammar and lack of general knowledge are a thorn in the side during courtship, it is bound to be a bone in the throat after marriage.

Often in my column I use the phrase "marriage is not a reform school." The notion that a man or woman can be made over after marriage is poppycock. A young woman from Sheboygan, Wisconsin, who wrote, "He drinks a little too much but promises to cut down after we are married," got this reply:

"If he drinks 'a little too much' now, he'll probably drink a lot too much after you marry him. A man who won't keep the cork in the bottle for his sweetheart certainly won't do it for his wife."

When I receive letters from girls who confide "my fiancé lost his temper and slapped me a few times—shall I have a word with him?" I tell them by all means, and the word should be "goodbye!" A woman who puts up with "a few slaps and punches" during courtship can expect loose bridgework and worse if she marries the man.

Superficial changes, however, are often made after marriage. A man may get his wife to cut her hair or let it grow, a woman may inveigle her husband into wearing more conservative neckties. But such minor triumphs have nothing to do with basic character. I urge engaged couples to take a good hard look at one another as they are *now,* because the husband or wife is going to be a great deal like the sweetheart, minus the halo and the wings.

In our society it is inevitable that people of different religious faiths fall in love and marry. Statistics support the theory that marriage works out best when both parties share the same religious faith. There was a time when I was strongly opposed to interfaith marriages, but I have changed my position in recent years. I have seen too many exceptions to the rule—on both ends of the spectrum. A great many marriages between individuals of the same faith have ended in the divorce courts. I am now seeing many marriages of mixed faiths doing extremely well.

If either the bride or groom has strong religious convictions I would not advise that individual to marry out of his faith. However, when neither bride nor groom has strong convictions about religion, it seems to make little difference in their lives.

I do feel, however, that the decision as to how to raise the children in regard to religious beliefs should be settled before marriage. The notion that "the kids can decide when they are old enough" is, to my way of thinking, not a sound approach. It goes without saying that if either husband or wife has promised at the time of marriage that all children from that marriage will be brought up in a certain faith, that promise should be kept—come what may.

To sum up:

(1) The more you have in common with the one you choose, the better your chances for a successful marriage. This means religious training, cultural, social and financial background. The old saying "opposites attract"

may be true in the field of electromagnetics, but it seldom works out in choosing a lifetime partner.

(2) Don't marry on the spur of the moment. If love is real, it will last. The tired line "marry in haste, repent at leisure" may be a cliché, but it still makes good sense.

(3) Don't marry a person whose chief attraction is sexual. A marriage based on sex will fall apart when the passions cool, and they'll cool a whole lot faster than you thought. The experts tell us that a male's peak of wow-power is at age seventeen. From then on—it's downhill, all the way.

(4) Don't marry with the intention of changing your beloved to meet your specifications. It won't work. If during courtship a person is unfaithful, a heavy drinker, a gambler or abusive, marriage will not provide the magic cure. In fact, he'll undoubtedly get worse as time goes on.

(5) Choose someone who wants the same things from life that you want. Discuss in detail your aims, goals and objectives. Marriage should mean companionship and building a life together.

(6) Approach marriage as a permanent relationship and not as an experiment which can be tossed aside if it doesn't work. Remember, a good marriage is not a gift—it's an achievement. It takes working at. You must repeatedly compromise. Forgive and forget. And then be smart enough to *forget* what you forgave. Often the difference between a successful marriage and a mediocre one is leaving four or five things a day—unsaid.

CREDIT: *Based on Ann Landers' book* Since You Ask Me, *Englewood Cliffs, New Jersey: Prentice-Hall.*

ANN LANDERS COOK?

DEAR ANN LANDERS: My wife hates housework and the place sure looks it. She says any idiot can clean a house, and she'd rather do something that requires brains. (Cooking is also for dummies, according to her.)

Whenever you print something about a sloppy housekeeper or a bum cook, I ask my wife if she read Ann Landers today. It burns her up. Yesterday it happened again. She said, "I'll bet Ann Landers doesn't do one lick of cooking or cleaning." I said I'd ask. How about it? MR. X

DEAR MR. X.: She's right. But I did for quite a few years. And my place always looked fairly presentable and nobody ever died from my cooking. Any more questions?

DEAR ANN: I read with great interest and mounting blood pressure the letter from the person who employs a "dumbbell" to do her ironing, although she did say that she was a nice person. Wasn't that sweet of her?

I have worked as a domestic in a household for several years, and if asked what qualifications you need to be able to do this type of work, I would say a degree in practically everything from psychology to nursing.

Also you should have your own teeth, because you will be grinding them a lot.

You will be working for women and men who don't have one ounce of common sense but are authorities on absolutely everything. They consider themselves BPs (Beautiful People). But the abbreviation really stands for Bitchy Phonies because that's what most of them are. P.S. If you think this letter is rough, you should see the ones I tore up. ANOTHER DUMB-BELL

DEAR FRIEND: Willie Washington is a wonderful woman who has done housework for me for 20 years. I read her your letter and asked for a comment. Willie said, "That woman is not going to like anybody she works for because she is mad at the whole world, including herself."

Interfaith Marriage

The Catholic Position

The position of the Roman Catholic Church on interfaith marriages is two-fold: It recognizes the positive aspects of such a marriage, but also is concerned about dangers of faith for both and the future marital stability of such a union.

In a broad sense, the Catholic Church is keenly aware of the role of religion in home and family life and also of the powerful and pervasive social conditions which threaten to undermine human dignity and marriage in America. Consequently, the Catholic Church is eager to join with all religious communions to bring the religious teaching of our respective faiths to bear upon our society and to join with all men of good will to create a healthier social climate in which family life in America can flourish.

In an interfaith marriage, permission is given primarily for the spiritual good of the couple. In the ecumenical climate following Vatican II Council, the bishops of the United States have taken action to promote among couples planning interfaith marriages better understanding and a respect for each other's faith.

In a statement of the National Conference of Catholic Bishops (January 1, 1971), the bishops emphasized some of the positive aspects of interfaith marriages, yet their concern for the faith of both parties and the inherent problems the couple realistically faces. They stated:

In order to aid these couples to come to this deep understanding of their married life together, when possible, the Catholic and other Christian pastors should jointly do all they can to prepare them for marriage and to support them and their families with all the aids their ministry can provide. They can, for example, enliven the couples' appreciation of the virtues of fidelity, mutual trust, forgiveness, honesty, openness, love and responsibility for their children. In this way the pastors of the different Christian communities can best bring the couple to a keen awareness of all that they have in common as Christians, as well as to a proper appreciation of the gravity of the differences that yet remain between their churches. (p. 4)

It is obvious, therefore, that in facing the prospect of interfaith marriage, preparation is paramount.

Presently, the marriage of a Catholic and non-Catholic is normally celebrated in the Catholic Church itself. However, for specific and valid reasons, permission is granted for the marriage to be celebrated in the church of the non-Catholic, especially if that person is the bride. Priests are permitted to participate in that marriage ceremony if invited to do so by their non-Catholic counterparts. Non-Catholic ministers also can participate with the priest in an interfaith marriage ceremony in the Catholic Church.

The problem of the faith of the children in an interfaith marriage continues to be a delicate one. The Catholic person is obliged not only to respect the freedom of conscience of his/her intended spouse, and in no way to violate his/her right and duty to follow his/her religious conviction, but the Catholic is expected to do everything possible to see that the children are reared Catholic. There is evidence, but not yet totally conclusive, that this problem and others related to it contribute to the religious indifference and the falling-away from religious practice by one or both parties.

One study indicates that 25 percent of such couples never attend church, and another 20 percent attend only occasionally. To the extent that the rate of desertion, separation or divorce is a criterion, the chance of failure has been found to be about three times greater in interfaith marriages than otherwise.

Realistically, when both parties approach an interfaith marriage, wisdom suggests that there should be a complete and free discussion on all factors involved prior to the marriage. Reasonable happiness in an interfaith marriage can be expected only when both parties have mature personalities, close affectionate ties, agree on goals and both want children.

CREDIT: *Most Rev. John J. Paul, D.D., Auxiliary Bishop of La Crosse, La Crosse, Wisconsin.*

The Historical Background
of Marriage Between
Jew and Gentile

There has never been and there is not now any Jewish religious law forbidding marriage between a Jew and one born a non-Jew. There have always been and there are now various shadings of opinions with regard to the conditions under which such a marriage may be considered religiously valid. These conditions have been and are determined largely by the historical and social circumstances and prejudices of the Jewish individual or the group making the determination.

From the earliest Bible times, the Jewish community has welcomed into its membership those who came voluntarily and sincerely, willing to accept its religious way of life. The only outsiders consistently denied such membership are polytheists (those who believe in many gods) and atheists.

Many who know not whereof they speak maintain that Deuteronomy 7:1–5 and Chapter 9 of the Book of Ezra forbid all marriages between Jews and non-Jews. This is not so. Both these passages merely proscribe marriages between Jews and the members of certain idolatrous Canaanitish tribes.

There is no mention, in the long list of biblical rituals, of any formal conversion rite beyond the circumcision required of all Jewish males. Like-minded non-Jews entered the biblical community, lived in it, worshipped with it, were accepted by it, married into it and became part of it. That was the truly spiritual, intelligent, efficient and practical way in which the biblical Jew handled the matter of intermarriage.

It was only in the post-biblical period, well along in the second Christian century, that circumstances of history stirred up strong Jewish opposition to intermarriage. The bitter persecution of the Jews by the Romans engendered in the Jews a violent dislike for the unlike. Also, as time went on, Christians and Muslims forbade their followers to marry Jews. As was only natural, the Jews retaliated in kind.

From the twelfth century on, hostility between Jew and non-Jew began to diminish. By the end of the eighteenth century, Christian and Jew were willing to admit that they had much in common. Jewish writers declared repeatedly in the later Middle Ages that Christianity and Islam are montheistic religions. Therefore, from the biblical point of view, there should have been no opposition to the marriage of Jews to Christians and Muslims. But there was and there continues to be such opposition. This opposition is more emotional than rational. It stems from the long record of Jewish maltreatment by Christians and Muslims, a sad saga of oppression, ghettoization, expulsion, pogroms, beating, robbing, murdering. Verily, "the fathers have eaten sour grapes and the children's teeth have been set on edge." To the majority of Jews, the idea of a son or daughter marrying a non-Jew is unwelcome because of a deeply embedded fear that even the best of non-Jews cannot be trusted to stand by the Jew when the chips are down.

How much of a threat is intermarriage to Jewish survival? Despite the hue and cry of professional Jewish propagandists, the realistic answer is: Not very much, at least at the present time.

In small communities with no synagogue and no rabbi, the Jew intermarries and disappears. In very large Jewish communities, with many synagogues and many rabbis, the Jewish intermarriage rate remains comparatively low. The most recent authentic study on Jewish intermarriages is that of Dr. Fred Massarik of the University of California at Los Angeles, completed in 1972 for the Council of Jewish Federations and Welfare Funds. For the years 1966–72, Massarik posited an intermarriage rate of 31.7 percent. At first sight, that figure would seem to be dangerously high, especially when one reads Dr. Massarik's finding that in 1920 it was only 2 percent. However, instead of becoming unduly alarmed by the 31.7 percent figure, the Jew should take just as seriously other statistics presented by Dr. Massarik, for example, that if the intermarrying Jew is a male, 63 percent of the children will be reared as Jews, and if the intermarrying Jew is a female, 98 percent of the children will be reared as Jews.

There are other important factors to consider. As has been indicated, the intermarriage rate in Jewish communities of twenty-five families or less is often close to 100 percent. In the largest Jewish communities (and most American Jews live in such), the intermarriage rate is somewhere between 12 and 20 percent. It is the very high proportion of intermarriages in the smaller communities that pulls the general average up to the 31.7 percent figure.

To understand this matter in true perspective, a distinction must be made between the person who happens by accident of birth to be a Jew and the one who is actively identified with Jewish religious life. Only about half the Jews in the United States belong to synagogues. With all due respect, the only Jews who really count as far as American Jewish survival is concerned are those who are members of the Jewish *religious* community. Every Jewish community study made to date shows that the rate of intermarriage among synagogue-identified Jews is much lower than among the non-identified. If one considers only those intermarriages in which a synagogued Jew marries a non-Jew who does not convert, the over-all intermarriage percentile dips to no more than 10 percent. If the study is narrowed even further to count only those Jews who are positively identified with the synagogue before marriage but who, after marriage, are lost to Jewish religious life because of the influence of the non-Jewish spouse, the loss to the American Jewish *religious* community is no more than 2 or 3 percent.

Traditional Jewish law states that no conversion to Judaism is valid that is based on any self-seeking motive, professional, educational, social or matrimonial. Yet most rabbis will not officiate at a marriage between a Jew and a born non-Jew unless the non-Jew converts prior to the marriage. In other words, the majority of rabbis deliberately choose to bypass the Jewish religious law in this area. They rationalize their conduct by saying they are choosing what they believe to be the lesser of two evils. About half the Reform rabbis of this country officiate at intermarriages without requiring the conversion of the non-Jew. Most of these Reform rabbis expect a commitment from the couple that its children will be reared in the Jewish faith.

How do Jewish intermarriages work out? Jewish prophets of doom proclaim ceaselessly in pulpit and press that all such marriages are ill-fated from the start. This is sheer nonsense. There is no firm proof that these marriages are much less stable than the average all-Jewish marriage. When a divorce does occur in a Jewish intermarriage, it is seldom based on grounds having to do with a difference in religions. The basic reasons are economic woes, sexual incompatibility, personality conflicts, etc., the same reasons that cause all-Jewish marriages to fail. It is also crystal clear that when the spouses-to-be arrive at a firm *pre-marital* determination regarding the religious rearing of their offspring, the possibility of religious difference causing friction in the marriage becomes almost nil.

Having written all this, how would I answer the questions: Do I encourage marriages between Jews and non-Jews? Do I look with favor on Jewish intermarriages? The answer to both questions would be: No. The most successful marriages are those in which husband and wife come from as similar backgrounds as possible, culturally, educationally, financially and religiously. Religious background is important but no more important than the other factors mentioned. But the marriage of a Jew to a non-Jew, when it occurs, must be viewed in the light of experience and common sense rather than in the shady recesses of prejudice and emotion. If a Jew who is ethnically oriented and synagogally affiliated marries a non-Jew, the odds are overwhelming that the non-Jew will be drawn into the Jewish orbit. If the Jew who marries the non-Jew is indifferent to his or her Jewish heritage both before and after the marriage, the Jewish community and religion have not lost much.

CREDIT: *Rabbi David Max Eichorn, Satellite Beach, Florida.*

Marriage Between Jew and Non-Jew

Intermarriage is the marriage of a Jew to a person who was not Jewish at the time the couple first met, though conversion may follow before or soon after the marriage. Where there is no conversion, the marriage should be termed a mixed marriage.

According to 1970–72 demographic study of the American Jewish community by Fred Massarik covering a sample of seven thousand interviews, 13 percent of marriages involving Jews were intermarriages in 1960, 29.7 percent in 1961–65, and 48.1 percent in 1966–72.

According to this survey, the combination of a Jewish husband and a non-Jewish wife is twice as common as the combination of a Jewish wife and a non-Jewish husband.

One out of four non-Jewish brides converts to Judaism; less for non-Jewish husbands.

According to the study, 98 percent of the children are reared as Jews if the mother is Jewish, and 63 percent if the father is Jewish.

Less than 1 percent of intermarrying Jews convert to Christianity, while 26.7 percent of non-Jewish females and 2.5 percent of non-Jewish males convert to Judaism. Further, more than 40 percent of non-Jewish marriage partners prior to marriage subsequently identify themselves as Jewish, even without formal conversion.

Statistics indicate that native-born Jews of the second generation tend to intermarry more than do the members of the immigrant generation. In the third generation the rate goes up even higher. College attendance doubles the intermarriage rate in the third generation.

Children born of a non-Jewish mother and a Jewish father are considered non-Jewish. And alternatively, children born of a Jewish mother and a non-Jewish father are considered Jewish. The former category of children will require conversion in order to be accepted in the Jewish group, though no restrictions are placed upon them once they have converted.

Neither Conservative nor Orthodox rabbis will officiate at a marriage between a Jew and an unconverted non-Jew, though both will officiate at the marriage of a Jew with one who has converted to Judaism prior to marriage.

Neither Conservative nor Orthodox rabbis will co-officiate with a non-Jewish clergyman, nor participate in a civil ceremony where one of the partners is not Jewish. While Reform Judaism is on record as opposing the participation of rabbis in a civil marriage or in a marriage between a Jew and one who is not a Jew, individual rabbis are granted the right to deviate from this ruling. The majority of Reform rabbis refuse to perform mixed marriages.

None of the three movements places any obstacle upon the marriage of a Jew to one who converts to Judaism prior to marriage.

Rabbis who will not participate in a marriage between a Jew and a non-Jew give the following reasons for their opposition:

(1) Religion is too important to be taken lightly.

(2) Rabbis have no right to impose their procedures upon one who may prefer to maintain his or her Christian identity.

(3) A sincere Christian cannot in good conscience recite or acquiesce to the phrase which sanctifies Jewish marriage and which the groom is expected to recite with the acquiescence of the bride: "With this ring I betroth thee as my wife in accordance with the Laws of Moses and the customs of the faith of Israel."

(4) The rabbi cannot conscientiously give his blessings to a marriage in which children born of that union may be torn between two religions and two parents. The emotional welfare of the child depends upon the religious integrity of the home.

(5) Withholding of rabbinic participation may be kinder than submission to the will of the bride and groom, in that non-rabbinic participation may influence the bride and groom to face up to the implications of their religious difference before bringing children into the world. Children who are left free to choose their religion may pit one parent against the other. Moreover, the preservation of the Jewish people depends upon households where both partners are committed to transmitting the faith of Judaism.

CREDIT: *Stanley Rabinowitz, rabbi; President, the Rabbinical Assembly (international organization of Conservative rabbis); rabbi of the ADAS Israel Synagogue, Washington, D.C.*

The Presbyterian View on Interfaith Marriage

On questions of marriage, Presbyterian churches throughout the country are guided for the most part by their statements of faith (generally called "Confessions") or by their denominational rules ("Forms of Government") or by the way they conduct their services and ceremonies ("Directories of Worship").

We use the word "guided" advisedly, because in the last resort, the decision about who can or should be married in a Presbyterian church is almost exclusively a decision arrived at by the local pastor. Sometimes this decision is made after consultation with the appropriate committee of the church's session—the official board of the church which locally controls all matters relating to a particular congregation.

Some Presbyterian ministers would make a distinction between an interfaith marriage and one which is interdenominational in character. As an example of an interdenominational marriage, we have the union of a man and a woman in holy wedlock who may be members of the Methodist, Baptist, Lutheran, Presbyterian churches, etc., or between members of the various Christian traditions, such as Roman Catholic, Orthodox, Coptic, Protestant. All of these being "Christian" in their confessions and beliefs, it is generally assumed that there is no barrier on the Presbyterian side for uniting two people coming from these backgrounds.

But supposing one or both is divorced? Obviously they can't get married in a Roman Catholic or an Episcopalian church without considerable difficulty. While in Presbyterian churches great care is required on the minister's part when he or she consents to the remarriage of divorced people, the barriers are not formidable. If there is true recognition of human frailty, failure and sinfulness, and a desire to begin again in the light of God's forgiveness, Presbyterians believe that this can happen with the blessing of the Church. Such blessing would not be withheld because people come from different Christian backgrounds, such as Protestant and Roman Catholic.

The interfaith issue calls for even greater thought and delicacy of approach. Here we are thinking, for instance, about the Christian faith and the Jewish faith, or the Moslem faith. It would be impossible to be dogmatic about a "Presbyterian position" on interfaith marriage in this sense, since

Presbyterians are divided in their convictions on some important issues relating to the union of a man and woman "in the holy bonds of matrimony." These divisions of opinion may arise from differences of theological belief, or conscience, or even from geographical location (north and south).

We must not assume, however, that since it is impossible to be dogmatic about interfaith marriage, Presbyterians act in a vacuum. Presbyterians hold definite beliefs about what is sometimes called the "sanctification of marriage."

In the marriage between two people of different faiths, such as Christian and Jewish, the Presbyterian minister is called upon to emphasize the privileges and obligations that would be assumed in a Christian marriage. This would involve a discussion of the meaning of baptism for the couple themselves and for their families.

It will be expected that at least one of the partners is a professing Christian. Where such a background is lacking, the minister and the man and woman will be asked to face frankly the jeopardy in which this lack may place both their marriage and the Christian nurture of their children, and shall take all such steps as may be possible to provide against the hazard.

In the light of these convictions, when "interfaith" means a marriage between a Christian and a non-Christian (that is, one committed in belief to another faith altogether), there may be no insurmountable barriers so long as one is a member of the Church and the other is a believer in God as he or she understands Him. This the officiating minister must decide, and considerable sensitivity and care are expected in interpreting to such a couple the expectations and obligations which are placed upon them by the sacramental nature of marriage.

A few specific examples may be helpful. Many Presbyterian ministers would officiate at the marriage of a member of their church to people of the Jewish faith, whether Reformed or Orthodox, so long as both partners had considered the implications of the "sanctification of marriage" and both believed that it is God who "joins them together." The same would apply with equal validity to a non-practicing Roman Catholic and a Presbyterian member. Some variations may be used in the wording of the marriage service, but there could be no surrender on the Presbyterian minister's side of the centrality of God's action in this union, and the living presence of Christ. How the latter phrase is understood by the non-professing Christian would be a matter for his or her conscience.

The issue of divorce of one or both partners in an interfaith marriage and their seeking remarriage in a Presbyterian church leads to many complications which only the minister can unravel in consultation with the parties concerned.

Greater care than ever is expected in the light of what Presbyterians believe, how they govern their churches and how they conduct their services and ceremonies. It would be impossible to generalize about "what most" Presbyterian ministers would do, and it would be fruitless to try to abstract guidelines from their Confessions of Faith. Some ministers, for instance, would marry a twice-divorced Presbyterian and a Roman Catholic in good standing, or not such good standing, if there was evidence of sincerity in seeking God's Will in their lives. Others would be adamantly opposed to this, not because they believe such people to be "beyond the pale" religiously, but because they would find it impossible to reconcile their beliefs concerning the teaching of the Scriptures, the intent of the teaching of the Church, and the repeated dissolution of marriage unions.

To sum up: The Presbyterian position tends to be inclusive rather than exclusive where there is a common belief in God, so long as one person in the marriage union is a committed Christian in terms of belief and practice. Where there is the possibility that religious differences would lead to increased tension and disharmony within the marriage relationship, extreme caution is urged on the minister (or session) in permitting such a service to be held in a Presbyterian church, or to receive the official blessing of the Church, whether the service were held in the chancel or in the minister's office. Further, where there is suspicion that there is failure on the part of one or both persons seeking marriage to understand the intent of lifelong union ("Till death do us part") in the Presbyterian marriage service, the caution demanded of the officiating minister almost borders on total prohibition.

CREDIT: *Elam Davies, pastor of the Fourth Presbyterian Church, Chicago, Illinois.*

Interfaith Marriage

Reform Jews and Gentiles

I am old enough to remember when the parents considered a son or daughter who married out of the Jewish faith dead. The Kaddish (prayer for the dead) was said and the picture of "the lamb who strayed" was turned to face the wall.

Reform rabbis today are permitted to marry couples "in accordance with their conscience." I always agree to marry couples, even though one may be non-Jewish. I realize they will be married, either by me or by someone else, so I try to work at keeping the family intact as best I can. When I see there is opposition from one set of parents or the other—as often there is—I make a special effort to get the Christian parents to accept the Jew and the Jewish parents to accept the Christian.

These days, many couples want to write their own marriage ceremony. This does not sit well with most rabbis or ministers with whom I have spoken. But we are agreeable, to a point, permitting them to use some of their own words, along with biblical passages and, of course, that which is required in order to make it a valid marriage ceremony.

Today more and more requests are made for a rabbi to officiate *with* a priest or minister. I had such a ceremony recently. The father of the young man was an Episcopal minister. How could I refuse? At this moment, I am the only rabbi in New Orleans who will officiate at such a service. One couple asked me to give the benediction in Hebrew which the Christian partner had prepared for me. He graciously left out any reference to his Savior.

Naturally, I prefer to marry a couple when both are Jewish, but these times are so rife with change, what shall we do? Deny what is real and live in the past? I say no—we cannot talk of brotherhood and refuse to co-operate with people of other faiths.

CREDIT: *Dr. Julian B. Feibelman, Rabbi Emeritus, Temple Sinai, New Orleans.*

Is Your Marriage Worth Saving?

The question "How do you find out whether your marriage is worth saving?" involves additional questions: "How long does it take when you are married to tell if it is worth it or not?" "Are these problems so serious that they would make the marriage impossible to save—or at least not worth the effort?" "What are the qualities that make a marriage worth saving?" "Under what circumstances are marriages likely to fail?"

The answer to all these questions is that you never know for sure. The best you can do is make an educated guess. Your guess may shape a portion of your life.

The questions asked above must be modified to: "What additional information or education can you give me so I can make a better informed guess, so the odds on being right will be better; the likelihood of being wrong will be less?"

Having redefined the question, the problem of the questioner is often seen as a fear of making a decision, a lack of trust in one's own judgment. For example, frequently individuals know there is a lot "wrong" before they get married, but they think they will change the other person "later." This is a very common and serious mistake. Instead of getting out soon after the marriage, when it becomes clear that no change will take place, they may spend the rest of their lives trying to change the mate and continue to wonder if the marriage is worth saving.

Another situation is one in which the woman is aware that the man was different from the other men she dated. He treated her "like a lady" during the courtship. He made no sexual advances. She interpreted this as a sign of "respect" and assumed that sex would come naturally after marriage. Or there is the man whose fiancée would not let him touch her before marriage and who attributed her rigidity to religious scruples. Then comes the marriage ceremony and the honeymoon. No sex takes place. The secret is out. The male continues with no sex or a very low sexual frequency. The decision must be made. Is sexual activity as important as other advantages offered by a sexless mate? If so, the individual must be capable of acting on this value system. If other advantages offered by the sexless mate are more important than sexual activity, the individual must be capable of forgoing sex.

Let us take another set of personal values to illustrate the principle of making choices. Suppose an individual believes marriage will offer an opportunity for development and fulfillment for both partners. After marriage, such a person may recognize that the marriage will be safe and stable but unstimulating with no growth potential. A decision must be made: to hold to one's values and get a divorce or to give up one's expectations as unrealistic and settle for what one has. The decision may be a good one either way. The people who have problems are those who can't make a decision or who say, "Why can't my mate change so I can have this marriage and what I want for myself, too?"

What the about-to-be-wed, or the newly wed, individual must realize is that there is little education or preparation for marriage. The two individuals involved do not know how to maximize their respective fulfillment, growth and development in a complex marital union. The marriage license requires less preparation, knowledge and money than are required for a driver's license.

Another preconception about marriage is that it is expected to be the most intimate, happy and successful relationship people will ever experience. For the fortunate ones this is true, but the rising divorce rate in America indicates how often this is not true. Our current culture accentuates another myth about marriage—that if the union fails, it is somebody's fault—that one of the parties is stupid, stubborn, evil or pathological.

The ideal of medicine is prevention. This is certainly true in the field of marriage. Pre-marital counseling should be a part of every pre-marital examination along with a physical examination, laboratory testing and birth control information. The difficulty that sometimes occurs is that even when told that a marriage will have serious problems and probably not work without counseling, the couple often get married anyhow and wait until the predicted troubles become painful before seeking the required professional help. There are also important problems of genetic counseling that should be discussed in the pre-marital examination.

Having responded to the question of how to find out if your marriage is worth saving by the establishment of general principles and describing the complexities of the problem, I can now answer the questions directly. How long does it take to tell if it is worth it or not?

At either end of the bell-shaped curve, the answer is: For some, they know immediately that it won't work, for others, they know immediately that this is what they want for a lifetime. These are not thought-out, intellectualized responses. They are gut responses that represent the basic feelings of the individual. In between these extremes marital strife and disruption take their toll.

Certain symptoms can occur soon after the marriage (even on the honeymoon), or they may develop through the years. They vary from mild or moderate phobias, depressions, anxiety attacks, psychosomatic illnesses, to the serious life-threatening stress-type illnesses, physical abuse, suicides and homicides. These would seem obvious clues as to whether the marriage is worth it or not. Yet many marital partners, even under these conditions, ask if it is worth it or how long they should wait before deciding.

How do you know if your marriage is worth saving? You are the *only* one who can tell, by getting in touch with your feelings. No one else knows how you feel. No one else can feel exactly the way you do. And no one else will take the consequences of your decision for you. So—get all the help you can to become knowledgeable about all aspects of the decision. Then make the decision.

In my experience there are only a few factors that would make a marriage impossible to save. One is the absence in both mates of the ability to feel sympathy for the other. This is usually accompanied by a deep and unchanging hatred. Another is the presence in one mate of a problem such as homosexuality or transsexualism. Even here if sympathetic understanding is present, free of destructive hostilities, such marriages are not impossible to save and for some individuals are worth trying to save. Marriages that provoke serious thoughts of suicide or homicide are *not* worth saving.

When we come to the question of what are the qualities that make a marriage worth saving, we come to the subjects of respect and love. Where there is the capacity within the marital partners of respect for another human being, we have a working basis of a marriage that is worth saving. Such an ability for sympathy and empathy for other individuals makes for successful solving of interpersonal problems. This is not identical with love but is related to the capacity for love of other people.

The capacity for love of the other person relates to the capacity to place the welfare of the mate on an equal (if not higher) level with one's own welfare. When this quality is present in one of the mates, the marriage is certainly worth saving.

Marriages which are most likely to fail are those where both mates are of the dependent, clinging type, each expecting the other to create an atmosphere in which he or she will be catered to and taken care of.

Up to this point, I have responded to the questions on the basis of a marriage without children for the purpose of simplification. However, these questions are often asked because the children are the complicating factor. Is the marriage worth saving for the sake of the children? Should a parent sacrifice personal values, goals and ambitions for the good of the children? Certainly children are traumatized by separation and divorce, but they also are traumatized by the atmosphere of hostility and destructiveness of parents living together when they hate each other.

Often the destructive effects of the divorce upon the children are the result of the manner in which the parents get the divorce and carry on their hostilities after the divorce. Marital and divorce counseling can be used to defuse the relationship between the parents so that the damage to the children is minimized. Children of divorce comprise a relatively high proportion of the child psychiatric population. Divorce is experienced differently by children at different developmental levels.

Mates who are tradition- and future-generation-minded will tend to emphasize maintaining the marriage more than those who are self-growth-oriented, and who may even feel that the divorce will be better for the future growth of their children.

The desirable role of the family is to provide a support system and growth center for each person within the family. Parents and children must be capable of recognizing their own deep needs for independence and growth. If this can be achieved, no matter how much work it takes, the marriage is worth saving. If this cannot be achieved, how much are you willing to sacrifice before you say, "Enough is enough. I've had it."

Many marital counselors are coming to believe that the goal is not to maintain, preserve or even increase the number of happy marriages, but rather to encourage couples to stay together only if marriage means maximizing the development of both partners, in which case it will surely benefit the children.

Regardless of the length of time a relationship has existed, symptoms of conflict are fairly clear. Usually when the warmth and closeness of a relationship begin to fade the overriding feeling is one of irritation, annoyance or disappointment at seeing or interacting with your partner.

The husband resists going home after work. The wife, if she works, finds it harder to get home and await her husband's arrival. She visits friends more than she used to and goes to more meetings. If she stays home, she no longer cooks with pride. She does not look as attractive as she could and she watches the clock matter-of-factly at bedtime rather than with a sense of excitement. Obviously in such a relationship, romance no longer exists, but the couple is not meeting one another's needs.

Conflicts tend to crystallize. The couple find it difficult to converse. There is a block in communication. Sensitive issues come up frequently and with almost no provocation: When will the bills get paid and who will pay them? How will the money be divided and to whom does it really belong? How much time should we spend with relatives? Sharing and allocating of responsibilities around the house become a problem. All external daily matters, which perhaps were not issues in better times, suddenly become major sore spots about which both partners may express irritation without focusing on the real problems of the relationship.

Both partners realize at some level that they are pessimistic about their future together, yet they cannot identify the core of their discomfort. Thus, each one looks to the other to account for their troubles. Yet there is the underlying feeling that something is wrong, that something must be changed to restore the excitement and sense of togetherness that the relationship previously held.

This seems to be happening all the time. Half the young people getting married are divorced or separated. There are multiple reasons. Large among them are changing economic conditions in society and changing expectations from within. Many men used to marry because they needed a woman to cook for them, to clean for them, to mend their socks and to have sex with. Romance, if it existed, was the frosting on the cake. Nowadays it's no trouble to cook for yourself. You buy ready-to-eat food in the supermarket or go to a fast food counter. No one mends any more. Who wears mended socks? Sex is readily available. So men don't need to get married and neither do women, except for one factor—loneliness.

Women needed men to support them, while they kept house. Now they can have careers. Housekeeping is so simplified they can cook and clean for themselves even with a nine-to-five job. When people needed each other they tended to stay together. Today they marry because they want each other. And when they stop wanting, there is no real reason to stay together, especially because when you stop wanting one person it's usually because you've started to want another.

If there are children, the parents don't care what harm comes to the children. Values have changed. The self is now more important than the child's welfare. As your growing sense of dissatisfaction continues, interaction between partners becomes worse. You may feel alone in this monumental decision which is to shape your future. External forces urge you to remain in your relationship and insinuate that if you cannot be happy there is something wrong with you. You feel unsure and doubtful, wonder whether you should pull out or settle for what you have. It's not very good but it's better than nothing.

This is a trying period. Guilt racks you. Confidence in yourself is lost. You feel hurt and angry at yourself for being where you are. You can't believe you could have made such a mistake in choosing a mate.

Feeling guilty and uncertain comes from not having your needs gratified. You are not sure you had a right to expect to be fulfilled. You feel guilty for the expectations you've built up.

However, feeling this new surge of emotion and experiencing the sense that you need and want *more* in a relationship is a healthy step. It is the first step toward affirmation of who you are—the first step toward realization of your full capacity to love and to be loved and valued for yourself. It is the first step toward realization in reality of yourself as an important and meaningful entity. You finally see yourself as a person with needs and rights—one who expects fulfillment and gratification in life. Confronting your situation in all its stark reality is the only way to learn about yourself and your needs.

When you are no longer willing to perpetuate ungratifying patterns, it means you are no longer willing to accept a position of weakness—a position which prevented you from having your needs met and enjoying your life to the full.

Part of the difficulty which you now face stems from your insecurity in standing firm and in fighting for what you feel you deserve. Remember, lack of success in marriage does not mean a deficiency in either person. To admit failure may mean to acknowledge faith in the future. One cannot close the door on a relationship unless one has enough of a sense of self to expect to find a better relationship. One cannot leave a relationship or risk changing it if one imagines being alone to be excruciatingly painful.

In changing or leaving a relationship one feels optimistic about the future. You expect to be responded to as a valuable, worthwhile human being. The key to the problem is the capacity for hope. Hope gives us the power to act in the present. The future is now.

CREDIT: *Peter A. Martin, M.D., Clinical Professor of Psychiatry, University of Michigan and Wayne State University Medical Schools, author of* A Marital Therapy Manual, *New York: Brunner/Mazel, 1976.*

HERE'S DESCRIPTION OF 'THE OTHER MAN'

DEAR ANN LANDERS: You recently had a column describing "The Other Woman." Why is it no one has ever described "The Other Man"? He is everywhere. Places you'd never suspect. I'd like to try my hand at it since I know him well. My wife knows him even better.

The Other Man is never seen in the morning, unshaven, with hair disheveled, in a ratty bathrobe, groping for his glasses. He appears in the morning (at work) or in the evening at a favorite rendezvous, looking perfectly groomed and very appealing.

The Other Man is not puttering around the house in torn trousers and an old shirt, trying to fix the plumbing or a garage door or a leak in the roof. No hint of perspiration from mowing the lawn or washing the car. He smells of cologne, toothpaste and aftershave.

The Other Man is always in a good mood. When he is with you he is out for a good time. He leaves his worries at home.

The Other Man invariably has a wife who has back trouble, is emotionally disturbed, frigid, and is a terrible nag. She doesn't understand him and talks of nothing but bills, unmanageable kids, bothersome relatives and things that are depressing. But he can't leave her to marry you—for awhile—because of financial circumstances, the children, his aging mother, his religion or his boss. His list of excuses is endless.

The Other Man doesn't care that he has caused his wife untold hours of anguish, that she has become a guilt-ridden nervous wreck, confused and unsure of herself. He doesn't give a thought to the fact that his children have heard rumors, or sense something is terribly wrong in the family. He is having a great big round ball—concerned only with himself, his pleasure and his ego, in spite of what he has led his playmate to believe. Do you know him? Look again. WATCHING IT ALL FROM UP CLOSE

DEAR WATCHING: Thank you for an insightful description. It's bound to hit a lot of people where they live—or at least visit.

A SEXUAL SCORECARD

DEAR ANN LANDERS: This morning when my neighbor came over for our regular 10 o'clock cup of coffee, she had in her hand a letter her husband had brought home from work. He thought it was pretty funny. We wonder how much kidding on the square was involved. Here's the letter, Ann. Please decide:

DEAR LOVING WIFE: During the past year, I have tried to make love to you 365 times. I recorded 320 excuses and 45 successes. I kept track of the reasons which accompanied the refusals. Here they are:

We'll wake the children	17
It's too hot	10
It's too cold	5
I'm too tired	32
It's too early	15
It's too late	23
Please, dear, I'm asleep	35
Windows open, neighbors might hear	9
Backache	18
Headache	16
Toothache	2
Drank too much	4
Ate too much	14
Not in the mood	21
Mud pack	2
New hairdo	17
Company in next room	11
Wouldn't you rather watch the late TV show?	40
Is that all you men think about	29

Thanks, dear.

YOUR LOVING HUSBAND
(BUT NOT ENOUGH)

How about it, Ann. Is it funny? PARADISE, CALIF.

DEAR PARADISE: Yes, it's funny, but like a great deal that passes for humor, I sense a lot of kidding on the square.

MAKE EXCUSES, NOT LOVE?

DEAR ANN: I'm one of the thousands (maybe millions) of wives whose husbands asked, "Did you read Ann Landers today?" The letter he wanted me to see was signed, "Your Loving Husband—But Not Enough." We both laughed and thought it was very clever.

How about equal time for a wife's rebuttal?

Dear Loving Husband:

During the last year I approached you to make love to me 365 times, but you had 329 excuses. You said "Yes" 36 times. Here's my tally on the excuses:

Hard day at the office—40 times.

Argument with the boss, too tense—35 times.

Important meeting tomorrow, have to get a good night's sleep—30 times.

It's too cold in here—5 times.

It's too hot in here—20 times.

I'm beat—30 times.

My back is acting up again—30 times.

I drank too much, couldn't hack it—15 times.

I can't tear myself away from this terrific movie (during which you fell asleep)—40 times.

As soon as I finish this article (during which you fell asleep)—35 times.

I was sleeping, what did you say?—30 times.

We aren't newlyweds anymore. What are you trying to prove?—10 times.

Why don't you go bowling with the girls or take a cold shower?—9 times.

Signed—Your Loving Wife, But Not Forever P.S. Ann, dear girl, will you please rush the name of "Loving Husband" and send it to my new address, which will be Siberia if my husband finds out I wrote this letter. ROCKFORD, ILL.

DEAR ROCK: My lips are sealed. I'll never never tell. Incidentally, I received dozens of tallies from other wives who had a similar tale of woe, but you told yours best.

Marriage*

An Overview

MARRIED LIFE
RULES FOR A HAPPY ONE

(1) Never both be angry at once.

(2) Never yell at each other unless the house is on fire.

(3) Yield to the wishes of the other as an exercise in self-discipline if you can't think of a better reason.

(4) If you have a choice between making yourself look good or your mate—choose your mate.

(5) If you have any criticism, make it lovingly.

(6) Never bring up a mistake of the past.

(7) Neglect the whole world rather than each other.

(8) Never let the day end without saying at least one complimentary thing to your life's partner.

(9) Never meet without an affectionate welcome.

(10) Never go to bed mad.

(11) When you've made a mistake, talk it out and ask for forgiveness.

(12) Remember, it takes two to make an argument. The one who is wrong is the one who will be doing most of the talking.

"If you had it to do over again, would you marry the person to whom you are now married?" This is the question I put to my readers.

Mr. and Mrs. John Q. Public responded with unprecedented speed and vehemence. Within ten days my office was buried under fifty thousand pieces of mail. Although I had requested "postcards only," more than seven thousand letters arrived—long ones—describing in detail how "terrific" (or "rotten") their marriage was.

My instructions were as follows: "Tell me (on a postcard, no letters please) if you had it to do over again, would you have married the person to whom you are now married? Write YES or NO. State whether you are male or female, and the number of years you have been married."

* Originally titled "If You Had It to Do All Over Again Would You Marry the Same Person?" Reprinted from July 1977 issue of *Family Circle* magazine, © 1977, The Family Circle, Inc.

Although my work has made me positively shockproof, I must confess the results of this survey rattled me. It was a devastating commentary on marriage, American style.

Seventy percent of the fifty thousand readers who responded did not sign their names. In my opinion, the unsigned responses reflected the true story. The final count—52 percent voted no; 48 percent voted yes. The breakdown of the unsigned mail: 70 percent from females and 30 percent from males. Of the signed mail, 70 percent said yes (many who signed their names also gave their addresses), 30 percent said no. Eighty percent of the signed mail came from females and 20 percent came from males.

We received forty-two postcards from homosexuals, who considered themselves "just as married as anyone else." They were all happy and voted yes.

I couldn't do a thing with "number of years married" because more than half who responded misunderstood the question and gave their ages instead. (Apparently Johnny isn't the only one in the family who can't read.)

Most respondents were candid about telling why they voted the way they did. One wife from Corning, New York, wrote: "Carl is one of those non-talkers you get so many complaints about. The last time he spoke a full sentence to me was Friday. He said, 'Pass the salt.' But actions speak louder than words, Ann. Today he brought home a dozen roses. I'm voting yes."

An Oakland male waxed philosophical: "We still love each other—physically, I mean—but we don't like each other. I vote no."

From Davenport, Iowa, I received a curious card with two votes—his and hers. She wrote: "I'm a female, married twenty-seven years. We are the happiest couple in town. I vote a great big yes." At the bottom of the card, hastily scrawled in pencil, was a word from her husband, who apparently had been asked to drop the card in the mailbox. He added: "That's what she thinks. I vote no."

One hundred and ninety women voted "Hell, no." One hundred and four men voted "Hell, no." Most of the "Hell, no"s were in extra-large block letters, heavily underlined and often followed by several exclamation points. A "Hell, no" from Omaha was written with such a heavy hand the pen went clear through the postcard.

From New Orleans, a male (age fifty-one, married thirty-four years) wrote: "No! No! A thousand times no. If I had any guts I would have called it quits twenty years ago. It's too late now. She's sick and I can't leave her."

A husband in Roanoke, Virginia (married fifty-six years), said: "Yes. She is a beautiful person . . . Women had character in those days."

A wife from Bonita Springs, Florida, made a point that turned up repeatedly among the negative responses. Reactions ran the gamut from quiet acceptance to angry resentment. The Florida woman wrote: "I would have voted yes during the first five years of our marriage, but I'm voting no now. He was 'Mr. Right' at the time, but somehow we didn't grow together and today we have very little in common. If I didn't have some outside intellectual stimulation, I'd go bananas. The man is dull, dull, dull."

A wife from a fashionable New Jersey suburb (she asked me not to pinpoint her residence) wrote: "When we were poor, our marriage was fun. Things changed when my husband started to make big money. We joined the country club, played golf and bridge. Then came the fancy clothes and expensive cars. Yes, we take glamorous trips and entertain a lot, but we haven't carried on a real conversation in years. I vote no. I'm sure he would vote no too."

One of the most heartwarming cards came from Mr. and Mrs. C. A. Jones of Santa Ana, California. It was Mr. Jones who wrote: "Yes! We've been married nearly sixty-six years. I am ninety; my wife is eighty-eight. See recent photo on reverse side." And there it was—two adorable, smiling faces, their white heads together; she wearing a double orchid corsage, he with a pink rose in his lapel. (I noted with interest that a great many yes votes came from couples who said they had been married over forty years.)

Thousands of no voters bluntly stated that sex was the major problem. Most women complained about the absence or infrequency of sexual relations, while the men were critical of the quality. ("She wants the lights out, the kids asleep and the phone taken off the hook. I have to shave and shower. All this for the deadest three minutes you can imagine.")

A man who voted "Hell, no" in Salem, Oregon, added, "Marriage is the only war where you sleep with the enemy. And sleep is all I get. I drew one of those cold fish you write about."

From Miami, Florida, a twenty-seven-year-old male and a twenty-nine-year-old female wrote: "Yes. We've been married five years. And we plan to stay happily married. We decided at the outset not to have any children."

A couple from Lancaster, Pennsylvania, both voted no—and it was the last election that did it. The wife wrote, "The fool is still defending Nixon and Agnew. It burns me up. Ford may be a nice guy, but he was picked by Nixon and that was enough for me. I vote no." The husband wrote on the same card, "We got along okay until my wife decided to go for that peanut farmer from Georgia. The day she came home wearing a Carter button, I knew I had married the wrong woman. I vote no."

At least one thousand no voters gave religion as the reason for sticking with a marriage that had gone sour. An eighty-one-year old woman from Dayton, Ohio, put it this way: "My marriage was a mistake and I knew it after two years, but I stayed with him because I am a Catholic. I'm glad to see the Church is becoming more human and moving away from some of the old nonsense. If I were twenty-five years younger, I would definitely get a divorce."

Several hundred widows voted yes (many from St. Petersburg, Santa Barbara, Monterey, Los Angeles and Honolulu). Almost every widow who voted yes extolled the virtues of her dearly departed. ("He was a saint.") Interesting how death improves people.

In-laws were mentioned in several responses. A male from Traverse City, Michigan, wrote: "Yes. She's a great girl. I would marry her again—but I'd poison her mother first."

An Indianpolis female (age forty-two) wrote: "I vote no four times. Once on account of him—he's a gutless wonder—and once for each of his miserable sisters."

Alcohol was mentioned by thousands of no voters. A Wichita, Kansas, wife said, "Put my vote in the no column. I could have handled his side affairs, the years of job-hopping and even the poker losses, but when the booze took over it destroyed all my love and respect. Whenever you mention A.A., I put the column where he can see it, but he's too pie-eyed to read."

Hundreds of writers took the opportunity to cast a belated vote for the first survey. They added a P.S. "And yes, I would have had every one of my children if I had it to do over again." But at least as many mentioned children as the reason they were voting no. A man in Louisville put it candidly: "The first five years of our marriage were great; then the children started coming. They ruined it for me. She became all mother, no wife. Long before they were teenagers they learned how to 'divide and conquer.' This house is an armed camp. The wife and kids are on one side and I'm on the other."

No one knows what a marriage is like except the two people in it—and sometimes one of them doesn't know. I arrived at this conclusion after having my ear—and eyes—bent by thousands of people whose marriages were considered "very good" by observers.

It is my firm conviction that a truly beautiful marriage—one that offers joy, fulfillment and genuine contentment with both parties operating on the same wave length as friends, partners and lovers—is very hard to find. I had such a marriage for many years, and it ended in divorce. Perhaps the lesson to be learned is, "No one knows what tomorrow will bring."

I believe if twenty-five couples were selected at random and their marriages examined under the glaring light of truth, it would be discovered that one marriage out of twenty-five is "very good." Four are "okay,"—which means they get along fairly well most of the time. Seven are bad—much bickering, many fights, poor communication—but the situation is tolerable. Eight of the twenty-five are unrewarding—a real drag, both parties fed up and wishing there were an easy way out. Five are disasters—they share nothing, not even a bed. Yet they plug along year after year, like a pair of matched mules, putting up a front, or not even bothering to pretend—needling each other at every opportunity, battling in the presence of family and friends. Or sadder still, they simply ignore each other: no sex; no conversation; no communication. They turn to hard liquor, white wine, work, hockey, golf, gambling or sleeping around. I've discovered, too, that millions of marrieds escape their boring—or punitive—partners by hooking their eyeballs into the TV set.

TV has had a stronger impact on our society than any single invention since the automobile. It has put the dead hand on conversation and provided countless couples with an excuse for not discussing what's on their minds. Worse yet, TV has become the electronic baby-sitter. How many young mothers who are reading this article are willing to permit their children to look at anything in exchange for a little peace and quiet? It can be successfully argued that TV is a wonderful tool for education, but unfortunately the overwhelming percentage of viewing time is devoted to trivia, nonsense and garbage—which includes smut, violence and offensive commercials.

The greatest natural resource in any country is its young people. What I see today that I didn't see before I became Ann Landers is a generation growing up in a sex-oriented culture. I'm convinced if we don't offer a first-rate program of sex education in all public schools no later than the fifth grade. we're headed for serious trouble. Of course the ideal place for children to learn about sex at home, but how many parents are well informed or emotionally equipped to do the job?

There were over one million teenage pregnancies in the United States last year. A report prepared by the Alan Guttmacher Institute in New York City revealed that at least eleven million teenagers in our country are sexually active. Venereal disease has reached epidemic proportions. Yet there are those who say we daren't give young people explicit information about sex because it will "encourage them to experiment."

When are the narrow, unrealistic vigilantes going to wake up and smell the coffee? Our teenagers are already experimenting—witness the Guttmacher statistics—and they won't stop just because their priest, rabbi, minister, parents, teachers or Ann Landers tells them to.

Some of my advice has changed over the years and I am not ashamed to admit it. There is a vast difference between abandoning one's principles and dealing with issues in a relevant manner. Change is essential to growth. The reversals in my advice reflect the changes in our society. It's a different world today than it was twenty-five years ago. To pretend otherwise is to hide one's head in the sands of time.

My position on virginity, for example, has been modified. In 1955 I held the firm conviction that every girl must hang on to her virginity until marriage or death—whichever comes first. I no longer believe this is true. I still believe that the young woman who can approach the marriage bed with hymen intact is to be admired, but today I would not call her a tramp if she failed to do so.

Lest there be a misunderstanding, I would like to make it clear that I do not condone high school sex. In my opinion, the majority of fifteen-, sixteen-and seventeen-year-olds are not sufficiently mature to deal with an intimate physical relationship. My opinion notwithstanding, recent surveys show that approximately 70 percent of the girls who graduate from high school have had sexual intercourse. So you can see they are not paying a great deal of attention to me in this regard.

My position on divorce has also changed. In 1976 there were over a million divorces in our country. It appears that 1977 will see at least as many splits, if not more. The bars and cocktail lounges are jammed with married men and women having "a quick one" before heading home. It's almost as if they were bracing themselves for the battle or anesthetizing themselves against the boredom that awaits them. Too often they end up seeing double and acting single. Women's magazines continue to print "helpful" articles on How to Hang on to Your Husband while thousands of wives write to me and complain that "hanging is too good for 'em."

According to a Gallup poll conducted in February 1977, the percentage of drinkers in the United States has reached a thirty-eight-year peak. The biggest gain was noted among women. Are more women drinking because their marriages have gone bad, or is it the other way around? Have the marriages gone bad because more women have taken to the bottle? If pressed for an answer, I'd say the booze came first.

What does all this mean? Is marriage on the way out? Has something occurred in our society these past thirty years to undermine this once-hallowed institution? Have people changed?

I think not. It is my firm conviction that marriage is here to stay. Moreover, human nature has changed very little in the last thousand years. Man is still capable of being the most base and the most magnificent of creatures. The seeds of everything—hate, anger, envy, malice, greed, selfishness, beauty, love, tenderness, generosity and nobility—are within all of us.

What then has gone haywire with the promise "Till death do us part"? Why were more couples divorced last year than were married?

One of the principal reasons is the economic independence and improved status of today's woman. Thirty-five years ago, if Grandma was galled by Grandpa's stinginess, his alcoholism, his roving eye or a tendency to crack her across the mouth when she spoke "out of turn," she hoped the neighbors didn't hear, and put up with the humiliation and abuse. In those days, Grandma had no marketable skills. She was dependent on her husband for the roof over her head and food for the table. If there were children, she stayed "for their sake."

What's more, the divorce laws were designed to make marriage permanent. Unless the wife had uncommon courage or family money to fall back on, she was hopelessly trapped.

Today, when a marriage turns sour, women have options. Vocational school, a college degree or on-the-job training can be her ticket to freedom. No longer is an exploited female forced to remain in a wretched, anxiety-producing situation for "room and board." She can tell the bum to get lost. And more and more women are doing that.

By the same token, the husband whose "dearly beloved" has turned into a shrew, a nag or a lazy slob who views him only as a meal ticket has a way out too. He can extricate himself without staging phony photographs to prove adultery. Can you believe adultery was the only ground for divorce in New York State until 1967? Thousands of women and men were forced to take this disgraceful route because it was the only way to legally terminate a terrible marriage.

No-fault divorce laws are among the most civilized pieces of legislation passed in the last twenty years. Today almost every state in the union has some form of no-fault divorce. I am ashamed to say own state, Illinois, is one of the few that does not. It was humiliating for me, in October 1975, to sue my former husband for "cruel and inhuman treatment" when he was neither cruel nor inhuman. But like thousands of others, I sought the least destructive grounds—and that was it.

Another reason for the increase in the divorce rate is the admission (at long last) that it is perfectly possible for well-intentioned, intelligent people to make a mistake. "He (or she) turned out to be very different from the person I thought I had married" is a line I've seen so often. People do change. The man or woman you took for better or worse in 1952 is not the same person you see across the breakfast table in 1977. If you don't believe it, just get out the old wedding album and take a good look.

Furthermore, the times have changed. Before World War II, a divorcée was considered—well, not exactly a scarlet woman, but she did pay a price. In small towns, particularly if she was Catholic or Jewish, she was made to feel like a pair of brown shoes worn with a tuxedo.

When the late Adlai Stevenson was being considered as a presidential candidate in 1953, there was grave concern about his chance for the nomination because he was a divorced man. When he received the nomination in 1954, it was a giant step toward making divorce "respectable." Interesting that in 1946 James M. Curley, the major of Boston, was elected while in jail. Had he been divorced, he wouldn't have had a chance.

Has the cultural shock knocked us crank-sided? Are we punchy from the radical changes that have occurred these past thirty years?

I don't know if these are the best of times or the worst of times, but I do know it is the only time we have. In my view, anything that allows people to be more honest and true to themselves is good. Life is too precious to waste years in a joyless marriage—or, worse yet, in a miserable one.

Divorce does not necessarily mean failure. In some instances it may be a victory, an indication that there has been growth, coupled with the courage to change one's life—to say, "We are no good for each other; let's not continue to cheat ourselves by putting up a false front for people who couldn't care less."

Do I sound as if I am championing the cause of divorce? No way. I am, however, making a strong plea in behalf of decency, integrity, courage and self-respect. This is what the good life is all about. Nothing is so joyous or energizing as a healthy marriage—nor as draining and nerve-racking as a sick one.

I believe in marriage. Man was made for woman and woman was made for man. This is the central theme of the Divine Plan. But it must be a straight-arrow partnership. They must be best friends as well as lovers—pulling together, giving one another emotional support, each sensing the other's needs and doing their best to fill them.

A healthy marriage means total trust, a long leash, respect for one another's privacy. Everyone needs room to breathe—time to reflect. Moments of silence can be the glue that holds the marriage together. Sometimes the best thing you can do for a tired, harassed mate is to leave him (or her) alone. This, in my view, is the true measure of maturity.

If your marriage does not embody the qualities I have mentioned, you have a piece of pop bottle instead of a diamond. How good and honest it is that more and more people are refusing to settle for shoddy substitutes. I vote yes for the real thing.

What Marriage Is All About

Nothing has been talked about or worked on more incessantly than the modern American marriage. The reason is simple. Americans want it to work. They don't set out to get divorced. But a successful marriage is a lot of trouble.

The notion that marriage solves life's problems, especially those of loneliness or of sexuality, is largely an illusion. Marriage doesn't solve anything. It is one long troublesome adventure filled with extraordinary possibilities for the peace and joy that all human beings long for. The big trouble is that joy does not come by itself nor is it marketed at a discount for those who want to avoid the risks involved in human closeness.

Marriage is a worthwhile kind of trouble because it is built on the efforts of two people who must continually work at it. It is an institution in which people have the opportunity to realize the best and the richest truths about themselves and others. It is the institution in which human beings feel that they have touched the core of existence and that they need not be afraid any more.

Taking the trouble to work at love makes the difference between successful and unsuccessful marriages. The most naive approach to marriage is that it will somehow take care of itself, that it is a special state that confers status, self-esteem and emotional security. There can be nothing but trouble for people who feel that marriage is a chamber of safety, and once having entered, the world will bother them no more.

The questions that all married people should ask themselves are: What does my marriage mean to me? Am I willing to pay the price to make it better? Or have things reached such a state that I am used to it and don't care to do anything more about it? Good will is not enough. We must take practical steps to nourish and deepen the sustaining love of the married state. It requires us to do something as well as to think beautiful thoughts. It demands that we invest ourselves and be able to meet each other freshly every day—to fight against letting life dull our responsiveness to one another.

A related mistaken expectation for married people is that their life together will always be like the life they shared in courtship and the early days of marriage. They are disappointed when this passionate, somewhat ethereal state begins to fade. They thought that fiery passion was love, and when its intensity is vastly diminished they don't know what to do about themselves or about their marriage. They are unprepared for the inevitable—that the way married people feel about each other changes steadily through the years.

The most practical thing that a married couple can prepare for is change. The effort to hang onto love in its original state can be disastrous. Change is the law that governs all other living things—and if your marriage is alive it will indeed undergo alterations.

This is not to say that love disappears when it changes. It evolves and transforms itself, demanding something new of husband and wife, allowing them to discover things they never suspected about each other. The learning that goes along with a man and a woman living closely together is never ended.

Marriage is filled with the glorious trouble of being alive. It is accepting this kind of trouble that allows people to know what it means to be human.

It is also helpful for people not to wait for something to happen to them. In marriage, as in almost everything else in life, if we want good things we must do something to make them happen. Nobody is going to do it for us and there is no way in which we can tease a happy life out of the fates if we are unwilling to take responsibility for it ourselves. We design our lives to a great extent, whether we admit it or not. Waiting for a change in one's spouse (or one's self) or a stroke of good luck is a deadly stance for a partner who wants a marriage to stay alive.

Unfortunately, many contemporary efforts to bolster marriage remain precisely at the surface level. That is the level at which people reach legal agreements about who will walk the dog and who will wash the dishes; these, of course, overemphasize the superficial aspects of their lifestyle. Too many people live on the surface, emphasizing the way they look and the things they have, and then wonder why they have so much trouble developing better and deeper relationships. An overriding concern of how the marriage looks to others is sure death.

As elsewhere, it helps if people are never surprised by anything that is genuinely human. This includes seven-year itches, wandering eyes and regrets about a wide variety of things. We should not be surprised to find that people who love each other very much can be distracted or that they can have bad days. The mistake comes when we interpret these as signs that the marriage is disintegrating or that we have become psychological wrecks and the only alternative is to abandon the conventional ways of life for something new and more exciting. This is precisely what many people do in a society which seems to be rushing to divorce courts in droves, convinced it will solve all of life's problems forever. While no one can argue the wisdom of pronouncing a marriage dead when it is indeed lifeless, one must resist the temptation to turn immediately to divorce whenever tensions or difficulties arise.

The acceptance of our human failings instead of misreading them as signals that the relationship is unsalvageable is essential for people who want to remain married. We must accept the fact that things don't "just happen" to us. We always contribute to their development. If a person begins to notice boredom, a need for a change, or finds he or she is beginning to flirt a little, it is time to examine the self. People sometimes engage in mildly seductive behavior because they enjoy the excitement, or they feel the need to prove something about their own attractiveness.

Husbands and wives should expect these things to happen and be prepared to withstand them rather than to pretend that they are of no consequence. When people get into this kind of trouble, it is because they want to.

Honest confrontation, not a frontal attack, is the way to deal with the truth of what is going on between us and others. When people try to ignore what is right before their eyes, and pretend it does not exist, they risk building up a reservoir of anger that finally cracks through any dam of control and washes away the marriage at the same time. Such situations do not become dangerous overnight. They acquire a devastating power when we ignore them or are afraid to face their implications. When a husband or wife first notices the small cracks in their relationship they should discuss them with an awareness that they are dealing with fissionable material. The "little things in life" carry a tremendous potential for destruction.

Husband and wife must be ready to understand each other in a practical way. To understand another person is a continuing journey into unfamiliar territory. We must not fool ourselves into believing that we already know everything there is to know about the person we married. We *never* have him (or her) all figured out.

Men and women must also look at fidelity as something that is highly significant in their relationship. The world has become careless about this. Fidelity is the willingness to live up to a commitment to another human being and there is nothing casual about it. Fidelity is not keeping an old promise as much as it is discovering what is new and fresh in life together.

Believers exchange extraordinary gifts in very simple ways. There is a special kind of faith that people who stay married have in each other. They know that what they do and think and how they act when they are apart have a lot to do with the strength of their commitment.

People who love each other and want to deepen their marriage should avoid feeling like victims. Men and women are not victims of life and there are many practical things which they can do to help see the fresh possibilities that continue to reside in their life together. There are no tired, old marriages. There are only tired and distracted people who have forgotten how to look at each other.

Perhaps the most central lesson for husband and wife to learn is that of respecting each other as separate, fully identified human beings. One can never live in the shadow of the other. One cannot be just the husband of somebody or the wife of some other personality. That is not the way marriages stay alive. People who love each other must learn to let each other be. They must have lives that are separate but in touch with one another. They must free each other for that existence, letting each other go, giving each other room, not in some faddish open-marriage style that insists on freedom, but rooted in each person's readiness to acknowledge the freedom of the other. They cannot do this if the identity of one is absorbed totally in the identity of the other. One must never sacrifice everything for the sake of the other. Later, blame sets in, and the sacrificing party plays that old familiar game—"If it weren't for you . . ."

Husband and wife are wise to recall that their relationship is not a reasonable one. How often man and woman, after a period of difficulty or strife, approach each other with the phrase "Let's be reasonable about this . . ." and, of course, when tempers flare, reason is the first thing to go.

This does not mean either or both parties are crazy—or illogical. It means that their relationship is highly personal and therefore exists on several levels besides that of intellect. There is no way to be reasonable about something that is fraught with emotion.

Married people should begin to worry if they have only logical problems to discuss. They should be deeply concerned if there is no overflow of emotion, no passionate concern about life or about each other. They should be properly upset if everything between them can be settled by the provisions of a legal document. It means there is something dusty and drought-season-dry about their relationship. It might be polite, perhaps platonic, the kind of relationship one might have with a schoolmate or bridge partner, but hardly the kind that should exist between people living intimately with each other. When passion is gone it is time for people to wonder why, to stand back and try to find out how their marriages became mummified.

Becoming sensitive and continually understanding requires concentrated effort and hard work. It also requires that people do something concrete, each day if possible, to express this sensitivity and to show one another that they are actively seeking to understand and respond at more than a surface level.

Resolve to do something special every day for the one you married. This doesn't take much. It doesn't mean a big present. It means a little thoughtfulness—something done freely rather than out of obligation. It should be the kind of thing that comes as a surprise and carries the message "you are treasured and loved because you are special."

Do something different once a week and do it together. Do things that bring you into the realm of new experiences and break the grip of routine and dullness. The cost of these adventures need not be high. They are, in fact, priceless because they provide the kind of setting in which people can revitalize their life together.

Stop immediately and get help of some kind if you note a growing conviction that whatever is wrong is all the fault of the other party. As soon as we are sure that we are the totally aggrieved one, it is time to take a closer look. No difficulty is caused totally by the other person. When we begin to believe this is true, it means we are in deeper trouble than we think.

This is also true when we are totally surprised by sudden difficulty which seems to have arisen from nowhere. Difficulties in marriage usually come from inside rather than from some distant place.

Sadly enough, many people hurt each other when they don't want to. They separate when, in truth, they still love each other but things went too far or got so out of hand that there is nothing left to do but move out of each other's range. There are many signals that, if noted, can move us to act before the roof falls in. Increasing our sensitivity to these signals is essential if we are to avoid disaster. Of course, a great deal of effort and energy is required to repair a relationship that has become damaged or sweeten one that has turned slightly sour, but it is nothing compared to the trouble it can spare us.

CREDIT: *Eugene Kennedy, Ph.D. From* The Trouble Book, *Chicago, Illinois: Thomas More Associates.*

WHY MARRIED COUPLES SHOULDN'T WORK TOGETHER

DEAR ANN LANDERS: This letter is for all couples who met at work, fell in love, married and continue to work together.

Please do yourselves a favor. One of you quit. I don't care which one, but for the sake of your marriage, the peo-ple who have to work with you, your boss, everybody, quit.

It's unhealthy for a couple to be to-gether 24 hours a day. You can't help but get on each other's nerves. Remember the old saying, "Don't bring your work problems home." Well, the reverse is true: "Don't bring your home problems to work." It's easy to tell when you've had a fight. You continue it on the job and make everyone uncomfortable.

So please take this suggestion in spirit intended. Quit—one of you—before both of you are replaced. IN THE KNOW

DEAR IN: Generally speaking, I agree with your admonition, but there are exceptions.

When the couple owns or runs the business there is less chance for the kind of trouble you describe. It's when they fight on somebody else's payroll that they run into problems.

HE CONSIDERS BATHROOM PRIVATE PLACE; SHE DOESN'T

DEAR ANN LANDERS: I recently retired from the Marine Corps after 30 years of service—never married, but lived with a number of women. Six months ago, I took unto myself a bride. She is wonderful, but—here's the problem:

I have always considered the bathroom a private place. Not so the Mrs. She thinks I'm a prude because I am not completely open about *all* human functions.

When I lock the bathroom door, she gets angry and screams, "When are you going to get over this ridiculous hang-up?"

I believe I am right. She insists I'm wrong—and says I need psychological help. You decide. IMPASSE IN LOUISVILLE

DEAR IMPASSE: There is no right or wrong about such matters. Each individual must decide for himself what is acceptable. Whatever is acceptable is "right."

In some marriages, the Open Door Policy operates in every room in the house. If both parties like it that way, it's nobody else's business.

Obviously you do *not* like it that way, and your wishes should be respected. You are not in need of psychological help. Your wife is. A woman who is so grossly insensitive—not to mention domineering—that she would deny her husband this basic fundamental privacy should get her head checked.

Masturbation

Masturbation is deliberate genital self-stimulation for the purpose of producing sexual pleasure. It is a natural and normal part of human development and human behavior for both sexes and all ages. A common practice in virtually every primitive human society, masturbation was usually regarded as an ordinary activity of life. In the animal kingdom, all mammalian species have been observed to masturbate both in captivity and in the wild.

Yet this natural activity has been subject to greater misunderstanding and has been responsible for the creation of more problems than any other aspect of normal human behavior. For thousands of years, particularly in Western society, masturbation has been blamed for nearly every conceivable mental and physical disorder—among which feeble-mindedness, insanity, heart attacks, pimples, dark circles under the eyes, brain degeneration, deafness, epilepsy, criminal behavior, sexual incompetence in women and impotence in men. Ghastly punishments and preventive measures have been developed and applied over the centuries, including tying children's hands to their beds, innumerable cage-like devices locked around genitalia and mutilating surgical procedures.

Normal masturbation is in no way injurious to one's health. It produces no physical disease and no direct psychological damage. But because it is judged within a moral framework rather than its normal physical and psychological functions, mild to very serious emotional consequences are not uncommon. The source of these problems is the traditional condemnation, not the activity. The fact that masturbation is frequently referred to as self-abuse is an indication of the dangerous and damaging role that society has assigned it. Hence, the greatest damage resulting from masturbation is the guilt, shame and loss of self-respect which are generated by these social taboos, usually laid on by parents.

Our society's atmosphere of conflict and secrecy about sex in general extends particularly to masturbation. Emerging sexuality is as natural in a child as the unfolding growth of speech or learning to walk. A child knows that masturbating produces pleasurable feelings that are quite real. Yet authority figures tend to treat masturbation as something evil and to communicate to the child that he or she is bad for engaging in the activity and wishing for pleasure. They threaten, nag and shame the child in an attempt to get him (or her) to stop it.

Children then become confused about their sexual feelings. They somehow get the notion it is wrong. The presence of these mixed emotions frequently leads to a wide range of psychological problems (not only sexual) in adulthood.

The normal pattern and purposes of masturbation should be understood. It first can be observed in nursing infants. Babies naturally explore their own bodies and soon discover that handling of the genitals produces pleasurable sensations. The stimulation provided in washing the babies' bodies reinforces this impression. At this early age, the random pleasure experienced with genital manipulation is equivalent to thumb-sucking as a source of pleasure. In the pre-schooler, masturbation continues to be a part of normal over-all self-exploration and self-stimulation. At this stage, exploration of surroundings and friends is an indication of healthy social development. So too, interest in masturbation increases as a part of this curiosity and early interpersonal awareness. Masturbation decreases somewhat (but remains common) in school-age children as other aspects of their expanding lives provide pleasurable outlets and absorb their attention. Adolescence is characterized by the emergence of intense sexual feelings and sexual interest in other people. Masturbation is a normal sexual tension reducer during this period and is characterized by a wide variety of fantasies.

In childhood and adolescence, then, masturbation is an aspect of development essential to the formation of a good image of oneself and healthy self-esteem as well as body pride in all dimensions. Essential groundwork for the capacity for mature sexual adjustment also is being laid. Absent or markedly diminished masturbation through the developmental years of childhood and adolescence tends to limit optimum development and to reduce the enjoyment of normal mature relationships and activities in adult life. Adults with sexual adjustment problems reveal a high incidence of absent early self-exploration and self-stimulation and a general inhibition of sexuality in childhood.

In adulthood, deprivation of regular sexual outlets leads to an increase in masturbation in both sexes. As an occasional sexual variant it is common in emotionally healthy adults after marriage but is more frequent during periods when the sexual partner is absent or ill. Only when masturbation is routinely preferred to intercourse or so frequent that it becomes an indication of an incapacity for sexual gratification with a partner is it considered to be abnormal in adulthood.

Many women and men remain sexually active well into late life. This period is also characterized by the likelihood of a sexual partner being no longer available or by an uneven rate of decline in sexual interest in a marital couple. For these reasons, masturbation is an important and normal part of sexual functioning in the elderly. This group may feel especially guilty and fearful of abnormalcy since prohibitions about sexuality and the myths about the harmfulness of masturbation were even more steadfastly maintained in their generation.

Excessive masturbation, on the other hand, is not in itself evil or damaging, but rather an indication of an underlying psychological disturbance. It is analogous to excessive eating. These activities are not themselves bad, but rather symptoms of problems that the individual is unable to handle in more appropriate and effective ways. Masturbation becomes excessive when it occurs several times daily, with a sense of a compulsion or a ritual.

Excessive masturbation in childhood most commonly indicates boredom, loneliness or some more specific emotional tension. It is used as a means of consolation or as a source of satisfaction and tension release in the absence of appropriate opportunities, activities and relationships. This situation requires not threats or punishments but an attempt to learn the reason for the activity and remove the causes that produce the need for this inappropriate gratification.

In adulthood, excessive masturbation can be an indication of one of several kinds of problems. People who tend to be immature and self-centered, whose personality development has not kept pace with their chronological age, may be unable to maintain a mature relationship with another person. In the same way that they are not able to be giving in other spheres, they can be more interested in masturbation than in intercourse. They have only themselves to please.

Secondly, unrelated emotional problems, for instance a sense of inadequacy or fear of rejection, produce anxiety which can be expressed as sexual tension. Excessive masturbation can be used in an attempt to relieve this tension.

Lastly, in a crisis of overwhelming stress an individual's normal adaptive adult coping mechanisms may be overloaded and fail. Return to use of a successful tension reducer from an earlier period is common, and excessive masturbation may be the result. In these latter two instances, masturbation tends to fail as a coping mechanism because the real problem is not in the sexual sphere. Uncovering the underlying problems through counseling and taking the appropriate steps to resolve them will lead to alleviation of the symptom.

CREDIT: *Patti Tighe, M.D., Assistant Professor of Psychiatry, Department of Psychiatry, University of Chicago, Pritzker School of Medicine. Daniel X. Freedman, M.D., Professor and Chairman of Psychiatry, Department of Psychiatry, University of Chicago, Pritzker School of Medicine.*

Masturbation as Practiced by Married Males

Thousands of women have written to me over the years and asked, "Why does my husband prefer to masturbate when he could have the real thing? I'm lying right next to him, but he'd rather take care of himself. I'm so disgusted I'm considering divorce."

These sexually hungry wives sometimes say, "My husband hasn't touched me in three months. He doesn't know I'm aware that he is getting satisfaction in this disgusting solitary manner," etc., etc. Sometimes they ask, "Is he a pervert?"

I tell them, "No, he is not a pervert. Unfortunately, he has been unable to make the normal transition from adolescent sex to mature married sex. You should talk to him openly about this. It's as big a problem to him as it is to you. If you can't work things out without professional counseling, then by all means go for outside help."

I wrote to Henry F. Gromoll, a psychiatrist and Chairman of the Department of Behavioral Sciences at Millikin University in Decatur, Illinois, and asked him for additional insight. Dr. Gromoll responded as follows:

"With reference to your question on male masturbation in marriage: We must first distinguish between two types of masturbation. One I would term compulsive, the other compensatory.

"My own clinical experience would indicate that many well-adjusted, mature, married males (and certainly some females) do masturbate throughout their lives. In situations where their partner is unavailable for a variety of reasons—illness, separation or temporary loss of one or the other's sexual interest—masturbation can be a satisfactory alternative. In some relationships where one partner's sexual needs are stronger masturbation (in addition to sexual intercourse) may be a reasonable solution.

"Damaging effects occur *not* as a result of masturbation, but as a consequence of the guilt, deception and feelings of alienation that can arise between the couple. If both partners are open and sharing about this activity and can make it an interpersonal experience, no negative consequences will result.

"Compulsive masturbation, on the other hand, is usually a symptom of some behavioral or interpersonal problem. The underlying motives can be varied but usually one or both partners are unable to share and communicate their sexual needs. Granted, masturbation is a highly personal act, shrouded in some degree of guilt. It does not require emotional involvement equal to that of sexual intercourse.

"Individuals who have difficulty establishing intimacy with their partner may find the sexual 'duet' more stressful than a solo performance. Other individuals may use compulsive masturbation to express feelings of resentment, contempt, hostility or fear.

"With regard to what partners can do about this problem: It would depend on the specific role that compulsive masturbation plays within the individual and the marriage relationship.

"To wives, I would suggest patience, honesty and openness about the situation. To ignore it, or to feel guilty or responsible for it, or to become hostile does nothing constructive—in fact, the opposite is true. Upon discovering that their husbands masturbate, most women respond by asking the question, 'How have I failed him?' Or worse yet, they regard the husband as some sort of pervert.

"The only healthy alternative is to openly and honestly try to understand where they both have failed to communicate their intimate needs to one another. This usually involves being willing to talk candidly about their sexual fears, fantasies, hopes and anxieties—a task that is often extremely difficult even for couples who have been married for many years.

"Should this approach fail, professional assistance from a competent sex therapist should be sought. In my own practice, I am impressed with how quickly caring couples can benefit from a few open, joint sessions, when the problem is handled supportively, objectively and non-judgmentally."

CREDIT: *Henry F. Gromoll, M.D., Chairman, Department of Behavioral Sciences, Millikin University, Decatur, Illinois.*

Maturity

Maturity is the ability to control anger and settle differences without violence or destruction.

Maturity is patience. It is the willingness to pass up immediate pleasure in favor of the long-term gain.

Maturity is perseverance, the ability to sweat out a project or a situation in spite of heavy opposition and discouraging setbacks.

Maturity is the capacity to face unpleasantness and frustration, discomfort and defeat, without complaint or collapse.

Maturity is humility. It is being big enough to say, "I was wrong." And, when right, the mature person need not experience the satisfaction of saying, "I told you so."

Maturity is the ability to make a decision and stand by it. The immature spend their lives exploring endless possibilities; then they do nothing.

Maturity means dependability, keeping one's word, coming through in a crisis. The immature are masters of the alibi. They are the confused and the disorganized. Their lives are a maze of broken promises, former friends, unfinished business and good intentions that somehow never materialize.

Maturity is the art of living in peace with that which we cannot change, the courage to change that which should be changed and the wisdom to know the difference.

CREDIT: *Ann Landers.*

Meditation

In recent years, Americans of all backgrounds have become increasingly aware of the importance of physical fitness. Runners and joggers seem to be everywhere. Gyms, spas, dance studios and health clubs have mushroomed across the country. Alongside this phenomenon has grown another, equally powerful and, in a way, complementary movement—the search for spiritual awareness and growth. In this regard, we hear a good deal about meditation. Terms such as Yoga, mantras, TM, gurus, Zen have all entered the common vocabulary. But what exactly is meditation?

Exercising—a means of developing the body—is a fairly straightforward (if sometimes boring) activity. Meditation, on the other hand—a means of developing the personality and the spirit—remains for many a mysterious process. How does one meditate? What are the benefits of meditation? Is it a religious activity? What is the role of the teacher? These are some of the questions we shall consider in this section.

Simply put, meditation is a disciplined attempt to focus on one object or activity to the exclusion of everything else. As an example, let's explore a technique called *breath control* which is widely practiced in the Far East. Place yourself in a comfortable position, either sitting or lying flat, in a room with few distractions (subdued light is preferable, but not necessary). Put a clock where you can see it without moving your head. Close your eyes and simply count your inhalations and exhalations. Count up to four and start over. It sounds easy, but now comes the difficult part: You must concentrate exclusively on what you are doing; keep your thoughts only on the breath counting.

Each time your mind wanders, bring yourself back to counting your breaths. Treat yourself, your thoughts, as you would a straying child, gently but firmly. Try this exercise for five minutes, peeking at the clock every now and then to see if the time is up.

Having tried a simple, five-minute exercise in meditation, you can understand why St. Theresa of Avila, a great mystic and teacher of meditation, compared the mind of an adult to an unbroken horse that will go everywhere except where the rider wants it to go.

Aside from breath counting, there are many other meditation techniques. Every school and teacher have a favorite, from staring at a candle flame to concentrating on an unanswerable riddle. Books describing the various tech-

niques abound. One especially popular method involves the use of a mantra
—a set phrase (usually short and meaningless) repeated aloud over and over
again during the period of meditation. As in breath counting, the goal here is
to have a heightened awareness of what you are doing and allow nothing else
to enter your consciousness. Try to catch yourself quickly when your mind
wanders and bring yourself back to the task at hand.

A wide variety of phrases has been used as mantras, ranging from "Christ,
have mercy" to the Eastern "om." It is my belief that a set of nonsense syllables is as effective as any other mantra and anyone who tells you that he can
prescribe a mantra with special meaning for you on the basis of a short acquaintance is pulling your leg—and frequently charging you a good price for
this disservice.

As with any disciplined activity, in order to reap the full benefits of meditation, you must make a firm commitment. Working out in a gym only occasionally will result in little if any improvement in your physical well-being.
The same holds true for meditation. Set up a reasonable schedule for yourself, one that you know you can keep. It would be counterproductive to plan
on meditating one hour a day, seven days a week, and wind up doing only
half as much on an irregular basis. Instead of reducing feelings of anxiety
and guilt, which is one of the prime goals of meditation, you will only increase them.

For the beginner working alone, a three- to five-week program is most
effective. At the end of that period evaluate your progress and design the
next phase accordingly, perhaps lengthening the daily meditation sessions.

In the ideal situation, you would meditate at the same time and in the same
place every day. In practice, of course, this is often impossible, and in fact it's
not even essential. Just stick to your schedule and don't skip a planned meditation session unless a major emergency arises. If you find that you keep putting meditation off until late at night, compel yourself to do it, even if you are
exhausted. You will be surprised at how easily you will find time for meditation earlier in the day.

The importance of meditating in a comfortable place and in a comfortable
position in order to cut down on distractions cannot be overemphasized. It is
to eliminate bodily distractions that many schools have developed certain positions ideally suited to meditation, such as the lotus position widely used in
the East. If, like most of us, you are more comfortable sitting or lying down,
by all means do so.

Do not be discouraged if you find yourself resisting meditation. The "unbroken horse" described by St. Theresa does not readily submit to discipline.
Just keep working at it and don't succumb to excuses, frustration at your lack
of progress or number of distractions. The latter, incidentally, can range anywhere from falling asleep and feelings of lightness or heaviness to rather
startling visions. No matter what it may be, ignore the distraction and concentrate on the meditative activity. A student once approached the great Zen

teacher Dogen and related how, deep in his meditation, he had suddenly seen
a great white light with "the Buddha behind it." To which Dogen replied,
"That's nice. If you keep counting your breaths, it will go away."

Above all, do not believe anyone who says, "There is only one way to
meditate, and it is my way." There are as many ways to meditate as there are
individuals. But remember that whatever method you choose, patience, discipline and work will be an integral part of it.

Just as there is no one "proper" way to meditate, the reasons for embarking on a meditation program and the benefits derived from it vary from person to person. Relaxation, both physical and emotional, is an obvious result
of meditation. The chance to shut out the world and its troubles and to focus
inwardly will give you a new perspective on the outer world and help you
cope more effectively with it. It is no accident that people who meditate on a
regular long-term basis have no need for drugs, alcohol or violence to increase the meaning of their existence or to reduce their sense of alienation
and loneliness. They are pleasant people to be with because they are at home
in the world and with themselves.

Meditation involves treating yourself gently and lovingly. When your
thoughts wander, bring them back to the object of meditation as you would a
straying child. Meditation means demanding the best of yourself, but with
compassion, humor and love. It also means accepting your failures as a part
of being human while trying at the same time to grow beyond them.

If much of the preceding two paragraphs sounds like a discourse on psychotherapy, it is because meditation and psychotherapy have the same objective. Psychotherapy was developed in the Western world at the beginning of
this century in response to the growing alienation of modern man who developed symptoms called neurosis. The origins of meditation are difficult, if not
impossible, to determine. In fact, man might almost be described as an animal that meditates. Meditation as a discipline has been "rediscovered" many
times through the centuries—in India 3,500 years ago, in Japan 600 years
later, in the deserts of the Middle East in the sixth century A.D., in twelfth-
century Christian monasteries and in the Hasidic communities of Poland and
Russia in the eighteenth century, to name only a few. But no matter how di-
verse their origins, meditation and psychotherapy share a common purpose:
the cultivation of the human personality to the point of its fullest development. Both seek to bring man into harmony with himself and his surroundings, to increase the fullness and efficiency of our lives.

It is an unfortunate fact that many people have never considered meditation because of its supposed "religious" content. It is true that almost all
religious groups incorporate some form of meditation and that, in the past,
schools of meditation and religious institutions (the only centers of advanced
thought in existence until relatively recent times) were closely linked. But
today things are different. We know that meditation is a natural process. We
all meditate to a certain degree without necessarily being aware of it. (Think

of the times you have lain on a beach, oblivious to everything except your own bodily sensations and the warmth of the sun.) Disciplined meditation is simply a means of developing inner harmony and self-awareness, totally devoid of religious significance, if you want it to be.

There is enough good written material available on the subject of meditation to enable you to tailor a style and program suited to your needs and circumstances. In other words, you can do it yourself, but a teacher can often prove invaluable. His role is to help you design and stick with a program of meditation that is right for you. An experienced teacher will almost instinctively know your state of development. He will be concerned about your goals and be willing to help you achieve them. But if for any reason you feel that your teacher is wrong for you (he may be indifferent to your needs, inexperienced or even a fraud, or there may be a lack of rapport between you and your teacher), head for the nearest exit. Remember that in meditation, as in other disciplines, having no teacher is preferable to having a poor one.

It is ironic that meditation and other spiritual disciplines have attracted so many Americans in recent years. Historically, we have been a nation of achievers in the material sense. And perhaps what we are trying to do by "turning inward" is strive for a better balance. Instead of putting all our efforts into external achievements, we must learn to put more of our energies into ourselves. We have learned how to accomplish, how to *do,* many things, but we have a long way to go in learning how to *be.*

NOTE: Older adolescents seem to benefit a great deal from meditation. However, since its effects on children under twelve years of age have not been properly evaluated, one should proceed cautiously in this area. If a child very much wants to experiment with meditation, by all means encourage him, but see to it that he stops if it produces anxiety or other problems.

CREDIT: *Lawrence LeShan, Ph.D., New York, New York, author of* How to Meditate: A Guide to Self-Discovery, *Boston, Massachusetts: Little, Brown & Co., 1974, and New York: Bantam Books, 1975.*

The Menopausal Woman

I recently met a woman whose goal in life is to "look forever twenty-nine." At the moment she is forty-two. She really *does* look twenty-nine—but so what? For one thing, I can think of few things I would dislike more than to be twenty-nine again.

When I was twenty-nine I was inexperienced, immature—and very dumb about a lot of things. I certainly wasn't having as much fun as I am now, in my late fifties. I know much more about my talents and limitations. I feel freer to live the life I want to live. Looking twenty-nine doesn't change the leaves on the calendar . . . and since the human experience of aging is unavoidable it seems to make more sense to deal with its advantages than to weep for its hazards.

There are understandable feelings of anxiety associated with reaching middle age. Most of us can remember grandmothers who seemed very old, often in their fifties and certainly in their sixties. We are an in-between generation, caught with one foot in the past when menopause meant looking and feeling like an elderly, displaced person, with nowhere to go but the cemetery. We need to remind ourselves that this image is a memory, not a fact of our times. With better medical care and nutrition, middle age has become a time for renewed vigor and personal fulfillment. Old age now begins in the eighties . . . if then. I know an eighty-two-year-old widower who is having a terrific love affair and I knew a woman who died at the age of one hundred and two still working at a job she loved.

Menopause is a physical fact simply meaning that there is a gradual diminution of the female hormone, estrogen, accompanied by the ending of the menstrual cycle. The average age at which this occurs has been changing in recent years. At one time the average age was about forty. Many women today continue to menstruate well into their fifties or even early sixties. Indications of hormonal changes, such as "hot flashes," fatigue, irritability or nonspecific aches and pains, ought to bring any intelligent woman to her doctor's office for a thorough medical checkup and some tender, loving guidance to quiet her anxieties.

At the present time there is a good deal of controversy about whether or not it is advisable for menopausal women to be given supplementary estrogen as nature's supply decreases. All one can do is find a specialist one trusts—a doctor with experience and wisdom and a balanced and flexible point of view —and follow his or her advice. An excellent source of general information on the physical aspects of menopause is the Information Center on the Mature Woman, 515 Madison Avenue, New York, New York 10019. Any librarian can help you find helpful books on the subject. If finances are limited, almost every hospital offers out-patient clinical services for consultation on such matters. These days there is no reason for any woman to feel that she cannot receive help with the physical symptoms of menopause.

It is my firm conviction that the problems of the middle years have to do primarily with how we feel about ourselves and what we are doing with our lives. Because menopause can appear anywhere from the mid-thirties to the mid-sixties, middle age is more a state of mind than a physical time slot. A woman is middle-aged when she begins to feel that life is slipping by too rapidly, and wonders if her life is going to have a sense of meaning and purpose.

I'm fond of the phrase "middlessence" to describe middle age, because it is very much like a second adolescence—only better! Teenagers are desperately struggling to discover their own identity—what makes them unique, what they want to do with their lives, what roles they want to play as they approach adulthood. However, since most of them are pathetically inexperienced, half frightened to death and mixed up, they tend to rebel against parental expectations and standards, only to find themselves even more rigidly trapped by the values and demands of their peers. It's too scary to "become your own person" during those tender years.

If we want to feel alive, if we are not willing to settle for the doldrums, letting the world go by as we crawl into some safe thirty-five- or forty-five- or fifty-five-year-old cocoon, we too must search out our identity and find out what is special and wonderful about each of us. It is our second chance to examine ourselves and the lives we have been leading. For most of us this means having the courage to discover new roles and continue to grow. I do not know a single middle-aged person who is "doing his or her thing" who has time to worry about growing old and dying.

Some years ago my husband went to a hospital to visit a woman who was terminally ill. She was weeping when he arrived. As he began to comfort her she sobbed, "Doctor, you don't understand. I'm not crying because I am dying—I'm crying because I have never lived."

The state of mind with which I associate middle age is when we reach a point in life when we do not want to die feeling that we have never lived. Menopause cannot be a downer unless we assume there are no new options for what we do with the rest of our lives. I know a woman who never learned to swim until she was sixty. I have a sixty-year-old friend who had the courage to quit a job she hated for thirty-five years to begin a new career. I know another woman who, at age fifty-five, decided she was going to take off sixty pounds and buy a Halston pantsuit. That woman was *me* and it was an upper like you wouldn't believe!

I know a couple in their mid-sixties who changed roles. She is now a college professor and he is the homemaker. They both love it. The wife told me, "The kids are gone, I always loved my work, Sam hated his . . . It's a shame we didn't think of this sooner. It blew my mind when I walked into the kitchen to make a cup of coffee and Sam said, 'Don't mess up my kitchen!' For the first time in over thirty years of marriage, we are both doing what we really want to do."

Of course some women love the lives they lead. They dread the empty nest or retirement. There are still choices to be made. A mother whose children have grown and gone can say to herself, "It's all over; I'm finished," or she can go back to school and become a nursery school teacher or a child therapist or get special training as a volunteer and work with handicapped children —all ways of going on with her capacities for nurturing the young.

I know one woman who was forced to retire at sixty-five. She sits around the house "kvetching," watching television . . . getting fat and mean. I know another woman who retired at sixty-three, and decided that her experience as a first-class secretary was excellent background for teaching office skills to street kids in an inner-city community center. She is having the time of her life. I know one retired schoolteacher who does absolutely nothing with her life and has become an unbearable bore. Another retired teacher tutors ex-convicts, helping them get their high school equivalency diplomas. She wrote me a letter recently saying, "June is a terribly busy month for me. I seem to be going to high school and college graduations every day, as my boys and girls start their new lives. You can imagine my pride and thanksgiving to have had the privilege of seeing these people reborn."

Each of us has unknown potentials. Each of us has dreams not yet fulfilled. Middle age is the time and the place to begin—even though it isn't easy to start new ways of thinking about oneself. We need to go through a good deal of introspection. Ask what you would give yourself for a birthday present if you were your own best friend. You may be surprised! I've known people to set off for an adult education center which gives courses in ceramics, or sign up to learn a foreign language, or go see the pyramids in Mexico, or maybe just take a day off alone and carry a picnic lunch to the beach or a nearby woods. A much tougher and more painful question is, "If I knew I was going to die in six months, would I go on doing what I'm doing right now?" If the answer is "No!" it is time to re-evaluate your life.

Most of us were badly trained as children. We were kept busy all the time. If we wanted to be alone, people worried about us. The truth of the matter is that being alone and liking it is a must for surviving and enjoying middle age. Oneself is the only companion always available . . . a friend we need to enjoy. It takes practice. In order to think through new possibilities, new challenges and adventures, we need to force ourselves to spend time alone, to reflect, to look at the world around us, to do quiet things . . . feed the ducks at the lake, watch a bird splash in a birdbath, plant a garden, maybe even paint some pictures.

There are problems in the middle years, of course. Our children grow up and have problems of their own, and too often we drown ourselves in guilt; what did we do wrong? We need to tell ourselves (the truth!) that we did the best we could, and grown-up children will have to find their own answers, aided and abetted by our love and support, but we must not allow them to rob us of our own fulfillment.

Aging parents become a responsibility just at a time when we thought we would be free. There are no easy solutions to the many problems that may emerge, but it is clear that total giving and succumbing to the guilt produced by unreasonable, demanding parents can be deadly.

If we are grown-up we can accept our realistic child-to-parent responsibilities but we need to set limits on the demands we can tolerate and the expectations we can live up to. If we try to please others at the expense of our own needs we end up hating them; worse yet, we get sick ourselves. We need to speculate on how we can give *quality* care which leaves time for our own essential and life-giving pursuits.

For example, one woman reported to her doctor that violent headaches were interfering with her ability to drive a car. She was traveling 100 miles twice a week to visit an aged father in a nursing home. Each time she arrived her father lashed out at her for being unfeeling, disrespectful, not caring what happened to him. Every hour spent together was full of anger and misery for both. But if the daughter skipped a visit her headaches were just as severe as those she had on the days she made the 100-mile round trip.

Her doctor suggested that if the old man was going to be angry no matter what she did, she might as well cut her visits to once a week and spend the second afternoon playing golf. The doctor also pointed out that producing guilt feelings in his children was nothing new—what's more, it was unfair because the daughter was doing her best to please him.

One day she decided to take a tape recorder along and ask her father to tell the story of his life in America, having arrived here as an immigrant eighty-five years before. One of the children had asked about Grandpa's early life, and this seemed a good way to collect stories to be handed down from generation to generation. Before her father could begin his berating, he was confronted with the tape recorder. The idea that his life was important to his grandchildren made him gratefully teary-eyed. The daughter now visits once a week and no longer feels resentful. The father pours out his memories, even though they are often repetitious, and he is glad to see his daughter. This is just one example of how a disagreeable duty was transformed into an enriching and mutually satisfying experience.

Often it helps if an adult child and an elderly parent can confront each other with the agenda of old hurts and angers. It clears the air. We need to understand that even a forty- or fifty-year-old woman can be made to feel like a ridiculous child by an infantilizing parent. A friend of mine telephoned her mother one day (she was forty, her mother was sixty-seven). Her mother told her to be sure and wear a sweater when she went out. My friend began to yell, "Mother! I'm really old enough!" Her mother laughed and said, "Okay, okay, you're right. I just talked to Grandma, she's eighty-eight, and she told *me* to wear a sweater!"

Middle age is often a time of crises and unrest in marriage. Most of us married when we were quite young and we have changed greatly in thirty or forty years. Personality changes cause friction and tension. With the children gone, there is more time for companionship—or the discovery that there hasn't really been any for a long time, but nobody noticed—what with the measles and report cards and sleepless nights with a feverish child and college tuitions. Suddenly, there you are—the two of you—totally different people than you were on your wedding day.

If you are lucky, you both will be open and honest in reassessing your marriage. You will have the courage to grow and to change . . . to find new bases for affection and friendship. It has been my experience that the most important step a middle-aged couple must take to save a faltering marriage is a step *away* from each other to allow more breathing space, to encourage each other to find new avenues of fulfillment. Feeling imprisoned in an unchanging relationship is a certain road to marital problems and eventual separation.

There are many reasons for the shaking-up of apparently unshakable marriages, not the least of which is that we live in a culture that values youth and beauty more than it values wisdom, inner strength and serenity. Women become depressed about unfulfilled dreams. Men become frightened of losing their sexual powers. Fear of the future, anxieties about finances and retirement, and boredom must be dealt with.

It is not easy to stay married to the same person for forty or fifty years. If one or the other cannot meet the test of facing change and giving freedom and autonomy to the other, the problems may become insoluble. There are times when all of us need the guidance and perspective that only an expert in marriage counseling can give. But the best of all possible antidotes to the middle-aged marriage blues is for each partner to search for the meaning of his or her *own life,* to live fully, to find new satisfactions and adventures, so that coming together can be refreshing rather than a duty or an obligation.

Many women have told me that they are ready to try their wings, to move on to new adventures, but their husbands are not. When better communication seems impossible it is still a good idea to pursue new interests. Emotional health is contagious. One woman confided, "My husband could not talk to me about what he was feeling. I knew he was depressed about his retirement and frightened of the future. I began to make my own plans. I took a course in real estate and got my license. I explored new places I wanted to see, places I wanted to consider where we might move. After a while my husband became excited about what I was doing. Slowly, but surely, he became involved. After a year, he liked the idea of our buying a mobile home. He sent for every available folder and went to every mobile home show he heard about. We began planning a new future together. If I'd done nothing but wait, nothing would have changed."

Divorce in middle age is becoming an increasingly common problem. When all one's resources fail, when counseling cannot help, the middle-aged woman again has a choice. She can become paralyzed by a sense of failure, unable to mobilize her own resources, or she can accept this painful and traumatic experience as a great challenge and opportunity. Taking one step at a time is the name of the game. One feels overwhelmed at first, and unable to make any choices. A recently divorced woman told me, "I think the day I moved the couch to a different wall was the beginning of my recovery! Then, each day, I found myself more and more able to make bigger and bigger decisions. I didn't push myself. I did a great deal of thinking and feeling and moved slowly. By the time I moved from the house to an apartment, from homemaking to a job, I was strong enough and sure enough to know my choices would be right for me." Very much the same kinds of adjustments are necessary when one becomes widowed. In either case, allowing ourselves to *feel all our feelings*—anger and sadness, rejection and terror—is the beginning of moving on.

The menopausal woman is in trouble only if she is afraid of change, afraid to make the most of her inner resources. The willingness to try to get in touch with one's feelings, to struggle towards genuine communication with others, gives one a sense of power and potential. Life can be an exciting adventure all the days of one's life if there is courage and curiosity—a sense of adventure and wonder and delight in the new opportunties that lie ahead.

CREDIT: *Eda LeShan, author of* The Wonderful Crisis of Middle Age, *Warner paperback.*

Male Menopause

Since males do not have uteruses and do not menstruate, they cannot stop (pause) menstruating; therefore, the label "menopause" is false and misleading.

The waning powers in both sexes are associated with decreases in the production of sex hormones. But men do not experience the abrupt cessation of hormonal function that women do. In fact, it is not uncommon for a man to father a child when he is in his sixties or seventies. Injecting sex hormones (estrogens in women; testosterone in men) is helpful in lifting the spirits of *some* middle-aged depressed people, but the emotional factors are probably more instrumental in producing the depression than the physical factors. The risks of possible cancer from prolonged treatment with hormones in this age group make it very questionable.

Mid-life crisis rather than male menopause is a far more accurate term for males who have come to the realization that they are slowing up sexually, have passed the point in life when they are going to be made president of the company—and, alas, can no longer beat their sons at tennis.

The necessity to face these facts can cause depression in some males. It does not happen to every man. And it does not always happen in the fifties. Sometimes it occurs in the forties or the sixties. But when the "I'm slipping" feeling takes over, some men try to compensate by switching to trendy clothes, tinting their hair to hide the gray—or they suddenly become physical culture buffs—or sexually aggressive, making a play for every skirt that passes. Some mid-life-crisis males decide they need a new (and younger) wife.

If the middle-aged man's behavior becomes markedly different it might be useful for him to discuss the changes with a therapist. Temporary medication to alleviate the depressed state can prove helpful.

CREDIT: *Gene Gordon, M.D., Senior Attending Psychiatrist, Children's National Medical Center, Washington D.C.; Faculty, George Washington University Medical School, Washington, D.C.; Supervising Training Analyst, Baltimore-District of Columbia Psychoanalytical Institute.*

Menstrual Cramps

Menstrual cramps, most of the time, are the result of the normal contractions of the uterus as it pushes out the blood and tissue of the menstrual period. Therefore, some degree of menstrual cramps is to be expected and is perfectly normal.

Sometimes, however, the cramps are so severe that help is needed to reduce the severity of them in order that the individual can go about her business. On still other occasions the cramps may be due to some inflammation or scar tissue near the uterus or ovaries, and treatment will be needed.

The medical term for menstrual cramps is dysmenorrhea. If the cramps come with the onset of menstruation or a little later, and are only an exaggeration of normal cramping, the condition is called *primary dysmenorrhea*. If a woman has painless periods or only mild cramps at first, and then the pains with her periods become more severe as she becomes older, the condition is called *secondary dysmenorrhea*.

When a woman has severe cramps she should be examined by her gynecologist so that he or she can determine whether they are of the primary or secondary type.

The cramps of primary dysmenorrhea can be treated with mild pain-killing medication, called analgesics. The medication used should be just strong enough to dull the pain without making the individual so groggy that she cannot work or study. Examples are Darvon compound or fiorinal with codeine.

Birth control pills will relieve cramps in about 80 percent of cases of primary dysmenorrhea. (Caution: Do *not* take these pills on your own. See your physician.) Pills may be prescribed if the pain is too severe to respond to mild analgesics. In a small percentage of cases the cramps are associated with emotional tension. These individuals usually do not get relief from mild analgesics or birth control pills. They might get relief from psychotherapy.

A still smaller percentage of individuals will receive no relief from pain-killers, birth control pills or psychotherapy. For them a surgical operation that cuts the sensory nerves from the uterus (a pre-sacral neuectomy) will provide relief.

Very few women should require surgery. Menstrual cramps have a tendency to become less severe as a woman grows older, particularly after marriage and childbirth.

Secondary dysmenorrhea, on the other hand, has a more serious potential. This comes on usually during the thirties after a woman has been free of cramps all her previous years of menstruation. It can be caused by scarring of the opening of the uterus (cervical stenosis), by the presence of tissue that has backed out of the tubes and spilled over the ovaries and uterus (endometriosis), by chronic inflammation of the tubes or by benign tumors of the uterus.

Your doctor will make the diagnosis and provide the appropriate treatment. Cervical stenosis is treated by dilating the cervix. Endometriosis is treated either by giving enough birth control pills to stop all menstrual periods for six to nine months, or by surgical removal of the endometriosis. Inflammation of the tube is treated with antibiotics and heat. Benign tumors of the uterus should be removed if they are causing sufficient symptoms.

CREDIT: *Melvin Taymor, M.D., Chestnut Hill, Massachusetts.*

Menstruation Problems*

IRREGULARITY:

Menstruation is often irregular during adolescence. Some adult women also find, however, that the duration of their menstrual cycle varies from month to month. Regular cycles can vary from between twenty-one to thirty-five days.

ABSENCE OF PERIODS (AMENORRHEA):

There are two types of amenorrhea—primary and secondary. If a girl reaches the age of eighteen without experiencing menstruation she is said to

* From *Woman's Body: An Owner's Manual* by the Diagram Group © 1977 The Diagram Group, published by Paddington Press.

be suffering from primary amenorrhea. This rare condition may be the result of an endocrine abnormality and must be investigated by a doctor.

Secondary amenorrhea is the term used to describe the absence of periods in a woman who has already begun to menstruate. This may be quite normal: Menstruation does not occur in pregnant women, and sometimes does not recommence until some weeks after the birth, especially if the mother is breast-feeding her child.

A missed period, however, can also be caused by emotional stress such as shock, fear, tension or depression and also by endocrine disorders, illness, drug-taking, traveling and poor general health.

HEAVY PERIODS

During a menstrual period, a woman usually sheds between two and four tablespoons of blood. Some women, however, discharge considerably more.

If menstrual bleeding is heavy or prolonged (and this often happens to women fitted with IUDs), iron-deficiency anemia can result. This can often be remedied by an iron-rich diet or a course of medicinal iron.

Heavy bleeding (and bleeding between periods) can sometimes be symptomatic of problems such as hormone disorders, fibroid tumors or cancer of the uterus. Also, occasionally heavy periods can be caused by psychological factors. Heavy bleeding should always be investigated by a physician.

Metropathia hemorrhagica is one of the conditions caused by hormonal imbalance which can result in very heavy bleeding. If the condition does not respond to curettage, a hysterectomy may be needed.

In all cases of excessive bleeding, a doctor should be consulted.

Mental Health

A National Priority

The very processes of living in America today seem increasingly stressful. At least one person in ten—an estimated twenty million people—suffers from some form of mental illness. Only one seventh of this number are receiving psychiatric care.

Perhaps as much as 80 percent of the symptoms Americans take to their doctors—colds, stomach upsets, back pains—are entirely or in large part of psychological origin—reactions to stress. One out of four people is anxious or emotionally tense, complaining of loss of appetite, insomnia, fatigue and difficulty in coping with everyday stress.

Many of the illnesses and symptoms of modern life cannot be cured by medication. Yet we have been programmed by an affluent society—by advertising bombardment, by easy availability of drugs—to seek instant relief for whatever ails us. Pills are being popped and people are running to doctors for the slightest complaint.

Most advertising today, especially on television, offers simple solutions for all manner of needs; it promotes the expectation of a pain-free, trouble-free, anxiety-free, inconvenience-free existence. The fact that this is not a reflection of life, as most humans live it, seems to make no difference.

Being healthy does not automatically ensure that man (or woman) will be happy. It takes more than the absence of symptoms for people to turn their disease-free state into a sense of worthwhileness. Instead of reaching for a tranquilizer to ease stress that is causing physical pain, we must learn better coping mechanisms to relieve the stress that caused the problem.

H. G. Wells' comment aptly describes the problem of prevention in psychiatry when he wrote: "Human history becomes more and more a race between education and catastrophe." Learning about ourselves—the ability of men and women to be in control of their lives, to be able to cope with everyday problems—this is the essence of good mental health.

The next several decades will witness the application of psychiatry to a variety of social ills. This is a focus that is based on the strength and quality of the treatment of the mentally ill. In this sense, our past is our prologue, yet it is our future as well.

Education and research must grow—no larger but stronger, wiser and more skillful—for it is from these areas that we derive our knowledge. With this strong base we will have the resources of talented people with extensive knowledge who can reach into every segment of society and offer knowledge and understanding which will help people manage their lives more effectively and experience a greater sense of personal worth.

CREDIT: *Roy W. Menninger, President, Menninger Foundation, Topeka, Kansas.*

Mental Retardation

One of the most common disorders of intelligence is mental retardation. It is found among all peoples all over the world, regardless of social class. Most experts agree that 3 percent of all school-aged children in the United States, or a total of over six million, are mentally retarded.

To be mentally retarded is to have a subnormal capacity for thinking, reasoning, problem solving, learning and remembering. This is measured by a standardized intelligence test. Here are the ratings, according to the Stanford-Binet scale:

IQ RANGE
90–100   Normal or Average
70–89   Slow learner
55–69   Mild *Retardation*
40–54   Moderate *Retardation*
25–39   Severe *Retardation*
Under 25 Profound *Retardation*

Most states and therefore school systems accept these classifications in order to place children in appropriate educational settings. Anyone with an IQ below 70 is considered retarded.

CAUSES OF RETARDATION

Just as mental retardation is broad in classification, it is broad in the factors that cause the disorder. There is rarely a single cause and in many cases a cause remains unknown. Mental retardation may be caused by a genetic abnormality or the effect of the environment.

GENETIC

Genetically caused mental retardation comes in many forms as well as gradations. The best-known and most common genetic disorder is Down's syndrome (formerly called mongolism). People affected by this disorder have an extra chromosome. One in every 660 births is an affected person and it is generally known to occur more frequently among children of very young mothers or mothers who are thirty-five or older. With the advent of pre-natal genetic diagnosis, Down's syndrome and other chromosomal or biochemical disorders can be predicted before birth. Other genetic syndromes have clinical names that stump the best of us, such as: Turner's syndrome, Klinefelter's syndrome, neurofibromatosis, cerebral angiomatosis and pseudohypoparathyroidism, to name a few.

PHYSICAL ENVIRONMENTAL FACTORS

What happens to a person's brain and central nervous system also affects his level of intelligence. People can be damaged before, during or after birth and the result could be retardation. Some examples of these environmental factors are:

(1) Lack of adequate pre-natal care to assure correct diet, good health for the mother, etc.

(2) A mother who takes too many drugs, is an alcoholic, has an illness (such as rubella, chickenpox, etc.), may have been exposed to radiation from X ray or has the RH blood factor incompatibility.

(3) A difficult labor and delivery or lack of oxygen for the infant at birth.

(4) Lack of appropriate nutrition after birth, child abuse or neglect.

(5) Direct injuries to head or brain (most common for children are injuries from automobile accidents).

(6) Brain tumors, infections causing inflammation of the brain or its lining membrane brought on by high fever.

(7) Ingestion of toxic substances (lead in paint, or mercury). More recently, food additives are being examined, as in the case of MSG (monosodium glutamate), which has been found to cause brain lesions in young rats and monkeys and is now banned from foods prepared for infants (evidence in humans is inconclusive at this writing—1978).

PSYCHOSOCIAL FACTORS

In addition to the list of environmental factors which cause retardation, research has demonstrated that infants in institutions (hospitals, orphanages, etc.) have shown increased levels of retardation if reared with little personal attention or cuddling love.

Children reared in deprived settings and homes often don't have enough verbal, visual or tactile stimulation necessary to develop adequate intellectual capacity and eventually are labeled "mentally retarded." Because educators, physicians, psychologists and sociologists are becoming aware of these factors, programs are being developed to help parents realize the importance of rearing children in a loving, stimulating environment. This does not require money—the poorest of homes can be loving, stimulating and encourage intellectual growth.

Although some causes of mental retardation are known, more are being investigated. Some recent and important discoveries emphasize the importance of avoiding rubella (three-day measles) during the first three months of pregnancy and how lead ingested from eating paint on walls or toys can cause retardation. Work is being done to study the effect of drugs (including aspirin), alcohol and smoking on unborn children. It is not likely that mental retardation can be eliminated in our lifetime or the next, but certain types of retardation can be reduced and environmental factors contributing to retardation can be altered.

CHARACTERISTICS OF RETARDATION

MILD RETARDATION

People who are mildly retarded are in the intelligence category of approximately 55–69 IQ. It is interesting to note that the IQ range for mildly retarded is sometimes considered 50–80. This depends on the state in which one lives.

The most widely accepted upper limit is an IQ of 69. Children in this category are usually classified as Educable Mentally Handicapped (EMH). They are significantly behind normal children in grade-level reading, writing, arithmetic and other academic subjects. Special education classes are usually provided throughout their grade school and high school years. Special curriculum is provided to allow the child to reach his maximum level of achievement.

There is a current trend nationally to integrate these children with normal children during the school day. This allows the retarded youngster to be viewed as "less strange" in spite of his handicap. This trend is called "mainstreaming."

An example of mainstreaming is the case of Rosie, who is EMH. She is with a regular third-grade class for every school activity except for one and a half hours in the morning spent with the special education teacher for reading and math. Rosie is an integral part of the normal class—same jobs, rules, etc. Her parents report she has an improved self-concept, better physical appearance, better health, additional interests and is willing to try new things more readily.

EMH children can be expected to hold jobs, manage their affairs and otherwise provide for themselves and their family at least at a marginal level during the adult years. Some consider this level of retardation to be a "six-hour-a-day disorder" because the individual may be academically retarded in school six hours each day and function quite well for the remaining hours. Some EMH people can and do become productive, independent members of society.

MODERATE RETARDATION

This category usually includes individuals with intelligence measures of 40–50 or 54. Most school systems call these children Trainable Mentally Handicapped (TMH). They cannot benefit from classes for Educable Mentally Handicapped and usually require their own class with a specifically trained special education teacher.

Some of these children may be "mainstreamed," but it is not a widespread practice. Emphasis is on self-care and adjustment to community, family and neighborhood. Most TMH individuals have the potential for community adjustment but will be semidependent throughout their lives. Adult TMH persons can be useful members of the community given the opportunity. Certain simple, non-competitive jobs in understanding environments allow many TMH persons a life in a community rather than in an institution.

SEVERE AND PROFOUND RETARDATION

Severe (IQ 25–39) and profound (below 25 IQ) retardation present additional and complicated problems to a family. Until recently, few services were provided within a community to assist parents with the demanding job of caring for these individuals.

Many folks at this level have severe communication problems (some are incapable of understanding as well as speaking) and often have severe physical handicaps as well. Some are not toilet-trained or capable of feeding themselves. While this group will be dependent throughout their lives, they can be taught certain skills and activities.

Many people in this category are institutionalized but the trend is to help the family maintain the person at home by providing public school programs, day-care programs, nursing care, home visitation and other related services. Institutions are being held more accountable for the progress of their retarded patients. Many are implementing educational programs to help patients learn behavior and skills that enable the patient to return to a community-based program. We have all heard horror stories about patients in institutions being tied to beds or sitting in corners in their own filth, doing nothing. Much of this is changing with the awareness that even the severely retarded can be taught something.

FUTURE DIRECTIONS

Each retarded individual presents his own set of problems. It is the goal of most mental health agencies, educational settings and medical agencies to encourage and assist retarded individuals to live full and productive lives.

The community must be prepared to accept these people and recognize their worth and human dignity. A model program in Libertyville, Illinois, is the Lamb's Farm. It is an innovative program for severe to moderately and mildly retarded adults which provides a work setting.

The retarded work in groups set up on a farm. They have a bakery, a restaurant, pet shop, kitchens where jam and jelly are manufactured, craft shops where they make lovely gifts and do an outstanding job of making silk-screen writing stationery. On the premises are shops which are open to the public for business. I have never seen a happier, more productive or healthier bunch of retarded people. Many ride the train to work every day from all parts of Chicago. The Lamb's Farm has provided a successful solution to a big problem—what to do when a retarded person grows up and there are no more school programs. It has proven that many retarded adults can lead useful lives and be much less dependent on their families.

Hopefully, with help for the retarded individual and his family through more understanding, compassion, interest and programs, we will allow the retarded to lead more normal lives. Perhaps we have just begun to realize the potential of our retarded citizens.

CREDIT: *Dale Layman, Ph.D., University of Illinois, College of Education, Chicago, Illinois.*

Moles

A mole is a spot or a fleshy bump in the skin. It can be brown, red, pink or blue. Moles contain pigment cells, blood vessels, hair or other appendages in the skin. The commonest use of the word "mole" is for a small raised or flat spot that is dark and may or may not have hair in it. These moles are also called nevi, or pigmented nevi. The medical name for a single mole is a nevus. When more than one mole is present the term used is nevi. Only 3 percent of people have pigmented nevi when they are born.

Most moles appear after three or four years of age. They increase in number and become darker until approximately 20 years of age. A large change in size and color often occurs at the time of puberty. Everyone acquires moles but the number varies and depends upon how small or light a spot one wants to include. For example, some people say that on the average an individual has twenty moles. The number would go up considerably if one counted little round dots, or very light-colored nevi. There are usually more moles on the upper parts of the body than on the lower. A single dark mole on the face is usually referred to as a beauty mark. Those who do not like the appearance of moles can have them removed surgically. (This is a simple procedure and can be done in a physician's office.)

Nearly all should be left alone. The exceptions are when they begin to darken, enlarge or bleed. When these changes occur, it is advisable to see a physician to make certain the mole is not developing into a melanoma. Melanoma is a cancer that comes from pigment cells in the skin or eyes. Most suspicious are those present from birth. The large flat freckles are generally of no concern. But those brown to black spots, with or without hair, that are somewhat raised and present from birth probably should be removed surgically.

Skin tags are small, soft stalks of skin that occur on the neck and under the arms especially in women during pregnancy. They never become malignant, but are a nuisance because clothing and jewelry catch on them. They can be snipped off easily by a physician.

From about thirty-five to fifty years of age many people develop small light to dark wart-like bumps on the face, neck and trunk. They are called seborrheic keratoses and they never become cancerous. People who do not like the appearance of these keratoses might want them removed. As one gets into the sixties, seventies and eighties, seborrheic keratoses can become very large and dark—like barnacles on an old hulk—as one eighty-year-old man called them.

CREDIT: *Aaron B. Lerner, M.D., Department of Dermatology, Yale University School of Medicine, New Haven, Connecticut.*

Money

How to Increase Your Salary

(1) *Believe that you can.* Many people think the only way to increase their income is to work hard and hope for a raise. The world is full of people waiting for that to happen. Others *make* it happen. Why shouldn't you be one of them?

(2) *Make yourself valuable.* Businesses exist to make a profit. Whatever or whoever helps achieve this goal becomes valuable to the business. Persons who help the business *make money* and persons who help the business *save*

money acquire a value that the business wants to protect and reward by paying them more than an employee who is just another cog in the machine and who can be easily replaced by another cog.

(3) *Learn about the business.* Don't confine your interests to the edge of your desk. First learn everything there is to know about all the "threads" that lead to and from your particular task. Then trace those threads to their next destination. Ask questions. Most people are only too happy to hold forth on something they know or do. If your supervisor or boss is reading a particular trade journal or paper, get yourself a copy. Don't come on like gangbusters but keep stacking up pieces of information about the interior workings of the firm as well as the general line of business it pursues.

(4) *Act.* When you're sure enough of your ground, however small it may seem in the over-all picture, make some waves. Be a problem solver—be the one who takes on a little extra load. Be a volunteer—but only to your boss or supervisor (not for a co-worker out to use your energy to supplement his or her own). Keep an eye out for the one thing that almost always seems to cause a problem—something that requires extra effort and knowledge. Become an expert in solving that problem or mastering the baffling details. Look for ways to save money and ways to make money.

(5) *Get full credit for what you do.* The rules here are the same as in competitive sports. You must develop a good defense and a good offense. Business offices are full of people who do most of the work and get the least credit—and money. They may gripe about it at home but they don't defend themselves against the co-worker or supervisor who may be taking bows for all their efficiency and sometimes their ideas. Offices shouldn't be jungles, but there are people who literally fatten their own positions by devouring others'. A good defense doesn't let this happen twice. On offense, look for ways to let your value be shown and known. If you've got a really good idea for making or saving money (and remember, as the cliché goes, time is money), don't test it out on a co-worker, take it as far up the ladder as you can get without overplaying your hand. It's usually possible to make a special appointment with the boss, or to put your ideas in memo form with copies sent to several people.

(6) *Don't be shy about money.* The person who is out to increase his or her salary has to be patient and flexible, but there comes a time to let it be known—directly or indirectly—that you are aiming for more money and a better position. Bosses don't take well to demands or ultimatums but there are more subtle ways of making it clear that you have expectations. There's a powerful myth in our society that it's not nice to talk about money. Management people are well aware of this shyness and will sometimes coast along until some signal is given that they can't ignore. It is sometimes necessary to take the initiative and convert the boss's appreciation of you into money. It may be as blatant as "Well, I hope there will be a raise in this for me soon" to "I'm glad you appreciate my work. I just don't know how much longer

I'll be able to hang on here at my present salary." But be careful not to threaten to quit unless you have another job in mind!

(7) *Risk and change.* Another social myth we've been raised on is that it's a sign of weakness or a terrible risk to change jobs. Sure, there's some element of risk in all of these steps toward increasing your salary. But there's risk in every part of life and the alternative of being forever stuck to a job you don't feel is worthy of your abilities is far grimmer.

If you really are worth more than the job you leave, statistics strongly favor your finding a far better job elsewhere. It's a big country.

CREDIT: *Helen Robison, White Plains, New York. Adapted from* Mademoiselle *magazine.*

The Mother/Daughter Relationship

The relationship between a woman and her mother is the most basic in her life. Understanding mother/daughter relations is the key to understanding what women are—and what we might be. Every woman is another woman's daughter. Should her mother die or leave her when she is a child, she is raised by society as a "daughter." Even if she becomes a mother, she remains a daughter. Of all the roles women are required to fill, the one we are least often excused from is that of mother.

Despite flowery seasonal tributes, mothers have a bad reputation. They are blamed for nearly all social ills by everyone, including their own children. Freudian-based psychology encourages us to condemn our mothers for thwarting us, repressing us, raising us for selfish motives, refusing to let us go and dominating our lives after their death.

The mother/daughter relationship, as it exists in a society which has devaluated women, prevents mothers and daughters from relating to each other with mutual love and support. Most mothers cast their daughters into female roles. In frustration, those daughters reject their mothers for their duplicity and incapacity—so the alienation grows.

As daughters, we believe mother love exists by definition and that this love includes acceptance, affection, admiration and approval. We want mothers like Marmee, in *Little Women,* whose self-sacrifice and unfailing, sympathetic understanding will never make us feel guilty. This view of motherhood is one in which Mother is always available (despite financial problems which may make it difficult or impossible or other children who may also need Mother at the same moment). What daughters usually expect from mothers (even when they become mothers themselves and should know better) is superhuman performance. Too many daughters expect not just loving—which many of us withhold from our mothers—but child care, cooking, cleaning, nursing and money, all of which most of us would resent if we were asked for it by our mothers.

The role of daughter, too, requires a false stance. Being a "good" daughter depends on how closely we hold to the current standards for women. No matter how loving we are, or how supportive—even financially—we are not meeting our mothers' expectations if we aren't *proper* women, in the now well-identified mode. We are expected to be passive, submissive, pretty, not too obviously intelligent and potential mothers and wives. This basic pattern remains the same throughout the culture, notwithstanding modifications on the basis of religion, class, race and ethnic group.

We learn how to be women from our mothers. They teach us, consciously and unconsciously, what women are. However, our mothers give us very little information on how to function as adults. They don't talk to us about the world, or tell us how to make our lives. In some instances, the reason for their silence is their own ignorance, compounded by inexperience, shame and discomfort. Generally, they seem not to remember the painful, frustrating aspects of their own lives. In their struggle, they have lost sight of their doubts and desires, and present to us the obvious facts of their lives, as if there is nothing more. They make the roles they fill seem to be what they had aspired to. They act and speak as if marriage and motherhood are all they ever dreamed of and reached for. (In some cases this may be true.)

Our mothers have almost never had the luxury some of us are now experiencing—support from other women. We can tell the truth about our fears and hopes without risking painful criticism. Our mothers have had to obscure the truth about their most intimate relationships with sisters, mothers and, of course, daughters. Women lie because we cannot face the truth. It is a fact that many women are coerced into having children, taught to believe that fulfillment and satisfaction will escape us if we do not become mothers. We daughters are made to feel if we don't live out the female role as our mothers have, we are rejecting them.

Ironically, some mothers tell very important truths to their daughters and are not heeded. If we have learned over the years not to trust our mothers, if we have been treated with disrespect or if our mothers have demonstrated no love for us, why should we believe their teachings? Why take their advice? One woman I interviewed said, "My mother told me everything she knew. She didn't know much." Another said, "My mother doesn't do anything. What could she teach me?"

We must begin with the assumption that babies need to be fondled and caressed, hugged and stroked, in order to be healthy and happy. Touching bonds mother to daughter and daughter to mother. If we are nursed lovingly at our mothers' breasts, or even held warmly and smiled at while being fed a commercial formula, we associate the pleasures of fulfillment and sensual gratification with the woman providing those services.

Unfortunately, most mothers don't stroke or fondle their small daughters very often, no matter what the successful advertising image of mothering might suggest. And it seems that even those mothers who did touch us when we were small stopped long before we wanted them to. The touching, as described by most women, decreases through the first few years we can remember and then stops around the age of nine or ten; most often it never returns. As adults, very few contemporary American daughters embrace mutually with their mothers, hold hands, walk arm in arm or kiss. Most of us describe, where physical contact does occur, the perfunctory social touching that is public affection, the cheek-laid-to-cheek greeting.

Just as we may try to overcome the loss of physical affection we suffered, some of us also attempt to understand and work out the anger we feel at our mothers' physical violence against us. This violence is born of the maternal role. Almost all of us were hit by our mothers as we grew up, primarily between the ages of two and twelve. This hitting usually took the form of spankings or slaps. Sometimes mothers use weapons—straps, belts or hairbrushes. Occasionally they use household objects—hangers, wet dish towels, electric cords—seized in passion.

Though discipline and punishment have traditionally been associated with the father's role, most physical punishment, like most of the responsibilities of parenting, falls to the mother. Even beatings are more frequently administered by mothers than fathers. But the violence our mothers vent upon us is a product of the frustration, pain, rage and desperation which the contemporary institution of motherhood creates and then seeks to suppress. It is not only those children whom the media now call "battered" who suffer the violence of the institution. These are only the most obvious, the proverbial tip of the iceberg. Below the water are the rest of us, daughters and sons, who receive the brunt of our mothers' grief and guilt. As Adrienne Rich points out in her book *Of Woman Born*, mothers in this society are not only made to feel that anger and frustration are unnatural, but we are isolated from each other, so that we have no way to share, and to thus differentiate the experience of mothering from the institution.

Many people make the assumption that all mothers and daughters compete fiercely, primarily for the affection of the husband-father. In fact, the competition is hardly on such a wholesale basis, and the mother/daughter relation is heavily influenced by other competitions within the family.

Some of the competition between daughters and their mothers is over the performance of "womanly" tasks. Can we cook and clean house, dress and act the role of gracious lady as well as or better than our mothers? Though they are generally the source of our skills and knowledge in these areas, often we (and they) feel that we have surpassed them at being the proper woman. Since mothers often must play that role as the sole basis for their identity, when a daughter usurps that place, the loss prompts alienation between mother and daughter. One woman put it this way:

"I was definitely categorized as the housekeeper in my family. I did everything she did. Unfortunately, I did it better because my mother didn't like housework and would read a lot. I could really whip up that house in ten minutes, and it looked like a target first thing in the morning, so you'd think I was real together. I used to win points that way."

Another said:

"Certainly I was a better cook. In fact, I have found out just recently that my mother used to like cooking, but it was just taken over by me. Now I am the family cook, and she doesn't even want to cook any more."

Others of us compete with our mothers in the areas of conversational wit and power. We try to stack up accomplishments against our mothers' totals, or belittle our mothers' lack of credits. No matter which—the daughter or the mother—initiates the rivalry, the fear is that one's rival will appear a more appealing woman. Many of us have felt that competition is initiated, or wholly carried on, by our mothers. Universally, daughters believe "she started it."

"My mother always had to feel that she did things better than I did. Things that she did real well, she'd always tell me that I couldn't do. She was competing with me; I wasn't competing with her."

"I learned from her, and I passed on to my eldest daughter, the competition to be the kid. Who was going to be the child, who was going to take care of whom? I did not feel competitive with her; I felt she was competitive with me."

It is apparent, however, that competition is mutual in most cases. Our mothers fear our maturing into women who will not only not be their little girls any more, but will simply be younger competition—especially when so many of us begin to separate from them by criticizing them and ignoring their advice.

Much of what they do in competition, their strongest weapon in fact, is to remind us of our weaknesses. For our part, daughters compete to surpass our mothers—perhaps out of the fear we have of "being" just like our mothers. We compete to go beyond them, so that we need not *be* this other woman, particularly, if her life is not what we want for ourselves. For most social purposes, we learn, women are interchangeable. When we perceive the role, demeaning as it is, we reject it; those of us who do consistently compete with our mothers do so to bypass them, to best them, to succeed where they have failed. *We* will be exceptional women. *We* will not be this degraded creature, woman.

> "I knew I would be a grown woman someday if I was lucky, but I knew I wasn't going to be like her."

> "Was my mother a role model? God, no, except in a negative sense. I didn't want to be like that."

The competition, despite efforts at repressing it, is conscious. Daughters may deny it, but it emerges in our (often rabid) fear of the similarity between ourselves and our mothers. Even those of us who don't or won't acknowledge the competition will talk about the fear of reproducing Mother's life pattern and her "peculiarities."

Rather than serving as love objects, many fathers compete with mothers for their daughter. In situations where the father competes openly, shows a preference for his daughter and criticizes or ridicules the mother, the daughter usually prefers him.

Some daughters—though fewer than one might imagine—have to compete with their brothers for their mother's love and attention. Most of these daughters come to understand that males are considered more valuable. (Interestingly, because we have been led to believe that mothers desire sons, this author discovered in the process of interviewing that the majority of women who wanted children preferred to have daughters or children of both sexes.)

Far more numerous than daughters who competed with their brothers are those whose rivals are sisters. Dismal enough to try to meet your mother's expectations and fail, without having to compete with another young woman, your sister, who seems to match your mother's dreams and meet her needs far better than you. In these situations, we not only lose our mothers' affection, but cannot love the sister-rivals who have won it.

Natural separation of daughter from mother, which allows the daughter to be whole, unto herself, and the mother to continue her life independently, is not easy. At the same time, a great majority of daughters are eager to move out of their mothers' homes. Leaving home, leaving mother, is the symbolic entry to one's majority, a sign of adult competence. Many of us leave our mothers when we marry; some of us go off to school and never come back. Others leave to make their way in the world. Very few of us stay with our mothers. Generally the leave-takings are crises. Many of our mothers are reluctant to have us go; they feel devastated and betrayed at our departure. Even in our desire to go, we may display ambivalence. Women who consider themselves "desperate" feel conflicted despite their urgency. Daughters who've waited years to escape suffer waves of guilt and fear.

We come to understand, though perhaps not consciously, that no one is going to support us, economically or emotionally; there is no societal source that provides shelter, food or love. Our mothers have taught us how to find and marry a man to take care of these needs. In so doing, they have taught us how to leave them, to supplant them with strangers. This explains our mothers' reluctance to let us go and our grief at going, even though we are eager to be independent, and they have accepted the dual nature of their role. We all understand, daughters and mothers, that we are not supposed to come back together; leaving is supposed to be final.

Our mothers' loss is more poignant than ours when we leave, for often we leave them *behind* and go beyond the lives they have lived. Though this is the purpose of all they have taught us, it still causes pain. They've prepared us to move ahead of them, to live "a better life" than they have. One of the ways many of us seek to lessen this pain and effect a return to our mothers is by becoming mothers ourselves. Whether we share love and ideas with our mothers or merely tolerate an unfortunate relationship, we all understand that having children is the ultimate attachment we can make to our mothers.

For when daughters become mothers, their own mothers are validated. The daughters are now *like them*—in a way no one can deny. This serves to mark the sameness daughters have tried to deny since early adolescence. "There it is, you see. We are alike. You shall do as I have done, be as I have been," mothers may say when their daughters become mothers.

When daughters become mothers, their stature increases in the eyes of their mothers and, in the great majority of cases, "adulthood" is attained.

Our mothers may never see us as full equals, but they must acknowledge the new position. The fact that our motherhood brings us the same painful struggle we experienced as children in our mothers' lives is a difficult irony to recognize.

Those adolescent women who bear babies and keep them, who say that they have no curfews now and they can see whomever they please, that their babies are the signs of their maturity, are the perfect symbol of this confusion of biological capacity with wisdom and life experience. Though the fact of our becoming mothers does, inevitably, bring us the opportunity to be closer to our mothers, it does not create the capacity—on either woman's part—to cease negating the truth of our similarity or the need for honest revelation of life experience.

Daughters who choose not to become mothers, holding out against the force of years of female socialization, may well inspire their mothers' disappointment, anger and secret envy. Neither do daughters who produce grandchildren, small second chances to love without guilt, escape the mother/daughter struggle. Our own maternity does not necessarily further the development of a satisfying mother/daughter bond.

When women go to libraries and bookstores, to colleges and universities, to counselors and doctors, we find either nothing at all which speaks of the mother/daughter relation, or literature which perpetuates the old lies and strengthens the "blame your mother" school of thought which keeps daughters apart from their mothers. Just now, in the middle of this decade, women are beginning to consider and investigate the issue of mother/daughter relations. There is a great deal of work to do. What we want is a telling of truths about women. We must redefine the mother/daughter relationship, learn to have realistic expectations and commit ourselves to acceptance of actual needs, so that expectations may be met, needs be satisfied. Then we can make this basic woman bond loving and fruitful, powerful and deep as once it was.

CREDIT: *Judith Pildes, author of* Our Mothers' Daughters, *Teacher of Women's Studies, Columbia College, The School of the Art Institute, New York.*

Mother Love

DEAR ANN LANDERS: I burned when I read your brutal statement to "Disturbed Mom." You said, "No mother loves all her children equally." It is obvious that you are not a mother. I am. I have four children and I KNOW I don't love one child more than another.

The mother who has a favorite or actually dislikes one of her brood must be mentally ill. Every normal mother loves her children the same, for they are all her flesh and bone.

If you wish to print this letter and state why you made such a barbaric attack on motherhood I would be interested in your explanation. And so would thousands of others who must feel as I do.   LOVE THEM ALL

DEAR LOVE THEM ALL: I don't think it's possible to feel exactly the same about any two humans, be they children, brothers or business associates. Love is an emotion. It cannot be weighed or measured for intensity.

We grow wiser, more patient (or less patient) depending on what happens in our lives. No woman is the same all through her childbearing years. The changes in her disposition, degree of stability and the knowledge she gains through experience all have an effect on her children.

An unwanted child, who senses a mother's hostility, is bound to react unfavorably. Children who do not receive ample love and attention often get into trouble and cause their parents grief. A mother who insists she loves a sullen, rebellious, antisocial child as much as the happy, well-integrated one is lying to herself to cover her guilt.

No one should feel guilty about his true feelings. Being able to recognize and face reality is a sign of good mental health.

Very often I hear from teenagers who say, "My mother is partial to my brother"—or "My sister gets all the attention. Mom likes her better." Children recognize this even if parents don't. Invariably it is the mother of such a child who insists at the top of her mistaken voice that she loves them "all the same."

Motherhood

Why I've Always Loved You Best

DEAR ANN LANDERS: It has been almost three years since you have had the article on an essay that put each child in his place. It was sent to you by a reader who found it in the library stuck between two books. I have had it on my refrigerator door and it's pretty tattered by this time.

Will you please give it a rerun. The date was September 26, 1974.

Many thanks.   MRS. T. IN HIALEAH, FLA.

DEAR FRIEND: Thanks for asking. The author of that lovely essay is my inimitable friend, that talented lady Erma Bombeck. Isn't she the greatest? Here it is—with pleasure:

DEAR FIRST BORN: I've always loved you best because you were our first miracle. You were the genesis of a marriage and the fulfillment of young love.

You sustained us through the hamburger years, the first apartment (furnished in Early Poverty), our first mode of transportation (1955 Feet) and the seven-inch TV we paid on for thirty-six months.

You were new and had unused grandparents and enough clothes for a set of triplets. You were the original model for a mom and a dad who were trying to work the bugs out. You got the strained lamb, the open safety pins and three-hour naps.

You were the beginning.

DEAR MIDDLE CHILD: I've always loved you best because you drew a tough spot in the family and it made you stronger for it.

You cried less, had more patience, wore faded hand-me-downs and never in your life did anything first. But it only made you more special. You were the one we relaxed with and realized a dog could kiss you and you wouldn't get sick. You could cross a street by yourself long before you were old enough to get married. And you helped us understand the world wouldn't collapse if you went to bed with dirty feet.

You were the child of our busy, ambitious years. Without you we never could have survived the job changes and the tedium and routine that is marriage.

TO THE BABY: I've always loved you best because while endings are generally sad, you are such a joy. You readily accepted the milk-stained bibs, the lower bunk, the cracked baseball bat, the baby book that had nothing written in it except a recipe for graham-cracker piecrust that someone had jammed between the pages.

You are the one we held onto so tightly. You are the link with our past, a reason for tomorrow. You quicken our steps, square our shoulders, restore our vision and give us a sense of humor that security, maturity and durability can't provide.

When your hairline takes on the shape of Lake Erie and your own children tower over you, you will still be our baby.   A MOTHER

Multiple Sclerosis

What is MS? Multiple sclerosis is a neurological disease—a disease of the central nervous system, the brain and the spinal cord. It is not a mental disease, nor is it contagious. Approximately 500,000 Americans now suffer from MS and related diseases.

The brain and spinal cord are directly related to such functions as walking, talking, seeing, eating, tying a shoelace, opening a door. These activities are controlled by impulses from the brain and spinal cord. The impulses travel along nerves in the brain and spinal cord, then to other parts of the body. The nerves are coated by a substance called myelin. When MS hits, patches of myelin disintegrate and are replaced by scar tissue. Why this happens, or how, is a mystery, but when it does happen, impulses have trouble getting by the scarred spots. There is interference. With interference come malfunctions —the danger signals of MS.

MS danger signals are varied and unpredictable. They are often mistaken for signs of other disorders. Each symptom, by itself, could be a sign of other ailments.

But, warns the MS Society's Medical Advisory Board, a combination of three or more symptoms such as those listed below, when they appear at once, or in succession, *could* be symptoms of MS. These symptoms should never be ignored. They are signals to see your doctor at once. It may very well *not* be MS. But let your doctor tell you—don't guess.

Here are signals that could mean MS:

(1) Partial or complete paralysis of parts of the body.

(2) Numbness in parts of the body.

(3) Double or otherwise defective vision, such as involuntary movements of eyeballs.

(4) Noticeable dragging of one or both feet.

(5) Severe bladder or bowel trouble (loss of control).

(6) Speech difficulties, such as slurring.

(7) Staggering or loss of balance (MS patients erroneously are thought to be intoxicated).

(8) Extreme weakness or fatigue.

(9) Pricking sensation in parts of the body.

(10) Loss of co-ordination.

(11) Tremors of hands.

(12) Hypersensation to sound.

Multiple sclerosis is usually progressive, proceeding in a series of unpredictable attacks, each attack usually causing further disability. However, this is not always the case. A number of patients may suffer mild and fleeting symptoms and enjoy long periods in which there is an absence or improvement of symptoms. There is no known cure. The cause is yet to be found. MS usually attacks people in their prime years, twenty to forty. Onset before eighteen or after forty-five is known but uncommon.

Unfortunately, no medication has been found to be successful as a treatment for MS. Virtually hundreds of drugs have been tried in an effort to influence the natural course of the disease—including antibiotics, vitamins, hormones and cortisone—but as yet no specific drugs or forms of treatment have proven consistently beneficial.

While no specific cure exists, the patient can and should be treated. Good general medical care designed to prevent upper respiratory and other infections is recommended. Braces may be prescribed for stabilizing usable limbs. The physician may recommend massage, passive or active exercise, and other measures suitable for promoting the greatest effort on the part of the patient to keep active.

Emotional support of MS victims by family and friends is extremely important. Keeping MS patients involved in day-to-day activity is vital. They must not be written off as invalids and permitted to withdraw or become reclusive. A positive, hopeful mental attitude can be immensely helpful.

When MS strikes, families can turn to their local chapter of the National Multiple Sclerosis Society for information, sympathetic help and guidance. Chapters can make available many specific services including aids to daily living, social, recreational and friendly visiting opportunities, professional counseling to alleviate social and psychological pressures, and medical guidance through the chapter's medical advisory committee.

The progress made in the Society's programs of basic and clinical research and professional education brings hope and help through the dissemination of accurate, valid, authentic information.

CREDIT: *National Multiple Sclerosis Society, 257 Park Avenue South, New York, New York 10010.*

How to Live with Multiple Sclerosis and Enjoy Life

In 1947, when my wife and I had just turned thirty, she began to notice a persistent numbness in her right foot. After trying to ignore it for a while, we went to a doctor to see what might be causing this minor problem. We were thunderstruck when he diagnosed it as the onset of MS. In what presumably was meant to be kindly reassurance, he hastened to add that there was no reason to panic because "She might live another twenty years."

Tests of spinal fluid and other examinations confirmed his diagnosis of MS. The confirmation was devastating. Imagine what it is like to be told in the prime of your life that you have a nerve disease with an unknown cause, one for which no cure has been discovered; a disease which may kill you quickly or incapacitate you in any or every way over a period of years. After the initial shock, our first resolution was to meet this crisis as a team—together all the way.

I had recently returned from military service in World War II. We were eager to resume civilian life, get back to an interrupted career, buy a home and start a family. On the final point, medical opinion was unanimous: Forget it.

We also were faced with other major adjustments. We could not foresee how badly or how soon my wife might be incapacitated. We didn't know how much of our savings might have to go for her treatment. We decided to defer buying a home so that we would be able to afford effective treatment if it should become available.

In the next five years we accumulated a medical fund and enough beyond that to enable us to make a down payment on a home in the suburbs. By the time we moved into it, my wife walked with slight difficulty and was losing the use of her right hand and arm. With quiet determination so typical of her, she trained herself to eat, write and perform other tasks with her left hand. (If it sounds easy, try tying your shoes that way.) She has done everything possible to maintain the regular schedule of any homemaker. What she cannot handle physically, I do. She has refused to be relegated to a wheelchair.

From the first intimation of her illness, my wife has shown indomitable courage, along with a beauty of character, grace and self-control that absolutely win me. Whatever her fears, she keeps them to herself. Whatever her pain—and there has been plenty of it—she refuses to buckle. There is never a hint of self-pity. It is a pleasure to be with her. She has great zest for life, a keen sense of humor, a fast mind and a presence that is comfortable and comforting.

From the first we have worked together to maintain as much of her strength and mobility as possible. For most of the time we have done it on our own. Our doctor has seemed to be content with maintaining her general health, providing low dosages of muscle relaxants and vitamins, and reviewing her condition annually. I have been concerned, in addition, with preserving joints and muscles so that a working structure will still exist when a way is discovered—as we pray it will be—to restore nerve function. For over twenty-five years we did the best we could at home with a series of exercise devices. Three years ago we discovered a dedicated physical therapist. We visit him weekly. In addition, we work together each morning and evening on an exercise program he has devised. The improvement has been slow but substantial—and thrilling. After ten years of using a walker for support she is learning to walk again without one.

Occasionally other couples who face MS ask us for suggestions on how to cope with it. The disease is so varied in its effects, and the temperament, needs and attitudes of individuals vary so widely, that generalizations may not apply. With those cautions, here are suggestions that have worked for us:

Consider MS as something to bring you together rather than to break you apart. The partner with MS needs reassurance, support, love, companionship, understanding and tenderness. The other partner has a real opportunity for personal fulfillment through being needed and responding to need.

Rework your lives to yield the greatest satisfaction within limitations imposed by MS. Outside of working hours I am at home with my wife. I have developed many kinds of recreation—music, writing, working in wood and metal, to name a few. They substitute for golf, bowling and other away-from-home kinds of recreation.

Make the MS partner part of the act. Over the years I have been invited to speak at many job-related conferences and seminars from Maine to Mexico, and from Florida to Alaska. I have always asked my wife to accompany me —and she has always accepted. She has won the admiration and friendship of all who have met her—and she has had more to think about and enjoy than if she had taken the easier option of staying at home. These trips give us something exciting to share and remember.

Forget what you're missing. Don't keep reminding yourself of what you must give up because of your MS or your partner's. Being physically sound is no guarantee of happiness. Many great physical specimens are also great at making themselves miserable.

If you have MS don't compare your case with others. Every individual is different. Don't borrow false hope from someone who has had a remission. Don't borrow terror from someone who hasn't.

Live one day at a time. Hope for the best. Exercise to your maximum capacity so you will still have joint mobility and muscle if the miracle of remission or nerve restoration should come to pass.

Hang tough. I'll never forget a young Marine who suffered battle wounds that resulted in the loss of a leg. "Okay, I'm a cripple," he said. "But I'm not disabled. Don't ever call me that!" That's the spirit that makes a winner, no matter what the scoreboard shows. As Ann Landers says, "It's not what happens to us, but how we take it that counts."

CREDIT: *Anonymous.*

Nails

Care and Treatment

Throughout history, long, carefully manicured nails have been a symbol of wealth and social status. In Asia, the well-to-do women let their nails grow so long it was obvious that they were incapable of performing simple household tasks. Even today, long manicured nails are status symbols of a sort. The assumption is that such hands couldn't possibly wash dishes, scrub floors or type.

The rate of nail growth varies according to the individual and can be influenced by many factors. Several diseases and infections slow up nail growth. Pregnancy, typing, piano playing and nail-biting make nails grow faster. Nail growth is greatest in youth and decreases slowly with age, dropping almost 50 percent between the ages of twenty-five and seventy-five. For some mysterious reason the middle fingernail grows the fastest, and the nails on the right hand of right-handed people grow more rapidly than those on the left hand.

COMMON NAIL PROBLEMS

Nails can be damaged by too much manicuring or improper manicuring. The most common error is cutting the cuticles.

The cuticle protects the nail fold from infection. A cuticle should not be cut unless it is torn and ragged. Trimming will prevent further tearing.

First the nails should be soaked in warm, soapy water to soften the cuticles. Then the cuticles should be pushed back gently with the fingertip or a towel—don't use another nail or a pointed file.

Hangnails are the most common cuticle problem. A hangnail is a ragged, often triangular, flap of dead skin. The best remedy is to remove it at the base with sharp clean scissors. If the area is inflamed, the attention of a doctor is advised. Nail infections can be painful and serious.

Nails that break and split are a common problem. The notion that eating large quantities of gelatin will make nails stronger is a myth. The best way to cope with fragile or splitting nails (when not caused by disease) is to protect them with several coats of nail polish.

Nail hardeners should be used with great care. Although such products do harden the nail, they can cause severe allergic reactions. Such preparations have been known to cause dryness of the nail, discoloration, discomfort, bleeding under the nail and eventually the nail may drop off.

CARING FOR YOUR NAILS

Nails respond best to kind, gentle treatment. Wear rubber gloves when scouring pans. Use a pencil when dialing. When gardening, put soap under your nails and wear gloves. Use the pads of your fingers for picking up things, never your nails. In general, if you pretend you are trying not to smudge wet nail polish, you will use your hands in such a way as to almost never break a nail.

TOENAILS

Any of the conditions that affect fingernails may also affect toenails. Several other conditions are peculiar to toenails.

An ingrown toenail forms when the soft tissue of the side of the toe is penetrated by the edge of the nail. The first symptoms are pain and redness, followed by swelling and pus. Without proper care, severe infection may follow.

Mild cases of ingrown toenails are best treated by applying wet dressings and lifting and paring off the excess nail. More severe cases may require removal of all or part of the nail by a physician. (Don't try to do this yourself.)

The main cause of ingrown toenails is shoes that are too narrow. Cutting the toenails too short and too far back at the corners is also a contributing factor. Flat feet, excessive curvature of the nail and an unusually large big toe are other possible causes. In any case, the first rule of treatment and prevention is that shoes must be wide enough and long enough so they will not put pressure on the toes. The nail must be allowed to grow until the edge is clear of the end of the toe before it is cut. Then it should be cut straight across with the sharp corners only slightly rounded.

CREDIT: *Committee on Cutaneous Health and Cosmetics, American Medical Association.*

Narcolepsy

ROCHESTER, MINN.—A housewife wrote a letter to the Mayo Clinic requesting an appointment. Her complaint:

"I fall asleep driving. I find myself on the wrong side of the road, off the shoulder, narrowly dodging parked cars or slamming on the brakes to avoid hitting the car in front of me.

"I have tried naps ahead of time, napping along the side of the road, singing, slapping myself, everything—to no avail. My children have been accustomed to saying, 'We'll wake you when the light turns green, Mom.'

"I've always welcomed red lights and trains at a crossing. Even a two-minute nap is a relief.

"I've slept washing dishes, washing clothes, fixing meals, eating meals. I've slept in restaurants, at dances, stage plays, concerts and in church. I've fallen asleep while taking dictation."

Dr. Robert Yoss, a Mayo Clinic neurologist, has been hearing such horror stories from truckers who've driven big semitrailers off into the ditch, executives who have lost jobs because they fell asleep in a business conference and people whose marriages have broken up because they fell asleep making love.

They are victims of the strange disorder known as narcolepsy, an uncontrollable desire to sleep. They can fall asleep anytime and any place. Some doze off ten or fifteen times a day. A quick nap will revive them, but only temporarily. The drowsy state soon returns.

"The best way to understand how a victim feels is to stay up two nights in a row, without sleep, then try to work as usual for the third day," says Dr. Yoss. "For you, it will be a temporary thing. For the narcoleptic, it is constant."

Dr. Yoss believes there is a little narcolepsy in all of us.

"It's a matter of degree," he explains. "Most of us can be reading a book after a heavy meal, when it is quiet, and begin to realize we are not getting much out of it. Then the head gets jerky and we find ourselves dozing off. The individual with a narcolepsy diagnosis does the same thing, only more often. It is a misconception that he is feeling fine at one moment and then at the next moment, whammo, he's unconscious."

For every sleepy person there is probably a philagrypneac (lover of wakefulness). These people seem to be able to get by on four or five hours of sleep, are always alert and enjoy an eighteen-hour production day.

"A philagrypneac wouldn't complain to a doctor because his wakefulness would not be considered a disease," commented Dr. Yoss. "Neither is narcolepsy a disease. It is just one end of the spectrum. Narcoleptics are just normal people who are not average in their ability to keep awake and alert."

The neurologist classified wakefulness in five levels—alert and sharp, alert but losing sharpness, tired but not drowsy, drowsy and very sleepy.

Whether one is at one extreme of the spectrum or the other is a matter of heredity, not a cultivated behavior pattern, Dr. Yost believes.

Fortunately, there is a good treatment for narcolepsy, he adds. Stimulant drugs are taken at prescribed intervals. The patient also is encouraged to get a good night's sleep.

"The key word is 'good,'" he emphasizes. "Eight hours of sleep with many interruptions is not good. Our goal is to have well-rested people during the day."

CREDIT: *Arthur J. Snider, Science and Medicine, Chicago Sun-Times.*

Nervous Habits and Compulsive Behavior

Nervous habit is a term used by laymen to describe repetitive movements which people make from time to time. The movements seem to have no apparent purpose or usefulness, and the person making them is partly or totally unaware of his actions. These repetitive movements are more likely to appear when the person is worried or anxious.

In the nineteenth century, anxiety and worry were thought to be caused by some kind of physical affliction of the nerves, the brain or spinal cord. We now know that in only rare instances are the nerves themselves actually affected when people are worried or anxious. Most of the time the nerves themselves are quite healthy and the worry or anxiety comes not from a physical disorder of the nerves but from disturbances in thought and emotion.

Nose picking and nail biting are probably the most common "nervous habits" of adults. They fall into a category of repetitive movements which might technically be called autoerotic; that is, they give bodily pleasure and you can do them yourself. They are partial pleasures which stem from infancy—islands of childhood in the personalities of people who otherwise may be quite mature. They represent unconsciously the kind of reassurance and pleasurable gratification that a kindly mother may once have given to an agitated infant. We have no good idea why they persist in some people. They are not usually nor ought they to be the reason for seeking professional psychiatric help, though they often spontaneously diminish or disappear in the course of psychotherapy which may be given for other reasons.

Nail biting often follows an earlier childhood experience of extensive thumb sucking. The thumb sucking may disappear and be replaced by nail biting; or in some instances the thumb sucking persists into adult life. When children suck their thumbs, they not infrequently pull or rub their ear lobes, their noses or their hair. Sometimes the hair pulling produces baldness; it goes so far that patches of the scalp are denuded. Any one of these associated movements (ear lobe pulling, nose touching or hair pulling) may become separated from the original thumb sucking and persist as a nervous habit by itself. The hair pulling may proceed from the hair of the head to the eyebrows, the eyelashes and even rarely to the pubic hair. People who have this habit feel no pain in removing their hair, and indeed are likely to say that it feels good.

Rhythmic rocking is another common nervous habit in infants. It may become severe enough to involve banging the head against the crib or wall. It also falls into the autoerotic category of giving bodily pleasure to the child, strange as this may seem to an adult observer because the head banging may be so intense as to produce bruises. Vestiges of this habit can be seen in adults who unconsciously rock themselves when they are disturbed, although head banging is likely to be seen only in extremely disturbed adults.

Nervous habits by themselves do not indicate severe psychopathology, but any of them may be associated with other disturbances, some severe. There is usually embarrassment about the activity itself or its effects. This embarrassment or shame usually leads the person to make some effort to stop the habit, but the efforts are likely to be unsuccessful because (1) the activity is pleasurable, (2) it allays anxiety and (3) it is often carried on more or less unconsciously. Efforts by parents and others to bring a stop to the activity are likely to make matters worse. In children, particularly where the approval of parents is so important a source of well-being, the parental criticism which is experienced by the child as disapproval simply makes him more anxious and unhappy, and is likely therefore to lead to intensification of the habit.

For nail biting and thumb sucking all kinds of devices have been used as deterrents—bad-tasting substances on the thumb or fingers, restraints of various kinds on the hands or arms, devices inserted in the mouth. Most often these fail, and in the instances where they succeed, the symptoms are likely to be replaced by others, such as nightmares. In older children or adults, these devices may be helpful in preventing nail biting or thumb sucking. The older child or adult may be willing to co-operate because he himself very much wants to stop, and he appreciates the fact that his habit is likely to go on outside of his awareness. He is willing, therefore, to use mechanical devices as a reminder, an aid to making him aware. In contrast to the young child, he may be able to make use of and may even solicit the assistance of other people to remind him without loss of self-esteem and intensification of anxiety.

Some habits are more worrisome to professionals than others. Hair pulling, for instance, is likely to be a manifestation of a somewhat more intense state of anxiety and inner loneliness than nail biting, especially when it involves the eyelashes or the pubic hair. Professional consultation should be sought.

Although they are not usually considered "nervous habits," two other types of repetitious actions should be noted: compulsions and tics. Both of these have a somewhat different significance than the autoerotic habits.

The compulsive acts have a ritual quality to them, and may seem excessive to the person involved or may seem natural and remain unquestioned. Hand washing is a good example. It may be necessary for a dentist or a nurse to wash their hands twenty or thirty times a day, but for the ordinary person four or five times a day is enough. If he washes his hands much more often than that, twenty or thirty times a day for instance, he may attempt to explain it in some way that seems plausible, but this explanation would likely seem to be farfetched, a rationalization to others. Indeed, the person himself may be aware that his hand washing derives not from reason but from anxiety.

There are ritual compulsions to touch or not to touch. There are procedures which seem almost ceremonial that have to be repeated in a certain sequence at certain times of the day, for instance before going to bed. Failure to perform any of these acts may produce great anxiety in the person, which is relieved only when the act is performed. These compulsive acts may have a simple repetitive character like the autoerotic habits noted above, or they may be a repeated series of separate acts. The person who displays this kind of behavior is less likely than the nail biter or hair puller to be aware of or disturbed by his "habit." For one thing, the compulsive habit is less likely to be offensive to others or embarrassing to the perform of the action. And secondly, it is more likely to go on outside the person's awareness. If he is aware of it at all, it seems natural and appropriate to him.

These compulsive ritual acts are not in themselves pleasurable like the first group of nervous habits that we considered. They are not remedial in the sense that they supply missing pleasure or reassurance. They are rather in the nature of guards against some kind of danger. The nature of the protection, its magical or symbolic significance are not usually known to the person; nor does he know what the danger is against which his ritual act protects him. The meaning of both the danger and the protective act lie in the unconscious mind and cannot usually be discovered except by special techniques of psychotherapy. In most instances, they do not need to be discovered because the compulsive behavior by itself is not necessarily a sign of pervasive psychopathology.

Most people have some compulsions just as most people have some autoerotic habits. For instance, most people feel compelled to knock on wood after commenting on some fortunate aspect of their lives, or they must say "God forbid" when they verbalize some gloomy possibility. These are magic ritual "protective" measures. They might indeed feel anxious if something prevented their doing them, but it is highly unlikely that these compulsions by themselves would move someone to seek professional assistance.

Yet another kind of "nervous habit" is the tic. The tic is a quick, jerky, usually purposeless movement, often of the face or head. The extremities or trunk may sometimes be involved. It has a spasmodic quality usually like a wink of the eye, or a flashing grimace of the face or part of the mouth, or a jerk of the head. It happens more often when one is upset or anxious. The person doing it is completely unaware and when it is called to his attention he is nonplused. In contrast with compulsions where the person can make up some kind of plausible excuse, the possessor of tics is at a total loss to explain the behavior. Nor does he have any control over it, in contrast with the two types of habits discussed above. Tics, like compulsive acts, are signs of unconscious worry and conflict. They usually represent both the forbidden wish and the protection against it. We do not understand why or how the mind chooses one kind of symptom rather than another; and in this sense, we do not understand why tics occur in some people. By themselves they are not usually sufficiently troublesome enough to interfere with the person's effective social functioning, and it is rare that someone seeks professional treatment simply because of the presence of a tic. Short of psychotherapy, there is no specific treatment, but anything which tends to lower the general level of anxiety in a person is also likely to ameliorate the tics.

There is a fourth category of "nervous habits" which do indeed warrant the designation "nervous"; that is, they stem from physical diseases of the nervous system, the brain and the spinal cord. Such diseases may give rise to repetitive acts or movements which can easily be confused with tics.

Tremors and tic-like movements which come from physical disorders of the nervous system may also be intensified by emotional upsets and anxieties, although they are less likely to be affected than psychologically caused tics.

In any case, the sudden onset of tic-like movements warrants a medical consultation to determine whether they are of emotional or neurological origin.

CREDIT: *Gene Gordon, M.D., Senior Attending Psychiatrist, Children's National
Medical Center, Washington, D.C.; Faculty, George Washington University Medi-
cal School, Washington, D.C.; Supervising Training Analyst, Baltimore-District of
Columbia Psychoanalytical Institute.*

Nipples

(*Inverted*)

There are two problems associated with inverted (turned in) nipples. The
most obvious problem is a cosmetic one, particularly if the opposite nipple is
not inverted. The second problem is the functional inability to breastfeed a
child.

This problem can be corrected surgically. The surgery is uncomplicated
and does not require an overnight stay in the hospital. It is usually performed
under local anesthesia and takes about an hour.

The scar is usually well hidden in the areola (dark area around the nipple). Each physician will place his/her own postoperative restrictions on the
patient, but generally they are few. There is little postoperative discomfort.

Depending on the cause of the inversion, it is possible for the nipple to retain sensation and the ability to breastfeed after surgery.

Since there is a definite functional need for this operation, most insurance
companies will reimburse the patient.

The various causes of inverted nipples are:

(1) Congenital: (You were born that way and when the breast developed,
the problem became apparent.)

(2) Scar tissue from previous surgery of the breast.

(3) Cancer. In some cases a woman with cancer of the breast will experience a pulling in, which results in an inversion of the nipple. Since cancer is a
possibility, any woman who has a new or sudden inversion of the nipple
should see a physician immediately.

A woman seeking correction of this problem should make sure that her
doctor is well qualified to correct inverted nipples. A qualified Plastic and
Reconstructive Surgeon may be researched by contacting your family physi-

cian, local medical society or the American Society of Plastic and Reconstructive Surgeons, Inc., 29 East Madison Street, Suite 807, Chicago, Illinois 60602. Many major cities have local chapters.

CREDIT: *David Ross, M.D., Plastic and Reconstructive Surgery, Chicago, Illinois.*

Nursing as a Career

Nursing plays a major role in health care. As important members of the medical care team, registered nurses perform a wide variety of functions. They observe, evaluate and record symptoms, reactions and progress of patients; administer medications; assist in the rehabilitation of patients; instruct patients and family members in proper health maintenance care; and help maintain a physical and emotional environment that promotes recovery.

Some registered nurses provide hospital care. Others perform research activities or instruct patients. The setting usually determines the scope of the nurse's responsibilities.

Hospital nurses constitute the largest group. Most are staff nurses who provide skilled bedside nursing care and carry out the medical treatment plans prescribed by physicians. They may also supervise practical nurses, aides and orderlies. Hospital nurses usually work with groups of patients that require similar nursing care. For instance, some nurses work with patients who have had surgery; others care for children, the elderly or the mentally ill. Some are administrators of nursing services.

Private duty nurses are self-employed and give individual care to patients who need constant attention in homes, hospitals or other convalescent institutions.

Office nurses assist physicians, dental surgeons and occasionally dentists in private practice or clinics.

Community health nurses care for patients in clinics, homes, schools and other community settings. They may also work with community leaders, teachers, parents and physicians in community health education.

Nurse educators teach students the principles and skills of nursing both in the classroom and in direct patient care.

Occupational health or industrial nurses provide nursing care to employees in industry and government and along with physicians promote employee health.

According to the most recent data from the Interagency Conference on

Nursing Statistics, there were 961,000 employed registered nurses on January 1, 1976. It is estimated that about 1.5 percent of the total employed registered nurses are male.

A license is required to practice professional nursing in all states and in the District of Columbia. To get a license, a nurse must be a graduate of a school of nursing approved by the state board of nursing and pass a written state board competency examination. Nurses may be licensed in more than one state, either by examination or endorsement of a license issued by another state.

Three types of educational programs—diploma, baccalaureate and associate degree—prepare candidates for licensure. However the baccalaureate program is preferred for those who aspire to administrative or management positions, and for those planning to work in research, consultation, teaching or clinical specialization, which require education at the master's level. In public health agencies, advancement is generally difficult for nurses who do not have baccalaureate degrees in community health nursing. It is important to consider future career goals as a nurse and to be aware of the career options available from each of the three different types of nursing education programs, because moving from one type of program to another is time-consuming and costly. Graduation from high school is required for admission to all schools of nursing.

Diploma programs are conducted by hospital and independent schools and usually require three years of training. Bachelor's degree programs usually require four years of study in a college or university, although a few require five years. Associate degree programs in junior and community colleges require approximately two years of nursing education. Varying amounts of general education are combined with nursing education in all three types of programs.

Students who need financial aid may qualify for federally sponsored nursing scholarships or low-interest loans.

Those who want to pursue a nursing career should have a sincere desire to serve humanity and be sympathetic to the needs of others. Nurses must be able to accept responsibility and direct or supervise the activity of others; they also should be able to follow orders precisely and to use good judgment in emergencies. Good mental health is needed in order to cope with human suffering and frequent emergency situations. Staff nurses need physical stamina because of the amount of time spent walking and standing.

A growing movement in nursing, generally referred to as the "nurse practitioner program," is opening new career possibilities. Several post-baccalaureate programs prepare nurses for highly independent roles in the clinical care and teaching of patients in such areas as pediatrics, geriatrics, community health, mental health and medical-surgical nursing.

Employment opportunities for registered nurses are expected to be favorable through the mid-1980s. Some competition for more desirable, higher paying jobs is expected in areas where training programs abound, but opportunities for full- or part-time work in present shortage areas, such as some southern states and many inner-city locations, are expected to be very good through 1985. For nurses who have had graduate education, the outlook is excellent for obtaining positions as administrators, teachers, clinical specialists and community health nurses.

Registered nurses who worked in hospitals in 1976 received average starting salaries of $11,820 a year, according to a national survey conducted by the University of Texas Medical Branch. Registered nurses in nursing homes can expect to earn slightly less than those in hospitals. Nurses employed in all federal government agencies earned an average of $15,500 a year in 1977.

Most hospital and nursing home nurses receive extra pay for work on evening and night shifts. Nearly all receive from five to thirteen holidays a year, at least two weeks of paid vacation after one year of service, and also some type of health and retirement benefits.

For information on approved schools of nursing, nursing careers and scholarships, contact:

Coordinator, Undergraduate Programs,
Department of Nursing Education
American Nurses' Association
2420 Pershing Road
Kansas City, Missouri 64108
         and
Career Information Services
National League for Nursing
10 Columbus Circle
New York, New York 10019

CREDIT: *Julie McGuire, Coordinator, Career Information Services, National League for Nursing, New York, New York. Based on a piece by Jean MacVicar, Director of Division of Hospital and Long-Term Care Facility Nursing Service, 1978–79. Edition of the Department of Labor's Occupational Outlook Handbook.*

The Licensed Practical Nurse

Practical (vocational) nursing is an occupation that provides many job satisfactions for those who have a genuine interest in helping others. Practical nursing programs prepare men and women to give nursing care under the supervision of a registered nurse or a physician, to patients in simple nursing situations. In more complex situations, the licensed practical nurse functions as an assistant to the registered nurse. The licensed practical nurse is employed in hospitals, extended care facilities, nursing homes, clinics and other health care facilities.

Practical nursing programs are approximately one year in length. In some states they are longer, and a few programs are shorter. Each program establishes its own admission requirements. The majority of programs accept both men and women who have good health and are interested in a service career. Academic requirements vary from state to state so it is important to contact the board of nursing in the state in which you wish to study in order to learn whether or not you need a high school diploma.

Scholarships are sometimes available for deserving students. Information about these may be obtained from the secondary school counselor.

Most practical nursing programs require full-time attendance. This will include classes, practice of nursing procedures and supervised learning experiences with real patients in a hospital, extended care facility or nursing home.

Satisfactory completion of a state-approved program in practical nursing is required before you are permitted to take the examination for licensure. The examination is given by the particular state board of nursing. Licensure as a practical or vocational nurse gives the person the legal right to practice as a licensed practical or vocational nurse in the state in which the license was issued.

Each state sets its own minimum licensing requirements. A practical nurse licensed in one state and wishing to practice in another must apply to the state board of nursing in the second state for licensure. Requirements vary slightly from state to state, however licensure in another state is not difficult to obtain and does not require the writing of an examination.

CREDIT: *Jean MacVicar, Director of Division of Hospital and Long-Term Care Facility Nursing Service, 1978–79. From* Practical Nursing Career, 1976–1977.

Nursing Homes

A Checklist of What to Look for

After deciding to place a parent, the next problem is finding the proper home. How does one go about checking out nursing homes?

Wetzel McCormick, administrator of the Warren N. Barr Pavilion on the

Near North Side in Chicago, lists some of the things that should be on your checklist (specifically, this relates to Illinois but can be applied to most states):

Check with your state Health Department or your local Health Department to find out if the home has had a record of problems.

Is the facility accredited by the Council for Long-Term Care Facilities of the Joint Commission on Accreditation of Hospitals? All nursing homes in Illinois must have a license. But not all are accredited by the JCAH, which means the facility has been evaluated (at its own expense) by the council, which states that it meets government standards in regard to quality of staff, health and food services, safety requirements, etc.

Be aware that in a nonprofit institution any operating surpluses are returned to the facility to upgrade patient care and services. For-profit homes may use the return on investment for outside purposes.

Does the home have a full-time medical director who is responsible for the staff and is answerable for the care of its residents.

Is the professional staff adequate? Are physicians on regular duty or on call at all times? There should be a registered nurse on twenty-four-hour duty on every patient floor. And there should be a nursing supervisor for every shift. Is there a social service staff? Are there plenty of nurses aides and social and rehabilitation aides? Is there regular review of all personnel? Ask these questions and keep your eyes open when you visit.

Is the home eligible for Medicare reimbursement?

Does it provide ancillary health care such as dental, optometric and podiatric services? Does it have physical and occupational therapists?

Are the social, recreational and religious programs suited to the prospective resident's needs?

Ask to see proof that the building meets safety and fire code standards. Are fire drills held regularly?

Visit the home at different times of the day to observe if it is kept clean. Find out if the bed linens are actually changed as regularly as you are told they are.

Are the rooms comfortable and orderly, and do they provide enough space?

Talk to residents (and those visiting them) to get their impressions. Observe the way residents are treated by the staff. Find out the views of staff members.

Does the facility have a selective menu that is posted, and are special diets available?

Does the home encourage meetings between the staff, residents and family members to establish lines of communication, to hear opinions and answer complaints?

McCormick maintains it is important for a person looking for a nursing home to communicate with the prospective resident. "It is important to minimize that person's fears by assuring him or her that you have found a comfortable place that provides the best of care," he says. "It should also be pointed out that there is a period of adjustment that varies for each resident in a controlled environment, such as a skilled nursing facility. Even though we try to motivate residents to get involved, every person has to adjust at his own pace."

CREDIT: *Illinois Masonic Medical Center, Warren N. Barr Pavilion, Wetzel McCormick, Administrator. Written by Barbara Varro, Chicago* Sun-Times.

Nutrition

What the Body Needs to Keep Well and Functioning

Nutritionally your body will do its best in growth, functioning and maintenance if it is properly nourished from birth until "death do us part." And nutrition for nine months before birth is also important.

Proper nourishment comes from eating a variety of foods and not eating too much in relation to one's weight and physical activity. This variety can include any foods—chocolate, sugar, Harvard beets, even so-called "junk foods"—but should be based on what nutritionists call the Basic Four Food Groups. They are:

1. Protein Group—meat, fowl or fish.
2. Dairy Group—milk (any kind), or anything made from milk, cheese, yogurt, ice cream, etc.
3. Fruits and Vegetables—any kind but always a variety.
4. Cereals—foods made from wheat, corn, rice, oats—again always a variety.

And don't eat too much of anything.

Unfortunately, we are surrounded today by a multitude of self-appointed "health and nutrition experts" whose only qualification is that they eat three times a day.

We hear of the glories of so-called "natural organic" foods, the benefits of megavitamin therapy, and the path to "revolutionary quick weight loss" through low carbohydrate diets. Newspapers repeatedly carry stories that are enough to make anyone's stomach churn: "Food Additives Linked with

Hyperkinesis," "Sugar is a Deadly Poison," "Chemicals in Bacon Cause Cancer."

Today we need all the help we can get in sifting food facts from food fads. The most serious problem is that rampant rumors and resulting anxiety distract you from the real nutritional guidelines—ones which have taken generations of scientific research to establish, which are very simple, and which you *should* be following in an effort to eat for good health.

Let's take a critical look at some of those food rumors and nutritional nonsense that are now circulating. We also will present some scientific facts to wise you up when your local food faddist comes calling.

"THOSE CHEMICALS" IN YOUR FOOD

Before you get caught up in the current wave of chemical phobia, remember that all foods, indeed all living things, are made of chemicals. A hot, steamy solution which contains, among other things, essential oils, butyl, isoamyl, phenyl, ethyl, hexyl and benzyl alcohols; tannin, geraniol and other chemicals, is not some artificially wicked brew, but a simple "natural" cup of tea. If you have rejected those new artificial egg substitutes because the ingredients include "lecithin, mono- and diglycerides, xanthum gums, tri-sodium and triethyl citrate," and a long list of other chemicals you can't pronounce, remember that 100 percent natural eggs, even organic ones laid by happy hens, contain, among other things, ovalbumin, conalbumin, mucin, lecithin, butyric and acetic acids, zeaxanthine and phosphates.

Not only will you find strange-sounding chemicals in natural foods, but there is no basis for the widely accepted assumption that natural is better than artificial.

In addition to occasionally being harmful, some perfectly safe natural foods contain deadly toxins. For example, a potato is a complex aggregate of more than 150 different chemicals, including solanine, oxalic acid, arsenic, tannin and nitrates. Solanine is a potent chemical which in high doses can interfere with nerve impulses. Each of us, on an average, eats about 119 pounds of potatoes a year containing enough solanine to kill a horse. However, when consumed in the small quantities present in a serving of potatoes, there is no adverse effect on the body.

Other examples: lima beans contain cyanide, a deadly poison, but not enough to worry about; nuts, wheat and other cereals may contain toxic substances called aflatoxins produced by contamination with certain types of molds, but not enough to harm us.

Additionally, natural foods quickly deteriorate with time, often developing molds and other growths which can cause disease. Thus, some preservative is necessary. Even wheat germ turns rancid if left unrefrigerated for a short time. So raise your eyebrows in healthy skepticism when you next encounter an advocate of the "back to nature" movement.

DO ADDITIVES CAUSE CANCER?

In the context of the misunderstanding about "chemicals," additives and modern food-processing techniques have been put on trial as the likely villains in the cancer "whodunit" mystery. Cancer has moved from being the eighth leading cause of death in 1900 to the second leading cause in 1970, but it still causes only a quarter of the deaths that heart disease does.

However, when you look more closely at the figures, you'll see no immediate reason for indicting food additives. Statistics clearly indicate that the rise in cancer deaths in the United States in the past forty years is largely attributable to an increase in lung cancer. The lung cancer death rate is now eighteen times as high for men and six times as high for women as it was forty years ago. There is no way to link food additives with lung cancer. Lung cancer mortality is directly related to the growth in popularity of cigarette smoking between 1900 and 1964. The frequency of other cancer deaths related to other sites—for instance, the stomach, which one might suspect could be affected by food—has declined or stabilized. Ironically, it is the use of certain food additives like the antioxidants BHA and BHT which may be responsible in part for the dramatic decline we have witnessed in stomach cancer deaths.

You will continue to read and hear stories about how additives are dangerous and not tested, put into our foods just so companies can make more money. The reality is, however, that we know more about additives (which make up less than 1 percent of our diet) than we do about the chemistry of food itself. Food additives, especially those introduced in the past ten years, have survived rigid testing procedures not applied to the great majority of natural products, and without the intelligent use of food additives, it would be far more difficult to feed all of us, food prices would be much higher, and most women would be back in the kitchen for many long hours!

ADDITIVES AND HYPERKINESIS

Dr. Benjamin Feingold, formerly the Chief of Allergy Department at the Kaiser Permanente Medical Center in San Francisco, has proposed in a popular book that additives, particularly flavoring and coloring agents, make children hyperactive (hyperkinetic). According to Dr. Feingold, all foods containing additives, dyes of any type, or compounds containing salicylates should be excluded from the diets of hyperactive children. But, to our knowledge, there is no basis for the Feingold theory. Recently an advisory committee of distinguished pediatricians, nutritionists, psychologists and many others with professional competence concluded that "no controlled studies have demonstrated that hyperkinesis is related to the ingestion of food additives. The claim that hyperactive children improve significantly on a diet that is free from salicylates and additives has not been confirmed."

SUGAR: A DEADLY POISON?

If you believed everything you read in recent popular books and magazines, you'd conclude that sugar was the "killer on the breakfast table" and the underlying cause of everything from heart disease to hypoglycemia.

In fact, however, sugar when used in moderation as part of a normal, balanced diet is a perfectly safe food. First, even in excess amounts, sugar is not a cause of diabetes (high levels of sugar consumption, though, may exacerbate this disease once you have it). Second, though for many people sugar may accelerate dental decay, it is actually the sticky and excessive sugar taken between meals that promotes decay, not sugar with meals. Third, there is no evidence that eating sugar increases your chances of developing heart disease. Fourth, sugar is not the "cause" of obesity. Obesity is caused by consuming more calories than are used up in physical activity. Too many calories are just too many, despite the source. Fifth, sugar is not the cause of hypoglycemia—"low blood sugar." Very low blood sugar is a once-in-a-million event and sugar is not the cause. So, enjoy that chocolate sundae or piece of candy but make it only a part of your total food intake.

THE NITRITE IN BACON

Sodium nitrite is used during the curing process and is responsible for the characteristic flavor, color, and texture of bacon, ham and sausage products. Without sodium nitrite, bacon would be salt pork and ham would look and taste like fresh roast pork. Most important, sodium nitrite provides protection against deadly botulism poisoning.

The concern over nitrite is based on the observation that under some circumstances it can combine with other components of our diet to form chemical compounds called nitrosamines. Some nitrosamines have been found to cause cancer when fed in large doses to test animals.

However, sodium nitrite is a normal component of human saliva and some 80 percent of the nitrite in the body comes from vegetables—celery, radishes, spinach, beets, etc. The potential conversion of nitrites to nitrosamines can happen as easily to the saliva's natural nitrite as it can to nitrite from hot dogs or bacon. So it seems a bit absurd to be panicking over small amounts of additives which prevent serious health threats while being unconcerned about naturally occurring nitrites.

Certainly nitrites should be further studied. We don't know everything we should about how they work, about what problems, if any, they may cause. But right now we have no other way of curing meats and preventing botulism in these foods and no evidence that nitrites in our foods are a health threat. So you can bring home the bacon (if you can afford it) and be confident that there is no hazard sufficiently great to cause alarm.

EAT, DRINK AND SUPPLEMENT?

The truth about vitamins is twofold: we do need them, but unless you have a medically diagnosed vitamin deficiency, you will get all the vitamins and other nutrients you need from a well-balanced diet. Indeed, you can cause yourself harm by self-medication with massive amounts of vitamins—particularly vitamins A and D, which are not excreted from the body.

But you are inevitably thinking, "What about vitamin C? Doesn't it prevent and cure colds?"

Unfortunately, it does not. The *Journal of the American Medical Association* recently published a nine-month study conducted at the National Institutes of Health in which volunteers took pills daily. Half of the subjects took three grams of vitamin C daily (three grams of the vitamin is roughly the amount you'd get from eating sixty oranges), while the other took "sugar pills." The dose was doubled whenever the volunteer thought a cold was coming on. The results showed that the effects of the vitamin on the number of colds "seem to be nil" . . .

Most physicians today do not recommend vitamin C overdosing. Not only do they feel it is a waste of money, but excessive use of vitamin C can cause serious kidney problems.

THE "LOW CARBOHYDRATES DIETS"

A severe limitation of carbohydrate intake can lead to a *temporary* weight loss. First, a diet low in carbohydrates tends to promote a temporary salt loss from the body, thus leading to dehydration, a condition which will temporarily send the scale indicator to the left.

Second, an individual avoiding carbohydrates soon finds that his diet becomes uninteresting. He will inevitably eat less, taking in fewer calories. Thus, it should be no surprise that he is losing weight. Studies have shown that people on low-carbohydrate diets consume 13 to 15 percent fewer calories than they usually would. This would be a good path to weight control except that the calories taken in are not nutritionally balanced.

When thirst makes up for the dehydration and the dieter—tired of a boring menu—returns to his regular overeating, the weight initially "lost" returns.

What is the point of such a diet? Essentially, it is planned malnutrition. There are indeed some potential problems here. We need foods with all types of nutrients, including carbohydrates. Each plays a role in developing our body and then keeping it in good operating condition. If we omit one of these important classes of food we sooner or later will be in nutritional trouble. If you want to lose weight safely and permanently there is only one way to do so: follow the if-you-want-to-lose-weight-you've-got-to-eat-less diet and exercise more.

To emphasize eating less and exercising more we have come up with the "Half plus Twice Diet." And what is this? It is very simple. Eat half of what you ordinarily eat, assuming you eat a varied diet based around the Basic Four Food Groups and get twice as much exercise. Simple, inexpensive, and it works! We call it the "Half Plus Twice Diet" or the "Stare-Whelan Diet."

EATING FOR GOOD HEALTH

The concerns about additives and vitamin regimens and fascinations with quick weight loss diets to some extent have blurred the understanding of what is important in good nutrition. Actually, it is not as complicated as you might believe. If you are truly interested in eating for good health, forget the latest fads and focus on the three areas which are important and over which you *should* exert control.

(1) *Variety*. It should come as no surprise that there is no one perfect food. The human body needs a variety of nutrients—proteins, carbohydrates, vitamins, minerals, fats and water—to function properly. Altogether there are some fifty known nutrients and no single food contains all of them. You get these by eating a balanced diet, choosing from the "basic four" food groups: *dairy products* (a glass of milk—preferably skim or low fat, some cheese, yogurt or ice cream—anything made of milk will do the job); the *meat* and other high-protein group (two servings daily, choosing from meat, fish or poultry); *cereals*—any foods made out of wheat, corn, rice or oats such as breads, breakfast cereals, noodles, spaghetti and, yes, even cake. *Vegetables and fruit*—any kinds but in variety (four servings daily will supply you with vitamins, minerals and sufficient roughage). Be sure to include in your variety of vegetables some dark green or yellow vegetables for carotene from which the body makes vitamin A, and some citrus fruits or tomatoes for vitamin C.

(2) *Calories and salt*. Instead of worrying about additives, pesticides and "overprocessing" of food, you should actually be concerned about America's number one nutritional problem, overeating. Obviously overindulgence in high calorie "junk food" (actually a food does not become a "junk food" unless it is overused and then any food can become a "junk food" because its overuse crowds out of the diet the variety of other foods that are necessary for good nutrition. Eat moderately and remember that the best exercise of all is pushing one's self away from the table.

Go easy on the salt shakers. It is an accepted medical fact that too much salt can promote heart trouble, hypertension and certain types of kidney diseases. Adding salt before you taste your food is not only an insult to the cook but a poor health habit. All food naturally contains some salt so if you must add salt, keep it to a minimum.

(3) *Fats*. In studying the consumption of fats, researchers have distin-

guished between three different types of fats and have shown a relationship between cholesterol and the intake of these fats.

Cholesterol is an organic waxy compound which is found only in foods of animal origin, but it is also made naturally by several body tissues, particularly the liver. Egg yolks are a highly concentrated form of cholesterol but there is none in egg whites. Meats, whole milk, butter, most cheese also contain cholesterol but much less than egg yolk; however, these foods contain *saturated* fats out of which the body makes cholesterol.

Two vegetable oils (coconut and palm) also have generous amounts of saturated fats and, hence, have the tendency to raise blood cholesterol even though they contain no cholesterol. *Polyunsaturated* fats (those of vegetable origin such as soybean, corn, cottonseed, sunflower seed and safflower oils) tend to lower blood cholesterol when they replace some of the saturated fats. *Monounsaturated* fats (like olive oil) tend to lower blood cholesterol when they replace saturated fats, but less so than the polyunsaturated fats.

An excessive amount of cholesterol is linked with atherosclerosis, a disease in which the arteries become narrow and obstructed. Atherosclerosis paves the way for the possibility of a heart attack or cerebral hemorrhage (stroke). It has long been known that cholesterol is one of the ingredients in the mushy deposits, or plaques, that block arteries. Evidence is accumulating to indicate that too much saturated fat and cholesterol also play an important role in your risk of developing certain types of cancer—of the ovary, colon, breast, uterus, and prostate—possibly by overstimulating the endocrine glands and by the development in the intestine of by-products of cholesterol that may have cancer-causing properties.

So what can you do? The best advice is to get your weight where it should be and keep it there, emphasize low saturated fat and low cholesterol main courses such as fish, poultry and veal instead of steak and roast beef. Use a polyunsaturated margarine instead of butter and eat fewer egg yolks, preferably no more than two "visible" eggs per week. The "visible" eggs are the ones you see (or they see you). Those used in cooking, that are not visible, we generally ignore because they don't amount to much in the total diet.

To summarize, let the kooks follow the kooky diets but not you. There are three basic rules for good nutrition.

(1) Watch those calories;

(2) Eat a variety of foods; and

(3) Cut down on all foods rich in saturated fat, cholesterol and salt. By following these simple rules you can eat well—and safely.

CREDIT: *Frederick J. Stare, M.D., and Elizabeth M. Whelan, Sc.D., Harvard University Department of Nutrition.*

Obesity

Humorist Gene Kerr once said, "You know you should do something about your excess pounds when you leave your seat on the subway or bus and two people rush to replace you."

It's been estimated that approximately 30 percent of the United States population is at least 10 percent overweight, and this includes school children. If you will stand on any street corner for ten minutes and look at the men and women as they pass, you will not doubt these figures for one moment.

Some people carry their excess baggage better than others. They dress to camouflage the bulges and are clever about selecting styles that accentuate the positive. Clothing may not completely eliminate the negative but it can cover a multitude of sins.

Obesity is often prevalent among middle-aged women of low socio-economic status. The level of fatness in adult females decreases as education and income rise.

Black women tend to be more overweight than white women, but black men are leaner than white men.

People of English, Scotch and Irish descent are the least likely to be overweight.

Among the members of various religious denominations, Episcopalians are the thinnest of all Protestants, Baptists the heaviest. Roman Catholics are more overweight in general than Protestants. Jews are usually more overweight than both Catholics and Protestants. This data (which has been disputed) applies only to white Americans, according to Dr. Albert Stunkard of the University of Pennsylvania.

So—how can you tell if you are really overweight? Obtain a Life Insurance weight chart. Remember that these charts give generous proportions and report the average, not the ideal. If you are 10 to 15 percent over the weight listed for your age, height and sex, then you are overweight. If you are 20 percent or more above the weight listed on the chart, you are obese.

A candid and critical look in the mirror will give you a pretty solid clue as to whether or not you need to do something about your weight. Your personal observation and the comparison between your weight at age twenty-five (that's when most people reach their ideal weight) and what you weigh *now* will provide the ultimate answer to your question.

WHAT CAUSES OBESITY?

A favorite defense of fat people is, "I have a glandular problem." Approximately two out of a hundred may, indeed, have a glandular problem, but the other ninety-eight are fat because they eat more than they need. The undeniable equation is this: When you take in more calories than you expend, fat deposits develop.

Perhaps you are thinking, "My body is different." It's true, some individuals are extremely energetic—they move quickly and prefer to run upstairs rather than take an elevator. These people, without realizing it, are burning up calories. They have what is known as an accelerated metabolism. If you are overweight, it is because you are eating more than your body needs or can handle. Unfortunately (and depressingly!) there is simply no way around that fact of life.

The main cause of obesity is eating too much. A related cause is lack of exercise. Obesity is a disease of a sedentary society. As former Surgeon General Jesse Steinfeld summarized it, "The only exercise some people get is jumping to conclusions, sidestepping responsibilities and pushing their luck."

Lack of exercise not only promotes excess weight (sitting at a desk or in front of the TV burns up very few calories) but it has been shown that lack of exercise can increase your appetite!

This may seem contradictory because you know that after a full day of hiking, swimming or playing tennis, you are absolutely ravenous. But it works the same way at the opposite end of the exercise spectrum. People who raise animals for slaughter have long known that penning up animals will fatten them up. Moderate exercise not only helps you use up calories but it also tames your appetite.

The primary causes of obesity are physiological, the result of internal imbalance of calories. But many of the *underlying* reasons are more "social-psychological." Generally, we have a built-in mechanism to avoid overeating —specifically, our appetite control system, commonly known as the "appestat." Our appetites prevent us from gaining weight by only "activating" when our bodies need food. But modern Man and Woman have found ways to circumvent the natural appestat control mechanism. For example, parents who continually pressure their children from the earliest age to "eat everything on your plate" may be interfering with the natural control system and laying the groundwork for obesity. For example:

Mothers sometimes say, "It's a sin to waste food. Think of all the little children starving in India." My advice to those mothers is simply this: Give the children smaller portions and no food will be wasted.

My heart goes out to men and woman trapped by social customs into eating more than they should because they must do business at luncheons and dinners. The All-American Business Lunch, complete with two martinis, a steak, potato and dessert, is murderous. Dinners are worse, since often there are appetizers and a cocktail or two before one sits down to order another cocktail before dinner.

The best way to beat this system is to establish the habit of ordering a salad for lunch and no booze. (You'll find your thinking will be a lot clearer without that martini and you will be able to do a day's work when you get back to the office.)

For dinner, when you must dine out, don't take that first hors d'oeuvre and you won't have to worry about the fifth or sixth.

And now we come to those unfortunate folks who reward or comfort themselves with food. They are not eating because their appestat tells them they are hungry. They are eating for comfort or pleasure.

WELL, WHAT'S WRONG WITH BEING FAT?

A few centuries ago being plump was considered downright sexy. The paintings of Raphael, Leonardo da Vinci, Michelangelo, Rubens and others depicted curvaceous, big-bosomed women with heavy thighs. Having a bit of extra weight was also considered a sign of social status and affluence, an indication that you were in good health, free from the ravages of diseases such as tuberculosis.

But today being overweight is both medically and socially undesirable. In terms of immediate effects, overweight people are generally more tired, short of breath, physically and mentally lethargic and likely to suffer from aching joints and poor digestion. Moreover, fat people tend to suffer from high blood pressure, heart disease, diabetes, kidney disorders, cirrhosis of the liver, pneumonia, inflammation of the gallbladder, arthritis, hernias, varicose veins and sterility. They also have more accidents and die more frequently during or after operations.

Some illness and death is explained by the sheer burden of carrying around extra weight. People who consume large quantities of alcohol are prone to being both overweight and victims of cirrhosis. Still other side effects of obesity, for instance, infertility and pregnancy problems, relate to the chemical impact of excess fat and the poor distribution of hormones over the great amount of body tissue.

Caesar may have wanted fat men around him, but most people—including employers and friends—don't. The 1947 song "Too Fat Polka" ("I don't want her, you can have her, she's too fat for me") carried a valid social message. Fat people have trouble being accepted. Prospective employers may relate their fatness to laziness or assume that their obesity is a sign of physical or psychological conditions which may interfere with work.

Being overweight is a problem that can have an undesirable effect at many stages of life. Beyond that, fat people often report that they are generally unhappy with their self-image, frustrated because they don't look well in clothes, and depressed about their inability to make friends. Happily, formerly fat people report increased self-confidence and pride in their appearance, pleasure at their new ability to move around more freely and a general sense of well-being that comes from meeting a challenge and emerging victorious.

OBESITY—WHAT CAN YOU DO ABOUT IT?

If you are overweight, you should have a thorough checkup by a competent physician to rule out any physical or metabolic problem. If your doctor pronounces you in good health, make up your mind that you are going to eat sensibly, eat less and exercise.

If you are not overweight but are living with someone who is (a spouse, a child, a friend) you can be helpful. First and most important, *don't nag the overweight person* to lose weight. You can suggest some meal-planning techniques, but harping on the subject often results in getting the fat one to eat more to assert his (or her) independence or seek comfort for being "scolded."

Friends who encourage you to eat fattening foods do not have your best interest at heart. You'll notice that most of them are on the chunky side. If you have this problem—hostesses, for example, who try to make you feel guilty for not eating that great food they worked so hard to prepare—simply say, "Sorry, I'm allergic to that." If they continue to press you might say, "If I eat it I will break out in fat."

Planning a diet and a new lifestyle is a highly individual matter. But here are some general tips:

First, some "don'ts":

—Don't be fooled by the fad diets. (There's a new one every week.) There are no short cuts. Most people who lose weight on fad diets regain the weight when they get off the diet and they are right back where they started—depressed, disgusted and discouraged.

You need a well-balanced diet, one which includes protein, vitamins, minerals *and* carbohydrates. Anyone who promises that you can shed excess pounds by eating a grapefruit, that marvelous yellow sparkplug, before each meal is giving you false information. If someone suggests starvation as the "last chance," inform them that your goal is to learn to live *with* food, not without it.

—Don't overdo diuretics—pills that take water out of the body. This is a highly deceptive solution to your weight problem. Your challenge is to remove fat, not water.

—Don't delude yourself by thinking that your problem is "not your fault." Stop saying things like "I'm big-boned" or "Fat runs in our family." Or "It's my thyroid or hormones." Bone density can account for about five extra pounds, but no more. Being overweight, while it can "run in families," is more the result of poor eating habits, which *also* run in families. Hormonal problems can cause weight gain, but this is another type of ailment, one which has manifestations in other ways than in excessive weight.

—Don't go out and buy reducing machines and diet apparatus. You don't need equipment or gadgets. All you need to diet successfully is will power, determination, awareness of basic facts of nutrition, and a mirror and a scale.

Second, some "do's":

—Adopt a definite diet plan prescribed by a physician and stick to it. Eat a variety of foods. Be sure your meals are balanced and, most important, eat moderately. If your daily intake includes food from the basic four categories (meats and fish, milk and dairy products, fruits and vegetables, cereals and breads), you will meet your nutritional needs. Get a book that lists caloric contents of foods and the desirable number of calories for your ideal weight and begin counting.

—Identify your "dietary enemies." Is it alcohol (which contains about 100 calories per shot of 80 proof liquor)? (Drinks mixed at home or by friends are usually doubles.) Is it mayonnaise and salad dressings? Desserts? You can't conquer your enemy until you know what it is.

—Serve yourself (or ask to be served) smaller portions. Sometimes you don't have to give up your favorite foods—just eat less of them.

—Set aside fifteen minutes to half an hour each day for moderate exercise. Some people find exercise extremely boring. A good solution is to exercise with music or in front of the TV and watch something that holds your interest. For those who are less disciplined, it may be advantageous to join an exercise class. Take up bike riding, jogging, swimming, tennis or just walking instead of hopping on the bus or getting into your car. Remember, exercise will help you use up some of the calories you consume and it will also depress your appetite. Another useful exercise to keep in mind is shaking your head vigorously from side to side when seconds are offered—and pushing yourself away from the table.

If none of the above works for you, consider joining a self-help group. One group may be terrific for your friend, but it won't work for you. It might be that Weight Watchers isn't your cup of tea, so perhaps you should go to Overeaters Anonymous, TOPS or Diet Workshop. The emotional support by these groups has done the trick for thousands of former fatties, both men and women, who swear by them.

—*Here are some tips to help stick to your diet when eating out:*

Don't look at a menu before ordering. Know what you are going to order in advance.

When eating with a group, be the first one to order, so you won't be tempted to order the same fattening pasta or sauce-drenched fish the person ahead of you just ordered. Don't become part of the "me too" syndrome.

Order clear soups such as consomme or broth instead of fattening cream soups.

Give the waiter specific instructions when ordering. For instance, request that the skin be removed from chicken breasts before having them broiled dry with lemon juice and a little seasoning such as oregano.

Order steak, lean meat, chicken or fish broiled dry, without butter, margarine or oil. Avoid breaded or fried meats or fish.

Request that sauces be left off meat and fish dishes.

Avoid anything stuffed—most stuffings are fried with butter.

Order a green vegetable without butter.

If you must eat a potato, order it baked without butter or sour cream.

Say, "No, thank you," when the hot rolls and butter are brought to the table.

Instead of fattening dressings, order a small glass of plain tomato juice and pour it over the tossed salad, or bring along your own low-calorie dressing.

Drink coffee or tea without sugar or cream.

After eating, ask the waiter to clear the table, so you won't be tempted to nibble on leftovers.

Request small portions of everything.

Recognize that a restaurant is a fat trap like the candy counter at a movie theater. If you are going to binge (and everyone does at some time or another), admit it and eliminate guilt feelings. Guilt feelings will make you go out and have a hot fudge sundae because you blew it. What keeps you fat is making resolutions you can't fulfill—so you just give up.

Losing weight can be extremely difficult but it doesn't need to be depressing and frustrating. It has taken you months or years to put on those extra pounds, so don't expect it to come off in a week or two. If you approach weight control scientifically and patiently (hopefully preventing the problem before it occurs), and if you make a lifelong philosophy of eating and drinking moderately, you will succeed. And if at first you don't recede, diet, diet again.

CREDIT: *Dr. Elizabeth M. Whelan, Research Association (Nutrition Education), Harvard School of Public Health and Executive Director, American Council on Science and Health. Additional material by Judy Moore, Feature Writer, the Chicago Sun-Times.*

Female Orgasm*

The female orgasm has possibly been the subject of more debate and literature than any other area of human sexuality. But fortunately, since the work of Masters and Johnson in the 1960s, many of the myths and mysteries surrounding it have gone. It is now known that, although the experience and in-

* From *Woman's Body: An Owner's Manual* by the Diagram Group © 1977 The Diagram Group, published by Paddington Press.

tensity of orgasm may vary considerably, the actual physical process of orgasm is always the same. The distinction between "vaginal" and "clitoral" orgasm is a myth.

REACHING ORGASM

Women vary greatly in what they respond to sexually, but the mons pubis, labia minora, clitoris and vaginal entrance are almost always important. The clitoris is the most sexually responsive part of a woman's body, and in most cases fairly continuous clitoral stimulation is needed for orgasm. However, since the tip of the clitoris is extremely sensitive, constant direct touch can become painful. So, for the majority of women, manipulation of the whole genital area is more pleasurable. During intercourse, movement of the penis in and out of the vagina provides continual clitoral stimulation by moving the labia minora backward and forward over the clitoral tip. The anus is another potentially erotic area, but it is not as easily penetrated as the vagina. For anal intercourse, lubrication—K-Y jelly, for example—is generally needed.

THE FEELING OF ORGASM

The time needed to reach orgasm varies from woman to woman and from occasion to occasion. Just before orgasm there is a feeling of tension lasting possibly 2 to 4 seconds when all the small muscles of the pelvis surrounding the vagina and uterus contract. This is followed by the orgasm itself, which may last 10 to 15 seconds. It is felt as a series of rhythmic muscular contractions, occurring every 0.8 seconds, firstly around the outer third of the vagina and spreading upward to the uterus. Both uterus and rectum also contract. In a mild orgasm there may be 3 to 5 contractions; in an intense one, 8 to 12. Also during orgasm the muscles of the abdomen, buttocks, arms, face, legs and neck may contract. Breathing is more rapid and blood pressure climbs. All these return to normal and orgasm is usually followed by feelings of relaxation and peace.

MULTIPLE ORGASM

Women, unlike men, are capable of multiple orgasm. That is, immediately or shortly after a first orgasm, if a woman maintains her sexual excitement at the plateau level, she can move directly into a second orgasm. Some women can experience 3 or 4 orgasms within a few minutes, and up to 12 in one hour have been recorded.

EXPERIENCE OF ORGASM

Virtually all woman are physically able to attain orgasm. But a recent survey, the Hite Report, suggests that as few as 30 percent regularly achieve orgasm through intercourse. Kinsey's data indicates that such orgasm does gradually become more frequent in long-term relationships but that even after twenty years of a relationship 11 percent of women never reach orgasm.

Nevertheless, it seems that the vast majority of women prefer intercourse to any other sexual activity because of the closeness and affection associated with it. Yet, despite the "sexual revolution" of the 1960s, women still seem to feel guilt about their own sexuality and are reluctant either to initiate sexual activity or to communicate their sexual needs to their partners.

BEDROOM ACTRESS SATISFIED WITH APPLAUSE

DEAR ANN LANDERS: Hurrah for the gal who signed herself "Honest." I'll bet the true number of bedroom Sarah Bernhardts in this world would be a shock—even to you. Yes, I am one of the vast army of actresses.

Why do we do it? Because we love our men and don't want them to feel inadequate. We accept the fact that we have been biologically short-changed by Mother Nature and that it isn't anybody's fault. No woman ever enjoys sex as much as a man does, and she never will. So we just go on doing our little act. Knowing that our men are satisfied is enough for us. Do you have the guts to print this? ENJOYING NOTHING BUT THE APPLAUSE IN KANSAS CITY

DEAR K.C.: If the applause is all you're enjoying, you are gypping yourself plenty. Your basic theory is incorrect, and I hope you will have the guts to discuss your problem with a therapist so you can begin to experience what is rightfully yours.

Male Orgasm

Orgasm in males is the experience of maximum pleasure in the genital area at the point of ejaculation (discharge of semen).

The normal male orgasm is a total experience involving both the body and the mind. To describe it adequately we must take up each aspect separately. First, the physical or body aspect. Orgasm in the male is a climax of a sequence that begins with erection. The penis has numerous nerve endings, which, when stimulated, cause the penis to fill with blood and become erect. (Stimulation of the penis is not the only way erection is achieved. Memories, fantasies, and seeing pictures of women and their bodies, reading erotic or pornographic literature also can produce an erection.)

Erections occur even in infant boys, as every mother has observed. Erections may also occur when the bladder is full. The penis frequently becomes erect during the night without direct stimulation.

Erections are most frequent during adolescence, when the capacity for sexual arousal is greatest, but they are experienced throughout the life of a man, although the frequency lessens with age.

If the exciting stimulation continues, there are changes in other parts of the body. There is more blood flow into the scrotum, prostate gland, and the testicles. The skin temperature rises. Blood pressure goes up, and the heart beats faster. There is also a reflex tendency to engage in regular pelvic to-and-fro movements, forward and back.

As the tension increases to the peak of pleasure, the orgasm itself (ejaculation of semen) occurs in a sequence of spasms involving the genital area and the pelvis especially, but may include the rest of the body, so that the trunk, legs and jaw may also be in spasm or at last be powerfully taut.

Pelvic to-and-fro movement may also be seen in infants. Sometimes boys before puberty experience erection and ejaculatory spasms, but only after complete sexual maturity at puberty is semen ejaculated at the point of orgasm.

At the end of the ejaculation, which occurs in several spurts along with the spasms, there is a total relaxation of the body, including the penis, which quickly loses its erection. The individual usually feels relaxed and may want to sleep.

Some young men sustain a partial erection and after 10 to 20 minutes begin the sequence which leads to another orgasm.

The emotional experience which accompanies the physical changes begins with the males being excited by sexual pleasure. The pleasure is aroused by direct touching of his penis or other sensitive parts of the body. The keenest pleasure is felt in the penis itself. But touching of the hair, neck, ear lobes, or the skin of almost any part of the body (by the "right" person) is exciting.

During the build-up phase, before the moment of orgasm, men may have fantasies of various kinds which are exciting. It does not matter what these fantasies (mental images) are as long as they are effective in maintaining the erection and achieving the orgasm. Sexual partners should not require that the fantasies be about themselves. Nor should the man feel it abnormal to fantasize about whatever arouses him.

Young males are highly excitable and are less able to keep from having the orgasm than older men, who have learned to sustain their erections and prolong the pleasurable period before orgasm and ejaculation.

The orgasm as the maximum of physical pleasure provides a strong motivation for engaging in sexual intercourse so that man can reproduce. The ejaculation of semen (which contains the sperm) into the vagina makes fertilization a likelihood, especially during the time of the menstrual cycle when the female has released the ovum (egg) into her uterus. But men do not have to be conscious of nature's purpose to want to have intercourse. They *are* conscious of their desire to experience the orgasm. Adolescent boys, not ready for the complexities of relationships with females, and men without women for various reasons may achieve orgasm through masturbation. Spontaneous orgasms may also occur at night (wet dreams). Usually, if orgasm is not reached by intercourse or masturbation, such spontaneous ejaculations at night are more frequent.

Masturbation is therefore an available means for achieving orgasm and releasing the tension that builds up from being aroused sexually. Tensions build up psychologically for many other reasons which are not sexual, and the pleasure of orgasm may be used to relieve these tensions, too.

In contrast to the belief of a century ago, we now know that masturbation to orgasm is beneficial psychologically. Masturbation prepares the young man for intercourse. Being able to gain pleasure by one's self prepares him to gain it with another. Of course, excessive masturbation (more than once or twice in a twenty-four hour period) may be a sign that the tensions which exist are not sexual and indicate emotional and psychological problems that require evaluation and perhaps treatment.

While orgasm is not essential for life itself, the desire to have it is often so strong that not achieving it, especially in youth and adulthood, may be extremely frustrating and depressing.

There may be physical diseases which interfere with having orgasm, and if failure to achieve it persists, a physical examination is called for.

But usually the failure to achieve orgasm is due to psychological causes.

Occasional failures should be expected by males and their partners and should not be considered a sign that something is seriously wrong in either partner or in the relationship. Young couples are usually frustrated and upset by failure. Older couples, while they may be frustrated, learn to accept these episodes more philosophically.

Continued inability to achieve orgasm either because of loss of erection or frequent prolonged erections without ejaculation should be considered a reason for investigation and possible treatment. Premature ejaculation (too early) is usually not accompanied by a full orgasm, and of course interferes with the achievement of satisfaction by the sexual partner. Again, occasional premature ejaculations are not to be considered a sign of physical or psychological disease.

One of the greatest advantages of a continued relationship with one sexual partner, as in marriage, is the partners learn about one another's special ways to reach orgasm. Persons who love each other and are comfortable and relaxed can be fully open and tell one another what works best in achieving orgasm. They can be considerate of each other's preferences, and accept each other's occasional failings.

It is *not* necessary for the male or the female to have orgasm at exactly the same moment. It is also not necessary for physical and psychological health that the male have an orgasm every time he has sexual intercourse. If a male is aroused nearly to the point of orgasm but does not reach climax, he may feel an aching sensation in the testicles which subsides within an hour or so. There is no danger to his health from such frustrating, aching experiences, though they cause him to wish for relief.

Consciously or unconsciously, reaching orgasm is felt as proof of maleness and therefore it is a source of masculine pride and self-esteem. Some males feel it necessary to make their sexual partners achieve orgasm before they do as proof of their ability to excite and satisfy a woman.

Males are often extremely sensitive about their sexual capacity. If their sexual partners make insulting or deprecating comments about it, they are deeply hurt and often angered. When males do poorly at school, or in their jobs or are frequent failures or losers in competitive sports, wherever their pride or self-esteem is tested, they may turn to orgasm to relieve their tensions. The orgasm is felt to be necessary. Under these circumstances, however, it is difficult to relax and the male is more apt to experience failure.

In some men, orgasm is necessary to keep them feeling alive and whole and prevents depression and mental disorganization. Needless to say, these men need psychological or psychiatric help. They act as if they are desperately in need of sexual satisfaction and they make their partners unhappy through their excessive demands for sex.

The male orgasm, as described so far, is the usual form in which orgasm takes place. However, there are many different ways that males use to achieve orgasm. These depend on the individual man and cannot be covered here.

Some men are "loners" who prefer to achieve orgasm by themselves, without partners. Others are "gay" and prefer partners who are male.

A man who cannot achieve orgasm in sexual intercourse should realize that he is not functioning according to nature's plan and should seek professional help so he can enjoy the full pleasures of his maleness. How and where does one obtain this help? First, as mentioned earlier, he should get a thorough checkup to make certain there is no organic problem. Then he should see a psychiatrist, psychoanalyst or psychologist for an evaluation and treatment. Mental health clinics can provide counseling for a modest fee— sometimes no fee, in special circumstances. These clinics can be found by contacting the state or county mental health societies.

One should beware of quack counselors who promise quick cures for sexual problems. In order to ascertain the reliability of a therapist, one should consult his own physician or the psychiatric department of a hospital. One may also call the Institute for Psychoanalysis if there is one in his city. They offer splendid referral service.

Social workers and sex therapists are often extremely useful in helping with these problems, but they must be trained in the treatment of emotional problems which include sexual dysfunctions. In order to check out any individual chosen to help with a sexual problem, one may contact the American Psychiatric Association, the National Association of Social Workers, the American Psychological Association, the American Medical Association, or the American Psychoanalytical Association. Their addresses may be obtained by calling the public library.

In rare cases, a patient seeking help for a sexual problem may encounter a psychiatrist, psychologist or therapist who suggests that the patient engage in sexual intercourse with him or her. Under no conditions should this be permitted. Such conduct is completely unethical and attempts at such bizarre behavior should be reported to the American Psychiatric Association, the American Psychological Association and the American Medical Association.

CREDIT: *Dr. Morris A. Sklansky, Training Analyst, Chicago Institute for Psychoanalysis.*

Pain

The New English Dictionary defines pain as "the sensation one feels when hurt in body or mind." However, most people use pain to describe a distressing discomfort occuring in the body. Historians tell us that pain has afflicted mankind since the beginning of time. Through the ages there has been great disagreement on not only the cause of pain but also the proper treatment of it. The Greek philosopher Aristotle, like Plato before him, spoke of pain as the opposite to pleasure. This was the accepted explanation of many centuries.

Interestingly, the word "pain" comes from the Latin word "poena," meaning punishment. It wasn't until 1840 that it was learned that specific nerve fibers carry pain messages. More recently pain was divided into two kinds, organic and psychogenic. The former was believed to be caused by a physical disorder of the body and the latter by a mental illness. Although this classification helped our understanding of pain by giving equal recognition to psychological as well as physical causes for the body distress, it also contributed to a great deal of misunderstanding.

Not infrequently when a doctor could not find a physical cause for a person's complaint of pain, he would assume that the cause was psychological and label the condition "psychosomatic." This diagnosis of pain when no organic disease could be found not only lacks scientific foundation, but also was frequently incorrect. The diagnosis of psychosomatic pain must be based on positive findings of emotional problems. Some doctors, and even lay people, through their own frustration in attempting to deal with a patient with a pain problem, would not only label it psychogenic, but would go further and sometimes in a hostile way tell the patient that his pain was "all in his head." The patient, feeling rejected by these remarks, would go from doctor to doctor looking for someone who understood his problem. Unfortunately, the patient, instead of finding an understanding, knowledgeable doctor, would often find someone who was willing to administer potentially destructive treatment (sometimes an operation) under the guise of "understanding" him.

This confusion within the medical society and the public in general led to an increase in the most common illness in our society, iatrogenic disease. This disease, or illness, develops in the patient as a result of treatment by a doctor. It may be obvious as surgical complications or side effects of medication. More frequently, however, it is manifested as fears, anxiety and depression instilled in the patient by a doctor who not only does not understand pain, but also does not understand the patient who is experiencing the pain. Fortunately misunderstandings about pain, in most cases, are not a part of modern day medicine. We now recognize that all pain is real.

The causes of the pain are varied and complex and may include complicated physical dysfunctions as well as multiple emotional reactions. To further complicate the problem, each person's reaction to pain is uniquely different. These reactions are as varied as personalities and are determined by all of the individual's past experiences with pain. It is not unlike a computer with a memory bank of painful experiences telling us how to react, what to expect from others, and even how to feel in response to the current painful condition. It is this complex pattern that makes it so difficult for one human being to understand another human being's pain. It is the most difficult symptom to evaluate because the doctor must depend solely on the report of the patient and cannot measure pain by laboratory tests or X rays. Our present understanding of the equal importance of the organic condition, the memory bank of painful experiences, and the current stress associated with the pain have led to the present classification of pain and a more realistic treatment approach to the patient experiencing pain.

There are two types of pain: acute or simple pain and chronic, complicated pain. Acute, simple pain is generally of short duration. There is very little stress associated with the cause and treatment of it. As a result, the individual's personal reaction is minimal and, for all practical purposes, the pain memory bank is not called upon. Therefore, the patient does not overreact to pain. Basically the pain is not part of a threatening situation. Therefore, there is minimal fear, anxiety, tension, worry, anger, frustration, depression or withdrawal. The doctor generally has little trouble diagnosing the cause of the pain, and even less difficulty treating it.

In many instances the body repairs itself without the need of medical intervention. Even when treatment is necessary, the response is excellent. In this type of pain there is very little if any risk in using the usual, customary treatment approaches to pain such as pain medications, surgery, immobilization of the part by splints, casts or bed rest, or other medical therapies. The reason these treatment approaches are almost always effective and seldom carry undue risk is because the patient's primary interest is relief of pain, recovery from illness and resumption of normal functioning as soon as possible. Acute simple pain serves a vital function. It tells us that something has gone wrong in the body or mind. Without it, we could not survive.

Chronic complicated pain generally is longer in duration. It takes over the individual's functioning, both physical and emotional, thus dictating by its agony and misery the way the person lives and relates to others. With this type of pain, an individual frequently becomes a zombie on drugs, a mass of scars from unsuccessful operations, as well as a "pain" to everyone around him.

It has been estimated that there are twenty million Americans living in chronic pain. Lost wages, medical expenses and workmen's compensation payments from this condition total somewhere between $35 billion and $50 billion a year. Back pain, the most common chronic pain condition, accounted for eighteen million physician office visits last year, while doctors spend twelve million hours of their time with patients having chronic headache. This adds up to a cost in suffering, dollars and physician time that we as individuals and as a nation cannot afford.

One of the main reasons chronic pain has caused so much suffering and expense is that we have failed to recognize its existence. Based on the assumption that all pain responded to the same approach given acute pain, chronic pain sufferers not only received improper treatment, but the treatment, in many instances, further complicated the condition and made it worse.

Pain always begins as a warning signal that something has gone wrong in the body or mind. If the signal is not heeded or is misperceived, in a very short time complications begin to develop. These complications lower the individual's tolerance to pain, thus increasing its intensity. As the complications multiply and expand, the initial pain, which was only a warning signal, becomes more intense and severe, affecting not only the person, but also those around him.

The pain is often described in agonizing terms and becomes the main topic of conversation. This fixation is one of the early complications and one of the most disabling. The sufferer cannot concentrate on his work or activities and therefore withdraws from his social contacts. The pain has now become a "disease" and, as it becomes more severe, the individual frequently finds it necessary to decrease his activities. Complications that increase the severity of the pain are physiological, psychological, interpersonal, social and vocational. The physiological complications are frequently secondary to medical treatment. They consist of drug dependence and addiction, muscle weakness through prescribed rest, postoperative complications and dependence upon braces, crutches, etc. The psychological complications consist of anxiety, tension, fear, worry, anger, frustration, depression, low self-worth and withdrawal.

The personal complications are further compounded by the reaction of others. Initially the patient receives understanding and sympathy. This, in a sense, "rewards" the patient for being ill. He is catered to by his family and compensated for by his employer. There may even be financial rewards related to pain caused by certain accidents. These secondary gains, as they are termed in the medical profession, may prolong the pain process without the patient's conscious knowledge. At this stage the patient has fallen into the vicious cycle of chronic pain. All of the above complications—physical, psychological, and interpersonal—lead to social withdrawal and a compounding of the pain syndrome.

Since all the focus up to this point has been on the person in pain, the significant other people in his life are often overlooked. These family members and friends are frequently hurting as much as the patient because of their own experiences in relationship to him. The other person has not only had a major upheaval in his life because of what has happened to the person with pain, but he has also had to suppress feelings of anger and guilt which could not be expressed openly to the patient. People are afraid to tell the person with pain how angry they are with him because of the unwritten law that you cannot "hit" a person who is already down. Even having these feelings produces guilt in the other person.

At this stage of the chronic pain syndrome, significant other people often reject the person with chronic pain, no matter how much they love him, in a desperate attempt to save themselves from further distress. Final and ultimate rejection felt by the person with chronic pain is the realization that society no longer wants or needs him as a worker no matter how effective he was at his job prior to the pain process. Compensation payments in dollars, although contributing to secondary gain, never compensates for the loss of self-worth experienced by the individual who is told he is no longer capable of making a contribution to society. Obviously, the best treatment of this chronic complicated pain syndrome is to prevent its occurrence. This can only be done if all of those involved with the person at the onset of pain, including the person himself, recognize that the potential for chronic pain exists in every pain process.

The physician's role in prevention is to treat the whole person and not just the painful part. With modern medical technology, there has been a tendency for doctors to specialize to the point where they fail to recognize that a human being is attached to part of the body that is in pain. Doctors should never treat a stranger. By spending time with the patient and his family, familiarizing himself with the patient's needs, his reaction to stress, his old pain patterns, and the family's reaction to the patient in his painful condition, the physician can prevent chronic pain.

Family members can play their part in avoiding chronic pain by dealing openly and honestly with the patient. He needs continued involvement in the family unit and in the role with which he is familiar to maintain his self-worth. The employer can play his role in preventing disability by providing a flexible work situation. This will allow the employee to maintain a positive attitude about his job. His return to work as a productive individual will help him maintain self-worth and avoid chronic pain. Most of all, the patient can avoid the development of chronic, complicated pain by keeping open communication with his family, friends, physician and employer. It is important for him to trust a competent physician and not doctor-shop when his physician tells him what he does not want to hear. He must also recognize that being cared for by others eventually leads to loss of independence and lowered self-worth. By resisting the temptation to go for the easy dollar through workmen's compensation, disability insurance or a court suit, dignity is maintained and chronic pain is avoided.

If, for whatever reason, prevention fails, and an individual develops chronic, complicated pain, all is not lost. There are now available, throughout the country, pain clinics that approach the pain problem by treating the whole person. The focus of treatment is to eliminate the complications and promote healthy living, thus decreasing the pain intensity. Therapeutic tools used in these clinics are those which increase relaxation, strengthen muscles, and increase activity, achieve healthy communication, and discontinue the use of addictive or habit-forming drugs. In these programs, healthy behavior is fostered while pain behavior is not rewarded.

The most essential force in these programs that leads to healthy living is a trust relationship built up between the patients and the staff. A strong bond also develops among the patients who are all working toward healthy goals. Family involvement is essential to develop healthy communication. A patient must spend weeks or months in a pain rehabilitation program to escape from the chronic pain syndrome, but this is a brief interlude compared to a lifetime of agony. God gave us pain to protect us from danger. It was never meant to be a disability.

The International Association for the Study of Pain and the American Society of Anesthesiologists are both compiling a catalogue of accredited pain clinics. This has become necessary because scores of pain clinics that offer nothing more than the old-fashioned, outdated treatment approach under a new name have sprung up around the country. Some pain control centers have gone so far as to offer the unwary public pain control methods administered by unskilled personnel without adequate medical supervision. Some of the so-called pain clinics have a medical doctor listed as director when he does no more than collect a fee for the use of his name.

Until an up-to-date list of reliable pain clinics is available, the unwary public is vulnerable to the quackery that will always be present when money can be made by dishonest people who exploit the suffering of others. A reliable pain clinic that approaches chronic pain by treating the whole person can generally be found by contacting the County or State Medical Society or the American Medical Association. An individual's family physician has frequently had other patients successfully treated in a comprehensive pain clinic and can also be of assistance. Listed below are accredited pain clinics that recognize the need to treat the whole person. If one of these clinics is not in your area, write to the nearest one and they can probably refer you to a similar clinic near you.

It is very important to adequately evaluate a pain clinic's treatment program before entering treatment. Investigate and ask questions. Persons suffering from chronic pain can ill afford another frustrating failure, with the added risk of more complications to intensify the pain even further.

COMPREHENSIVE PAIN CLINICS

Arizona
The Center
Mesa Lutheran Hospital
501 West Tenth Place
Mesa, Arizona 85201
Telephone: (602)834-1211, Ext. 2175
Chief of Center: Neal Olshan

California
Pain Center
City of Hope National Medical Center
1500 East Duarte Road
Duarte, California 91010
Telephone: (213)359-8111
Directors: Benjamin L. Crue, M.D.,
and Jack J. Pinsky, M.D.

Pain Treatment Center
Hospital of Scripps Clinic
La Jolla, California 92037
Telephone: (714)459-2390
Directors: Richard A. Sternbach,
Ph.D., and Donald J. Dalessio,
M.D.

UCLA Pain Management Clinic
UCLA School of Medicine
10833 Le Conte Avenue
Los Angeles, California 90024
Telephone: (213)825-0779
Director: Verne L. Brechner

Georgia
Emory University Pain Clinic
Clifton Road
Atlanta, Georgia 30322
Telephone: (404)377-9111, Ext. 375
Director: Steven F. Brenna, M.D.

Illinois
Pain Center
Rush Medical College
Rush Presbyterian St. Luke's Medical
Center
1725 West Harrison Street
Chicago, Illinois 60612
Telephone: (312)942-6631
Director: Max S. Sadove, M.D.

Maryland
Pain Clinic
Johns Hopkins University School of
Medicine
Baltimore, Maryland 21205
Telephone: (301)955-6405
Directors: Donlin M. Long, M.D., and
Richard G. Black, M.D.

Massachusetts
Pain Unit
Massachusetts Rehabilitation Hospital
125 Nashua Street
Boston, Massachusetts 02114

Telephone: (617)523-1818
Director: Gerald M. Aronoff, M.D.

Minnesota
Minneapolis Pain Clinic
4225 Golden Valley Road
Minneapolis, Minnesota 55422
Telephone: (612)588-0661
Director: Loran F. Pilling, M.D.

Pain Rehabilitation Program
Metropolitan Medical Center
900 South Eighth Street
Minneapolis, Minnesota 55404
Telephone: (612)347-4506
Director: Loran F. Pilling, M.D.

Pain Clinic
University Hospital
University of Minnesota
Mayo Building
Minneapolis, Minnesota 55455
Telephone: (612)373-8205
Directors: Donald Erickson, M.D.,
    and Allan Roberts, Ph.D.

Pain Management Center
Mayo Clinic–St. Mary's Hospital of
    Rochester
Rochester, Minnesota 55901
Telephone: (507)282-2511
Director: David W. Swanson, M.D.

Nebraska
The Nebraska Pain Rehabilitation
    Unit
University of Nebraska

College of Medicine
42nd Street and Dewey Avenue
Omaha, Nebraska 68105
Telephone: (402)541-4301
Director: F. Miles Skultety, M.D.

Oregon
Portland Pain Rehabilitation Center
Emanuel Hospital
3001 North Gantenbein Avenue
Portland, Oregon 97227
Telephone: (503)280-4404
Director: Joel L. Seres, M.D.

Virginia
Nerve Block and Pain Studies Clinic
University of Virginia Medical Center
Charlottesville, Virginia 22903
Telephone: (804)924-5581
Director: Harold Carron, M.D.

Washington
Pain Clinic
University of Washington School of
    Medicine
Seattle, Washington 98195
Telephone: (206)543-2672
Director: John J. Bonica

Wisconsin
The Pain and Health Rehabilitation
    Center
615 South Tenth Street
LaCrosse, Wisconsin 54601
Telephone: (608)786-0611
Director: C. Norman Shealy, M.D.

CREDIT: *Loran Pilling, M.D., Minneapolis Clinic of Psychiatry and Neurology, Director of the Minneapolis Pain Clinic and Metropolitan Pain Rehabilitation Center, Minneapolis, Minnesota.*

Back Pain

Although the term "Oh, my aching back" is attributed to the servicemen of World War II, people have been afflicted with low back pain for as long as people have been standing erect. It is, in fact, believed that this is the penalty humans must pay for standing on their two hind feet.

Usually people who have low back pain have more anxiety about it than the condition actually deserves. Because of the myths, legal problems and work problems relating to the back, there is a poor understanding of the medical aspects of back pain. Because the spine performs the principal function of body support, any problems relating to it may result in considerable anxiety. They can usually be controlled, however—especially conditions that deal with posture, exercise, obesity and emotional turmoil in our daily lives.

To best understand spinal pain, it is necessary to know something about anatomy.

The spine is made up of twenty-six bones stacked like blocks (these are called vertebrae) separated by a cushion or shock absorber (intervertebral disc). This forms the support beam for the rest of the erect body, to which is attached muscles, ligaments and ribs. These vertebra are divided into areas of the body, seven are involved in the neck, (cervical spine), twelve in the chest (dorsal or thoracic spine), five in the low back (lumbar spine), and the rest into the sacrum and tail bone (coccyx). Within the canal that runs through all of the bones (spinal canal), there is a tube, in which there is fluid and nerves (spinal cord). Between each set of vertebra, there is a pair of spinal nerves that go out to appropriate parts of the body. These nerves perform the function of supplying the muscles for movement and sensation to the skin as well as other parts of the body. Also connecting between the vertebra are ligaments which help to support the body along with the muscles which cause the body to move. Because the cervical spine and lumbar spine are more mobile, they are subject to the increase of stresses and, consequently, account for most of the pain involved in the spine. When the nerve endings to muscles, skin, bone, joints, etc., are irritated in an abnormal way, sensations are sent back to the nerves, then to the spinal cord, and to the brain itself. The brain gets the message of irritation or injury, and it causes the body to react in such a way as to protect it. All of the parts involved in the spine can likewise be irritated. All can react to these abnormal irritations. Regardless of cause of back strain, most of the discomfort that one experiences comes from stretching the ligaments, irritated joints, spasm of muscles, and pressure on nerves.

Specifically, most of us have these symptoms because of back strain due to poor habits of bending or picking up objects, poor body mechanics in walking and sitting. The same mechanics that cause pain in the above methods can result from injuries of any sort but may be even more pronounced because they are sudden in nature.

Another common cause of back pain is due to excess weight which is often accompanied by poor posture. Poor posture in those who are not overweight can cause chronic back pain if the abdominal muscles are weak. In today's society very few of us concentrate on abdominal muscle strength. We sit at desks, walk and work with our bellies literally hanging out. It is to this area that we must concentrate most of the treatment of back pain.

The term that most of us are accustomed to hear is a "slipped disc." This is not a common cause for back problems, although most back pain is blamed on the "slipped disc." When one actually has a "slipped disc" (herniated nucleus pulposus) it is most likely to be accompanied by radiation of pain down the back of the thigh and leg and often to the foot, itself. It must be remembered that very few cases require surgery.

The wear and tear of normal living may cause osteoarthritis, also known as degenerative arthritis. Most often this cannot be avoided, but this does not necessarily have to cause pain if one continues to observe the good practices of normal living.

Anxiety is a common penalty for being alive. No one escapes it. Any sort of emotional stress can cause pain in various parts of the body, the back being one of the more common areas afflicted. When the doctor can find no organic reason for your back pain, it is wise to look for emotional reasons and work at eliminating the anxiety-producing problem.

When looking for causes of pain in your back, your doctor will also look for the less frequent sources of pain. These include tumors (both benign and malignant), metabolic disorders, infections, congenital diseases and inflammatory arthritis. If the back pain persists, it is wise to periodically recheck for any disease that might have developed since the first check. This is especially true where there has been a change in symptoms as well as a persistence or an increase in severity of symptoms.

Because there are so many types of and causes for back ache, you must be aware of the doctor you turn to for an examination. Most commonly, this can be done through your own doctor, who, if he feels that he cannot find the cause, will probably refer you to a specialist. The specialist may be an orthopedic surgeon, a neurological surgeon, a neurologist or a physiatrist.

It is important in an examination that the doctor obtain a thorough history of the problem, the nature of the pain, the severity of the pain, the length of time it has been present, as well as a history of previous X rays, laboratory work and treatment. After this is done, the physical examination can help the physician determine whether or not the pain involves the nervous system or is a mechanical type of painful problem. This not only includes examination of the muscles and bone structure, but must also involve other sources of back pain. Because the history and physical examination alone cannot give the final diagnosis, it is necessary for the doctor to have various blood and urine tests and X rays in order to make an accurate diagnosis. It might be necessary to proceed to other types of special studies such as electromyography to test whether the muscles of the body are involved, or the insertion of a dye into the spinal column (myelogram) to see if there is pressure on a nerve. Other tests that can be performed are bone scans, computerized axial tomography (CAT scan) and lumbar venograms. More than likely, the end result of the examination will be that of a chronic or acute back strain or irritation or arthritis, or some benign growth. It is to these areas that we direct our recommendations for treatment. The more one understands the *principles* of treatment, the better he will be able to cope with the periodic or constant discomfort.

In acute back pain, relief is usually obtained from bed rest, mild sedatives for a short period of time, a firm mattress and occasionally the injection in the painful areas with local anesthetics and/or steroids. The corset, or back brace, is meant to be used only for the acute phase of the pain. Wearing it beyond that point promotes muscle weakness. The time limit is generally no more than six weeks.

As soon as the acute pain phase is over, exercises can be started and it is to this point that I would like to direct the *principle* of treatment. This may cause a controversy between various doctors and physical therapists. I firmly believe that *sit-ups and toe-touching exercise should not be done*. There are many substitutes for these exercises and one can achieve the same results without taking the risk of rekindling the original irritation. Almost anyone who walks, stands, gets in and out of cars, or exhibits any other normal back support system does not have to develop the "back" muscles but must concentrate on the abdominal muscles. These can be done *isometrically*. That is, by tensing the muscles without going through the great range of motion of the spine.

Included in the exercise program are those activities of daily living that one must learn how to do. For example, when lifting, one must bend from the knees and lift with arms and legs, rather than with the back. In standing or walking, it is good to walk with the pelvis tilted forward. When standing for long periods of time one should elevate one foot by using a foot stool or other device to relieve the stress on the back.

For people who work at desks one must regulate the height of the desk and the height of the chair so that the feet, knees and hips are comfortable when sitting for long periods of time. This also applies to driving. The bucket seat position is often uncomfortable, whereas with the car seat moved forward and the knees bent properly, drivers are more comfortable.

Since one third of our lives is spent in bed, the importance of a firm mattress cannot be overemphasized. Too often, we compensate for mattresses by telling patients to use a bedboard. It is more important to have the firmness next to the patient's body and not eight or ten inches away from it. If additional support is needed, it is probably wise to use a pillow under the knees or to sleep on the side in a knees-up position. Sleeping on one's abdomen often causes additional stress on the back.

Women who wear high heels (often the slender "fashionable" kind) for long periods of time risk falling down stairs. They also throw their bodies out of line in a way that creates back aches.

Exercises for the back should be done with regularity. It is better to do the exercises briefly three times during the course of a day than to do them violently a few times during the week. Exercises should become a permanent feature in one's daily lifestyle.

One of the best back-strengthening exercises is to lie on one's back and place a small sponge in the low back area. When one can press the sponge down to the floor, thereby completely flattening out the "sway-back," the abdominal muscles will tense up noticeably. It is this exercise that will help most in building up strength in this area and eliminate a good many back aches.

CREDIT: *Robert G. Addison, M.D., Rehabilitation Institute of Chicago, Northwestern University Medical School, Director of Low Back and Pain Clinic.*

Paranoia

Literally, this word of Greek derivation means a state of being "beside one's mind." The term denotes a disease also known as true paranoia and is fortunately very rare. It manifests itself in gradual development of an intricate, complex and elaborate, often logical system of thought based on a false premise.

An illustration of paranoia is the story of the farmer who loved his animal stock dearly and one day decided to wean his horse from eating. Each day he diminished the horse's ration of oats while he continued to take excellent care of the animal. He kept congratulating himself on how well the horse looked while it still worked every day. When the animal finally dropped dead, the farmer could not understand what happened. After all, he followed the procedure of weaning to a tee. Why did the horse die?

A good case of paranoia is rare and difficult to find even for teaching purposes. St. Elizabeth's Hospital in Washington, D.C., usually has a few cases at hand because the city, being the seat of the United States Government, attracts paranoiacs who have developed a "better system" of governing and in their zeal to promote it come to the Capitol and eventually land in a psychiatric hospital. They often have intelligent, persuasive and charismatic personalities and easily attract followers, are extremely sensitive, jealous, suspicious and consider themselves endowed with unique and superior abilities. Once in power, they are ruthless. Despite their particular paranoid system, their thinking and personality traits remain intact. The history of mankind is full of despots, tyrants and dictators who were or are paranoids.

A true paranoiac can be recognized by his "cause," very often political or religious. He needs people to follow him and is often seen in public places and squares proselytizing, discussing and arguing his point of view. He is rigid, self-righteous and cannot accept opposing views. He often loses his temper and gets into fights. He participates in plots and counterplots which may involve murder. This is how he comes to the attention of the police and is sent for psychiatric examination. Those whose diagnosis is true paranoia are kept in mental hospitals and those who are dangerous may, after trial, be sent to prisons for the insane where a program of treatment and rehabilitation is designed for them.

Treatment is difficult because as a rule they do not co-operate, simply because they cannot accept the fact that they are sick. Therapy consists of tranquilizing medication, electroshock and individual and group psychotherapy, usually a combination of all these modalities. Occasionally lobotomy (cutting of certain pathways in the brain) is recommended in some violent cases when everything else has failed.

In addition to paranoia as a disease one must be aware of paranoid trends and symptoms in other psychiatric conditions and pathological states and even in non-pathological conditions.

There is a type of schizophrenia (split personality) in which paranoia trends predominate in the form of persecutory or grandiose delusions. Persecutory hallucinations are a frequent companion. Excessive religiosity may be an important factor. These people are usually hostile and aggressive. The paranoid schizophrenic does not show the usual personality disorganization and deterioration present in other forms of schizophrenia. It is as if their paranoia serves as a unifying factor which holds the personality together.

Paranoid states occur frequently in the older age group and are completely reversible with proper help. Irritability, accusatory trends, ideas of persecution, stubbornness, suspiciousness of friends and relatives are the main symptoms. They may appear after the loss of an important person. Once these symptoms show up, professional help is indicated.

Lastly, it is worthwhile mentioning that even in emotionally healthy and functioning individuals an occasional transitory paranoid episode may take place that does not require professional intervention. Any person under stress may develop a nagging suspicion lasting for hours and even days that he has been betrayed by a friend, lover, even spouse because an untoward event took place in his life, such as losing a job or not getting a promotion, etc. Brooding and exaggeration of a "case" against the alleged perpetrator follow. Plans of revenge are put together. But as the stress abates the person realizes that his suspicions and schemes were without foundation. What all this indicates is that paranoid mental mechanisms are an important way to protect the oneness of the self and are automatically used by the individual when flooded by stress and anxiety.

The important thing about paranoia in general is to remember that besides becoming at times a severe mental illness which may endanger the life of the carrier as well as the lives of people at large, it also has the function of holding the personality together and avoiding its complete disintegration.

An outstanding characteristic of the paranoid symptom is that an unpleasant and threatening situation which is too much to handle is put outside of the individual and projected onto another individual. It is not I who hate him but it is he who hates me. In a simplified way, it is the pot that calls the kettle black.

Finally, though the severe paranoid disorders are difficult to treat, they constitute a tiny minority compared with the huge majority of benign paranoid states and conditions which either subside on their own or can readily be treated in a brief period of time.

CREDIT: *Samuel L. Safirstein, M.D., New York, New York, Associate Clinical Professor of Psychiatry, Mount Sinai School of Medicine, New York, New York; Associate Attending, Department of Psychiatry, Mount Sinai Hospital, New York, New York.*

Parenthood: Guidelines to Help You Live Through It*

All parents believe in heredity until a child of theirs begins to act a little goofy. If your children are beautifully adjusted, totally reliable, consistently obedient, co-operative, respectful, courteous, considerate and have never caused you a moment's trouble, you should be on display at the Smithsonian.

* Reprinted from June 1968 issue of *Family Circle* magazine, © 1968 The Family Circle, Inc.

If, on the other hand, there are times when your children annoy you, exhaust you, worry you and cause you to wonder what in heaven's name you're doing wrong, join the club.

The painfully embarrassing truth is that we are living in a child-dominated society. We have allowed our kids to take us over. Those of us who are past forty have witnessed a dazzling historical triple pass. In *our* growing-up years Father was the undisputed head of the house. With the advent of World War II, Mother displaced Father. And now, in far too many families, the kids are clearly in control. They direct the family's activities to an alarming degree. Whole communities are geared to their "needs." The junior members, more often than not, decide where the family will live, where it will vacation, what kind of car Dad will buy, and what brand of cereal, soap and toothpaste Mother will put in her shopping cart. Child guidance has taken on a new meaning: Parents are being guided by children.

This is a strange phenomenon indeed, when one views the sociological history of man. The concept of a child-centered family was virtually unheard of until recently. What is the reason for this unnatural chain of command? Parents are afraid to say no, afraid to give orders, afraid to punish because they fear the loss of love or they want to avoid an unpleasant confrontation. Moreover, the shakier the marriage, the more marked the abdication of parental responsibility. The woman who feels that her husband does not love her tries to get her children to love her twice as much by being permissive and wildly generous. The husband who feels rejected plays the same game, particularly with his daughters. Children are acutely sensitive to these machinations and learn quite promptly how to make parental insecurity pay off in gifts and unearned privileges.

We have before us the depressing spectacle of millions of frightened and groveling parents, haunted by the ghosts of Adler and Freud, knocking themselves out to be "nice" trying to relate to their kids in Meaningful Ways, competing for approval, and making incredible financial sacrifices so *their* children will have every known advantage—and some advantages never heard of outside the United States.

Show me a family run by children, and I will show you a set of embattled parents trying to buy love. What a sorry sight—and some of us need go no farther than the mirror. Love, as viewed by the poets, may be a many-splendored thing, but the quest for love can result in considerable heartache. When we try to buy love, the price goes up, as it does with other commodities. The child who senses that his parents feel guilty about leaving him with a sitter and a TV dinner will not hesitate to raise the price of "forgiveness." Then, after he has collected his ransom, he will think up something else to be angry about so he can collect again. Emotional blackmail can be a profitable business.

In my opinion the theory of permissive upbringing was the most damaging concept ever latched on to by a generation of mixed-up parents. This "experiment" produced a shocking number of disturbed kids, plus countless nervous wrecks who had hoped to be teachers but turned to other careers because they couldn't stand the spoiled brats.

In Dr. Lee Kanner's book for laymen entitled *In Defense of Mothers,* he describes permissive upbringing as an unnatural and antihuman scheme. Writes Dr. Kanner: "There is no air-raid shelter to protect us from the verbal bombs that rain down on contemporary Mom and Dad. At every turn they are assaulted by unfamiliar words and phrases which confuse and frighten them. Words such as Oedipus complex, maternal rejection, sibling rivalry, schizoid personality, regression, aggression, blah-blah-blah, and more blah."

I applaud Dr. Kanner's statement and wish to add to it. My comments, however, are for *both* Mother and Father: Remove the rose-colored glasses, folks. They contain no correction for parental myopia. What the vast majority of American children need is to stop being pampered, stop being indulged, stop bing chauffeured, gifted, catered to and made to feel the world belongs to them and they are doing their parents a favor by letting them live in it.

Don't be afraid to be boss. Children are continually testing, attempting to see how much they can get away with—how far you will let them go—and they secretly hope you will not let them go too far. Be aware of this testing mechanism the next time you are locked in bitter debate with your teenager. And don't bug out when the crunch comes.

The parent who tries to curry the favor of his child by giving him everything he asks for and letting him do as he pleases loses out on all fronts. He does not gain his child's goodwill or affection. He is despised for his gutlessness and in the end blamed when there is trouble. "Why did you let me do it?" the child demands to know. "Because you begged me—you wanted to" is the feeble response. Then comes the most devastating blow. "You should have said no. What kind of parent are you, anyway?"

Accept the fact that there will be moments when your children will hate you. This is normal and natural. But how a child handles hate may determine whether he will go to Harvard or San Quentin. A child should be taught to vent his anger in socially acceptable ways—ways that will not injure others, damage property or hurt his own self-esteem. Rules should be established and limits set—in writing, if necessary. I cannot emphasize too strongly the importance of setting limits. The child who knows just exactly how far he can go is relieved of a heavy burden.

In our family the rules were simple: Get as mad as you like but there must be no hitting, no yelling, swear-words (so loud that the neighbors will hear) and no breaking anything you aren't prepared to pay for.

Finally, remember that parents have rights and, like other rights, they must be exercised or they will be lost by default. If there is a question as to whether you should give the edge to your child or take it for yourself, I say take it for yourself. And don't feel guilty. Rank hath its privileges. Children need to practice the art of giving—and who is more deserving of consideration than one's own parents?

An important parental right is privacy. Teach your children to mind their own business. If you want them to grow up with integrity and high principles, demonstrate these qualities in your daily life, and your youngsters will follow in your steps.

The most important parental right is to have a life of your own. A man and his wife should enjoy a special relationship separate and apart from their children. Parents should have fun together, evenings—just the two of them. They must never lose sight of the fact that they started together as sweethearts, and one day their children will be gone, and they will be alone.

Parents who genuinely love their children will insist on their rights and will give their children the rights that are theirs. Love is not a grasping, greedy thing that hangs on. It is a generous, lovely thing that lets go.

In the final analysis, it is not what you do for your children but what you have taught them to do for themselves that will make them successful human beings.

A PRAYER FOR PARENTS

Oh, God, make me a better parent. Help me to understand my children, to listen patiently to what they have to say and to respond to their questions kindly. Keep me from interrupting them, talking back to them and contradicting them. Make me as courteous to them as I would have them be to me. Give me the courage to confess my sins against my children and ask them for forgiveness when I know I have done wrong.

May I not vainly hurt the feelings of my children.

Forbid that I would laugh at their mistakes, or resort to shame and ridicule as punishment. Let me not tempt a child to lie or steal. Guide me hour by hour that I may demonstrate by all I say and do that honesty produces happiness.

Reduce, I pray, the meanness in me. May I cease to nag; and when I am out of sorts, help me, O Lord, to hold my tongue. Blind me to the little errors of my children and help me to see the good things they do. Give me a ready word for honest praise.

Help me treat my children as those of their own age.

Let me not expect from them the judgment of adults. Allow me not to rob them of the opportunity to wait upon themselves, to think, to choose and to make their own decisions.

Forbid that I should ever punish them for my selfish satisfaction. May I grant them all their wishes that are reasonable and have the courage always to withhold a privilege which I know will do them harm.

Make me so fair and just, so considerate and companionable, that they will have genuine esteem for me.

Fit me to be loved and imitated by my children. Oh, God, do give me calm and poise and self-control.

Ann Landers

Parenthood: What Do You Owe Your Children?*

If I were asked to select the one word that best describes the majority of American parents, that word would be guilt-ridden. Every day I receive an unending stream of mail and each family has a different story to tell. But the message is almost always the same: "We blew it."

Beleaguered Mom and Dad, in their hairshirts from Saks and Sears, tell me they did their best but "something went wrong."

A mother from El Paso confesses, "I was too permissive."

A father from Kansas City laments, "I was too strict."

From Scarsdale, both parents write: "We paid over $22,000 for psychiatric help for our three daughters. Now two of them aren't speaking to us. I wish we'd spent the money on a boat instead, and raised our kids the way we were raised."

Wherever you look you see parents walking on eggshells, bending over backward to relate to their children in "meaningful" ways. They hunger for approval, make outrageous financial sacrifices so their children will have every known advantage and some advantages never before heard of outside of the United States.

Love's magic spell may be everywhere, but when you try to buy it, the price goes up, as it does with any other commodity. Emotional blackmail can be a highly profitable business, especially when the buyer is loaded with guilt. How sad it is to see parents turning into willing victims of the "gimmee" game, complying with every request, large and small, only to discover that no matter what they do, it isn't enough. Attempts to curry favor lead only to a barrage of new requests. In the end, parents are despised for their gutlessness and blamed when there's trouble.

The results of the General Mills American Family Report (1976–77) conducted by Yankelovich, Skelly and White, Inc., would have knocked the average reader cranksided, but it produced no surprises for me. The study was based on interviews with 1,230 families who are raising children in a changing society. It dealt with a re-examination of lifestyles and traditional values

---

* Reprinted from November 1977 issue of *Family Circle* magazine, © 1977 The Family Circle, Inc.

that place greater emphasis on sexual freedom, self-fulfillment, the blurring of the male and female roles, less conformity and more openness and frankness.

Fifty-seven percent of parents interviewed fell into the category of "Traditionalists." They firmly believe in religion, marriage as an institution, saving money and hard work. These parents want their children to be outstanding and are willing to make sacrifices in order to help them.

Not far behind (43 percent) were the "New Breed Parents." They do not consider the institution of marriage all-important. They do not put as much weight on such values as religion, saving money, patriotism and success. "New Breed Parents" favor a permissive approach to child rearing and believe that children should be free to make their own decisions. They do not feel that their children have any obligation to them later on in life. (This blew my mind.)

Several authorities were asked to comment on the results of the study. Verle L. Nicholson, Director of Information for the President's Council on Physical Fitness and Sports, said, "The failure to provide discipline and direction and the anxiety about guiding children has created terrible problems." (He seems to have a firm grasp of the obvious.)

Fred Hechinger of the Editorial Board of the New York *Times* said, "The general disappearance of widely agreed upon standards and values is extremely dangerous to secure family life. It sets everyone adrift. Children have the least capacity to fashion their own rules." (Hello, Fred. So what else is new?)

Precisely what did the study say to me? It said the same thing that I've been saying to everyone these past twenty years: Parents had better get back to the traditional values and hang together . . . or they will hang separately.

With these unsettling facts as a backdrop, I'll get down to the basic question: What do parents owe their children? It would be easier to start by telling you what you do not owe them.

You do not owe them every minute of your day or every ounce of your energy. Nor do you owe them round-the-clock chauffeur service, baton-twirling lessons, horseback-riding lessons (and $90 boots), singing lessons, summer camp, ski outfits and ten-speed bikes, a Honda or a car when they turn sixteen. You don't owe them a trip to Europe when they graduate from high school.

I take the firm, unpopular position that parents do not owe their children a college education, medical school, dental school or law school. If Bob or Betsy are serious students and have well-defined goals, if they consider higher education a privilege and not a right, by all means send them to college if you can afford, it, but don't feel guilty if you can't. They don't have it coming. If they really want to go, they'll find a way. Student loans are available on a massive scale, and scholarships are plentiful for the bright and eager who can't afford to pay.

After children marry, you do not owe them a down payment on a home or money for furniture. Nor do you have an obligation to baby-sit with their kids or take over when they go on vacation. If you want to do any of these things, it should be considered an act of generosity—but they have no right to take it for granted.

Parents do not owe their progeny an inheritance no matter how much money they have. One of the surest ways to produce loafers and freeloaders is to let children know that their future is assured. The child who is goal-oriented and highly motivated will make it on his or her own, but there is no incentive like knowing it's the only way he or she is going to get there. Necessity is the best self-propelling agent of all.

Unfortunately, the tax burden for the well-to-do makes trust funds a highly attractive alternative. Estate planners who work overtime (at $80 an hour) tell us one of the neatest devices to keep from giving it all to Uncle Sam is to set up a trust fund for the children. In my opinion, a far saner approach is to make a modest inheritance available when the child becomes thirty or thirty-five—with a stipulation that larger sums are available before that time in case of catastrophic illness or grave financial hardship. If the money is not used, it should be held over for educating the next generation—if there is a need—or given to a worthy charity.

At this point you're probably wondering whether parents owe their children anything. My answer is, yes, they owe them a great deal.

One of the chief obligations parents have to their children is to give them a sense of personal worth. Self-esteem is the cornerstone for good mental health. A youngster who is continually criticized and "put down," made to feel stupid and inept, constantly compared with brothers, sisters or cousins who do better, will not try to improve. On the contrary, he or she will become so unsure, so terrified of failing, that he or she won't try at all. When report cards are sent home, they'll read: "unmotivated, lazy—not working up to potential."

The child who is repeatedly called "bad" or "naughty" or "no good" will have such a low opinion of him- or herself that he or she will behave in a way that justified the parent's description. Children have an uncanny way of living up—or down—to what is expected of them.

Of course, they should be corrected and set straight—this is the way children learn—but criticism should be heavily outweighed by praise. To a child, parents are the most important people in the world. Pleasing them and looking good in their eyes is the greatest satisfaction. To fail them is the worst punishment of all.

I once suggested to a mother whose bright but "unmotivated" eleven-year-old son was flunking nearly every subject that she listen carefully, for one full day, to every word she said to him. The mother reported, after her experiment, that she was appalled . . . and ashamed of herself. "I had no idea I never spoke to Jimmy except to admonish him or order him to do something. Now I know why my husband keeps telling me to 'get off the boy's back.'"

Some parents find it difficult to verbalize approval of their children, even though they do think well of them. (My own dear mother was like that, but Poppa made up for it.) Parents who cannot praise with words should show their approval in other ways—with a smile or a caress. Touching is very important. Children need to be taken on a lap and held long after they have gone to school.

Parents owe their children consistency in discipline and firm guidelines. Youngsters continually try to split the ranks, working one parent against the other, testing to see how far you will let them go. Behind the bold front they secretly hope you won't cave in and let them go too far, no matter how much they beg. It's frightening to a youngster to discover that he is in charge of himself; it's like being in a car with no brakes. Even a very young child is aware that discipline is a special kind of love. When you say, "No, you can't go," he may put on a long face, but deep down he will be greatly relieved. The parent who has the courage to say no when other parents are saying yes sends out a double message. He is also saying, "I love you, and I am willing to risk your wrath because I don't want you to get into trouble."

Parents owe their children some religious training, if they had it themselves and it provided comfort and strength and a sense of identity. On the other hand, if your religious training filled you with fear and guilt and you don't want to hand down such a punishing legacy to your offspring, you should search for a substitute. I'm convinced that children need the emotional support of religion today more than ever. The fact so many kooky cults enjoy such success in our country is irrefutable evidence that children feel the need for something spiritual in their lives.

Parents owe their children a comfortable feeling about their bodies and sufficient information about sex to counteract the garbage they will inevitably pick up on the street. Most—yes, I said most—parents are too poorly informed or hung up to give their children adequate sex education. Ironically enough, these parents are the very ones who scream the loudest in an attempt to keep sex education out of the public schools. They are also the ones who write letters to the editor and complain when Ann Landers runs a letter about you-know-what.

Parents owe their children privacy and respect for their personal belongings. This means not borrowing items without permission and not snooping in diaries, rooting through bureau drawers, wallets and purses. Ditto, not listening in on the extension telephone. Parenthood does not give you the inalienable right to play CIA and FBI. When mothers insist it's for the child's "own good," I tell them that if they must read a daughter's diary to find out what's going on, the lines of communication are pretty bad.

Parents owe their children a set of decent standards and solid values around which to build a life. This means teaching your children to respect the opinions and rights of others. It also means being respectful of elders, their teachers and the law.

Values are not only taught, they are caught. When parents keep their promises, no matter what the cost, they teach their children the importance of honoring a commitment. A father who brings home tools from the factory and a mother whose linen closet is stocked with towels from the Holiday Inn or the Hilton let their children know it's all right to steal. A child who is lied to will lie. A child who is slapped and punched will slap and punch others. A youngster who hears no laughter and sees no love in the home will have a difficult time laughing and loving.

No child asks to be born. If you bring a life into this world, you owe him or her something. And if you give your youngster their due, they'll have something of value to give to your grandchildren.

A PECULIARITY OF DAD'S THAT CAN BE KISSED OFF

DEAR ANN LANDERS: Thirteen months ago I had my first child, a beautiful baby boy. My husband, Chris, is a wonderful husband and father but he has never kissed the child.

I mentioned this to him recently and he said he'd feel funny—that he's never kissed a guy before. I've told him how much this bothers me but it doesn't do any good.

My father kissed my brothers and they never lost their masculinity because of it. Some of Chris's male friends have kissed our child on the cheek, which I've pointed out to him.

Still no change.

He is a warm, affectionate person and this hang-up has me terribly confused. Can there be a deeper problem? MAMA

DEAR MAMA: A father who considers a 13-month-old son "a guy" has a little strudel in his noodle. I'd say Chris has a deeper problem all right.

But if he holds the child, plays with him and "is a wonderful father," overlook this peculiarity. Kissing isn't essential to healthy development.

TEN WAYS TO BREAK UP A MARRIAGE

DEAR ANN: Please repeat that great column "Ten Ways to Break Up a Marriage." I need it now.   SOS

DEAR SOS: Here it is. Thanks for asking.

(1) When sons or daughters let you know they plan to be married, show open hostility to the person of their choice. After all, marriage means less love and attention for parents, and they have a right to resent it.

(2) Expect your married children to

spend every Sunday and holiday at your home. Act hurt if they have other plans.

(3) If your married children have problems with their mates, encourage them to come home, no matter what. Listen attentively to all complaints and point out additional faults which may have gone unobserved. Remember, single drops of water can wear away a rock if the drops keep falling long enough.

(4) When your married children

have financial problems, rush in with the checkbook. If you are having financial problems yourself, borrow, if necessary, but let them know they'll never have to do without anything so long as you are around.

(5) If a married child has a drinking problem, tell him his mate drove him to it. It will make him feel better. Everyone needs someone to blame.

(6) If your married son gets an opportunity for advancement which takes him to another city, tell him, "Family is more important than money." If he leaves anyway, remind him that God punishes those who ignore the commandment "Honor thy father and thy mother."

(7) If there are grandchildren, smother them with gifts. If the parents object, tell them to keep out of it. After all, grandchildren are to spoil. Sneak money to the little ones secretly if you have to. They'll love you for it.

(8) If your married child has a difference of opinion with his mate, get into the act and give them both a sample of your wisdom, born of years of experience. What do THEY know? You've lived!

(9) When your married sons or daughters visit with their children, make a point of how thin and tired the kids look. Get across the message that you don't like the way your beloved grandchildren are being cared for. Ask repeatedly what they eat and why they have so many colds. If a kid breaks a tooth or is injured during play, get all the details and place the blame on lack of maternal supervision.

(10) If your son has a button off his shirt, say something. Also mention the hole in his sock or the spot on his coat. It will fan the flames of self-pity and could start the final fight that ends in the divorce court.

Parenthood: What Do Your Children Owe You?*

"What is your mother doing these days?" I asked a friend who recently returned from a visit with her family in New York.

"Mother is very busy doing what she does best," was the reply. "She's the East Coast distributor for guilt."

I often hear this sentiment expressed by young marrieds—who are irritated and resent their invisible burden. There's a tremendous amount of guilt around these days and many of the victims don't know if it is being laid on them by self-centered, punitive parents, or if they are really rotten kids.

* Reprinted from September 1978 issue of *Family Circle* magazine, © 1978 The Family Circle, Inc.

What *do* children owe their parents, anyway? Not just married children, but *all* children—from six years of age to sixty-six. No one can speak for everyone, but since this question has been raised by many people groping for answers, I shall try to respond.

First, let's start with teenagers. Here are the basics: You owe your parents consideration, loyalty, and respect. The Biblical injunction "Honor thy father and thy mother" is simple and clear.

But what if they are drunks and abusive and failures, not only as parents but as human beings? Are we still supposed to "honor" them? Do we still owe them consideration, loyalty and respect? This question is often put to me.

"Yes" is my answer. Honor them because they gave you life. Give them consideration and loyalty for the same reason.

Consideration is a word that needs no definition, but loyalty as it relates to the family is sometimes vague. What does it mean? It means hanging in there when things go wrong. It means keeping family matters inside the family. The child who speaks ill of his parents and runs them down to outsiders, says more about himself than he says about them.

Respect is difficult to bestow when it has not been earned—and sad to say, some parents have not earned it. If you feel your parents have not earned your respect, try to find it in your heart to substitute understanding and compassion. Granted, this is a great deal to ask of a teenager, but if you can do it, it will help you grow as a person. Look beyond the brittle façade and you'll see people who are bitterly ashamed of their inability to measure up. They're insecure and shaky—struggling with unresolved problems stemming from their childhood. To fail as a parent is extremely painful. They suffer a lot.

But most parents are not drunks, nor are they abusive. They are plain, ordinary people, with good intentions and feet of clay—trying desperately to survive in a dangerous, untidy world. They are out there every day, on the front lines, battling inflation, obesity, chronic fatigue, obsolescence, and crabgrass.

Nearly 48 percent of the work force in America today is female. This means great numbers of mothers are wearing two hats, or three. They're working at part-time (or full-time) jobs, trying to run a house, raise children, and participate in community activities. What do children owe parents who fit this description?

Here are the fundamentals: They owe them prompt and honest answers to the following questions:

Where are you going?
Who are your companions?
How do you plan to get there?
When will you be home?

Teenagers frequently write to complain that their parents want to pick their friends. Do they have a right to do this? The answer is "No." I never fail to point out, however, that when parents are critical of a teenager's friends, they usually have a good reason. Bad company can be bad news. But, in the final analysis, the choice of friends should be up to the individual. If he or she makes poor selections, he or she will have to pay for it.

Parents have the right to expect their children to pick up after themselves and perform simple household chores. For example, every member of the family over six years of age should clean the bathtub and the sink so it will be in respectable condition for the next person. He or she should also run errands and help in the kitchen if asked—in other words, carry a share of the load without feeling persecuted.

The days of "hired help" are, for the most part, gone. And this is good. Boys as well as girls should be taught to cook and clean, do laundry and sew on buttons. This is not "sissy stuff." It makes for independence and self-reliance.

What do teenagers and college students owe their parents in terms of time and attention? There's no pat answer. It depends on the temperament, the expectations and the desires of the individuals involved. Some parents are extremely demanding—others are loose hangers. Some children can't wait to move out of the house. Others must be pushed out. A college student should not be expected to write home every day, but certainly a postcard once a week is not asking too much if parents wish this. A phone call (collect, of course) on Sunday should not be impossible to manage if parents want it.

What about vacations? Do children owe it to their parents to come home, rather than go to Fort Lauderdale or to a ski resort? Yes, they do, if the parents want them home and are footing the bills for education and transportation.

What do working children who live at home owe their parents in terms of financial compensation? The following letter is typical of what I read at least two dozen times a week:

"Dear Ann Landers: Our daughter is twenty-six years old. She chose business school over college and is now number one secretary to the president of a large firm. We are pleased that Terry still lives with us and doesn't want an apartment of her own like so many girls these days, but I feel we are being taken advantage of.

"Terry has no savings account. She buys very expensive clothes, has her own car, takes vacations in Europe, and doesn't give us one cent for room and board. She pays the telephone bill, mainly because the long-distance calls are hers. I do her laundry, keep her room clean, fix her a big breakfast every morning and dinner whenever she wants it.

"Our home is paid for and Terry knows we are not hard up for money, but it would be awfully nice to have a little extra coming in. My husband says not to 'rock the boat' or she might move. What do you say? If you believe she should pay—how much? Thanks for your help, Ann.—A Pittsburgh Mom."

I replied, "Dear Mom: Terry should give you 20 percent of her paycheck. If she thinks she can get lodging, breakfast, laundry, and maid-service elsewhere for less—let her try it.

"The fact that you are not hard up for money is no excuse for your daughter's selfishness. Share this letter with your husband, and I hope together you will muster up the courage to talk to Terry promptly."

When sons and daughters marry, things change considerably. Even though parents have a tendency to forever think of their children as "children," they should be granted a totally different status when they establish a family unit of their own.

Should Mom be forever and always the Number One woman in Sonny's life? Does he owe her that? No, he does not. A wise and loving mother willingly relinquishes that place to her daughter-in-law. She remembers how she felt about *her* husband's mother when *she* married. By the same token, a kind and thoughtful daughter-in-law will be considerate of her husband's mother so she will not feel displaced or abandoned. Life's cycles have an ironic way of evening up the score. The woman who finds herself with a mother-in-law problem might do well to think ahead a few years when *her* son will marry and *she* will become the mother-in-law.

Getting down to specifics, what do married children owe their parents in terms of time and attention? According to my readers, this is a major problem among marrieds in their thirties and forties. Here are some questions from this week's mail bag:

From Lubbock, Texas:

"My mother telephones me at least four times a day. She wants to know if the children ate a good breakfast, who wore what at a party last night, what am I fixing for supper, has my husband's boss said anything about a raise . . . ?"

From Nashville, Tennessee:

"My husband's mother asks me every two weeks if I am pregnant yet. She keeps reminding me that I'm not getting any younger and she would give anything to have a grandchild. The woman is getting on my nerves."

From Richmond, Virginia:

"My husband's parents are in their mid-seventies. He spends at least five hours every Saturday driving them to the supermarket, the dentist, the doctor, the pharmacy, the optometrist, the greenhouse, the dry cleaners, and so on. My in-laws have two daughters who live in town but they never bother *them*. My husband is the one they run ragged. Does he owe them this kind of service?"

From San Diego, California:

"My mother is sixty-four, a widow, attractive and well read. When we have guests for an evening, she is hurt if she isn't included. I love her dearly, but Mom has strong opinions and I have the feeling our friends resent her. Am I obligated to include her because she is my mother?"

There are no hard and fast rules to cover every situation but here are some suggestions that can be tailored to fit a great many:

Countless people are victims of not only in-laws but friends who have black-cord fever—also known as telephonitis. The best protection against these types is to develop a technique for getting off the phone after a reasonable period of time—or sooner, if you wish. The victim should have prepared sentences handy and read them when the need arises. Sample: "Sorry, dear. I have a million things to do this morning and I must hang up now. We'll talk again soon."

People have no right to complain about being trapped or taken advantage of if they don't have the gumption to assert themselves. I tell them repeatedly, "No one can exploit you without your permission." This includes refusing to answer "nun-uvyer-bizniz" type questions. Sample comeback: "Now why in the world would *you* be interested in *that?*"

No woman owes her in-laws grandchildren. Any person who presumes to put pressure on a woman to "give us a grandchild" should be put in her place.

Running errands and chauffeuring aged parents can be time- and energy-consuming, but it may be essential when no alternatives exist. If there are other children (or nieces and nephews) who might help out, they certainly should be asked to do so. Where time is more valuable than money, a paid driver may relieve a lot of tension in an emergency.

Including parents in social activities is not essential and parents should not expect it. No apologies or excuses are necessary.

Perhaps the most anxiety-producing problem is one that hits in the late forties or early fifties—about the same time some adults are going through the mid-life crisis. What to do with Mama when Papa dies. Or, if Mama goes first, what should be done with Papa?

Circumstances alter cases. Some mamas wouldn't live with their children on a bet. The same goes for some papas. Many factors should be considered at the outset; first: How would Grandma or Grandpa fit in with the family? Is she or he too bossy? Would there be trouble in the kitchen? Would the children feel that too many people are telling them what to do?

Finances are another major consideration. Does the surviving parent have sufficient money to maintain his or her own place? The issue of health is also important. Is Mama or Papa well enough to live alone? The answers to these questions should be carefully reviewed when attempting to reach a decision.

Strictly from a standpoint of morality and decency—do you owe your parents a place in your home if he or she would like to move in? I say, "No." If they need housing or care, it goes without saying, you should provide it, but you do not owe them a place under your roof if it would create dissension and conflict in your family.

The ideal solution is to keep the surviving parent in his or her own home or apartment if it is economically feasible.

When money is a problem, all the children should ante up and share the cost. (Often this is easier said than done.) Endless family fights have resulted because brother George or sister Mabel say they can't help out with the old folks because they have kids in college. Yet they manage to go to Florida or Arizona every winter, belong to the country club, and drive new cars.

The most serious crisis arises when Mama and Papa become ill or too old to take care of themselves. Nursing homes are expensive and many old people don't want to go there. What then? Some heroic women have taken in a parent or an in-law (or both) at tremendous personal sacrifice. This can be the most physically exhausting and emotionally draining job in the world, since old folks tend to be senile, incontinent, ill-tempered and in need of constant watching. I implore daughters and daughters-in-law not to feel guilty if they are unable to do it. The woman who does make this sacrifice, in my opinion, deserves a place at God's right hand come reckoning time.

In the final analysis none of us goes through life debt-free. We all owe something to somebody. But the most noble motivation for giving is not prompted by a sense of duty. It flows freely from unselfish love.

Parents: Possessive and Strict

Parents' difficulties in adjusting to their teenagers' "adolescent turmoil" is a fact of life. This difficulty reflects the many changes, up, down and sideways that the parent must adjust to in the teenager. The difficulty is made greater by the fact that many parents have blocked out memories of their own teenage years because of the emotional pain of that period. The struggles of the teenage years are centered around resolving his excessive attachments to his family, finding a sense of who he is, as well as dealing with his emerging sexual feelings and impulses.

The physical changes of the teenager are visible and develop at a relatively consistent rate toward physical adulthood. The emotional changes are less clear-cut, and tend to go backward and forward as the child strains toward emotional adulthood. Parents as a rule have a difficult time understanding when and where the teenager develops inner conflicts and is pulled backward.

The parents' understanding and ability to respond properly to these different fluctuations are important in offering the teenager a family climate in which he can move toward adulthood with greater ease.

Parents who have resolved their own problems regarding the ties to *their* parents and who handle their own sex lives satisfactorily will be better able to tolerate their teenager's struggles and help him in his effort to grow up and move into the adult world.

Some of the characteristics of the teenager that parents find difficult to tolerate are rebelliousness, self-centeredness, moodiness and rapid changes in the teenager's view of who he values and admires. These characteristics make it difficult for a parent to be supportive at a time when the teenager needs as much support as he can get.

While it is difficult to recommend a specific list of guidelines for being an effective parent for all teenagers, we will try to describe policies that reflect understanding of the important elements of the teenage period.

It is important to remember that every child is an individual who grows both physically and emotionally at a different rate. Each family environment reflects different styles as influenced by parental experiences, religious and ethnic background, as well as family size, quality of the marriage and whether the child is the first-born, boy or girl, and other factors too numerous to mention.

We will discuss the two main tasks of adolescence and the needs expressed by the child, as well as the parental reactions.

The two main tasks to be mastered are (1) emerging sexual feelings and impulses without excessive inhibitions or lack of self-control, and (2) breaking away from the old-style attachment to the family. These developmental tasks affect one another and cannot be separated. We will address them separately in order to discuss the issues more clearly.

The period of development prior to adolescence is called the latency period. The child of this age period is usually at relative peace with himself and family. He is a "good kid," dependent on and needful of both parents. From this peaceful state there is a gradual and increasing intensity of swings between the youngster showing signs of greater self-reliance and a return to the previous child-like attachments.

At this point, the teenager begins to deny the importance of the standards and values imposed by the parents and adheres to his peer group views and pressures. The further the peer group point of view is from the parents' positions, the greater the stress. The teenager's break from the family leads to a confused and confusing situation for both the parents and the teenager. This is partly due to the fact that while the teenager is becoming a "physical" adult, he is still dependent on the parents for clothing, bed and board.

He is given more responsibility for making decisions about staying out later, selecting his own clothes, driving a car, working part-time, etc. At the same time, parents become anxious about the teenager's unpredictable behavior. Concern about unpredictable behavior shows itself in the exaggerated way parents react to the issue of what time the teenager is supposed to return from a party or a date. The fear that forbidden behavior is taking place is a common source of anxiety, as if no forbidden behavior can take place before the agreed time for the teenager to return home. Anxiety about the teenager's ability to stay out of trouble can lead to excessive and irrational "rules and regulations." This inconsistency leads to further confusion in the teenager's mind about what is expected of him.

The teenager's mood swings are at first very difficult for the parents to adjust to. This is especially true because the heightened sensitivity of the teenager makes communication between parent and child more difficult. The parents need to be more supportive of the movements away from them. They must be tolerant of the child's lapses into "babyish" behavior and not make him feel ashamed.

These changes in the teenager have a potential for stirring up other anxieties in the parents. If the parents recognize these anxieties they will be able to be more supportive in helping the teenager deal with growing up.

Parental anxieties about the changing teenager are present in all parents to some degree. They represent remnants of previous ties to their own parents that have not been completely resolved. The teenager's breaking of ties to the parents has a potential for rekindling the feelings of anxiety around the parents breaking away from their own parents during their adolescence. If these unresolved anxieties are strong, they may hinder the parents' effectiveness in helping their teenager move ahead. Sometimes the term "possessiveness" is used to describe this lack of freedom in the parent in supporting the teenager's separation from the family.

Some degree of possessiveness is present in all relationships where people care about one another. The appearance of possessiveness is seen in most child-parent relationships when the child is starting to change, but the changes at first are not recognized by the parent. It appears that the parent is holding on to the child. In these situations, as soon as the parent recognizes that change is taking place, the parent should loosen the reins. The signs of real possessiveness are those that inhibit the child's natural growth. Because of the parents' anxiety about the child breaking away, they need to diminish the sense of confidence that the child has in himself and insist that he is not ready to break away. Sometimes the parent conveys to the child that the parent needs him to remain close, producing a sense of guilt in the child for his desire to grow up and leave.

Another form of possessiveness is seen in parents who refuse to allow their teenagers to pick their own friends. Such possessiveness is usually associated with overindulgence and the underlying feeling that "no boy is good enough for my daughter" or "my child should be going with a better class of people."

This kind of behavior may be rationalized by the parent as "caring," but, actually, it inhibits the normal distancing that must take place between parent and teenager during this developmental phase. The child must find satisfactions in relationships outside of the home to meet the real needs of growing up.

The teenager needs positive support in breaking away from parental ties to be free to enter the outside world. If this permission is not granted, the child will experience guilt about his wishes to change and move on. A lack of confidence will produce a clinging kind of attachment in some children and an excessive rebelliousness in others as they feel conflicted about the restrictiveness of their environment.

The issues of excessive strictness or parental possessiveness are not the critical points for the parent-teenager relationships. It is more important to accentuate the teenager's need for guidance, limit-setting and consistency from the parent to help the teenager deal with the inner confusion and uncertainty which the teenager struggles with during this period. The teenager will openly complain about the rules and regulations and appear to be demanding free reins, but at a deeper level, he feels more secure with firm, friendly guidance. The understanding of this paradox is the crucial issue for the parent.

CREDIT: *Leon Diamond, M.D., Director, Graduate Education, Department of Psychiatry, Northwestern University Medical School, Chicago, Illinois.*

STARVED FOR AFFECTION

DEAR ANN LANDERS: I'm an 18-year-old girl who would like to say a few words to "Smothered In Topeka." Her folks "embarrassed" her in front of her friends because they insisted on kissing her good-by whenever she left the house. She said it made her feel like a baby.

I can truthfully say I cannot recall being kissed by either my mother or father. Dad died when I was 13 and I can't remember him ever touching me. It was as if there was a wall between us.

When I mentioned this to my mother, she said, "He wasn't a person who could show his feelings." I then asked, "How about you, Mom?" Her answer was, "I guess I am pretty much the same way but that doesn't mean your father didn't love you—or that I don't."

Her explanation never convinced me. All I know is I felt isolated—starved for affection. It left a mark on me, a bad one. When I was 14, I started to sleep with any guy who asked. By the time I was 16 I was pregnant, lost the baby and a social worker (bless her) got me into therapy.

I understand a lot more now than I did then. But still there's that emptiness. When I marry and have children, I'm going to hug and kiss them to pieces. They'll KNOW I care. HAZARD, KY.

DEAR KY.: Here's your letter. It contains a ton of information for both children and parents. Thanks for unloading.

Parents: Twelve Rules For Raising Children

(1) Remember that a child is a gift from God, the richest of all blessings. Do not attempt to mold him in the image of yourself, your father, your brother or your neighbor. Each child is an individual and should be permitted to be himself.

(2) Don't crush a child's spirit when he fails. And never compare him with others who have outshone him.

(3) Remember that anger and hostility are natural emotions. Help your child to find socially acceptable outlets for these normal feelings or they may be turned inward and erupt in the form of physical or mental illness.

(4) Discipline your child with firmness and reason. Don't let *your* anger throw you off balance. If he knows you are fair you will not lose his respect or his love. And make sure the punishment fits the crime. Even the youngest child has a keen sense of justice.

(5) If you have a spouse, present a united front. Never join with your child against your mate. This can create in your child (as well as in yourself) emotional conflicts. It gives rise to destructive feelings of guilt, confusion and insecurity.

(6) Do not hand your child everything his little heart desires. Permit him to know the thrill of earning and the joy of deserving. Grant him the greatest of all satisfactions—the pleasure that comes with personal achievement.

(7) Do not set yourself up as the epitome of perfection. This is a difficult role to play twenty-four hours a day. You will find it easier to communicate with your child if you let him know that Mom and Dad can err too.

(8) Don't make threats in anger or impossible promises when you are in a generous mood. Threaten or promise only that which you can live up to. To a child a parent's word means everything. The child who has lost faith in his parents has difficulty believing in anything.

(9) Do not smother your child with superficial manifestations of "love." The purest and healthiest love expresses itself in day-in, day-out training which breeds self-confidence and independence.

(10) Teach your child there is dignity in hard work, whether it is performed with calloused hands that shovel coal or skilled fingers that manipu-

late surgical instruments. Let him know that a useful life is a blessed one and that a life of ease and pleasure-seeking is empty and meaningless.

(11) Do not try to protect your child against every small blow and disappointment. Adversity strengthens character and makes us compassionate. Trouble is the great equalizer. Let him learn it.

(12) Teach your child to love God and to love his fellow man. Don't *send* your child to a place of worship—*take* him there. Children learn from example. Telling him something is not teaching him. If you give your child a deep and abiding faith in God, it can be his strength and his light when all else fails.

CREDIT: *Ann Landers.*

Parents: What to Do with the Old Folks

IN-LAWS VS. PARENTS

DEAR ANN LANDERS: I've never written to you before, but I couldn't resist commenting on your answer to "Ignored In San Jose."

It will be a deep-freeze day in hell when I put my in-laws ahead of my parents. I respect my wife's mother and father, but my own Mom and Dad come first—after my wife, of course.

Please don't print that corny poem again that says, "A son is a son till he takes a wife, but a daughter's a daughter all of her life." It's not true. A.S.

DEAR A.S.: About 400 others wrote to tell me the same thing. Nice to know there are so many loyal sons around.

You made a lot of mothers happy today.

There is an old Greek saying that states: "When the gods are angry with you they give you what you want." Human beings have always wanted long life, and now we have it.

However, we are not yet able to celebrate this triumph of long life. We have not come to grips with the considerable social changes resulting from the increase in the absolute numbers and relative proportions of older Americans. At the moment, we often tend to view the aged as a problem; we are just beginning to enter a necessary stage of adjustment in which we are learning "What to Do with the Old Folks."

The most important principle to follow in your interactions with the old is that *they must have as much control over their own lives as possible.* Throughout life, we strive to learn and develop independence. Legally and morally we always have that right and one's age should not affect it. Most aged individuals wish to remain in their homes as long as possible and while they want and need a close relationship with their children they do not wish to be a burden to them. It is for these reasons that adult children might think about their style of interaction with their parents from three perspectives:

(1) How can I tell if my parents are okay?

(2) How do I know when to intervene and when to keep out of their lives?

(3) What should my interventions be?

It is of great value if adult children and older people have discussed these issues well in advance of any developing problems so that each can find straightforward ways of signaling to the other and not have to rely on subtleties and hints.

Communicating one's needs and concerns is always a delicate matter. It is often difficult for the older person to know when to call on the children for help and for the children, in turn, to know when not to intrude. Neither parent nor child can always evaluate the situation appropriately and the best relationships are built as a result of much trial and error.

Before we can even begin to assess the issues and problems of our aging parents we must get our own emotional houses in order. When a parent suddenly becomes dependent on his/her children, stored-up feelings of anger, conflict and fear begin to surface. Nothing can divide a family more. When adult children experience the great anxiety that accompanies the shocking realization that their all-powerful, advising parents are no longer the omnipotent beings they once were, the old sibling rivalry returns. Long-buried problems in our relationships with our parents and our siblings suddenly flare up and we find brothers and sisters fighting with each other. Angry emotions and feelings of conflict between parents and children must be recognized and dealt with.

In times of stress, our memory often fails us. It amazes me how frequently adult children forget the seventeen to twenty-two years of care they received from their parents and will often say things like, "I just can't give up so much of my life taking care of my folks—it could be three years." It is equally surprising to see parents caught up in these same feelings of ingratitude. They forget how preoccupied they were in their own early and mid-adult years and how they felt about their mothers and fathers at that time in their lives.

Parents and children cannot always set aside these conflicts easily, but by openly acknowledging and dealing with them we can begin to steer a moral course. Remind yourself of those great injunctions of the Judeo-Christian tradition regarding mutual indebtedness. Often, with the help of outside counseling from clergymen, family agencies and/or the physician, those longstanding conflicts can be set aside and brothers, sisters and parents can work together to maintain well-being for all.

Parents and children should recognize the need for a period of evaluation. Long before we recommend changes in our parents' lifestyle, we should spend some time with them assessing the many aspects of their social, medical and environmental needs. Again, keep in mind that old people must have as much control over their own lives as possible.

From my twenty-plus years of clinical and research experience, I have observed a common tendency to underestimate the capacities of our older people. We often unwittingly contribute to the weakening of their spirit, spunk and reserve by doing too much for them or by implying that they are no longer capable of doing things for themselves. We must be absolutely sure to give "old folks" plenty of opportunity to do what they *can* do.

It is crucial that we encourage our parents and older relatives to become or to remain self-starters. It is necessary for them to develop a social life in order to retain their independence. At any age, going out and meeting people keeps us vibrant and active. The older man or woman must not be denied the opportunity to establish new relationships. Also, children must keep quiet about any mixed and uneasy feelings they might have about their parents' remarriage, if the possibility should arise.

The maintenance of good health in the older individual is like the maintenance of good health in individuals at any other stage of development. We must encourage our "old folks" to take care of themselves by fueling their bodies through decent nutrition and by maintaining their physical "equipment" through a sensible exercise program.

A good diet for an old person is the same as a good diet for a middle-aged person—less meat, plenty of fruit and green vegetables and a lot of fiber to reduce intestinal problems. Frequently, old people who live alone become apathetic and careless about meal preparation. Proper nutrition helps to insure old people against those forms of so-called "senility" which are brought about by inadequate nourishment and a reduction of the oxygen flow to the brain. Indeed, anything that reduces adequate oxygen and food supply to the brain can cause various states of intellectual confusion.

Physical fitness for the old person means exercising (modestly at first) to maintain muscle strength, body flexibility, and heart and lung endurance under some measure of stress. Good physical fitness can reduce the likelihood of falls and minimize the thinning of bones (osteoporosis) which frequently occur with age. This in turn enhances recovery from any unexpected illness or heart attack. Appropriately prescribed, and alternated with necessary rest, physical exercise is a vital part of treating many diseases which affect the elderly, including rheumatoid arthritis and Parkinsonism.

In recent years, physicians have noted that many drugs have different effects on older individuals than on other age groups. Because some drugs or combinations of drugs can cause opposite and/or adverse reactions in old people, geriatric patients should keep in close contact with their doctors. If patients and their families would report physical and emotional changes (such as confusion, depression, loss of appetite, nausea, decreased sexual function) to their doctors, it is possible that a variation in medication would remedy some of the unpleasant side effects.

We must learn to recognize the beginnings of an illness. It is important for old people to seek medical advice early and not delay a visit out of fear of what the diagnosis might be. As we get older our responses—pain and fever and our heart rate—can vary. Be suspicious whenever someone doesn't seem "quite right," when there is a mood change or when there is some sign of breathing difficulty. Always look for early symptoms of disease—it may be an easily treatable infection.

As individuals approach old age, serious consideration should be given to selecting a competent physician. If friends or relatives cannot help, call the County Medical Society and ask for the names of one or two practitioners who have had experience treating old people. Try to find a doctor who is willing to make house calls or visits to the nursing home. It is not unusual for people in their young or mid-adult years to select a physician and expect to remain with him through old age. In many instances, the patient outlives the physician. Consequently, many of this nation's old people have no doctor at all. It is advisable to find a replacement for your physician when you both reach old age.

Evaluating an older person's surroundings is especially difficult. You want to create a living situation which will be secure and also afford a maximum opportunity for independent activity. When does it become important for your parents or older relatives to move from their own home into a more protected or sheltered environment? When should they move in with you, if at all? And, what are the conditions that point to hospital or nursing home admission?

Bearing in mind that most old people wish to remain in their own home (70 percent of America's aged people own their own homes), find out about the variety of services available to them. Often with state or federal support, communities may offer various services such as visiting nurses, part-time help, meal delivery, and extra police protection to the older citizen. There are non-profit organizations concerned with the aged that provide free legal assistance, and many religious groups which keep a roster of friendly visitors for aged individuals in their community. An old person's place of residence would ideally be:

(1) in a neighborhood which is low-risk for crime or well patrolled by the local police,

(2) close to shopping, friends and recreational activities or to transportation for all of the above, and

(3) close to one's physician or health care facility.

Should your parent(s) feel that their present residence is no longer suitable and the possibility of their moving in with you arises, then all options should be considered. It may be preferable for your parent(s) to live in an apartment nearby. Don't just put Grandma in the basement or the attic unless it's a mighty attractive basement or attic. In some cases, adult children may be able to build a comfortable addition onto their homes to accommodate a parent.

In actuality, only about 20 percent of old people and children live together. When parents do move in with their children (or the reverse) there is usually no reason for the older family members to be viewed as burdensome. The older person wants responsibilities in the household so that she (or he) too has a sense of participation and belonging. It is important to set up an open line of communication between young and old family members. The family should set aside regular times, perhaps once or twice a week, when grievances, worries, aspirations and concerns can be discussed. In addition to these planned talk sessions, it should be understood that when any family member has the desire, he/she will initiate a talk.

Privacy is another issue of prime importance. Everyone, regardless of age, needs time alone and a place to go to spend that time. In addition to these reasons for privacy, we must not forget that older people still need and have a right to emotional closeness, including sex. Adult children should be careful not to discourage their parents' love-making by ridiculing or being insensitive to these normal needs.

I have saved the problem of institutionalization for last because this issue is often the most painful for everyone, and, in fact, should be and usually is the last option. Institutionalization is a compound of two sorrows—sadness upon relegating the older person to a long-term care institution as the final step before death and then, of course, grief at the time of passing. Everything must be done to minimize the extent to which admission to the home is seen as a social death. Continued visits and contacts help make this period of transition as pleasant as possible. Otherwise, the family will develop feelings of conflict and guilt which then make the actual death even more painful.

Sometimes, institutionalization becomes the only realistic alternative. Fortunately, this is now the case for only 5 percent of this nation's old people (nearly a million at any given point in time). When an old person begins to wander confused in the streets at night, becomes incontinent and cannot control excretion of urine and feces or seriously disrupts the family life because of emotional instability or senility, then institutionalization may be the only answer.

A decent institution must not be seen automatically as something bad, but as a place that can contribute to the quality of life of an old person—a place where that person might find affection and camaraderie. Before placing any relative in a nursing home, the family should check carefully the availability of physicians and nursing staff, the quality of food, housekeeping and maintenance, recreational activities and visiting rules. Because so many nursing homes are subsidized through our Medicare and Medicaid programs, your local Social Security office keeps inspection reports and records of any complaints filed against such homes in your area. Request a copy of this information for any home you may be considering.

Until such time as modern medicine can eliminate some of the devastating and often dehumanizing conditions that affect our old people, we must not turn our backs in horror. The same compassion that enabled our parents to give so much to us as children—changing diapers, cleaning up bloody noses —must be practiced by you now.

Although the financial burdens associated with caring for one's aged parents and relatives may sometimes seem unbearable, we must not direct our anger at them. The adult children should work out the money problems among themselves. Pride should not overshadow reality. Families should take advantage of all federal and state funding available to them for this purpose. At the beginning of each year, it should be determined which family member will claim the parent as a dependent and benefit from the tax deduction. Both you and they have paid their taxes for years and have every right to take advantage of entitlements and benefits—whether in housing or Medicaid (the state-federal plan for helping the medically indigent), either for ambulatory care or for expensive nursing home and long-term care. Our Medicaid policies require older people to use up their own funds in order to be eligible for free nursing home care. Sadly, this means the other parent can become pauperized while supporting the spouse in a nursing home. It is useful to know that children are no longer legally responsible for the support of parents. The children can stand back and hold their finances in reserve to provide some big and little extras that may be needed later.

"What to Do with the Old Folks" is now a major issue which tests the very cohesion of the American family. In another fifty years, as the young Americans from the post-World War II "baby boom" enter their seventies and eighties, these problems will take on even more horrendous proportions. Instead of 23 million old people, this nation will have 53 million people over sixty-five years of age.

CREDIT: *Robert N. Butler, M.D., Director, National Institute of Aging, National Institutes of Health, Bethesda, Maryland; author of* Why Survive? Being Old in America, *New York: Harper & Row. This book won the Pulitzer Prize in 1976.*

Parkinson's Disease

. . . involuntary tremulous motion with lessened muscular power in parts not in action and even when supported; with a propensity to bend the trunk forwards, and to pass from a walking to a running pace: the senses and intellect being uninjured.

"An Essay on the Shaking Palsy,"
James Parkinson, 1917

Parkinsonism, paralysis agitans or shaking palsy was first described by James Parkinson in 1917. It is a combination of symptoms, the principal ones being tremor, stiffness or rigidity of the muscles and difficulty carrying out voluntary movements. These symptoms may be seen individually or in various combinations. Often they may be accompanied by one or more additional symptoms which are seen less often but occur often enough to be considered part of the overall picture of Parkinsonism.

Possible causes of Parkinsonism include some type of brain fever (encephalitis) caused by a virus infection with a twenty- to twenty-five-year dormant period before signs appear. How this development comes about is a mystery. Onset of Parkinsonism in the elderly has been attributed to hardening of the arteries with decreased blood supply to certain areas of the brain; however, it is just as likely that it may be produced by aging changes in certain brain cells. A small percentage of cases may follow injury to the nervous system by trauma, carbon monoxide poisoning, manganese and other metallic poisonings and intoxication with tranquilizing drugs over a period of time.

Most cases of Parkinsonism have no well-defined cause and are referred to as idiopathic Parkinsonism. Studies have shown degenerative changes in some cases. This form occurs most often in the sixth to eighth decades of life. The incidence in the two sexes is approximately equal. It is not usually considered to be an inherited disease. At the present time it is estimated that thirty-six thousand new cases of Parkinsonism occur annually in the United States. The overall incidence is about 1 percent of the population over the age of fifty years. This means that the condition is a major public health problem especially with the increasing numbers of people aged fifty years or older in North America.

The most common symptom is involuntary shaking or tremor which is usually present when the patient is at rest. It is a rhythmic, alternating tremor more prevalent in the hands. As the tremor progresses it may involve the arm, the feet and legs and at times the head and neck. While the tremor may be increased by excitement or emotional stress, it usually occurs with relaxation and quiet surroundings. It may build up in public places or in the presence of strangers. This is common and should not be considered reacting poorly to stress.

Stiffness or muscle rigidity is present in most cases of Parkinsonism and may be more incapacitating than tremor. There may be a feeling of lack of flexibility of the muscles causing a decrease in finger dexterity which may progress to board-like rigidity of the entire body. All movement is affected, arm swing will decrease and disappear, eating will be slower and facial expression will become blank. The expressionless face is characteristic and may be the first sign noted by the family.

Slowness and difficulty of movement (bradykinesia) along with a feeling of muscular weakness become troublesome for patients with walking difficulties developing. A leg may drag, steps become shorter, patients lean forward and may begin running, involuntarily. This phenomenon is called festination. At times the patient can't turn and feels as if his feet are rooted to the floor.

Parkinsonism sometimes causes the patient's handwriting to become smaller, with shaky lines caused by tremor. Minor symptoms may be related to vegetative nervous system dysfunction, e.g., excessive sweating, excessive salivation, increased oiliness of the skin, constipation and urinary difficulties in some males. Voice volume may be diminished, speech slowed with some slurring noted. Psychological reactions include depression, self-consciousness, and the patient may become reclusive and withdrawn. This reactive depression lifts as symptoms are relieved.

Treatment of Parkinsonism includes medical therapy, physical therapy, good dietary and hygienic habits and wholesome physical and social activity. Since the advent of effective drugs surgery is seldom used. The drug of choice is L-dihydroxyphenylalanine (L-dopa). L-dopa is transformed into dopamine after passage into the brain, alleviating the deficiency of natural dopamine in certain parts of the brain (substantia nigra and corpus striatum). Improvement includes a feeling of well-being, facial mobility, decrease in rigidity and bradykinesia and finally decrease in tremor. Up to 80 percent improvement has been attained compared to 20 percent before the advent of L-dopa. Sometimes, other of the earlier anti-Parkinson "anticholinergic" drugs may be used concurrently such as Artane, Kemadrin and Cogentin. Amantadine may be effective in combinations. Anyone taking L-dopa may have some side effects. If such unpleasant symptoms as nausea, dizziness, involuntary movements, feeling of extra heartbeats or mental disturbance occur they should be reported to one's physician. The proper doses and combinations should be determined by the physician. Many persons in all walks of life now function with great improvement over their previous state due to the current improved therapy.

CREDIT: *Calvin L. Calhoun, Sr., B.S., M.S., M.D., Professor of Neurology and Director, Division of Neurology, Meharry Medical College, Nashville, Tennessee.*

How to Improve Your Personality

Nobody goes through life wearing the same clothes day after day, year after year. Even the least clothes-conscious person glances in the mirror from time to time to check on appearance. Yet many people still "wear" the same personality they've had for years—the same mannerisms, the same responses, the same way of presenting themselves to the world. Unlike clothing, personalities don't wear out, but contrary to common belief, personalities can be changed, improved, updated, made more attractive and positive.

We all know men and women of whom it is always being said, "What a great personality!" And we know just as many of whom the opposite is true. But few take time out to inventory their own personality even knowing that a pleasing, positive, confident self-presentation is one of life's most valuable assets in terms of both personal and business success. A good personality rises out of a sound self-image. It builds confidence in one's ability to deal with others and has been the key to success for many.

There is no magic formula for improving your personality but there are concrete steps that can improve it dramatically and permanently.

First, take a long, close look at yourself. Make a list of what you consider your strong points and your weaknesses. Be honest and ask yourself if you have trouble relating to others. Do you make friends easily? Do people seek you out, or tend to avoid you?

Next, consider the following five steps that make for a pleasing personality:

(1) Voice: People react to the quality and tone of your voice. If it has a shrill or nasal sound, start working to change it immediately. Listen for irritating habits such as nervous laughter and compulsive phrases like "you know." Buy or borrow a tape recorder and listen to yourself. Wait till you're

in a conversational setting. Forget the machine is on. If what you hear upsets you, use the tape to practice making your voice pleasing.

(2) Posture: Walk as if you are proud of yourself. Sit, gesture, stand in front of a mirror until you like what you see. Eliminate the slouch. Don't sprawl when you sit. Kill off choppy, nervous gestures. Watch what you do with your hands. All this will make you self-conscious for a while, but that is the point.

(3) Poise: All the world likes a relaxed, interested person who seems to have time to listen. The person who talks too fast, swallows words, hops from foot to foot, glances at his watch, and seems harried and ill at ease gives a negative image. The unspoken message is: "He's letting me know he has better things to do than talk to me." There is also a verbal and mental pause which people with good personalities practice. It amounts to thinking before they speak. This takes practice, and it may slow you down a bit (usually a good thing, anyway), but thinking before you speak is as important as looking before you leap. A final filter installed just behind the vocal cords could improve the most offensive personality 100 percent.

(4) Tact: This means never hurting another person's feelings unnecessarily. Remember the times you've been made to feel uncomfortable or just plain hurt when someone passed a thoughtless remark and belittled you. Sensitivity to the other fellow's feelings can be acquired with practice. The rule "When in doubt, shut up" is a good one.

(5) Output: You are with yourself constantly. You are with others for periods of time which range from seconds to hours. Others experience you only in those periods. You may be thinking the kindest of thoughts about them but they will never know it if you don't say so or show it. Don't be a backslapper or an offensive spouter of phony compliments, but a good word, a smile, a nod, a genuine expression of concern or a deserved compliment can work wonders in the way your personality is perceived—and, strangely enough, the reaction will work wonders in making you feel better and more confident about yourself.

Finally, Dale Carnegie was in the business of teaching people how to "win friends and influence people" for a long time. His list of "Twelve Ways to Win People to Your Way of Thinking" can be used to improve personality and confidence as well:

(1) Avoid arguments.

(2) Never tell a person he/she is wrong; respect his/her opinion.

(3) If you are wrong, admit it quickly.

(4) Begin a discussion in a friendly way.

(5) Phrase your questions so people must answer yes.

(6) Let the other person do a great deal of the talking.

(7) Let the other person feel that the idea is his own.

(8) Try honestly to see things from the other person's point of view.

(9) Listen sympathetically to the ideas and desires of others.

(10) Appeal to the person's nobler motives.

(11) Dramatize your ideas.

(12) When nothing else works, throw down a challenge.

CREDIT: *Helen Robison, White Plains, New York. Adapted from* Mademoiselle *magazine.*

Perspiration

Perspiration is a normal process and fulfills an important and at times vital function. Its major purpose is to control the heat flow from the body and to contribute to the stability of the body temperature. If the body temperature exceeds the relatively narrow limits of 106° to 108° F., life is in danger, since a number of vital functions cannot be adequately carried out.

The skin acts as a radiator somewhat on the same principle as the radiator in an automobile. If the internal temperature is elevated either due to environmental heat from the outside or due to disease such as infections from the inside, the blood vessels just below the surface of the skin expand greatly to permit more blood to be brought to the skin surface in order to give off heat, and then return as cooler blood to the inside of the body. When the external temperature is high, the blood flowing through the skin cannot be adequately cooled by mere dissipation of heat to the outside. In order to increase the heat loss through the skin and thereby the cooling of the blood just under its surface, the body secretes a watery fluid. This perspiration or sweat evaporates on the skin surface. In rare instances some individuals are born with very few or no sweat glands. They are in grave danger when the body temperature is elevated, either in a hot climate or due to illness. Death may result from heatstroke. When sweating or evaporation of the perspiration is inadequate due to other causes in persons who have normally developed sweat glands, heatstroke, also with potentially fatal outcome, may occur.

Nevertheless, perspiration has social and psychological significance beyond its major biological function. The degree and type of perspiration is affected by a number of factors other than heat and cannot be controlled by the individual. Emotional factors and environmental circumstances can affect the amount and rate of flow of perspiration.

Three types of glands are responsible for perspiration. The most widely distributed type of gland, known as the eccrine sweat gland, is principally responsible for the secretion of fluid over the entire body surface. While the eccrine sweat glands are distributed all over the body surface, they are more numerous on the forehead, the palms of the hands, and the soles of the feet. The less common so-called apocrine sweat glands are less widely distributed and predominate in the armpits, around the nipple and in the area around the genitals and the anus.

While the eccrine sweat glands secrete a clear fluid, the apocrine glands secrete a more milky-appearing fluid. The third type of gland, the oil gland or sebaceous gland, which is not a sweat gland in the true sense, secretes fluid which mixes with the fluid secreted by the eccrine and the apocrine glands. As the temperature of the skin increases, the activity and thereby the flow of the oily secretions from the sebaceous gland is also increased and thus contributes to the total amount and quality of the perspiration.

The perspiration that poses personal psychological and social problems is the type that is excessive, particularly under nervous or emotional stress. This is called hyperhydrosis. It becomes a vicious cycle in that the perspiration causes embarrassment to the individual which in turn increases the state of nervousness thus resulting in more perspiration and consequently more embarrassment.

There is relatively little known of the mechanisms by which excessive perspiration is brought about and consequently even less is known about how to control or reduce it. From a practical point of view antiperspirants which usually contain aluminum chloride or other aluminum salts are reasonably effective. They act by blocking the outlets of the sweat glands and, at least temporarily, reduce the flow of the perspiration. Unfortunately, these preparations are not entirely effective, may act for a short time only, and cease to work altogether after variable periods of weeks, months and sometimes years of continued use. It is not known why they cease to be effective. It is also not known why, when they stop being effective, perspiration may become even more of a problem than it had been before. Apparently the quality of the perspiration fluid is changed in such a way that the aluminum complexes either do not form or do not form to an adequate degree to block the outlets of the glands or are being removed by the perspiration fluids.

There are several medications that can be taken by mouth which may reduce secretory activity of the sweat glands and the amount of perspiration. Some of these agents are derivatives of the belladonna alkaloids, such as atropine, or agents with atropine-like action. They have unpleasant and sometimes serious side effects and should be used only under the close supervision of a physician. As a rule, their use is not indicated except under unusual circumstances because of the possible hazards associated with the side effects. One of the common side effects of these agents is that it may interfere with the activity of other glands, such as the salivary glands, leading to dryness of the mouth and throat with uncomfortable and sometimes dangerous consequences.

Antiperspirants are available in many forms and under many brand names. Sufferers from excessive perspiration should be advised to try a number of these agents either as single preparations or a number of them in combination and be prepared to rotate their use when one agent or a combination of several begins to lose its effectiveness. One should be careful not to confuse antiperspirants with deodorants. While antiperspirants will reduce body odor, they should be labeled specifically as antiperspirants. Conversely, however, dcodorants as a rule do not reduce the flow or the amount of perspiration. They only reduce the odors resulting from the action of the bacteria on the perspiration.

Individuals plagued by excessive perspiration should consult a physician, preferably a dermatologist, who will be able to advise on the use of local antiperspirants and guide the administration of medication for the control of perspiration if and when indicated. Also, the physician may be able to reduce the nervous tension by prescribing tranquilizers or sedatives in addition to exploring the possibility of psychotherapy. A psychiatrist may be able to reduce the nervous or emotional elements as factors contributing to excessive perspiration or at least help the individual to accept the inevitable and live with it.

Finally, there are simple measures which may be taken such as dress shields (to protect against excessive underarm perspiration) and air conditioning or ceiling fans. A simple device which I advise when my patients are embarrassed by "clammy hands" is to carry absorbent materials such as tissue paper in their pockets, so that they can unobtrusively remove the fluid secreted. In severe cases, pretreatment of the absorbent material with aluminum chloride may serve the dual purpose of absorbing the perspiration from the palms or the forehead and at the same time deliver a fresh dose of antiperspirant to the involved area. Wearing of cotton gloves or their availability in the handbag or in the pockets of trousers or a dress or a sweater can be enormously helpful. In this connection, new types of pliable materials have been developed especially for the purpose of increased absorption and retention of perspiration. This can be a boon to those individuals who suffer from excessive perspiration.

CREDIT: *Edmund Klein, M.D., Research Professor, School of Medicine, State University of New York; Associate Chief of Dermatology, Roswell Park Memorial Institute, Buffalo, New York.*

Phobias

DEAR ANN LANDERS: I nearly laughed myself sick when I read the letter from the woman who was so clean she washed a banana before she ate it, even though she had peeled it herself.

Then I remembered a neighbor I had a few years back. She was even wackier. This woman used to cash her paycheck every Friday, bring the money home and wash it with soap and water and hang it in the bathroom to dry. She said money had germs on it and she didn't want to be responsible for anyone's illness.

It takes all kinds of people to make a world, doesn't it? LIVE AND LEARN

DEAR LIVE: It sure does. And the woman who washed the money so people wouldn't get sick had a sickness herself. It is called molysmophobia.

A phobia is an exaggerated, uncontrollable and sometimes disabling fear of perfectly natural situations or objects. According to Dr. Freud, phobias may be divided into two groups:

(1) A common (or normal) phobia, such as a fear of something that many people experience, in varying degrees.

Examples: fear of darkness, fear of being alone, fear of death, illness and old age.

(2) Unusual phobias that inspire no fear in the normal person.

Examples: A fear of falling into the toilet, a fear of certain colors, a fear of being buried alive, or a fear of calling someone by his given name.

Most phobics believe they are the only ones in the world who have their "special" fears. They cannot explain why they are afraid and are often too ashamed to reveal their fears, even to a doctor.

Phobics must be encouraged to talk openly about what bothers them. This can be done only in a climate of complete trust and tranquility. Fearful people need reassurance from family and friends that with proper outside help they can overcome their phobias.

The most common phobias, according to my mail, are the following:

Animals, bees, being alone, being stared at, blood, blushing, cancer, cats, choking, corpses, crowds, darkness, death, deformity, demons, dirt, dogs, dreams, elevators, enclosed space, flying, germs, height, horses, illness, insanity, insects, lightning, mice, nakedness, noise, pain, poverty, pregnancy, robbers, school, sexual intercourse, sleep, smothering, snakes, spiders, strangers, surgical operations, syphilis, thunder, travel, vomiting, work, and worms.

Here are some addresses that might be useful to phobics who would like help:

Look for Recovery, Inc., in your local phone book. If it is not listed, write to the National Headquarters. The address is:

Recovery Inc.
116 South Michigan
Chicago, Illinois

For private treatment in New York:

Institute for Behavior Therapy
354 E. 76th Street
New York, New York 10021

Behavior Therapy Center of New York
111 East 85th Street
New York, New York 10028

Hospital Treatment
White Plains Hospital Phobic Clinic
41 East Post Road
White Plains, New York 10601

Payne Whitney Clinic Behavioral Services
New York Hospital
525 East 68th Street
New York, New York 10021

Long Island Jewish Hospital at Hillside Phobia Clinic
New Hyde Park
New York, New York 11040

For private treatment in California:

Behavior Therapy Institute of Sausalito
Sausalito, California 94965

Behavioral Therapy Institute of Beverly Hills
Beverly Hills, California 90212

For private treatment in Chicago:

The Institute for Psychoanalysis
180 North Michigan
Chicago, Illinois 60601

Michael Reese Hospital and Institute for Psychosomatic and Psychiatric
    Research and Training
2959 South Ellis Avenue
Chicago, Illinois 60616

For addresses of other places to seek help, write to

The American Psychiatric Association
1700 18th Street, N.W.
Washington, D.C. 20009

CREDIT: *Ann Landers.*

Poisoning of Children

What is the number one poison to children? A twentieth-century miracle
drug? A potent new insecticide? Lead? Arsenic? No, it is aspirin, a medication so common that Americans take over seventeen billion tablets a year.

Fifty aspirin tablets can kill a two-year-old child. Every year 100,000 children are poisoned by aspirin. Of this number approximately 144 die.

HOW TO AVOID POISONING

If you have preschool children, remember they love to put everything in
their mouths. Mouthing is part of normal growth and a way of learning about
things. Toddlers will eat or drink anything. A child can drink a pint of
kerosene, without minding the taste.

If your child sucks or chews "on everything" provide him with safe chewa-
ble objects such as carrot or celery sticks.

Be aware that that "Candy flavored" aspirin can be dangerous. Unlike
other poisons such as ammonia or floor polishes, "candy" aspirin tastes good
and a child will not only eat it if it's lying around, but also search it out on

high shelves or in the medicine chest. When urging a feverish child to take baby aspirin, don't tell him it's "just like candy." Say it's "medicine."

If you have preschool children, be sure to store all potential poisons out of reach. Put your medicines away after using them. Most children get poisons from these four places:

(1) Under the sink or on kitchen shelves (polishes, cleaning agents).

(2) Bedside or living room table tops (medicines, lighter fluid).

(3) The bathroom (lotions, medicines).

(4) The basement, back porch or garage (insecticides, paint thinners).

Be particularly careful when you are moving or going on vacation. Medicines and other poisons are apt to be in different places.

Young children love to explore pocketbooks. If you carry pills in your pocketbook, be careful where you leave it.

WHAT IS POISONOUS?

Today there are over 250,000 potential poisons which you can buy in your neighborhood stores. Many poisonous substances in your home are not labeled "poison." They are particularly poisonous to children because their small bodies can't absorb as much as adults. If taken in large enough doses, anything can be poisonous, even milk. Poisoning really depends on the amount swallowed and the size of the person who swallows it, which is why children are so vulnerable.

Aspirin is by far the most common poison. The next nine most common are: insecticides (because parents frequently store insect killer concentrates in pop bottles), bleach, detergents and cleaning agents, furniture polish, kerosene, vitamin and iron pills and syrups, disinfectants (iodine, etc.), strong acids and alkalies (lye), and laxatives.

LYE AND PETROLEUM   If your child has swallowed any of the following substances DO NOT MAKE HIM VOMIT. (Lye may rupture the esophagus; kerosene may pass into the lungs and damage them.)

L—contains lye   K—contains kerosene

HOUSEHOLD ITEMS

ammonia	metal cleaner (K)
bleach	typewriter cleaner (K)
drain cleaner (L)	gun cleaner (K)
oven cleaner (L)	grease remover (L or K)
toilet bowl cleaner (L)	carbolic acid disinfectants
corn and wart remover (L)	strychnine rat poison
furniture polish (K)	

L—contains lye   K—contains kerosene

PAINT THINNERS AND FUEL OIL

turpentine (K)   lighter fluid (K)
paint thinner (K)   wood preservatives (K)
kerosene (K)   brush cleaner (L or K)
gasoline (K)

OTHER POISONS These substances are poisonous to children, but may
be vomited. If a child swallows any of these, call your doctor or hospital for
advice. He will probably ask you to make your child vomit.

HOUSEHOLD ITEMS

antifreeze   permanent wave solution
camphor   nail polish
arsenic rat poison   hair dye
D.D.T. insect poisons   perfume
denatured alcohol   liquor or beer
after shave lotion

MEDICINES

aspirin   iodine
"pep" drugs   eye medicine (atropine)
iron pills and syrup   heart medicines
reducing medicine   rheumatism medicine
some douche preparations   vitamins
sleeping drugs   paregoric
laxatives

SPECIAL POISONS

LEAD PAINT tastes like candy and is poisonous if swallowed in small
doses over a long period. Poisoning occurs because children chew on window
sills or other painted areas. If your child "chews on everything," check with
your doctor because lead poisoning must be treated before any symptoms appear.

BORIC ACID is not valuable for treating diaper rash or any common ailment. Poisoning occurs because it is mistaken for a baby's formula mix, or
used to treat diaper rash. DO NOT KEEP BORIC ACID IN THE HOUSE.

THE JEQUIRITY BEAN is a small, red bean with a black spot. Its inner
meat is highly poisonous. It is used in beads or decorations from the Carib-
bean, Mexico or South America. If you have any jequirity beans, flush them
down the toilet immediately.

VOMITING METHODS

(1) Give syrup of ipecac. Dose: 1 tablespoon (one to four years old).

(2) Give him a glass of milk, then put a blunt spoon handle down his throat while you hold him face down across your lap.

After he has vomited, have him drink milk and take him to the nearest doctor or hospital. If he doesn't vomit give him milk and take him to the hospital anyway. *Always take with you the bottle or box that contained the poison.*

SAFETY CHECK LIST

(1) Do you put all medicine (particularly candy aspirin and tranquilizers) safely away after using them?

(2) Do you read the label on medicine before you give any to your child?

(3) Do you keep all drugs, household chemicals and detergents on shelves where no food is stored?

(4) Do you throw away old containers that once held poison without reusing them?

(5) If you transfer drugs, pills or poisonous substances, do you label the new containers?

(6) Do you flush old medicines down the toilet instead of throwing them in the trash can?

(7) Do you tell children that aspirin is "medicine," not "candy"?

(8) Do you always give or take medicines with the lights on, never in the dark?

(9) Have you checked your jewelry to be sure you have no jequirity beans?

(10) Do you take extra precautions with poisons in times of illness or stress?

If you have answered no to any of these questions, make some changes. Your house may have other dangers.

Keep syrup of ipecac on hand at all times. It is available through a doctor's prescription.

CREDIT: Dangers to Children and Youth *by Jay Arena, Chief of Pediatrics, Duke University School of Medicine, Durham, North Carolina: Moore Publishing Company.*

Politics

(*As a Career*)

ADVICE TO A YOUNG POLITICIAN
(FROM BRITISH INTELLIGENCE)

(1) NEVER TELL A LIE.

(2) NEVER TELL THE WHOLE TRUTH.

(3) NEVER MISS A CHANCE TO GO TO THE BATHROOM.

(1) A FEW PEOPLE WILL BE FOR YOU . . . ALWAYS.

(2) A FEW PEOPLE WILL BE AGAINST YOU . . . ALWAYS.

(3) MOST PEOPLE DON'T GIVE A DAMN.

The framers of the Constitution left no doubt where the concentration of power was to be in our government.

"We, the People," they wrote. Not we the rich, or we the poor, or we the blacks, or we the whites, or we the politicians, or we the corporate executives, but "we, the People." There are no words more beautiful in our heritage than these.

Vast power is concentrated in this phrase, "We, the People." In it lies an enormous gift, a monumental challenge, and a charge to the citizens of this great land to make their government what it ought to be.

How will we secure the blessings of liberty for all Americans? How will we harness the resources of this land and put them to work for the common good? How will we guide our inefficient democracy towards the goals we share? The answer to all these questions is—you.

And whether you like it or not, the name of the game is politics. Dirty word though it is to some people, particularly after Watergate and other problems in recent years, politics is the way to get things done in our system of government.

It is the lifeblood of representative democracy. It is the vehicle of change. It is the means by which conflicts and competing interests can be resolved peacefully. It enables us to choose leaders who will represent and protect our rights and interests and to remove them when they fail.

But remember that we have no perfect people—no saints to make and administer the decisions adopted by a majority. Elected officials are human beings, with ample faults and strengths.

This, of course, is why the ultimate decisions must rest with all the people. We have no single sovereign in America, no one source of power, no final single arbiter. Every citizen must be that final judge and, in a sense, a politician.

So if you care about your government, if you care about your own future, get off the sidelines and participate. If you think politics is dirty—and if you're clean—get in there with your own brand of political soap and clean it up.

I learned politics at a young age from my father. I went with him to city council meetings, to county Democratic gatherings and to state party conventions. I learned that politics offers solid opportunities for public service. It can challenge the best that is in a man or a woman to work and help make this country, this world, a better place in which to live.

A major reason people often become discouraged about politics is because society's most difficult and important problems inevitably are solved through the political process. None of the issues that reach the President's desk are easy. Very few of the problems which are addressed in legislation passed by Congress are simple.

And almost all of these issues involve fundamental values of how people live, the justice which is available to them, the rules by which our economic system functions and the relationships between the United States and foreign nations.

But if young men and women are seeking a real challenge, if they want to do things with their lives that matter, then a career in politics and government has a potential that cannot be matched in any other endeavor.

While there are great frustrations and disappointments along the way—and I have known both—the rewards are also great.

Because we are engaged with problems of the moment, we often forget how much is accomplished through politics. Many young people today literally know nothing of the civil rights problems which plagued our country until the mid-1960s.

Black Americans living or traveling in the South were forbidden, by law, from eating in white-only restaurants, from sleeping in white-only hotels and motels; they could not play or relax in tax-supported white-only parks and playgrounds.

In many states blacks found it nearly impossible to register and vote. Only the most exceptional blacks could get meaningful and satisfying jobs. And even though the Supreme Court outlawed segregated education in 1954, educational opportunities for white and black children were grossly unequal.

Today problems of overt discrimination and segregation based on race are relegated to the history books. To be sure, problems of unequal opportunity still exist in America, but segregated restaurants, hotels, parks and swimming pools have disappeared. Blacks vote, and their political decisions often decide elections. Job opportunities for blacks improve every year. Today black students have a much better chance to obtain a meaningful public education.

Positive action through political action can bring results. The Civil Rights Act of 1964 and the Voting Rights Act of 1965, both of which I helped guide through Congress, achieved their goals to a degree that exceeded our most optimistic hopes.

Dr. Martin Luther King, Jr., and countless others, both black and white, worked decades to achieve the results. Some even gave their lives to this cause. But they accomplished, through politics, what they set out to do. And our country is far better because of it. There are few material rewards, if any, that can match such accomplishments.

The most distinguishing mark of American character since the first colonists arrived on this continent has been a profound faith in progress, in our ability to create a better life for ourselves and for future generations. Our progress as a nation has been a constant process of becoming, of constant motion and growth, of evolving aspirations and ideals.

What was declared in 1776 was not the fullness of American freedom, but the privilege of laboring for its fulfillment—and that task will never be finished. Each generation has its own summons to the cause of life, liberty and the pursuit of happiness.

The record of America in the last two hundred years reflects the gradual evolution of individual liberty, an idea that was revolutionary at its birth and remains so today.

The American dream is a metaphor for the creation of a truly open society. Such a society is one in which men and women are free to develop their talents and pursue their dreams. It is one that is free of the nightmares that have haunted generations of mankind—hunger, disease, ignorance, fear, racial prejudice, slavery and political oppression and religious persecution.

Instead, the open society is based on the idea, set forth in our Declaration of Independence, of the inherent dignity of man, endowed by our creator with a soul and with certain rights that cannot be taken away. This emphasis on the dignity and rights of man gives sense and reason to the system of the government we call democracy. Without it, men and women become pawns to be manipulated and controlled, rather than humans to be respected as democracy requires.

Like our forebears, we must be willing to experiment, to risk failure and to bear the consequences of our mistakes, both past and yet to come. We must be prepared to do the things we ought to do, because they are right. We must be willing to make some sacrifices now in order to protect and preserve what we most cherish in American life for the benefit of future generations.

We must accept the burdens of leadership as the strongest nation of the free world and set a good example of adhering to our principles both at home and abroad. We must accept responsibility for our actions, both as individuals and as a nation. We must continue to chart our progress by the liberation of the human spirit and to work for its fulfillment.

We live by hope. We do not always get all we want when we want it, but we have to believe that someday, somehow, someway it will be better and that we can make it so.

You cannot tell a poor boy from a small country town on the plains of South Dakota who has had the opportunity to be a teacher, a mayor, a senator and Vice President that America is not a nation of promise.

You cannot tell a people whose ancestors were a handful of pioneers settling in a new land, and descendants who have forged the most prosperous and successful democracy in history, that America is not a country of hope, promise and opportunity.

So, as you look to your individual futures and to our collective futures, keep in mind the wise advice of Victor Hugo.

"The future has many names," he said. "For the weak, it is the impossible. For the fainthearted, it is the unknown. For the thoughtful and the valiant, it is ideal. The challenge is urgent, the task is large, the time is now."

Go to it!

CREDIT: *This essay was prepared especially for the encyclopedia by the late Honorable Senator Hubert H. Humphrey, Democrat of Minnesota.*

Population

Or Where Is Everybody?

According to the 1975 edition of the United Nations Demographic Year Book, the population of the world is 3.968 billion. This means there will soon be 4 billion people in the world. The population is doubling every thirty-seven years.

2.256 billion people live in Asia.

473 million in Europe.

401 million in Africa.

324 million in Latin America.

255 million in the Soviet Union.

237 million in North America.

21.3 million in the South Sea Islands.

Shanghai is the world's largest city—10.8 million people.

Tokyo—8.06 million.

Mexico City—8.5 million.
New York—7.6 million.
Peking—7.5 million.
London—7.2 million.
Moscow—6.9 million.

Sweden has the lowest infant mortality rate—8.3 per 1,000 births—followed by Iceland, Denmark, France, Switzerland, Spain, Singapore, Luxembourg and Canada. The United States ranks 20th, with 16.7 deaths for every 1,000 live births.

As regards longevity, women in Sweden enjoy the longest life expectancy —77.6 years—with 13 other countries reporting female life expectancy at birth to be over 75. Among them are Norway, France, the Netherlands, Canada, Japan, Denmark, the United States (76.4), England and Wales.

Sweden reports the life expectancy of its men at 72.1 years, ranking No. 1 in the world. The life expectancy of U.S. males is 68.5 years.

CREDIT: Parade *magazine, April 10, 1977.*

Pornography

According to Webster's Third International Unabridged Dictionary, pornography is "art or literature that panders to man's basest appetites and desires. It depicts the lewd, licentious and obscene."

And this is where the problem lies. The 1970 American Commission on Obscenity was surprised to discover that no federal statute prohibiting "obscene" material ever defined the term.

In 1964 Justice Stewart Potter of the U. S. Supreme Court came up with what I consider the best definition yet. He said, "I know it when I see it."

It is generally agreed that pornography applies to pictures, magazines or movies that show nudity or sexual activity in a manner that violates contemporary standards of propriety. Yet no lawyer, judge, clergyman, artist, critic or vice-squad officer has ever been able to describe those "contemporary standards" in a way that satisfies society at large.

While the experts agree that the idea behind pornography is to excite people, they cannot agree on whether the results of this excitement are good or bad. What you and I consider pornographic, may be viewed as "real" and "honest" to the educated young. Each generation shapes its own moral sense of the community. Change is inherent in every civilized society.

The present generation's avant-garde has opted to take sex out of the bedroom and put it on the coffee table. Photographs of every conceivable variety of kinky sex can be purchased at almost any bookstore and newsstand in the country.

Will this lead to decadence, rape and the collapse of morality? There is no evidence to support those charges. I have always believed that censorship eventually leads to problems far worse than the damage done by pornography—if indeed any damage is done by it at all. The violence on TV and in the films and the live war scenes from Vietnam viewed by millions of Americans on the six o'clock news was, in my view, far more obscene than anything for sale in the bawdiest bookstore.

Adults should be free to decide for themselves what movies they want to see, what magazines and books they want to read and what kind of pictures they want to look at. This is what a democratic society is all about.

I would like to make it clear that I do not consider "kid porn" (photographs of children between the ages of six and sixteen) pornography. This is child abuse. I have seen some of this material—little girls and boys, posing in lewd positions, both alone and with other children—or worse yet, engaging in sex acts with adult men and women. I am in favor of harsh criminal action against anyone involved in this activity. All such photographs should be considered illegal.

Parents who permit their children to pose in this manner should be taken into custody and put under psychiatric treatment. They are ill.

The forbidden has always been immensely appealing. The sure way to get people to want something is to tell them they can't have it. And so it is with pornography. I am in favor of making the rotten (and boring) junk available to any adult who is foolish enough to throw away his money on it. After a while, in America, as in the Scandinavian countries, it will sit on the shelves and they won't be able to give it away.

CREDIT: *Ann Landers.*

PIOUS PORNOGRAPHER

DEAR ANN LANDERS: Recently a dearly loved, much-admired and respected man died. He was an ideal husband and father, a community leader, financially successful and the sort of person everyone looked up to. After his death, his wife and adult children went through his personal belongings—together. What they found was shattering and heartbreaking. They discovered a collection of pornographic magazines and books, stacks of obscene pictures and a suitcase filled with stag movies.

The family is crushed. They now feel his life was a sham—that he was a hypocrite. No one can understand it. How could a person have kept his true character so completely hidden from those who were so close to him? A prurient interest in sex is as unlike this man as night is from day. Please explain. STUNNED IN CONNECTICUT

DEAR STUNNED: It is not unusual for a person to have a private, kooky compartment in his life—ranging from the slightly offbeat to the wildly bizarre. This needn't mean the person was evil or sinister. It merely means that, in THIS particular area, he had strudel in his noodle.

SHE SHOULD HAVE KEPT HER HOT HANDS OFF

DEAR READERS: Pass the humble pie, or the crow, or whatever you want to call it. Ann Landers has her fork ready. There's nothing like 54,000,000 daily readers to keep a girl on her toes.

Every now and then I reverse my advice, usually because the readers have persuaded me I was wrong. And so it was in the case of the mother who found a collection of nude pictures in a box under her son's bed. She wrote to say she had cured her 17-year-old son by pasting the nudes on the living room wall and shaming him. "That," she crowed, "ended his career as an art collector."

I thought it was ingenious and amusing, and I said so. Hundreds of readers let me know it wasn't funny. Hundreds more said it was a destructive thing to do to a 17-year-old boy. They said the lad's behavior was normal, and Mom should have kept her hot little hands off the pictures and said nothing.

The following letter is a fairly representative example of what made me change my advice.

DEAR ANN LANDERS: The mother who discovered pictures of nudes under her son's bed and plastered them on the living room wall was guilty of a cruel and insensitive act. Your applauding her left me disappointed and mystified. I have read your column for several years and I know you are not a cruel and insensitive woman. I can only conclude that you were unthinking in this instance.

It is not easy for a boy to deal with adolescent sex drives. Add to this the problem of a mother who makes him feel guilty and you have a very mixed-up kid.

Here is a mother who, while snooping no doubt, seized on what she thought was a challenge—in the form of "other women." She then displayed her find in a manner calculated to increase his guilt and bare his most secret emotions. Because the boy was embarrassed and tore the pictures down, she thought she had taught him something and "won a victory."

All she did was fill the boy with resentment for her lack of consideration for his private feelings.

Too bad you didn't tell the mother, and ALL mothers, that collecting girlie pictures is not uncommon, that such pictures are a source of stimulation for immature males and when the boy grows up to be a man he no longer needs his paper dolls. BEEN THERE.

DEAR BEEN: Thank you for setting me straight. You, of course, are right, and I appreciate your letter.

Posture

What is it? Posture is the relative position of the movable parts of the body. Good posture depends on the correct alignment of these parts, or the way you hold yourself. This has a tremendous effect on your figure, your health and the impression you make on others.

How to test posture: Stand in front of a full-length mirror, in the nude, and look at yourself sideview. A hand mirror should be used. Do your hips swing out in the back, or does your abdomen protrude? Do your ribs sink down and in? Do your shoulders round, or does your chin jut forward? Any one of these is a sign that you are not posture-perfect. Also imagine a straight line drawn from the middle of the ear down to the floor. It should pass through shoulder, hip, knee and end over the front of your foot.

What to do: Most people never think about how they hold themselves and therefore have no defense against the downward pull of gravity and fatigue. It is of prime importance to learn how the body should stack up and to get the feeling of correct posture. Then you can check many times during the day on the way you carry yourself.

Poor posture cannot always be corrected immediately. For instance, if shoulders have been rounded for a long time, the chest muscles will have shortened and the back shoulder muscles will have stretched and weakened. If the condition is extreme, the chest muscles must be stretched and the shoulder muscles strengthened with exercise before good posture is possible. If the abdominal muscles have protruded habitually they may be too weak to pull the abdomen in and hold it there. Abdominal exercises will be necessary. Here is one of the best: Pull the abdominal muscles in toward your backbone as far as possible and hold the contraction for a slow count of six. Do this several times during the day.

Try to do this: Stand with feet pointing forward, weight evenly divided. Pull your abdominal muscles in and *up* and tuck your hips under. Lift your rib cage and straighten your spine all the way. Shoulders should be down and back but be *sure* they are relaxed. The knees should also be relaxed. The chin should not protrude forward or duck into the neck. Hold it parallel to the floor. Feel as though you are pushing gently toward the ceiling with the *top* of your head. Body weight should be forward, not back over the heels.

When walking, assume the same posture and swing the legs straight forward from the hips, not from side to side. Knees should not be hyperextended at the end of each step. When sitting, the hips should touch the back of the chair and the spine should be straight. If it is necessary to lean forward toward a desk or bench, lean from the waist. Do not round the shoulders.

Effects of posture on figure: Fat and bones and muscles make up the figure, but habits in posture are constantly molding it into the shape it becomes. Poor posture can cause a double chin, creases in the neck, a dowager's hump (the bump at the back of the neck), spinal curvature, swayback, round shoulders and a protruding abdomen. It can thicken the waist and take inches from the bust measurement. Exercises for a spinal curvature should be prescribed and supervised by an orthopedist.

The effects of poor posture on health and figure are slow, treacherous and far-reaching. For this reason, training should be started early in life, at school and at home. By teenage the shadow of things to come in maturity are often plainly visible. Children and young people should be taught not to slump in chairs, or stand with the weight on one foot and the opposite hip thrust forward. They should not always carry school supplies with the same hand or slung over the same shoulder. Alternate.

Effects of posture on health: Incorrect posture can damage one's health. It makes the work of the heart more difficult and decreases our intake of oxygen because it crowds the heart and lungs. It does not provide adequate support for other organs and causes prolapsus (downward slump of internal organs). This can lead to chronic fatigue, indigestion and constipation. The majority of backaches are due to weak muscles and poor posture. Improved posture means improved health.

How your posture impresses others: Nothing creates such an aura of youthfulness as good posture. Wrinkles and gray hair lose their impact when the spine is straight, the chin is up and the walk is lively.

One's mental attitude, his feelings about himself and others are often reflected in posture. Round shoulders and dragging feet, head ducked and eyes fixed on the ground, bespeak a lack of self-confidence and pessimism. Head up, ribs lifted and spine straight, say, "Hello, I'm glad to be alive and going places."

CREDIT: *Josephine Lowman, author of the column "Why Grow Old?", Des Moines Register and Tribune Syndicate.*

Pregnancy

The Last Month

The last month of pregnancy can be very trying. There are psychological, physical and social stresses which come to bear on the pregnant woman.

As the end of pregnancy approaches, concern about the outcome increases. "When will this pregnancy end?" "Will I be okay?" "Will the baby be normal?" "Will I suffer?" Even such frightening thoughts as "Will I die?" or "Will the baby die?" creep into the woman's mind. These concerns are normal. Every woman in this day and age is exposed to obstetrical horror stories by friends, radio, TV and the press. Since she can't close herself off from the rest of the world, the pregnant woman must endure and worry.

A calm discussion with the obstetrician can do much to relieve a woman's anxieties. Often she will learn that her fears are normal. The vast majority of pregnancies turn out well for both mother and infant. Defusing a potentially frightening experience can be extremely helpful. Knowledge of what to expect can go a long way towards alleviating fear.

Added to a woman's emotional burdens as the pregnancy nears its end are the persistent inquiries about her condition, her size and her due date by well-intentioned family, friends, neighbors, sales clerks, fellow workers, etc. Ultimately, these solicitous inquiries make the woman feel as though something might be wrong, and that the pregnancy will never end. One thing is certain: all pregnancies do end! Only 10 percent (one in ten) of pregnancies last more than two weeks past term. Only elephants carry a pregnancy for two years. In some cases, being overdue merely means a miscalculation of dates. In other cases, being overdue means that baby is being well nourished in utero and will continue to grow and gain weight. Rarely, the placenta (afterbirth) may age, resulting in a lack of nourishment of the fetus which may be harmful. Modern obstetrical care includes techniques for monitoring the effects of being overdue and taking corrective measures when necessary.

As the pregnancy progresses, the increasing size of the uterus adds to a woman's physical discomfort. She becomes big and bulky, as a result of which she feels clumsy and unattractive. Swelling of the legs is common due to pressure on the pelvic veins, gravity, and fluid retention. This is a normal phenomenon. Formerly, the swelling was thought to be indicative of the beginning of toxemia of pregnancy and was vigorously treated with diuretic agents (water pills). Now, it is recognized that edema (swelling of the legs) is not necessarily bad, and that the potential disadvantages of diuretic pills outweigh the advantages. To eliminate troublesome swelling, the simplest and most effective method is to stay in bed, off the feet, for twenty-four hours. While lying in bed, for physiological reasons, it is best to lie on one's side rather than flat on one's back.

Since the large uterus presses the stomach up under the diaphragm, eating large meals may cause discomfort. Part of the stomach may actually be pushed through the diaphragm (hiatus hernia), causing regurgitation of acid which results in heartburn. This is aggravated when the woman goes to bed since when she lies down, the uterus can push the stomach through the diaphragm more easily. Relief can be obtained by taking non-sodium-containing antacids (consult your doctor first). Sometimes sleeping propped up on cushions helps.

Perhaps the most frequent discomforts of late pregnancy are due to the pressure of the baby's head on the inlet of the pelvis. This generally causes sensations of pressure on the bowel and bladder in addition to aching in the lower abdomen and upper thighs. It is a normal phenomenon of late pregnancy.

In most cities (and certainly in rural areas) many women live some distance from the hospital. This poses the question of when to notify the obstetrician and start out for the hospital. Although no general rules can apply for everyone, the following will apply for most women: If there is a question about what to do, call your doctor. Remember, it is better to have gone to the hospital for a false alarm than not to have been there in time for the delivery.

Since many obstetricians now do internal examinations to evaluate the condition of the cervix (mouth of the womb), your doctor may tell you just how quickly you should head for the hospital.

In general, you should call if the water bag breaks, if there is vaginal bleeding or regular uterine contractions. In the latter part of pregnancy, women frequently have painless contractions (Braxton-Hicks contractions) which can be described only as a tightening sensation of the uterus. Real labor pains are generally regular in frequency and become more and more intense as time passes.

Facing labor for the first time, you will hear all sorts of horror stories, but face it with confidence. Remember, for hundreds of thousands of years, the human race has been reproducing successfully. Under all sorts of conditions, in all climates, women have successfully borne and delivered normal children. Why not you?

CREDIT: *Allan G. Charles, M.D., attending physician, Obstetrics/Gynecology, Michael Reese Hospital. Clinical Professor, Obstetrics/Gynecology, Pritzker School of Medicine, University of Chicago.*

Pregnancy Test

A new blood-serum test that can detect pregnancy as early as ten days after conception is gaining popularity.

The Biocept-G test (or RRA for radio-receptor assay) measures the amount of a hormone called Human Chorionic Gonadotrophin (HCG), which is released when conception occurs. The test provides diagnosis of pregnancy much earlier than the conventional urine test, which generally isn't reliable until twenty-five to thirty days after conception.

Chicago obstetrician-gynecologist Dr. Leon Carrow says the new test is an important medical find because it is more accurate than older tests (it is more sensitive to the patient's HCG hormones), as well as permitting earlier detection of pregnancy.

The test, developed by Birj B. Sexana, Professor of Endocrinology at Cornell University, involves taking a small amount of blood from a patient's arm. The blood serum is added to a test tube containing part of the ovary membrane from a cow and purified HCG with radioactive iodine that can be measured with a gamma counter. Then the mixture is incubated.

If the patient is pregnant, her own HCG molecules will adhere to the membrane, displacing some of the radioactive HCG already present. If the patient is not pregnant, she will not produce HCG, and only the original hormone will be present on the membrane.

Doctors who support use of the new test say it gives pregnant women the opportunity for earlier medical treatment. By indicating hormonal levels, the test also can give early warning of abnormalities such as ectopic pregnancy (which develops outside the uterus) and the woman can be told to expect a miscarriage.

CREDIT: *Ann Landers.*

Sexual Behavior During Pregnancy

Sexual intimacy is an important part of the total lives of most couples. The need for this intimacy does not diminish for either partner during pregnancy or right after delivery, but the woman's sexual interest and responsiveness may decrease somewhat.

Two common questions women ask about sex and pregnancy are:

(1) When is it all right to have intercourse while I'm pregnant?

(2) How can I keep my husband happy and sexually satisfied while I'm pregnant?

There is no simple answer to the first question. Some obstetricians permit intercourse at any time during pregnancy until labor begins, so long as it is comfortable and acceptable to both partners, no uterine bleeding is occurring and the membranes have not ruptured. Before making a decision about her own sexual behavior during pregnancy, a woman should discuss the situation with her partner and her physician. An exploration of new coital positions may be appropriate at this time, if the couple's usual positions are uncomfortable. There are some conditions, such as habitual abortion, that may necessitate limiting sexual activity.

A recent study involved interviews with women who were admitted to the hospital in labor. They were asked when they last had intercourse. The majority had their last contact within one week prior to labor, a small percentage stopped six weeks prior to labor. Our thinking has changed, and intercourse is allowed up until the last two weeks—the reason for this prohibition is that the baby's head is low in the pelvis at that time and there is a mechanical difficulty.

A few doctors still ask all women, regardless of their condition, to refrain from intercourse during the last two or three months of pregnancy. Many couples fail to follow this advice, which often leads to feelings of guilt and fear that their sexual activity might harm the baby. These feelings are unnecessary since, according to recent findings, there is no medical reason for severe restrictions of sexual activity.

Intercourse is allowed six weeks after delivery except where no episiotomy is involved—in that case four weeks is recommended. (An episiotomy is an incision made to ease the baby's passage through the vagina.)

There is a story of the father of his firstborn asking a father who just had his sixth baby, "How soon after delivery is intercourse allowed?" The second father replied, "Is she in a private room or a ward?"

Since pregnancy can occur again before the first menstrual period following delivery, a decision on contraception should be made before resuming intercourse.

Many women become concerned about keeping their husbands sexually satisfied, especially during later stages of pregnancy. The romantic notion is that the relationship of expectant parents becomes increasingly warm and close as the day for baby's birth grows nearer. This may be the case in some relationships, but by no means in all.

Masters and Johnson found that the majority of men interviewed did not understand or agree with the prohibitions placed on sexual activity by physicians. Many thought their wives invented the story as an excuse for avoiding sex, and several men reported having extramarital affairs during their wives' pregnancies.

If the physician recommends abstinence or restraint in sexual activity for a certain length of time before or after delivery, the condition should be explained to both husband and wife, thus avoiding unnecessary strain on their relationship. The couple should also be encouraged and possibly helped to communicate openly with each other about their sexual feelings and desires. Alternative forms of sexual gratification can be recommended. Oral-genital sex and manual stimulation can be satisfying and rewarding without physiological ill effect.

CREDIT: *John S. Long, M.D., American Board of Obstetricians and Gynecologists, F.A.C.S., F.A.C.O.G.; Associate Professor of Obstetrics and Gynecology at Rush-Presbyterian-St. Luke's Hospital; attending obstetrician-gynecologist at Rush-Presbyterian-St. Luke's Hospital, Chicago.*

Premature Ejaculation

Premature ejaculation is defined by Masters and Johnson as the inability to delay ejaculation long enough for a regularly orgasmic female to achieve orgasm 50 percent of the time. Hurried or clandestine sexual experiences are often evident in the history of these men. To avoid being "caught" in their youth, they learned to ejaculate quickly in cars, on couches, etc. Later in life, when getting caught was no longer a hazard, these men discovered they were unable to delay ejaculation.

Obviously, a man experiencing premature ejaculation or other problems in sexual functioning should check out his health first. He should also consult with his physician regarding any prescribed drugs he may be taking on a regular basis. Some drugs used to treat illnesses, certain tranquilizers, along with alcohol and heavy smoking have been known to decrease sexual desires and performance. After having been checked out by a physician and given a clean bill of health, behavioral therapy is the treatment of choice. Hormone therapy and chemotherapy in the treatment of ejaculatory incompetence have generally been unsuccessful and often obscure or have nothing to do with the relationship problems within the marriage. In essence, the treatment of premature ejaculation involves more than a shot of hormones and a reassuring pat on the back.

There is no absolute scale against which to evaluate male performance. Obviously the male must maintain an erection long enough to reach climax. Beyond this it is difficult to judge prematurity in anything other than a relative way, and within the particular interpersonal relationship

Men are physically able to achieve orgasm within two minutes following insertion and most of our mammalian cousins are even quicker. Although it is impossible to set exact time limits to define normal sexual functioning, a significant number of men and their partners complain of inability to delay ejaculation until some degree of mutual enjoyment has been achieved.

When orgasm occurs before penetration, the whole aim of intercourse may seem lost. The feelings of inadequacy, loss of masculinity, as well as the partner's frustration, can create a vicious circle that sets up both partners for failure in the future.

Rather than recognizing that adequate sexual interaction takes time, practice and awareness of each other's needs and responses, the couple may blame themselves or each other for their lack of adequate performance. Instead of enjoying *what* they are doing together, such a couple concentrate on *how* they are doing. The sexual interaction thus becomes a deadly serious game, with both partners keeping score.

Chronic, premature ejaculation can produce serious marital conflicts. It is readily and successfully treatable, but sadly enough, few couples, and especially males, seek therapy. Shame, guilt, anger and marital conflicts secondary to the sexual dysfunction often hamper the couple in honestly seeking help. Medical care stressing physical dysfunction and often treating the male via hormones can further complicate the problem.

Using the term "premature ejaculation" to denote occasional instances, often caused by fatigue or tension, when the man "comes" sooner than the woman wishes, should be avoided. Belittling comments can increase anxiety and feelings of inadequacy.

Behavioral treatment is simple and successful (80 percent success, in most cases). Apart from joint counseling of husband and wife, specific procedures developed by Semens, and elaborated by Masters and Johnson, may be included. This involved preventing the ejaculation by pressure on the penis, followed by a return to foreplay or reinsertion (the so-called "squeeze technique"). Following reinsertion, there is a gradual increase in the male's activity so that he may slowly experience and grow accustomed to the stimuli present. Should he then approach ejaculation, withdrawal and squeezing is again instituted, until greater confidence and "staying power" is developed. By means of successive approximations then, the male is trained to maintain erection without ejaculation for increasing periods of time.

The first point demonstrated by these details is that treatment is direct relearning. The second is that therapy can only take place in an honest, open and supportive interpersonal relationship involving both husband and wife. Like dancing, sexual interaction is complex and requires mutual understanding of the other person's feelings, responses and movements.

All males experience at some point in their lives, or in some intimate relationship, premature ejaculation. It is sometimes called "buck fever" . . . getting ahead of one's self or one's partner, passion or inexperience. Given the patience, concern and commitment that often accompany love, most males do learn that "nice guys finish last" . . . or preferably . . . "together."

CREDIT: *Henry F. Gromoll, Ph.D., Department of Behavioral Sciences, Millikin University, Decatur, Illinois.*

Procrastination

> "The tide is running,
> The sails are set straight,
> You've dallied your hour
> So fish or cut bait."

If to forgive is divine, then to delay is human. It is a universal trait attested to by the Latino's "mañana" and to the Puritan's framed needlepoint maxim: "Never put off till tomorrow what can be done today."

Most of these sayings equate delay with plain old-fashioned laziness. But in our experience, much true procrastination is not the fruit of sheer sloth so much as it is of indecisiveness born of fear or uncertainty of outcome. Another cause is ignorance or confusion about how to set about doing what needs to be done. Complexity, awkwardness, unpleasantness associated with the deferred task accounts for delay, as well.

Most of us carry around a mental notebook, the last page of which is filled with a list of things we've been meaning to do, we should do and eventually know we must do, and somehow never quite get around to doing for one reason or another.

It may be something as simple as putting off painting the garage because you hate working on ladders, or it may be avoidance of an overdue physical exam because you fear the results. Whatever, we tend to put certain things on the back burner.

Unless it becomes an all-encompassing way of dealing with life—when there are more things added on the back burner than get done in the course of a week—there is nothing sinister about procrastination in and of itself. Sometimes, in fact, delay is a form of prudence. Circumstances change or problems solve themselves. What is dangerous about becoming a habitual procrastinator is the gradual diminishment of all priorities to the least common denominator where all things deferred seem of equal importance—or lack of it.

This can cause problems and pain. The unpainted garage will probably survive another winter but a delay in making out that will may cause countless hardships for your family. The reconciliation, too painful to confront today, may come too late to save a friendship (or a marriage).

The way to beat procrastination is to get at what is causing you to delay and label it honestly for what it is—fear of inability to do the job well, a dislike for the job, not understanding the job or hostility against someone who requests the job done. Once you understand why you are procrastinating you may be surprised at how quickly you handle the priority items on that cluttered back burner, and how much better you'll feel when you do.

CREDIT: *Joel Wells, Editor of* The Critic. *From the newsletter* You *published by the Thomas More Association, Chicago, Illinois.*

Promiscuity

The psychiatric definition of promiscuity is "indiscriminate, casual sexual encounters, high frequency of sexual relationships with a large number of partners . . ."

This definition should be kept in mind because the word promiscuity is often used loosely, particularly by parents who have yet to adjust to the new sexual freedom of the current generation. Sexual promiscuity is often the result when a person lacks self-esteem or feels rejected. It is not abnormal sexual behavior by oversexed girls as is commonly thought.

If one were to describe the classic sexually promiscuous boy or girl, man or woman, homosexual or heterosexual, one would point to a person who is sleeping around, going in for one-night stands in a compulsive search to satisfy some inner need. Unfortunately, most one-night stands are not sexually or emotionally gratifying since there is no romantic investment either by the partner who precipitated the encounter or by the object of the search. As a result, the longing for fulfillment is not satisfied nor will it ever be in these body-oriented rather than feeling-oriented people.

We need not concern ourselves here with transient promiscuity, which is usually either a manifestation or an early sign of emotional illness, such as depression or severe neuroses. Hysterics or individuals with a high level of frustration from a number of causes often use sexual promiscuity to give them a sense of well-being and gratification despite the fact that they are almost always short-lived. Ultimately, one way or another, usually because their needs are not fulfilled, and their level of frustration increases, they end up seeking therapy.

Our concern here is primarily with the teenager or the young adult and how parents cope with what seems to them to be an unresolvable problem.

First, parents should realize that promiscuous behavior, as with other unacceptable behavior, which is repeated time after time, must indicate some deep need. This emotional deprivation may be a result of a lack of communication between parents and son or daughter. It is essential that parents be aware of this failing in themselves, painful as it is to acknowledge.

Once you make an effort to establish communication, both verbally and non-verbally, you have overcome the first hurdle.

Remember to be careful not to set boundaries and rules that cannot be enforced. Talk to your child, but don't show anger or call names. This leads only to hurt feelings and frustration. Refrain from saying things that might make a child afraid—such as the dire consequences if he, or she, doesn't shape up. Appeal to his or her rational and better self. It is amazing how often acting-out can be helpful if it ends in talking-out.

Patience, understanding, a non-judgmental attitude and, most important, your time are what the child needs. Offer this four-way therapeutic approach and the searching for emotional fulfillment will *gradually* pay off and the child's self-esteem will be raised. Note that the word "gradually" is underscored. Don't expect a complete reversal of behavior because you've had one heart-to-heart talk. You must establish a feeling of trust over a period of time, so that your child will come to believe that you love her or him regardless of what he or she has done. Remember the child who is least "lovable" needs love the most.

You will find that what the child needs is not sex, but a feeling of personal worth. So many young girls—twelve, thirteen, fourteen—in search of the male attention that they desperately desire from their fathers, end up in the arms (and the beds) of young boys—or older men.

Promiscuous husbands or wives in some strange way have the same problem. They mistake sex for love and try to substitute one for the other. They want to be held by a man (or woman), to feel the closeness of another person. If parents didn't cuddle their children when they were little, they grow up emotionally deprived.

Such a person rarely receives sexual gratification and almost always there is no emotional investment when he or she has sex with the spouse. In the case of the promiscuous married woman, there may be more anger than confusion. Her catting around may be to punish her husband for ignoring her or treating her more like a thing than a person.

As in the case of the promiscuous child, the spouse should give himself or herself a month or two to find out the reasons for the other's behavior. There is no substitute for a good, heart-to-heart talk. If all else fails, the couple should consult a family therapist or marriage counselor.

In the case of the child, the action is more complex. An appointment with a psychotherapist may be viewed by the child as punishment for wrongdoing. Outside therapy should never be forced on a child. If it is, you are wasting your child's time, the therapist's time and your money. It should be resorted to only if the child realizes his or her life is not going in the direction he wants it to go. If the child is unhappy (and promiscuous children *are*) they will almost invariably welcome the opportunity to discuss the problem with a "mediator" with whom he or she can communicate freely. Then, and only then will genuine progress be made.

CREDIT: *Shervert H. Frazier, M.D., Psychiatrist-in-Chief, McLean Hospital, Belmont, Massachusetts, Professor of Psychiatry, Harvard Medical School.*

Prostitution

Like everything else in our society, prostitution ain't what it used to be. There is a strong possibility that the reason for this is that amateurs have ruined it for the professionals.

While most of the twenty-dollar hookers are still as busy as they want to be in the large cities, their clientele is vastly different from that of the call girl who charges $100 an hour—and up.

Dr. Sam Janus, Clinical Assistant Professor of Psychiatry at New York Medical College, in his book *A Sexual Profile of Men in Power* (written with the help of psychiatrist Dr. Barbara Bess and Carol Saltus) makes it abundantly clear that the customers of the higher-priced ladies of the night (or morning or afternoon) are more interesting than the run-of-the-mill types who buy love at a cheaper rate. The majority of the customers are top politicians and business executives. The conclusion is that the power drive and the sex drive are so closely linked they become inseparable.

Most of the customers of the high-priced prostitutes are middle-aged to elderly married men who need reaffirmation of their power and youth. They need to dominate a woman, to make her do what they want. They are not able to exercise that power over their wives.

Call girls are a superb alternative because they have the expertise, perform the required services and keep their mouths shut. A social friend may want an emotional relationship and there is always the chance that she might tell. Moreover, men who like kinky scx are more likely to get it from a prostitute than from a secretary or the wife of a golf partner.

About 80 percent of all call girls are asked to perform oral sex. Many men in positions of power, such as politicians, want kinky sex, such as bondage, flagellation, etc. Some men who enjoy being whipped have told prostitutes that they feel the need to be punished for their "bad" behavior.

Women from various socio-economic levels become professional prostitutes for a number of reasons. College girls, for example, earn money to pay their way through school. Suburban housewives and single secretaries consider it a lucrative part-time job that makes it possible for them to buy more expensive clothes or a new car. Liberal members of contemporary society whose motto is "If that's the way I want to make a living, it's my own business" no longer view prostitution as a fate worse than death.

The average call girl who works for a madam considers herself much more "respectable" than the streetwalker who works for a pimp. She is of above-average intelligence and many have had one year or more of college. Her "career" as a call girl usually began when she was in her late teens or early twenties. The so-called "elite" call girls do not fit the conventional stereotype of the common hooker. They dress fashionably, travel "first class" and appear as refined as the wives of the city's leading businessmen.

Prostitution becomes more of an addiction than an option with women who make it a full-time job. In a three-year study tracing those who renounced prostitution, it was discovered that two thirds of the women who left the business for a year or more returned to it, at least part-time.

Most prostitutes were sexually abused during adolescence. They often fail to make the connection between being sexually exploited by their fathers, brothers or mother's boyfriends and their chosen profession. They just grow up doing to men what men did to them. Instead of viewing themselves as victims, they see their customers as victims who have to pay for services.

Money and the sense of power their bodies give them are major motivations for engaging in prostitution. Prostitutes have learned at an early age to relate through their bodies, which they consider "equipment" for commanding money from men. They consider the faking of pleasure a type of manipulation of men who are duped into believing they are proving their masculinity through sexual performance.

Though busy call girls in major cities can earn as much as $200,000 a year, very few save or invest the money they earn. Those who work for a madam get only 50 or 60 percent of the take. And there is a subculture of people who live off prostitutes. Also, in some cities there are police officers who have to be paid off, and doctors who take care of problems such as pregnancies and bruised bodies. The doormen and bartenders and taxi drivers who steer customers their way must also be paid. Call girls who operate out of their own apartments often pay two to three times the normal rent so the landlord will keep quiet.

It has been estimated that about 60 percent of the high-priced prostitutes prefer women as sexual partners for their own personal enjoyment. They tolerate men but admit they get very little sexual pleasure when they have intercourse with males.

Some prostitutes tell about regular customers who pay $100 an hour just to talk. They say they are lonesome (though married) and need to tell someone they trust exactly how they feel without fear of being laughed at, criticized or told they are crazy.

This is a pretty sad commentary on the state of some so-called "successful" marriages.

CREDIT: *Ann Landers. Material taken from* A Sexual Profile of Men in Power *by Sam Janus, M.D., New York, New York: Warner Books, Inc.*

Psoriasis

THE SCALING DISEASE

Psoriasis (pronounced so-*ri*-ah-sis) is a skin disease that affects at least one out of every fifty persons in the United States. This stubborn affliction remains something of a "mystery." Neither its cause nor its cure is known. It attacks both sexes equally, and most often appears between the ages of fifteen and thirty, although it may appear at any age.

The person with psoriasis may be deeply distressed by his appearance. It is essential to know that psoriasis is not contagious and what once was considered a hopeless, incurable condition can now be viewed as controllable when treated properly.

Signs and Symptoms: The skin of the person with psoriasis appears as silver or gray scaling, with red patches, usually on the elbows, knees, trunk or scalp. The underarm and genital areas also may be involved.

The borders between the psoriatic patches and normal skin are usually sharp. The appearance may differ slightly in various parts of the body. The elbows, knees and trunk most frequently are the areas with the characteristic thick, red, scaling patches. In the scalp, red patches with sharp borders usually are visible at the hairline. These shed large quantities of silvery white scales that resemble severe dandruff.

When acute psoriasis is present, many small, raindrop-like sores appear. There may be a severe flare-up in which there is a painful reddening and cracking of the skin around the joints, chills and a generalized shedding of large areas of scaling skin. Patients with this form of the disease often need to be hospitalized promptly and given intensive treatment.

Although arthritis may be associated with psoriasis, involvement of the vital internal organs does not occur. Thus psoriasis does not threaten or shorten the lives of those who have it.

The Cause: Although researchers have not discovered the exact cause of psoriasis, more is known about it than in the past. The development of psoriasis is thought to be inherited because it tends to occur in families. Not every person with this problem can recall blood relatives who have had the disease; however, at least 30 percent of patients are able to give a family history of the disorder.

Many of the factors that aggravate and set off an outbreak of psoriasis have been recognized in recent years. Several of these factors:

(1) Injury to the skin is perhaps the most common factor. A cut, burn or minor abrasion may "trigger" the appearance of a new lesion in about eight to eighteen days. Occasionally this phenomenon has been noted to occur in surgical scars, on severely sunburned skin and in scratch marks.

(2) Changes in the seasons commonly cause a variation in the severity of psoriasis. It often improves during the summer and worsens during the winter. However, in some cases, the opposite is true.

(3) General health factors may influence psoriasis. Many patients note flare-ups during periods of physical and emotional stress.

(4) Infections as well as certain medications used in the treatment of other diseases can aggravate psoriasis. Frequently a flare-up of psoriasis can be triggered by severe viral or bacterial infections of the upper respiratory

tract. This has been particularly true following severe streptococcic infections of the throat.

(5) As in almost all skin problems, there is an emotional factor, and psoriasis is no exception. People who have traumatic experiences or whose life patterns are disturbed by disappointment, failure, unhappiness—or if something is getting under their skin—it can reactivate an old case of psoriasis, or trigger a fresh outbreak.

Case histories of people who have psoriasis indicate that when their lives flow along tranquilly, the psoriasis improves or disappears. When emotional problems occur, the psoriasis returns.

Treatment. The degree of the discomfort is a factor in determining the form of treatment.

In many instances, psoriasis responds well to sunlight. Often time spent at the beach or outdoors, particularly during the summer, is the best single treatment available.

Some patients find that the daily use of a sun or ultraviolet lamp will sustain the improvements for several months. However, if these lamps are to be used safely, the user must adhere strictly to the manufacturer's recommendations and the physician's instructions. Many serious burns have resulted from improper use of these lamps. Falling asleep under a sun lamp can be particularly hazardous.

Many ointments, creams and lotions are available for the external treatment of psoriasis. Some require a physician's prescription, others do not. Most of these medications contain a variety of tar (distillates of petroleum) combined with other ingredients designed to remove scales. Shampoos, cleansers and bath oils containing tar are readily available without prescription. If these preparations cause irritation, their use should be discontinued and a physician should be consulted for further recommendations as to treatment.

In recent years, dermatologists have used a number of newer approaches in treating stubborn psoriasis. Cortisones and the newer steroids when applied to the skin will give temporary relief. Some of these steroids can be injected directly into the lesion, and are also available as lotions and creams. Corticosteroid creams and lotions have caused significant improvement, particularly when the treated areas are covered with thin plastic film wrappings.

Therapy with tar and ultraviolet light often is recommended in addition to treatment with the steroid creams.

When patients develop extensive and resistant lesions, it has been a common practice to hospitalize them for intensive use of tar preparations and therapy with light.

In crises of psoriasis, methotrexate is sometimes prescribed. This medication requires careful and continuous supervision by your physician.

Psoriasis is a common skin disorder. Some patients have "given up" after years of searching for a "cure." It is hoped that one day such a cure will be available, but until then, proper treatment by a competent skin specialist can provide very good control of psoriasis.

CREDIT: *Eugene M. Farber, M.D., Professor and Executive Head, Department of Dermatology, Stanford University School of Medicine, Stanford, California. Samuel Bluefarb, M.D., Professor and Chairman of Dermatology; Northwestern University, Chicago, Illinois.*

Psychiatry

How to Choose the Right Psychiatrist

How do you choose the right psychiatrist for yourself, a family member or a friend? Because psychiatry is at least as much of an art as a science, the choice of therapist is vitally important to the successful outcome of psychiatric treatment. The anguish that usually brings about the decision to seek psychiatric help does not normally favor a complicated selection process, yet the choice of the right psychiatrist is all-important.

If one has a broken arm it will probably heal quite well even if we dislike the orthopedist who sets it. Even though we don't communicate well with our family doctor, he or she can be helpful in spite of the fact that we may tend to forget to take the pills, omit reporting recent symptoms and will generally lack the faith which could speed recovery.

With a psychiatrist, however, the patient/doctor relationship (often called the therapeutic alliance) is a major factor in successful treatment. The therapeutic alliance needs to be strong in order that therapy be of real benefit. Often people who have made relatively poor connections with the key figures in their lives seek therapy. The first and often principal goal of psychotherapy is to learn to "connect" with the therapist.

I urge the person seeking help to be specific in determining what kind of psychiatrist is needed. What personality factors have been important in helping this person in the past? With what kinds of people does he tend to be most comfortable? What kinds of people can he not stand to be around for very long? All these factors are important in the selection of the right psychiatrist.

Under special circumstances, one cannot be too choosy. For example, if the person needing help is suicidal, in a state of panic or in the middle of a nervous breakdown, it is imperative to get to a psychiatrist immediately—one who is geared to emergency treatment and able to hospitalize the patient if it is necessary. Problems with street drugs such as heroin or amphetamines usually require a specially trained psychiatrist. Most psychiatrists do not like to treat people with drug problems and tend to do poorly with them.

Children are best treated by child psychiatrists or general psychiatrists who are skilled at meeting the special needs of children. A patient desiring a specific type of therapy such as psychoanalysis, should look for people who have the special expertise that these approaches require. There is also the matter of medication. Is the patient seeking a therapist who uses psychiatric medications, or one who avoids them? Another consideration is money. Psychiatrists are expensive and a great deal of time is required for psychotherapy. Some Beverly Hills and Park Avenue doctors charge $100 for a fifty-minute hour. A range of $30 to $55 is common. Some problems can be resolved in a few sessions. Others take months or years. Medicaid is available to some people needing therapy. Others who neither qualify for Medicaid nor can afford full fees need to consider other options. Community mental health centers throughout the nation offer psychotherapy on a sliding scale fee according to what one may be able to afford. Non-medical psychotherapists such as psychologists, social workers, psychiatric nurses and ministerial counselors charge a smaller fee and can be excellent.

It is highly recommended that a thorough physical examination looking for possible physical causes for the emotional distress be undertaken before therapy. If the psychotherapy is long-term or if the patient is not responding well, a repeat physical and possibly a psychiatric consultation to determine whether medication might be of help are indicated.

It is important to select a psychiatrist whose personality is compatible with that of the patient. The psychiatrist who is fantastic for one's spouse may not be right for one's self. It helps to think of the kinds of people who have been supportive in one's life. It may be someone "just like Mom or Dad" or exactly the opposite. Some individuals need an articulate, verbal therapist. Others should have a warm, outgoing personality. A quiet introspective therapist may be necessary for maximum trust and open communication in certain instances.

Is it important that the therapist be male or female? Is race important? Has the person seeking help been in therapy before? If so, did he get the help he needed? What factors does he or she think might make additional therapy more helpful in the future? Sometimes switching to a psychiatrist of the opposite sex—or one with a different personality—can make a great deal of difference.

The medical licensing board in your state can tell you if the therapist is licensed to practice medicine. The psychiatric society and medical association can tell you whether the therapist is a member of those organizations.

The high regard of his or her medical colleagues (such as your family physician) tends to be a more sensitive measure of the psychiatrist's overall competence.

How does one sort out and explore all of these factors? Several different avenues are possible. Most optimally a trusted matchmaker who knows you and also knows several psychiatrists should be consulted. It could be your priest, rabbi or minister, family physician, school counselor or a close friend. A friend or relative's referral to a psychiatrist with whom they had a good experience tends to be trustworthy.

There are often referral agencies in a community as well. The local medical society or state psychiatric society can direct you to the available psychiatrists in your community. They often also know who works with children, does forensic work (medical-legal work), speaks languages other than English or has a special area of focus such as psychoanalysis or group therapy. They often can give some direction in finding a psychiatrist of a given sex, race or ethnic group. If not, and such a psychiatrist is needed, the American Psychiatric Association has committees on women, blacks, Asian-Americans, American Indians and Spanish-speaking therapists who could be helpful. If a non-medical therapist is sought, check the telephone directory for listings of their specialty groups (such as the American Nursing Association) for referral help.

Finally, there remains the task of interviewing the psychiatrist. The interview should be a two-way exchange. After therapy has been in progress a while a therapist will tend to want to know why a particular question is important to you before answering it. But in the first interview I urge people to ask for and expect straight answers to their questions.

Probably more basic than the answers to questions is the feelings of the patient during his hour with the psychiatrist. Was it easy to talk? Did you feel empathy and caring from the psychiatrist? Do you feel you can trust him or her with your most intimate secrets?

If you sense an immediate "click," stay with that therapist. If you find yourself uncertain, make an appointment with another therapist—and if necessary, a third, and a fourth. Then exercise the same diligence and energy used in the initial selection to get as much as you can out of your therapy.

CREDIT: *Ann Laycock Chappel, M.D., Instructor, University of California in San Francisco, Psychiatric Department.*

SOME GOOD COUNSEL

DEAR ANN LANDERS: I read your column every day and think your advice is very good. That's why I hate to see you cop out and suggest "counseling."

I've been to many counselors, analysts, psychologists, etc. None of them did me any good. The first few visits they listen, look at the ceiling a lot, nod their heads and ask about your childhood.

The next few visits they ask what you think should be done. After several visits they tell you to do what you think is best. This is advice? If I could depend on my own judgment why would I need them?

Several months ago I called my doctor in the middle of the night. I was desperate. I begged him to help me. Do you know what he said? "Come see me tomorrow."

Finally I got smart and realized that for $50 an hour I could have a terrific vacation and it would do me a lot more good.

So please, Ann, when people write for advice, give them your best shot. You might be the only one who is willing to speak out.   AN ADMIRER

DEAR AD: I "speak out" plenty, and I'll continue to do so. Many people who write for advice know what they ought to do. They just need someone to tell them to go ahead and do it. Others need a lot more than advice. They should have continuing help. And this is when I suggest counseling.

I realize one's chances for getting a first-rate counselor are the same as getting a first-rate doctor, lawyer, plumber, auto mechanic or hairdresser. No better than 50-50.

Psychiatry, Psychoanalysis and Psychotherapy and Other "Helpers"

(*The Differences*)

Psychiatry is the medical specialty dedicated to the study of human behavior and the treatment of conduct that is troublesome to the individual or to society.

This study of human behavior includes:

Genetic predispositions, which means inherited tendencies and weaknesses, birth injuries, emotional problems developed in childhood, physical problems that might influence behavior, toxicities and infections that might affect the brain and other organic factors.

The character-forming influences of family, education, sexual, social and cultural experiences.

How favorable physical and environmental factors can result in socially acceptable "normal" behavior for some individuals and how stressful or difficult life situations can cause others to develop anxieties, irrational fears (phobias), persistent obsessions, destructive thoughts and actions, bizarre behavior and depression with suicidal impulses, often accompanied by imaginary illnesses.

In the treatment of such deviations, psychiatrists attempt to relieve a person's discomfort by developing his/her integrity, dignity and creativity.

The therapy may include:

Physical: Advice as to diet, exercise, rest periods, environmental or occupational changes, medication, surgery (when necessary for brain tumors or in similar rare instances) and other medical procedures.

Psychological: (1) Re-education of the patient by encouraging him to talk freely about his innermost, often suppressed feelings and by so doing enable him to better understand himself and how he relates to others. (2) Family or group conferences during which all the parties involved, hopefully, come to realize that deviant patterns of conduct when replaced by improved behavior give all concerned greater and more lasting satisfaction.

Existential: Restoration of trust in humanity and the enjoyment of the values and beauties of life.

Psychiatrists are M.D.s who have taken three years of specialized study in psychiatry after their internship. Only M.D.s may prescribe drugs. Most are not analysts. Look for one whose residency was in a university-affiliated program, who has a valid state license and who is either certified by the American Board of Psychiatry and Neurology or "board eligible."

Psychoanalysis: A qualified psychoanalyst is a psychiatrist who has been further trained in a Psychoanalytic Institute approved by the American Academy for Psychoanalysis and the American Psychoanalytic Association. This training comprises a personal analysis averaging four hourly sessions a week for four or five years of intensive study of the theories and techniques of Sigmund Freud (in advanced Institutes, also those of Alfred Adler, Carl Jung, Karen Horney, Melanie Klein, Sandor Rado, Franz Alexander and others). During the course of psychoanalytic training the student must undertake the psychoanalytic treatment of a minimum of three patients—under the supervision of an experienced analyst.

Psychoanalytic Therapy: This involves the psychoanalyst talking with or listening to the patient during fifty-minute sessions, three to five times per week. These sessions cover the discussion of childhood experiences, fears and hopes. They are examined and analyzed and the patient then better understands who he is and why he is the way he is. This type of self-understanding enables the patient to alter his conduct in ways that make him more secure, more productive and less anxious.

Psychotherapy: This is a vague term applied loosely to all methods intended to influence thought, feeling and behavior. Professionally these range from the expert practices of psychiatrists and psychoanalysts to the nonmedical and less comprehensive but valid advice and guidance offered by academically sanctioned psychologists (M.A. or Ph.D.) as to career potentialities or methods of improving verbal skills, or by qualified social workers.

Psychologists may have only a master's degree or may have taken additional training to obtain a doctorate. Not all treat patients; some do only testing or research. Look for one with a state license and certification by the American Board of Examiners in Professional Psychology or with a listing in the National Register of Health Service Providers in Psychology.

Social Workers do many of the same kinds of individual and group therapy that psychologists and psychiatrists do. Most work for hospitals and clinics but a few are in private practice. Look for at least a master's degree (M.S.W. or M.S.S.W.) and accreditation by the Academy of Certified Social Workers (A.C.S.W.).

Pastoral Counselors are members of the clergy who have taken special training in social work or psychology, sometimes enough to qualify for degrees in their fields. Such persons can be extremely helpful to troubled people, but untrained members of the clergy are often not effective psychotherapists.

Paraprofessionals are a mixed bag of individuals offering psychotherapy of one sort of another but without sufficient training to qualify for another title. They are usually not licensed or accredited but may have completed two-year associate degree courses to be called "mental health assistant," "psychiatric counselor," "activity therapist" or "nurse's aide."

Individuals who undertake extensive treatment should be certain that they are working with qualified professional people. If there is any doubt, they should contact the American Medical Association, American Psychiatric Association, the American Psychological Association or the National Association for Social Workers. The addresses can be obtained from any public library with a telephone call.

Be aware that any individual can call himself a therapist even though he has had no professional training or credentials. At this moment there is no law to protect the public against such practitioners.

CREDIT: *Jules Masserman, M.D., Chicago, Illinois, President, American Psychiatric Association and Professor Emeritus, Psychiatry & Neurology, Northwestern University, Chicago.*

Psychology

(Help for Your Head—Where to Get It)

The National Accreditation Association and the American Examining Board of Psychoanalysis, Inc., a group of several bodies that certifies psychoanalysts, maintains a registry of those who meet certain minimum requirements of training and experience. The registry chiefly includes analysts who are not psychiatrists. Most are social workers.

This group's national registry can be purchased for $4 by writing the organization at 80 East 11th Street, New York, New York 10003. People may also call (212) 677-5455 to ask whether a given analyst is listed.

Psychoanalysts whose basic training is in psychiatry and whose qualifications exceed certain minimums are listed in two directories.

The American Psychoanalytic Association maintains a roster of members which is available in many larger libraries. In the current directory, persons listed as "active members" have been certified as meeting a second, higher set of criteria. To learn how and whether an analyst is listed, people may call the association headquarters in New York at (212) 752-0450.

The American Academy of Psychoanalysis, also headquartered in New York, has a similar roster and will answer questions about whether someone is a member at (212) 477-4250.

By far the largest profession providing psychotherapy services is that of social work.

The largest compendium of social workers who meet certain minimum standards set by the National Association of Social Workers is the N.A.S.W. Clinical Register. Copies, which cost $25 from the association office in Washington, D.C., may be consulted in larger libraries and schools of social work.

Another listing of social workers who offer psychotherapy and meet certain minimal criteria is the National Registry of Health Care Providers in Clinical Social Work.

The National Registry is available for consultation in some clinics or may be purchased for $8.50 from the publishers, the Board of the National Registry of Health Care Providers in Clinical Social Work, 1025 Dove Run Road, Lexington, Kentucky 40502.

Additional sources of information include the following:

American Psychological Association will answer questions about whether and how psychologists are listed in its national directory at (202) 833-7581. A.P.A.'s national office is at 1200 17th Street, N.W., Washington, D.C.

American Psychiatric Association provides similar information at (202) 232-7878. Ask for background information. Headquarters are at 1700 18th Street, N.W., Washington, D.C.

American Association of Marriage and Family Counselors, 41 Central Park West, can give information on therapists specializing in this field at (212) 725-5290.

American Association of Sex Educators, Counselors and Therapists, 425 East 79th Street, will provide information at (212) 535-5520.

CREDIT: *Boyce Rensberger, Psychotherapy:* "Finding More Shrinks to Fit," *from the New York* Times, *Wednesday, January 18, 1978, page C-9.*

Quackery

Barnum was right. There's a sucker born every minute. And two to take him. How do I know? Because they write to me—by the thousands. The victims, that is.

"How can they be so stupid?" I ask myself. And then I answer the question. It's not merely stupidity. It's desperation and wishful thinking that wipe out all reason and common sense. I became furious at the exploitation of these good people whose only crime is ignorance and vulnerability.

Here are some examples of some of the letters:

DEAR ANN LANDERS: Is it true that musk oil will turn a man on? My husband is forty-six years old and sexually dead as a doornail. I've seen this musk oil advertised, but $11 is a lot of money for a little bottle. If you say it will help I will buy it.

DEAR ANN: I'm a career girl, twenty-eight years old, and haven't had more than three real dates in my life. The reason is because I am flat-chested. I mean I don't have any bust at all. All my life I've wanted to have nice round bosoms. Please tell me if this cream will help. (Advertisement enclosed.) As you can see, the "before" and "after" pictures are very convincing. What do you say?

DEAR ANN: Is it true that cooking in aluminum will cause cancer? A man came to the door yesterday selling cookware. He scared the life out of me.

His utensils cost $450 for the complete set. If what he says is true, about cancer, I mean, it sure would be worth it. But I hate to throw out these perfectly good pots and pans I've used for ten years.

One after another the letters come—from the "exotic dancer" who wants to grow "gorgeous nails in twenty days"—from the overweight housewife who will do *anything* to get thin except quit eating the things she loves. Then there are the females with bags under their eyes and extra chins who are sure they will look ten years younger if they use the enriched cream (secret formula) for thirty days. The trouble is—it's awfully expensive. "But it would be well worth the money if it works," writes Mrs. W. from Sheboygan. "Cheaper than a face lift. And no pain."

When men write and ask if the pomade and treatments guaranteed to grow hair will help, I often reply, "Yes. It will help the manufacturer and the man who sells it. They will get rich. As for you, it will help flatten your wallet, but it won't do anything for your bald head."

The letters from teenagers are especially pathetic. "My skin is such a mess of pimples and blackheads no girl would go out with me, so I don't even ask. Please don't suggest a doctor. I can't afford one. This soap and cream combination promises results within ten days. What do you think, Ann? And while I'm at it, Ann, maybe you can tell me if this mail-order speech course will help my brother. He stutters. His grades are awful. He's not dumb, he's just ashamed to speak up in class."

DEAR ANN: Our sex life is blah after fifteen years. My husband wants to try a sex clinic, but some friends of ours went and you wouldn't believe the things they were asked to do. I don't go for that far-out stuff like changing partners. Frankly, I'm scared. What do you think?

The saddest letters of all come from relatives of the desperately ill, those who are dying of cancer, or kidney disease. "Our family doctor said there was nothing more he could do, so we took Mom to this wonderful chiropractor. She seems a little stronger today. Do you think, Ann, that we should have brought her to the chiropractor from the beginning and not wasted all that time and money on a specialist with a fancy diploma from Harvard hanging on his office wall?"

Every letter gets a personal reply in the mail, if there's a name and an address. I urge my readers to beware of quacks and phonies. I warn them against the charlatans and fakers. More often than I care to admit, I have received in return a seething reply: "How dare you take away our hope! I'll bet you are on the payroll of the American Medical Association. The medical doctor didn't do anything but send us big bills. Jesus Christ is the greatest healer of them all. Now that we have put our child in His hands, we know everything is going to be all right."

How can the public be protected against phonies, quacks and unscrupulous money-grabbers who prey on the insecure, the frightened and the sick? The answer is education.

I recommend a book called *The Health Robbers,* a compilation of material by several outstanding physicians and authorities in the field of health and public information.

Some of the chapter titles are:

"The Cruelest Killers—Exploiting Cancer Victims"

"The Pill Pushers—Do You have 'tired blood'?"

"The Misery Merchants—Exploiting Arthritis Sufferers"

"Weight Control and Diets—Facts and Fads"

"The Make-Believe Doctors—Medical Imposters"

"Phony Sex Clinics"

"The Genuine Fake—Organic Rip-Off"

"The Eye Exorcisors—Can You Throw Away Your Glasses?"

"Dubious Dentistry"

"The Miracle Merchants—Does Faith Healing Really Work?"

The Health Robbers was edited by Stephen Barrett, M.D., and Gilda Knight, and published by George F. Stickney Company.

CREDIT: *Ann Landers.*

Rape

Avoiding Rape

During a discussion in the Israeli parliament on the increasing rate of rape, a male member suggested that there be a curfew on women. Golda Meir, then Prime Minister, countered by saying that there should be a curfew on men. They, after all, were the ones doing the raping.

This story illustrates my mixed feelings in having to tell *women* how to change their awareness and behavior because of what *men* do. Since many men in today's society confuse power, aggression and sex, we must educate women so they can protect themselves. Here are some short-range suggestions based on other studies of rape avoidance, primarily those of Medea and Thompson (*Against Rape* [1974]) and *Rape Prevention and Resistance,* a study reported by the Queens Bench Foundation in San Francisco (1976). I have learned a great deal from an ongoing study during which I talked with women who were attacked and avoided being raped as well as women who were raped.

There is no way to guarantee that you will not be raped. Women of all ages from three-month-old babies to eighty-year-old great-grandmothers have been victims. Women have been raped in their homes and on the streets, in prisons and in mental hospitals, by their fathers, stepfathers, uncles, husbands (although this is not illegal in most places), their boyfriends, as well as by strangers. Hopefully, this information will decrease your *probability* of being raped.

I spoke with two women recently (not part of the study). One was a victim and one avoided a rape or a mugging. The difference in attitude and behavior of the two illustrates an important point. The avoider, while waiting alone on an El platform, noticed a man get off on the other side, look at her and then appear on her side of the platform. When he started to walk toward her, she immediately started running to the exits. He followed her but did not follow her down the stairs. She escaped into the street. She did not worry about his thinking she was crazy for running or that he might have taken the wrong train by mistake and was trying to correct it. She thought about herself—not about offending him. The other woman, when her doorbell rang, opened the door and allowed a strange man to come into her apartment because he said that he had car trouble and needed to use the phone. She was nice. She was helpful. She trusted. In short, she exhibited all the traits most of us were taught were "feminine." She was raped.

The Queens Bench study finds that "attempted rape victims were more than twice as likely as rape victims to respond in a rude or unfriendly manner." Moreover "attempted rape victims were more likely than rape victims to be suspicious of their future assailants" and to trust these feelings even though they didn't know why they felt uneasy. The moral of the story is *trust your feelings*. You may have picked up cues you are not consciously aware of. These feelings may arise in the course of an apparently friendly conversation (prior to the attacker becoming aggressive), since in over half the cases both victims and offenders reported that the attack was preceded by casual conversation.

People always ask what strategy to use if they are attacked. They falsely assume there is one magic strategy. The Queens Bench study found that the attempted rape victims employed *more* resistance measures than did the rape victims—for example, screaming, physical resistance, talking, fleeing when the opportunity arose. If you can delay the rape by screaming it is *possible* that someone will call the police and the noise of the siren will frighten him so he will either flee or lessen his grip on you so you can get away. If it is a street situation, a passerby may appear and frighten the would-be rapist. There is no one strategy that works in all situations. But even if the attack seems imminent keep watching for an opportunity to get away.

Learn as much as you can about rape and rape prevention. A large percentage of attempted rape victims say they remembered advice or information about rape prevention.

Learn self-defense or street fighting through a special course designed for and preferably taught by women. These courses do more than teach you a martial art such as karate or judo. They teach you how to confront men who hassle you in the street, in public transportation, in theaters—men who make obscene phone calls. These courses heighten your awareness and ability to cope with the "little rapes" that occur in our daily lives. Such training is useful in dealing with more serious situations. While at this point I have only spoken with five women who had taken such courses, all of them avoided attempted rapes. They did not necessarily use the techniques they were taught. My analysis is that in order to take such a course you have to have a more realistic view of the world, and the course validates that view. (This view is *not* paranoid. It is realistic.) It develops your confidence and skills through practice. The support of other women encourages you to believe that you, too, can do it. And your awareness is heightened so that you are more likely to respond like the woman on the El platform than like the woman who let the man into her apartment to use her phone.

You can find out if courses on self-defense are available in your area and how to contact the organizers by calling the local YWCA, the Women's Center or Women's Studies office at a local college or university, a women's bookstore or newspaper if you are lucky enough to live in a community that has such resources. Or you can ask your librarian to obtain a copy of *Black Belt Woman,* a journal for women involved in self-defense for women. If there is no listing or advertisement in that magazine for courses in your area, write to them and ask where the nearest course is and whom to contact.

Probably over half the rapists are men who know their victims. They may not define themselves as rapists, but in fact they have forced the woman to have sex (of any kind) against her will. Medea and Thompson found that the largest category of these known rapists was friends of friends or of relatives. One woman told me she had just been raped by two of her husband's friends. She let them into the house since they said they wanted to wait for him and she made the mistake of being too trusting.

We have been taught to be hospitable, never to turn away from our door someone we know, even if we know them ever so slightly. But rape is worse. And once you have let someone in your house not only is it more difficult to avoid rape than if you were assaulted on the street, but it is more difficult to press charges and obtain a conviction. Never let any man into your house unless you can completely trust him, especially if you are alone. If he wants to use the phone and you feel obligated to meet his need, keep the chain on the door and get the number, telling him you will make the call for him. Similarly if someone you do not know asks you for something on the street keep on walking or answer in an abrupt manner. After reading *Against Rape,* I was out alone late one night when a man asked me if he were walking in the correct direction to get to the El station. I nodded yes even though the directions he needed were more complicated. But my car was parked on a dark street near a vacant lot and I didn't want to take a chance. Because I was raised to be polite and helpful I felt guilty about that incident for months. But I did the correct thing under the circumstances.

Medea and Thompson also suggest that when you go out, at night, dress so that you can flee easily. That means wear flat-heeled shoes and avoid long skirts. It also means avoid having your arms encumbered with purses and packages. Backpacks are very useful. You won't look glamorous, but you'll be safer. And since some rapists look for women who appear vulnerable, dressing sensibly, particularly if you walk with confidence and seem to know where you are going, may deter such men. I should point out that we know very little about rapists. So far, we have been unable to put them in any particular category. A rapist can be anybody.

Here is more common-sense advice from people who work in the field of sexual assault:

(1) Car: Always keep all your doors locked. Even if they were locked when you parked your car, check the inside of your car before you get in. If possible, keep the windows closed, particularly when you stop at intersections. Keep plenty of gas in your tank so you won't run out and have to leave your car and walk to a station. If you have car trouble, unless you can fix it yourself, raise your hood, lock your door, turn on your flasher and wait for a patrol car. If the neighborhood is safe, lock the car and phone for assistance. Do not accept help from passing motorists.

(2) Apartment or house: Carry your keys in your hand as you approach your house or apartment so you can enter immediately. A woman in a corridor is easy prey. When you select an apartment avoid the ground floor or one that has a balcony that can be reached from the street. If you live on the ground floor have bars on your window or window locks. Have dead-bolt locks on your doors. The Queens Bench study reports that "often the assailant illegally entered the woman's home through an *open* window or unlocked door."

(3) Street: Think of the street as enemy territory. If financially possible, take a cab if you are out alone at night, or try to share a ride with a friend, rather than walking or taking public transportation.

Conclusion: Some readers may resent the suggestions presented in this article. No woman wants her life restricted. But until we change society (and if we don't, who will?) women are not free. To pretend that we are is only a delusion, it is dangerous.

CREDIT: *Pauline B. Bart, Ph.D., Associate Professor of Sociology, Department of Psychiatry, Abraham Lincoln School of Medicine, University of Illinois in Chicago; and principal investigator of "Avoiding Rape: A Study of Victims and Avoiders."*

Rape

(*What to Do if It Happens to You*)

If you are raped, what you should do depends on the community resources available to you as well as your personal resources at this particular time of crisis in your life. It also depends on what you feel you can manage. All rape victims need to know that it is a crime of violence, not a sexual crime. Though many women feel guilty about being raped and think of all the things they might have done to have prevented it, it is important to remember that being raped is not your fault any more than being robbed. Whatever you did, or did not do, no one has the right to have sex with you against your will.

How long it takes to recover from being raped depends on the quality of support you get from your family and friends, how you are treated by the institutions you deal with (such as police and the courts) and your past history, notably any prior sexual exploitations such as incest or child abuse as well as prior history of violence, such as battering. In addition, the circumstances of the rape may have a relationship to the length of time it takes you to recover from "the rape victim trauma."

You should also remember that it may take a year to get over even the main side effects, although some women are able to recover quite quickly. If it takes you a long time, it doesn't mean something is wrong with you any more than there would be something wrong with you if you healed slowly after major surgery. Your body was invaded. You felt powerless. Your trust may have been violated. You may have been in a life-threatening situation and thought you were going to be killed. If, after rape, you are especially cautious, this does not mean you are paranoid. You may, in fact, be thinking more rationally than you were before the attack when you were too trusting.

Ideally you should know in advance what resources are available to a rape victim in your community. Let us assume, however, that you do not have the information. Let us also assume that the police are not present, as they may be if someone heard you scream and called them. First, telephone the person you trust the most. A friend, a relative, a lover or a spouse. Ask that person to come to be with you. It occasionally happens that a person you thought you could count on does not react supportively to the news of your rape. This is not a reflection on you but on them. Call another person. Then contact a rape crisis line. If you do not have the number, get it from Information. If you are fortunate, you will be put through immediately to a trained counselor who can tell you what options are available. For example, in Seattle you can obtain treatment in a hospital that has a special program for rape victims and the hospital does not have to report your name to the police. They tell the police only the technique the rapist used so they can check the information you give with other information. The more information the better the chances of picking him up.

The crisis line can tell you which hospitals have rape victim treatment programs, and suggest one nearest you. Sometimes you will speak to a tape or an answering service and be told you will be called back. If you don't want to wait, call the hospitals yourself and find out if they have a special rape treatment program with rape victim advocates.

If you are able to reach the crisis center usually a woman from the crisis center will accompany you to a hospital and stay with you and function as an advocate, at least until the advocate arrives. She or the advocate will give you moral support, explain the hospital procedures and try to make sure the hospital does not break "the chain of evidence" so if you should decide to press charges, the evidence will be there.

Do not take a shower or douche before going to the hospital even though you may feel unclean. It will destroy valuable evidence. The reasons for going to the hospital are as follows: First, you can be examined for internal or external injuries. These are not only important in court cases, but also important for all women because they may not be aware of injuries due to the psychological shock of the rape. For example, on occasion anal intercourse will pierce the wall between the anus and the vagina, allowing feces to pass from the former to the latter, causing infection. If you are multiply raped (either by one person or by a group) you may have internal injuries. The rape victim advocate or nurse who has been trained to act as an advocate will be particularly useful at this point. The pelvic examination may feel like another rape, particularly if the resident or specialist is not sympathetic. Unfortunately they have lagged behind other segments of our society in their treatment of rape victims, according to not only the victims with whom I have spoken, but scholars who have studied hospital care.

You can get a preventive VD shot, although you should return in two weeks and ask for what is called a GC culture, as well as a test for syphilis to make certain you are not infected. Be sure and tell them if you are allergic to any antibiotics.

You should be told of the various methods of avoiding pregnancy. First a test should be taken to determine if you are pregnant. Then you should be told that the alternatives are D.E.S. (the morning-after pill), menstrual extraction about the time your period should arrive, which would remove the contents of the uterus so that a pregnancy will be prevented, and abortion.

You should be given D.E.S. only with informed consent. This means not only should you be told that you may become nauseated, but that the drug has been banned for most other uses (except for victims of rape and incest) because it has caused cancer in daughters of women who have taken it during their pregnancies. Some women would like to take D.E.S. even after having been given the information and you may be one of these (e.g., if you do not feel you could go through an abortion if you became pregnant as a result of the rape). Should you decide to take D.E.S. be sure and take it for the full five days or you may become pregnant and the fetus may be affected. The rape victim advocate should explain this to you. If your mother had D.E.S. when she was pregnant with you, you should not take it.

Mention any sore places even if bruises haven't shown up yet. If black and blue marks show up in the next few days you should report them to the rape victim advocacy program at the hospital. This should be added to your record.

You have a right to be treated sensitively by the hospital. If you are not, remember the specific people and incidents and either you or the antirape movement in your city will notify the hospital administrator.

If your city or town does not have a special program for treating rape victims and you have a private physician, call him or her.

Most hospitals have to call the police, but that does not mean you must prosecute.

If your city or town does not have a rape crisis center or crisis phone line, try to locate one in a city near you so you will have somebody with whom you can talk about your feelings. Your best bet is a city or town that has a university. If not, try a general "hot line." The Information operator can often help you locate these services.

POLICE

Many women do not want to call the police because they have heard about the insensitivity of the police to rape victims. But in the past few years police attitudes, at least to rape by strangers, have improved. The rape crisis line can tell you what to expect from the police. In New York City, for example, the police are for the most part extremely sensitive to rape victims. Many police programs now include policewomen trained to deal with victims of sexual assault. Ask for a policewoman if you prefer to see one. It is your right to decide whether or not to call the police. An advantage of calling the police is that you then have the option of prosecuting. Sometimes you may not feel like it at the time, but you may feel like it later. Have your friend or advocate with you for the police questioning. You may be asked to repeat your story several times. As soon as possible after the rape, write down or tape the account of what happened. If you decide to go to court and the state's attorney or district attorney decides to prosecute, you will have a record to refresh your memory. The assailant's attorney may try to trick and trap you. The attorney may try to talk to you outside of court. Do not speak with him or her outside of court. Having a record will keep you from "changing your story," which may be used against you.

Whether you should prosecute or not depends on the amount of support available to you from your family and friends or from any victim assistance program in your community and what the laws in your state are. For example, can your past sexual history be brought up? The laws are changing and are now somewhat better for victims of rape than they were. Should you decide to prosecute, be aware that there will be many delays (called continuances) in the procedures and you must be prepared to come back again and again. Bring a friend, relative or advocate each time. You will have to see your assailant. It makes most women uncomfortable to do so and that is why it is important to have somebody with you for emotional support.

The prosecuting attorney is the state's attorney—not yours (if you want your own attorney, you may file a civil suit for damages). He or she may want to "plea-bargain" to lower the charge from rape to some lesser crime. This does not mean that he/she does not believe you were raped. It means that the attorney does not think the case can be won on a rape charge and is willing to compromise so the assailant will be found guilty.

At various stages in the judicial process the case may be dropped or the charges changed. You may not have much power over this process. It is in no way a reflection on you or an invalidation of your suffering, although you may think otherwise. For this reason it is useful to be accompanied at all stages through the judicial system by a person who understands the process. Your city may also have a victim witness assistance project that will give you help. But you must be persistent and determined. Of all felonies, rape has the lowest rate of conviction. While women whose assailants are found guilty and sentenced feel that justice has been done, the others feel disappointed.

COUNSELING

Most mental health professionals have not had special training in dealing with rape victims. Many women have nightmares, and trouble sleeping. They think they need to move out of their apartments or houses. They feel guilty and anxious and have sexual problems, especially anger toward all men. If these or other symptoms last, and if they are disturbing you, ask an antirape group or a women's center for a list of therapists who specialize in helping women who have been raped. Do not see anyone whom you do not like, even if he or she is recommended. Go on to the next person on the list. The people on the list should have a sliding fee scale. If you are upset after being raped, that does not mean you are crazy. It is normal to have such feelings.

If you are in therapy and your therapist is helpful in regard to the rape problem, you should continue to see that person. You might also find it useful to read some of the books on rape, such as Medea and Thompson's *Against Rape,* Susan Brownmiller's *Against Our Will,* Diana Russell's *The Politics of Rape* or Burgess and Homstum's *Rape and Its Victims.*

Some women find it therapeutic to join the antirape movement, becoming counselors, giving talks or testifying before official groups. Others find writing about their experience helpful.

Attitudes and behavior towards rape victims are changing. Hopefully, if you are raped, your treatment will reflect these changes.

CREDIT:　*Pauline B. Bart, Ph.D., Associate Professor of Sociology, Department of Psychiatry, Abraham Lincoln School of Medicine, University of Illinois in Chicago; Associate Professor of Sociology, University of Illinois, Chicago Circle; principal investigator of "Avoiding Rape: A Study of Victims and Avoiders."*

Rebellion—Child Against Parents

Most people in our society will, during early and late adolescence, engage in behavior or attitudes which are clearly displeasing to their parents. Usually their actions conflict with values their parents hold to be important. It is difficult to know whether these conflicts are simply a normal part of growing up or if they actually represent a powerful attack on the parents or a turning away from their parents' influence.

A certain amount of conflict over values between parents and children is normal and probably even desirable. It should not be considered a problem, and the wise parent should welcome his child's efforts to find a sense of individuality and identity. For the purpose of this discussion, it would be better to consider the child's conflict with the parent as rebellion only when it is prolonged and troubling to family members. Rebellion may be an appropriate term when a youth seems motivated to attack his parents' values. It is also likely to be appropriate when there is concern that the child's behavior and attitudes will ultimately be destructive or when the child's actions are causing the parents great embarrassment or grief.

A number of value conflicts between parent and child can escalate to a level of tension that can make a family feel they are at war. The most common value disagreements between youth and parents these days relate to practices and attitudes regarding drugs, sex and religion. Many of our young people take a far more permissive attitude toward the use of illegal drugs and toward premarital sex than their parents did at a comparable age. If neither parents nor child can reach a compromise on this issue, the child's behavior will eventually be seen as rebellion.

More recently, serious value conflicts have been developing between adolescents and their parents around the issue of religion. A number of youths have insisted upon adopting religious practices which their parents find offensive and potentially dangerous to their child's welfare. It is again difficult to determine whether the child is exercising independence or simply expressing resentment and antagonism toward his parents. One kind of rebelliousness, which seems to have diminished since the late 1960s and the early 1970s, is political. These days, fewer youths seem to be questioning the political values of their parents.

Youths who are truants, run away from home, refuse to work, and steal or commit other antisocial acts are likely to be expressing some element of rebellion toward their parents. Here it is important to note that such behavior should not be called rebellion unless it meets with the parents' strong disapproval, and unless the parents themselves are law-abiding citizens. Sometimes delinquent youths are merely imitating behavior patterns observed at home.

There are a number of explanations for rebelliousness among youth. It is important to understand that no single explanation is ever sufficient. Usually several factors are involved in rebellious behavior. Each case must be studied separately. Some explanations may be satisfactory and helpful in understanding one youth, and other explanations would be more useful in understanding another. The major explanations focus on social change, problems in the family and problems related to the mental health of the child.

In a rapidly changing society, youths are exposed to daily experiences which are quite different than those which their parents knew. These experiences may contribute to shaping a value system which is alien to their parents. New technologies, such as birth-control pills, television and computers, influence the growing child's life in a manner which parents may have difficulty understanding. Youths are also influenced by media which their parents know little about. Magazines, books, television, movies and even music are often directed specifically at the youth market. All of these media influences can lead to the child's developing attitudes which are in clear conflict with those of the parents. Youths are also deeply influenced by peers. A child's rebelliousness may be determined by his belief that it is more important for him to meet the expectations of his friends than to meet the expectations of his parents.

Most behavioral scientists agree that rebelliousness is more likely to occur if the parent raises the child in an extreme manner. Too much overprotectiveness and strictness is harmful. Too little guidance, concern and lovingness toward the child are equally damaging. The child who is given little opportunity to develop on his own, to experiment or to feel independent may have to assert himself through a rebellious act. On the other hand, the child who knows no limits or who is unloved may rebel as a way of calling attention to his feeling that no one cares about him. Sometimes the rebellious youth is responding to inconsistent value messages from his parents. One parent may be strict, while the other is permissive. Other rebellious youths may be responding to problems between the parents. Parents who are not getting along with one another often turn to their children for satisfaction, or they insist that the child take his or her side. This places a heavy responsibility on the child. Often the child is not ready to assume the burden and will rebel as a means of escaping it.

Sometimes youths are rebellious because of severe personal problems. A child may have a neurological disorder which prevents him from putting the kind of control on his impulses which enables him to function in school or in society. His actions will appear as rebellious, although he actually lacks the emotional capacity to control his behavior. Sometimes children with learning difficulties will be especially prone to turn to rebellious behavior. Because they cannot succeed at tasks which other youths accomplish easily and because they have difficulty in gaining praise from others, they may turn to rebellious behavior in an ill-advised effort to gain some sense of belonging, prestige or status. These youths are particularly susceptible to the influence of other delinquent youths. There is also the possibility that the youth has some neurological problems that is affecting his behavior. These illnesses are fortunately rare; but when the child becomes so difficult to handle that he disrupts the family and you suspect he may be heading for serious trouble, he should be taken to a neurologist, who will test him.

In dealing with mild to moderate rebelliousness, it is wise for the parent to acknowledge the existence of the problem but to begin by doing as little as possible. Too often, making a big fuss about a minor rebellion only makes the situation worse. The first thing parents should do is question themselves. Are they being too hard on the child? Are they failing to provide enough guidance? Are they being consistent? Sometimes the very process of reviewing one's own role as a parent will help remedy the situation; and often it will provide clues as to what action might be helpful. Parents should make a concerted effort to understand their child's point of view. It is useful to sit down and talk about their differences with their child in an open, honest, non-condemning way.

None of this means that the parents should allow their children to run wild. When parents feel they cannot tolerate a particular aspect of a child's behavior, they need to inform the child of this and communicate as clearly as possible how far they are willing to go in tolerating rebellious behavior. If attempts to understand the child and to talk with him are unsuccessful, the setting of firm limits will often work. It is absolutely essential that both parents be in agreement as to what limits will be set and how they will be enforced.

Unfortunately, conflicts between parents and youths often escalate these days to the point where communication, understanding and limit-setting are not sufficient to remedy the problem. When this happens, professional help is needed. One of the easiest ways to go about seeking such help is for the whole family to present their problem to a counselor. The rebellious child does not like to be labeled as the person in need of counseling and is more likely to accept help if the problem is defined as a *family* problem and if all members are willing to admit that they need guidance. Usually it is difficult to simply take the child in hand and dump him in a psychiatrist's office. The counselor will make the decision to work with the entire family or to work alone with the rebellious youth. A decision to work alone with the child is more apt to be accepted if the child knows his parents have been concerned enough to look at their own roles in creating the problem.

In summary, it is useful to remind ourselves that rebellious behavior is usually harmless and can disappear as quickly as it appears. For the overwhelming majority of youths rebelling, it is a phase which may cause a great deal of temporary difficulty for parents, but which will pass without permanently harming anyone. For a few youths, in fact, rebellion may be a pathway to their finding themselves and becoming more innovative and creative.

Rebelliousness is only a serious problem if it leads to repetitive antisocial behavior. When a child becomes delinquent, it is common for parents to first become angry at the child and then to blame themselves. Self-blame on the part of parents is neither rational nor useful.

There are many causes of antisocial behavior. Parents may be partly to blame for a child's antisocial conduct, but there are so many forces influencing such behavior that it is totally irrational for the parents to assume a major burden of guilt. It is best for parents to simply ask themselves what they can do to help the situation, try to change whatever it is they are doing that is harmful and stop blaming themselves.

The troubled youth needs parents who are willing to do everything possible to seek help. He does not need parents whose own guilt is so strong that it prevents them from dealing with the youth's antisocial behavior.

CREDIT: *Seymour L. Halleck, M.D., Professor of Psychiatry, University of North Carolina School of Medicine, Chapel Hill, North Carolina.*

Reconciliation

We are referring here to an attempt to repair a marriage that has fallen apart. It is a problem with many sides and there are no solutions that will work for every couple.

Reconciliation is best approached by understanding the strength of the desire of each partner to save the marriage and the intensity of effort each one is willing to commit. It will not work if one mate needs the other desperately and will do anything to patch things up while the other partner is merely going through the motions.

The interest in reconciliation does not have to be the same in each partner (one can have a greater desire than the other) but they both must be sincere in their wishes that the effort succeed.

People grow at different rates and in different directions through the years. They also change in regard to their values and interests. Moreover, marriages have a life of their own. They do not remain the same. They also go through stages. Marriage brings changes. The honeymoon is over—along comes the first child, a new job, etc. Life keeps changing and the mates may react differently to the changes. For example, our present culture has been called the "narcissistic age." These new values direct the individual to take care of himself. The family (past, present and future) becomes secondary to gratifying his or her personal pleasures. Both mates may adopt this new set of values or one may and the other may not. Either way, this force from the culture, as well as the different marriage stages mentioned above, contributes to the falling apart of marriages.

It it is obvious that not all marriages are worth saving and not all couples should be reconciled. This, however, is not for the "expert" to decide (with one possible exception which I will mention later). It is up to the individuals who must live with the consequences of the divorce. Let me illustrate.

Two women had idential situations. Both marriages turned out to be shams. Their husbands were skirt-chasers who had lost physical, emotional and intellectual interest in their wives after the birth of the children. The husbands provided nothing beyond financial support. They left all other responsibilities to their wives. Both women had been overprotected and sheltered by their parents. When their own children grew up and left home they suffered from the "empty nest syndrome." They became depressed and had to seek psychiatric help. Both their psychiatrists asked to see their husbands. Both husbands refused to come. Finally both women sought and received divorces with adequate financial settlements. They went through the typical post-divorce period with anxiety and depression. One of the wives, however, found herself. She obtained a job and began to experience the joy of being alone and free. She spoke of never having been happier in her life and no longer mourned the loss of her husband.

The other wife was incapable of living alone. Separation and freedom were no joy to her. She missed the safe position of being a married woman. The agonies she suffered when her husband was running around were easier to bear than being alone. She complained that her therapist had misled her, that he should have insisted that she not get a divorce. She misread his sympathy as a personal interest. She did not tell him of her fantasy that he would take her husband's place and make up for all the years when she was neglected.

No therapist should tell a woman *not* to reconcile if she wants to. The one exception is where there is physical abuse. These women, who are willing to experience repeated beatings to keep the marriage together, run the risk of being beaten to death. The advice to these women can be compared to the efforts to prevent a person from committing suicide. The same is true when the husband is a repeated child beater. Then the effort is to prevent the death of the child. Of course, the husbands should be urged to get treatment, but often they refuse and separation is a life-saving measure.

Let us take another example that illustrates additional principles. The husband was an anxious, dependent, hard-working man, very much in love with his wife. He was a "one-woman" man, a kind and loving father who spent time with and enjoyed his children. But the wife was the leader of the family. She was a bright, cheerful, active person, knowledgeable in the arts and humanities. She was also a fine mother, an excellent sex partner, kind and caring, and she brought excitement into her husband's life.

However, she was also interested in almost everything and everybody with whom she came in contact. She had many women friends and many men friends with whom she may or may not have had sexual affairs. His family and friends began to talk about her, which contributed to his jealousy. He separated from her and was miserable. He dated many women and was alternately bored and depressed by them. Finally, with help, he made the decision to ignore the gossip. He wanted his wife back and would accept her as she was. He knew she loved him in her own way and that was good enough for him. The point of this example is that partners match up. They have unconscious collusions on how to get along together. The match-up need not be perfect for the marriage to work. One must always respect this unconscious collusion that makes for lasting marriages or contributes to successful reconciliations.

There are other relationships known as unconsummated marriages. These involve wives who, from childhood, fear sexual relations. The husbands are kind, gentle men who accept the situation and live without sex. When the wives finally come for medical help and are ready for sex, the husbands turn out to be quite appreciative of the added pleasure. Again, when both mates want to live together, they find a way to do so. They make match-ups that are mutually gratifying.

Couples who want to live together and are willing to work out their problems should be encouraged to do so. If what brought them together in the first place is still present, but has been tarnished, it needs polishing. If the changes that took place have destroyed the original bond, a new bond must be found. Professional help is advisable.

There are three main approaches that help remedy such problems. One is where anger seems to be the most obvious cause of the problem. This calls for sitting down together and saying to one another, "Help me with my anger. I become very angry when you make critical remarks about me (fill in the specifics). Please help me get rid of my anger."

The second is where hurt is uppermost, followed by withdrawal or anger. Here the mutual help starts with "Help me with my hurt. Please help me to be free of my pain." Mutual working together on an important problem is already a good start towards reconciliation.

The third approach needs professional help. When the problem appears to be mainly sexual (marital and sexual problems merge but some are mainly sexual), then sexual therapy by trained, qualified sexual therapists is needed. These are educational problems more than relational problems. When deep seated relational problems are present, sexual therapy without marital therapy won't work.

Those who use any or all of the above approaches successfully are negotiating a new, up-to-date and workable marriage contract. Mutual commitment to the new contract bodes well for success. It may be a renewal of old marriage vows for the first time, or a commitment to a new, future-oriented contract.

The willingness and the capacity for change in both mates are the most important ingredients in a successful reconciliation. There must be genuine and continuing commitment and not false promises made in order to get the other mate back—and then business as usual. Also they must not be based on the understanding that one mate was wrong and the other was right. Each contributed in his or her own way to the marriage failure and should admit it. Reconciliation must not be considered a fifty-fifty effort, with both mates watching to see if the other is doing an equal share. It takes a 100 percent individual responsibility and effort by both. With such an effort each mate will be a more mature person than before, and the marriage will be stronger than it was before the break. The result will be a healthier union with greater respect and appreciation than ever.

The preceding paragraphs indicate theoretically the way in which any type of couple should try a reconciliation. The analogy could be made to a broken bone. Theoretically with every type of broken bone an attempt should be made to heal it. Theoretically it will be stronger at the healing line than it was before the break. In practice, however, some bones are shattered in too many pieces to heal straight or to become functional again. In some instances the pain of healing will be too intense or may even produce complications that might endanger the life of the individual. The same goes for some marriages. They are too shattered. Too much harm and hurt have been done to either or both parties. The reconciliation process can be too traumatic, endangering emotional health in the process.

In some marriages, hatred and vindictiveness have been the single bond which kept the marriage together and there are no areas of agreement or compatibility with which to work. These marriages had a poor chance from the beginning because respect for the rights of the mate had never been present. But again, this is up to the individuals involved to decide, since for some, a poor relationship with all its agonies may *for them* be better than nothing.

It is difficult to describe a couple who had better not attempt a reconciliation but one classic example is the following: a marriage between two strong individuals with each one needing to be the dominant personality. This is an obvious mismatch. They cannot get along together. They would both do better alone or with someone else. The qualification I have to throw in is that they tend not to admire or respect a person they can dominate and are attracted to other dominant personalities who resist their need for control.

There are circumstances, of course, where the disadvantaged one wants a divorce but cannot get one. For example, in some religious orders the women give up their legal rights in signing a marriage contract and become victims of abuse by husbands. They want out but cannot get a divorce unless they give up the children and/or rights to property. The only way the woman can get a divorce is if she accepts her husband's conditions, which leave her without children, property or self-respect. These are social injustices which need to be changed. At present, divorce laws are being re-examined in America to prevent such inequities and progress is being made.

A less bizarre and more common type of marital disorder where reconciliation is better for one mate than for the other is where one mate can never admit to being wrong and blames the other for everything that doesn't go right (the way he or she wants it to go). This type of marriage may continue for years. The criticized one often becomes convinced that he or she is totally at fault. The brainwashing is successful.

He or she would be better off without the criticizing mate but doesn't know it. Sometimes the "criticizers" make a mistake. They believe what they have been saying, and get a separation or a divorce. Now the criticized ones are forced to get along on their own. After an initial anxiety stage they often do beautifully. They find new friends who admire and appreciate them. They also find a new freedom which is exhilarating—if nothing else, a freedom from criticism.

The "criticizer," meanwhile, with no mate to blame, is in trouble. No one else will take from him or her what the former mate took. They often ask for reconciliation or remarriage, but it is too late. Some become tragic figures living with their mistakes. Others, after a difficult adjustment period, successfully effect a change in themselves which allows true self-respect and self-confidence for the first time.

In summary, reconciliations are workable by a large majority of sincere marriage couples if they are willing to work at it. Separation and divorce, on the other hand, can be turned into a good thing if the individuals make a virtue of a necessity and continue to grow and develop through the experience.

CREDIT: *Peter A. Martin, M.D., Clinical Professor of Psychiatry, University of Michigan and Wayne State University Medical School; author of* A Marital Therapy Manual, *New York: Brunner/Mazel, 1976.*

Religion

Its Meaning in Our Troubled Times

Religion. Scholars have long debated the origins of this word. Innately, there is a deep sense in every man and woman that turns us toward that which is "the holy," toward the source and goal of our religious instinct.

But if we are to understand the meaning of religion in our troubled times, perhaps it is best to go back to the Latin roots of *religio*. The three verbs *relegere, religari* and *re-eligere* are considered the possible derivations.

Relegere—to "constantly turn to" or "conscientiously observe." In the swift-paced, often changing, sometimes fickle world that we experience as our home in this last quarter of the twentieth century, there is an inner drive, a deep need for someone or something to which we can constantly turn. We have our friends, our loved ones. We have our strong influences and supports. We have strengths both within and without our own person. But is there someone to whom we can constantly turn? Is there a someone who answers the dilemma of our human journey? Is there indeed a safe place in our troubled times? It is to religion that mankind naturally turns when faced with these questions. This response is not a purely speculative reaction. To "conscientiously observe" is another of the root derivations of the word "religion." Throughout the history of religious experience, mankind has been aware of the responsibilities implicit in such a response. Religion is not an opiate, a way to relieve the tensions of unanswered basic questions. When a person turns to religion for an answer, he finds himself in a situation that demands personal involvement in the religious response. Ethical expectations, moral demands, a call to self-realization and self-development flow naturally from the structures of the great religions of mankind. In the "conscientious observance" of religious laws and/or ideals, again we find the relevance of religion in our troubled times.

The second derivation of the word "religion" is found in the verb *religari* —to bind oneself—to bind oneself back to one's origin and goal. It is in recalling our roots and our destiny that the individual is empowered to experience the joy of the human journey and to bear with the pain, loneliness, sickness and death that are part of this journey. In binding oneself to his origin and goal, the individual binds himself to the source and end point of his life as well. This absolute beginning and end are what mankind understands as the divine. The alpha and omega points of man's personal history are that same creative force that underpins all of reality. In binding himself to that reality, the individual finds that common bond which binds him with all other men and women—for that matter, with all of creation. It is in the discovery of this unifying principle that we find the greatest potential for true peace and harmony. Man is bound not only to the Absolute Being but he is bound as well to all other members of the human family and to this universe that is our home and life-support system. When an individual realizes and accepts this fact, the deepest act of personal integration ensues. In binding himself to the Eternal, he is bound as well to the fragile, volatile uncertainties of the human condition. Thus, he is integrated within himself and learns the deepest lesson that religion can teach.

Finally, since this task set before us by the word "religion" is so difficult, speaking to us of origins and goals, deep questions of human existence, mankind can *re-eligere*. He can "choose again." The process of religious experience is not a once-and-forever event. As we proceed through life, we are constantly wrestling with questions of our origin and goals. Each day, each year, each peak experience of life can give us new insights, new answers— and, at times, new questions related to our deepest search. We are called upon to choose, to choose again and again and again. In so doing, we are guided by our personal and social religious history. At the same time we are constantly shaping our personal religious response.

Hopefully, this response, as it deepens in maturity, becomes a stronger determinant in our personality—and so teaches us how to live and find meaning in these troubled times.

CREDIT: *John Cardinal Cody, Archbishop of Chicago, appointed to cardinalate by Pope Paul VI in 1967.*

A Religion For Today

I had nothing to do with my coming into this world, I will have nothing to do with my leaving it. My responsibility is to live in such a way that some child, some dumb animal or old, broken person, somebody who is having a hard time will be glad because I lived. For that gladness I would trade all your theology—all your outgrown, dead mythology.

There is no page of human history that does not reveal that man had some kind of religion. Through the centuries man has been developing, gradually and honorably, at times with severe setbacks, toward a satisfactory religion that might answer his intellectual needs, conform to the finest of scientific achievements and at the same time preserve a sense of harmony with the universe.

Hold fast to the simple principles of integrity of the self and respect for others. I am interested in a religion which is founded on a fine awareness of individual and social values in human society, which inspires us to the cultivation of a higher standard of values in our relations with one another; in a religion which constantly holds up before the individual the ideal concept that he possesses a deep possibility for becoming better than he is now; a religious life that leads the individual to strive toward the attainment of that ideal and, in striving, to do more good for himself and for society; a religious life that inspires enjoyment and love of life.

We must be more than good—we must be good for *something*. We must not be satisfied merely to be moral. We must see morality as our responsibility to respond to the needs of others, to love and help our fellow man.

Let us find a religion for today. What will it be? How shall we know it? First of all, it must be a religion that will have intellectual courage. It must be a rational religion. It must have social courage. It must be a religion that will address itself to unemployment, poverty, injustice, war—all the modern disasters of society.

The religion of today must be a religion that is not afraid to attack social injustice. Above all, it must have moral courage which in the presence of customs and traditions will maintain the integrity of a free spirit. Find that religion and you have found a religion for today. The labels and the creeds will not matter.

CREDIT: *Dr. Preston Bradley, pastor of the People's Church, Chicago, Illinois.*

Religious Cults

A Trap for the Young? What Parents Can Do

This is the age of messiahs, a time when new religions are prospering. Each campus has its share of gurus. Young people are flocking to join religious movements that are often cults.

There are enough leaders of new religions around, commandeering the time and energy of thousands of disciples, to make a definition of the most dangerous type of cult a necessary part of the education of young people.

Here are some criteria a person may use to determine the legitimacy of a new religion:

The cult has a living leader. Cult doctrine is based on his (or her) revelations, which either supplant or supplement traditional doctrine and scripture.

The cult leader enjoys absolute authority over the members. He often lives in kingly splendor while his subjects live in poverty.

A cult promises a system in which a convert may work to save the world and humanity but actually sponsors no community-improvement programs.

The daily work of nearly all cult members is demeaning and utilizes little of their potential, in terms of intelligence, training or education.

Religious cults are exclusive social systems, claiming that their members will achieve salvation (or happiness). Members are taught to believe that they are superior to those outside the group.

To be a member of a cult a person must cut himself off from job, education, friends and family.

Methods of ego destruction and thought control are part of a religious cult's recruiting and indoctrination practices.

Cults discourage critical analysis by dictating the suppression of negative thoughts, therefore fostering a dependency on the cult's authority that arrests the maturation process.

The cult rituals and practices are psychologically unwholesome and in some cases physically dangerous when they involve the use of drugs or perverse sexual rites.

The cults concentrate on recruiting the sons and daughters of the middle class, preying on the vulnerabilities of this particular generation of young adults. In our efforts to profile the cult member, we hurtled into blind alleys each time we groped for a simple solution or a pat generalization. As a group, these young disciples could be part of any crowd of idealistic college-age kids. As individuals, each is unique. Judging from the hundreds of religious-cult members we have met we can say they could be anyone's son or daughter, your best friend or the kid next door.

Religious cults exploit youth and ought to be held accountable for the techniques they use to convert and control their members. But the cults cannot be blamed for the cultural conditions that make today's young people especially vulnerable. Society must accept this responsibility.

When we started to write our analysis of the religious-cult experience, we could see that young people's minds and actions were changed significantly once they adopted fervent religious beliefs. But we had trouble believing cult critics who told us, "Thousands of brainwashed American young people are running around this country carrying out the orders of malicious false messiahs who have programmed them and robbed them of their minds."

Parents who feel they've lost a son or daughter to a religious cult often want desperately to believe their children have been unwitting victims of insidious plots to separate them from their real personalities. But as fantastic as the allegations may seem, our observations validated the fears of coercion and brainwashing.

The process is not nearly as dramatic as the mystery that surrounds it suggests. The mechanics are subtle. Victims often don't even know they are being manipulated. The change is gradual and it begins long before the recruit starts to believe.

But the condition of ego destruction and coercive persuasion, mystical manipulation, the need of purity, confession, the separation of the group through the aura of sacred science, the development of a new language and the belief that all outsiders are unworthy and unfit for salvation—all must be present in order for the subject to be brainwashed.

Rick Heller, a college student from Dallas, told us how he surprised himself when he started behaving like a Moonie. Rick went to spend a night in the Unification Church at their center in Austin, Texas. His older brother was a member of this group and Rick thought he might like to be one too. "I was in my sleeping bag on the floor of a room with about twenty other guys. At about five-thirty in the morning this guy comes in with a guitar and starts playing and singing 'You Are My Sunshine.' I thought, 'Oh, brother.' I rolled over, buried my face and tried to go back to sleep.

"But all of a sudden I realized all the other guys were singing and rolling up their sleeping bags. It was weird, like a private production of *Hair* or something. I thought, 'They're crazy, a bunch of fanatics.' But then I realized that I was the only one in the room who wasn't singing . . . so I started to sing too."

Rick explains that then he had to rationalize and justify his behavior to himself. "I had thought they were behaving like fanatics. But I was behaving just like them. Either they weren't crazy, or I was. So I decided they were okay. I was behaving like a Moonie before I knew what hit me," he says.

Brainwashing? Hardly. But like Rick Heller, we attended religious-cult recruiting workshops and experienced and observed the process of conversion. Our inside look at what can happen during the initial contact with religious cults convinced us that the common sequence of events that precedes these "conversions" is similar in many ways to the coercive techniques used by the Chinese Communists during their revolution and the North Koreans in their prisoner-of-war camps.

The issue of brainwashing in religious cults cannot be discounted.

What conditions in religious-cult recruiting are similar to brainwashing techniques?

Unrelenting group pressure, combined with a young subject's inherent need to conform, produces the same result as imprisonment. During their indoctrination programs the groups use various techniques to heighten the emotions while at the same time they often keep their identities as religious groups carefully hidden.

(When we were recruited by the Unification Church, all potential members were told the group was a community service project. Not only was the Reverend Moon's name never mentioned, but when we repeatedly asked if the group had an affiliation to any religious group the answer was no.)

The second stage in adopting the belief system of a religious cult is the *increased suggestibility* of the mind. Now the recruit is "softened up" and is high on both emotion and the idea of adopting lofty new goals.

While the mind is suggestible, *new beliefs are introduced* to supplant old ones. Here is where one of the most dangerous of the cult's philosophies is introduced: "Skepticism is negativism," and you must not question our beliefs until you understand all. Since "understanding all" is clearly an impossible goal, the young converts are trained not to question but to accept on face value all they are taught.

In the final stage of conversion, the new convert's *mind is controlled.* During this conversion, his behavior has been changed, his consciousness has been altered, and ultimately, his mind and his behavior are controlled by the cult, by members who have themselves undergone the identical process and have become true believers.

There are many avenues open to parents of cult members. Here are some of those choices:

There is the rescue (kidnap and snatch, as it is sometimes called) and deprogramming, a debriefing session where the young cultist listens to information he has often not had the chance to hear. Most of this information is carefully gathered by the deprogrammer and his assistants and organized as opposed to cult involvement. Those who favor deprogrammings say that only in this way can young people be returned to personal choice and freedom of thought.

Legal removal of a young person from a cult is often accomplished by a court order, demanding that a young person (whether legally a child or an adult) be turned over to the custody of his parents. This is usually carried out in conjunction with a formal deprogramming.

The bargain (or contract) between parent and child. Here, a parent might say to the child, "If you plan to spend the rest of your life in this group, you owe us one week (or month or any reasonable period of time) to hear our side of the story and to explain to us the other side of your story." Then an informal, well-organized series of talks with authorities on cults and former members might take place.

Wait and work. Some parents feel it is unscrupulous to remove a child from the cult without his consent, but at the same time they are opposed to their child's commitment to the new religion so they work at accumulating information about the religious cult. There is a danger here that positions will become hardened and communication will be impossible. But if parents attempt to listen and ask non-threatening questions, and adopt a neutral or low-key attitude, there may be the possibility of accomplishing informal deprogramming without losing contact with a son or daughter.

Wait and hope for the best. Like the proverbial ostrich with its head in the sand, some parents wait and do nothing, hoping the son or daughter will "come to his senses" and leave the group on his own. One mother tells of spending a year drinking and praying. With her subsequent feeling of loss of control over both her own and her son's life, it is not surprising that she now considers that year a waste of time. She has since had her son legally removed and deprogrammed from the Church of Armageddon, the Love Israel Family, in Seattle.

Conditional approval. There are parents who, in fact, condone a son's or daughter's cult membership because it has ended a pattern of drug experimentation, brushes with the law, psychiatric care and institutionalization or just general aimlessness. This is a parent who might say, "He's better off there than he was on drugs."

Complete approval. There are many parents who think being a member of the Unification Church, or the Children of God, or any other religious cult is a constructive way of life. One set of parents, the Dwayne Blacks of northern California, attended a Creative Community Project meeting and said they were amazed at how different and clean the young Unification Church members look within weeks of "conversion." Mrs. Black told us that church members' attitudes are so vastly improved, their general demeanor so much more wholesome than before, that she and her husband fully approve of son Dwight's involvement and do not understand other parents' negative attitudes.

It is the responsibility of each family to respond in its own way to the threat of the religious cult that separates parents from sons and daughters. Members of families can call on the major institutions in society for help.

The countercult parents' groups are doing just that, and many of them are doing it well.

Here are the names of several such parents' groups:

Committee Engaged in Freeing Minds, Box 5084, Arlington, Texas 76011

Citizens Engaged in Reuniting Families, Box 348, Harrison, New York 10052

Citizens Freedom Foundation, Box 256, Chula Vista, California 92012

Free Minds, Inc., Box 4216, Minneapolis, Minnesota 55414

Individual Freedom Foundation, Box 48, Ardmore, Pennsylvania 19003

CREDIT: *Carroll Stoner, author of* All God's Children, *Radnor, Pennsylvania: Chilton Book Company, co-author Ann Clarke*

Retirement—How, When and Where

How to retire? The secret of retirement planning is to start planning *now*. No matter what your age or stage of living, you'll enrich your present as well as assure your future. For instance:

It's not *where* you live but *how* that determines your cost of living. Simplify your life today, and you'll have more money today and tomorrow.

Start *now* on a program of enjoyable exercise, proper diet and sufficient rest. You'll be happier and healthier—today and tomorrow.

Start *now* to develop a hobby, service project, second career. You can enjoy it today and perfect it tomorrow.

Planning invites a challenge. But someone once said, "Challenges are opportunities in work clothes." Challenges *create* opportunities. We don't get much out of life unless we respond to a challenge. Retirement gives you that sort of challenge—something to aim at and strive for. And the secret of a full response to a challenge is to *plan* for it.

How do you go about planning? Base your plans on knowledge—knowledge of yourself, and of the retirement world. In seeking knowledge of yourself, analyze what kind of a person you are, what you want from retirement and what resources you have to realize these wants.

In seeking knowledge of the retirement world, discover what possibilities are open to that person you discovered through self-analysis. Here are some of the challenges you'll find in the retirement world:

Health. Consult your doctor and learn how to maintain and improve your health to prevent or postpone physical and mental changes: to find enjoyable activities . . .

Finances. Plan ways to reduce expenses and increase income . . . to protect savings from inflation and to invest surplus cash in safe investments . . . to take advantage of special retirement tax deductions and to make maximum use of Medicare and Social Security . . .

Leisure. Find *meaningful* activities that pay you tangible rewards . . . travel with a purpose and in ways that suit your pocketbook and personality . . . find new values in activities involving self-expression, participation, learning, contemplation . . .

Housing. Plan well in advance to find housing that is as personal as your dreams and as practical as your pocketbook . . . to improve your lifestyle in your old community or find a new lifestyle in a new location . . . to reduce the expense and maintenance of housing to give yourself more freedom . . . to make your housing suitable for all stages of retirement living (activity, privacy, convalescence) . . .

Legal matters. Learn how the law affects you in Social Security, Medicare, buying and selling retirement housing, starting a retirement business, a late or second marriage, taking care of an ill or incompetent relative or friend, types of ownership, making a will, estate planning . . .

A good guide to help you resolve the challenges and take advantage of the opportunities of the above is *The Complete Retirement Planning Book* by Peter A. Dickinson (E. P. Dutton, 1976).

When can you retire? The average retirement age is dropping, and many employees and employers are anticipating early retirement. Some 96 percent of pension plans have "escape hatches" for early retirement, and over half of those now collecting Social Security are under age sixty-five. On the other hand, Congress early in 1978 passed a law eliminating the mandatory retirement age of sixty-five.

Regardless of at what age you retire, it would be very comforting if you have:

An income of at least $10,000 (from all sources) for yourself and spouse, and proportionately more in succeeding years to keep ahead of inflation.

Major financial obligations (mortgages, children's education, installment payments) either paid off or under control.

At least $10,000 in savings or investments.

Counseling or some study in advance of retirement.

A second career or socially useful part-time occupation, preferably one that pays.

This last point is important, because you get a second wind through a second career. If it's deeply satisfying, you'll find that making money is no longer of paramount importance. By organizing your life around your own standards, you can cut down on expenses without sacrificing lifestyle, and you can always earn enough money to bridge the gap between the present and the time when you can start drawing Social Security and a pension (if you retire early). Most important, you can start preparing yourself *now* for the opportunities that lie ahead—both psychological and financial.

Where to retire? Finding retirement housing is like selecting a spouse: There are many possibilities, but few that are right. Ideally, the "right" housing should take care of us rather than require us to take care of it. It should give us shelter, security, privacy; allow us freedom; keep us near friends, relatives—and a grocer who delivers.

The fact remains that 70 percent of us retire in the place we now live. Of those who move, about 25 per cent move to a smaller place in the same general area, and only about 5 percent actually leave their home state. But even those who don't move often dream of it. A recent study showed that about 60 percent of retirees consider moving.

What parts of the United States are "best" for retirement? While no place is perfect, here are some generalizations you can make about each region of the United States according to:

Cost of living. Recently, the U. S. Bureau of Labor Statistics compared retirement living costs in various parts of the United States using a scale on which 100 represents the average retirement budget for the urban United States (places with populations of 2,500 or more). The Bureau determined that for metropolitan areas with populations of 2,500 to 50,000, the average index is 106. For non-metropolitan areas with populations of 2,500 to 50,000, the average is 82. By regions, the non-metropolitan indices are: Northeast, 95; North Central, 85; West, 84; South, 77. Among selected individual metropolitan areas, Boston at 130 was the highest; Baton Rouge, Louisiana, the lowest at 87.

Taxes. Generally, taxes are highest in the Northeast and lowest in the North Central states. Taxes are generally higher in the West than in the South. Most states have homestead and property tax exemptions for seniors, but you must meet residency requirements and you must apply for them. Also, lower taxes generally mean a lower level of services.

Health care. The availability of hospital beds and doctors tends to reflect the general population trend. Thus, you'll find the largest number of hospital beds (general medical and surgical plus nursing homes) in the Northeast, with 9 beds per 1,000 population. There are 7.5 beds per 1,000 in the North Central states, 7.4 in the South, and 6.2 in the West.

Climate. Your body functions best at about 66 degrees F. with a relative humidity of about 55 percent. The older we get, the less we can stand extremes of temperature or humidity. Doctors say localities below the snowline are frequently recommended for arthritis, rheumatism, emphysema, sinus, respiratory problems, hypertension and heart disease. Stress diseases—ulcers, certain heart problems and hardening of the arteries—are less frequent in warm zones. Diabetes appears to be more controllable in the tropics. Sometimes an arid, warm climate helps sufferers who have hay fever and allergies.

Safety. No place is completely "safe," but generally the South is the safest region of the United States, followed by the North Central, Northeast and West. Here, for example, are some popular retirement towns rated in terms of safety (in order): Provo, Utah; Albany, Georgia; Midland, Texas; Odessa, Texas; Wichita Falls, Texas; Fort Smith, Arkansas; Lakewood, California.

Adding together safety, climate, health facilities, cost of living and availability of retirement housing, where are retirees settling? Most who do move go to the so-called "retirement belt," which lies south of a line between San Francisco and Norfolk, Virginia, or to the area west of the Cascades-Sierra range. Here snow is relatively rare, weather is mild and sunny, with an average annual temperature of 55 degrees F. or higher.

Homes in this belt usually don't require furnaces, basements, heavy insulation, etc. You can save on fuel, clothing, car operation and doctor bills.

Many of these "ideal" retirement towns are covered in detail (climate and environment, medical facilities, cost and availability of housing, cost of living, culture and recreation, special services to seniors) in the book *Sunbelt Retirement* by Peter A. Dickinson (E. P. Dutton, 1978).

But remember this important lesson: It's not *where* you live but *how* you live that determines your cost of living. If you want the same services and facilities you have now, it will cost you about the same no matter where you locate. While some state taxes may be lower, some local taxes may be higher. And you may have to pay for services that are covered by taxes where you now live.

Now is the time to explore those places you might like to live, and to experiment with different ways of life. Retirement can be the most enjoyable and productive time of your life—if you *plan* for it. You'll have many happier tomorrows—if you start planning today!

CREDIT: *Peter A. Dickinson, retirement planning consultant, Larchmont, New York; Editor of "The Retirement Letter."*

Rhinoplasty ("Nose Job")

Definition: "Rhino" is from the Greek, meaning "nose." "Plasty," also Greek, means "to mold." Therefore, rhinoplasty is an operation to change the shape or structure of the nose and thereby improve its appearance and possibly its function.

Synonyms: A rhinoplasty is frequently spoken of by lay people as a "nose job"; "a plastic on the nose"; "a nose bob," etc.

HOW TO SELECT A DOCTOR FOR YOUR RHINOPLASTY

Most people see a nose job they like on a friend or relative, ask, "Who did it?" and then go to that doctor. Or you can ask your family doctor or another doctor in whom you have confidence to recommend one to you. Or get in touch with your County Medical Society or the Executive Office of the American Society of Plastic and Reconstructive Surgeons, Inc., 29 East Madison, Suite 607, Chicago, Illinois 60602.

Beware of the plastic surgeon who advertises in newspapers. Many of these surgeons have had little or no training in plastic surgery.

Inquire of any doctor if he has been certified by the American Board of Plastic Surgery. Some otolaryngologists may perform rhinoplasties also. If you go to one, ask to see pictures of some of his patients with noses similar to yours.

WHO WOULD BE A GOOD CANDIDATE FOR A RHINOPLASTY OPERATION?

The person who has an obvious deformity of the nose and is unhappy because of it and simply wishes to have it corrected. The alert plastic surgeon will be wary, however, of the patient who comes in with a deformity but is sure that having a "nose job" will assure her success and popularity which she has not experienced previously. In other words, unrealistic expectations are likely to result in disappointment and dissatisfaction with the operation. Furthermore, the wise plastic surgeon will reject the patient who complains of very slight defects or the patient who has had previous plastic operations on the nose and still complains of imperfections that the surgeon cannot see.

In considering the patient's face, the plastic surgeon may note that the chin is retruding and may advise building out the chin by inserting a small plastic implant either through a small incision under the chin or a small incision just inside the lower lip. This additional surgery may change a good result to a marvelous over-all result.

COSMETIC OR CORRECTIVE RHINOPLASTY

This is the most common plastic operation on the nose. It is usually done for removal of a hump or bump on the bridge of the nose. It is usually a condition inherited from one of the parents and begins to develop sometime after puberty. Aside from the hump, other complaints are that the nose is too large or too wide, the tip is too bulbous or the nose is crooked—or the tip hangs down or pulls down when the person is smiling, the skin is too thick and oily or the nose is too flat; the nose is crooked and breathing on one or both sides is difficult; the columella (middle part) hangs down too much or is too high.

Almost all of these problems may be satisfactorily corrected, although the nose with a thick, oily skin is difficult to correct.

Timing: Most surgeons prefer to wait until the nose is fully developed (girls fifteen to sixteen, boys sixteen to eighteen). The theory is that if the nose is reshaped before growth is completed, continued growth after the operation might result in a change in the shape of the nose.

ANESTHESIA

This may be a local anesthetic plus proper sedation to calm the patient, or a general anesthetic with the patient being put completely to sleep. The doctor and patient agree beforehand as to what anesthetic is to be used. A local anesthetic is the safest and with an adequate dose of sedatives is quite satisfactory for the majority of patients. Immature persons or extremely nervous persons may do better under a general anesthetic. A general anesthetic, although extremely safe, still carries a slightly greater risk than a local anesthetic.

THE OPERATION

The operation is performed through the nostrils without any external incision. The hump is removed with a saw or chisel or scissors according to the preference of the surgeon. To prevent the nose from looking flat a cut is made through the nasal bones on each side so that they can be pushed together to narrow the nose. As a rule the nasal tip will require refinement by removal of some cartilage.

Where is the operation performed? Most rhinoplasties are done in a hospital operating room. Some doctors may have a well-equipped operating room set up in their office where the surgery may be performed satisfactorily. Perhaps the most common routine would be admission to the hospital one afternoon with surgery on the following day. Many doctors prefer this arrangement in the interest of postoperative care and patient comfort.

Other doctors are willing to operate in their own office operating room or on an out-patient basis at the hospital with the patient going home the same day of surgery. The main advantage of this routine is a reduction in expense.

The postoperative course: There is surprisingly little pain associated with a rhinoplasty. Usually a metal or plaster of Paris splint will be applied to the nose to be worn for about one week. Swelling and discoloration of the lower eyelids is to be expected, but this usually clears up in about two weeks. The nose will likely be more or less stuffy for a week and there is usually some clear or slightly blood-tinged drainage for a few days. Rarely a "nose bleed" or hemorrhage may occur on the day of surgery or a week after the surgery. Most of the swelling of the nose disappears in about two weeks but there will be a slight residual swelling in the skin which may require several weeks or months to subside.

The submucous resection (*SMR*): If the nasal septum is deviated markedly to one or both sides of the nasal cavity it may cause obstruction to breathing. Most plastic surgeons would probably do a submucous resection of the septal cartilage or a septoplasty (straightening of the septum). Some surgeons prefer to do the septal operation either before or after the rhinoplasty even though this means another operation.

RECONSTRUCTIVE RHINOPLASTY

Sometimes all or part of the nose may be destroyed by accident, cancer or disease. In such cases reconstruction usually requires the use of skin flaps from the forehead, cheek or arm and may require more than one operation.

CONCLUSION

A rhinoplastic operation, when performed by an experienced and artistic plastic surgeon on a properly selected patient, can be a most satisfying procedure. On the other hand, when poorly done it can be a disaster. The importance of carefully selecting your surgeon is, therefore, obvious.

CREDIT: *Thomas D. Cronin, M.D., Clinical Professor of Plastic Surgery, Baylor College of Medicine, Houston, Texas; and Director of Plastic Surgery Residency Training Program at St. Joseph Hospital, Houston, Texas.*

Runaway

Perhaps your youngster has just run away and you are looking to these pages for counsel. If so, you may well be experiencing a bewildering mixture of fear, hurt and rage, and guilt and depression. The fear, of course, is because your child could be in danger. It is an agonizing worry even though the chances are better than ten to one that he or she will come to no harm, and might be enjoying his travels. Nevertheless, awful things do happen, and parents face the unknown until their child returns. It is worse when the runaway is a girl.

The hurt and rage are because a runaway is considered a slap in the face to the family. It is an assault. Parents sometimes bury their rage until just after a tearful and relieved reunion, when anger pours forth unchecked. This should be guarded against.

The guilt and depression are because most parents, deep inside, sense that somehow they have "failed." Some parents wonder, "What did we do wrong?" Others know clearly how they got off the track. Some parents feel innocent, even righteously indignant, and blame the runaway youngster. If you are in this last category, a little soul-searching may be in order. Some families respond to runaways with a sense of shame and shun friends who wish to help. Friends will rally around and can be a source of strength and support.

It is crucial to know that the task for the family, when the lost is found, is to be emotionally ahead of where they were when the young person sought the runaway solution. By this I mean that when the child comes home, it is time to be constructive, a point I will return to at the end.

Why do kids run? In childhood, runs are usually brief. The angry stomp down the block, or the adventurous explorer. Here every effort should be to understand, to empathize, to get the message of distress. But most runs are by adolescents. Hall, in 1904, wrote, "At the dawn of adolescence the impulse to migrate or wander shows a great and sudden increase. The restlessness of spring is greatly augmented." This very impulse, then, presents itself to the adolescent as a possible solution for a problem. We know the Beatles' song "She's Leaving Home After Living Alone All of These Years." The Beatles sensed what is so often a part of running—a psychological twist from passive to active. "She" abandoned those she had felt abandoned by. In many cases, the runaway is somehow doing to the family what he or she feels the family has done to him or her.

Anger, a disappointment, unhappiness, vengeance, the need to escape from an intolerable situation, the wish for independence, the need to separate from an overly close family, the desire to be with someone else, a run "to something" are but a few of many motives. Sometimes, of course, youngsters are kicked out openly or subtly. However, the "why" is often never really understood until long after return—or maybe never. The reasons are often not well formed, and the young person can only say, "I just wanted to—or had to."

Young people run away from all kinds of families—rich, poor, close, distant. Most commonly, they run from families in which there is tension; tension between them and their parents, and more important for the parents to reflect on, tension between the parents about something, either overt or hidden. Some runs are from intolerable, abusive homes, or broken and remarried families where the young person may not really be welcome. Such families have great difficulty bringing themselves to seek help. Some young people who run are seriously emotionally disturbed. The run is but the latest sign of trouble—a cry for help. However, a run can be a first obvious sign of trouble. When in doubt, seek advice.

These days young people run into a world "out there" where an underground exists that is much more intricate than it was a generation ago. The runaway may be sheltered and nurtured in a crash pad or commune, or by well-meaning but perhaps questionable families that take young people in. Some religious groups, of which there are both good and evil examples, take young people in. Unhappily, some parts of the underground are brutally exploitative and dangerous and are fronts for entry into the hideous life of the flesh market. Please know that the psychological injury from a very bad experience is healable. Parents of children who have had bad experiences need to discipline themselves not to think of their young person as ruined, but as needing their help in healing and in seeking counsel. Do not bury a secret that will explode later—like a buried time bomb.

As the incidence of runaways has increased, and it did strikingly during the late 1960s and has remained high, public agencies such as the police, local mental health agencies and ministers have become much more knowledgeable and can be very helpful. Even though police deal with a tremendous number of cases and often suffer manpower shortages, they can be a source of wise counsel. Parents need to know that no agency can do everything a family might wish. Regulations in some instances even protect privacy and prevent certain kinds of investigation and search.

To search themselves or not to search? When to search? How much to search? These are questions which plague the family. There are no "right" answers to these questions. Each family must proceed in ways that make them feel best. For what it is worth, it has seemed to me that runaways tend to get found when they are ready to be found. However, the family that searches not at all or preoccupies itself totally with search may well need help in gaining perspective.

Sometimes, particularly after days or weeks or months, it is useful to get a message to the underground: "Come home, all is forgiven." Everything gets negotiable and then there can be peaceful re-entry. But parents don't always feel that way. Parents can "abandon back" with retaliatory angry rejection. When this is true, and the returnee himself is a reluctant dragon, a destructive battle may follow. Parents are encouraged to seek help to avoid battle and do what emotional work they can during the period of runaway so that the time of return can be constructive. Strong words may need to be said, but they should be spoken, not shouted.

It is here that I would repeat my key advice. Parents will do best if they accept the runaway as a sign of a family problem and not just a child problem. Whether you choose to deal with the issues within the privacy of the home, or with outside help, it is best if parents and child each work to accept their share of responsibility. This prevents the returnee from finding himself an outcast within the home. Honest facing of the issues will tell the family if they need professional help. If the family cannot face the issues, they need help in doing so. Unhappily, such families rarely seek help.

As a last thought, I would suggest that you realize that the act of running away can be a growth-promoting, creative, even healing effort on the part of the young person. Through it he can gain distance, rethink issues, develop perspective and perhaps make it possible for all to understand things they did not understand before. Like any crisis, a young person's running away can be an opportunity—the very basis—for an improvement in family life.

CREDIT: *Edwin Z. Levy, M.D., Director, Therapy Service, the Menninger Foundation, Topeka, Kansas.*

Safety Checklist for Parents

Do you store all drugs and chemicals (insecticides, bleaches, detergents, etc.) away from food and where children can't reach them?

Do you put all medicines—particularly flavored aspirin—safely away after using them?

Do you double-check labels on medicines before you give or take them? Do you turn on the lights when giving your child medicine at night?

Do you keep substances in their original containers and never store poisons —such as kerosene and cleaning fluids—in pop bottles?

Are all glasses used by children unbreakable?

Do you turn pot handles towards the back of the stove? If possible, do you remove the burner knobs when the stove is not in use?

Do you keep your baby and his toys off the kitchen floor when you are cooking? Is the high chair or playpen at least two feet away from your working counters in the kitchen?

Do you keep the fireplace screen in place?

Are electric cords of movable appliances (fry pan, toaster, etc.) out of reach so they can't be tripped on and the baby can't chew the cord?

Are all of your baby's toys free of splinters and too big for him to swallow?

Do you stay with your pre-school child when he is in the bathtub?

Do you keep knives, pointed scissors, needles, pins, tacks, matches, table lighters, nuts out of the reach of pre-school children?

Are furniture and lamps heavy enough so that they can't be pulled over easily?

Are hot radiators and pipes covered or insulated?

Are all unused electric outlets fitted with dummy plugs? Are all electrical cords in good condition, neither frayed nor damaged?

Do you keep electrical appliances—especially TV sets—away from the bathtub? (A TV that falls into a tub can electrocute you.)

Are attic and basement free of oily cloths?

Is there a gate at the head and the foot of the stairs to keep your child from falling down or climbing up?

Are all stairs well lit and fitted with firm handrails and treads? Are all stair- and porch-railings secure?

Are second-story windows properly screened or barred to prevent the child from falling out?

Are clotheslines strung out of children's reach?

Do you slow down and take extra precautions in the 4–7 P.M. hours when everyone is tired and hungry?

Read this questionnaire carefully. Is everything as it should be in your house? You may save the life of your child because you were willing to expend a little extra time and energy. Can you think of anything better to do today?

Safety in the Kitchen

In 1977 alone, kitchen accidents (especially prevalent during the frantic holiday seasons) resulted in 2,500 deaths and another 1 million disabling injuries. A tragic statistic, made even more so by the fact that most of these mishaps could have been prevented by a little foresight and advance preparation.

Trying to make a complicated, holiday or special occasion meal from scratch on the day it is to be served exposes the cook/host not only to a case of frazzled nerves but to a number of potentially fatal accidents (burns, cuts, shocks and poisonings head the list). The trick to avoiding both is simple: Do as much of the preparation as possible ahead of time and don't try to do everything yourself—assign jobs to other members of your family.

Take an inventory of what you need and do your shopping well ahead of time. Get out your good dishes, silver and utensils, wash everything in advance and keep clean with plastic wrap. Recruit your older children to polish the silver. (Note: In rummaging for seldom-used dishes or utensils, be sure to use a sturdy stepladder to reach those items stored on high shelves. Never resort to a chair or a combination of chair and phone books.)

Kitchen appliances should be checked regularly for defects and since the holiday season usually calls for the heaviest usage of the year, it is a good idea to take a thorough appliance inventory several weeks before—cleaning, oiling and checking parts for wear. If servicing is needed, have it done now. Appoint the resident electrical genius to the task of inspecting your electric and battery-powered portable appliances such as mixers, knives, blenders, roasters, etc. Cords with worn, crumbled or cracked insulation should be replaced. Also, be sure to use appliances only with a cord made especially for that appliance to ensure adequate current flow. A tingle or slight shock when handling an appliance means that the appliance should be inspected by a qualified repairman. Motor-driven appliances that are not permanently lubricated need regular oiling and servicing even though they are not in daily use. Refer to the instruction manual, and oil according to the manufacturer's directions.

Prepare and freeze as much food ahead of time as possible. Cookies, pies, breads, rolls, cakes and casseroles all keep well in the freezer.

By the day of the meal, all the shopping, chopping, measuring, stirring, mixing, cleaning and polishing should have been done. That leaves the stationary activities such as roasting and baking, as well as plenty of time for creating the super salads, appetizers, relish trays, flower arrangements that only a refreshed and relaxed cook can do well.

As you cook, try to keep the kitchen as clean as possible. This not only makes for a better appearance, but facilitates your work and can protect you from possible injuries and food poisoning.

Keep all non-essential personnel out of the kitchen during the final meal preparation time. Guests, young children and pets can entertain themselves in another room. Anyone working in the kitchen should resist the temptation to join in the drinking until the dinner is on the table.

Wait until just before your guests arrive to don any fancy attire. Dangling sleeves, bows and other frills near sources of direct heat such as range burners can spark painful clothing fires.

When the moment comes to transport foods to the table, carry only what you and your assistants can safely handle. If you have any heavy dishes—such as a turkey, large ham, soup tureen, casserole, etc.—avoid the possibility of back strain and an accidental spill by asking for help in toting these foods to the table. Older children who want to help may be assigned to table setting (well in advance) or taking small, light items to the table.

The happy conclusion to all this careful preparation will be a beautiful table laden with wonderfully fragrant, well-prepared food. The best result of all is a relaxed host or hostess who can enjoy a marvelous—and safe—holiday with family and friends.

CREDIT: *National Safety Council, Chicago, Illinois.*

Safety on the Streets

Suggestions for Women

BEFORE GOING OUT

(1) Plan your route. Take well-lighted, busy streets if possible and try to arrange for a companion.

(2) Dress with discretion so as not to provoke attention, but avoid unrelieved dark clothing that may make you difficult to see as you cross a street.

(3) Do not leave a key in the mailbox, under a mat or in any other hiding place. If you must, leave a key with a trusted neighbor.

(4) Items to carry with you:

    (a) emergency phone numbers (local police, sheriff, etc.);

    (b) a flashlight, if you are going out at night)

    (c) an alarm device such as a whistle or battery-powered horn, if you are required to enter a dangerous area;

    (d) a solid or sharp instrument to ward off a possible attacker (suggested by some authorities, not all).

(5) Do not carry valuables or large sums of cash. Rely instead on checks, credit cards and charge plates. Keep a list of all your credit cards at home.

(6) Leave some lights on at home both for illumination when you return and to discourage a potential burglar.

(7) Close and lock all doors and windows in both house and garage.

(8) If you are going on an extended trip:

    (a) Tell a trusted neighbor (and the building superintendent, if you live in an apartment) of your plans (including hour of arrival at destination and hour of return) and leave a key so an emergency or unusual activity in your house can be investigated.

    (b) Notify police of your absence and tell them of your arrangement with your neighbor.

    (c) Cancel newspaper deliveries and have mail held; or ask a neighbor to receive them for you.

    (d) Leave shades and blinds in their normal position.

    (e) Have the lawn mowed or snow shoveled in your absence.

LEAVING AND RETURNING HOME

(1) It bears repetition: Lock the doors of your residence when you leave it.

(2) Avoid going into unlighted yards alone at night. To avoid falls, be sure loose or broken pavements, rocks or stones are reported or, if you own your own home, repaired promptly.

(3) Install lights at dark walkways or driveways and in the yard to lessen chance of falls and assault. Leave these lights, as well as entrance and garage lights, on if you plan to return after dark.

(4) Use a flashlight going to and from house and garage if there is no yard light.

(5) Do not stop to pick up your mail when entering your apartment building after dark if you sense that someone is following you, if it is very late or if you live in a dangerous area. Enter the apartment door quickly but cautiously. If anything seems wrong, do not go in. Go elsewhere and call police, a neighbor or the janitor. Many women who live in apartment complexes ring their own buzzers when coming home alone to an empty apartment on the theory that it gives an intruder a chance to escape and prevents possible attack by a surprised prowler.

WALKING ON THE STREETS

(1) If possible, walk with another person and vary your schedules and routes.

(2) Be on the lookout for uneven sidewalks, broken curbs and holes in the street that might cause falls.

(3) Do not jaywalk. When crossing a street, especially at night, allow plenty of time to move with caution and avoid falls.

(4) Walk near the curb rather than close to buildings and keep on the side of the street nearest oncoming traffic. You will be better able to react to a suspicious car if you are facing it than if it slips up from behind you. Facing traffic also gives you an added measure of protection where there is no sidewalk and you are forced to walk on the road.

(5) Avoid walking on the street late at night. If you must go out after dark, note shadows which can alert you to a person some distance away. Never take a short cut through poorly lighted areas.

(6) Areas to avoid:
    (a) narrow walkways between buildings (at all times);
    (b) alley entrances or shrubbery;
    (c) deserted, poorly lighted areas;
    (d) parks;
    (e) public facilities such as restrooms (at night).

(7) Watch for loiterers at all times.

(8) Carry purse close to the body or under your coat. If your purse has a shoulder strap, be aware that many purse-snatchers come from behind, snip the straps, grab the purse and run.

(9) *Never* accept a ride from a stranger.

(10) Be wary if people in a car stop to ask directions. If accosted by a motorist, run in the direction opposite that in which the car is headed.

(11) If pursued by anyone, do not run to your own home. A pursuer would then know where to find you. Instead, run to the nearest dwelling or place of business and summon help.

DRIVING

(1) Be the best driver possible. Drive defensively. Fasten your seat belt at all times. Before driving, avoid alcohol and determine your reaction to certain medicines or drugs in case of accident. Keep a list of such drugs where they may be easily found by a doctor or paramedic. Know your car and its care.

(2) Be prepared: Make sure that you have ample gasoline, a good battery and safe tires before embarking on a trip. Keep a flashlight and flares in the passenger compartment, but if children ever ride in the car, put flares in the trunk.

(3) Do not carry car license number or your name and address in your key case.

(4) Always lock the car and keep keys in your possession whenever possible. Take driver's license, credit cards, receipts and ID cards with you when you leave your car. Remove trunk, house and other keys from key case when having car serviced or parked in a public lot or garage. Remember: Keys are easily duplicated.

(5) Never leave valuables on the car seat; store them in the trunk. However, do not put any valuables in the trunk after you have parked your car and intend to leave it for some time. Instead, when you are en route, pull off the road, transfer your materials to the trunk, then proceed to your destination.

(6) Leave car in a well-lighted area when parking on the street at night. Use an attended parking facility whenever possible.

(7) Check back seat of your car for intruders before getting in.

(8) Lock all car doors and put windows up high enough so that no one can put an arm and hand through any of them. If you must ventilate the car, roll windows up when stopped at intersections or stalled in traffic.

(9) Should anyone try to enter your car, sound the horn in short blasts until police or others come to your aid. Do likewise if two cars hem you in with an obviously threatening intent.

(10) Leave space between your car and the cars ahead for maneuverability in the event of an attack and for safety from collision.

(11) If you think a suspicious-looking car is following you, drive to a police,

fire or gas station and report it. If that is impossible, stop at a populated curb and let the car pass you. If a car follows you into your driveway at night, stay in the car with doors locked until you can identify the occupant or ascertain the driver's intent. If necessary sound the horn to attract the attention of your neighbors. The noise may also scare the pursuer away.

(12) If you have a flat tire in a questionable area, drive on it until you reach a safe or well-lighted spot.

(13) In the event of car trouble, lift the hood, attach a white handkerchief to the antenna or left door handle as a signal for help. Get back in the car promptly and lock the door. At night, leave lights and emergency flasher on. If someone stops, lower your window a crack and ask him to call for assistance. Do not let him into the car.

(14) A woman driving alone should not stop to aid others as long as public safety is as uncertain as it is today. If you do stop, keep the doors locked, quickly find out what assistance is needed and drive on to a well-lighted area (if at night) or service station and notify the police or emergency service.

(15) Keep car in gear during brief stops at night. Be ready to move instantly.

(16) Never pick up hitchhikers.

(17) Have keys in hand so that you can quickly unlock garage and house doors.

USING PUBLIC TRANSPORTATION

(1) Plan to travel with one or more companions when using mass transit at night and during slack hours.

(2) If possible, sit near the driver, conductor or motorman. Do not sit near a rear door, where your purse or other valuables can be snatched just as the vehicle is about to move. In such a situation, the thief can escape easily before the door closes. If you must sit near a window or door, hold on to your possessions tightly.

(3) Never sleep on public transportation.

(4) If you are going to a dark or questionable neighborhood, take a taxi instead of mass transit. Request that taxi doors be locked. When you arrive at your destination, ask the taxi driver to wait while you enter the building or ask him to walk to the entrance with you.

MISCELLANEOUS SAFETY TIPS

(1) Do not invite trouble by placing your purse or valuables on a store counter, in a grocery cart or on the floor or an empty seat in a theater or restaurant.

(2) Be careful in a store or office at street level. Keep valuable possessions

out of sight. Costly purchases too bulky to conceal should be delivered by the store.

(3) Be unobtrusive when writing a check or handling money. Watch for anyone following you after transacting business in a bank.

(4) Be wary of giving your name, address or place of business in restaurants or other public places.

(5) Sit near the aisle in a theater; avoid dark corners and vacant rows in the balcony or at the rear of the theater.

(6) Patronize a cocktail lounge only with a friend or escort.

(7) Be wary of women in washrooms.

(8) Keep a hotel or motel door locked. Use the chain if there is one. Put valuables in the safe. When entering your accommodations, check the room before locking the door and cutting off your escape.

YOUR CHILD'S SAFETY

(1) Do not permit youngsters (under thirteen) to go out at night if possible. Enforce a curfew for your teenagers.

(2) Check the route your children take to and from school. If you are concerned about hazards along the way, show them a safer route. Call their attention to any danger spots. If they are late getting home, find out why.

(3) Tell children that adults can sometimes be dangerous. Ask them to report unusual incidents. Warn them against accepting rides or gifts from strangers.

(4) Know the names of your children's playmates, where they live and how they can be reached.

(5) Instruct your child in traffic laws. See that your child knows the safety rules if he rides a bicycle.

(6) Instill in your child a respect for policemen, the school patrol and crossing guards. If your child's school does not have a patrol or guards, work to get them.

(7) If your child rides a school bus, see that he knows about proper behavior, that the bus driver is competent and that the bus is inspected for safety.

IF YOU ARE ATTACKED

These suggestions, a digest of materials produced by many civic groups and law-enforcement agencies, are all subject to circumstances and the judgment of the person involved in a dangerous situation. In all circumstances, however, it is important to estimate quickly the motives of a suspicious person and then act.

(1) Screaming. Many law-enforcement authorities emphasize that the best protection a woman has is her voice. A scream may frighten an attacker into

flight, or startle him into hesitation that will gain precious moments in which to run away. However, there are other considerations:

(a) If the assailant is a robber, screaming may cause him to hurt you when his intention was only to steal.

(b) If threatened with a weapon such as a club or knife in the presence of other people, you are advised by some authorities not to scream at once. The attacker might kill you before bystanders could help. Keeping quiet could make him think you are too frightened to scream. Then when you do scream at a more opportune time, you may catch him off guard.

(2) Running. Scream first if that seems the thing to do, but run and keep running. Do not run in high heels. Kick your shoes off and if there is time, pick them up for use as weapons. Then continue running. If your accoster is in a car, immediately run in the direction opposite to that in which the car is headed. Run to where a car would be unable to follow (but avoid running into a blind alley or street).

(3) Hiding. If you hide, make sure you can get away if you are spotted. Protective coloration can work to your advantage. If you are dressed in dark colors, hide against dark walls.

(4) Counterattack. Most authorities agree that it is best to try to avoid physical combat, but if necessary you should do the following:

(a) Strike fast and violently in assailant's vital areas with the intention of making it hurt.

(b) Scratch hard with your fingernails, gouge eyes with your thumbs and jab a knee into the assailant's groin.

(c) Strike with purse or heavy object at the Adam's apple or bridge of the nose.

(d) If grabbed from behind, smash down hard on the attacker's instep with your heel, throw your head back into his face, bite or bend his fingers, kick his shin, gouge his ribs with your elbows.

(e) Some authorities suggest using any of the following as weapons: pencil, nail file, tweezers, corkscrew, hat pin, aerosol hair spray, umbrella, rolled newspaper or magazine, key ring, metal comb, book. Some women have carried black or red pepper. Battery or gas-operated personal alarm devices that emit a piercing sound are available commercially. (Note: Guns and other commercial weapons are not effective without basic training or instruction. Some of them may be illegal. Many state laws prohibit carrying weapons such as a blackjack, a switchblade knife, tear gas. Some states prohibit the use of police whistles. Check with your local authorities before investing in weapons or devices of this sort.)

CREDIT: *National Safety Council, Chicago, Illinois.*

Scars

When a wound heals, a permanent scar takes its place. A scar is the inevitable result of the healing process. In some instances it may be inconspicuous; in others it may be very disfiguring.

In considering the realities of scars, the discussion will be divided under three headings: (1) the linear scar from wounds without skin loss; (2) the scar from tissue loss such as occurs in burns, accidental tearing off of tissue or surgical removal of skin lesions; and (3) scars from surgical incisions.

The various factors with which we can forecast the quality of a scar following the healing of a wound is of great importance, yet there is much misconception by the lay public.

It is logical to assume that by using meticulous care, along with fine threads and small needles, a hairline scar can be obtained when stitching up a wound. A hairline scar may be the result, but that is not the full story. The first question a young surgeon is likely to ask an experienced plastic surgeon is, "What material do you use?" He asks the question thinking this factor is important in obtaining a fine scar, somewhat analogous to using good ingredients in baking a cake. Nothing could be further from the truth. A fine scar depends less on the type of material and technique in sewing up the wound than on the region of the body where the wound is situated and the direction it was inflicted.

So-called plastic surgery of a skin wound is nothing more than skillful sewing. But the surgeon and the patient should keep in mind that even the finest technique cannot entirely undo the damage of the injury nor guarantee a satisfactory result. Many unsightly scars are not the result of poor surgical technique.

The part of the body where the wound lies is perhaps the most important factor in the quality of a scar. Places where the formation of bad scars is notorious are the breastbone region and the shoulder region. Scars in the back and the arms and legs also tend to widen and at times become dense and elevated above the surrounding skin level.

When a wound is inflicted on the skin, the tension in the skin is the force that separates the borders of the wound. Skin tension also is the force that pulls on the scar of a healed wound and tends to widen it, and at times this pulling may stimulate the scar, causing it to become thick, hard and raised.

All factors being equal, some patients heal better than others. Individual tendencies may be responsible for unattractive scars. Some patients have a "keloid tendency." Their abdominal scar or a scar on the shoulder turns out to be thick and raised when in most normal persons the scar is barely noticeable.

There are other factors which tend to lessen or increase the skin deformity of operative or accidental wounds. These factors are pattern or design (curved or U-shaped scars are notoriously unsightly because the scar contracts towards the center becoming depressed and the unscarred circumscribed area tends to bulge), the angle of wound to skin surface, depth of wound, degree of blunt injury to the skin borders, healing with or without complications (infection, bleeding) and age of patient (older persons tend to have less visible scars than younger patients).

Although a fresh scar will soften and fade after a year or two, surgeons with experience on scar repair know which scars will eventually require "fixing up." Why, then, submit the patient to the prolonged mental anguish of disfigurement when it can be corrected earlier than traditional practices suggest? Most scars may be improved two months following injury. By then, the depth of the wound has healed sufficiently, and the soft tissues have reacquired adequate circulation.

TECHNIQUES FOR CORRECTING UNSIGHTLY SCARS

Surgical abrasion or planing consists in removing the top layer of the skin with a wire brush or a motor-driven cylinder of sandpaper. It is specially useful for acne scars but also may be used following any of the three scar repair techniques. In linear scars it has a very limited effect if used without first performing surgical revision.

Most of the time skin grafts are required to treat burn deformities. Even if the surgeon is capable of closing the wide skin defect with sutures and obtain a hairline closure, the scar will eventually become wide and raised regardless of the effort to counteract this tendency.

The keloid represents one of the plastic surgeon's most trying challenges. Despite many recent discoveries it remains one of the most vexing problems.

A keloid is a scar that may continue to enlarge beyond the original size and shape of the wound. Though seen most frequently among blacks it may be found in patients of any race if the person has a tendency to keloid formation.

Surgical removal of a keloid creates injury to the tissues. As the wound heals a new keloid may develop which is larger than the one that was removed.

Keloids are best treated by X rays or cortisone injections. Local cortisone injections may make the scar undergo softening, flattening and relieve the symptoms of itching and discomfort. Injected locally, cortisone is well tolerated and has little or no effect on the rest of the body.

CREDIT: *Albert F. Borges, M.D., F.A.C.S., plastic surgeon, The Fairfax Hospital, Falls Church, and Arlington Hospital, Arlington Virginia. Formerly Chief of Plastic and Reconstructive Surgery, Havana University Hospital, Cuba.*

Schizophrenia

The term "schizophrenia" was first coined by Eugen Bleuler, a Swiss psychiatrist, at the turn of the century to define a particular pattern of mental illness. The term does not mean, as is popularly supposed, "a split or multiple personality." Rather, Bleuler intended it to describe individuals whose thinking is persistently disturbed. They may hear voices (hallucinations), have strange or bizarre ideas (delusions). Often they are flatly unemotional or inappropriately or overly emotional. They may be uncommunicative and withdrawn. Individuals with a combination of these symptoms who have no organic (physical) disease are schizophrenic.

Most patients diagnosed as schizophrenic show persistently disturbed thinking, incoherent, disconnected thought patterns and bizarre ideas. The single most characteristic symptom of this form of mental illness is loss of contact with reality.

Some examples of schizophrenic behavior are as follows:

A forty-year-old bank teller whose salary is $21,000 a year writes a check for $2 million, as a down payment on a 747 which he insists he is buying from American Airlines.

A thirty-eight-year-old housewife buys a new outfit and gets her hair fixed at the most expensive beauty salon in Chicago because she thinks she has a dinner date with Perry Como. She goes to the hotel where she read Mr. Como is registered and waits in the lobby for him.

No amount of reasoning can persuade a schizophrenic that the situation is not exactly as he perceives it.

Schizophrenia most commonly makes its first appearance in late adolescence and in the early twenties. However, schizophrenia may occur any time during and after adolescence up to about the forties. A first episode of schizophrenia in the middle and later years of life is relatively rare.

Schizophrenia afflicts approximately .05 to 1.0 percent of the population. About 25 percent of the admissions to mental hospitals are for this condition and female patients slightly outnumber the males. The frequency with which it occurs appears to be the same in cultures—regardless of complexity or level of industrial development. The symptoms are definitely influenced by cultural factors.

Although schizophrenia was not formally diagnosed until the nineteenth century, there is evidence in both the Old and New Testaments and in Shakespeare's plays that schizophrenia has existed throughout much of human history.

Recent research indicates that schizophrenia in the industrialized countries is more common among individuals of lower educational and economic status. It is well established that this is because disabling symptoms of the illness prevented individuals from succeeding in school or making progress in their chosen fields of endeavor.

The time course of this illness varies considerably from individual to individual. Some experience only a single, brief episode. Others may experience a series of episodes interspersed with intervals of "normalcy." For still others in whom the onset of the illness is typically gradual, the symptoms persist without interruption (unless removed by treatment) for long periods of time with devastating results which make educational, occupational and social life extremely difficult, if not impossible.

It is worth noting that contrary to popular belief, schizophrenic patients are no more criminally dangerous than the population at large—indeed probably less so.

Until the early fifties no reliable or curative treatment of schizophrenic illness was known. The majority of schizophrenics in the United States languished in state mental hospitals and received no more than custodial care. In 1952 it was discovered both in France and in the United States that a class of drugs known as major tranquilizers (phenothiazines) was capable of reducing or totally removing the symptoms of schizophrenia in the great majority of patients. It has also been discovered, unfortunately, that these drugs do not cure the illness. When the medication is stopped, the symptoms usually reappear.

The discovery of the tranquilizing drugs developed public policy which led to a shift from treatment of mental illness in remote mental hospitals to centers in the community.

The treatment of schizophrenia often includes residential treatment in the hospital, designed to create a comfortable, simple, consistent, predictable non-threatening environment mainly through dedicated and trained people. As the demands for living are structured and simplified, this has the effect of reducing excessive anxiety in the patient and helps restore the individual's equilibrium. In a therapeutic setting, in addition to treatment needs, ordinarily everyday needs such as proper nutrition, health care and recreation are also provided. Various recreational, occupational and art therapy programs are also utilized as tools for treatment.

The use of megavitamins has been tried in the treatment of schizophrenia, but there is no conclusive evidence that this treatment is effective. In some settings electroshock therapy is also used, but this is not employed routinely.

Work with the families is important not only for emotional support of ongoing treatment, but also in modifying the home environment in order to prepare for return to the home after completion of treatment.

Another important approach is psychotherapy, which is a "talking treatment" carried out with a trained psychotherapist. Effort is made by the therapist to develop a trusting relationship with the patient. He slowly learns to deal with his frightening feelings, his fantasies, wishes and conflicts.

These twin developments in the last twenty-five years have made for dramatic changes in prospects of individuals afflicted with schizophrenia. The resident populations of chronic schizophrenics in state mental hospitals have been sharply reduced. Some states, such as California, have closed most of their public mental hospitals and are relying almost exclusively on public and private community resources to care for schizophrenic individuals. Both by virtue of drug treatment and community support, large numbers of schizophrenic individuals are now able to lead relatively productive lives outside the confines of mental hospitals.

There are, however, a number of patients who do not respond to drug treatment in a dramatic way. They may be able to live in the community and care for themselves, but they are unable to lead productive lives. Research is currently going on to determine whether combination of drug treatment with psychosocial forms of treatment (such as psychotherapy or social case work) may improve the quality of their community adjustment.

The largest proportion of research efforts devoted to this illness is, however, concerned with determining its causes and the conditions under which it develops. The causes of this illness are still largely unknown, and we will probably have to wait on the discovery of the underlying causes before a cure treatment can be developed.

The genetic hereditary factors in schizophrenia have been clearly demonstrated. Based on studies of families, twins and adopted children, it has been shown that the incidence of illness in biologically related people is significantly higher than in others. However, family history alone does not determine the onset of the illness. Research in this area is sufficiently well advanced so that married couples in whose family there is a history of schizophrenic illness, or one or both of whom are schizophrenic themselves, are well advised to seek genetic counseling if they plan to have children.

Current research concerned with the causes of schizophrenia, while not yet close to a breakthrough, is much more promising than it was even twenty years ago. The number of scientists studying the biochemical and neurochemical processes in schizophrenia has increased in recent years, and the methods of study in this area have become greatly refined. Hopefully, the next twenty years will produce the key to unlock the mysteries of this baffling mental illness.

CREDIT: *Herbert E. Spohn, Ph.D., Senior Research Psychologist, Menninger Foundation. Mrs. Jean Hahn, secretary to Dr. Spohn. Material by Harcharan Sehdev, M.D., Menninger Foundation, revised and supplemented by J. Cotter Hirschberg, M.D., Professor of Psychiatry, Menninger Foundation, Topeka, Kansas.*

School Phobia

A number of youngsters starting kindergarten or first grade may complain of sudden stomach pains, headache, dizziness or vomiting.

The symptoms appear on school mornings but disappear mysteriously if the child misses the school bus and is permitted to stay home. The pains rarely occur during weekends, during summer vacations or at Christmas time.

The symptoms are real. The child is not faking. The mother becomes worried and calls the doctor. Almost always careful examination, including laboratory tests, shows no organic reason for the distress.

In most cases, the diagnosis is "school phobia," according to Dr. Barton D. Schmitt, a pediatrician who teaches at the University of Colorado at Denver. Symptoms are due to anxiety and the fear of school.

It is the fear of leaving home that leads to the fear of going to school. School phobia could also be called "separation anxiety."

Normally, separation fears in a child should be resolved by age five. When school phobia surfaces, the problem is an overprotective parent and an overdependent child.

The oversolicitous parent is the mother in more than 90 percent of cases. She wants her child to suffer no physical or emotional distress. She tries to shield him from any and all unpleasant experiences by constantly anticipating and meeting his every need.

Mama worries that physical harm may befall the child on the way to school or on the playground. She fears that he will be overwhelmed by the demands of the classroom, or that he will be treated badly by the other children.

Sometimes the child initiates the fear. School is society's first test of a youngster's independence. Many children feel unsure of themselves. So they simply refuse to go to school.

The parent should reassure the child about his fears rather than overreact to them. The child will not be able to cope with separation if the parent allows him to cling and stay safely in his nest at home.

The dependent relationship is only the backdrop. It usually takes an additional stress (sometimes a mild one) to trigger the phobia. It could be the end of summer, changing schools, a new teacher, the loss of a pet, an illness in the family or a marital crisis.

If untreated, school phobia can continue into adolescence. Sometimes it subsides as the child becomes accustomed to a specific teacher as a mother substitute, but the phobia may flare up again in junior high school when the child suddenly has several teachers and no special one to lean on.

Treating school phobia requires forceful measures. If the child says he doesn't feel well, take his temperature. If it is not higher than 99, tell him he must go to school anyway. Reassure him that there is a school nurse who will take care of him should be begin to feel worse—and that if he becomes really ill, she will send him home. It must not be a subject for debate. Daily school attendance must be an irrevocable rule. The best treatment of any fear is to face it and overcome it as soon as possible. Staying home has a corrosive effect on the ability to return.

Mother should *not* ask the child who seems to be sluggish in the morning how he feels. Such a question presents the perfect opportunity to say, "I don't feel good." If the child is well enough to be up and around—watching TV—he is well enough to be in school. If he pokes around complaining until he is late, he should be told to take public transportation or walk if it isn't too far—or be driven, if it is convenient.

School phobia can be prevented by encouraging independence. When a child is six months old, the parents should be having evenings out alone. By age two, every child should be left at home with a baby-sitter while he is still awake. By age three, every child should experience being left somewhere other than his home—such as with neighbors while the mother shops, or in the home of a friend or relative.

By age four, a child should be allowed to play in the yard by himself, but an adult should keep an eye on him.

High-risk youngsters can often be identified. He is usually the only child, the last child, a child the parents consider "delicate" or the child with a chronic disease who arouses overprotective tendencies in the parents.

Parents should encourage their child to make friends with his peers. Inviting children to the house and sending your child to the homes of playmates are good ways to promote this.

An overprotective mother should be encouraged to become involved in rewarding activities of her own, doing volunteer work or taking a part-time job.

The father must make an effort to fulfill some of his wife's needs for companionship so that she will not need an overly close relationship with her child to compensate for what she is not getting from him.

CREDIT: *Arthur J. Snider, medical and science writer, Chicago* Sun-Times.

Self-Confidence

How to Be in Charge of Your Life

Most people are not in control of their lives. The average person's actions are based on dangerous foundations—random choice (chance) or the choice of others. If you aren't basing your actions on rational self-choice, you're out of control, and anything out of control is a menace both to itself and its surroundings.

What's the payoff for basing your actions on rational self-choice? In simple terms, more pleasure and less pain—a better life for you. Acting rationally, and thus being in control, translates into having a clear mind instead of one that is cluttered and confused. It means enjoying love relationships instead of longing for them. It means experiencing warm friendships instead of concentrating your thoughts on people for whom you harbor negative feelings. It means making enough money to be able comfortably to afford the material things you want in life instead of being bitter about not having them.

A person in control is a person who usually can perceive realities correctly. And one of the most important realities to understand is that absolutely everything in life has a price: love, friendship, material gain, a relaxed mind, the freedom to come and go as you please—anything which adds pleasure to your existence. All things worth obtaining must be paid for. If you delude yourself into thinking otherwise, you only open the door to endless frustration.

Whether the required payment be in money, time, energy, discomfort, or any other form, try not to kid yourself. And once you've decided that something is worth the price, don't prolong the payment. The sooner you get it out of the way, the sooner you can enjoy the rewards of a clear mind and a happier life.

Many, if not most, price-paying decisions involve other people, because people are at the root of most of life's complications. And it's those who are closest to you who have the potential to do the most damage. Remember: Friends, lovers, parents and children are people, too. They are all subject to human imperfections, but because of their relationship to you, they're in a position to cause you more grief than others—if you allow them to.

Eliminating people problems requires that you face the reality that people possess an unlimited number of potentially harmful traits, that you learn the art of spotting these qualities and—the supreme test—that you develop the ability and self-discipline either to ignore their neurotic actions or, in extreme cases, to eliminate from your life those individuals responsible for actions that are harmful to you.

Intimidation—motivation through fear—is one of the ploys people most commonly use to cause others problems. If you give it some thought, you might be surprised to discover that a large percentage of your actions are motivated by fear. You may be motivated by the fear of physical harm, by the fear of losing someone's love or by the fear of being embarrassed, to name just a few.

Intimidation comes in a variety of packages and isn't easy to spot if you are not aware how it is camouflaged. Whenever you have the feeling you're being intimidated, ask yourself one simple question: Why am I doing what I am doing? If you can trace the reason for your action to any kind of unfounded fear, you're being intimidated.

You're intimidated when you do something just because it's a custom or tradition. You're intimidated when you go along with a new idea that has gained wide acceptance, or the latest "in" things, just to conform. And, worst of all, you're intimidated when you feel guilty. Don't be so ready to accept criticism and blame and, whether justified or not, remember that guilt is a state of mind you needn't endure. Through rational analysis, you must decide what is right and wrong for you, then live your life accordingly.

If you do engage in behavior that you later decide is wrong by your standards, admit it, apologize, then forget it. On the other hand, if you haven't done anything wrong, skip the apology and just forget it. You must overcome the fear of being condemned for refusing to do what others want you to do. Don't accept a responsibility just because someone thinks you should. An important rule to remember is: Learn to say no politely and pleasantly, but immediately and firmly.

Does this mean you should be wary even of friends? To put it in a better perspective, too many people destroy friendships by forgetting that friends are people and people aren't perfect. All friends possess, to some degree, every negative human trait. They'll disappoint you; they'll hurt you; they'll let you down. Depending on the degree and frequency, this doesn't necessarily mean that a person isn't a good friend; it just reaffirms the fact that human beings have faults. If the friendship is worthwhile from your standpoint, then the key to surviving negative human actions on the part of a friend is forgiveness.

Should you put up with any amount of irritation a friend throws your way? Of course not. You put up with it in relation to the value you place in the friendship. So long as what you derive from the relationship is worth it, you forgive. When it is not worth it, it's time to get out.

When someone bugs you with irrational rhetoric and/or neurotic actions, always remember that you have one weapon that can wipe out his entire arsenal: Ignore him. You have no obligation to deal with irrational people. You needn't accept nagging or coercion for the sake of keeping the peace. You have a right to live your life as you please, so long as you're not bothering anyone.

Most of the principles which apply to friendship also apply to love relationships. First, remember that no matter how close your relationship with a lover, you are, and will remain, an entity unto yourself. Your every desire is not identical; your every thought is not parallel; your every need is not the same. A lover can be a part of your life, but not a literal part of you.

Loneliness too often is a major motivating factor in love relationships. Too many people are in the wrong kind of relationships because they have chosen, at least subconsciously, to spend their lives in misery out of the fear of dying alone. Loneliness for love is a potential panic situation. But panic is something you must avoid at all costs if you wish to retain the hope of finding that someone special.

When you do find someone who can bring you happiness, don't forget that he or she doesn't owe you a thing—especially not love. How much love can you expect from a lover? The exact amount you earn. You can never be free to enjoy the goodies in life unless you seek to earn everything you receive. That goes for money; it goes for friendship; it goes for self-respect; it goes for love.

Another common problem in love relationships is the refusal to face the reality of who and what your lover is. This can lead to one of two irrational actions on your part. The first is to try to imagine him to be something other than what he really is. The second is to try to mold him into what you want him to be. The first is a matter of lying (to yourself), the second a matter of tampering with the impossible. And the latter is based on the rather arrogant assumption that you have some sort of right to "improve" someone.

As with friendships, the easiest way to ruin a love relationship is to forget that your lover is a human being. Once again, remember that people will hurt you, disappoint you and let you down. Your lover is a person, so if you expect him never to do these things, you're expecting the impossible and are likely to get the probable: trouble.

If you happen to be in the unenviable position of having a lover who is irrational, you're probably in a can't-win situation. If so, heed this advice: Don't beg, don't argue, don't try to reason. It won't work. The hassle-oriented person has the deck stacked against you before you even open your mouth. You must avoid can't-win situations—and rid yourself of existing ones—if you are to be successful in being in control of your life.

Compromising is probably the worst solution to a bumpy love relationship. Too much compromising is not good for either party. Both you and your mate should be spending the majority of your time doing those things which bring you pleasure. If you're not, the solution isn't to continue compromising, but to find someone whose interests are similar to yours. It's better to lose love now—temporarily—than to wake up years from now and realize that you never had the Real Thing to begin with. Don't yield to the tormenting myths that would have you believe you should continue to invest valuable years in a relationship which has caused you mostly pain. Don't try to hide the truth or smooth over it. As always, ignoring the realities will only cause them to get worse.

If you do decide that your love relationship no longer meets the requirements necessary to your living a happy life, and if you've rationally made the decision to split, let me suggest you do one thing with regard to looking back: don't! There's only one thing worse than the painful search for a lover, and that is a continued life of dull, nagging nothingness with a person who causes you mostly unhappiness.

Whether you're just getting out of a bad romance or are still in the process of looking for the right partner, beware of the Better Dealers. Every person probably has the Better Deal instinct to some extent, but in the true Better Dealer it is totally out of control.

It's human nature, once you have a "deal" sewn up, to wonder about the possibility of there being a better deal down the road. And theoretically there probably is—simply because there is a huge prospective-mate pool. But the question is, how far down the road is it practical to travel before reaping the rewards of a meaningful love relationship, and how much of your life are you prepared to spend on such an illusory search?

An even bigger question: After you find your mythical Better Deal, how can you be sure that down the road a piece there isn't one still better? The answer is that you can't. One would have to be omnipotent to know such a thing, so it's not a human possibility. The seriously afflicted Better Dealer is an individual hopelessly chasing his tail, cheating himself of happiness within his reach by conducting a lifelong impossible search for the ever Better Deal.

Work hard at trying to keep this instinct as dormant as possible. When you engage in Better-Dealing, you're flying blind. You're assuming there are greener pastures that can satisfy you, and you'll probably continue to assume it all your life, no matter how many green pastures you find, unless you learn to control the illusion of the Better Deal. And every instinct, every emotion, everything about yourself over which you gain control will bring you that much closer to being in charge of your life.

CREDIT: *Robert J. Ringer, author of* Looking Out for Number One, *New York, New York: Funk & Wagnalls.*

Self-Esteem

Self-esteem is an objective respect or realistically favorable impression we ought to have of ourselves. It is accompanied by a feeling of well-being and can be the thermometer for measuring one's mental health.

Evaluate your self-esteem by asking: Do I feel compatible with—and good about—myself most of the time? Can minor slurs (often unintentional) and insignificant failures catapult my self-esteem thermometer to way below normal? Or am I healthy enough to keep the temperature steady except for severe disappointments in my performance? How easily am I thrown off balance? Do I become unhappy or depressed when things don't go my way? Do I feel like a complete flop if I am not the "main attraction"?

A more subtle clue for measuring self-esteem is discovered in the nature of one's relationships. Many people are able to maintain self-esteem only when they are attached to (or bask in the reflected glory of) someone they see as a "superstar" (lover, friend, teacher, parent, etc.). As long as the desired relationship is operative, self-esteem is high, but when the "star" no longer provides an emotional high, the level of self-esteem tumbles. This may occur if the "star" fades, leaves or simply doesn't shine because he is otherwise involved.

The less one depends on outside sources for self-esteem, the better equipped he is to stay in psychological balance. Each of us should be his own "star" shining from within.

How does one develop the capacity for self-esteem? The seeds are sown early in childhood and continue to flower throughout life as new challenges surface. Since all children think the world centers around them, frustrations are inevitable as they begin to deal with the real world. If we imagine that the caretaking adult regulates the frustration so that it is not too painful we view that adult as "caring." An empathic parent lets the child struggle a bit, but not too much, and then stands aside and compliments him or her for some small accomplishment.

For example, the empathic parent will admire the toddler's efforts to dress himself even though it takes a long time. He is learning co-ordination and developing a new, important skill. The same parent will admire the child's ability to sing a song or recite a poem. He will make a fuss over the kindergartener's crayon drawings. As the child grows, the admiration from the parent becomes more selective but always in relation to praising some aspect of an attempt. "Gee, that is nice art work! Tell me about it and we'll tack it on the wall." Never say, "Your brother could draw much better when he was your age."

At a three-to-four-year-old level the child who failed at jumping down the staircase may try to fly. We should not respond by becoming hysterical and humiliating the youngster. She/he has not yet successfully bridged the gap between reality and the all-powerful, "I can do anything" attitude. An understanding parent will patiently explain why children cannot fly and the child's mortification will be brief. In this way the parent soothes and helps to restore his self-esteem.

In an empathic atmosphere, the child is learning the beginning of self-esteem regulation, still extremely dependent on surrounding adults to protect and admire his efforts. An interesting technique healthy children use to handle their failure to do what they aren't ready to do is to feel that, "I can't, but my mommy or daddy can do anything." At some later point this changes inside the child's mind to, "I can't do it *now,* but I will be able to when I'm grown up like Mom and Dad." The parent becomes the ideal and this ideal is reshaped to lifelong goals and ambitions.

There are two major compensating techniques used by people who suffer from the lack of self-esteem. Both reflect the parents' negative impact if the parent is unable to respond sensitively and consistently. If there are two parents available, the child may turn from one parent who may be (temporarily or permanently) insensitive to the other parent who is more empathic. Of course, the unempathic parent suffers from damaged self-esteem himself. (A person who has little self-esteem cannot give it to others.)

Compensating techniques can produce a great deal of anxiety in the person who finds that his substitute method of bolstering his self-esteem is not working. The first of these substitutes (already mentioned) is the attachment to a "superstar." This results when the child finds that he is unable to use his own parent as an ideal. So . . . he seeks another "superstar." The degree of this maladaptation can run the gamut from mild overidealization (highly characteristic of adolescents) to masochistic surrender to the leader of a bizarre cult.

The second major maladaptation resulting from low self-esteem is seen in people who have an inflated view of their capacities and are constantly looking to others for compliments and praise. If this substitute for genuine self-esteem is not forthcoming, a single aspect of the person may become "the big thing." Examples vary from the "macho man" and the "sex-symbol woman" to the more severely disturbed exhibitionistic male who exposes himself publicly and the promiscuous woman who will go to bizarre lengths to be reassured of her desirability. If these outlets don't bolster the shaken self-esteem, maintaining a sense of self may require more bizarre substitutes such as drug addiction, kleptomania or child molestation.

Modern psychoanalytic psychotherapy is often able to re-establish a healthier sense of self-esteem for those individuals who are aware they need or want changes, or for those who suffer from chronic depression as a reflection of the absent star not shining within.

There are two approaches for getting professional help. One is short-term counseling to help bolster your self-esteem after a sudden setback, such as being fired from a job or left at the altar. The second approach requires a great deal more time, energy and money. It is called psychoanalysis.

CREDIT: *Brenda Clorfene Solomon, M.D., Glencoe, Illinois; faculty-teacher, Education Program, Chicago Institute for Psychoanalysis.*

Senility

Many people fear "senility" as much as they fear cancer. The thought of growing old, losing your mind and ending up in an institution is one of the most frightening specters of old age. The truth is that "senility" is not one condition but a group of symptoms with a number of causes, many of which respond to prompt and effective treatment.

The symptoms that are characteristic of what we call "senility" are serious forgetfulness; disorientation relating to time, places and people; and the inability to concentrate. These symptoms vary in severity. In fact, many people experience them momentarily. Mild symptoms are not "senility" and should not cause undue anxiety.

There are two types of "senility," with important differences. One is functional "senility," which may result from depression or boredom. The other is "senility" caused by a variety of underlying physical conditions. A correct diagnosis is essential for effective treatment.

It is a shame that many people, including doctors, sometimes fail to recognize that depression can mimic "senility." An older person caught up in worries about finances, grief over the loss of a loved one or simply a depressed state for one of many reasons can be misdiagnosed as "senile."

By reviewing and assessing his life in order to come to terms with approaching death, an old person may be viewed as dissociating himself from the present—showing all the signs of "senility."

Although it doesn't happen to everybody, many people who retire fall into a "use it or lose it" syndrome and develop an emotional problem mistaken for "senility." They are no longer able to compute figures or function well in social situations. They lose their sense of calendar and become confused about work schedules and time. Eventually, they begin to feel they exist outside the mainstream of life.

Still another cause of functional (non-organic) "senility" is created by the programming of life itself. When a person develops skills in his formative years and goes through life without opportunities for retraining or renewal, he may become obsolete in the same way as a refrigerator or an automobile. "Newer models" come along and the old ones are out-of-date.

Perhaps the final form of functional "senility" is brought on by boredom. People who have not developed areas of interest—a second or third career, a sense of civic participation, an interest in art, music, sports or hobbies—may find themselves with nothing to do.

Those who suffer from these non-organic forms of "senility"—depression, obsolescence or boredom—can be helped, but only if their condition is promptly recognized and efforts are made to help them to help themselves.

As important as it is to distinguish the cause of functional "senility," it is crucial to diagnose the organic forms. A number of these are also reversible with treatment. There may be as many as one hundred organic causes of "senility." These causes usually show themselves in physical discomfort but more importantly affect the circulation and the oxygen supply, which nourishes the brain.

One common physical condition that can produce symptoms of "senility" is anemia. Because poor eating habits can result from depression and anxiety —or from the feeling that cooking for one is too much trouble—the so-called tea-and-toast syndrome which may cause anemia can affect the well-to-do elderly as well as the poor. Unrecognized infections, congestive heart failure or alterations in the body's metabolism can also affect the brain and cause "senility." Some of these physical conditions pose a threat to the patient's life as well. Thus it is crucial that apparent "senility" be treated as a medical emergency. If the underlying physical condition is diagnosed and promptly treated, the patient may not only avoid "senility" but enjoy a longer, healthier life.

Unfortunately, other organic brain diseases which produce symptoms of "senility" have no specific treatment and cannot be reversed, although much can be done to lessen discomfort and slow deterioration and help the patient make use of residual strengths. The two most common disorders are cerebral vascular disease and primary degenerative disease of the brain. These conditions have various names—the first commonly is referred to as cerebral arteriosclerosis and the second as senile brain disease or senile dementia. Simply stated, cerebral arteriosclerosis is caused by the hardening of the arteries in the brain. Senile brain disease, which appears more frequently in old age, results from an obscure dissolution of the central nervous system cells.

These conditions make it necessary for a substantial number of older people to be in nursing homes and other institutions. Perhaps as many as 500,000 people out of 23 million older Americans suffer from organic brain disease, making it a shatteringly significant illness.

HOW TO PREVENT "SENILITY"

With proper consideration given to physical fitness and keeping actively involved in business, volunteer work or an interesting hobby, and remaining in the mainstream of life, it may be possible to prevent the non-organic forms of "senility." Older people should never feel they are beyond learning and doing and contributing. They must continually strive to maintain a lively and spirited mind.

Social fitness is also of great importance. This means developing a strong social network within the family and neighborhood as well as society at large. People need close relatives and intimate friends but also a larger circle of acquaintances.

I think of physical fitness in terms of maintaining stamina and working at muscle flexibility, co-ordination and strength. Daily exercises and walking, jogging and swimming all aid in retaining intellectual ability and certainly increase morale and high spirits. Good nutrition through a balanced diet is also an essential part of physical fitness.

WHAT TO DO FOR SEVERE "SENILITY"

If symptoms of "senility" become severe, an individual or his family should not put off seeking professional help from a family agency, social worker, psychologist or psychiatrist. Since a physical problem can play a role in these disorders, a medical checkup is also necessary.

For those who are diagnosed as being severely depressed rather than "senile," psychiatric treatment is required. Patients who have organic brain diseases may not be cured but they may secure some benefit from a simplified environment, social and personal support, good nutrition and the judicious use of tranquilizers and antidepressants. Depending on the strength, size and character of the family and the availability of space, it may even be possible for the patient to remain at home.

Unfortunately some 25 percent of older people have no close family and those who have no family substitutes are more apt to be institutionalized. If the individual is reasonably docile, this may mean a home for the aged. If he suffers from some of the more severe agitated and confused forms of "senility," it can mean a nursing home or mental hospital.

Some families struggle to keep a "senile" patient at home even when incontinence, nighttime agitation and daytime wandering and confusion make it virtually impossible for a person to remain at home. Then family and friends must face the difficult task of finding the right place for the person. They should seek help from private physicians, psychiatrists and family agencies in choosing the facility that will be most appropriate for the patient.

ATTITUDES TOWARD "SENILITY"

I have put the word "senility" in quotes throughout this article. In many ways the term is a poor one and yet we are probably stuck with it. It is a wastebasket term for many evils, some of them treatable and some not. Our society must learn to deal realistically and sensitively with these conditions and to provide emotional support for those who suffer from them. With proper planning and research and support of the biomedical studies which will lead to an understanding of these conditions, it may be possible to someday eliminate these devastating and dehumanizing disorders.

CREDIT: *Robert N. Butler, M.D., Director, National Institute on Aging, Department of Health, Education and Welfare, Bethesda, Maryland; author of* Aging and Mental Health, *co-author Myrna I. Lewis, St. Louis, Missouri: C. V. Mosby Company.*

Sex After Sixty

Every day five thousand Americans turn sixty. Altogether over thirty million people, or one out of every seven of us, is sixty or older. What happens to sex at this time of life? Many persons—not only the young and the middle-aged, but older people themselves—simply assume that it is over. This is nonsense. It is well known that healthy older people who enjoy sex are capable of experiencing it often until very late in life. Moreover, those who do have sexual problems can frequently be helped. Sex and sexuality are pleasurable, rewarding and fulfilling experiences that enhance the later years.

Those who have had a lively enthusiasm and capacity for sex all their lives sometimes need various kinds of treatment suggested by their physician in order to continue their sexual activity as the years go by. In addition, people for whom sex may not have been especially satisfying in their younger days may find it possible to improve its quality despite long-standing difficulties if they do seek guidance.

It is crucial that people realize sex after sixty is appropriate, normal and decent, and not a sign of senility or an embarrassing inability to adjust to aging with proper restraint and resignation. There is no need to accept the folklore of cookie-baking grandmothers who bustle about the kitchen making cookies for their loved ones while rocking-chair grandfathers puff on their pipes and reminisce. Nor are the prejudices appropriate. Our language is full of telltale phrases: older men become "dirty old men" or "old fools" where sex is involved; older women are depicted as "hags." Most of this "humor" implies the impotence of older men and the assumed ugliness of older women.

The truth is that sex can remain interesting and exciting after forty, fifty or sixty years of adulthood. Older people themselves have testified that it can. Affection, warmth and sensuality do not have to deteriorate with age, and may in fact increase. Sex in later life is sex for its own sake: pleasure, release, communication and shared intimacy. When people are young and first getting accustomed to sexuality, their sex tends to be urgent and explosive, involved largely with physical pleasure and, in many cases, the conception of children.

This is the first phase of sex. It is biological and instinctive, with wonderfully exciting and energizing potentialities. But sex is not just a matter of athletics and "production." Some young people recognize this early on and simultaneously develop a second and more mature phase of sex. It is emotional and communicative, as well as physical. The second phase is largely learned, rather than instinctive. It is often vastly underdeveloped since it depends upon one's ability to recognize and share feelings in words, actions and unspoken perceptions, and to achieve a mutual tenderness and thoughtfulness between two people. In its richest form, the second phase becomes highly creative and imaginative, with bountiful possibilities for new emotional experiences.

There are, of course, normal physical changes in sex and sexuality with age and information pertaining to these changes will reduce groundless fears that sex is over.

The menopause, or change of life, in the woman under normal conditions is not nearly as disturbing as some women make it out to be. Various symptoms, including the "hot flashes" and changes in the vagina, are treatable in brief periods of low-dosage estrogen. With men, allowing for the individual variations, a number of gradual and fairly predictable processes are associated with chronological aging. The older man ordinarily takes longer to obtain an erection than a younger man. The difference is often no more than a matter of minutes.

Perhaps more important than knowing the normal physical changes that occur with age is understanding the illnesses and drugs that can make an impact on sex. In the case of illnesses, fear and discomfort are the main problems. Men may fear returning to sexual activity after a heart attack, for instance. And yet sex can usually be carried out safely following the doctor's guidance.

On the average, couples take ten to sixteen minutes for the sex act. The oxygen usage during this time approximates climbing one or two flights of stairs or walking rapidly at a rate of two to two and a half miles per hour. Understanding the nature and treatment of strokes, diabetes, anemia, arthritis, backaches, hernia, Parkinsonism, prostatitis, incontinence, etc. can help to resume sexual activity.

Surgery, such as hysterectomy and mastectomy, while understandably troublesome to the woman, need not and usually does not interfere with sexual activity.

Many drugs, particularly antihypertensives, tranquilizers and antidepressants, can affect libido (desire) or potency. Often reductions in dosage or selection of a different drug may solve the problem.

In some persons, the following drugs *may* reduce libido in men and women, reduce potency in men and delay orgasm in women:

alcohol
amphetamine—stimulant
guanethidine—antihypertensive
haloperidol—tranquilizer
lithium—psychoactive
methyldopa—antihypertensive
phenothiazines—tranquilizer
reserpine—antihypertensive
sedative and sleep-inducing drugs (hypnotics) when
    used on a regular basis
thiazide diuretics
tricyclic antidepressants

There are common emotional conflicts associated with sex. Perhaps 80 percent or more of the problems in sexual activity in men and women are related to emotional difficulties which can be aided by consultation with clergy, family agencies, physicians or psychotherapists.

Taking care of one's self through diet and regular exercise will help keep you sexually active. Such habits obviously contribute to good health as well as to good looks. There is time, too, in the later years to learn new patterns of lovemaking through the use of self-help books now available.

One of the most difficult situations in later years is that statistically women live an average of eight years longer than men. Many have husbands who are four or five years older than themselves, so many women can expect to live eleven years as widows. As self-starters, older women can and should develop new relationships. The later years are those during which one should seek experiences that are satisfying, pleasurable and sustaining. Time earns us that right.

CREDIT: *Adapted from* Sex After Sixty: A Guide for Men and Women for Their Later Years *by Robert N. Butler, M.D. and Myrna I. Lewis, A.C.S.W. Copyright © 1976 by Robert N. Butler, M.D. and Myrna I. Lewis. Courtesy of Harper & Row, Publishers, Inc. (Paperback edition published 1977 under the title* Love and Sex After Sixty.*)*

WHEN THE FIRE'S OUT

DEAR ANN LANDERS: I am in agreement with your "Atlanta Reader" who is in his 60s. He criticized you for printing too many letters about sex and referred to himself as "one who had been neutered by time." He asked that you print fewer letters in your column dealing with problems of frigidity, impotence, incest, homosexuals, truck drivers who wear pantyhose, and Funny Uncles.

You told him time doesn't necessarily have to "neuter" anybody—that it was mostly in his head, etc. Although you are probably correct I would like to tell you that I'm a woman, and I agree with him. I'm glad to be free of "that old feeling." I'd have a real problem if the fires were still burning. I'm a widow (also in my 60s) and although I'm still hale and hearty I no longer need sex.

There are so many of us, Ann (some married to men who can't perform). We consider ourselves fortunate that Mother Nature has dealt with us in this manner. It's like losing your appetite for caviar when you can no longer afford it. So, as the kids say, "Cool it, honey." BASTA AMOUR

DEAR BASTA: If you consider it a blessing that you no longer need sex because it is not available to you through respectable and moral channels, I have no argument with that. But to request that I no longer print letters dealing with sex because it has no interest to YOU is grossly unfair. This column deals with human problems and is read by a wide variety of people, many of whom are still interested in sex.

AT WHAT AGE SHOULD A WIFE TURN OFF SEX?

DEAR ANN LANDERS: After reading your column for a few years, I am convinced that the kids from 14 to 22 (and single) are having more sex than the married couples over 35.

What I'd like to know is this: At what age is it OK for a wife to say to her husband, "We are too old for sex. Please leave me alone."

Last night I heard that line for the hundredth time. Rather than have a fight all the neighbors could hear, I decided to keep my mouth shut and write to Ann Landers for an answer.

Before you reply, I want to make it clear that I am not talking about husbands who are 50 pounds overweight, or the slobs who never take a bath, or the ones who get drunk every night. I'm talking about husbands who are clean, sober and turn over their paychecks regularly.

So many decent men get shut off sexually by their wives in the prime of life and don't know what to do about it. Small wonder there were more divorces last year than marriages. I'm signing myself—Just Another Animal (My Wife's Name For Me)

DEAR JUST: The erogenous zone is between the eyebrows and the hairline. (In case of baldness, let's just say, "the mind.") This is where all sex begins or ends—whichever the case may be.

There is no physical reason for terminating sex solely because of age. Couples can and do make love in their 70s and 80s—and this is as it should be.

Naturally, couples in their 80s are not apt to have sex as frequently (nor as intensely) as couples in their thirties, but the physical expression of love can still be immensely satisfying in the twilight years.

SEX AFTER 60

DEAR ANN LANDERS: I've been reading letters from women who think sex should end at 50. May I share my experience with them?

My husband is 61 and I am almost 64. We have been married only five months. My man could give some of those young fellows lessons on love. Most "frigid" women could be cured by his method.

For one thing, he still makes his living by hard physical labor and comes home covered with tar, sawdust and other disagreeable substances. Before we go to bed he bathes, shaves, uses a good deodorant and puts on clean night clothes. He doesn't drink anything stronger than coffee.

When we retire, I lie quietly in his arms and we discuss the day's activities or our past lives. I'd been a widow for six years and never believed I would ever be able to enjoy sex again. But the combination of my love for him and a chance to relax before love-making has proved miraculous.

Husbands sometimes forget that women are not as easily aroused as men. Young wives who rassle with children all day or are worn out from housework or a second job, need a quiet time before they can respond to their husbands. Many husbands find fault with their wives at the supper table and then expect them to be ready for romance the moment the lights go out. My husband compliments my cooking and my hair style. These things help me forget I am almost 64. Our love grows stronger every day. Please sign me YOUNG AT HEART

DEAR HEART: Beautiful! Your husband sounds like a prize—and so do you. I'm glad you found each other. Bless you both.

Sex and the American Male

The feminists accuse today's modern male of being exploitative, egotistical and obsessed with indiscriminate sexual gratification. Writers of popular psychology books describe him as uncommunicative, insensitive and driven by machismo. But how does the average American male really feel about his sexuality? To learn the truth, Anthony Pietropinto, M.D., and Jacqueline Simenauer conducted a nationwide survey of more than four thousand men, aged eighteen to sixty-five, encompassing all occupational groups, income groups and education levels. Their findings are reported and analyzed in *Beyond the Male Myth,* a book that explodes many of the prevailing myths about modern man.

The authors learned that, far from being threatened by women who express their sexual desires and take the initiative in sexual relations, men now prefer an aggressive, active partner who likes to experiment. A majority reported that the most unpleasant aspect of sex for them is an unresponsive or disinterested woman, and nearly half said such a partner could render them impotent. Women have been led to believe that men are "turned off" by women who make known their lovemaking preferences, yet there were only one tenth as many men who objected to a woman who "tried to control things" or even criticized them as those who cited impassive females as the greatest "turn-off."

Male orgasms, like female, differ profoundly in intensity and quality. Men have been accused of being concerned only with their own gratification; yet it was found that nearly all men felt it was important for a woman to have an orgasm, and more than half were self-critical if their partners failed to reach orgasm.

Four out of five men try to delay their orgasms as long as possible, and two thirds use the woman's gratification as the end point of a sex act. Nearly one third succeed in bringing their partners to orgasm almost all the time, and more than half are successful at least 60 percent of the time, in sharp contrast to Shere Hite's contention that only 30 percent of women can reach orgasm regularly through intercourse.

Despite their reputation for being unaffectionate, American men are more interested in sex than they ever were. Most would like it on an average of four times a week. More men selected kissing and caressing as their most enjoyable foreplay activity than any other practice, including oral sex. Female nudity is not a big "turn-on." Less than 2 percent said they disliked foreplay. Most men enjoy hugging and kissing even without subsequent intercourse. Although men have been frequently accused of wanting to have intercourse in the traditional way, more than half of the men said that the thing they would most like to do more often is employ different sexual positions.

Men are still strongly in favor of marriage. Asked what they would consider the ideal sex life, half of them chose marriage with the wife as the only sex partner, and, if those who wanted outside partners are included, the number opting for marriage exceeded two thirds. Less than one third of men living with a partner to whom they were not married felt that their arrangement was ideal, and, including those who wanted outside partners, there were more such men who would rather be married than who wished to continue their status quo. Less than one man in ten felt that many sexual partners constituted the ideal sex life.

Only one man in five considered sex to be the most important pleasure in life. More than a third felt that being in love was the most important thing in life, and less than one in ten said that love was an old-fashioned idea or that sex was better without it. Nearly one third of them would be so upset by a broken love affair that they would either avoid women for a while or their work would suffer.

Despite the contention of many psychologists that men will not confront their own dependency, the type of woman most men desired for a long-term relationship was one with concern for their needs. Intelligence was more valued than sexiness, and sincerity and affection ranked even higher. Nearly half of men today would marry primarily for companionship and marriage for the purpose of regular sex was the least chosen answer.

Whereas only one third of men over fifty-five have ever cheated on their partners, more than half of the men under thirty have already done so. While a third of men said they would never cheat, only half as many said they would not even be tempted.

One quarter of all single men would want to marry a woman with no previous sexual partners. And, regardless of the man's age or marital status, only 2 percent would choose a wife who had been intimate with many men.

These are only a few of the revelations that emerged from this unique study. Pietropinto and Simenauer depict modern man in transition, a creature of surprising sensitivity and self-insight, sharing for the first time his innermost feelings about sex, love and life.

CREDIT: *Anthony Pietropinto, M.D., Medical Director, Mental Health Program, Lutheran Medical Center, New York, co-author of* Beyond the Male Myth, *with Jacqueline Simenauer, New York: Quadrangle Books.*

Sex

Answers to the Most Frequently Asked Questions

(1) How can I get my mate to please me sexually without requesting or telling him or her how?

You can't. How could a mate read your mind? Love is not magical. People place restrictions on sexual relationship that are totally unrealistic. Couples should set aside special occasions if it's necessary to explain in detail what is most pleasurable, to express wishes, fantasies of what would be nice to try. Hopefully, these become incorporated in the awareness of each person so that the activity or behavior emerges spontaneously in sexual play.

In the best of relationships there is a place for sexual signals—more of this and less of that.

(2) Can alcohol and marijuana cause impotence?

Of all the chemicals that interfere with good sex life in our culture, alcohol is the greatest single culprit. The seeming aphrodisiacal effect of initial use of alcohol in relaxing tensions and blocking inhibitions is deceptive. Continuous drinking on a long-time basis has a depressing effect on the glands and hormones of men and women. It interferes with sexual life by destroying both tissue and chemical functioning.

Early in life the sex drive may be great enough to override the depressing influence of alcohol. But as drive diminishes naturally through the years, as personality conflicts become activated and relationship problems develop, alcohol becomes destructive. A man cannot perform as a lover if he has an excessive amount of alcohol in his system. He cannot maintain an erection and almost certainly will ejaculate prematurely. In women, alcohol interferes with the buildup of readiness for climax.

One of the most frequent syndromes with couples whose sex lives have gone to pot: Husband comes in from work and has several drinks before and after dinner. What happens is that this fatigue causes a need for his body to let down and then the alcohol provides more of a letdown, so his system goes inert.

Marijuana also creates problems with sexuality. Studies have indicated that because marijuana is not water-soluble, it is residual in the system, particularly in soft tissues of the glands and brain, for about three months.

Although marijuana has a similar effect as alcohol—relaxing inhibitions—it is tricky. Heavy use of marijuana can inhibit and then paralyze the ejaculatory mechanism. It has caused total lack of sex interest among heavy users.

(3) What are the best aphrodisiacs, or how can I increase my sexual desire?

In terms of chemicals and other products, forget it. Aphrodisiacs (such as drugs, food, etc.) are largely the product of fertile imaginations, sensuous longings and economic exploitation.

The best and only continuously effective sexual stimuli are a healthy body and mind and a meaningful and challenging relationship.

Conversely, the greatest enemies of sexuality are failure to share, failure to take care of oneself, lack of communication and the carelessness and neglect attendant to boredom.

(4) How acceptable or dangerous is oral sex?

Oral sex is a natural sexual exchange. The erotization of the mouth is normal. The subject is fear-ridden because of brainwashing by culture, which has said it is perverted, sinful, illegal, taboo, infectious. It seems to be more prevalent among today's youth, but some of them still ask about possible infection.

Some diseases can be passed back and forth, but others cannot. Syphilis and gonorrhea can be passed by any exposed tissue. But many medical specialists say that different strains of disease, such as herpes simplex (cold-sore type), will not grow in the vagina, nor will herpes vaginalis grow in the mouth.

With normal bathing, if you want to make a comparison, the mouth contains far more bacteria and viruses than the genitals. So you can't arbitrarily rule oral sex out. Two sensible partners should refrain from it if they know one of them has a disease.

What I am most concerned about is mutuality. I sometimes hear of a one-sided desire—he wants it and she can't stand it. Any individual who wants it for him- or herself and does not reciprocate for the mate is creating an unhealthy situation.

(5) How does a woman learn to climax in intercourse if she has never had an orgasm, or if she has orgasms only with mechanical or manual stimulation?

If the problem is related to major personality difficulties, only intensive psychotherapy accompanied by instruction in self-stimulation and response is likely to resolve it. This usually involves instruction in learning to respond to stimulation so her body can become involved.

If a never-responsive woman's failure is based on lack of information as well as prohibitions against sexual response, then a supportive counseling relationship coupled with instruction in self-exploring will usually make her orgasmic in a short period of time.

The next step is having a caring mate who joins in stimulation other than intercourse until she learns to respond in that situation, but short of intercourse. In order to transfer what she knows to intercourse, several conditions must be met: Anxiety about pregnancy or disease must be minimized. Trust of self and mate must be maximized. Sexual play must be sufficient to build her up at least to what is known as the plateau stage of arousal before coitus.

Coital activity must last long enough for the woman to yield her body spontaneously to normal orgasmic response. Remember, the determination to be orgasmic is one of the greatest enemies of being orgasmic.

(6) Will hormone pills or shots help a person to become more sexually responsive?

Not if the body already has an adequate hormonal level, which is true in about 98 percent of younger and middle-aged people. Even most people with sexual problems have a very high hormonal level.

If the male with adequate androgen has his supply artificially increased, though it may temporarily increase rate of sexual desire, it is likely to cause premature ejaculation. That person usually needs individual or couple counseling, and giving him drugs is playing into his needs to pretend that his problem has nothing to do with his personality problems.

We know more about male response to hormones. But I'm concerned about females who resort to hormonal treatment to increase sexual desire. If a woman's estrogen level is high in contrast to androgen level, increasing her estrogen may reduce sexual desire rather than increase it.

(7) Can antihypertensive medication be a factor in causing sexual failure or impotence?

Now that studies show that one adult in five is hypertensive and should be on medication, this is a vital issue. Every compound being used today to lower blood pressure has one or more of these possible side effects:

(a) Reduction of sex drive.

(b) Aspermia (lack of ejaculation).

(c) Impotence.

(8) What can a postmenopausal woman do to keep sexually alive now that hormonal replacement is thought to cause cancer?

The most important way to keep sexually alive is to keep sexually active. Body glands that are kept in tune should respond optimally. Supplemental lubrication can counter postmenopausal dryness of vaginal tissue.

(9) What causes coital pain in an experienced woman where no medical problem can be found?

Pain from depth of penetration can be caused if the uterus is bumped during coitus. If the uterus is sensitive, intercourse can be painful. Cure is change of position or type of penetration.

Some women are not getting stimulated sufficiently prior to penetration to allow the uterus to lift. Inadequate lubrication or pent-up tension from friction can also cause irritation and pain. Residual pain from frequent stimulation and engorgment never released through orgasm is a common source of ache and spasmic pain among non-orgasmic women. Sexually related fears can cause a woman to tighten up.

CREDIT: *Arnold Rutledge, Ph.D., Director of the Grosse Pointe Psychological Center, Grosse Point, Michigan. Reprinted from the Chicago* Sun-Times, *November 27, 1977.*

IS BISEXUALITY COMMON AMONG COLLEGE STUDENTS?

DEAR ANN LANDERS: I am a sophomore at a highly respected college who is confused about something. When I enrolled last year I knew of no bisexual relationships among my friends. Now, it seems, bisexuality is not only accepted but widely practiced among my peers. Male students I could have sworn were straight date members of their own sex just as often as members of the opposite sex. This goes for jocks, cheerleaders and officers of student government. Young people with tendencies for both sexes tell me they consider this an advantage, not a handicap. They call it "the best of both worlds."

I'm a 19-year-old guy and I've never had any desire to try anything with a member of my own sex. The moral values I learned as a child tell me it's wrong. Yet, if it is accepted by my peers and doesn't do me any harm, isn't it worth experimenting with?

Please print my letter because I'm sure many college students are just as confused as I. STRAIGHT AND NARROW

DEAR S AND N: Don't mess around. There is more involved here than "right" or "wrong." What it shakes down to is "natural" or "unnatural."

It's dumb to try something for kicks if it violates your sense of decency. What's more, it can get you involved with a bunch of weirdos.

In spite of the facts presented in your letter, let me assure you that a really straight person would have a devil of a time going the other way unless he were bombed, stoned, kinky or a little cuckoo.

THEY ENJOY WHIPPING EACH OTHER BEFORE SEX

DEAR ANN LANDERS: Thanks for running the letter about the couple who enjoyed beating each other as a prelude to sex. Please add two more to the list. My wife and I have been whipping each other for several years and it is a highly emotional experience.

Your Delaware reader noted that the centers of pain and pleasure are not far apart. Surely you know that pain and sex are often inseparable. We tried straight sex at the beginning and it left us exhausted, frustrated and unfulfilled.

Now we have great fun expressing our primitive feelings. We look forward to these lively encounters. Even though we end up with scratches, teeth marks and purple bruises, life is much more exciting.

I'm sure you don't approve but I hope you'll print my letter so the couple in Delaware will know there are others. WE LOVE CUPID'S STING

DEAR STING: There are MANY others and I've heard from dozens. As for "approval," what I think is not important. I only give advice when asked.

I'm not a judge or jury. If people enjoy scratching, biting and bruising one another (and call it love, yet), that's their business. But I'll tell you what I told the other couple. How nice that you two found each other. You belong together.

DEAR ANN LANDERS: I've been hoping someone with the same problem would write in and save me the embarrassment. Since no one has, I decided to muster the courage and ask you myself.

My husband and I are both 31. We married when we were 18 and have been passionate lovers from the beginning. Bill works the night shift so most of our lovemaking takes place during the day.

The problem is the children. We lock our bedroom door and try to be as quiet as possible. The question: Are the sounds of parents making love harmful to children? I know this is a dumb question but I need an answer and I can't ask anyone else. Help me, please, Ann. TOO MUCH NOISE IN MUNCIE

DEAR T.M.N.: It is better that children NOT hear their parents making love because it may not sound like "love" to them.

Do you have a TV or a radio in your bedroom? If not, get one and turn it up LOUD. I suggest this not only to protect the children, but to relieve you of the anxiety that surely must inhibit your lovemaking.

Sex Clinics

by William H. Masters, M.D.

The main stimulant to sexual quackery seems to be money. Whenever you have thousands of people who are willing to spend money, begging somebody to take it, somebody will oblige—at a minimum of $25 an hour. Thus, sexual quackery. The current field of sexual therapy is dominated by an astounding assortment of incompetents, cultists, mystics, well-meaning dabblers and outright charlatans.

I had a nightmare several years ago. It was while my associate, Virginia Johnson, and I were preparing our second book, *Human Sexual Inadequacy.*

That book described more than eleven years of clinical experience with couples who had visited us at the Reproductive Biology Research Foundation, in St. Louis, Missouri, seeking help in solving various kinds of sexual problems. Before we began our work it was rare that any physician would offer to treat sexual problems in the direct, specific, intensive way that we developed; and in my nightmare I saw this new branch of medicine growing suddenly into a major public fascination.

I saw it becoming a subject of television interviews and cocktail-party conversations. I saw hordes of prospective patients going to their doctors and asking, "Where can we get this kind of treatment? Is there a clinic nearby?" And I saw the doctors sadly shaking their heads: "Sorry. The field is still too new. There aren't enough trained people yet. . . ."

Warnings were issued that a deluge of patients might be forthcoming: patients demanding a type of help which would not be readily available unless the medical profession had been adequately prepared to give it. The point was made that a fourth of American medical schools failed to include in their curricula even a cursory discussion of sexual functions. It was urged that training of competent professionals begin right away.

Not many took the warning seriously—back then. Today, everything feared has come true. In fact, the situation is even worse than we expected. The deluge of patients has materialized, and the medical profession hasn't been able to handle it. What wasn't predicted is the enormous size and sustained insistence of the public demand for sexual therapy. The would-be patients, frustrated in their search for legitimate treatment, understandably haven't been willing to wait until it becomes available. They have gone in search of paradise wherever it was promised, looking for a happiness and satisfaction bound to sexual fulfillment. But, too often, instead of the garden of earthly delights they found only their own private nightmares.

In the less than five years since *Inadequacy* was published, approximately 3,500 to 4,000 new "clinics" and "treatment centers" devoted to sex problems have been established in the United States. Of these, the most charitable estimate cites perhaps 100 that are legitimate. Our instinct says that 50 would be a better guess. Only 50 out of a possible 5,000 offer treatment methods that have been developed with proper scientific care; have been subjected to long, conscientious testing and evaluation; and are administered by trained, fully competent personnel.

The rest of the clinics give nothing more than a superficial sex education at best and dangerous quackery at worst. They offer unevaluated theories, mystical cant, pop-psychology remedies and simplistic pseudoscience. Although the untested approaches sound imaginative, appealing and interesting, and some of the practitioners present seductively logical-sounding justifications for their theories, few or none can offer a truly believable promise that they will lighten your sexual difficulties. They can promise only to lighten your wallet.

Let me support these pessimistic remarks with another set of statistics. *Inadequacy* reported that 48 percent of the patients seen in the prior decade plus had experienced failure in previous therapy. In the past two years, among new patients visiting the foundation, the record of prior therapeutic failure has risen to 85 percent.

What do these figures tell us? Either that many more people are visiting therapists than had been previously, or that more of the therapists are inept —or both. We suspect that both are true.

Many men and women in the medical professions share our pessimistic view of the current sex-therapy scene. Among them are Louis Lefkowitz, Attorney General, and Stephen Mindell, Assistant Attorney General, of New York State. A little less than two years ago, they conducted an undercover investigation of what they called "unregulated therapists"; public hearings followed.

"We have found," said Mindell, "what appears to be a shockingly widespread pattern of 'sex therapy' wherein male therapists encourage female clients . . . to engage in sexual activities with them, under the guise that this is necessary for the client's well-being." Lefkowitz reported that the roster of self-styled therapists in his state included "criminals and mentally ill persons" as well as unqualified practitioners.

A physician came to the hearing and told of a therapist who induced a woman to engage in mutual masturbation with him, because this would cure her "mistrust" of men. A college professor reported that at one institution men and women gathered in encounter groups and screamed "Hate, hate, hate!" at each other. The institution not only accepted patients for a fee, said the professor, but offered to train apprentice therapists and give them diplomas and degrees—although the school wasn't accredited by the state. An undercover investigator for the state reported on a group-therapy "community" in which the patients "are urged and advised by therapists to leave their homes and move in with others in the group."

Some clinics advertise or privately assure prospective patients that their therapists have been trained at the St. Louis foundation. The phrase "Masters-and-Johnson-trained therapists" often crops up in promotional material. In most cases, this is a patent falsehood. The foundation's training methods are necessarily time-consuming. It takes anywhere from four months to a year or more to complete a course of training, depending on the man's or woman's previous clinical experience. To date, we have only eight therapy teams that have been trained in St. Louis and are practicing elsewhere in the country. When a non-authorized clinic uses the "M-J-trained" gimmick, the phrase often means only that somebody there has read one of the foundation's textbooks.

Other therapy shops advertise that they offer treatment based on "the M-J technique." This, too, is usually less than true. There is no "M-J technique." We follow no formula. We preach no dogma. We certainly aren't wedded to any therapeutic fad such as nude group encounters or punching people to relieve anger. We treat each couple as a unique relationship, and we don't know what approach will be followed until we know what the particular problems are.

When somebody tries to hook patients with "M-J technique" as the bait, he may mean that his approach bears some outward procedural similarity. The foundation accepts only couples for treatment, not individual men or women. The relationship, rather than separate individuals, is treated. Each couple stays at a local hotel and visits the foundation daily for two weeks of intensive treatment after which comes five years of follow-up—for a total cost of $2,500 per couple. A minimum of 20 percent are treated at reduced fee or at no cost.

You may wonder why there is such concern about the sorry state of this field. What harm do sex charlatans render, after all? It isn't as though they endanger people's lives or even, in most cases, physical health. Although the Lefkowitz-Mindell investigation turned up some cases of severe mental disturbance and even suicide as apparent results of bad therapy, such cases are relatively rare. On the surface, it may seem that sexual quackery is fairly benign: that it takes people's money but in other respects is usually harmless.

Not so. Sex-therapy quacks can make it more difficult for legitimate therapists to help a person. Having once been in the hands of an incompetent therapist a patient may experience special difficulties in any later treatment. For instance, the foundation staff has seen many couples who claim that either one or both partners had been seduced by self-licensed therapists. Some of these seductions have been homosexual. One troubled woman told us that a female "therapist" had induced her to co-operate in a series of sexual acts, under the pretext: "Maybe your trouble is that you're a latent homosexual. Let's check it out." Having lived through this, the woman was frightened of what might be done to her in St. Louis.

An obverse kind of problem also can arise. Instead of being frightened as a result of past encounters, some people seem disappointed to learn that seduction isn't a part of our approach. Whether apprehensive or dissatisfied, such patients represent frustrating difficulties. Time must be spent undoing the results of past blundering.

Another kind of problem, less measurable but perhaps even more serious, arises from the delicate, intensely personal nature of sex therapy. It takes courage to go through such therapy. If the initial experience is bad—if it yields unsatisfactory results or, worse, is actually frightening or depressing— that man and woman may never again seek help. They are doomed to live the rest of their lives with a sexual problem that might have been handled quite simply if they had only sought legitimate help from the beginning.

There is no way to measure this kind of damage. We can't count the numbers of people who, after disappointments and scares, thenceforth shy away from what could be genuine help. There are no statistics. We can say only that the problem exists and that it is widespread and serious.

You ask: All right, why not drive all these frauds and blunderers out of the field? Why not sue them, prosecute them, expose them by name?

We have now arrived at the very heart of the problem. Legal action is next to impossible because there is no legal definition of who is and who is not a legitimate sex therapist.

No state, to my knowledge, has any law requiring that a self-styled sex therapist be licensed, that he conform to any minimum standards of education or experience or that he observe any special code of professional ethics. The states license and regulate various professional titles such as "psychiatrist" or "psychologist." If you go into practice and call yourself a psychiatrist, you must be one and prove it. But should you call yourself a "sex therapist" or "psychotherapist" you can operate in most states with no restrictions beyond those that would apply to a candy-store proprietor or any other business person. So long as you behave yourself, pay your taxes, don't perpetrate provable fraud and avoid the trap of practicing medicine without a license—avoid prescribing medicines, for example, or giving advice about a patient's kidney functions—you can probably count on a peaceful and profitable career.

This lack of standards, this absence of either government controls or professional self-regulatory mechanisms, was the focal point of the Lefkowitz-Mindell investigation in New York. The Attorney General sadly pointed out that in his state, as in most others, there is no way to protect the public from therapeutic quacks as long as they are careful. "They are within the law," he said. "Or more accurately—the non-law."

The main purpose of the New York hearings was to determine, in effect, whether the fields of sex counseling and general psychotherapy could or should be more strictly regulated. Some witnesses said yes and some said no, and of those who said yes, no two agreed on exactly how the purpose might be accomplished. So things remain at a standstill not only in New York but nearly everywhere else. Mrs. Johnson and I feel a direct and heavy responsibility for this new field of medicine, but, to date, have been frustrated in almost all attempts to protect it. Casting about for legal weapons with which to attack charlatans, we find our corner virtually empty.

Unless and until your state protects the field with a strong wall of law, there is only one man or woman who can effectively guard you against sexual quackery: That is yourself. The best advice is this: Before signing up for any course of sexual therapy, seek counsel from four separate sources:

Your physician. At the outset, he is probably the man best qualified to help you judge your personal needs. From talking to patients and other local physicians, he also may know of a nearby clinic that he can recommend.

Rely on your city or county medical society. Either organization will probably be able to recommend a clinic or at least some sources of further advice. Also, as a local medical listening post, the society will know of at least some charlatans in the area and can help you avoid them.

Your local family and children's service. This is the focal point of social work in the area and serves as a listening post much like the medical society. Its workers will have dealt with troubled people who have had both good and bad experiences with sex therapists.

Your minister, priest or rabbi. As a counselor to the troubled, he is likely to have helped other people grapple with marital and sexual problems, some perhaps similar to yours. He may know which local treatment centers produce results and which don't.

Even with these four sources to guide you, you still will need to tread warily. As bad as things are we are optimistic about the future. History is on our side. Back in 1910, most branches of medicine were in the same state as sexual therapy is now. There was a chaotic lack of standards. It took a lot of time and a lot of struggle, but today most branches are fairly firmly regulated by both law and self-imposed ethics. You are reasonably safe in assuming that a man who calls himself "M.D." really is one, and that the degree means he went through a specified amount of training. The same is true of specialist titles such as "gynecologist" or "ophthalmologist." One day, hopefully, it will also be true of "sex therapist."

CREDIT: The Health Robbers, *George F. Stickley Company, Publishers.*

Sex Education in Our Schools

Most people assume that, in the absence of direct instruction, no sex education takes place. Actually the parents' reaction to themselves and to each other as sexual beings, their feelings toward the child's exploration of his own body, their attitudes toward the establishment of toilet habits, their response to his questions and his attempts to learn about himself and his environment, their ability to give and express their love for each other—and for him—are among the many ways in which they profoundly influence the child's sexual conditioning.

Avoidance, repression, rejection, suppression, embarrassment and shock are negative forms of sex education. That fact cannot be escaped. Parents cannot choose whether or not they will give sex education. They can choose only whether they will do something positive or negative about it, whether they will accept or deny their responsibility.

Sex education must be thought of as education—not moral indoctrination. Attempting to indoctrinate young people with a set of rigid rules and ready-made formulas is doomed to failure in a period of transition and conflict. Instead, the time-tested principle accepted in other areas of education must be applied: to equip youngsters with the skill, knowledge and attitudes that will enable them to make intelligent choices and decisions.

Most people seem to operate on the false assumption that the more a child knows about sex, the more likely she/he will be sexually active. Virtually all opposition to the sex education of parents and their children is based on the belief that information stimulates inappropriate behavior. We must explode the myth that knowledge is harmful.

We need only look at the startling figures in front of us. More than 1 million teenage girls—that's one out of every ten—become pregnant each year. Over 600,000 of these pregnancies result in births. Over half the 21 million fifteen- to nineteen-year-olds in America are estimated to have had sexual intercourse. The venereal disease statistics reflect a public health problem of alarming magnitude.

Despite all the talk about a sexual revolution in this country, the actual truth is that a lot of young people still don't know the facts about sex. Contrary to the claims that the "pill" is the cause of the increase in sexual activity among teens, less than 20 percent of sexually active adolescents use any form of birth control. And even if they wanted to use them, most birth control methods would not be available to them.

Although most adults favor sex education in the schools and availability of contraception for unmarried teenagers, only a handful of states require any form of family life or sex education classes in their schools. Moreover, even where sex education is a part of the curriculum, only 40 percent of the programs include information about birth control. Given the lack of comprehensiveness of such education, it is not surprising that studies show "sex education" makes little difference in measures of sexual responsibility, such as avoiding VD and unwanted pregnancy. Research does indicate, however, that teens who have the right kind of knowledge about sexuality tend to behave more responsibly.

It has only been recently that our laws and legislative policies have begun to change to provide adolescents who want them with effective family planning services. It is still estimated, however, that half of the 3.7 million fifteen- to nineteen-year-olds are not receiving family planning help from either organized clinics or private physicians. This factor alone may help to explain why in 1975 there were at least 300,000 unintended pregnancies and 325,000 abortions by teenage women.

In its report, the Alan Guttmacher Institute suggested a national program to cope with this silent but serious epidemic. It included:

(1) Realistic sex education through schools, churches, youth agencies and the media.

(2) An expanded network of preventive family planning programs and adequate pregnancy counseling service.

(3) Equal availability and accessibility of legal abortions to all women, regardless of their income, where they live and other factors.

(4) Adequate medical care—before, during and after pregnancy—for those who choose to have their babies.

(5) Educational, employment and social services for adolescent parents and day-care facilities for their children.

(6) Greater research to discover safe and effective birth control techniques that fill the need of young people.

A child can't be told too much, contrary to the beliefs of some parents who feel that too much knowledge may lead to inappropriate behavior. If you tell a child more than he/she can understand, he will either ask another question or tune you out.

Adequate sex education and information is essential for today's youth. We cannot hide behind fears and myths. We must pass on to tomorrow's family the notion that correct information about sexuality promotes responsible behavior. Parents must work toward being *askable*. We need to teach our children what they want and need to know.

OBJECTIVES OF SEX EDUCATION ARE:

(1) To provide for the individual an adequate knowledge of his own physical, mental and emotional maturation processes as related to sex.

(2) To eliminate fears and anxieties relative to individual sexual development and adjustments.

(3) To develop objective and understanding attitudes toward sex in all of its various manifestations—in the individual and in others.

(4) To give the individual insight concerning his relationships to members of both sexes and to help him understand his obligations and responsibilities to others.

(5) To provide an appreciation of the positive satisfaction that wholesome human relations can bring in both individual and home life.

(6) To build an understanding of the need for the moral values that are essential to provide rational bases for making decisions.

(7) To provide enough knowledge about the misuses and aberrations of sex to enable the individual to protect himself against exploitation and against injury to his physical and mental health.

(8) To provide an incentive to work for a society in which such evils as prostitution and illegitimacy, archaic sex laws, irrational fears of sex and sexual exploitation are non-existent.

(9) To provide the understanding and conditioning that will enable each

individual to utilize his sexuality effectively and creatively in his several roles, e.g., as spouse, parent, community member and citizen.

CREDIT: *Sol Gordon, Ph.D., Institute for Family Planning and Education, Syracuse, New York.*

DEAR ANN LANDERS: Today's column was the last straw. Another letter about sex. And kinky sex, at that. I have four teenagers who fight for your part of the paper. I just die when you print such garbage and it gets worse every day.

I am a mature, broad-minded person, but enough is enough. Like the woman whose husband wanted her to wear black nylon stockings and a garter belt to bed. My kids just roared.

Today the 14-year-old daughter had a sore throat and we were afraid she might develop rheumatic fever. She didn't have the slightest idea what rheumatic fever was, but she knows all about VD—thanks to Ann Landers. Cool it, will you please? A MOTHER WHO LOVES HER KIDS

DEAR MOTHER: I love your kids, too, and that's why I'm trying to acquaint them with the real world which includes black nylons and garter belts.

A teenager's chance for getting VD today is at least 100 times better than getting rheumatic fever. You should be grateful that somebody is doing your job—and that somebody is me.

There is no need to hide my column from the kids, Mother. If the subject matter is beyond a child's ken, it will have no meaning. If he understands, all the better. Ignorance is dangerous. Information can help kids stay out of trouble.

THOSE CRAZY AMERICANS

DEAR ANN LANDERS: I enjoy your column very much. It has helped me, but not in the same way it has helped most other people. I came from a foreign country and learned how to read English from your articles. Your true-to-life writing is easy to follow. You don't use big words like many other writers.

I hope you will accept a suggestion from me because I see the world through the eyes of a newcomer. I happen to know your column appears in many foreign cities because I have seen it in my travels to Tokyo, Bangkok, Hong Kong, Mexico City and Caracas.

Would you please not publish letters about teen-age girls getting with child, married women who have love affairs with the boss, husbands who ask their wives to wear black stockings to bed and other things that make Americans look immoral and crazy? Thank you very much. YOUR GOOD FRIEND

DEAR FRIEND: The letters that appear in my column are human problems. They come from every one of the 50 states, as well as from Canada, Bermuda, Nassau—in fact from all over the world. There is no such thing as "an American problem" or "American craziness." Trouble and strange behavioral pattern are universal. Thank you for writing.

Sex for the Handicapped

DEAR ANN LANDERS: I was the eldest girl and devoted my life to helping my widowed mother raise a big family. I'm 43 now and all the others are married but me.

I work as a dietician in a hospital and have fallen in love. The man has been a patient here for several months. Vince is a diabetic who had a leg amputated.

He is a retired farmer, fairly well-to-do and has grown children. His wife died two years ago and he treats me like a queen. Vince will be discharged in May and wants me to marry him in June. A close friend of mine says I'd be crazy to marry a diabetic with one leg—that all he's looking for is a nurse. She has been divorced three times and says she knows men a lot better than I do (which is true). I need advice. LOVE HIM

DEAR FRIEND: Your signature says it all. Go ahead and marry Vince. It's that three-time loser with the big mouth who doesn't have a leg to stand on.

Sex, by all society, is viewed as the most dramatic and immediate means of expressing and receiving love and affection and/or physical pleasure. Great concern about sex may occur in handicapped people because of realistic fears that the presence of a visible "deformity" will make them less sexually desirable.

In addition to the problem of unattractiveness, there are also problems resulting from the physical disability to perform sexual acts. Serious deterrents are paralysis, pain, inability to have erections, inability to have orgasms, contracted joints and muscles, and involuntary movements. Other problems that make sexual expression difficult are spinal cord injury (paraplegia, quadriplegia), arthritis, multiple sclerosis, cerebral palsy, hemiplegia (stroke, brain tumors), polio, Parkinson's disease, as well as other diseases of muscles, nerves and bones that can limit movement, cause pain and impair sensation.

The handicapped do *not* need to feel incapable of sexual expression. Primarily they must realize that sexuality involves more than genital contact. Secondly they must realize that in almost all physical disabilities genital involvement *is* possible. The first avenue to solution is communication. Even able-bodied sexual partners are not particularly open in regard to expressing their feelings, preferences, degrees of satisfaction or in making suggestions.

Also, health professionals to whom the disabled turn for advice frequently are not well informed and may be too embarrassed to discuss sex at all.

The handicapped need intelligent, free and specific advice on sexual activity. Also they must have a sufficient sense of their own sexuality, capabilities and needs so that they can talk candidly with their partners about their sexual feelings. They must communicate openly and let one another know if they are receiving pleasure and satisfaction. Moreover, they must overcome the burdens of unnecessary fear of rejection.

People in general are likely to take the lead from handicapped people themselves in relation to attitude. If the handicapped feel pitiful, unworthy, rejected and unattractive, others are apt to see them in this light. If they have a healthy sense of self-esteem, feel attractive and desirable, others will respond more positively.

Sexual intercourse can almost always be accomplished by the handicapped. It may be necessary to experiment with positions and oral considerations. Patience, care and thoughtfulness and more attention to foreplay is important. This can be done only if there is openness and frank discussion.

It is important to realize that sexual satisfaction does not necessarily involve actual contact of the genital organs. Closeness, embracing, stroking, kissing, even just nearness and "glances" of affection can fill the void when more vigorous sexual expression such as intercourse or orgasm is not possible.

Many rehabilitation centers are now educating staff in regard to how they can be better sex counselors. Most major rehabilitation centers have specific people and/or programs that can give practical advice. A handicapped person seeking help can contact the medical director of a rehabilitation hospital, especially those dealing with spinal cord injuries.

I am listing here several specialists in this field who can be contacted for more detailed advice and/or discussion. My apologies for those who have been excluded; it would be virtually impossible to list them all.

The "pioneer" physician in this field is Ted Cole, M.D., Professor and Chairman, Department of Physical Medicine and Rehabilitation, University of Michigan, Ann Arbor.

Dorothea Glass, M.D., Professor and Chairman, Department of Physical Medicine and Rehabilitation, Temple University, Moss Rehabilitation Center, Philadelphia.

Sanders Davis, M.D., Institute of Rehabilitation Medicine, New York University Medical Center, New York.

Joel Rosen, M.D., Rehabilitation Institute of Chicago—Northwestern University, Chicago.

Lauro Halstead, M.D., Associate Professor, Baylor University, Texas Institute for Rehabilitation and Research, Houston, Texas.

Scott Manley, Ph.D., Craig Rehabilitation Hospital, Englewood (Denver), Colorado.

Dan Mayclin, Ph.D., Santa Clara Valley Medical Center, San Jose, California.

George Hohmann, Ph.D., V. A. Hospital, Tucson, Arizona.

CREDIT: *Henry Betts, M.D., Executive Vice President and Director of the Rehabilitation Institute of Chicago.*

Oral Sex

DEAR ANN LANDERS: I realize you are Jewish. Armed with this knowledge and my familiarity with the culture from whence you emerge, it all figures.

I take strong exception to the column about canker sores on the lips of girls (I assume) who were engaging in oral sex. You stated that this type of VD is on the increase and warned your readers to "be aware." That column would have been better had it never seen the light of day. What's more, I believe you could enhance your reputation (maybe it's too late now) and increase your readership if you devoted your efforts toward uplifting the nature of man rather than publicizing his frailties.

This is an age of deterioration. Why should you contribute to the erosion just because you have a job on a newspaper? Why not use your power to uplift rather than pull people down? Our goal in life is to assist in the development of society. That's why those who don't do their bit, no matter how little, always get it in the neck sooner or later. A REAL AMERICAN

DEAR READER: You call yourself "A Real American"? Not in my book. Your opening sentences disqualify you. It's perfectly OK to tell me my advice is lousy, but to say, "it figures"—because I'm Jewish—reflects some pretty warped logic.

I view this column as an opportunity to educate, and I tell it like it is. To suggest that I am contributing to the deterioration of this country when I warn people about a relatively new disease that few people know anything about is sheer lunacy. You say, "Our goal in life is to help assist in the development of society." I know what I've been doing for the last 20 years. What have YOU been doing—besides dishing out ethnic slurs?

Oral-genital sex, which is the stimulation of the partner's genitals by using the mouth and tongue, was once considered extremely "far out," but attitudes are changing. The person who felt ashamed to admit his wish for oral-genital sex, even to his wife or girlfriend, much less to acknowledge the practice to others, has learned it is commonly practiced. Prostitutes were often solicited because the man was ashamed to ask his wife to perform the act.

Oral stimulation of the man's genitals is called fellatio, and that of the woman's is called cunnilingus. Kinsey (1948) many years ago found that 60 percent of the better-educated population acknowledged oral sex, while some recent sampling and surveys indicate that oral-genital sex is even more widely practiced. In one under-thirty-five age group, 91 percent considered oral-genital activity as a regular part of normal sex.

This is true whether oral-genital stimulation is used as foreplay, a prelude to genital intercourse, or as an occasional or even habitual act leading to full gratification. There is no rule that every sex act must end in intercourse. Many couples enjoy such activity as an occasional variation. At any rate, many find oral-genital stimulation pleasurable and effective, both as foreplay and as a primary means to orgasm.

Nonetheless, many people suffer conflicted feelings about oral-genital sex. They think it is "taboo," "dirty," "perverse," "abnormal," "dangerous," etc. From the psychiatric point of view, no sexual behavior acceptable to both partners need be considered abnormal.

The "perverse" label springs from two factors: (1) Many have been brought up to consider sexual behavior for anything but procreation and reproduction as sinful and wrong, and non-genital contacts, they figure, must be queer beyond belief. (2) Oral-genital activity is often the preferred act of homosexuals.

Similarly, the feeling of "taboo" comes from our traditions which extolled the non-responsive woman, the missionary position and the sexual hang-ups of childhood in which examining, touching and exploring genitals, one's own or another's, was considered "naughty," prohibited and a cause for punishment.

The "dirty" idea also has a dual origin. First, some of us were reared to believe the genital area forbidden, off limits and "dirty." Then there are the anatomical-physical aspects. The urethra and anus are in close proximity to the female genitals, and of course the penis is also used in urination. However, with normal hygiene, the genitals are as clean and appetizing as any part of the body, without the assistance of cosmetics, deodorants or special hygienic products. (In fact, some vaginal douches, and the practice of repeated douching, can be quite harmful). Actually, the mouth is a dirtier organ than the genitals. The mouth is swarming with a variety of bacteria—as any TV mouthwash ad will assure you.

But we develop strange, unreal biases and aversions. The same lover who will passionately devour the lips and explore with his tongue the interior of his beloved's mouth and have her do the same to him may recoil in horror at the idea of using her toothbrush!

It may be mentioned that the lips, tongue and mouth are highly erotic or erogenous zones, and that their use on any part of the body—face, mouth, neck, nipples, genitals or toes, etc.—can be very pleasurable.

Some wonder if oral-genital sex is "dangerous," that is, it will take precedence over penis-in-vagina activity. Afraid of finding oral-genital sex highly pleasurable, they fear that they will get carried away into a sea of uncontrollable, abnormal, sensuous pleasure. As we said before, any way can be the right way. Each couple must decide what is best and most pleasurable. The method best suited for a particular occasion may be adopted, with each striving to bring about maximum gratification to the other. Open communication, discussion and experimentation will let each couple know what brings the greatest erotic pleasure.

As to other kinds of danger, there is none to healthy genitals, but infections can be transmitted—such things as herpes, a kind of fever blister sometimes found on the lip, or the usual venereal diseases.

We have dealt with most of the myths surrounding oral sex, but one that persists is that it is degrading and debasing. In themselves, none of the oral-genital activities should be considered as such. If it is in the mind of one partner (his fantasy) to force upon the other an act of submission and degradation, that attitude will color this and any other sex activity or behavior. People who feel this way have mixed their concepts of sexual pleasure (and general relationships) with themes of submission and power, or, if you will (to get fancier), sadism and masochism.

Couples who are tender and loving with each other will find genital kissing one more expression of their mutual pleasure-giving. Couples who are loving and supportive don't hurt or humiliate one another, nor are they prey to guilt and shame instilled by some of our cultures. They utilize without fear or doubt all parts of their bodies. There are no concerns about being deviant or disrespectful, immodest or "wicked." Instead they readily communicate wishes and desires in this intense manner.

Mutuality of desire, or at least a willingness by both parties, should be of prime consideration. In some instances only one party wants it—almost always the male—and the other party doesn't want it or expresses a frank revulsion to it. If the party who doesn't enjoy it (but can tolerate it) will go along, it will surely help the total sexual relationship. If one party simply loathes it, there should be no excessive pressure exerted.

Any individual who wants oral sex for himself or herself and is not willing to reciprocate is selfish, emotionally unhealthy and exploitive.

CREDIT: *Jerome B. Katz, M.D., Menninger Foundation, Topeka, Kansas.*

Sexual Fantasies

IF HE'S IN YOUR ARMS BUT NOT YOUR MIND, HUSH

DEAR ANN LANDERS: If I didn't know better, I'd think you hit the bottle occasionally because some of your advice is really off the wall. For example: That wife who imagines her husband is Kirk Douglas when he makes love to her.

According to you, it was perfectly "normal"—nothing to be concerned about—so the dumbbell went and told him about her mental substitution!

If a wife has to think about Kirk Douglas when her own husband is right there, the least she can do is keep it to herself. I wouldn't be very flattered if I learned the reason my husband was enjoying himself so much was because he imagined I was Ann-Margret. If he confessed such a thing to me, I'd tell him to get lost.

We hear too much these days about switching, swapping, nude shows and weird sexual practices of every con-ceivable type. What this country needs is someone to stand up for decency and morality. I thought you were it, but I see I was wrong. DEEPLY DISAPPOINTED

DEAR D.D.: The human mind is such an intricate piece of machinery that no one knows exactly how it functions—or why—particularly in the area of sexual responses.

What turns some people on is a mysterious mix of everything they have ever seen, read, heard, dreamed about, plus assorted bits and pieces that are so private they are shared with no one.

I agree with you that not every person can tolerate complete openness and candor. In such cases, it is best to keep your mouth shut. The wisdom lies in knowing the emotional temperament of your partner and behaving accordingly.

It ought to be easy to write about sexual fantasies. Everyone has them, and some are extremely vivid. They are the basis of all pornography and much great art, music and literature (implicitly if not explicitly) in the course of human history.

The current merchandisers of sexual fantasy show surprisingly little sophistication compared with many of their predecessors. As camera work, the photographs in *Playboy* may be excellent, but the fantasy aspect is crude, gross and unimaginative.

If sexual fantasy is universal, appealing and powerful, it is also an awkward subject for discussion. Most people are ashamed of their fantasies, or they do not understand them. Many feel so guilty that they must vigorously deny them and launch angry attacks on those who hint of their existence. Some of the opposition to pornography, for example, is probably based on guilt about one's own imagination.

The fantasy world is disordered and chaotic. It draws the line at no sexual behavior, because it has not learned, like the ego, that certain kinds of sex destroy relationships, society and civilizations. Incest, rape, homosexuality, bestiality, sadomasochistic orgies are all completely undifferentiated in the raw and primal imagination.

Are sexual fantasies evil? As fantasies, surely not. They become evil when we attempt to accomplish all of them (which happens usually only among the unbalanced), or when we permit them to substitute for relationships in the real world. Some fantasies can be safely carried out, others give us critical hints about our personality and our needs. Still others can provide a richness and variety in our sexual relations that may substantially improve our emotional life and our psychological well-being. Finally, sexual fantasy has profoundly religious overtones. It is part of the pre-conscious self that produces both sexual and religious images.

Sexual fantasies are part of the human condition. To pretend they are not is to ignore the facts. They tell us something about the nature and destiny of humankind. A theology which ignores such data is a theology with blinkers on.

I will confine my discussion to heterosexual fantasies because for most people they are the most frequent and the most pertinent to the subject of marriage and sexual play. Still it must be noted in passing that a sexually mature man is confident enough in his own maleness that he does not need to hide from himself the fact that he sometimes finds the bodies of other men in a shower room sexually appealing. Nor need a woman feel that she is perverted because she occasionally feels an urge to touch the breasts of another woman. Such urges are normal statistically and psychologically. To acknowledge them is merely to concede the complexity of human sexuality. Mature heterosexuals do not take such urges as a norm for action. They do not feel constrained to give in to such longings, and they are not shaken by insecurity or guilt simply because they discover such desires in themselves.

As far as one can judge from the sparse, confused and uneven psychiatric and social scientific literature on the subject, there are four general kinds of frequent sexual fantasies. Each is as prevalent in men as in women, although they may take different forms in the different sexes.

(1) Fantasies of nakedness. Dressing and undressing are an aspect of human behavior filled with sexual overtones beginning with the earliest childhood memories. To be exposed is to be seen, enjoyed, possessed. Clothes are designed both to conceal and to reveal, to hide and to display. The sexual implications of clothes are so obvious that one should not have to mention it.

But the very hint that dressing and undressing are highly sexual activities is enough to send Puritans into fits of anger.

A good criterion of a sexual relationship is the richness, the excitement and the significance that a husband and wife permit the ordinary but highly charged activity of putting on and taking off clothes. It is a behavior that is inherently playful with an almost limitless variety of possibilities. When all play is gone out of it, there can be little play left in the relationship.

(2) Rape and being raped. I hesitate to use the word, because real rape is a sordid, violent, ugly act. It may occasionally be so in fantasy life too, but fantasy "rape" is transformed and has little in common with the ugly violation of another human being that occurs all too frequently in the real world. It is the essence of fantasy rape that one is forced to do something that one desperately wants to do, or that one forces the other to do something that the other deeply wants to do. There may be violence in fantasy rape but not violation. One may be powerless (or render another powerless) but it is a pleasurable and not a brutalized powerlessness. To the extent that brutality may be involved, it is a brutality that brings delight and not shame. The essence of fantasy rape is that resistance, inhibition, hesitancy are firmly and completely swept away. One either becomes powerless and is completely at the whim of the other or renders the other powerless and has complete control of him (or her).

(3) Seduction and being seduced. Rape fantasies concentrate on the direct, forcible and, if need be, violent reduction of resistance. Seduction fantasies focus on the slow, gentle art of taking possession of or being possessed by the other. Instead of the process being quick, firm, even harsh, it is long, teasing and leisurely. The end is the same, of course, but the important fact of the imagery is not the end but the style. In both the rape and seduction fantasies one conquers or is conquered. In the former one's effort is directed at immediate conquest, in the latter it is directed at slow, gradual, agonizingly delightful surrender.

(4) Fantasies that have to do with a variety of positions, places and organs. Given that there is an endless variety of places where sex can occur and a considerable number of positions and techniques for obtaining sexual satisfaction with one's partner, there are countless possibilities for fantasies on this subject. Most marital sex takes place in one position, in one place and with one technique, but this does not prevent the imagination from contemplating a wide variety of interesting possibilities.

Such a list of fantasies is bound to be inadequate and incomplete, but to sketch some of the fantasies that are apparently so frequent as to be universal may tell us something extremely important about human sexuality.

Let us now consider the fantasies of a relatively typical (composite) upper-middle-class American couple. I wish to emphasize that these fantasies are "normal" both in the statistical sense of being commonplace and in the psychological sense of not indicating emotional disturbance. On the contrary, such fantasies (or similar fantasies) are typical to the point of being almost universal among physically healthy adults.

The wife imagines herself being brought to a party of her husband's friends. The men are wearing evening clothes and she is wearing a black strapless gown and black lace underthings. Her husband begins to describe quite clinically her sexual attributes. His friends demand evidence and he compels her to remove her clothes. He makes appropriate descriptive comments as she undresses, and his friends applaud in appreciation. Completely naked, she is then compelled to walk among the men while they touch and caress her, leaving not a part of her body untouched. Finally, her husband makes love to her while his friends cheer him on. Her fantasy ends as he turns her over to one of his friends for his pleasure.

Another fantasy: The husband is on an airplane on a business trip. He is seated next to an attractive, shapely woman with pale white skin, dark hair turning slightly gray and a deep, seductive voice. In his fantasy she strikes up a conversation, letting her hand wander to his thigh and leaning her body suggestively against his. As they get off the plane, she invites him to her hotel room. In the room he becomes completely passive and she is the aggressor, teasing him to uncontrollable desire. She then kneels astride him and screams with joy as she brings the two of them to a dazzling climax. (In the real world, of course, she gets off the plane without saying a word.)

The wife is in the kitchen finishing the dishes in early afternoon. She imagines a man entering the room. He is dark, muscular, and wears only a scanty loincloth. Without saying a word he comes up behind her and locks his arms around her in a fierce embrace. She tries to break away, but her struggles are useless. He kisses the back of her neck and her shoulders, squeezes her breasts and tightens his grip. She stops struggling. Still silent, he unzips her dress, tears away her panties and bra and forces himself into her—quickly, skillfully and insistently. She has never before responded so completely and totally to a man. She is utterly helpless and totally transformed. She can almost feel his hot breath on her face when the phone rings and her nine-year-old says, "Mom, it's raining awfully hard. Can you come and get me?"

Note well that we are dealing with two responsible, self-possessed adults. They are good parents, good spouses. They are not sick or dirty people. Their fantasies—vivid, exciting and compelling—come out of their experiences and imaginations and are stored up in their unconscious minds. If they were hypnotized (which is in itself another fantasy) and compelled to live out their fantasies, they would find it a delightful experience (who wouldn't?) only because they could then be dispensed from freedom of choice, responsibility and guilt.

What then are fantasies besides entertaining ways of passing the time? They are first of all a way to release emotional and psychic energy, dangerous only if they become so compulsively important that real human relationships and responsibilities are ignored, or if one seriously begins to turn the fantasies into reality.

But these fantasies also reveal to us, if we are not ashamed to consider their implications, that we are creatures with powerful, deep, complex hungers. We can restrain and control these hungers, but we cannot eliminate them completely. It is a mistake to try. Fantasies can be safety-valve mechanisms in which some of the raw force of our primal hunger can be discharged in a framework of safety and support.

Fantasy, then, does not provide a detailed outline for reality, but it does open up some interesting possibilities. What possibilities will be pursued depends on the people involved.

To what extent can one share fantasies with another? Some fantasies are intensely private and can't be shared. Others can be shared or not, depending on the strength of the relationship. Some can be shared with relative ease. There are no hard and fast rules. Much depends on the taste, sense of humor, self-possession and emotional strength of the people involved. Certainly the direct encounter group strategy, "Let's sit down now and communicate with each other about our fantasy lives. You tell me yours, and I'll tell you mine," is both foolish and harmful.

Fantasy-sharing is an option, not an obligation. There is no all-purpose formula for what ought to be shared or how. Given the fact that most people are so ashamed and so guilty about their fantasy lives, it is likely that fantasy-sharing in most relationships will be minimal. I would be suspicious, indeed, of married couples who contend that they have a big and very easy fantasy-sharing thing going. My inclination would be to suspect that there is something profoundly wrong with such a marriage and the huge fantasy success is a cover-up. Slow, gradual, tasteful, witty sharing of daydreams is probably a sign of a healthy development. Anything else ought to be considered dubious.

CREDIT: *Andrew M. Greeley, author of* Love and Play, *Chicago: Thomas More Press.*

LA, LA, LA, LA, LA, LA, LOVELY LINDA

DEAR ANN LANDERS: Last May my husband asked me if he could wear one of my housedresses while painting the kitchen. He said it would be more comfortable. I said OK. He did look awfully cute, and I told him so. Ever since that time he has been wearing my dresses and wigs and makeup when we are alone. He has asked me to call him Linda when we "play girl friends," as he calls it.

I can truthfully say I don't mind. The only thing that bothers me is that he is prettier than I am. If we went out in public together, he would get more whistles. Yesterday I read an article on sex deviation. It said men who enjoy dressing up in women's clothes are transvestites. I do not consider my husband abnormal. He is very manly in every way. He just happens to enjoy playing this little game. Is there anything wrong with it? I'd like your opinion. HAPPY WOMAN WHO LOVES HER HUSBAND

DEAR WOMAN: My opinion is of no consequence. The only thing that matters is what you think, and apparently you think it is just fine. If you and your husband enjoy "playing girl friends," it's nobody's business. Just make sure the doors are locked and the shades down. And say hello to Linda.

A MISSOURI WIFE HAS NO TIME FOR THE KINKY LIFE

DEAR ANN: In the past you have been willing to admit it when you have made a mistake. I hope you will do so again. I refer to your advice to the woman whose husband wanted her to spice up their night life on occasion by wearing black nylons and a garter belt to bed. Your counsel was absolutely rotten.

Obviously the wife felt uncomfortable about it or she wouldn't have written to ask if it was "all right." Why didn't you tell her to ask her husband how he would feel if she asked him to wear a leopard-skin jock strap and beat on his chest before jumping into bed?

It is obscene to impose one's crazy fantasies on other people. I believe it's high time men and women put an end to the glorification of kinky standards set by pornographic magazines and dirty movies and got in touch with their own feelings. A WIFE FROM MISSOURI

DEAR WIFE: The question put to me was, "Is it all right?" My reply was, "Yes. If you enjoy it."

What goes on between a man and his wife, behind closed doors, is nobody's business but theirs. They decide what is "right." I don't agree that my advice was rotten, but if you think so, I respect your right to ignore it.

Teenage Sex

The shock that many adults register when confronted with teenage sex is understandable but unrealistic, understandable because sex is a loaded dynamite issue for most people, unrealistic because a few seconds of listening to almost any rock song, a few minutes of viewing most commercial television, a sidelong glance at the covers displayed at the corner newsstand (to say nothing of a peek inside one of these magazines) is sufficient to convince all but the mindless that our economy is powered by sex and teenagers are also consumers.

What else sells cologne in *TV Guide?* What else sells cars, deodorant, toothpaste, wine? Teenagers are not immune to Madison Avenue's efforts to promote our way of life by using sex as the underlying theme. You can be sure Madison Avenue didn't select this theme without complete confidence that it would be effective.

One of the major reasons for the increase of sexual activity among the young is that children are maturing physically at an earlier age, because of better nutrition and advances in health care. A thirteen-year-old girl today is as physically developed as a fifteen-and-a-half-year-old was thirty years ago. This means our society, which views adulthood as somewhat near twenty, requires millions of adolescents to endure as much as seven years of physical maturity with no acceptable sexual outlets.

Teenagers respond to their sexual drives just like adults. Moreover, they are encouraged to do so by what they read, see and hear. More likely than not, their parents avoided discussing sex with them when they were still young enough to accept it as a neutral issue—anywhere from age seven to ten. Their parents' parents did not discuss sex with them and they were reared with the notion that the children will ask "when they are ready." Somehow, they never get "ready" because the climate is not conducive to asking questions about things that create feelings of discomfort.

By the time a child reaches puberty, sex, because of body changes, is so important to the child that it is no longer a neutral topic. It is loaded with conflicting messages. Every embarrassed response of a parent, every lewd rock song, every advance of the opposite sex creates confusion, ambivalence and feelings of guilt. It is not surprising that many teenagers, filled with misinformation about sex (which is worse than no information), make their own decisions without the correct facts that might help them make responsible decisions. They feel it is not necessary to follow the dictates of parents or church because not only do they sense the turmoil this topic creates within those camps, but also their messages cannot beat out the competition—TV, movies, magazines, music ads, peer pressure, etc.

Myths play an important role in teenage sex. They are accepted as facts because most teenagers are not getting sex education—at home or at school. Myths are what teens pass on to each other as proof of their superior knowledge and experience. Myths are what many boys are not afraid to use to convince girls to have sex. Myths are lines like these:

You can't get pregnant if you do it standing up.

You can't get pregnant the first time.

You can't get pregnant if you don't have an orgasm.

You can't get pregnant if the boy pulls out before he ejaculates.

You can't get pregnant if you don't do it very often.

You can't get pregnant if you take the pill right before you have intercourse.

The facts are, you *can* get pregnant in every one of these situations—and many girls do.

American teens are not alone. Early sexual activity, followed by early childbearing is increasing worldwide. Bulgaria, East Germany, New Zealand all rank ahead of the United States in teenage pregnancies.

Some girls do manage to get to Planned Parenthood before it's too late for good factual information and counseling, but many get caught and find 99 percent of their life's script written for them.

Sociologist F. Ivan Nye, in a booklet published by Washington State University, points out some grim consequences of too early parenthood:

For mothers. Among mothers thirteen to fifteen years of age, only 11 percent go on to graduate from high school. Many feel rejected by other students. One third live below the poverty line, and lacking education and job experience, they are unlikely to break out of that wretched category.

Of those under eighteen, only 40 percent marry the fathers—and 65 percent of these marriages end in divorce within the first five years. Suicide attempts by school-age mothers are seven times the national percentage for teenage girls without children.

For fathers. If the boy marries the pregnant girl, he often has to interrupt his schooling and job training. If there is an abortion or adoption, he may feel guilt. Legally he is obliged to support his child until the child is of legal age, in some states, eighteen, others, twenty-one—unless the child is adopted. (Boys as young as fourteen have been successfully sued to establish legal obligation for eventual support of their children.)

For babies. Babies born to mothers seventeen or younger face greater health hazards. The mortality rates for babies whose mothers are under fifteen are more than twice as high as for those who were born to mothers in their twenties.

Because young teenage mothers have not yet reached full biological maturity, and because they tend to have poorer diets and inferior medical care (if any), their babies are more likely to be born prematurely. Birth defects such as breathing difficulties, neurological impairment, epilepsy and mental retardation are more frequent. Child abuse is also believed to be more common among very young fathers and mothers, who tend to react impatiently to a baby's demands.

The Alan Guttmacher Institute of Planned Parenthood has studied the numbers.

(1) Babies born to adolescents are two to three times as likely to die during the first year of life as is normal.

(2) 72 percent of young mothers whose babies arrived between their fifteenth and eighteenth birthdays are on welfare.

(3) 60 percent of the girls seventeen years and younger who become preg-

nant before marriage are separated or divorced within six years of marriage. Eleven million U.S. teenage girls are sexually active. Only 30 percent of them use contraception. Of the 11 million teenagers, 1 million get pregnant and of these, 590,000 have babies, 140,000 have miscarriages and 270,000 have abortions.

It is not true that all of these teenagers have frequent or promiscuous sex. Some teenage girls, according to a recent study, have had sex with only one boy and said, "We were in love." Many more who reach the Planned Parenthood teen clinics get the kind of information and support they need to start saying no. As pure survival course information, the girls need their own lines to give back to the guys. Parents must wake up to the fact that there is more teenage sex because there is more sex in everything around us and very little sex education to put it in its proper perspective.

Some parents and clergy believe the availability of contraceptives is to blame for so much sexual activity among the young. This is another myth. Birth control in the form of condoms (rubbers) has been available for a good many years—for those who wanted them. Many surveys have shown that teenagers do not want to use contraceptives because it "spoils the naturalness," or "I didn't want to be prepared. I'd look cheap," or "It's too much trouble."

Most teens are reluctant to seek out clinics where they can get information for fear of being found out. ("My mother would kill me if she knew I was into sex!") Furthermore, a high proportion of teen girls who do find their way to birth control clinics come in with a pregnancy scare or a late period. They are terrified. That's when the counselors hear the recitation of those awful lines: "He told me I couldn't get pregnant if . . ."

If the schools taught sex education the way they teach driver education, more teenagers would emerge from their adolescent years unscarred by early childbearing. Many teenagers think it is cool to be free and easy when the truth is they are more often than not awkward, uncomfortable and anxious. Those who begin sexual activity early have a difficult time later when they try to tell themselves that sex is an expression of love. After years of fooling around for sheer pleasure it is not simple to shift one's emotional gears.

So what are parents of teenagers to do? First they must start at an early age to keep the lines of communication open. They must never be shocked or judgmental—no matter what the child says, reports or confesses. The best place for sex education is at home, but unfortunately, too few parents are equipped with the proper information and too many parents are uncomfortable talking to their children about sex. So the next best place is in school.

In spite of the fact that teenagers account for more than 20 percent of all births and produce more than one half of the country's illegitimate children, and have one third (350,000) of all abortions each year, sex education in the schools is not permitted in twenty-nine states at this very moment.

We must accept the fact that once a teenager becomes sexually active he (or she) will not stop because someone says it "isn't right." We must educate these children in the areas of venereal diseases and unwanted pregnancy and tell them how to prevent both. The notion that they will "go do it" if we give them the information is absurd. Information is good. It is ignorance that is bad—and dangerous—and expensive, in terms of tax dollars, emotional and physical health and peace of mind.

If your daughter wants information on birth control—even though you still think of her as a child, send her to your family doctor or to Planned Parenthood. (Look in the phone book for the address.) If you have no chapter in your city, write for information. The address of the national headquarters is 810 Seventh Avenue, New York, New York. Education is the answer.

CREDIT: *Deborah M. Roach, Vice President for Public Education, Planned Parenthood Association, Chicago, Illinois.*

Dear Readers: I hate to admit it but I'm giving in. I wasn't too crazy about the Sex Test for Teenagers (composed by a teenager in 1966) but I printed it because I believed it had some redeeming features.

The response was incredible. Teens (and their parents) had plenty to say, both pro and con. Four years later, four Memphis teenagers "updated" the Sex Test and I printed it. Again, the ceiling fell in.

Since 1970, I have received over 5,000 "updated" Sex Tests. Each contributor insists I owe it to my young readers to print a new one. They say anyone who digs cats between 13 and 19 has got to know times have changed and if I really want to help teenagers, I'd better tell it like it is NOW. So—here's the 1978 Teenage Test, submitted by five teenagers (three girls and two boys, ages 15 to 17). They attend a public high school in Dayton, Ohio. The scoring guide is at the end.

Instructions for scoring: For each yes answer, give yourself the number indicated. Ready? Here it is: Have you:

Ever been out with a member of the opposite sex? 2

Ever engaged in light making-out? Kissing but no intimate touching? 2

Ever gotten or given a hickey? 2

Ever said I love you? 3

Ever said I love you to more than one person in the same week? 4

Ever removed part of your clothing while making out in a car? 4

Ever masturbated? 2

Ever gone all the way with a member of the opposite sex? 5

Ever done so without using a contraceptive? 6

Ever tried sex with a member of your own sex? 8

Ever tried cigarets? 1

Do you smoke regularly? 3

Do you smoke pot regularly? 5

Ever mix pot with pills? 6

Ever tripped on LSD? 7

Ever done Angel Dust, cocaine, or heroin? 8

Ever had an abortion or been responsible for one? 8

Ever wake up and not been able to remember what you did? 7

Ever get a girl pregnant? 8

Ever considered getting pregnant so you could hook a guy? 8

Ever had group sex? 8

SCORING GUIDE:

7 or under Candidate for Sainthood

8 to 16 Normal and Decent

17 to 30 Heading for Serious Trouble

30 to 40 In Serious Trouble and Plenty Messed Up

41 or over Either You Are a Damned Fool or Completely Freaked Out

Note From Ann Landers: Maybe I'm a wiggy antique, but in my opinion, anyone who scores more than 12 is not "Normal and Decent."

HERE ARE THE 'LINES' GIRLS HEAR THESE DAYS

DEAR FRIENDS: Recently I asked my female teen-age readers what "lines" the boys were using these days to break down their resistance. The response was staggering. Would you believe over 18,000 letters? To my surprise (although I should have learned long ago never to be surprised at what turns up on my desk) I received a handful of letters from boys telling me what "lines" the girls had used on THEM.

I received a few critical letters admonishing me for putting out a "how-to" list for beginners. "Young boys are plenty aggressive these days," wrote the mother of three daughters in Wheeling, W. Va. "It's foolish to supply them with alternate 'lines' should theirs fail."

I hastened to inform "Wheeling mother" that the purpose of printing the "lines" was to wise up the naive and vulnerable who, too often, are snowed by cool cats on the make. Hopefully, if the girls see it in print, they will recognize it for what it is—just a line. And a fairly standard one at that.

I promised to share my findings with you. Here they are:

Sharon, Pa.: "Come on. What are you afraid of? Don't be a baby. It's just part of growing up."

Louisville, Ky.: "If you really loved me you would. That's the way people express their true feelings. It's been going on since the world began."

Honolulu: "It's very painful for a guy to be in this condition and not get relief. You got me all heated up; now if you're any kind of a woman you'll take care of me."

Marshalltown, Iowa: "It will be good for your complexion. You should have seen my face before I did it. Honest, it's better than any medicine."

Carbondale, Ill.: "You're the most exciting chick I've ever met in my whole life. I have never wanted anybody the way I want you."

Fort Lauderdale: "Life is so uncertain. Who knows whether you'll be alive tomorrow? It would be awful if you died in an accident or something without experiencing the greatest thrill of all."

Mexico City: "You're awfully uptight. Sex is a great tension-breaker. It will make you feel relaxed."

Gatineau, Quebec: "I want to marry you some day. Now we have to find out if we are sexually compatible."

Rochester, N.Y.: "I've heard rumors that you're 'lezzie.' If you aren't, prove it."

Nassau, The Bahamas: "I promise we won't go all the way unless you want to. We'll stop whenever you say."

Harrisburg, Pa.: "You have nothing to worry about. I'm sterile."

Toronto, Canada: "I know you want

it as much as I do but you're afraid of your reputation. I swear I will never tell anybody. It will be our secret."

Shrewsbury, N.J.: "It isn't sex I'm after. I'm really in love with you. If you get pregnant I'll marry you right away."

Durham, N.C.: "You have the body of a woman. Mother Nature meant for you to have sex. You're ready for it."

And now that most unique approach in the handful of letters from boys who had been propositioned by girls: From Greenwich, Conn.: "I have a terrible time with cramps every month. The doctor said I should have sexual intercourse. Of all the guys I know, you're the one I want to help me with this medical problem." (P.S. The guy said no.)

AFTER THE 'MEANINGFUL RELATIONSHIP'

DEAR ANN LANDERS: Where are all those advocates of premarital sex when it comes time to pick up the pieces after a "momentary mistake"? And what do the advocates do to help prevent such "mistakes"?

Do they tell the kids that though a relationship may be "meaningful" to one partner, it may be purely self-satisfaction, an ego trip or mere condescension on the part of the other?

Do they tell the kids that a "meaningful relationship" may be so meaningful that one partner may have an overwhelming desire to cement that relationship with a child?

Do they tell the kids they should never count on the other person to take precautions—and that to be perfectly safe, both parties should count on themselves?

Do they tell the kids that a girl's most intense desires are very likely to accompany her most fertile time? ("Just this once?")

Do they tell the kids that a person's "love" might be severely dampened by resentment and turn to full-fledged hate should that person feel trapped?

Do they tell the kids that alternative solutions to an unwanted pregnancy are vastly more difficult to handle than coping with the challenges of virginity?

Do they tell the kids that the legality of abortion is insignificant compared to the emotional trauma?

Do they tell the kids that giving up a child for adoption is no simple matter for anyone who has had a "meaningful relationship"?

Do they tell the girls that keeping an out-of-wedlock baby goes far beyond the enjoyment of having a cute little bundle of joy to cuddle and take for a stroll in the perambulator?

Where are those advocates of premartial sex when it's time to mend lives suffering from their advice? A SHOULDER TO CRY ON

DEAR SHOULDER: Thank you for a good letter. I'm glad you offered your shoulder to "cry on." Mine is already the wettest in the U.S.A. (Are you listening, students?)

PUTOUTS AND HOLDOUTS

DEAR ANN LANDERS: Please print this letter for every boy between 15 and 17 years of age who reads your column.

I am a girl of 15. All these boys think about is sex and who they can get it from. If a girl says no, she is shunned and made fun of. The boy will never look at her again. He tells all his pals she is a "dead number," and they give her the get-lost treatment. In other words she is a social outcast, doomed to sit home until she becomes more "cooperative" and loosens up.

This happened to me and two of my girl friends. Why don't these immature and selfish boys realize they are being unfair? If they are all so fond of marrying virgins, why don't they leave a few around? A HOLDOUT

DEAR H.O.: Sorry, I don't agree that all boys between 15 and 17 shun and ridicule girls who say no. In fact, the opposite is closer to the truth. It's the put-outs, not the hold-outs, who are shunned and ridiculed. (You ought to read my mail, dear.)

Shoplifting

SWEATING OVER A SWEATER

DEAR ANN LANDERS: I stole a sweater from a store. It cost $19.85. I feel rotten and want to pay for it but I'm afraid to turn myself in. I have saved $12 so far and I need your advice on what to do. Please tell me. NEVER AGAIN

DEAR NEVER: Send a $10 bill and two singles (well-wrapped) to the credit manager of the store with a note of explanation. Make it clear the balance will be sent as soon as you can get it together. Congratulations on going straight. I admire you.

Almost everyone has been involved in some kind of stealing behavior at some point in his life, usually in childhood. A natural tendency exists in all of us to take what we want, like or think we need.

Prohibitions against taking things are built up, as we develop ethical standards and learn the consequences of breaking the law. Thus, most grown-ups are reasonably protected from the impulse to steal by outer and inner controls, although lapses may occur.

Certain individuals are inclined to steal without acknowledging to themselves that they are lawbreakers. Shoplifters generally fall into this category. A common experience in childhood is to take money from Mother's purse. The rationalization is, "She doesn't need it," or "She has so much she won't miss this small amount."

The child may be angry at the mother and retaliate by helping himself to something that is hers. At times stealing is subtly condoned by the parents, especially if they feel guilty about not giving to the child in other ways—such as time and attention.

Shoplifting or other forms of stealing have little to do with poverty or the lack of basic necessities. Evidence for this is the large number of poor people who do not steal and the frequency with which stealing is indulged in by people who could well afford to pay for whatever it is they steal.

Psychiatry in the past made a strong distinction between kleptomania and stealing. Kleptomania referred to the taking of objects that in themselves were largely worthless and had only a symbolic value. Stealing was seen as taking something for gain. More recent evidence suggests that the distinction is not valid. Even when someone steals for gain, the act of stealing has symbolic significance. It satisfies unconscious psychological needs and does not represent simply the realistic desire to acquire the good things in life.

Stealing appears to have a great deal to do with the issue of *entitlement*—what the person feels is due him. The individual who steals sees the act of stealing not as taking something that does not belong to him but rather making up for something which is rightfully his, but which was denied because of life's unfairness. These people say to themselves, "I have this coming to me."

Typically, the person who steals thinks that, at some point in the past, something that belonged to him was taken away. Thus, the person who steals sees himself as the *victim,* rather than the perpetrator of a theft.

Related to the desire to get even is a conscious feeling of defiance and a wish to "beat the system." The associated feeling is one of victory rather than guilt.

Shoplifters often report a sense of excitement when they get away with a small trinket. In other cases the stealing may involve many expensive items. The excitement comes from the feeling that the person is "putting one over" and is willing to take a risk to achieve this feeling. Such individuals are very much like the gambler who also plays the odds for the sake of the big win and risks "getting caught."

This sense of excitement contributes to the shoplifter's willingness to take a chance.

Shoplifters are aware that the security systems in some stores are not very good and that if they are caught, they probably can get off by offering to pay for the merchandise. They often speak with contempt about store detectives.

Some shoplifters and others who steal have a grossly exaggerated view of their own cleverness and invulnerability. Thus they often react with surprise and shock when they are caught. They frequently insist, "It's all a mistake."

A patient of mine who had been involved in stealing (and was very nearly caught several times) had a strong sense of being smarter than everyone else. As a child this patient discovered he could talk rings around his immigrant parents, who were not knowledgeable about American ways. (Actually they were less intelligent than he.) As a result of his relationship with his parents this young man grew up thinking he could outsmart everybody.

At times shoplifters are quite daring. One woman reported with a sense of pride that she once walked out of a store carrying a huge garbage can and "got away with it."

Often shoplifting is done by persons who are submissive in their social relations and use stealing as a way of asserting themselves or presenting a courageous image—even if only to themselves.

Many people who steal are not psychopaths or hardened criminals. They are just ordinary people who have "a failure of conscience" which they do not recognize for what it is.

People who steal usually have very little guilt about it. This is seen commonly among shoplifters, who rationalize their behavior, as in the case of taking from Mother's purse. They say to themselves, "The store will not miss it," or "They charge too much and I am only getting even."

A very real consequence of the lack of guilt is that these people are not likely to seek treatment. It simply does not bother them. Therefore, they are seen by psychiatrists mainly when they seek help because of other problems. The psychiatrist learns about the stealing only incidentally.

Occasionally someone who has shoplifted may present himself for treatment because of the stealing behavior, but this takes place usually if the person is caught and has some anxiety about having been discovered. As soon as the heat is off and the legal problem has been settled (typically without real penalty), the patient's motivation for treatment disappears and treatment is discontinued.

Similar comments can be made about patients whose treatment is ordered by a court as part of the "sentence." Again, the motivation for treatment is superficial.

I believe that psychiatric treatment does not have much to offer for one who steals unless the stealing is part of a larger psychiatric problem which causes the patient continuing distress and makes him more responsive to treatment.

From the standpoint of society, in the great majority of cases, instances of shoplifting and other forms of stealing should be regarded as legal, not medical, problems. Prevention requires that shoplifting be recognized by the public as having real legal consequences. The public, instead, knows that very often these situations can be "fixed" simply by agreeing to pay for the stolen merchandise.

CREDIT: *Pietro Castelnuovo-Tedesco, M.D., and James G. Blakemore, Professor of Psychiatry, Vanderbilt University School of Medicine, Nashville, Tennessee.*

MANY HAPPY RETURNS

DEAR ANN LANDERS: I read with amazement your suggestion that shoplifters mail to the store credit manager (anonymously, of course) cash to pay for at least part of the merchandise they pilfered. You must be kidding.

You don't believe the credit managers will actually turn over the money to the store, do you? Most people are dishonest and credit managers are only human. Cash, sent anonymously, is too great a temptation. So, why don't you wake up and smell the coffee? SURPRISED AT YOUR STUPIDITY

DEAR SUR: Thanks for your vote of no confidence in the human race. The following letters might be of interest to you:

QUINCY, ILL.: Received today $1.25 as a direct result of your column. Thanks, Ann.
CARL FAIN, Manager,
Woolworth Store

YOUNGSTOWN, OHIO: Shortly after Christmas I received a $5 bill for a pair of scissors. The person signed the note "New Leaf," the same signature as the shoplifter in your column.
D. W. SMITH of McKelveys'

FRANKLIN PARK: For the first time that anyone in this store can remember, we received payment for stolen merchandise. Two $1 bills came wrapped in your column.
W. T. GRANT CO.,
Mannheim Rd.

LONG ISLAND, N.Y.: I am enclosing the note which accompanied payment for some personal items which were stolen from our store. This should make you feel good.
GEORGE K.,
Manager of Nassau 5 & 10

KANSAS CITY: What a surprise when folding money fell out of an envelope—no name, no address. A note attached said, "Ann Landers says to pay for what I shoplifted. Here it is."
KATZ DRUG CO.

MINNEAPOLIS: I sent the Dayton Co., part-payment for cosmetics I took in November. I will send them the rest when I can. Thank you for helping me go straight.
J.G.

FROM CHICAGO: I hope Goldblatt's let you know I sent them $1 for the lipstick I swiped.
ASHAMED AND CURED
And there were many others—but the space is gone. Thank you all.

Shyness

What It Is—What to Do About It

Do you consider yourself to be shy? If so, you're in good company. About 40 percent of all Americans we have asked label themselves as currently shy. This figure escalates to over 80 percent when we add those who report that they used to be but are no longer shy. Only 1 percent of the entire sample of four thousand Americans surveyed tell us they have never experienced shyness. Thus shyness is widespread enough to deserve the classification of "social epidemic." That designation is earned not only because shyness is so prevalent, but in addition, it is so damaging to the human spirit.

Shyness is thought to be cute by some, but rarely by the person who is shy. It may connote the bashfulness and awkwardness of adolescence or the modest demeanor of the middle-aged introvert. But to the majority of shy people, shyness represents a serious personal problem. It can be an incapacitating form of social anxiety that limits freedom of action, speech and association. Indeed, we can think of shyness as a self-imposed psychological prison. The shy person is inhibited from acting spontaneously despite his ability and motivation.

Under some conditions shyness can develop into a powerful "people phobia." The fear of others, their negative evaluation and rejection, may lead to total withdrawal from all social contact and create a life of painful loneliness. Isolation from the warmth of human contact contributes to many forms of psychopathology—depression, alienation, neurosis and sometimes suicide. For this reason, shyness should not be thought of as merely a passing phase of mild distress experienced by some overly sensitive souls. It can be a lifelong source of intense anxiety suffered by many people regardless of age, sex, education or social class.

A particularly insightful definition of shyness is given by poet Pablo Neruda:

> Shyness is a kink in the soul, a special category, a dimension that opens out into solitude. Moreover, it is an inherent suffering, as if we had two skins and the one underneath rebelled and shrank back from life. Of the things that make up a man, this quality, this damaging thing, is a part of the alloy that lays the foundation, in the long run, for the perpetuity of the self.

A more formal approach to the concept that has guided our research specifies shyness as a tendency to avoid social situations, to fail to participate in social encounters, to feel anxious and uncomfortable during interactions with others and to undervalue one's self-worth. Shyness thus may involve four components: (1) thoughts ("I'm gonna make a fool of myself"), (2) feelings (anxiety, nervousness, etc.), (3) physical reactions (blushing, heart pounding, butterflies in stomach, etc.), (4) behavior (failing to smile, or avoiding eye contact with others).

The shyness trigger is pressed by certain types of people or social situations. Often shyness is specific to special situations, such as blind dates, public speeches, cocktail parties. The situationally shy person reacts the same as the chronically shy person, but his outlook is different. For the situationally shy, the problem is viewed as being brought on by anxiety-producing situations and not as a personal trait or handicap. The person says, "The problem is out there, it's not me."

In general, shyness tends to be turned on by people and situations that are unfamiliar, demanding or vague. When we must initiate some social action rather than react to someone else's initiative, and when a person does not know how he is expected to respond, shyness becomes more pronounced. Individuals who must talk in public or deal with authorities or those who find themselves in a potentially intimate situation are all likely candidates for shyness.

While shyness is revealed in people through overt behavior, our research has uncovered an unexpected type of shy person—the shy extrovert. Many celebrities in the public eye report being shy, even though they know what to do and do it well when playing their public role. The shy extrovert is privately shy. The basis of his shyness lies in a lack of self-confidence and anxiety about being accepted if others "really" knew his private real self and not merely the public role self. In my book *Shyness,* many public personalities describe the causes and adverse effects of their shyness. Among them are Carol Burnett, Phyllis Diller, Robert Young, Johnny Mathis, Barbara Walters and others whose public masks conceal the dimensions of their secretly experienced shyness.

Beyond the obvious problems, shyness can impair memory when the shy person feels he or she is being evaluated. Shy people, as compared to non-shy people, report less sexual experience. Moreover, when they do connect sexually, they don't like it much. There is also reason to believe that shyness plays a role in recruiting people into alcoholism and maybe drugs—in an effort to relieve inhibitions and social anxieties. We have found that many sudden murderers (a first and only offense) were overcontrolled, well-behaved shy children and obedient, never assertive grown-ups.

Our research in eight different cultures reveals that shyness is perhaps universal. There is a core of shyness reactions common to very different societies. Some interesting variations, however, suggest a social programming.

Shyness is engendered in societies that: promote a cult of the ego (introspection and self-consciousness); emphasize individual rather than communal goals; overvalue competition, with failure a source of personal shame and success underplayed by modesty training; make love and respect of children contingent upon fluctuating, vague and critical standards of performance; provide little room for expression of emotions and sharing of intimate feelings.

Shyness is highest in Japan, Taiwan and Germany, where shame for failure is the price one must pay for trying, while rewards for success are minimized by modesty. In Israel, where shyness is relatively low, the opposite is true. Minor successes are great personal victories while failures are externalized and blamed on the situation, not on the person. Thus Israelis take chances and develop "chutzpah" while Japanese keep a low profile and develop an inscrutable façade.

Shyness can be overcome and its adverse effects minimized. Attempts can also be made to prevent its recurrence in future generations. Shyness must first be recognized as a serious personal problem. Because it is a learned reaction, we must realize it can be unlearned and new, more effective reactions substituted. People can change even a lifetime of ingrained habits if they make a commitment to change and are willing to put forth the effort to do so.

Four areas of change are possible for the shy person: (1) social skills, (2) anxiety management, (3) self-esteem building, (4) social responsiveness. There are many basic social skills to be learned and practiced by the shy. They form the nuts and bolts of the social machinery of human interaction. How to start a conversation, keep it going, interrupt effectively and terminate the contact are necessary skills. Shy people are often thrown by receiving a compliment (they usually disown, degrade or ignore it).

Simple Rule 1. Beginner: Say, "Thanks."

Simple Rule 2. Intermediate: "Thanks," and add a comment, "I wasn't sure it was my color so I'm pleased you like it!"

Simple Rule 3. Advanced: "Thanks"+comment+question to make conversation, "Where do you buy your clothes?" and/or a soft stroke returned, "Coming from you that's a lovely compliment since you are one of the best dressers I know." Social skills mean not only learning what to say, how and when, but also mastering simple non-verbal skills. One formula (proposed by Seattle shyness counselor Art Wassner) tells the shy person to *soften: smile; open* up your posture (don't be hunched over and wrapped in your arms and legs); *forward* leaning toward the other person; *touch,* make physical contact whenever appropriate; *eye contact* is crucial for relating; *nodding* gives approval and keeps the contact flowing. Many other specific social skills recipes are given in my book to enhance one's sociability quotient.

Anxiety feelings can be brought under control by learning how to relax (using any of a variety of techniques). While your body is in a state of relaxation, imagine the shyness-inducing setting and call forth images of a competent, assertive you. This approach can go far to weaken the inhibiting grip that anxiety exerts on behavior.

Self-confidence is boosted when we *stop* saying negative things about ourselves, especially chronic irreversible statements (such as, "I'm dumb," or "I'm ugly"). Instead, *start* thinking, saying and believing positive things about yourself. Take inventory of your personal assets and keep noticing what is good, special, admirable about what you are and do.

Shyness is weakened to the extent that the shy person breaks out of his self-imposed isolation and becomes more socially responsive. By paying attention to the needs of others and feeling responsible to make other people hurt less and be happier there is less mental energy left to devote to preoccupation with one's own shyness. Reach out to help someone. Be something special to him or to her. In doing so you become a more special, less shy person yourself.

To *prevent* shyness requires a major overhaul in how parents relate to their children, teachers to their students, employers to workers and friends to one another. In general, it involves being less competitive, less critical and less rejecting of others. Social values that promote co-operation, constructive feedback and acceptance of others help to undermine the foundations of shyness.

"Caring," "sharing," "daring" and "swearing" are vital aspects of the parent-child relationships that must be practiced to head off the appearance of shyness.

Parents must openly show that they care for, love, like and respect their children. This positive regard must not be made contingent on good behavior, but freely given because of what the child is—a unique human being— and not because he has made good grades or won a contest. The fear of negative evaluation haunts shy people. This probably occurs because the integrity of their ego has been tied too closely to successful performances. Soon everything in life becomes a performance being evaluated by some unseen super-critic.

Parents should teach children the joy of sharing, because it is the way to give to and receive from others valuable human gifts. This means the sharing of food and toys and possessions as well as the sharing of ideas and feelings. It will bring a child from the isolation of "mine" to the communal trust of "ours."

Shy people tend to be passive, to play it safe, not take chances. Daring is an attitude that can be encouraged by parents in very young children. Help them first by encouraging little risks, such as jumping into your arms. Then go on to intellectual risks, such as stating their own opinions and defending unpopular points of view. Equally important is teaching children to feel responsible for taking an active part in the life of the social community.

Swearing does not mean use of obscenity or profanity but being able to say no, to disagree, to dissent openly and, if justified, to disobey on occasion.

This is difficult for parents, who often prefer blind obedience rather than reasoned evaluation and activism, that is not in line with what the parents believe in.

After five years of research on shyness, my perspective has broadened considerably. Shyness, for me, is a code name for all the forces within each of us as well as the pressures from society that combine to isolate us from each other. In overcoming shyness we reaffirm the social contract and nourish the human connection so essential for survival of our community. Whatever we do collectively to prevent shyness from stilling the spontaneous laughter in the next generation of our children gives us more reason to live fully and love freely in our time.

CREDIT: *Philip G. Zimbardo, Stanford University, Stanford, California, author of* Shyness, *Wesley Publishing Company.*

Sibling Rivalry

It is natural for people to observe differences between themselves and others, make comparisons, feel superior or inferior and strive to get the better of a competitor. That's rivalry. Sibling rivalry is a special form of competition and what makes it special is that it is rivalry between children who share the same parents. The prize: first place in their parents' affections.

Animosity, envy and hatred between brothers and sisters are as old as family life. The stories of Cain and Abel, Jacob and Esau, Joseph and his brothers, Cinderella and her envious stepsisters have fascinated children and adults for generations. This is so because these stories deal with a universal problem—sibling rivalry. Deep down, every one of us wants to be the best loved.

It is true that most people get over this wish, or at least it becomes less intense, and they are capable of sharing the ones they love with others. But very few of us ever reach the point of rising above jealousy, nor do we get beyond feeling entitled to the exclusive love and loyalty of at least one other human being.

Where does the idea come from that we have the right to be loved best? It comes from experience, since each of us has had what feels like the exclusive attention and love of our mothers during the earliest months of our lives. This experience is deeply imprinted upon our personalities, even though we can't remember those earliest months. Even if we were the second or third or fourth child, we still felt loved exclusively during those early times simply because the mind of an infant is too immature to include the presence of others.

In some ways all of us try to get back to that time when we were loved best —perhaps that is why we enjoy stories about the poor boy who competed with princes in daring deeds and won the hand of the King's daughter as his prize; or why we love to see athletes compete and imagine ourselves the winners. Or why winning second prize is less enjoyable than first.

The feelings of sibling rivalry begin when a baby who has enjoyed the mother-baby world as if nothing else existed gradually begins to sense that there is someone else Mother pays attention to, and that this person's gain is his loss.

Sibling rivalry starts with a sense of losing the mother, and holding the brother or sister responsible for the loss. So in order to talk sensibly about sibling rivalry, we must talk about what it means to a baby and to a young child to be separated from its mother. The feelings about physical separation from Mother are not very different from the feelings of losing some of Mother's attention and love. One is merely a milder version of the other.

Rene Spitz, a psychoanalyst who made careful observations of babies in foundling homes and nurseries, discovered that babies can be separated from their mothers for longer or shorter periods and cared for by a substitute without showing any ill effects up to the age of about four to eight months. It is as though babies at this very early age cannot tell the difference between the mother and other people that take care of them. They thrive as long as they get good care, no matter who gives it to them.

Around about four to eight months of age, however, a significant change takes place in the baby: He begins to show differences in his reactions to Mother as compared to other people, and gets shy or upset when somebody other than Mother comes near. This so-called "stranger anxiety" is an indication that the baby's mind is maturing so that it can now make a clear discrimination between Mother and other people. It is at this point that the baby is extremely vulnerable to the loss of the mother. If Mother is ill or goes away on a vacation at this point, and is gone for more than a week or so, babies have been observed to stop eating, to become limp and motionless, unresponsive to others and they cry a great deal. This reaction is reversed when the mother returns.

It is rare for a baby to get a younger brother or sister during this very sensitive age of four to eight months, but it can happen: Mothers who apply for adoptive babies very often become pregnant shortly before their adopted baby arrives, and they give birth to their natural child when the adoptive baby is less than a year old. Because of such a young child's vulnerability to separation and to the partial loss of Mother's attention when she must focus her interest onto the new baby, it is especially stressful for children under a year of age to have a younger sibling.

They experience the rival in a vague but real way as threatening their lifeline. Competition between children this close together in age tends to be deep and perhaps more complicated than it is for children born farther apart. For one thing, if one of them becomes noticeably stronger, better co-ordinated or quicker intellectually, the children do not understand that the difference is due to one being older. This increases the difficulties both children have in dealing with the differences between them.

It is common for a younger sibling to arrive when the first-born is between one and a half and two and a half years of age. Mothers have a tendency either to go back to work or to have another baby when their first-born reaches the toddler stage. Their babies have gone through a period of independence around age ten months when they are busy learning to crawl and walk. They often almost ignore their mothers while practicing their new skills. At this point Mother may feel the need for another baby to cuddle. That wish may grow stronger as the toddler begins having temper tantrums, insisting on having his way and being difficult.

From the toddler's point of view, getting a younger brother or sister in the midst of the "terrible two's" is no privilege. Too young to understand about pregnancy and babies, but old enough to be increasingly clear about how much he needs Mother, and indeed to be worried about losing her, the toddler has a good deal of trouble, inwardly at least, accepting a new baby.

Eager to please Mother, the one-and-a-half- to two-and-a-half-year-old may put on a convincing act of "loving" the new baby. At the same time he may show the strain by losing some of his recently acquired skills. He may go back to baby talk, or start to wet the bed again.

The toddler may also show his feelings about the new baby through open expressions of anger and rejection that may either upset his parents or strike them as funny. Either reaction can make the older child feel more threatened than ever by a sense of being out in the cold. In time he will take this out on the younger one in the form of teasing, pinching or hitting. This usually results in the mother rushing to the defense of the younger child and punishing the older one, thus "proving" that his worst fears were correct: She really *does* love the little one best. This in turn makes the envy and anger of the older child all the stronger, and the vicious cycle is in motion.

When a child of three to five gets a brother or sister, he can be prepared for the event in advance since, unlike the younger toddler, the nursery school child can understand some explanations about what is going on, and feel a part of the family's new venture. All the same, a child at this age must cope with some difficult reactions to the new baby.

A boy of nursery school age will be strongly attached to his mother and will have romantic feelings about her. His dad will be viewed as a competitor for his mother's affections. If he now gets a baby brother, he has not *one* but *two* males to share his mother with. If the new baby is a girl, a lot of the boy's worries about sex differences may be stirred up by observing how different he is from her. Most boys this age when confronted with a baby sister will suspect she has had a bad accident and lost her penis. He fears the same thing might happen to him. In the long run, however, he will likely take a protective if somewhat condescending attitude toward the little sister. Rivalry between them may be less intense than if she had been a boy.

For children five years of age or older, a new baby does not seriously threaten the lifeline to Mother, the sense of security with Mother (as it does in the case of the toddler) or their security about who they are as a boy or a girl. Siblings this far apart in age may never be as close emotionally as those born nearer together, but neither will they be as rivalrous.

Rivalry between twins tends to begin at that stage of their lives when, shortly after learning to walk, they begin to have a sense of how little they really are by comparison with adults, and of how much they need the protection and concern of Mother. All children, in fact, seem to find upright locomotion a pretty sobering experience. With it comes a difficult period of their lives which some researchers regard as a crisis—a period when children try to sort out how much independence they can allow themselves, how much they need Mother and how much they can really count on her. In a way it's like an early version of adolescence. In any event, when twins reach this point they begin to compete openly and fiercely with each other for their mother's attention. Often, however, they are able to give a good deal of emotional support to one another at this time.

The greatest pain of rivalry for twins may occur as they become old enough to compare their talents and attributes, strengths and skills, and to suffer the pain of inferiority when they don't measure up to one another. This means that parents have particularly difficult tasks with twins who are markedly different in their capabilities, although even twins who are very evenly matched will detect small differences between themselves and magnify these into large ones.

Identical twins often solve some of their competitive feelings by shifting the battle from between themselves to between the two of them and the outer world, taking pleasure in fooling people and making it even harder for others to tell them apart. Twins can be so interesting to each other and can give each other so much that this can dilute the problem they have in needing to share the affection and attention of parents between them. Nevertheless, like all children, twins have to struggle with the eternal question of which one of us do the parents love the most?

For an older child with several younger brothers or sisters, each succeeding new brother or sister has less impact emotionally because the eldest child gets used to babies showing up in the household, learns to share the parents' affection with others and gets compensatory satisfaction from having the status of the eldest. The eldest learns leadership, caretaking, and has a tendency to wind up as a leader in later life. This eldest child is likely to be particularly competent as a wife or husband and parent, especially if she or he has had the advantage of having both brothers and sisters. It helps to get ready for marriage and parenthood if one has had experience with peers of the opposite sex in the family while growing up.

For children who have older siblings, rivalry involves having from the beginning of their lives someone near in age and yet bigger, smarter and more competent in every way. The good side of this is that the older child teaches the younger one a great deal, and speeds the young child's development. The disadvantages are that the younger one is often pushed by the older one to achieve things before he is ready, and is constantly confronted with his inferiority, for which he has to learn how to compensate.

Often younger children overcompensate by becoming intensely ambitious and competitive. Or they may accept a role of inadequacy and dependence and never fulfill their potentialities entirely. If a younger sibling is also the youngest, with no brothers or sisters younger than himself, he is handicapped as a parent because he lacks the experience in his formative years of looking after children younger than himself. His parents may compensate for this by providing younger playmates or pets for this youngest child to be responsible for.

Rivalry between brothers and sisters is intensified and complicated by such events as the loss of a parent, the breaking up of the family, serious illness or the death of one of the siblings. Such events inevitably decrease the amount of energy a parent has to spend on the children, and children react to any decrease in the amount of parental love they feel by becoming more competitive with each other for what is left.

Of course there are other reactions to family crises as well. Brothers and sisters may be drawn together by crises. They may learn to love and help each other more—especially if trouble comes when they are over the early years when rivalry is the most intense, and have entered the period of later childhood where genuine co-operation has become psychologically possible. Parents who understand how their children feel about their brothers and sisters can help them develop the strength they will need in meeting the challenges life inevitably deals out to them.

In summary, sibling rivalry is competition among siblings for being the best-loved by the parents. The form it takes depends on the age of the child.

When a child under one and a half gets a brother or sister, it will show its sibling rivalry by becoming depressed, like a child who has lost its mother.

When a child between one and a half and three gets a sibling, it may show sibling rivalry by trying to interfere with Mother's care of the new baby, or by open hostility to the baby—sometimes physical. The child may compete with the new baby by going back to more babyish behavior. Or he may try to hold his position of best-loved by making a special effort to be "good."

When a child of three to five gets a baby brother or sister, rivalry may show up in disguised ways at first, and later it may develop into open fighting and teasing. A child of this age can deal with his or her rivalrous feelings by imitating the parent of the same sex and feeling "fatherly" or "motherly" toward the new baby.

In general, the younger you are when you first face sibling rivalry, the harder it is for you.

HOW PARENTS CAN HELP CHILDREN WITH SIBLING RIVALRY

Toddlers cannot tell their parents clearly in words about their feelings of jealousy, envy and insecurity. They speak through their actions. For example, one fifteen-month-old twin who had been a stable and happy little boy all along began to have trouble going to sleep, and started waking up several times during the night when his mother went back to work three or four hours a day. The little boy's sister showed no sign of upset with the change. Observing the children over a period of several days, the mother noticed that when she came home from work the little girl rushed joyously toward her, climbed on her lap and wanted to be read to, while the little boy sat where he was, apparently busy with his blocks or his book. It occurred to the mother that the girl was able to ask for the attention and love that she needed, while the boy was not. Therefore the mother began going immediately to her son upon returning, showing her joy at seeing him even though he didn't ask for it. On the first day that she changed her behavior, he slept soundly through the night, and as she continued initiating contact with him rather than waiting for him to come to her, he had no further difficulties with his sleep.

What is hard for parents to do is direct their love to a child who is naughty or cranky, having tantrums or being openly aggressive toward a younger child. Here the only thing that can help is for the parents to be aware that the child who is the worst behaved is the one who feels the most left out—and that he is also going to have to cope with his guilt for his bad behavior. The aggressor needs more comforting and help than the victim at moments of sibling rivalry.

Faced with the inevitable teasing and persecuting that go on between competing siblings, parents may worry that the bigger, stronger child may seriously injure a smaller one. Actually, it is rare for children to get badly hurt while under adult supervision. It may be that supervising warring siblings without interfering too much in their battles is the best way to help children deal with the problem. If not protected too much by the parents from the older child, a younger child can generally battle his way to a position of feeling reasonably strong and competent. If defended too much, he or she may grow up with the feeling of being unable to fight his own battles, of needing outside help, and in general, of being inadequate and incompetent.

For an older child, it is helpful for a parent to acknowledge how hard it is for him sometimes to see the younger one get so much attention, and how bad he feels about teasing and being hard on the younger one.

How easy or how difficult it will be for a parent to understand a child's problem with a brother or sister depends a great deal on the kind of experience the parent himself or herself had in growing up. For example, a parent who is an only child may find it quite difficult to understand how children feel about brothers and sisters. When both parents are only children they may be inclined to have only one child themselves so that the problem of sibling rivalry does not come up.

A mother who was the youngest in her own family and who was protected so as not to have to fight her own battles may feel excessively protective toward her own youngest child and, without meaning to, help that child to grow up feeling inadequate by rushing to his defense in any sibling battle. In general, parents may notice that the easiest of their children to understand is the one who has the same sibling position that the parent has: A father who was an oldest son may feel that he understands his own oldest son the best of all his children, although he may feel closest to his younger daughter, having had a younger sister himself while growing up. Since the key to helping children with their feelings of sibling rivalry is understanding how the children feel, parents may find it rewarding to notice which ones of their children they find easy to understand, and then ask themselves why this might be.

Some families have found family therapy extremely helpful when the children seem to be suffering from their competitiveness with each other and the parents have not found a way to help them.

In many communities courses are given in Parent Effectiveness Training. When parents understand their own feelings and those of their children better, the feelings tend to get easier to manage.

Can sibling rivalry be prevented? Only by having no children or only one child. If you want to minimize sibling rivalry in your family, space your children about four years apart. The advantages of having brothers and sisters far outweigh the pain of sibling rivalry. Childhood is our practice ground for adulthood, and having brothers and sisters to practice living with is a tremendous advantage. In many ways children learn more from each other than they do from adults. One of the great lessons children learn from their sibling rivalries is that human conflicts, even very intense and bitter ones, can be worked out, though it may take years and many hard knocks and hurt feelings to accomplish it.

CREDIT: *Ann Halsell Appelbaum, M.D., psychiatrist and psychoanalyst at the Menninger Foundation, Topeka, Kansas; consultant to the Child Development Center, Topeka State Hospital.*

Sickle Cell Anemia

Sickle cell anemia is an inherited disease characterized by lifelong anemia and complicated by intermittent painful crises and by obstruction of blood flow to various parts of the body.

The disorder involves a specific abnormality in the structure of human hemoglobin. Hemoglobin is the iron-containing protein in red cells which gives blood its red color. This protein is composed of chains which contain sequences of building blocks called amino acids strung out in a specific arrangement. Hemoglobin S or sickle hemoglobin differs from normal hemoglobin A by a substitution of one of the amino acids at a specific position. The structural abnormality causes sickle hemoglobin to stick together when oxygen is released from red cells. These cells assume an elongated or "sickle" shape, becoming extremely rigid.

Sickle cell anemia is found almost exclusively among people of African ancestry. It is probably the most important cause of severe anemia among black people. In order for a child to inherit this disorder it is necessary that both parents be carriers of the abnormality. The carriers are usually entirely healthy and without any symptoms but nevertheless have an abnormality called sickle *trait*. In the red cells of individuals with sickle trait about half of the hemoglobin is normal and the remainder has the structural abnormality known as hemoglobin S. The presence of the normal hemoglobin protects these individuals from any significant problems associated with the sickle hemoglobin. But when two parents with sickle trait have a child, there is a 25 percent chance that the baby will have sickle cell anemia. This child has inherited one sickle gene from each of his parents, and has no normal hemoglobin A in his red cells. On the average, half of the children of these parents will have sickle trait (not anemia) and the remaining quarter of the children will be entirely normal without any sickle hemoglobin in their red cells. Individuals who have sickle trait should be reassured that they have no significant medical or surgical problems and should have a normal life expectancy. Most physicians consider these individuals perfectly fit for insurance and employment purposes. The condition sickle cell trait can be diagnosed by special tests done on a blood specimen. The presence of the abnormal sickle hemoglobin can be demonstrated by a separation technique called electrophoresis.

In addition, there are specific solubility tests which will enable a screening clinic to discover individuals who may have sickle trait. Those who find that they do have sickle trait may want to consult a physician or some other well-qualified individual for counseling on the significance of this condition. This is particularly important if two individuals with sickle trait are contemplating marriage and are making possible plans for having children.

In the United States about one out of every ten black people has sickle trait. Therefore, in about one out of one hundred black couples, both partners have sickle trait. Among babies born to black couples in general about one in four hundred will have sickle cell anemia.

It is important to remember that sickle cell anemia is something that a child is born with. It is inherited from both parents. Sickle cell anemia is not caused by any type of infectious agent such as a germ or a virus and cannot be passed through contact from one person to another. Furthermore, it cannot be transmitted to another person by means of a blood transfusion.

The clinical picture of sickle cell anemia does not declare itself until the child is about eight to twelve months old. This is because it takes time for the sickle hemoglobin to replace the fetal hemoglobin that a baby has when it is born. Young infants and children with sickle cell anemia may develop pain crises which are often mistaken for other abnormalities such as appendicitis or rheumatism. Some children with sickle cell anemia develop what is called the hand-foot syndrome in which there is acute redness, swelling and pain in the hands and/or feet accompanied by an increase in temperature. This complication does not develop after a child outgrows late infancy.

Those children who are born with the full form of the disease known as SS disease or homozygous sickle cell anemia generally have a considerable degree of difficulty during their lifetime. These children remain moderately to severely anemic during their entire life. The anemia is due to the fact that the red cells containing the high proportion of sickle hemoglobin are readily distorted or "bent out of shape" during the circulation of these cells throughout the small blood vessels of the body. The stiffening of the red cell is aggravated by removal of oxygen from the cell as the blood passes through the capillary circulation. In this way the rigid blood cell obstructs blood flow and causes a local area of oxygen deficit. In some cases this obstruction of blood flow can result in the development of pain in various parts of the body. The attack is often quite severe and sudden in onset, causing the patient to seek medical help. Often these patients have to come to the hospital to receive adequate pain medication as well as other types of supportive care. The pain crises that plague individuals with sickle cell anemia are highly variable and unpredictable. A patient may have several severe pain crises in a month requiring almost continuous hospitalization. More often, however, the pain crises are spread out and sometimes a patient may go six months, a year or even several years between pain crises. During this time, the patient with sickle cell anemia may be entirely without symptoms and be able to have a perfectly normal life including the ability to hold down a full-time job.

In addition, the obstruction by sickle cells of flow in the small blood vessels can cause damage to specific organs in the body. For example, patients with sickle cell anemia often have permanent damage to selected organs such as the kidneys resulting in impairment of kidney function. The obstruction of blood flow to an area of tissue can result in a process called infarction in which there is not enough oxygen and nutrients delivered to the tissue to keep it alive. This can result in a significant amount of damage to the organ that is involved. Other organs besides the kidney that may be affected in this manner include the bones, the eye, the brain and the lungs.

Various symptoms can result from damage to specific organs. For example, infarctions in the innermost part of the kidney can result in the passage of red blood cells in the urine, giving a red or smoky color to the urine. Impaired blood flow to the hipbone can result in pain and eventual dislocation of the hip joint and in some patients can cause a considerable degree of disability. If the sickling phenomenon affects the circulation to the eye, varying degrees of visual disturbances may be encountered. Some patients with sickle cell anemia get skin ulcers over the ankle bones. These ulcers are sometimes difficult to manage because the sickled red cells do not supply enough oxygen to the skin in this area to allow for adequate healing. Rarely patients with sickle cell anemia may develop strokes, from which recovery is highly variable. Patients with sickle cell anemia have frequent problems with lung infection, sometimes complicated by the obstruction of blood flow to major portions of the lung.

Patients with sickle cell anemia have a slow rate of development during childhood. They may be somewhat small and slender for their age. Furthermore they have an increased tendency to develop serious infections. Probably the leading cause of death among children with sickle cell anemia is overwhelming infection. For this reason, it is very important for a child to seek medical attention at the first sign or symptom of an impending infection such as sore throat, pneumonia or infection of the urinary tract.

The clinical course and outlook of patients with sickle cell anemia is highly variable. There are some children who do not survive into adulthood. There are some adults with a severe form of the disease who develop significant complications due to the damage to vital organs mentioned above. However, it should be emphasized that there are a number of individuals who nowadays survive well into middle or late adulthood without significant organ damage. These individuals will have a severe anemia and may have occasional pain crises but nevertheless remain productive and lead useful lives despite their lifelong disability. There are even patients with homozygous or full-blown sickle cell anemia who are almost totally asymptomatic. Thus it is a great mistake to assume that once a diagnosis of sickle cell anemia is made the individual will necessarily be an invalid and be faced with a series of life-threatening complications. It is important that both children and adults with sickle cell anemia should feel free to take part in any play, recreation or occupation which does not tax the limit of their strength and energy. Usually the patient is the best judge of how much he or she can or cannot do.

The treatment of sickle cell anemia is largely supportive. Most patients require a liberal amount of pain medication in order to control symptoms due to painful crises. It is very important that patients with sickle cell anemia maintain adequate fluid intake and do not get dehydrated, particularly in the summer months or when living in an overheated dwelling during the winter. Some patients occasionally need to have supplementary fluid administered by the intravenous route. It is sometimes helpful to give oxygen to patients who have sickle crises, since the sickling is worsened by the removal of oxygen from the red cells. As mentioned above infections should be diagnosed promptly so that appropriate treatment can be given.

Although there is a great deal of knowledge about the molecular basis of sickling, there is no effective therapy which prevents the polymerization of sickle hemoglobin molecules within the red cell. However, a considerable amount of progress is being made in a number of research laboratories, in attempts to design a drug which will cross the red cell membrane and interrupt the sickling process. A number of such agents look promising as a result of laboratory experiments, but none are yet ready for use as therapy. A great many claims of cures for sickle cell anemia have been made during the last decade. Many of these reports have to be taken with a considerable degree of caution. At this time there is no cure. However, the outlook for patients with sickle cell anemia is improving steadily because of the improved quality of medical care in the United States and elsewhere. An increasing number of individuals are diagnosed at an early age and are followed regularly in clinics around the country. There is a reasonable chance that within the next ten years a specific and hopefully definitive treatment for sickle cell anemia will be developed.

CREDIT: *H. Franklin Bunn, M.D., Director of Hematology, Peter Bent Brigham, and Associate Professor of Medicine, Harvard Medical School, Boston, Massachusetts.*

SIDS (Sudden Infant Death Syndrome)

(*Crib Death or Cot Death*)

SIDS is a disease which causes from eight thousand to ten thousand infant deaths annually in the United States. SIDS has been with us since biblical times, but only in recent years has it been recognized to be a "specific disease."

It is best defined by describing a typical case. An apparently healthy infant, usually between the ages of three weeks and seven months, is put to bed without the slightest suspicion that things are out of the ordinary. He may have signs of a slight cold. Some time later the infant is found dead. Often there is no evidence that a struggle took place, nor did anyone hear the baby cry.

Often the autopsy reveals no evidence of illness. In about 15 percent of crib death cases careful examination does demonstrate a previously unsuspected abnormality or a rapidly fatal infectious disease, such as meningitis or pneumonia.

UNEARNED GUILT

Virtually every parent feels responsible for the death of his child, until the facts are known. In thousands of cases much needless blame has been placed by one parent upon the other, on relatives, on the baby-sitter who happened to be with the infant at the time or on the family doctor who pronounced the infant healthy shortly before it died.

SIDS cannot be predicted, and in the light of present knowledge SIDS cannot be prevented.

The disease has no specific symptoms and occurs in the best families, to the most competent, careful and loving parents. The victims of SIDS are usually robust, healthy and obviously well cared for. SIDS can occur in hospitals, and many physicians and nurses have lost their own babies to SIDS.

DID THE BABY SUFFOCATE?

It is not uncommon for victims to be found wedged into the corner of their cribs or with their head covered by blankets. Sometimes their faces are turned down into the pillow or mattress or are discolored. Under such circumstances, it is natural to assume the baby smothered. However, SIDS also occurs under conditions where there is *no* possibility of smothering. The baby can be found without any articles of bedding, clothing, toys or pets around or near the face. The autopsy findings are identical in both types of cases. Investigators have found that even when infants are covered by bedding, the amount of oxygen is not reduced to the point of causing suffocation. Thus it is possible to say with certainty that SIDS is not caused by external suffocation.

COULD MY BABY HAVE CHOKED AFTER HIS LAST FEEDING?

SIDS is not caused by vomiting and choking. Sometimes milk or even blood-tinged froth is found around the mouth or on the bedding. This has been shown usually to occur after death, and at autopsy is found not to block the internal air passages.

CAN SIDS BE PREVENTED?

There is no known way to prevent its occurrence. No symptoms exist, so extreme anxiety will serve no useful purpose.

WHAT CAUSES SIDS?

There have been many theories through the years as to the cause of SIDS. None of these have yet been proven. Years ago it was believed that an enlarged thymus gland blocked off the infant's airway, but this has been disproven.

Allergy to cow's milk has been suspected by some to bring on sudden reaction severe enough to cause death. However, recent studies on antibodies in SIDS cases have failed to support this theory. Many SIDS babies have been entirely breast-fed.

Theories that have been discounted are: bacterial infection, radiation fallout, use of modern machines and drugs, smoking, adding bleach to the diaper wash, "whiplash" injury to the spinal cord, air pollution and fluoridation. It is important to emphasize that SIDS is not a new disease and is no more frequent now than it was centuries ago.

DID MY BABY SUFFER?

SIDS can occur within five minutes and is probably almost instantaneous. There may be some movement during the last few seconds of life, accounting for the displaced blankets or unusual positions that are sometimes evident. However, the babies do not cry out and very often show not the slightest trace of having been disturbed in their sleep. Therefore, it is safe to conclude that SIDS does not cause pain or suffering to the baby.

WAS IT SOMETHING INFECTIOUS? IS THE IMMEDIATE FAMILY IN DANGER?

SIDS is not contagious. For example, if one of twins in the same bed is taken by SIDS, the other is usually spared.

There are seasons during which SISD is more commonly seen but there is no reason for concern in cases where an infant is exposed to a SIDS case. SIDS virtually never happens after the first year of life, so older children are not at risk. There is no need to be concerned about contamination from clothing, bedding or furniture of a SIDS baby. The common viruses which might cause SIDS do not survive outside living bodies.

WHAT ABOUT BABIES WE MIGHT HAVE IN THE FUTURE?

According to the best available data, SIDS is not hereditary, and any future babies in a family will run no more of a risk than any other baby. More harm than good may be done to a subsequent child by excessive anxiety over SIDS.

PROBLEMS OF GRIEF

After the initial shock and the numbness of the first few days begin to wear off, parents find that they are left with a prolonged depression. There will be ups and downs that can be brought on by a thoughtless or innocent remark from someone who doesn't understand the disease.

At these low points, it is often helpful for parents to talk to a member of the NSIDSF, referred to later in this piece. Only another parent who has had this same experience can convincingly say that things won't always look as they do today, that time really does make a difference. If there is no such person available, the family physician or clergyman can be reassuring.

SOURCES OF HELP AND INFORMATION

National Sudden Infant Death Syndrome Foundation
310 South Michigan Avenue
Chicago, Illinois 60604
(312) 663-0650

This is a national organization with chapters in many areas of the United States. It maintains contact with and makes referrals to other groups and individuals concerned about Sudden Infant Death Syndrome, some of whom are not directly affiliated with it.

The purpose of the NSIDSF is to assist parents, educate the community about SIDS and promote SIDS research.

Scientific information: Two major sources of scientific information regarding SIDS are:

"Sudden Death in Infants: Proceedings of the Conference on Causes of Sudden Infant Death in Infants" (1963), National Institute of Child Health and Human Development, Bethesda, Maryland 20014.

"Proceedings of the Second International Conference on Causes of Sudden Infant Death in Infants" (1970), University of Washington Press, Seattle, Washington 98105.

CREDIT: *The Sudden Infant Death Research Team of Children's Orthopedic Hospital and Medical Center in co-operation with the University of Washington, Seattle, Washington. Washington State Chapter, National Foundation for Sudden Infant Death, Inc. National Sudden Infant Death Syndrome Foundation, 310 South Michigan Avenue, Chicago, Illinois 60604.*

Silence

How unsporting it seems to say nothing when public curiosity snaps up every tidbit of gossip and rumor. How unfair not to tell what you know about yourself or about others, especially the famous, if you have had a privileged look at them. The public's right to know—yes, of course, how could we have forgotten? We forget that this shaggy maxim is balanced by the private person's right to remain silent.

Silence is not just a discipline for monasteries and library reading rooms, not a regulation to safeguard others from distractions. Silence is not a void but a world of its own. Modern persons will never get in touch with themselves with a transistor radio plugged into their ears. And the crackle of CB radios won't help much either.

There is a silence that matches our best possibilities when we have learned to listen to others. We can master the art of being quiet in order to be able to hear clearly what others are saying. This is vital for friends and lovers, for parents with their children and teachers with their students. We need to cut off the garbled static of our own preoccupations to give to people who want our quiet attention.

And there are times when there is nothing to say, nothing that could fit the occasion. There are times when silence is the most sacred of responses.

Other times our wordy clichés break like brittle swords in frozen weather. That is why, as Emily Dickinson once wrote, "There is a hush in a home on the morning after death, a silence that would be violated by too many words."

Even those who love each other deeply must master the lessons of silence and its meaning in their relationship. There are moments—after hurt, intended or not—when only silence will do. Is it too great a gift to ask, too much respect for the way things heal, to expect silence when saying something, saying anything at all, only makes things worse? Remaining silent even when one longs to apologize and buy release from the pain or tension of wounding a loved one: This is as hard a discipline as we know. How hard it is for any of us to master it. But it is in silence that love speaks softly; it is in such sacrificed silences that forgiveness finds its voice.

Silence has been a traditional choice, not for itself, but because it is the medium for so much that is powerful and significant for human beings. Silence is a choice not for the fearful and the timid who are afraid of the world but for the brave and loving who wish to deepen their relationship with the world. It is what we hear in the silence with each other and with God that gives us more to share and more to say in all the other moments of life.

CREDIT: *Eugene Kennedy, Ph.D., Loyola University, Chicago, author of* Living with Everyday Problems, *Chicago, Illinois: Thomas More Association.*

Sleep Talking

Somniloquy, or sleep talking, is quite prevalent in the entire population in varying degrees—from a simple groan, to unintelligible mutterings, to cries for help, to minor monologues. Most of what we hear from a person who is talking in his sleep makes no sense because we do not know what the child or adult is dreaming about.

Often the sleep talker, if prodded, can recall his dream, but then again he may be unable to remember it. Also, many persons are unaware of talking in their sleep, and will deny that any such activity has taken place when questioned about it.

Sometimes a very distressing or frightening experience can be relived in a dream, complete with talking. Such incidents are known as nightmares—with or without talking. The person who has frequent nightmares (especially the same one over and over again) should be seen by a psychiatrist. Something is bothering him and he needs to find out what it is so he can talk about it and get it out of his system.

It is often very difficult to get into a conversation with sleep talkers because they have their own stream of thought which occupies their attention. Individuals who have tried report no success and great frustration.

It is thought by some that guarded secrets can be obtained either by listening to spontaneous sleep talking or by asking questions of the sleep talker. Others believe that secrets are never betrayed in sleep talking. More research needs to be done in this area, but as of now, sleep talkers are not thought to be a good source of illicit information. That "Julia" about whom he spoke so admiringly in his sleep may be his first-grade teacher!

Sleep talking, then, is a fairly normal manifestation of rather normal sleep, and is not to be construed as a source of reliable information, or a dangerous and abnormal symptom. It is sometimes annoying, perhaps, but is not a serious problem.

CREDIT: *William K. Keller, M.D., Emeritus Professor and former Chairman, Department of Psychiatry, University of Louisville, Kentucky.*

Sleepwalking

Sleepwalking has been going on for centuries, and it's still anyone's guess why some people walk in their sleep and others do not. It has been attributed to many causes, from being possessed by demons to eating too much for dinner. Like many disorders, when the cause is unknown, specific treatment is also unknown. Now, since the brain itself can be studied in many of its various functions, more and more is being learned about sleep, sleepwalking and talking when asleep.

A great deal of research and investigation on these subjects has been carried out in sleep laboratories in clinical settings. Such competent investigators as Anders, Aserinsky, Broughton, Dement, Guilleminault, A. Kales, J. D. Kales, Kleitman and many others have contributed to the literature on this and related subjects such as bedwetting and nightmares. These researchers and their colleagues have shown that there is a certain rhythm to the brain in sleep, deep sleep, light sleep and various gradations in between.

Somnambulism, or sleepwalking, occurs at one time or another in approximately 1 to 6 percent of all people, mostly in children. All of us have sleep patterns which can be examined by as simple a method as observation, to complicated research into brain wave studies.

Sleepwalking may last from a few minutes to as long as a half hour or more. People who are subject to such occurrences are difficult to awaken and they do not remember their actions. The fact that this is not an uncommon occurrence should be reassuring, and the further fact that such manifestations become less frequent as the child grows older should be a greater comfort.

The gravest danger in sleepwalking is that the child, or occasional adult, might fall or be injured. Simple safety precautions should be taken such as locking windows and screens, keeping furniture in the same place, and the use of uncomplicated devices like a child's gate at the top of the stairs.

One bit of superstition is that something serious will happen to an individual if awakened suddenly while sleepwalking. This bit of folklore probably originated when someone startled a sleepwalker on a bridge and he fell off.

Any sleepwalker should be awakened gently, reassured and led quietly back to bed. No one likes to be awakened suddenly with a shove or a shout.

It is generally agreed that sleepwalkers are not acting out a dream. If this phenomenon continues night after night, however, a physician should be consulted in case there is some other reason for the sleep disturbance. Specific treatment may be needed. It goes without saying that one should never take medicine of any kind from a friend who claims he has had success with it. One should take only those medicines prescribed by his doctor.

If someone you know walks in his or her sleep, remember that about 15 percent of all children have sleepwalked at least once. Sometimes the eyes are open, with a glassy stare. The individual may walk around the room, about the house and even down the stairs, if measures have not been taken to prevent it. In general, however, be assured that, if you have taken all necessary precautions to protect the sleepwalker against injury, time will probably take care of the problem.

Keep in mind that sleepwalkers do not know what they are doing, so fussing or scolding them because they have awakened you and interfered with *your* rest will not help. In the meanwhile, remember that the person who walks in his sleep needs patience, understanding and love.

CREDIT: *William K. Keller, M.D., Emeritus Professor and former Chairman, Department of Psychiatry, University of Louisville, Kentucky.*

Smile

SMILE

DEAR ANN LANDERS: That letter from the guy who was called a "sourpuss" because he didn't smile much hit close to home.

Ever since I can remember my mother nagged me to "turn up the corners of my mouth." Once she paid an artist to sketch a picture of me with a glum look on my face. After that I made an effort to smile as seldom as possible.

When I was in my 20s I was walking down the corridor of the office where I worked. A woman I'd never seen before was heading toward me. Suddenly she stopped and said, "Cheer up. Things can't be THAT bad!" I caught my reflection in the window and was shocked at how downhearted I looked.

That very day I began to practice smiling in the mirror and I vowed I'd keep a smile on my face no matter how glum I felt. Know what? That pleasant expression felt ever so much better. All it took was relaxing the frown lines between my eyebrows and bringing up the corners of my mouth a quarter of an inch.

The rewards have been tremendous. I now drive a school bus and one of the kids said just last week, "You make us all feel good because you look so cheerful. You're not like the other driver who always looked so grumpy." Sign this KALAMAZOO

DEAR ZOO: A beauty expert once told me, "A smiling face looks years younger. It lifts everything." And it does! Well, almost. Thanks for sharing.

A smile costs nothing but its value is priceless.

It enriches the one who gives it, yet it impoverishes him not.

It happens in a flash but the memory may last for days.

No one is so rich that he can get along without it. No one is so poor that he cannot afford to give it.

A smile generates happiness in the home and goodwill in business because it says, "I like you. You pleasure me."

If you meet an acquaintance or a friend who is too busy to give you a smile —leave one of yours.

No one needs a smile so much as the person who has none to give.

Smoke

(*Secondhand Smoke*)

DEAR ANN LANDERS: The letter from "I Feel Better Already" made me write to you.

A few years ago, I, too, was hacking, coughing and sneezing. I had watery eyes, chapped lips and a red nose. Food tasted awful. I was a "chronic asthmatic," so short of breath at times I had to sleep sitting up. When our young son began to develop the same symptoms, I became frantic.

We moved to another city, and I had to start with a new doctor. The first thing he said to me was, "You'll never get any better until you stop smoking."

The doctor was shocked when I told him I didn't smoke—and never had. He then asked if my husband smoked. When I replied, "Only three packs a day," he informed me that I was allergic to smoke and secondhand smoke was making me sick.

I could write a book on what happened after I got that news, but this is enough for one letter to Ann Landers. Please print it for others who might have a similar problem and not know it. BREATHING EASY IN BERMUDA

Because the health hazards of smoking cigarettes had not been clearly defined until approximately ten years ago, little attention was paid to the effects of tobacco smoke on the non-smoker. However, with the overwhelming evidence that smoking is harmful, it became necessary to study the physiological and pharmacological effects of cigarette smoke upon those who unwittingly and involuntarily are exposed to the products of tobacco smoke.

This is nowhere more true than in the case of the unborn child exposed to tobacco through the bloodstream of the pregnant mother. In this instance, however, the mechanism of exposure is different from that of the individual sitting in an automobile or in a room filled with tobacco smoke.

While it will undoubtedly take a number of years to collect more data regarding the effects of tobacco smoke on the non-smoker, there is much we already know and I should like to review that information now.

The smoking of a popular-brand cigarette releases approximately 70 mg. of dry particles and 23 mg. of carbon monoxide into the air. Additional amounts of these materials are absorbed by the smoker himself, but the former is the contribution of the average cigarette to contaminating the air around the smoker.

Several recent studies indicate that a number of compounds found in cigarette smoke are produced in higher quantities in the sidestream smoke from the burning of the cigarette as compared to the mainstream smoke which is inhaled by the smoker. More specifically, there is four times as much carbon monoxide in sidestream smoke as in mainstream smoke. As the cigarette is smoked more and more, there is a greater proportional production of carbon monoxide. I should add that the pipe and cigar smoker is even less considerate than the cigarette smoker in that he does not himself absorb nearly as much of the noxious products, but rather leaves it for his non-smoking companions to inhale.

About the only well-ventilated area, in terms of air exchange and removal of contamination, is the modern jet airplane, which exchanges the air volume several times per minute. Many of the rooms in which we work or in which we hold meetings, also the automobiles in which we ride, have a very low rate of exchange of air—and in some instances none at all.

The results in levels of carbon monoxide which are well above those found to be hazardous for working conditions by the U. S. Environmental Protection Agency of the U. S. Department of Labor. It is not only levels of carbon monoxide which may be hazardous, but sidestream cigarette smoke may contain three times as much benzopyrene as mainstream smoke and may contain up to three times the level of tars as well as significant amounts of nicotine. Another group of contaminants are the nitrous oxides which are present in smoke-filled rooms. These compounds are quite toxic to the lungs.

Sidestream smoke can lead to serious impairment of health in the individual who already has cardiac or pulmonary disease. Studies prove that psychomotor function, such as the ability to discriminate sound levels or the ability to distinguish relative brightness, can be impaired by carbon monoxide. The same applies to the ability to co-ordinate muscular function and "put on the brakes rapidly."

Individuals suffering from chronic heart and lung disease are not the only victims of cigarette smoke. A significant portion of our population is allergic to one or another compound. Even non-allergic non-smokers report discomfort and respiratory symptoms when exposed to tobacco smoke. Tobacco smoke can precipitate allergic attacks, headaches, eye irritation, nasal symptoms, coughing and wheezing.

In a free society, individuals who choose to smoke should certainly be permitted to do so, but the right of the non-smoker to inhale clean air must not be denied him, especially now that we know other people's smoke can be harmful to his health.

CREDIT: *Jesse L. Steinfeld, M.D., former Surgeon General, U. S. Army, 1969–73.*

Snakes

What to Do if You Are Bitten

If you are a hiker, a serious backpacker or just enjoy an occasional walk in the woods, you have probably come across a snake at one time or another. Even if you knew that 85 percent of the world's snakes are not poisonous, you would still be terrified if you stumbled over one. You would probably envision eight-inch, dripping fangs, protruding from the mouth of an innocuous nine-inch garter snake.

This is perfectly natural. What's more, it pays to be cautious when you don't know. It doesn't pay, however, not to enjoy the woods because you are afraid. The degree of danger of succumbing to a venomous snake depends upon two things: One, you must be in an area where venomous snakes are known to inhabit, and two, you must provoke an attack. After you are bitten the results depend to a large degree upon the severity of the bite, the immediate treatment and the availability of medical facilities adequately equipped.

Let's take a look at the first factor, distribution. Probably the safest place to be if you want to avoid being bitten by a venomous snake in the continental United States is the Northeast. Only the timber rattlesnake, which still roams areas in Pennsylvania, New York and New Jersey, is a real danger. The ill-reputed copperhead is actually a secretive snake whose bite has a very low fatality record. If you really want to be safe, go to Hawaii. There is not a single species of snake on that island! (Alaska has very few poisonous snakes, also.)

The snakes that concern us most in America are the pit vipers—rattlesnakes, cottonmouths and the copperheads. Although here and in other parts of the world there are snakes with more potent venoms, nowhere is the apparatus for injection of venom so well developed. This makes the pit vipers truly among the most feared and dangerous snakes in the world.

The long, hollow fangs of these animals may be voluntarily moved into position for a strike. Hinged with the upper jaw at the rear, these natural hypodermics stab the victim with a rapid thrust.

All snakes, virtually without exception, prefer flight to fight. The way to avoid being bitten by any snake, venomous or not, is to leave it alone. Except for the rare and unfortunate instance when your cold big toe connects with a resting rattlesnake at the bottom of your sleeping bag, or when you reach down with a bare hand to retrieve a baseball which has landed on top of a prowling copperhead, accidents happen as the result of provocation or carelessness.

Carelessness does not only mean the joking of an overconfident zoo keeper. Often carelessness and provocation are one and the same. If you stick your hand in a crevice on a rocky ledge while trying to scale a cliff, that's carelessness (if you're in venomous snake country). The provocation end of it is clamping your fingers down on his lung. The best course of action is to buy a field guide for your area and become familiar with identifying features and preferred habitats of venomous serpents in your area. Here are some general rules:

Never turn a stone over or move a heavy branch (on the ground in front of you) with your bare hands. Don't hang out on rocky ledges, or tramp through dense undergrowth crouched over if you're in snake country. If you are hiking, or birdwatching, keep your eyes on the ground a few feet ahead of you. Stay on the beaten track and don't go out alone or get separated from your companions by more than shouting distance. If there is some urgent need to go prowling in the woods or in high grass or rocks (maybe you dropped your camera or see a fresh, new hundred-dollar bill), make sure you are wearing high boots. In lieu of this, beat the bush or grass in front of you and tap rocks with a heavy stick. Remember that most snakes are harmless and can barely break your skin if they try to bite you. Don't let my treatment of the venomous snake problem scare you. Be informed, not petrified.

Earlier I mentioned pit vipers and quoted their potential for inflicting a serious bite. There is one other group of snakes in the continental United States which is also potentially extremely hazardous. These are the coral snakes, which can be found from the coast of the Southeast to the Gulf states and over into Arizona and New Mexico. Coral snakes are different in many ways than the rattlers and their relatives. Generally small and shy, they belong to the same group as the cobras, venomous sea snakes and many other dangerous Asian and Australian species. The corals are less likely to be aggressive than pit vipers. As a matter of fact, their diminutive size combined with their small, blunt fangs make them almost harmless. The "almost" is the key word in this phrase. Heaven help you if you get a finger or toe snagged on the fang of a coral snake! Unlike the pit viper, the coral snakes have a comparatively primitive apparatus for venom injection. The fangs are in the front and have an enclosed groove for the passage of venom like the vipers'. The fangs, however, cannot protrude and thus do not function like hypodermics. To compensate for this, the coral snakes have venom that is extremely deadly drop for drop.

Out of all these remarks and grim descriptions of snakes and their venoms should come the best obvious advice. Don't get bitten. But what if you do? The bite of a poisonous snake can be recognized by one or more punctures caused by the fangs. The poison quickly causes severe stinging. Soon the area around the bite begins to swell and turn purple. The victim becomes pale and weak and often nauseated. His pulse becomes rapid. The first objective is to get competent medical attention immediately. If there are more than two people in the party, one should go at once to a telephone and get in touch with the nearest Poison Control Center. A telephone operator will put you in touch with the emergency room of the nearest hospital and you can receive instructions from them. A snake bite victim should not be allowed to walk. He should be kept motionless and quiet. Activity causes the poison to spread. Have the operator put in a long-distance call to the Center for Disease Control, United States Public Health Service, Atlanta, Georgia. Their lines are open day and night. It is a great help if you can tell the physician on the phone the identification of the snake that bit you. If you are unable to identify the snake, describe it to the best of your ability.

If no doctor can be reached and summoned to the victim, the best course of action is to get the victim to a medical facility as soon as possible.

If medical attention is more than a half hour away, other treatment is recommended. This consists of a tourniquet and cutting and suction. The tourniquet need only be tight enough to stop the superficial blood flow. If you can slip your finger underneath it, it is probably all right. It should be tied a few inches above the bite on the nearest major limb. An incision is recommended to get out as much of the poison as possible. Remember, these procedures are only applicable if medical aid is more than half an hour away. The incision should be made not deeper than is necessary to assure getting a good blood flow. If you have a knife or razor blade and matches, sterilize the knife or blade by putting it in the flame. Then make an X-shaped cut through each fang mark. After the incision has been made, apply a suction cup (if you have a snakebite kit). It is not recommended that you suck the wound with your mouth except in an emergency, as venom may enter the system through a cut in the mouth. When not being sucked, cover the wound with a wet dressing. As swelling increases, move the band upward. Give the victim plenty of water, but *no* alcohol. If the victim stops breathing, use artificial respiration.

The necessary materials to do this are available in commercial snakebite kits. These kits are a must for anyone inhabiting or penetrating an area infested with venomous snakes.

Again, I stress, the chances of being bitten by a venomous snake and seriously poisoned are less than being struck by lightning. Take ordinary precautions and feel free to enjoy nature. Buy a field guide to your area if you live in dangerous-snake country. The nasty part is getting treatment after you are bitten. Don't let your apprehension be worse than the real thing.

CREDIT: *Arthur Rosenfeld, undergraduate in biology, Yale University, New Haven, Connecticut.*

Snoring

WHEN HUBBY SNORES, THEN ALL IS WELL

DEAR ANN LANDERS: I was shocked to read the letter from the wife who wanted her husband to sleep with a bicycle horn strapped around his head, so that when he lay on his back and snored the horn would blow and wake him up.

Maybe I'm crazy but the sound of my husband snoring is the sweetest music in all the world. When I hear that familiar snore I know he's at home where he belongs—and all is well.

Not only do I love to hear him snore but I love to look at his face when he's asleep. You know, Ann, men are a lot like little boys, and when they sleep their hair is all tousled, and their faces are angelic and innocent.

When my husband is asleep he looks so much like our 5-year-old son that it tickles me. Of course I'd never let him know, so please don't give me away by printing my initials or the name of my city. Just call me. HUSBAND WATCHER

DEAR WATCHER: Only a lady in love could write such a warm and sweet letter. How lucky—for both of you!

There's a lot of "little boy" in every man, and the woman smart enough to understand this usually has a solid marriage. You've got it taped, Honey.

An estimated thirty-five million people in this country snore and they are evenly divided as to sex. As many women snore as men. The real victims of snoring (sometimes called the "listener's disease") are spouses, lovers, relatives, roommates, dorm occupants, fellow campers, barracks buddies, shipmates and members of the same cell block.

The victim, not the snorer, is the one who loses sleep, his temper and may eventually be driven to do things which are completely out of character. The snoring has led to separate bedrooms, mayhem, divorce and even murder.

This story was reported by the Associated Press, dateline Silver Spring, Maryland.

Luther G. told the court this sequence of events took place when he arrived home around midnight after attending a lodge meeting.

His wife, E., was in bed snoring. He climbed into bed without disturbing her and fell asleep. He was awakened a short time later when his wife kicked him in the leg.

She got up, jerked a sheet and blanket from him and said, "I'm not going to sleep with anybody who snores like that." Then she struck him on the head with a billy club.

This led to his obtaining a warrant. Luther charged his wife with assault and battery. During her trial, before Judge Ralph Miller of People's Court, Mrs. G., a school bus driver, testified that he smelled of beer when he came home at 2:30 A.M., slammed a door, dropped his shoes, made all kinds of noise, fell into bed and started to snore.

"I asked him three times to turn over," she said. "Suddenly he sat up and slapped me. I then tapped him lightly with a billy club."

The judge ruled that, although Luther had slapped her, she could easily have walked away instead of hitting him. E. was found guilty as charged. The judge, however, suspended the sentence and made this statement: "Apparently, you two should not have gotten married in the first place."

This is only one of hundreds of cases heard by judges across the country from distraught victims who cite snoring as the "last straw."

The Canadian Medical Association did extensive research into the cause and "cure" of snoring and admitted it didn't learn much.

A variety of experiments were conducted. For example, wads of cotton were sewed into the shoulders of snorers' pajamas and nightgowns so they couldn't sleep on their backs. Unfortunately, many snorers continued to shake the fixtures while sleeping on their sides, stomachs and even sitting up.

Adhesive tape was used to keep the snorer's mouth shut but some people snored even then.

The Association's researchers concluded that the only solution was to isolate the snorer. One of the researchers (an admitted snorer) was outraged at this suggestion. He said, "As one who runs up and down a few scales myself after I hit the sack, I resent this so-called 'solution.' I do not wish to be moved into a specially constructed, soundproof, bomb-proof shelter just because I disturb the little woman. It would be better to reinforce the walls so the vibrations don't shake the plaster loose and stuff some wadding around the windows so they won't rattle—then go to bed peacefully."

The inference, of course, is that the victim of the snorer is on his own and it is up to him (or her) to do whatever he can to deal with the problem.

A snore is what happens when breathing during sleep causes various structures in the respiratory tract to vibrate. The tongue slips to the rear of the mouth, and the soft palate and muscles in that area relax as air goes in and out. The resulting vibrations frequently infuriate the listener. Snoring tends to become worse with age as the muscles lose their tone.

Snores are infinite in variety. There are laryngeal and nasal snores, neurotic and physiological snores, lyrical snores and "fixture-shakers."

Since snoring has many causes it also has many possible cures. But first somebody, usually the ear-witness to the stentorian roar (named after the mythical herald Stentor, whose voice in *The Iliad* equaled that of fifty ordinary men), must convince the snorer that the problem exists. This takes time, tact and a firm assertion that the snoring, not the snorer, is intolerable.

Next a physician should check the respiratory tract to determine whether enlarged tonsils and adenoids, gross nasal deformities, nasal polyps, allergies, inflamed sinuses or congestion is causing the problem.

Snoring may also be caused by loose dentures, smoking, obesity, drinking, emotional tension and lack of exercise.

So what is a person to do when her (or his) bed partner's nocturnal racket-making interferes with her ability to get a good night's sleep? Here are several suggestions. Some work better than others.

You can sew a couple of Ping-Pong balls on the back of the snorer's pajamas or nightgown to discourage the snorer from sleeping on his back. This technique has helped in about 50 percent of the experiments.

Mouthpieces designed to prevent a sleeper from breathing through the mouth have been on the market for quite some time. Originally they were invented for individuals who slept with their mouths open and awakened with throat infections, inflamed adenoids, sclerosis of the eardrum, defective hearing and a fly or two in the mouth. For individuals who snore *only* when their mouths are open, this contraption can be useful.

There are also chin straps and "beauty caps" for sale but the same results can be accomplished by taking strips of gauze (or any fabric) and bandaging the mouth shut.

Earplugs have proven a boon for some, but many individuals are reluctant to use them because they must hear the children if they should call out at night, or the telephone if it should ring.

Behavior modification has worked in some instances—in other words, the snorer is psyched out. One technique is to make a tape recording of the snoring and play it back to him every evening for several weeks. He sometimes becomes so ashamed he actually stops snoring.

Some doctors suggest behavior modification for the listener. The concept is as follows: The mate of the snorer should develop a sympathetic approach, an earnest desire to help bolster the snorer's self-esteem. He must look upon his tolerance as a contribution toward the snorer's mental health. "This generosity of spirit," said one psychologist, "can do wonders for a marriage." (Personally, I think it's asking a great deal.)

Autosuggestion has worked for some. A man from Toledo wrote to say he repeated one hundred times every night before retiring, "I will not snore. I will not snore." After two weeks, he did not snore, according to his wife.

Charles W. Eliot, president of Harvard, says the best way to cope with a snorer is to fall asleep ahead of him. Another logical suggestion is soft music to distract the victim from the snoring.

Occasionally snoring is caused by conditions inside the mouth, such as a small jaw and a large tongue or a marked overbite. The latter problem can be corrected by an orthodontist.

When a nasal obstruction is the cause for snoring, surgery can solve the problem. It is a simple procedure and helps the person breathe in a healthier manner and often eliminates the snoring. The surgical removal of nasal polyps (small growths) puts an end to snoring.

One of the most unusual letters I ever received was from a twenty-six-year-old woman who lived in Rock Island, Illinois. She told me she was just about to divorce her husband because of his intolerable snoring when she discovered it was not he who snored, but his German shepherd, who shared their bed. Her husband refused to put the dog in the back hall, nor would he take the animal to a vet to see if the dog's snoring could be remedied. Counseling was out. She suggested it (so did her physician), but he refused to go.

The woman went to her clergyman for guidance. He said, "Throw the bum out." And that, my friends, is where I first picked up the phrase.

CREDIT: *Marcus H. Boulware, author of* Snoring, *American Faculty Press.*

DEAR ANN LANDERS: This is for the crazy lady who wrote to say she loves to watch her husband sleep at night because he looks so much like a little boy. Then she added, "I adore listening to him snore. It's such a comfort to know he's right there beside me." (That broad must sleep in the daytime.)

For 24 years I have been married to a man who snores. If I turn on the light to look at him I'm sure the only thought that would come to my mind is murder. His snoring, under ordinary circumstances, is enough to shake the fixtures, but when he's had a few drinks he makes such a racket the people in the next apartment bang on the floor with what must be a sledge hammer.

Several years ago we took *The City of San Francisco* (a great train) to the west coast. The people in the next compartment knocked on our door and asked if I could do something to quiet my husband. I said, "Yes, but it's against the law."

Last year our family doctor suggested either a sedative for me, earplugs or separate bedrooms. I am now using all three. Pass the word to my sister sufferers, Ann. PEACE IT'S WONDERFUL

DEAR PEACE: Consider it passed. I can't imagine worse punishment than being up all night, while the mate is snoring up a storm, depriving you of a night's sleep. Your suggestions all sound good. Too bad it took you so long to get relief.

Sterilization

Emotional Impact of Voluntary Sterilization

In most discussions pertaining to voluntary sterilization, the thoughts, motives and feelings of the patient are extremely important. I would like to stress that any surgical procedure involves two people—the patient and the doctor.

No generalizations should be made about why a person chooses sterilization. Reasons for the choice have changed over the years along with changes in public information and attitudes. The decision "to be or not to be" is based on thinking that is both rational and emotional.

The rational factors vary. To mention a few: age, economic circumstances, careers and lifestyle, health, degree of enjoyment of children. (Some women look upon having children as a disaster. Others view it merely as an inconvenience.) How does a person perceive the possibility of later regret? For some, it would be very sad indeed not to be able to have a child in a second marriage, for others it would be a blessing. Some couples look forward to adopting interracial or otherwise unwanted children. Others wouldn't consider it.

What are the feelings about contraceptives? Fears of side effects of the pill are mounting. Millions of women have gone off the pill within the last two years. On the other hand, the discomfort or inconvenience of using a condom or diaphragm is a factor that must be reckoned with also. Feelings about abortion run to both extremes. Some women have no guilt whatever about the procedure and are therefore willing to risk pregnancy. These women tend to steer clear of sterilization.

Others feel that abortion is murder and need more certainty in their contraceptive method. They tend to favor sterilization—when they can get an okay from their clergyman, which is often not easy.

A woman may be more or less aware of her own ambivalence about having another baby. Dr. Hans Leyfeldt has described the syndrome he calls "Willful Exposure to Unwanted Pregnancy," in which a woman unconsciously forgets her pill or her diaphragm. She may enjoy pregnancy, but not children. She may be afraid of no longer having babies to keep her busy. She may feel the need of a pregnancy, to hold her husband. In agreeing to a sterilization for either herself or her husband, a woman may be unwittingly protecting herself from her irrational thinking.

To turn to less rational motives for sterilization, especially among young people, there may be fear of the responsibilities of raising children, or an overconcern with money. A fairly common motive is the hope of improving sexual pleasure, and this also has its rational and irrational sides. It is perfectly true that the fear of pregnancy may inhibit enjoyment of sex and reduce its frequency. But any hope of a magic cure for sexual problems must be extinguished by the doctor before surgery.

In theory, other unconscious irrational motives may be imagined: hostility to the spouse and a wish to deprive him or her of a baby, self-punishment and so on. A number of psychiatrists have let their fantasies roam widely, because of their high index of suspicion, and possibly because of their own feelings.

The patient may also have both rational and irrational reasons to be reluctant to have a sterilization. There may be a possible worry about a later change of heart in wanting a baby. Sometimes there are anxieties—the most common mentioned in surveys is pain.

In the most recent survey of men having vasectomies, about one third of the men spoke of some worry about "less sex drive" and one sixth about less masculinity. Clearly, any surgery interferes to some extent with body image, and surgery on the reproductive organ is even more significant. But this impact varies in degree, and cannot be assumed to be important in all cases.

I will turn now to the decision by the doctor. After a patient requests a sterilization, the doctor of course goes through the same process of weighing the factors. Since he is taking some risks, however small, and since his support is important to the patient, he has the right to refuse to perform the procedure. He should not, however, project onto the patient his own feelings about having children, his own sexual anxiety or his own satisfaction with other contraceptive methods. He should be so well informed that he recognizes whether his fears are irrational. This includes the fear of lawsuits, the fear of being held responsible for some neurotic problem in the patient, or for later regret.

A doctor generally asks himself: What could go wrong if I do this? The chances of something going wrong are well under 5 percent. He should ask himself: What could go wrong if I *don't* do this? The chances are far greater. They include continued discontent with present contraceptive methods, chronic anxiety about their failure, possible side effects of the pill or IUD and of course the chance of an unwanted child or abortion. The doctor cannot avoid a responsibility for saying no any more than for saying yes. If a doctor does not feel good about the procedure, he should send the patient to another physician.

Various papers about vasectomy clearly reveal the prejudices of many doctors. In some the writer assumes that all men will confuse vasectomy with castration. Another writer assumes that the motives are always neurotic. I read one paper in which the doctor deplored the performance of surgery on the man for the benefit of the wife. He stated, "In the male mind an unwanted pregnancy is still woman's misfortune alone." The erroneous assumption is often made that vasectomy must inevitably lead to lower self-esteem, and that the low incidence of regrets indicates overcompensation and denial.

In the case of tubal ligation for women (having tubes tied), the decision is complicated by the frequent addition of medical reasons, sometimes increasing conflict in the patient. An occasional doctor, unfortunately, has been influenced in his decision by emotions such as resentment against the cost of welfare. I should perhaps add sexism as well; for example, who ever heard of a male doctor advocating compulsory vasectomy for men who have fathered too many children?

I will briefly discuss what has been reported about the results of sterilization, as they affect attitudes and decisions.

The results of vasectomy have been described in many surveys which have been taken after the operation, generally by questionnaires and occasionally by interviewers.

I will simply mention the two largest and most recent reported studies, one of 1,012 men in England done by the Simon Population Trust in 1969, and the other of 401 men in Canada done in 1970. In England, 99.4 percent of the men had no regrets, 73 percent enjoyed increased sex pleasure and 1.5 percent decreased pleasure. In the latter group, many of these men still had no regrets. This important point has been made in other surveys also. In the Canadian study, the figures are very similar: 98 percent of the men would have the operation again, the same 73 percent had increased sexual pleasure, and 2 percent decreased. The health and sexual enjoyment of the wives improved even more than the husbands'. Very rarely a wife will report a new sexual problem for her after her husband's vasectomy. The work done by Drs. Ziegler and Rodgers covered a period of four years, and compared forty-two couples choosing vasectomy with forty-two couples choosing the pill. After one year, psychological tests revealed increased unconscious disturbance in the vasectomy men, though they were consciously very satisfied. Later this difference disappeared. Two of the vasectomy couples regretted their decision, but nearly half the women who were on the pill stopped taking it and chose another form of contraception.

We turn now to the results of female sterilization. Some sterilizations were by hysterectomy, some by tubal ligation. Many of the women were sterilized because of medical reasons, which rarely are an indication for vasectomy. In some cases the sterilization of women was combined with abortion, and it would be difficult to sort out the results. If a group has a high proportion of women for whom sterilization is recommended for psychiatric reasons, the results will probably be different. A well-educated person would undoubtedly respond differently than an ignorant one.

To get down to figures: When asked, "Do you regret the operation?" the "yes" responses ranged from 1 to 10 percent, except for one study in Sweden where the sterilizations were done mostly with abortions, and many for psychiatric reasons. Generally, regrets were higher after a hysterectomy. One possible explanation is that then there is no opportunity to fantasize a reversal, which many women otherwise do, and the absence of a menstrual period may increase a feeling of damage.

It's important to recognize that a women may regret her inability to have a child, but she still may not want more children. The survey with the lowest incidence of regret, 1 percent, was of one thousand women in Hong Kong studied by Lu. Apparently in Hong Kong sterilization is supposed to affect your temper and your memory, and 18 percent of them said that their tempers and memories and general health were worse, but this was a price they seemed willing to pay.

As far as sexual activity among women is concerned, diminished enjoyment in one form or another ran from about 3 percent to 24 percent. This rate was much higher than that in men. This seems to contradict a popular conception that males are more threatened by sterilization, and supports the assumption that the childbearing function is more important to women. In general, the large majority of women report improved health, better sex life and happier marriages. In any couple, which partner should be sterilized should be determined by individualized counseling, and the role relationships in the family also should be taken into consideration.

Any pressure by spouse or doctor must be avoided. Psychological aspects are as important as medical or practical ones.

CREDIT: *Helen Edey, M.D., treasurer of the Association for Voluntary Sterilization, New York, New York, also former Staff Psychiatrist at the Margaret Sanger Research Bureau, now retired.*

Stomach

The Nervous Stomach

The nervous stomach is more properly called irritable bowel syndrome. It is also known as "spastic colon," "spastic colitis," "mucous colitis" and "functional dyspepsia." This is not a diseased bowel but it can cause worrisome and even frightening symptoms. Fortunately, this condition is not life-threatening nor is it a sign that you are coming down with a serious illness.

In spite of the fact that all tests show the patient to be normal, he may have some very distressing symptoms. These symptoms are real and not "all in the head." If the upper intestinal tract is especially involved in the "nervous stomach" the individual may vomit or belch excessively. If the small bowel seems to be chiefly involved, the pain can be cramp-like or of almost any character, but often moves from one area of the abdomen to another.

If the lower bowel is involved with the irritable bowel symptoms (no disease) the individual may have loose and watery stools. These often occur soon after meals and perhaps may even interrupt a meal. In other instances, however, the patient may be constipated. Individuals who suffer excessively from these problems may need treatment by a trained physician if the pain becomes severe and interferes with the person's ability to work or enjoy life.

While the cause is not known, possible explanations are reasonable. The body is controlled by two types of nerves: (1) The conscious nervous system causes specific actions; for example, if one picks up a pencil from a table it may require the use of fifty muscles. The act is consciously performed. This is a function of the conscious nervous system. (2) The unconscious nervous system is just as important in the functions of the body and yet the individual can't control this nervous system. For example, if you should go to a funeral and the sermon is sad, you may weep. If you give a speech before a thousand people, your heart may beat fast, your hands may become moist and the paper might shake. You may even need to empty your bladder before going on the podium.

The gastrointestinal tract from our mouth to our rectum is controlled by the unconscious nervous system. We consciously have a little to do with chewing and swallowing our food. Actually, even this is for the most part unconscious, for we don't have to wonder where our tongue is while chewing. We do have a little control over emptying the bowel, but not total control. We have all heard the vulgar expression "It scared the ——— out of me." During World War II, pilots and crews of bombers on the way home from bombing Berlin often had diarrhea to such a degree that they would soil their clothing. Yet these men were chosen because they were considered the most emotionally stable individuals in our armed services.

At the other extreme it is not unusual to go on a trip and become constipated for a few days. The constipation was likely the result of the worry and tension of arranging the 101 little details that must be managed prior to leaving home, and after a few days, the bowel rights itself.

Another example: A perfectly healthy person may suddenly vomit if he comes upon an accident and sees blood and brains scattered over the sidewalk. Again—the body behaves in an "unusual way," but this does not represent disease.

It is important to know that these things can and do occur at times to all individuals. When, however, troublesome symptoms *persist* the patient has an irritable bowel syndrome. Sometimes this in inaccurately called spastic colitis.

The treatment of the irritable bowel syndrome is difficult and varies with the way the unconscious nervous system is having its effect. First, and perhaps most important, is that the patient understand and be assured that the problem is not due to disease. This is usually the major helpful factor and can be convincingly done after a thorough examination with history, physical examination, laboratory tests and X rays have proved normal. Second, everything possible must be planned to help the bowel perform normally. The individual should eat slowly, chew his food well, avoid eating when nervous, tense or tired, and eat three moderate-sized meals each day, at approximatly the same time. This helps give the intestinal tract a regular and consistent amount of work to perform. The type of food is usually not important. One day any food may cause trouble while the next the patient can eat anything without difficulty.

Six to eight glasses of water should be drunk each day, not more than one glass of liquid with each meal, so that the digestive juices will not be unduly diluted. The water should be drunk between the meals and not after 6 P.M. or the patient will have to get up to empty the bladder. The patient should plan to sit on the toilet each day at a regular time, preferably fifteen to thirty minutes after a meal.

The patient should be encouraged never to try to belch. The "belcher" will usually swallow consciously or unconsciously three times or so before belching. When he belches two swallows of air come up, but he is actually retaining one swallow. This occurs each time he belches and eventually the patient becomes distended, bloated and very uncomfortable from the swallowed air. This is called aerophagia.

It is very important for the individual with the irritable bowel syndrome to recognize that he is not very different from other individuals. If he is worried about his nervous stomach, the symptoms tend to increase. They do not, however, develop into cancer or any other serious disease.

A word of warning, however. While these symptoms do not turn into disease, the patient must be aware that he is not immune from getting something serious. If his symptoms change noticeably, he should consult a well-trained physician, preferably a gastroenterologist.

CREDIT: *James C. Cain, M.D., Gastroenterology and Internal Medicine, the Mayo Clinic, Rochester, Minnesota.*

Stress

Like death and taxes, everyone complains about the stress in their lives, yet few people understand what it is; much less do they attempt to reduce its ravages.

Dr. Hans Selye, a Vienna-born endocrinologist, is perhaps the world's foremost authority on stress—in fact, he is called "Dr. Stress." According to this renowned authority, the only way to avoid stress completely is to be dead. "Stress," he claims, "is part of the human condition."

The most frequent causes of stress are psychological, though our primitive ancestors had stress from physical causes and nature—like the fear of being eaten or carried away in a flood.

Modern stress comes from an inability to adapt to our surroundings and the demands of work or family. It can also come from setting up for ourselves standards which are unrealistic—impossible to attain. When we don't "measure up" we feel inadequate and even depressed.

Stress is often associated with the jobs of high-powered executives and professionals. As more and more women move into these roles, it is already evident that they will begin to suffer the same consequences as men, in terms of ulcers and coronary problems.

Stress itself is not a bad thing, but too much stress can shorten your life. The secret of coping with stress is not to avoid it but to alleviate it. Drugs can help if the stress is caused by a temporary problem or life change (divorce, death of a loved one, the loss of a job), but drugs can create additional stress if used as a cop-out.

In some instances, the answer may be change jobs—or careers. Too many people are doing things they really don't want to do or aren't equipped to do —simply because it makes sense economically or because they think it is expected of them by parents, spouses or peers.

Physical activity—tennis, swimming, squash, handball, bicycling, etc.—can help relieve stress, but it is seldom a solution to the problem. "The most important thing," says Dr. Selye, "is to have a code of life, to know how to live. Find yourself a port of destination—and practice what I call altruistic egoism." This means—set up goals which please your ego and yet have a redeeming or worthwhile element. Then go after goals that make you happy and perhaps help others as well. When you're sure of what you want, avoid distractions, detours and frustrations. Keep your eye on your goal and don't let anything sidetrack you.

Dr. Selye admits to being an egoist in this sense, but his altruistic goal is to acquire "as much goodwill and as many friends as possible." Too many people today measure their worth and self-esteem on making money. Consequently, they find themselves in stressful situations in pursuit of a goal that may be rubbing them the wrong way almost all of their lives.

But "you can invest in goodwill and friendship, too," says Dr. Selye. "If you are desired, if you are necessary, then you are safe."

Asked what he would say if he had to give a single piece of advice to people about stress, he replied: "I would offer the wisdom of the Bible translated into terms a scientist can easily accept today: 'Earn thy neighbor's love.'"

CREDIT: *Eugene Kennedy, Ph.D., Loyola University, Chicago, author of* Living with Everyday Problems, *Chicago, Illinois: Thomas More Association.*

Stretch Marks

The medical term for stretch marks is striae distensae—but no matter how fancy the handle, millions of women (and some men) hate the sight of the darned things and are willing to do almost anything to get rid of them.

There is no known way to get rid of stretch marks, but it might be of some comfort to know that time can be a friend. When they first appear they are purplish in color or pink—but after a few months the marks become lighter and lighter and eventually they are faint whitish streaks that can scarcely be seen.

Stretch marks can develop on the stomach (especially during and after pregnancy). They can show up on the breasts of nursing mothers, the buttocks, thighs and sometimes across the lower back, knees and elbows. They sometimes appear after a sudden weight gain or rapid growth and with the onset of Cushing's syndrome (a glandular problem). Any illness for which cortisone is used might produce this much dreaded "scarring."

About one out of three adolescents between ten and sixteen years of age develop stretch marks on the thighs, hips or stomach. Approximately three times as many girls get them as boys.

No one knows exactly how stretch marks are formed. The loss of the skin's elasticity has something to do with it. Hormones must also be a factor because of the frequent connection with pregnancy, puberty and cortisone. Heredity undoubtedly figures in somewhere. If stretch marks run in your family, you'll probably have them.

A common misconception is that you have to be fat and put tension on the skin to develop stretch marks. This is not true, witness the fact that many thin people have them also.

CREDIT: *Harry J. Hurley, M.D., Upper Darby, Pennsylvania.*

Stroke

Stroke and heart attack have much in common. The immediate cause of each is the same: The blood supply is reduced or cut off. If this occurs in the area of the heart, it's a heart attack. If it occurs in the head, it's a stroke.

A stroke may occur when the blood supply to a part of the brain is reduced or cut off for any reason—such as a blood clot, or a blood vessel becoming clogged or bursting.

The brain controls all bodily functions, from walking and talking to thinking and feeling. Therefore, a stroke can affect any part of the body, depending on the area of the brain deprived of an adequate supply of blood.

Common results of a stroke are paralysis of one side of the body and/or loss of speech. These and other effects may vary according to the individual and the kind of stroke.

The problems resulting from stroke may be slight or severe, temporary or permanent.

Stroke is a major killer and an even more serious crippler. It is estimated that about 700,000 persons in the U.S.A. suffer serious new strokes each year. About one third of these people die, and about half of those who survive suffer aftereffects that limit their lives. Fortunately, new treatments and preventive treatments in recent years have reduced some of the serious aftereffects and modern research promises even more hope for stroke victims in the future.

TYPES AND CAUSES OF STROKE

Strokes are of two main types, medically called ischemic and hemorrhagic.

Ischemic strokes are two or three times more common than hemorrhages. Ischemia means that the blood supply to the tissue becomes insufficient to meet the tissue's need for oxygen. When this occurs, the tissue dies. With ischemia, the individual usually suffers only a temporary neurological loss from which he may recover. This explains the improvement some people may show following a stroke.

Global ischemia results when the heart stops or the blood pressure falls to very low levels so that the circulation drops below what the whole brain needs to function. Although with a duration too brief to produce stroke, this is what happens when a person faints. To put it simply the blood pressure falls suddenly after an emotional or painful crisis and he loses consciousness. Because *some* circulation always continues during a fainting spell, the circulation to the brain almost immediately restores itself as soon as the patient becomes horizontal. More serious global ischemia occurs, however, during temporary standstill of the heart due to heart attacks, during severe blood loss or injury causing profound shock, or in the course of certain rare blood diseases where small clots plug the majority of blood vessels leading to the brain.

Regional ischemia to the brain occurs when one or more of the larger blood vessels become plugged and no longer can carry the brain's vital nourishment or drain its waste products. Trauma, inflammation or clotting abnormalities can sometimes cause such obstructions. Much more commonly, however, such closures result from arteriosclerosis, also known as hardening of the arteries, a process which thickens the arterial wall and piles up cholesterol and other chemicals in plaques on the inside of the wall so as to narrow and eventually close the opening. Blood products normally designed to provide for the healing of wounds fasten themselves onto the area of arteriosclerotic plaques and sometimes contribute the final step in closure. In this special instance, the intent on healing actually makes matters worse: The vessel itself can completely close off or a piece of the plaque plus the repair products can break off. Such pieces can then wash downstream to a smaller artery and plug it off. These fragments drifting through the arterial stream to a distant artery are called *emboli*. The most common source of emboli causing stroke probably is from these plaques in the large arteries in the neck that lead to the brain. Removal of such plaques reduces the risk of such emboli and stroke.

Cerebral hemorrhage occurs mainly in older persons and results when a once normal artery in the brain ruptures. Such arteries gradually lose their resistance as the result of years of wear and tear caused by arteriosclerosis, hypertension and aging. As the artery leaks, blood escapes into the brain under more or less pressure, depending on the size of the hole in the artery and the efficiency of local repair factors.

Occasionally, as in hemophilia or leukemia, abnormalities in the blood itself may cause a hemorrhage. Less often, such hemorrhages can result from inborn abnormalities in the arteries, called aneurisms. The seriousness of the accompanying stroke depends on where the hemorrhage occurs, that is whether it damages critical neurological centers such as those controlling speech, movement and consciousness and how big it becomes. Large cerebral hemorrhages often are fatal. Although hemorrhages into the brain sometimes are treated surgically, there is little evidence that such procedures are helpful.

Cause of stroke. Most strokes occur in persons over fifty years of age and are due to the interrelated disorders of atherosclerosis and hypertension. Atherosclerosis is caused by diabetes, certain inherited abnormalities of fat metabolism, and some mysterious factors which may cause the blood vessels to overreact to infections and aging. High blood pressure also produces its own special damaging effects on blood vessels, since the arteries must gradually thicken to meet the higher pressure and this thickening can eventually lead to closure. As one might expect, hypertension accelerates the time when weak vessels blow out. Both cigarette smoking and the use of contraceptive pills contribute in a small but important way to the risk of stroke. These risks are substantially accentuated in persons with a history of diabetes, heart attack, high blood pressure or migraine headaches.

There are many less frequent causes of stroke including congenital and acquired heart disease, diseases of the blood cells or blood coagulation mechanisms, inflammation of the arteries and, rarely, even severe migraine.

BEHAVIORAL CHANGES

A patient who has had a recent stroke will often show partial loss of his emotional control. He may switch from laughing to crying without apparent reason. The most frequent problem seems to be crying. Sometimes the stroke patient will cry because he is depressed.

Certainly most stroke patients will have considerable reason to be depressed. Depression is a natural response to loss of ability or any abrupt change in life. Often excessive crying by the stroke patient is due to the brain damage he has experienced and is not directly connected with his perceived losses.

It is usually possible to tell the difference between loss of emotional control due to brain damage and sadness due to depression. When brain damage is the cause, the patient may begin weeping for no reason whatsoever. He will stop weeping abruptly if his attention is diverted. Diversion can be accomplished by snapping the fingers and calling his name—or asking him a simple question. Unexpected laughter, flares of angers or moaning usually can be interrupted by using the same tactics. On the other hand, crying caused by depression is not easy to interrupt.

Do not make the mistake of thinking that when the stroke patient is crying he is terribly sad or when he is laughing he is particularly happy. Even patients who behave as if they were angry will later express surprise that they "flew off the handle."

HOW YOU CAN HELP

Some memory problems can be expected in most stroke patients. When working with memory deficits, you can often increase the patient's ability to perform if you:
(1) Establish a fixed routine whenever possible.
(2) Keep messages short to fit his retention span.
(3) Present new information one step at a time.
(4) Allow the patient to finish one step before proceeding to the next.
(5) Give frequent indications of effective progress; he may forget his past "successes."
(6) Train in settings that resemble, as much as possible, the setting in which the behavior is to be practiced.
(7) Use memory aids such as appointment books, written notes and schedule cards whenever possible.
(8) Use familiar objects and old associations when teaching new tasks.

TREATMENT

Treatment of acute stroke is based on three principles: (1) prevent the stroke from enlarging or recurring; (2) correct or prevent complications; (3) aid in the restoration of neurological function.

Preventing strokes from enlarging is largely a matter of medical therapy. Appropriately selected patients with evolving strokes are given intravenous anticoagulants to stop the progress of the thrombotic process. The same treatment generally is employed for patients with progressive vertebro-basilar strokes. If the blood pressure is high, it should be brought to ranges more near normal. When transient ischemic attacks are present, oral anticoagulants usually help, assuming no complicating illness sets in. Drugs that counteract the aggregation of platelet cells in the blood also may be useful. Most patients with acute stroke receive oxygen to aid the threatened brain. Few, if any, acute strokes can be treated surgically.

Prevention. The single most important measure in preventing stroke is to treat hypertension. At all ages, the presence of hypertension correlates with an increased incidence of stroke and, usually, the higher the pressure the greater the risk. Effective treatment that reduces the blood pressure back toward normal reduces this risk, no matter at what age the treatment is begun. Some evidence even suggests that lowering the blood pressure after the first stroke prevents against future strokes.

Obesity is a risk almost equal to hypertension. For one thing, being overweight brings on both high blood pressure and diabetes prematurely. Put another way, how many healthy fat old people do you know?

Those who smoke face an increased risk of stroke at all ages as opposed to those who do not. Women taking contraceptive pills, especially if there is a history of migraine, should recognize that if they also smoke their risk of stroke is four to six times higher than that of their contemporaries who avoid these risks.

Other risk factors are harder to counteract. Evidence is controversial, but other than keeping the weight down and exercising regularly there probably is little one can do to stave off the ravages of diabetes and inherited diseases of fat metabolism. Nevertheless, even these steps are important, and together with attention to the ones above they have already begun to reduce the incidence of stroke in this country.

CREDIT: *Fred Plum, M.D., Department of Neurology, New York Hospital-Cornell Medical Center, New York.*

Stuttering

Stuttering is the act of speaking with involuntary, spasmodic halts, breaks, repetition of syllables and sounds. Over two million people in the United States stutter—approximately 1 percent of the population.

The stutterer is often embarrassed by his inability to get his words out smoothly, and for this reason, some stutterers are reluctant to speak. This handicap can create serious employment problems as well as social problems.

According to Dr. Dorvan Breitenfeldt, a speech pathologist at Eastern Washington State College in Cheney, Washington, Winston Churchill, one of the greatest orators of our time, was once a stutterer. So was Moses, Aristotle and Demosthenes. Historically, stutterers come from all social and economic classes. Dr. Breitenfeldt claims that 85 percent of all stutterers can conquer the handicap for life. The major determinant is the stutterer's wish to do so. (Dr. Breitenfeldt himself is a former stutterer.)

The cause of stuttering has been a matter of continuing controversy among the specialists for a long time. Some say it is the result of an organic brain disease or a psychological defect. Others say it is a psychic condition produced by anxiety or the fear of not being permitted to speak one's mind. It occurs more frequently in males, in individuals who are twins and in those who are left-handed.

According to Linda Swisher, Ph.D., director of Northwestern University Speech and Language Clinics in Chicago, many children go through a normal stage of stuttering when they first learn to speak. They often outgrow it as they acquire better speaking skills. During this time, parents and siblings should treat the stutterer naturally and wait for him to complete his sentences.

Dr. Swisher added that brothers and sisters should be prohibited by their parents from laughing at a stutterer. It should be viewed as a handicap, and not funny. The stuttering child should *not* be told, "Stop stuttering," or "Start again and speak more slowly." No notice should be taken of his stuttering. He should be protected against interruption by others, especially in school and at the dinner table. The teacher or parent should say, "Please let Johnny finish what he is saying."

If, however, a child (as early as age three) begins to exhibit symptoms of serious frustration, he should be taken to a speech therapist. The goal of the therapist would be to decrease the stuttering behavior before secondary characteristics develop. Secondary characteristics are blinking of the eyes, or a refusal to look at the person to whom he is speaking, stamping of feet and the failure to properly control breathing.

If a child's stuttering persists beyond twelve years of age, he needs speech therapy. The best way to contact a speech therapist is by calling the speech department of the nearest college or university.

If there is no college or university in your vicinity, write to: American Speech and Hearing Association, 9030 Old Georgetown Road, Washington, D.C. 20014. The telephone number is: (301) 530-3400.

CREDIT: *Ann Landers*

Success

Success is a word for which there could be a thousand definitions. A great many people equate success with money. Almost always, these people are of modest means. My mail bears strong testimony to the fact that there are millions of affluent "failures" and an equal number of "successes" who have nothing in the bank.

This definition for success was written in 1904 by Bessie Anderson Stanley from Lincoln, Kansas. She was paid $250 for this prize-winning essay.

"He has achieved success who has lived well, laughed often and loved much; who has enjoyed the trust of pure women, the respect of intelligent men and the love of little children; who has filled his niche and accomplished his task; who has left the world better than he found it, whether by an improved poppy, a perfect poem or a rescued soul; who has never lacked appreciation of earth's beauty or failed to express it; who has always looked for the best in others and given them the best he had; whose life was an inspiration; whose memory a benediction."

CREDIT: *Ann Landers.*

Suicide Among Adults

Each year twice as many Americans kill themselves as kill each other. Currently suicide is listed as the tenth most common cause of death. Experts estimate the number of deaths caused by suicide to be approximately 25,000 a year. They say, however, that the incidence is undoubtedly far higher because it is so difficult to obtain accurate data. For a suicide to be recorded, there must be undeniable evidence that the person intentionally killed himself. It is well known, however, that numerous "accidents" have earmarks of at least unconscious self-destruction. Many experts estimate that the actual figures for suicide may be more than twice the number recorded.

The World Health Organization places the United States far behind world suicide leaders—Hungary, Austria, Czechoslovakia, Sweden, Finland, Denmark and West Germany. The WHO qualifies this placement by noting that these countries may simply be keeping the most unbiased and accurate records.

There are certain trends in the statistics that should be mentioned. For many years, it was noted that men were three times more likely to commit suicide than women. Recent research indicates that this trend may be changing, moving toward a more equal proportion between the sexes.

The suicide rate rises steadily with men as they increase in age, while the rate for women levels off by about age seventy. Another particularly vulnerable age group is those fifteen to twenty-four years of age. In the past the rate of Caucasian suicides far outnumbered the Negro, and Gentiles far outnumbered Jews, but again, there is evidence that these groups seem to be moving closer together in this regard.

In our society, it is the most affluent, and presumably most "successful," who show the highest suicide rates. They are professional and managerial people, businessmen and executives. Doctors and dentists have more than double the rate of the general population (no doubt in part because they have easier access to large doses of fatal drugs). The rate for married people is far lower than for single, widowed or divorced—in fact, one fourth of all suicides had been living alone, compared with only 7 percent of the general population who live alone.

Contrary to popular belief, about 70 percent of persons who threaten suicide actually make the attempt; the warning is a cry for help, and not merely a bid for attention. Only about 15 percent leave suicide notes. In most cases, these notes express love or hate, the desire for revenge and the wish to be loved after death.

Suicide which is disguised and attributed to some other cause can take many forms. Self-destructive behavior can be manifested through starvation, excessive eating, excessive smoking, alcoholism and refusal to take prescribed medication. It is often impossible to tell whether a person fell or jumped from a high place. In this same category are drowning, reckless automobile driving, unskilled use of potentially dangerous tools, failure to carry out lifesaving medical procedures, inviting murder in any number of bizarre ways, burning to death in a fire and inviting lethal bites by poisonous snakes or spiders.

Most people who try to kill themselves are rescued by friends and treated by the family doctor, if at all. They return to their routines hoping to avoid the public record—with good reason. Suicide is still a crime in eight states; and the religious still regard taking one's life as a sin against God; and whether or not suicide can occur among mentally healthy persons is still a debate within the medical profession.

Helen Epstein, a member of the journalism faculty at New York University, wrote in the New York *Times Magazine* in a piece titled "Suicide—A Sin or a Right?":*

"The traditional profile of the American suicide has been . . . a relatively successful, white, middle-aged man with a wife and children whose chances of killing himself rose gradually through middle age and then precipitously after the age of sixty. This kind of man committed suicide in droves in 1933 and set the all-time American record. But, like all composites, the profile obscured a more complex reality. The incidence of suicide has always been greatest among people of any sex, age or racial group who have made previous attempts on their lives. Women (using drugs, poisons, gas) have traditionally attempted suicide three times as often as men. Men (using violent means like hanging, jumping or shooting) have actually died by suicide three times as often as women. Traditional explanations for the 3 to 1 ratio of male to female suicides have centered around the theme of men being both more decisive and more efficient than women. The highest-risk age group has been the elderly, who account for about 25 percent of all suicides in the United States. Among ethnic groups, the American Indian has led all others with a rate that is twice the national average, and on some reservations, five or six times that.

* Copyright © 1974 by The New York Times Company. Reprinted by permission.

"These trends have not been difficult for researchers to explain. Suicide among the elderly has been attributed to decline in status, income, power, health and mobility in a culture which glorifies all these qualities. The desire to end a serious illness, or to die before succumbing to one, swells the ranks of elderly suicides."

Because suicide is a complex human act and because it can touch everyone's life at one time or another, both laymen and professionals constantly search for understanding.

No one really knows why human beings commit suicide. They have been doing so for as long as history has been recorded. Edwin Shneidman, Ph.D., one of the foremost suicidologists in the country, has noted, "A dozen people can shoot themselves through the head and subsequent psychological autopsies would reveal that they participated in a dozen different descriptive events. One was escaping from pain, another was afraid of going insane, a third acted on impulse after a quarrel, a fourth hoped to join a loved one in the hereafter, a fifth was punishing his parents and so on. But every case of overt self-destruction involves the presence of unbearable anguish."

Some of the more familiar psychological theories regarding suicide have been listed by Herbert Hendin, M.D. These include:

(1) *Death as retaliatory abandonment.* In such instances, the suicide is a way of getting back—the suicide "leaves" or abandons the loved or cherished person in order to pay back a felt rejection by that person. "You leave me, I'll leave you by killing myself. Then you'll be sorry."

(2) *Death as retroflexed murder.* This involves situations where the person says, "I'm so angry at you I could kill you. However, that's unacceptable so I'll kill myself." Then he or she does.

(3) *Death as a Reunion.* Here the emphasis is not so much on dying, but on how pleasant the reunion with the deceased loved one will be after death is accomplished. Fantasies of this kind are often verbally expressed by psychotic individuals and should be taken very seriously.

(4) *Death as rebirth.* One's life may be so tragic and miserable that dying may be seen as a way to "start over with a new life."

(5) *Death as self-punishment.* This occurs when a person fails to achieve a goal or level of success which he considers extremely important in his life's plan. The person feels like a failure, and decides that he or she needs to be punished. The ultimate punishment is death.

How do average laymen deal with the possibility that one of their associates or close family members may be experiencing such thoughts? There are a few basic principles that are well known among professionals and others who have worked with suicidal persons. The first is that (1) some people who commit suicide (they are a small percentage, but they cannot be ignored) do not give off *any* signals that they are contemplating suicide; and (2) if a person truly wants to kill himself he will find a way to do it despite the efforts of those around to save him.

There are specific clues to a potential suicide with which the average person should have some familiarity. The professional evaluates suicidal risk in terms of a number of factors. As these factors weigh more heavily, the risk is thought to be greater.

(1) *Age and sex*. The potential is greater for men than women and greater over age fifty.

(2) *Marital status*. The potential is greater for divorced, widowed and single persons than for married, especially those married who have children. In other words, the less interpersonal support, the greater the potential.

(3) *Symptoms*. The potential is greater if the person is depressed, has severe insomnia, is alcoholic or has homosexual conflicts.

(4) *Stress*. The potential is greater if the person is under severe stress.

(5) *Acute versus chronic*. The potential is greater if there is a sudden onset of specific symptoms.

(6) *Suicidal plan*. If the person has a detailed plan, the potential is greater than if the suicidal thoughts are vague.

(7) *Previous suicide attempt*. The risk is greater if the person has acted on suicidal impulses previously.

(8) *Medical status*. If the person is suffering from a chronic disease or has the potential of a chronically debilitating illness, the risk is greater.

(9) *Communication aspects*. If the person feels rejected by others or feels there is no outlet for his distress, the potential is higher.

(10) *Family history*. If there is a history of suicide in the family— especially a same-sexed parent—the risk increases.

The evaluation of suicidal potential is a risky business for even the experienced professional. The basic principle is that if a person has serious reason to suspect that someone may commit suicide, he or she should attempt to get the person to accept professional help during the critical period. Since most people are ambivalent about taking their own lives, strategic care can be most helpful and even lifesaving. A certain few will say no to any efforts to help them, and this also must be recognized. This is the most frustrating aspect of dealing with suicidal persons. Moreover, suicide can occur even among those who get help.

It is for most people literally unthinkable that someone close to them would feel the need to take his own life. It is, in fact, difficult for most people even to acknowledge that they themselves have had suicidal thoughts.

How then can one comfort oneself and those persons who are close after a suicide has occurred? The natural response to any major life event, whether it is failing an examination, experiencing a divorce or suffering a severe business loss, is to go over in one's mind again and again the particulars of the event, in an attempt to make sense out of it, and make it a "part" of one's self. Negative events are far more difficult to integrate because the pain is so great.

The most difficult and painful emotion subsequent to a suicide or suicidal attempt is the feeling of guilt engendered in those who are left. It is generally an irrational feeling. A survivor may have read some of the signs, consulted, urged treatment and, in fact, may have seen that the person was hospitalized in a protected environment, but the suicide occurred anyway. At this point, survivors must strive to be more kind and less self-punishing toward themselves. This is, in fact, the most reasonable and constructive response to a suicide.

A great many spouses, parents and siblings suffer tremendous guilt when a suicide occurs, believing that they were insensitive to the "signs." They torture themselves with the thought that had they been more caring or alert, they could have prevented the loved one from committing suicide.

When these individuals find life joyless—when they isolate themselves from others, refuse social invitations and avoid seeing persons who remind them of the deceased—in other words, when depression hangs on and cannot be shaken, professional help should be sought.

Survivors often need outside counseling so that they can verbalize their feelings and obtain emotional support that comes from ventilation. Moreover, the feedback from the professional, hopefully, will help them understand that they were not responsible for the tragedy, and that life is for the living.

CREDIT: *Sara Charles, M.D., Assistant Professor of Psychiatry, Abraham Lincoln School of Medicine, University of Illinois in Chicago.*

SUICIDE AS FAST RELIEF . . .

DEAR ANN LANDERS: I disagree with the person who referred to suicide as a planned maneuver to cause suffering or punish others. Suicide is an uncontrollable gut-level emotional urge to find relief. It is saying, "I'm not good enough. I'm trouble. My loved ones would be better off without me."

To those who are contemplating suicide, let me say this: Nothing is worth killing yourself over. Give yourself time. Remember that old cliché, "There is nothing to fear but fear itself." Almost always the fear is worse than the problem. Any problem. ONE WHO KNOWS

DEAR ONE: The next letter may be of interest to you. Please read on.
. . . OR FAIR SOLUTION

DEAR ANN LANDERS: This is for the person who said, "Those who commit suicide are full of hate (often self-directed), and they want to put an end to their lives in order to punish someone for a real (or imagined) injustice. ('You'll be sorry for the way you treated me.')" That writer was violently one-sided in his appraisal.

I have contemplated suicide many times. I'm in my 50's now, and I hate nobody. Nor would I kill myself to make someone sorry they treated me badly. In fact, I can't think of anyone who has. My family and friends always have been patient and considerate.

I've had a great deal of counseling over a period of years, but it hasn't helped. I guess I'm just tired of swimming against the tide. I'm exhausted and depressed because I can't seem to make anything work. I seem to be fighting a losing battle on every front. Life is joyless. I'm not being fair to my family because I'm a drag—a pessimist, a kill-joy. I believe the world would be better off without me. I contribute nothing.

So please, Ann, print this letter in case I do it one day. I'd hate to have those near and dear to me think I took my life to punish them. They don't deserve to carry such guilt. A LONG-TIME READER.

DEAR READER: Get a little more counseling, please, and a physical examination as well. There might be an organic reason for your depression. You sound like such a gentle soul. The world does need you—whether you think so or not. Stick around. I care.

DECEPTIVE PRACTICES

DEAR ANN LANDERS: The letter about suicide stirred many emotions in me. I identified strongly with the writer because many years ago I seriously considered suicide. Thank God I came to my senses in time.

Every now and then someone we know takes his (or her) life and all the relatives, friends and neighbors are shocked. That individual appeared to be so content, so fortunate. He seemed to have everything a person could want or hope for.

Will you please print this poem by Edward Arlington Robinson? It has a lesson in it for all of us.

Whenever Richard Cory went
  downtown,
  We people on the pavement looked
  at him.
He was a gentleman from sole to
  crown,
  Clean favored, and imperially slim.
And he always was quietly arrayed,
  And he was always human when he
  talked;
  But still he fluttered pulses when he
  said,

"Good morning," and he glittered
  when he walked.
And he was rich—yes, richer than a
  king.
  And admirably schooled in every
  grace;
In fine, we thought that he was
  everything
  To make us wish that we were in
  his place.
So on we worked, and waited for the
  light,
  And went without the meat, and
  cursed the bread;
And Richard Cory, one calm, summer
  night,
  Went home and put a bullet
  through his head.

A FRIEND OF YOURS

DEAR FRIEND: I first came across that poem when I was a high school freshman. It stopped me dead in my tracks. It did so again 40 years later and I thank you for the enriching experience.

Suicide in Children and Adolescents

American children and adolescents enjoy better health today than ever before in our history because of improved living standards and advances in medical care. With the gradual elimination of many of the dread diseases of the past, the major threats to life in the 1970s are deaths from violence: accidents, homicide and suicide. Throughout the age span from one to twenty-four, accidents are by far the leading cause of death, accounting for approximately one half of all deaths.

Suicides are rare before age ten, still quite uncommon from ten to fourteen, but for the age range from fifteen to twenty-four, suicides are the third leading cause of death for males (after accidents and homicides) and the fourth for females (after accidents, cancers and homicides). The over-all death rate between fifteen and twenty-four for males (192 out of 100,000) is much higher than that for females (69 out of 100,000), primarily because of much higher rates for violent deaths (four times higher for accidents and three times higher for homicide and suicides).

Particularly alarming is the fact that suicide rates for both males and females have been steadily increasing for the last twenty-five years as indicated in the following table based on the latest data from the National Center for Health Statistics. (Suicide rates for the age range five to nine are not tabulated separately in national mortality statistics; the relative rarity of suicide in this age group results in too high an unreliability in computed rates.)

MALE SUICIDE RATES PER 100,000

Year	Age Group		
	10–14	15–19	20–24
1950	0.5	3.5	9.3
1960	0.9	5.6	11.5
1970	0.9	8.8	19.3
1975	1.2	12.2	26.4

FEMALE SUICIDE RATES PER 100,000

Year	Age Group		
	10–14	*15–19*	*20–24*
1950	0.1	1.8	3.3
1960	0.2	1.6	2.9
1970	0.3	2.9	5.7
1975	0.4	2.9	6.8

It should be emphasized that these tables present *minimum* incidence figures. For a death to be officially designated a suicide, proof that the suicide was intentional is required. Thus, a death from a poisoning, "falling" out of a window, gunshot or deliberate automobile accident will not be included in the statistics if a suicidal note or statement is not noted by—or reported to—authorities. Moreover, well-meaning physicians and coroners may label a known suicide as an accident in order to spare the family embarrassment. It has been estimated that actual suicide rates may be twice as high as reported rates.

In all age groups, in all countries, and for all periods for which data are available, males consistently outnumber females by about three to one in *completed suicides*. On the other hand, reports of *suicide attempts* are consistently higher for females by three to one or more. The reports of attempts are based primarily on records from hospital emergency rooms. Consequently, they grossly understate the frequency of suicide attempts since those which can be managed out of the hospital (probably the majority) are not included. It has been estimated that the ratio of attempts to completions in young people is one hundred to one.

Efforts to understand why young people kill themselves are mostly based on unsuccessful suicides since the individuals are still alive to be interviewed. When death has occurred, the attempt to reconstruct motives is limited to written notes, reported conversations with friends and relatives, and medical records, for those individuals under care prior to death.

In such psychological autopsies, the investigator frequently discovers a history of suicide in family members or close friends. In part, this indicates a family pattern of reacting to failure or disappointment. Most suicides have displayed a recent change in behavior (despondent mood, inability to concentrate, truancy from school). Careful inquiry usually identifies a precipitating event such as school failure, rejection by a lover or a humiliating disciplinary episode. Finally, completed suicide requires access to lethal means: poisons or weapons in the household and a long enough period without supervision to make their use possible.

Children do not fully comprehend the permanency of death. Suicide attempts are sometimes intended to "change things"—to make parents or others regret the error of their ways in the fantasy that he will be treated better when he awakens. The thought process resembles Mark Twain's account of Tom Sawyer attending his own funeral. However unrealistic the premises on which it is based, the suicide attempt is a statement of personal agony. Moreover, it carries a serious risk of death because children (and adolescents) are poor judges of the permanency of the act. The relative rarity of suicide under age ten reflects, among other facts, limited access to means of suicide, less ability to plan ahead and to manage lethal instruments, and fewer long periods of despondency.

Among adolescents, a frequent motive for the suicide attempt is the effort to manipulate or punish significant others (parents, boyfriends or girlfriends, teachers). A common fantasy is: "You'll be sorry you were so mean to me after I'm dead." Anger as a prominent element in adolescent suicide has been emphasized by studies in England and in the United States. Many of the children whose histories were studied had exhibited behavior disorder, school difficulties and runaways *prior* to the attempt. Most had either talked about suicide or threatened suicide in the days and weeks before the event. Among the older adolescents, depression, similar in nature but different in its manifestations to depression among adults, was a prominent underlying feature. Such youngsters feel unwanted and unloved, come to regard themselves as bad or "inferior." They decide that death is the only way out.

There is no "treatment" for suicide. What is needed is a program for prevention; that is, (1) the creation of conditions which will minimize misery and despair and (2) the prompt response to threats and attempts at suicide by acting to change the feelings which provoked the behavior. Because the majority of attempters do give warning, there is almost always an opportunity to intervene. It may be difficult to predict risk accurately, but there are general principles which appear to be valid. Since the hazard is great if risk is underestimated, it is far better to err on the side of caution.

Talk of suicide or threats of suicide should always be taken seriously. At the least, they represent an important message from the child about the intensity of experienced despair; at the most, they warn of an impending event. As noted earlier, *most suicides do give warning.* We must not deceive ourselves into believing that most people who talk about suicide don't actually try it, and be fooled by the fact that most who try it fail. The warning must be heeded because it is from among this group that fatalities occur. If a youngster's attempt at suicide leads to a family response which manifests love and concern, peace of mind and a sense of well-being can be restored. This opens a new opportunity for growth toward health.

Every suicide attempt is a medical emergency. Once medical measures have removed the immediate threat to life, the next pressing question that must be answered is whether hospitalization is necessary. The decision rests upon weighing the balance between two sets of factors: the degree of risk in the youngster and the family's ability to provide emotional support. The degree of risk can be estimated from (1) the deadliness of the method the patient had employed, compared to (2) the evidence for a wish to be rescued.

(1) Thus, the use of guns, rope or major poisons indicates a more serious wish to die than the taking of aspirin or superficial cuts at the wrist with a kitchen knife. However, one must be careful not to mistake an objective assessment of the lethality of the method for the logic of the youngster's decision. That is, the child's ignorance of risk may dictate a choice that does not reflect his intent. He may use a drug which is fatal without realizing its toxicity; or he may survive when death was intended because the amount used was insufficient.

(2) Most suicides are ambivalent; that is, along with the wish to die, there is a hope of being saved. The wish for rescue can be estimated from the extent to which warning had been given and the choice of circumstances to permit discovery in time. For example, the patient who chooses a time when the family is out of the home and not likely to return for several hours has a more serious intent than the one who makes a dramatic gesture when parents are home and who calls attention to his actions.

If the weight of the risk/rescue ratio is on the rescue side of the fraction *and* the parent or parents show understanding and concern, psychiatric treatment on an out-patient basis without hospitalization can be undertaken. But if the parents are indifferent, or worse yet, if they are angry and show no understanding of the youngster's distress and fail to be supportive, then hospital treatment will be urgent even if the first suicide attempt appeared relatively minor. The failure of the gesture to arouse genuine concern may serve to confirm the patient's worst fears—that he is unloved. This often brings on a repetition of the attempt—with a fatal outcome.

After the acute suicidal situation has been dealt with, the focus must be placed on treatment. For those patients in whom depressive disease is diagnosed (a minority of the young) antidepressant medication will be necessary. But medication, even when it is indicated, is only one element in the treatment process. What is essential is the rebuilding of hope and self-confidence and the establishment of healthier ties among family members. Because the patient feels unloved and unworthy of love, the task of treatment is to convey a sense of caring and to restore faith in the possibility of a satisfying future.

SUMMARY

Threats of suicide and attempts at suicide are cries for help. If heard, they offer a major opportunity to reverse a potentially lethal situation. When family and friends rally to the side of the previously despondent individual and provide a network of emotional support, good mental health can be restored with psychiatric help. That suicide rates among adolescents are increasing can only reflect our failure as a society to meet the psychological needs of our young people. Fundamental remedies will require: (1) social supports to preserve the integrity of the family, (2) improvements in educational and vocational opportunities for the young and (3) re-creating a sense of national purpose so that young people feel needed and wanted.

CREDIT: *Leon Eisenberg, M.D., Harvard Medical School, Children's Hospital Medical Center, Boston, Massachusetts.*

An Additional Thought by Ann Landers

I cannot imagine a more tragic experience than to lose a child. We expect our parents to die before we do. The loss of a brother or a sister can be heartbreaking. To lose a beloved spouse can be extremely difficult. But to lose a child must be the most wrenching experience of all.

When that child dies by his own hand the agony and the feelings of guilt—the unanswered questions—the list of "if only's" must be a mile long.

Suicides among young people are on the increase (over four thousand last year) and the reasons are many. The majority of teen suicides are in some way related to drug abuse and alcohol. Then there is the pressure of school—feeling that it is *so* important to get good grades in order to gain admittance to the so-called "better" colleges, medical and law schools. How sad. In many instances, a less prestigious school would have been the "better" choice.

Whatever the reason, the parents of a suicide child need all the emotional support they can get. If I could speak to these parents I would tell them that no one knows for sure why some children can live through the most harrowing experiences, unscarred, and others cannot face the stresses of everyday life without cracking up.

We have known for a long time that children have different thresholds of pain. And so it is with stress. I believe that some children have a death wish from an early age on—and nothing you could have done would have changed the situation. So stop punishing yourselves with afterthoughts of what you did wrong. All parents make mistakes, and strangely enough, some parents who make the worst mistakes have the best-adjusted children. Their kids turn out just fine. In fact, they became stronger and tougher because they were knocked around and had no one to lean on.

The parents I have known whose children were suicides were all fine people who loved their children and gave them a great deal of themselves—maybe too much. Almost all of these children had professional help. In the final analysis nothing could save them because they did not want to be saved. No one knows why. And they never will.

More on Teenage Suicide

According to the U. S. Public Health Service, the rate of suicide among fifteen- to twenty-four-year-olds has risen by almost 300 percent in just twenty years. It has almost doubled in the past ten years. Between 1974 and 1975—the latest statistics available—the suicide rate rose by a walloping 10 percent.

According to the Federal Bureau of Vital Statistics, more than four thousand teenagers kill themselves every year. Officials make it clear that at least twice as many go unreported—hidden by parents and disguised as accidents.

Drug abuse, alcoholism, increase in violent crime, the ever-rising divorce rates, disintegration of the family, pressure to engage in sex at an earlier age, competition for places in the so-called "better schools"—all this has placed a great deal of added pressure on teenagers.

Studies of youthful victims who died by their own hand show that only a small proportion are psychotic or medically insane. Most of them suffer from loneliness, feelings of hopelessness and despair. Suicidal people are torn between wanting to live and feeling they have nothing to live for.

How can you tell when an adolescent is becoming suicidal? The most obvious clue is severe and continuing depression. They become gloomy, uncommunicative, down in the dumps, despondent, preferring to be by themselves for hours or days at a time—or even weeks.

The best way to help such a person is to let him (or her) know you are aware of a change in behavior—and are concerned. Ask if he wants to talk about something that is troublesome. Try to break through the wall of isolation. Maybe he will reject you completely, but then again, he may open up.

Try to get such a person to seek professional help. Temporary medication may be immensely useful. Or perhaps some minor physical problem, unattended, has caused at least part of the depression. The important thing is not to ignore such a person. Let him know he is not alone—that somebody cares.

The most difficult aspect of teenage suicide is the guilt felt by parents and often brothers and sisters. They ask themselves, "Why didn't I see the signs? If only I knew he (or she) was so desperate I could have helped." Some of the most heartbreaking letters I receive are from parents whose children have taken their own lives.

I tell these parents that they must accept in life that which they cannot change. Often the child harbored dark notions of suicide in the deepest recesses of his mind from an early age, and nurtured a sick preoccupation with death. In such instances, nothing could have changed the course of that child's life.

A great many things occur that do not add up. They make no sense. We must accept them and not drive ourselves crazy looking for logical answers to questions relating to senseless behavior.

Some of the finest people I know have lost children through suicide. They were devoted and loving parents—and their lives were torn apart by the tragedy. I can only say, there are some mysteries in life that are and will remain forever unsolvable. You did your best—and all of us, being imperfect, make mistakes. Carry on—look forward, not back.

CREDIT: *Ann Landers.*

Sunburn

Does soaking up the rays of a blazing sun make you feel healthy, young and full of vitality? Are you a sun worshiper who regards bronzed skin as a status symbol of the leisure life? There are countless reasons for exposing oneself to the sun. Some must do it as part of a job—lifeguards, farmers, fishermen, etc., but those who do it for cosmetic reasons rarely realize that in the long run, unless they are extremely careful, they will pay a heavy price for that "healthy" glow.

Carefully weigh the facts about sunlight and your skin. You may become convinced (as are most medical experts) that the benefits of the sun's rays are mostly psychological and heavily outweighed by the damage. Too much sun during the teen years and early twenties can make a woman, at forty, look like sixty. It can also cause skin cancer, which resulted in the deaths of 5,300 people in 1977. Know the facts and decide just how much sun is best for you.

Consider the time of day if you decide to sunbathe. The sun's rays are most potent between 10 A.M. and 2 P.M. when the sun is directly overhead. During these hours you are most likely to tan or burn. On the other hand, there is little chance of doing either if your sun exposure is before 8 A.M. or after 4 P.M.

Atmospheric conditions also play a role in determining how the sun affects your skin. Many people feel they won't burn if the sun isn't shining brightly. Not true. The most vicious sunburns occur on overcast days, particularly in a fog, when people believe the sun isn't very hot because they can't see it.

Altitude is a factor, too. At high altitudes there is less atmosphere to filter the sun's ultraviolet rays. This is important for skiers to remember. Snow can act as a reflector and intensify the rays' penetration. Sand on the beach can do the same thing.

It is a mistake to think a covering such as a beach umbrella will protect you from the sun. Because of sky radiation, ultraviolet waves radiate from all sides, and can easily get at you even if you are under an umbrella. To make matters worse, the heating rays of the sun, which ordinarily warn of too much overexposure, are reduced under an umbrella and you could get burned without realizing it.

The environmental factors mentioned above are important in determining how the sun affects you, but they are only part of the story. The rest depends on what type of skin you have.

The more pigment in your skin, the more protection you have against sunburn. (But blacks can and do get sunburned if they expose themselves to too much sun.)

If your first exposure of the season is too long, sunburn will occur before you get a tan. Furthermore, if the burn is hot enough to raise blisters and cause peeling, some surface skin is lost. For this reason gradual daily doses are far more sensible than long stretches on weekends. This is particularly important for fair-skinned people who get a two-week vacation and want to show up at the office on Monday morning looking like bronzed beauties and Adonises.

Use common sense. Experiment cautiously to find out how long you can safely stay in the sun. Try to get out of the sun *before* you are lobster-red. Don't wait until you *feel* you're getting too much. By then it's too late. The best method is to follow the clock. If it's between 10 A.M. and 2 P.M. give yourself ten minutes the first day, fifteen the second, twenty the third, etc.

Cancer. The threat of skin cancer is not a concern of the occasional sunbather, but the evidence is clear that repeated and persistent exposure to sunlight can be one of the major factors in causing cancer of the skin in susceptible persons.

Evidence shows that:

(1) Skin cancer has long been observed to be an occupational hazard to the farmer, the sailor and the rancher. Ardent outdoor sportsmen and sun worshipers share the same risk.

(2) Cancer of the skin occurs more often in the South and Southwest— areas noted for their sunny climates.

(3) Skin cancer occurs most frequently on the exposed parts of the body. One study showed that more than 90 percent of skin cancers originate on the face, ears, hands or neck.

(4) Skin cancer occurs more frequently in light-skinned than in dark-skinned persons.

(5) Skin cancer can be produced in mice 100 percent of the time by using ultraviolet light.

Aging skin. I repeat, the teenage girl who bakes in the sun to attain a glorious tan may find when she is forty that her skin looks fifteen to twenty years older. Years of overexposure are likely to result in wrinkles, skin folds and sagging.

Once this type of destruction has occurred, no cream, lotion or series of facials can undo the damage.

Allergies. Some people have allergic reactions to the sun, which can result in skin rashes, blotching and a wide assortment of annoying problems. Often the problem begins after a severe sunburn. Or sometimes the skin becomes sensitive to sunlight after repeated contact with various plants, perfumes, cosmetics or some skin creams or suntan lotions. These problems can be persistent and may increase in severity with repeated exposure.

Certain medications can help people who are "allergic" to the sun, but a permanent cure has not yet been discovered. Fortunately, some cases are limited to childhood or appear only during certain times of the year. As with other allergies, the best treatment is to avoid whatever is causing the trouble —in this case the sun.

What about the suntan lotions and other preparations sunbathers use to anoint their bodies? Are the benefits real or imagined? Acutally, properly applied suntan lotion can be somewhat helpful in preventing a burn and promoting a tan if you use one suited to your needs. Here's why:

Certain commercial suntan preparations contain chemicals called sunscreens. They absorb some of the ultraviolet rays of the sun while letting others through. The better lotions allow you to stay in the sun longer with less risk of burning. However, do not expect even the best lotions to protect you from unlimited exposure. It is possible to burn through a tan.

Most suntan preparations also contain a lubricant. This helps to keep your skin from drying out too quickly.

Suntan lotions must be reapplied at least every two hours during exposure and whenever the protecting film may have worn off or washed off.

Some people claim that mineral oil or baby oil mixed with iodine makes a good suntan lotion. The fact is that these preparations do not contain sunscreens and therefore will not help you tan, nor will they prevent burning. Their only benefit is that they provide lubrication to cut down on the drying effects of the sun.

Recently artificial tanning preparations known as "bronzers" have become available. These contain a water-soluble stain. They simply *color* the skin, but the color comes off when you shower or bathe.

Although artificial tanning lotions appear to be safe, remember that they do not protect you from the sun (unless they also contain a sunscreen agent), and their prolonged use may cause your skin to become dry and scaly.

If you have stayed in the sun too long, don't expect a quick "cure" for the problem. You can, however, get relief from the discomforts of painful sunburn. Ointments, wet compresses and soothing lotions can be helpful. A bland cold cream or lightweight mineral oil may also give relief.

A word of caution about commercial sunburn medications: These products contain ingredients which are intended to relieve pain, but they can cause allergic skin reactions. If the pain becomes unbearable or if extensive blistering occurs, see your physician.

The most widely advertised benefit of the sun is that it gives you more vitamin D. The average American, however, gets enough vitamin D in his diet and does not need a supplement from the sun.

Certain skin disorders, such as acne, eczema and psoriasis, can be helped by the sun, but check with your doctor before trying the sun as a treatment for any skin problems.

I repeat, for normally healthy people, anything beyond moderate and careful exposure to the sun can do you more harm than good.

If you will forgive a personal reference, I have studiously avoided the sun since I was thirty years of age and people tell me I look many years younger than I am. The secret of course is the skin.

CREDIT: *Ann Landers with information from the American Medical Association: Department of Health Education, Committee on Cutaneous Health and Cosmetics.*

Sunlamps

This year at least twelve thousand people who used sunlamps were burned so badly they required hospital emergency-room treatment. Almost half of the victims said they "fell asleep."

Why do people use sunlamps? Many insist the heat makes them feel better. Others like to look "sun-kissed" all year round. These psychological benefits are understandable, but according to a spokesman from the American Medical Association, sunlamps have very little, if any, therapeutic value.

Barbara Shea, of *Newsday* (Long Island), did some investigating to learn why so many people are burned year after year by sunlamps. She reported as follows:

(1) Most were sold without control devices or timers.

(2) Only 10 percent came with protective goggles.

(3) Instructions for proper use usually were in the form of printed material that could be lost or mislaid.

(4) Information on exposure time and safe distance from lamp to user was not included in some instructional material.

(5) In only a few cases was any safety warning affixed permanently to the lamp.

The government is exploring the feasibility of requiring the sunlamp bulbs to be made so that they cannot be screwed into an ordinary lamp that is not equipped with a timer.

If you must use a sunlamp, buy only the type that has a timer with an automatic turn-off. And be aware that your body is being cooked even if you don't feel a *thing*. If you overdo it, you'll feel plenty within an hour and then it will be too late.

Don't ever get under a sunlamp without protective goggles. Heat dries the eyes and causes cataracts and other eye problems.

CREDIT: *Ann Landers with information from the American Medical Association: Department of Health Education, Committee on Cutaneous Health and Cosmetics.*

Surgery

Few subjects are as fascinating to the teller and as boring to the listener as details of an operation.

But when the doctor says, "You need surgery," the words can be very frightening. People worry about everything from size of the scar to the possibility of dying on the table. Some patients are very proud of their scars. (Remember that famous photograph of Lyndon B. Johnson lifting his pajama top after his gallbladder surgery?) At the other extreme, a San Francisco stripper was very distressed by hers. She claimed the scar from her hysterectomy had ruined her career. The woman applied for permanent disability.

Surgery should never be taken lightly. Any operation, with the accompanying anesthetics and drugs, involves hazards that a patient must be willing to face in return for the benefits of the surgery.

An operation affects each patient differently—according to his ability to stand pain, his general physical condition and his understanding of the operation that is to be performed. Every patient should be told in advance exactly what to expect. Fear of the unknown is probably the most upsetting part of surgery.

First, your doctor must evaluate the problem. He will carefully question you about symptoms and collect data from X-ray studies and laboratory tests. From this he will make a diagnosis of what appears to be wrong and what treatment is called for.

If your doctor tells you you need an operation and you do not trust his judgment, by all means seek a second opinion. If the second doctor's evaluation is not in accord with the first doctor's, get a third opinion and then make up your mind.

PREPARATION

Except in emergencies, surgical patients go through a tedious preparation period before an operation. The prompt action required in an emergency prevents lengthy observation and preparation, but the greater hazard is justified by the urgency of the treatment required. Normal preparatory procedures may be inconvenient and uncomfortable, but they help put the patient in the best possible physical condition for both anesthesia and surgery.

Preparation usually calls for an overnight stay in the hospital during which time you will be asked many questions, usually by a medical student or an intern. It is very important that you answer all questions honestly and not for reasons of false pride and vanity withhold information. (Example: Some people do not wish to admit that they wear dentures. A patient who undergoes surgery with dentures or partial plates may choke to death while under an anesthetic.)

The skin surfaces around the site of the operation are shaved and cleansed to reduce the chance of infection. The lower bowel is cleansed with an enema to reduce postoperative discomfort. If food is allowed, it is limited to a light supper. A relaxed sleep is assured with sedatives. You will be told not to take any liquids or eat any food after midnight. This advice should be taken seriously. A patient who has surgery with particles of food in his stomach could choke while vomiting.

The anesthesiologist usually visits his patient the evening before the operation to explain what he or she will do and what the patient should expect. He will ask about recent colds and other respiratory infections, possible allergies, dentures that might interfere with breathing and other factors that could cause problems. The anesthesiologist, who is a physician just like your doctor, often orders the sedatives that set the stage for smooth anesthesia by keeping the patient relaxed and quiet before surgery.

A surgical patient may never remember seeing the operating room, because the medication given to him while still in his bed will make him so drowsy he will not be able to recall anything that happened. When a local anesthetic is used, such as an injection in the spinal canal or into the tissues involved in the operation, the patient may be awake in the operating room and be aware of what is going on, but he will probably be under heavy sedation and feel no pain. Even in cases where general anesthesia is used for complicated surgery the patient may be semi-conscious but he will feel no pain.

A surgical operation involves three teams.

First, the anesthesiologist and his assistants. They administer the anesthetic, drugs and other substances, measure pulse, respiration and blood pressure and keep the surgeon informed about the patient's condition.

Second, the surgeon and his assistants. They perform the operation while a surgical nurse or technician keeps the operating team supplied with the instruments needed.

The third team is made up of nurses, orderlies and aides who remove and account for used instruments, gauze packs and sponges.

The type of operation being performed determines the nature of the operating theater. A room for operations on the ear, nose or throat under local anesthesia will be equipped quite differently from one used for setting a broken bone.

Heart and lung surgery that requires a heart-lung machine to maintain circulation will be equipped much differently than the room for an abdominal operation.

Equipment also will differ according to the position of the patient on the operating table. Some operations require one to lie flat, others use a tilted table. In a few instances, the patient is required to be in a sitting position.

When surgery is completed and the wound is closed and protected with dressings and supporting binders, the anesthetic is discontinued, and postoperative care begins.

RECOVERY

Depending on the patient's need, he will be taken to an intensive treatment center, a recovery room or his own hospital room. When he recovers from the anesthetic, he may be surprised at the array of bottles, tubes and equipment attached to various parts of his body.

If the patient is receiving a blood transfusion, a bottle of blood will be connected to a vein in his arm or leg by a tube through which the blood flows. Liquid food and medication are administered the same way from a different bottle.

After abdominal operations, gas may accumulate in the bowel and cause discomfort. To prevent this, a small suction tube may be passed through the nose and throat and into the stomach and upper bowel. This picks up gas bubbles, and aids the patient's comfort.

Other tubes, electronic equipment and a host of devices may be used in special situations. All of these, though unfamiliar to the patient, have important functions.

The patient who comes to the hospital expecting to spend all his time in bed may be in for a surprise. In many cases he will be encouraged to sit up and walk soon after the operation. Even while wearing an array of tubes, the patient may be asked to sit up and dangle his legs over the side of the bed to stimulate circulation. The day after the operation, or sometimes the same day, the tubes may be disconnected long enough for a short walk or a trip to the toilet.

Exercise promotes rapid recovery and is started as soon as possible. It improves circulation and helps to prevent the clots and vein inflammations that used to plague surgery patients. Exercise also makes the patient feel stronger and shortens the hospital stay.

The length of the recovery period varies with the operation and the physical condition of each patient. Abdominal operations such as uncomplicated appendectomies may heal quickly enough for the patient to go home after three or four days, sometimes even before the stitches are removed.

Once a patient returns home, he may have to visit his surgeon or personal physician for subsequent care, but often he may go about his business in two or three weeks and be unrestricted after two months.

REHABILITATION

Following bone or joint surgery, neurological surgery, extensive skin grafting or other complex operations, the patient may require rehabilitation through physical therapy and other procedures. When surgery involves an amputation, an artificial limb must be fitted and the patient must be taught how to use it.

Patients with less dramatic problems may also need help in readjusting to a normal life after illness and surgery. This is all part of rehabilitation—and the patient's co-operation is very important. A positive mental attitude can be his most valuable asset. The doctor can do only so much. Each patient must be an active participant in his own recovery.

The person who is determined to recover rapidly and get back into the swing of things will probably do so. The chronic complainer who enjoys poor health will use his operation to get sympathy and avoid responsibility. He will also recover slowly and feel "lousy" for a long, long time.

CREDIT: *American Medical Association; Dr. David Skinner, Professor and Chairman of the Department of Surgery, University of Chicago.*

Tattoos

If I am to believe my readers, nine out of ten people who have had themselves decorated with tattoos were drunk at the time and wish they hadn't done it.

Every week I receive letters asking for advice on how to remove a tattoo. Usually it's a male who wants the name of a girlfriend taken off his arm or hand because he is now going with (or is married to) someone else.

Sometimes the man writes and says he wants to get rid of the battleship on his abdomen because he has joined a health club and gets too many questions.

Recently, an architect wrote to say he was interested in a young lady but the tattooed snake around his arm was "hurting his sex life." He had to get rid of it because his girl hated it and it "turned her off."

Women sometimes write about tattoo marks. Usually it's a man's initials they want taken off a thigh or a shoulder. Occasionally, women who went in for peacocks and butterflies write to say they are embarrassed when they go swimming and wish they hadn't been so foolish. "How can I get rid of it?" they ask.

There are several techniques. The most satisfactory is dermabrasion. This is the removal of the outer layers of skin with a sandpaper wheel which is run by electricity. In the hands of a skilled technician, preferably a dermatologist (skin specialist), this procedure is excellent. Sometimes salt is used instead of sandpaper. In both instances, the area is anesthetized, but when the anesthetic wears off there is some pain until the healing takes place. While the pain is not excruciating, it may last for days.

If an individual has an obscene word or picture he wishes to obliterate, he can have a tattoo artist tattoo a skin-colored pigment over the word or scene. Even with a near-perfect color match (it is never perfect) the skin-colored tattoo generally looks different than the surrounding skin. Of course, it doesn't tan, which can be a problem.

Surgical grafting is another technique. The physician can remove the tattoo with a scalpel, and graft a piece of skin (taken from another part of the body) over the area. Often this technique leaves an unsightly scar, but it is preferable to the tattoo if a patient wants to be rid of it.

If I were to give some advice in regard to tattooing, I would say, "Don't do it. The chances are very good—like nine out of ten—you'll regret it."

CREDIT: *Harry J. Hurley, M.D., Upper Darby, Pennsylvania, President of the Dermatology Foundation, 1976–77.*

Teenage Drinking

Approximately 1.3 million American teenagers have a serious drinking problem, according to the National Institute on Alcohol Abuse and Alcoholism.

A survey of high schoolers revealed that 80 percent of the males and 75 percent of the females drink alcoholic beverages and about 15 percent of them drink enough to be considered abusers.

Drinking is started at an earlier age than ever—twelve is not unusual. Experts predict that 20 percent of early drinkers will become alcoholics. It is likely that the number of adult alcoholics twenty years from now will be increased considerably.

Many teenagers who drink only beer fail to realize that beer can be just as harmful as hard liquor. There is more alcohol in a twelve-ounce bottle of 5 percent beer than in a cocktail containing one ounce of 90-proof liquor. Put another way, drinking a six-pack of 5 percent beer is equivalent to drinking almost a third of a fifth of whiskey or gin.

Three fourths of the students surveyed admitted that they drank. Consumption ranged from very little to astonishing quantities of alcohol. About 50 percent said they started with booze and then turned to drugs. Multiple drug use was common among the students. About 55 percent admitted using two drugs, and 44 percent said they used three or more drugs, including alcohol.

Health professionals warn against the hazards of mixing alcohol and drugs. "Everyone should be aware of the potentially lethal interaction of alcohol and barbiturates, which can cause serious physical distress and even death," says pharmacologist Joe Graedon. "The simultaneous consumption of a couple of drinks and a few tranquilizers can produce an effect greater than either one alone. The result can be unintentional suicide by causing a big fall in blood pressure and breathing failure." Even aspirin should not be mixed with alcohol. When alcohol is introduced, the stomach becomes supersensitive to the irritating effects of the salicylates in aspirin and serious bleeding can result.

Authorities believe that today's teenagers are turning to alcohol more frequently because of several factors:

Peer pressure. Young people who want to feel like "part of the crowd" are apt to go along with others who are drinking even though they may not like the taste of alcohol or the effect it has on them.

Easy availability. Almost anyone under age can buy alcoholic beverages by faking an identification card or by having someone older buy it for them. Alcohol is also cheaper than most other drugs, and in many ways the high it offers is more predictable. A person knows that if he drinks a six-pack of beer he will really "feel it." On the other hand, drugs such as marijuana sold on the street are often so adulterated and weak that the high isn't as strong.

Role Models. Many youngsters see their fathers and/or mothers come home from their jobs and have a few drinks. Drinking has become an accepted part of the home scene in many families.

Advertising. Drinking is depicted as glamorous and sophisticated. It is equated with having a good time. In recent years many of the commercials and print ads, particularly those touting wines that taste like fruit drinks and milk shake-flavored liquor, have been aimed at the youth market.

Feeling of alienation. Teenagers who feel alienated from the world in general and their families in particular frequently seek an escape from their fears and frustrations through drugs. They believe that the high they get from drugs (including alcohol) will help them cope with life's pressures.

A Gallup youth survey backed up the findings of the authorities on youth and behavioral problems. Teenagers listed the major reasons for using alcohol as: peer pressure, escape from their problems, to have a good time and feel good, showing off to look grown-up, boredom, rebellion and parental indifference. The survey also revealed that only 57 percent of the nation's teens have received any kind of instruction about the dangers of alcohol abuse.

Many youth experts maintain there is a need for more prevention programs designed to stop the growth of alcohol abuse among teenagers. They believe that early education combined with parental understanding is the key to the prevention of alcohol abuse among the young.

"Because studies show that drinking is starting at an earlier age, it is crucial to begin the educational process in elementary schools," says Mary Brennan, director of the Central States Institute of Addiction's alcohol and drug abuse programs for the schools in the Chicago area.

The Institute's program begins at the fifth-grade level with lectures, films and discussions of alcohol abuse. In high schools the program is offered as an alternative to expulsion. Students identified as having a drinking problem are required to attend six sessions at the Institute accompanied by parents.

Miss Brennan contends that not enough parents understand the seriousness of the teen drinking problem. "We feel it is vital to increase family communication, lack of which is at the core of most drug abuse," she says. "When told about their child's problem, many parents say, 'Thank God, it isn't drugs.' They don't understand that alcohol *is* a drug."

She says teens have to learn that it is okay not to drink. They have to learn that not giving in to peer pressure shows strength. They have to be taught that chemical solutions to problems are not effective and it is better to keep busy with productive, creative activities such as athletics and the arts.

Education should focus on giving students the facts about alcohol, which puts the responsibility on them for abusing it or not. Among the facts to be pointed out:

Alcohol can be dangerous to a person's health. It can be detrimental to the development of healthy cells, particularly in young bodies that are still in the state of development.

Driving while under the influence of alcohol is a leading cause of accidents, many of which are fatal. Do they want the responsibility of injuring or killing someone?

Studies indicate that young people have become physically addicted to alcohol more quickly (six months to two years) than adults (five to fifteen years). Do they really want to become alcoholic?

The teenager who abuses alcohol often does not get the help needed because of a protective family that will not admit the problem. Because it is ignored, the teenager continues to drink and the problem becomes intensified.

"If someone protects the teenaged alcoholic, he is protecting that person to death," says Dr. John Steffek, a professor of psychiatry at the University of Illinois College of Medicine. "Professional help is essential because the problem is apparently too big to be handled inside the home."

It is vital for the teen who abuses alcohol to admit that he has a problem so he can seek help. These are some of the questions to ask yourself to determine whether you have a drinking problem:

Do you lose time from school because of drinking?

Are your grades slipping because of your drinking?

Do you drink to build up self-confidence, such as before you go out on a date?

Do you drink because you have difficulty facing up to stressful situations like problems at home or in school?

Do your friends drink less than you do?

Do you drink until the bottle is empty?

Have you begun to drink in the morning before going to school or work?

Do you often prefer to drink alone than with others?

Have you lost friends since you started drinking?

Does it bother you if someone says you drink too much, and do you lie about the fact that you drink?

Have you ever had a loss of memory from drinking?

Do you get into trouble when you are drinking?

Have you had an automobile accident while under the influence of alcohol?

Do you think you have a problem with liquor?

If you answer yes to three or four of the questions, that is an indication that you have a problem with drinking. Affirmative answers to half of the questions or more indicate your problem is acute.

Males and females of any age are welcome to become members of Alcoholics Anonymous, according to a spokesman for the group. Because teens may be inhibited about attending meetings with older members, several A.A. chapters throughout the country have special youth groups where teens may feel more comfortable meeting with those of their own age. (For information about groups in your area, write to: A.A., P. O. Box 459, Grand Central Station, New York, New York 10017.)

Alateen (an auxiliary of Al-Anon, an organization which helps families of alcoholics) is not associated with Alcoholics Anonymous. Members are children of alcoholic parents who share their experiences and learn how to deal with problems. Al-Anon believes that alcoholism is a family illness and that changed attitudes within the family group can aid in the alcoholic member's recovery. For information write to: Al-Anon and Alateen, P. O. Box 182, Madison Square Station, New York, New York 10010.

CREDIT: *Barbara Varro*, Chicago Sun-Times.

Teeth

Capping Teeth

Have you ever marveled at the beautiful, gleaming, perfectly shaped teeth that smile at you from the stage, TV, movie screen, political podium, or across the room at a cocktail party? "How lucky she (or he) is to have such wonderful teeth," you may say to yourself enviously. Well, it may be more than luck. The person with the gorgeous smile may have had a little help from his friendly dentist. Capping is now a widely used technique for people whose teeth were chipped, cracked, discolored, mishapen, unattractively spaced or knocked out in an accident.

The term "cap" means to cover or replace the outer surface of the tooth. In dentistry, the term can be interchanged with the word "crown." A cap should look natural and not interfere with the normal positioning of the lip.

The decision to cap one or more teeth is based on the following:

(1) Appearance: The teeth may be badly stained or have large, unsightly fillings. They may be broken, jagged or poorly spaced.

(2) Strength: A tooth may have too many fillings or too much decay, leaving its biting edge unsupported and fragile.

(3) Mobile teeth: When bone structure has weakened, caps may be necessary to splint or join one tooth to another for additional stability.

(4) Missing teeth: A fixed bridge (non-removable) can be made to replace a missing tooth by adjoining an artificial tooth to the adjacent capped teeth on either side of the space.

(5) Twisted teeth can be capped and splinted to prevent further movement.

Once the decision to cap the teeth has been made, the dentist must concern himself with two primary issues: root canal therapy and gum disease.

In the center of a tooth is a pulp chamber which houses blood vessels and nerves. These vessels connect at the base of the tooth to the blood supply of the body. The shape and size of this chamber is an important consideration in making the cap. If the chamber is encroached upon, either by decay or by the depth of the preparation necessary to create a well-contoured crown, the chamber must be sterilized and sealed. This process is called root canal treatment. It prevents infection from going into the bloodstream.

The strength of the tooth in the jawbone must also be considered. If disease of the gum and bone is present, special treatment is required before caps can be put on.

To prepare for a cap, enough structure is removed from the outer surface of the tooth to allow for the required bulk of the selected capping material. All decay is removed and, if necessary, the remaining tooth structure is medicated and strengthened. A temporary plastic cap is made so the person will look presentable and have a "working" tooth. An impression is taken, from which a model is made to duplicate the prepared tooth outside of the mouth. The dentist or technician then makes the cap in the laboratory.

There are several types of caps being used today. The two most common caps for front teeth are the porcelain jacket crown and the porcelain veneer crown. The porcelain jacket is formed from powdered porcelain which is baked in an oven. The porcelain is very strong and, when used properly, there should be no breakage. The porcelain jacket is not gold-reinforced and thus has superior color characteristics. It is not, however, generally considered strong enough for replacing missing teeth.

The porcelain veneer crown is a cast gold crown with porcelain fused directly to the gold in an oven under high heat and vacuum. The porcelain to gold combination is very durable and quite good-looking. The gold backing provides extra strength, which is ideal for supporting loose teeth and replacing missing teeth with a bridge.

The caps generally used in the back of the mouth are made of gold, gold and acrylic, and porcelain. Processed plastics have a tendency to lose their luster and are susceptible to physical or chemical wear. The gold caps are probably the best choice when no consideration is made for cosmetics. Gold is the easiest material for the dentist to work with and the most durable. The porcelain fused to gold is also excellent for capping back teeth when appearance is important.

Depending on the work load and proximity of the technician, the laboratory procedures may take one to two weeks. A single cap may be completed in two visits, and a splint or large bridge usually takes longer.

How long will a cap last? A well-made cap will generally last for many years with proper home care (good oral hygiene) and the avoidance of any unusual accident.

Gums tend to recede with time. When this occurs, a dark line may appear around the upper rim of the cap. This may bother some people for cosmetic reasons, in which case they can have the cap replaced.

Capped teeth should be cared for as if they are natural teeth. They should be cleansed with dental floss or dental tape and a toothbrush, after each meal if possible, but surely every morning and every night.

People who want their teeth capped for appearance's sake only should be aware of the extent to which healthy teeth must be changed in order to make the transition. Those with dental reasons for caps or crowns should understand the long-term benefits of this procedure.

CREDIT: *Jordan C. Block, D.D.S., Chicago, Illinois.*

Straightening Children's Teeth

STRAIGHTENING TEETH—WHAT DOES THAT MEAN?

Straightening teeth means the repositioning of teeth within the dental arches. This is done to enhance the appearance of the face and the teeth, to improve the ability to chew or both. Repositioning of teeth is known as orthodontics.

HOW IS IT POSSIBLE TO STRAIGHTEN TEETH?

Changing the positions of teeth is possible because (1) teeth can be moved (within limits) and (2) the bone which holds the teeth can be changed in shape by applying pressure to the teeth. In other words, a tooth does not remain tightly fixed in its original position throughout life.

Changes in position of teeth occur with growth of the arches, the eruption of new teeth and biting and chewing and sucking habits. Changes are also made by pressure applied in orthodontic treatment.

HOW DOES ONE KNOW THAT TEETH NEED TO BE STRAIGHTENED?

If teeth are unattractive because of their position it is time to ask questions of a qualified person. A children's dentist will inform parents at the time of regular visits. If your child has not had "regular visits" to a dentist and it is obvious to him or her or to you that the second teeth are coming in crooked, by all means take the child to a dentist for evaluation. If you don't know of a dentist, call the County Dental Society (look in the phone book) and one or two will be recommended. If you are not satisfied with the dentist's appraisal, go to another dentist.

In evaluating the mouth of a child one must look ahead to the distant future, not merely the next few years. This has to do, primarily, with the areas of the mouth which support the teeth.

Problems with gum tissue and supporting bone are the dental problems of the adult. There are times when the entire mouth of a child may look quite satisfactory, but in spite of the acceptable appearance there may be a bite problem which will not be disturbing until the patient is in middle age.

One example is a closed bite in which the upper front teeth close over the lowers beyond the desirable limit. After many years the heavy stress on the lower front teeth may cause severe wear to the teeth or damage to the bone which supports the teeth.

Another example is the positioning of the teeth near the outer surface of the bone of the arch with only a thin layer of bone covering the roots of the teeth. This may look and feel all right at twelve or fourteen years, but at thirty-five or forty the too-thin bone may gradually disappear, and the patient will have real trouble.

Dentists and patients need not always insist on the toothpaste-ad perfect line-up look. Often they are willing to settle for satisfactory appearance and efficient function. When function is acceptable, bony support is good and no future harm is predicted, the dentist should thus inform the patient. The patient and parents then can make the decision regarding treatment, based on their standards of acceptable appearance. People's values differ. Economic resources and financial obligations vary. Patients must feel free to ask, "Is it essential that my child have treatment now or may we postpone it or avoid it?"

WHAT HAPPENS IN SUCCESSFUL ORTHODONTIC TREATMENT

Briefly, the teeth become properly aligned and fit correctly, top to bottom.

The aim in orthodontic treatment is to properly align the teeth so they produce a good, solid bite. A variety of straightening problems may occur.

A few teeth or many teeth may overlap, or be out of line. The teeth may have been moved out of position by a prolonged pressure habit. There may be extra teeth present. There may be teeth missing, never formed, or lost when they should have been retained. The arches and teeth may close over farther than is desirable—closed bite. The lower teeth may fail to reach the upper teeth when closure is complete—open bite.

AT WHAT AGE SHOULD A PATIENT HAVE ORTHODONTIC TREATMENT?

There is no set age for orthodontic treatment. Early treatment, when not actually preventing problems, may make later treatment easier and shorter in duration. Adults, even after growth has been completed, can have orthodontic treatment, though the scope may be limited. The decision about timing for treatment is important. If there is a choice, treatment should be done in a stage of growth when the most can be accomplished in the shortest period of time.

WHO IS QUALIFIED TO STRAIGHTEN TEETH?

Any licensed dentist can make and place appliances for the purpose of straightening teeth. All dentists have had some training in this area, some more than others.

There are many degrees of difficulty in the correcting of dental problems— from the simplest band and loop for the maintenance of space, to the improvement of a severe facial deformity. There is much variation in training and experience in the professional persons permitted to straighten teeth. The dentist who has accepted the responsibility for the dental care of the patient, whether he is a general dentist or a pedodontist (pediatric dentist), will suggest that he do the orthodontic treatment himself or he will refer the patient to an orthodontist.

Orthodontics is one of the recognized specialties in dentistry. Every qualified orthodontist has had specialized training in the use of appliances for correction. His practice is limited to the exclusive practice of this specialty.

The choice of the professional person to treat the problem, should hinge on: (1) The established reputation of the dentist; (2) the ability and willingness of the dentist to teach and explain; (3) faith on the part of all participants.

WHY ARE SOME KIDS SO LUCKY? NO CROOKED TEETH.

What determines whether or not teeth are straight (properly aligned) or crooked? Let's look at personal characteristics which are set before birth:

(1) *Jaw size*. Large or small; wide or narrow. This determines the space available for the lining up of the teeth in each dental arch.

(2) *Tooth size*. Wide or narrow. Add one or two millimeters to the size of each of fourteen or sixteen teeth in one arch and we add perhaps more than an inch to the over-all measurement. Envision that for yourself. It's a lot! Or, subtract the same amount.

(3) *Tooth number*. There may be extra teeth, more than the usual number. An extra tooth is called a *supernumerary*. Some teeth which are expected to appear may never have formed. These are called congenitally missing teeth.

(4) *Jaw or arch relation*. An upper or lower arch may appear to be set back or set forward or shifted to one side in relation to its partner.

(5) *Muscle strength and tone*. Lips, cheeks, tongue pressures exert force on teeth. There are many possible variations.

The above factors are inherited from one parent or the other in varying combinations. Of six children of the same parents, there may be *none* with problems, *all* with problems, or *some* with problems.

HOW SIGNIFICANT IS THUMB-SUCKING?

The answer is: It depends.

First, thumbs are not the only things that are sucked. There are various one-finger, two-finger positions, also lips, tongue, pacifier, pencil, blanket corner, etc. Thumbs do win out, though, in a poll.

The age of the sucker is important. The bone of the infant, the three-year-old, even the four-year-old is quite pliable. Remove the sucked object and the bone that holds the teeth resumes its original contour because of the pressure from the lips, the cheeks, the tongue. If the habit continues to six, seven, ten, the return to the desired shape is less likely.

The amount of force exerted in the sucking is important. A resting thumb or finger does not move teeth or bone. A thumb that pushes does damage. If, in addition to the push, there is a strong sucking pull, putting in motion cheeks and swallowing muscles, as is sometimes seen in enthusiastic ten-year-old habits, the problem obviously becomes complicated.

Brief advice about managing thumb-suckers—advice more easily given than followed: Don't hassle your young thumb-sucker. Leave him alone until you can both talk about the problem in a reasonable manner. Identify your reason for wanting the habit stopped. Refer to it as a dental problem, not a behavioral problem. Get a kind, reasonable, professional person to help you if you aren't sure when to ignore, to go easy or to insist. Another person may be helpful, but remember that you know your own child best.

BRACES

Pressure on teeth is created by what professional persons call orthodontic appliances. We call them orthodontic appliances instead of "braces," not to make a more important sounding term but because the idea is *not* to hold the teeth but to move them, not to *support* them but to apply pressure to them.

There are many types of orthodontic appliances. Some are fastened to the teeth with cemented bands or brackets bonded directly to the tooth surfaces. Some are removable, not fastened to the teeth, and can be removed by the patient. Both metals and plastics are used.

WHAT INFORMATION IS NECESSARY BEFORE TREATMENT MAY BEGIN?

All the patient's questions about treatment are usually not answered at the first visit. For diagnosis and the planning of the treatment considerable information must be collected and a period of time for study must follow.

Dental X rays. Films which show all the teeth, including the roots. These films answer many questions: Are there missing teeth? Are there extra, unerupted teeth? Is the bony support healthy? Is infection present? Are there cavities to be filled?

Cephalometric films. Films of the head made at intervals which show growth direction as well as the relationships of the bony parts of the face and head.

Study Models. Hard plaster models poured from dental impressions. These models show positions of the crowns of the teeth, duplicating the patient's dentition. They enable the dentist to study the dentition from every angle.

Photographs. Over-all views of the face and teeth, used to show change and progress.

Case History. A detailed questionnaire, a medical and dental history, essential for correct, carefully thought-out treatment.

After the essential diagnostic aids are put together and carefully studied, the orthodontist is ready to present information to the patient and to answer the patient's questions. Some patients and parents want to know a great deal more than others and the presentation of the treatment plan can be a pleasure to the orthodontist. Others ask very few questions.

WHAT IS THE MINIMUM INFORMATION NEEDED BY THE PATIENT, PARENT?

Is treatment necessary?
Is now the proper time to begin?
What appliances will be used?
How long is treatment anticipated?
How much will it cost?

A WORD ABOUT HOME CARE—ORAL HYGIENE

Orthodontic appliances do not cause tooth decay. They do increase the hazard, however. Dental cavities are caused by acid excreted by bacteria which live in plaque—gook—which sits on the tooth surfaces. Anything foreign in the mouth which is not kept meticulously clean can contribute to plaque formation. If there is no plaque, there can be no cavity. Many patients with complicated appliances in their mouths maintain plaque-free teeth. It is not easy, but it is certainly possible. Optimum fluoride, conscientious hygiene, the minimum of sugar will prevent decay or keep it at a minimum. Patients with appliances must continue regular dental checks.

A WORD ABOUT PATIENT CO-OPERATION

The dentist must diagnose as accurately as is possible; he must communicate to the patient his plan of treatment. He will construct and place the appliances and make the adjustments for the correct amount of pressure in the specific areas at the proper time. Tooth movement and progress in treatment, however, is impossible without the patient's co-operation. The presence of mechanical devices in the mouth is obviously a bother. There may be some soreness, though this is minimal. Patient co-operation includes the consistent keeping of appointments, the minimum of breakage of appliances, good oral hygiene, attention to regular dental care and checking for possible decay.

EDUCATIONAL INFORMATION

There is much information available about good dental care, including the straightening of teeth. Contact your dentist for material, the local dental society or a school of dentistry. Inform yourself and enjoy good dental health for yourself and your children.

CREDIT: *Mary Lynn Morgan, D.D.S., Atlanta, Georgia.*

RULES YOU CAN GET YOUR TEETH INTO—BY GUM!

DEAR ANN LANDERS: Is there a Code of Ethics for Gum Chewers? I've never seen one and I think it's time some courageous soul wrote one. Will you stick your neck out, Ann Landers? M.J.A.

DEAR M.J.A.: Of course I will. Don't I always?

I know of no Code of Ethics for Gum Chewers, but I agree there is need for one in American culture, so here's a start:

First, let it be known to one and all that I am neither endorsing nor am I bum-rapping gum chewing. Some dentists claim it's not the best thing in the world for the teeth. On the other hand, some psychologists say it's a good way to release tension. Each individual must decide for himself it it's more important to soothe his jangled nerves or protect the enamel.

Rule Number One: Gum should never be seen. Chewers who talk and display the wad while so doing commit a grievous social blunder.

Rule Number Two: Gum should never be heard. Snap, crackle and pop are fine for breakfast cereals, but sound effects with chewing gum are verboten.

Gum cracking is particularly annoying to office workers. I read recently where a gum popper in an insurance office was clobbered with a 9-pound weight by a fellow employe who said he had been "pushed to the brink." (I was not surprised and must admit I was faintly sympathetic.)

Rule Number Three: Once gum is chewed it should be disposed of permanently. Sticking the wad on a piece of paper or on a dinner plate for later is out. Also, don't put gum behind the ear (don't laugh, I've seen it done).

The song entitled, "Does the Spearmint Lose Its Flavor on the Bedpost Overnight?" gave many people the mistaken notion that stashing gum for future chewing is socially acceptable.

Rule Number Four: It is impolite to take a stick of gum for oneself without offering it to others. If you happen to have only one stick, offer to split it. If there are several people in the group, wait until you are alone.

Gum sneaks (those who pop gum into their mouths furtively) are in the same category as cigaret or candy-mint sneaks. One minute you look at them and they are doing nothing. The next minute they have a cigaret, a mint, or a piece of chewing gum going. I have always thought that I would not care to play cards with people who are such experts at sleight of hand.

Rule Number Five: Disposing of gum is an art. It is also an index to a person's character and upbringing.

A considerate, well-bred person wouldn't think of spitting out gum on the sidewalk where unwary pedestrians are bound to step in it. Nor would they dream of sticking gum under a theater seat, or, heaven forbid, under a dining room chair or a table.

The proper way to dispose of chewing gum is to wrap it in a piece of paper and deposit it in a trash container—or in your purse or pocket, if no container is handy.

Unsightly Teeth

We do not know of a time in history when people did not use mirrors. The first mirrors were polished stones. Then came metal. Glass was invented in the fifteenth century. One's reflection always causes a reaction either pleasant or unpleasant. Concepts of beauty have varied from race to race and time to time. But to be pretty or handsome, by whatever standards, has always been important to youth.

In modern American these standards have become related to perfection in the body and especially the face. It is a rare young person whose self-esteem is not damaged if he has an unsightly problem.

With modern technology there is little that cannot be corrected or at least improved.

Unsightly teeth disturb teenagers even more than acne. With acne they have lots of company. Not so with defective teeth. Talking makes the teeth appear and disappear and therefore they are more noticeable. Teeth that protrude or are crooked, discolored, decayed, broken or absent—as well as swollen or infected gums—come into view as one speaks. Efforts to cover do not work well and the affected person becomes shy and withdrawn.

Teenagers have a natural inclination to become depressed because of the loss of childhood. They worry about the future. Unsightly teeth may increase that depression to a state of severity. With basically healthy personalities they can accept what cannot be changed, but they feel angry if told, "It doesn't look so bad" (not true to them) or, "We can't afford it," when they are stuck with a defect that can be corrected.

What to do about it? First one must appreciate the importance of looks to young people. Parents sometimes forget how they felt when they were young. They must be willing to give the situation some priority for whatever funds there are.

Consult a general dentist for referral to the appropriate specialist. This might be an orthodontist, who straightens teeth, a prosthodontist who caps and replaces teeth, a periodontist who takes care of gums and other structures around the teeth, or an oral surgeon. The work will be expensive but in most cases will cost far less than many of the large items you already own, for example, your car.

Check your medical insurance. It may cover part of the cost. Most dental specialists will arrange manageable terms. If one will not, try another. If your income does not permit putting out the price of private care, your dentist can refer you to a dental school or hospital clinic where excellent work will be done. It is a good bet that your teenager will be more than happy to help to ease the financial burden by working to earn part of the cost. Your concern for their feelings will be evident in later years and you will be gratified to see the outgoing personality that emerges.

CREDIT: *Marita D. Kenna, M.D., Child Psychiatrist, Assistant Professor, University of Pittsburgh.*

Teething

Teeth usually begin to erupt between six and eight months of age. However, there is an extremely wide variation in the time of initiation of teething. It may normally be delayed until as late as twelve to fifteen months, or begin very early in life. In fact, occasionally an infant is born with one or two teeth already erupted. (Ann Landers was born with two teeth. Her twin sister, Dear Abby, was born with one.)

In general, premature infants' teeth erupt somewhat later than full-term infants. It is not true that early tooth eruption indicates advanced mental ability or that delayed eruption is a sign of mental retardation.

Infants sometimes pass a few loose stools during the time of teething. They also may be irritable for a day or two and occasionally teething is preceded by excessive drooling or chewing. On rare occasions a bluish discoloration may appear on the gum a few days before the eruption of a tooth. This is due to a collection of blood in front of the erupting tooth and disappears when the tooth finally erupts. It has no significance and should not be of concern to parents.

Teething does not cause fever, vomiting or other signs of any illness. If an infant appears sick, it should not be attributed to teething, and professional assistance is indicated.

A teething ring may be offered if the infant is irritable during the teething period. Applying medication on the gums is not effective in relieving irritablity and is not recommended.

CREDIT: *David Van Gelder, M.D., FAAP, president of the American Academy of Pediatrics 1977–78, Baton Rouge, Louisiana.*

Telephone Calls

What to Do About Annoying Calls

KINDS OF ANNOYING CALLS

There are, in general, three types of annoying calls:
  (1) Indiscriminate or thoughtless "sales" or "survey" calls.
  (2) Nuisance calls designed to irritate you.
  (3) Abusive, harassing or obscene calls.

INDISCRIMINATE "SALES" OR "SURVEY" CALLS

When used correctly, with proper selection of prospects and careful choosing of the time to call, selling and surveying by phone provide useful services for companies and their customers. In addition, these services may give employment to handicapped people who cannot work at other jobs.

People often become annoyed when telephone pitches are made at inconvenient or inappropriate times.

The telephone company is in a difficult position. It is required to provide telephone service for any legitimate use. However, the phone company does not condone thoughtless and indiscriminate sales or survey calls to its customers. Here are some suggestions as to how to handle such calls.

WHAT YOU CAN DO:

(1) Remember, a telephone call is just as personal as a face-to-face conversation. Don't feel obligated to answer questions just because the questioner sounds "official." Don't answer questions on the phone you wouldn't answer if they were asked by a stranger on the street.

(2) Always find out who is calling. Ask for the name of the person and the company he or she represents.

(3) If the caller is a sales person and you're not interested, say so. One response is to ask the caller to send you all the information in a letter so you can consider it at your leisure.

(4) If you don't recognize the name of the company conducting the survey, offer to call back or ask the caller to call you again after you've had time to check the firm with the Better Business Bureau.

(5) Remember, it's your phone service and your time. If the caller is rude and persistent and will not let you go graciously, hang up.

NUISANCE CALLS

Experience has shown that nuisance calls don't come only from strangers. They also come from acquaintances, neighbors or business associates.

A relatively small group—unsupervised youngsters, misguided or frustrated people, those who are mentally ill—have a tendency to make nuisance calls.

Generally, such calls are made at random. If you receive such a call, and give the caller no satisfaction, the person will usually give up after one or two attempts.

If you get anonymous calls or calls that try to obtain information you don't want to give, here are some suggestions:

(1) Always use the telephone on your terms, not those of the caller. Don't talk to anyone unless you want to.

(2) Ask the caller to identify himself or herself. If the caller asks, "Who is this?" don't give your name. Instead ask, "What number did you call?" or "Whom do you want?" If the call isn't legitimate, that very likely will end it.

(3) Instruct your children and the baby-sitter never to talk on the phone to anyone they don't recognize. An innocent comment like "Daddy's out of town" could be helpful to a burglar. Teach them to ask for the number so someone can call back later.

(4) If the caller remains silent or breathes hard into the phone after you answer, HANG UP. It is no fun listening to a dead line.

ABUSIVE, HARASSING OR OBSCENE CALLS

Calls such as these often are meant to infuriate or terrify you.

WHAT YOU CAN DO:

(1) As with the milder nuisance calls, this caller may remain silent for a while. Don't give the person a chance to get started. *Hang up*.

(2) If a caller makes an obscene or suggestive remark, hang up. The person would like nothing better than for you to demand to know who he is, or to ask repeatedly what he wants.

HARASSING PHONE CALLS FOR DEBT COLLECTION

Improper use of the telephone for debt collection is also a concern to the phone company. This includes calls from store owners and collection agencies who make annoying or threatening calls to obtain money which may be owed to them. Improper calls could include:

Calling at hours when most people are asleep.

Repeated calls without appropriate justification.

Calls to third parties offering information about the person who owes money in an attempt to embarrass the debtor so he will pay up.

Calls threatening bodily harm or property damage.

Calls asserting falsely that the matter will be referred to credit rating agencies and damage the reputation of the debtor.

Calls asserting falsely that legal action is about to be taken.

If debt collection calls are being made in a manner that violates legal restrictions, the telephone company will take appropriate measures. These may include suspension of service after written notice.

WHAT YOU CAN DO

Notify the telephone company. Give the name of the calling party, the date and time of the calls and the ways in which the calls were abusive, harassing and so on.

THREATENING CALLS

Calls in this category include the extreme cases—bomb threats, threats to life and property, threats of kidnapping, robbery or bodily injury to members of your family.

Sometimes these calls are repeated over an extended period of time to harass and frighten a family. If you are unfortunate enough to be a victim of such a campaign, the techniques suggested here are not sufficient. Call the police and the telephone company immediately. The phone company will work with you and the police to eliminate the problem.

CREDIT: *A.T.&T. Courtesy Joseph P. O'Brien, Assistant Vice President, Illinois Bell, Chicago, Illinois.*

DEAR ANN LANDERS: People are always complaining about telephone operators, calling them "dumb" and "rude." May I say a word about the public, please? As a telephone operator in charge of directory assistance for more years than I would care to own up to, I have had ample opportunity to form some firm impressions.

Here are the major sources of irritation:

(1) The customer who calls Information for help with a number and does not have a pencil to write it down. He then asks the operator to wait until he can find "something that will write" and leaves the phone for five minutes.

(2) The customer who is too lazy to make the call himself and asks his 7-year-old son to do it, then hollers instructions from the next room.

(3) The customer who has his stereo or hi-fi turned up so loud it just about cracks the equipment. He invariably yells at the operator, "I can't hear you. Can't you talk louder?"

(4) The customer who does not know how to spell the name of the party he is trying to locate, has no idea where he lives, can't remember his first name or initials. (I once had a caller who started to describe the appearance of the party he wanted to reach, and ended up saying, "You'd know him if you saw him.")

(5) The customer who gets mad and swears when told the party has an unpublished number and keeps insisting "you could give the number out if you wanted to."

(6) The customer who eats celery or potato chips while he's on the phone.

(7) Customers who are stoned or drunk (or both) and use obscene language because they cannot make themselves understood.

If you print this letter, Ann Landers, thousands of telephone employes will rise and call you blessed. MORE THAN JUST TALK

DEAR MORE THAN: Here it is. Let 'em rise. I've been called lots of things lately but not blessed. Thanks for a welcome change.

PLEASE HOLD WHILE WE CHECK IF THERE'S LIFE ON EARTH

by Art Buchwald

WASHINGTON—A recent nationwide survey has just revealed that there were 789,345,678 unreturned telephone calls made in 1977, an increase of 10 per cent over 1976. Phone experts believe that at the present rate the figure of 1 billion could be reached by 1980.

Mark Stampel is the head of a non-profit organization named The Unreturned Telephone Call Institute, whose main function is to investigate all unreturned telephone calls and decide on the basis of this information whether there is life on Earth.

He told me at the UTC Institute's plush estate in Middleburg, Va., that the fact that someone does not return a telephone call doesn't mean that the person called does not exist. "It only means that the person who made the call doesn't exist for the person who didn't call back."

It took me a few minutes to digest this.

Stampel tried to spell it out in layman terms. "Let us assume Pleeder calls Arragant to get a job. Arragant's secretary says that Arragant is in a meeting and will get back to Pleeder as soon as possible.

"Arragant has no intention of calling back Pleeder. Pleeder waits by the phone

—1 hour, 24 hours, a week. No word from Arragant. He calls back again. This time Pleeder can't get through the switchboard to even speak to Arragant's secretary."

"Arragant's a cruel man," I said.

"Aha," said Stampel. "You would think so. But the reason Arragant has not called back Pleeder is that he is waiting for a call from Byer. Arragant keeps asking his secretary if Byer has called."

"Byer hasn't?" I asked.

"Of course not. He doesn't want Arragant's railroad ties."

"Why doesn't Byer call and tell him so?"

"Because he doesn't want to tie up the phone. He's waiting to hear from his girlfriend, who hasn't returned his call for three days."

"Why?"

"Because Byer won't get a divorce from Mrs. Byer, and the girl friend has decided that she has had it with him."

"That's reasonable."

"After the girl friend made the decision to give up on Byer, she calls Altman, whom she met at a party, and leaves word she's available for dinner. Now she's waiting by her phone for Altman to call back."

"Why doesn't Altman call her back?"

"He can't remember what the girl looked like and he's afraid to take a chance that she may be a dog."

"Altman sounds like a male chauvinist."

"He is, except that he's afraid of his mother. He's particularly frightened because she hasn't answered his call."

"Why not?" I wanted to know.

"Because Altman didn't call her the week before, and his mother is going to make him pay for it. Besides, she's waiting to hear from the Board of Health to complain because the furnace in her apartment house is on the fritz."

"And of course they don't call back."

"You have to be kidding. The heating inspector for the board of health is sitting by his phone waiting to hear from the mayor's deputy assistant on whether he can hire more people to handle telephone complaints."

"The mayor's deputy doesn't call him back?"

"No, because he's waiting for a call from Washington, which will never come, telling him whether the city can have the funds it needs, not only for the health inspector but for Pleeder, who still doesn't have a job because Arragant never answered his call."

"On the basis of what you just told me," I said to Stampel, "does your institute really believe there is life on Earth?"

"Well, there's *something* out there," Stampel said. "And I have to believe they're trying to communicate with us, even if they refuse to do it by telephone."

Television

How to Get More Value from TV for You and Your Family

Television stands at the pinnacle of the electronic communications evolution. While radio is able to reach more Americans, TV alone has the unique appeal and impact of sound, sight, motion and color. Only a handful, 2 percent, of our homes are without sets, while nearly half have two sets or more.

Standing front and center as the primary leisure time companion of the American family (sets are in use over six hours per day in the average home), television now offers at least seven channels to two thirds of our homes while hardly any receive fewer than three.

Through these channels come drama and comedy, music and news, sports and documentaries and discussions. Some of the benefits these provide are obvious: entertainment, information about local, national and world news. For most viewers, young and old, television is their sole contact with places, people and events that few people can hope to confront directly. The value of this wider view of our world is immeasurable. It has affected our politics and economics, our perspectives on ourselves and our neighbors on a planet which television has brought so close.

Other benefits, more specific and novel, are being developed through the joint efforts of broadcasters, educators and parents. These range from simple do-it-yourself activities to more elaborate plans that involve entire school systems. All of them depend on the new and exciting ingredient of viewer participation and use. Here are some examples:

Planned family viewing. Shared viewing experiences bring families closer together, not just physically, but in discussion and even in the planning process itself. As a first step, check local TV guides or newspaper listings each week. Make a group decision on what looks interesting, then post the list near the TV set and follow through.

Parent Participation TV Workshops: Developed by *Teachers Guides to Television* (P. O. Box 564, Lenox Hill Station, New York, New York 10021), this project starts with meetings of parents and their children at a school or other convenient place where a trained leader guides discussion after a program is viewed. Both generations learn to exchange ideas and to come to better understanding of themselves, each other and of the issues raised by the program. Hard-to-deal-with subjects like death, sex, drugs and personal relationships can be spoken of more freely and frankly when the starting point is a television program. The techniques learned at the workshop can then be applied at home.

Publications like *Teachers Guides to Television* make it possible for schools and parents to multiply the values in regularly available programs. Some creative teachers have incorporated their students' TV interests into their classroom activities to enhance language arts skills, vocabulary enrichment, written and oral expression and development of logical thought and reasoning ability. Others have had similar success in history, current affairs and the performing arts.

Stations and networks underwrite and offer special projects for improving reading skills by employing scripts of popular programs.

Teacher Rosemary Lee Potter urges teachers to capitalize on the positive offerings of commercial television. She speaks of its sustained interest for young viewers, points out that it "furnishes a common body of information for [their] early socialization," and believes that the true worth of television depends not only on the content of the programs, but "on how we extract and refine what resources of TV we have and how we put them to use."

Parental responsibility for children's better use of TV is being given new importance by educators, child psychologists and parent groups as well as broadcasters. Dr. Louise Bates Ames, President of the Gesell Institute of Child Development, calls parental involvement the key to productive viewing by children. She offers these basic principles: (1) Know what your children are watching. Suggest programs you feel they'd like. Set limits to their viewing if you think that's necessary. And share their viewing experience with them when you can. (2) Explain the things your children don't understand. They'll surprise you by what they know and also by what they don't. You can help them understand what's real and what's make-believe. (3) Discuss the program. Let the discussion lead to whatever interests or puzzles them. Listen to their points of view. This can help unlock feelings. (4) Consciously set out to let television help you get to know your children better. You'll learn about their values and their tastes *and* they'll learn about yours.

The shared viewing experience not only stimulates the interplay of thoughts and feelings, but also helps the child to understand himself and his parents better and to build a solid set of moral values.

Another positive effect of popular entertainment programs has been their effect on library circulation and book reading. Novels and historical works on which programs are based become best-sellers. School libraries stay abreast of television schedules, knowing the rush that will follow the broadcast of a book-related special or series.

While the entertainment and relaxation television provides are important contributions to our social fabric, the best is yet to come as the audience itself gains greater media literacy and learns to make the most of what is at its fingertips.

CREDIT: *Roy Danish, Director, Television Information Office of the National Association of Broadcasters, New York, New York.*

TV or Not TV

The influence of TV was vividly brought home to me a number of years ago. The previous evening I had just read Aldous Huxley's warning about the powers held by the mass media in contemporary society. He stated that one of the most dangerous aspects about this situation is that a child is unable to differentiate between reality and unreality on the screen.

I read this and it registered—but vaguely. The following evening my four-year-old boy came racing into my study, screaming at me to come into the other room immediately. We went together where he had been watching a western on TV. He shouted: "Daddy, that man is going to *kill* the other man!" To him that was reality.

All of us have read news stories about children who murder, and then are very sad when they discover that the victim is not going to get up and appear later, the way they do on TV. (He has seen the same actor who was killed on one show appear safe and sound on another.)

Dr. Michael Rothenberg analyzes just what the average child is taking in: "On the basis of the Nielsen Index figures, the average American child will have viewed some 15,000 hours of television by the time he has been graduated from high school, as compared with his having been exposed to some 11,000 hours of formal classroom instruction. He will have witnessed some 18,000 murders and countless highly detailed incidents of robbery, arson, bombing, forgery, smuggling, beating and torture—averaging approximately one per minute in the standard television cartoon for children under the age of ten. There is six times more violence during one hour of children's television than there is in one hour of adult television."

Rothenberg then turns to the effect upon the child of the advertising battering ram: "Twenty-five percent of the television industry's profit comes from the 7 percent of its programming directed at children. While the Code of Hammurabi in 2250 B.C. made selling something to a child or buying something from a child without the power of attorney a crime punishable by death, in A.D. 1975 our children are exposed to some 350,000 commercials by the time they reach age eighteen, promising super-power, sugar-power and kid-power.

Advertising develops in the child premature cynicism. Children of previous generations became cynical only with age. Now children of four and five already are disillusioned by extravagant promises about the products that fail to materialize: the little wooden train that careened so merrily around the track on the TV ad, when purchased, barely makes its way around once. This loss of youthful trust and idealism is a tragedy. Broken promises raise serious questions in the minds of the young. Who can they believe?

We wonder about the escalating divorce rate, free love, and the loss of fidelity within marriage. How can a child grow up with virtue intact when he is subjected to a constant barrage of sexually oriented ads and programming, prematurely exposed to sexual innuendo, double and triple entendres with a barracks twist.

In these silver screen presentations he sees marriage ridiculed, and adultery and free love as valid substitutes. He is programmed to believe that no love relationship can be permanent. He learns that what is important is "kicks"— to drain like a honeybee all the sweetness from each flower and then go on to the next. He is taught that true love is for squares. Sexual compatibility is all that counts.

The game shows which give away obscene sums of money and gifts have given us the idea that one should not have to work for a living, that greed is natural and honesty is old-fashioned junk left around by the Puritans.

While we are on the subject of game shows, have you ever noticed that about 95 percent of the questions asked deal with trivia? Those who watch game shows waste a staggering amount of time learning almost nothing of value. Sample gems of knowledge one can pick up are these: "In 1934 who played the part of the maid for the leading lady in the South Seas unforgettable classic filmed by the great director Mr. X?"; "What hit tune came from an obscure Broadway show which began in 1942 and then . . . ?" et cetera.

And let's not minimize the effects of televised sports. It does little good to indoctrinate your child with sportsmanlike ideals, then subject his consciousness to the brutalizing arena of professional football, hockey and baseball, where winning means everything, and the way the game is played— unless caught by the umpire—means very little. When we hear our children discussing the Sunday football game and gleefully reveling in the possibly permanent maiming of the other team's quarterback, then I believe we have cause for serious soul-searching.

I'll have to admit to an inconsistency here, for I greatly enjoyed televised sports myself, but it is this winning at any cost, cripple your opponent when the ump isn't looking, the mockery of the fair play principle that disturbs me.

TV VERSUS THE FAMILY

Of all modern inventions, with the possible exception of the automobile, TV has battered the family more than any other. The problem is that the one-eyed monster, instead of being subservient to its owner, ends up dominating in far too many cases. Just deciding what program to watch can create a family fight. Because most of us are one-track minds, we get testy when interrupted. Thus children who have questions that need to be answered—and may never be asked again—are treated rudely by the adults glued to the box. Recently, one of my students told her class how delighted she was when the TV broke down. "The family actually spoke to one another!" she said. How disappointed she was when the set was repaired.

In TV-dominated homes there is very little reading together, hiking together, participating in hobbies together, laughing and crying together, asking and answering the important questions of life. Without these there is no real home; it is merely a glorified motel.

TV breeds discourtesy. Even when company comes the guests, forced to compete with the TV, must shout to be heard. TV also breeds laziness. Work is left undone because it's much easier to vegetate in front of the tube.

TV is destructive to our physical well-being in that we sit instead of exercise. One tends to snack a lot while watching the set, which results in obesity. TV ruins holidays. Thanksgiving used to mean thoughtful meditation on our many blessings, a good dinner, followed by horseshoes, baseball or volleyball. Now it means a huge dinner ruined by eight hours of televised football.

Another liability of television is its almost unbelievable waste of our most precious commodity—time. In all fairness, not all TV is evil; nevertheless, much of the time spent watching it is wasted. Every moment of life is precious.

In summary: It is clear that TV stifles creativity, destroys family togetherness, wrecks reading and writing habits, shortens the attention span, encourages greed and laziness, deifies trivia, ignores great ideas, warps concepts of love and marriage, pre-empts needed silence, weakens the physical body, and wastes vast amounts of irreplaceable time.

On the other hand, TV does offer some good programs. The news usually is well presented, though it is more predigested and preselected than in newspapers. There have been some excellent documentaries and literary works shown. Educational TV has pioneered a new approach to learning, and the Church is just beginning to tap TV as a means of spreading the word of God.

But we still come back to this: Either we rule TV or it will destroy us and those dear to us—now and forever!

CREDIT: *Joe Wheeler, Ph.D., Professor of History, Southwestern Adventist College, Keene, Texas.*

Television, Violence and the Public Interest

Television is one of the most powerful forces that humanity has ever unleashed against itself. And the quality of human life may ultimately depend on our ability to comprehend and control that force.

Now there are 71.2 million homes in the United States, and over 97 percent of them are equipped with a television set. (In fact, more homes in America have TV than have indoor plumbing!) The television is turned on for more than six hours every day. The average male viewer, between his second and sixty-fifth birthday, watches roughly 72,000 hours of television. That translates into 3,000 full days, or approximately nine full years of his life. Every weekday evening nearly one half of all Americans can be found silently glued to the TV screen.

With that much of our lives spent in front of the TV, it is no wonder that psychologists, academicians and media analysts have, for years, been arguing about the impact of television on the attitudes and behavior of those who watch it. The television industry has been accused of employing racist, sexist and ageist stereotypes in its programming—stereotypes that perpetuate false myths about minorities, women and the elderly. It has been charged with ignoring the needs of America's children, choosing to baby-sit them, rather than educate and inform them. Critics complain that television promotes alcoholism and drug use by depicting actors and actresses incessantly consuming liquor to solve their emotional dilemmas, or popping pills to unwind after a hard day at the office.

To each of these charges, and others, the industry has attempted to respond.

But there is one issue which has engendered the most severe public outrage and rigid resistance by the network and programming executives: the impact of TV violence.

For almost twenty-five years experts have debated the pros and cons of televiolence. The assassinations of President Kennedy, Senator Robert Kennedy, and Martin Luther King, Jr., the campus uprisings, the ghetto riots— all were evidence that violence was becoming an increasingly acceptable way of venting one's dissatisfaction with the American system. But the question

was "Why?" Why had Americans chosen this sort of outlet for their grievances?

To quote from the National Commission on the Causes and Preventions of
Violence:

> A large body of research on observational learning by pre-school children
> confirms children can and do learn aggressive behavior from what they see in a
> film or on a TV screen. The vast majority of experimental studies . . . have
> found that observed violence stimulates aggressive behavior rather than the op-
> posite.

But this outcry against televised violence has not been limited to govern-
ment-appointed committees. It has involved dozens of private groups as well.
Educators, psychiatrists, pediatricians and, most recently, the American Medical Association have called for action. Dr. Richard Palmer, then AMA President, called upon the television industry to re-examine its policies regarding
violence, charging that: "TV violence is a mental health problem and an environmental issue which may be creating a more serious problem of air pollution than industrial plants."

The International Association of Police Chiefs is appalled at the amount of
crime and violence on prime-time entertainment programming—enough so
that it now considers television a college of criminal instruction. Police blot-
ters record that tonight's television crime will be tomorrow's crime statistic.
In fact, criminals have confessed to watching TV's "action/adventure" shows
with pen in hand, jotting down innovative crimes and abuses dreamed up by
Hollywood's best writers.

Religious leaders of virtually every denomination have spoken out. The academic, research and foundation communities are involved in the struggle to
reduce television violence. Most major magazines and newspapers have written about the issue.

But with all the brouhaha over television violence, the most important
question must not be forgotten: What are the documented dangers?

For starters, over 146 published papers representing 50 different studies
involving 10,000 people all independently concluded that violence-viewing
produces increased aggressiveness, both immediately after the viewing experience and later in life as well. These studies confirm that aggressive behavior
is observed and remembered but whether it is actually carried out depends on
a number of things: the similarity between the TV setting and the viewer's
real setting; the effectiveness of the observed aggression in accomplishing its
goal; whether or not the aggressive behavior in the TV show goes un-
punished.

Secondly, televiolence desensitizes the audience to the cruelty of real violence in society, making confrontation and combat acceptable social behavior. The result is an increased willingness to use violence as a problem-solver.

Third, criminals and potential criminals stalk the nightly crime dramas, searching for new ways to commit old crimes, and vice versa. If college credits were offered, TV might become a back alley "open university" with nightly courses in arson, rape, murder, burglary and other forms of human depravity.

Finally, and possibly the most serious charge leveled against televiolence, is that it creates a climate of fear. Stimulated by the excessive portrayals of crime and violence on TV's "action adventure" shows (the industry's euphemism for violence) TV addicts become nervous wrecks worrying about what will happen to them on the street.

The networks have tended to respond to this information with a string of mutually inconsistent and unpersuasive arguments. By and large, these claims bear no relation to reality. A point/counterpoint examination reveals how lacking in substance these claims actually are:

POINT: Nobody has yet proved that televiolence does any real harm.

COUNTERPOINT: More than 500 studies conducted over the last 26 years all singled out television violence as, at a very minimum, a contributing factor in the growing tide of violent behavior that has swelled up in America.

POINT: Children know that TV is not real, and they are not affected by its messages.

COUNTERPOINT: Particularly for young children, who know little of external realities and have nothing with which to compare TV, the TV screen becomes their reality, substituting its portrayal of events for those that are going on in the real world. Indeed, programmers, designers and writers do everything possible to duplicate the real world environment. To conclude that "seeing is *not* believing" contradicts the basic tenets of Madison Avenue advertising.

POINT: Violence on TV is only a reflection of the violence in society at large.

COUNTERPOINT: The problem here is deeper than one might suspect. Television has so inundated us with crimes against humanity that people now believe most crimes are of this nature. The truth is that the majority of crimes recorded by the police involve money or property. More often than not, the criminal never sees his victim. Secondly, the assertion that violence on TV reflects the violence in real life, is patently false. The crimes that are routinely committed on TV nightly drama are relatively infrequent in real life. An FBI Crime report showed that while 14 percent of television crimes were murder, only 0.65 percent of the crimes actually committed that year were homicide. In addition, the role of law enforcers is grossly misrepresented. In real life, most police officers rarely, if ever, fire their guns. On TV, however, over 75 percent used their guns.

POINT: We are giving the public what it wants.

COUNTERPOINT: Only when someone can prove there is a biological need for sadism will this argument make sense. People do not write the networks and plead for more brutality on television. Rather, the programming executives know the ease and frugality with which they can turn out carbon copy killings and force it upon viewers. And when these "shoot-em-up" dramas get good ratings, the smug network people remark with satisfaction, "See, we're giving them what they want." To paraphrase a parable which illustrates the absurdity of their position: If you tie a cow to a post, she will eat the grass she can reach. This does not mean she prefers it.

Broadcasting today is run by corporations which have a virtual lease in perpetuity on the right to broadcast. These corporations are like all other businesses—they are interested in profits. This is not to be viewed as a hostile judgment of these corporations. America has been served well by the profit motive in a competitive system. It does suggest, however, that the system is different today from the way it was envisioned by the pioneers in the industry.

In order to completely understand the programming incentives, it is imperative to examine the economic incentives as well. Broadcasters strive to gain as large an audience as possible—and the audience is attracted or repelled by the broadcasters' programming. Programming is therefore chosen for the number of people it can deliver. The incentive to get the largest audience possible, regardless of good taste, has on occasion driven the networks to arrogant indifference to "what the public wants." Likewise, "what the public will watch" has driven broadcasters to air some extraordinarily putrid shows. The prevailing sentiment among broadcasters is best expressed by Hollywood producer's line, "If people would watch autopsies, we'd put them on."

However, there are some groups who are trying to hold the networks accountable for their deplorable practices.

One such group is the National Citizens Committee for Broadcasting, 1028 Connecticut Avenue NW, Washington, D.C. 20036. With a grant from the American Medical Association, the NCCB prepared a violence profile, listing not only the most violent programs, but naming the sponsors. This information is made available, free to advertisers, networks, producers, shareholders and viewers so that each may take whatever action he thinks most appropriate.

The National PTA has also joined the fight against televiolence, urging its members to boycott products of those manufacturers who sponsor programs with excessive violence.

TV violence is a cheap trick, a gimmick. It costs networks less to produce television programs that will hold an audience's attention if they hire unimaginative writers who follow tested formulas. One of the best tested, surest producers of a quick rating point is violence. The only alternative is to pay America's finest writers to create quality drama. TV has seldom, if ever, been willing to pay this price.

It has now been two and a half decades that experts have been discussing the impact of televiolence on the attitudes and behavior of viewers. And by now the dangers involved have been proved in hundreds of different studies.

We can conclude, at a minimum, that the potential of television to do harm is great, and that it may be doing considerable harm. Dr. Wilber Schramm describes the situation accurately: "We are taking a needless chance with our children's welfare by permitting them to see such a parade of violence across our picture tubes. It is a chance we need not take. It is a danger to which we need not expose our children any more than we need to expose them to tetanus, or bacteria from unpasteurized milk."

CREDIT: *Nicholas Johnson, former Commissioner of the Federal Communications Commission, 1966–73, and since then chairman of the National Citizens Committee for Broadcasting, 1028 Connecticut Avenue NW, Washington, D.C. 20036.*

Temper Tantrums

Temper tantrums are storms which beset young children when frustration or anger overtakes them and they can't express their feelings in words. The pent-up emotion has nowhere to go and the child loses control of himself, flailing, fighting and sometimes holding his breath until his face turns purple. The younger the child, the more violent the tantrum because language ability is still so primitive.

Rare is the parent whose child has never had a temper tantrum. And rarer still is the parent who has been successful in stopping one once it has begun. The child behaves as if he's been seized by demons. All attempts to calm him seem to make matters worse.

What can a parent do? How does one handle a rage that seems to come from nowhere? The first thing to do is remove the child to a quiet place where he can't hurt himself or others. If he seems bent on hurting himself, stay with him. Say, even if you must shout to be heard through his screaming, "I won't let you hurt yourself." He may be pummeling you with his fists. (Stop him by holding his wrists.) He may be banging his body violently. (Toss pillows under him.) He may be crying, screaming or spitting.

Sit quietly in a corner of the room and wait for the storm to subside. Recognize that it will take time for him to defuse and that he himself is frightened by the bombastic nature of his feelings and his lack of control.

This is no time to lecture or threaten or take disciplinary action. This is the time to wait out the storm bolstered by the understanding that he really is unable to help himself. The fury must subside before reason can return.

Often the end of the tantrum is marked by sobs and a rush for affection from you. Be as comforting as you can. It's easier to be non-judgmental about the tantrum when you accept the fact that it is not a deliberate flouting of authority, but rather an inability to cope with rage.

When all is quiet—even the next day perhaps—try to learn what sparked the conflagration. The older the child the more words he has at his command, and the better you will be able to understand what he is trying to tell you. But often he can't say—and even when he tries you may find it hard to understand why his complaint had to erupt in so volatile a fashion.

Be aware that the tantrum is not the real issue. What you have seen is the tail end of the build-up of feeling. For very young children, anger needs to be expressed at the time it is felt.

To prevent or at least neutralize the tantrum, one should encourage the expression of anger in peacemeal fashion. Small verbal outbursts when they are felt can help. For the child who is a non-talker, punching pillows or kicking stools are non-verbal alternatives when he is so angry he must do something. For the four- and five-year-olds words are best. Certainly he should not be allowed to beat up anyone. You can say to him, "It is all right to say it or feel it, but you cannot hurt other people."

The school-age child who is subject to tantrums can be helped to find more appropriate ways of letting off steam. He can walk around the block, complain to a friend or hit a punching bag. The younger child has fewer alternatives and parents need to be clever in finding ways to help him release the pressure.

If the tantrum is of the milder sort (the child is stamping his foot or shouting furiously) you can send him to his room by himself and encourage talk later. Often he starts to play in his room and calms down. Sensible rules must be explained. You could say to him: "I won't let you hurt me, yourself or the house."

It helps to remember that the child is often in conflict with himself about many things as he is growing up. He wants to be big; he wants to be small. He loves the new baby, he hates the new baby. He wants to be clean; he likes to make messes. He wants to be the boss; yet he fears his imaginary power and hides from thunder. Such conflicts are part of normal development and if you know this, you will be less threatened by normal growth clashes.

In the larger context of family life, what can one do to avoid or at least reduce the intensity of the tantrum? It may be helpful to allow the child to make some decisions that affect his life. It helps diminish the power struggle with you when he is allowed to decide some issues that really have no great importance. For example: What hat to wear, whether he gets chocolate milk or not, whether to invite over a friend or not. These small matters of assertiveness (and they would vary from family to family depending on what your own priorities are) modify his power wishes and make him more amenable to your having the final word on the big issues. Yielding on things that don't really count is not a retreat from discipline but a recognition of the child's emotional immaturity. It diminishes struggle rather than escalates it. The adult can then save his ammunition for what is genuinely important.

Finally it should cheer everybody up to know that in the normal course of events, temper tantrums decrease as the child gets older. When they occur try to find out what is creating the additional pressure on the child. By so doing you can help him deal with his feelings so he can find the road to greater self-control and self-acceptance.

CREDIT: *Eleanor Weisberger, Child Therapist, Beachwood, Ohio, author of* Your Young Child and You, *New York, New York: E. P. Dutton & Co.*

Tennis Elbow

Tennis elbow is a form of bursitis. It is nearly always caused by an inflammation, strain or injury.

Tennis elbow usually occurs in very aggressive individuals who attempt to "kill the ball," play and work with great intensity, and therefore it is believed that emotions may be a precipitating factor.

Symptoms and findings of tennis elbow are:

(1) Elbow joint motion is painless, no swelling of the elbow joint is present.

(2) There is a localized tenderness of the bony part of the forearm.

(3) Turning the forearm and hand upward is extremely painful.

(4) One notices weakness of the wrist and pain when the wrist is moved upward.

Tennis elbow is not limited to tennis players. It may result following any injury or activity that involves the back muscles of the forearm and other muscles nearby.

X rays of the elbow are of no value in the diagnosis except to eliminate other causes. Tennis elbow is not a life-threatening disease. It can affect persons of all ages and either sex.

Treatment includes:

(1) Heat.

(2) Rest—avoidance of the source of the injury or irritation.

(3) One or more injections of a local anesthetic agent and cortisone into the precise area of local tenderness, which is known as the trigger spot.

(4) If symptoms persist in spite of the above measures, it may be necessary

to put the forearm and wrist into a cast for a few weeks to completely rest the arm.

(5) On rare occasions it has been necessary to operate on the affected elbow and cut the attachment of the muscles at their site of origin.

CREDIT: *Daniel M. Miller, M.D., F.A.C., Omaha, Nebraska, Associate Professor of Surgery, University of Nebraska College of Medicine, Omaha, Nebraska.*

Thin People

A forgotten minority, the thin people who long for a filled-out figure but look to themselves like ninety-eight-pound weaklings, had best forget the curves and muscles.

Unlike the very fat, who can lose weight if they are placed on a low-calorie diet, the very thin are almost impossible to fatten up, said Dr. Jean Mayer, Harvard nutritionist.

They are products of genetic determination. They lack adipose tissue, the storage vaults for fat. While a pound of fat accumulates when 3,500 more calories are eaten than expended, if there are no adipose cells there is no place for the fat to accumulate.

The lean who worry about their wispy appearance are usually young men and women between seventeen and twenty-five. The men want over-all weight and bigger muscles. The women want rounder arms and thighs, a bustier chest and a little more derrière.

When they consult a physician they usually say they want to gain weight to make them feel better. But all data from insurance statistics agree that the thinnest people live longer and are least affected by the degenerative diseases, Dr. Mayer said.

Trying to get more food into them is virtually impossible. They say they eat huge meals, but when it is measured the daily intake is quite small.

"Our work at Harvard's nutrition department suggests that persons with very limited fat deposits have sudden and complete feelings of satiety," Dr. Mayer wrote in *Family Health*. "Unlike most of us who can usually be persuaded to have a little more of a favorite dish, these constitutionally thin people stop feeling hungry quite abruptly and would gag at another mouthful."

The very thin have ectomorphic frames—elongated skeletons, narrow hands and feet, long fingers and toes. They are to be distinguished from endomorphs, who are often thin during their youth but take on weight in middle age.

"The inability of constitutionally very thin to gain weight is an excellent example of the complexity of the problem of weight control," Dr. Mayer noted. "Very complex mechanisms regulate food intake and the rate of fat synthesis and utilization."

"The difficulty—indeed the near impossibility—for many thin people to gain weight, even temporarily, is an indication of the difficulty that many fat people have in losing weight, at least permanently."

After a checkup to be sure that the thinness is not due to a chronic disease, the best advice Dr. Mayer had for thin folks is to concentrate on good posture, choose clothes, colors and patterns that do not emphasize the appearance of slenderness and, for the ladies, some padding here and there in strategic places.

CREDIT: *Arthur J. Snider, Science and Medicine, Chicago* Sun-Times.

Thumb-sucking

Thumb-sucking and its equivalents, such as sucking fingers, toes or the corner of a towel or blanket, are common in infancy.

During the first three or four months of life, sucking is the sole method by which the infant gets nourishment. It is also one of his first co-ordinated acts from which he gets pleasure. Choice of the thumb as a sucking object is natural, since it is the most likely appendage to come into contact with the mouth in random movements of the hand.

The thumb-sucking habit usually becomes established during the early months of life. When it persists beyond infancy, into the preschool years, the possibility of a deeper problem must be examined.

Thumb-sucking is most likely to occur when the child is about to go to sleep, when he is watching television or when he is hungry, tired or ill. It may occur if he feels displaced by a younger child or otherwise senses withdrawal of parental interest. The message can be one of many. It could also mean the child is overfatigued, bored or unhappy.

Thumb-sucking is usually harmless. If it persists continuously and intensely, it may cause mal-positioning of the teeth and require lengthy and expensive orthodontal care. Ordinarily, the habit is dropped at about two years of age, but not infrequently it may continue until five or six, or even into adult life.

Treatment should be directed toward correcting the symptom rather than the thumb-sucking itself. In the case of an infant, if he is taking his feedings too rapidly and has too little sucking pleasure it might be wise to lengthen the feeding periods.

In older children threats of punishment, shaming and constant reminders to "take your thumb out of your mouth" are usually of no avail. In fact, they tend to reinforce the habit.

Applying bad-tasting substances to the thumb and using thumb covers, metal mittens or elbow splints are equally ineffective and may create additional emotional problems.

The thumb-sucking child should have ample rest and play outlets. He should, if the habit persists beyond two years of age, be given more time and attention, and extra assurance of parental love.

CREDIT: *Jay M. Arena, M.D., Chief of Pediatrics, Duke University Medical Center, Durham, North Carolina; author of* Child Safety Is No Accident, *with Miriam Bachar, M.A., Duke University Press, Durham, North Carolina. Reviewed by: David Van Gelder, M.D., FAAP, president of the American Academy of Pediatrics 1977–78, Baton Rouge, Louisiana.*

Tickling

Tickling in its earliest stages is a form of body contact between a parent and a child that evokes a pleasurable emotional response in both. It is a normal response of the parent to the young baby and is a conduit for transmitting the parent's love and affection to the baby as well as eliciting a happy response from the baby, thus reassuring the tickling parent that the baby loves the parent also. When the baby grows up and in turn becomes a parent, he will then tickle his own child in order to convey and receive the same emotional and physical contact that he once experienced.

If the child is stimulated inappropriately by excessive tickling, then the pleasurable feeling becomes one of pain. In addition, the child may feel that he is losing control of his body and this can be very frightening to him. The knowledge that excessive tickling can be painful and frightening has been known since ancient times, when tickling was used as a method of torture.

A parent, in addition to his wish to have pleasant body contact with a child, may also have angry feelings toward the child. These angry feelings may stem from the fact that the parent may feel troubled by the dependency needs of the baby when his own dependency needs have not been fully met. Or the angry feelings may be due to the fact that unwittingly the child reminds the parent of someone in the parent's background toward whom he felt anger. Or the anger may really be toward the other parent but is projected onto the baby.

If the parent is aware of the fact that he is feeling angry towards the baby, he will then deal with his own anger in an appropriate way. However, if the parent cannot allow himself to be aware of these angry feelings, then the parent will not know consciously that he is feeling angry toward the baby. Instead, the anger will come out indirectly. It may be in the way the parent physically handles the baby, such as when he tickles him. The tickling may become rough or excessive without the parent realizing it. The baby now feels a painful and frightened reaction to the parent's tickling and will associate tickling with pain and unpleasantness and fright.

When the baby in turn grows up and becomes a parent and experiences anger toward his own baby, he may tend to express his own angry feelings toward the baby also through tickling. Thus the pattern continues from generation to generation. In a more severe form, the same pattern shows itself in the area of child abuse.

When one parent (for example, the mother) realizes that the other parent (for example, the father) is causing the baby pain and panic by the way he tickles him, the mother can handle this in the following way:

(1) Realize that it is not a deliberate act by the father and that he does not realize that he is inflicting pain on the baby.

(2) Point out to her husband that the tickling is not really an expression of affection, though it may be intended as such. Explain that the baby really feels pain and fear.

(3) Suggest to her husband that when he feels affectionate toward the baby he not show it through tickling but instead find another way of showing it, for example, spending more time with the baby.

(4) Ask herself if there are any marital problems for which the baby is serving as a scapegoat.

(5) If she feels it is appropriate and that her husband is prepared to listen she may tactfully suggest to him that, without realizing it, he sometimes feels angry at the baby and perhaps he should think about this and ask himself what this anger is all about.

CREDIT: *Jack Scofield, M.D., Associate Professor, Department of Psychiatry, Indiana University, School of Medicine, Indianapolis, Indiana.*

TICKLING

DEAR ANN LANDERS: I wrote to you several months ago to ask what to do about my husband's tickling our three-year-old son. We had many arguments about it. I felt he was subconsciously antagonizing the child because Timmy always ended up crying. My husband said I was crazy—that it was all in fun and the child was crying from exhaustion, but he really liked it.

Your response was, "Tell your husband to knock it off. Tickling can be an expression of hostility. The one being tickled may laugh—at first—but soon the frustration becomes too much and anger sets in. One of these days your son might retaliate with a knuckle sandwich."

Today, Ann, we both won our point. Enclosed is the clipping that tells the story. When my husband read the story in the paper his face went white. Love you, Lady!   TO THE VICTOR

DEAR VIC: I must let my readers in on "the enclosed." Here it is—a UPI wire service story from Zanesville, Ohio. Dateline Cleveland:

"If Edward Bruening could talk these days you can bet he'd be bragging about his seventeen-month-old son, Jamie, who packs quite a punch.

"Bruening needed three hours of surgery Monday to repair a broken jaw suffered in a tickling session with his twenty-three-pound offspring.

"'Every morning he goes to wake his daddy up,' said Mrs. Bruening. 'They were on the bed tickling each other. Both of them relaxed on the pillow for a moment, then Eddy tickled him again.

"'James came around with a quick right and hit him on the left side of the jaw.'

"Bruening, who weighs 147 pounds, said his jaw hurt and ten minutes after the punch he couldn't hold a cigarette in his mouth. He went to Lutheran Medical Center on the advice of his sister, Janice, a clinician at the hospital.

"The doctors told him he had a fractured jaw apparently because his son hit him just right. They then used twenty wires to keep his jaw shut for the next six weeks."

TICS (Nervous Twitching)

Tics (nervous twitching) are a common and usually temporary disorder of children, especially at ages eight and nine. These must be differentiated from motor tics and motor-verbal tics which may be of greater significance.

By definition tics are any involuntary muscular movement. Most tics are of the eyelids, face and shoulders, but they may occur also in any voluntary muscle and may form complicated patterns.

Tics tend to be short-lived and they vanish in the normal child by the age of ten, to appear again in later life at times of stress. A good night's sleep will often suffice for the temporary tics to disappear.

When tics continue for longer than a month, they should be evaluated by a neurologist with a trained eye. Prolonged tics may be related to physical illnesses for which the patient should be treated without delay.

The treatment of tics depends on the diagnosis. Tics which are reflective of tension may require the services of a mental health expert, but often thoughtful inquiry by a concerned friend or teacher into the reasons for tension can relieve the condition. Special consideration should be given to the symbolic meaning of the movement for clues.

Medication has been found useful for people who have had encephalitis and Gilles de la Tourette's disease. A physician should supervise a course of treatment, including the use of Haldol, L-Dopa, Cogentin and Artane as the condition warrants. The physician-supervision is necessary for monitoring the condition, as well as for control of medication.

Tics are of historical interest. Sam Boswell suffered from what was probably Gilles de la Tourette's disease: "He is forever dancing the devil's jig, and sometimes he makes the most driveling effort to whistle some thought in his awkward paroxyms." Other contemporary witnesses confirm the fact that Johnson had a whole complex of tics that kept him jerking, kicking and flailing about in his chair. (From *Samuel Johnson: His Friends and Enemies* by Peter Quennell.)

In literature, tics are often used to convey implicit tension and evidences of guilt, as, for example, in the works of Sherlock Holmes. Historically, tics have been seen as conveying the ebbing of power.

Through the centuries the *maladie de tiques* has been the harbinger of anxiety and the symbol of discontent.

CREDIT: *Mary Giffin, M.D., Medical Director of the Irene Josselyn Clinic, Northfield, Illinois.*

Time

How to Manage It
(*Advice from the head of America's largest corporation, based on his own methods*)

What success I have had in parceling out the too-few hours of each day I attribute to three factors:

First, I am not a brooder.

Second, the people I work with are the best in the world at what they do.

Third, I like my work.

In my experience, most decisions are best made now. There are not many problems that solve themselves, nor do they get any easier if shifted to the bottom of the pile.

There are, of course, problems too complex and too crucial for immediate decision. Faced with these, I decide *not* to decide. But after all the facts are in, all the angles have been aired and all the possibilities and ramifications considered, I like to haul off and decide. I don't brood over a problem, preferring instead to confront it and act on it and move on to the next one.

I am uncertain whether my preference for dealing with problems on the spot is an ingrained personal characteristic or a practice developed over the years in response to the pressures of business. I suspect it is both. At any rate, I seldom relegate a problem, no matter how complex, to the bottom drawer for consideration at a later time. I like to tackle it now.

That leads me to factor number two: delegation. In a business as large and as complicated as A.T.&T., the delegation of major responsibilities is a management must. There is no other way to operate this business successfully. In order to accomplish this you must have people with proved ability to do the jobs you delegate. And we have. As a result, it isn't necessary for me to spend much time second-guessing. If you match the right people with the right responsibilities, you will get the right results. In fact, so important is that principle that I never begrudge the time I spend identifying and developing future managers. It's the most important thing I do.

Delegation gives me time for activities that require my personal attention.

Spokesman on behalf of my business—and of Business—is one such activity. Accordingly I try to do my part in such organizations as The Business

Council, The Business Roundtable, United Way, etc. In addition to these activities, I serve on a number of corporate boards.

Of course, one must be selective. Organizations that simply want my name on their letterheads are of no interest to me. I am attracted to organizations that are doing important serious work to which I can contribute something.

Similarly one must be selective with respect to invitations to speak. I probably accept too many, but there is one criterion I apply to all invitations to speak: Do I have something to say worth saying? Beyond that, the demands on my time require that I ask whether it is a significant national audience and whether my appearance will help the operating telephone company serving that particular area of the country. I check this out with the company president and if he feels my presence might benefit the business in its operations there. If he says yes, I accept the invitation if possible.

The trick is to keep internal and external duties in proper balance so they complement one another and contribute to the positive management of time.

The third factor I credit with contributing to my own management of time is what I will call, simply, the joy of the job. This may be the most critical element of all. Without it, you're sunk.

I truly love what I do. And I have felt that way about every job I have held in this business, all twenty-three of them, over a period of forty-one years. When you feel good about your work, it is really not all that difficult to get the most out of each day. I feel very fortunate to have been in a business and to have held jobs in it that have been so satisfying. There is no question in my mind that my use of time over the years has been a reflection of the way I have always felt about the work I have done.

Finally, some general comments about getting things done:

I work in the car, on planes and trains, and in helicopters, too. I take a briefcase home every night. Normally I spend a few hours working on Sundays as well. I arrive at the office a little after eight in the morning, and usually leave by six P.M. It is rare when I do not attend a business-related dinner during the week. Mrs. De Butts attends many of these dinners with me. We have an apartment in New York and manage to meld our social and business lives very comfortably.

I don't want to leave the impression that I am a business grind, a workaholic. I'm not. When there is work to be done I like to get it done so I have time to enjoy life—family and friends, a round of golf, skeet shooting. The pressure of work left over weighs heavily on my conscience.

There are only so many minutes and hours in a day. To get the most out of them I try to stay pretty loose, both in personal style and in terms of my schedule. I don't like to rigidly structure every day. Of course, when one meeting comes on the heels of another, it is difficult to keep a schedule as open-ended as I would like. But in general I remain flexible rather than mechanical. It is the only way I can deal with developments that pop up unexpectedly . . . and they always do.

Do I think my way of managing time is best? It seems to be for me, although I seldom feel at the end of a day that I have accomplished all that I wanted to.

I don't think this is a bad way to feel. I think, in fact, it is a good way. It means I've managed my time pretty well but I could probably do better.

CREDIT: *John deButts, Chairman, American Telephone and Telegraph Company, New York, New York.*

Tipping

STINGY, MESSY WOMEN

DEAR ANN: I have a few words for that idiot who thinks women should not be expected to tip when they eat out. I'm a waitress who has worked most of my life and I'd 10 times rather serve men.

Women are stingy tippers. They demand more service and request a lot of substitution. (Two vegetables, no potato.) They almost always leave the table in a mess. I think they're getting even with their kids who leave messy tables for THEM to clean up.

I'd rather serve males any day. SOUTH DAKOTA

DEAR S.D.: In your field you are the authority, and I'll take your word for it. I hope your message gets across to the females out there who recognize themselves.

According to most experts on etiquette, the practice began back in medieval England when pubs installed collection boxes inscribed with the words "To Insure Prompt Service." The slogan later was shortened to "tips."

The policy gradually spread to most parts of the globe in one form or another. Militant non-tippers may take heart that the situation is even worse in many other countries than here in the United States.

In England, for example, the usher who shows you to your seat in a theater usually expects a shilling or two for his service. The same principle applies in most of Europe as well. Here it applies mostly to major sports events in stadiums and arenas.

In Morocco, guides have been known to leave tourists stranded in the winding marketplace if they are not given a few dirhams for their shopping advice.

And in Romania, surgeons expect a large payment if they gave only a small scar following an operation. Most patients are afraid not to shell out for fear they may need further medical care.

Americans have made sporadic efforts to curb tipping without much luck.

During the early 1900s, six states passed laws prohibiting tipping, but they later were declared unconstitutional by the U. S. Supreme Court.

Since then, efforts have been aimed at educating the consumer on alternatives to mindless straight 15-percent tipping.

The Non-Tipping Society of the United States, a California-based group, for example, advises its members to leave a card saying "thank you" instead of a tip. Waiters rarely say, "You're welcome."

Taking another approach. Tippers International, which began in Wisconsin, suggests that diners tip 15 to 20 percent only if the service is totally satisfactory.

Many consumers seem to approve of tipping. Some more than others. In fact, a lot more than others.

Although the *Guinness Book of World Records* does not include figures on the "biggest tip ever given," stories of enormous gratuities often pop up in the nation's newspapers.

In 1969, for example, a waitress in Pueblo, Colorado, served a customer a bowl of soup and received a 1959 Cadillac for her trouble.

And in 1972, an English cab driver received a $47,000 tip for chauffeuring an elderly woman around town several times a week.

Although few people exhibit such largesse, workers in service-related fields generally agree that there are certain "big-tip" types.

Among them are businessmen who are on expense accounts, businessmen who have had a few drinks too many and businessmen who are trying to make time with the waitresses.

The biggest of all are people who have worked for tips themselves.

CREDIT: *Kathleen Begley, Chicago* Daily News *reporter.*

WOMEN'S WAITRESS WOES

DEAR ANN LANDERS: I have a few words for that waitress in South Dakota who chastised women for being "stingy tippers." She said she would rather wait on men any day. I have had to endure many waitresses who ignored my presence, except to slap some food in front of me while they were asking my husband if he'd like more water, more coffee, or, "Was the food OK?" If waitresses gave women the same attention and courtesy they give men, the tips might be bigger. IRATE IN OKLAHOMA

DEAR OKLA: I received dozens of letters from women who wrote to express the same sentiments. The volume of mail and the intensity of their wrath convinced me there's something to it. There's got to be a lesson in here someplace.

BELEAGUERED TIPPER

DEAR ANN LANDERS: May I have the last word on tipping? For those who are interested, "tips" originated in England. It stands for "To Insure Proper Service."

With unions, minimum-wage laws and the outrageous prices these days, it seems to me that waiters and waitresses should be paid a decent wage by the employer. The already beleaguered customer ought not to have to leave an additional 15 or 20 percent "to insure proper service." He is entitled to it, along with the meal. N. S. HAMPTON BAYS

DEAR HAM: Of course you're right, but waiters and waitresses depend on those tips for a decent living. Although I agree with you in principle, until the system is changed, we've got to go along with something I personally deplore, and hope will be changed one day.

Tipping—a Word from Ann Landers

Most people resent tipping, but it is part of the "system" and since we know there are people whose livelihood depends on it, we do it.

In restaurants, a 15-percent tip is considered good. For special service a 20-percent tip is considered very generous.

A doorman who hails you a taxi should get at least twenty-five cents. If it is raining or snowing, fifty cents is fair. If it's pouring or a snowstorm is in progress, a dollar is a nice way to say, "Thank you."

Usually the captain (in a swanky restaurant) expects two dollars for seating you and making sure you have a good table. If the table isn't good or if you are not inclined to tip him, forget it. It is not essential.

If the wine steward has given you some help with your selection of wine, he should get two dollars.

Skycaps at the airport expect and should get at least fifty cents a bag.

A bellman in a hotel should get a dollar for a single bag, when he carries it to your room. If there are more bags, he should receive more money. The hotel doorman who takes your bags inside should receive a dollar for his trouble. When you check out, and he helps put the bags in the car or taxi, another dollar, please. Maids in hotels are usually forgotten. This is ironic— and unfair—since they do the dirtiest work. A dollar tip (left in the glass in the bathroom) for a one-night stay is always a pleasant surprise. If you are vacationing and spending several days at a resort, increase the gratuity accordingly.

Hairdressers expect to be tipped. In salons, the tip should be 15 percent of the bill. The manicurist—ditto. If they do an exceptionally good job, make it 20 percent.

The boys who deliver your newspaper should get a "reward" at Christmas time. If the service has been faithful and good, five dollars is a lovely gift—if you can afford it. Also, the postman should be remembered. Also, the garbageman—if you live in a home. The employees of your apartment building should also be remembered—if you are a "cliff dweller" as I am.

And now—for rotten service. *Don't tip anything*. The notion that a small tip will "give them the message" is absurd. You are throwing away your money. The best message is *no tip*.

Toilet Training

Toilet training seems to be one of the most vexing challenges of child rearing. While some parents find their children take to it easily, most parents often find it a battleground that is upsetting to everyone.

One explanation is that when you undertake toilet training you are asking your child to do something *your* way for the very first time. Before this, you asked very little of him. When you undertake toilet training you become a requester, a "do it in the pot, please" person. The child acquires a power he never had before. He can say no emphatically. As a matter of fact, a child tends to be in his most negative stage just about the time you decide to toilet train him. Often he behaves as though being asked to *give* means being asked to *give in*. So the issue of conflict must be faced.

In an effort to avoid a battle, some parents attempt to train early. Others, to avoid conflict, procrastinate and start the training later. It has been found that neither of these is as constructive as the training that starts when the child is ready. Experience has shown that he is ready when the following conditions are met:

(1) The sphincter muscles are fully developed (at about eighteen months) so he can control himself.

(2) He can walk fairly well.

(3) He has some words at his disposal.

(4) He has shown some ability to be dry for several hours at a time.

This happens at about eighteen months or so, so that's a good time to begin. You can start by naming the functions several months before if you like—sixteen months or so—leading him to the potty, showing him where he is to go, even emptying his diaper into the potty. This is regarded as preliminary to the training.

At around eighteen to twenty months you take the plunge and buy the following: training pants, a pail for soaking and a wire brush. You already have the potty or seat attachment. The latter is actually not as helpful because often he is afraid he will fall in. When you put him in training pants and announce that this is what big boys (and big girls) wear he gets the idea that he is getting to be big and this is a step toward growing up.

To make it easier on yourself, have clean-up supplies available so you can keep your cool in the face of accidents, which are inevitable. Club soda is helpful in cleaning stains and removing odor. A mixture of one quart of warm water and two tablespoons of white vinegar and two tablespoons of detergent makes an even more effective spot remover.

Take him to the potty twice a day, especially when he looks like he is about to perform. When you catch him in time, he makes the connection between need and place. For several months you do the changing as you did when he was in diapers. In this interval, teach him how to pull his pants up and down. (Boxer type shorts for both girls and boys make this easier.) What you are doing is showing him how to manage independently. The potty chair is a help here because he can get to it by himself and it can be moved to the floor you are on.

Obviously, there will be greater messing than when he was neatly tucked into diapers and plastic pants. This is how he learns. He feels what is happening. The benefits of this step are great as he begins to learn that he is responsible for what he does. You bring that idea home to him when you start on clean-ups, at about twenty-two or twenty-four months of age. From then on it is he who must rinse out his pants in the toilet (the wire brush is helpful here) and soak them in the pail. If time passes and he is slow to use the pot, you can step up the pressure, a number of months later, by having him wash his pants out with soap.

The training then is not really a training at all—it is education in body mastery. When you view it in this light you will see that becoming "clean" early or late is of less importance than how it happens. Gradual increase in expectations works with the child's increasing intelligence. (He gets smarter as well as older.) It also allows for swings of feeling that seem to go with the age. "Yes?" "Now?" "Later?" "Why Should I?" Also "I like to be messy." "No, I like to be clean."

Knowing that toddlers are conflicted people (often they can't even agree with themselves) should help you be less combative as you recognize this as something they will outgrow. But your insistence that they accept responsibility for what they do—even in the face of childish resistance—is important in character development. It slowly teaches the lessons of responsibility and self-control and it sets a precedent for future learning.

Many feelings, worked out in toilet training, have an influence on a child's response to future tasks in life. In school it is he who must study and complete his work. On the job it is he who must perform. The boost in self-sufficiency is the effort's best reward. It is a process that takes time and it is important that you not become too elated with successes or too downcast by failures. If you are too involved emotionally, he has the ultimate weapon when he chooses to do you in. Fundamentally it is *his* business, therefore, *his* failure and *his* success. When he finally succeeds, his self-esteem increases enormously. It is a victory of self over self—not *you* over *him*. That is why punishment, rewards, threats, stories and all the things parents have used to "win the battle" are useless.

Consistency is important but not always possible. There are times when you go visiting or when your child has "the runs" and it isn't easy to be calm. At these difficult times use two pairs of training pants, or plastic pants over the training pants. Carry an extra pair for emergencies. This is better than going back to diapers—which would be regarded by him as a retreat.

It is not a good idea to perform your body functions in front of your child. Youngsters often find this confusing. Sex differences and size differences seem to mix them up. Better for everyone to have bathroom privacy. Other tips which help include the encouraging of water play and the use of Play-doh, clay or sand (in the summer). Little children love to mess and these are socially acceptable ways of doing so.

Funny things happen when children toilet train. One child may mess in his pants yet is terribly neat about his toys. (Hard to believe, but he is training.) Another child may be dry but messes everything in sight. (He is also training.) This is the clean-dirty struggle that only the child can work out. Insist that he be responsible for his pants. Also, it is better not to press him too hard on other issues when he is training. Meeting one big expectation at a time is as much as he can stand. Neatness about clothes, rooms, etc. can come later.

For those of you with children four and five years of age and up who haven't yet trained, the message is the same. Start now. Insist on clean-ups. Make it plain with the remark "You can't make my house a toilet." Don't punish for resistance. Having to do the clean-ups is the greatest incentive for hitting the pot eventually.

Jealousy may play a part in keeping an older child from training. "You clean her up," he says about the baby. "Why not me?" Acknowledge that it's hard for him but he must be responsible for himself even if sometimes he still wishes he were a baby. You can be sympathetic about his feelings but continue to be firm about the responsibility. The ultimate reward is his own good opinion of himself. You can say, "How proud you must be that you are so grown-up now!"

CREDIT: *Eleanor Weisberger, Child Therapist, Case Western Reserve University, School of Medicine, Cleveland, Ohio, author of* Your Young Child and You, *New York, New York: E. P. Dutton & Co.*

Transsexualism

MEET OUR OFFSPRING

DEAR ANN LANDERS: This is no phony from Yale. I live in Hartford and I don't drive a car. My problem is real and I need an answer.

How do parents introduce a 27-year-old son who has had a sex-change operation? Do we say, "This is our son Bob," or, "This is our daughter Roberta?"

We are trying to be broadminded about the whole thing and it hasn't been easy. Please give us some assistence. STRUGGLING DESPERATELY TO BRIDGE THE GAP

DEAR FRIEND: Since Bob has gone to considerable lengths to be "Roberta," he surely must be dressing in feminine attire. To introduce him as "Bob" would be ludicrous. It seems to me that you are being extremely cooperative and he (or she) should help you out of the tight spots by introducing himself—or herself.

Transsexualism is a rare condition characterized by the conviction on the part of a person that he (or she) is of the opposite sex. Thus a transsexual man might say, "I am a mistake of Nature. I am a woman locked in a man's body." The transsexual woman would say the same thing in reverse.

Both statements would carry the fervent desire to be let out of the "wrong" body by a surgeon—an operation that would change the body, insofar as it is feasible, to resemble that of the desired sex. This is called "sex-reassignment surgery."

For the transsexual man this would mean surgical removal of the penis, testicles and scrotum and the formation of an artificial vagina. It would also mean taking female sex hormones for life. For the transsexual female, surgery would remove breasts, ovaries, tubes and uterus and would mean the construction, by plastic surgery, of an artificial penis. It would also mean taking male sex hormones for life (which might, for example, produce a beard).

Transsexualism is often described as a reversal of gender identity. This means the person's concept of his sexual self does not match what he sees when he looks in a full-length mirror.

In 1953 the United States and the civilized world were startled to read of an American soldier who was "changed into a woman" by an operation in Denmark. When he returned to the United States he went on the stage under the name of Christine Jorgensen. While a few such operations have been done without fanfare during the several decades before 1953, the Christine Jorgensen case created worldwide publicity and intense curiosity as to how such a thing could happen. It was the beginning of an era that would see, twenty years later, sex-reassignment surgery being done in a dozen major American medical centers.

The causes of this strange condition are not known. Guesses range all the way from speculation having to do with how the child was raised by parents (particularly by the mother) to guesses at the other end of the yardstick that have to do with physical or constitutional factors of genetics, body chemistry and the like. However, it must be kept in mind that as of 1977 no one can give a scientific explanation about the causes of transsexualism. They are simply not known.

Nor is it known how often this rare condition occurs in the population. Unlike Public Health surveys of cancer, for example, which quite accurately predict how many cases of various cancers (breast, bladder, colon, etc.) will occur in each 100,000 members of the population, no similar information exists for transsexualism (or for homosexuality and transvestism either). There is no way to send out a questionnaire asking the public to describe themselves sexually, nor could one have much confidence in the accuracy of the results of such a questionnaire if it were attempted.

A typical history of a twenty-year-old transsexual person would read something like this: His (or her) earliest childhood memories give clues of gender confusion. As a little boy, he could not be interested in "boy" sports such as baseball, playing with toy guns and fire trucks or riding on the tractor with his father if they lived on a farm. Rather, this little fellow would prefer to play with dolls, hang around with girls his own age, and play house with them. In his mind, he would be the mother, and try to help his mother in the kitchen. As he grew older, he would, if he could, play "dress-up" in the clothes of a sister which would make him feel "natural and comfortable." He would impress everyone as an extremely feminine boy and be regarded as a "sissy." Later on, others would regard him as "queer" or a "homo." At no time in his life would dressing as a woman cause him to get "charged up" sexually and become so excited that he would have to masturbate to relieve the tension. Such feelings are characteristic of the *transvestite,* who experiences intense sexual urges on cross-dressing. The transsexual dismisses the matter of cross-dressing simply by saying that it makes him feel more comfortable.

The homosexual, on the other hand, has no problem with gender identity. If you ask a male homosexual, for example, if he is a man or a woman, and if he takes you seriously, he will answer, "Of course, I am a man. Why do you ask?" If you go further and ask him if he would like to have surgery to remove his penis and testicles, the homosexual male would look at you in astonishment and indicate that you are asking a crazy question that does not deserve a serious answer. "Why would anyone want his genitals cut off when they give so much pleasure?" is the obvious intent of such a response. This stands in stark contrast to the attitude of the transsexual, who regards his genitals as hated symbols of his despised anatomy. (The transsexual female regards her breasts as similarly hated symbols.)

The transsexual female would give corresponding replies but in the opposite direction. As a little girl she would have been interested in boys' activities: baseball, toy guns, fire engines and the like. She would have had nothing to do with dolls and little-girl play, but if she had "played house" she would have been, in her fantasy, the father. As she reached her teens, fantasy would see her imagining herself to be a man with a penis and having sexual relations with a "straight" female and fathering her children.

Please note that many normal young girls are tomboys who outgrow their preference for boys' activities and parents should not become alarmed unless this preference persists beyond the midteens.

As to treatment, the ideal therapy (if it existed) would be to change the mind to match the body. All sorts of treatments have been tried in an attempt to accomplish this—psychoanalysis, persuasion, behavior modification including aversion techniques, hormones, electric shock and tranquilizers. None has been successful.

Perhaps one day future research will show the way to make the mind fit the body, but as of 1977 no such solution is in sight. At present only one treatment method exists, and that is to change the body surgically, insofar as this is feasible, to match the mind. It is on this basis that sex-reassignment surgery is done, and the long-term results are quite good in carefully selected cases. There is no other treatment known for the transsexual condition as of this date.

CREDIT: *Donald W. Hastings, M.D., Department of Psychiatry, University of Minnesota, Minneapolis, Minnesota.*

DEAR ANN LANDERS: Your letter to the mother who wanted to know what her children should call their dad after a sex change operation was too low-key. Why, after all these years, do you still insist on advising kooks as if they were rational people? Give up, Doll. It won't work.

Can you imagine what life would be

like for those kids at school? You should have suggested that the woman either threaten to have a sex change operation herself so the children would still have both a mother and father, or better yet, she should have the nut declared legally dead. ALSO CONCERNED

DEAR ALSO: Your "advice" wouldn't play in Peoria—or anyplace else. (a) An empty threat is meaningless. (b) The law would not permit a man who is alive to be declared "legally dead."

But thanks a lot. I know you meant well.

A Transsexual Tells What It's Like to Be Changed from a Man to a Woman

The John Wayne Tennis Club in Newport Beach, California, is a tasteful blend of tradition and today: Whites only, with television consoles monitoring the court action, and the latest in instructional equipment.

And the club's best player, perhaps, is Renee Richards, M.D., formerly Richard Raskind, M.D., who provoked an uproar when she unsuccessfully tried to enter the women's division of the U. S. Open tennis championships.

Dr. Richards said she is taking a one-year leave of absence from her ophthalmology practice to hit the tennis tournament trail and "keep transsexualism in the news. I want people to know we're people, that we have feelings, that we have rights—and that we're not two-headed psychotics or freaky."

"I've found the hard way," Dr. Richards said, "that people in sports or entertainment can have a public impact far greater than other people. I am a talented tennis player, and I plan to take advantge of this to enlighten people about transsexualism."

Dr. Richards, forty-two, was leaving for La Costa, California, for two weeks of tennis training under Pancho Segura, who trained men's champion Jimmy Connors, among others. In the future she was expecting to win or place high in several of the major women's championships, including the Australian, French and Italian opens, and Wimbledon. Such a record, she believed, would bring her an invitation to the U. S. Open, which, ironically, was held at Forest Hills, New York, where the former Dick Raskind grew up into the epitome of male success.

"In the abstract," Dr. Richards said, "it might well have appeared that I had it all as Dick Raskind—a big career, big income, big professional reputation, beautiful wife and son, considerable success as a tennis player. But I was miserable. I wanted to be a woman. I had always wanted to be a woman."

Dr. Richards was always a star athlete as Dick Raskind. In high school she recalls, "I was a star pitcher on the baseball team, good enough to attract attention from major league scouts. And I was a good end on the football team. I had great anticipation, hands like glue and good eye and hand co-ordination. But I couldn't stand the physical contact, which is why I gave up wrestling, at which I also excelled."

Tennis was her real game and as Dr. Richards remembers, "I was always captain of the tennis team, at Yale, in the Navy, during the Maccabiah Games (the Jewish Olympics).

"I was a very good tennis player as a man," Dr. Richards said, "but I certainly did not become a woman so that I could become the best woman player."

In 1973, Dr. Raskind was a finalist in the U.S. national finals for those thirty-five and older. "I was the only one of the top ten who did not make his living from tennis." He was a highly successful ophthalmologist. "I had been on female hormones for about eight years and looked pretty strange. Many people thought I had cancer or something and had to take the hormones as therapy."

Dr. Richards traces her quest for fulfillment as a woman. "My mother was a Freudian psychiatrist," she said, "and when I was sixteen, my freshman year at Yale, I told her about my psychosexual difficulties. Well, Freudian interpretations were the vogue then, and she suggested analysis, which I started during my senior year at Yale. When I entered medical school at Rochester, New York, I went into full-scale analysis. I was very innocent, very naïve about transsexualism, but I learned that psychiatry had little to offer me and that this particular therapist had scarcely a clue as to what my problem was.

"During my internship, I declared a moratorium on therapy because of the rigors of the internship year. After completing it, however, I took four and a half years of therapy with a prominent New York psychiatrist, Robert Bak, M.D. He thought I was a normal young man except for a compartmentalized, isolated crazy wish to be a woman. Because of all the disappointments—nine years of futile psychotherapy, the pullback at Casablanca, the reluctance of Johns Hopkins to act on my case—I was distraught. In the backlash, I married. I can recall going to Chicago once in 1969 on a cold, cold day to visit a private hospital and having to be furtive, dressing one way on the flight, another for the hospital interview, trying to sell them on my need, seeing that they knew little about the problem—the hiding, the furtiveness and the pain of it all. I gave up and got married in 1970 and fathered a son. Since the age of eighteen I had always been living with one girlfriend or another. They were all aware of my dilemma, but thought they could talk me out of it. However, since 1965 I had been on female hormones and looked a little peculiar in men's clothing. In many ways, I looked then just as I do now, except that I dressed as a man. Once, in 1969, I was visiting a state park with a girlfriend and when I came out of the men's room a state trooper wanted to know what the devil did I think I was doing.

"I was married for four years, but by 1974 I knew I couldn't continue as a man. I went back to Dr. Laidlaw and Dr. Benjamin, who was in his eighties by then. They decided, 'You know, Richards, the last thing you need is the screening program offered by a university gender identity clinic. You've had that ad nauseam. You need three things: skilled surgery, minimum red tape, and anonymity.'

"I was thinking of going to Stanford, but I found all three requirements in New York. Three days later my surgical reassignment was performed by Roberto Granato, M.D., at a private hospital in Queens.

"God, the postoperative recovery was painful, unbelievably so, but I was happy, wonderfully happy that it was done. I'm not so foolish as to think I'm a total woman, like one with a uterus and ovaries, but I'm happy being 80 percent woman, or 75 percent, or 25 percent. It's better than zero, and I'm as much of a woman as one who has had a hysterectomy.

"You know, some psychiatrists think that transsexualism is caused by a castration complex, that the cross-dressing is symbolically, ceremoniously acting out the fear, so as to be relieved to find later that the male genitals are intact. Well, after I had my surgery (August 4, 1975), I thought, God forbid, that that would be the case with me, that I'd miss my male genitals, break down, become psychotic—and it certainly hasn't been the case. I don't regret for one moment becoming a woman. Except when I reach back for that extra power on a first serve and wish I still had Dick Raskind's strength."

CREDIT: *Dennis Breo,* American Medical News, *October 18, 1976.*

Transvestism

As used in this article the term "tranvestism" means fetishistic cross-dressing; it therefore refers only to people who become sexually excited by garments of the opposite sex. It almost never occurs in females, so this discussion will focus on males in whom women's clothes produce sexual excitement, leading usually to masturbation and orgasm.

Within the category are two different styles of behavior. People in the first group are excited by wearing a single garment or a few garments, and the preference for these particular items remains constant throughout life. Individuals in the second group start in the same manner, but over the years there is a gradual spread to the use of more and more garments, until finally the man enjoys dressing from the skin out in the clothes of the opposite sex. When this stage is reached, the pleasure in cross-dressing is not simply erotic but also a more generally felt enjoyment in imagining oneself to be a woman.

The man who does this wishes to be successful in appearing as a member of the opposite sex. He will go to great lengths to select the most feminine apparel available. Moreover, he tells himself that he is a woman when he is cross-dressed, though he is aware of his male genitals and receives intense pleasure from them. It should be noted that women who cross-dress (usually transexuals or masculine lesbians) do not become sexually excited by the garments they put on.

Most tranvestites are married, prefer intercourse with women (that is, they are not homosexual), and have children. It is rare for homosexual men to be sexually excited by women's clothes.

Transvestites, except when cross-dressing, are masculine. They are found in all the masculine professions and rarely in the professions preferred by effeminate homosexuals. Their behavior, quality of vocal expression, choice of language and style of clothes when not cross-dressing are masculine.

For these men, not only are their penises the source of the greatest erotic pleasure but they also consider themselves men (not just males). Their excitement is expressed through their penises; more important, the presence of the penis, as sensed beneath the women's garments, is exciting. They never quite forget the trick they are trying to put over—that they are hiding their penises. The thought that they are fooling the world is surpassed in enjoyment only by the moment when they can reveal the secret. Since this may be a dangerous secret to tell, it can only be shared with a co-operative wife or girlfriend.

Thus, maleness and masculinity are not only an unavoidable part of the masquerade but an essential ingredient.

Case One: This patient, in his thirties, married, the father of three children, and a precision machine operator, remembers his first cross-dressing as a tremendously exciting sexual experience in which, as a punishment, an aunt forced him to cross-dress at age seven. Although he has no conscious memory of it, he has learned that he was first cross-dressed by another aunt at age four.

From puberty on, sexual excitement was invariably and intensely induced by putting on women's shoes. As the years passed, he added a few more feminine pieces of clothing. Now he dresses completely as a woman and, with proper makeup to hide his beard, passes in society as a woman for a few hours at a time. He has never had a homosexual relationship and has no interest in male bodies. Although looking at women excites him, lying next to a woman is more complicated. He can then only maintain full potency either by putting on women's garments or by fantasizing that he has them on.

Most transvestites, when questioned about the first experience, report it was a girl or woman who cross-dressed them. When a man was responsible, it was generally the father who made the child cross-dress, as a punishment.

Transvestites, however, do not always report that their first cross-dressing was done to them by another person. Some with no memory of having been cross-dressed in childhood discover it nonetheless did occur. They learn this by seeing photographs in the family album that go back before their memories began, or on having it reported to them later by their mothers, or sisters, or aunts, etc.

It seems, therefore, that transvestism usually follows an attack on the boy's masculinity by someone, usually a woman, who puts females' clothes on him in order to humiliate him (demean his masculinity). In addition, one finds that tranvestites do not have loving and warm relationships with their fathers. What is reported, instead, is disruption: a father who is distant and passive or a father seen by his son as a cold, rigid, powerful, usually an unreachable man who punctuates his distance with moments of all-too-close rage. At times transvestites' fathers, whether distant and passive or distant and angry, introduce rare amounts of tenderness with their sons. And so the boys hunger for their fathers, loving them despairingly and with an almost sexual tinge; that is, with a yearning so intense that there is created an eroticized state of frustration.

Other conditions in which cross-dressing occurs can be differentiated from transvestism: (1) transsexualism, in which one feels oneself to be truly a member of the opposite sex and would like his body changed by surgery; (2) effeminate homosexuality, in which one cross-dresses in order to mimic women; (3) intersexuality, in which a biological abnormality of sex (for instance, abnormal sex chromosomes) induces cross-dressing; (4) psychosis— or severe mental illness. In none of these other conditions does cross-dressing produce sexual excitement.

Children occasionally try on the clothes of the opposite sex without sexual excitement, and without thoughts of changing sex. Such behavior should be treated casually since it falls in the same category as "play acting."

Adults may behave similarly under carnival conditions, such as costume parties and Mardi Gras.

In summary, transvestites are heterosexual men who put on woman's clothes because that is their preferred, indeed often necessary way of becoming sexually excited. They do this, however, with full knowledge that, beneath the clothes, they are males. They are not erotically interested in people of the same sex. Because they do not need a partner who must be physically harmed, humiliated or otherwise damaged, this condition is not dangerous.

CREDIT: *Robert J. Stoller, M.D., Department of Psychiatry, University of California, Los Angeles. Excerpted from Dr. Stoller's article which appeared in* Archives of Psychiatry, *March 1971.*

Tubal Ligation

(*Tying the Tubes*)

A METHOD OF BIRTH CONTROL

Recent widespread demand for a simple, effective and inexpensive method of female sterilization has resulted in the adoption of several traditional operations for ligation of the fallopian tubes. This is commonly referred to as "having the tubes tied." The use of a local anesthetic, for example, has reduced problems and shortened the recovery time. New equipment permits a variety of approaches. Simpler procedures have brought the number of tubal ligations up to equal the number of vasectomies (male vas ligations) done each year (approximately 600,000 each, in the U.S.A.).

The first technique of tubal ligation was described in 1880 and involved simple ligation (tying) of the tube. A standard four- to six-inch vertical incision (opening) was made in the lower abdomen, and extended from the belly button to just above the pubic area. This early technique had a high failure rate (up to 20 percent), so in 1919, Madlener both ligated and crushed the fallopian tube in an effort to increase its effectiveness. Further refinements have included ligation, and division and burial of the tube, as well as ligation and resection. The most popular is the Pomeroy technique, in which a loop of the tube is tied and then the top of the loop is cut off. The failure rate for this method is less than 0.5 percent. This is the most frequently recommended technique when the traditional abdominal incision is used, and is usually done immediately after delivery.

In the past fifteen years, the operative procedure (laparotomy) has been reduced to a smaller operation (mini laparotomy). Instead of an incision, and scar that is five to six inches long, the incision is now only one inch long. A further reduction of the incision size has been accomplished with the use of an endoscope (a viewing scope) inserted below the belly button into the abdomen (laparoscopy), or through the cervix into the uterus (hysteroscopy), or through the vaginal cul-de-sac (culdoscopy). These techniques, however, make direct ligation difficult, so the fulguration (coagulation) technique was developed. Fulguration involves using a special instrument for grasping the tube, and then a small point of burning heat is applied by a concentration of electric current. Electro-coagulation of the tubes, with or without division or excision, is very effective with failure rates of less than 1 percent. Unfortunately, there is a risk of burn or perforation of nearby structures, such as the bowel. Done through the uterus (hysteroscopy) into the orifices of the tubes, electro-coagulation is quick and does not require an incision, but it carries a risk of perforating the uterus and has a high failure rate (10 to 35 percent). Finally, all methods of fulguration usually burn the entire tube, which causes irreversible sterilization.

Chemicals such as Quinacrine and silver nitrate, have been used to solidify the tube. These chemicals are dangerous, with varying degrees of effectiveness, and usually result in irreversible occlusion of the tubes.

With all the current problems associated with the simpler, less permanent, contraceptive methods, many women are turning to other techniques, including "temporary" tubal ligation. The "pill" increases (a) the rate of thrombophlebitis (blood clots in legs), (b) the rare development of liver tumors, (c) uterine cancers (1 percent), and (d) coronary artery disease, especially in smokers. The I.U.D. (intrauterine device) has failure rates of 4 percent and can cause uterine perforation and infection if pregnancy occurs. Therefore, the possibility of "temporary" or reversible tubal sterilization has stimulated interest in these methods for contraception.

Two easy techniques of "temporary tubal obstruction" use clips and bands. The clips (tantalum, spring-loaded stainless steel, or plastic) are effective and can be applied by either laparoscopy or culdoscopy procedures. Clips are potentially reversible by removing the clipped segment and having the two remaining ends of the tube sewed together during an operation. The bands are made of silicone rubber and can be applied during an outpatient procedure, as can the clips. Bands have a low failure rate and are potentially reversible (15 to 20 percent successful reversals with surgery).

The most unique method of fertility intervention has been the use of solid plugs (silastic, polyethylene, ceramic, Dacron, and Teflon) placed into the fallopian tubes, either directly from inside the uterus (hysteroscopy) or through a mini laparotomy. Although these plugs appear to be effective and reversible, the necessary specially designed instruments and specially trained operators will probably prevent their widespread acceptance.

At the present time the most common technique of tubal ligation is a clip or band placed during laparoscopy or electro-coagulation through the laparoscope. However, if the patient has had multiple surgical procedures in the past, or had pelvic inflammatory disease (gonorrhea) or peritonitis (inflammation in the abdomen with adhesions), then a mini laparatomy with band-ing or clipping is a safer procedure than the use of a laparoscope. The Pomeroy technique is used commonly as an additional procedure during some other operation and is the most preferred for permanent tubal ligation after delivery.

CREDIT: *John Najarian, M.D., Chairman, Department of Surgery, University of Minnesota, Minneapolis, Minnesota.*

Twins*

Years before I dreamed of becoming an advice columnist, I promised myself I would one day write a book on rearing twins. I know how it looks from the inside, because my twin sister and I were practically Siamese from the day we were born to the day we married (and naturally it was a double wedding).

As Ann Landers, I receive a great many letters from twins. It is disturbing to me that in the past twenty-three years I have encountered so few twins whose parents are doing an enlightened job of raising them. I do not say this critically. If the parents *knew* better, they would *do* better. But unfortunately there has been precious little information available to help parents raise twins.

The most common (and damaging) mistake is to assume that because twins came into the world together they must be dressed alike, encouraged to do the same things, and instructed to stick together, come what may. This is precisely what should *not* be done.

It is of course easier to treat twins as a single unit rather than as two individuals. Extra time, energy and imagination are required to steer children of the same age in separate directions. It is infinitely simpler for the parents if the twins go everywhere together, share each other's friends, clothes and interests. And then, too, twins boost the parental ego. It makes them feel "special" (for Dad, a better word is virile). A multiple birth falsely suggests extraordinary sexual prowess. So how do you let the world know? By dressing your twins alike, parading them as a unit and keeping them together. This may do wonders for Mama and Papa, but it triggers serious problems for the twins.

The chances of having quintuplets are 1 in 57 million, so it's unlikely that anyone who reads this will be faced with that problem. The chances of hav-

* From *Since You Ask Me* by Ann Landers © 1961 by Prentice-Hall, Inc., Englewood Cliffs, New Jersey.

ing twins, however, are about 1 in 87. If it happens to you, the most important thing to keep in mind is this: Remember that each is a person. Each has an ego. Encourage them to be individuals.

RULE NUMBER ONE FOR REARING TWINS: DO NOT DRESS THEM ALIKE!

Dressing twins alike is an exploitative and attention-getting device to accentuate their similarities. This defeats the prime objective: to encourage the development of separate personalities.

When I have suggested in my column that twins not be dressed alike, irate mothers let me know that their twins *want* to dress alike. Of course they do. But it should not be permitted.

A mother in Madison, Wisconsin, wrote to say her twin daughters made a great effort to look as much alike as possible. One had a natural mole on her left cheek. The other twin penciled in a matching mole with a crayon. "They spend hours pinning up their hair exactly alike," the mother wrote. "I don't think this is good. Why do they do it?"

I gave the mother this answer:

"Your twins are using their twinhood as a gimmick to attract attention. It works. It sets them apart from the crowd at once. Identical twins are on stage at all times. The average singleton hasn't a chance in a room with a pair of identically dressed twins. Don't let your twins use an accident of nature to put themselves over. Encourage them to develop individual personalities. They may resist your efforts at first, but in the long run they will be much happier because you laid down the law."

RULE NUMBER TWO: SEPARATE YOUR TWINS IN SCHOOL IF IT IS POSSIBLE.

Twins in a classroom (a) get more than their share of attention, (b) confuse the teacher, (c) lean on one another for support, (d) work less effectively than if they were strictly on their own.

My twin sister and I were in our second year at North Junior High School in Sioux City, Iowa, when two enlightened teachers decided that we should be split up. No teacher had thought of it before. When we received our home-room assignments and discovered we were to report to different rooms, we kicked up such a fuss that one would have thought the school officials had plotted to send one twin to Siberia and the other to Venezuela.

Hand in hand we marched to the principal's office and presented a picture of solidarity that would have made Damon and Pythias look like strangers. "You can't separate us," we sobbed. "We'll just die!"

The principal was a gentle soul. He listened patiently and made a major concession. We could be together for two subjects, but we had to remain in separate home-rooms. This was a partial victory but we were less than jubilant. However, during the first week of separation, my twin was elected president of her home-room. This was the first time either of us had been given individual recognition, and I'm sure it was one of the happiest days of her life.

When we entered Central High School, we had the privilege of selecting subjects and teachers, and I am sorry to say we slipped back to the sure-fire, attention-getting tricks. We selected every course together, once more casting ourselves in the roles of Kate and Dupli-Kate. For the next three years we were side by side in every class—confusing the teachers, overwhelming the boys, antagonizing the girls, and playing the double exposure for all it was worth.

RULE NUMBER THREE: ENCOURAGE TWINS TO FOLLOW SEPARATE INTERESTS AND DEVELOP THEIR INDIVIDUAL TALENTS.

Because two people may look alike to the casual observer does not mean they think alike or that they have identical personalities, work habits or talents.

My twin sister and I both studied the violin. Half of our dear father's money was wasted. The half spent on lessons for *me* went down the drain. I had little interest in the violin, but it takes two to make a duet and I guess we looked pretty cute playing our violins together. Small wonder my sister played the violin better than I. In addition to having a natural talent for the instrument, which I lacked, she took a good many more lessons. My twin frequently substituted for me because I didn't like to practice.

I realize now that I lacked the initiative in my teen years to develop my own special talents—writing and public speaking. Instead of fiddling around with the fiddle and being part of a duet, I should have been on the debating team, working on the yearbook, or writing editorials for the school paper. I loved to write, I loved to talk, and I loved to crusade for causes. But it wasn't until many years later that I was able to break up the vaudeville act and function as my own person.

RULE NUMBER FOUR: SEPARATE FIELDS OF ENDEAVOR WILL AVOID HEAD-ON CLASHES OR—WORSE YET—BELOW THE SURFACE HOSTILITIES.

In my opinion, twins should not compete in the same field. Such competition may produce a champion, but it is far more important to produce two healthy personalities.

The following letter from a mother of twin sons was interesting because she wrote for help with a problem which was actually only a symptom of the main trouble.

She wrote:

DEAR ANN LANDERS: My twin sons are seventeen years old and if I say so myself, they are handsome. I am worried about them because they have no interest in girls.

It seems my twins have only one interest in life—golf. They are on the golf course almost every day after school until it is too dark to see the ball. Both boys are excellent golfers, but one twin has won more tournaments and cups than the other."

The mother added a telling P.S.:

My twins are devoted to each other. There is no rivalry between them. They haven't had a fight in years. I'm so happy that they love each other so dearly, but I do wish they would get interested in girls before they go to college in the fall. Can you suggest something? MOTHER

Mother was, of course, off in Disneyland. She had no understanding of what was going on in the minds and hearts of her sons. She did not realize that her twins who "have not had a fight in years and love each other dearly" were fighting it out daily on the golf course. They had no interest in girls because their energies were directed into another channel. Both boys were consumed with a single interest—to beat out the other one. This was more fun than girls.

I advised the mother to send the twins to different colleges. I went further. I told her, if necessary, *forbid* them to go to the same school. I explained that they were too tied up with one another, and too competitive. Separated, I suggested, their interests would fan out in a variety of healthy directions— including girls.

Mother shot back a reply informing me that I was "out of my mind." She said I had a lot of nerve suggesting that *her* sons were trying to outdo each other. Furthermore, my recommendation that they be sent to different colleges was downright cruel. She wrote, "God meant them to be together. He sent them to us together. It would be a sin to separate them."

I replied:

"God did not join these two at the hip. He gave them separate bodies, separate minds and separate nervous systems. God sent you *two* human beings. He meant them to be individual personalities. I hope you will co-operate with Him and help each of your sons to lead his own life."

RULE NUMBER FIVE: DO NOT COMPARE ONE TWIN WITH THE OTHER AND DO NOT PERMIT FRIENDS AND RELATIVES TO DO IT.

I grew up with a pair of dimples. My twin sister had no dimples. Thoughtless people often said to her, "How does it happen that your twin has dimples and you don't have any?" I can't say for certain how my twin felt about this inane question, but I can imagine.

No mention should be made of differences between twins. If one twin boy is smaller than his brother, you can bet he is sensitive about it. On one occasion I heard an adult ask a nine-year-old who was noticeably smaller than his twin brother, "Why don't you grow faster and catch up with your twin brother?" The child was crestfallen and stood silent. My blood pressure shot up about forty points. I turned to the adult and said, "What's so special about being bigger than somebody? I always went for the short fellows myself. What counts is not being short on brains."

The nine-year-old looked at me with the most grateful eyes I'd ever seen. "Gee," he beamed, "I'll have to remember *that* one!"

On another occasion, when I spoke in San Bernardino, California, several young people crowded around after the speech. A pair of identically dressed twin girls asked for my autograph. One of the girls said with an air of false bravado, "We're twins—but my sister is prettier." My heart went out to her because I knew she had heard it from others many times and had learned to protect herself against the hurt by saying it first.

I told the little twin that I would give her my autograph in exchange for hers—and to write down her address because I wanted to drop her a note. She was delighted. The following week I sent her a four-page typewritten letter on "twinship" and told her never again to mention her sister's better looks or to feel that it made her second-best. I told her that looks don't matter to people who are worth knowing. It's how we treat others and what we make of ourselves that counts.

Parents can protect their twins against thoughtless comparisons by stopping people dead in their tracks. Sample sentence: "We never compare our children—if you don't mind."

RULE NUMBER SIX: ENCOURAGE YOUR TWINS TO BE HONEST AND OPEN ABOUT THEIR FEELINGS.

There is competition between all brothers and sisters. This is natural and normal. Twins can be twice as competitive—and they usually are. Parents who fail to understand this can make big trouble for their twins. Twins should not be made to feel guilty or disloyal if they don't stick together on all things.

I remember the sense of guilt I suffered when, at the age of eleven, I screwed up the courage to express a preference for shredded wheat over puffed rice. I had been brought to feel that "everything with twins should be alike." I knew my sister preferred puffed rice and she knew I preferred shredded wheat—so one day both of us would eat puffed rice and the next day we'd both have shredded wheat. It was a momentous morning when I announced, "Look, you can eat puffed rice every day if you want it, but I'm having shredded wheat." She was perfectly agreeable, but I'm sure she felt, as I did, that somehow we were letting our mother down.

Twenty-three years later, in 1952, I supported Adlai Stevenson for President. My sister supported General Eisenhower. We reminded each other of the shredded wheat and the puffed rice and laughed about it. In spite of the passing of many years, however, there were still twinges of guilt because we were not "sticking together." It was nobody's fault. The early training had left its mark—and the roots were deep.

Twins should develop their own likes and dislikes. They should cultivate their own friends, hobbies and interests. Every twin should paste this motto where he can look at it every day: *"The one thing that I can do better than anyone else is be myself."*

Ulcers

"Doctor, is my problem an ulcer or do I have an ulcer because I have a problem?" This is a question heard frequently in consulting rooms. Certainly some people are so obsessed by the pain that the cure of the ulcer can renew their lives. In other instances, new complaints follow the disappearance of the ulcer symptoms. Nevertheless, few people joke about an ulcer when they really have one.

Ulcers are common in most parts of the world among the rich and poor alike. Each year more than three million people develop an ulcer. More than 15 percent of our population probably will have an ulcer at some time in their lives. Deaths from ulcers and their complications exceed 12,000 each year. Recent figures showed ulcers to be the thirteenth most common cause of death in white males in this country.

The true cause of peptic ulcers is believed to be an excess of gastric juice acting on a damaged mucous membrane and actually digesting tissue so as to leave a hole in this membrane and the underlying tissues. Why the conditions exist that lead to the digestion of a part of one's own stomach and intestine is somewhat obscure.

Heredity is thought to be a factor, but the familial character of peptic ulcer may be due to living in the same physical and emotional environment with other family members who develop ulcers. The genetic factor also is evidenced by the observation that people of blood group O are more prone to ulcers than people with other blood groups.

The excessive amount of hydrochloric acid in the stomachs of peptic ulcer patients is probably of nervous origin. Environmental stress and the hormone changes in emotional states ultimately stimulate the vagus nerve, which causes the lower part of the stomach to secrete the hormone gastrin into the bloodstream. This hormone causes the stomach glands to put out increased amounts of hydrochloric acid. The same occurs when the stomach is stretched by food or irritated by alcohol or caffeine.

Other illnesses seem to be related to peptic ulcer. At least 20 percent of rheumatoid arthritis patients also have a peptic ulcer. Ulcers are frequent in patients with chronic pulmonary disease, including emphysema and tuberculosis. Ulcers may coexist with gastric cancer, although it is believed that most ulcers do not become cancers.

The major complications of peptic ulcer which occur are bleeding, perforation and obstruction. Most ulcers bleed more or less. Erosion of a major blood vessel in the wall of the stomach or duodenum may produce enough bleeding to necessitate immediate surgery. Likewise, an ulcer that perforates through the full thickness of the wall of the stomach or duodenum also requires immediate surgical care.

ULCER SYMPTOMS

Pain is the most common symptom of an ulcer. Typically it begins an hour or so after a meal or wakes a person out of a sound sleep at 3 A.M. It is described as a dull ache, exaggerated by hunger, or a mild to severe burning sensation in the upper part of the abdomen. In severe cases the mid-back may hurt as well. Other symptoms include nausea, frequent belching, heartburn and a feeling of fullness and weakness. Usually the pain is rhythmic. It is worse when the stomach is empty (except before breakfast).

Internal bleeding may be indicated by the passage of black tarry stools or in severe cases by vomiting bright red blood. The latter is a frightening symptom and may signal a life-threatening emergency.

Acute perforation of an ulcer is heralded by a severe upper-abdominal pain. If allowed to progress without treatment there may be temporary improvement, but soon a deadly infection called peritonitis sets in. When this occurs the abdomen becomes stiff as a board and shortly thereafter there is collapse and death. The development of a perforated ulcer is a grave emergency. A delay of only a few hours before hospitalization may make the difference between life and death.

Repeated attacks of vomiting indicates there is an obstruction. X rays will show that the barium given by mouth will not leave the stomach. This symptom also signals an emergency. Eventually most patients with an obstruction require surgery for relief.

Compared with the number of patients who have had the severe complications of bleeding, perforation, obstruction or agonizing pain, many more patients go to see their physicians for a month or two, then they disappear until the pain gets bad again.

Strangely enough in this country ulcers usually become more bothersome in the spring or in the fall. As the years roll along the pain gradually tends to become more severe and persistent. If these patients are followed by barium X rays, increasing deformity of the duodenum or stomach will show up and serious complications become more common.

When a patient complains of pains that sound as if an ulcer might be present, the diagnosis can be confirmed by either X-ray studies or an endoscopy. The X ray is a simple procedure. The radiologist gives a barium mixture by mouth, and as it reaches the stomach or duodenum an ulcer crater or a deformity due to the formation of scar tissue may be seen.

An endoscopy is the passing of a lighted tube down the esophagus into the stomach and duodenum. The ulcer usually can be seen and, if necessary, photographed. Specimens are then taken to determine whether or not the ulcer is benign or malignant. The technique of endoscopy has developed rapidly in the past few years. The flexible endoscope has increased the safety of the procedure. With it many more ulcers can be diagnosed than can be seen by the radiologist.

Once the diagnosis has been made, the patient's chief concern is to get rid of his symptoms. Essentially this means that some way must be found to eliminate gastric irritants and reduce the amount of acid in the stomach by any of the numerous drugs that are available. For many years this meant strict dietary treatment. Half milk, half cream (the Sippy diet) taken every half hour was the old standby. It was unpleasant and fattening but it did alleviate the ulcer pains. Today physicians are inclined to rely less on diet as a method of control. Patients, however, learn it is wise to avoid highly spiced foods and that they should eat regularly, especially a light snack before bedtime. They learn, too, that nicotine aggravates an ulcer. Aspirin and related drugs are also irritants and can increase the chances of bleeding. Caffeine such as is found in coffee, tea or cola drinks should be avoided by an ulcer patient. Alcohol is a definite no-no.

Two important factors that increase acid output have to do with the vagus nerve and a substance called gastrin. Two vagus nerves run from the brain to the stomach. Pavlov, the great Russian physiologist, discovered years ago that hungry dogs secreted a great deal of hydrochloric acid when they saw food. This effect was abolished after the vagus nerves were cut. In humans the vagus nerves are active night and day. It is the pathway by which the stomach responds to emotions. A life free of worry (is there such a life?) would greatly reduce this cause of hyperacidity. Ulcer patients who insist they have no emotional problems and that ulcers are caused by their diet, are told, "It's not what you eat, but what's eating you."

The second important cause of hydrochloric acid secretion is gastrin, an important hormone. Though its actions still are not fully understood, there are at least five kinds of gastrin that have variable importance insofar as acid secretion is concerned. The active forms of gastrin are poured into the blood-stream, where they last for only about ten minutes. By that time they are ab-sorbed by the acid-bearing cells in the upper part of the stomach which are then stimulated to produce hydrochloric acid.

The output of acid due to the vagus nerves can be reduced by using drugs that block nerve impulses. These drugs include belladonna (atropine) and Banthine. In a more effective way the surgeon can cut and remove short sec-tions of the vagus nerves so that their effects are abolished. Reducing the out-put of gastrin is achieved with difficulty by medical measures but can be re-duced to low levels by the surgical removal of the portion of the stomach from which it comes.

In recent years a promising new series of drugs that block the output of hydrochloric acid from the acid-secreting cells has been developed. The first of them—metiamide—unfortunately had side effects that caused depression of the bone marrow. The most recent—cimetidine—is now undergoing tests in this country. It apparently is safe and presumably will be made available by the FDA. This drug has been available in England for many years. Ap-proximately two thirds of all patients treated with this drug have shown prompt relief. Whether or not it is the final wonder drug is not certain at this time. At any rate, there is hope that eventually some drug will be discovered that will be safe and effective for the treatment of peptic ulcers.

One of the major questions that must be faced by the ulcer patient who has suffered for many years but never has had a severe complication is whether or not to abandon medical therapy and have an operation. Such patients are said to have "intractable" ulcers. Two points should be recognized. One is that the stomach after surgery is rarely as good as the stomach was prior to the development of the ulcer. The second is that relief of severe symptoms can be dramatic and one's entire outlook may be changed for the better by an operation. The advice of a trusted physician is exceedingly important in the decision.

When surgery is used to control an ulcer, removal of the vagus nerves is usual when the ulcer is in the duodenum. Removal of a portion of the stom-ach is usually done for gastric ulcers and for most duodenal ulcers. Surgeons are continually in search of a procedure that will leave the patient as free of postoperative symptoms as possible. In some parts of the world operations that remove only a portion of the vagus nerves are now used in the hope that symptoms that occur after surgery will be reduced to a minimum.

Some of the unusual features of ulcers deserve mention. For example, an extremely severe type can be produced by the Zollinger-Ellison syndrome. In this disease an enormous amount of gastrin is secreted by a pancreatic tumor so that numerous ulcers in unusual locations are involved. Oddly enough, it appears that even this type can be controlled by cimetidine. This substitutes drug therapy for a disease so severe it usually requires surgical removal of the entire stomach.

Many mysteries remain. Why has the number of peptic ulcers diminished dramatically in recent years? Why do they seem to be less severe than they were twenty years ago? Why can ulcers be prevalent in one province in India and rare in other parts of the country? Can the decline in the occurrence of peptic ulcer be connected with the decline in the number of cases of cancer of the stomach in this country? Nobody knows the answers, but if you worry about such questions night and day you may get an ulcer.

CREDIT: *Claude Welch, M.D., Clinical Professor of Surgery Emeritus, Harvard Medical School and/or Senior Surgeon, Massachusetts General Hospital, Boston.*

Values

The Missing Link

Somehow, a large proportion of our people have lost their way. They are confused about goals, standards, relationships with other people and how to cope with the vexing problems of life.

Respect for governments, schools, churches, law, custom, personal integrity, property and the rights of others has deteriorated. Even more serious is the increase in crime. In a survey sponsored by the National Commission on Marijuana and Drug Abuse more than one third of all subjects in a representative sample indicated that they, or someone close to them, had been attacked, mugged or robbed. One third of the respondents also reported that they had had experience with someone breaking into their homes or place of work to steal property.

From these considerations it seems logical that we are concerned less with the absence or presence of mental disorder than with the deterioration of values, standards and loss of self-respect as well as respect for others.

Traditionally we have assumed that the values we live by have been derived from the experience of family living, shaped by contact with other people in schools, work and recreational activities.

During the past few decades, particularly since the advent of rapid travel and communication, the family, the church or synagogue and the school have been losing out in the influence they wield among the young. Older people have consoled themselves with the idea that values will in some way be transmitted from one generation to another. As a result, the task of indoctrinating the young (and altering our own values as well) has fallen by default to peer group influences and pressures, the movies, radio, television, newspapers and magazines and advertising in all these media. I leave it to you to reflect upon whether the massive exposure to these stimuli has resulted in higher standards of taste, behavior or satisfaction.

Over and over again our young people have indicated that what they appreciate most are parents who exhibit firmness and direction without dictation, and have rules which make sense. They value being taught how to make decisions, thinking for themselves, and having the privilege of being able to defend their own decisions. Above all, they appreciate parents who spend time with them and set good examples rather than parents who simply tell them what to do.

What do children really need if they are to grow up into citizens who enjoy life and are able to work effectively, love their fellow man and attain a state of humility and independence? From my vantage point as one who has spent his entire professional life studying this problem, I think of these needs as (1) developing the capacity to give and receive love and affection, (2) firm and friendly discipline with emphasis on developing independence as rapidly as they can handle it, and (3) parents (or surrogates) who treat and respect them as separate individuals rather than extensions of themselves, and who explain the reasons for what they do rather than acting arbitrarily. In addition, they need regular alternation between contact with other children and sufficient privacy to develop their capacity to sort out all the elements of active living and apply them to their own needs and desires.

If the great majority of our children are to grow up and develop the ideal qualities of maturity, they need either an intact family or the nearest thing to it. They must have teachers who love and understand children, role models to emulate and policemen who promote order by methods that enhance human dignity rather than degrade it. They need contact with members of the clergy who have the goals I have been describing as well as loyalty to their own organizations.

The list is endless, but I hope my point is made that children can mold their lives only by absorbing those qualities they see and admire. Very few of them can emulate an ideal they have never known or seen applied in real life.

Why do we not have the will to learn how we could more effectively aid our young in improving the society in which they see so many flaws? That problem itself could be the subject of fruitful research. Perhaps we do not want to make the major effort required to become concerned in productive ways with the vast wasteland of false values which we have so long tolerated.

As a chronic optimist, I believe it might be possible in the next few years to capitalize on the righteous indignation (as well as frustration) that so many of us presently feel about the discrepancy between principles and practices now so evident at all levels of society. We have nowhere to go but up.

CREDIT: *Dana L. Farnsworth, M.D., Consultant on Psychiatry, Harvard School of Public Health, Cambridge, Massachusetts.*

Vasectomy

NO-COUNT VASECTOMY

DEAR ANN LANDERS: I am 37 years old. My husband is 42. We have four healthy children who are a handful. My husband and I decided "no more." So three months ago, he had a vasectomy.

Last week, I began to feel queasy in the morning. Today the doctor told me I am PREGNANT! I screamed, "Impossible, my husband has had a vasectomy!" The doctor gave me a wry look and asked, "Do you have a lover?" I was shocked at his question and told him I didn't go in for that sort of thing. He replied, "Ask your husband if he went back and had his seminal fluid checked six weeks after his surgery."

Well, I asked him, Ann, and his answer was, "No, I forgot." Yesterday, he returned to his doctor (furious that the doctor's office hadn't reminded him about the checkup) and sure enough, the sperm count was high enough to make me pregnant.

So please tell your readers that having a vasectomy is not enough. They must make sure it "took." NUMBER 5 COMING UP

DEAR NUMBER 5: Thanks for a letter that can make a great deal of difference to a lot of readers. (P.S. I hope you haven't given away the crib and high chair.)

The "vas," or more accurately the "vas deferens," is a small but tough-walled pipeline which conducts sperm cells from their point of production in the testicle to their point of delivery at the time of ejaculation.

There is one vas on each side. They may become blocked as a result of infection or injury, and if this happens on both sides no sperm cells can come through. The result is sterility. By the same token, if sterility is the objective, the vas may be cut and tied by a surgeon. This prevents the delivery of sperm at the time of intercourse. It has become a widely used form of sterilization because it involves a relatively simple operation for the male as compared with a more complicated technique of tying off or otherwise blocking the fallopian tubes in the female.

When a surgeon performs a "vasectomy" for this purpose it is generally done as a simple office procedure. Local anesthetic is injected in the skin of the scrotum on each side, and through a short incision, the vas is located, cut and tied. Many doctors actually cut out and remove a half inch or more of the vas for two reasons. The first is so that it can be double-checked in the laboratory to make sure it is the vas which has been cut and not a blood vessel or something else. The second reason is that nature makes a valiant effort to put things back together again. If the cut ends are significantly separated this is much less likely to occur.

Healing is generally uneventful and there is minimal discomfort. If the vas is not cut but merely tied, the proper term is "vas ligation," but there is greater risk of things opening up after the operation if the vas is merely tied.

A vasectomy is not instant sterilization. Sperm cells which have traveled up the vas, before the operation, are stored in two spongy reservoirs at the upper end of the vas near the prostate gland just behind the bladder. There they may survive for a relatively long period of time. This means the fluid which is expelled at intercourse may contain sperm cells which got there before the surgery was performed. No male should regard himself as "safe" until an examination of his seminal fluid shows that sperm are no longer present. In any case one should not presume sterility until he has had a dozen or more ejaculations to empty the storage reservoirs.

A vasectomy performed by a competent surgeon is a minor operation and quite safe. Almost the only risks are possible bleeding or infection, neither of which is likely to be serious. Very rarely, it may happen that the lower end of the vas will become untied or open up and some of the sperm cells will leak into the surrounding tissues. This can set up a troublesome irritation and swelling called "spermatic granuloma" which may require further treatment. The only other risk is that if it was *not* the vas which was tied off on either side, the individual has not been sterilized. This again is a good reason for a final check on the seminal fluid to be sure no sperm are coming through.

The successful vasectomy does not ordinarily affect the male adversely in any way except that it ends his ability to father a child. His sexual desires should remain unchanged. He should still be able to get an erection. In other words, he is *potent,* even though he is sterile. Intercourse should proceed precisely as before, with unaltered sensations as soon after the operation as the man feels up to it. Some men have reported that they had intercourse within twenty-four hours of the surgery, but most vasectomy patients prefer to wait a few days.

The doctor will occasionally be consulted by the man who has reacted badly from the psychological point of view. In his mind he has not cheerfully accepted the fact that he is now sterile, and because of this he may develop feelings of inferiority, insecurity or some other manifestation of mental disturbance. The problem is, of course, more psychiatric than surgical. It merely points up the importance of having a complete understanding of what a vasectomy is (on the part of both husband and wife) before the procedure is undertaken. The man should be absolutely certain that he wants it done. Moreover, he should assume that his sterility will be permanent.

If, however, the vasectomy patient should have a change of heart (or of mind) and he decides he would like to become fertile again (children may have died, a new wife may wish to have a baby) it is sometimes possible to grant his wish. In any event, if he is sincere it is worth a try.

The expert doctor in this field (the urological surgeon) can attempt to join the two ends of the vas and sperm may again begin to flow. This is a very delicate operation performed by some surgeons with the aid of magnifying lenses. Its success depends on two factors. The two ends must be accurately joined so that the channel is restored, and the testicle must still be in the business of manufacturing sperm cells.

Over a period of time, following blockage to the vas, the testicle will reduce and perhaps stop its production of sperm. If substantial time has elapsed since the vasectomy, say several years, it is good judgment on the part of the doctor, as the first step in the operation, to clip out a tiny piece of the testicle itself (biopsy) and request that the laboratory do an immediate microscopic examination to be sure it is making sperm cells. If it is obviously out of production it would be useless to proceed with the operation. With careful selection of patients and improving surgical techniques a higher percentage of successful restorations of fertility is being achieved, but at best it is still a gamble with only slightly favorable odds.

There are religious aspects to all forms of sterilization or contraception, for both males and females. The Roman Catholic Church does not condone them. Vasectomy may commonly be done for purposes other than sterilization, and in such circumstances the Church appears to have no objections. But the Church does oppose vasectomy for sterilization. There may well be religious denominations or sects other than Catholicism which reject the morality of sterilization procedures, but the writer is a urologist, not a theologian. Certainly the individual who considers himself to be a candidate for vasectomy should explore this matter with his spiritual advisors if there is any chance of conflict.

In short, there is no 100 percent instantaneously effective form of birth control save for complete surgical removal of the sex organs of the male or female. Among the less radical, more acceptable approaches to the achievement of sterility, tying off the tubes in the female is undoubtedly the most effective. Close behind this is the vasectomy, if proper attention is paid to a postoperative danger period as we have discussed it, and if a small allowance is made for the perversity (or persistence) of nature in endeavoring to put together that which man hath put asunder.

CREDIT: *The piece was written especially for this encyclopedia by Russell B. Roth, M.D., attending urologist, Saint Vincent Health Center, Erie, Pennsylvania, and past President, American Association of Clinical Urologists.*

Venereal Disease (VD)

A case of VD is caught every eleven seconds. Over three million cases of VD are caught in the United States each year. Over 75 percent of all *reported* cases of VD occur in people between fifteen and thirty years of age. It has been estimated that there are approximately a half million cases of untreated syphilis in the United States today.

A recent survey indicates that private physicians treat 70 percent of this nation's venereal disease cases but report only 10 percent of the cases they treat. The actual number is therefore unknown.

The cost of untreated syphilis can be measured not only in death and human suffering but also in tax dollars. In 1973, costs for the hospitalization of the syphilitic insane exceeded $58,000,000. Add this to the cost to our economy in man hours to industry, insurance payments and welfare costs spent for the permanently crippled, and you can see the impact that this disease has on American society.

Gonorrhea can kill. While death from this infection is rare, it killed more people than polio last year. There is evidence in some areas that gonorrhea is not responding to penicillin. While other drugs are available, the verification of adequate treatment may become a difficult and complex problem. Imagine the impact if an infection already this widespread became incurable!

In almost every major city in this nation, venereal disease is the number one communicable disease. Chicago is no exception. From our population of 3,369,359 over 40,000 cases of VD were treated and reported last year alone. This figure represents more than one out of every hundred Chicagoans and, remember, all cases are not reported.

HISTORY OF VD

The term "venereal" was first used around 1500. For two hundred years gonorrhea and syphilis were thought to be the same disease. In 1793, Benjamin Bell of Edinburgh proved they were not. But it wasn't until eighty-six years later (1879) that Albert Neisser, a German bacteriologist, isolated the bacteria that causes gonorrhea.

Gonorrhea is one of the earliest diseases known to mankind. It was familiar to the Chinese five thousand years ago. The Bible refers to "running issue" believed by medical historians to be gonorrheal discharge. It has been said, facetiously, that Moses was the first Public Health Officer. He set down rigid rules of behavior (Leviticus 15; Numbers 31) for those who had symptoms for what may well have been gonorrhea.

During the period of discovery and exploration, gonorrhea spread all over the world. In 1687, it was brought to the South Pacific islands by traders and sailors. By 1800, every island in the South Pacific had some gonorrhea.

There were no known drugs to combat the disease until 1935, when the sulfonamides appeared. They were called "miracle drugs" and produced extremely impressive results. The curative effects were temporary, however, and physicians went back to the ineffective remedies.

Penicillin was used against gonorrhea in 1943 and the results were hailed as among the most spectacular in medical history. Hundreds and thousands of cases of gonorrhea were cleared up in a few months. Penicillin was truly the "miracle drug" that richly deserved the name.

Some historians claim syphilis was unknown in Europe and Asia until Columbus and his men brought it back from their first trip to America in 1492. It was known as the "Indian measles."

In 1495, a serious epidemic of syphilis hit Europe and spread throughout the world. Thousands died in this scourge, which lasted for approximately fifty years.

Royal families were not immune. Charles VIII of France fell victim to syphilis and left no heirs. Henry VIII was thought to have had syphilis before he married. His children, Mary Tudor (Bloody Mary), Edward VI and Elizabeth I, all manifested signs of congenital syphilis.

At the height of the epidemic, each country blamed its neighbor. The French called it "the Italian sickness," the English called it "the French pox," the Germans called it "the French malady" and the Japanese called it "the Portuguese sickness."

In 1905, Fritz Schaudinn isolated the *treponema pallidum,* the syphilis germ. In 1906, August von Wassermann developed a blood test which clearly identified infected persons.

The first effective agent used against syphilis was an arsenic compound. In 1909, Paul Ehrlich's 606th experimental combination, Salvarsan, was produced. It was called "Magic Bullet Number 606" and gave a promise of cure to millions of syphilitic victims.

Gold and mercury continued to be used. Other techniques were tried, such as giving syphilitic patients malaria, hoping the high fever might kill the syphilis "germs." Of course, it was unsuccessful.

The tremendous increase in syphilis during World War I made it impera-
tive that something be done to control this rampant disease. In 1918,
Congress passed legislation which gave funds to each state through the U. S.
Public Health Service to set up VD control and treatment programs.

This move was considered "revolutionary," considering that only ten years
earlier, Bernarr Macfadden was sentenced to two years in prison and fined
two thousand dollars for mailing a magazine which contained an article on
venereal disease.

In 1909, President William Howard Taft saved Macfadden from prison,
but Macfadden had to pay the fine.

In 1943, Dr. John Mahoney of the Public Health Service reported that
penicillin "may be the answer to syphilis." He was proved to be right. That
statement revolutionized the treatment and control of VD.

FACTS ABOUT SYPHILIS

How can you tell if you have it?

Symptoms are the same for males and females. The incubation period—ten
to ninety days—is somewhat of a blessing because it allows a detected victim
to alert recent sex partners.

The first symptom may be a chancre (pronounced "shanker"), a sore appearing where the germ entered the body, usually in or around the sex organs, the mouth or an open wound. The chancre doesn't hurt but often it
produces itching. It resembles a pimple, blister or ulcer and is highly infectious. In some cases no chancres appear, or they look so innocent they are ignored. Sometimes the chancre may be hidden deep within a woman's sex organs and not seen at all. A chancre will heal within weeks, even without
treatment.

Soon, however, the germs spread throughout the body, and the secondary
stage occurs when a rash appears, looking very much like heat rash, hives or
a rash caused by allergy. The germs thrive in the warm, moist areas of the
body. Sores may form in the mouth, and other symptoms can include sore
throat, fever, headaches or an unusual loss of hair. Sores frequently appear in
the mouth or on the palms of the hands and the soles of the feet. The palm
and sole sores are frequently mistaken for callouses.

Even without treatment, these symptoms of syphilis disappear. The un-
knowing syphilitic may outwardly appear and feel healthy for as long as
twenty years, while billions of syphilis germs thrive in the body. Like a land
mine, they can become activated at any time, damaging the heart, brain and
spinal system beyond restoration. This could result in heart failure, blindness,
paralysis, insanity, crippling arthritis and even death.

Today the treatment for syphilis is a series of injections of penicillin or
other antibiotics. The shots are painless. It is not unusual for a patient to
have a negative blood test after one or two shots. This does not mean he is

cured and can discontinue treatment. It does mean, however, that he cannot pass the disease on to someone else. The full treatment for syphilis is a minimum of ten shots; these shots may be given within a period of ten days or spaced three or four days apart.

After the treatments have been concluded most doctors insist on a blood test every three or four months for two or three years. This is to ensure against a recurrence of the infection. Sometimes the disease will be arrested and not show up in a blood test for several weeks, then suddenly it may become active again.

ARE VENEREAL DISEASES HEREDITARY?

Venereal diseases are not hereditary if the mother has been cured. But VD can be passed from an infected mother to her child before or at the time of birth. With some forms of VD, if the expectant mother is given proper treatment soon enough, the child will not have VD. With other forms of venereal diseases, if the disease is detected soon enough, precautions can be taken to ensure that the venereal disease doesn't pass to the child. In all cases of venereal disease, if the infection isn't detected soon enough and the proper medical care isn't given, the newborn infant could suffer serious damage, even death.

FACTS ABOUT GONORRHEA

Gonorrhea is almost always contracted through sexual relations, but physicians have reported exceptions. There have been recorded cases of virgins who have been blinded by gonorrhea. The eyes are especially susceptible to this infectious germ.

The incubation period of gonorrhea is short—three to five days. It can be passed on quickly to many partners by sexually active men and women who may not be aware they have become infectious.

Heart trouble, blindness and even death can be caused by gonorrhea if not treated by a physician. The germs can get into the bloodstream and cause arthritis. By no means am I suggesting that everyone who suffers from arthritis got it from gonorrhea! There are many other causes.

The first symptoms for an infected male involve his penis. There may be pain while urinating, accompanied by a discharge of pus. Urination is also more frequent and urgent. If not treated, gonorrhea spreads to a man's glands along the urinary tract of his penis, and he can become sterile.

It has been estimated that eight out of ten women experience *no* symptoms. Any evidence of pus can pass unnoticed while urinating. An excessive amount of pus will have a noticeable odor. Often the symptoms are not recognized until the gonococcus germs spread throughout the womb and into the fallopian tubes and pelvic inflammatory disease (PID) results.

Then the woman experiences serious pain and hospital treatment may be required. As a result of advanced gonorrhea, she may be unable to bear children. If she is pregnant, gonorrhea may be transmitted to the baby in the birth canal during delivery. It can get into the child's eyes and make the infant blind.

There is no blood test to determine if a woman has gonorrhea; other laboratory tests can be made, however. Health authorities urge women to have cervical cultures taken during their annual gynecological checkups, or more frequently if they are sexually active.

Gonorrhea is treated by injections of penicillin or other antibiotics. Two or three shots may cure an active case. For chronic gonorrhea, the treatment is more intense.

HOW TO PROTECT YOURSELF AGAINST VD

There is a chance that syphilis can be picked up by *kissing*. A person who is infected may have a chancre in his (or her) mouth or on the tongue or lips. Be on the alert for "cold sores." Some chancres look very much like an ordinary cold sore—the difference is the cold sore goes away within a few days, but the syphilis chancre hangs on and on. If you know of someone who has an extremely stubborn "cold sore," by all means suggest that he (or she) see a doctor about it and you might even mention the possibility that it could be a symptom of a "blood infection."

If you have sores on your lips, in your mouth or on your tongue—even though you may think it's nothing more than a canker sore—note, not *chancre*—canker sore—do not kiss anyone, relatives, friends or sweetheart. If the sore does not disappear within four or five days, see a doctor.

People who read about symptoms often imagine they have the disease, be it polio, TB or VD. If you have never had sexual relations, the chances are about one thousand to one that the cold sore you are worrying about is *only* a cold sore and nothing more.

Once cured, does the cure last forever? No. A person once cured can become reinfected every time he is exposed to the disease.

I have received hundreds of letters from teenagers and adults who describe VD symptoms but insist they couldn't possibly have it because their friends are so "nice."

I cannot emphasize this point strongly enough. Germs do not respect class lines and many "nice" people get VD and pass it on to other "nice" people.

A fourteen-year-old girl who lives in Harrisburg, Pennsylvania, wrote that she had little sores on the private parts of her body and the itching drove her crazy. "But," she added, "I just couldn't have a venereal disease because I've gone all the way with only one boy in my whole life and he is my steady. Bill is very refined and comes from a good family. He couldn't possibly have given me anything like *that*."

A seventeen-year-old boy from Memphis wrote:

"I am writing to you because I can't talk to my folks about this problem. I've heard the guys in the locker room laugh about gonorrhea. They always make a big joke of it. I'm afraid I may have it but I can't figure out how it happened. I've had quite a lot of pain. At first, I thought I strained myself playing football, but other things have happened which make me sure it must be something else. I only take out respectable girls—no tramps—and I have never been with a prostitute. The four girls I have had relations with all attend my church and are very high-class."

Just as venereal disease doesn't recognize social-economic barriers, neither does it respect age. For instance, an article in *Seventeen* magazine tells of a high school coed who was the first link in a chain of syphilis involving 198 persons, some of them students in each of her city's high schools and leading citizens, including a physician and a clergyman.

Children under nine are not immune to VD. More than two thousand were treated in 1971 in the state of California. Approximately five thousand California boys and girls, between ten and fifteen, were infected.

Every day my mail brings me dozens of similar letters from teenagers and adults alike who suspect they might have VD and ask, "What do you think?" I tell them by return mail that I am not a physician and I certainly am not qualified to diagnose through the mail. I urge everyone who inquires about *any* illness to go immediately to his family doctor, a clinic, or the city, county or state Board of Health and be examined.

Here are some facts everyone should know about VD:

Gonorrhea and syphilis are the most common venereal diseases, but there are others which usually remain local and do not spread through the body, as do gonorrhea and syphilis. These three local types of VD are called chancroid, lymphogranuloma venereum (LGV), and granuloma inquinale.

Like gonorrhea, the early symptom of lymphogranuloma venereum (LGV) is also elusive. A small lesion appears on the sex organs five to twenty-one days after infection, but is transitory. The glands in the male groin become enlarged, while the female rectal area swells internally. There also may be pain in the joints, headaches, fever and chills. Debilitation and invalidism occur in the late states of untreated LGV.

Chancroid is especially common in tropical and subtropical regions, and more prevalent where substandard sanitary conditions prevail. Chancroid destroys body tissue, and its first symptom is a painful sore on the sex organs much like a soft chancre. The germs in the sores spread and attack the groin, often enlarging the glands in that part of the body.

The symptoms of granuloma inquinale are evidenced by small bumps breaking out on the sex organs after an incubation period of eight days to twelve weeks, sometimes up to one hundred days after infection. The germ-laden bumps do not heal easily. They contain pus which spreads across the penis or vagina, then the rectal area, accompanied by an unpleasant odor.

Pain and fever accompany a secondary infection, and untreated cases can result in debility, then death.

The VD rate is higher among the poor—both white and black.

VD *can* be cured. The earlier the treatment is begun the better the chances for a complete cure.

It is possible to have both gonorrhea and syphilis at the same time. Having one does not immunize against the other.

Once cured, a patient can contract the disease again if he is exposed to someone who has it. The records show that 80 percent of those who are infected will become reinfected in the future—probably *one fourth* within six months.

It is *not* true that VD is passed on only one way—through sexual relations. The overwhelming majority of VD cases *do* result from sexual intercourse with an infected person, but medical journals have recorded many exceptions.

It is extremely unlikely that VD will be caught from towels, toilet seats, contaminated drinking glasses, silverware and so forth, but no one can say for sure that it is impossible. There are recorded cases of virgins who have contracted syphilis and gonorrhea.

HOW YOU CAN HELP OTHERS

If you have been diagnosed and are receiving treatment for syphilis or gonorrhea, inform your sex partners immediately. Chances are that one of them infected you or that they were infected by you. They deserve the benefit of treatment. You will be doing them an enormous favor by telling them you are infected and urging them to get in touch with a doctor or the city Board of Health. They will receive quick, confidential treatment.

WHAT TO DO IF YOU THINK YOU HAVE VD

It is essential that you know VD will not go away by itself. Even if the symptoms disappear, you still need to be treated.

The first line of defense is the family physician. If you are a teenager and fear that your parents will be told, I can tell you most family doctors will keep your secret. Many years ago it was against the law for a physician to treat a minor without parental consent. That stupid law is no longer in effect.

If you simply cannot bring yourself to go to your family physician, go to the school nurse. She will give you the word regarding the city or county health clinics. Most of them will treat you free. And they too will keep your secret.

Do not be afraid that you will be lectured on "morality," or made to feel like a sinner. Medical people are not interested in the moral aspects of VD. They view it as a disease and want only to help you get well.

HOW TO PROTECT YOURSELF AGAINST VD

There is no vaccine for VD or 100 percent safe protection if a person is exposed to the germ. However, if the male uses a condom (a sheath, commonly called a "rubber," that fits over the penis), the chance of infection can be greatly reduced for the uninfected partner. Hopefully, the public will soon realize that these items are a vital disease preventive and should be easily available to anyone who wants them.

Thorough washing of the genitals and urinating soon after sexual intercourse may reduce chances for infection, but by no means is this to be considered reliable protection.

You may have heard that "The Pill" can prevent VD. It's not true. "The Pill" can prevent nothing but pregnancy.

The major roadblocks to the eradication of venereal disease are ignorance and apathy. Thank God, there are now cures for syphilis and gonorrhea. An informed and concerned public could do much in eradicating these diseases.

The greatest need is a new public attitude toward VD. Private physicians and public health agencies cannot do the job alone. Every responsible citizen has a role. This means *you* and *me*.

CREDIT: *Ann Landers. Material obtained through the help of Murray C. Brown, M.D., Commissioner, City of Chicago Department of Health. Control Disease Center of Communicable Diseases, Atlanta, Georgia. American Medical Association.*

Veterans

Help on Benefits, Training and Placement

As a veteran of one of our nation's wars, you have many rights written into law. You are entitled to help in finding a place for yourself in the job market, furthering your education, obtaining loans, securing medical assistance and obtaining various kinds of insurance.

In getting a job, here are some special aids:

Unemployment compensation. If you can't find a job right away you may be entitled to this.

Local veterans employment representatives. You may go to a nearby office at the state employment service offices to receive priority in referrals to jobs, training and filing of claims.

Priorities on federal job contracts. If you are a disabled or Vietnam veteran, you are entitled to extra help with federal job contractors holding government contracts of $10,000 or more. They must take affirmative action in employing veterans.

Discrimination. If you feel you are not being treated fairly, you have the right to file a discrimination complaint with the Veterans Employment Service, Veterans Administration or the Civil Service Commission.

Job seniority retention. If you left a job to enter the armed services, you may have a right to return to that employment with seniority credit, pay hikes and promotions you would have received if you had stayed.

On-the-job training. You can get on-the-job training for a new career and be paid while learning.

You can get many different types of financial help to study for a higher education and work toward a degree.

Employment training programs, under the Comprehensive Employment and Training Act programs in your area. The local veterans employment representatives in your state employment service offices can tell you about other employment-training opportunities. Bring your armed forces separation Form DD214 and your Social Security card with you for quicker service.

Just started in 1977 is a new program, HIRE, to place veterans in private industry on-the-job training, raise the number of veterans in public service employment and assist disabled veterans through a special outreach program within the employment service.

State employment service offices. With about 2,400 local offices, one is probably near you. These are staffed with professionals who are acquainted with the laws, know where the jobs are, the kind of training available and who will help you plan and find a job. Ask for the local veterans employment representative. You are entitled to priority in job referral, training, counseling and testing.

U. S. Veterans Assistance Centers, located in various cities within the VA regional centers. These provide you with a one-stop center for facts on the range of your benefits, including job referral, placement, employment and educational benefits. These centers are strictly for veterans, serve as a central point to inform you on affirmative action programs and help you with discrimination complaints. Look in your phone book under U. S. Government, VA, for a nearby center.

U. S. Civil Service Commission, the federal government's central personnel office to provide exams, job referrals and facts on federal jobs. It gives preferences to qualified veterans. There are thirteen federal job information centers, plus one in Washington, D.C. Consult your phone book under U. S. Government, Civil Service Commission.

Office of Veterans Re-employment Rights, Labor-Management Services Administration. That office helps you, a qualified veteran, obtain your legal rights to return to your former employer with the position and benefits you would have obtained had you not been in service. You also might get back pay for earnings lost and protection against discharge without cause for a year. For locations, write the Office of Veterans Re-employment, Room N5469, U. S. Department of Labor, 200 Constitution Avenue, N.W., Washington, D.C. 20216.

Other sources of help include your state employment service office; the Employment and Training Administration, Department of Labor, Washington, D.C. 20213; or the ten Offices of Regional Administrators for Employment Training.

CREDIT: *Sylvia Porter, Field Newspaper Syndicate, Chicago, Illinois.*

Violence

Family Fighting

Violence in the American home has been an invisible problem. Only in the past decade has the true situation come to light.

When the subject of family violence is raised, people tend to think of a family living in poverty, a number of illegitimate children, a mother on welfare, a father who has left home and a boyfriend living with Mom. This is a false picture. Family violence occurs at all economic and social levels.

People are ashamed when they abuse their children or spouse, thus incidents are not reported until the level of violence reaches the crisis stage. Spouse abuse is the single most unreported crime in the country. The word "crime" is emphasized, because most people think that what occurs in the home is a private matter between family members. This is the viewpoint of the perpetrator and the victim, as well as the police and court system. Recent studies, police reports and files at crisis shelters all concur with the following facts:

(1) Approximately one fourth of all murders in the United States occur within the family. Half of these are husband-wife killings.

(2) At least one fourth of all American couples engaged in an episode of violence during their relationship. Many studies indicate the percentage

may be as high as 60 percent. Ten percent involve extreme and recurrent physical abuse.

(3) Twenty percent of all Americans approve of hitting a spouse, but among college-educated the percentage rises to 25 percent. In cases of child abuse in lower income groups financial and environmental pressures increase frustrations that lead to aggression. All kinds of people batter children. There is no typical offender.

(4) Violence begets violence. Family violence is learned. Aggression is seen as the normal response to frustration in some families. As the children grow up, boys will beat their wives; girls will think it is "normal" to be beaten. When these children become adults they are more likely to beat their children. At least 10 percent of the children who witness parental violence eventually become adult batterers themselves.

(5) More children die of child abuse than any childhood disease. There were more than one million runaway children last year. Many left because of physical child abuse or sexual exploitation.

(6) Patriarchal society asserts that the man is in charge. Many boys are raised to believe they must "control" women to prove their masculinity.

(7) Pregnant women appear to be battered more often. The woman is usually hit in the stomach. The added burden of a first or an additional child sometimes pushes an angry (or drunk) male beyond the point of endurance.

(8) Alcohol and drugs are often involved in family violence. Research has not confirmed whether the person uses these to excess to justify the physical abuse or whether it causes the abuse. Alcohol-related violence is almost exclusively male.

(9) The existence of handguns in the home makes severe or fatal injury more likely.

(10) There is a relationship between violence and the level of frustration. When unemployment increases in a particular community, so does the violence.

How can this situation exist in a country which prizes the family as its most cherished institution? It is noted in the history of Western civilization.

Women and children were considered the property of the male. In the Middle Ages, men were encouraged to beat their wives. Women grew to expect this behavior. Laws condoned such treatment. It was not until 1880 in England that severe physical abuse was considered legal reason for a woman to separate from her husband. During this past decade, women began to realize that they were not "property" but independent human beings.

The cliché "a man's home is his castle" implies that men are more owners of their home than their wives; that their homes are inviolate, and they can do anything they like at home.

Violence in America is an accepted manner of behavior. A favorite activity of children is the re-enactment of battles between cowboys and Indians or of

World War II. Studies indicate that the amount of violence in television programs adversely affects the behavior of the viewer. Most parents approve of spanking their children as a means of discipline. Most battering of wives has been the subject of "humor"—Richard Reeves recently told a "joke": "Wives, like politicians, should be beaten once in a while." And we all recall the frequently used line of Jackie Gleason to his wife: "One of these days, POW, right in the kisser."

American life is filled with tension and frustrations. Violence is a release. A husband comes home from the office; it has been a hard day. He has been put down by his superiors. His wife makes a simple error (forgetting to buy cigarettes at the store). This triggers a violent explosion. All the frustrations of his job are taken out on his wife. A man is laid off work and can't find a job. He is ashamed of his loss of manhood and takes it out on his family.

Battered children feel the same guilt and shame. They are totally dependent on their parents for emotional and financial support. Most children will deny that they have been beaten and will fabricate stories to explain their bruises, burns and broken bones. For children, often removing the child from the home is the only way to prevent further violence. Although many state laws require reporting of child abuse, many doctors and neighbors still refuse to get involved.

The deaths and injuries that result from violence in the home can be reduced. Society must play a long- and short-term role in this problem. The first step is to acknowledge that violence is widespread in the American home. Communities must insist that a higher priority be given to proper training of the police and that funding for programs to aid the abused and the abusers be supported.

Some communities have shelters and counseling services for battered wives. Hotlines to aid women in distress are being established by local mental health groups. Look under Community Referral in the phone book. Call that number and explain the problem you need help with. A group named Parents Anonymous has been organized for parents who want to stop abusing their children. Another organization is called CALM. National headquarters are in Santa Barbara, California. The address is: CALM, P.O. Box 718, Santa Barbara, California, 93102. They have chapters around the country.

Police and courts must be educated to view severe violence as a crime. Schools should teach boys and girls that hitting is not appropriate behavior. Men, women and children must learn that regardless of the behavior of a child or spouse, no one has the right to physically abuse another human being.

People aren't for hitting!

CREDIT: *Barbara A. Mikulski, member of the United States House of Representatives, Third District, Maryland.*

Virginity

DEAR ANN LANDERS: I'm a 19-year-old virgin and I'm sure I'm not as much of a freak as the girls I work with make me out to be. I hope you will print this letter in support of all of us who have decided that sex belongs in marriage.

I have dated at least 20 men in the last three years and I'm proud to say I never let anyone talk me into anything. I've been called "abnormal," "too religious," "chicken," "square," "frigid" and "just plain crazy." When the arguments got heavy I told a few clowns to buzz off. I never figured I had lost anything of value when a high-pressure make-out artist didn't ask me out again.

I knew one day I'd meet a man who would accept my view and not try to change me to suit his "needs."

It happened a few months ago and we plan to be married in the fall. There is no hassling about how far to go. He knows my rules and is willing to abide by them.

I feel good about myself and what's more, I'm not worried to death from month to month like some girls I work with. Also, I'm not concerned about the side-effects of the Pill (as so many women are these days) because I'm not on it. The peace of mind and self-respect make up for whatever I might be missing, and I can wait a few months to find out what it is. ALL TOGETHER

DEAR FRIEND: I applaud a young woman who knows what she wants and what she doesn't want and has the courage to stick by her convictions. I've never received a letter from a girl who said she was sorry she saved herself for marriage, but I've received hundreds from those who didn't and were heartsick. Thanks for writing.

The hymen, or maidenhead, is a thin membrane that partially covers the external opening of the vagina. It is untrue that when a male does not have a somewhat difficult time penetrating upon intercourse that the hymen has been ruptured by someone else and the girl (or woman) is not a virgin. Before a woman becomes sexually active, the hymen may be stretched by using tampons. Horseback riding or other strenuous sports can also rupture the hymen. So can a pelvic examination.

In most cases the hymen will usually stretch or tear without much difficulty during the first act of intercourse. Slight bleeding may occur. There may be some discomfort, but the pain is not excruciating. A small percentage of females may have unusually thick maidenheads. If this is the case, and the couple has waited until marriage to have sex, the long-anticipated wedding night can be a nightmare. The bride who encounters this problem should see a gynecologist, who will remove the membrane surgically and make entry by the husband possible.

Can a virgin become pregnant? The answer is no. The word virgin means "untouched" or "undiscovered by man." Can a girl with a maidenhead become pregnant? The answer is yes, although such occurrences are extremely rare. Medical literature has recorded instances of pregnancy when the hymen was intact. What happened was the sperm were ejaculated on the vulva, made their way through perforations in the hymen into the vagina and upward through the uterus to the fallopian tubes, and conception took place.

A question that comes up frequently in my mail, almost always from teenagers, is this: Can a girl get pregnant the very first time she has sexual intercourse? The answer is *yes*. Many thirteen-, fourteen-, and fifteen-year-olds discover this—much to their astonishment.

Through the years some of my ideas have changed. Virginity is one of the subjects about which I have done some rethinking. Twenty-five years ago I held the firm conviction that a girl should hang on to her virginity until marriage or death—whichever came first. I no longer believe this.

I am still opposed to high school sex since I believe very few girls under eighteen years of age are emotionally equipped to handle a sexual relationship. If, however, the girl who goes on to college (or to work), is mature and has her head together, meets someone with whom she becomes emotionally involved, and there is a genuine sense of mutual caring, respect and commitment, it seems to me that a physical relationship would not be inappropriate. In fact, for a young, in-love couple nearing twenty years of age *not* to express their feelings in this way would be somewhat unusual, if not unnatural.

I do not recommend sexual expression, however, for all nineteen- and twenty-year-olds. A great deal depends on the individual. Some girls at twenty are too immature to handle sex. It would overload the circuits and might produce enormous guilt feelings if premarital sex is against her religion. But one thing is certain, no girl should consider sex, regardless of age, without being well informed in advance of the methods of protecting herself against VD and pregnancy. And remember this—according to a recent study, slightly over 55 percent of the boys interviewed said they would prefer to marry a virgin.

CREDIT: *Ann Landers.*

DEAR ANN LANDERS: You asked teenage girls to write and tell you the "lines" that were used on them by boys who were after sex. What a great idea!

I'm no teenager (I'm 22) but I thought you might be interested in the "lines" pitched at me over the past several years. Some of them were hilarious, others downright pathetic.

The adolescent, nonserious passes started in the seventh grade with games like Spin-the-Bottle and Post Office. Then there were those unforgettable Scavenger Hunts—with kids pairing off and wandering around in search of pink toilet paper and vegetable sieves.

The serious, for-real lines started in the ninth grade. My favorite boyfriend was best pals with a guy who dated the most popular girl in school. He told me she "did it." That, of course, meant "it" was the thing to do. When he discovered that strategy didn't work, he promptly switched to, "if you loved me you'd prove it." I told him if he loved ME he wouldn't make such demands on me.

Finally he became adamant and said I HAD to give in because my stubbornness was lousing up his maturing process and giving him pimples. When I told him to buzz off he threatened to kill himself. The threat turned out to be as ridiculous as the rest of his garbage.

Then I started to date a fellow who was extremely considerate of my feelings but also very affectionate. When I made my position clear, he didn't pester me about sex. We necked a little, but he never tried to step beyond the boundaries I set up. After a few blissful months, Mr. Well-Behaved in-

formed me I was going to have to share him with "Winnie" (a hot number) who wrote notes that made it plain she was ready, willing and able to "fulfill" him.

Off I went to college—still intact but getting curiouser and curiouser. The second day on campus I met Claude. He told me on our second date that dozens of girls had followed him from the swimming pool to his apartment, lusting after his bod. Others were so aggressive (and hungry) they knocked on his door with bottles they couldn't open, dresses that needed to be zipped, furniture they couldn't move—anything to get past his front door and hopefully into his bed.

Then there was Horace, two years my junior, who wanted me to "teach him" . . . and Bernie, who was dying to know if a political science major had anything that worked besides her brain. And Orval, a religious nut who had been instructed by God to "show me the way."

Funny thing, nothing wore down my resistance. The lines just made me run in the other direction. No girl wants to feel used, fooled or easy.

When I finally said yes, it was because a sensitive and caring young man made me feel valuable as a human being. He applied no gimmicks, no hogwash, no sales talk. I made up my own mind. It was beautiful. I'm glad I waited. HAPPY PAST AND PROUD TO TELL IT

DEAR HAPPY: I hope every young virgin out there who reads your letter will pay close attention. Ah! The more things change—the more they are the same!

Vitamins

(Or: Ponce de Leon, Where Are You?)

During the past twenty-five years, Americans have been bombarded with propaganda regarding the beneficial effects of vitamins as an adjunct to our normal daily diet.

In the field of medicine, however, the philosophy is reversed. We are conscious of the concept of malnutrition among the poor, the chronically ill, the aged and the emotionally disturbed as well as the "fadists" and emotional complexes restricting the normal intake of food. Note, we have not mentioned destructive diseases which precipitate malnutrition for one reason or another, because of the inability to absorb and ingest normal food stuffs and receive proper nutrition through our daily eating habits.

Society has reversed this image and is looking to vitamins as "super-gods" through a new form of "drug pushers." We have all heard of the super "wonders" of vitamin E, vitamin C, B complex, natural elements such as rose hips, kelp, seaweed, yeast, etc., which, we are told, if consumed in large quantities will delay the aging process, add energy, enhance virility, provide resistance against illness and give us "beautiful bodies."

Unfortunately, there is no reliable evidence in clinical literature that super vitamin ingestion is the secret key to a longer or healthier life. The prime folklore of our society that vitamin E in massive doses adds physical endurance, produces sexual potency, longevity, affects cardiac status, skin care, prevents sterility and has a multitude of other benefits has been proved to be a myth. For individuals with normal serum alpha tocopherol (vitamin E), taking increased doses of vitamins has no benefits or effects, nor will it help any of the above-mentioned. The folklore and fadism of our nutritional society that vitamin C taken in massive doses prevents infection and colds has also been disproved. A person can get all the vitamin C his body needs by drinking a glass of orange juice daily, or eating a piece of lime rind. Nor do vitamin B-12 injections give pep, zest, or a sense of well-being. Any "beneficial" effects derived from B-12 are purely psychological.

Who, then, really needs vitamins as a supplement to normal intake? There are very few. The premature baby, the infant, the chronically sick (as mentioned above), senile patients who do not feed themselves, the emotionally disturbed, alcoholics who "forget" to eat and, last but not least, those who are unfortunately afflicted with chronic destructive diseases—the hospital in-patient. These are primarily the only individuals who require supplementary vitamins in normal doses in conjunction with normal foodstuffs, along with mineral intake, so they may maintain physiological balance. Those of us who do not fall into the above categories do not require vitamin substitutes, pro-viding we eat three well-balanced meals a day with total adequate caloric in-take to maintain the body weight in relationship to age, sex, and bone struc-ture.

So you may ask: What is "adequate"? Daily ingestion of fruit (some of which are citrus), vegetables, protein in the form of meat, fish or soft organs (liver, kidney), milk products and fresh vegetables (some of which are green and properly cooked) will give the average person adequate intake of all vi-tamins required for the human body. This includes vitamins A, D and E, which are fat soluble and found in liver, fish, vegetable oil, wheat, egg yolk and butter, B complex, derived from milk products, bread containing yeast, liver, fish, meat, green leafy vegetables (cooked or raw); vitamin K, derived from the same; and vitamin C, derived from citrus fruits, tomatoes, potatoes, green pepper, cabbage, etc. If the above are consumed with normal eating habits, one never really requires vitamin substitutes in any form and espe-cially in super dosage, unless you are afflicted with the emotional problem of our society called "junk foods," which depress one's appetite and deny one the privilege of eating a normal selection of foods at mealtime.

Many fadists believe that vitamins are a food substitute. While on a weight reduction diet, which is near starvation, vitamins for super energy add noth-ing to one's sense of well-being, nor do vitamins prevent people from the complications of strenuous dieting. This brings us to the most frequently talked-about use of vitamins, which is "Dieting for Our Overweight Society." Propaganda has again plagued us with the grapefruit diet, egg diet, pure star-vation diet (that is, eating nothing), the liquid diet or bouillon diet, the car-bonated drink diet, and last but not least, the latest fad, the liquid protein diet. When examined carefully, the liquid protein diet is really destructive to the body unless managed with great care, and under the supervision of trained professionals.

Dr. Hilde Bruch, who is a leading authority on the emotional aspects of eating disorders as they relate to obesity, anorexia, and personality problems within these disorders, writes that eating habits relate to the most difficult and primitive characteristics engrained in our personality. They are formed early and are difficult to change. For the most part, the culture we live in deter-mines what we eat! Eating habits may be altered temporarily through cult, fadism and persuasion, but they return to the engrained "mother-taught" likes and dislikes. The old adage "You cannot make a Chinaman eat like an Irishman" holds true. If one toys with these deeply engrained patterns, psychopathology may be precipitated, followed by an associated organic destructive process. The extreme example of this is anorexia nervosa (self starvation).

So, heed this lesson well. If you wish to lose weight, eat the same food you have been brought up on. But, eat less of it, in small frequent feedings—with discipline. And exercise, along with the eating. Make it part of your daily routine. There is no substitute for will power, and this does not come in a capsule. It takes determination and wisdom. The dieting patient derives no nutritional benefit from taking excess vitamins. He may take small amounts of iron substitute and mineral substitute during this period of trial, but once stabilized in weight, these substitutes are no longer required.

Our society is plagued with many fragments of idolatry—copper bracelets to cure arthritis, vitamin E to cure everything, vitamin C to prevent everything. None of these concepts is valid. Vitamins are essential and important to good health. A person who eats well-balanced meals gets his daily requirement of vitamins in his food.

So, a word to the wise: If you are basically healthy, there is no substitute for good food. Super vitaminosis is of no avail. It is only beneficial to the man who sells it.

CREDIT: *Edward A. Newman, M.D., Senior Attending Physician, Department of Medicine, Michael Reese Hospital, Associate Clinical Professor of Medicine, University of Chicago.*

Voyeurism

Voyeurism is the practice of obtaining sexual satisfaction by looking at sexual objects or viewing sexual acts, especially secretively. It is the secretive aspect of this behavior that produced the name *Peeping Tom*.

During the reign of Edward the Confessor (1042–66) the inhabitants of Coventry, England, offended the Earl of Mercia, the lord of an English kingdom in central Britain. They were ordered to pay an additional tax. If there were no relief from this oppressive debt, the community would be left destitute.

In desperation, the villagers appealed for help to the Earl's wife, the compassionate and modest Lady Godiva. She consented to intercede for them and asked the Earl to rescind the tax. He was in a difficult spot and cleverly decided to attach what he thought would be an impossible provision. He said he would rescind the tax on the condition that his wife would ride naked through the streets of Coventry. She surprised him by accepting his condition.

When the townsfolk learned of her bravery, they responded to the willingness of their Lady to suffer humiliation by agreeing that no one should leave his house before noon on the appointed day of Lady Godiva's ride. Furthermore, they stipulated that all the windows were to be closed and darkened so no one would violate Lady Godiva's modesty. True to her promise, Lady Godiva rode naked through the streets of Coventry that day. Tom was the only villager whose lustful curiosity overwhelmed him. He yielded, looked and was struck blind.

This incident is commemorated by a stained-glass memorial in St. Michael's Church, Coventry, Warwickshire.

There is an even more ancient legend of the punishment meted out to a voyeur. On the authority of the great Homer, the blind Theban wiseman, Tiresias, is reputed to have lost his sight for having looked on the Goddess Athena while she was bathing. Inasmuch as his mother was Athena's friend, the penalty of death for this violation was reduced to blindness. And as an ironic act of compensation, she also gave him the power of prophecy—foresight.

However, voyeurism need not be considered a perversion. Indeed, merely looking at the opposite sex with admiring appreciation, which, up to recently, has been thought of as an exclusively male preoccupation, has become a normal activity for both sexes in our Western society.

A recent example of "just looking" was given wide public notice during the Presidential Campaign in the fall of 1976. The then-future President of the United States, a devout and moral man, was quoted in the November issue of *Playboy* magazine as saying, "I've looked on a lot of women with lust," and added significantly, "I have committed adultery in my heart many times. This is something God recognizes I will do—and I have done it . . ."

The public response was clamorous, but divided. As many people were shocked as were approving of the candidate's honest admission of his private thoughts.

This frank exposure provides a public recognition of what is widely acclaimed and deplored as the revolution in moral values.

As a diagnosed psychiatric condition, the label "voyeurism" is restricted to that behavior in which a man compulsively seeks opportunities to look at unsuspecting women who are either naked, in the act of undressing, or engaging in sexual activity. The setting in which voyeuristic behavior takes place often lends itself to a sense of superiority, inasmuch as the woman being looked at is perceived as if she were passive and helpless. Rarely is this accompanying feeling the prelude to rape. Most often, the voyeur is restricted from acting out those ravishing impulses by his emotional immaturity and the fear of its consequences.

Professionals who have studied the psychological makeup of voyeurs have concluded that their peeping behavior is an expression of infantile sexuality.

In our society, exposure of certain parts of the body is forbidden and therefore a prime focus of erotic curiosity. Despite shifts of fashion in dress, there persists the basic childhood mystery concerning the anatomical difference between the sexes and their sexual function. The psychological factors responsible for what is perceived as a mystery provide an irresistible attraction. Stimulated by such stressful experiences as loneliness, rejection and frustration, the recalled experience of the infantile attraction leads to a compulsive need to repeat the peeping behavior. This is of course an attempt to replace anxiety tension with satisfying erotic fantasy.

It appears that opinions are equally divided between two attitudes. The conservatives see pornography as pandering to latent voyeuristic impulses and harmful to the public. The other point of view (supported by data obtained from studies undertaken by the Commission on Obscenity and Pornography) indicates that the degree of exposure to erotica is only a surface manifestation of sexual development.

Society's concern would be better served in an atmosphere that avoided the secrecy about sex that shrouded the nineteenth century's Victorian attitudes. Any serious student of the Victorian era will tell you that the most bizarre orgies and wildest episodes of every conceivable kind took place during those days when sex was suppressed—and driven underground.

CREDIT: *Howard Rome, M.D., Professor of Psychiatry (Emeritus), Mayo Graduate School of Medicine; Staff Psychiatrist, Rochester State Hospital, consultant, C. B. Wilson Center, Faribault, Minnesota.*

Warts

There are many varieties of warts. All warts are caused by a virus.

(1) The common wart appears most often on the hand, especially on the back of the hand, and around and under the fingernails. Common warts rarely occur in early childhood. They become more of a problem during the school years, and then decrease in frequency.

Fortunately, many warts disappear for no apparent reason within two years and need not be treated by a physician. But most people find them a nuisance, unsightly, sometimes painful, and want them removed.

The forms of removal therapy are numerous and varied. Traumatic destructive and mutilating treatment should never be used on children.

"Suggestion therapy" is very often successful. Examples of "suggestion therapy" are: (a) Rubbing the wart with a slice of potato, which is then tossed over the left shoulder and allowed to rot in the earth. (b) Urinating on the warts three nights in a row, after which the warts fall off in ten days. (Urine from a virgin will cause the warts to fall off in five days—but where can you find a virgin who will co-operate?) (c) Rubbing the wart with a piece of string and then burying the string at midnight under a full moon.

Obviously, none of the three "cures" have anything to do with logic or science, but such crazy stunts have caused warts to disappear.

In older patients, the physician might use acids or other chemicals which are destructive, or electrosurgery usually with local anesthesia. These procedures will leave some scars.

(2) The flat or juvenile wart is smooth, and flesh-colored. It usually appears on the face and backs of the hands, in groups ranging in number from just a few to hundreds. They are most often seen in young children. These warts usually can be peeled off chemically so the scarring and painful freezing techniques and electrosurgery need not be used.

(3) The plantar wart is found on the sole of the foot. A wart anywhere else on the foot other than the sole is not a plantar wart. It appears most frequently in school-aged children. It may be related to walking barefoot in showers, locker rooms and around swimming pools. A true plantar wart can be painful and should be removed "root and all" or it will grow back.

In some cases, many small warts develop close together, forming a mosaic pattern. As stated above, the therapy will vary from one dermatologist to another. A group of chemicals can be used successfully in many cases. Any surgical operation is liable to be followed by painful scarring. Therefore, if the wart does not cause pain, it is best for the patient to forget it and wait for the darned thing to disappear on its own.

(4) The venereal wart usually occurs in the ano-genital area and is therefore now considered a sexually transmitted disease. The virus causing venereal warts is a completely different virus from that which causes common warts. In fact, there is no connection whatever between the two. Anyone who develops venereal warts should be examined and tested for other sexually transmitted diseases, especially gonorrhea and syphilis. Most of these warts respond to drugs. Only infrequently will surgery be necessary. Recurrence is not unusual and is often due to the fact that the sexual partner has the same condition and has not been treated. To put it bluntly, the only way to get rid of venereal warts permanently is to make sure your sex partner gets rid of his (or hers), then, refrain from getting intimate with anyone else who has the "problem."

CREDIT: *Leslie Nicholas, M.D., Philadelphia, Pennsylvania.*

Wet Dreams

(*Nocturnal Emissions*)

Any time after the male becomes able to produce semen, usually about a year after pubertal changes get under way, he may have a sexual climax while asleep. The semen is ejaculated just as would occur in masturbation or later in intercourse. This is called nocturnal (nighttime) emission; in common language, a wet dream.

Not every male has this experience. If he does not, it doesn't necessarily mean he has a problem.

Most boys have the experience sooner or later. Of those who are headed for college, 90 percent are having nocturnal emissions by the age of fifteen. Of those not college bound, a little more than 50 percent are having them. Why the difference? Generally those who aspire to a college education plan on postponing marriage, and their value system may call for delaying any form of direct sexual experience, lest it interfere with educational plans.

With all other outlets avoided, the body takes care of the sexual need with an automatic ejaculation during sleep, with or without the aid of a sexual dream.

The youth who is not college bound generally gives himself a right to some sex expression at a much earlier age. If the boy is masturbating or having other sex experience which leads to orgasm, there is little need for nocturnal relief.

There is some evidence that the differences in sexual expectations for the two levels of educational aspiration are leveling off. When all youth are taken into account, approximately 80 percent of boys are having nocturnal emissions, peaking at the mid-teens.

As other forms of sex life are utilized, the frequency of these emissions diminish. By the age of thirty, few are having them. Yet, even a happily married, sexually fulfilled male may have an occasional emission as the climax of an erotic dream.

Just how is the wet dream caused? Semen has collected in the ducts. In the young male, an erection tends to occur every ninety minutes while asleep. During this ebb and flow of sexual readiness, a dream, or the pressures of clothing, may trigger the climax.

After the ejaculation, everything is as before, except the pajamas and bedclothes feel as though they have egg white on them. Within a brief time the clothing and sheet dry out, leaving a slightly yellow stain which disappears with laundering.

Since girls do not have an emission with sexual climax, usually we do not say that they have nocturnal emissions. They do have the same rhythmic readiness for sexual experience during sleep, accompanied by engorgement of the genitalia and lubrication. Sexually or affectionally charged dreams may accompany the experience, along with orgasm at times. Her lubrication may be great enough to dampen clothes.

Nocturnal dreams which are sexually charged are not harmful in any way, either to boys or to girls. Rather, it is a normal happening for any time in life, especially in youth, when sexual relief is not occurring in any other form.

The only problem attached to nocturnal emissions is that the boy may worry about it, including wondering what parents or others will think should they find the evidence. Knowing that it is a healthy manifestation of sexuality, the boy or girl should be pleased that they can have sexually related dreams.

CREDIT: *Aaron L. Rutlege, Ph.D., Grosse Pointe Psychological Center, Grosse Pointe, Michigan.*

Widowhood

A Personal View

My husband thought he would live forever. He didn't. In 1971 Martin died of cancer, leaving me with two small children: Buffy, our five-year-old daughter, and Jon, our nine-year-old son.

Martin and I had a beautiful marriage. We both worked hard. He had his law practice and I had my job in publishing. We had each other and our children. We considered ourselves a very special couple. Martin was not only my husband and lover, he was my best friend. And he had more courage than anyone I ever knew. "I'm going to die, darling," he told me after his illness was diagnosed. "I'm going to die. The prognosis is zero. And it's going to be harder on you than on me."

But I never quite accepted the fact. Though I knew for fourteen months that he was going to die, I was totally unprepared for the finality of death. The months of Martin's dying, however, were only a painful prelude to what followed: the grief, the confusion, the rage, and perhaps the greatest penalty of widowhood, the loneliness. With no preparation, I found myself in a new world, a world that was like living in a country where nobody speaks your language, a country that considers you a pariah. Widows tend to become invisible women. They are constant reminders of mortality and grief, sexual threats to married women.

Census figures show that one out of every six women over the age of twenty-one is a widow. At any given moment, there are about 174,000 women under the age of forty-five who have been widowed and who have not remarried. Eventually some of them will. Most won't. Some will make a healthy adjustment to widowhood. Others will be defeated by it. But in every case, their adjustment will be affected by how well others understand their special needs.

Often it is assumed that widows, particularly young widows, can pick up the pieces of their lives as easily as the millions of their contemporaries who have undergone divorces. This is not true. Our distaste for death is so great that society at large, including doctors, clergymen, members of the so-called helping professions, fail to appreciate that widows, unlike divorcées who can begin to make a new life as soon as their husbands are out of the house, must go through a period of mourning and predictable stages of grief.

Now, almost three years after my husband's death, I am convinced that if I had understood the facts of grief before I had to experience them, it would not have made my grief less intense, lessened my misery, minimized my loss or quelled my rage. Knowledge would have given me hope and courage. I would have known that once my grief was worked through, once I could accept my loss as permanent, I would be my joyful self again. Not my old self, but a stronger, more self-reliant woman. A woman I like better. But it was a difficult process—unnecessarily difficult.

I hope that my experience will give other women strength and hope, relieve their alienation, dispel the fear and ignorance that prolongs and intensifies bereavement, and help them find their true identities so they can regain their zest for life.

The first stage of grief is merciful—numbness that comes with shock. It carries a built-in anesthesia that gets you through a lot. I don't know how I could have functioned without that anesthesia. When dying was over and the little ceremonial flurry subsided, friends withdrew to get on with their own lives. I would have been lost without that blessed numbness. I didn't feel the grief gnawing at me and wondered in a dazed way when I would begin to hurt. I found out soon enough. Feeling crept back nerve by nerve. Five months after Martin died I was a quivering wreck.

I fought against the pain. I became self-protective and spent a lot of time in bed with a heating pad. I craved warmth and softness. My refrigerator was stocked with "mommy" food—custard, vanilla ice cream, vanilla yogurt. But there was no escape. I began to feel, began to hurt.

When the protective fog of numbness finally dissipated, life became truly terrifying. I was full of grief, choked with unshed tears, overwhelmed by the responsibility of bringing up two children alone, panicked about my financial situation, almost immobilized by the realization that I was alone. My psychic pain was such that putting a load of dirty clothes in the washing machine, taking out the vacuum cleaner, making up a grocery list, all the utterly routine chores, loomed like Herculean labors.

I was alone. Alone. And I didn't know what to do. I was beset with problems, some real, most imagined. I did not know how or where to start to put my life in order. If only I had known that the wisest course of action was inaction. Doing nothing at all. At least until I had regained the ability to cope with the essentials of everyday life.

If that hypothetical wise person had existed, he would have told me about grief's seasons. He would also have stressed that the widow has no conception of what she is doing for many, many months after her husband's death. That few of her actions have much to do with reality. She is inconsistent. Extreme. Crazy. I was not prepared for craziness, but it was inevitable. Folk wisdom knows all about the crazy season. Friends and acquaintances tell the widow, "Sit tight. Do nothing. Make no changes. Coast for a few months. Wait . . . wait . . . wait." But the widow, while she hears the words, does not get the message. She believes that her actions are discreet, deliberate, careful, responsible. I certainly did. I believed that every step I made was carefully thought out, wisely calculated. But the record shows otherwise.

One bizarre caper of mine was to write to a rich politician. "You are fat and rich. I am poor and thin," I wrote. "My husband died leaving me with no life insurance and two small children to support on a publishing salary. Would you please send me $500,000. I met you at a literary cocktail party in Washington last year and you drove me to the airport. I look forward to hearing from you."

This was just the tip of the iceberg. My craziness went deep. I was a lost child. I yearned for someone to take care of me, to love me. It took me a long time to undo some of my ridiculous and expensive mistakes.

Another stage of grief is anger. My anger shot out in all directions. At old friends. At my family. At my neighbors. Even at my children. But most of all at my husband. At the beginning I was full of compassion, but then as the dying went on and on, fury crept in. I was helpless. I couldn't save Martin. Helplessness was too much to bear, so I became angry. And after he died, my rage took possession of me, just as Martin had warned me when he said, "You're going to shake your fist at my photograph."

Through all the months of nightmares and anxiety attacks, the woman I presented to the world was calm, coping, cool. Part of it was pride, but more of it was a dread of letting people sense my vulnerability. Close friends, I know now, were concerned about me. They sensed my strain, my confusion. But my refusal to talk inhibited them from probing, from helping.

One of the chores of grief involves going over and over in one's mind the circumstances that led to the death, the details of the death itself. Endless dwelling on the dead person. Memories are taken out and sifted. Finally the widow accepts the fact that her husband is dead. This is reality, and talking about it helps make it real. Judith Viorst, writer, and a supremely articulate spokeswoman on this subject, suggests: "Maybe we all should begin to talk about death. The silence I've met on this subject shows we've been more frightened than we know. This deprives us of each other's consolation and takes from us the gift of comforting . . . So let us talk about death."

There *are* people to talk to, although it may not be easy. There are relatives, friends, religious leaders, widow organizations, and professionally trained therapists. I wish I had known about the therapeutic value of talk when my husband was dying. I know now it is what you don't talk about that terrifies you. Talking dispels the phantoms. And after Martin died I would have talked about him. And talked about him. And talked about him. Until I finally knew that he was dead and I was alone—starting a new life. I would have emerged from grief sooner.

"Widow" is a harsh and hurtful word. It comes from the Sanskrit and it means "empty." I do not want to be pigeonholed as a widow. I am a woman whose husband has died, but I am not a second-class citizen—a lonely goose. I am a mother and working woman and a friend. I am a sexual woman and a laughing woman and a concerned woman and a vital woman. I am a person. And I am very much alive. I owe the person I am today to my husband's death. If he had not died, I am sure I would have lived happily ever after as a twentieth-century child-wife. But today I am someone else. I am stronger, more independent. I have more understanding, more sympathy. A different perspective.

Perhaps the single bit of advice I can give to other widows is this: Keep your job if you have one, and find one if you don't. A full-time job, a part-time job, a volunteer job, anything that will provide you with a routine and stability. I can't stress how important my job was to me, and not only in terms of money coming in. It gave structure to my life. Even in my lowest times, the very fact of having a job gave me emotional security. I belonged somewhere. I had a place to go to every day. I had work to do.

Why should any woman face deprivation and anxiety and financial terror because her husband dies? Women must learn to protect themselves and their children. And that means becoming responsible now for their own personal futures.

CREDIT: *Lynn Caine, author of* Widow, *New York, New York: William Morrow & Co., and* Lifelines, *Garden City, New York: Doubleday & Company.*

Wills

The Importance of Wills

A WIDOW'S THIRD

DEAR ANN LANDERS: I am a fairly intelligent woman (or so I thought) in a state of shock. Why? Because I didn't know the first thing about inheritance laws. I sit here dumbfounded at my ignorance and angry at my deceased husband for not educating me. (Maybe he didn't know any better either, but he should have.)

John and I were married 33 years. We have two children. Five years ago our son ran off with a girl we never liked. We haven't heard from him since. Our daughter is living in California with some hippie—weaving baskets. We wrote her off in 1972 when she wrote us a nasty letter about our "crass materialism."

Two weeks ago John died of a heart attack. He was 57 and in the best of health. No history of a coronary problem, ever. He had a physical in December and was pronounced fit as a fiddle.

John left no will. When the lawyers told me I am entitled by law to only one-third of my husband's estate and our daughter and son will divide the other two-thirds I almost keeled over. Yes, that's the way the law in Illinois reads and I am helpless.

I am writing in the hope that you will print this letter and wake up others who are as stupid as I was. DON'T KNOW WHAT HIT ME

DEAR DON'T KNOW: Here's your letter and I hope it gets a few million people to thinking.

Do you women out there know what would happen if your husband dropped dead tomorrow? If you don't, call a lawyer or your insurance agent and find out.

Without a will, the possessions accumulated by a person over a lifetime go to that person's heirs under the laws of intestacy of the particular state where the person lived at death. This can result in the distribution of your property in ways that might not be to your liking. Here are some examples:

(1) A husband dies, leaving his widow with a four-year-old child. In many states, the wife would receive no more than a third of his estate. The rest of his estate would go to the child. The mother would not be able to use

any of the child's portion for herself even if she had a desperate need due to illness. Moreover, she may not be able to use the child's portion for the child's needs without court approval—sometimes a clumsy and expensive procedure.

(2) A husband dies leaving a wife and no children. His wife has never worked but has been solely dependent upon him for twenty-five years. His father, who is wealthy, is still alive. In many states, the wife would receive no more than one half of the husband's estate; the father would receive the rest. (In some states, the father's portion would be shared with the deceased's sisters and brothers.)

(3) Sam and Matilda lived together for many years. They were never legally married, even though people who knew them assumed that they were. Sam had no known relatives. One day he died suddenly. In most states, all of Sam's possessions would go to the state.

State laws of intestacy usually provide a right of inheritance only for "blood" relationships, roughly following the ancient line of descent of the kingship to English sovereigns, except for the addition of the spouse as an heir. Only a few states still recognize "common-law" marriages under which a valid marriage results not from a ceremony performed, but from a mutual agreement to live together as husband and wife.

The difference between having the distribution of your property determined by a will, rather than by the laws of intestacy of your particular state, is the difference between the state deciding what happens to everything you have managed to accumulate during your lifetime, and you deciding.

It makes a lot of difference what the future needs of your children are likely to be, whether the wife is self-supporting or totally dependent, the state of the wife's health and of the husband's wealth, the neediness of your own parents, the degree to which you feel that your spouse will act caringly and responsibly toward your children after you are dead, how much life insurance is carried—a myriad of such questions have to be weighed to decide intellectually the best way to provide for your family.

Since men are usually the principal breadwinners of the family, and women as a group have a longer life-expectancy, estate planning ordinarily revolves around providing financial security for the wife and children. However, all possible contingencies are provided for in a well-drawn will.

Another reason a will is important is to anticipate an event that occurs not frequently in our modern society—death in a common disaster. Should the decision as to the custody of your children in that situation be made by a judge hearing testimony by your relatives after the tragedy occurs, or by you now, together, in a will? The two of you not only can decide who among your family and friends could best rear your children; you could talk to them or leave instructions to them in a letter that would be kept in the same place you leave your will about particular things they should know that would help them in raising your children. Also, if you have more than one child, you might want to specifically provide in the will that the children are not to be parceled out, but are to remain in a single family.

A will affords you an opportunity to leave specific instructions as regards burial or cremation and other aspects of funeral arrangements. You can also donate your organs for transplant to enable another human being to see with your cornea or to survive with your kidney. You can also make provisions for your favorite charity, or give a treasured item of personal property that will be particularly meaningful to a certain person.

A will once made may be modified by the formal execution of what is called a "codicil." A marriage or divorce of a person, an annulment of a marriage, or the birth of a child after a will has been executed, ordinarily revokes or modifies the will unless the events were anticipated in the will itself.

A will *never* takes effect until a person's death. For this reason, it can be changed or destroyed by you at any time prior to death. (This is a good reason for *not* signing duplicate copies of a will, for if you do so and later destroy the original copy, there will still be a signed copy of that will to invite confusion or even fraud.)

The signed original of the will ought to be kept by you in a safe place such as a safe deposit box, or by your lawyer. The usual way of canceling a will is by the execution of a new one. The latest valid will is the one that counts. If there is a desire to disinherit a particular member of the immediate family—a step that should not be taken lightly—the will should mention that person's name to show that the omission was a deliberate decision, and not a mere oversight.

Much ill will can be engendered among children by the action of parents in vindictively favoring one over the other in a will. In addition, there is much to be said for bequeathing property in such a way that it will not necessitate joint use. "Say not you know another entirely until you have divided an inheritance with him," said Johan Kaspar Lavater, an eighteenth-century writer. The only time a will cannot be changed is where two people—usually a husband and wife—execute "a joint and mutual will." In this situation, upon the death of one of them, the other may no longer be able to change the will. For that reason, such a will should never be utilized except with the utmost care and caution. A "joint and mutual will" may destroy the very flexibility that has made the will such an invaluable device for meeting human needs over the centuries.

Some people shy away from writing a will because of fear or distaste of the subject of death. Since all of us now have accepted death as a reality by our willingness to purchase life insurance, we can do the same by having our estate plans in readiness.

Another reason some don't prepare wills is the mistaken notion that this may avoid probate costs and death taxes. On the contrary, the costs are likely to be higher. The requirements for the probating of an estate—that is, proving and establishing the validity of a will—are imposed so that a court will make sure that the deceased's wishes are carried out (at that point, the deceased isn't there to speak for himself).

In each state, the law requires the probating of every estate that exceeds a certain minimum amount, whether or not the person left a will. If you left a will, however, you may save some costs by yourself designating the person who will be in charge of probating your estate (called the "executor") rather than leaving it to the statute and judge to select that person; you can also provide for the waiver of a surety bond, which will save some costs. Moreover, especially in larger estates, the lawyer whom you consult for the drawing of a will, being familiar with federal and state tax laws, may make suggestions to you that can result in reducing considerably the taxes your estate and beneficiaries will pay. However, the first question of the lawyer is *whether* you need a will. Such a question requires individual consideration. There are no universal rules that fit every situation. For example, many couples have believed that by placing funds or property in "joint tenancy," they automatically save money. While joint tenancy can reduce probate costs, it can result in increased taxes. The drawing of a will offers an excellent time to consider with legal help the advisability of many alternative ways of protecting your estate and carrying out your wishes.

The law varies from state to state as to the formalities required for a person (called a "testator") to make a valid will. In general, the person must understand that he is by the written instrument disposing of his property upon death. He must so acknowledge in the presence of disinterested witnesses (persons who do not inherit under the will), two or three in number, depending on the particular state. (It is better to err on the side of caution by using three.) These witnesses usually must also acknowledge in the presence of each other that they are witnessing the execution of a will. Notarization is not a requirement.

The person making the will must be "of sound mind"; there must be no fraud or undue influence being perpetrated upon him; he must be acting of his own free will. However, courts do not lightly set aside a will unless the incapacity of the person signing it is clear.

Some states permit an individual to make a valid will without witnesses if the entire will is written in his or her own handwriting (called a "holographic will"), and some states even permit in limited situations an oral will to be validly made. Because the laws of each state can change at any time, this article will not list the states in each category. A lawyer in your state is the only reliable source of such information.

The characteristic feature of the probate field of law is that a mistake once made is not usually discovered until it is too late to correct. By then, the person whose will is in issue has departed. A classic example of how the failure to meet legal technicalities can invalidate a will occurred some years ago when the will of a member of the Supreme Court of Connecticut—drawn by himself—was after his death thrown out because it failed to meet the technical requirements of the laws of Connecticut! (It also demonstrates the wisdom of the ancient legal aphorism that "a man who acts as his own lawyer has a fool for a client.")

There is no better way to close than by reciting some lines from a ballad written by a British jurist, Lord Neaves:

> He writes and erases, he blunders, and blots,
> He produces such puzzles and Gordian Knots,
> That a lawyer, intending to frame the thing ill,
> Couldn't match the testator who makes his own will.
> Testators are good, but a feeling more tender . . .
> Springs up when I think of the feminine gender!
> No customer brings so much grist to the mill
> As the wealthy old woman who makes her own will.

CREDIT: *Harold A. Katz, attorney, Chicago, Illinois.*

TAKE THE MONEY AND RELAX

DEAR ANN LANDERS: My wife's mother lived with us for 14 years. She helped with the housework and cooking, and she was wonderful with our children. We never considered her a burden. The only time I ever became annoyed with her was when she cut your column out of the paper and I'd find a big hole when I went to read Ann Landers.

My wife has a sister and two brothers. They never gave us a nickel toward Grandma's expenses. We bought her clothes, paid her medical insurance and saw to it that she had a little money in her purse. The last year of her life was very expensive. She was gravely ill.

Grandma's will was probated a few days ago. We didn't know she had any-thing. To our surprise she owned some blue-chip stocks and had a pile of war bonds from World War II.

The estate is not huge, but to people like us it looks like a million.

The big question: Grandma left everything to us. The brothers and sister are closing in. They say Grandma wasn't "all there" and it's up to us to "do the right thing."

So, Ann, what is "the right thing?" Should Grandma's other children share equally in the inheritance? R&L

DEAR R & L: The money isn't Grandma's. It's yours.

She left it to you—all of it. If you want to share it with a swarm of locusts, go ahead.

Living Will—The Right to Die

To: My Family, My Executor, My Physician and My Lawyer:

If the time comes when I can no longer take part in decisions for my own future, I want you to be guided by this expression of my views.

If there is no reasonable expectation of my recovery from physical or mental disability, I request that I be allowed to die, preferably at home, and that no artificial means or heroic measures be employed to prolong my life. Death is as much a reality as birth, growth, maturity and old age. I do not fear death as much as I fear the indignity of deterioration, dependence and hopeless pain. I ask that drugs be mercifully administered to me for terminal suffering even if they hasten the moment of death. I have no desire to be kept alive by machines in a hospital if there is no sound medical hope of a recovery which will permit me to participate meaningfully in life.

The language quoted above is a good example of a "Living Will," sometimes referred to as a "Right to Die" statement or a "Death with Dignity" declaration. The development of such documents has been stimulated by modern medical techniques and devices. Artificial respirators, mechanical heart pumps and intravenous feedings can extend the life of a patient's body long after "brain death" has occurred.

The medical and legal professions and the courts are working to find an acceptable definition of death. One thoughtful physician, Dr. Donald W. Seldin (Chairman, Department of Internal Medicine, Southwestern Medical School, University of Texas), observes that there are three levels of life: (1) biochemical life, in which the metabolic processes of a cell are intact; (2) vegetative life, in which the functions of the organs and organ systems are intact; and, (3) human life, in which there is the capacity of intentionality and purposeful behavior. Dr. Seldin suggests that if a person has irretrievably lost the capacity of human life, the situation may be an appropriate one for carrying out the Living Will. The decision would be made jointly by the person's family and physician.

If a person wishes to have a Living Will, he or she should sign and execute the document with the same formalities used for a Will disposing of property.

Living Wills today are legally questionable. Many lawyers and doctors are rightfully concerned about charges of malpractice and even criminal conduct if every effort to extend and preserve life is not pursued.

Some states are struggling to create laws to deal with these issues. The Karen Ann Quinlan case is an example of the many legal, moral and ethical problems involved. Some people believe it would be wise to continue to rely on the good sense and compassion of families and doctors rather than writing detailed rules and regulations on the right to die. Each of us, while in good health, should discuss these questions calmly and reflectively with our loved ones.

CREDIT: *Newton N. Minow, attorney, Chicago, Illinois.*

Women

How and Where They Are
Treated Unfairly by the Law

In some states, a widow loses all right to any share of the family estate if her husband leaves her out of his will.

Elsewhere, the woman whose husband unmercifully beats her probably will find she can't count on police or courts for help.

In Louisiana, a husband controls his wife's earnings.

In practically all states, women have no way to enforce support laws when husbands refuse to take financial responsibility for their families. Contrary to myth, American divorce settlements are meager.

The laws discussed here apply equally to women employed outside the home and in most cases to men; however, the laws' harshest impact is on the homemaker not working for pay.

INHERITANCE

Unfair inheritance laws appear to be widespread in the United States.

A South Dakota husband can completely disinherit his wife except for the right to live in the family home for her lifetime.

Likewise, a Georgia husband can completely disinherit his wife; however, a court may, on her petition, grant her one year's support, to be paid by his estate.

Children in Alabama rank above their mother in inheriting real estate and personal property from their father if there is no will. A husband, on the other hand, has much greater priority in inheriting from his wife. The majority of states will require division of the estate among children, parents, grand-children, brothers and sisters, nephews and nieces—in addition to the spouse —if there is no will.

In Louisiana, a wife cannot receive her husband's half of community property even if he wishes to will it to her. If the husband has children or living parents, these surviving relatives are "forced heirs," and they must receive a share of the husband's estate *regardless* of provisions in a will.

If a New Jersey husband dies without a will, title to all real estate that is in his name alone, including the family residence, passes to the children, rather than the wife. She is entitled only to the income from one half the real estate during her lifetime.

Vermont courts may prevent a woman from breaking her husband's will. The court has no right to prevent such action when the surviving spouse is male.

Under South Carolina law, a married man who owns only personal property (bonds, stocks, cash) can make a valid will leaving his wife nothing. He can leave up to one fourth of his property and an unlimited amount of life insurance to his mistress or illegitimate children.

Where there is no will, the wife in South Carolina may forfeit her "dower rights" and her part of her husband's estate if she is guilty of "misconduct." There is no similar provision depriving a man of his wife's property if he "misbehaves."

On the positive side, a surviving spouse in Arizona, California, Idaho, Nevada and Washington inherits all the community property when there is no will; in Arizona, the surviving spouse inherits separate property as well.

PROPERTY RIGHTS

Arkansas is one of the states that appears to hold homemakers in lowest esteem. In that state, homestead rights belong to the husband, not the wife. The Arkansas husband can choose, abandon and sell homesteads at will without the wife's consent, since state law presumes that all personal property including household furnishings belongs to him.

To protect her personal property from sale by her husband without her consent, or from seizures by his creditors, a married woman in Arkansas must file a schedule of her separate property with the county recorder. If she does not, she must prove that she bought the property with her separate money. No such burden is ever placed on the husband.

In Louisiana, the husband has the power to sell and mortgage community property, including the home, without consent or knowledge of the wife. In West Virginia, the courts have decided that when a wife earns money working in her husband's business, those earnings belong to the husband. If a Maine couple jointly run a business, the profits belong to the husband.

SUPPORT

The nationwide homemaker survey reveals that the right to support is a myth. A husband's legal duty to support his wife is not enforceable. Few states will interfere in an ongoing marriage to ensure support for a wife and children. Generally, courts will become involved in "support" cases only when the marriage has ended by separation or divorce.

In three states, judges cannot award alimony: Pennsylvania, Texas and Indiana. A divorced wife is completely dependent on the goodwill and decency of her former husband.

In most states, courts generally do not award alimony; in fact, only 14 percent of divorced wives in America are ever awarded alimony. In 90 percent of the divorce cases that come before the Iowa courts, no alimony is awarded.

Alimony is very difficult to collect even when awarded; fewer than half of the awards are collected regularly.

In many states (for example, Virginia and Louisiana as well as the District of Columbia) a wife may not receive alimony if she is at fault. However, a husband is not penalized for being at fault.

In 1973, 83 percent of all Iowa child-support payments were between $10 and $20 per week; in 20 percent of the cases involving children, no child support of any kind was awarded. Such meager or non-existent awards are typical, according to the state studies.

Child support awards typically cover less than one half the support of the children and are also very difficult to collect. National data collected in 1975 by the National Commission for the Observance of International Women's Year showed that child support was awarded to 44 percent of divorced mothers, and that fewer than half were collecting regularly.

A study in Jefferson County, Alabama, showed that court-ordered child support falls far below welfare assistance available to dependent children. The average amount of support ordered for a woman and two children was $80 monthly; whereas a woman with children on welfare would receive cash and services worth $300 per month, plus free medical care. The welfare payments are, of course, more dependable and regular than court-ordered support.

In a number of states, including Florida, Georgia, New York, Pennsylvania, Rhode Island, South Carolina, Virginia and Utah, the court cannot divide property titled in the husband's name even if the wife's money contributed to the purchase. In many states where the judge can divide the property, there is no requirement that a spouse's contribution as homemaker be taken into account in dividing the property.

Even in Kentucky, where divorce courts are required to consider the domestic services and economic contribution of the wife, the prevailing rule of thumb awards a homemaker approximately one third of jointly held property. Only if she has been a wage-earning participant in the household may she receive up to a maximum of one half the property.

Alaska law does not provide for temporary alimony pending divorce, so that a wife with no independent resources cannot seek a divorce unless she can go on welfare.

Women face other inequities in divorce proceedings:

In Kansas, Texas and Washington state, a woman who cosigns for a debt with her husband is liable to the creditor, even if a divorce decree orders the husband to pay the debt.

RAPE AND ABUSE

Women are protected from rape by their husbands in only six states: Iowa, Wisconsin, Michigan, Minnesota, Ohio and Pennsylvania. However, laws in five of these states specify that parties must be living apart.

Iowa is the only state to allow a wife to charge her husband with rape regardless of his domicile. She may bring charges if he forces sexual intercourse through injury or threat with a weapon.

The state studies show a pattern of inaction by officials who do not regard abuse of a wife as seriously as they regard violence against any other person. Such rulings reflect the old idea that a wife is her husband's property, and he has a right to sexual relations with her, even if he must use force.

In Utah, for example, laws against assault are systematically not enforced when violated in a family context. Courts and police officials do not want to interfere in what they call "family disputes," "family quarrels," "personal matters" or "domestic squabbles."

Wife beating in Delaware is referred to the family court, where these cases are considered only third-degree assault (legally, the least serious type of assault), no matter how extensive the injuries.

The indifference of officials to assault against women by their husbands is evident in Alaska, where an accused wife beater is likely to be released quickly on $25 bond. The sentence for a convicted wife beater is usually a fine of $25–$50, which may be suspended. In Alaska, the average total time spent by police in Alaska on wife-beating complaints is seventeen minutes.

In New Hampshire, the penalties for wife beating or simple assault range from a verbal warning to a small fine.

In Nevada, police do not arrest a wife abuser unless the battering is severe enough to charge the husband with a felony (assault with a deadly weapon). In Virginia, Montana and many other States, as well as in the District of Columbia, a married woman may not sue her husband for physically abusing her.

In Pennsylvania, a recent court decision held that a wife who has been beaten by her husband cannot sue him for medical expenses required to treat her injuries.

In South Carolina, if a woman flees home because of abuse and then files for divorce, she must prove that the physical cruelty endangered her life and also that she did not provoke the abuse. South Carolina courts instruct the wife that she has the obligation to be tolerant, within reason, of her husband's shortcomings.

In Texas, a conviction depends on proof of "substantial physical injury" to the wife. In New York, isolated cases of wife abuse are not grounds for divorce; evidence of a pattern of violence or a "concerted course of conduct" by the husband against the wife must be shown. In Oregon, police departments view domestic quarrels skeptically and hesitate to appear on the scene unless a divorce proceeding has begun and a restraining order has been secured.

PENALTIES RELATED TO ADULTERY

In Alabama, a man who finds his wife in the act of adultery and immediately kills her is not guilty of murder (punishable by death or life imprisonment) but of manslaughter only (punishable by one to ten years' imprisonment). There is no such defense for a woman who murders her husband under similar circumstances.

This double standard in the law is also evident in Vermont, where the husband who is granted a divorce because of the wife's adultery may be awarded property that is owned separately in the wife's name. But an adulterous husband can't be deprived of his separate property.

In South Carolina a woman is *absolutely* denied alimony if she is found guilty of adultery.

Here are some state laws that are fair to homemakers:

Arizona, California, Idaho, New Mexico and Washington: In these "community property" states women have always been considered to own half the property acquired during marriage, but until recent revisions in the law in these states, the husband was the "manager" and generally could dispose of or mortgage community property without his wife's consent.

Montana: Lawmakers passed comprehensive legislation in 1975 to implement the equal rights provision in the new state constitution. The new legislation explicitly recognizes the economic worth of the homemaker and it reads:

> Duties of husband and wife as to support: Insofar as each is able, the husband and wife shall support each other out of their property and labor. As used in this section, the word "support" includes the nonmonetary support provided by a spouse as homemaker.

The new legislation also provides a more effective means of collecting child support, and allows a woman to choose her legal residence.

Nebraska: Courts dividing property at divorce must consider each party's contributions to the care and education of the children, and the interruption of other careers.

Texas: A share of a husband's retirement benefits, including any to be received in the future, may be awarded to a wife in a divorce settlement.

Alaska, New Mexico and Washington: Some jurisdictions have informally adopted a child-support schedule pegged to the net salary of the parent who works for pay; for example, a person making $900 a month in King County, Washington, would pay $315 per month for two children, $378 for three. The schedules provide for modifying the amount because of other considerations. The New Mexico and Washington schedules are more liberal than the Alaska schedule.

New York: This state, while among the worst in many respects, has a new strict disclosure law requiring that both parties in a divorce case disclose their full assets.

Pennsylvania: This state, also among the worst for homemakers, recently enacted a Protection from Abuse statute, which allows an abused wife to seek a temporary court order requiring her husband to leave the family home.

Wisconsin: The legislature has just passed, as a result of a long and intensive effort by a women's coalition, a greatly improved divorce bill. The statement of intent includes the following sentences:

It is the intent of the legislature that a spouse who has been handicapped socially or economically by his or her contributions to a marriage shall be compensated for such contributions at the termination of the marriage, insofar as this is possible, and may receive additional education where necessary to permit the spouse to become self-supporting at a standard of living reasonably comparable to that enjoyed during the marriage. It is further the intent of the legislature that the standard of living of any minor children of the parties be maintained at the level the children would have enjoyed had the marriage not ended, so that insofar as is possible, the children will not suffer economic hardship. It is the intent of the legislature to recognize children's needs for close contact with both parents, to encourage joint parental responsibility for the welfare of minor children and to promote expanded vistation.

CREDIT: *National Commission on the Observance of International Women's Year, Office of Public Information, U. S. Department of State, Washington, D.C.*

The Workaholic

The term "workaholic" has crept into our contemporary vocabulary as an analogy to "alcoholic." Obvious similarities are relevant if one does not push the comparison too far. Both work and alcohol are part of the social scene and considered "good" in moderation. But both are often misused and overused. One can, in a sense, become addicted to work as well as to alcohol.

Differences are obvious also. Work is necessary, alcohol is not. Work is vocational, alcohol is generally recreational. Work requires self-discipline and responsibility, while alcohol in varying degrees diminishes self-discipline and responsibility. Work is morally good. Alcohol is morally suspect.

There are understandable explanations for hard work and for what, measured by average behavior, is called overwork. Some individuals have a personality characterized by drive and energy and they need to invest themselves vigorously in challenging tasks. By expending a great deal of psychic energy they manage to maintain psychological balance. Hard work is a gratification. It is even a wholesome necessity. Workaholics may adjust poorly to enforced idleness. When convalescing from an illness, for example, they become tense and nervous from inactivity. On vacation or in attempting to pursue a hobby, they manifest the same enthusiasm and drive as in work performance. When such persons are exceptionally talented they can contribute significantly to humanity.

Some people work overtime in response to social or family pressures. They want to get ahead, to achieve, and are highly competitive. This type of workaholic assumes, often correctly, that if he exerts more energy than is expected and does more than is required, spends more hours at the office or takes work home, he will probably beat out the competition. He then gets caught up in the rat race and reacts in response to outer pressure rather than inner drives. A son who is competing with his father in a family business—or worse yet, a son-in-law—can become a workaholic. Brothers—or sisters or cousins—who are competing in the same business (or field) can also fall into this trap. If the competition were to disappear, so would the compelling drive to do more and more.

Some persons devote long hours to work for essentially moral reasons. The austere Protestant ethic in which many of us were reared labeled work as "moral" and idleness as "sinful." In the belief that the devil finds mischief for idle hands, the virtue of working long hours, combined with the controlling of impulses, is still preached from some pulpits, taught in some homes and encouraged in the marketplace. The morally motivated worker's primary goal is psychological—it protects him from feeling guilty.

The healthy hard worker and the neurotic workaholic have noticeable differences. The "diagnosis" of workaholism does not rest on the excessive number of hours worked but the motivation for such a schedule. The crucial difference is the freedom to choose. The workaholic is not free. He is compelled by inner forces he does not understand.

A prominent psychologist, Abraham Maslow, suggested two fundamental motives—desire for growth and a feeling of inadequacy. The individual influenced primarily by the growth motive works vigorously to maintain a healthy self-esteem and self-respect. His work is stimulating, growth-promoting, creative and gratifying.

The person influenced primarily by feelings of inadequacy senses himself deprived of love, approval and acceptance. He misuses work in an unconscious effort to attain a feeling of personal security and to appease his gnawing neurotic hungers. Frequently he accomplishes little. He expends energy but ends up running in place because his strivings are not reality-based and realistically goal-directed. Since his efforts bring him only temporary relief from his voracious inner cravings and his irrational fears, he compulsively repeats and repeats his superworking behavior in order to feel comfortable. His performance is characterized more by grim determination than gratification. If he does not work he becomes anxious and has difficulty justifying any of his non-work activity.

DIAGNOSIS

Workaholics, like alcoholics, are not all alike. They have many similar characteristics but also several differences.

The aggressive personality. Aggressiveness can be advantageous in coping with everyday life. However, the individual who uses aggression as his chief approach to life situations has a psychological problem. His acquaintances and colleagues consider him extremely competitive, impatient, restless and often hostile. Pushed by a compelling sense of time urgency, he lives by self-imposed deadlines. He feels stressed by the pressures of commitment and responsibility, yet he frequently takes on additional "projects." He cannot let go of his overcommitment to work. Whenever not aggressively striving he feels uneasy.

The obsessive-compulsive personality. Orderliness, careful attention to detail and uncompromising standards of excellence are worthy traits, but if they persistently dominate an individual's behavior they can be a limiting, handicapping personality disorder. The person with the obsessive-compulsive personality is emotionally constricted, obstinate, orderly to a fault, persevering, rigid—a perfectionist. He can be a problem to his employer, his colleagues and his family because of his insistence on overperformance. He cannot put off until tomorrow what could better be done tomorrow.

The constricted personality. Work seems for certain persons almost the whole of life. If not at work such a person considers himself worthless. Only when immersed in work can he find meaning in life and the desired approval for devotion to duty. Typically, he has no hobbies or community interests and is periodically a victim of "weekend neurosis" or "holiday depression." He feels inadequate and lost when he is suddenly faced with a few extra hours. He is at loose ends because he never learned to play.

Another type of workaholic is married to a woman who nags and complains incessantly when he is at home. She is frustrated and discontented and may have many imaginary illnesses. She follows him from room to room to porch to garage to lawn, all the while confiding to and imposing upon him her every thought, suspicion, fear, disappointment, symptom and concern. Her monologue intrudes on his reading of the newspaper, his listening to music or TV, writing a letter or figuring his income tax.

He is a decent man, monogamous and non-violent. To escape his wife's relentless vocalizing he returns to the silent haven of his office or to the briefcase he has brought home. His productivity is thus increased, his earnings grow and he becomes accustomed to working for long periods. After a time his habit is his chief pleasure. He becomes a workaholic instead of a wife beater or divorced.

TREATMENT

The workaholic does not consider himself psychologically ill or odd. Although he is often vaguely dissatisfied with the lack of fulfillment in his life and dimly aware that his accustomed work pattern stems from compulsion rather than free choice, he considers himself "normal." However, when confronted with his excessive work behavior, like the alcoholic, he protests, becomes adept at denying, excusing, minimizing and rationalizing his excesses. If challenged, he may admit to non-gratifying, even self-harmful aspects of his affliction and promise or resolve to change, but soon he returns to his addiction. Since his behavior is a response to subconscious neurotic drives, all efforts to get him to change are futile.

The best hope lies in getting the workaholic to seek professional help.

His only chance for a "cure" hinges on his ability to recognize that he is missing out on some of the best things in life and that his family is suffering because of his one-dimensional approach. This awakening cannot be achieved by nagging. It must be arrived at by the workaholic whose uncomplaining wife goes about her own hobbies and interests and leaves him alone.

The workaholic will need professional help to get to the root of his compulsive behavior. (Why is he the way he is? With whom is he competing?

Why does he feel so inadequate that he must do twice as much as anyone else?) A good therapist can help him identify the cause of his drivenness and, once discovered, he can hopefully examine his neurosis and see that he has turned out to be the slave rather than the master and that the multifaceted life is by far the richer and more rewarding.

CREDIT: *Herbert C. Modlin, M.D., Psychiatrist, the Menninger Foundation, Topeka, Kansas.*

Xanthelasma and Other Skin Problems

XANTHELASMA: Patches of skin, yellowish in color, found on the eyelids. They may or may not be related to high blood cholesterol. A physician may remove the patches by the use of a chemical, or minor surgery.

XANTHOMA: A condition that produces irregular patches or nodules on the skin, usually on the neck, back or elbows. The presence of these patches indicates that there may be a disturbance in the cholesterol balance. In some instances, with a low-fat, low-cholesterol diet, the patches will disappear.

XANTHOSIS: A yellow discoloration of the skin from abnormal causes. Malaria and hepatitis are two of the most common diseases that cause xanthosis.

XERODERMA: A disease of the skin characterized by a dry roughness and sometimes scaling. It may be hereditary or acquired. Creams or oils may help alleviate the discomfort.

CREDIT: *Ann Landers.*

Xenophobia

A fear or hatred of strangers or foreigners or of anything that is different from what the individual is accustomed to.

For the last ten years I have received at least three signed letters a week from a man in California who suffers from this illness. He is literate and intelligent, informs me in great detail of his social activities and particularly about what he eats.

In every letter, he makes some mention of the Mexican check-out clerk in the supermarket who insulted him, or a small group of Mexican women who were staring (or glaring) at him and tried to obstruct his entrance to the bus or a doorway. This week I heard about the Mexican women who followed him into a drugstore and whispered derogatory statements behind his back.

Although it is dangerous to attempt to diagnose through the mail, I am certain that my California correspondent has xenophobia.

CREDIT: *Ann Landers.*

X Ray

X ray is a form of electromagnetic radiation which has the power to penetrate solid substances to varying degrees. X ray was discovered by Wilhelm Conrad Roentgen on November 8, 1895. The extraordinary value of Roentgen's discovery has been most notable in the field of medicine.

Radiology is the branch of medicine which deals with the use of X rays. Diagnostic radiology employs X ray as an aid in the diagnosis of disease and injuries. An example of the use of X ray is when a child swallows a safety pin. The doctor will order an X-ray picture to locate the object. The pin may be in the throat or even the stomach. By seeing exactly where it lies, the doctor can determine the best way to remove it. Another example is when a person has a fall or is injured in a car accident. He is in pain, but the doctor does not know whether or not there are broken bones. The X-ray picture can tell precisely where the break is (if there is one) and the doctor can determine the best way to treat the injury. If there is a break, another X ray after the bone is set will tell whether or not it has been set in the correct position so that it will heal properly.

Therapeutic radiology employs higher-energy X rays for the treatment of disease. This is frequently referred to as a cobalt treatment, but it is actually a form of X ray. Another form is the treatment by the linear accelerator. These therapeutic radiology treatments are one of medicine's ways of holding back the growth of cancer, in some cases curing it.

Nuclear medicine is still another branch of radiology. Tiny amounts of radioactive substances are introduced into the body, creating an image of different organs. With an X ray, the radiologist can see and evaluate certain functions of the organs and diagnose a variety of disease processes.

ARE X RAYS DANGEROUS?

Much has been written in the press on this subject and a great deal of controversy exists. (Some physicians say they have evidence that too much X ray can cause cancer.) The center of this storm currently is the risk of mammography (X ray of the breasts) to the younger woman. It has been established that only in cases where the physician has fully evaluated the risks against the knowledge to be gained should X-ray mammography be done on the patient under the age of thirty-five.

Overall, standards have been set which allow that when an X-ray examination supervised by a qualified radiologist and conducted by a qualified technologist is performed, it involves risks smaller than the risks one would encounter every day at home, at work or on the street. The physician who orders the examinations has weighed any risks and determined that the risk is smaller than the risk of not having the examination.

To protect the patient, many safeguards are used. The X-ray tube is shielded by a metal casing, the X-ray beam comes through an opening in the tube and metal filters are placed in its path to select the useful energies. For the patient's protection, a device called a collimator is added to the tube. This confines the beam so that it is directed only to the area to be studied. Another protective measure is the use of high-speed X-ray film which requires less radiation to make a useful picture.

HOW IS AN X-RAY EXAMINATION USED?

The initial examination may be a direct aid to diagnosis and treatment of a specific disease or condition. After the diagnosis is made, further films may be taken on a follow-up basis to show progression of the disease or correction of the condition.

In many cases, contrast studies may be necessary. Contrast is the dye that is placed in the body to outline an organ, such as the stomach or the gallbladder. Contrast materials may be swallowed, as in the case of barium, which is used in the examination of the stomach and intestinal tract. By the use of a fluoroscope, the radiologist can see these organs at work and check for any malfunction. Contrast can also be injected into the veins, where it is carried to organs such as the kidneys or the gallbladder and its bile ducts.

More complex contrast procedures called angiograms visualize the blood vessels. After contrast is injected through a catheter or tube inserted into the vessels of almost any one of the organs of the body, the radio-opaque dye can be seen on an X-ray picture or through a fluoroscope and the doctor can tell whether the organ is diseased and if surgery is necessary. Angiography has been especially useful in diagnosing disease of the heart and central nervous system. With angiography it is possible to map out the vessels of the heart and brain, which might lead to corrective surgery when narrowed vessels are present. This technique can also be useful in the evaluation of other parts of the circulatory system and various organs such as the kidneys. The status of the lymphatic system can be determined by injecting radio-opaque dye into the very small lymph vessels.

DEVELOPMENTS IN RADIOLOGY

Ultrasound has become an important branch of radiology. In an ultrasound examination, sound waves are directed into the body, where they reflect back from organs and are converted electronically into a picture. These images are interpreted by the radiologist and can reveal information which cannot be seen on regular X rays. Since ultrasound uses only sound waves and not radiation, it can be used with complete safety. An example of the use of ultrasound is its use with the pregnant patient. It can aid the physician in detecting multiple births, predicting birth dates, determining the position of the baby and also detecting abnormalities.

Recently a great deal of attention has been attracted by a form of X ray where the machine is linked to a computer. This computed tomography, or CT as it is popularly known, uses a brain or whole body scanner to diagnose human ailments by methods never before possible. A CT scan of the brain can show its anatomy in great detail. It can demonstrate congenital abnormalities, tumors, blood clots and other abnormalities. It can also rule out the presence of disease and confirm a healthy condition without the complex contrast studies which previously were the only method available to study the circulation of the brain.

Body scanners give clear images of the organs in the chest and abdomen, which may eliminate the need for performing other diagnostic studies. In some cases, scanning may even eliminate the need for exploratory surgery.

While a conventional X-ray machine sends a focused beam of radiation through the body, during computed tomography, a penlike X-ray beam scans across a layer of tissue in many different directions. After the beam has passed through the tissue, its intensity is measured by a sensitive detector. This information is analyzed by a computer and calculated according to complex mathematical formulas. These calculations form a picture of the tissue layer which is displayed on a TV screen. Photographs are taken from the screen of these different layers of tissues and these are evaluated by the radiologist. He makes his diagnosis based on his analysis of these scans and information gathered from the other tests the patient may have had.

The field of radiology (X ray) is a branch of medicine that is fast moving into space-age technology. New methods and techniques are being researched constantly. Not only are there more and more exacting techniques for diagnosing disease, but safety to the patient is being constantly updated so that the person facing a series of X-ray examinations recommended by his doctor does not need to be any more apprehensive than he would be if he were facing any other type of diagnostic study.

CREDIT: *Peter E. Weinberg, M.D., Department of Radiology, Northwestern Memorial Hospital, Chicago.*

BIBLIOGRAPHY:

Publications of the American College of Radiology, 20 North Wacker Drive, Chicago, Illinois.
X Ray: An Inside Look.
Computers, X Rays and You: A New Insight (1977).
Seeing with Sound: Diagnostic Ultrasound (1977).

Encyclopaedia Britannica. Vol. 18, "Radiology," pp. 898–905; Vol. 23, "X Ray," pp. 842–58. Chicago: Wm. Benton, 1971.

Youth

Youth is not a time of life; it is a state of mind; it is not a matter of rosy cheeks, red lips and supple knees; it is a matter of the will, a quality of the imagination, a vigor of the emotions; it is the freshness of the deep springs of life.

Youth means a temperamental predominance of courage over timidity, of the appetite for adventure over the love of ease. This often exists in a man of sixty more than a boy of twenty. Nobody grows old merely by living a number of years. We grow old by deserting our ideals.

Years may wrinkle the skin, but to give up enthusiasm wrinkles the soul. Worry, fear, self-doubt bow the heart and turn the spirit back to dust.

Whether sixty or sixteen, there is in every human being's heart the lure of wonder, the unfailing childlike curiosity of what's next and the joy of the game of living. In the center of your heart and mine there is a wireless station; so long as it receives messages of beauty, hope, cheer and courage, you are young.

When the aerials are down, and your spirit is covered with the snows of cynicism and the ice of pessimism, then you have grown old, even at twenty. But so long as your aerials are up, to catch the optimism, there is hope you may die young at eighty.

CREDIT: *Family of Samuel Ullman.*

Zoonoses

Diseases Humans Get from Animals

Zoonoses are those diseases of man which are transmitted to him from animals. They have afflicted mankind since before recorded history and are found everywhere on earth where man and animals exist together. Many of these diseases are nothing more than a mild irritation while others can wipe out whole civilizations.

Zoonoses can be caused by a variety of "germs," such as bacteria, viruses, fungi, Rickettsia, spirochaetae, protozoa; and by larger parasites such as worms, flukes, fleas, lice, flies and mosquitoes.

Some zoonoses such as polio, rabies, influenza, trichinosis and the common cold are seen in all parts of the world. On the other hand, other zoonoses are very much confined to specific areas. Examples of these are: Bwamba fever, found only in Uganda; and a disease of the liver from a fluke found only in Japan (a fluke is a wormlike parasite).

The kinds and numbers of animals that spread diseases to humans are too numerous to list here. Any animal on the face of the earth can be a carrier of disease to man.

Diseases are spread to humans in many different ways. Some are the result of direct contact, such as tularemia from rodents, the common cold, infectious hepatitis, measles, mumps, diphtheria, tuberculosis, leptospirosis (a kidney disease) and many fungus infections. Some diseases are spread through a bite. These diseases include hundreds of so-called "fevers." For example: Colorado tick fever, Rocky Mountain spotted fever, yellow fever, equine encephalitis, malaria and bubonic plague.

Rabies is probably the most common zoonosis we see today. It is a disease spread to humans by the bite of a rabid animal. The disease can be reduced by vaccinating domestic animals against it. Once a person is bitten by a rabid animal, he will die if not treated promptly. Rabies is one of the oldest diseases in recorded history, having been discussed by ancient Greek physicians over three thousand years ago.

Bubonic plague is the most devastating zoonosis known to mankind. It is a bacterial disease spread to humans by the bite of the rat flea. Today we have medicine that will cure a person of the plague, but when it ran wild through Europe in the Middle Ages it killed millions of people because there were no antibiotics. In fact, man didn't even know the cause of the disease. The plague wiped out whole countries and changed the course of world history.

A disease that was once almost epidemic is polio. This crippling illness is caused by a virus that can be transmitted to humans by parakeets, monkeys and chimpanzees as well as humans. Fortunately, there are now vaccines to protect humans from polio.

Fungus infections often can be spread by dogs, cats and horses, as well as other animals. "Athlete's foot" is a name for a type of fungus infection of the foot. This same general type of fungus can cause infection over the entire body. Usually it can be controlled by medicine applied to the diseased skin and by medicine taken by mouth at the same time. These fungus infections are not usually serious problems even though they can be spread easily and are irritating to the victim.

Of a more serious nature are the so-called systemic fungi, those that attack the internal organs. These can be found most commonly in the lung, liver and spleen. If not caught in time, they can lead to death. We now have medication that can control most of these fungus infections.

A very common and worldwide problem of humans is internal parasites which are gotten from lower animals. There are hundreds of different kinds of worms that can cause human disease: tapeworms, roundworms and hookworms to name a few. Some parasites can attack almost all vital organs of the body. Blood-sucking leeches can be enormously debilitating to the person who is attacked by them.

Besides spreading disease, animal life can be a source of pain to mankind. Mosquitoes, flies and fleas cause mild irritation when they bite. Bees, wasps and scorpions can inflict more painful and serious wounds, while some spiders can even cause death.

The animal that has caused more problems through the ages is the flea. As noted earlier, the flea is the carrier of bubonic plague as well as other diseases. Wherever soldiers have gone into the field of battle, the flea has joined them.

"The flea," a noted scholar once wrote, "has affected the course of more wars than have all the great generals and admirals the world has produced. It has spread disease among the troops in the field and among civilians at home and has done more to change history than almost any other phenomenon of nature."

In so short a discussion we cannot even begin to approach the magnitude of the field of zoonoses. Zoonoses are found on every continent, in every temperature zone, in every ocean on the face of this earth. There are three hundred recognized zoonoses listed today. Perhaps there are more that we don't yet known about. There is no animal on earth that does not spread some disease to man. The wonder is that, in spite of all his enemies, man has managed to survive.

CREDIT: *David I. Epstein, D.V.M., Director, Northbrook Animal Hospital, Northbrook, Illinois.*